Great World Atlas

Great World Atlas

An Illustrated and Informative View of the Earth

Mosaik

Photographic Credits

Cover illustrations
(Small photographs – from left to right)
Carlo Lauer, Rainer Kiedrowski, Erik Lieber-mann, Rainer Kiedrowski, (World map)
ZEFA/IMTEK IMAGINEERING

Inside illustrations
B & U Int. Picture Service/ Herman Scholten, Huizen (NL): 98/99
Prof. Dr. Jürgen Bähr: 117, 122, 125, 136, 139, 140/141, 142, 144/145, 146, 148/149, 150/151
Dr. Ambros Brucker: 93, 96, 104

Deutsche Forschungs- und Versuchsanstalt für Luft- und Raumfahrt e.V., Oberpfaffen-hofen: 82/83
Ingrid Eckhardt-Heinert: 133
Prof. Dr. Eckart Ehlers: 116
Ina Grill: 146
Prof. Dr. Hartwig Haubrich: 122
Hans-Georg Herrnleben: 102, 107, 113, 120, 151
Hungarian Pictures/Kossuth: 95
Dr. Jörg Janzen: 130/131, 132
Rainer Kiedrowski: 84, 88/89, 99, 102, 111, 116, 121, 123, 125, 126, 130, 140, 141
Dr. Werner Klohn: 142

Prof. Dr. Heinrich Lamping: 117, 120
Carlo Lauer: 102, 128, 129, 134, 135, 136, 138/139, 140, 141
Erik Liebermann: 99, 106
Christoph Lutze: 93
Photo Press: 92/93, 96 97; Brucker: 114; Pago: 99; Pape: 95, 100; Schweitzer: 108, 109, 112/113
Prof. Dr. Ulrich Pietrusky: 84, 88/89, 94, 95, 110, 124, 125, 126, 128, 129, 130/131, 132, 143, 144, 146, 148/149, 150/151, 152
Erika Rieger: 135
Peer Schmidt-Walther: 83, 90, 115, 117

Prof. Dr. Wulf-D. Schmidt-Wulffen: 82, 92/93, 124/125, 129, 132
Ernst Schneider: 86, 138, 139
Prof. Dr. Fred Scholz: 110, 111
Urs Schweitzer: 87, 101, 102/103, 104, 106, 107, 108, 110/111, 118, 120/121, 145, 148, 149, 151
Dr. Christoph Stein: 131
ZEFA/Damm: 94/95

Aerial photograph (88/89) by permission of the regional council of Düsseldorf
38 V 10

Cartography: Kartographisches Institut Bertelsmann, Gütersloh
Text and photograph editor: Carlo Lauer
Cover design: Bärbel Jehle
Texts to »The Earth — Its Continents and Countries«: Dr. Ambros Brucker, Munich
Translation: GAIA Text (Lonnie Legg), Munich
Book design and production: Hubertus Hepfinger, Freising

Typesetting: Buchmacher Bär, Freising
Reproduction: Repro Ludwig, Zell am See
Printing and bookbinding: Mohndruck Graphische Betriebe GmbH, Gütersloh
Printed in Germany
ISBN 3-575-16772-9

Contents

Abbreviations used in the Maps

A....;...	Alpes, Alpen
ad.	adası
Ág.	Ágia, -ios
Aig.lle	Aiguille(s)
AK	Alaska
Akr.	Akreotérion
AL	Alabama
AO	Autonome Oblast
AR	Arkansas
Arch.	Archipelago
Arr.	Arroyo
Austr.	Australia
Aut.	Autonomous
AZ	Arizona
B.	Bad, Basin, Bay
Ban.	Banjaran
Bat.	Batang
-b.	-bach
Bel.	Belyi, -aja-, -oje, -yje
Bg(e).	Berg(e)
-bg(e).	-berg(e)
-bğ.	-burg
B.io	Balneario
Bol.	Bol'šoj, -aja, -oje, -ije
Bos.	Bosanski, -a, -e
Bras.	Brazil
-br(n).	-brücke(n)
B.t	Bukit
C.	Cape
Č.	Český, -ká, -ké
CA	California
Can.	Canal
C.bo	Cabo
C.d	Ciudad
Chan.	Channel
Chin.	China
chr.	chrebet
C.(ke)	Coll(e)
C.ma	Cima
CO	Colorado
Col.	Colombia
Coll.s	Collines
Cor.	Coronel
Cord.	Cordillera
C.po	Capo
Cr.	Creek
C.Rica	Costa Rica
C.ro	Cerro
ČSFR	Czechoslovakia
CT	Connecticut
Cuch.	Cuchilla
D.	Danau
Dağl.	Dağlari
DC	District of Columbia
DE	Delaware
Den.	Denmark
Dép.	Département
-df.	-dorf
Ea.	East
Ec.	Ecuador
Eción	Estación
E. G.	Equatorial Guinea
f.	fontein
Fd.	Feld
-fd(e)	-felde(e)
-fdn.	-felden
Fed.	Federal
F.êt	Forêt
Fj.	Fjord
-fj.	-fjord
FL	Florida
Fr.	France, French
F.rte	Fuerte
F.t	Fort
F.tin	Fortín
G.	Gölü (lakes); Gulf (bays, gulfs)
GA	Georgia
G.a	Gora
G.d	Grand
G.de(s)	Grande(s)
-geb.	-gebirge
G.fe	Golfe
Gl.	Glacier
-gl.	-gletscher
-gn.	-ingen
G.ng	Gunung
G.ng-g.ng	Gunung-gunung
Gr.	Groß, -er, -e, -es
-gr.	-gruppe (mountains); -graben (waters)
G.ral	General
G.t	Great
-h.	-hafen
-hav.	-haven
H.d	Head
-hfn.	-hofen
-hgn.	-hagen
HI	Hawaii
-hm.	-heim
-h.n	-horn
Hon.	Honduras
H.s	Hills
-hsn.	-hausen
Htr.	Hinter
-hvn.	-hoven
...I.	Insel, Island
I....	Isle
Î	Île
IA	Iowa
I.a	Ilha
Î.a	Îsola
ID	Idaho
IL	Illinois
I.la(s)	Isla(s)
IN	Indiana
Ind.	India
I.s	Islands
Î.s	Îles
Isr.	Israel
It., Ital.	Italy
J.	Jabal
-j.	joch; joki
Jap.	Japan
Jord.	Jordans
Juž.	Južnyj, -aja, -oje
-K.	-kopf
-kan.	-kanal
-kchn.	-kirchen
Kep.	Kepulauan
-kfl.	-kofel
Kgl.	Kogel
-kgl.	-kogel
km.	Kilómetro
Kl.	Klein
Kör.	Körfezi
Kr.	Krasno, -yj, -aja, -oje
KS	Kansas
KY	Kentucky
L.	Lake
LA	Lousiana
-lbn.	-leben
L.d	Land
-l.d	-land
Lim.	Limnē
L.le	Little
L.oa	Lago(a)
L.una(s)	Laguna(s)
M.	Monte
MA	Massachusetts
Mal.	Malyj, -aja, -oje
M.as	Montanhas
Mc.	Mac
MD	Maryland
ME	Maine
Mex.	Mexico
M.gne(s)	Montagne(s)
MI	Michigan
MN	Minnesota
MO	Missouri
MS	Mississippi
MT	Montana
Mt.	Mount
M.t	Mont
M.ti	Monti
Mt.n	Mountain
Mt.s	Mountains
M.t(s)	Mont(s)
n.	nos
Nat.	National-
Nat.-P(ark)	Nationalpark
NC	North Carolina
ND	North Dakota
N.do	Nevado
Ndr.	Nieder
NE	Nebraska
Neth.	Netherlands
NH	New Hampshire
Nic.	Nicaragua
Niž.	Nižnij, -'aja, -eje, -ije
nizm.	nizmenost'
NJ	New Jersey
NM	New Mexico
Norw.	Norway
Nov.	Novo, -yj, -aja, -oje
NV	Nevada
N.va	Nueva
NY	New York
N. Z.	New Zealand
o.	ostrov
Ob.	Ober
Obl.	Oblast
OH	Ohio
OK	Oklahoma
OR	Oregon
Ou	Ouèd
o-va	ostrova
oz.	ozero
P.	Port (cities, towns); Paß (passes); Pulau (islands)
PA	Pennsylvania
Pan.	Panama
Pass.	Passage
P.c	Pic
P.co	Pico
Pen.	Peninsula
per.	pereval
P.it(e)	Petit(e)
P.k(s)	Peak(s)
Pl.a	Planina
Pl.au	Plateau
-pl.au	-plateau
Port.	Portugal
p-ov	poluostrov
P.-p.	Pulau-pulau
Pr.	Prince
Prov.	Province, Provincial
P.rto	Puerto
P.so	Passo
P.t	Point
P.t(e)	Point(e)
P.ta	Punta
P.to	Porto
P.zo	Pizzo
R	Rio
Ra.	Range
Ra.s	Ranges
R.ca	Rocca
Reg.	Region
Rep.	Republic
Res.	Reservat
RI	Rhode Island
Riv.	River
-riv.	-rivier
S.	San
...(-)S.	(-see) See
S. Afr.	South Africa
S.ai	Sungai
SC	South Carolina
Sd.	Sund
S.d	Sound
SD	South Dakota
S.ei	Sungei
Sev.	Severnyj, -aja, -oje
S.i	Sidi
Sl.	Slovenski, -a, -e
S.nia	Serrania
Sp.	Spitze
-sp.	-spitze (mountains); -sperre (waters)
S.ra(s)	Sierra(s)
Sred.	Srednje, -ij, -'aja, eje
S.rra	Serra
St.	Sankt
S.t	Saint
-st.	-stadt (cities, towns); -stein (mountains)
S.ta	Santa
Star.	Staryj, -aja, -oje
S.te	Sainte
S.th	South
-stn.	-stetten
st.n	stein
S.to	Santo
Str.	Street
Tel.	Teluk
Ter.	Territory
TN	Tennessee
T.ng	Tanjung
TX	Texas
U. K.	Unitede Kingdom
Unt.	Unter, -ere
USA	United States
UT	Utah
V.	Volcán
V.a	Vila
VA	Virginia
V.an	Volcán
vdchr.	vodochranilišče
Vel.	Veliki, -aja, -oje
Ven.	Venezuela
Verch.	Verchne, -ij, -'aja, -eje, -ije
V.ey	Valley
V.la	Villa
vozvyš.	vozvyšenost'
VT	Vermont
W.	West
(-)W.	(-wald) Wald
-w	-witz
WA	Washington
-wd(e).	-wald(e)
W.di	Wadi
WI	Wisconsin
-wlr.	weiler
WV	West Virginia
WY	Wyoming
zal.	zaliv
Zap.	Zapadnaja
zapov.	zapovednik

UNITED KINGDOM

AND NEIGHBOURING COUNTRIES

Shetland (Zetland)

Shetland

Foroyar (Færøerne) (Den.)

Orkney

Orkney

UNITED KINGDOM

NORTH SEA

Dogger Bank

Devil's Hole

1 : 2,500,000

100 Kilometers

75 Statute Miles

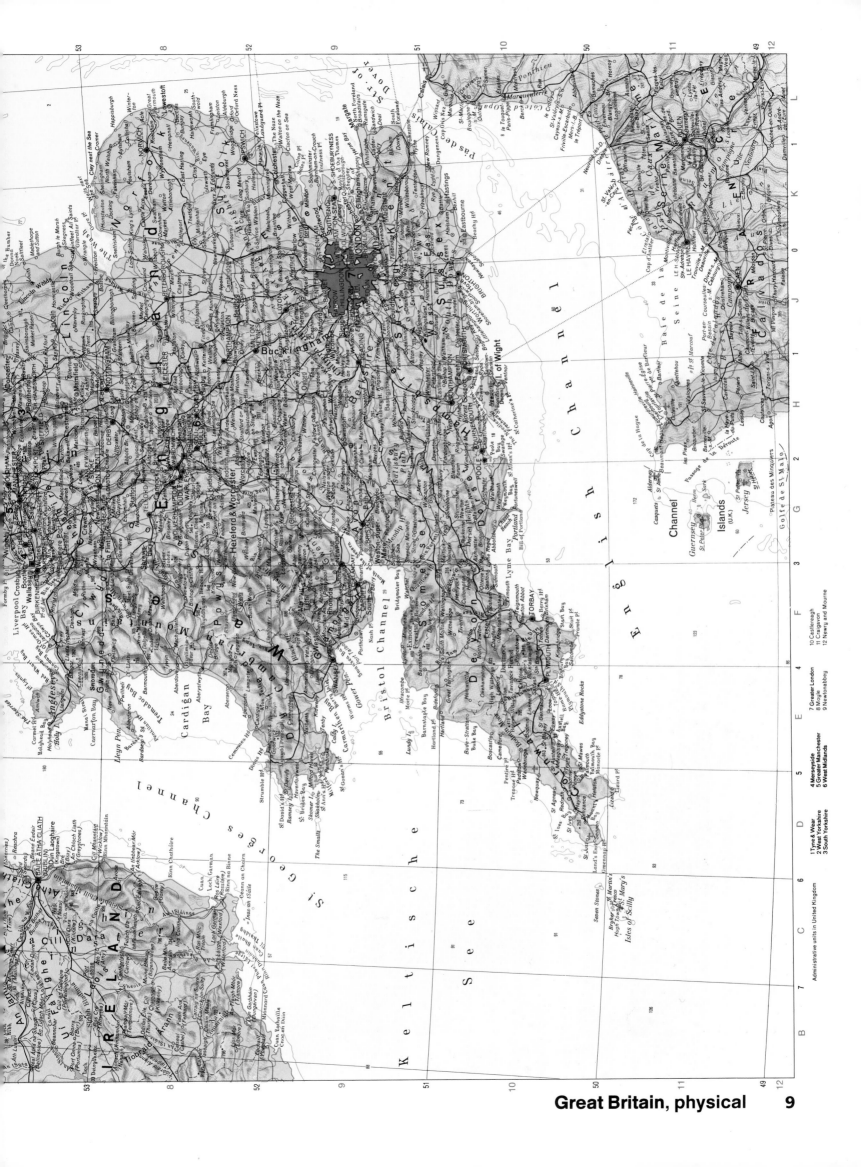

Great Britain, physical   **9**

1 : 5 000 000

0   50   100   150   200 Kilometers

0   50   100   150 Statute Miles

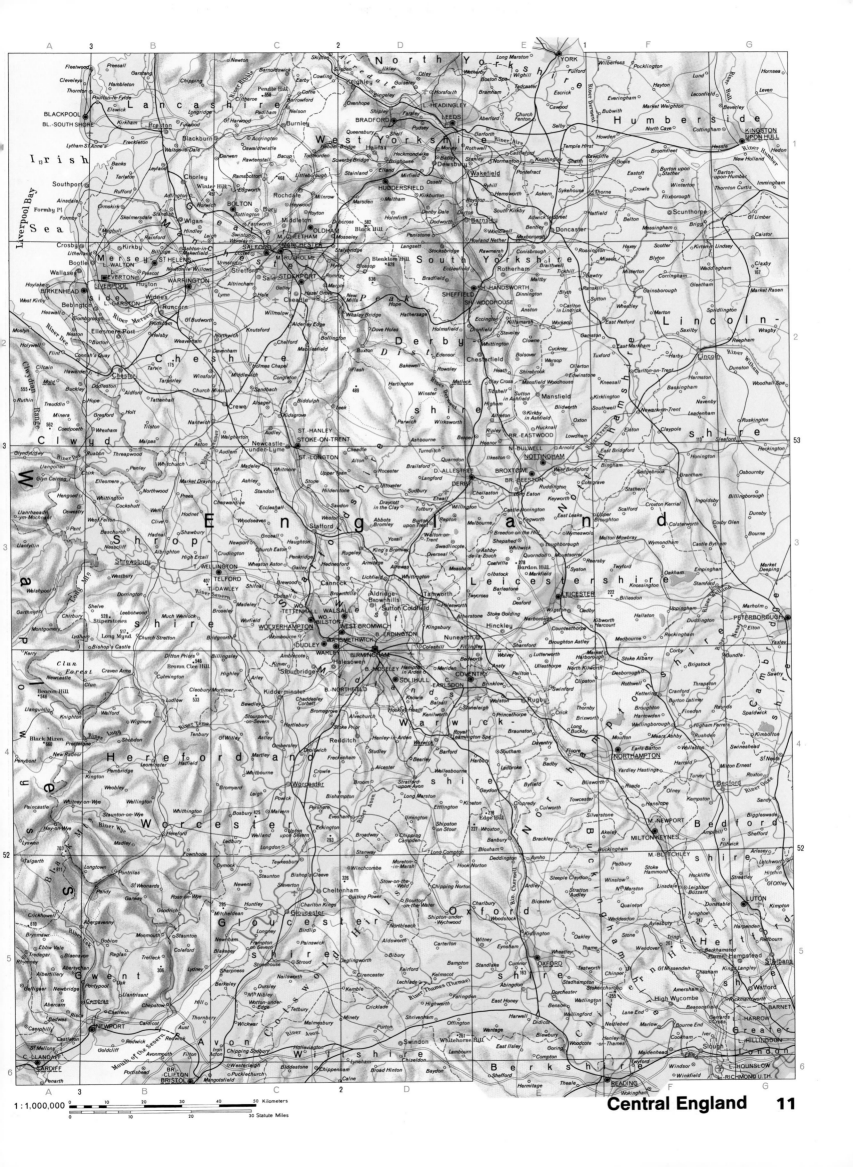

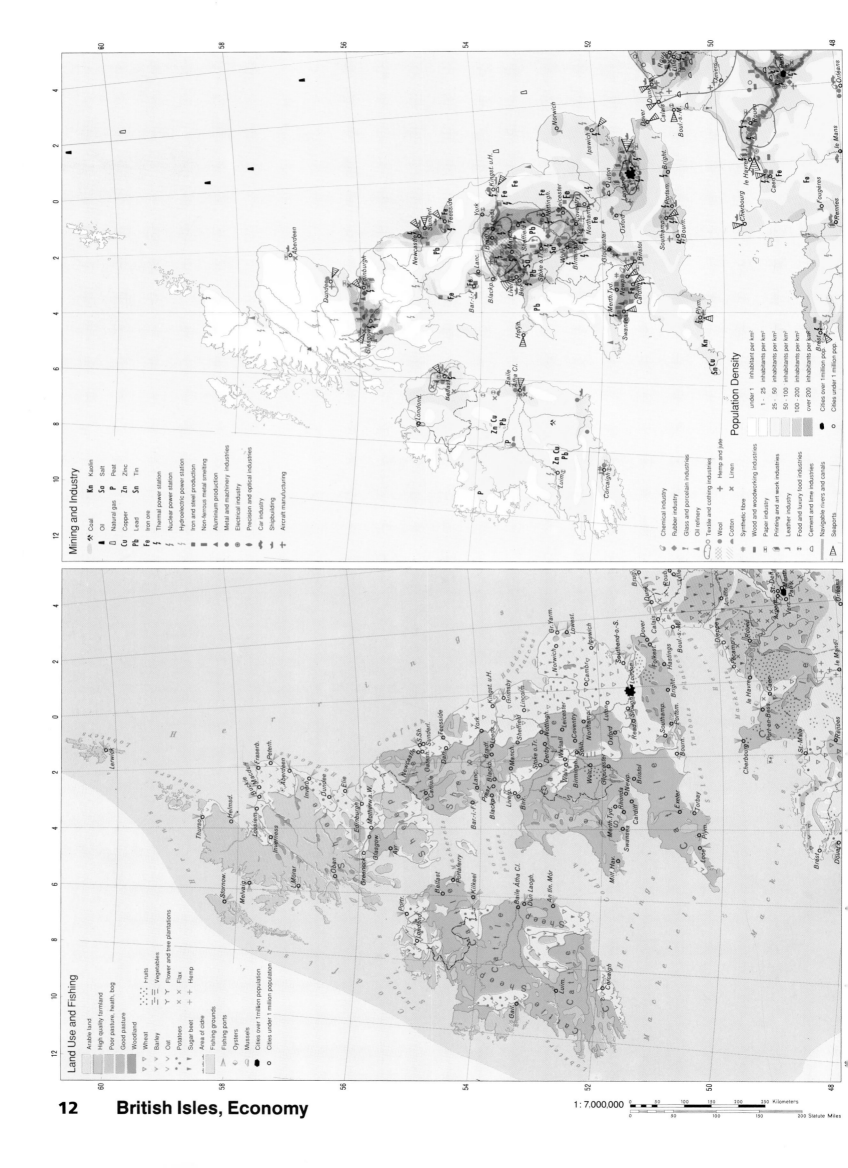

Mining and Industry

⚒ Coal	**Kn** Kaolin
◢ Oil	**Sa** Salt
◹ Natural gas	**P** Peat
Cu Copper	**Zn** Zinc
Pb Lead	**Sn** Tin
Fe Iron ore	

- ⚡ Thermal power station
- ⚡ Nuclear power station
- ⚡ Hydroelectric power station
- ■ Iron and steel production
- ◣ Non-ferrous metal smelting
- ● Aluminium production
- ◉ Metal and machinery industries
- ◐ Electrical industry
- ◗ Precision and optical industries
- ⬟ Car industry
- ⚓ Shipbuilding
- ✈ Aircraft manufacturing

- ◔ Chemical industry
- ◆ Rubber industry
- ▽ Glass and porcelain industries
- ◠ Oil refinery
- ⊞ Textile and clothing industries
  - Wool
  - Cotton
  - Hemp and jute
  - Linen
- ▦ Synthetic fibre
- ▤ Wood and woodworking industries
- ◫ Paper industry
- ⊟ Printing and art work industries
- ▱ Leather industry
- ⚐ Food and luxury food industries
- ⌂ Cement and lime industries

Population Density

▢ under 1	inhabitant per km²
▢ 1 - 25	inhabitants per km²
▦ 25 - 50	inhabitants per km²
▦ 50 - 100	inhabitants per km²
▩ 100 - 200	inhabitants per km²
■ over 200	inhabitants per km²

- ● Cities over 1million pop.
- ○ Cities under 1 million pop.
- ⏁ Seaports
- ▱ Navigable rivers and canals

Land Use and Fishing

▢ Arable land	
▨ High quality farmland	
▦ Poor pasture, heath, bog	
▩ Good pasture	
▥ Woodland	

- ▽ Fruits
- ▷ Wheat
- ⫶ Vegetables
- ⩔ Barley
- ⩔ Oat
- Y Flower and tree plantations
- • Potatoes
- ▾ Sugar beet
- Y Flax
- + Hemp
- ⚓ Area of cidre
- Fishing grounds
- ⏁ Fishing ports
- ◆ Oysters
- ✚ Mussels
- ● Cities over 1 million population
- ○ Cities under 1 million population

1 : 7,000,000

0 50 100 150 200 250 Kilometers

0 50 100 150 200 Statute Miles

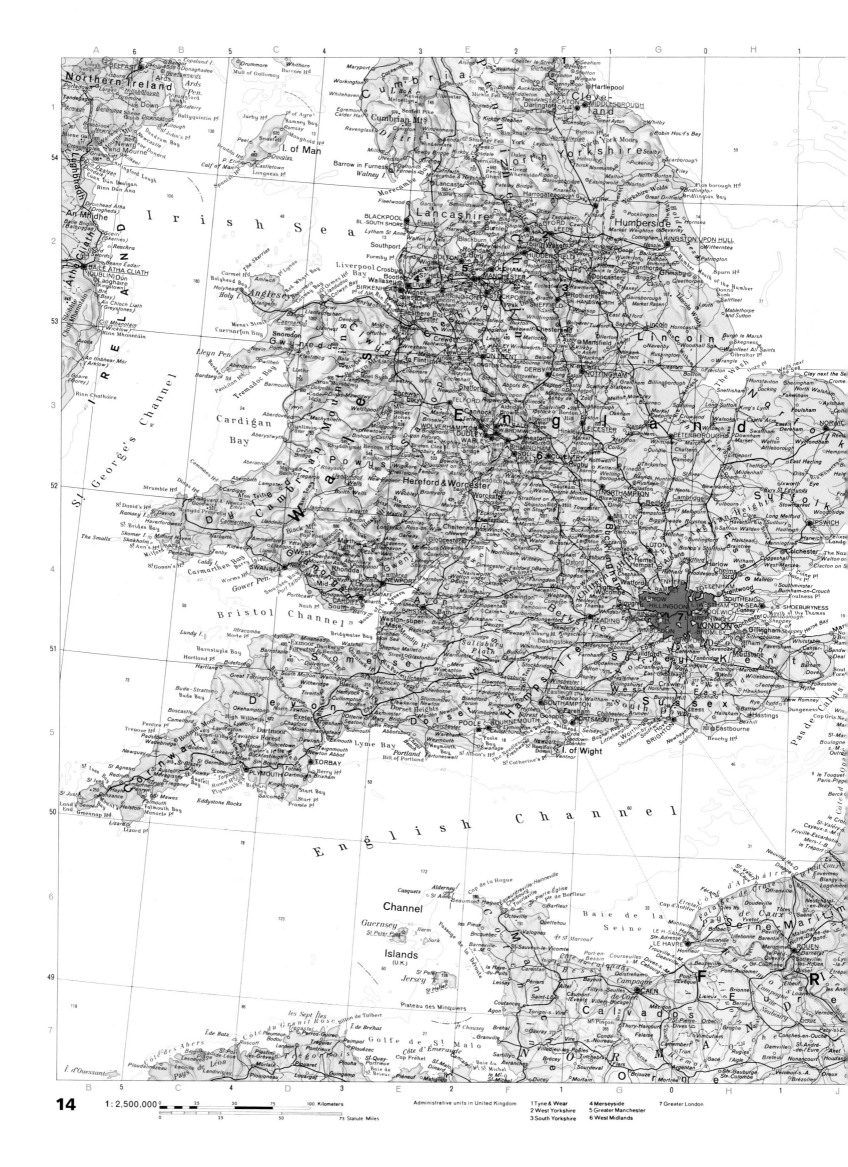

1 : 2 500 000

25   50   75   100 Kilometers

0   25   50   75 Statute Miles

Administrative units in United Kingdom

1 Tyne & Wear
2 West Yorkshire
3 South Yorkshire
4 Merseyside
5 Greater Manchester
6 West Midlands
7 Greater London

Administrative units in France.   1 Ville-de-Paris   3 Seine-Saint-Denis
                                  2 Hauts-de-Seine   4 Val-de-Marne

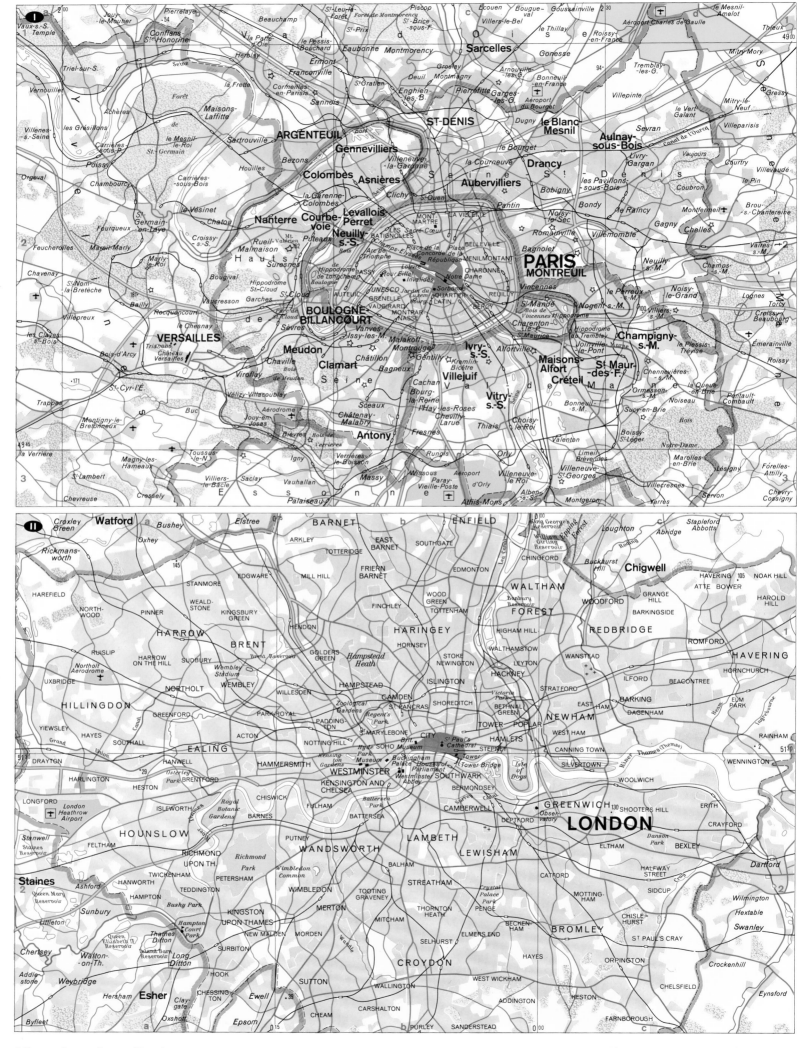

1 : 250,000

0   2,5   5   7,5   10 Kilometers

0   2,5   5   7.5 Statute Miles

THE EARTH

Symbols

River, stream		Railroad	
Drying river, stream		Primary railroad	
Intermittent river, stream		Secondary railroad	*on larger scale maps*
Canal		Suspended cable car	
Canal under construction		Railroad under construction	
Waterfall, rapids		Train ferry	
Dam		Tunnel	
Fresh-water or salt-water lake with permanent shore line		Major highway	
Fresh-water or salt-water lake with variable or undefined shore line		Expressway	*on larger scale maps*
Intermittent lake		Expressway under construction	
Well in dry area		Caravan route, path, track	
Swamp, Bog		Ferry	
Salt marsh		Pass	
Flood area		Airport, Airfield	
Mud flat			
Reef, Coral reef			
Glacier		International boundary	
Average pack ice limit in summer		Boundary of autonomous area	
Average pack ice limit in winter		Boundary of subsidiary administrative unit	
Shelf ice		MADRID — National capital	
Sand desert, gravel desert, etc.		Salem / Nachičevan' — Principal cities of subsidiary administrative units	

Place

⬭	LONDON	over 1,000,000 Inhabitants
◼	BRISBANE	500,000 - 1,000,000 Inhabitants
●	ROSTOCK	100,000 - 500,000 Inhabitants
◉	Segovia	50,000 - 100,000 Inhabitants
⊙	Douglas	10,000 - 50,000 Inhabitants
○	Ansó	unter 10,000 Inhabitants

Locality

L.-HARROW	
BR.-IPSWICH	
R.-WARNEMÜNDE	

•	Inhabited spot, station
∴	Ruins
♜	Castle, fort
⛪	Monastery, church
⊥	Monument
☀ ⚓	Lighthouse
	Nature reserve

Type Styles

VENEZUELA	Independent country
Tirol	Subordinate administrative unit
(Port.) *(Port.)*	Political affiliation
VALENCIA / Cáceres / *Dover*	Places
ATLAS / Causses	Mountain
Snowdon	Mountain, cape, pass, glacier

G O B I / *Mallorca* / *Devon*	Physical regions and islands
OCÉANO / North Sea / *Volga*	Hydrography
Devil's Hole	Ocean basin, trench, ridge etc.
2834	Altitude and depth in meters
164	Depth of lakes below surface

Altitudes and Depths

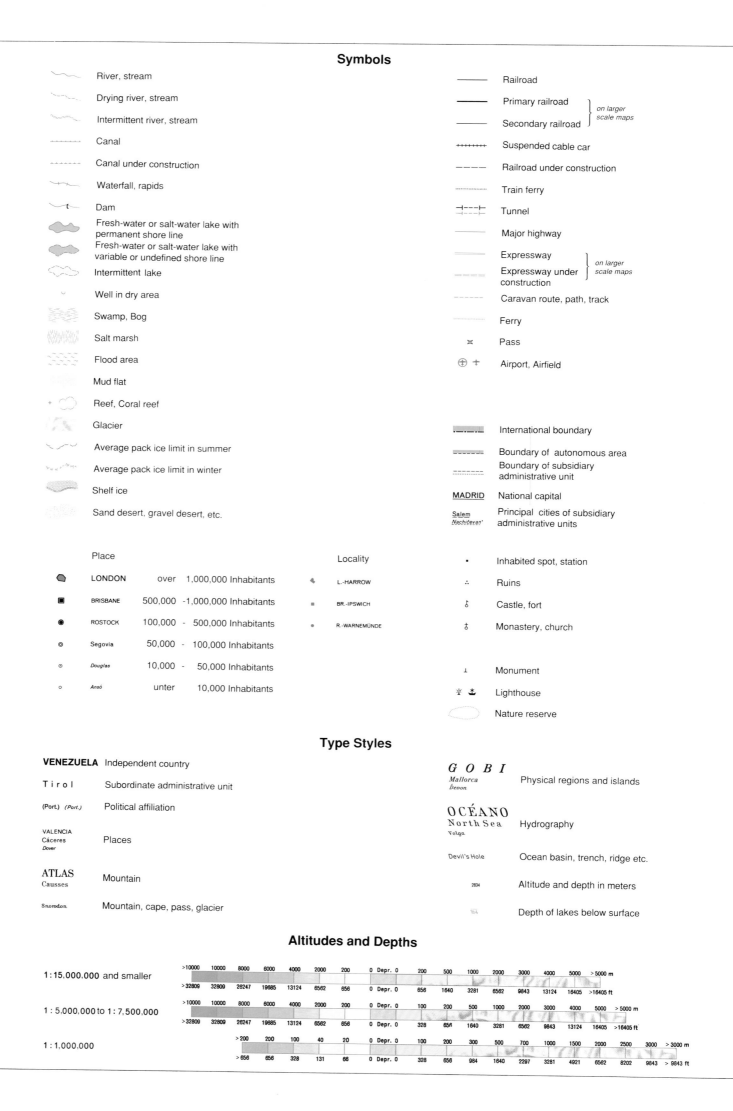

| 1 : 15,000,000 and smaller | >10000 | 10000 | 8000 | 6000 | 4000 | 2000 | 200 | 0 Depr. 0 | 200 | 500 | 1000 | 2000 | 3000 | 4000 | 5000 | > 5000 m |
| | >32809 | 32809 | 26247 | 19685 | 13124 | 6562 | 656 | 0 Depr. 0 | 656 | 1640 | 3281 | 6562 | 9843 | 13124 | 16405 | >16405 ft |

| 1 : 5,000,000 to 1 : 7,500,000 | >10000 | 10000 | 8000 | 6000 | 4000 | 2000 | 200 | 0 Depr. 0 | 100 | 200 | 500 | 1000 | 2000 | 3000 | 4000 | 5000 | > 5000 m |
| | >32809 | 32809 | 26247 | 19685 | 13124 | 6562 | 656 | 0 Depr. 0 | 328 | 656 | 1640 | 3281 | 6562 | 9843 | 13124 | 16405 | >16405 ft |

| 1 : 1,000,000 | > 200 | 200 | 100 | 40 | 20 | 0 Depr. 0 | 100 | 200 | 300 | 500 | 700 | 1000 | 1500 | 2000 | 2500 | 3000 | > 3000 m |
| | > 656 | 656 | 328 | 131 | 66 | 0 Depr. 0 | 328 | 656 | 984 | 1640 | 2297 | 3281 | 4921 | 6562 | 8202 | 9843 | > 9843 ft |

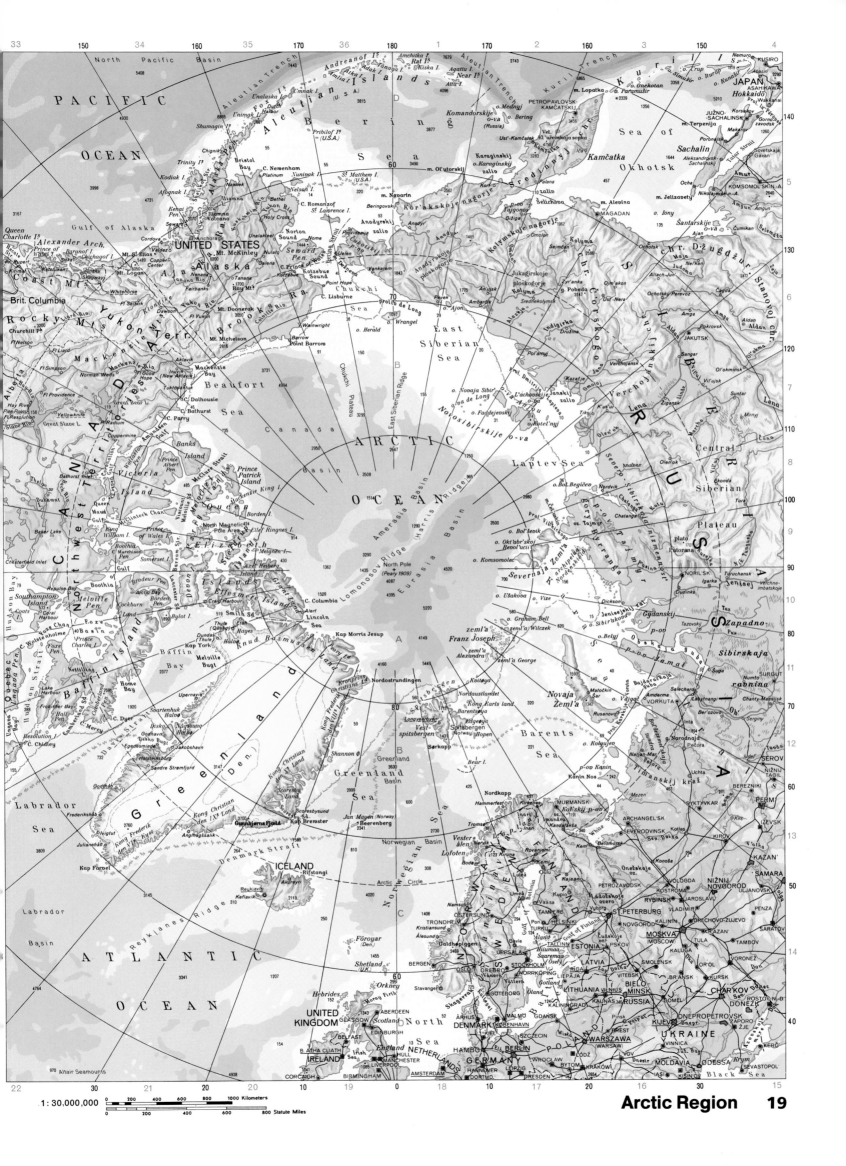

Arctic Region 19

A. = Andorra
AFGHAN. = Afghanistan
ALB. = Albania
AR. = Armenia
AU. = Austria
AZ. = Azerbaijan
B. = Belgium
BA. = Bangladesh
BE. = Belorussia
BH. = Bhutan
BULG. = Bulgaria
CAM. = Cameroon
CAMB. = Cambodia
CR. = Croatia
CZECH. = Czechoslovakia
DEN. = Denmark
DJ. = Djibouti
DOM.REP. = Dominican Republic
EQUAT.GUINEA = Equatorial Guinea
E. = Estonia
Fr.-G. = French Guiana
G. = Germany

• Cities over 1,000,000 Population
○ Cities under 1,000,000 Population
— Shipping trade routes

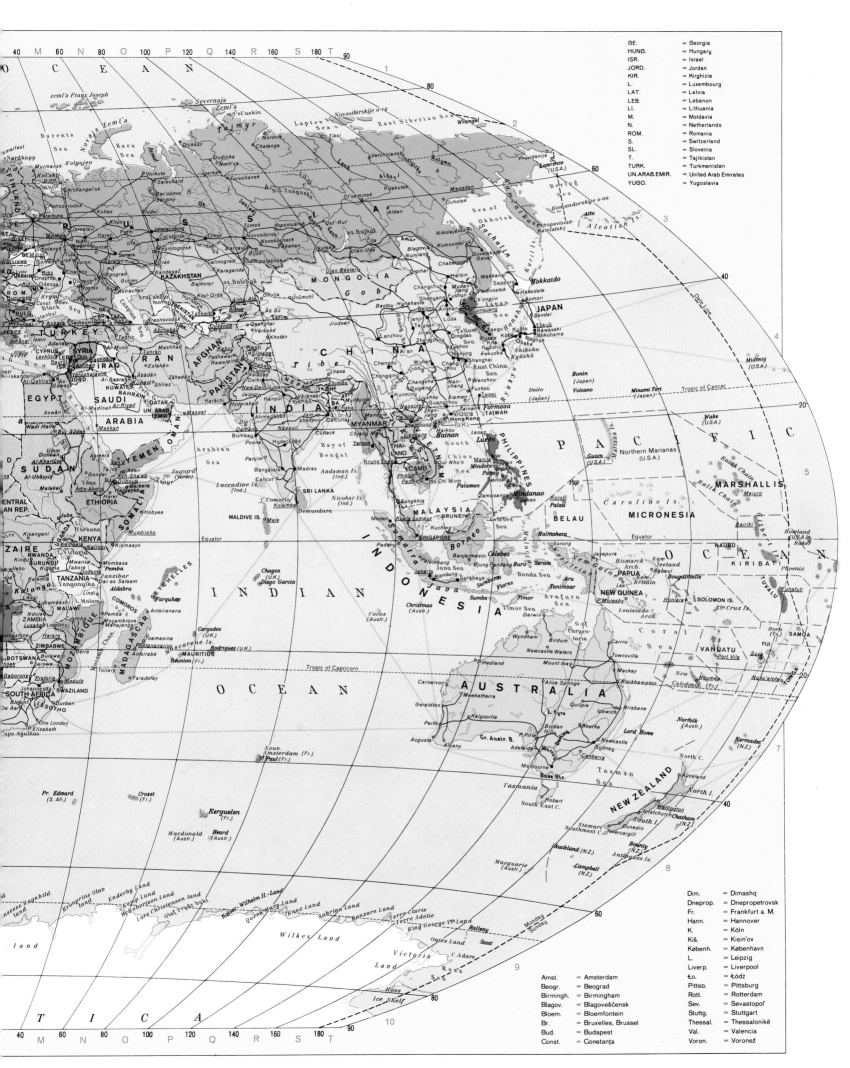

GE. = Georgia
HUNG. = Hungary
ISR. = Israel
JORD. = Jordan
KIR. = Kirghizia
L. = Luxembourg
LAT. = Latvia
LEB. = Lebanon
LI. = Lithuania
M. = Moldavia
N. = Netherlands
ROM. = Romania
S. = Switzerland
SL. = Slovenia
T. = Tajikistan
TURK. = Turkmenistan
UN.ARAB.EMIR. = United Arab Emirates
YUGO. = Yugoslavia

Dim. = Dimashq
Dneprop. = Dnepropetrovsk
Fr. = Frankfurt a. M.
Hann. = Hannover
K. = Köln
Kiš. = Kisin'ov
København. = København
L. = Leipzig
Liverp. = Liverpool
Ło. = Łódź
Pittsb. = Pittsburg
Rott. = Rotterdam
Sev. = Sevastopol'
Stuttg. = Stuttgart
Thessal. = Thessalonikē
Val. = Valencia
Voron. = Voronež

Amst. = Amsterdam
Beogr. = Beograd
Birmingh. = Birmingham
Blagov. = Blagoveščensk
Bloem. = Bloemfontein
Br. = Bruxelles, Brussel
Bud. = Budapest
Const. = Constanța

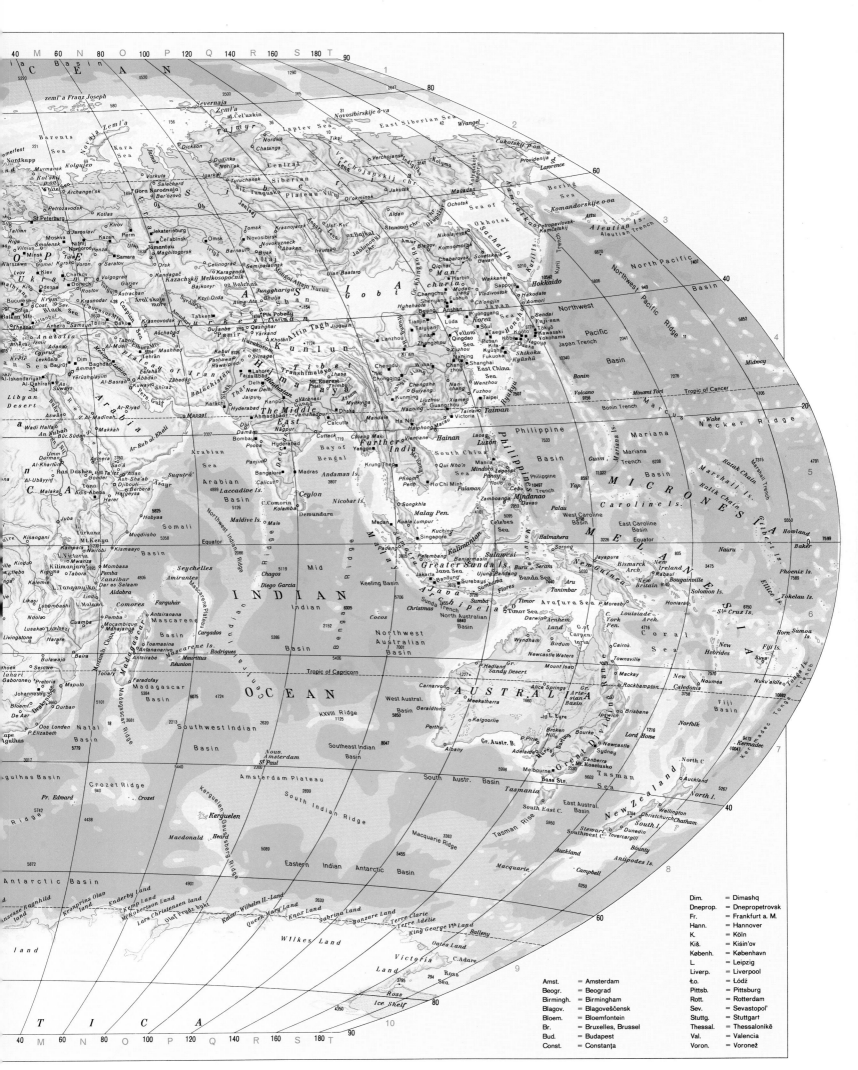

Dim. = Dimashq
Dneprop. = Dnepropetrovsk
Fr. = Frankfurt a. M.
Hann. = Hannover
K. = Köln
Kiš. = Kišin'ov
Københ. = København
L. = Leipzig
Liverp. = Liverpool
Ło. = Łódź
Pittsb. = Pittsburg
Rott. = Rotterdam
Sev. = Sevastopol'
Stuttg. = Stuttgart
Thessal. = Thessalonikē
Val. = Valencia
Voron. = Voronež

Amst. = Amsterdam
Beogr. = Beograd
Birmingh. = Birmingham
Blagov. = Blagoveščensk
Bloem. = Bloemfontein
Br. = Bruxelles, Brussel
Bud. = Budapest
Const. = Constanţa

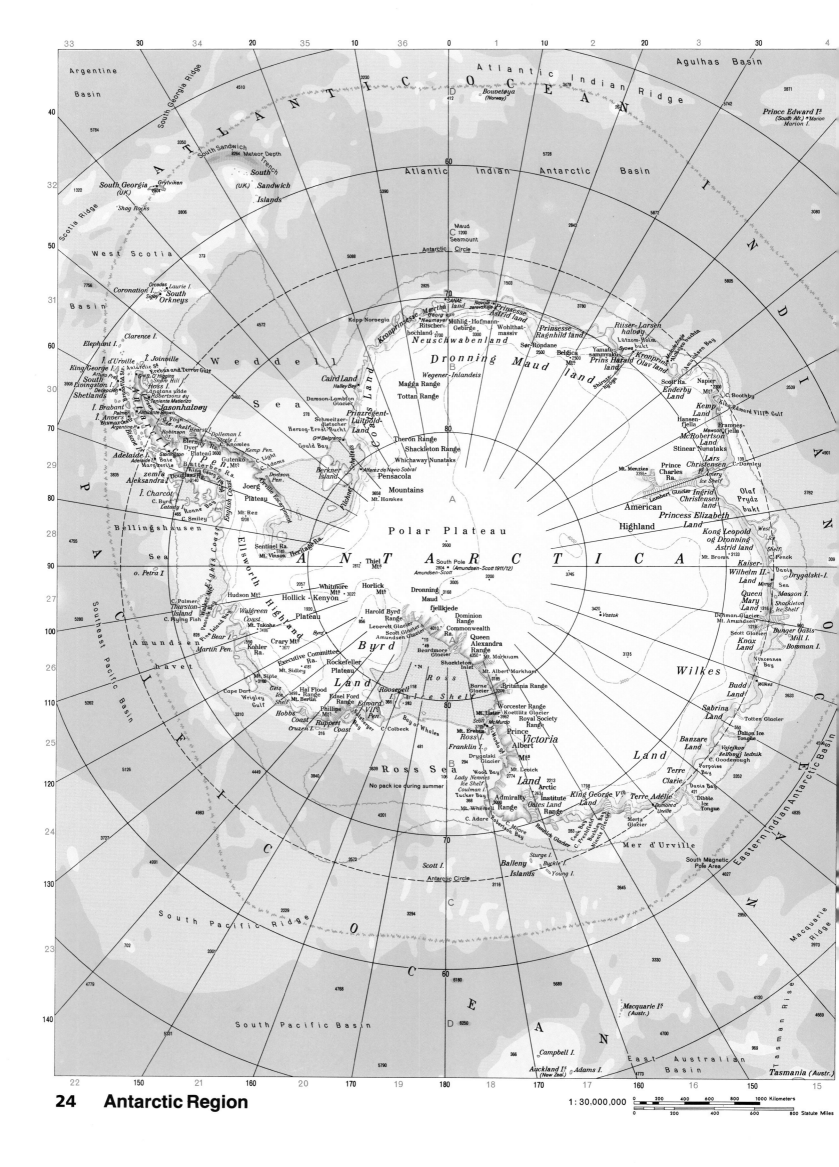

1 : 30,000,000

0 200 400 600 800 1000 Kilometers

0 200 400 600 800 Statute Miles

EUROPE

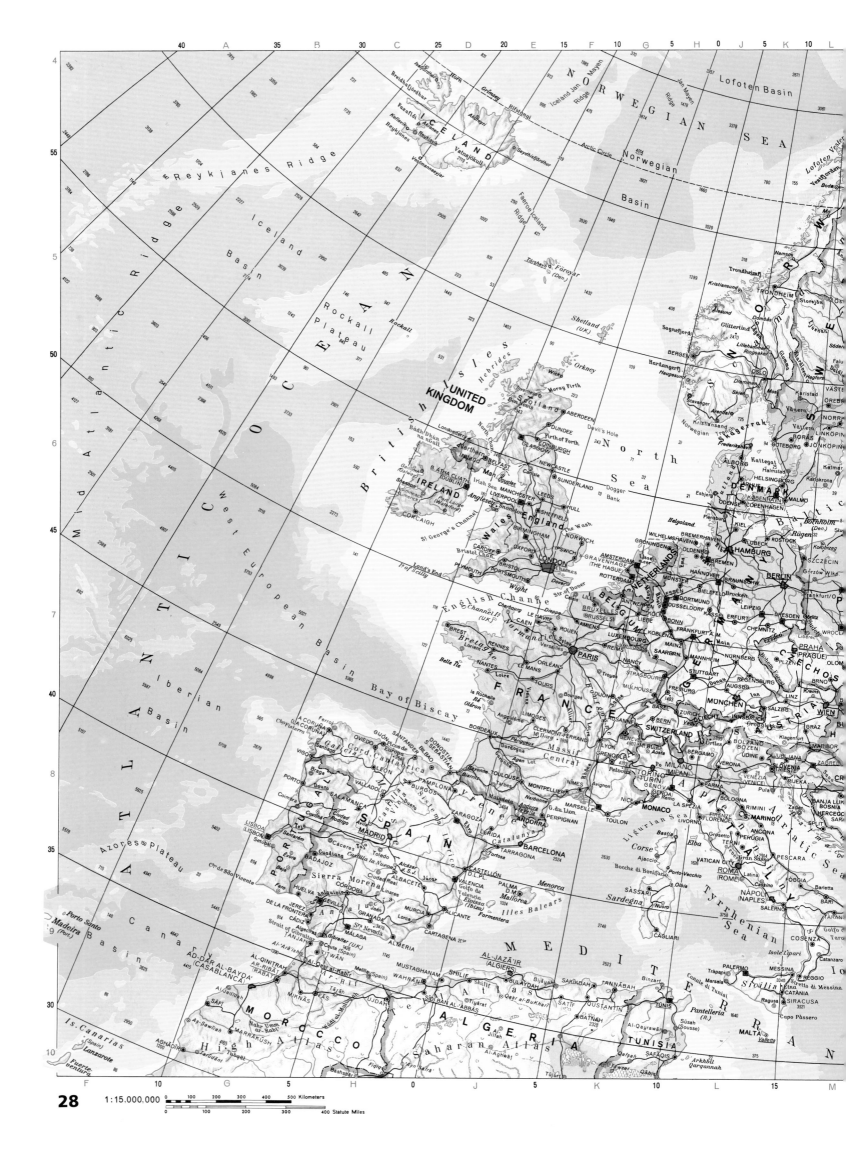

1:15.000.000

100 200 300 400 500 Kilometers

100 200 300 400 Statute Miles

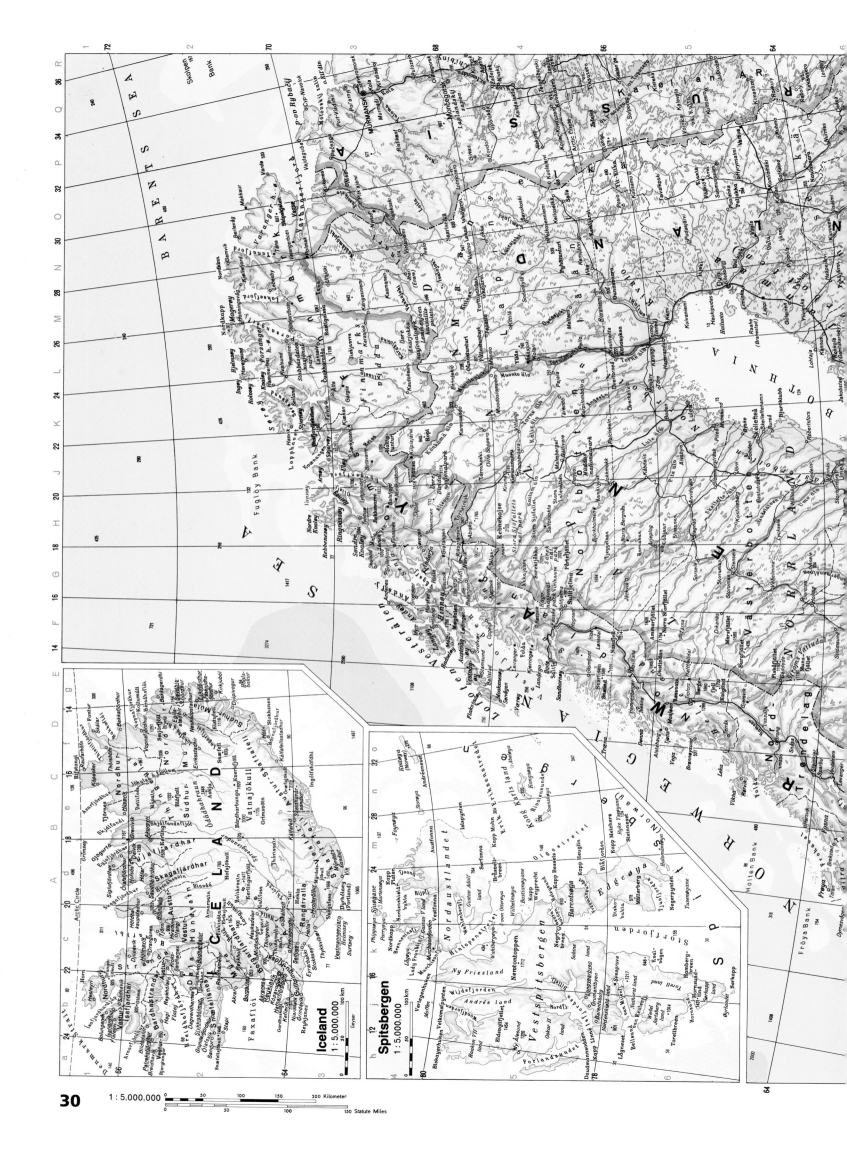

Iceland
1 : 5,000,000

Spitsbergen
1 : 5,000,000

1 : 5,000,000

0   50   100   150   200 Kilometer

0   50   100   150 Statute Miles

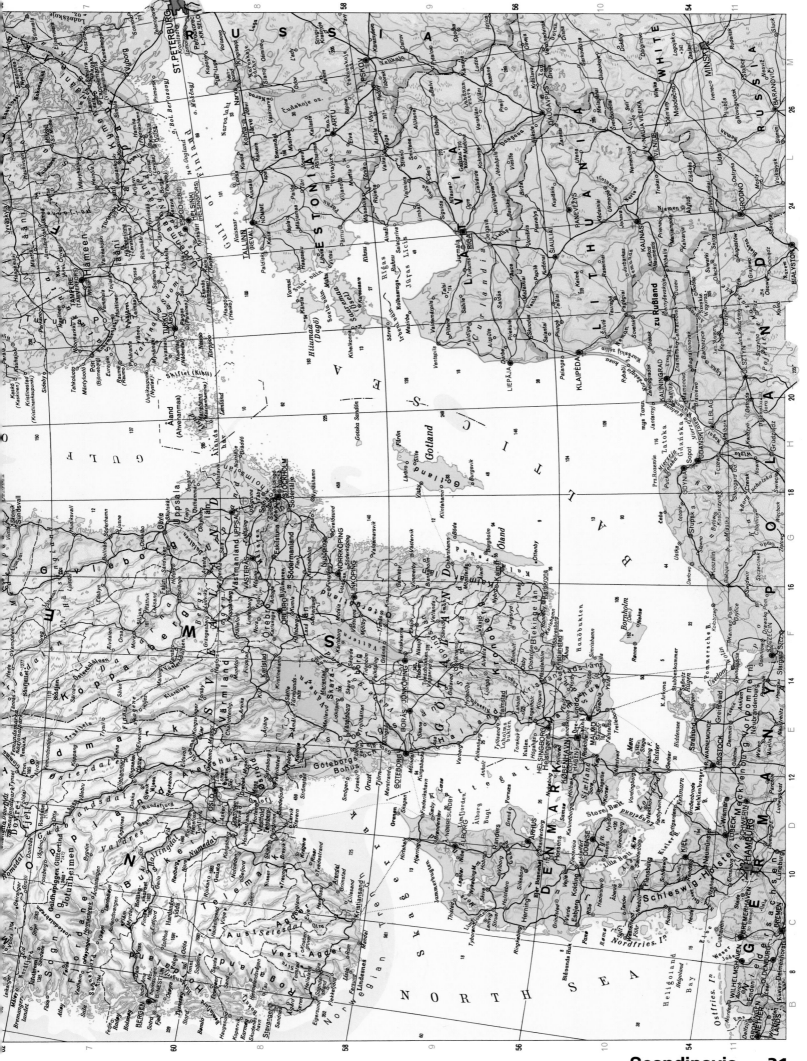

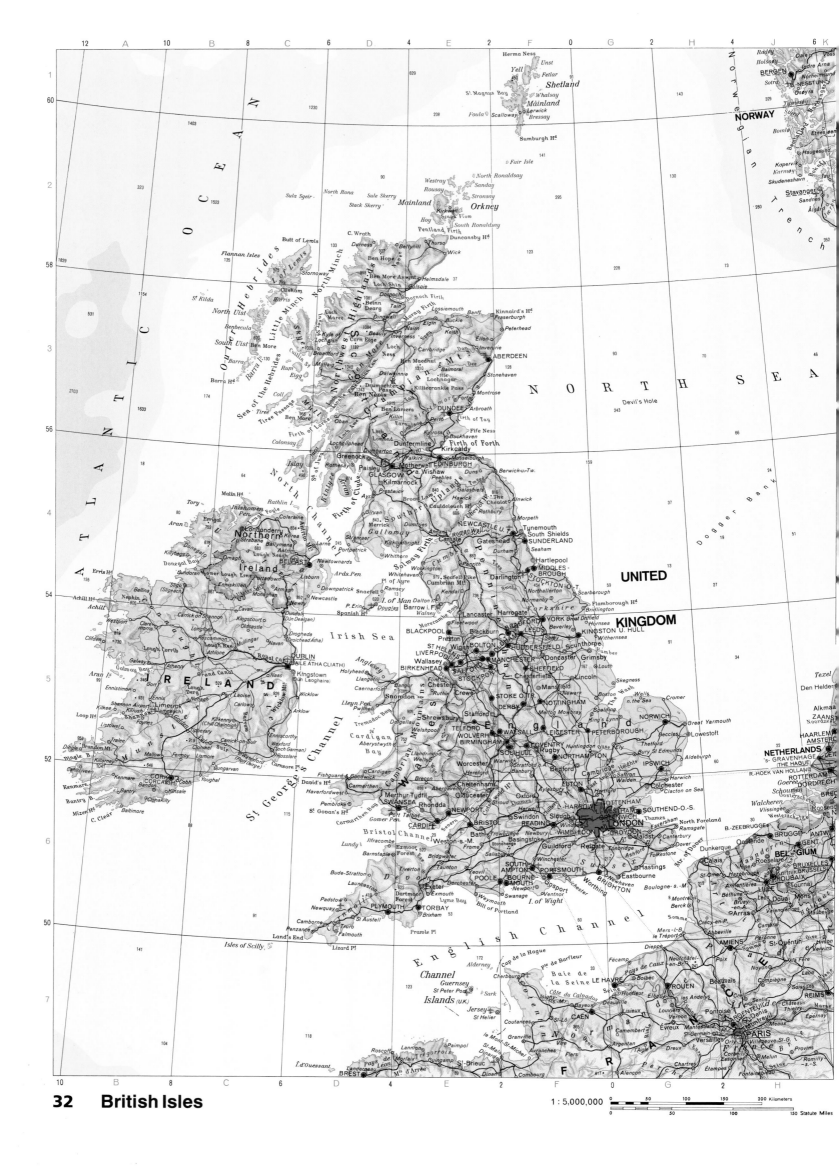

1 : 5,000,000

| 0 | 50 | 100 | 150 | 200 Kilometers |

| 0 | 50 | 100 | 150 Statute Miles |

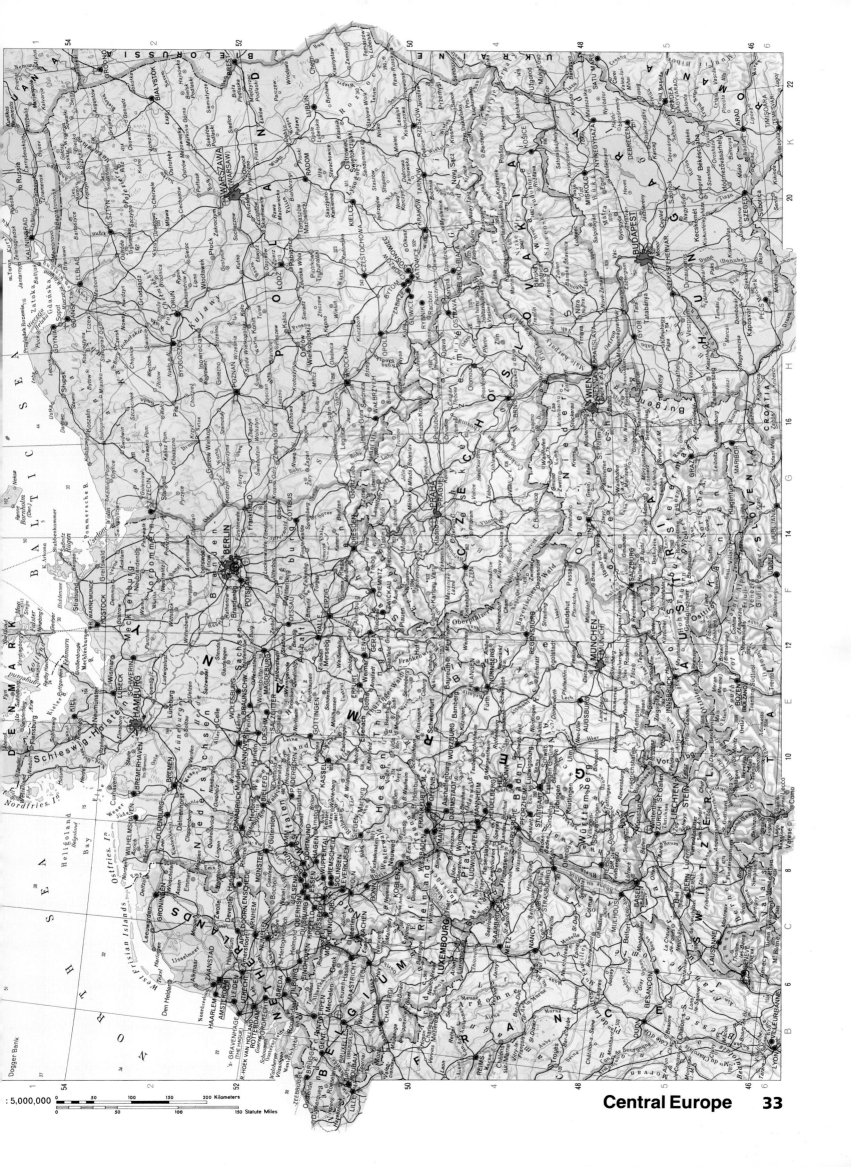

: 5,000,000

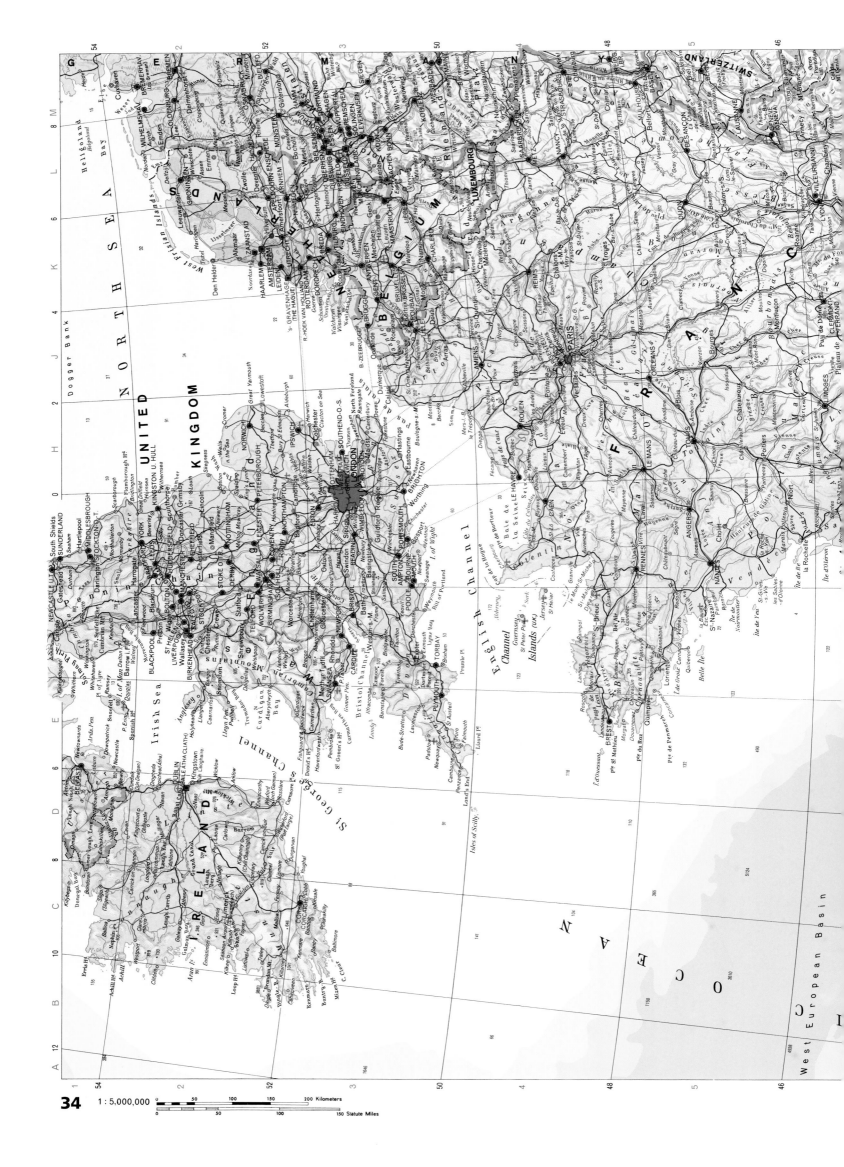

1 : 5,000,000

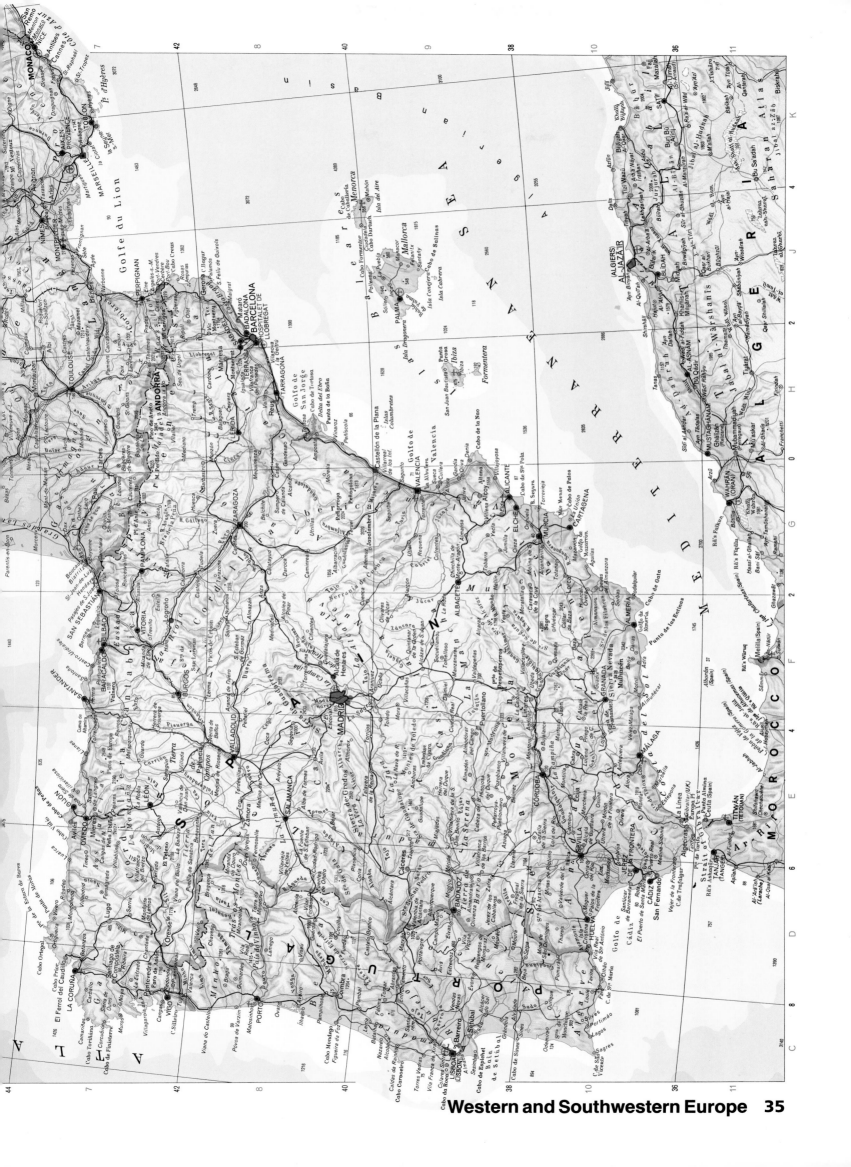

1 : 5.000.000

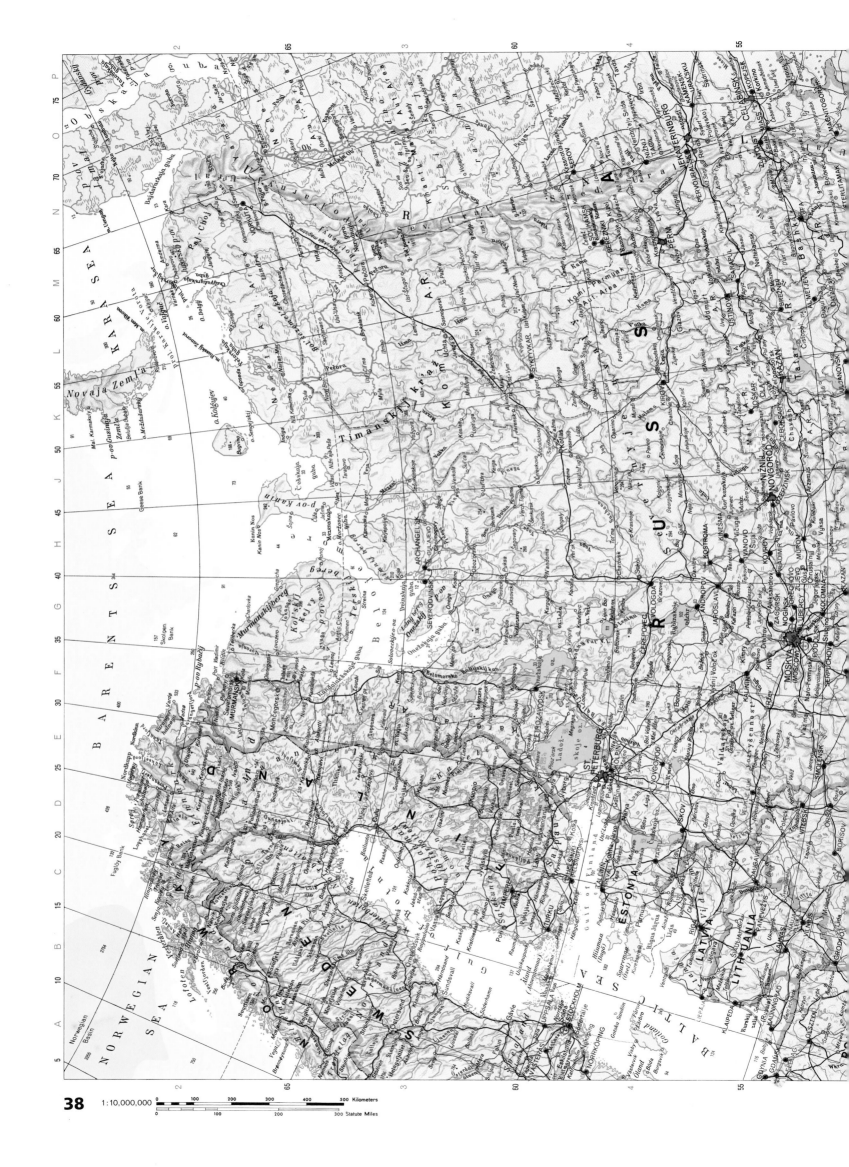

38 1:10,000,000

0 100 200 300 400 500 Kilometers

0 100 200 300 Statute Miles

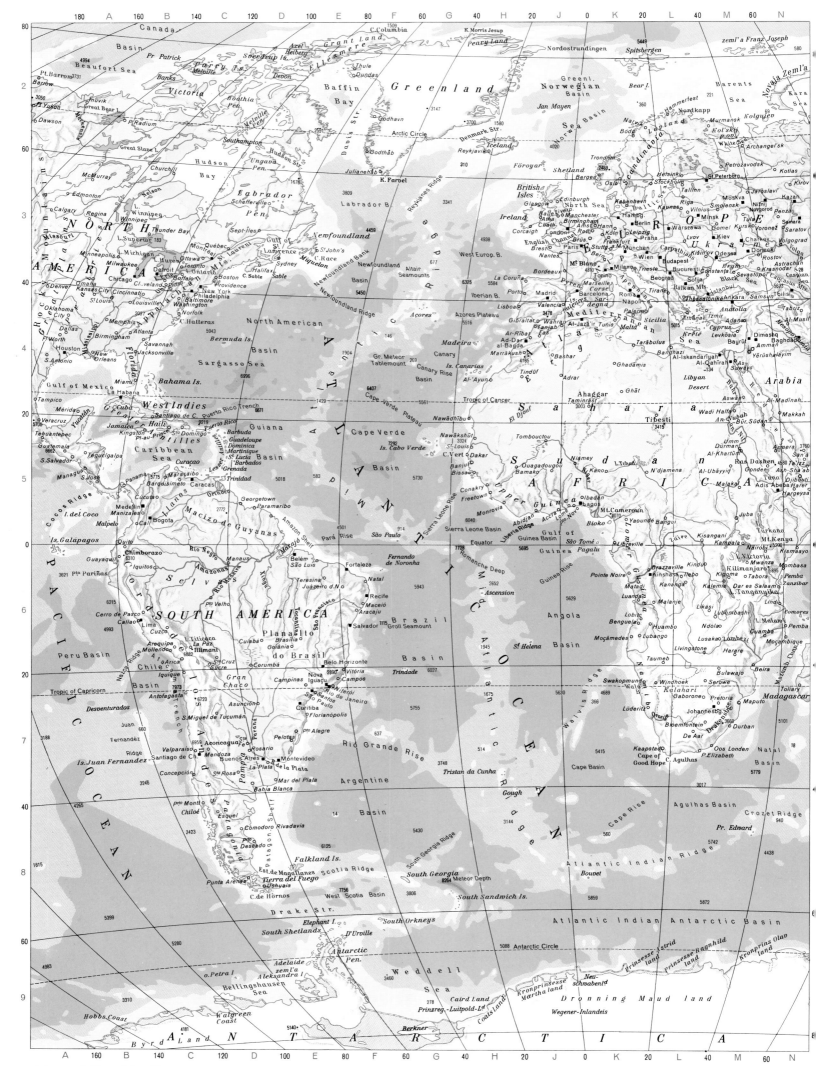

ASIA

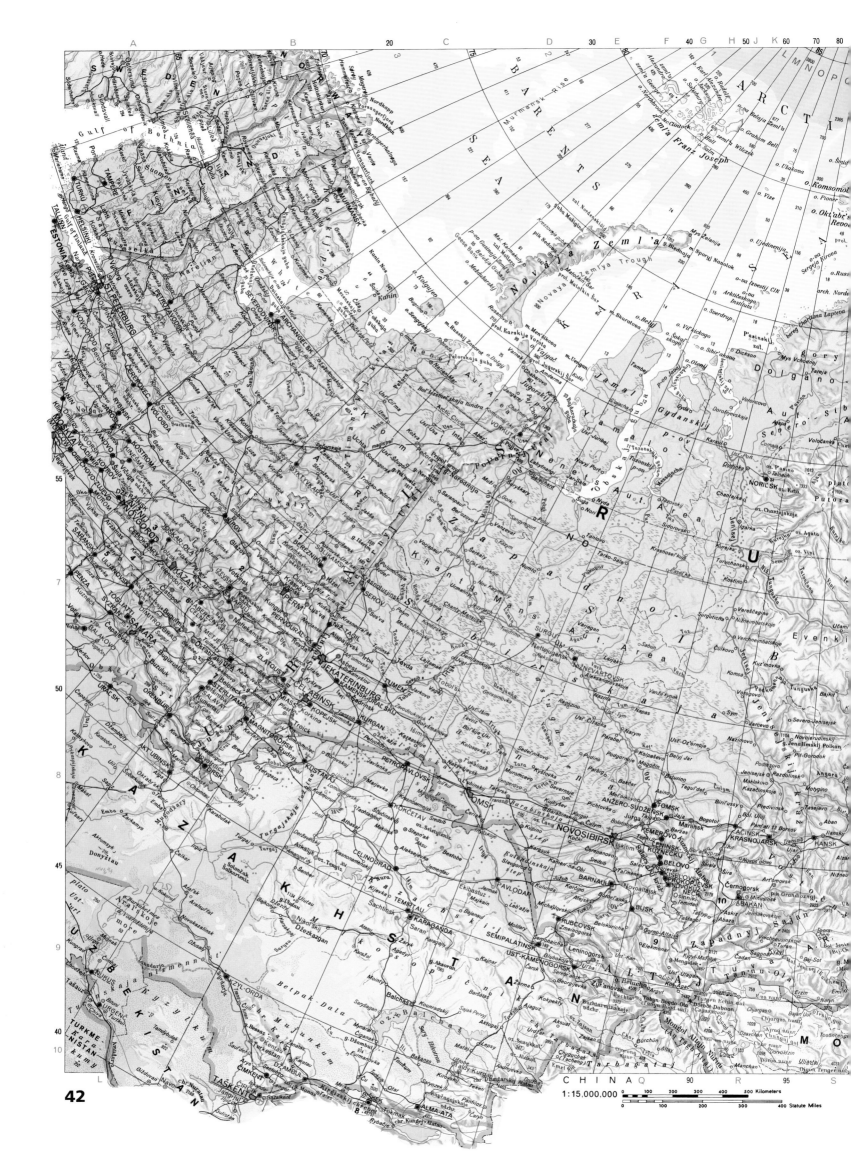

42

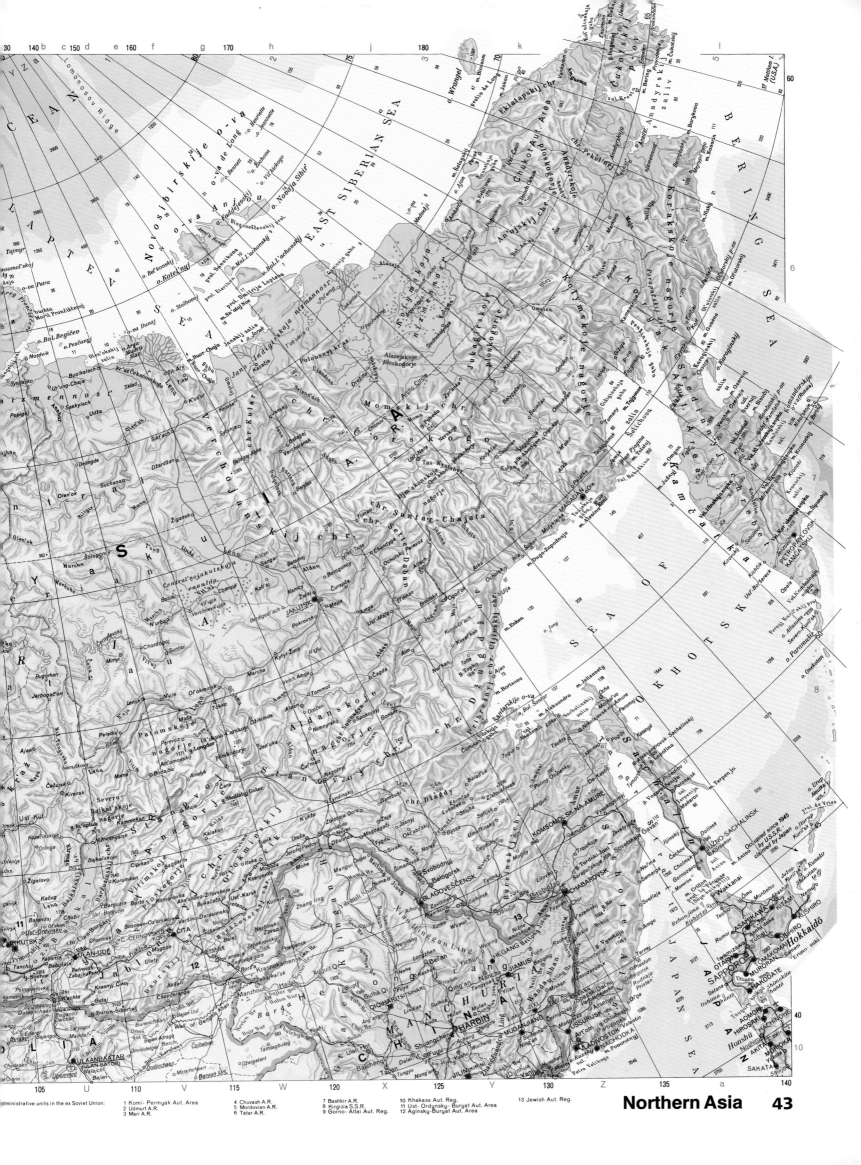

Administrative units in the ex Soviet Union:

1 Komi- Permyak Aut. Area	4 Chuvash A.R.	7 Bashkir A.R.	10 Khakass Aut. Reg.	13 Jewish Aut. Reg.
2 Udmurt A.R.	5 Mordovian A.R.	8 Kirgizia S.S.R.	11 Ust- Ordynsky- Buryat Aut. Area
3 Mari A.R.	6 Tatar A.R.	9 Gorno-Altai Aut. Reg.	12 Aginsky-Buryat Aut. Area

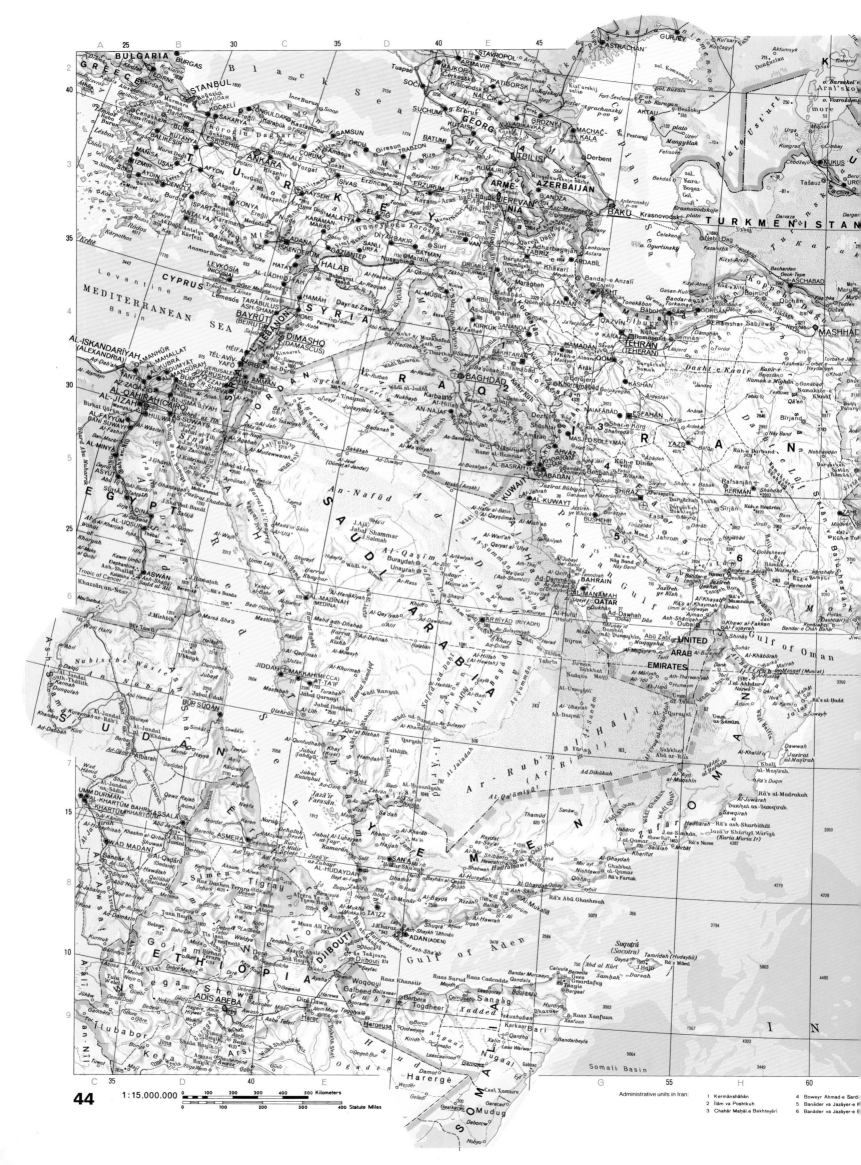

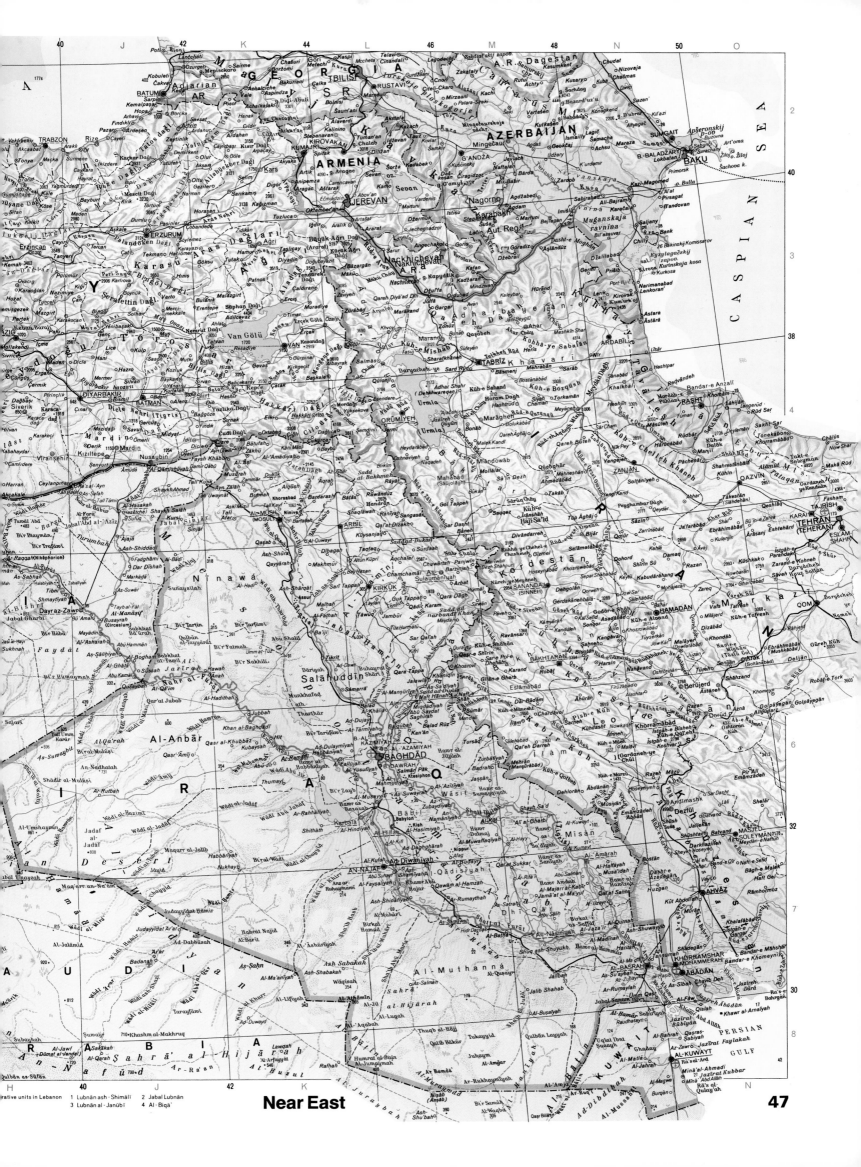

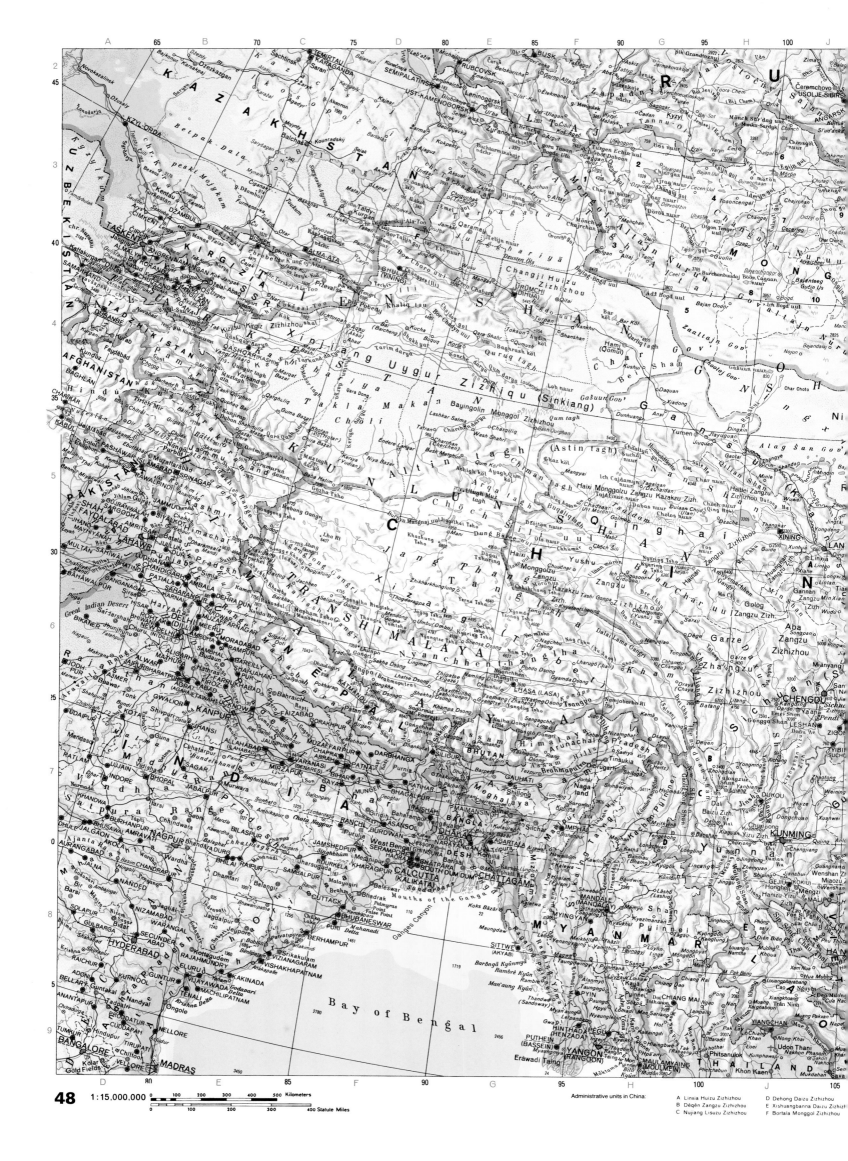

48 1:15,000,000

0 100 200 300 400 500 Kilometers

0 100 200 300 400 Statute Miles

Administrative units in China:

A Linxia Huizu Zizhizhou
B Dêqên Zangzu Zizhizhou
C Nujiang Lisuzu Zizhizhou
D Dehong Daizu Zizhizhou
E Xishuangbanna Daizu Zizhizhou
F Bortala Monggol Zizhizhou

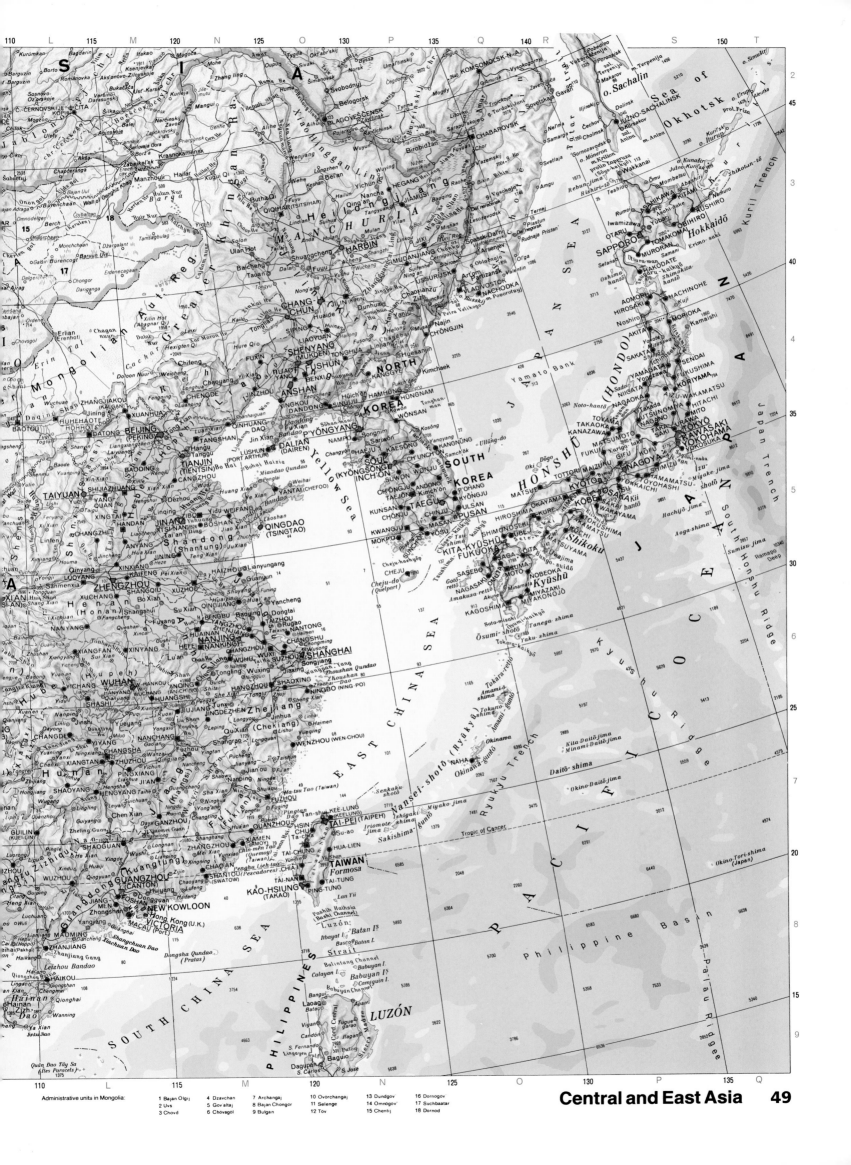

Administrative units in Mongolia:

1 Bajan Ölgij	4 Dzavchan	7 Archangaj	10 Övorchangaj	13 Dundgov	16 Dornogov
2 Uvs	5 Gov'altaj	8 Bajan Chongor	11 Selenge	14 Ömnögov	17 Suchbaatar
3 Chovd	6 Chövsgöl	9 Bulgan	12 Töv	15 Chentij	18 Dornod

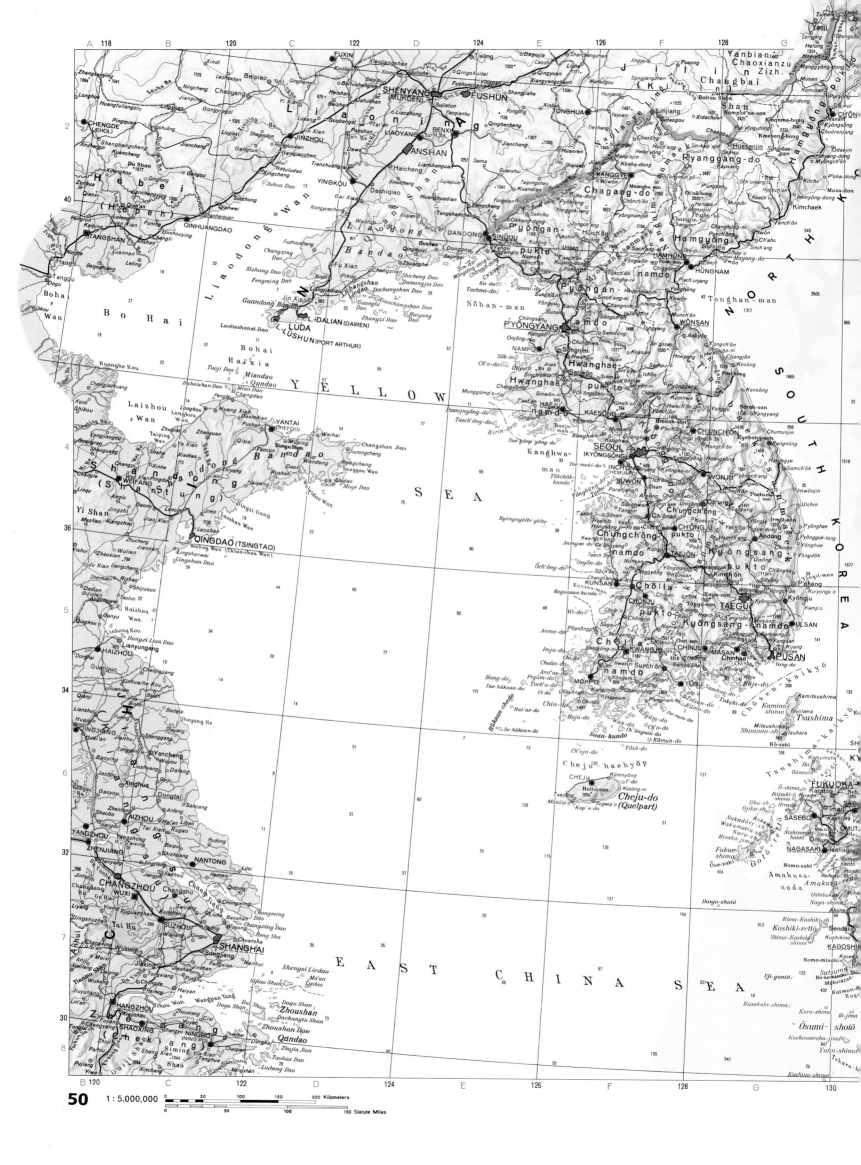

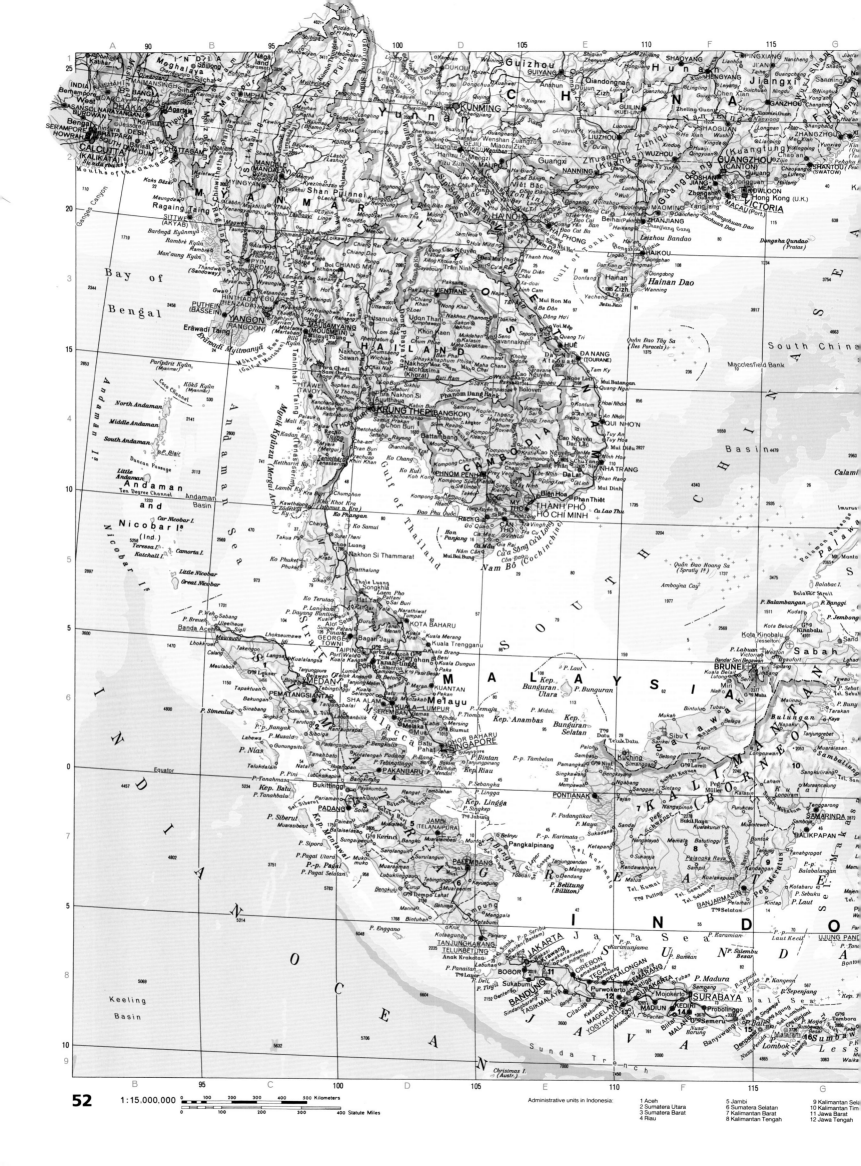

Southeast Asia 53

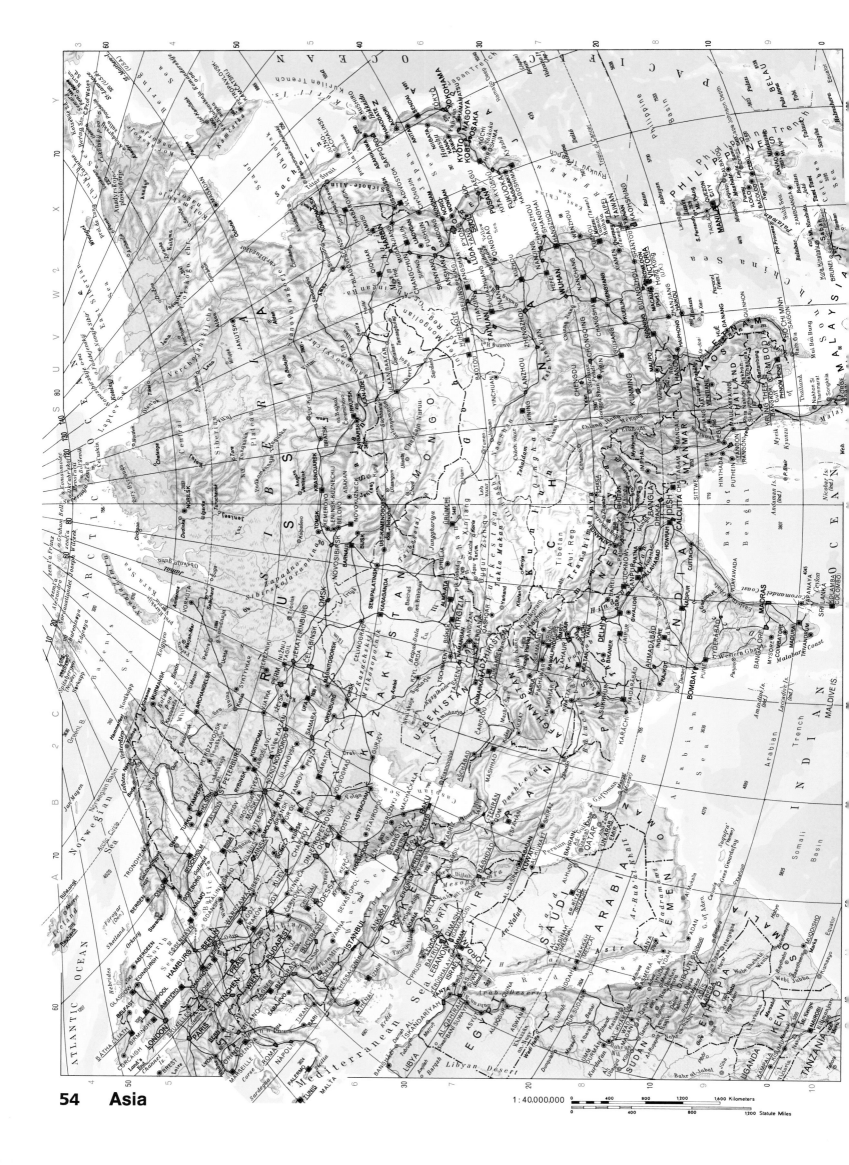

1 : 40,000,000

400   800   1,200   1,600 Kilometers

400   800   1200 Statute Miles

AUSTRALIA

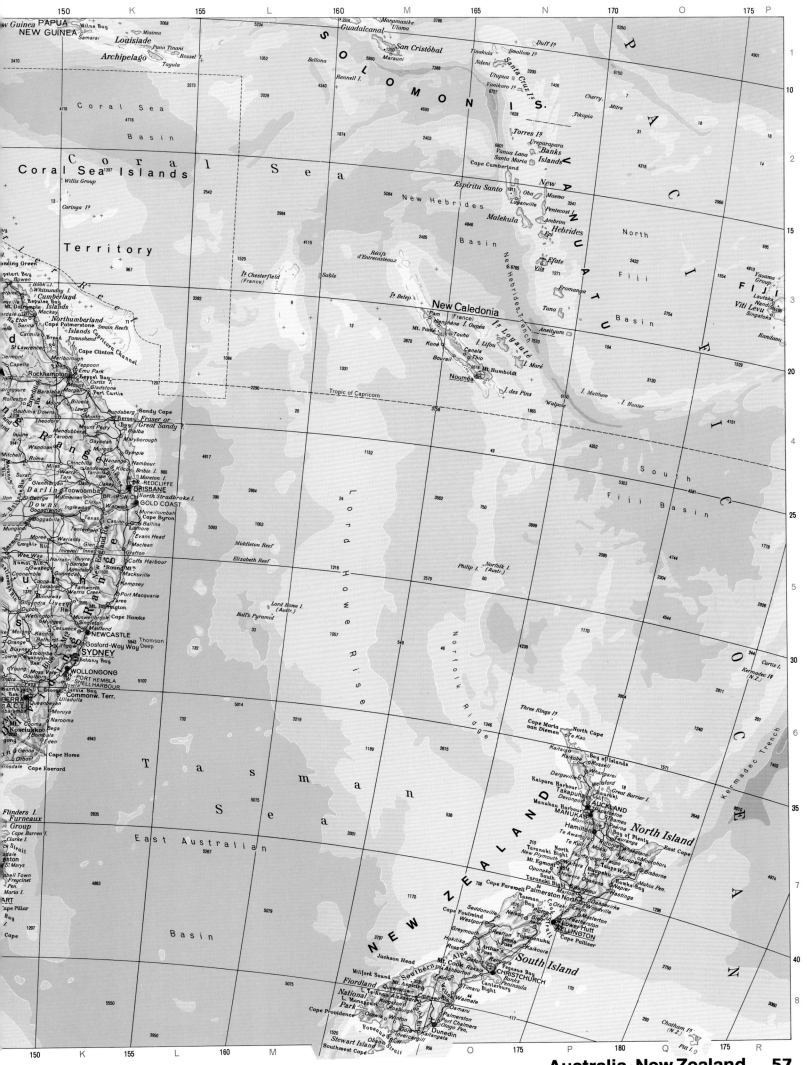

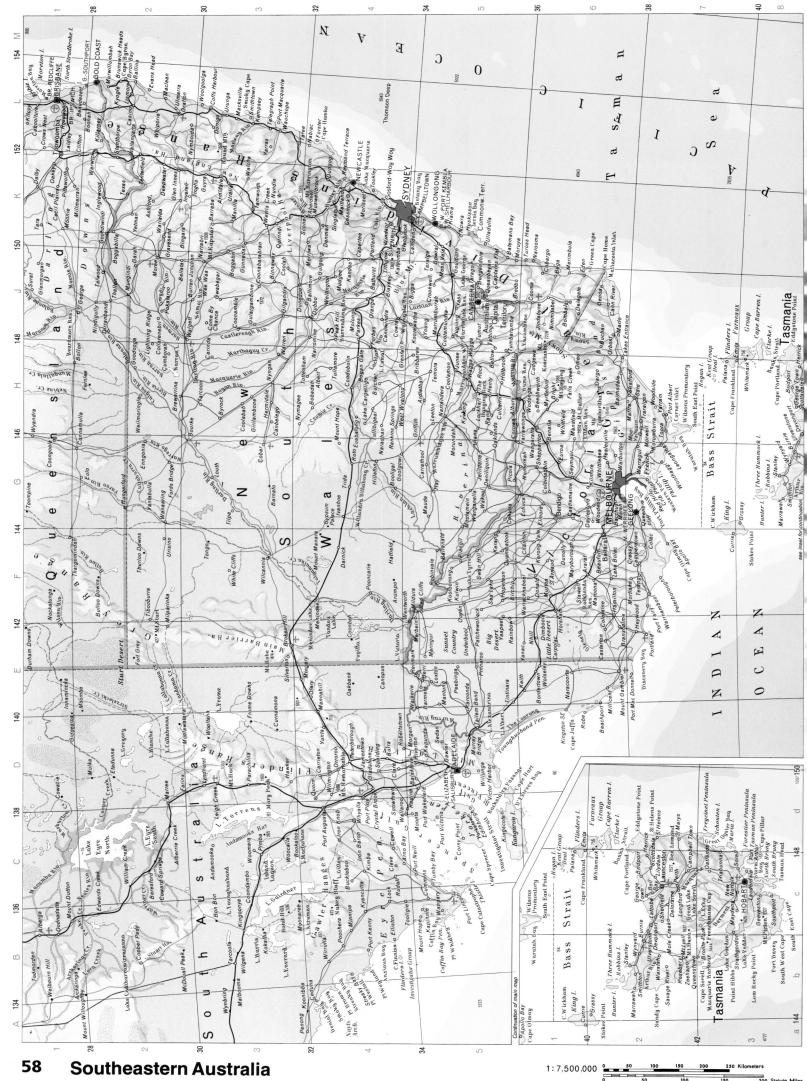

58 **Southeastern Australia**

1 : 7,500,000

0   50   100   150   200   250 Kilometers

0   50   100   150   200 Statute Miles

AFRICA

Administrative units in Somalia: 2 Banaadir   4 Jubbada Hoose
3 Shabeellaha Hoose   5 Shabeellaha Dhexe

Somalia

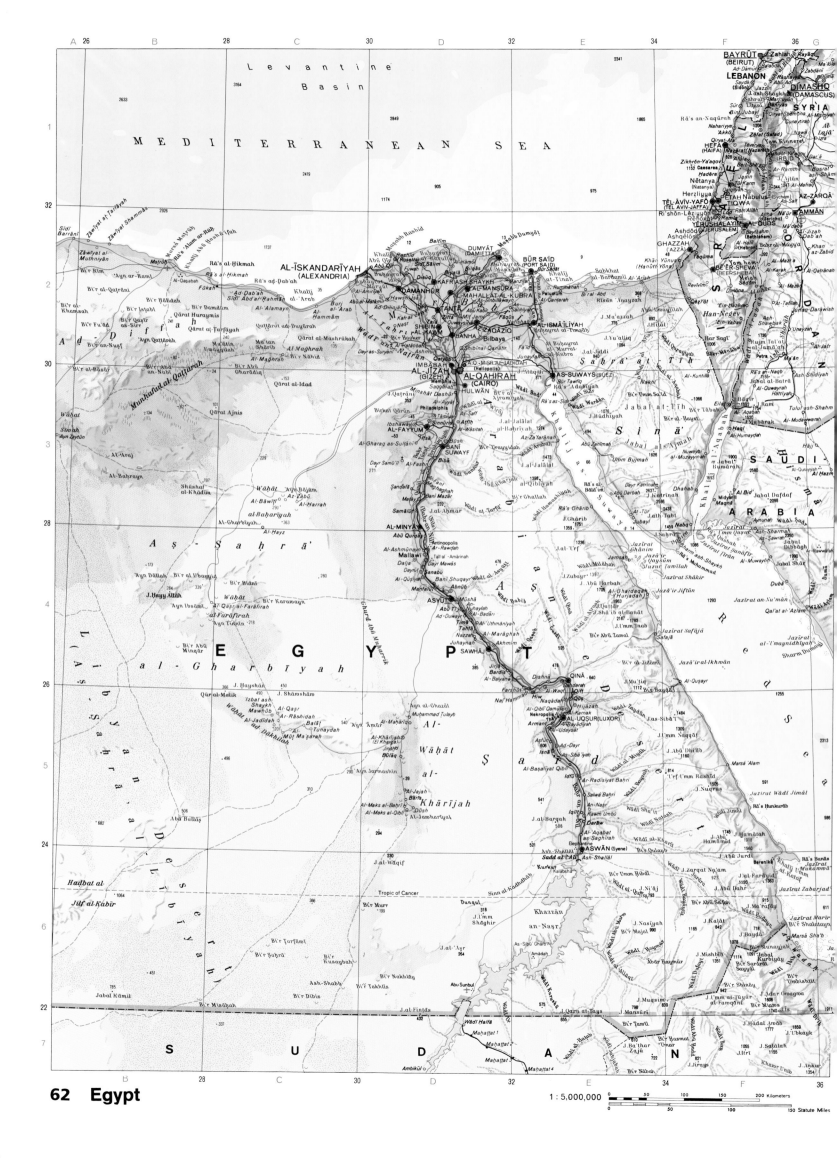

1 : 5,000,000

0   50   100   150   200 Kilometers

0   50   100   150 Statute Miles

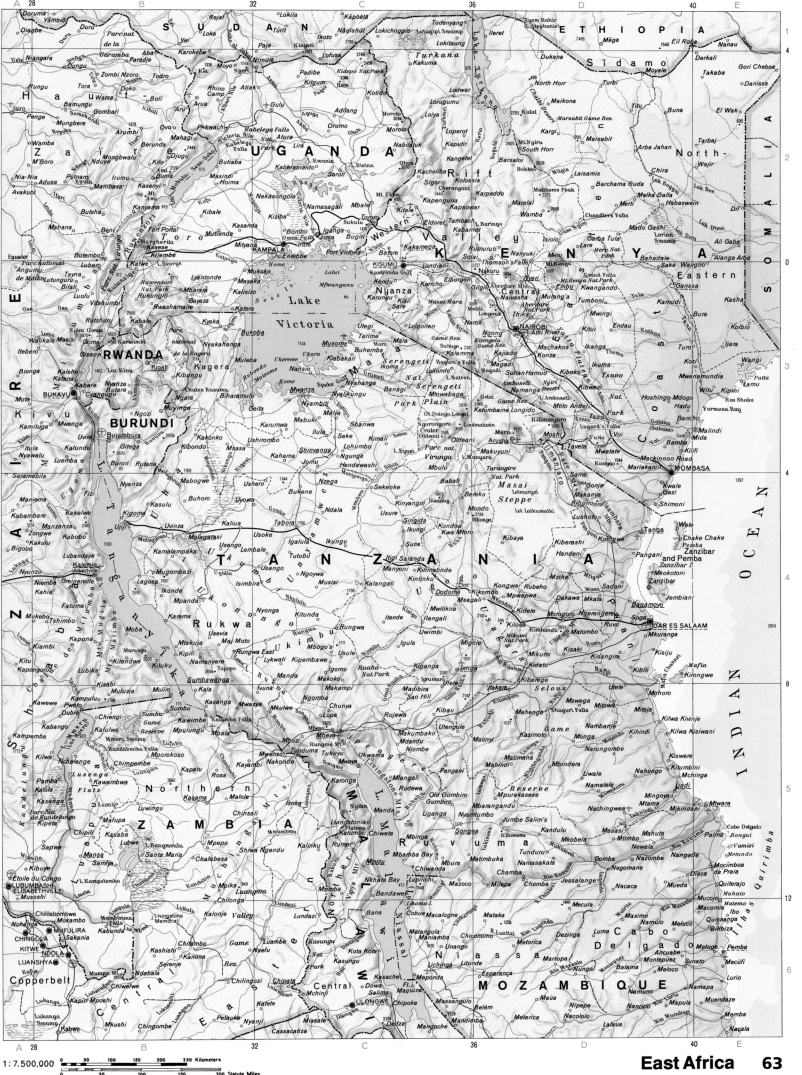

East Africa 63

1 : 7,500,000

0 50 100 150 200 250 Kilometers

0 50 100 150 200 Statute Miles

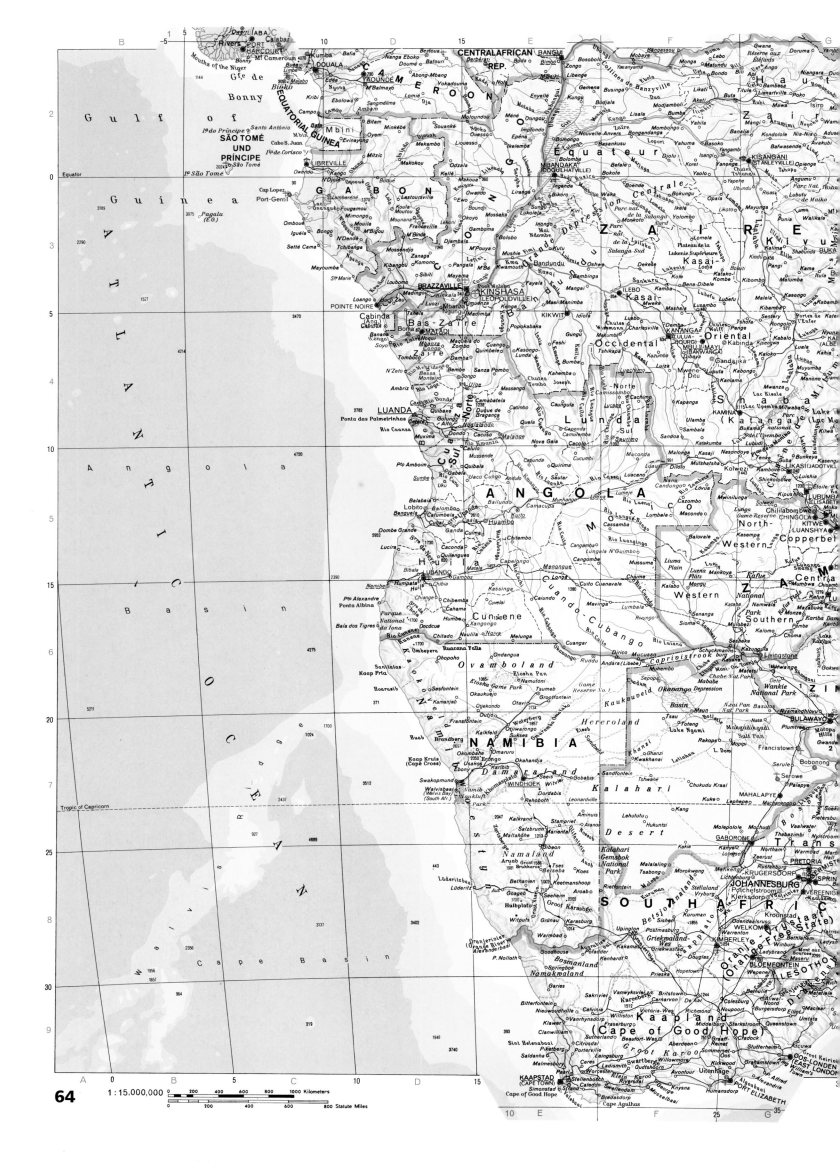

Administrative units in Zimbabwe
1 Matabeleland North   4 Manicaland   7 Mashonaland West
2 Matabeleland South   5 Mashonaland East   8 Midlands
3 Masvingo   6 Mashonaland Central

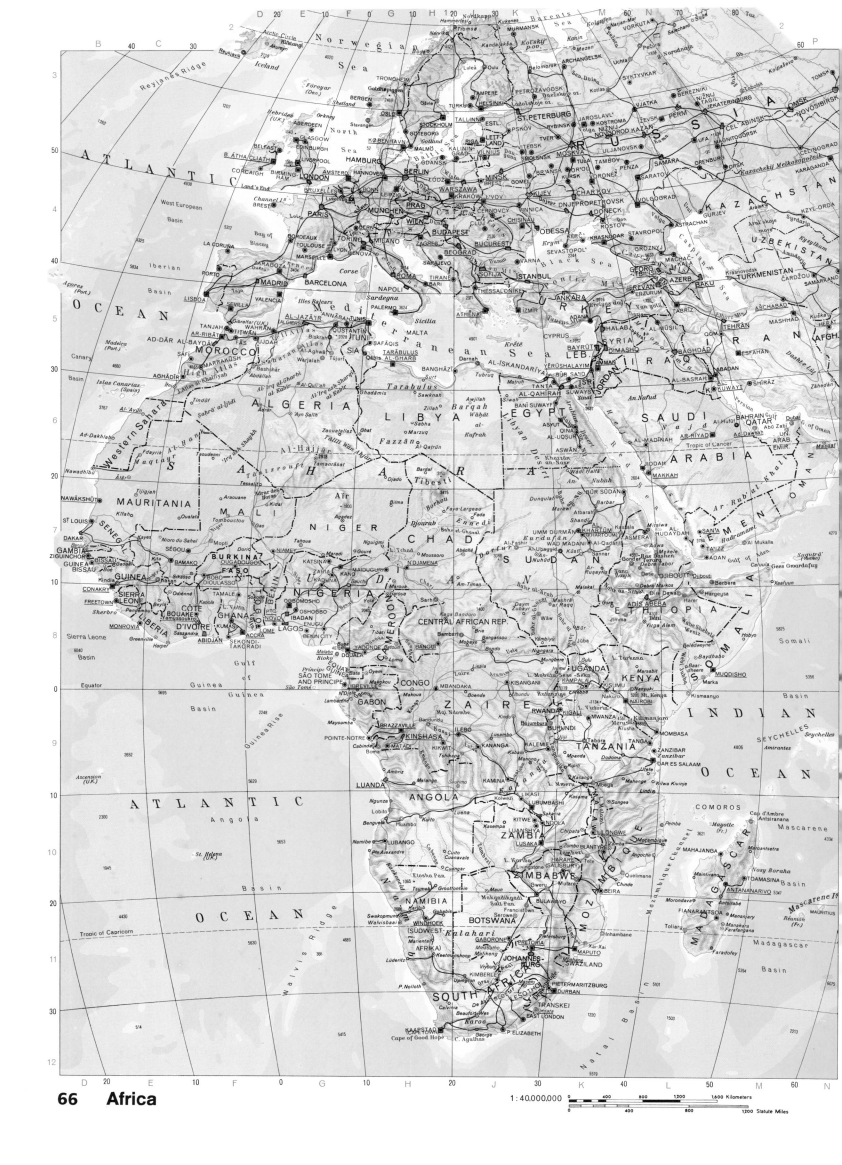

66 **Africa**

1 : 40 000 000

AMERICA

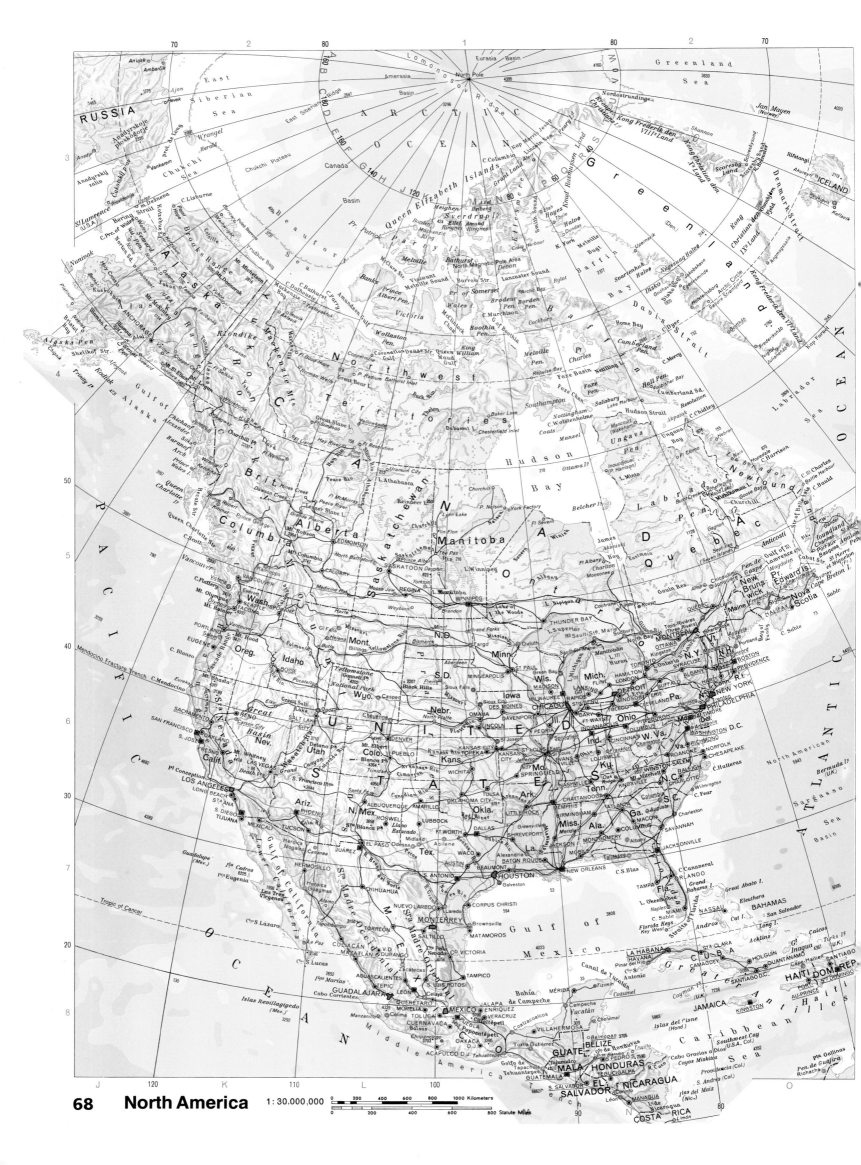

North America   1:30,000,000

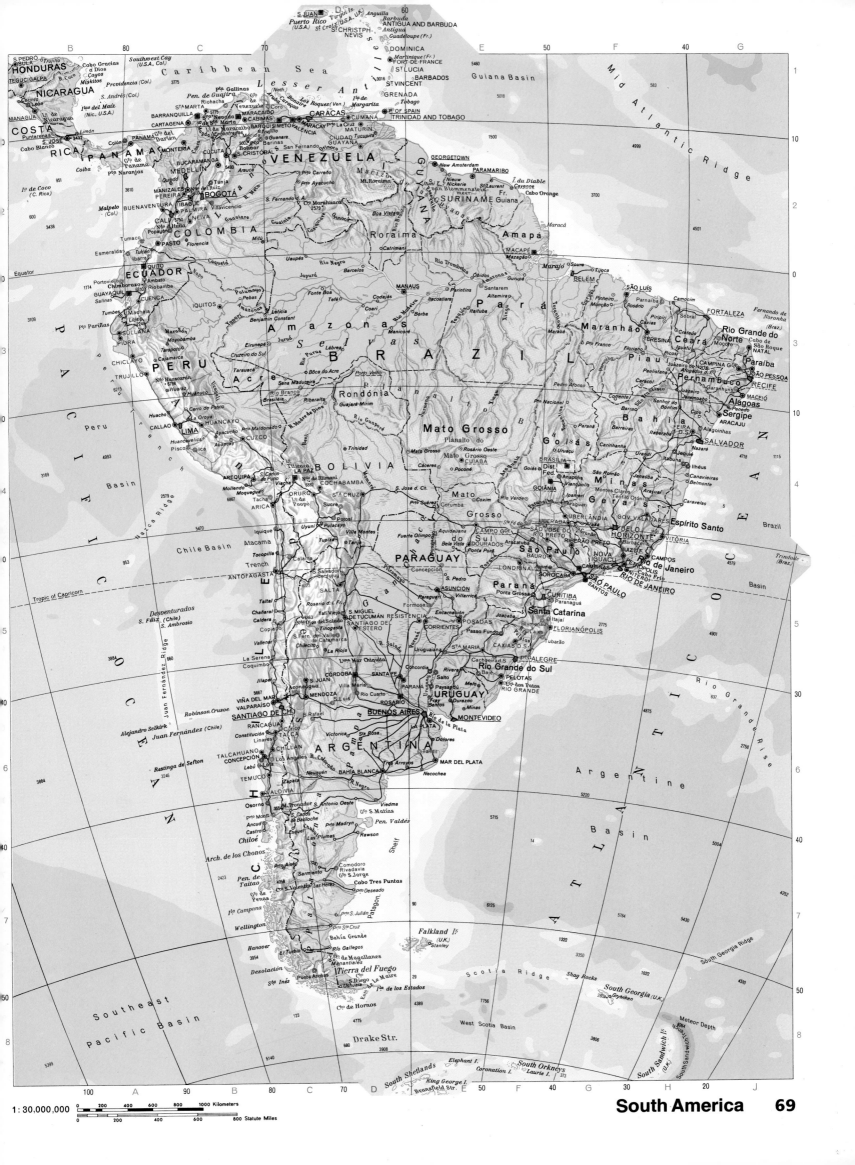

Panama Canal
1:1,000,000

Caribbean Sea

PACIFIC OCEAN

72   1:15,000,000

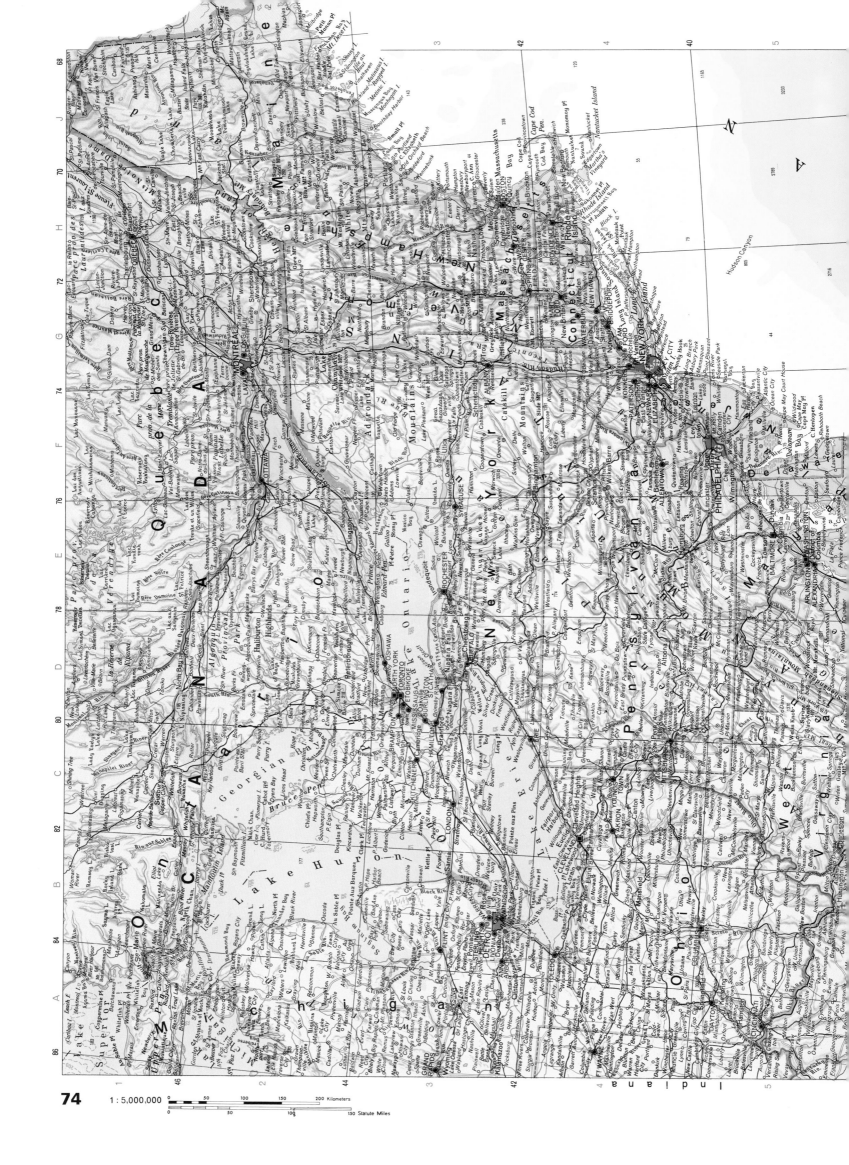

1 : 5,000,000

50   100   150   200 Kilometers

0   50   100   150 Statute Miles

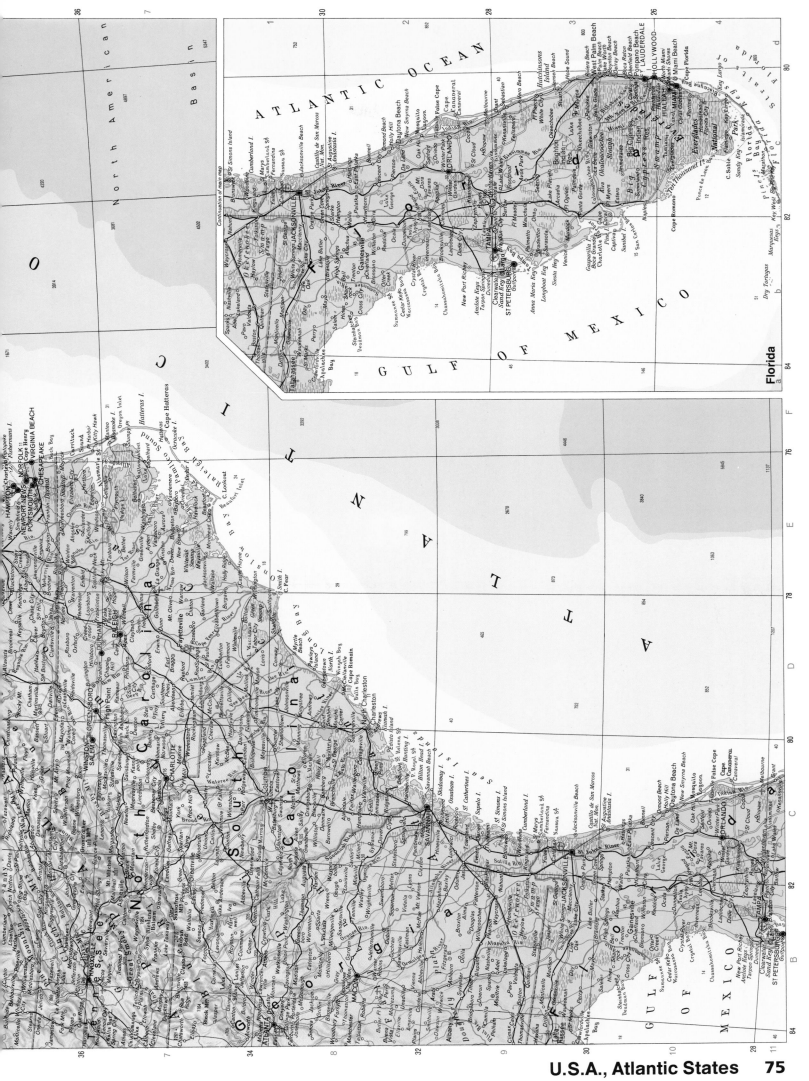

1 : 5,000,000

0   50   100   150   200 Kilometers

0   50   100

150 Statute Miles

Northern South America 79

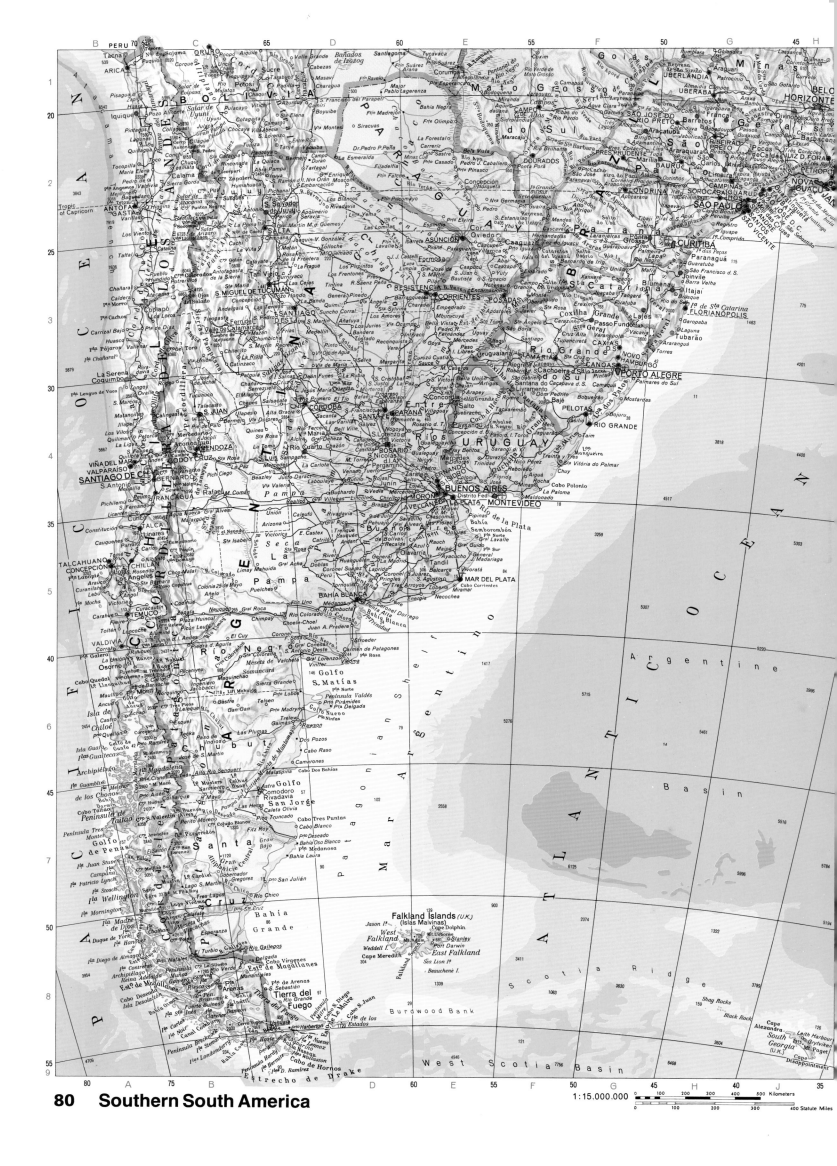

80 **Southern South America**

1:15,000,000

THE EARTH
Its Continents and Countries

The Earth
NATURAL ENVIRONMENT AND BIOSPHERE

Unique in every respect, our planet earth is the only planet in our solar system with an atmosphere containing water. Thus, it alone provides a suitable environment for organic life.

The continents and the surrounding oceans give our planet earth its unmistakable face. The water masses cover around 71 per cent of the total surface area – with oceans taking up 60 percent of the northern hemisphere and even 81 percent of the southern hemisphere. The Pacific alone is larger than all the land masses on earth. Although the individual oceans constitute a single continuous body of water, they vary considerably in terms of salt content, temperature and ocean currents – as well as due to the topographic differences in their ocean beds. This submarine landscape is made up not only of vast seabed plains at a depth of approx. 5,000 metres, but also includes deepsea trenches ringing the Pacific (the deepest point being the Witjas Deep at -11,034 metres within the Mariana Trench) and, above all, it features the largest continuous system of mountain ranges on earth, the Midoceanic Ridge. Wherever these ridges rise above sea-level, we find signs of volcanic activity – such as on Iceland.

As far as the land masses are concerned, the mountain ranges in their various configurations pro-

duce the sharpest contours in the everchanging topography of the continents. Here we distinguish two major forms. On the one hand: the latitudinal chain of mountain ranges from the Pyrenees via the Alps, the Caucasus and the Himalayas to the Southeast Asian chains; on the other hand, the circumpacific mountain ranges interlinked with the alpidic mountain chains in Southeast Asia. Compared with the horizontal dimensions of the earth surface, the mountain ranges and trenches are but faint wrinkles on the face of the planet – the greatest difference in elevation being only some twenty kilometres. The Dead Sea is the lowest visible depression on our planet (-403 m), whereas the bed of Lake Baykal (-1158 m) is actually the lowest point on any continent. The Himalayas rise to an elevation of 8,848 metres at Mount Everest, the highest place on earth; but the largest mountain in terms of its surface area is the Kilimanjaro (5,895 m) in Africa; and, in terms of absolute elevation, the highest mountain is the Chimborazo in Ecuador, rising from an ocean depth of 6,600 metres to 6,310 metres above sea-level.

Enclosed by these high mountain ranges, or flanking them, there are highlands and lowlands of varying widths. They are covered by the planet's major belts of ve-

Centre: »The earth is a shining oasis amidst the infinite vastness of space,« proclaimed one of the astronauts on his return flight from the moon. Without warmth and water, however, that same earth remains desolate, as in the Sahara Desert.

Left: The middle latitudes with their moderate climate are the granaries of the earth. Today industrial farming is a widely practiced form of agriculture in this part of the world.

Right: The German research ship »Polarstern« plowing its way through the earth's ›icy desert‹.

getation, such as the northern coniferous forests, the vernally greening deciduous forests and the tropical rainforests. This is where the large rivers systems, such as the Amazon or the Zaire, arise. These regions, moreover, were the original habitat of that adaptable species: the homo sapiens.

The human population distribution, largely due to regional climatic and topographic differences, is highly uneven. Extremely cold or arid climates make some regions virtually uninhabitable; whereas others with damp, mild climates and fertile soil are densely populated. Latter conditions exist within the moderate or subtropical zones ans in large oases along the major rivers. Initially, a thriving agriculture was responsible for the early development of advanced civilizations in these regions. Although they make up only seven per cent of the total land area, these zones of dense population are inhabited by three quarters of the over five billion human beings. This is also where most of the cities with over a million inhabitants are located: in southern and eastern Asia, in Europe and the eastern half of the United States. Compared to the other centers of agglomeration, the European zone lies remarkably far to the north. This shift can be largely attributed to the favorable influence of the warm North Atlantic stream on the climate of Western Eurasia – even in the remote North.

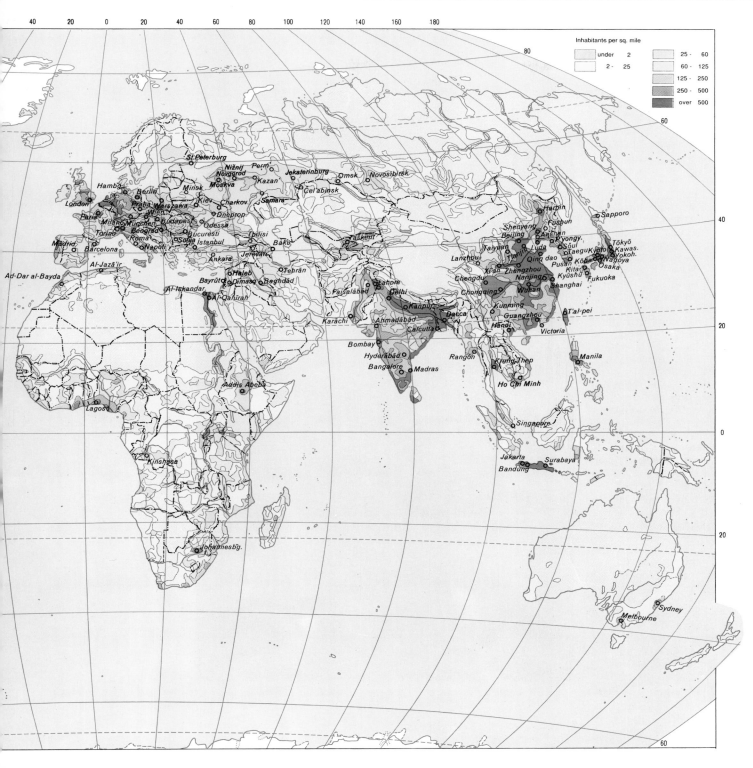

Inhabitants per sq. mile

under 2	25 - 60
2 - 25	60 - 125
	125 - 250
	250 - 500
	over 500

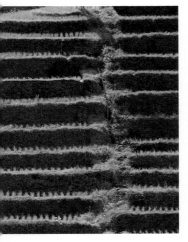

Left: Tulip fields near Amsterdam (Netherlands).

Center: Rice terraces in Southeast Asia. Rice is the major agricultural crop in the world – feeding around a third of the human population.

Right: The Paraguay flows through a forested flood savanna, the Pantanal, a huge swamp area in Southern Brazil.

85

Left: Vast areas of Canada and Alaska in northern North America are deserted. The summers are too short for higher plants to develop.

With conditions more hostile at higher altitudes, some nine tenths of the world population is crowded into the elevation range between zero and 1,000 metres. Conversely, it is only in the tropics that population densities increase at higher altitudes – where the air is less muggy.

Due to the wide range of natural conditions prevailing within the largest countries – such as the former USSR, India, Australia and Egypt – there is also great variance in population density between regions. Generally industrial nations are more densely populated than developing countries, but here, too, India and China are the exceptions. The populations of these two most populous countries in the world alone make up two thirds of the human race.

Since population growth is not linear but exponential – that is, the human race doubles in number within shorter and shorter intervals – the development of the human population is one of mankind's most urgent problems. In order to meet their growing needs – e.g. for food and raw materials – human beings continue to tamper more and more extensively with nature. We do not yet know how far we can tax this planet's resilience – i.e. how much more strain the earth can bear.

Earth Statistics

Surface area: 510,100,934 sqkm

Equatorial circumference: 40,076 km

Meridial circumference: 40,009 km

Equatorial diameter: 12,757 km

Equatorial radius: 6,378 km

Polar radius: 6,357 km

Volume: 1083,000,000,000 ckm

EUROPE

Looking at the map of the earth it seems as if Europe was a subcontinent of the huge land mass of Eurasia. Due to its independent historical and cultural development and distinctive topographic features, Europe is nevertheless considered a separate continent, the smallest populated one.

Its tightly interlocking contours of land and sea, its highly differen-tiated topography, its predominately temperate and mild climate and its central location with respect to the other populated continents are all characteristic features of the Occident. The political fragmentation and cultural differentiation – manifest, for example, in the former division of the continent into two opposing political and ideological blocs – are also typical.

Europe
NATURAL ENVIRONMENT

The second smallest continent on earth is also the lowest, with an average elevation of only 300 metres. The marginal seas of the Atlantic, such as the North Sea, the Baltic Sea and the Mediterranean penetrate deeply into the continent. Europe, due to the large number of peninsulas and islands, has nearly 40,000 kilometres of coastline.

The traditional demarcation line between Europe and Asia runs from the Ural Mountains along the Ural River and the northern edge of the Caucasus, through the Bosporos to the Dardanelles.

The topography of the continent is characterized by a diversity of landscapes within a small area. A chain of mountains stretching from the Pyrenees via the Alps (Montblanc, 4,807 m) to the Balkans separates Southern Europe from the rest of the continent.

From time immemorial, however, people have discovered numerous passes, using these chinks in the wall of mountains to maintain close ties with the inhabitants on the other side. Enclosed within the young mountain chains of the Mediterranean region, we find old continental masses like the mesetas in Spain and young lowlands like the Po Plain. The western and central European peneplain spreading out north of the Alps is made up of ›broken-up‹ bevelled uplands. This landscape's abundance of forms is further enhanced by the various manifestations of former volcanic activity: the volcanic columns in the French central massif, the volcanic lakes in the Eifel Mountains, the lava caps in Vogelsberg and the rounded basaltic cupolas in the Rhön.

The western, central and eastern European lowland, the most uniform and expansive landscape in Europe, fans out to the east. Its broad glacial valleys, the chains of hilly terminal moraines and the rounded ground moraines were all caused by the glaciers which reshaped the region during the Ice Ages (approx. 600,000 to 12,000 years ago).

Scandinavia's sharply indented fjord coastline, the Scandinavian »fjells« (Glittertind 2,472 m), the skerry coast and the Finnish lake-filled lowland plain are also products of ice-age remodelling. Dur-

ing the Ice Ages over half of the European region was reshaped by glacial activity!

Located within the Northern Temperate Zone with exposure to the Atlantic Ocean, Europe – with the exception of the North – has an extraordinarily favorable climate. Besides providing Europe with sufficient moisture, the Atlantic Stream with its northern-most branch, the Gulf Stream, and the west-wind drift have the effect of ›shifting‹ the cool-to-warm Variable Zone northward to include the continent. There are nevertheless noticable differences in climate between the north and the south, the east and the west. The seasonal temperature variation increases as one moves East: from the even Atlantic climate of Western Europe with its mild winters and cool summers to the continental climate of Eastern Europe with its typical hot summers and very cold winters. Hot, predominately dry summers and mild, damp winters are characteristic of the subtropical climate in southern Europe.

One remarkable feature of European climates is distinctive local

Page 87: Schönbrunn Palace, the 18th-century imperial summer residence in Vienna, surrounded by a splendid palace park.

Above: North Sea lighthouse amidst mud-flats which dry up each time the tide goes out. The mud-flats are scored with an even grid of »Gruppen«, or ditches.

Far left: Tuscany, one of the most colorful landscapes in the world.

Top left: View of Mount Watzmann (2,713 m) in the Salzburg Alps.

Bottom left: Iceland, the Island of Fire and Ice, is composed entirely of volcanic rock. Hot springs are scattered throughout the island.

Right: Since prehistoric time men have been cutting the fine-grained stone in the famous Carrara (Tuscany) marble quarries at the foot of the Apuanic Alps.

winds; e.g. the Alpine föhn, the mistral of the Lower Rhone Valley or the bora in Yugoslavia and the etesia in the Aegean region. Before humans began to settle here, the continent was largely covered by forests. Today, the only uninterrupted belt of coniferous forest lies north of the 60th parallel – where the unfavorable climate prevents any other utilization of the land. Land cultivation has displaced the mixed woodlands throughout the rest of Europe except on the wooded mountain ridges. In the Mediterranean region, however, these ridges generally bear a secondary vegetation of sclerophyllous evergreens.

Although not the longest European river, the Rhine is certainly the major economic artery, because it connects several industrial areas before emptying into the North Sea; whereas the Danube and the Volga flow into the »remote« Black Sea.

Above: Rügen, the largest German island in the Baltic Sea, is surrounded on all sides by steep, chalky cliffs battered by the sea.

Cultivated land (arable land, plantations and irrigated land)

Grassland of the temperate zone

Forest of the temperate zone (predominant exploitation of forest)

Mediterranean scrub (Maquis; partly low trees with leathery leaves)

Semi-desert and desert

Tundra, fell and swamp taiga

Rock, snow and ice areas of mountain regions

1:15 000 000

0   100   200   300   400   500 km

Europe
PEOPLE AND CULTURE

Unlike all other continents, Europe is very evenly populated. With an average of 66 inhabitants per square kilometre, it is one of the most densely populated regions in the world. Except in Eastern Europe, the terrain is tightly structured – which explains the variety of different peoples inhabiting the region. 120 languages are spoken across this small continent – forty of them in the Caucasus alone. Over thirty countries have evolved in Europe. The powerful forces emanating from the »hotbed of human activity« on this planet have had a crucial affect on all the other continents: the colonization of nearly all the so-called southern continents; the settlement of the »New World«; industrialization and mechanization; and the dissemination of religions, ideologies and European civilization. In the course of discovering and conquering the world, the Europeans spread their languages to all parts of the globe. 95 per cent of all Europeans speak Romance, Germanic or Slavic languages – 7 of these being world languages spoken by over 50 million people: English, French, Spanish, Russian, German, Portuguese and Italian. Even after their independence many former colonies have kept English or French as their official languages. Portuguese or Spanish are spoken throughout South and Central America. In most parts of the world, European technical terms are widely used in technology and banking.

The europeanization of the earth has been closely connected with the spreading of European religions. In Europe proper (without the former Soviet Union) about half the population belongs to the Roman Catholic Church, around a quarter to the Protestant and about one tenth to one of the various Orthodox Churches. As the center of world Catholicism, Rome is the site of both the politically independent Vatican State and St. Peter's, the largest ecclesiastical building in the world. The church buildings from the various architectural periods are distinctive features in the skylines of most European cities. Aside from villages, towns are the typical form of settlement in Europe. Some were erected on ancient foundations. Others simply evolved out of trading settlements, grew in the shelter of forts or were established by royal incorporation during the Middle Ages – then expanded and changed during the period of industrialization. They have always, however, served as the economic and cultural centers of the various states. They also cover a considerable portion, nearly three per cent, of the entire land area of Europe.

For centuries Europe was the dominant economic center of the world. With fertile soils and a mild climate favorable to intensive cultivation, a large portion of the total land area could be made agri-

Top left: Prague with the former royal castle, Hradschin, (now the seat of the President of Czechoslovakia) and the Gothic St. Vitus Cathedral overlooking the Vitava River.

Lower left: Malbork (German: Marienburg) on the Nogat. The castle, once occupied by the Teutonic Order, dominates the town.

Top right: St. Petersburg is famous for its baroque (here: Smolny Cloister) and classicist architecture.

Bottom right: The 16th-century Basilius Cathedral dominates the southern end of the Red Square in Moscow, the capital of Russia.

Netherlands
Koninkrijk der Nederlanden

Amsterdam

41.548 sqkm

Pop.: 14.560.000

Dutch (in Friesland Province: Frisian)

Dutch Guilder

Belgium,
Royaume de Belgique Koninkrijk België

Brussels

30.518 sqkm

Pop.: 9.910.000

French, Dutch, German

Belgian Franc

Luxembourg
Grand-Duché de Luxembourg Grousherzogdem Letzebuerg

Luxembourg

2.586 sqkm

Pop.: 370.000

Luxembourgian, French, German

Luxembourgian Franc

France
République Française

Paris

547.026 sqkm (incl. Corsica, w/o overseas territorities)

Pop.: 55.390.000

French (German, Breton, Basque Corsican and other regional languages)

French Franc

Germany
Bundesrepublik Deutschland

Berlin

357.040 sqkm

Pop.: 77.811.000

German (partially school language in Schleswig-Holstein: Danish; by a regional minority: Sorbian)

Deutsche Mark

Poland
Rzeczpospolita Polska

Warsaw

312.683 sqkm

Pop.: 37.660.000

Polish

Zloty

Czechoslovakia
Česká a Slovenská Federativní Republika

Prague

127.869 sqkm

Pop.: 15.570.000

Czech, Slovak

Czech koruna

93

culturally productive. Other assets were abundant mineral resources, convenient means of transportation and a population trained in a tradition of skilled craftsmanship. These factors all contributed to the evolution of the first major center of industrial production in the world: within the triangle between the English Midlands, Paris and the Ruhr area. Other industrial centers were to follow, such as the Ukraine, Upper Silesia and Northern Italy.

The various European countries are divided up into groups according to geographic location.

Central Europe includes the German-speaking countries Germany, Switzerland and Austria. As a whole this area, with its high degree of industrialization and increasing urbanization, is comparable to the Northeastern United States or Japan.

Because of their location and historic development Hungary, Czechoslovakia and Poland are considered part of Eastern Central Europe, which also includes the Baltic states Estonia, Latvia and Lithuania – now that they have broken away from the former Soviet Union.

The Western European countries are all strongly oriented toward the Atlantic and the adjoining seas. They largely owe their former status, in fact, as mother countries of colonial empires to this geographic blessing. France, the Benelux states (Belgium, the Netherlands and Luxembourg), Great Britain and Ireland make up this »Atlantic Europe«. The cosmopolitan cities Paris and London have remained important centers of culture, the insurance business, commerce and major finance to this day.

Southern Europe comprises the co-called Mediterranean countries: Portugal and Spain on the Iberian Peninsula, Italy on the Apennine Peninsula and Greece. Owing to the favorable Mediterranean climate and the physical heritage of their rich past, mass and educational tourism together are a dominant economic factor in these countries.

In Southern Europe there is a marked contrast between population centers with their urban culture and the agrarian regions with open and concealed unemployment. In Italy this has given rise to a conflict between

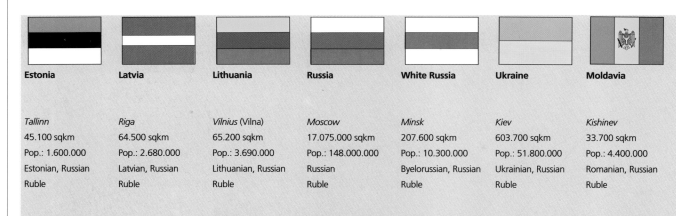

Estonia	Latvia	Lithuania	Russia	White Russia	Ukraine	Moldavia
Tallinn	Riga	Vilnius (Vilna)	Moscow	Minsk	Kiev	Kishinev
45.100 sqkm	64.500 sqkm	65.200 sqkm	17.075.000 sqkm	207.600 sqkm	603.700 sqkm	33.700 sqkm
Pop.: 1.600.000	Pop.: 2.680.000	Pop.: 3.690.000	Pop.: 148.000.000	Pop.: 10.300.000	Pop.: 51.800.000	Pop.: 4.400.000
Estonian, Russian	Latvian, Russian	Lithuanian, Russian	Russian	Byelorussian, Russian	Ukrainian, Russian	Romanian, Russian
Ruble	Ruble	Ruble	Ruble	Ruble	Ruble	Ruble

Top: One result of German Unification: the Reichstag Building in Berlin (built by Paul Wallot) is again available for sessions of the Bundestag, the German parliament.

Center left: Even today Iceland lives to a large extent from fishing and whaling.

Center right: Istanbul (Constantinople, Byzantium) sprawls on the hills to either side of the Bosporus.

Top right: 384 metres long and built from 1840-49, this chain bridge in Budapest is still considered a technical masterpiece. It connects Buda on the right bank of the Danube with the newer district, Pest.

Lower right: The Holstentor in the old Hanseatic city of Lübeck – located in the Holstein-Mecklenburg hills country. The gate, erected from 1466-78, is a typical example of Northern German brick Gothic architecture.

the industrial North and the agrarian Mezzogiorno South – the upshot being the migration of workers to the industrial areas in Northern Italy and Central Europe. Southeastern Europe is a diverse mosaic of peoples, confessions and states. As a result, the region is considered the »European powderkeg« – where hatred and prejudice keep rekindling century-old conflicts. The collapse of Communist rule in Yugoslavia, Albania, Bulgaria and Rumania in 1989/1990 sparked the revival of ancient Balkan conflicts: the most dramatic example being the civil war between Serbs, Croatians and Slovenes, and the resulting disintegration of the Yugoslavian multi-national state. The border between Slovenia and Bosnia-Herzegovena marks an old cultural boundary: the region to the north and west was proselytized

Right: The Campanile (12th century), or »Leaning Tower« of Pisa, is over four metres askew.

Sunflowers are grown as a source of oil, as green fodder and as ornamental plants. The plant attains heights of up to 3.5 metres. Its seeds contain lecithin and cholesterine, as well as protein and fat.

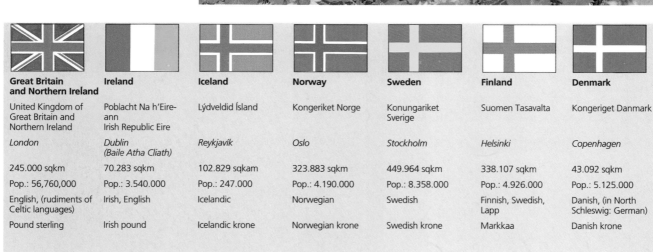

Great Britain and Northern Ireland	Ireland	Iceland	Norway	Sweden	Finland	Denmark
United Kingdom of Great Britain and Northern Ireland	Poblacht Na h'Eire-ann Irish Republic Eire	Lýdveldid Ísland	Kongeriket Norge	Konungariket Sverige	Suomen Tasavalta	Kongeriget Danmark
London	*Dublin (Baile Atha Cliath)*	*Reykjavík*	*Oslo*	*Stockholm*	*Helsinki*	*Copenhagen*
245.000 sqkm	70.283 sqkm	102.829 sqkam	323.883 sqkm	449.964 sqkm	338.107 sqkm	43.092 sqkm
Pop.: 56,760,000	Pop.: 3.540.000	Pop.: 247.000	Pop.: 4.190.000	Pop.: 8.358.000	Pop.: 4.926.000	Pop.: 5.125.000
English, (rudiments of Celtic languages)	Irish, English	Icelandic	Norwegian	Swedish	Finnish, Swedish, Lapp	Danish, (in North Schleswig: German)
Pound sterling	Irish pound	Icelandic krone	Norwegian krone	Swedish krone	Markkaa	Danish krone

by Rome before coming under Central European influence until the last century, as part of the Austro-Hungarian Empire. Initially under Eastern Roman rule, the region to the south and east later fell to the Islamic Ottoman Empire. To fend off this Ottoman threat, a wide strip of fortified farms was set up along the »military border« between the two spheres of control – farmed by armed Croatian and Serbian refugees. Even today a diverse array of separate social groups lives side by side within this small area.

During the national wars of liberation against the Turks which began in 1804, Orthodox Christians fought against Moslems, during the Balkan Wars of 1912/1913 the Serbs and Bulgarians battled on opposing sides and during the Second World War the Catholic Croatians clashed with Orthodox

Top right: Sevilla, the southern Spanish port on the Guadalquivir and the old capital of Andalusia, was once the center of trade with the Americans. The heritage of that period includes an array of prestigious buildings – like these here on Plaza de España at the edge of the expansive Parque de Maria Luisa.

Below: The Tower of Belém is the symbol of Lisbon, the capital of Portugal. To defend the entrance to the harbor, it was built in Emanuel style from 1515-21.

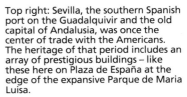

Spain	Andorra
Reino de España	Principat d'Andorra Principauté d'Andorra Principado de Andorra
Madrid	*Andorra la Vella*
504.782 sqkm	453 sqkm
Pop.: 38.830.000	Pop.: 45.000
Spanish (Castilian), Catalan, Galician, Basque	Catalan, French, Spanish
Peseta	Peseta French Franc

Serbs. Today, the bloody rifts crisscrossing the Balkans seem insurmountable.
Rumania, Albania and Bulgaria have their own smouldering minority conflicts. Is a disintegrating Yugoslavia merely the first in a series of regional conflicts to shake the Balkans?
Eastern Europe encompasses the area of White Russia, the Ukraine, Moldavia and Russia – whose remaining territory also makes up all of northern Asia. Prior to the tremendous upheavals in Eastern Europe in 1989/1990, the largest state in the world was controlled from Moscow with the Kremlin being the central seat of Soviet power. Moscow was also the headquarters of a number of central authorities both of the former Soviet Union and of the former »Eastern bloc« countries.

An old city in the province of North Holland, Alkmaar is known for the long tradition of its cheese market, which is held at the old town scales every Friday from ten to twelve a.m. (May through September).

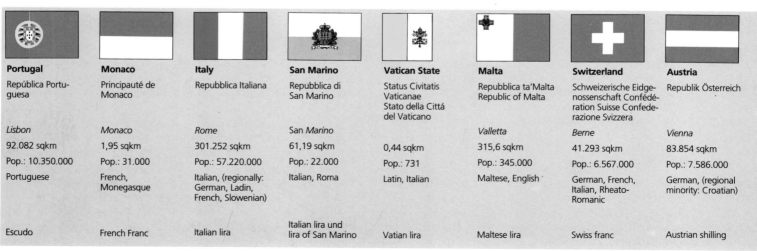

Portugal	Monaco	Italy	San Marino	Vatican State	Malta	Switzerland	Austria
República Portuguesa	Principauté de Monaco	Repubblica Italiana	Repubblica di San Marino	Status Civitatis Vaticanae Stato della Città del Vaticano	Repubblica ta'Malta Republic of Malta	Schweizerische Eidgenossenschaft Confédération Suisse Confederazione Svizzera	Republik Österreich
Lisbon	Monaco	Rome	San Marino		Valletta	Berne	Vienna
92.082 sqkm	1,95 sqkm	301.252 sqkm	61,19 sqkm	0,44 sqkm	315,6 sqkm	41.293 sqkm	83.854 sqkm
Pop.: 10.350.000	Pop.: 31.000	Pop.: 57.220.000	Pop.: 22.000	Pop.: 731	Pop.: 345.000	Pop.: 6.567.000	Pop.: 7.586.000
Portuguese	French, Monegasque	Italian, (regionally: German, Ladin, French, Slowenian)	Italian, Roma	Latin, Italian	Maltese, English	German, French, Italian, Rheato-Romanic	German, (regional minority: Croatian)
Escudo	French Franc	Italian lira	Italian lira und lira of San Marino	Vatian lira	Maltese lira	Swiss franc	Austrian shilling

Before the »Silent Revolution« and the overthrow of the Communist Party in 1990, a monolithic political and economic system had held the former Soviet Union together. Since its disintegration all the republics of the former state have declared their independence and united to form the Community of Independent States (CIS).

The location of one of the oldest industrial regions in Russia on both sides of the Ural Mountain Range – i.e. the European and the Asian slopes – clearly demonstrates how immaterial the ›boundary‹ between Europe and Asia was in the former Soviet Union, let alone in the Russia of today.

Northern Europe includes the countries Norway, Sweden, Finland and, because of its old historic affiliation, Denmark. It is the most sparsely populated portion

Top: These neat town houses are typical of Flanders. In the Middle Ages its textile industry and trade made this Belgian province on the North Sea Coast one of the wealthiest regions in Europe.

Bottom: Snowbound alpine cabins. The buildings are only used during the summer when the cattle is driven up to the alpine pastures.

Lower right: Loch Maree in Scotland (loch meaning 'lake' or 'bay' in Scottish Gaelic). The lake fills a basin enclosed by a soft rounded ridges.

Liechtenstein	Hungary	Yugoslavia	Slovenia	Croatia	Bosnia-Herzegovina
Fürstentum Liechtenstein	Magyar Köztársaság	Socijalisticka Federativna Republika Jugoslavija			
Vaduz	Budapest	Belgrade	Ljubljana	Zagreb	Sarajevo
160 sqkm	93.032 sqkm	127.886 sqkm	20.251 sqkm	56.538 sqkm	51.129 sqkm
Pop. 28.000	Pop.: 10.610.000	Pop.: 12.775.000	Pop.: 1.890.000	Pop.: 4.467.000	Pop.: 4.278.000
German	Madjarish (Hungarian)	Serbian, Macedonian, Albanian (other minority languages)	Slovenian	Croatian	Serbo-Croatian
Swiss Franc	Forint	Dinar	Dinar	Dinar	Dinar

On its lower reaches in the Rhone-Alpes region, the Ardeche (a right tributary of the Rhone) has carved deeply into the massive layers of limestone, creating this picturesque gorge. The Ardeche is popular with canoers.

of Europe. Until recently rich deposits of iron ore, an abundance of wood and rich fishing grounds were the lifeblood of this region. Today, however, the inhabitants have come to depend more and more on Norway's oil reserves and on the processing industries. For the inhabitants of Iceland, the »Island of Fire and Ice«, fishing provides still the main livelihood.

Istanbul and its hinterland are actually located on the European continent – with a bridge only recently connecting them to Asia Minor. Because of its cultural differences, however, Turkey is not considered a part of Europe.

Albania	**Rumania**	**Bulgaria**	**Greece**	**Cyprus**
Republika Popullóre Socialiste e Shqipërisë	Republica România	Republika Bǎlgarija	Helleniki Demokratia	Kypriaki Dimokratia Kibris Cumhuriyeti Republik of Cyprus
Tirana	*Bukarest*	*Sofia*	*Athens*	*Nikosia*
28.746 sqkm	237.500 sqkm	110.912 sqkm	131.944 sqkm	9.251 sqkm
Pop.: 3.080.000.	Pop.: 23.170.000	Pop.: 8.950.000	Pop.: 9.970.000	Pop.: 670.000
Albanian	Rumanian, (colloquial minority languages)	Bulgarian, (colloquial minority languages)	Greek (modern Greek)	Greek, Turkish, English
Lek	Leu	Lew	Drachme	Cypriot pound

ASIA

This »Giant among the Continents« covers almost a third of the earth's land surface. More people live here than on all other continents combined. From the western to the eastern end of Asia, there are eleven time zones. Its territory includes every type of climatic and vegetation zone: from perpetual ice to tropical rain forests. Asia is a continent of superlatives – boasting the mightiest mountain range and the highest peak, the most landlocked region and the largest area undrained by rivers; but also a unique diversity of peoples, religions and cultures: with the most populous country in the world, with wealthy industrial nations and miserably poor developing countries.

Asia
NATURAL ENVIRONMENT

At an average elevation of 925 metres, Asia is the highest continent on earth. With islands and peninsulas making up a quarter of its total surface area, it has over 70,000 kilometres of coastline. Asia stretches 11,000 kilometres from west to east, 8,500 from north to south. Piercing the isthmus between the Mediterranean and the Red Sea, the Suez Canal is considered the boundary between Asia and Africa. The dividing line between Asia and Europe runs along the Ural Mountains, the Ural River, the Caspian Sea, the northern edge of the Caucasus, the Black Sea through the Bosporos and the Dardanelles to the Aegean Sea. This division is highly arbitrary, however, since large parts of Northern Asia have strong political and cultural ties with Eastern Europe. For the better part of this century, in fact, these countries – now members of the Community of Independent States (CIS) – were parts of the one nation: the Soviet Union.

The European mountain chains extend by way of the Mediterranean islands to Asia, where they converge at the Ararat (5,156 m) and in the clusters of mountains in the Hindukush and Pamir (7,495 m) – enclosing the highlands of Anatolia, Iran and Tibet – before finally extending into the Indo-Chinese Peninsula. Covering some eight million square kilometres, the inner Asian mountain block – including the Himalayas with the tallest mountain in the world, Mount Everest (8,848 m) – is the largest raised land mass on earth. To the south the topography changes, giving rise to the tablelands of Arabia and Southeast Asia. To the east, the continent drops away in several steps to the Pacific. The arched garlands of islands fringing the coast are bordered by deep-sea trenches (Mariana Trench: -11,022 m). Separating individual seas from the open Pacific, the Kurils, Japan, the Ryukyu (Nansei) Islands, the Philippines and Indonesia are all part of the Pacific »Ring of Fire«. The earthquakes and volcanic eruptions (Fujisan 3,776 m) caused by the shifting earth's crust in this tectonicly active zone are a threat to human life.

East of the Ural, the vast expanses of western Siberian lowland are broken up by the central Siberian mountains and the eastern Siberian mountain range.

Mighty rivers issuing from the Central Asian mountains flow in all directions. In most of these rivers, the discharge fluctuates considerably throughout the year. The rivers of Siberia (Ob/Irtysch, Jenissej, Lena) drain into the Arc-

Page 101: Indian street scene at sunset. The sari, a wrapped garment frequently made of silk, is the typical dress of Indian women.

Lower left: The cones and spires of the karst landscape along the Li River near Guilin in subtropical southern China.

Center: With its blossom and multiple fruits (bunches), this is how bananas grow in tropical countries all over the world.

Lower right: The harvesting of natural latex, the thickened milky liquid of the rubber tree, which grows to a height of 30 metres.

tic Sea. With thaws setting in earlier in the south than in the north, huge floods are regular events. The Amur, the Huang, the Chang Jiang (or Yangtze) and the Mekong empty into the Pacific; the Brahmaputra, Ganges and Indus rivers, the Euphrates and Tigris flow into the Indian Ocean. With an area of 370,000 square kilometres, the Caspian Sea is the largest undrained lake on earth. The Dead Sea is the lowest visible point on earth (-400 m), and Baykal Lake is the largest freshwater lake in Asia with a depth of 1,620 metres.

Their distance from the nearest ocean and their location in the lee side of huge chains of mountains are the causes of the deserts at the edge of or within the Central

Top: Nepal, a kingdom on the southern slope of the Himalayas, is the country with the largest number of mountains over 8,000 metres.

Lower left: Ladakh, the mountainous region between the Himalayas and the Karakorum, lies on either side of the upper Indus. Livestock is the main source of livelihood, since irrigated agriculture is only possible in some of the lower valleys.

Lower right: Palm grove in Malaysia.

Asian Massif; e.g., the Kyzyl-Kum, the Gobi (or Shamo) or the Takla-makan in the Tarim Basin. Tropical deserts like those in Arabia, on the other hand, developed from tropic deserts. Whereas winter rains are features of Asia Minor's Mediterranean climate, the climate in Southern and Eastern Asia is dominated by monsoons: the southwestern monsoon bringing summer rains, the northeastern monsoon winter dryness. The largest rainfall of 10,800 millimetres was measured in Cherrapunji (India). With its varying climatic zones, Asian is covered by the following belts of vegetation: northern Asia with its distinctly continental climate is covered with tundra in the North, followed by a belt of coniferous forests, then by steppes and desert areas. The deciduous and mixed forests of ancient China have been almost entirely cleared, as have the Indian monsoon forests. Large areas of Indonesia are still covered with rain forest.

Top: Loess landscape near Yenan in northern China. The river has gouged deep valleys with steep walls, whereas the higher slopes have been terraced. Erosion is a major problem in China.

Bottom: Camel market in Rajastan (India).

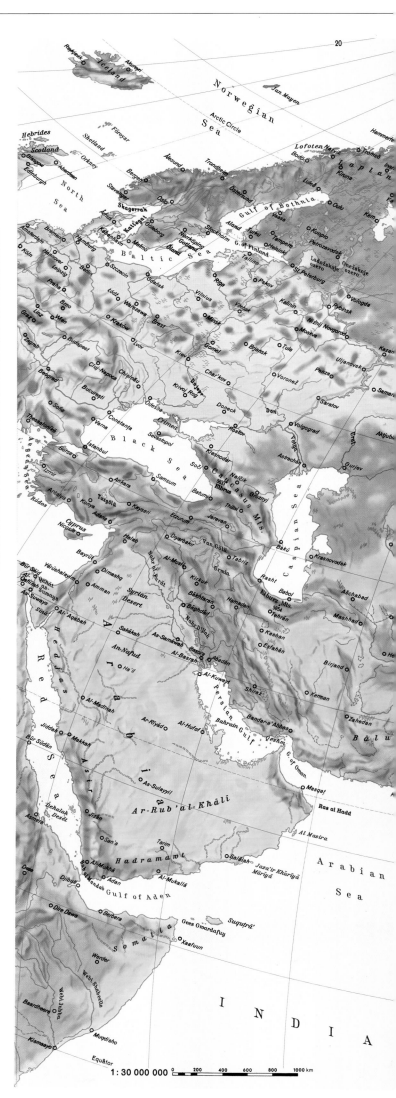

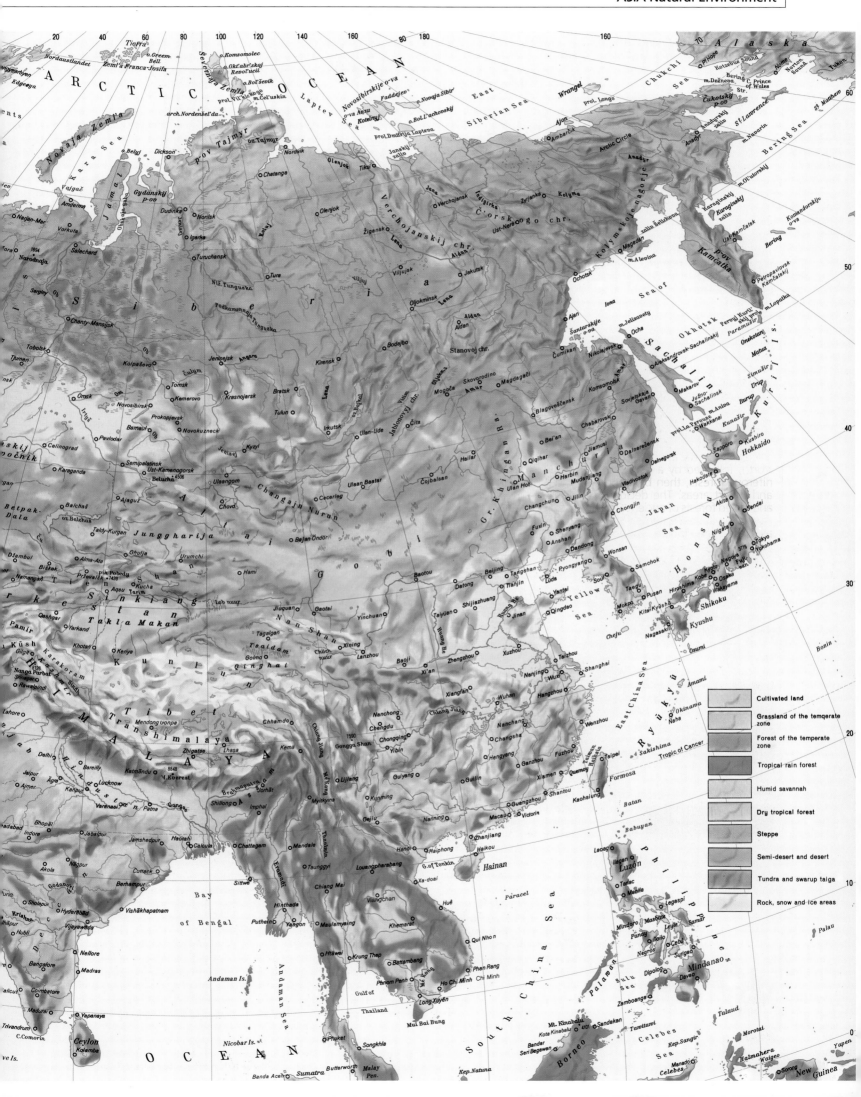

Cultivated land

Grassland of the temqerate zone

Forest of the temperate zone

Tropical rain forest

Humid savannah

Dry tropical forest

Steppe

Semi-desert and desert

Tundra and swarup taiga

Rock, snow and ice areas

Asia
PEOPLE AND CULTURE

Asia's cultural diversity and its colorful mosaic of ethnic and racial groups are the result of a long historical process. In Asia one can encounter almost every cultural stage in the history of human evolution: from the game hunters in the subarctic North (Archaic Siberians) to the nomads in the arid regions to the land-cultivating peoples of Mesopotamia, India, East Asia and the East Indies.

In Asia, the average population density is 65 inhabitants per square kilometre. On a continent with such varied topography, however, this does not tell us very much about the actual population distribution. In the tundra or taiga with their permafrost, in the vast desert regions of India and Central Asia, in the mountainous regions or rain forests of Southeast Asia, for example, the population density is extremely low. Yet Asia is also the continent with largest densely-populated agricultural regions in the world. 90 per cent

	Georgia	Armenia	Azerbaijan	Kazakhstan	Uzbekistan	Turkmenistan	Kirgiziya	Tadzhikistan
	Tbilisi (Tiflis)	Erevan	Baku	Alma Ata	Tashkent	Ashkhabad	Pishpek (Frunze)	Dushanbe
	69.700 sqkm	29.800 sqkm	86.600 sqkm	2.717.300 sqkm	447.400 sqkm	488.100 sqkm	198.500 sqkm	143.100 sqkm
	Pop.: 5.500.000	Pop.: 3.300.000	Pop.: 7.100.000	Pop.: 16.700.000	Pop.: 20.300.000	Pop.: 3.600.000	Pop.: 4.400.000	Pop.: 5.200.000
	Georgian, Russian	Armenian, Russian	Azerbaijani, Russian	Kazakh, Russian	Uzbek, Russian	Turkoman, Russian	Kirgisian, Russian	Tadzhik, Uzbek, Russian
	Ruble	Ruble	Ruble	Ruble	Ruble	Ruble	Ruble	Ruble

of all Asians – that is, nearly three fifths of the world population – live on a mere third of the continent's surface area: the fertile plains and estuaries of the large rivers between the Indus and the Huang. In the last 300 years alone, the population here has grown to five times its size. This silent »explosion« – the combined result of traditionally high birth rates and advances in medical care – is so dramatic that by the year 2000 this region will be inhabited by some 3,5 billion Asians! So far family-planning programs have been successful only in Japan, Singapore and, to some extent, in China. There are already 70 cities in Asia with populations of over a million – after only 13 in 1935. The majority of population, however, still subsists on agriculture and, hence, lives in the country. Only around one fifth of the total area of Asia is cultivated – the al-

pine regions, deserts, tundras, marshes and forests are all non-arable land.

Struggling with the elements, farmers were forced to irrigate fields artificially or control flooding, to organize and intensify their efforts. This process, leading to the development of the first of Asia's advanced civilizations, took place around 4000 B.C. wherever soils were good and climates favorable: e.g. within the Near Eastern »fertile crescent« – including the large-scale oases along the Euphrates and Tigris rivers – that crescent-shaped arc joining Asia and Africa, which stretches from the Persian Gulf via Mesopotamia, Syria and Palestine to the Nile Valley. Or in Hither India, a subcontinent separated from the rest of Asia by towering mountain ranges where the monsoon-belt agriculture is dictated by the biannual succession of dry and rainy

Far left: Buddhism, the world religion, was founded by Buddha (560-480 B.C.) in northern India. It then spread to China and Japan, Ceylon and Southeast Asia, as well as to the Himalayan countries.

Top center: Female tea pickers.

Center: A boy at a candy stand in Sri Lanka (Ceylon).

Top right: A cremation in India. Hindus believe that the soul continues to roam about after death until it has found redemption throuth purification.

Lower right: The Omar Mosque or Rock Dome, finished in 691. To followers of Islam, it is one of the most important shrines in Jerusalem – the Holy City of Jews, Christians and Moslems alike.

Turkey	**Syria**	**Lebanon**	**Israel**	**Jordan**	**Iraq**	**Iran**
Türkiye Cumhuriyeti	El Dschamhurija el Arabija es Surija	El Dschumhurija el Lubnanija	Medinat Yisrael	Al Mamlakah Al Urdunniyah Al Hashimiyah	Al Dschumhurijah al Iraqija ad Dimukratija asch-Sha'abija	Dschumhuri-i-Islami Iran
Ankara	*Damascus*	*Beirut*	*Jerusalem*	*Amman*	*Bagdad*	*Teheran*
780.576 sqkm	185.180 sqkm	10.400 sqkm	20.770 sqkm	97.740 sqkm	438.446 sqkm	1.648.000 sqkm
Pop.: 50.800.000	Pop.: 10.970.000	Pop.: 2.710.000	Pop.: 4.370.000	Pop.: 3.660.000	Pop.: 16.450.000	Pop.: 49.760.000
Turkish, (colloquila languages of other nationalities)	Arabic, (Kurdish, Armenian)	Arabich, English, French, (Kurdish, Armenian)	New Hebrew, Arabic	Arabic	Arabic, Kurdish (additional colloquial languages)	Persian (Farsi), (various Iranian dialects)
Lira	Pound	Pound	Shekel	Jordan Dinar	Iraq Dinar	Rial

seasons; and, above all, in China, where rice, the most important crop throughout the monsoon belt, is planted with a plow, like in India.

These spheres of cultural progress not only fostered the development of numerous languages, but also the cultivation of a variety of alphabets. Chinese, now spoken by one out of three Asians, has become the most important language in Asia. Written Chinese, with its ideographic system of representation, has exerted a formative influence far beyond the borders of China – in Japan, in particular. Asia as a whole has played a pre-eminent role in the history of religion as the continent which spawned and nurtured such major world religions as Islam, Buddhism, Hinduism, Judaism and Christianity. It is only with some reservation that Chinese Universalism – including Confucianism and Taoism – with its roots in nature worship can be considered a religion. The strong link between religion and all aspects of daily life and culture is

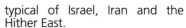

typical of Israel, Iran and the Hither East.

In spite of all the cultural differences between the various larger Asian regions, since World War II, the combined influence of industrialization and western civilization has succeeded in bringing them closer together – these influences being more pronounced, however, in urban centers than in rural areas.

In the former socialist republics of the Soviet Union people have begun to resist any form of ideological, cultural or economic control or »levelling« – having suffered all that for nearly 70 years. The demise of communism brought on by politics of openness and restructuring (»Perestroyka« and »Glasnost«; introduced around 1985), was sealed in 1990 when all the republics of the former Soviet Union formally declared their independence.

As early as the 16th century, Cossacks in the service of the Czar began conquering that sparsely populated »sleeping land«, Siberia. During the 18th and 19th

Top left: The Gilgit Valley, near the Kashmir town of the same name, is 1,500 metres above sea level. The lofty mountain ranges framing it on both sides, the Hindukush, Karakorum and Himalayas, ascend to elevations of up to 6,000 metres.

Top: At the top of Swayambhunath Hill we find the oldest and most important shrine in Nepal: the main stupa Chaitya. Resting on the white dome representing the vault of heaven there is a square tower bearing the pairs of Buddha eyes and the golden point with the 13 heavens.

Bottom left: Russian-style houses in Irkutsk, the regional capital of South Siberia, located on the Transsiberian Railway and the Angara River.

Below: A detail of Permual Temple in Singapore. The »City of Lions« is situated on an island off the southern tip of the Malay Peninsula. The numerous Chinese temples, mosques and churches are a typical feature of the city's Old Town.

Bottom right: Saddhu in Nepal. These Hindu holy man lives off the alms he receives from the faithful.

centuries the Czar signed defensive treaties with the kings of Georgia and Azerbaijan, annexing these territories to his empire. At the outset of the 20th century, Russia ruled both the Black Sea and the Caspian Sea. In 1847 the Cossacks began conquering the area around the Aral Sea and Lake Balkhash. By the turn of the century they had reached the borders to India and Afghanistan. In the aftermath of the October Revolution of 1917, the Russian Empire converted into the Union of Soviet Socialist Republics, the most diverse multi-national state on earth. Although the individual union republics were promised cultural self-administration, the central policy was actually one of across-the-board Russianization.

The Asian portions of the former Soviet Union were radically transformed by the systematic development of industrial complexes; e.g., in the Ural, the Kuzneck Basin, along the upper Angara and in the Fergana Basin. Local industrial centers were set up along the 7,525 kilometres of Transsiberian Railway, built from 1891-1904, and along the Baykal-Amur Magistral (BAM). Another major step, accomplished by developing more resistent varieties of cereals,

was the creation of a new granary: the Siberian Grain Belt. So far, only a fraction of the area's tremendous hydroelectric potential has been harnessed.

In addition to cultural self-determination, the peoples of Grusia, Armenia, Azerbaijan, Uzbekistan, Kazakhstan, Kirgiziya, Tadzhikistan and Turkmenia have demanded jurisdiction to plan the expansion of their economies and infrastructure. In claiming the rights of disposal, they will also hopefully end the rampant over-exploitation of natural resources. In Uzbekistan, for example, water was diverted from rivers to irrigate vast cotton fields, thus causing the Aral Sea to dry up – threatening the entire region with an ecological disaster of horrendous proportions.

In the autonomous regions within Russia, voices are growing, demanding more freedom – evidence that this part of the world has far from settled down. Benefitting from its highly developed traditions of agriculture and craftsmanship Japan managed to overcome its two main handicaps – the crippling damage it suffered during the Second World War, and its lack of coal and iron – accomplishing a

Saudi-Arabia	Yemen Yemen Arabic Republic	Oman	United Arab Emirates	Bahrain	Qatar	Kuwait
Al Mamlaka Al 'Arabiya As-Sa'udiya	Al Dschumhurija al Jamanija	Saltanat aman	Al- Imārāt al-'ArabTya al-Muttahida United Arab Emirates	Dawlat al-Bahrain	Dawlat al Qatar	Dawlat al Kuwait
Riyadh	*Sanaa*	*Maskat*	*Abu Dhabi*	*Manama*	*Doha*	*Kuwait*
2.149.690 sqkm	527.968 sqkm	212.457 sqkm	83.600 sqkm	622 sqkm	11.437 sqm	17.818 sqkm
Pop.: 13.610.000	Pop.: 11.634.000	Pop.: 1.190.000	Pop.: 1.380.000	Pop.: 430.000	Pop.: 330.000	Pop.: 1.870.000
Arabic	Arabic	Arabic, Persian, Urdu	Arabic, English (commercial language)	Arabic, English (commercial language)	Arabic, Persian, English (commercial language)	Arabic, English (commercial language)
Saudi Riyal	Yemen-Rial	Rial Omani	Dirham	Bahrain Dinar	Katar-Riyal	Kuwait Dinar

Top: The Taj Mahal in Agra (India). Built from 1630 to 1652, this mosque-like marble mausoleum was erected by a king in memory of his favorite wife.

Center: Natural gas being burnt off an oil well in the United Arab Emirates on the Persian Gulf.

Top right: Terraced rice fields in northern Luzon (Philippines). Created some 2,000 years ago, these »sky terraces« can comprise up to 80 tiers of paddies.

Lower right: Irrigated seedlings in the United Arab Emirates.

Afghanistan

De Afghánistán Djamhuriare

Kabul

647.497 sqkm

Pop.: 18.630.000

Pashto, Dari (Persian)

Afghani

Pakistan

Islamic Republic of Pakistan Islami Jamhuriya-e-Pakistan

Islamabad

803.943 sqkm

Pop.: 102.240.000

Urdu, English, regional languages

Pakistan Rupee

India

Bharat Juktarashtra

New Delhi

3.287.590 sqkm

Pop.: 66.140.000

Hindi (15 main languages, as well as 24 independent languages and more than 720 dialects)

Indian Rupee

Maledives

Republic of Maldives Divehi raajje

Malé

298 sqkm

Pop.: 195.000

Devehi, English

Rufiyaa

Sri Lanka

Sri Lanka Janarajaya

Colombo

65.610 sqkm

Pop.: 16.360.000

Sinhalese, Tamil, English

Sri Lanka Rupee

Nepal

Nepal Adiradscha Sri Nepalá Sarkár

Kathmandu

140.797 sqkm

Pop.: 17.130.000

Nepali, (additional languages and dialects)

Nepalese Rupee

Bhutan

Druk-Yul

Thimphu

47.000 sqkm

Pop.: 1.450.000

Dzongkha, (additional regional languages)

Ngultrum

Bangladesh

Ghana Praja Tantri Bangla Desh

Dhaka

143.998 sqkm

Pop.: 102.560.000

Bengali (additional regional languages)

Taka

rapid process of extensive industrialization. The region also includes several upwardly mobile economies gradually emerging from Japan's shadow; particularly the four »Little Tigers«: South Korea, Taiwan, Hong Kong and Singapore. Obviously, close international trade relations are vitally important in an area which has become the hub not only of the Pacific realm, but of the entire world economy.

Although still mainly an agricultural society, the People's Republic of China has begun to accelerate industrialization – capitalizing especially on its abundant reserves of hard coal. Back in colonial days, in fact, the western powers had already begun to set up heavy industry in Manchuria, as well as textile mills and other light industrial plants in the major ports. Currently, the main priorities are the improvement of the deficient transportation infrastructure and the exploitation of China's abundant mineral resources. Initially, the state was entirely in charge of planning and administering the economy. As of 1978, however, »systems of autonomous responsibility« were introduced – first in the country, then in the cities – coupled with free-market elements. This has created a widening, unbridgeable rift between the political and economic

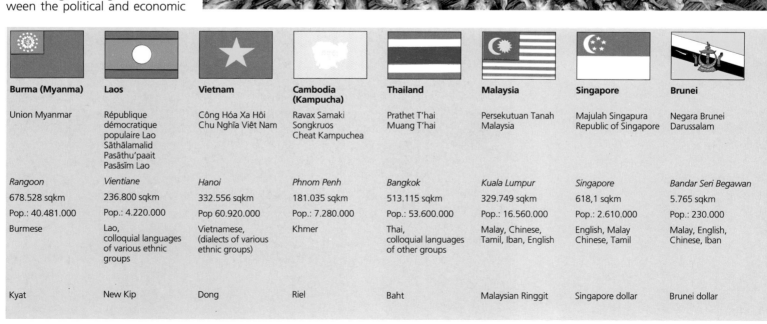

Burma (Myanma)	Laos	Vietnam	Cambodia (Kampucha)	Thailand	Malaysia	Singapore	Brunei
Union Myanmar	République démocratique populaire Lao Sāthālamalid Pasāthu'paait Pasāsīm Lao	Công Hóa Xa Hôi Chu Nghĩa Viêt Nam	Ravax Samaki Songkruos Cheat Kampuchea	Prathet T'hai Muang T'hai	Persekutuan Tanah Malaysia	Majulah Singapura Republic of Singapore	Negara Brunei Darussalam
Rangoon	*Vientiane*	*Hanoi*	*Phnom Penh*	*Bangkok*	*Kuala Lumpur*	*Singapore*	*Bandar Seri Begawan*
678.528 sqkm	236.800 sqkm	332.556 sqkm	181.035 sqkm	513.115 sqkm	329.749 sqkm	618,1 sqkm	5.765 sqkm
Pop.: 40.481.000	Pop.: 4.220.000	Pop 60.920.000	Pop.: 7.280.000	Pop.: 53.600.000	Pop.: 16.560.000	Pop.: 2.610.000	Pop.: 230.000
Burmese	Lao, colloquial languages of various ethnic groups	Vietnamese, (dialects of various ethnic groups)	Khmer	Thai, colloquial languages of other groups	Malay, Chinese, Tamil, Iban, English	English, Malay Chinese, Tamil	Malay, English, Chinese, Iban
Kyat	New Kip	Dong	Riel	Baht	Malaysian Ringgit	Singapore dollar	Brunei dollar

Top left: Coastal fishermen spreading their catch out to dry near the port of Puttalam on the west coast of Sri Lanka. Fish and rice are basic foodstuffs on Sri Lanka.

Right above: A torii, a Japanese Shinto monument. Positioned 160 metres off the coast, it is part of the Miyajima Island Temple Shrine in the Bay of Hiroshima.

Lower left: The city of Amritsar in Punjab (India) is the religious capital of the Sikhs. The Golden Temple, the tallest Sikh shrine, towers over the Pool of Immortality, where Sikhs come to cleanse themselves.

systems. Unable to participate in the achievements of the new economic system, the Chinese intellectual class, for example, is at a disadvantage. There are also islands of industrial development within the agricultural societies of Indonesia, the Indo-Chinese peninsula and India – with their huge ›dormant‹ reserves of manpower and vast mineral resources. Some of these countries are western-influenced, while others have an eastern, communist orientation. The communists have gained the upper hand in Vietnam, Laos and Cambodia. India is the most populous democracy on earth.

The Arab states pursue a course of industrialization based on their abundant oil reserves. Striking contrasts between intensively cultivated arable land and desert, between traditional craftsmanship and modern industry are characteristic features of the Near Eastern economies.

38 metres tall, the Heavenly Temple is one of the symbols of both Peking and China. The most beautiful temple in China, it was first erected in 1420. A gilded sphere tops the three-tiered roof. The wooden temple was built without a single nail.

Indonesia	Philippines	Taiwan	China	Mongolian People's Republic	Democratic Peoples Republic of Korea	Republic of Korea	Japan
Republic of Indonesia	Republika Ñg Philipinas República de Filipinas	Chung-Hua Min-Kuo	Zhonghua Renmin Gonghe Guo	Bügd Nairamdach Mongol Ard Uls	Tschosson Mintschu tschu-i-Jinmin Konghwa-Guk	Dähan-Minkuk Han Kopk	Nihon-Koku Nippon
Jakarta	*Manila*	*Taipeh*	*Peking*	*Ulaan baatar*	*P'yong yang*	*Seoul*	*Tokyo*
1.919.443 sqkm	300.000 sqkm	36.188 sqkm	9.560.779 sqkm	1.565.000 sqkm	120.538 sqkm	98.484 sqkm	372.313 sqkm
Pop.: 170.530.000	Pop.: 56.980.000	Pop.: 19.135.000	Pop.: 1.072.220.000	Pop.: 1.940.000	Pop.: 20.880.000	Pop.: 42.030.000	Pop.: 120.047.000
Bahasa Indonisia (Malay), (Indonesian regional languages)	Filipino, Cebuano, Tagalog, Ilocano, Panay Hiligayon, Bicol et al	Mandarin Chinese, Fukien (Amoy) dialects	Mandarin Chinese, (regional official languages)	Khalkah Mongolian	Korean	Korean	Japanese
Rupiah	Philippine Peso	New Taiwan dollar	Renminbi Yuan	Tugrik	Won	Won	Yen

AUSTRALIA OCEANIA

The smallest continent on earth is also the furthest removed from the others. Moreover, it is the only inhabited continent located entirely in the southern hemisphere – an island continent within the earth's watery hemisphere. This geographic separation from the other continents is responsible for the unique development of its unique flora and fauna.

One of the reasons for its late discovery is its antipodal (= ›opposite foot‹) location with respect to Europe. The »empty continent« is home to less than half of one per cent of the world population. Over three quarters of the some 16 million inhabitants live in the metropolitan areas in Australia's southeast – due to its favorable climate.

Australia/Oceania
NATURAL ENVIRONMENT

Surrounded on three sides by »empty« oceans, this southernmost continent is 13,000 kilometres from South America and 9,000 kilometres from Africa. The Southeast Asian archipelago to the north, the only ›connection‹ to another continent, was an actual land bridge to Asia at an earlier stage of the earth's development. Australia owes its relatively short coastline (20,000 km) to its compact form – the only indentation being the Carpentaria Gulf to the north. Off the eastern and northeastern shores of Australia there are coral reefs; the most important being the Great Barrier Reef off the eastern coast.

The average elevation of Australia is similar to that of Europe, but otherwise there are considerable topographic differences. The continent of wide open spaces, Australia is basically a vast tableland ringed almost entirely by raised rims bordering narrow coastal plains. The western Australian plateau covers over two thirds of the surface area, rising to elevations between 200 and 500 metres – punctuated only by individual worn-down mountain ranges or by »mountain islands«, isolated mountains rising abruptly from the plains. The most striking of these ridges is Ayers Rock in the center of Australia, the eroded

sandstone remains of a larger ancient geological formation.

The central Australian lowland surrounds the salt-flat-ringed depression of Lake Eyre at twelve metres below sea level. Eastern Australia and Tasmania are covered by the Australian cordillera, the Great Dividing Range. The only rugged formations in this low, eroded range are the Australian Alps (Mount Kosciusko, 2,228 m). During the summer, the north of Australia is part of a zone with tropical zenithal rains. The resulting narrow strip of marshy mangrove along the northern coast borders on evergreen rain forest.

Page 115: The »road trains« on Australia's highways can be over 50 metres long. Most of them haul livestock (sheep, cattle) to the coast.

Lower left: The scrub, or brushland, in the interior of this dry continent.

Top right: Coral reefs and islands in the Pacific.

Right: The Great Barrier Reef off the eastern coast of Australia is 2,000 kilometres long and 300 to 2,000 metres wide. For a long time this coral barrier represented a major obstacle to the exploration of Australia.

Further south, this gives way to the so-called »scrub« or brushland, a dry savanna covered with thorny brushwood.
The southeasterly trade wind sheds abundant rain on the slopes of the mountains in the southeast. The typical plant of this sub-

Top: Ayers Rock in the center of Australia. The largest monolith on earth, it is a sacred site to the Aborigines.

Center: The elements have carved this hollow out of Ayers Rock – which rises 350 metres above the plain with a circumference of 9,000 metres.

Lower left: Devil's Marbles in the Australian interior. These ›bales of wool‹ are also products of erosion.

Lower right: A herd of sheep in the Australian Alps.

tropical forest, the eucalyptus tree, can grow to heights of up to 160 metres. The only area with considerable winter precipitation is the extreme southwestern tip of the continent. Here, the typical vegetation consists of sclero-phyllous evergreens. The rest of the area between the slope of the cordillera and the west coast, however, is part of a dry region. Nevertheless, aside from the »dead heart« of the continent, there is hardly any actual sandy desert. The Australian fauna includes mammals of the lowest orders, such as marsupials (kanga-roos, opossums) and the egg-laying duckbilled platypus. The koala, a tree-climbing marsupial indigenous to eastern Australia, feeds on eucalyptus leaves. Some rivers contain lungfish, creatures which survive the dry season buried in sand, using their swim-ming bladders as a sort of lung to breathe with. Domestic animals did not exist before the arrival of the Europeans, yet recently the semi-wild dingo and the rabbit

have begun to reproduce at an unpleasant rate.
The groups of Pacific islands to the north and east of the Austra-lian continent are known as Oceania. Oceania is made up of an inner and an outer arc of is-lands – the inner one comprising New Zealand and Melanesia, whereas the outer one includes Micronesia and Polynesia. From a geological point of view, New Guinea, the second largest island in the world (2,100 km long, up to 800 km wide), is considered part of Australia because it rises from the same continental shelf. The remaining islands are composed of either vulcanic rock or coral limestone. They mark the edges of the submarine rises, which are staggered in wide, sweeping arcs across the South Pacific.
The most distinctive features of the twin islands of New Zealand are its young chains of mountains (Mount Cook, 3764 m), the active volcanoes on the North Island (Ruapehu, 2,797 m), the deep fjords and U-shaped valleys.

Above: Tree ferns in New Zealand – one of numerous species which owe their unique evolution to the isolated conditions on this island.

Cultivated land (arable land, plantations and irrigated land)

Grassland of the temperate zone

Forest of the temperate zone

Tropical rain forest

Humid savannah (open eu-calyptus forests in Australia)

Dry savannah

Scrub

Semi-desert and desert

Rock, snow and ice areas of mountain regions

PACIFIC OCEAN

Mariana Isl.
Pagan
Rota
Guam

Legaspi
Samar
Leyte
Cebu
Surigao
Mindanao
Davao
2953

Palau

C a r o l i n e   I s .

Mortlock

Kep.Sangir
Morotai
Manado
Halmahera
Waigeo
Sorong   Cenderawasih
Yapen
Sula   Obi   Misool
Buru   Ceram
Ambon
Buton
Banda Sea
Wetar
Timor   Babar
Tanimbar
Yos Sudarsa
Tng Vals

Admiralty Is.
New Guinea
Jayapura
5030
G. Jaya   Peg. Maoke (Central Ra.)
Lae

Bismarck
Bismarck Sea
Arch.   Rabaul
New Britain   G.of Papua
Port Moresby

New Hanover
New Ireland

Bougainville
Choiseul
Santa Isabel
Malaita
Guadalcanal
San Cristobal
Sta Cruz Is.
Rennell

Nauru

Equator   Gilbert Is.

M E L A N E S I A
Solomon Islands

Ellice Is.

Timor
Sea
Arafura Sea
Torres Str.
C. York

Cobourg Pen.
Melville I.
Croker
Bathurst
Darwin
Arnhem Land
Tasman Land
Wyndham
Kimberley

G. of
Groote
Eylandt
Carpentaria
C. York
Pen.
Barkly Tableland
Tennant Creek

Gr.Sandy
Desert
Gibson Desert
AUSTRALIA
Macdonnell Ra.
Alice Springs
1580

Mount Isa
Cairns
Townsville
Mackay

Coral
Sea

Santo
Malekula
New
Hebrides

New Caledonia
Lifou
Maré

Vanua Levu
Viti Levu
Is.Fiji

Esperance
Gr.
Victoria Desert
Nullarbor Plain
Australaian Bight
Kangaroo I
Mount Gambier

oorlie
L. Eyre
L. Torrens
Broken Hill
Adelaide
Murray
Mt. Kosciusko
2230
Melbourne

Rockhampton
Bundaberg
Fraser
Brisbane
Grafton
Darling
Newcastle
Sydney
Canberra

Great Dividing Range

Norfolk

Lord Howe

Tropic of Capricorn

T a s m a n
S e a

King Bass Str. Flinders
Launceston
Tasmania
Hobart
C.Sudeste

North C.
North I.
Auckland

C. Farewell
South I.
Hastings
Wellington
Mt. Cook
3764
Southern Alps
Christchurch
Dunedin
Southwest C.
Chatham

New Zealand

1 : 30 000 000   0   200   400   600   800   1000 km

119

Australia/Oceania
PEOPLE AND CULTURE

Australia was not discovered and opened up to colonization until quite late, in the early 17th century. Aside from being extremely far from Europe, in the era of seafaring exploration, Australia's largely inaccessible coastline posed a major obstacle.

Prior to its invasion by whites, the vast continent was populated solely by Native Australians. Frequently erroneously called »Austral negroes«, the most common term today is »Aborigines«. At the time of their ›discovery‹, they still lived in the manner of stone-age hunters and gatherers, equipped with a simple array of implements (spear, boomerang, bone and stone tools). After a long period of persecution had finally reduced their population to around 7,000, they were assigned reservations in the arid interior. In the meantime, their numbers have increased to 50,000, or 160,000 including half-castes.

Today Australia is a continent of whites with strict immigration laws designed to make sure it remains that way. The Briton James Cook was the first white to set foot on this southern continent. Subsequently the British used the remote island continent for a while as a penal colony. In the middle of the 19th century the discovery of gold near Coolgardie and Kalgoorlie brought droves of settlers to the country. When the pay dirt proved to be poorer than expected, many a prospector settled down as a farmer. Finally one began to discover the con-

tinent's economic potential. Within a few decades the population grew from one to over ten million. Around 95 per cent of the inhabitants are Australians of British ancestry, a fifth of the population was born abroad – an

indication that Australia still draws a large number of immigrants. In 1988 the white population celebrated the 200th anniversary of the first European settlement in Australia – despite protests from the Aborigines. To-

Australia	**New Zealand**	**Papua New Guinea**	**Vanuatu**	**Fiji**	**Tonga**	**Samoa**	**Tuvalu**
The Commonwealth of Australia	New Zealand	Papua New Guinea	Republic of Vanuatu République de Vanuatu	Fiji Matanitu Ko Viti	Kingdom of Tonga Pule' anga Tonga	Malotutuo' atasi o Samoa i Sisifo	Tuvalu
Canberra	Wellington	Port Moresby	Port Vila	Suva	Nuku' alofa	Apia	Vaiaku
7.686.420 sqkm	269.063 sqkm	461.691 sqkm	14.763 sqkm	18.272 sqkm	699 sqkm	2.842 sqkm	24,6 sqkm
Pop.: 16.028.000	Pop.: 3.280.000	Pop.: 3.400.000	Pop.: 140.000	Pop.: 714.000	Pop.: 110.000	Pop.: 163.000	Pop.: 8.000
English	English, Maori	English, Melanesian Pidgin, various Papua-languages	Bislama, English, French	English, Fiji, Hindi	Tonga, English	Samoan, English	Tuvalu
Australian dollar	New Zealand dollar	Kina	Vanuatu franc, Australian dollar	Fiji dollar	Pa'anga	Tala	Australian dollar

day the Commonwealth of Australia, comprising six states and two territories, is still a constitutional monarchy and part of the British Commonwealth – with the English Queen as chief-of-state. The seat of government is Canberra. Founded in 1927, the city is purely an administrative center. Five sixths of Australia's inhabitants live within the narrow fringe along the southwestern and southeastern coasts – the areas where the first whites settled. The vast interior, on the other hand, is almost entirely uninhabited.

Large portions of the continent can only be used, due to the arid climate, for grazing sheep. As the basis for its wool production and meat exports, however, sheep breeding – until a century or two ago – brought the country considerable wealth. »Australia rides to prosperity on the back of a sheep,« was a frequently quoted slogan. As one approaches the wetter edges of the continent, the sheep farms give way to cattle ranches. The main areas for cultivating wheat, citrus fruit, fruit and other agricultural products are in the southeast and southwest where land has been made arable through irrigation. The most important irrigation project was carried out in the Australian Alps. The purpose of the Snowy Mountains Scheme was to re-channel unused waters flowing off the damp east side of the range to the dry west side. Although Australia still produces considerable amounts of wool and other animal products for the world market, the importance of agricultural products as export items has been dwindling ever since the discovery of Australia's rich mineral deposits. Several mountains of ore are currently

Top left: In the dry interior, reservations were set up for the Aborigines, the original inhabitants of Australia. Many of them find work on cattle ranches.

Lower left: The Polynesian inhabitants of Samoa, a group of islands in the Pacific, raise coconuts (copra) as their staple commodity.

Top center: Most Australians live in their own homes in vast housing areas in the southeast of the continent. The moving of entire homes is one expression of the population's high mobility.

Center: This geothermal power station on New Zealand harnesses the forces at work in the bowels of the earth – steaming evidence of volcanic, tectonic and thermal activity.

Right: This view of Sydney shows the modern opera building erected at the entrance to the harbor. Its principal architectural elements symbolize the hulls of ships.

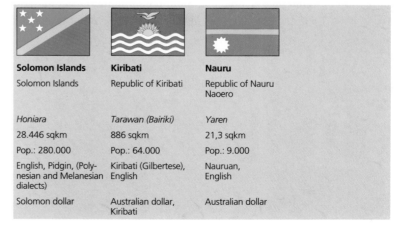

Solomon Islands	Kiribati	Nauru
Solomon Islands	Republic of Kiribati	Republic of Nauru Naoero
Honiara	Tarawan (Bairiki)	Yaren
28.446 sqkm	886 sqkm	21,3 sqkm
Pop.: 280.000	Pop.: 64.000	Pop.: 9.000
English, Pidgin, (Polynesian and Melanesian dialects)	Kiribati (Gilbertese), English	Nauruan, English
Solomon dollar	Australian dollar, Kiribati	Australian dollar

being stripped in open-pit mining operations in the Kimberley District in the northwest. Initially, the textiles industry and the food, beverages and tobacco industry (mills, canning) played a major role, but for some time heavy industry, processing plants, and the consumer goods industry have been gaining importance. The latter industries are concentrated in the metropolitan regions around Sydney, Melbourne and Adelaide.

New Zealand is one of the major exporters of agricultural products for the world market. Its inhabitants are almost entirely of English, Scotch or Irish ancestry. Some 80 percent of the New Zealand population lives in the cities. In addition, there are around 300,000 Aborigines. Whereas the western portion of New Guinea is under the political jurisdiction of Indonesia, the eastern section, Papua New Guinea is independent. The island is inhabited by pygmy tribes and by the dark-skinned Papua.

In 1959 Hawaii, the most important group of islands in Micronesia and Polynesia, became the 50th state of the USA. Three quarters of the population (totalling around one million, mainly Polynesian, inhabitants) live in the capital city, Honolulu. Huge plantations – mainly sugar cane, coffee and especially pineapple – take advantage of the fertile, weathered soil of the mightiest volcanoes in the world – rising from a depth of 5,000 metres below sea level to an elevation of 4,000 metres. Hawaii also flourishes on its revenues from tourism and as a major naval base.

Top: Native Australian rock paintings inspire the bark paintings of contemporary Aborigine artists, in which they represent episodes from their tribal history.

Below: Coober Pedy in Southern Australia, where opals were first found in 1915. To escape from the unbearable heat many of the 4,000 local inhabitants live in underground dwellings.

Islands under United States Trusteeship

Palau	Micronesia	Marshall Islands
Republic of Palau	Federated States of Micronesia	Republic of the Marshall Islands
Koror	*Kolonia*	*Uliga*
458 sqkm	720,6 sqkm	181 sqkm
Pop.: 15.000	Pop.: 115.000	Pop.: 35.000
English, Micronesian dialects	English, Micronesian dialects	English, Micronesian dialects
US dollar	US dollar	US dollar

AFRICA

In contrast to Eurasia with its complex contours, Africa is often called a »giant torso without limbs«. The second largest continent on earth, it covers a fifth of the entire land mass – but is inhabited by only a tenth of the world population. This »torrid continent without winters« lies almost entirely within the Tropics. The largest desert on earth, the Sahara, separates »White Africa«, the oriental Islam-influenced north, from »Black Africa« in the south. Nearly all the 52 sovereign African states are considered to belong to the group of developing countries. The exception in every respect is South Africa, where the Apartheid rule of a white minority has excluded the black majority from government.

Africa
NATURAL ENVIRONMENT

Africa has the shape of a trapezium to the north resting on an upside-down triangle to the south – with the equator marking the dividing line between them. The »Dark Continent« extends 8,000 kilometres from the north to the south and 7,300 kilometres from east to west. Not counting Madagascar, islands and peninsulas make up only two per cent of the total area, so that the largely unindented coastline measures only 30,000 kilometres.

The Suez Canal severs the land bridge between Africa and Asia at its narrowest point and is considered the demarcation line between the two continents. At its nearest point, the Straights of Gibraltar, Africa is only 14 kilometres from Europe.

With the exception of the young ridges at the very northern and southern ends of the continent, it is composed almost entirely of primitive rock strata. Thus, the continent not only lacks the long chains of mountains which normally create meteorological and cultural barriers, but also sizable lowlands. Instead, the topography comprises extensive, gentle undulation basins – such as the Western Sahara basin, the Chad, Zaire and Kalahari basins – interrupted by dividing rises and sweeping highlands. The rises entirely ringing the continent reduce the navigability of most rivers. Where they overcome rises like the Asande and the Lunda rises, the rivers often form waterfalls – the most famous being the Victoria Falls on the Sambesi with a drop of 120 metres.

The chains of volcanoes in East Africa are part of the extensive East African/Syrian system of rifts and faults. The highest point in Africa is the Kilimanjaro rising to 5,895 metres. Lying in the recess of a rift valley, Lake Tanganyika reaches a depth of 1,435 metres. The Ethiopian highland (Ras Daschan 4,620 m) with its deep gorges is also largely of volcanic origin. A line drawn from Port Sudan on the Red Sea to Luanda on the Atlantic Ocean roughly divides the continent into ›Low Africa‹ to the north and ›High Africa‹ to the south.

Bisected virtually in the middle by the equator, Africa comprises an almost archetypal sucession of climatic and vegetation zones. The equatorial areas typically have

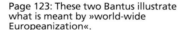

Page 123: These two Bantus illustrate what is meant by »world-wide Europeanization«.

Top left: The baobab or monkey-bread tree is a typical savanna plant. It loses its leaves in the summer. The natives cook its young leaves as a vegetable and make oil from its seeds.

Lower left: These basalt columns, once the chimney fillings of active volcanoes, jut up from the Tassili Highland – the natural environment of the Tuareg.

Top : The approaching front of a Saharan sandstorm.

Center: Once covered with tropical mountain forest, these steep slopes have been cleared and cultivated by mountain farmers in eastern Zaire.

Far right: Deep canyons gouged out of the East African highland plateau.

Lower right: A sailboat near Assuan on the Nile, the main artery of Egypt.

two rainy seasons, spring and autumn – in addition to precipitation in other months – with high humidity and little variation in average monthly temperatures. Thus, one refers to the climate in the ever-humid tropics as being diurnal. The characteristic regional vegetation is tropical rain forest with its abundance of species. To the north and to the south, this zone borders on the tropics with their periodical changes in humidity: with a marked dry season following a distinct period of (northern or southern) summer rains. Beyond the tropical rain forest, there are the well-watered savannas, giving way to dry savannas, followed by thorny savannas. The East African savannas are the location of the wildlife reserves – famous for their big game (antilopes, zebras, giraffes, elephants, rhinoceros, lions, etc.). In the region between the Tropics, there are also large arid areas, including the Kalahari salt and clay basins in

South Africa and, in the north, the largest desert on earth: the Sahara. The Namib, a desert along the coast of southwestern Africa, is caused by offshore trade winds and the cold upward currents from the Benguela Stream. A third of the African continent is covered by desert-like terrain – yet even in the Sahara itself, no more than about one fifth of the area is actual sandy desert. Predominately one finds a gravel and rock desert etched with deep dry valleys, or wadis, produced during earlier pluvial periods. Oases are found either where ground water surfaces, or where allogenous rivers bring in water from rainier regions.

Top: Smoke from fire-clearing in the Zaire Basin in Central Africa. More and more tropical rain forest goes up in flames to create arable land where tropical fruits can be grown for personal consumption and trade – temporarily relieving the strain of a growing population.

Bottom: The East African savanna is the only remaining animal paradise on earth. Extensively protected, they serve as national parks.
From left to right: Elephants, the largest mammals on earth; a bufallo herd at a watering hole; long-nosed rhinoceros, hunted for the medicinal powder from their horns and thus threatened with extinction; lions; a leopard; and zebras.

Cultivated land (arable land, plantations, oasis and irrigated land)

Grassland of the temperate zone and of the tropical highlands

Forest of the temperate zone and of the tropical higlands

Tropical rain forest

Humid savannah

Dry tropical forest (Miambo) and dry sahannah

Steppe

Semi-desert and desert

MEDITER RANEAN SEA

ATLANTIC OCEAN

INDIAN OCEAN

Arabian Sea

Red Sea

Gulf of Aden

Persian Gulf

G. of Oman

Mozambique Channel

Madagascar

Mascarene Islands

Seychelles

Tropic of Cancer

Tropic of Capricorn

Equator

1 : 30 000 000   0   200   400   600   800   1000 km

Africa
PEOPLE AND CULTURE

2,000 kilometres wide, the hostile range of the Sahara Desert looks like a natural barrier, separating White Africa in the north from Black Africa to the south. The population to the north of this line is made up of light-skinned peoples – predominately Hamites and Arabs – belonging to the large Caucasian race, whereas the South is populated by Negro peoples. The Ethiopians of Eastern Africa, on the other hand, are unique in that they bear traits of both these major races. Then there are the few remaining survivors of the original African native peoples: the pygmy tribes of Zaire (Congo) and the bushmen of the South African Kalahari. The Hamite and Negro races have been mingling ever since the Hamites began moving south into the northern fringe of Black Africa, conquering the Negro population. The resulting tribes, the cattle-breeding Fulbe (Fulah) and the trade-oriented Hausa built mighty empires long before the arrival of the Europeans.

Distinguishing according to language, there are two major groups of black-skinned Africans: Sudanese Negros and Bantu Negros. Each individual African belongs to one of many nations or tribes – each having their own characteristic forms of industry and commerce, types of settlement, language and culture, customs and religion. Generally speaking, the animistic religions are on the wane, whereas Islam –

considered to be free of any association with the former colonial rulers – continues its triumphal sweep through the Sahel Zone south of the Sahara.

Based on its black-majority population, South Africa is also considered a part of Black Africa – even though a white minority still controls the political and economic system.

Until 500 years ago, Europeans thought of Africa as the »Dark Continent« – having explored only the narrow strip along the Mediterranean coast. They did not reach the Cape of Good Hope until 1487. Operating from support bases along the coast, the

Europeans then began to extend their influence into the hinterland. Even today, several sections of the West African coast still bear the names of the fundamental commodities which once lured the colonial powers: the Pepper, Ivory, Gold and Slave Coasts. After the discovery of the Americas, slave labor was needed there to work the fields. The resulting slave hunts in Black Africa lasted well into the middle of the 19th century. Entire regions were brutally depopulated. The Portuguese and Spanish, but above all the English, French and Belgians and, for a while, the Germans and Italians divided up Africa by means

Morocco	**Algeria**	**Tunesia**	**Libya**	**Egypt**	**Sudan**	**Ethiopia**	**Djibouti**
Al Mamlakah al Maghrebia	République Algérienne Démocratique et Populaire El Dschamhurija el Dschasarija el demokratija escha'abija	El Dschumhuri ja et Tunusija République Tunisienne	Al-Jamahiriyah Al-Arabiya Al-Libya Al-Shabiya Al-Ishtirakiya	El Dschumhurija Misr El Arabija	El Dchumhurijat ed Demokratijat es Sudan Jamhuriyat as Sudan Al Demokratia	Ye Ethiopia Hizebawi Democraciyawi Republic	République de Djibouti
Rabat	*Algiers*	*Tunis*	*Tripoli*	*Cairo*	*Khartoum*	*Addis Ababa*	*Djibouti*
458.730 sqkm	2.381.741 sqkm	164.150 sqkm	1.759.540 sqkm	1.001.449 sqkm	2.505.813 sqkm	1.221.900 sqkm	22.000 sqkm
Pop.: 22.480.000	Pop.: 22.420.000	Pop.: 7.460.000	Pop.: 3.740.000	Pop.: 50.740.000	Pop.: 22.180.000	Pop.: 46.180.000	Pop.: 460.000
Arabic, Berber dialects, French, Spanish	Arabic, French, Berber dialects	Arabic, French, Tunesian (Arabic dialect)	Arabic, Berber dialects	Arabic, (English, French)	Arabic, English, Hamitic, Nilotic and Sudanic languages	Amharic, English, Italian, ca. 50 additional languages	French, Arabic, Kushitic languages (of the Afar and Issa tribes)
Dirham	Algerian dinar	Tunesian dinar	Libyan dinar	Egyptian pound	Sudanese pound	Birr	Djibouti franc

Far left: Massai women with their typical jewelry and clothing. The huts are built by flinging cow dung onto frames of interwoven branches and twigs.

Top: A tannery in Fez (Morocco). The animal hides are tanned by dipping them in the various vats filled with diluted vegetable tanning agents.

Center: The grading of roads with heavy machinery like this inflicts unhealable wounds upon the tropical forest.

Right: A native village, or kral, in Uganda.

of a ruler – not taking into consideration the tribal boundaries. These borders have been upheld to this day.

Up to 1950 the only independent countries were Liberia and Ethiopia. In the years from 1956 to 1961, the »African era« reached its climax as 30 countries gained their independence. Today Africa has more UN members than any other continent. Seeking combined solutions to their political and economic difficulties, most African states have joined the »Organization for African Unity« (OAU). The Republic of South Africa is barred from OAU membership because of its policy of Apartheid – which still excludes the black majority population from sharing political power. The African national borders of today – and thus the mixture of peoples in each country – are a legacy of the colonial era. Thus, many countries are frought with deeply-rooted tribal conflicts. Many of these nations are headed by military regimes or are ruled by a single party.

European influence and the resulting spread of western civilization has set off tremendous upheavals in the economy and medical care, as well as in social and cultural matters. Efforts to improve the infrastructure – designed, as they were, mainly to promote the export of mining and plantation products to European industrial countries – were in the first place focussed on the coastal

Cape Verde	Mauretania	Senegal	The Gambia
Républica de Cabo Verde	République Islamique de Mauritanie El Dschumhurija el Muslimija el Mauretanija	République du Sénégal	Repúblic of the Gambia
Praia	Nouakchott	Dakar	Banjul (Bathurst)
4.033 sqkm	1.030.700 sqkm	196.192 sqkm	11.295 sqkm
Pop.: 330.000	Pop.:1.950.000	Pop.: 6.610.000	Pop.: 660.000
Portuguese, Crioulo	Arabic, French, (Hassanya, Ful,Berber and Sudanic languages)	French, Wolof, (Sudanic languages)	English, Mandinka, Wolof, Ful, Arabic
Cape Verde escudo	Ouguiya	CFA-Franc	Dalasi

regions – thus leaving the interiors of the various countries undeveloped. In a continent of this tremendous size, the lack of infrastructure facilities, particularly the lack of roads, is an acute problem. The slums of the modern cities are inhabited by a new urban proletariat: masses living outside the traditional forms of tribal order; without education or employment. The search of work caused huge streams of migrant workers to pour into the cities – losing those original tribal ties which constitute both a network of mu- tual social security as well as a family defence alliance. Aside from the ports, the main population magnets are industrial regions like the Copper Belt in Zambia and Zimbabwe, Katanga/ Shaba in Zaire, or the industrial centers in the Republic of South Africa. The transition from a self-reliant subsistence economy to a free market economy and the attendant social revolution have caused the disintegration of the traditional tribal society. With a small educated leadership, on the one hand, and an unstructured

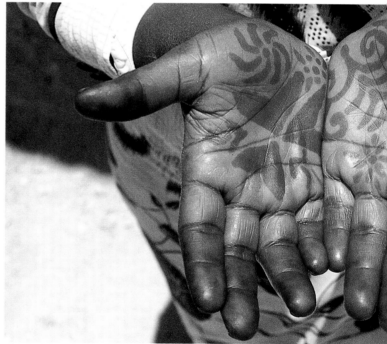

Mali	**Burkina Faso (Upper Volta)**	**Niger**	**Chad**	**Guinea-Bissau**	**Guinea**	**Sierra Leone**	**Liberia**
République du Mali	Burkina Faso	République du Niger	République du Tschad Djoumhourîyat Tschâd	República da Guiné-Bissau	République de Guinée	Republic of Sierra Leone	Republic of Liberia
Bamako	Ougadougou	Niamey	N'djamena	Bissau	Conakry	Freetown	Monrovia
1.240.142 sqkm	274.200 sqkm	1.267.000 sqkm	1.284.000 sqkm	36.125 sqkm	245.857 sqkm	71.740 sqkm	111.369 sqkm
Pop.: 8.680.000	Pop.: 6.750.000	Pop.: 6.608.000	Pop.: 5.140.000	Pop.: 935.000	Pop.: 6.339.000	Pop.: 3.670.000	Pop.: 2.350.000
French, Bambara, Songhai Djerma, Arabich, Ful	French, Volta semi Bantu languages, Foulani, western sudanic languages	French, Songhai Djerma, Arabic dialects, Foulani, Hausa, Tamashagh	French, Arabic, Chad-Arabic	Portuguese, Sudanic languages	French, Mandinka languages, Foulani	English, Sudanic languages, Krio	English, Mande, Kru, Golla, Kpelle
CFA franc	CFA franc	CFA franc	CFA franc	Guinea peso	Guinea-Franc	Leone	Liberian dollar

proletarian mass, on the other, what is largely missing is a middle class. There is a lack of skilled labor in agriculture, industry and the administration. Thus, the fight against illiteracy is one of the major goals in all African countries. The high birth rates characteristic of all African states, moreover, literally eat up any increase in productivity.
Compared with the two other developing regions, Latin America and Southern Asia, Africa is at the lowest level of economic development.

Far left: This Massai woman is wearing typical glass beaded jewelry. The Massai, a nomadic cattle-herding people, lives in the savannas of Kenya and Tanzania.

Top: A view out over the roofs of Cairo. On top of its crippling traffic and housing problems, the Egyptian capital is plagued by extreme environmental pollution.

Center: An ancient African cosmetic application: hennah-painted hands.

Right: The harvesting of long-fibred sisal leaves on a plantation in East Africa.

	Ivory Coast	Ghana	Togo	Benin	Nigeria	Cameroon	Gabon	Congo
	République de Côte d'Ivoire	Republic of Ghana	République Togolaise	République Populaire du Bénin	Federal Republic of Nigeria	République du Cameroun / Republic of Cameroon	République Gabonaise	République Populaire du Congo
	Abidjan	Accra	Lomé	Porto-Novo	Lagos	Yaoundé	Libreville	Brazzaville
	322.463 sqkm	238.537 sqkm	56.785 sqkm	112.622 sqkm	923.768 sqkm	475.442 sqkm	267.667 sqkm	342.000 sqkm
	Pop.: 10.160.000	Pop.: 14.040.000	Pop.: 3.050.000	Pop.: 4.153.000	Pop.: 98.520.000	Pop.: 10.860.000	Pop.: 1.170.000	Pop.: 1.790.000
	French, Kwa	English, Twi, Fante, Ga, Ewe, Foulani and other west African languages	French, (native languages and dialects)	French, (and over 60 African dialects)	English, Sudanic and Bantu languages, (in the North; Foulani and Hausa))	French, English, Bantu,Semi-Bantu, Sudanic languages	French, Bantu languages	French, Lingala Kikongo, Teke, Sanga, Ubangi
	CFA franc	Cedi	CFA franc	CFA franc	Naira	CFA franc	CFA franc	CFA franc

131

Left: The rich palette of African peoples ranges from the light-skinned Arabs in the North to ebony-skinned Negros in Black Africa. The continent also abounds with languages and cultures, religions, customs and traditions, as well as supporting a wide variety of archetypal forms of industry and commerce. – Self-adornment is one of the human being's primal instincts.

Equatorial Guinea

República de Guinea Ecuatorial

Malabo
28.051 sqkm
Pop.: 390.000
Spanish, Bubi, Fang

CFA franc

São Tomé and Principe

República Democrática de São Tomé e Principe

São Tomé
964 sqkm
Pop.: 110.000
Portuguese, Crioulo

Dobra

Central African Republic

République Centralafricaine

Bangui
622.984 sqkm
Pop.: 2.740.000
French, Sangho, Bantu and Sudanic languages

CFA franc

Zaire

République du Zaïre

Kinshasa
2.345.409 km˝
Pop.: 30.850.000
French, Tshiluba, Kikongo, Lingala, Suaheli

Zaïre

Rwanda

Republica y'u Rwanda
République Rwandaise

Kigali
26.338 sqkm
Pop.: 6.270.000
French, Kinyarwanda, Kiswahili

Rwanda franc

Burundi

Republika y'Uburundi
République du Burundi

Bujumbura
27.834 sqkm
Pop.: 4.927.000
Kirundi, French, Kiswahili

Burundi franc

Tanzania

United Republic of Tanzania
Jamhuriya Mwungano wa Tanzania

Dar es Salaam
945.087 sqkm
Pop.: 22.460.000
Swahili, English, Bantu and Hamitic languages

Tanzania franc

Uganda

Republic of Uganda

Kampala
236.036 sqkm
Pop.: 16.020.000
English, Kiswahili,

Uganda shilling

Kenya

Republic of Kenya
Dschamhuri ja Kenia

Nairobi
582.646 sqkm
Pop.: 22.940.000
Swahili, English, languages of the Bantu and Nilotic tribes

Kenya shilling

Somalia

Al-Jumhouriya As Somaliya Al-Domocradia

Mogadishu
637.657 sqkm
Pop.: 4.760.000
Somali, Arabic, English, Italian

Somalia shilling

Seychelles

Republic of Seychelles
République des Seychelles

Victoria
404 sqkm
Pop.: 70.000
Creole, English, French

Seychelles rupee

Comores

Republique fédérale et islamique des Comores

Moroni
1.862 sqkm
Pop.: 440.000
French, Comoran Arabic

Comoran franc

Madagascar

Repoblika Demokratika Malagasy
République Démocratique de Madagascar

Antananarivo
587.041 sqkm
Pop.: 10.300.000
French, Malagasy, (native idioms like Howa)

Madagascar franc

Mauritius

Mauritius

Port Louis
2.045 sqkm
Pop.: 1.034.000
English, Creole, French, East Indian languages

Mauritius rupee

Angola

República Popular de Angola

Luanda
1.246.700 sqkm
Pop.: 8.980.000
Portuguese, Bantu languages

Kwanza

Zambia

Republic of Zambia

Lusaka
752.614 sqkm
Pop.: 6.900.000
English, Bantu languages

Kwacha

Malaŵi

Republic of Mala^wi

Lilongwe
118.484 sqkm
Pop.: 7.500.000
English, Chichewa, Nyanja, Chitumbuca, Chiyao

Malaŵi Kwacha

Moçambique

República Popular de Moçambique

Maputo
799.380 sqkm
Pop.: 14.550.000
Potuguese, Bantu languages

Metical

Botswana

Republic of Botswana

Gaborone
600.372 sqkm
Pop.: 1.170.000
Setswana, Bantu languages, English

Pula

Zimbabwe

Republic of Zimbabwe

Harare
390.622 sqkm
Pop.: 8.410.000
English, Bantu languages

Simbabwe dollar

South Africa

Republic of South Africa

Pretoria
1.221.037 sqkm
Pop.:22.761.000
Afrikaans, English, Bantu languages, East Indian languages

Rand

Swaziland

Umbuso we Swantini Ngwane

Mbabane
17.364 sqkm
Pop.: 670.000
Si-Swati (Isi-Zulu), English

Lilangeni

Lesotho

Kingdom of Lesotho
Muso oa Lesotho

Maseru
30.335 sqkm
Pop.: 1.560.000
Southern Sotho, English

Maloti

Namibia

Windhuk
823.168 sqkm
Pop.: 1.590.000
Afrikaans, English, German, Bantu languages

NORTH AND CENTRAL AMERICA

Stretching 16,000 kilometres from north to south, the Americas are the world's longest continent and the second largest in land size (40 million square kilometres). The two halves are connected by the narrow land bridge of Central America, as well as semi-connected by the ›bridge piles‹ of the West Indian Islands. The natural demarcation line between North and South America is the Isthmus of Panama.

Canada, the second largest country in the world, and the USA, the leading economic power, together make up the Anglo-American portion of the »New World«. Latin America, the romanicly-oriented part of the continent, begins directly at the northern border of Mexico.

North and Central America
NATURAL ENVIRONMENT

With islands and peninsulas making up a quarter of its surface area, this continent has the longest coastal circumference of any continent: 75,000 kilometres. Greenland is also considered part of this northern land mass. At the Bering Straight there are only 92 kilometres separating North America from Asia. The continent stretches 6,000 kilometres from Alaska in the west to Novia Scotia in the east and measures 8,700 kilometres from north to south. Mountain ranges basically divide the continent meridionally into three parts: the Atlantic maritime region to the east of the low Appalachian Mountains, a central lowland including the Canadian Shield in the middle, with the high mountain region of the western cordillera to the west.

The Appalachians, a soft, rolling range of parallel ridges, rise to their highest point at Mount Mitchell (2,037 m). The slopes are still largely covered with their original vegetation of mixed and summer-green deciduous forest.

On the adjoining plains to the west, however, the natural flora has been largely decimated. The woodlands of this temperate zone were cleared by the early settlers who proceeded to till the inland plains. In Florida and on the coastal plain along the Gulf, parts of the subtropical moist forests and marshlands (Everglades) have been protected as national parks. The Mississippi, the third longest river in the world, drains the central lowland, before emptying into the Gulf of Mexico. The Canadian Shield with the Hudson Bay in the middle is the tectonic keystone of North America. It gets its name from the shield-like bulge running around its edges. The glaciated valleys and fjords, landscapes covered with smoothed round humps, and the long chains of lateral moraines provide visible evidence that this region was once covered by glaciers. The string of lakes running along the rim of the shield starts at the Great Lakes, the largest freshwater lakes in the world, and stretches up to Great Bear Lake in the far North. With the exception of the icy desert of the Arctic archipelago and the lichen and moss-covered tundra in the marshy permafrost areas, the North is covered almost entirely by vast, virtually untouched, boreal coniferous forests. To this day, trappers and hunters continue to stalk the animals of these woodlands for their fur.

The Rocky Mountains (Mount McKinley, 6,193 m), a young range of longitudinal ridges, make up the Continental Divide, the mighty watershed dividing the areas draining into the Pacific and the Atlantic Ocean. The twin chains of the Rockies are separated by vast elevated basins, such as the Colorado Plateau, the Great Basin and the Mexican highland. In the rain shadow of the Rockies, highland steppes and even semi-deserts and deserts have evolved (Mojave Desert).

Cutting their way through this range, rivers have gouged spectacular ravines, or canyons, through the mountains and highland plateaus. Due to the low precipitation, except in Alaska, there are no glaciers or major lakes. The Mexican highland, bounded by a mighty string of volcanoes to the south, is typical cactus country. It was from here that these prickly plants began their successful proliferation around the world.

Page 133: To find an outlet, the Colorado River had to carve its way through 350 kilometres of plateau, cutting a vari-colored fissure up to 1,800 metres deep: the Grand Canyon.

Top left: Calc-sinter terraces formed by the geysers in Yellowstone National Park.

Far left: Moose in Yellowstone National Park.

Left: Originally indigenous only to the Americas, the triumphant cactus has spread around the world.

Top: The Canyon de Chelly in Arizona (»arida zona«; Spanish = arid area).

Center: Alpine landscape in the Canadian Rocky Mountains.

Right: Redwood National Park in the Sierra Nevada. These giant Sequoia trees, which can grow to a height of 100 metres, yield a fine-grained soft timber valued by the furniture industry.

Parallelling the coast and flanked by the Pacific Mountains, the long Californian valley marks the position of the earth-quake-prone San Andreas Fault. In fact, all of western North America makes up part of the circumpacific »Ring of Fire«. This was dramaticly demonstrated by the eruptions of Mount St. Helen (1980) and is constantly visible in the spectacular display of volcanic phenomena in Yellowstone National Park.

With its arching chains of mountains, its strings of volcanoes and the lowlands opening out onto the Caribbean, the Central American land bridge comprises highly varied topography within a small area. 4,000 kilometres long, the curved string of islands including the Greater Antilles (Cuba, Jamaica, Hispaniola, Puerto Rico), the Lesser Antilles and the Bahamas is partially of volcanic origin and partially evolved out of karstified limestone tables or coral limestone deposits. The Cayman Trench, including the Puerto Rico Trench (-9,219 m), marks the Atlantic edge of Central America. The na-

tural vegetation on the windward slopes consists of rain forests, whereas the leeward sides are covered with dry savanna. Both types of vegetation have been reduced through chop-and-burn clearing for plantations.

North America owes much of the temperateness of its climate to the meridional structure of its tectonic elements. Mountain ranges along the coasts limit the areas affected by oceanic influences. Well on into late spring, cold air sweeps in from the arctic North, reaching as far as the southern coast. In the summer, conversely, hot, damp air floods north from the Gulf of Mexico, spreading a blanket of unbearable humidity all the way up into Canada. Even mountains are no obstacle to the tornadoes racing north. The cold Labrador Stream lowers temperatures as far south as the New York area, and the Hudson Bay functions like an ice cellar. The 100th meridian marks the beginning of an arid zone where rain crops fail to grow.

Taken as a whole, North America's climate is distinctly more continental than Europe's.

Top: Mesas and spires in Bryce Canyon National Park. The splendid array of rugged forms was produced by the erosion of red clays and marl in this elevated, arid zone.

Left: Monument Valley in Arizona.

Lower right: With its 50-metre-high steaming spout, Old Faithful is the largest geysir in Yellowstone National Park.

Cultivated land (arable land, plantations, irrigated land)

Grassland and grassland farming

Forest of the temperate Zone

Tropical forest

Savannah

Steppe

Semi-desert, desert

Boreal forest

Tundra

Rock, snow and ice areas of mountain and polar regions

1:30,000,000   0 200 400 600 800 1000 Kilometers

North and Central America
PEOPLE AND CULTURE

On 12 October, 1492 when Columbus landed on San Salvador (part of the Bahama group), he thought he had discovered India. Today, this misconception lives on in our use of the word »Indian« (or Spanish: »indio«) to refer to Native Americans, as well as in the name »West Indies«. The Native Americans were almost displaced by wave upon wave of immigrants. Finally, reservations were set up in relatively unattractive parts of the country, where some eleven million Indians live today.

Since its discovery, North America's population has not only witnessed an extraordinary growth in terms of numbers. The first settlers were from Great Britain, Ireland, Holland and Sweden. Then the United States of America first admitted the Germans and Irish during the second half of the 19th century, and then, as of the turn of the century, let immigrants from southern and eastern Europe into its ›melting pot‹. Today, the descendants of those immigrants make up ninety per cent of the population of Anglo-America. And then there were the black slaves ›imported‹ to the South before slavery was abolished in 1865. Many of the freed slaves migrated to the North and West. Today they account for some ten per cent of the Anglo-Americans. Particularly since the Second World War, increasing numbers of Chinese, Japanese and Philippinos have settled in the western United States, while in the East the immigration of Puerto Ricans continues unabated. Although Puerto Rico is autonomous, its inhabitants have Ame-

rican citizenship. The largely Polynesian Hawaiian Islanders did not receive US statehood until 1959. Last but not least, there are the some 55,000 native inhabitants of the arctic North, the Eskimos who are considered to be of Mongoloid extraction.

Whereas English is the dominant language in most parts of the continent (Anglo-America), Canada has French as its second language. After all, the French language and traditions play a key role in the French-Canadian's strong sense of independence. French is also spoken on the Lesser Antilles and in Haiti.

In the rest of Central America, however, Spanish is spoken. With the aboriginal West Indian population nearly extinct, these islands are now relatively densely populated by mulattoes and blacks. Mexico and Guatemala are generally thought of as countries with largely Indio populati-

Top left: The Dalton Highway north of Fairbanks in Alaska, USA.

Lower left: Dawson City, a typical small North American town, whose mainstreet shops largely supply the population of small settlements scattered throughout the surrounding region.

Top right: Virginia City (Nevada, USA), once a center of commerce and of the livestock trade, is now a museum town.

Center: Manhattan, New York, as seen from the Hudson River. This unique amassment of skyscrapers is the most important financial center and stock market in the world. Each of the twin towers of the World Trade Center is over 400 metres high.

Far right: Flowing above ground through heavily insulated pipes, oil from the northernmost state of the USA is pumped south through the Transalaska Pipeline.

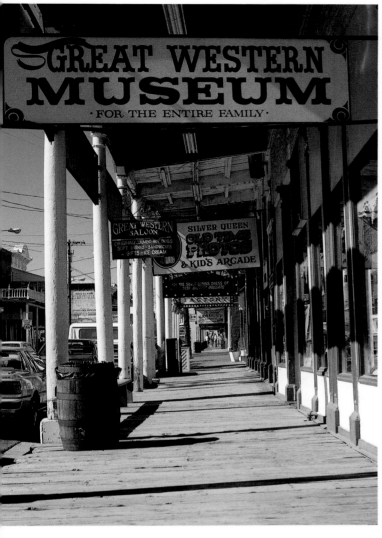

ons, whereas Honduras, El Salvador and Nicaragua are considered mestizo countries.

The continent's average population of 13 inhabitants per square kilometre says little about the actual population distribution. With an average density of 200 people per square kilometre, the most populous region in North America, an area favored by its climate, stretches from the Great Lakes on the north to the Gulf of Mexico on the south, from the Atlantic on the east to the rainfall boundary (approx. the 100th western meridian) on the west. Beyond the adjoining zone of sparse population, there is another populous zone to the west (California).

In Central America the highest concentration of people is found in the Central Mexican Highland. There are twenty million people living in Mexico City alone! In fact, urbanization is very high throughout North and Central America. Some two thirds of the total population are found living in cities.

Most of the Anglo-American population belongs to one of the various Protestant denominations, while approximately a quarter are Catholics – plus the some six million Jews and three million Orthodox Christians. In Central America, as in the rest of Latin America, the Catholic Church is dominant.

There is a sharp dividing line separating the industrial from the developing countries – cutting right across North and Central America and coinciding here with the boundary between the Anglo-American and the Latin American countries: the border between the USA and Mexico.

North of this boundary, there are readily accessible rich deposits of all the mineral resources in commercial demand. This was one of

the natural prerequisites for the development of the most important economic region – not just of North America, but of the world – and the home of eighty million people: the American Manufacturing Belt. Already blessed with good natural harbors, the building of transcontinental transport systems – the Central Pacific, in 1869, being the first rail connection between the East and West Coasts – was a major boon to the economy, as was the productive, material and capital-intensive methods of farming the abundant fertile land. These endeavors were supported by the inhabitants' Protestant-Calvinist work ethic coupled with a capitalist economic system with its inherent incentives to private enterprise. The most obvious manifestations of this so-called »American Way of Life« are a generally prosperous, highly motorized population with increasing leisure time. Success is measured in terms of material prosperity. Streams of commuters are but one product of American mobility. The emigration from agrarian to industrial regions, frequently changed jobs and places of residence, the relocation of companies, as well as the migration of retired elderly to the Sunbelt in the South (especially Florida) and West (California) have had a major effect on American society.

New industrial zones have evolved at the southern edge of the Appalachians, in the Gulf region, in California and in the northwestern USA, as well as

Top left: From the eleventh to thirteenth centuries, the Anasazi, precolumbian Pueblo Indians, built these cliff dwellings into the sandstone rock (Mesa Verde, Colorado).

Left center: Sugar cane harvest in Central America. The cane is topped, defoliated and chopped off near the ground, and then processed immediately.

Lower left: Richmond, the capital of Virginia (USA), was founded in 1737. During the American Civil War (1861-1865) it was the capital of the Southern Confederacy.

140

Top center: An Indian woman working her loom in Mexico City. She sells her hand-crafted products to tourists.

Center: With its splendid mosaic façades, the Central Library in Mexico City is the symbol of the university.

Top right: A show in Disneyland, the fantasy and adventure park for young and old built in 1955. The film producer Walt Disney (1901-1966) invented Mickey Mouse and Donald Duck.

Lower right: Rum is a brownish-yellow brandy distilled from molasses and sometimes also from the sugar foam of cane sugar. The English word »rum-bullion« means »large commotion«.

between Montreal and Toronto. In the USA, the world's leading economic area, tertiar-sector economic growth has entailed the steady development from an industrial society to a service-oriented one.

In Central America, on the other hand, the dominant factors characterizing social and economic structures are: a sharp contrast between the impoverished masses and a small, affluent upper class; a relatively high illiteracy rate (up to 50 per cent); explosive population growth; high unemployment; a low level of industrialization as well as the absence of a middle class. The only area of economic concentration in Central America is the Mexican highland. In the coastal regions of the Central American land bridge and archipelago, tropical plants and fruits are grown for the world market.

Whereas the Anglo-American countries are all constitutional democracies, most Central American states are headed either by the military or by a dictator; Cuba is a »Socialist« Republic.

Human industriousness has left a strong imprint on the Anglo-American landscape. The most visible example is the partitioning of cities and the countryside into grids of squares. In large parts of rural USA, the landscape – dotted with single-family homesteads – is dominated by this geometric organization of square plots. The central market towns evolving at the traffic junctions have the same checker-board layout as the surrounding countryside.

Canada	United States of America	Mexico	Guatemala	Belize	El Savador	Honduras	Nicaragua
Canada	United States of America	Estados Unidos Mexicanos	República de Guatemala	Belize	República de El Salvador	República de Honduras	República de Nicaragua
Ottawa	*Washington*	*México*	*Guatemala*	*Belmopan*	San *Salvador*	*Tegucigalpa*	*Managua*
9.976.139 sqkm	9.363.123 sqkm	1.958.128 sqkm	108.889 sqkm	22.963 sqkm	21.041 sqkm	112.088 sqkm	130.000 sqkm
Pop.: 25.610.000	Pop.: 242.080.000	Pop.: 81.160.000	Pop.: 8.430.000	Pop.: 170.000	Pop.: 5.010.000	Pop.: 4.510.000	Pop.: 3.380.000
English, French	English	Spanish, Indian languages	Spanish, Maya-Quiche dialects	English, Spanish Creole, Carib, Maya	Spanish, Indian dialects	Spanish, English, Indian dialects	Spanish, English, Chibcha
Canadian dollar	US dollar	Mexican peso	Quetzal	Belize dollar	El Salvador Colón	Lempira	Córdoba

High-rise buildings, a product of functional American architecture, dominate the skylines of America's major cities, whereas historic buildings are largely missing. Metropolitan suburbs are typically composed of sprawling settlements of individually-owned homes.

In the world of music, jazz – a blend of African-American and European musical elements – has spread triumphally around the world from its birthplace in the American South.

Top left: Bananas, one of the main agricultural and export products of Central America.

Lower left: Indian children in Mexico.

Top right: Fruit plantations (orange groves) in California, the »fruit garden« of North America.

Lower right: Las Vegas (Nevada), the amusement capital of the USA.

Costa Rica	**Panama**	**Cuba**	**Bahamas**	**Jamaica**	**Haiti**	**Dominican Republic**	**Antigua and Barbuda**
República de Costa Rica	República de Panamá	República de Cuba	The Commonwealth of the Bahamas	Jamaika	République d'Haïti	República Dominicana	Antigua and Barbuda
San José	Panamá	Havanna	Nassau	Kingston	Port-au-Prince	Santo Domingo	St. John's
50.700 sqkm	75.650 sqkm	114.524 sqkm	13.935 sqkm	10.991 sqkm	27.750 km²	48.734 sqkm	443 sqkm
Pop.: 2.670.000	Pop.: 2.270.000	Pop.: 10.300.000	Pop.: 240.000	Pop.: 2.370.000	Pop.:5.440.000	Pop.: 6.720.000	Pop.: 82.000
Spanish	Spanish, English, Indian dialects	Spanish	English	English	French	Spanish	English, Creole
Costa Rica Colón	Balboa	Cuban peso	Bahama dollar	Jamaican dollarr	Gourde	Dominican peso	East Caribbean dollar

Staint Cristopher and Nevis	 **Dominica**	**Saint Lucia**	**Saint Vincent and the Grenadines**	**Barbados**	**Grenada**	**Trinidad and Tobago**
Federation of Saint Cristopher and Nevis	Commonwealth of Dominica	St. Lucia Sainte-Lucie	St. Vincent and the Grenadines	Barbados	State of Grenada	Republic of Trinidad and Tobago
Basseterre	Roseau	Castries	Kingstown	Bridgetown	Saint George's	Port of Spain
262 sqkm	751 sqkm	616 sqkm	389 sqkm	431 sqkm	344 sqkm	Pop.:5.128 sqkm
Pop.: 60.000	Pop.: 80.000	Pop.: 140.000	Pop.: 100.000	Pop.: 250.000	Pop.: 115.000	1.200.000
English	English, Creole French	English, Patois (Creole French)	English, Creole English	English	English, Creole English or French	English
East Caribbean dollar	East Caribbean dollar	East Caribbean dollar	East Caribbean dollar	Barbados Dollar	East Caribbean dollar	Trinidad and Tobago dollar

SOUTH AMERICA

South America is the most tropical continent with the corresponding climate and vegetation, as well as the world's largest river basin and the most complex river system. There is great disparity in the levels of economic development among the South American countries. The fourth largest continent is one of the world's major developing zones with all the familiar symptoms: from exploding populations migrating to expanding city slums to unemployment, housing shortages and national debt. The unbalanced population distribution – its heterogenous population crowding into the Atlantic coastal region while large portions of the interior remain nearly deserted – is an aftermath of South America's colonial past.

South America
NATURAL ENVIRONMENT

The triangular southern continent has a very regular, unindented outline without a single major bay. With islands and peninsulas making up only one per cent of its total surface area, its coastline measures a mere 28,700 kilometres. Its maximum width is 5,100 kilometres, its maximum length 7,500 kilometres. The Central American land bridge connects it to North America to the north; it is joined with the Antarctic by the South Antilles and South Georgia to the south. Whereas deep ocean trenches (Peru Trench, Atacama Trench: -8,066 m) parallel the Pacific coastline, on the Atlantic side the continent slopes gradually, spreading out to form a broad shelf base – upon which the Islas Malvinas (Falkland Islands) rest.

The surface of South America displays a structure similar to that of its continental neighbor, North America.

Like the North American Rocky Mountains, the Andes are a part of the circumpacific fault zone and include several chains of volcanoes, such as the Cotopaxi (5,911 m), the Chimborazo (6,310 m) and the Aconcagua (6,958 m). This young mountain range, consisting of an east and a west cordillera, has been frequently shaken by earthquakes. The coastal chain and the eastern chain are separated – e.g. in the central Andes – by highlands (the Bolivian Altiplano) at elevations of 3,500 to 4,000 metres. Lying in the rain shadow of the coastal ridges, these highlands are very arid. As a result, most of the lakes, with the exception of Lake Titicaca, have a very high salt con-

tent. In Patagonia the Cordilleras lose some of their height, taking on the more subdued forms of secondary mountains. The fjords penetrating the western coastline and the finger-shaped lakes surrounded by moraines are signs of Patagonia's glacial past.

Over half the surface of South America is covered by lowlands. The largest, the Amazon lowland, was built up out of alluvium from rivers and lakes. With a drainage area of over seven million square kilometres, it is comparable only to the Zaire basin (Congo). Most of this lowland is at an elevation below 200 metres above sea-level. The Amazon carries more water than any other river and,

measuring 250 kilometres at the mouth, it is also the widest river in the world.

Parts of the broad fluvial plains of the Orinoco (Llanos) and the Parana/Rio de la Plata are as flat as a table. Benchlands (cuestas) and lava plateaus (Mato Grosso) are characteristic features of the highlands in the eastern mountainous regions of Guyana (Pico da Neblina, 3,014 m) and Brazil (Pico da Bandeira, 2,890 m). In Brazil the Atlantic coastline rises sharply like a wall to meet the eastern edge of the Planalto, which then descends gradually toward the interior. South America's tropical climate manifests itself in monthly normal temperatures which never vary

Page 143: The floodplain of the Rio Negro, just above where it empties into the Amazon.

Top left: Ravaged tropical rain forest: robbed of its protective vegetation, the soil of this sloping terrain is totally exposed to erosion.

Lower left: To the Incas, Lake Titicaca in the central Andean highland was a holy lake. Today, it is not only the largest standing body of water in South America, but also the highest lake (3,812 metres) in the world on which steamboats ply.

Top: This sort of barren mountain steppe is typical of the »tierra helada« in the Peruvian Andes.

Center: South America's Cordilleras rise to an elevation of 6,958 metres at Mt. Aconcagua. Unlike high mountain regions in temperate zones, in the tropics they are islands of aridity.

Right: Iguacu Falls: shortly before flowing into the Rio Parana, the roaring Iguacu River plunges over basalt steps into the depths 60 to 80 metres below.

more than one degree (»diurnal climate«) from the annual temperature average (in Manaus: 27°C). Another tropical ›blessing‹ is year-round precipitation. On the northwestern flank of the Colombian Cordillera northeasterly and southeasterly trade winds shed an average of over 8,500 millimetres of rain per year. The meridional arrangement of the cordilleras blocks major air currents. There are regions affected by periodic aridity beginning just above and below the equator; such as the Mato Grosso (1,300-1,400 mm) and the Gran Chaco (less than 500 mm). On the western side of the continent where the cold waters of the Humboldt Stream rise to the surface, the air currents shed their moisture before reaching land. As a result, the central Pacific coast includes one of the most arid deserts in the world, the Atacama. In the continent's remote South, the distribution of rainfall is just the opposite with westerly winds blessing the Pacific maritime region with plenty of rain, while Patagonia to the east remains dry. A third of the continent is covered with tropical rain forest (»selva« or »hyläa«), which are bordered by savannas with scattered forest formations, like the Venezuelan »llano«, the Brazilian »caatinga« and »campo«, as well as the Argentinean Gran Chaco and »pampa«.

Among the abundant species of South American wildlife, the most spectular varieties are the some 200 types of hummingbirds and multi-hued parrots. Another of this continent's »character animals« is the llama, the tamed version of the South American camel.

Top: In tropical rain forests, the various plants compete for what little light there is – and even it rarely reaches the forest floor.

Center: Settlers set up homesteads along the new roads, burning down the rain forest, only to reap a meagre harvest for a few years before moving on – leaving behind irreparably destroyed terrain.

Lower left: With its long limbs and prehensile tail, the death's-head monkey is well-adapted to the conditions of its environment.

Lower right: Sheep grazing on the vast Patagonian pampa.

ATLANTIC OCEAN

PACIFIC OCEAN

ATLANTIC OCEAN

Caribbean Sea

Equator

Tropic of Capricorn

La Habana
Sta Clara
Cuba
Bahamas
Gt Inagua I.
Canal de Yucatán
C. S. Antonio
I. de la Juventud
Guantánamo
Mérida
Cozumel
Pen. de Yucatán
Great
Greater
Antilles
Kingston
Jamaica
Port-au-Prince
Sto Domingo
S. Juan
Puerto Rico
Is Virgin Is.
Anguilla
Hispaniola
Guadalupe
Antilles
Dominica
Martinique
Fort de France
Barbados
Lesser Antilles
Tobago
Port of Spain
Trinidad
Ila de Margarita

Golfo de Honduras
Cabo Gracias a Dios
Tegucigalpa
Managua
L. de Nicaragua
S. José
Cabo Blanco
Coiba
Pta Naranjas
Golfo de Panamá
Panamá
Colón
Golfo del Darién
Monteria
Cúcuta
Cartagena
Barranquilla
Golfo de Venezuela
L. de Maracaibo
Mérida
Valencia
Caracas
Maturin
Pta Gallinas

I. de Coco
Malpelo
Buenaventura
Cali
Medellín
Manizales
Bogotá
Santa
Pasto
Esmeraldas
Llanos
Meta
Pto Carreño
Orinoco
Cto Bolívar
Georgetown
Paramaribo
Cayenne
van Blommesteinmeer
Macizo de las Guyanas
Mt. Roraima 2812
Boa Vista
Brazo Casiquiare
Orinoco
Maracá

Galápagos
S. Cristóbal
Ila Española
Equator
Quito
Chimborazo 6267
Guayaquil
Golfo de Guayaquil
Tumbes
Pto Pariñas
Cuenca
Mitú
Caquetá
Río Negro
Japurá
Amazonas
Manaus
Santarém
Macapá
Marajó
Belém
São Luís
Camocim
Fortaleza
Fernando de Noronha

Chiclayo
Trujillo
Huascarán 6768
Huánuco
Callao
Lima
Pisco
Moyobamba
Marañón
Iquitos
Amazonas
Selvas
Juruá
Río Purus
Río Branco
Pto Velho
Guajará-Mirim
Guaporé
Madeira
Tapajós
Juruena
Xingu
Teresina
Floriano
Natal
Recife
Maceió
Aracaju
São Francisco
Caatingas
Brasileiro

Cuzco
Trinidad
Mato Grosso
Planalto do Mato Grosso
Cuiabá
Campos
Planalto
Diamantina
Rio Verde
Goiânia
Brasília
Paranaíba
Uberaba
Ilhéus
Salvador

L. Titicaca
La Paz
Ilimani 6882
Cochabamba
Sta Cruz
Sucre
Potosí
L. de Poopó
Arica
Iquique
Arequipa
Tupiza
Corumbá
Campo Grande
Araçatuba
Ribeirão Preto
Bauru
Campinas
Londrina
São Paulo
Santos
Rio de Janeiro
Campos
Vitória
Trindade

Antofagasta
Salta
Pilcomayo
Chaco
Gran
Asunción
Concepción
Paraná
Ponta Grossa
Curitiba
Blumenau
Florianópolis
Passo Fundo

Desventurados
S. Félix
S. Ambrosio
Copiapó
S. Miguel de Tucumán
Resistencia
Corrientes
R. Salado
Sta Maria
Pto Alegre

Coquimbo
Córdoba
L.na Mar Chiquita
Santa Fe
Paraná
Rosario
Salto
Bajé
Pelotas
Rio Grande
Durazno

Aconcagua 6960
Mendoza
Valparaíso
Santiago
S. Rafael
Pampa
Buenos Aires
Rio de la Plata
La Plata
Montevideo
Dolores
Mar del Plata

Juan Fernández
Alejandro Selkirk
Robinson Crusoe
Talca
Concepción
R. Colorado
Temuco
Sta Rosa
Andes
Bahía Blanca
Restinga de Sefton
Valdivia
R. Negro
Osorno
Golfo S. Matías
Pen. Valdés

Castro
Chiloé
Archipiélago de los Chonos
Pen. de Taitao
Comodoro Rivadavia
Golfo de S. Jorge
Cabo Tres Puntas
Patagonia
Golfo de Penas
Campana
Wellington
Hanover
Falkland Is.
Stanley
Bahía Grande
Rio Gallegos
Desolación
Sta Inés
Punta Arenas
Est. de Magallanes
Tierra del Fuego
C. S. Diego
Ushuaia
C. de Hornos
I. de los Estados
Est. Le Maire
South Georgia

Legend:
- Cultivated land (arable land, plantations and irrigated land)
- Grassland of the temperate zone
- Forest of the temperate zone
- Tropical forest (predominant tropical rain forest)
- Savannah (Campos and Llanos)
- Dry tropical forest and dry savannah (Chaco and Caatinga)
- Steppe (Grassland and shrub; Pampa)
- Semi-desert and desert
- Alpine vegetation (Puna and Paramo); Subantarctic shrub and moss tundra
- Rock, snow and ice areas of mountain regions

1 : 30 000 000
0 200 400 600 800 1000 km

South America
PEOPLE AND CULTURE

The dominant influence of the discoverers and explorers from the Iberian Peninsula – and of their Spanish and Portuguese descendants – is still evident in all forms of South American culture today. One of their main instruments, of course, being their respective languages: both so-called Romance languages. This is why South America, along with Central America, is considered part of the cultural sphere called Latin America, or Ibero-America. There are only a few actual »Indio countries« remaining; such as Ecuador, Peru and Bolivia. Mestizos, the ›mixed-blooded‹ offspring of European and American Indian parentage, make up 24 per cent of the Latin American population. 43 per cent are whites – who in the so-called »white countries«, Argentina, Uruguay and Chile, in fact, make up the majority. Twelve per cent are mulattoes, of mixed European and African extraction, and eight per cent are blacks. The some 100,000 Brazilian Indians live in isolated groups – with probably no long-term prospects of preserving their cultural identities. Once they had discovered America in 1492, the Spanish and Portuguese powers set about exploiting their overseas wealth. Destroying the advanced Indian civilizations, they divided up the continent between them; Portugal claimed Brazil, leaving the rest to Spain. As a result, Spanish is spoken in all the countries of Latin America except in Brazil where Portuguese is spoken. The vernacular versions spoken in the various countries of course vary to a greater or lesser degree from the language spoken in their respec-

tive mother country. Since missionaries were busy spreading their faith wherever the European colonists settled, today, South America is the Roman Catholic continent – with only five million Protestants. A more recent trend, however, is the proliferation of cults mixing African traditions with elements of Christian religion.

The European powers divided their colonies up into viceking-doms and provinces, distributing the land among wealthy aristocrats, merchants or military leaders in the form of latifundia, or large estates; thus preventing peasant colonization from the outset. Until 1888, when slavery was abolished, blacks were brought in as slave labor from Africa.

Here, unlike North America, the dominance of large haciendas made it difficult for immigrants to settle as farmers. So even the mass immigration of Italians, Spanish and Portuguese during the 19th century was no real stimulus to agricultural development in Latin America. Hampered by this barrier to mass settlement, the colonies were reduced to suppliers of raw materials (sugar, tobacco, cotton, gold, diamonds, etc.) and markets for European goods. This established South America's economic and political dependence upon the industrial countries. Foreign investment policies reinforced this development, with Europeans and Americans pouring capital into the cattle industry in the Rio de la

Top left: The Copacabana, the famous bathing beach of Rio de Janeiro. The buildings in the background belong to the upper class.

Lower left: In Latin America, the Catholic continent, devout Christian religiousness mingles with traditional Indian customs.

Top center: This view of Brasilia from the television tower shows the business and entertainment center in the midground with the crown-shaped cathedral (to the right) and the congressional high-rises and government buildings behind it, on either side of the Square of the Three Powers.

Lower center: A road through the Pantanal, a vast marshland in southern Brazil.

Top right: Picturesque painted façades, such as these in a poor quarter in Buenos Aires, often distract from the misery of the inhabitants.

Lower right: The tango, originally a West Indian folk dance, was turned into a social dance in Argentina prior to its introduction in Europe in 1911.

149

Plata district, as well as into sugar, cotton and coffee production, and Andean mining ventures – investments geared exclusively toward promoting the export of raw materials and agricultural products.

In the early 19th century, the South American colonies gained their independence – within national borders largely adhering to the lines of the former Spanish-American administrative districts. Independence did nothing, however, to change the traditional social order. Feudal and semi-feudal social structures, large-scale land-holding and slavery remained, as sources of the extreme social tension still unresolved today – and particularly evident in the visual contrast between the manor houses of rural landlords and the miserable hovels of their tenant farmers. The military continues to play a crucial role in the power strucures of these countries. Since the early sixties alone, military juntas have gained power through coup d'états in Brazil in 1964, in Peru and Panama in 1968, in Bolivia in 1969, in Ecuador in 1972, in Chile in 1973 and in Argentina in 1976 – some of them still in power today. Alternately, the heads of state are frequently authoritarian rulers, so-called caudillos, supported by loyal members of the military forces.

All South American countries have one factor in common: a growing population. Once a result of the large influx of immigrants (around 13 million since 1850), this growth is now due to

Top left: São Salvador da Bahia, the capital of Bahia State (Brazil).

Bottom: A market on Antigua, one of the Lesser Antilles with a predominately mestizo population.

Top center: The opera house of Manaus – the capital of the Brazilian state of Amazon. Its gilded cupola testifies to the city's former wealth as a center of the rubber trade.

Center: A smallholding in the rain forest of the Amazon basin. Once the jungle has been burnt down and stripped, it takes but a few crops to deplete the forest soil.

Top right: São Salvador da Bahia, with its array of baroque churches, is the seat of a Catholic archbishop.

Lower right: Rio de Janeiro sprawls around the Bay of Guanabara (left). The unmistakable Sugar Loaf Mountain (center) separates the bay from the open Atlantic to the right.

high birth rates – which, in turn, can be partly attributed to high illiteracy rates: over fifty per cent in Bolivia, Brazil, Peru and Ecuador; just under ten per cent in the ›white‹ South American countries. The gross disparity in the distribution of property between the rural poor and the landed class has caused many of the landless to emigrate to the cities in search of work, better living conditions and a more promising life. Today, therefore, nearly half the South American population lives in the cities, i.e. in the major centers of commerce and industry. Cities like Rio de Janeiro, São Paulo, Montevideo, Buenos Aires, Santiago de Chile, Caracas, Bogotá and Lima; cities with skylines dominated by the huge skyscrapers of multinational corporations. Instead of solving the problems, though, this migration has merely shifted them.

The result: growing slums within the »primate cities«, as well as at the edges of metropolises – with all their negative symptoms, such as criminality, poverty, unemployment, undernourishment, chronic lack of education, prostitution, etc.

Half the South American population still subsists on agriculture – under property and market conditions equivalent to those prevailing under the old colonial plantation systems. Economic development is impeded by the uneven population distribution, which in turn counteracts attempts to improve the transport and communications infra-

Colombia	**Venezuela**	**Guyana**	**Suriname**
República de Columbia	República de Venezuela	Cooperative Republic of Guyana	Republiek van Suriname
Bogotá	*Caracas*	*Georgetown*	*Paramaribo*
1.138.914 sqkm	912.050 sqkm	214.969 sqkm	163.265 sqkm
Pop.: 29.730.000	Pop.: 18.270.000	Pop.: 970.000	Pop.: 380.000
Spanish, Indian languages	Spanish, Indian languages	English	Dutch, Sranan Tongo (Creole) Saramaccan (mixed languages) English
Colombian peso	Bolívar	Guyana dollar	Suriname guilder

structure. South America lacks efficient transportation systems, with the large, navigable rivers often the only access to the remote interior. The population is concentrated along the coastal fringe area; particularly within the maritime provinces ›facing‹ Europe, i.e. along the Atlantic coast, where the extensive industrial regions around São Paulo and along the Rio de la Plata developped. Brazil even resorted to building its new capital, Brasilia, inland – in a largely failed attempt to focus the attention of the public and industry upon the development of the interior.

South America is still heavily dependent on foreign capital for all major endeavors – whether they be Venezuelan or Colombian oil drilling operations, mineral-mining in the Guyanan mountains, for extracting copper, zinc, lead or silver from the Peruvian or Bolivian Indian highlands, or for Argentinian farms in the pampas.

In spite of deeply rooted national differences, culturally, the countries of South America have a great deal in common, starting with the various Iberian influences. Other common denominators are the checker-board layout of Latin American cities around central squares, as well as the dominant ecclesiastical and secular buildings in the ubiquitous quasi-baroque »Jesuit style«. Like Anglo-American jazz, Latin American folk music – along with such rhythmically accentuated dances as the rumba, samba and tango – has become popular throughout the world.

Left: This road cutting straight through the tropical rain forest gets its rich red color from laterite – an iron-rich deposit typical of many tropical soils.

Ecuador	**Peru**	**Bolivia**	**Chile**	**Brazil**	**Paraguay**	**Argentina**	**Uruguay**
República del Ecuador	República del Perú	República Bolivia	República de Chile	República Federativa do Brasil	República del Paraguay	República Argentina	República Oriental del Uruguay
Quito	*Lima*	*Sucre*	*Santiago de Chile*	*Brasilia*	*Asunción*	*Buenos Aires*	*Montevideo*
283.561 sqkm	1.285.216 sqkm	1.098.581 sqkm	756.626 sqkm	8.511.965 sqkm	406.752 sqkm	2.767.889 sqkm	177.508 sqkm
Pop.: 9.650.000	Pop.: 20.730.000	Pop.: 6.550.000	Pop.: 12.540.000	141.450.000	3.920.000	31.500.000	2.980.000
Spanish, Quetchua (colloquial language)	Spanish, Quetchua (colloquial language)	Spanish, Quetchua Aymara	Spanish	Portuguese	Spanish, Guaraní	Spanish	Spanish
Sucre	Inti	Boliviano, (Peso?)	Chilean peso	Cruzado	Guaraní	Austral	New peso

Index

The index contains all the names that appear within the international map section (p. 9 - 14 and p. 16 - 80). It is ordered alphabetically. The umlauts ä, ö and ü have been treated as the letters a, o and u, and the ligatures æ, œ, as ae and oe.
The first figure after the name entry is the page number of the single or double page where the name being looked up is to be found. The letters and figures after the page reference refer to the grid in which the name is located or those grid sections

through which the name extends. The location of settlements is indicated by the grid number of the symbol for places. The names that have been abbreviated on the maps are listed unabbreviated in the index. Only with U.S. place names have the official abbreviations been inserted accorded to common U.S. practice, e.g. Washington, D.C. The alphabetical sequence includes also prefixes, e.g. Fort, Saint. The determinative element of geographical names follows behind, e.g. Mexico, Gulf of –;

Wight, Isle of – or the name of the city behind that of a suburb, e.g. Fremantle, Perth –. Official supplements to place names are included in the alphabetization. They may follow to the name proper, e.g. Châlons-sur-Marne or be added in parenthesis, particularly in German speaking areas, e.g. Kempten (Allgäu).
To a certain extend official second name forms, linguistic versions, renamed places and other secondary designations are listed in the index with reference to the name form used in the map, e.g.

Kamien Pomorski = Cammin in Pommern; Meran = Merano; Siam = Thailand.
To differentiate identical name forms mainly motor vehicle nationality letters for the respective countries have been added in brackets following these names:

A	Austria	ETH	Ethiopia
AFG	Afghanistan	F	France
AL	Albania	FJI	Fiji
AND	Andorra	FL	Liechtenstein
AUS	Australia	GB	United Kingdom
B	Belgium	GCA	Guatemala
BD	Bangladesh	GH	Ghana
BDS	Barbados	GR	Greece
BG	Bulgaria	GUY	Guyana
BH	Belize	H	Hungary
BOL	Bolivia	HK	Hong Kong
BR	Brazil	HY	Burkina Faso
BRN	Bahrein	I	Italy
BRU	Brunei	IL	Israel
BS	Bahamas	IND	India
BUR	Burma	IR	Iran
C	Cuba	IRL	Ireland
CDN	Canada	IRQ	Iraq
CH	Switzerland	IS	Iceland
CI	Ivory Coast	J	Japan
CL	Sri Lanka	JA	Jamaika
CO	Colombia	JOR	Jordan
CR	Costa Rica	K	Cambodia
CS	Czechoslovakia	KWT	Kuwait
CY	Cyprus	L	Luxembourg
D	Germany	LAO	Laos
DK	Denmark	LAR	Libya
DOM	Dominican Republic	LB	Liberia
DY	Benin	LS	Lesotho
DZ	Algeria	M	Malta
E	Spain	MA	Morocco
EAK	Kenya	MAL	Malaysia
EAT	Tanzania	MC	Monaco
EAU	Uganda	MEX	Mexico
EC	Ecuador	MS	Mauritius
ES	El Salvador	MW	Malawi
ET	Egypt		

N	Norway	SCV	Vatican City
NA	Netherlands Antilles	SD	Swasiland
NIC	Nicaragua	SF	Finland
NL	Netherlands	SGP	Singapore
NZ	New Zealand	SME	Suriname
P	Portugal	SN	Senegal
PA	Panama	SP	Somalia
PAK	Pakistan	SU	former Sovjet Union
PE	Peru	SY	Seychelles
PL	Poland	SYR	Syria
PNG	Papua New Guinea	T	Thailand
PY	Paraguay	TG	Togo
Q	Qatar	TJ	China
RA	Argentina	TN	Tunisia
RB	Botsuana	TR	Turkey
RC	Taiwan	TT	Trinidad and Tobago
RCA	Central African Republic	USA	United States
RCB	Congo	VN	Vietnam
RCH	Chile	WAG	Gambia
RFC	Cameroun	WAL	Sierra Leone
RH	Haiti	WAN	Nigeria
RI	Indonesiea	WD	Dominica
RIM	Mauritania	WG	Grenada
RL	Lebanon	WL	Saint Lucia
RM	Madagascar	WS	Samoa
RMM	Mali	WV	Saint Vincent
RN	Niger	Y	Yemen
RO	Romania	YU	Yugoslavia including Slowenia, Croatia, Bosnia Herzegowina
ROK	South Korea		
ROV	Uruguay	YV	Venezuela
RP	Philippines	Z	Zambia
RSM	San Marino	ZA	South Africa
RU	Burundi	ZRE	Zaire
RWA	Rwanda	ZW	Zimbabwe
S	Sweden		

To differentiate identical name forms among others the following symbols are used	▲	Mountain	⊙	Island
	∪	Bay, Gulf	∧	Cape
	–	River	≅	Landscape, Region
	▲▲	Mountain Range	●	City, Town, Locality
	∩	Peninsula	⇄	Pass

Ø	Ruin
≈	Lake
★	State
☆	Administrative Unit

A

Aachen 33 C 3
Aalen 33 E 4
A'ālī an-Nīl 60-61 KL 7
Äänekoski 30-31 L 6
Aar, De – 64-65 F 9
Aarau 33 D 5
Aare 33 D 5
Aavasaksa 30-31 KL 4

Aba [WAN] 60-61 F 7
Aba [ZRE] 64-65 GH 2
Abā' al-Qūr, Wādī – 46-47 J 7
Abā ar-Rūs, Sabkhat – 44-45 GH 6
Abad 48-49 E 3
Ābādān 44-45 F 4
Ābādān, Jazīreh – 46-47 N 7-8
Ābādeh 44-45 G 4
Abagnar Qi = Xilin Hot 48-49 M 3
Abai 80 E 3
Abajo Peak 76-77 J 7
Abakan 42-43 R 7
Aban 42-43 S 6
Abancay 78-79 E 7
Abanrherit, I-n- 60-61 F 5
Abā Sa'ūd 44-45 EF 7
Abashiri 48-49 RS 3
Abashiri-wan 50-51 d 1-2
Abasiri = Abashiri 48-49 RS 3
Abau 52-53 N 9
Abay 60-61 M 6
Abaya Hayiḳ 60-61 M 7
Abaza 42-43 R 7
Aba Zangzu Zizhizhou 48-49 J 5
Abbeville 34-35 HJ 3
Abbeville, GA 74-75 B 8-9
Abbeville, SC 74-75 B 7
Abbottabad = Ebuṭṭābād 44-45 L 4
Abchazische Autonome Republiek = 6 ◁ 38-39 H 7
'Abd al-'Azīz, Jabal – 46-47 HJ 4
'Abd al Kūrī 44-45 G 8
'Abdāllah 60-61 D 2
'Abd Allāh, Khawr – 46-47 N 8
'Abd Allāh, Khawr – 46-47 N 8
Ābdānān 46-47 M 6
Ābdānān, Rūdkhāneh-ye – 46-47 M 6
Abd an-Nabī, Bi'r – 62 B 2-3
Abdulino 42-43 J 7
'Abdullah = Minā' 'Abd Allāh 46-47 N 8
Abéché 60-61 J 6
Abécher = Abéché 60-61 J 6
Abed-Larache, El – = Al-Ādib al-'Arsh 60-61 F 3
Abeg, I-n- 60-61 D 4
Abeløya 30-31 n 5
Abengourou 60-61 D 7
Åbenrå 30-31 C 10
Abeokuta 60-61 E 7
Abercorn = Mbala 64-65 H 4
Aberdare Mountains 64-65 J 2-3
Aberdare National Park 63 D 3
Aberdeen [AUS] 58 K 4
Aberdeen [GB] 32 EF 3
Aberdeen [ZA] 64-65 F 9
Aberdeen, ID 76-77 G 4
Aberdeen, MD 74-75 E 5
Aberdeen, NC 74-75 D 7
Aberdeen, SD 72-73 G 2
Aberdeen, WA 72-73 B 2
Aberdeen Lake 70-71 R 5
Abergavenny 32 E 6
Abert, Lake – 76-77 CD 4
Aberystwyth 32 D 5
Abez' 42-43 L 4
Abhā 44-45 E 7
Ābhār 46-47 N 4
Abhē Bid Hayiḳ 60-61 N 6
Abiaḍ, Râss el – = Rā's al-Abyaḍ 60-61 FG 1
Ābīd al-'Arsh, Al- 60-61 F 3
Abidjan 60-61 CD 7
Abilene, TX 72-73 FG 5
Abingdon, VA 74-75 BC 6
Abingdon = Isla Pinta 78-79 A 4
Abisko 30-31 H 3
Abitibi, Lake – 70-71 UV 8
Abitibi River 70-71 U 7-8
Abjasia, República Autonóma de – = 6 ◁ 38-39 H 7
Abkhaz Autonomous Republic = 6 ◁ 38-39 H 7
Abkhazie, République Autonome d' = 6 ◁ 38-39 H 7
Abnūb 62 D 4
Åbo = Turku 30-31 K 7
Abomé = Abomey 60-61 E 7
Abomey 60-61 E 7
Abong-Mbang 60-61 G 8
Aborigen, pik – 42-43 cd 5
Abou-Deïa 60-61 H 6
Aboû eḍ Ḍouhoûr = Abū aẓ-Ẓuhūr 46-47 G 6
'Abr, Al- 44-45 F 7
Abrantes 34-35 CD 9
Abra Pampa 80 CD 2
Abreojos, Punta – 72-73 CD 6
'Abrī 60-61 L 4
Abrolhos, Arquipélago dos – 78-79 M 8
Abruzzes = Appennino Abruzzesa 36-37 E 4-F 5
Abruzzi 36-37 EF 4
Absaroka Range 72-73 D 2-E 3
Abu 44-45 L 6
Abū 'Ajāj = Jalib Shahab 46-47 M 7
Abū al-Ḥaṣīb 46-47 MN 7
Abū al-Maṭāmīr 62 CD 2
Abū 'Aweiqīla = Abū 'Uwayjīlah 62 EF 2
Abū aẓ-Ẓuhūr 46-47 G 5
Abū Ballâṣ 60-61 K 4
Abū Ḍahr, Jabal – 62 F 6
Abū Dârah, Rā's – 62 G 6
Abū Darbah 62 E 3
Abū Dhi'āb, Jabal – 62 F 5
Abū Durba = Abū Darbah 62 E 3
Abu Gharādiq, Bi'r – 62 C 2-3
Abū Ghashwah, Rā's – 44-45 G 8
Abū Ḥādd, Wādī – 62 F 7
Abū Ḥaggâg = Rā's al-Ḥikmah 46-47 BC 7
Abū Ḥajār, Khawr – 46-47 L 7
Abū Ḥamad 60-61 L 5
Abū Ḥamāmīd, Jabal – 62 F 5
Abū Ḥammān 46-47 J 5
Abū Ḥarbah, Jabal – 62 E 4
Abū Ḥashūifah, Khalīj – 62 BC 2
Abū Ḥjār, Hôr – = Khawr Abū Ḥajār 46-47 L 7
Abū Hujar 60-61 LM 6
Abuja 60-61 F 7
Abū Jābirah 60-61 K 6
Abū Jaḥaf, Wādī – 46-47 K 6
Abū Jamal 60-61 M 5
Abū Jamal, Jabal – 60-61 M 6
Abū Jīr 46-47 K 6
Abū Jīr, Wādī – 46-47 K 6
Abū Jurdī, Jabal – 62 F 6
Abū Kabīr 62 D 2
Abū Kamāl 44-45 DE 4
Abū Khârga, Wâdî – = Wādī Abū Kharjah 62 DE 3
Abū Kharjah, Wādī – 62 DE 3
Abukuma-sammyaku 50-51 N 4
Abū Marīs, Sha'īb – 46-47 L 7
Abū Marw, Wādī – 62 E 6
Abū Minqār, Bi'r – 60-61 K 3
Abū Muḥarrik, Ghurd – 60-61 KL 3
Abunā 78-79 FG 6
Abuná, Río – 78-79 F 7
Abū Qīr 62 D 2
Abū Qīr, Khalīj – 62 D 2
Abū Qurqāṣ 62 D 4
Abū Rijmayn, Jabal – 46-47 H 5
Abū Sa'fah, Bi'r – 62 F 6
Abū Ṣaida = Abū Ṣaydat Ṣaghīrah 46-47 L 6
Abū Salmān 46-47 M 7
Abū Ṣaydat Ṣaghīrah 46-47 L 6
Abū Shalīl 46-47 K 5
Abū Shīl = Abū Shalīl 46-47 K 5
Abū Sinbil = Abu Sunbul 60-61 L 4
Abū Ṣkhair = Abū Ṣuhayr 46-47 L 7
Abū Ṣuhayr 46-47 L 7
Abu Sunbul 60-61 L 4
Abū Tīj 60-61 L 3
Abū 'Uwayjīlah 62 EF 2
Abū Zabad 60-61 K 6
Abū Ẓabī 44-45 G 6
Abū Zanīmah 60-61 L 3
Abū Zawal, Bi'r – 62 E 4
Abū Zenīma = Abū Zanīmah 60-61 L 3
Abyaḍ 60-61 K 6
Abyaḍ, Ar-Rā's al- 60-61 A 4
Abyaḍ, Rā's al- 60-61 FG 1
Abyay 60-61 K 7
Abymes, les – 72-73 O 8
Abyssinie = Éthiopie 60-61 MN 7

Acadia National Park 74-75 J 2
Acadie 70-71 XY 8
Acajutla 72-73 HJ 9
Acámbaro 72-73 FG 7
Acandí 78-79 D 3
Acaponeta 72-73 EF 7
Acapulco de Juárez 72-73 FG 8
Acará 78-79 K 5
Acaraí, Serra – 78-79 H 4
Acaraú 78-79 LM 5
Acarigua 78-79 F 3
Accomac, VA 74-75 F 6
Accra 60-61 DE 7
Aceh = 1 ◁ 52-53 C 6
Achacachi 78-79 F 8
Achaguas 78-79 F 3
Achaïa 36-37 JK 6
Achalciche 38-39 H 7
Achao 80 B 6
'Achârâ, El – = Al-'Asharah 46-47 J 5
Acharnai 36-37 K 6
Achegour 60-61 G 5
Achelõos 36-37 J 6
Acheng 48-49 O 2
Acherusia = Zonguldak 44-45 C 2
Achigh Köl 48-49 F 4
Achill 32 A 5
Achill Head 32 A 4-5
Achter-Indië 22-23 OP 5
Achtuba 38-39 J 6
Achtubinsk 38-39 J 6
Achtyrka 38-39 F 5
Aci Göl 46-47 CD 4
Ačinsk 42-43 R 6
Acıpayam 46-47 C 4
Acireale 36-37 F 7
Acklins Island 72-73 LM 7
Acomayo 78-79 E 7
Aconcagua [RCH, ▲] 80 C 4
Acopiara 78-79 M 6
Açores 66 D 5
Açores, Seuil des – 22-23 HJ 4
Acqui Terme 36-37 C 3
Acraman, Lake – 56-57 FG 6
Acre 78-79 EF 6
Acre = 'Akkō 46-47 F 6
Acre, Rio – 78-79 F 6
Acri 36-37 G 6
Acton 74-75 C 3
Acton, CA 76-77 D 8
Açu, Rio – = Rio Piranhas 78-79 M 6
Acworth, GA 74-75 A 7

Achacachi 78-79 F 8
Achaguas 78-79 F 3
Achaïa 36-37 JK 6
Achalciche 38-39 H 7
Achao 80 B 6
'Achârâ, El – = Al-'Asharah 46-47 J 5
Acharnai 36-37 K 6
Achegour 60-61 G 5
Achelõos 36-37 J 6
Acheng 48-49 O 2
Acherusia = Zonguldak 44-45 C 2
Achigh Köl 48-49 F 4
Achill 32 A 5
Achill Head 32 A 4-5
Achter-Indië 22-23 OP 5
Achtuba 38-39 J 6
Achtubinsk 38-39 J 6
Achtyrka 38-39 F 5

Ada [GH] 60-61 E 7
Ada, OK 72-73 G 5
'Adabīyah, Rā's – 62 E 3
Adado, Raas – = Raas Cadcadde 60-61 b 1
Adafir 60-61 BC 5
Adakale = Ardanuç 46-47 K 2
Adak Island 19 D 36
Adale = Cadale 60-61 b 3
Adalia = Antalya 44-45 C 3
Ādam 44-45 H 6
Adam, Monte – = Mount Adam 80 DE 8
Adam, Mount – 80 DE 8
Adama = Nazrēt 60-61 M 7
Adamana, AZ 76-77 HJ 8
Adamantina 78-79 JK 9
Adamaoua 60-61 G 7
Adamaua = Adamaoua 60-61 G 7
Adamello 36-37 D 2
Adamovka 38-39 LM 5
Adam Peak 76-77 E 5
Adams, MA 74-75 G 3
Adams, NY 74-75 EF 3
Adams, Cape – 24 B 30-31
Adams, Mount – 72-73 B 2
Adams Island 24 D 17
Adam's Peak = Samanalakanda 44-45 N 9
'Adan 44-45 F 8
Adana 46-47 F 4
Adapazarı = Sakarya 44-45 C 2
Adare, Cape – 24 B 18
Adavale 56-57 HJ 5
Adda 36-37 C 3
Addâr, Râss – = Rā's aṭ-Ṭīb 60-61 G 1
Addis Alem = Alem Gena 60-61 M 7
Addison, NY 74-75 E 3
Addison = Webster Springs, WV 74-75 C 5
Addy, WA 76-77 E 1
Adel, GA 74-75 B 9
Adel, OR 76-77 D 4
Adelaide [AUS] 56-57 GH 6-7
Adelaide Island 24 C 29-30
Adelaide Peninsula 70-71 R 4
Adelaide River 56-57 F 2
Adelanto, CA 76-77 E 8
Adélie, Terre – 24 C 14-15
Adélie Land = Terre Adélie 24 C 14-15
Ademuz 34-35 G 8
Aden = 'Adan 44-45 EF 8
Aden, Golfe d' 44-45 F 8
Adén, Golfo de – 44-45 F 8
Aden, Golf van – 44-45 F 8
Aden, Gulf of – 44-45 F 8
Adghar = Adrār 60-61 DE 3
Ādhār, Rā's – 60-61 G 1
Ādharbayejān-e- Bākhtarī 44-45 EF 3
Ādharbāyejān-e-Khāvarī 44-45 EF 3
Adi, Pulau – 52-53 K 7
Adib al-'Arsh, Al- 60-61 F 3
Adige 36-37 D 3
Adigej Autonome Oblast = 1 ◁ 38-39 H 7
Adīgrat 60-61 MN 6
Adiguey, Oblast Autónoma de – = 1 ◁ 38-39 H 7
Adī Keyih 60-61 MN 6
Adilang 63 C 2
Adilcevaz 46-47 K 3
Adin, CA 76-77 C 5
Adiriyāt, Jabal al- 46-47 G 7
Adirondack Mountains 72-73 M 3
Adīs Abeba 60-61 M 7
Adīs Dera = Dirē 60-61 M 6
Adī Ūgrī 60-61 M 6
Adıyaman 46-47 H 4
Adjarian Autonomous Region = 8 ◁ 38-39 H 7
Adjarie, République Autonome d' = 8 ◁ 38-39 H 7
Adler, Soči- 38-39 G 7
Admar, Irq – 60-61 F 4
Admer, Erg d' = 'Irq Admar 60-61 F 4
Admiralty Gulf 56-57 DE 2
Admiralty Inlet [CDN] 70-71 TU 3
Admiralty Inlet [USA] 76-77 B 1-2
Admiralty Island 70-71 K 6
Admiralty Islands 52-53 N 7
Admiralty Range 24 B 17
Admont 33 G 5
Adonara, Pulau – 52-53 H 8
Ādoni 44-45 M 7
Adour 34-35 G 7
Adra 34-35 F 10
Adramúttion = Edremit 44-45 B 3
Ādrār 60-61 DE 3
Adraskan, Daryā-ye – = Hārūt Rōd 44-45 J 4
Adré 60-61 J 6
Adrī = Idrī 60-61 G 3
Ādria 36-37 E 3
Adrian, OR 76-77 E 4
Adrianopel = Edirne 44-45 B 2
Adriatic Sea 36-37 E 3-H 5
Adriatische Zee 36-37 E 3-H 5
Adua 52-53 J 7
Adua = Adwa 60-61 M 6
Adusa 64-65 G 2
Adventura, Banco – 36-37 DE 7
Adventure Bank 36-37 DE 7
Adwa 60-61 M 6
Adyča 42-43 a 4
Adygei Autonomous Region = 1 ◁ 38-39 H 7
Adyghéens, Région Autonome des – = 1 ◁ 38-39 H 7
Adž Bogd uul 48-49 GH 3
Adzharia, República Autónoma de – = 8 ◁ 38-39 H 7
Adzjarische Autonome Republiek = 8 ◁ 38-39 H 7

Aegean Sea 36-37 L 5-M 7
Ærø 30-31 D 10

'Afag 46-47 L 6
Afallah 60-61 B 5
Afántu 36-37 N 7
Afars et Issas = Djibouti 60-61 N 6
Afganistán 44-45 J 4-L 3
Afgooye 60-61 ab 3
Āfhjalar = Āqchalar 46-47 L 5
'Afif 44-45 E 6
Afikpo 60-61 F 7
Aflāj, Al- 44-45 F 6
Afmadow 60-61 N 8
Afogados da Ingàzeira 78-79 M 6
Afognak Island 70-71 F 6
Afrēra Ye-Tyew Hayiḳ 60-61 N 6
Africa 22-23 J-L 5
África 22-23 J-L 5
África del Sudoeste = Namibia 64-65 E 7
African Island 64-65 M 3
'Afrīn 46-47 G 4
Āfrīneh 46-47 M 6
Afrique 22-23 J-L 5
Afrique du Sud 64-65 F-H 8
Afşin 46-47 G 3
Afton, WY 76-77 H 4
Afuá 78-79 J 5
'Afūla 46-47 F 6
Afyon 44-45 C 3

Aga = Aginskoje 42-43 VW 7
Ağaçören 46-47 EF 3
Agadem 60-61 G 5
Agades = Agadez 60-61 F 5
Agadez 60-61 F 5
Agādīr = Aghādīr 60-61 BC 2
Agadyr' 42-43 N 8
Agaie 60-61 F 7
Agalega Island 64-65 N 5
Agalta, Sierra de – 72-73 J 8-9
Agan 42-43 O 5
Agapa 42-43 Q 3
Agarā = Agra 44-45 M 5
Agartala 44-45 P 6
Agata, ozero – 42-43 R 4
Agathonēsion 36-37 M 7
Agats 52-53 L 8
Agatti Island 44-45 L 8
Agattu Island 19 D 1
Agboville 60-61 D 7
Agdam 38-39 J 7-8
Agde 34-35 J 7
Agen 34-35 H 6
Agere Ḥiywer = Hagerē Hiywet 60-61 M 7
Aghādīr 60-61 BC 2
Āghā Jarī 44-45 FG 4
Aghwāṭ, Al- 60-61 E 2
Ağın 46-47 H 3
Agin-Boerjatmongolen, Autonome Gebied der – 42-43 V 7
Aginskoje 42-43 VW 7
Aginsky-Buryat Autonomous Area 42-43 V 7
Ágios Geṓrgios 36-37 KL 7
Ágios Iōánnēs, Akrōtḗrion – 36-37 LM 8
Ágios Nikólaos 36-37 LM 8
Ağlasun 46-47 D 4
Agnew 56-57 D 5
Agnone 36-37 F 5
Agochi = Aoji 50-51 H 1
Agout 34-35 J 7
Agra 44-45 M 5
Agrachanskij poluostrov 38-39 J 7
Ağrı [TR] 44-45 E 3
Agrigento 36-37 E 7
Agrínion 36-37 J 6
Agròpoli 36-37 F 5
Agryz 42-43 J 6
Agua Caliente Indian Reservation 76-77 E 9
Água Clara [BR] 78-79 J 9
Agua Fria River 76-77 G 8-9
Aguán, Río – 72-73 J 8
Agua Nueva 80 BC 4-5
Agua Prieta 72-73 DE 5
Aguascalientes [MEX, ●] 72-73 F 7
Aguascalientes [MEX, ☆] 72-73 F 7
Águas Formosas 78-79 L 8
Águeda, Río – 34-35 D 8
Aguga 63 C 2
Aguila, AZ 76-77 G 9
Águilas 34-35 G 10
Aguja, Punta – 78-79 C 6
Agujas, Cabo – 64-65 F 10
Agujas, Cuenca de – 22-23 L 8
Agulhas, Cape – 64-65 F 10
Agulhas, Kaap – 64-65 F 10
Agulhas Basin 22-23 L 8
Agulhasbekken 22-23 L 8
Agulhas Negras 78-79 K 9
Agung, Gunung – 52-53 G 8
Agusan 52-53 J 5

Ahaggar = Al-Hajjār 60-61 EF 4
Ahaggar, Tassili Oua n' = Tāsīlī Wān al-Hajjār 60-61 E 5-F 4
Ahar 46-47 M 3
Ahar Chāy 46-47 M 3
Ahar Chāy 46-47 M 3
Ahır Dağı 46-47 G 4
Ahırlı = Karaburun 46-47 B 3
Ahlat 46-47 K 3
Ahlat = Yusufeli 46-47 J 2
Ahmadabad [IND] 44-45 L 6
Aḥmadābād [IR] 46-47 M 4
Aḥmadī, Al- = Mīnā' al-Aḥmadī 46-47 N 8
Ahmadnagar 44-45 LM 7
Aḥmadpūr Sharqī 44-45 L 5
Aḥmar, Jabal al- 62 D 3
Ahmednagar = Ahmadnagar 44-45 LM 7
Ahogayegua, Sierra de – 72-73 b 2-3
Ahoskie, NC 74-75 E 6
Ahtopol 36-37 MN 4
Āhūrān 46-47 M 6
Åhus 30-31 F 10
Ahvāz 44-45 F 4
Ahvenanmaa = Åland 30-31 HJ 7
Aḥwar 44-45 F 8
Ahwaz = Ahvāz 44-45 F 4

Āībak = Samangān 44-45 K 3
Aibetsu 50-51 c 2
Aichi 50-51 L 5
Aidin = Aydın 44-45 B 3
Aigina [GR, ⊙] 36-37 K 7
Aigina [GR, ●] 36-37 K 7
Aigion 36-37 JK 6
Aigle, Chaîne de l' 33 GH 3
Aigle, Chaîne de l' 33 GH 3
Aigle, l' 34-35 H 4
Aiguá 80 F 4
Aigues-Mortes 34-35 JK 7
Aiguilles, Bassin des – 22-23 L 8
Aiguilles, Cap des – 64-65 F 10
Aigun = Aihun 48-49 O 1
Ai He 50-51 E 2
Ai Ho = Ai He 50-51 E 2
Aihsien = Yacheng 48-49 K 8
Aihui 48-49 O 1
Aija 78-79 D 6
Aikawa 50-51 LM 3
Aiken, SC 72-73 K 5
Aileron 56-57 F 4
'Ailī, Sha'īb al- = Sha'īb al-'Aylī 46-47 H 7
Aim 42-43 Z 6
Aimorés 78-79 L 8
Aimorés, Serra dos – 78-79 L 8
Ain 34-35 K 5
'Ain, Wādī al- = Wādī al-'Ayn 44-45 H 6
'Ainabo = Caynabo 60-61 b 2
'Ain al Mugshin, Al- = Al'Ayn al-Muqshin 44-45 GH 7
Ainaži 30-31 KL 9
Aïn-Beïda = 'Ayn Baydā' 60-61 F 1
Aïn-ben-Tili = 'Ayn Bin Tīlī 60-61 C 3
'Aïn Dîouâr = 'Ayn Dīwār 46-47 K 4
Aïn Galakka 60-61 H 5
Aïn-Salah = 'Ayn Ṣāliḥ 60-61 E 3
Aïn-Sefra = 'Ayn Ṣafrā 60-61 DE 2
Aïn-Témouchent = 'Ayn Tamūshanat 60-61 D 1
Aioi 50-51 K 5
Aiquile 78-79 F 8
Aïr 60-61 F 5
Airan Köl = Telijn nuur 48-49 F 2
Aire, Isla del – 34-35 K 9
Air Force Island 70-71 W 4
Aisch 33 E 4
Aisega 52-53 g 6
Aishihik 70-71 J 5
Aisne 34-35 J 4
Aitana 34-35 G 9
Aitape 52-53 M 7

154 Aache

Aiud 36-37 K 2
Aiun, El – = Al-'Ayūn 60-61 B 3
Aix-en-Provence 34-35 KL 7
Aix-les-Bains 34-35 KL 6
Āīzāl = Aizawal 44-45 P 6
Aizawal 44-45 P 6
Aizpute 30-31 J 9
Aizu-Wakamatsu 48-49 QR 4
Aizu-Wakamatu = Aizu-Wakamatsu 48-49 QR 4

Aj 38-39 L 4
Ajā, Jabal – 44-45 E 5
'Ajabshīr 46-47 L 4
Ajaccio 36-37 C 5
Ajaguz 42-43 P 8
Ajaj, Wādī – 46-47 J 5
'Ajājā 46-47 J 4
'Ajam, Al- 46-47 G 6
'Ajam, El- = Al-'Ajam 46-47 G 6
Ajan [SU, ~] 42-43 R 4
Ajan [SU, ● Pribrežnyj chrebet] 42-43 a 6
Ajan [SU, ● Sibirskoje ploskogorje] 42-43 U 6
Ajana 56-57 BC 5
Ajanka 42-43 g 5
Ajanta Range 44-45 M 6
Ajax Mountain 76-77 G 3
Ajdābīyah 60-61 J 2
Ajedabya = Ajdābīyah 60-61 J 2
Ājī Chāi = Rūd-e Āqdogh Mīsh 46-47 M 4
Ājī Chāi = Rūd-e Āqdogh Mīsh 46-47 M 4
Ajigasawa 50-51 MN 2
Ājīn 46-47 M 5
Ajjer, Tassili n' = Tāsīlī Wan Ahjār 60-61 F 3
Ajkino 38-39 J 3
'Ajlūn 46-47 FG 6
'Ajlūn, Jabal – 46-47 FG 6
'Ajmah, Jabal al- 60-61 L 3
'Ajmān 44-45 GH 5
'Ajmī 46-47 L 5-6
Ajnis, Qārat – 62 BC 3
Ajo, AZ 76-77 G 9
Ajo Mountains 76-77 G 9
Ajon, ostrov – 42-43 g 4
Ajrag nuur 48-49 GH 2
'Ajramīyah, Bi'r al- 62 DE 3
Ajtos 36-37 M 4

Akabira 50-51 c 2
Akademii, zaliv – 42-43 a 7
Akaishi-sammyaku 50-51 LM 5
Akalkot 44-45 M 7
Akan ko 50-51 cd 2
Akantarer, I-n- 60-61 E 5
Akanyaru 63 B 3
Akasaki 50-51 J 5
'Akāsh, Wādī – = Wādī 'Ukāsh 46-47 J 5-6
Akashi 50-51 K 5
Akasi = Akashi 50-51 K 5
Äkäsjoki 30-31 KL 4
Akayu 50-51 N 3
Akbulak 38-39 L 5
Akcaabat 46-47 H 2
Akçadağ 46-47 GH 3
Akçakale 46-47 H 4
Akçakoca 46-47 D 2
Akçakoyumla 46-47 G 4
Akçan = Sakavi 46-47 J 3
Ak Çay 46-47 C 4
Akchar = Āqshar 60-61 B 4
Ak Dağlar 44-45 BC 3
Akdağlar 46-47 FG 3
Akdağmadeni 46-47 F 3
Akershus 30-31 D 7-8
Aketi 64-65 F 2
Akhḍar, Jabal al- [LAR] 60-61 J 2
Akhḍar, Jabal al- [Oman] 44-45 H 6
Akhisar 46-47 BC 3
Akhmīm 62 DE 4
Aki 50-51 J 6
Akik = 'Aqīq 60-61 M 5
Akimiski Island 70-71 UV 7
Akıncı Burnu 46-47 F 4
Akıncılar 46-47 B 2
Akita 48-49 QR 4
Akjoujt = Aqjawajat 60-61 B 5
Akkajaure 30-31 G 4
Akka-mori 50-51 N 2
Akkeshi 50-51 d 2
Akkeshi wan 50-51 d 2
'Akkō 46-47 F 6
Akköy 46-47 B 4
Akku = Çaldere 46-47 G 2
Akkuş 46-47 G 2
Aklavik 70-71 J 4
Akmal'-Abad = Gižduvan 42-43 L 9
Ak-Mečet' = Kzyl-Orda 42-43 M 9
Akmolinsk = Celinograd 42-43 MN 7
Akō 50-51 K 5
Akōbō = Akūbū 60-61 L 7
Akola 44-45 M 6
Akonolinga 60-61 G 8
Akordat 60-61 M 5
Akören 46-47 E 4
Akpatok Island 70-71 X 5
Akpınar = Çınar 46-47 J 4
Akranes 30-31 bc 2
Akrar 30-31 b 2
Akre = 'Āqrah 46-47 K 4
Akritas, Akrōtērion – 36-37 JK 7
Akron, OH 72-73 K 3
Akrōtēri 36-37 L 8
Akrōtēriu, Kólpos – 46-47 E 5
Akša 42-43 V 7
Akşar 46-47 K 2
Aksaray 46-47 EF 3
Akşehir 44-45 C 3
Akşehir Gölü 46-47 D 3
Akseki 46-47 D 4
Aks'onovo-Zilovskoje 42-43 VW 7
Aksoran, gora – 42-43 O 8
Aksu [SU] 42-43 N 7
Aksu [TR] 46-47 G 4
Aksu = Aqsu 48-49 E 3
Aksuat 42-43 P 8
Aksu Çay 46-47 D 4
Aksum 60-61 M 6
Aktogaj 42-43 O 8
Akt'ubinsk 42-43 K 7
Aktumsyk 42-43 K 8
Akūbū 60-61 L 7
Akulurak, AK 70-71 CD 5
Akune 48-49 OP 5
Akure 60-61 F 7
Akureyri 30-31 de 2
Akyab = Sittwe 52-53 B 2
Akyaka 46-47 K 2
Akyazı 46-47 D 2

Ål 30-31 C 7
Alabama 72-73 J 5
Alabama River 72-73 J 5
Alaca 46-47 F 2
Alacadağ 46-47 DE 4
Alacahan 46-47 G 3
Alacahöyük 46-47 F 2
Alaçam 46-47 F 2
Alachua, FL 74-75 b 2
Aladağ 46-47 K 3
Ālādāgh, Reshteh – 44-45 H 3
Ala Dağlar [TR, ▲▲] 46-47 F 4
Alagoas 78-79 M 6-7
Alagoinhas 78-79 M 7
Alagón 34-35 D 9
Alag Šan Gov' 48-49 J 4
Alajuela 72-73 K 9-10
Alakol', ozero – 42-43 P 8
Alalaú, Rio – 78-79 G 5
'Alamar-Rūm, Rā's – 62 B 2
'Alamayn, Al- 60-61 K 2
Alameda, CA 76-77 BC 7
Alameda, ID 76-77 G 4
Alamo, NV 76-77 F 7
Alamo, Cerro – 76-77 EF 10
Álamo, El – [MEX, Baja California] 76-77 EF 10
Alamogordo, NM 72-73 E 5
Alamo Lake 76-77 G 8
Alamo River 76-77 F 9
Alamos 72-73 E 6
Alamosa, CO 72-73 E 4
Ālāmūt 46-47 O 4
Åland [SF, ⊙] 30-31 HJ 7
Åland [SF, ☆] 30-31 HJ 7
Åland, Fosa de – 30-31 H 7
Åland, Fosse d' 30-31 H 7
Ålandsdiep 30-31 H 7
Ålands hav 30-31 H 7-8
Alanga Arba 64-65 JK 2
Ālanmyō 52-53 C 3
Alanya 44-45 C 3
Alaotra, Lac – 64-65 L 6
Alapaha, GA 74-75 B 9
Alapaha River 74-75 B 9
Alapajevsk 42-43 L 6
Alaplı 46-47 D 2
Ālappi = Alleppey 44-45 M 9
Alāq 60-61 B 5
Alarcón 34-35 FG 9
Alas, Selat – 52-53 G 8
Alaşehir 46-47 C 3
Alašejev buchta 24 C 5
Alashtar 46-47 MN 6
Alaska, Golfe d' 70-71 GH 6
Alaska, Golfo de – 70-71 GH 6
Alaska, Golf van – 70-71 GH 6
Alaska, Gulf of – 70-71 GH 6
Alaska Highway 70-71 H 5
Alaska Peninsula 70-71 DE 6
Alaska Range 70-71 F-H 5
Alàssio 36-37 C 3-4
Alatri 36-37 E 5
Alatyr' [SU, ●] 42-43 H 7
Alausí 78-79 D 5
Alava, Cape – 76-77 A 1
Alaverdi 38-39 H 7
Alayunt 46-47 D 3
Alazani 38-39 J 7
Alazeja 42-43 d 3-e 4
Alazejskoje ploskogorje 42-43 c 4
Alba 36-37 C 3
Albacete 34-35 FG 9
Alba de Tormes 34-35 E 8
Alba Iulia 36-37 K 2
Albanese Alpen = Alpet e Shqipërisë 36-37 HJ 4
Albania 36-37 H 4-5
Albanië 36-37 H 4-5
Albanie 36-37 H 4-5
Albany 56-57 C 6-7
Albany, CA 76-77 B 7
Albany, GA 72-73 K 5
Albany, NY 72-73 LM 3
Albany, OR 72-73 B 3
Albany River 70-71 U 7
Albarracín 34-35 G 8
Albatros Island 64-65 NO 6
Albatross Bay 56-57 H 2
Albayrak 46-47 KL 3
Albemarle, NC 74-75 C 7
Albemarle = Isla Isabela 78-79 A 5
Albemarle Sound 74-75 EF 6
Albenga 36-37 C 3
Alberche 34-35 E 8
Alberga 58 B 1
Alberga, The – 56-57 FG 5
Alberrie Creek 58 C 2
Albert [AUS] 58 H 4
Albert, Lake – 56-57 GH 7
Albert, Parc national – = Parc national Virunga 64-65 G 2-3
Alberta 70-71 NO 6
Alberta, VA 74-75 E 6
Albertkanaal 34-35 J 3
Albert Lea, MN 72-73 H 3
Albert Markham, Mount – 24 AB 17-15
Albert Nile 64-65 H 2
Alberton, MT 76-77 F 2
Albertville 34-35 L 6
Albertville = Kalemie 64-65 G 4
Albi 34-35 J 7
Albina 78-79 J 3
Albino 36-37 CD 3
Albion, NY 74-75 DE 3
Alborán 34-35 F 11
Ålborg 30-31 CD 9
Ålborg Bugt 30-31 D 9
Alborz, Reshteh Kūhhā-ye – 44-45 G 3
Albufera, La – 34-35 GH 9
Albuquerque, NM 72-73 EF 4
Alburquerque 34-35 D 9
Albury-Wodonga 56-57 J 7
Alcácer do Sal 34-35 C 9
Alcalá de Guadaira 34-35 E 10
Alcalá de Henares 34-35 F 8
Alcalá la Real 34-35 F 10
Àlcamo 36-37 E 7
Alcañiz 34-35 G 8
Alcántara 34-35 D 9
Alcântara [BR] 78-79 L 5
Alcantarilla 34-35 G 10
Alcañiz 34-35 F 9
Alcaraz 34-35 F 9
Alcaraz, Sierra de – 34-35 F 9
Alcarria, La – 34-35 F 8
Alcázar de San Juan 34-35 F 9
Alcázarquivir = Al-Qaṣr al-Kabīr 60-61 C 1
Alcester Island 52-53 h 6
Alcira 34-35 G 9
Alcira [RA] 80 D 4
Alcobaça 34-35 C 9
Alcobaça [BR] 78-79 M 8
Alcolea del Pinar 34-35 FG 8
Alcoota 56-57 F 4
Alcoy 34-35 G 9
Aldabra Islands 64-65 L 4
Aldağ [TR, ▲] 46-47 F 4
Aldağ [TR, ●] 46-47 F 4
Aldan [SU, ~] 42-43 Z 6
Aldan [SU, ●] 42-43 XY 6
Aldano-Učurskij chrebet 42-43 Y 6
Aldanskoje nagorje 42-43 X-Z 6
Aldeburgh 32 GH 5
Alder, MT 76-77 GH 3
Alderney 32 E 7
Alder Peak 76-77 C 8
Alduş = Temsiyas 46-47 H 3
Aleg = Alaq 60-61 B 5
Alegrete 80 E 3-4
Aleï, I-n- 60-61 D 5
Alejandra, Cabo – = Cape Alexandra 80 J 8
Alejandría = Al-Iskandarīyah 60-61 KL 2
Alejandro Selkirk 69 B 6
Alejsk 42-43 P 7
Aleksandra, mys – 42-43 ab 7
Aleksandrov 38-39 GH 4
Aleksandrov Gaj 38-39 J 5
Aleksandrovsk = Belogorsk 42-43 YZ 7
Aleksandrovskoje [SU, Zapadno-Sibirskaja nizmennost'] 42-43 OP 5
Aleksandrovsk-Sachalinskij 42-43 bc 7
Aleksandrów Kujawski 33 J 2
Aleksandry, zemľa – 42-43 FG 1
Aleksejevka [SU, Kazachskaja SSR] 42-43 N 7
Aleksejevsk = Svobodnyj 42-43 YZ 7
Aleksinac 36-37 JK 4
Ålem 30-31 G 9
Alem Gena 60-61 M 7
Alem Maya 60-61 N 7
Além Paraíba 78-79 L 9
Alençon 34-35 H 4
Alenquer [BR] 78-79 HJ 5
Alentejo 34-35 C 10-D 9
Alenuihaha Channel 52-53 ef 3
Alenuihaha Channel 52-53 ef 3
Alenz 46-47 J 4
Aleoetentrog 11 D 35
Aléoutiennes, Fosse des – 19 D 35
Alert 19 A 25
Alerta 78-79 E 7
Alès 34-35 K 6
Alessàndria 36-37 C 3
Ålesund 30-31 AB 6
Aleuten Trench 19 D 35
Aleutianas, Fosa de las – 19 D 35
Aleutian Islands 19 D 35-1
Aleutian Range 70-71 E 6-F 5
Aleutka 48-49 T 2
Alevina, mys – 42-43 cd 6
Alevisik = Samandağ 46-47 F 4
Alexander, Kap – 70-71 WX 2
Alexander, Point – 56-57 G 2
Alexander Archipelago 70-71 J 6-K 7
Alexanderbaai 64-65 DE 8
Alexandra [NZ] 56-57 N 9
Alexandra, Cape – 80 J 8
Alexandra, zemľa – = zemľa Aleksandry 42-43 FG 1
Alexandra Fiord 70-71 VW 2
Alexandra land = zemľa Aleksandry 42-43 FG 1
Alexandretta = İskenderun 44-45 D 3
Alexandrette = İskenderun 44-45 D 3
Alexandria [AUS] 56-57 G 3
Alexandria [BR] 78-79 M 6
Alexandria [R] 36-37 L 4
Alexandria [ZA] 64-65 G 9
Alexandria, LA 72-73 H 5
Alexandria, VA 72-73 L 4
Alexandrië = Al-Iskandarīyah 60-61 KL 2
Alexandrie = Al-Iskandarīyah 60-61 KL 2
Alexandrina, Lake – 56-57 GH 7
Alexandrúpolis 36-37 L 5
Alfambra 34-35 G 8
Alfarez de Navio Sobral 24 A 32-35
Alfatar 36-37 M 4
Alfeiós 36-37 J 7
Alföld 33 J 5-L 4
Ålfotbreen 30-31 A 7
Alfred, ME 74-75 H 3
Alga 42-43 K 8
Ålgård 30-31 A 8
Algarve 34-35 CD 10
Algeciras 34-35 E 10
Algēna 60-61 M 5
Alger = Al-Jazā'ir 60-61 E 1
Algeria 60-61 D-F 3
Algerian Basin 28-29 J 8-K 7
Algérie 60-61 D-F 3
Algerije 60-61 D-F 3
Algerijns-Provençaals Bekken 28-29 J 8-K 7
Alghero 36-37 C 5
Algiers = Al-Jazā'ir 60-61 E 1
Algoabaai 64-65 G 9
Algoa Bay = Algoabaai 64-65 G 9
Algodones 76-77 F 9
Algoma, OR 76-77 C 4
Algonquin Provincial Park 70-71 V 8
Alhambra, CA 76-77 DE 8
Alhucemas = Al-Ḥusaymah 60-61 D 1
Alhucemas, Islas de – 34-35 F 11
'Ālī, Sadd al- 60-61 L 4
Aliákmon 36-37 JK 5
'Alī al-Gharbī 46-47 M 6
Ali-Bajramly 38-39 J 8
Alibardak = Mermer 46-47 J 3
Alibej, ozero – 36-37 O 3
Alibey Adası 46-47 B 3
Alibunar 36-37 J 3
Alicante 34-35 GH 9
Alice, TX 72-73 G 6
Alice, Punta – 36-37 G 6
Alice Springs 56-57 FG 4
Alicudi 36-37 F 6
Ali Gabe 63 E 2
Aligar = Aligarh 44-45 M 5
Aligarh 44-45 M 5
Alīgūdarz 46-47 NO 6
Alihe 48-49 N 1
Alima 64-65 DE 3
Alindao 60-61 J 7-8
Alingsås 30-31 E 9
Alipur Duar 44-45 O 5
Aliquippa, PA 74-75 C 4
Alisal, CA 76-77 C 7
Aliwal-Noord 64-65 G 9
Aliwal Suid = Mosselbaai 64-65 G 9
Alkali Desert 76-77 EF 5-6
Alkali Flat 76-77 DE 5
Alkali Lake 76-77 D 5
Alkmaar 34-35 K 2
Allach-Jun' 42-43 a 5
Allada 60-61 E 7
Allagash, ME 74-75 J 1
Allagash River 74-75 J 1
Allahabad [IND] 44-45 N 5
Allaire, Banc – 72-73 BC 7
Allakaket, AK 70-71 F 4
Allaküekber Dağları 46-47 K 2
Allanmyo = Ālanmyō 52-53 C 3
'Allāqī, Wadī al- 62 E 6
Alleghenies = Allegheny Mountains 72-73 K 4-L 3
Allegheny Mountains 72-73 K 4-L 3
Allegheny Plateau 74-75 C 5-F 3
Allegheny River 74-75 D 4
Allemagne 33 D-F 2-4
Allemagne, Baie d' 33 C 1
Allendale, SC 74-75 C 8
Allentown, PA 72-73 L 3
Alleppey 44-45 M 9
Aller 33 D 2
Allerheiligenbaai = Baía de Todos os Santos 78-79 M 7
Alliance, NE 72-73 F 3
Alliance, OH 74-75 C 4
Allier 34-35 J 6
Alligator Sound 74-75 EF 7
Alliston 74-75 D 2
Alma [CDN, Quebec] 70-71 W 8
Alma, GA 74-75 B 9
Alma-Ata 42-43 O 9
Almada 34-35 C 9
Almadén 34-35 E 9
Almalyk 44-45 KL 2
Almanor, Lake – 76-77 C 5
Almansa 34-35 G 9
Almanzora 34-35 F 10
Almazán 34-35 F 8
Almeida 34-35 D 8
Almeidia Campos 78-79 K 8
Almeirim [BR] 78-79 J 5
Almenara [BR] 78-79 LM 8
Almendralejo 34-35 D 9
Almería 34-35 F 10
Almería, Golfo de – 34-35 F 10
Al'metjevsk 42-43 J 7
Älmhult 30-31 F 9
Almirante Brown [Antarctica] 24 C 30-31
Almo, ID 76-77 G 4
Almodóvar del Campo 34-35 E 9
Almonte [CDN] 74-75 E 2
Almorox 34-35 E 8
Almota, WA 76-77 E 2
Almuñécar 34-35 F 10
Almuñécar 34-35 F 10
Almus 46-47 G 2
Almyrós 36-37 K 6
Alnwick 32 F 4
Alofi 52-53 b 1
Aloha, OR 76-77 B 3
Alonnêsos 36-37 KL 6
Alor, Pulau – 52-53 HJ 8
Álora 34-35 E 10
Alor Setar 52-53 CD 5
Alotau 52-53 NO 9
Aloysius, Mount – 56-57 E 5
Alpena, MI 72-73 K 2
Alpercatas, Rio – 78-79 KL 6
Alpes 28-29 KL 6
Alpes Albaneses = Alpet e Shqipërisë 36-37 HJ 4
Alpes Cárnicos 36-37 E 2
Alpes Carniques 36-37 E 2
Alpes Cottiennes 34-35 G 6
Alpes Dolomíticos = Dolomiti 36-37 DE 2
Alpes Graies 34-35 L 6
Alpes Julianos 36-37 EF 2
Alpes Juliennes 36-37 EF 2
Alpes Maritimes 34-35 L 6
Alpet e Shqipërisë 36-37 HJ 4
Alpha 56-57 J 4
Alphonse Island 64-65 M 4
Alpine, AZ 76-77 J 9
Alpine, ID 76-77 H 4
Alpine, TX 72-73 F 5
Alpi Transilvanici 36-37 KL 3
Alps 28-29 KL 6
Alpu 46-47 D 3
Alqūsh 46-47 K 4
Alroy Downs 56-57 G 3
Als 30-31 C 10
Alsace 34-35 L 4-5
Alsasua 34-35 FG 7
Alsea, OR 76-77 B 3
Alstahaug 30-31 DE 5
Alta 30-31 K 3
Altaelv 30-31 K 3
Alta Gracia [RA] 80 CD 4
Altagracia [YV] 78-79 E 2
Altaï = Altaj 48-49 EF 1
Altair, Cima del – 22-23 H 2-3
Altair-Ondiepte 22-23 H 2-3
Altair Seamounts 22-23 H 2-3
Altaj [Mongolia, Altaj] 48-49 H 2
Altaj [Mongolia, Chovd] 48-49 G 2
Altaj [SU] 42-43 PQ 7
Altajn Nuruu = Mongol Altajn nuruu 48-49 F-H 2
Altamaha River 72-73 K 5
Altamira [BR] 78-79 J 5
Altamira, Cueva de – 34-35 EF 7
Altamont, OR 76-77 BC 4
Altamont, WY 76-77 H 5
Altamura 36-37 G 5
Altanbulag 48-49 K 1-2
Altar Valley 76-77 H 10
Altavista, VA 74-75 D 6
Altay 48-49 F 2
Altdorf 33 D 5
Altenburg 33 F 3
Alter do Chão [BR] 78-79 HJ 5
Alter do Chão [BR] 78-79 HJ 5
Altevatn 30-31 H 3
Altınekin 46-47 E 3
Altınhisar 46-47 F 4
Altınkaya Barajı 46-47 F 2
Altınözü 46-47 G 4
Altin Tagh 48-49 EF 4
Altıntaş 46-47 CD 3
Altiplanicie Mexicana 72-73 E 5-F 7
Altiplano 78-79 F 8
Altmühl 33 E 4
Alto Anapu, Rio – 78-79 J 5
Alto Egipto = Aṣ-Ṣa'īd 60-61 L 3-4
Alto Garças 78-79 J 8
Alto Longá 78-79 L 6
Alto Molócuè = Molócuè 64-65 J 6
Alton, IL 72-73 HJ 4
Altoona, PA 72-73 L 3
Alto Parnaíba 78-79 K 6
Alto Piquiri 80 F 2
Alto Río Senguerr 80 BC 6-7
Altunhisar = Ortaköy 46-47 F 4
Āltūn Kūprī 46-47 L 5
Alturas, CA 76-77 C 5
Altus, OK 72-73 G 5
Altyn Tagh = Altin tagh 48-49 EF 4
Alucra 46-47 H 2
Alūksne 30-31 M 9
Aluminé 80 B 5
Alung Gangri 48-49 E 5
'Aluula = Caluula 60-61 c 1
Alva, FL 74-75 c 3
Alvalade 34-35 C 9-10
Alvand, Kūh-e – 44-45 FG 4
Alvar = Alwar 44-45 M 5
Alvarado 72-73 GH 8

Alvar 155

Alvarães 78-79 G 5
Álvaro Obregón = Frontera 72-73 H 8
Alvdal 30-31 D 6
Älvdalen 30-31 F 7
Alvesta 30-31 F 9
Alvord Lake 76-77 D 4
Älvsborgs län 30-31 E 8-9
Älvsbyn 30-31 J 5
Alwar 44-45 M 5
Alys = Kızılırmak 44-45 D 3
Alytus 30-31 L 10
Alzamaj 42-43 S 6

Allach-Jun' 42-43 a 5
Allada 60-61 E 7
Allagash, ME 74-75 J 1
Allagash River 74-75 J 1
Allahabad [IND] 44-45 N 5
Allaire, Banc – 72-73 BC 7
Allaire, Banco – 72-73 BC 7
Allakaket, AK 70-71 F 4
Allaküekber Dağları 46-47 K 2
Allanmyo = Ālanmyō 52-53 C 3
'Allāqī, Wadī al- 62 E 6
Alleghenies = Allegheny Mountains 72-73 K 4-L 3
Allegheny Mountains 72-73 K 4-L 3
Allegheny Plateau 74-75 C 5-F 3
Allegheny River 74-75 D 4
Allemagne 33 D-F 2-4
Allemagne, Baie d' 33 C 1
Allemania 33 D-F 2-4
Allendale, SC 74-75 C 8
Allentown, PA 72-73 L 3
Alleppey 44-45 M 9
Aller 33 D 2
Allerheiligenbaai = Baía de Todos os Santos 78-79 M 7
Alliance, NE 72-73 F 3
Alliance, OH 74-75 C 4
Allier 34-35 J 6
Alligator Sound 74-75 EF 7
Alliston 74-75 D 2

Amada = 'Amādah 62 E 6
Amadabad = Ahmadabad 44-45 L 6
'Amādah 62 E 6
Amadeus, Lake – 56-57 F 4
Amādī 60-61 KL 7
'Amādīyah, Al- 46-47 K 4
Amadjuak Lake 70-71 W 4-5
Amagasaki 50-51 K 5
Amahai 52-53 J 7
Amakusa nada 50-51 G 6
Amakusa-rettō 48-49 O 5
Amakusa syotō = Amakusa-rettō 48-49 O 5
Åmål 30-31 E 8
Amalfi 36-37 F 5
Amaliás 36-37 J 7
Amalyk 42-43 W 6
Amami-guntō 48-49 O 6
Amami-ō-shima 48-49 O 6
Amami-Ō sima = Amami-ō-shima 48-49 O 6
Amandola 36-37 E 4
Amangel'dy 42-43 M 7-8
Amanos dağları = Nur dağları 46-47 G 4
Amantea 36-37 FG 6
Amapá [BR, Amapá ●] 78-79 J 4
Amapá [BR, Amapá ☆] 78-79 J 4
Amara 60-61 M 6
'Amārah, Al- 44-45 F 4
Amaramba, Lagoa – = Lagoa Chiuta 64-65 J 5
Amarante [BR] 78-79 L 6
Amaravati = Amravati 44-45 M 6
Amargo, CA 76-77 E 8
Amargosa Desert 76-77 E 7
Amargosa Range 76-77 E 7-8
Amargosa River 76-77 E 8
Amarillo, TX 72-73 F 4
'Amarina, Tel el- = Tall al-'Amārinah 62 D 4
'Amārinah, Tall al- 62 D 4
Amarna, Tell el – = Tall al-'Amārinah 62 D 4
Amaro Leite 78-79 JK 7
Amarume 50-51 M 3
Amarúsion 36-37 KL 6-7
Amasra 46-47 E 2
Amasya 44-45 D 2
Amatique, Bahía de – 72-73 J 8
Amauã, Lago – 78-79 G 5
Amazon = Amazonas 78-79 F-H 5
Amazonas [BR] 78-79 F-H 5
Amazonas, Estuário do Rio – 78-79 JK 4
Amazonas, Plataforma del – 22-23 G 5-6
Amazonas, Rio – [BR] 78-79 HJ 5
Amazonas, Rio – [PE] 78-79 E 5
Amazone, Plateau Continental de l' 22-23 G 5-6
Amazoneplat 22-23 G 5-6
Amazon Shelf 22-23 G 5-6
Amba Alagē 60-61 MN 6
Amba Alaji = Amba Alagē 60-61 MN 6
Ambajogai 44-45 M 7
Ambala 44-45 M 4
Ambalavao 64-65 L 7
Ambam 60-61 G 8
Ambanja 64-65 L 5
Ambarčik 42-43 fg 4
Ambaro, Baie d' 64-65 L 5
Ambato 78-79 D 5
Ambatoboeny 64-65 L 6
Ambatolampy 64-65 L 6
Ambatondrazaka 64-65 L 6
Ambatosoratra 64-65 L 6
Ambelau, Pulau – 52-53 J 7
Amber, WA 76-77 E 2
Amberg 33 EF 4
Ambergris Cay 72-73 J 8
Ambikapur 44-45 N 6
'Ambikūl 62 D 7
Ambilobe 64-65 LM 5
Ambodifototra 64-65 LM 6
Ambohibe 64-65 K 7
Ambohimahasoa 64-65 L 7
Amboim = Gabela 64-65 DE 5
Amboina = Pulau Ambon 52-53 J 7
Amboise 34-35 H 5
Amboland = Ovamboland 64-65 DE 6
Ambon 52-53 J 7
Ambon, Pulau – 52-53 J 7
Amboseli, Lake – 63 D 3
Amboseli Game Reserve 64-65 J 3
Ambositra 64-65 L 7
Ambovombe 64-65 L 8
Amboy, CA 76-77 F 8
Amboyna Cay 52-53 F 5
Ambrakikòs Kólpos 36-37 J 6
Ambre, Cap d' 64-65 LM 5
Ambre, Montagne d' 64-65 L 5
Ambridge, PA 74-75 CD 4
Ambrim 56-57 N 3
Ambriz 64-65 D 4
Ambrizete = N'Zeto 64-65 D 4
Amchitka Island 19 D 1
Am Dam 60-61 J 6
Amderma 42-43 L 4
Ameca 72-73 F 7
Amedabad = Ahmadabad 44-45 L 6
Amelia Court House, VA 74-75 DE 6
Aménas, In – = 'Ayn Umannās 60-61 F 3
Amenia, NY 74-75 G 4
Amer, Lac – = Al-Buḥayrat al-Murrat al-Kubrá 62 E 2
Amerasia Basin 19 A
América, Meseta de – = American Highland 24 B 8
América del Norte 22-23 DE 3
América del Sur 22-23 FG 6
American Falls, ID 76-77 G 4
American Falls Reservoir 76-77 G 4
American Fork, UT 76-77 H 5
American Highland 24 B 8
American River North Fork 76-77 C 6
Americus, GA 72-73 K 5
Amérique du Nord 22-23 DE 3
Amérique du Nord, Bassin de l' 22-23 FG 4
Amérique du Sud 22-23 FG 6
Amersfoort 34-35 K 2
Amery Ice Shelf 24 BC 7-8
Ames, IA 72-73 H 3
Amesbury, MA 74-75 H 3
Amfilochía 36-37 J 6
Ámfissa 36-37 K 6
Amga [SU, ~] 42-43 X 6
Amga [SU, ●] 42-43 Z 5
Amgar, Al- 46-47 L 8
Am Géréda 60-61 J 6
Amghar, Al- = Al-Amgar 46-47 L 8
Amgu 42-43 a 8
Amguèma 42-43 k 4
Amgun' [SU, ~] 42-43 a 7
Amgun' [SU, ●] 42-43 a 7
Amhara = Amara 60-61 M 6
Amherst 70-71 XY 8
Amherst, MA 74-75 G 3
Amherst, VA 74-75 D 6
Amhurst, Mount – 56-57 E 3
Ami, Mont – 63 B 2
Amiata, Monte – 36-37 D 4
Amiens 34-35 J 4
'Āmij, Wādī – 46-47 J 6
Amik Gölü 46-47 G 4
Amindivi Islands 44-45 L 8
Amino 50-51 K 5
Aminuis 64-65 E 7
Amirantes 64-65 M 4
Amirauté, Îles de l' = Admiralty Islands 52-53 N 7
'Amīrīyah, Al- 62 CD 2
Amisós = Samsun 44-45 D 2
Amlia Island 19 D 36
'Ammān 44-45 D 4
Ammarfjället 30-31 FG 4
Ammersee 33 E 5
Amnok-kang 48-49 O 3
Amnyemachhen Gangri 48-49 HJ 5
Amol 38-39 K 8
Amores, Los – 80 DE 3
Amorgós 36-37 LM 7
Amos 70-71 V 8
Amos, CA 76-77 F 9
'Âmoûdâ = 'Āmudā 46-47 J 4
Amoy = Xiamen 48-49 M 7
Ampanihy 64-65 K 7
Ampasindava, Baie d' 64-65 L 5
Ampato, Nevado de – 78-79 E 8
Amphipolis 36-37 K 5
Amposta 34-35 H 8
Ampurias 34-35 J 7
Amravati 44-45 M 6
Amrawati = Amravati 44-45 M 6
Amritsar 44-45 LM 4
Amroha 44-45 M 5
Amsīd, Al- 60-61 B 3
Amsterdam 34-35 K 2
Amsterdam, NY 74-75 FG 3
Amsterdam, Plateau d' 22-23 NO 8
Amsterdamdrempel 22-23 NO 8
Amsterdam Plateau 22-23 NO 8
Amstetten 33 G 4
Amt'ae-do 50-51 EF 5
Am Timan 60-61 J 6
'Āmūdā 46-47 J 4
Amudarja 44-45 J 2
Amund Ringnes Island 70-71 RS 2
Amundsen, Mount – 24 BC 11
Amundsen Bay 24 C 5
Amundsen Glacier 24 A 23-20
Amundsen Gulf 70-71 L-N 3
Amundsen havet 24 BC 25-26
Amundsen-Scott 24 A
Amur 42-43 Z 8
Amur = Heilong Jiang 48-49 P 2
'Āmūr, 'Ayn – 62 CD 5
Amurang 52-53 H 6
Amursk 42-43 a 7
Amurskij zaliv 50-51 H 1

Anabar 42-43 V 3
Anābīb an-Naft 44-45 DE 4
Ana Branch 56-57 H 6
Anabuki 50-51 K 5-6
Anacapa Island 76-77 D 9
Anaconda, MT 72-73 D 2
Anaconda Range 76-77 G 2-3
Anacortes, WA 76-77 B 1
Ana Deresi 46-47 B 2
Anadyr' [SU, ~] 42-43 hj 5
Anadyr' [SU, ●] 42-43 j 5
Anadyrskaja nizmennost' 42-43 j 4-5
Anadyrskij zaliv 42-43 j-l 5
Anadyrskoje ploskogorje 42-43 h 4
Anáfē 36-37 LM 7
Anagni 36-37 E 5
'Ānah 46-47 JK 5
Anaheim, CA 76-77 DE 9
Anáhuac, Mesa de – 72-73 FG 7-8
Anaiza, Jebel – = Jabal Unayzah 44-45 DE 4
Anajás 78-79 JK 5
Anak 50-51 J 6
Anakapalle 44-45 N 7
Anakāpalli = Anakapalle 44-45 N 7
Anak Krakatau, Pulau – 52-53 DE 8
Analalava 64-65 L 5
Anamã 78-79 G 5
Anambas, Kepulauan – 52-53 E 6
Anambra 60-61 F 7
Anamur 44-45 C 3
Anamur Burnu 44-45 C 3
Anan 50-51 K 6
Ananjev 36-37 NO 2
Anantapur 44-45 M 8
Anantnag 44-45 M 4
Anápolis 78-79 K 8
Anār 44-45 GH 4
Anarak 38-39 K 9
Anārak 44-45 G 4
Anārdara 44-45 J 4
Anastasia Island 74-75 c 2
Anatolia 44-45 C 3
Anatolië 44-45 C 3
Anatolie 44-45 C 3
Anatone, WA 76-77 E 2
Añatuya 80 D 3
Anbār, Al- 46-47 J 6
Anbyŏn 50-51 F 3
Ancenis 34-35 G 5
Anceny, MT 76-77 H 3
An-ching = Anqing 48-49 M 5
Anchorage, AK 70-71 FG 5
Anchuras 34-35 E 9
Anclote Keys 74-75 b 2
Ancober = Ankober 60-61 MN 7
Ancona 36-37 E 4
Ancuabe 64-65 J 5
Ancud 80 B 6
Ancud, Golfo de – 80 B 6
Ancyra = Ankara 44-45 C 3
Anda 48-49 NO 2
Andalgalá 80 C 3
Andalousie = Andalucia 34-35 D-F 10
Åndalsnes 30-31 BC 6
Andalucia 34-35 D-F 10
Andaman, Bassin des – 52-53 BC 4-5
Andamán, Cuenca de – 52-53 BC 4-5
Andamán, Mar de – 52-53 C 4-5
Andaman, Mer des – 52-53 C 4-5
Andaman and Nicobar Islands 44-45 OP 8
Andaman Basin 52-53 BC 4-5
Andamān Dvīp = Andaman Islands 44-45 P 8
Andamanenbekken 52-53 BC 4-5
Andaman et Nicobar = Andaman and Nicobar Islands 44-45 OP 8
Andaman Islands 44-45 P 8
Andaman Sea 52-53 C 4-5
Andamanse Zee 52-53 C 4-5
Andamán y Nicobar = Andaman and Nicobar Islands 44-45 OP 8
Andamooka 56-57 G 6
Andamooka Ranges 58 C 3
Andant 80 D 5
Andara 64-65 F 6
Andarīn, Al- 46-47 G 5
Andelys, les – 34-35 H 4
Andenes 30-31 G 3
Andermatt 33 D 5
Anderson, CA 76-77 BC 5
Anderson, IN 72-73 J 3
Anderson, SC 72-73 K 5
Anderson Ranch Reservoir 76-77 F 4
Anderson River 70-71 L 4
Andes 78-79 D 3
Andes, Cordillera de los – 78-79 E 3-F 9
Andes, Los – 80 B 4
Andhra 44-45 M 8-N 7
Andhra Pradesh 44-45 M 8-N 7
Andidanob, Jebel – = Jabal Asūtarībah 62 G 7
Andīmashk 46-47 N 6
Andırın 46-47 G 4
Andižan 44-45 L 2
Andkhoy 44-45 JK 3
Andoas 78-79 D 5
Andong 48-49 O 4
Andong = Dandong 48-49 N 3
Andørja 30-31 GH 3
Andorra 34-35 H 7
Andorra la Vella 34-35 H 7
Andorre 34-35 H 7
Andover, OH 74-75 C 4
Andøy 30-31 FG 3
Andra = Andhra 44-45 M 8-N 7
Andradina 78-79 J 9
Andreanof Islands 19 D 36
Andréba = Ambatosoratra 64-65 L 6
Andrée land 30-31 j 5
Andréeneset 30-31 n 4
Andrejevka [SU, Kazachskaja SSR] 42-43 OP 8
Andrews, OR 76-77 D 4
Andrews, SC 74-75 D 8
Andrews, TN 74-75 B 7
Ándria 36-37 FG 5
Andriba 64-65 L 6
Andringitra 64-65 L 7
Androka 64-65 K 8
Ándros 36-37 L 7
Androscoggin River 74-75 H 2
Andros Island 72-73 L 7
Androth Island 44-45 L 8
Andr'uškino 42-43 de 4
Andsfjord 30-31 G 3
Andújar 34-35 EF 9
Andulo 64-65 E 5
Anegada 72-73 O 8
Anegada Passage 72-73 O 8
Aného 60-61 E 7
Aneityum 56-57 N 4
Añelo 80 C 5
Aneto, Pico de – 34-35 H 7
Aney 60-61 G 5
An-fu = Linli 48-49 L 6
Angamos, Punta – 80 B 2
Ang-ang-ch'i = Ang'angxi 48-49 N 2
Ang'angxi 48-49 N 2
Angara 42-43 S 6
Angarsk 42-43 T 7
Angarskij kr'až 42-43 S-U 6
Ånge 30-31 F 6
Angel, Salto del – 78-79 G 3
Ángel de la Guarda, Isla – 72-73 D 6
Ángeles, Los – [RCH] 80 B 5
Ängelholm 30-31 E 9
Ångermanälven 30-31 G 5-6
Ångermanland 30-31 GH 6
Angermünde 33 FG 2
Angers 34-35 G 5
Ängesån 30-31 K 4
Angka, Doi – = Doi Inthanon 52-53 C 3
Angkor 52-53 D 4
Anglesey 32 D 5
Angleterre 32 E-G 5
Angmagssalik = Angmagssaliq 70-71 de 4
Angmagssaliq 70-71 de 4
Ango 64-65 G 2
Angoche 64-65 JK 6
Angoche, Ilhas – 64-65 JK 6
Angol 80 B 5
Angola 64-65 EF 5
Angola, NY 74-75 D 3
Angola, Bassin de l' 64-65 BC 5-6
Angola, Cuenca de - 64-65 BC 5-6
Angola Basin 64-65 BC 5-6
Angolabekken 64-65 BC 5-6
Angora = Ankara 44-45 C 3
Angostura = Ciudad Bolívar 78-79 G 3
Angostura I, Salto de – 78-79 E 4
Angostura II, Salto de – 78-79 E 4
Angosturas 78-79 E 5
Angoulême 34-35 H 6
Angoumois 34-35 GH 6
Angrapa 33 KL 1
Angra Pequena = Lüderitzbaai 64-65 DE 8
Angren 44-45 KL 2
Angrenšachtstroj = Angren 44-45 KL 2
Anguila = Anguilla 72-73 O 8
Anguilla 72-73 O 8
Angumu 64-65 G 3
Anholt 30-31 D 9
An-hsi = Anxi 48-49 H 3
Anhuei = Anhui 48-49 M 5
Anhui 48-49 M 5
Anhumas 78-79 HJ 8
Ani 50-51 N 2-3
Aniaĭ = Ani 50-51 N 2-3
Anie, Pic d' 34-35 G 7
Animas, NM 76-77 J 10
Animas Peak 76-77 J 10
Anina 36-37 JK 3
Anita, AZ 76-77 G 8
Aniva, mys – 42-43 b 8
Aniva, zaliv – 42-43 b 8
Anjar 44-45 KL 6
Anjou 34-35 G 5
Anjou, ostrova – = ostrova Anžu 19 B 4-5
Anjouan = Ndzuwani 64-65 KL 5
Anju 48-49 O 4
Ankara 44-45 C 3
Ankara Çayı 46-47 DE 3
Ankaratra 64-65 L 6
Ankazoabo 64-65 K 7
An Khe 52-53 E 4
Anklam 33 F 2
Ankober 60-61 MN 7
Ankūr, Jabal – 62 FG 7
Anlong 48-49 JK 6
Anlung = Anlong 48-49 JK 6
Anma-do 50-51 E 5
Ann, Cape – 74-75 H 3
Annaba = 'Annābah 60-61 F 1
'Annābah 60-61 F 1
Annai 78-79 H 4
Annam = Trung Bô 52-53 D 3-E 4
Anna Maria Key 74-75 b 3
Annan 32 E 4
Annapolis, MD 72-73 L 4
Annapolis Royal 70-71 XY 9
Ann Arbor, MI 72-73 K 3
Annecy 34-35 L 6
An Nho'n 52-53 E 4
Anniston, AL 72-73 JK 5
Anqing 48-49 M 5
Anṣāb 44-45 F 8
Anṣāb = Niṣāb 44-45 EF 5
Anṣārīyah, Jabal al- 46-47 G 5
Ansbach 33 E 4
Anshun 48-49 K 6
Ansó 34-35 G 7
Anson Bay 56-57 EF 2
Anšong 50-51 F 4
Ansongo 60-61 E 5
Ansonia, CT 74-75 G 4
Ansted, WV 74-75 C 5
Anta [PE] 78-79 E 7
An-ta = Anda 48-49 NO 2
Antabamba 78-79 E 7
Antakya = Hatay 44-45 D 3
Antalaha 64-65 M 5
Antália = Antalya 44-45 C 3
Antalya 44-45 C 3
Antalya körfezi 44-45 C 3
Antananarivo 64-65 L 6
Antarctica 24 B 28-9
Antarctic Peninsula 24 BC 30-31
Antarctic Sound 24 C 31
Antarctique 24 B 28-9
Antártida 24 B 28-9
Antelope, OR 76-77 C 3
Antelope Hills 76-77 J 4
Antelope Island 76-77 G 5
Antelope Range 76-77 E 6
Antequera 34-35 E 10
Anthony Lagoon 56-57 FG 3
Anti-Atlas = Al-Aṭlas aṣ-Ṣaghīr 60-61 C 2-3
Anti Atlas = Al-Aṭlas aṣ-Ṣaghīr 60-61 C 2-3
Antibes 34-35 L 7
Anticosti, Île d' 70-71 Y 8
Antigua 72-73 O 8
Antigua and Barbuda 72-73 OP 8
Antigua en Barbuda 72-73 OP 8
Antigua et Barbuda 72-73 OP 8
Antigua Guatemala 72-73 H 9
Antigua y Barbuda 72-73 OP 8
Antikýthēra 36-37 K 8
Anti Lebanon = Jabal Lubnān ash-Sharqī 46-47 G 5-6
Anti Liban = Jabal Lubnān ash-Sharqī 46-47 G 5-6
Antilibano = Jabal Lubnān ash-Sharqī 46-47 G 5-6
Antilles, Mer des – 72-73 K-N 8
Antilles du Sud, Bassin des – 22-23 G 8
Antillas 72-73 LM 7
Antímēlos 36-37 KL 7
Antimony, UT 76-77 H 6
Antinopolis 62 D 4
Antioch, CA 76-77 C 6-7
Antiócheia = Antakya 46-47 FG 4
Antiokia = Antakya 46-47 FG 4
Antioquia [CO, ●] 78-79 D 4
Antiparos 36-37 L 7
Antitauro = Güneydoğu Toroslar 44-45 DE 3
Anti Taurus = Güneydoğu Toroslar 44-45 DE 3
Antofagasta [RCH, ●] 80 B 2
Antofagasta de la Sierra 80 C 3
Antongila, Helodrano – 64-65 LM 6
Antonibe 64-65 L 5-6
Antrim 32 C 4
Antrim Mountains 32 CD 4
Antsalova 64-65 K 6
Antsirabé 64-65 L 6
Antsiranana 64-65 LM 5
Antsla 30-31 M 9
Antsohihy 64-65 L 5

156 Alvar

An Tuc = An Khe 52-53 E 4
Antung = Dandong 48-49 N 3
Antwerpen 34-35 J 3
Anũi 50-51 F 5
An'ujsk 42-43 f 4
An'ujskij chrebet 42-43 fg 4
Anuradhapura = Anuradhapuraya 44-45 MN 9
Anuradhapuraya 44-45 MN 9
Anvers = Antwerpen 34-35 J 3
Anvers, Île – 24 C 30
Anxi [TJ, Gansu] 48-49 H 3
Anxious Bay 56-57 F 6
Anyang [ROK] 50-51 F 4
Anyang [TJ] 48-49 LM 4
Anzá [CO] 78-79 D 3
Anzarān, Bi'r – 60-61 B 4
'Anz ar-Ruḥaymāwī 46-47 K 7
Anžero-Sudžensk 42-43 PQ 6
Ānzio 36-37 E 5
Anžu, ostrova – 42-43 a-d 2
Añatuya 80 D 3
Añelo 80 C 5
Aoba = Oba 56-57 N 3
Aoga-shima 48-49 Q 5
Aoga sima = Aoga-shima 48-49 Q 5
Aoji 50-51 H 1
Aomen = Macau 48-49 L 7
Aomori 48-49 QR 3
Aonae 50-51 a 2
Aosta 36-37 B 3
Aouk, Bahr – 60-61 HJ 7
Aouker = Āwkār 60-61 BC 5
Aoya 50-51 JK 5
Aozou 60-61 H 4
Apa, Rio – 80 E 2
Apache, AZ 76-77 J 10
Apalachee Bay 72-73 K 6
Apaporis, Rio – 78-79 EF 5
Aparri 52-53 H 3
Apat 70-71 ab 4
Apatity 42-43 EF 4
Apatzingan de la Constitución 72-73 F 8
Apeldoorn 34-35 KL 2
Apeninos 28-29 K 7-M 8
Apennine 28-29 K 7-M 8
Apennins 28-29 K 7-M 8
Apennijnen 28-29 K 7-M 8
Apex, NC 74-75 D 7
Api [ZRE] 64-65 G 2
Apia 52-53 c 1
Apiacás, Serra dos – 78-79 H 6-7
Apiaí 80 G 3
Apiaú, Serra do – 78-79 G 4
Apo, Mount – 52-53 HJ 5
Apodi, Chapada do – 78-79 M 6
Apodí, Chapada do – 78-79 M 6
Apolda 33 E 3
Apolinario Saravia 80 D 2
Apollo Bay 58 F 7
Apollonia = Sūsah 60-61 J 2
Apolo 78-79 F 7
Apolyont Gölü = Uluabat Gölü 46-47 C 2
Apopka, FL 74-75 c 2
Aporé, Rio – 78-79 J 8
Apostle Islands 72-73 HJ 2
Apóstoles 80 E 3
Apostolovo 38-39 F 6
Apoteri 78-79 H 4
Appalaches = Appalachian Mountains 72-73 K 5-N 2
Appalachia, VA 74-75 B 6
Appalachian Mountains 72-73 K 5-N 2
Appennino Abruzese 36-37 E 4-F 5
Appennino Toscano 36-37 D 3-4
Appennino Umbro-Marchigiano 36-37 E 4
Appleton, WI 72-73 J 3
Appomattox, VA 74-75 D 6
Apposai 44-45 K 4
Apšeronsk 38-39 G 7
Apšeronskij poluostrov 38-39 K 7
Apsley Strait 56-57 EF 2
Apucarana 80 F 2
Apucarana, Serra de – 80 F 2
Apure, Rio – 78-79 F 3
Apurimac, Rio – 78-79 E 7
'Aqabah, Al- [IRQ] 46-47 KL 7
'Aqabah, Al- [JOR] 44-45 CD 5
'Aqabah, Khalīj al- 44-45 C 5
'Aqabah, Wādī al- 62 EF 2-3
'Aqabat aṣ-Ṣaghīrah, Al- 62 E 5
Āqā Jarī = Āghā Jarī 44-45 FG 4
Āqchalar 46-47 L 5
Āq Chāy 46-47 L 3
Āq Chāy, Al- 46-47 L 3
Āqdogh Mīsh, Rūd-e – 46-47 M 4
'Aqeila, el – = Al-'Uqaylah 60-61 H 2
'Aqīq 60-61 M 5
Aqjawajat 60-61 B 5
'Aqrah 46-47 K 4
Aqshār 60-61 B 4
Āq Sū [IRQ] 46-47 L 5
Aqsu [TJ] 48-49 E 3
Aq Tagh altai = Mongol Altajn Nuruu 48-49 F-H 2
Aquarius Plateau 76-77 H 6-7
Aquidauana 78-79 H 9
Aquila, L' 36-37 E 4
Ārā = Arrah 44-45 N 5
'Arab, Bahr al- 60-61 K 6-7
'Arab, Khalīj al- 62 C 2
'Arab, Shaṭṭ al- 44-45 F 4
'Arabah, Wādī – 62 E 3
'Arabah, Wādī al- 46-47 F 7
Araban 46-47 G 4
Arabatskaja Strelka, kosa – 38-39 FG 6
'Arabestān = Khūzestān 44-45 F 4
Arabi, GA 74-75 B 9
'Arabī, Al-Khalīj al- 46-47 N 8
Arabia 22-23 LM 4
Arabian Basin 22-23 N 5
Arabian Desert 60-61 L 3-4
Arabian Sea 44-45 JK 7
Arabia Saudí 44-45 D 5-F 6
Arabië 22-23 LM 4
Arabie 22-23 LM 4
Arabie, Bassin d' 22-23 N 5
Arabie, Mer d' 44-45 JK 7
Arabie Saoudite 44-45 D 5-F 6
Arabisch Bekken 22-23 N 5
Arabische Woestijn 60-61 L 3-4
Arabische Zee 44-45 JK 7
Arabistan = Khūzestān 44-45 F 4
Araç 46-47 E 2
Aracaju 78-79 M 7
Aracati 78-79 M 5
Araçatuba 78-79 JK 9
Araceli = Dumaran Island 52-53 GH 4
Aracena, Sierra de – 34-35 D 10
Arachthós 36-37 J 6
Araçuai 78-79 L 8
Arad 36-37 J 2
Arada 60-61 J 5-6
Arafura, Mar de – 56-57 FG 2
Arafura, Mer d' 56-57 FG 2
Arafura Sea 56-57 FG 2
Arafurazee 56-57 FG 2
Arago, Cape – 76-77 A 4
Aragón 34-35 G 7-8
Aragón, Rio – 34-35 G 7
Araguacema 78-79 K 6
Aragua de Barcelona 78-79 G 3
Araguaia, Parque Nacional do – 78-79 JK 7
Araguaia, Rio – 78-79 J 7
Araguari 78-79 K 8
Araguari, Rio – [BR, Amapá] 78-79 J 4
Araguatins 78-79 K 6
Arai 50-51 M 4
'Araîch, el – = Al-'Arā'ish 60-61 C 1
Araioses 78-79 L 5
'Arā'ish, Al- 60-61 C 1
Araito = ostrov Altasova 42-43 de 7
'Araiyida, Bîr – = Bi'r 'Urayyiḍah 62 DE 3
'Araj, Al- 62 B 3
Arak [DZ] 60-61 E 3
Arāk [IR] 44-45 F 4
Arakamčečen, ostrov – 42-43 I 5
Arakan = Ragaing Pyinnei 52-53 B 2
Arakawa 50-51 M 3
Araklı 46-47 HJ 2
Araks 38-39 J 8
Araks = Rūd-e Aras 46-47 L 3
Aral, Mar de – = Aral'skoje more 42-43 KL 8-9
Aral, Mer de – = Aral'skoje more 42-43 KL 8-9
Aralık 46-47 L 3
Aralmeer = Aral'skoje more 42-43 KL 8-9
Aral Sea = Aral'skoje more 42-43 KL 8-9
Aral'sk 42-43 L 8
Aral'skoje more 42-43 KL 8-9
Aralsul'fat 42-43 L 8
Aramac 56-57 HJ 4
'Aramah, Al- 44-45 F 5-6
Aran 32 B 4
Aranda de Duero 34-35 F 8
Arandjelovac 36-37 J 3
Aran Islands 32 AB 5
Aranjuez 34-35 F 8-9
Arao 50-51 H 6
Araouane 60-61 D 5
Arapey 80 E 4
Arapkir 46-47 H 3
Arapongas 80 F 2
'Ar'ar 46-47 J 7
'Ar'ar, Wādī – 46-47 J 7
Araranguá 80 G 3
Araraquara 78-79 K 9
Araras [BR, Pará] 78-79 J 6
Araras [BR, São Paulo] 78-79 K 9
Araras, Serra das – [BR, Mato Grosso] 78-79 J 8
Araras, Serra das – [BR, Paraná] 80 F 2-3
Ararat [AUS] 56-57 H 7
Ararat = Büyük Ağrı Dağı 44-45 E 2-3
Arari, Cachoeira do – 78-79 K 5
Araripe, Chapada do – 78-79 LM 6
Araripe, Chapada do – 78-79 LM 6
Arariúna = Cachoeira do Arari 78-79 K 5
Aras, Rūd-e – 46-47 L 3
Ārāsanj 46-47 O 5
Aras Nehri 44-45 E 2
Arato = Shirataka 50-51 MN 3
Arauan = Araouane 60-61 D 5
Arauca [CO, ●] 78-79 E 3
Arauca, Rio – 78-79 F 3
Arauco 80 B 5
Aravaipa Valley 76-77 H 9
Ārāvaḷā Parvata = Aravalli Range 44-45 L 6-M 5
Aravalli Range 44-45 L 6-M 5
Arawa 52-53 j 6
Araxá 78-79 K 8
Araxes = Rūd-e Aras 46-47 L 3
Arba Jahan 63 D 2
Arbaj Cheere = Arvajcheer 48-49 J 2
Arbaj Cheere = Arvajcheer 48-49 J 2
Arba Minch = Arba Minty 60-61 M 7
Arba Minty 60-61 M 7
Arbat 46-47 L 5
Arbīl 44-45 E 3
Arboga 30-31 F 8
Arbon, ID 76-77 G 4
Arbroath 32 E 3
Arbuckle, CA 76-77 B 6
Arcachon 34-35 G 6
Arcadia, FL 74-75 c 3
Arcadie = Arkadía 36-37 JK 7
Arcata, CA 76-77 A 5
Arc Dome 76-77 E 6
Archangaj = 7 ◁ 48-49 J 2
Archangel'sk 42-43 G 5
Archenū, Gebel – = Jabal Arkanū 60-61 J 4
Archer River 56-57 H 2
Arches National Monument 76-77 J 6
Arciz 36-37 N 3
Arckaringa 56-57 FG 5
Arckaringa Creek 58 B 1-2
Arco 36-37 D 3
Arco, ID 76-77 G 4
Arctic Bay 70-71 TU 3
Arctic Institute Range 24 B 16
Arctic Ocean 19 C 19-B 17
Arctic Ocean 19 AB 32-5
Arctic Red River [CDN, ~] 70-71 K 4
Arctic Red River [CDN, ●] 70-71 K 4
Archipiélago Malayo 22-23 O 5-Q 6
Arḍ, Rā's al- 46-47 N 8
Arda 36-37 L 5
Ardabīl 44-45 F 3
Ardahan 46-47 K 2
Ardakān 44-45 G 4
Ardakān = Ardekān 44-45 GH 4
Ārdalstangen 30-31 BC 7
Ardanuç 46-47 K 2
Ardar Gwagwa, Jabal – 62 F 6
Ardasa = Torul 46-47 H 2
Ardebil = Ardabīl 44-45 F 3
Ardèche 34-35 K 6
Ardekān 44-45 GH 4
Arden, NV 76-77 F 7
Ardennes 34-35 K 4-L 3
Ardennes, Canal des – 34-35 K 4
Ardeşen 46-47 J 2
Ardestān 44-45 G 4
Ardila 34-35 D 9
Ardlethan 58 H 5
Ardmore, OK 72-73 G 5
Ards Peninsula 32 D 4
Ardud 36-37 K 2
Åre 30-31 E 6
Arecibo 72-73 N 8
Areia Branca 78-79 M 5-6
Arena, Point – 76-77 AB 6
Arenales, Cerro – 80 B 7
Arenas, Punta de – 80 C 8
Arendal 30-31 C 8
Arequipa [PE, ●] 78-79 E 8
Arere 78-79 J 5
Åreskutan 30-31 E 6
Arévalo 34-35 E 8
Arezzo 36-37 DE 4
Arfayyāt, Al- 46-47 K 8
Arğa = Akçadağ 46-47 GH 3
Argachtach 42-43 d 4
Arga-Muora-Sise, ostrov – 42-43 XY 3
Argel = Al-Jazā'ir 60-61 E 1
Argelès-sur-Mer 34-35 J 7
Argelia 60-61 D-F 3
Argenta 36-37 D 3
Argentan 34-35 GH 4
Argenteuil 34-35 J 4
Argentia 70-71 Za 8
Argentina 80 C 7-D 3
Argentine 80 C 7-D 3
Argentine, Bassin d' 22-23 GH 7-8
Argentine Basin 22-23 GH 7-8
Argentine Islands 24 C 30
Argentinië 80 C 7-D 3
Argentijns Bekken 22-23 GH 7-8
Argeş 36-37 M 3
Arghandāb Rōd 44-45 K 4
Argolikós Kólpos 36-37 K 7
Argonne 34-35 K 4
Árgos 36-37 K 7
Argostólion 36-37 J 6
Arguello, Point – 76-77 C 8
Argun' [SU, ~ ◁ Amur] 42-43 WX 7
Argungu 60-61 EF 6
Argut 42-43 Q 8
Arguvan 46-47 H 3
Arhavi 46-47 J 2
Arhli 60-61 F 5
Århus 30-31 D 9
Ariake kai = Ariakeno-umi 50-51 H 6
Ariakeno-umi 50-51 H 6
Ariake-wan = Shibushi-wan 50-51 H 7
Ariano Irpino 36-37 F 5
Aribinda 60-61 D 6
Arica [CO] 78-79 E 5
Arica [RCH] 80 B 1
'Āriḍ, Al- 44-45 F 6-7
Arid, Cape – 56-57 D 6
Ariège 34-35 H 7
Ariel, WA 76-77 B 3
Arīha 46-47 F 7
Arikawa 50-51 G 6
Arimā [BR] 78-79 G 6
Arimo, ID 76-77 GH 4
Arinos 78-79 K 8
Arinos, Rio – 78-79 H 7
Aripuanã, Rio – 78-79 G 6
Ariquemes 78-79 G 6
'Arīsh, Al- 60-61 L 2
'Arīsh, Wādī al- 62 E 2-3
Arismendi 78-79 F 3
Arita 50-51 K 5
Arivaca, AZ 76-77 H 10
Ariza 34-35 FG 8
Arizaro, Salar de – 80 C 2
Arizona [RA] 80 C 5
Arizona [USA] 72-73 D 5
Årjäng 30-31 E 8
Arjeplog 30-31 GH 4
Arjona [CO] 78-79 D 2
Arka 42-43 b 5
Arkadak 38-39 H 5
Arkadía 36-37 JK 7
Arkalyk 42-43 M 7
Arkansas 72-73 H 4
Arkansas River 72-73 F 4
Arkanū, Jabal – 60-61 J 4
Arkenu, Jebel – = Jabal Arkanū 60-61 J 4
Arklow 32 CD 5
Arkona, Kap – 33 F 1
Arktičeskogo Instituta, ostrova – 42-43 OP 2
Arlanzón 34-35 EF 7
Arlberg 33 E 5
Arlee, MT 76-77 F 2
Arles 34-35 K 7
Arlington, OR 76-77 CD 3
Arlington, VA 72-73 L 4
Arlington, WA 76-77 BC 1
Arlit = Arhli 60-61 F 5
Arlon 34-35 K 4
Armadale 56-57 C 6
Armagh 32 C 4
Armagnac 34-35 GH 7
Armand, Rivière – 70-71 W 6
Armant 62 E 5
Armavir 38-39 H 6-7
Armenia 38-39 H 7-J 8
Armenia 78-79 D 4
Armenië 38-39 H 7-J 8
Arménie 38-39 H 7-J 8
Armentières 34-35 J 3
Armero 78-79 E 4
Armevistḗs, Akrōtḗrion – 36-37 M 7
Armidale 56-57 K 6
Armstead, MT 76-77 G 3
Armuña, La – 34-35 DE 8
Armuña, La – 34-35 DE 8
Arnarfjördhur 30-31 ab 2
Arnarvatn 30-31 cd 2
Arnávtē, Akrōtḗrion – 46-47 DE 5
Árnes 30-31 cd 2
Arnhem 34-35 KL 2-3
Arnhem, Cape – 56-57 G 2
Arnhem Bay 56-57 G 2
Arnhem Land 56-57 FG 2
Arno 36-37 D 4
Arno Bay 58 C 4
Arnold, PA 74-75 D 4
Arnøy 30-31 J 2
Arnsberg 33 D 3
Arnstadt 33 E 3
Aroab 64-65 E 8
Arōmā = Arūmā 60-61 M 5
Aroostook River 70-71 X 8
Arpaçay 46-47 K 2
Arpa Çayı 46-47 K 2
Arqa tagh 48-49 FG 4
'Arqūb, Al- 60-61 AB 4
Arrah [IND] 44-45 N 5
Arraias 78-79 K 7
Arraiján 72-73 b 3
Arran 32 D 4
Arras 34-35 J 3
Arrecife 60-61 B 3
Arrecifes, Gran Barrera de – = Great Barrier Reef 56-57 H 1-K 4
Arrée, Monts d' 34-35 EF 4
Arriaga 72-73 H 8
Arriola, CO 76-77 J 7
Arroyo Grande, CA 76-77 CD 8
Arroyo Seco [USA] 76-77 F 9
Arša Nuur = Chagan nuur 48-49 L 3
Arsenjev 42-43 Z 9
Arsī 60-61 M 7
Arsuz = Uluçınar 46-47 F 4
Árta 36-37 J 6
Artaki = Erdek 46-47 B 2
Arṭāwīyah, Al – 44-45 EF 5
Artesia, CO 76-77 J 5
Artesia, NM 72-73 EF 5
Arthur 74-75 C 3
Arthur River 58 b 2
Arthur's Pass 56-57 O 8
Arti 38-39 L 4
Ártico Central, Cuenca del – 19 A
Artigas [ROU, ●] 80 E 4
Artjärvi 30-31 LM 7
Artois 34-35 J 3
Art'om 42-43 Z 9
Art'omovskij [SU, Rossijskaja SFSR] 42-43 R 7
Art'omovskij [SU ↗ Bodajbo] 42-43 VW 6
Art'omovskij [SU ↗ Sverdlovsk] 42-43 L 6
Artova 46-47 G 2
Artur de Paiva = Capelongo 64-65 E 5
Arturo Prat 24 C 30-31
Artvin 44-45 E 2
Aru 64-65 H 2
Aru, Kepulauan – 52-53 KL 8
Arua 64-65 H 2
Aruab 64-65 E 8
Aruanã 78-79 J 7
Aruba 72-73 N 9
Arumā [BR] 78-79 G 5
Arūmā [Sudan] 60-61 M 5
Arumbi 64-65 G 2
Arumpo 58 F 4
Aruṇ 44-45 O 5
Arunachal Pradesh 44-45 P Q 5
Arunta Desert = Simpson Desert 56-57 G 4-5
Arusha 64-65 J 3
Arusī = Arsī 60-61 M 7
Aruwimi 64-65 G 2
Arvajcheer 48-49 J 2
Arvidsjaur 30-31 H 5
Arvika 30-31 E 8
Arvin, CA 76-77 D 8
Arys' 42-43 M 9
Arzamas 42-43 GH 6
Arzgir 38-39 H 6
Åsa [S] 30-31 E 9
Aša [SU] 38-39 L 4
Asadābād [AFG] 44-45 L 4
Asadābād [IR] 46-47 MN 5
Aşağıçıgıl 46-47 DE 3
Aşağı Pınarbaşı 46-47 E 3
Asahi 50-51 N 5
Asahi dake [J, Hokkaidō] 48-49 R 3
Asahi dake [J, Yamagata] 50-51 M 3
Asahigava = Asahikawa 48-49 R 3
Asahi gawa 50-51 J 5
Asahikawa 48-49 R 3
Asalē [ETH, ●] 60-61 MN 6
Asalē [ETH, ≈] 60-61 N 6
Asam 44-45 P 5
Asángaro = Azángaro 78-79 EF7
Asansol 44-45 O 6
Asante = Ashanti 60-61 D 7
Åsarna 30-31 F 6
'Asayr 44-45 G 8
Asayta 60-61 N 6
Asben = Azbine 60-61 F 5
Asbest 42-43 L 6
Asbe Teferī 60-61 N 7
Asbury Park, NJ 74-75 FG 4
Ascensión [BOL] 78-79 G 8
Ascension [GB] 66 E 9
Ascensión, Bahía de la – 72-73 J 8
Aschabad 44-45 HJ 3
Aschaffenburg 33 D 4
Ascoli-Piceno 36-37 E 4
Aseb 60-61 N 6
Asela 60-61 M 7
Åsele 30-31 G 5
Aselle = Asela 60-61 M 7
Asenovgrad 36-37 L 4-5
Asfī = Ṣāfī 60-61 C 2
Asfūn 62 E 5
Ashanti 60-61 D 7
Ashāqif, Tulūl al- 46-47 G 6
'Asharah, Al- 46-47 J 5
Ashburn, GA 74-75 B 9
Ashburton 56-57 O 8
Ashburton River 56-57 C 4
Ashdōd 46-47 F 7
Asheboro, NC 74-75 CD 7
Asheville, NC 72-73 K 4
Ashe Yōma 52-53 C 3
Ashford 32 G 6
Ashford [AUS] 58 K 2
Ashford, WA 76-77 BC 2
Ash Fork, AZ 76-77 G 8
Ashibetsu 50-51 c 2
Ashikaga 50-51 M 4
Ashizuri-zaki 50-51 J 6
Ashkelon = Ashqĕlōn 46-47 F 7
Ashland, KY 72-73 K 4
Ashland, ME 74-75 J 1
Ashland, OH 74-75 BC 4
Ashland, OR 76-77 B 4
Ashland, VA 74-75 E 6
Ashland, WI 72-73 H 2
Ashland, Mount – 76-77 B 4
Ashmūn 62 D 2
Ashmūnayn, Al- 62 D 4
Ashqĕlōn 46-47 F 7
Ashshur = Assur 44-45 E 3
Ashtabula, OH 74-75 C 3-4
Ashton, ID 76-77 H 3
Ashuanipi Lake 70-71 X 7
'Āshūrīyah, Al- 46-47 K 7
'Āṣī, Al- 46-47 K 4
'Āṣī, Nahr al- 46-47 G 5
Asia 22-23 N-P 3
Asia, Kepulauan – 52-53 K 6
Asie 22-23 N-P 3
Asike 52-53 LM 8
Asinara 36-37 BC 5
Asinara, Golfo dell' 36-37 C 5
Asi Nehri 46-47 G 4
Asino 42-43 PQ 6
'Asīr 44-45 E 7
Asiut = Asyūṭ 60-61 L 3
Aşkale 46-47 J 3
Askalon = Ashqĕlōn 46-47 F 7
Asker 30-31 D 8
Askersund 30-31 F 8

Asker 157

Askī Muṣil 46-47 K 4
Askiz 42-43 R 7
Askja 30-31 e 2
Askol'd, ostrov – 50-51 J 1
Aṣlāndūz 46-47 M 3
Asmaca = Feke 46-47 F 4
Asmara = Asmera 60-61 M 5
Asmera 60-61 M 5
Asnām, Al- = Shilif 60-61 E 1
Asosa 60-61 LM 6
Asotin, WA 76-77 E 2
Aso zan 50-51 H 6
Aspen Hill, MD 56-57 E 5
Aspiring, Mount – 56-57 N 8
Aspromonte 36-37 FG 6
'Aṣr, Jabal al- 62 D 6
Assab = Aseb 60-61 N 6
Assad, Buhayrat al- 44-45 D 3
Assaitta = Asaita 60-61 N 6
Assal, Lac – = Asalē 60-61 N 6
Assale = Asalē 60-61 MN 6
Assam = Asam 44-45 P 5
Assam Hills 44-45 P 5
Assam Himālaya 44-45 OP 5
Assateague Island 74-75 F 5
Assen 34-35 L 2
Assens 30-31 CD 10
Assiniboine, Mount – 70-71 NO 7
Assiniboine River 70-71 Q 7
Assis 78-79 J 9
Assisi 36-37 E 4
Assiut = Asyūṭ 60-61 L 3
Assuan = Aswān 60-61 L 4
Assumption Island 64-65 L 4
Assur 44-45 E 3
Astakós 36-37 J 6
Āstāneh 46-47 N 6
Astara 38-39 J 8
Āstārā [IR] 46-47 N 3
Astin tagh = Altin tagh 48-49 EF 4
Astorga 34-35 DE 7
Astoria, OR 72-73 B 2
Astove Island 64-65 L 5
Astra 80 C 7
Astrachan 38-39 J 6
Astrida 64-65 G 3
Astrolabe Bay 52-53 N 7-8
Asturias 34-35 DE 7
Astypálaia 36-37 LM 7
Asunción [PY] 80 E 3
Asunción, La – 78-79 G 2
Asūtarībah, Jabal – 62 G 7
Aswa 64-65 H 2
Aswān 60-61 L 4
'Aswân, Sad el – = Sadd al-'Ālī 60-61 L 3
Asyūṭ 60-61 L 3
Asyūṭī, Wādī al- 62 D 4

Atacama [RA] 80 BC 3
Atacama, Desierto de – 80 B 3-C 2
Atacama, Fosa de – 22-23 F 6-7
Atacama, Fosse d' 22-23 FG 7
Atacama, Salar de – 80 C 2
Atacama Trench 22-23 F 6-7
Atacamatrog 22-23 F 6-7
Atakor = Atākūr 60-61 F 4
Atakora, Chaîne de l' 60-61 E 6-7
Atakora, Chaîne de l' 60-61 E 6-7
Atakpamé 60-61 E 7
Atākūr 60-61 F 4
Atalaya [PE, ●] 78-79 E 7
Ataleia 78-79 L 8
Atami 50-51 M 5
Ataniya = Adana 44-45 D 3
Ataouat, Day Nui – 52-53 E 3
Atapupu 52-53 H 8
'Atāqah, Jabal – 62 E 2-3
Āṭār 60-61 B 4
Atarque, NM 76-77 J 8
Atascadero, CA 76-77 C 8
Atasu 42-43 N 8
Atatürk Barajı 46-47 H 4
Atauro, Pulau – 52-53 J 8
'Aṭbarah 60-61 L 5
'Aṭbarah, Nahr – 60-61 LM 5
Atbasar 42-43 M 7
Ātbu Ṣāliḥ 46-47 M 7
Atenas = Athēnai 36-37 KL 7
Atessa 36-37 F 4-5
Atfārītī 60-61 B 3
Aṭfīḥ 62 D 3
Athabasca 70-71 O 7
Athabasca, Lake – 70-71 OP 6
Athabasca River 70-71 O 6
'Athāmīn, Al- 46-47 K 7
Athena, OR 76-77 D 3
Athēnai 36-37 KL 7
Athene = Athēnai 36-37 KL 7
Athènes = Athēnai 36-37 KL 7
Athenry 32 B 5
Athens, GA 72-73 K 5
Athens, OH 74-75 B 5
Athens, PA 74-75 E 4
Athens = Athēnai 36-37 KL 7
Atherton 56-57 HJ 3
Athi 64-65 J 3
Athi River 63 D 3
Athlone 32 C 5
Athol, ID 76-77 E 2
Áthos 36-37 L 5
Ati 60-61 H 6
Atiak 63 BC 2
Atico 78-79 E 8
Atil 76-77 H 10
Atitlán, Volcán – 72-73 H 9
Atka 42-43 d 5
Atka Island 19 D 36
Atkarsk 38-39 H 5
Atlanta, GA 72-73 K 5
Atlanta, ID 76-77 F 4
Atlantic City, NJ 72-73 M 4
Atlantic Coastal Plain 72-73 K 5-L 4
Atlantic Indian Antarctic Basin 22-23 J-M 9
Atlantic Indian Trench 22-23 J-L 8
Atlantic Ocean 22-23 G 4-J 7
Atlántico Norte, Dorsal del – 22-23 H 5-3
Atlántico Sur, Dorsal del – 22-23 J 6-8
Atlantische Oceaan 22-23 G 4-J 7
Atlantisch-Indische Rug 22-23 J-L 8
Atlantisch-Indisch Zuidpolairbekken 22-23 J-M 9
Aṭlas al-Khalfīyah, Jabal- 60-61 C 2-3
Aṭlas al-Wasṭī, Jabal- 60-61 CD 2
Aṭlas aṣ-Ṣaghīr, Al- 60-61 C 2-3
Atlas Medio = Al-Aṭlas al-Mutawassiṭ 60-61 CD 2
Atlas Medio = Al-Aṭlas al-Mutawassiṭ 60-61 CD 2
Atlasova, ostrov – 42-43 de 7
Atlas Sahariano 60-61 D 2-F 1
Atlas Saharien 60-61 D 2-F 1
Atlas Tellien 60-61 D 2-E 1
Atlas Telliano 60-61 D 2-E 1
Atlin 70-71 K 6
Atlin Lake 70-71 K 6
Atlixco 72-73 G 8
Atløy 30-31 A 7
Atomic City, ID 76-77 G 4
Atouat, Massif d' = Day Nui Ataouat 52-53 E 3
Atrāk, Rūd-e – 44-45 H 3
Aṭrash, Wādī al- 62 E 4
Atrato, Río – 78-79 D 3
Atrek 38-39 K 8
'Aṭrūn, Al- 60-61 K 5
Atsumi 50-51 M 3
Atsumi-hantō 50-51 L 5
Atsunai 50-51 cd 2
Atsuta 50-51 b 2
Atsutoko 50-51 d 2
Attalea = Antalya 44-45 C 3
Attaléia = Antalya 44-45 C 3
Attawapiskat River 70-71 TU 7
Attopo' = Attopu 52-53 E 3-4
Attopu 52-53 E 3-4
Attu Island 19 D 1
Atūwi, Wād – 60-61 B 4
Atwater, CA 76-77 C 7

Auati Paraná, Rio – 78-79 F 5
Aubagne 34-35 K 7
Aube 34-35 K 4
Aubrac, Monts d' 34-35 J 6
Auburn, AL 72-73 J 5
Auburn, CA 76-77 C 6
Auburn, ME 74-75 H 2
Auburn, NY 74-75 E 3
Auburn, WA 76-77 B 2
Auburndale, FL 74-75 c 2-3
Aucanquilcha, Cerro – 80 C 2
Auce 30-31 K 9
Auch 34-35 H 7
Auckland 56-57 OP 7
Auckland, Ramal de – 24 D 17
Auckland, Seuil des – 24 D 17
Aucklanddrempel 24 D 17
Auckland Islands 24 D 17-18
Aude 34-35 J 7
Aue 33 F 3
Auenat, Gebel – = Jabal al-'Uwaynāt 60-61 K 4
Auf, Ras el- = Rā's Banās 60-61 M 4
Augathella 56-57 J 5
Augila = Awjilah 60-61 J 3
Augrabies Falls = Augrabiesval 64-65 EF 8
Augrabiesval 64-65 EF 8
Augsburg 33 E 4
Augusta [AUS] 56-57 BC 6
Augusta [I] 36-37 F 7
Augusta, GA 72-73 K 5
Augusta, ME 72-73 N 3
Augusta, MT 76-77 G 2
Augustów 33 L 2
Augustus, Mount – 56-57 C 4
Augustus Downs 56-57 GH 3
Augustus Island 56-57 D 3
Auja, El- = Qēẓī'ōt 46-47 F 7
Auk = Bahr Aouk 60-61 HJ 7
Auki 52-53 k 6
Aulander, NC 74-75 E 6
Auld, Lake – 56-57 D 4
Aunis 34-35 G 5
Auob 64-65 E 8
Aurangabad [IND, Maharashtra] 44-45 LM 6-7
Aurich 33 C 2
Aurignac 34-35 H 7
Aurillac 34-35 J 6
Aurlandsvangen 30-31 B 7
Aurora [CDN] 74-75 D 2-3
Aurora, IL 72-73 J 3
Aurora, NC 74-75 E 7
Aurora, OH 74-75 A 5
Aurukun 56-57 H 2
Aus 64-65 E 8
Ausangate = Nudo Ausangate 78-79 E 7
Ausangate, Nudo – 78-79 E 7
Ausiait 70-71 Za 4
Äußere Mongolei = Mongolische Volksrepublik 48-49 H-L 2
Aust-Agder 30-31 BC 8
Austfonna 30-31 m 4
Austin, MN 72-73 H 3
Austin, MT 76-77 GH 2
Austin, NV 76-77 E 6
Austin, OR 76-77 D 3
Austin, TX 72-73 G 5
Austin, Lake – 56-57 C 5
Australia 56-57 C-J 4
Australia Meridional, Cuenca de – 22-23 PQ 8
Australia Noroccidental, Cuenca de – 22-23 OP 6
Australia Occidental, Cuenca de – 22-23 P 7
Australia Oriental, Cuenca de – 22-23 RS 8
Australia Septentrional, Cuenca de – 56-57 C 2
Australië 56-57 C-J 4
Australie 56-57 C-J 4
Austria 33 E-G 5
Austur-Bardhastrandar 30-31 bc 2
Austur-Húnavatn 30-31 cd 2
Austur-Skaftafell 30-31 ef 2
Austvågøy 30-31 F 3
Autlán de Navarro 72-73 EF 8
Autriche 33 E-G 5
Autun 34-35 K 5
Auvergne 34-35 J 6
Auvergne [AUS] 56-57 EF 3
Auxerre 34-35 J 5
Auyuittuq National Park 70-71 XY 4

Avadh 44-45 N 5
Āvaj 46-47 N 5
Avakubi 64-65 G 2
Avalon, CA 76-77 D 9
Avalon Peninsula 70-71 a 8
Avān 46-47 M 3
Avanos 46-47 F 3
Avaré 78-79 K 9
Aveiro [BR] 78-79 HJ 5
Aveiro [P] 34-35 C 8
Avej = Āvaj 46-47 N 5
Avellaneda [RA, Buenos Aires] 80 DE 4-5
Avellino 36-37 F 5
Avenal, CA 76-77 CD 7-8
Averøy 30-31 B 6
Aversa 36-37 EF 5
Avery, ID 76-77 F 2
Avesta 30-31 G 7
Aveyron 34-35 HJ 6
Avezzano 36-37 E 4-5
Avignon 34-35 K 7
Ávila 34-35 E 8
Avilés 34-35 DE 7
Avión, Faro de – 34-35 CD 7
Avis 34-35 D 9
Avlije-Ata = Džambul 42-43 MN 9
Ávola 36-37 F 7
Avon, MT 76-77 G 2
Avondale, AZ 76-77 G 9
Avon Downs 56-57 G 4
Avon Park, FL 74-75 c 3
Avontuur 64-65 F 9
Avranches 34-35 G 4
Avşa Adası 46-47 B 2

Awadh = Avadh 44-45 N 5
Awādī 60-61 B 4
Awaji-shima 50-51 K 5
'Awānah 60-61 C 5
Awasa 60-61 M 7
Awasa Hayik 60-61 M 7
Awash [ETH, ~] 60-61 M 7
Awash [ETH, ●] 60-61 MN 7
Awa-shima 50-51 M 3
Awaso 60-61 D 7
Awaya 50-51 K 5
Awbārī 60-61 G 3
Awbārī, Dahnā' – 60-61 G 3
Awdah, Hawr – 46-47 M 7
Awdheegle 60-61 N 8
Awe, Loch – 32 D 3
Aweil = Uwayl 60-61 K 7
'Awjā', Al- 46-47 M 8
Awjilah 60-61 J 3
Āwkār 60-61 BC 5
Awlaytīs, Wād – 60-61 B 3
Awsart 60-61 B 4
Awsaṭ, Al- 60-61 L 6
Awul 52-53 h 6

Axarfjördhur 30-31 e 1
Axel Heiberg Island 70-71 ST 1-2
Axim 60-61 D 8
Ax-les-Thermes 34-35 HJ 7

Ayabaca 78-79 CD 5
Ayabe 50-51 K 5
Ayacucho [RA] 80 E 5
Ayacucho [PE, ●] 78-79 E 7
Ayagh Qum köl 48-49 F 4
Ayamonte 34-35 D 10
Ayancık 46-47 F 2
Ayas [TR] 46-47 E 2
'Ayāshī, Jabal – 60-61 CD 2
Ayaviri 78-79 E 7
Aybastı 46-47 G 2
Ayden, NC 74-75 E 7
Aydın 44-45 B 3
Aydıncık 46-47 E 4
Aydın Dağları 46-47 B 4-C 3
Aydınkent 46-47 DE 4
Aydin köl 48-49 F 3
Aydınlık Dağları 46-47 J 3
Ayers Rock 56-57 F 5
'Aylay 60-61 L 5
Aylesbury 32 F 6
'Aylī, Sha'īb al- 46-47 H 7
Aylmer [CDN, Ontario] 56-57 C 3
'Ayn, Wādī al- 44-45 H 6
'Aynabo 60-61 O 7
'Ayn al-Ghazal [LAR] 60-61 J 4
'Ayn al-Muqshīn, Al- 44-45 GH 7
'Ayn 'Ayssah 46-47 H 4
'Ayn Azzān 60-61 G 4
'Ayn Dīwār 46-47 K 4
'Ayn Qazzān 60-61 EF 5
'Ayn Ṣafrā 60-61 DE 2
'Ayn Ṣāliḥ 60-61 E 3
'Ayn Tādīn 60-61 E 4
'Ayn-Umannās 60-61 F 3
Aynunāh 42-43 D 5
'Ayn Zālah 46-47 K 4
Ayōd = Ayūd 60-61 L 7
Ayr 32 D 4
Ayr [AUS] 56-57 J 3
Ayrancı 46-47 E 4
Ayre, Point of – 32 DE 4
Ayrig Nur = Ajrag nuur 48-49 GH 2
Aysha 60-61 N 6
Ayu, Kepulauan – 52-53 K 6
Ayūd 60-61 L 7
'Ayun, Al- 60-61 B 3
'Ayūn al-'Atrūs 60-61 C 5
Ayvacık [TR, Çanakkale] 46-47 B 3
Ayvalık 46-47 B 3
'Ayyāṭ, Al- 62 D 3

Azafal 60-61 AB 4
'Azair, Al- = Al-'Uzayr 46-47 M 7
'Aẓamīyah, Baghdād-Al- 46-47 L 6
Azángaro 78-79 EF 7
Azaoua, I-n- 60-61 F 4
Azaouâd 60-61 D 5
Azaouak, Vallée de – 60-61 E 5
Azare 60-61 FG 6
Āzar Shahr 46-47 LM 4
Azawak, Wadi – = Azaouak 60-61 E 5
A'zāz 46-47 G 4
Azbine 60-61 F 5
Azdavay 46-47 E 2
Azéfal = Azafal 60-61 AB 4
Azerbaïdjan 38-39 J 7
Azerbaijan 38-39 J 7
Azerbaiján 38-39 J 7
Azerbajdzjan 38-39 J 7
Azië 22-23 N-P 3
'Azīzīyah, Al- [IRQ] 46-47 L 6
'Azīzīyah, Al- [LAR] 60-61 G 2
Aẓlam, Wādī – 62 FG 4
'Azmātī, Sabkhat – 60-61 DE 3
Aznā 46-47 N 6
Azogues 78-79 D 5
Azorendrempel 22-23 HJ 4
Azores = Açores 66 D 3
Azores, Plataforma de – 22-23 HJ 4
Azores Plateau 22-23 HJ 4
Azov 38-39 G 6
Azov, Mar de – = Azovskoje more 38-39 G 6
Azov, Mer d' = Azovskoje more 38-39 G 6
Azov, Sea of – = Azovskoje more 38-39 G 6
Azovskoje more 38-39 G 6
Azraq, El- = Azraq ash-Shīshān 46-47 G 7
Azraq ash-Shīshān 46-47 G 7
Azroû = Azrū 60-61 CD 2
Azrū 60-61 CD 2
Aztec, AZ 76-77 G 9
Azuaga 34-35 E 9
Azucar, Pan de – 78-79 D 4
Azuero, Península de – 72-73 K 10
Azul [RA] 80 E 5
Azuma-yama 50-51 MN 4
Azurduy 78-79 G 8-9
Azza = Ghazzah 44-45 C 4
'Azzān 44-45 F 8
Azzel Matti, Sebkra – = Sabkhat 'Azmātī 60-61 DE 3

B

Baa 52-53 H 9
Ba'abdā 46-47 F 6
Baalbek = Ba'labakk 46-47 G 5-6
Ba'an = Batang 48-49 H 6
Baardheere 60-61 N 8
Baargal 60-61 c 1
Bāb, Al- 46-47 G 4
Baba Burun [TR, Çanakkale] 44-45 B 3
Baba Burun [TR, Zonguldak] 46-47 D 2
Babadag 36-37 N 3
Babadag, gora – 38-39 J 7
Babaeski 46-47 B 2
Baba Hatim 48-49 E 4
Babahoyo 78-79 CD 5
Babajevo 42-43 F 6
Babar, Kepulauan – 52-53 JK 8
Babati 63 C 4
Babb, MT 76-77 G 1
Babbit, NV 76-77 D 6
Babel = Babylon 44-45 EF 4
Babelthuap 52-53 KL 5
Babia Góra 33 J 4
Bābil 46-47 L 6
Bābil = Babylon 44-45 EF 4
Babinda 56-57 J 3
Babine Lake 70-71 L 6-7
Babine Range 70-71 L 6-7
Bābol 44-45 G 3
Baboquivari Peak 76-77 H 10
Baboua 60-61 G 7
Bābul = Bābol 44-45 G 3
Babuškin 42-43 U 7
Babuškina, zaliv – 42-43 de 6
Babuyan Channel 52-53 H 3
Babuyan Channel 52-53 H 3
Babuyan Island 52-53 H 3
Babuyan Islands 52-53 H 3
Babylon 44-45 EF 4
Babylon, NY 74-75 G 4
Bacan, Pulau – 52-53 J 7
Bacău 36-37 M 2
Bắc Bô 52-53 DE 2
Bacchus Marsh 58 G 6
Bacerac 76-77 J 10
Bacharden 44-45 H 3
Bachchār = Bashshār 60-61 D 2
Bachkirs, République Autonome des – = 7 ◁ 42-43 K 7
Bachmač 38-39 F 5
Bachu = Maral Bashi 48-49 D 3-4
Bačka 36-37 H 3
Bačka Palanka 36-37 H 3
Bačka Topola 36-37 HJ 3
Back Bay 74-75 F 6
Back River 70-71 R 4
Backstairs Passage 56-57 G 7
Bac Lio' = Vinh Lo'i 52-53 E 5
Bacoachi 76-77 J 10
Bacolod 52-53 H 4
Bacuit = El Nido 52-53 G 4
Bad', Wādī – 62 E 3
Badajos, Lago – 78-79 G 5
Badajoz 34-35 D 9
Badakhshān 44-45 L 3
Badalona 34-35 J 8
Badanah 44-45 E 4
Badārī, Al- 60-61 L 3
Badayun = Budaun 44-45 M 5
Baddūzzah, Rā's al- 60-61 BC 2
Bad Ems 33 C 3
Baden [A] 33 H 4
Baden [CH] 33 D 5
Baden-Baden 33 D 4
Baden-Württemberg 33 D 4
Badgastein 33 F 5
Bad Hersfeld 33 D 3
Bad Homburg 33 D 3
Bādī, Al- [IRQ] 46-47 J 5
Badī', Al- [Saudi Arabia] 44-45 F 6
Badīn 44-45 K 6
Badin, NC 74-75 C 7
Bad Ischl 33 F 5
Bad Kissingen 33 E 3
Bad Kreuznach 33 CD 4
Badlands [USA, North Dakota] 72-73 F 2
Badlands [USA, South Dakota] 72-73 F 3
Bad Mergentheim 33 DE 4
Bad Nauheim 33 D 3
Bad Neuenahr 33 C 3
Baḍoḍēṅ = Vadodara 44-45 L 6
Ba Đôn 52-53 E 3
Badong [TJ] 48-49 KL 5
Badr 44-45 E 7
Badrah 46-47 L 6
Bad Reichenhall 33 F 5
Badr Ḥunayn 44-45 D 6
Bad Tölz 33 E 5
Badu Danan = Denan 60-61 N 7
Badu Island 56-57 H 2
Badulla 44-45 N 9
Bad Wildungen 33 D 3
Bafang 60-61 G 7-8
Bafatá 60-61 B 6
Baffin, Bahía de – 70-71 W-Y 3
Baffin, Baie – 70-71 W-Y 3
Baffin, District of – 70-71 T-V 3-4
Baffinbaai 70-71 W-Y 3
Baffin Bay 70-71 W-Y 3
Baffin Island 70-71 V 3-X 5
Baffin Island National Park 70-71 XY 4
Baffinland = Baffin Island 70-71 V 3-X 5
Bafia 60-61 G 8
Bafing 60-61 B 6
Bafoulabé 60-61 BC 6
Bafoussam 60-61 G 7
Bāfq 44-45 GH 4
Bafra 46-47 FG 2
Bafra Burnu 46-47 G 2
Bafwasende 64-65 G 2
Bagabag Island 52-53 N 7
Bāgalakōṭṭē = Bagalkot 44-45 LM 7
Bagalkot 44-45 LM 7
Bagalpur = Bhagalpur 44-45 O 5-6
Bagamojo = Bagamoyo 64-65 J 4
Bagamoyo 64-65 J 4
Bagan Jaya = Butterworth 52-53 D 5
Bagase Burnu = İncekum burnu 46-47 EF 4
Bagdad, AZ 76-77 G 8
Bagdād = Baghdād 44-45 EF 4
Bagdarin 42-43 VW 7
Bağgöze 46-47 JK 4
Baghdād 44-45 EF 4
Baghdādī, Rās – = Rā's Ḥunkurāb 62 F 5
Baghelkhand 44-45 N 6
Bāgh-e Malek 46-47 N 7
Bagheria 36-37 E 6

Baghlān 44-45 K 3
Baghrash köl 48-49 F 3
Bagirmi = Baguirmi 60-61 H 6
Bağlum 46-47 E 2
Bagnères-de-Bigorre 34-35 H 7
Bagnères-de-Luchon 34-35 H 7
Bagoé 60-61 C 6
Bagrationovsk 33 K 1
Baguio 52-53 H 3
Baguirmi 60-61 H 6
Bagur, Cabo – 34-35 J 8
Bagzane, Monts – 60-61 F 5
Bahadale 63 D 2-3
Bahamas, Banc des – 72-73 L 6-7
Bahamas, Gran Banco de las – 72-73 L 6-7
Bāhār 46-47 N 5
Baharāich = Bahraich 44-45 N 5
Baharampur 44-45 O 6
Bahar Assoli = Beraisolē 60-61 N 6
Baḥarīyah, Wāḥāt al- 60-61 K 3
Bahāwalpur 44-45 L 5
Bahçe 46-47 G 4
Bahçesaray 46-47 K 3
Bahia 78-79 LM 7
Bahia = Salvador 78-79 M 7
Bahía, Isla de la – 72-73 J 8
Bahía, Islas de la – 72-73 J 8
Bahía Blanca [RA, ∪] 80 D 5
Bahía Blanca [RA, ●] 80 D 5
Bahía de Caráquez 78-79 CD 5
Bahía Grande 80 C 8
Bahía Laura 80 CD 7
Bahía Negra 80 E 2
Bahía Oso Blanco 80 CD 7
Bahía Solano [CO, ●] 78-79 D 3
Bahir Dar 60-61 M 6
Baḥrah, Al- 46-47 MN 8
Bahraich 44-45 N 5
Bahrain 44-45 G 5
Baḥrayn, Al- 62 B 3
Bahr Dar Giorgis = Bahir Dar 60-61 M 6
Baḥreh, Āb-e – 46-47 N 7
Baḥr-e 'Ommān, Banāder va Jazāyer-e – = 6 ◁ 44-45 H 5
Bahrgān, Ra's-e – 46-47 N 7-8
Baḥrīyah, Barqat al- 60-61 JK 2
Bahu-mbelu 52-53 H 7
Bai 48-49 E 3
Baía = Salvador 78-79 M 7
Baía dos Tigres 64-65 D 6
Baia Mare 36-37 KL 2
Baião 78-79 JK 5
Baia Sprie 36-37 KL 2
Baïbokoum 60-61 H 7
Baibū = Baybū 46-47 KL 4
Bai Bung, Mui – 52-53 D 5
Baicheng 48-49 N 2
Baicheng = Bai 48-49 E 3
Baihe [TJ, ●] 48-49 KL 5
Ba'ījī 46-47 K 5
Baïkal, Lac – = ozero Bajkal 42-43 U 7
Baikal, Lake – = ozero Bajkal 42-43 U 7
Baikalmeer = ozero Bajkal 42-43 U 7
Baile Átha Cliath = Dublin 32 CD 5
Băileşti 36-37 K 3
Bailundo 64-65 E 5
Baing = Tanahkadu Kung 52-53 H 9
Bain-Tumen = Čojbalsan 48-49 L 2
Baiqibao = Baiqipu 50-51 D 2
Baiqipu 50-51 D 2
Bā'ir 44-45 D 4
Bā'ir, Wādī – 46-47 G 7
Baird Mountains 70-71 DE 4
Bairnsdale 56-57 J 7
Baïse 34-35 H 7
Baitou Shan 50-51 FG 2
Baitou Shan = Changbai Shan 48-49 O 3
Baituchangmen 50-51 CD 2
Baja 33 J 5
Bājā [Sudan] 63 C 1-2
Baja California 76-77 F 10
Baja California Norte 72-73 CD 6
Baja California Sur 72-73 D 6
Bājah 60-61 F 1
Bajan [Mongolia] 48-49 K 2
Bajan Adraga 48-49 KL 2
Bajanaul 42-43 O 7
Bajan Char uuul 48-49 H 5
Bajan Chongor = 8 ◁ 48-49 HJ 2
Bajan Choto 48-49 JK 4
Bajan Char uuul 48-49 H 5
Bajan Chongor = 8 ◁ 48-49 HJ 2
Bajan Choto 48-49 JK 4
Bajandaj 42-43 U 7
Bajandalaj 48-49 J 3
Bajangol [Mongolia] 48-49 K 2
Bajan Gol [TJ] 48-49 K 3
Bajan Obo 48-49 K 3
Bajan Ölgij = 1 ◁ 48-49 FG 2
Bajan Öndör 48-49 H 3
Bajan Sum = Bajan 48-49 K 2
Bajanteeg 48-49 J 2
Bajan Tümen = Čojbalsan 48-49 L 2
Bajan Ulaa = Bajan Uul 48-49 H 2
Bajan Uul [Mongolia, Dornod] 48-49 L 2
Bajan Uul [Mongolia, Dzavchan] 48-49 H 2
Bajawa 52-53 GH 8
Bajčunas 38-39 K 6
Bajdarackaja guba 42-43 M 4
Bajé 80 F 4
Bajio, El – 72-73 F 7
Bajirge = Esendere 46-47 L 4
Bajkal, ozero – 42-43 U 7
Bajkal'skij chrebet 42-43 U 6-7
Bajkal'skoje 42-43 UV 6
Bajkit 42-43 S 5
Bajkonur 42-43 M 8
Bajmak 42-43 K 7
Bajo Baudo 78-79 D 3
Bajram-Ali 44-45 J 3
Bajšint = Chongor 48-49 L 2
Baj-Sot 42-43 S 7
Bajtag Bogd uul 48-49 G 2-3
Bājūm, 'Ayn – 62 C 3
Bakal 42-43 K 6-7
Bakala 60-61 HJ 7
Bakal'skaja kosa 36-37 P 3
Bakanas 42-43 O 8-9
Bakčar 42-43 P 6
Bakel [SN] 60-61 B 6
Baker, CA 76-77 E 8
Baker, ID 76-77 G 3
Baker, NV 76-77 FG 6
Baker, OR 72-73 C 3
Baker, Canal – 80 B 7
Baker, Mount – 76-77 C 1
Baker Foreland 70-71 ST 5
Baker Lake [CDN, ●] 70-71 R 5
Baker Lake [CDN, ≈] 70-71 R 5
Bakersfield, CA 72-73 C 4
Bakhmah, Sadd al- 46-47 L 4
Bākhtarān [IR, ●] 44-45 F 4
Bākhtarān = 1 [IR, ☆ ◁] 44-45 F 4
Bakhtegān, Daryācheh – 44-45 G 5
26 Bakinskich Komissarov 38-39 K 8
Bakır Çayı 46-47 B 3
Bakırdağı 46-47 F 3
Bakırköy, İstanbul- 46-47 C 2
Bakkafjördhur 30-31 fg 1
Bakkaflói 30-31 f 1
Bakkagerdhi 30-31 g 2
Baklan 46-47 C 4
Bakongan 52-53 C 6
Bakony 33 HJ 5
Bakool 60-61 a 3
Baku 38-39 JK 7
Bakwanga = Mbuji-Mayi 64-65 F 4
B'ala 36-37 L 4
Bala [CDN] 74-75 D 2
Balâ [TR] 46-47 E 3
Bala, Cerros de – 78-79 F 7-8
Balabac Island 52-53 G 5
Balabac Strait 52-53 G 5
Balabaia 64-65 D 5
Ba'labakk 46-47 G 5-6
Balabalangan, Kepulauan – 52-53 G 7
Balachna 38-39 H 4
Balad 46-47 L 5-6
Bal'ad = Balcad 60-61 b 3
Balad'ok = Bolod'ok 42-43 Z 7
Balad Rūz 46-47 L 6
Balagansk 42-43 T 7
Balaghat 44-45 N 6
Balaguer 34-35 H 8
Balā'im, Rā's al- 62 E 3
Balaiselasa 52-53 CD 7
Balaklava 56-57 G 6
Balakovo 42-43 HJ 7
Balama 63 D 6
Balambangan, Pulau – 52-53 G 5
Balangan, Kepulauan – = Kepulauan Balabalangan 52-53 G 7
Ba Lang An, Mui – = Mui Batangan 52-53 EF 3
Balangir 44-45 N 6
B'ala Slatina 36-37 K 4
Balasore = Baleswar 44-45 O 6
Balašov 38-39 H 5
Balāṭ 62 C 5
Balaton 33 HJ 5
Balboa 72-73 b 3
Balboa Heights 72-73 b 3
Balcad 60-61 b 3
Balcanes 36-37 K-M 4
Balcarce 80 E 5
Balchaš 42-43 N 8
Balchaš, ozero – 42-43 NO 8
Balčik 36-37 MN 4
Balcones Escarpment 72-73 F 6-G 5
Bald Butte 76-77 D 4
Bald Head 56-57 C 7
Bald Knob, WV 74-75 C 6
Bald Mountain 76-77 F 7
Baldwinsville, NY 74-75 E 3
Baldy, Mount – 76-77 H 2
Baldy Peak [USA, Arizona] 72-73 DE 5
Balē 60-61 N 7-8
Bâle = Basel 33 C 5
Baléares, Îles – = Illes Balears 34-35 H 9-K 8
Baleares, Islas – 34-35 H 9-K 8
Balej 42-43 W 7
Bālēshvara = Baleswar 44-45 O 6
Baleswar 44-45 O 6
Balḥāf 44-45 F 8
Bali [RI = 15 ◁] 52-53 F 8
Bali, Mar de – 52-53 FG 8
Bali, Mer de – 52-53 FG 8
Bali, Pulau – 52-53 FG 8
Balīh, Nahr – 46-47 H 4
Balikesir 44-45 B 3
Balikpapan 52-53 G 7
Balintang Channel 52-53 H 3
Balintang Channel 52-53 H 3
Bali Sea 52-53 FG 8
Balizee 52-53 FG 8
Balkan Mountains 36-37 K-M 4
Balkans 36-37 K-M 4
Balkh 44-45 K 3
Balkh Āb 44-45 K 3
Balkhach, Lac – = ozero Balchaš 42-43 NO 8
Balla Balla = Mbalabala 64-65 GH 7
Balladonia 56-57 D 6
Ballarat 56-57 H 7
Ballard, Lake – 56-57 D 5
Baḷḷāri = Bellary 44-45 M 7
Ballé 60-61 C 5
Balleine, Rivière à la – 70-71 X 6
Balleny Islands 24 C 17
Ballimore 58 J 4
Ballina 32 B 4
Ballina 56-57 K 5
Ball's Pyramid 56-57 L 6
Ballstad 30-31 EF 3
Ballymena 32 C 4
Balmoral 32 E 3
Balombo 64-65 D 5
Balovale 64-65 F 5
Balqā 46-47 F 6-7
Balranald 56-57 H 6
Balsas [BR] 78-79 K 6
Balsas, Río – 72-73 F 8
Balsfjord 30-31 HJ 3
Balta 36-37 MN 3
Baltic Sea 30-31 G 10-J 8
Baltijsk 33 J 1
Balṭīm 62 D 2
Baltimore [GB] 32 B 6
Baltimore, MD 72-73 L 4
Bāltistān 44-45 M 3-4
Bāltit 44-45 L 3
Balūchistān 44-45 J 5-K 4
Balvi 30-31 M 9
Balwin Aboriginal Reserve 56-57 E 3-4
Balya 46-47 B 3
Balyanā, Al- 60-61 L 3
Balygyčan 42-43 d 5
Ballenas, Dorsal de las – 22-23 K 7
Bam 44-45 H 5
Bama 60-61 G 6
Bamaco = Bamako 60-61 C 6
Bamako 60-61 C 6
Bamba [EAK] 63 D 3
Bamba [ZRE] 64-65 E 4
Bambari 60-61 J 7
Bamberg 33 E 4
Bamberg, SC 74-75 C 8
Bambesa 64-65 G 2
Bambinga 64-65 E 3
Bambuí 78-79 K 8-9
Bamenda 60-61 G 7
Bamingui 60-61 HJ 7
Bamingui, Parc national de la – 60-61 HJ 7
Bamingui-Bangoran 60-61 HJ 7
Bāmiyān 44-45 K 4
Bampūr, Rūd-e 44-45 HJ 5
Ba mTsho 48-49 G 5
Bamum = Foumban 60-61 G 7
Bamungu 63 B 2
Bana [MW] 63 C 6
Baña, Punta de la – 34-35 H 8
Banaadir [SP, ≅] 60-61 ab 3
Banaadir [SP, ☆ = 2 ◁] 60-61 O 8
Banāder va Jazāyer-e Baḥr-e 'Ommān = 6 ◁ 44-45 H 5
Banāder va Jazāyer-e Khalīj-e Fārs = 5 ◁ 44-45 G 5
Banadia 78-79 E 3
Banagi 63 C 3
Banalia 64-65 FG 2
Banámichi 76-77 H 10
Banana 64-65 D 4
Bananal, Ilha do – 78-79 J 7
Bananeiras 78-79 M 6
Banat 36-37 J 3
Banatului, Munţii – 36-37 JK 3
Banaz 46-47 C 3
Banaz Çayı 46-47 C 3
Banbury 32 F 5
Banco, El – 78-79 E 3
Bancroft 74-75 E 2
Bancroft, ID 76-77 H 4
Banda = Sainte-Marie 64-65 D 3
Banda, Cuenca Meridional de – 52-53 J 8
Banda, Cuenca Septentrional de – 52-53 HJ 7
Banda, Kepulauan – 52-53 J 7
Banda, La – 80 D 3
Banda, Mar de – 52-53 JK 8
Banda, Mer de – 52-53 JK 8
Banda, Punta – 72-73 C 5
Banda Aceh 52-53 BC 5
Bandama 60-61 CD 7
Banda Méridional, Bassin de – 52-53 J 8
Bandar = Machilipatnam 44-45 N 7
Bandāra = Machilipatnam 44-45 N 7
Bandar Banhâ = Banhâ 62 D 2
Bandarbeyla 60-61 c 2
Bandar-e 'Abbās 44-45 H 5
Bandar-e Anzalī 44-45 FG 3
Bandar-e Būshehr 44-45 G 5
Bandar-e Chāh Bahār 44-45 HJ 5
Bandar-e Chāh Bahār 44-45 HJ 5
Bandar-e Khomeynī 44-45 FG 4
Bandar-e Lengeh 44-45 GH 5
Bandar-e Māhshar 46-47 N 7
Bandar-e Shāh 44-45 G 3
Bandar Lampung 52-53 DE 8
Bandar Maharani = Muar 52-53 D 6
Bandar Murcaayo 60-61 bc 1
Bandar Penggaram = Batu Pahat 52-53 D 6
Bandar Seri Begawan 52-53 FG 5-6
Banda Sea 52-53 JK 8
Banda Septentrional, Bassin de – 52-53 HJ 7
Bandawe 64-65 H 5
Bandazee 52-53 JK 8
Band Bābā, Kuh-i- 44-45 J 4
Bandeira, Pico da – 78-79 L 9
Bandeirante 78-79 JK 7
Band-e Qir 46-47 N 7
Bandera 80 D 3
Banderas, Bahía de – 72-73 E 7
Bänd-e Turkestān = Selselae-i-Band-i-Turkestān 44-45 JK 3
Bandiagara 60-61 D 6
Bandırma 44-45 B 2
Band-i-Turkestān, Selselae-i- 44-45 JK 3
Bandjarmasin = Banjarmasin 52-53 F 7
Bandon 32 B 6
Bandon, OR 76-77 A 4
Bāndra, Bombay- 44-45 L 7
Bandundu [ZRE, ●] 64-65 E 3
Bandundu [ZRE, ☆] 64-65 E 3-4
Bandung 52-53 E 8
Bāneh 46-47 L 4-5
Banes 72-73 L 7
Bañeza, La – 34-35 DE 7
Banff [CDN] 70-71 NO 7
Banff [GB] 32 E 3
Banff National Park 70-71 NO 7
Banfora 60-61 D 6
Bangâl Khārī = Bay of Bengal 44-45 N-P 7
Bangalore 44-45 M 8
Bangassu 60-61 J 8
Bangassu = Bangassou 60-61 J 8
Bangfou = Bengbu 48-49 M 5
Banggai 52-53 H 7
Banggai, Kepulauan – 52-53 H 7
Banggai, Pulau – 52-53 H 7
Banggala Au = Bay of Bengal 44-45 N-P 7
Banggi, Pulau – 52-53 G 5
Banghāzī 60-61 HJ 2
Bangka, Pulau – 52-53 E 7
Bangka, Selat – 52-53 E 7
Bangkinang 52-53 D 6
Bangko 52-53 D 7
Bangkok = Krung Thep 52-53 D 4
Bangladesh 44-45 OP 6
Bangor 32 DE 5
Bangor, ME 72-73 N 3
Bangor, PA 74-75 F 4
Bangui [RCA] 60-61 H 8
Bangui [RP] 52-53 GH 3
Bangweulu, Lake – 64-65 GH 5
Banhâ 62 D 2
Banī [DOM] 72-73 M 8
Banī [RMM] 60-61 C 6
Banī, Jabal – 60-61 C 2-3
Banī 'Abbās 60-61 D 2
Baniara 52-53 NO 8
Banī Mallīlah 60-61 C 2
Banī Mazār 60-61 L 3
Banī Sa 'd 46-47 L 6
Banī Shuqayr 62 D 4
Banī Suwayf 60-61 L 3
Banī Walīd 60-61 G 2
Banī Wanīf 60-61 D 2
Bāniyās [SYR, Al-Lādhiqīyah] 44-45 D 3
Bāniyās [SYR, Dimashq] 46-47 FG 6
Banjak, Kepulauan – 52-53 C 6
Banja Luka 36-37 G 3
Banjar 52-53 E 8
Banjarmasin 52-53 F 7
Banjermassin = Banjarmasin 52-53 F 7
Banjo = Banyo 60-61 G 7
Banjul 60-61 A 6
Banjuwangi = Banyuwangi 52-53 F 8
Bank 38-39 J 8
Banka = Pulau Bangka 52-53 E 7
Banks, ID 76-77 E 3
Banks, OR 76-77 B 3
Banks Island [CDN, British Columbia] 70-71 KL 7
Banks Island [CDN, District of Inuvik] 70-71 MN 3
Banks Islands 56-57 N 2
Banks Lake 76-77 D 2
Banks Peninsula 56-57 O 8
Banks Strait 56-57 J 8
Banks Strait = MacClure Strait 70-71 MN 2-3
Banmau 52-53 C 2
Ban Me Thuôt 52-53 E 4
Ban Muang = Pong 52-53 CD 3
Bannack, MT 76-77 G 3
Banning, CA 76-77 E 9
Banningville = Bandundu 64-65 E 3
Bannockburn [CDN] 74-75 DE 2
Bannockburn [ZW] 64-65 GH 7
Bannock Range 76-77 G 4
Bannū 44-45 KL 4
Ban Phai 52-53 D 3
Banská Bystrica 33 J 4
Banská Štiavnica 33 J 4
Banta Eng 52-53 GH 8
Bantam = Banten 52-53 E 8
Banten 52-53 E 8
Bantry 32 B 6
Bantry Bay 32 AB 6
Bantyū 60-61 KL 7
Banyak, Pulau-pulau – = Kepulauan Banjak 52-53 C 6
Banyo 60-61 G 7
Banyuwangi 52-53 F 8
Banzaburō-dake 50-51 M 5
Banzare Land 24 C 13
Banzystad = Yasanyama 64-65 F 2
Banzyville = Yasanyama 64-65 F 2
Banzyville, Collines des – 64-65 F 2
Baña, Punta de la – 34-35 H 8
Bañeza, La – 34-35 DE 7
Baoding 48-49 LM 4
Baoji 48-49 K 5
Baojing 48-49 K 6
Baoqing 48-49 P 2
Baoshan [TJ, Yunnan] 48-49 HJ 6
Baotou 48-49 KL 3
Baoulé 60-61 C 6
Baoying 48-49 M 5
Baptiste 74-75 DE 2
Bāqir, Jabal – 46-47 F 8
Ba'qūbah 44-45 EF 4
Baquedano 80 BC 2
Bar 36-37 H 4
Baraawe 60-61 N 8
Barabinsk 42-43 OP 6
Barabinskaja nizmennost' 42-43 O 6-7
Baracaldo 34-35 F 7
Bărăganul 36-37 M 3
Bārah 60-61 L 6
Barahī = Barhi 44-45 O 6
Barahona [DOM] 72-73 M 8
Barā'ij, Al- 46-47 G 5
Barak = Karkamış 46-47 G 4
Baraka 60-61 M 5
Barakī [AFG] 44-45 K 4
Baralaba 56-57 JK 4
Bārāmūlā 44-45 L 4
Barā Nikōbār = Great Nicobar 44-45 P 9
Baranof Island 70-71 JK 6
Baranoviči 38-39 E 5
Barão de Grajaú 78-79 L 6
Barbacena 78-79 L 9
Barbade 72-73 OP 9
Barbar 60-61 L 5
Barbastro 34-35 GH 7
Barberton 64-65 H 8
Barberton, OH 74-75 C 4
Barborá = Berbera 60-61 O 6
Barbosa [CO, Boyacá] 78-79 E 3
Barca = Al-Marj 60-61 J 2
Barcaldine 56-57 HJ 4
Barcellona Pozzo di Gotto 36-37 F 6
Barcelona [E] 34-35 J 8
Barcelona [YV] 78-79 G 2
Barcelone = Barcelona 34-35 J 8
Barcelonnette 34-35 L 6
Barcelos [BR] 78-79 G 5
Barchama Guda 63 D 2
Barchöl Choto = Bar köl 48-49 G 3
Barcoo River 56-57 H 4-5
Barchöl Choto = Bar köl 48-49 G 3
Bardaï 60-61 H 4
Bardarash 46-47 K 4
Bardawīl, Sabkhat al- 62 E 2
Barddhmān = Burdwan 44-45 O 6
Bardejov 33 K 4
Bárdharbunga 30-31 e 2
Bardīs 62 D 4
Bardīyah 60-61 K 2
Bardiz = Gaziler 46-47 K 2
Barduba 72-73 O 8
Bareilly 44-45 MN 5
Barēlī = Bareilly 44-45 MN 5
Barents, Mar de – 19 B 14-15
Barents, Mer de – 19 B 14-15
Barentsburg 30-31 jk 5
Barentsøya 30-31 l 5
Barents Sea 19 B 14-15
Barentszzee 19 B 14-15
Barentu 60-61 M 5
Barfleur, Pointe de – 34-35 G 4
Barga [TJ] 48-49 M 2
Barguzin 42-43 UV 7
Barguzinskij chrebet 42-43 U 7-V 6
Barhampura = Berhampur 44-45 NO 7
Bar Harbor, ME 74-75 J 2
Barhi [IND, Bihar] 44-45 O 6
Bari [I] 36-37 G 5
Bari [SP] 60-61 bc 1
Baricho 63 DE 3
Barīm 44-45 E 8
Barinas [YV, ●] 78-79 EF 3
Baring, Cape – 70-71 MN 3
Baringo, Lake – 63 D 2
Bārīs 62 D 5
Barisal 44-45 OP 6
Barīt, Al- 46-47 K 7
Barito, Sungai – 52-53 F 7
Barkā' 44-45 H 6
Barka = Al-Marj 60-61 J 2

Barka 159

Barka = Baraka 60-61 M 5
Barkan, Rās-e – = Ra's-e Bahrgān 46-47 N 7-8
Barkly Tableland 56-57 FG 3
Bar Köl [TJ, ●] 48-49 G 3
Bar köl [TJ, ≈] 48-49 G 3
Barla Dağı 46-47 D 3-4
Bar-le-Duc 34-35 K 4
Barlee, Lake – 56-57 C 5
Barletta 36-37 G 5
Barlovento, Islas de – 72-73 OP 8-9
Barmer 44-45 L 5
Barmera 56-57 H 6
Barnabus, WV 74-75 BC 6
Barnato 58 G 3
Barnaul 42-43 P 7
Barnegat Bay 74-75 FG 5
Barne Glacier 24 A 17-18
Barnesville, OH 74-75 C 4-5
Barney Top 76-77 GH 7
Barnstable, MA 74-75 H 4
Barnstaple 32 D 6
Barnwell, SC 74-75 C 8
Baro 60-61 F 7
Baroda = Vadodara 44-45 L 6
Barôngā Kyûnmya 52-53 B 3
Barpeta 44-45 P 5
Barqa = Al-Marj 60-61 J 2
Barqah [LAR] 60-61 J 2
Barqah, Jabal al- 62 E 5
Barquisimeto 78-79 EF 2-3
Barra 32 C 3
Barra [BR, Bahia] 78-79 L 7
Barraba 56-57 K 6
Barracão do Barreto 78-79 H 6
Barra do Bugres 78-79 H 7-8
Barra do Corda 78-79 KL 6
Barra do Garças 78-79 J 8
Barra do São Manuel 78-79 H 6
Barrage 60-61 C 6
Barra Head 32 BC 3
Barra Islands 32 C 3
Barranca [PE] 78-79 D 5
Barrancabermeja 78-79 E 3
Barrancas [YV, Monagas] 78-79 G 3
Barranqueras 80 DE 3
Barranquilla 78-79 DE 2
Barra Velha 80 G 3
Barre, VT 74-75 G 2
Barreiras 78-79 KL 7
Barreirinha 78-79 H 5
Barreirinhas 78-79 L 5
Barreiro 34-35 C 9
Barreiros 78-79 MN 6
Barren Grounds 70-71 O 4-S 5
Barrenland = Barren Grounds 70-71 O 4-S 5
Barren Sage Plains 76-77 E 4
Barretos 78-79 K 9
Barrie 70-71 UV 9
Barrier Range 56-57 H 6
Barrington Tops 56-57 K 6
Barro Colorado, Isla – 72-73 b 2
Barros, Tierra de – 34-35 D 9
Barrow [IRL] 32 C 5
Barrow, AK 70-71 E 3
Barrow, Point – 70-71 EF 3
Barrow Creek 56-57 FG 4
Barrow in Furness 32 E 4
Barrow Island 56-57 BC 4
Barrow Strait 70-71 RS 3
Barṣā' 46-47 H 4
Barsakel mes, ostrov – 42-43 KL 8
Barsaloi 64-65 J 2
Baršatas 42-43 O 8
Bārshī = Barsi 44-45 M 7
Barsi 44-45 M 7
Barstow, CA 72-73 C 4-5
Bar-sur-Aube 34-35 K 4
Barṭallah 46-47 K 4
Bartica 78-79 H 3
Bartın [TR] 46-47 E 2
Bartın çayı = Koca ırmak 46-47 E 2
Bartle, CA 76-77 C 5
Bartlesville, OK 72-73 G 4
Bartolomeu Dias 64-65 J 7
Bartoszyce 33 K 1
Bartow, FL 74-75 bc 3
Barú, Volcán – 72-73 K 10
Barun-Šabartuj, gora – 42-43 UV 8
Baruun Urt 48-49 L 2
Barwon River 56-57 J 5
Barwon River = Darling River 56-57 H 6
Barykova, mys – 42-43 jk 5
Barylas 42-43 Z 4
Barzanja = Barzinjah 46-47 L 5
Barzas 42-43 Q 6
Barzinjah 46-47 L 5
Başalīyat Qiblī, Al- 62 E 5
Basankusu 64-65 EF 2
Basco 48-49 N 7
Basel 33 C 5
Basharrī 46-47 G 5
Bashi Haixia = Pashih Haihsia 48-49 N 7
Bāshim = Bāsim 44-45 M 5
Bashkir Autonomous Republic = 7 ◁ 42-43 K 7
Bashkiria, República Autónoma de – = 7 ◁ 42-43 K 7
Bash Kurghan = Bash Qurghan 48-49 G 4
Bash Malghun 48-49 F 4
Bash Qurghan 48-49 G 4
Bashshār 60-61 D 2
Basiano 52-53 H 7
Basilan Island 52-53 H 5
Basilan Strait 52-53 H 5
Basilicata 36-37 FG 5
Basilio 80 F 4
Basim 44-45 M 6
Basin, MT 76-77 G 2
Basingstoke 32 F 6
Basīṭ, Rā's al- 46-47 F 5
Basjkiren, Autonome Republiek – = 7 ◁ 42-43 K 7
Başkale 46-47 KL 3
Baskil 46-47 H 3
Başköy = Aralık 46-47 L 3
Bāsmenj 46-47 M 4
Basoko [ZRE, Haute Zaïre] 64-65 F 2
Başrah, Al- 44-45 F 4
Bass, Détroit de – = Bass Strait 56-57 HJ 7
Bassac = Champasak 52-53 DE 4
Bassano del Grappa 36-37 D 3
Basse Californie 76-77 F 10
Basse-Guinée 22-23 K 5-6
Bassein = Puthein 52-53 B 3
Basse Kotto 60-61 J 7-8
Basseterre [Saint Kitts und Nevis] 72-73 O 8
Basse-Terre [Guadeloupe, ●] 72-73 O 8
Bassett, VA 74-75 C 6
Bassin Algéroprovençal 28-29 J 8-K 7
Bassin Antarctico-Indien 22-23 O-Q 8
Bassin Arctique Central 19 A
Bassin Atlantique Indien Antarctique 22-23 J-M 9
Bassin Australien Méridional 22-23 PQ 8
Bassin Australien Occidental 22-23 P 7
Bassin Australien Oriental 22-23 RS 8
Bassin Australien Septentrional 56-57 C 2
Bassin Brésilien 22-23 H 6
Bassin Canadien 19 AB 32-33
Bassin Caraïbe 72-73 MN 8
Bassin Central Indienne 22-23 NO 6
Bassin Chinois Méridional 52-53 FG 3-4
Bassin Corallien 56-57 K 2
Bassin Chinois Méridional 52-53 FG 3-4
Bassin Eurasiatique 19 A
Bassin Ibérique 22-23 HJ 3
Bassin Ionien 36-37 GH 7
Bassin Islandais 28-29 CD 4
Bassin Norvégien 22-23 JK 2
Bassin Océanique japonais 50-51 J-L 2
Bassin Rouge = Sichuan Pendi 48-49 JK 5-6
Bass Strait 56-57 HJ 7
Bastia 36-37 C 4
Bastianøyane 30-31 l 5
Bastogne 34-35 KL 3-4
Bastrop, LA 72-73 H 5
Bastuträsk 30-31 HJ 5
Bāsūr, Bi'r al- 62 AB 3
Basutoland = Lesotho 64-65 G 8
Basutos 64-65 G 6
Basyurt Tepesi 46-47 D 3
Bas-Zaïre 64-65 DE 4
Bata [Äquatorial-Guinea] 60-61 F 8
Batabanó, Golfo de – 72-73 K 7
Batac 52-53 GH 3
Batagaj 42-43 Za 4
Batagaj-Alyta 42-43 YZ 4
Batajsk 38-39 GH 6
Batala 44-45 M 4
Batalha 34-35 C 9
Batam, Pulau – 52-53 D 6
Batamaj 42-43 YZ 5
Batang [TJ] 48-49 H 6
Batangafo 60-61 H 7
Batangan, Mui – 52-53 EF 3
Batangas 52-53 H 4
Batan Island 48-49 N 7
Batan Islands 48-49 N 7
Batanta, Pulau – 52-53 JK 7
Bāṭās 46-47 L 4
Batatchatu = Chulaq Aqqan Su 48-49 G 4
Batavia, NY 74-75 DE 3
Batavia = Jakarta 52-53 E 8
Batbakkara = Amangel'dy 42-43 M 7
Batemans Bay 58 K 5
Batesburg, SC 74-75 C 8
Batesville, OH 74-75 A 5
Bath 32 E 6
Bath, ME 74-75 J 3
Bath, NY 74-75 E 3
Batha 60-61 H 6
Baṭḥa, Al- 46-47 L 7
B'athar Zajū, Jabal – 62 E 7
Bathurst [AUS] 56-57 JK 6
Bathurst [CDN] 70-71 XY 8
Bathurst = Banjul 60-61 A 6
Bathurst, Cape – 70-71 KL 3
Bathurst Inlet [CDN, ∪] 70-71 P 4
Bathurst Inlet [CDN, ●] 70-71 P 4
Bathurst Island [AUS] 56-57 EF 2
Bathurst Island [CDN] 70-71 R 2
Batié 60-61 D 6-7
Bāṭin, Al- [IRQ ↙ As-Salmān] 46-47 K 7-L 8
Bāṭin, Al- [IRQ ↘ As-Salmān] 46-47 M 8
Baṭin, Humrat al- 46-47 KL 8
Bāṭin, Wādī al- 44-45 F 5
Bāṭinah, Al – 44-45 H 6
Batlow 58 HJ 5
Batman 44-45 E 3
Batna = Batnah 60-61 F 1
Batnah 60-61 F 1
Batoche 70-71 PQ 7
Baton Rouge, LA 72-73 H 5
Batouri 60-61 G 8
Batrā, Jabal al- 46-47 F 8
Batrūn, Al- 46-47 F 5
Battambang 52-53 D 4
Batterbee Range 24 BC 30
Batticaloa = Maḍakalapūwa 44-45 N 9
Battle Creek, MI 72-73 J 3
Battle Creek [USA ◁ Owyhee River] 76-77 E 4
Battle Harbour 70-71 Za 7
Battle Mountain, NV 76-77 E 5
Battle River 70-71 OP 7
Battonya 33 K 5
Batu 60-61 M 7
Batu, Kepulauan – 52-53 C 7
Batu Arang 52-53 D 6
Bāṭūfah 46-47 K 4
Batumi 38-39 H 7
Batu Pahat 52-53 D 6
Baturaja 52-53 D 7
Baturi = Batouri 60-61 G 8
Baturino 42-43 Q 6
Baturité 78-79 M 5
Batutinggi = Kasongan 52-53 F 7
Batvand 46-47 N 6-7
Baubau 52-53 H 8
Bauchi [WAN, ●] 60-61 FG 6
Baudh 44-45 N 6
Baudouinville = Moba 64-65 G 4
Baudwin 52-53 C 2
Bauhinia 56-57 J 4
Baukau 52-53 J 8
Baúl, El – 78-79 F 3
Bauld, Cape – 70-71 Za 7
Baule-Escoublac, la – 34-35 F 5
Bā'ūrah, Sabkhat – 46-47 J 5
Baures 78-79 G 7
Bauru 78-79 K 9
Bauska 30-31 L 9
Bautzen 33 G 3
Bauya 60-61 B 7
Bavispe, Rio de – 76-77 J 10
Bawean, Pulau – 52-53 F 8
Bāwīṭī, Al- 60-61 K 3
Bawku 60-61 D 6
Bawlagè 52-53 C 3
Baxter State Park 74-75 J 1-2
Bay 60-61 a 3
Bayāḍ, Al- [DZ] 60-61 E 2
Bayāḍ, Al- [Saudi Arabia] 44-45 F 6
Bayāḍīyah, Al- 62 E 5
Bay al-Kabīr, Wādī – 60-61 GH 2
Bayamo 72-73 L 7
Bayat [TR, Afyon] 46-47 D 3
Bayat [TR, Çorum] 46-47 F 2
Bayāzeh 38-39 KL 9
Baybay 52-53 HJ 4
Bayboro, NC 74-75 E 7
Baybû 46-47 KL 4
Bayburt 44-45 E 2
Bay City, MI 72-73 K 3
Bayḍā', Al- [LAR] 60-61 J 2
Bayḍā', Al- [Y] 44-45 EF 8
Bayḍā', 'Ayn al- 46-47 GH 7
Bayḍā', Barqat al- 60-61 HJ 2-3
Bayḍā', Bi'r – 62 FG 4
Bayḍā', Jabal – 62 F 6
Baydāh, 'Ayn al- 46-47 GH 5
Baydhabo 60-61 a 3
Bayerischer Wald 33 F 4
Bayern 33 E 4
Bayeux 34-35 G 4
Bayḥān al-Qaṣab 44-45 F 8
Bay Ḥasan 46-47 L 5
Bayındır 46-47 B 3
Bayingolin Monggol Zizhizhou 48-49 FG 4
Baykan 46-47 J 3
Bay Mountains 74-75 B 6
Bayonne 34-35 G 7
Bayraktar = Karayazı 46-47 JK 3
Bayramiç 46-47 B 3
Bayreuth 33 E 4
Bayrūt 44-45 CD 4
Bays, Lake of – 74-75 D 2
Bay Shore, NY 74-75 G 4
Bayt al-Faqīh 44-45 E 8
Bayt Laḥm 46-47 F 7
Baytown, TX 72-73 GH 6
Bayyūḍ, Bi'r al- 46-47 H 5
Bayyūdah, Ṣaḥrā' – 60-61 L 5
Bayzaḥ, Wādī – 62 E 5
Baza 34-35 F 10
Bazar Dere 48-49 D 4
Bazard'uzi, gora – 38-39 J 7
Bāzargān 46-47 L 3
Bazaruto, Ilha do – 64-65 J 7
Bazas 34-35 G 6
Bāzdar 44-45 JK 5
Bazias 36-37 J 3

Beachport 56-57 G 7
Beacon, NY 74-75 G 4
Beagle, Canal – 80 C 8
Beagle Bay 56-57 D 3
Bealanana 64-65 L 5
Beara 52-53 MN 8
Bearcreek, MT 76-77 J 3
Beardmore Glacier 24 A 20-18
Beardmore Reservoir 58 HJ 1
Beardsley, AZ 76-77 G 9
Bear Island 19 B 16-17
Bear Island 24 B 26
Bear Lake [USA] 72-73 D 3
Béarn 34-35 G 7
Bearpaw Mountain 76-77 J 1
Bear River [USA] 72-73 D 3
Bear River Bay 76-77 G 5
Beata, Isla – 72-73 M 8
Beatrice 64-65 H 6
Beatrice, NE 72-73 G 3
Beatrice, Cape – 56-57 G 2
Beatty, NV 76-77 E 7
Beaucaire 34-35 K 7
Beauce 34-35 HJ 4
Beauchene Island 80 E 8
Beaudesert 58 L 1
Beaufort [AUS] 58 F 6
Beaufort, NC 74-75 E 7
Beaufort, SC 74-75 C 8
Beaufort, Mar de – 19 B 32-33
Beaufort, Mer de – 19 B 32-33
Beaufort Inlet 74-75 E 7
Beaufort Sea 19 B 32-33
Beaufort-Wes 64-65 F 9
Beaufort West = Beaufort-Wes 64-65 F 9
Beaufortzee 19 B 32-33
Beauharnois 74-75 FG 2
Beaujolais 34-35 K 5
Beauly 32 D 3
Beaumont, CA 76-77 E 9
Beaumont, TX 72-73 GH 5
Beaune 34-35 K 5
Beauvais 34-35 HJ 4
Beaver, UT 76-77 G 6
Beaver Creek [USA ◁ Milk River] 76-77 J 1-K 2
Beaverdam, VA 74-75 DE 6
Beaver Falls, PA 74-75 C 4
Beaverhead Range 76-77 G 3
Beaverhead River 76-77 G 3
Beaver River 70-71 P 7
Beaverton 74-75 D 2
Beawar 44-45 LM 5
Beazley 80 C 4
Bebedouro 78-79 K 9
Bebra 33 D 3
Beccles 32 G 5
Bečej 36-37 HJ 3
Béchar = Bashshār 60-61 D 2
Becharof Lake 70-71 EF 6
Bechtery 36-37 P 2
Beckley, WV 72-73 K 4
Beclean 36-37 KL 2
Beda 60-61 M 7
Beddington, ME 74-75 JK 2
Bedelē 60-61 M 7
Bedford 32 F 5
Bedford [CDN, Quebec] 74-75 G 2
Bedford, PA 74-75 D 4
Bedford, VA 74-75 D 6
Bedirli 46-47 G 3
Bèdja = Bājah 60-61 F 1
Bedourie 56-57 GH 4
Bedshar 38-39 K 8
Beech Creek, OR 76-77 D 3
Beechworth 58 H 6
Beegum, CA 76-77 B 5
Beerenberg 19 B 19
Bē'ēr-Mĕnūḥa 46-47 F 7
Beersheba = Bĕ'er-Sheva' 44-45 C 4
Bĕ'er-Sheva' 44-45 C 4
Beeville, TX 72-73 G 6
Befale 64-65 F 2
Befandriana-atsimo 64-65 K 7
Befandriana-avavatva 64-65 L 6
Bega [AUS] 56-57 JK 7
Bega, Canal – 36-37 J 3
Begemdir-na Simen = Gonder 60-61 M 6
Begičeva, ostrov – = ostrov Bol'šoj Begičev 42-43 VW 3
Begna 30-31 C 7
Begorītis, Límnē – 36-37 JK 5
Behagle, De – = Laï 60-61 H 7
Behágue, Pointe – 78-79 J 3-4
Behara 64-65 L 7
Behbahān 44-45 G 4
Behn, Mount – 56-57 E 3
Bei'an 48-49 O 2
Beibei 48-49 K 6
Beibu Wan 48-49 K 7-8
Beiḍa, Bīr – = Bi'r Bayḍā' 62 EF 4
Beidá', El – = Al-Bayḍā' 60-61 J 2
Beida, Gebel – = Jabal Bayḍā' 62 F 6
Beihai [TJ, Guangxi Zhuangzu Zizhiqu] 48-49 K 7
Beijing 48-49 LM 3-4
Beijingzi 50-51 DE 3
Beipa'a 52-53 N 8
Beipiao 50-51 C 2
Beira 64-65 HJ 6
Beira [P] 34-35 CD 8
Beiroet = Bayrūt 44-45 CD 4
Beiroût = Bayrūt 44-45 CD 4
Beisan = Bēt Shĕan 44-45 F 6
Bei Shan 48-49 GH 3
Beishanchengzhen = Caoshi 50-51 E 1
Beitbridge 64-65 GH 7
Beit Laḥm = Bayt Laḥm 46-47 F 7
Beit Shĕ'an 44-45 F 6
Beizaḥ, Wâdî – = Wādī Bayzaḥ 62 E 5
Beizhen [TJ, Liaoning] 50-51 C 2
Beja 34-35 D 9-10
Béja = Bājah 60-61 F 1
Bejaïa = Bijāyah 60-61 EF 1
Béjar 34-35 E 8
Bejestān 44-45 H 4
Bekabad 44-45 KL 2
Bekasi 52-53 E 8
Bek-Budi = Karši 44-45 K 3
Bekdaš 44-45 G 2
Békés 33 K 5
Békéscsaba 33 K 5
Bekily 64-65 L 7
Belā [PAK] 44-45 K 5
Bela Crkva 36-37 J 3
Belaga 52-53 F 6
Belagām = Belgaum 44-45 LM 7
Belaia = Beleye 60-61 b 2-3
Bel Air 34-35 F 4
Bel Air, MD 74-75 E 5
Belaja [SU, ~] 42-43 J 6
Belaja Cerkov 38-39 F 6
Belaja Glina 38-39 H 6
Belaja Zeml'a, ostrova – 42-43 L-N 1
Bel'ajevka 36-37 O 2
Belang 52-53 HJ 6
Bela Palanka 36-37 K 4
Bela Vista [BR, Mato Grosso do Sul] 78-79 H 9
Bela Vista [Moçambique] 64-65 H 8
Bela Vista, Cachoeira – 78-79 J 5
Bela Vista de Goiás 78-79 K 8
Belawan 52-53 C 6
Belcher Channel 70-71 RS 2
Belcher Islands 70-71 U 6
Belchite 34-35 G 8
Belcik = Yavi 46-47 G 3
Bel'cy 38-39 E 6
Belcher Channel 70-71 RS 2
Belden, CA 76-77 C 5
Belebej 42-43 J 7
Beledweyne 60-61 O 8
Belém [BR, Pará] 78-79 K 5
Belém [Mozambik] 63 CD 6
Belen, NM 72-73 E 5
Belep, Îles – 56-57 M 3
Beleye 60-61 M 6
Belfair, WA 76-77 B 2
Belfast 32 CD 4
Belfast, ME 74-75 J 2
Bèlfodyo 60-61 LM 6
Belfort 34-35 L 5
Bēlgāṅv = Belgaum 44-45 LM 7
Belgaon = Belgaum 44-45 LM 7
Belgaum 44-45 LM 7
Belgica 34-35 JK 3
Belgica Mountains 24 B 3-4
België 34-35 JK 3
Belgique 34-35 JK 3
Belgium 34-35 JK 3
Belgorod 38-39 G 5
Belgorod-Dnestrovskij 38-39 EF 6
Belgrade, MT 76-77 H 3
Belgrade = Beograd 36-37 J 3
Belgrado = Beograd 36-37 J 3
Belhaven, NC 74-75 E 7
Belīkh, Nahr – = Nahr Balīh 46-47 H 4
Beli Lom 36-37 LM 4
Belinyu 52-53 E 7
Beli Timok 36-37 K 4
Belitung, Pulau – 52-53 E 7
Belize [BH, ●] 72-73 J 8
Belize [BH, ★] 72-73 J 8
Bel'kovskij, ostrov – 42-43 Za 2
Bell, FL 74-75 b 2
Bella Coola 70-71 L 7
Bellaire, OH 74-75 C 4-5
Bellary 44-45 M 7
Bellata 58 J 2
Bella Unión 80 E 4
Bella Vista [BOL] 78-79 G 8
Bella Vista [RA, Corrientes] 80 E 3
Bell Bay 58 c 2
Bellefonte, PA 74-75 DE 4
Belle Glade, FL 74-75 c 3
Belle Île 34-35 F 5
Belle Isle 70-71 Za 7
Belle Isle, Strait of – 70-71 Z 7
Bellemont, AZ 76-77 GH 8
Belleville [CDN] 70-71 V 9
Bellevue, WA 76-77 BC 2
Bellin [CDN] 70-71 WX 5
Bellingham, WA 76-77 BC 1
Bellingshausen Sea 24 BC 28
Bellinzona 33 D 5
Bell Island = Wabana 70-71 a 8
Bello [CO] 78-79 DE 3
Bello Horizonte = Belo Horizonte 78-79 L 8
Bellona 52-53 j 7
Bellota, CA 76-77 C 6
Bellows Falls, VT 74-75 G 3
Bell Peninsula 70-71 U 5
Belluno 36-37 DE 2
Bell Ville [RA] 80 D 4
Belmez 34-35 E 9
Belmont, NY 74-75 DE 3
Belmonte [BR] 78-79 M 8
Belmopan 72-73 J 8
Belogorsk [SU, Krym'] 38-39 FG 6
Belogorsk [SU, Rossijskaja SFSR] 42-43 YZ 7
Belogradčik 36-37 K 4
Belo Horizonte [BR, Minas Gerais] 78-79 L 8
Beloit, WI 72-73 J 3
Beloje, ozero – 42-43 F 5
Belokuricha 42-43 PQ 7
Belomorsk 42-43 EF 5
Belomorsko-Baltijskij kanal 38-39 F 3
Belopolje 38-39 F 5
Belopúla 36-37 K 7

160 Barka

Beloreck 42-43 K 7
Belören 46-47 G 4
Belorussia 38-39 EF 5
Belo Tsiribihina 64-65 K 6
Bel'ov 38-39 G 5
Belovo 42-43 Q 7
Beloz'orsk 42-43 F 5-6
Belpre, OH 74-75 C 5
Belsund 30-31 j 6
Belt, MT 76-77 H 2
Belted Range 76-77 E 7
Belton, SC 74-75 B 7
Belucha, gora – 42-43 Q 8
Beluchistan = Balūchistān 44-45 J 5-K 4
Belumut, Gunung – 52-53 D 6
Belušja Guba 42-43 HJ 3
Belyj, ostrov – 42-43 MN 3
Belyj Byček = Čagoda 42-43 EF 6
Belyj Jar 42-43 Q 6
Bemaraha 64-65 KL 6
Bembe 64-65 DE 4
Bembèrèkè 60-61 E 6
Bemidji, MN 72-73 GH 2
Benāb = Bonāb 46-47 M 4
Bena-Dibele 64-65 F 3
Benadir = Banaadir 60-61 ab 3
Benalla 56-57 J 7
Benares = Varanasi 44-45 N 5
Benas, Ras – = Rā's Banās 60-61 M 4
Benavente 34-35 DE 7
Benbecula 32 BC 3
Bend, OR 72-73 B 3
Bendel 60-61 F 7
Bender Abas = Bandar 'Abbās 44-45 H 5
Bender Bayla = Bandarbeyla 60-61 c 2
Bendery 38-39 EF 6
Bendigo 56-57 HJ 7
Beneden Egypte = Aṣ-Ṣa'īd 60-61 L 3-4
Beneden Trajanuswal = Nižnij Trajanov val 36-37 N 3
Benevento 36-37 F 5
Benga 64-65 H 6
Bengal, Bay of – 44-45 N-P 7
Bengala, Dorsal de – 22-23 O 5-6
Bengala, Golfo de – 44-45 N-P 7
Bengale, Dorsale du – 22-23 O 5-6
Bengale, Golfe du – 44-45 N-P 7
Bengalen, Golf van – 44-45 N-P 7
Bengalenrug 22-23 O 5-6
Bengalore = Bangalore 44-45 M 8
Bengal Ridge 22-23 O 5-6
Bengalūru = Bangalore 44-45 M 8
Ben Gania, Bir – = Bi'r Bin Ganīyah 60-61 J 2
Bengasi = Banghāzī 60-61 HJ 2
Bengbu 48-49 M 5
Benge, WA 76-77 D 2
Benghazi = Banghāzī 60-61 HJ 2
Bengkalis, Pulau – 52-53 D 6
Bengkayang 52-53 EF 6
Bengkulu [RI, ●] 52-53 D 7
Benguela 64-65 D 5
'Ben Guerîr = Bin Gharīr 60-61 C 2
Beni [ZRE] 64-65 G 2
Beni, Río – 78-79 F 7
Beni-Abbès = Banī 'Abbās 60-61 D 2
Benicia, CA 76-77 BC 6
Benî Mazâr = Banī Mazār 60-61 L 3
'Benî Mellâl = Banī Mallīlah 60-61 C 2
Bénin 60-61 E 6-7
Bénin 60-61 E 7-8
Bénin, Baie de – 60-61 E 7-8
Benin, Bight of – 60-61 E 7-8
Benin City 60-61 F 7
Benî Shigeir = Banī Shuqayr 62 D 4
Béni Souef = Banī Suwayf 60-61 L 3
Benî Suêf = Banī Suwayf 60-61 L 3
Benito Juárez 80 DE 5
Benjamim Constant 78-79 EF 5
Benkulen = Bengkulu 52-53 D 7
Bennett, Lake – 56-57 EF 4
Bennetta, ostrov – 42-43 cd 2
Bennettsville, SC 74-75 D 7
Bennington, VT 74-75 G 3
Bénoué 60-61 G 7
Benqi = Benxi 48-49 N 3
Bensheim 33 D 4
Benson, AZ 76-77 H 10
Bentinck Island 56-57 GH 3
Bentiū = Bantyū 60-61 KL 7
Bent Jebaïl = Bint Jubayl 46-47 F 6
Benton, CA 76-77 D 7
Benton City, WA 76-77 D 2
Benué = River Benue 60-61 F 7
Benue, River – 60-61 F 7
Benue Plateau 60-61 F 7
Benxi 48-49 N 3
Beograd 36-37 J 3
Beppu 50-51 H 6
Beqâ', El- = Al-Biqā' 46-47 FG 5-6
Beraïje = Al-Barāij 46-47 G 5
Beraisolè 60-61 N 6
Berat 36-37 H 5
Berau, Teluk – 52-53 K 7
Berber = Barbar 60-61 L 5
Berbera 60-61 b 1
Berbérati 60-61 a 1
Berch 48-49 L 2
Berchtesgaden 33 F 5
Berck 34-35 H 3
Berd'ansk 38-39 G 6
Berdičev 38-39 E 6
Berdigest'ach 42-43 XY 5
Berea, OH 74-75 C 4
Beregovo 33 L 4
Bereku 63 CD 4
Berenda, CA 76-77 CD 7
Bereneiland 19 B 16-17
Berenike 60-61 LM 4
Berens River [CDN, ~] 70-71 R 7
Berens River [CDN, ●] 70-71 R 7
Beresford 58 C 2
Beresniki = Berezniki 42-43 JK 6
Beretău 36-37 JK 2
Berezina 38-39 E 5
Bereznik 38-39 H 3
Berezniki [SU, Perm'] 42-43 JK 6
Bergama 44-45 B 3
Bèrgamo 36-37 CD 3
Bergen [DDR] 33 F 1
Bergen [N] 30-31 A 7
Bergerac 34-35 H 6
Bergslagen 30-31 F 7-8
Berhampore = Baharampur 44-45 O 6
Berhampur 44-45 NO 7
Berhampur = Baharampur 44-45 O 6
Béring, Détroit de – 70-71 B 5-C 4
Bering, Estrecho de – 70-71 B 5-C 4
Bering, Mar de – 19 D 35-1
Béring, Mer de – 19 D 35-1
Bering, mys – 42-43 k 5
Bering, Straat – 70-71 B 5-C 4
Beringa, ostrov – 42-43 fg 7
Bering Glacier 70-71 H 5
Beringovskij 42-43 j 5
Bering Sea 19 D 35-1
Bering Strait 70-71 B 5-C 4
Beringzee 19 D 35-1
Beris = Bārīs 62 D 5
Berja 34-35 F 10
Berjozovo = Ber'ozovo 42-43 LM 5
Berkeley, CA 72-73 B 4
Berkner Island 24 B 31-32
Berkovica 36-37 K 4
Berlevåg 30-31 N 2
Berlin 33 FG 2
Berlin, MD 74-75 F 5
Berlin, NH 72-73 M 3
Berlin = Berlin 33 FG 2
Berlin, Mount – 24 B 23
Berlijn = Berlin 33 FG 2
Bermejo [BOL] 78-79 G 9
Bermejo [RA] 80 C 4
Bermejo, Río – [RA ◁ Río Paraguay] 80 D 2
Bermeo 34-35 F 7
Bermuda Islands 72-73 NO 5
Bern 33 C 5
Bernardo de Irigoyen 80 F 3
Bernburg 33 EF 3
Berne, WA 76-77 C 2
Berne = Bern 33 C 5
Berner Alpen 33 C 5
Bernier Bay 70-71 ST 3
Bernier Island 56-57 B 4
Bernina 33 D 5
Bĕroia 36-37 JK 5
Beroroha 64-65 KL 7
Beroun 33 FG 4
Berounka 33 F 4
Ber'oza 38-39 DE 5
Ber'ozovka 36-37 O 2
Ber'ozovo 42-43 LM 5
Berri 58 E 5
Berry 34-35 HJ 5
Berryessa, Lake – 76-77 B 6
Berryville, VA 74-75 DE 5
Bersâ' = Barṣā' 46-47 H 4
Bersabee = Bĕer Sheva' 44-45 C 4
Berseba 64-65 E 8
Bertiskos 36-37 K 5
Bertolinia 78-79 L 6
Bertoua 60-61 G 8
Bertua = Bertoua 60-61 G 8
Berunda 63 B 2
Beruni 42-43 L 9
Beruri 78-79 G 5
Berwick, PA 74-75 E 4
Berwick-upon-Tweed 32 EF 4
Beryl, UT 76-77 G 7
Berytus = Bayrūt 44-45 CD 4
Besalampy 64-65 K 6
Besançon 34-35 L 5
Besarabia = Bessarabija 38-39 E 6
Besarabia = Bessarabija 38-39 E 6
Beşîré, El- = Buṣayrah 46-47 J 5
Beşiri 46-47 J 4
Beskidy 33 JK 4
Beşkonak 46-47 D 4
Besna Kobila 36-37 K 4
Besni 44-45 D 3
Beşparmak Dağı 46-47 BC 4
Bessa Monteiro 64-65 D 4
Bessarabie = Bessarabija 38-39 E 6
Bessarabija 38-39 E 6
Bessarabka 38-39 E 6
Bessaz gora 42-43 M 9
Bessels, Kapp – 30-31 lm 5
Bessemer, AL 72-73 J 5
Bessemer City, NC 74-75 C 7
Besshi 50-51 J 6
Bessŏky, gora – 44-45 G 2
Bestamak 38-39 L 6
Bestobe 42-43 N 7
Bêt = Okha 44-45 K 6
Betaf 52-53 L 7
Betafo 64-65 L 6
Betanzos 34-35 CD 7
Bétare-Oya 60-61 G 7
Betchouanaland = Botswana 64-65 FG 7
Bethal 64-65 G 8
Bethanië = Bethanien 64-65 E 8
Bethanien 64-65 E 8
Bethel, AK 70-71 D 5
Bethel, ME 74-75 H 2
Bethel, NC 74-75 E 7
Bethel, VT 74-75 G 3
Bethlehem 64-65 G 8
Bethlehem, PA 74-75 F 4
Beth Shaan = Beit Shĕ'ān 44-45 F 6
Bethulie 64-65 G 9
Béthune 34-35 J 3
Betioky 64-65 K 7
Betlehem = Bayt Laḥm 46-47 F 7
Betpak-Dala 42-43 MN 8
Betroka 64-65 L 7
Bēt Shĕ'ān = Beit Shĕ'ān 44-45 F 6
Betsiboka 64-65 L 6
Betsjoeanaland 64-65 F 8
Bette, Pic – 60-61 HJ 4
Bettyhill 32 DE 2
Betvā = Betwa 44-45 M 6
Betwa 44-45 M 6
Beulah, OR 76-77 D 4
Beverley 32 F 5
Beverly, MA 74-75 H 3
Beverly, WA 76-77 D 2
Beyābān, Kūh-e- 44-45 H 5
Beyce = Orhaneli 46-47 C 3
Bey Dağları 46-47 D 4
Beydili 46-47 D 2
Beykoz, İstanbul- 46-47 C 2
Beyla 60-61 C 7
Beylikova 46-47 D 3
Beypazarı 46-47 DE 2
Beypınarı 46-47 G 3
Beyrouth = Bayrūth 44-45 CD 4
Beyşehir 46-47 DE 4
Beyşehir Gölü 44-45 C 3
Beyt = Okhā 44-45 K 6
Beytişebap = Elki 46-47 K 4
Bežeck 38-39 G 4
Beziers 34-35 J 7
Bezwada = Vijayavada 44-45 N 7
Bhadrak 44-45 O 6
Bhagalpur 44-45 O 5-6
Bhairab Bazar 44-45 P 6
Bhamo = Banmau 52-53 C 2
Bhandāra 44-45 MN 6
Bharatpur [IND, Rajasthan] 44-45 M 5
Bharuch 44-45 L 6
Bhātgāṅv = Bhātgaon 44-45 O 5
Bhatgaon 44-45 O 5
Bhatinda 44-45 L 4
Bhātpara 44-45 O 6
Bhaunagar = Bhavnagar 44-45 L 6
Bhavānīpāṭnā = Bhawānipatna 44-45 N 7
Bhavnagar 44-45 L 6
Bhawānipatna 44-45 N 7
Bhelsā = Vidisha 44-45 M 6
Bhilainagar 44-45 N 6
Bhilsa = Vidisha 44-45 M 6
Bhima 44-45 M 7
Bhīr = Bir 44-45 M 7
Bhivānī = Bhiwani 44-45 M 5
Bhiwani 44-45 M 5
Bhopal 44-45 M 6
Bhor 44-45 L 7
Bhoutan 44-45 OP 5
Bhubanēshvara = Bhubaneswar 44-45 O 6
Bhubeneswar 44-45 O 6
Bhuj 44-45 KL 6
Bhusāvaḷ = Bhusawal 44-45 M 6
Bhusawal 44-45 M 6
Biābān, Kūh-e – = Kūh-e Beyābān 44-45 H 5
Biak, Pulau – 52-53 L 7
Biała Podlaska 33 L 2-3
Białobrzegi 33 K 3
Białogard 33 GH 1-2
Białystok 33 L 2
Biar = Bihar 44-45 NO 6
Biaro, Pulau – 52-53 J 6
Biarritz 34-35 G 7
Biasso = Bissau 60-61 A 6
Bibā 62 D 3
Bibai 50-51 bc 2
Bibala 64-65 D 5
Biberach 33 D 4
Bībūr 60-61 L 7
Bībūr, Nahr – 60-61 L 7
Bicaner = Bikaner 44-45 L 5
Bickerton Island 56-57 G 2
Bickleton, WA 76-77 CD 2-3
Bicknell, UT 76-77 H 6
Biḍ = Bir 44-45 M 7
Bid', Al- 62 F 3
Bida 60-61 F 7
Bidar 44-45 M 7
Bidara = Bidar 44-45 M 7
Biddeford, ME 72-73 MN 3
Bidele Depression = Djourab 60-61 H 5
Bidnī, Bi'r – 62 C 4
Bié = Kuito 64-65 E 5
Bieber, CA 76-77 C 5
Biebrza 33 L 2
Biel 33 C 5
Bielawa 33 H 3
Bielefeld 33 D 2
Biele Karpaty 33 HJ 4
Biella 36-37 BC 3
Bielorrusia 38-39 EF 5
Biélorussie 38-39 EF 5
Bielsko-Biała 33 J 4
Bielsk Podlaski 33 L 2
Biên Hoa 52-53 E 4
Bienne = Biel 33 C 5
Bienville, Lac – 70-71 W 6
Bifuka 50-51 c 1
Biga 46-47 B 2
Bigadiç 46-47 C 3
Big Arm, MT 76-77 FG 2
Big Baldy 76-77 F 3
Big Bell 56-57 C 5
Big Belt Mountains 76-77 H 2
Big Bend, CA 76-77 C 5
Big Bend National Park 72-73 F 6
Big Chino Wash 76-77 G 8
Big Creek, ID 76-77 F 3
Big Cypress Indian Reservation 74-75 c 3
Big Cypress Swamp 74-75 c 3-4
Big Chino Wash 76-77 G 8
Big Delta, AK 70-71 GH 5
Big Desert 58 E 5
Big Falls 76-77 E 1
Bigfork, MT 76-77 FG 1
Bigga 58 J 5
Biggar [CDN] 70-71 P 7
Bigge Island 56-57 DE 2
Biggs, OR 76-77 C 3
Bigha = Biğa 46-47 B 2
Big Hole River 76-77 G 3
Bighorn Mountains 72-73 E 2-3
Big Island [CDN, Baffin Island] 70-71 WX 5
Big Lost River 76-77 G 4
Bigobo 63 A 4
Big Pine, CA 76-77 DE 7
Big Pine Key, FL 74-75 c 4
Big Piney, WY 76-77 HJ 4
Biğrān 44-45 G 6
Big Salmon Range 70-71 K 5
Big Sandy, WY 76-77 J 4
Big Sandy River 76-77 G 8
Big Smoky Valley 76-77 E 6
Big Spring, TX 72-73 F 5
Big Springs, ID 76-77 H 3
Big Stone Gap, VA 74-75 B 6
Big Sur, CA 76-77 BC 7
Big Timber, MT 76-77 J 3
Big Trout Lake [CDN, ≈] 70-71 T 7
Big Wood River 76-77 F 4
Bihać 36-37 F 3
Bihar [IND, ●] 44-45 O 6
Bihar [IND, ☆] 44-45 NO 6
Biharamulo 64-65 H 3
Bihor 36-37 K 2
Bihor, Munţii – 36-37 K 2
Bihoro 50-51 d 2
Bijagós, Arquipélago dos – 60-61 A 6
Bijapur [IND, Karnataka] 44-45 LM 7
Bijāpura = Bijapur 44-45 LM 7
Bījār 44-45 F 3
Bij-Chem = Bol'šoj Jenisej 42-43 S 7
Bij-Chem = Bol'šoj Jenisej 42-43 S 7
Bijie 48-49 K 6
Bījistān = Bejestān 44-45 H 4
Bijnoṭ 44-45 L 5
Bijrān 44-45 G 6
Bijsk 42-43 Q 7
Bikaner 44-45 L 5
Bikin [SU, ~] 42-43 a 8
Bikin [SU, ●] 42-43 Za 8
Bikoro 64-65 E 3
Bilaspur [IND, Madhya Pradesh] 44-45 N 6
Bilati 63 B 3
Bilbao 34-35 F 7
Bilbays 62 D 2
Bildudalur 30-31 ab 2
Bileća 36-37 H 4
Bilecik 46-47 C 2
Bili [ZRE, ~] 64-65 FG 2
Bili [ZRE, ●] 64-65 FG 2
Bilibiza 63 E 6
Biliran Island 52-53 H 4
Billefjord 30-31 k 5
Billings, MT 72-73 E 2
Billiton = Pulau Belitung 52-53 E 7
Bill Williams River 76-77 FG 8
Bilma 60-61 G 5
Biloela 56-57 K 4
Bilo gora 36-37 G 2-3
Biloxi, MS 72-73 J 5
Bilqās 62 D 2
Bilqas Qism Auwal = Bilqās 62 D 2
Biltine 60-61 J 6
Bilugyn = Bīlū Kyûn 52-53 C 3
Bīlū Kyûn 52-53 C 3
Bimbéreké = Bembèrèkè 60-61 E 6
Bimbo 60-61 H 8
Bimlipatam 44-45 M 7
Binalbagan 52-53 H 4
Binboğa 46-47 G 3
Bindloe = Isla Marchena 78-79 AB 4
Bin Ganīyah, Bi'r – 60-61 J 2
Bingara 58 K 2
Bingen 33 C 4
Bingerville 60-61 D 7
Bingham, ME 74-75 J 2
Bingham Canyon, UT 76-77 GH 5
Binghamton, NY 72-73 LM 3
Bin Gharīr = Bin Jarīr 60-61 C 2
Bingo Bay = Hiuchi-nada 50-51 J 5
Bingöl 46-47 J 3
Bingöl Dağları 46-47 J 3
Binjai 52-53 C 6
Bin Jarīr 60-61 C 2
Binnaway 56-57 JK 6
Binnen-Mongolië 48-49 K 3-M 2
Binnenzee = Seto-naikai 48-49 P 5
Bintan, Pulau – 52-53 DE 6
Bint Jubayl 46-47 F 6
Bintuan 52-53 D 7
Bintulu 52-53 F 6
Bintuni 52-53 K 7
Binzart 60-61 FG 1
Binzert = Binzart 60-61 FG 1
Bío Bío, Río – 80 B 5
Biograd 36-37 F 4
Bioko 60-61 F 8
Biola, CA 76-77 CD 7
Bionga 63 AB 3
Biqā', Al- = 4 ◁ 4 46-47 G 6
Biqā', Al- = RL [≅] 46-47 FG 5-6
Biqā', Al- = Sahl al-Biqā' 46-47 FG 5-6
Bir 44-45 M 7
Bira 42-43 Z 8
Birāk 60-61 G 3
Bi'r al-Abd 62 E 2
Bī'r 'Alī 44-45 F 8
Birao 60-61 J 6
Birchip 58 F 5
Birch Mountains 70-71 O 6
Birdsville 56-57 G 5
Birecik 46-47 GH 4
Birganj 44-45 NO 5
Birhan Terara 60-61 M 6
Birigui 78-79 J 9
Biril'ussy = Novobiril'ussy 42-43 QR 6
Birimşe = Sincik 46-47 H 3
Bīrjand 44-45 H 4
Birkenhead 32 E 5
Birket Fatimé 60-61 HJ 6
Birkīm 46-47 L 4
Bîrlad [R, ~] 36-37 M 2-3
Bîrlad [R, ●] 36-37 M 2
Birma 52-53 BC 2
Birmania 52-53 BC 2
Birmanie 52-53 BC 2
Birmingham [GB] 32 EF 5
Birmingham, AL 72-73 J 5
Birnin Kebbi 60-61 EF 6
Birni N'konni 60-61 EF 6
Birobidžan 42-43 Z 8
Birrie River 58 H 2
Birrindudu 56-57 EF 3
Birsk 42-43 K 6
Birskij = Oblučje 42-43 Z 8
Birtavarre 30-31 J 3
Bi'r Umm Qarayn 60-61 B 3
Biruni = Beruni 42-43 L 9
Bir'usa 42-43 S 6
Biržai 30-31 L 9
Bisa, Pulau – 52-53 J 7
Bisaliya, El – = Al-Başalīyat Qiblī 62 E 5
Bisbee, AZ 76-77 HJ 10
Biscaje, Golf van – 34-35 EF 6
Biscay, Bay of – 34-35 EF 6
Biscayne Bay 74-75 c 4
Biscéglie 36-37 G 5
Bischofshofen 33 F 5
Biscoe Islands 24 C 30
Biscra = Biskrah 60-61 F 2
Biševo 36-37 F 4
Bīshah, Wādī – 44-45 E 6-7
Bīsheh, Īstgah-e – 46-47 N 6
Bishenpur 44-45 P 6
Bishop, CA 76-77 D 7
Bishopville, SC 74-75 C 7
Bishrī, Jabal al- 46-47 H 5
Bisina, Lake – 64-65 HJ 2
Biskayerhuken 30-31 hj 5
Biškek 42-43 NO 9
Biškek 42-43 NO 9
Biskrah 60-61 F 2
Bisling 52-53 J 5
Bismarck, ND 72-73 F 2
Bismarck, Archipel – 52-53 NO 7
Bismarck, Archipiélago de – 52-53 NO 7
Bismarck, Mar de – 52-53 NO 7
Bismarck, Mer de – 52-53 NO 7
Bismarck Archipel 52-53 NO 7
Bismarckburg = Kasanga 64-65 H 4
Bismarck Range 52-53 M 7-N 8
Bismarck Sea 52-53 NO 7
Bismarckstraße 24 C 30
Bismarckzee 52-53 NO 7
Bismil 46-47 J 4
Bīsotūn 46-47 M 5
Bissau 60-61 A 6
Bistcho Lake 70-71 N 6
Bistōnis, Límnē – 36-37 L 5
Bistriţa [R, ~] 36-37 M 2

Bistr 161

Bistrița [R, ●] 36-37 L 2
Bitam 64-65 D 2
Bitlis 44-45 E 3
Bitlis Dağları 46-47 JK 3
Bitola 36-37 J 5
Bitonto 36-37 G 5
Bitter Creek 76-77 J 5
Bitterfeld 33 F 3
Bitterfontein 64-65 E 9
Bittermeer = Al-Buḥayrat al-Murrat al-Kubrá 62 E 2
Bitterroot Range 72-73 C 2-D 3
Bitterroot River 76-77 F 2
Bitung 52-53 J 6
Biu 60-61 G 6
Biviraka 52-53 M 8
Biwa-ko 48-49 Q 4
Biyāḍ, Al- = Al-Bayāḍ 44-45 F 6
Biyalā 62 D 2
Bizerta = Binzart 60-61 FG 1
Bizerte = Binzart 60-61 FG 1

Bjargtangar 30-31 a 2
Bjelovar 36-37 G 3
Bjelowo = Belovo 42-43 Q 7
Bjelucha = gora Belucha 42-43 Q 8
Björkholmen 30-31 H 4
Björna 30-31 H 6
Björneborg = Pori 30-31 J 7
Bjuröklubb 30-31 JK 5

Blackall 56-57 HJ 4
Black Belt 72-73 J 5
Blackburn 32 EF 5
Blackburn, Mount – 70-71 H 5
Black Canyon 76-77 F 8
Black Diamond, WA 76-77 BC 2
Black Duck 70-71 ST 6
Black Eagle, MT 76-77 H 2
Blackfeet Indian Reservation 76-77 G 1
Blackfoot, ID 76-77 GH 4
Blackfoot, MT 76-77 G 1
Blackfoot Reservoir 76-77 H 4
Blackfoot River 76-77 G 2
Black Hills 72-73 F 3
Blackleaf, MT 76-77 G 1
Black Mesa 76-77 H 7
Black Mountain [USA] 74-75 A 7
Black Mountain, NC 74-75 BC 7
Black Mountains [USA] 72-73 D 4-5
Black Pine Peak 76-77 G 4
Blackpool 32 E 5
Black River [USA ◁ Henderson Bay] 74-75 F 3
Black River [USA ◁ Salt River] 76-77 HJ 9
Black Rock 80 H 8
Black Rock, UT 76-77 G 6
Black Rock Desert 72-73 C 3
Blacksburg, VA 74-75 C 6
Black Sea 38-39 E-G 7
Blackshear, GA 74-75 BC 9
Black Springs, NM 76-77 J 9
Blackstone, VA 74-75 DE 6
Blackville, SC 74-75 C 8
Black Waxy Prairie 72-73 G 5
Bláfjall 30-31 e 2
Blåfjorden 30-31 lm 5
Blagodarnoje 38-39 H 6
Blagoevgrad 36-37 K 4-5
Blagoveščensk [SU, Belaja] 38-39 KL 4
Blagoveščensk [SU, Rossijskaja SFSR] 42-43 YZ 7
Blagoveščenskij proliv 42-43 c 2-d 3
Blaine, WA 76-77 B 1
Blainville 56-57 FG 2
Blair Athol 56-57 J 4
Blairsden, CA 76-77 C 6
Blairsville, PA 74-75 D 4
Blanca Peak 72-73 E 4
Blanche, Lake – [AUS, South Australia] 56-57 GH 5
Blanche, Lake – [AUS, Western Australia] 56-57 D 4
Blancos, Los – [RA] 80 D 2
Blandá 30-31 d 2
Blanding, UT 76-77 J 7
Blankaholm 30-31 FG 9
Blantyre 64-65 HJ 6
Blåvands Huk 30-31 BC 10
Blavet 34-35 F 4-5
Blaye 34-35 G 6
Blayney 56-57 J 6
Blaze, Point – 56-57 EF 2
Blazon, WY 76-77 H 5
Blednaja, gora – 42-43 M 2
Blejeşti 36-37 L 3
Blekinge län 30-31 F 9
Blenheim [CDN] 74-75 C 3
Blenheim [NZ] 56-57 O 8
Blida = Bulaydah 60-61 E 1
Blīdah = Bulaydah 60-61 E 1
Bliss, ID 76-77 F 4
Blitar 52-53 F 8
Blitong = Pulau Belitung 52-53 E 7
Blitta 60-61 E 7
Blitzen, OR 76-77 D 4
Block Island 74-75 H 4
Block Island Sound 74-75 GH 4
Bloemfontein 64-65 G 8
Blois 34-35 H 5
Blönduós 30-31 cd 2
Bloody Falls 70-71 NO 4
Bloomington, IL 72-73 HJ 3
Bloomington, IN 72-73 J 4
Bloomsburg, PA 74-75 E 4
Blosseville Kyst 70-71 ef 4
Blossom, mys – 42-43 jk 3
Bloxom, VA 74-75 F 6
Blūdān 46-47 G 6
Blue Bell Knoll 76-77 H 6
Blue Creek, UT 76-77 G 5
Bluefield, VA 74-75 C 6
Bluefield, WV 74-75 C 6
Bluefields 72-73 K 9
Bluejoint Lake 76-77 D 4
Blue Knob 74-75 D 4
Blue Lake, CA 76-77 B 5
Blue Mountain [USA, Pennsylvania] 74-75 EF 4
Blue Mountain Pass 76-77 E 4
Blue Mountains [JA] 72-73 L 8
Blue Mountains [USA, Maine] 74-75 H 2
Blue Mountains [USA, Oregon] 72-73 C 2-3
Blue Mud Bay 56-57 G 2
Bluenose Lake 70-71 N 4
Blue Ridge [USA, New York] 74-75 F 3
Blue Ridge [USA, North Carolina] 72-73 KL 4
Blue Ridge, GA 74-75 A 7
Blue River 76-77 J 9
Bluff 56-57 N 9
Bluff, UT 76-77 J 7
Bluffton, IN 74-75 A 4
Blumenau [BR] 80 FG 3
Bly, OR 76-77 C 4
Blythe, CA 76-77 F 9
Blytheville, AR 72-73 HJ 4

Bo [WAL] 60-61 B 7
Boali 60-61 H 8
Boa Nova [BR, Bahia] 78-79 LM 7
Boardman, OR 76-77 D 3
Boa Vista [BR, Roraima] 78-79 G 4
Bobadah 58 H 4
Bobbili 44-45 N 7
Bòbbio 36-37 C 3
Bobo-Dioulasso 60-61 D 6
Bobo-Diulasso = Bobo-Dioulasso 60-61 D 6
Bobonong 64-65 G 7
Bóbr 33 G 3
Bobrujsk 38-39 E 5
Boca, La – 72-73 b 3
Boca del Pao 78-79 FG 3
Boca do Acre 78-79 F 6
Boca do Jari 78-79 J 5
Boca do Tapauá = Tapauá 78-79 FG 6
Boca Grande, FL 74-75 b 3
Bocaiuva 78-79 L 8
Bocaranga 60-61 H 7
Boca Raton, FL 74-75 cd 3
Bochina 33 K 4
Bocholt 33 C 3
Bochum 33 C 3
Böda 30-31 G 9
Boda [RCA] 60-61 H 8
Bodajbo 42-43 VW 6
Bodega Head 76-77 B 6
Bodélé 60-61 H 5
Boden 30-31 JK 5
Bodensee 33 D 5
Bodø 30-31 EF 4
Bodoquena 78-79 H 8
Bodoquena, Serra – 78-79 H 9
Bodrog 33 K 4
Bodrum 46-47 B 4
Boé 60-61 B 6
Boedapest = Budapest 33 J 5
Boekarest = Bucureşti 36-37 LM 3
Boende 64-65 F 3
Boerjaten Autonome Republiek 42-43 T 7-V 6
Boerundi 64-65 GH 3
Boffa 60-61 B 6
Bōfu = Hōfu 50-51 H 5-6
Bogalusa, LA 72-73 HJ 5
Bogandé 60-61 DE 6
Bogan Gate 58 H 4
Bogan River 56-57 J 6
Bogarnes 30-31 bc 2
Boğaziçi 44-45 BC 2
Boğazkale 46-47 F 2-3
Boğazköprü 46-47 F 3
Boğazlıyan 46-47 F 3
Bogd 48-49 J 2
Bogdanovič 38-39 M 4
Bogdo uul 48-49 FG 3
Bogd uul, Ich – 48-49 J 3
Bogd uul, Ich – 48-49 J 3
Boggabilla 56-57 JK 5
Boggabri 58 JK 3
Boggai, Lak – 63 D 2
Bogham, Al- 46-47 J 5
Boghari = Qasr al-Bukharī 60-61 E 1
Bogia 52-53 MN 7
Bogo [RP] 52-53 H 4
Bogong, Mount – 56-57 J 7
Bogor 52-53 E 8
Bogorodick 38-39 G 5
Bogotá 78-79 E 4
Bogotol 42-43 Q 6
Bogučany 42-43 S 6
Bo Hai 48-49 M 4
Bohai Haixia 48-49 N 4
Bohême = Čechy 33 FG 4
Bohemen = Čechy 33 FG 4
Bohemia = Čechy 33 FG 4
Böhmerwald 33 FG 4
Bohol 52-53 H 5
Boibēĭs, Límnē – 36-37 K 6
Boigu Island 52-53 M 8
Boim 78-79 H 5
Bois, Lac des – 70-71 M 4
Bois Blanc Island 74-75 A 2
Boise City, ID 72-73 G 3
Boise River 76-77 E 4
Bois-le-Duc = 's-Hertogenbosch 34-35 KL 3
Bojador, Cabo – = Rā's Bujdūr 60-61 AB 3
Bojarka 42-43 S 3
Bojnūrd 44-45 H 3
Bojuru 80 F 4
Boké 60-61 B 6
Bokhona River 58 J 1
Bokkol 63 D 2
Boknfjord 30-31 A 8
Bokoro 60-61 H 6
Bokote 64-65 F 2-3
Bokovskaja 38-39 H 6
Bokungu 64-65 F 3
Bolaiti 64-65 FG 3
Bolama 60-61 A 6
Bolān, Kotal – 44-45 K 5
Bolangir = Balāngīr 44-45 N 6
Bolan Pass = Kotal Bolān 44-45 K 5
Bólbē, Límnē – 36-37 K 6
Bolbec 34-35 H 4
Bole 60-61 D 7
Bole, MT 76-77 GH 2
Boles, ID 76-77 E 3
Bolesławiec 33 GH 3
Bolgatanga 60-61 D 6
Bolgrad 38-39 E 6
Boli [TJ] 48-49 P 2
Boli [ZRE] 63 B 2
Boliden 30-31 J 5
Bolissós 36-37 L 6
Bolívar [PE] 78-79 D 6
Bolívar, Pico – 78-79 E 3
Bolivia 78-79 FG 8
Bolivie 78-79 FG 8
Bolkar Dağları 46-47 F 4
Bollnäs 30-31 G 7
Bollon 56-57 J 5
Bolobo 64-65 E 3
Bolod'ok 42-43 Z 7
Bologna 36-37 D 3
Bologne = Bologna 36-37 D 3
Bologoje 42-43 EF 6
Bolomba 64-65 E 2
Bolonia = Bologna 36-37 D 3
Bolor = Bāltistān 44-45 M 3-4
Bolo-retto = Penghu Lieh-tao 48-49 M 7
Bólos 36-37 K 6
Bolotnoje 42-43 P 6
Boloven, Cao Nguyên – 52-53 E 3-4
Bol'šaja = Velikaja 42-43 h 5
Bol'šaja Višera 38-39 F 4
Bolsena, Lago di – 36-37 DE 4
Bol'ševik, ostrov – 42-43 T-V 2
Bol'šezemel'skaja tundra 42-43 JK 4
Bol'šije Uki 42-43 N 6
Bol'šoj An'uj 42-43 fg 4
Bol'šoj Balchan 38-39 K 8
Bol'šoj Ber'ozovyj, ostrov – 30-31 MN 7
Bol'šoj Jenisej 42-43 S 7
Bol'šoj Oloj = Oloj 42-43 f 4
Bol'šoj Šantar, ostrov – 42-43 ab 7
Bol'šoj Uluj 42-43 R 6
Bol'šoj Uzen' 38-39 J 5-6
Bolton 32 E 5
Bolton, NC 74-75 D 7
Bolu 46-47 D 2
Bolucan 46-47 GH 3
Bolukābād 46-47 M 4
Bolungarvík 30-31 ab 1
Bolvadin 46-47 D 3
Bolzano 36-37 D 2
Boma 64-65 D 4
Bómba, Khalig – = Khalīj al-Bunbah 60-61 J 2
Bombaim = Bombay 44-45 L 7
Bombala 56-57 JK 7
Bombay 44-45 L 7
Bomberai 52-53 K 7
Bombetoka, Baie de – 64-65 KL 6
Bombo 63 C 2
Bom Comércio 78-79 F 6
Bom Despacho 78-79 KL 8
Bomi Hills = Tubmanburg 60-61 B 7
Bom Jesus [BR, Piauí] 78-79 L 6
Bom Jesus da Gurguéia, Serra – 78-79 L 6-7
Bom Jesus da Lapa 78-79 L 7
Bømlafjord 30-31 A 8
Bømlo 30-31 A 8
Bomokandi 64-65 G 2
Bomongo 64-65 E 2
Bomu 64-65 F 2
Bonāb [IR ↖ Tabrīz] 46-47 LM 3
Bonāb [IR ↙ Tabrīz] 46-47 M 4
Bonaire 72-73 N 9
Bonancita 76-77 GH 10
Bonanza, ID 76-77 F 3
Bonaparte, Mount – 76-77 D 1
Bonaparte Archipelago 56-57 DE 2
Bonavista 70-71 a 8
Bon Bon 58 BC 3
Bondeno 36-37 D 3
Bond Hill 58 B 3
Bondo [ZRE] 64-65 F 2
Bondoc Peninsula 52-53 H 4
Bondoukou 60-61 D 7
Bondurant, WY 76-77 HJ 4
Bône = 'Annābah 60-61 F 1
Bone = Watampone 52-53 GH 7
Bone, Teluk – 52-53 H 7
Bonga 60-61 M 7
Bongandanga 64-65 F 2
Bongo 64-65 CD 3
Bongolave 64-65 L 6
Bongor 60-61 H 6
Bonifacio 36-37 C 5
Bonifàcio, Bocche di – 36-37 C 5
Bonin 54 RS 7
Bonin Trench 22-23 R 4
Bonintrog 22-23 R 4
Bonita, AZ 76-77 HJ 9
Bonitas, Las – 78-79 FG 3
Bonn 33 C 3
Bonne-Espérance, Cap de – 64-65 E 9
Bonner, MT 76-77 G 2
Bonners Ferry, ID 76-77 E 1
Bonneville, OR 76-77 C 3
Bonneville Salt Flats 76-77 G 5
Bonnie Rock 56-57 C 6
Bonny 60-61 F 8
Bonny, Golfe de – 60-61 F 8
Bonnyville 70-71 O 7
Bō-no misaki 50-51 GH 7
Bonthe 60-61 B 7
Bontongssunggu = Jeneponto 52-53 G 8
Bookabie 56-57 F 6
Bookaloo 56-57 G 6
Booligal 56-57 H 6
Boonah 58 L 1-2
Böön Cagaan nuur 48-49 HJ 2
Boone, NC 74-75 C 6
Boonville, NY 74-75 F 3
Boorama 60-61 a 2
Boosaaso 60-61 bc 1
Boothbay Harbor, ME 74-75 J 3
Boothby, Cape – 24 C 6-7
Boothia, Gulf of – 70-71 ST 3-4
Boothia Isthmus 70-71 S 4
Boothia Peninsula 70-71 RS 3
Booué 64-65 D 3
Boqueirão [BR, Rio Grande do Sul] 80 F 4
Boqueirão, Serra do – [BR, Bahia] 78-79 L 7
Bor 36-37 K 3
Bor [TR] 46-47 F 4
Bōr = Būr 60-61 L 7
Bor, Lak – 64-65 J 2
Boraha, Nosy – 64-65 M 6
Borah Peak 72-73 D 3
Borås 30-31 E 9
Borāzjān 44-45 G 5
Borba [BR] 78-79 H 5
Borborema, Planalto da – 78-79 M 6
Bor Chadyn uul 48-49 EF 3
Bor Choro uul 48-49 E 3
Borçka = Yeniyol 46-47 JK 2
Borcu = Borkou 60-61 H 5
Bor Chadyn uul 48-49 EF 3
Bor Choro uul 48-49 E 3
Bordeaux 34-35 G 6
Borden Island 70-71 NO 2
Borden Peninsula 70-71 U 3
Bordertown 58 E 6
Bordighera 36-37 BC 4
Bordzongijn Gov' 48-49 K 3
Bóreioi Sporádes 36-37 KL 6
Bóreiron Stenòn Kerkýras 36-37 HJ 6
Borgå 30-31 LM 7
Borgarfjardhar 30-31 c 2
Børgefjell 30-31 EF 5
Borger, TX 72-73 F 4
Borgholm 30-31 G 9
Borgomanero 36-37 BC 3
Borgoña = Bourgogne 34-35 K 5-6
Borisoglebsk 38-39 H 5
Borisov 38-39 E 5
Borisova, mys – 42-43 a 6
Borja [PE] 78-79 D 5
Borkou 60-61 H 5
Borku = Borkou 60-61 H 5
Borlänge 30-31 FG 7
Borlu 46-47 C 3
Bòrmida 36-37 C 3
Bornemouth 32 F 6
Bornéo = Kalimantan 52-53 F 7-G 6
Bornholm 30-31 F 10
Borno = Bornu 60-61 G 6
Bornou = Borno 60-61 G 6
Bornu 60-61 G 6
Borogoncy 42-43 Z 5
B'or'ol'och = Susuman 42-43 cd 5
Boron, CA 76-77 E 8
Borovići 42-43 EF 6
Borovl'anka 42-43 P 7
Borovskoj 42-43 LM 7
Borroloola 56-57 G 3
Borşa 36-37 L 2
Borščovočnyj chrebet 42-43 W 7
Bortala Monggol Zizhizhou = F ◁ 48-49 E 2-3
Bor Talijn gol 48-49 E 3
Borto 42-43 V 7
Borūjerd 44-45 FG 4
Borz'a 42-43 W 7
Bosa 36-37 C 5
Bosanska Gradiška 36-37 G 3
Bosanska Krupa 36-37 G 3
Bosanski Novi 36-37 FG 3
Bosanski Petrovac 36-37 G 3
Bose 48-49 K 7
Bósforo = Karadeniz Boğazı 44-45 BC 2
Boshan 48-49 M 4
Bosmanland 64-65 E 8
Bosna [BG] 36-37 M 4
Bosna [YU] 36-37 GH 3
Bosna i Hercegovina 36-37 GH 3-4
Bosnia Hercegovina 36-37 GH 3-4
Bosnia y Hercegovina 36-37 GH 3-4
Bosnie-Herzégovine 36-37 GH 3-4
Bosobolo 64-65 E 2
Bōsō hantō 50-51 N 5
Bosphore = Karadeniz Boğazı 44-45 BC 2
Bossangoa 60-61 H 7
Bossembélé 60-61 H 7
Bossier City, LA 72-73 H 5
Bosso 60-61 G 6
Bostān [IR] 46-47 MN 7
Bostānābād 46-47 M 4
Boston [GB] 32 FG 5
Boston, GA 74-75 B 9
Boston, MA 72-73 MN 3
Boston Mountains 72-73 H 4
Bosveld 64-65 G 7
Botan Çayı 46-47 K 4
Botany Bay 56-57 K 6
Botev 36-37 L 4
Bothia Gulf of – 30-31 H 7-K 5
Botletle 64-65 F 7
Botnia, Golfo de – 30-31 H 7-K 5
Botnische Golf 30-31 H 7-K 5
Botoşani 36-37 M 2
Botswana 64-65 FG 7
Botte Donato 36-37 G 6
Bottnie, Golfe de – 30-31 H 7-K 5
Botucatu 78-79 K 9
Botulu 42-43 W 5
Bouaflé 60-61 C 7
Bouaké 60-61 CD 7
Boû 'Amaroû = Bu 'Amarū 46-47 HJ 5
Bouar 60-61 H 7
Bouca 60-61 H 7
Boucau 34-35 G 7
Boudeuse Cay 64-65 M 4
Boudewijnstad = Moba 64-65 G 4
Boû Djébéha 60-61 D 5
Bougainville 52-53 j 6
Bougainville, Cape – [AUS] 56-57 E 2
Bougainville, Fosse de – 52-53 h 6
Bougainvilletrog 52-53 h 6
Bougie = Bijāyah 60-61 EF 1
Bougouni 60-61 C 6
Bougtob = Bū Kutub 60-61 E 2
Boukān = Būkān 46-47 LM 4
Bou-Ktoub = Bū Kutub 60-61 E 2
Boulder, CO 72-73 EF 3-4
Boulder, MT 76-77 GH 2
Boulder, WY 76-77 HJ 4
Boulder City, NV 72-73 CD 4
Boulder Creek, CA 76-77 B 7
Boulder Dam = Hoover Dam 72-73 D 4
Boulia 56-57 G 4
Boulogne-sur-Mer 34-35 H 3
Boumba 60-61 H 8
Bouna 60-61 D 7
Bouna, Réserve de Faune de – = Parc national de la Komoé 60-61 D 7
Boundary Mountains 74-75 H 2
Boundary Peak 72-73 C 4
Bounday, WA 76-77 E 1
Boundiali 60-61 C 7
Boundji 64-65 E 3
Boundou 60-61 B 6
Bountiful, UT 76-77 H 5
Bourail 56-57 MN 4
Bourbonnais 34-35 J 5
Bourem 60-61 DE 5
Bourg-en-Bresse 34-35 K 5
Bourges 34-35 J 5
Bourgogne 34-35 K 5-6
Bourgogne, Canal de – 34-35 K 5
Bouriates, District Nacional des – = 11 ◁ 42-43 T 7
Bouriates, République Autonome des – 42-43 T 7-V 6
Bouriates-Mongols, District National des – 42-43 V 7
Bourke 56-57 J 6
Bouse, AZ 76-77 FG 9
Bouṣrá ech Châm = Buṣrat ash-Shām 46-47 G 6
Bouṣrá ech Châm = Buṣrat ash-Shām 46-47 G 6
Bousso 60-61 H 6
Boutilimit = Bū Tilimīt 60-61 B 5
Bouvard, Cape – 56-57 BC 6
Bouvetøya 24 D 1
Bovenmeer = Lake Superior 72-73 HJ 2
Boven Trajanuswal = Verchnij Trajanov val 36-37 N 2
Bovill, ID 76-77 E 2
Bow Bridge 56-57 C 6-7
Bowdoin, Lake – 76-77 K 1
Bowen [AUS] 56-57 J 3-4
Boweyr Aḥmad-e va Sardsīr Kohkīlūyeh = 4 ◁ 44-45 G 4
Bowie, AZ 76-77 J 9
Bowling Green, KY 72-73 J 4
Bowling Green, VA 74-75 E 5-6
Bowling Green, Cape – 56-57 J 3
Bowman Island 24 C 11
Bowmanville 74-75 D 3
Bowral 58 JK 5
Bow Rover 70-71 O 7
Bo Xian 48-49 LM 5
Boyabat 46-47 F 2
Boyalık = Çiçekdağı 46-47 F 3

162 Bistr

Boydton, VA 74-75 D 6
Boykins, VA 74-75 E 6
Boynton Beach, FL 74-75 cd 3
Boyuibe 78-79 G 9
Bozburun 46-47 C 4
Bozcaada [TR, ⊙] 46-47 AB 3
Boz Dağ [TR, ▲▲] 46-47 D 2-3
Boz Dağı 46-47 C 4
Boz Dağlar 46-47 C 3
Bozdoğan 46-47 C 4
Bozeman, MT 72-73 D 2
Bozen = Bolzano 36-37 D 2
Bozkır 46-47 E 4
Bozkurt 46-47 F 1-2
Bozok Yaylâsı 46-47 F 2-3
Bozoum 60-61 H 7
Bozova 46-47 H 4
Bozqūsh, Kūh-e – 46-47 M 4
Bozüyük 46-47 CD 3
Bozyaka = Beşkonak 46-47 D 4

Bra 36-37 B 3
Brabant, Île – 24 C 30
Brač 36-37 G 4
Bracciano, Lago di – 36-37 DE 4
Bracebridge 74-75 D 2
Bräcke 30-31 F 6
Braço Menor de Araguia 78-79 JK 7
Brad 36-37 K 2
Bràdano 36-37 G 5
Bradenton, FL 72-73 K 6
Bradford 32 F 5
Bradford [CDN] 74-75 D 2
Bradford, PA 74-75 D 4
Bradley, CA 76-77 C 8
Brady, MT 76-77 H 1-2
Braga 34-35 C 8
Bragado 80 D 5
Bragança 34-35 D 8
Bragança [BR, Pará] 78-79 K 5
Bragança Paulista 78-79 K 9
Brahestad = Raahe 30-31 L 5
Brahmani 44-45 O 6
Brahmaputra 44-45 P 5
Brăila 36-37 M 3
Brainerd, MN 72-73 H 2
Bramaputra = Brahmaputra 44-45 P 5
Brampton 74-75 CD 3
Branchville, SC 74-75 C 8
Brandberg 64-65 D 7
Brandenburg [DDR, ≅] 33 FG 2
Brandenburg [DDR, ●] 33 F 2
Brandon [CDN] 70-71 Q 8
Brandon, FL 56-57 b 3
Brandon, VT 74-75 G 3
Brandon Mount 32 AB 5
Brandywine, MD 74-75 E 5
Branford, FL 74-75 b 1-2
Braniewo 33 JK 1
Bransfield Strait 24 C 30-31
Br'ansk 38-39 FG 5
Brantford 74-75 CD 3
Branxholme 58 EF 6
Brásc = Birāk 60-61 G 3
Bras d'Or Lake 70-71 YZ 8
Brasil 78-79 F-L 6
Brasil, Macizo da – = Planalto Brasileiro 78-79 KL 8
Brasiléia 78-79 F 7
Brasília 78-79 K 8
Brasília Legal 78-79 H 5
Brașov 36-37 L 3
Bråsvellbreen 30-31 lm 5
Bratislava 33 H 4
Bratsk 42-43 T 6
Bratskoje vodochranilišče 42-43 T 6
Brattieboro, VT 74-75 G 3
Braunau 33 F 4
Braunschweig 33 E 2
Brawley, CA 72-73 C 5
Bray, CA 76-77 C 5
Bray Island 70-71 V 4
Brazil 78-79 F-L 6
Brazil Basin 22-23 H 6
Braziliaans Bekken 22-23 H 6
Brazilian Plateau = Planalto Brasileiro 78-79 KL 8
Brazilië 78-79 F-L 6
Brazos River 72-73 G 5-6
Brazzaville 64-65 DE 3
Brčko 36-37 H 3
Brdy 33 FG 4
Brechin [CDN] 74-75 D 2
Brecknock, Peninsula – 80 B 8-9
Břeclav 33 H 4
Brecon 32 E 5-6
Breda 34-35 K 3
Bredasdorp 64-65 F 9
Bredbo 58 J 5
Bredy 42-43 KL 7
Bregalnica 36-37 K 5
Bregenz 33 DE 5
Bregovo 36-37 K 3
Breidhafjördhur 30-31 ab 2
Breidhavik 30-31 a 2
Brejinho do Nazaré 78-79 K 7
Brekstad 30-31 C 6
Bremangerlandet 30-31 A 7
Brême = Bremen 33 D 2
Bremen 33 D 2
Bremerhaven 33 D 2
Bremerton, WA 72-73 B 2
Brenne 34-35 H 5
Brenner 33 E 5
Brennero = Brenner 33 E 5
Brennevinsfjord 30-31 k 4
Brèscia 36-37 D 3
Brésil 78-79 F-L 6
Bressanone 36-37 DE 2
Bressay 32 F 1
Bresse 34-35 K 5
Bressuire 34-35 G 5
Brest [F] 34-35 E 4
Brest [SU] 38-39 D 5
Bretagne 34-35 F 4-G 5
Breton, Cape – 70-71 Z 8
Breton Sound 72-73 J 6
Breueh, Pulau – 52-53 B 5
Brevard, NC 74-75 B 7
Breves 78-79 J 5
Brevik 30-31 C 8
Brewarrina 56-57 J 5
Brewer, ME 74-75 J 2
Brewster, WA 76-77 CD 1
Brewster, Kap – 19 BC 20-21
Bria 60-61 J 7
Briançon 34-35 L 6
Brian Head 76-77 G 7
Briare 34-35 J 5
Bribbaree 58 HJ 5
Bribie Island 56-57 K 5
Briceland, CA 76-77 AB 5
Brickaville = Vohibinany 64-65 LM 6
Bridge, ID 76-77 G 4
Bridgeboro, GA 74-75 AB 9
Bridgeport, CA 76-77 D 6
Bridgeport, CT 72-73 M 3
Bridger Basin 76-77 HJ 5
Bridgeton, NC 74-75 E 7
Bridgeton, NJ 74-75 F 5
Bridgetown [AUS] 56-57 C 6
Bridgetown [BDS] 72-73 OP 9
Bridgton, ME 74-75 H 2
Bridgwater 32 E 6
Bridlington 32 FG 4
Bridport [AUS] 58 c 2
Brie 34-35 J 4
Brig 33 CD 5
Brigham City, UT 72-73 D 3
Bright 58 H 6
Brighton 32 FG 6
Brighton [CDN] 74-75 DE 2
Brighton, NY 56-57 E 3
Brighton Indian Reservation 74-75 c 3
Brijuni 36-37 E 3
Brilon 33 D 3
Brindakit 42-43 a 5-6
Brindisi 36-37 GH 5
Brisbane 56-57 K 5
Brisbane River 56-57 K 5
Bristol 32 EF 6
Bristol, RI 74-75 H 4
Bristol, TN 74-75 B 6
Bristol, VA 72-73 K 4
Bristol Bay 70-71 DE 6
Bristol Channel 32 DE 6
Bristol Channel 32 DE 6
Bristol Lake 76-77 F 8
Britannia Range 24 AB 15-16
British Columbia 70-71 L 6-N 7
British Isles 28-29 F 5-G 4
British Mountains 70-71 HJ 4
Britse Eilanden 28-29 F 5-G 4
Britstown 64-65 F 9
Brive-la-Gaillarde 34-35 H 6
Brixen = Bressanone 36-37 DE 2
Brixham 32 E 6
Brno 33 H 4
Broach = Bharuch 44-45 L 6
Broadford 32 CD 3
Broad Law 32 E 4
Broad River 74-75 C 7
Broad Sound 56-57 JK 4
Brochet 70-71 Q 6
Brocken 33 E 3
Brock Island 70-71 N 2
Brockman, Mount – 56-57 C 4
Brockport, NY 74-75 DE 3
Brockton, MA 74-75 H 3
Brockville 70-71 V 9
Brockway, PA 74-75 D 4
Brodeur Peninsula 70-71 T 3
Brodnax, VA 74-75 DE 6
Brodnica 33 J 2
Brody 38-39 E 5
Brogan, OR 76-77 E 3
Broken Hill 56-57 H 6
Broken Hill = Kabwe 64-65 G 5
Brokopondo 78-79 HJ 3
Brønderslev 30-31 CD 9
Brønnøysund 30-31 DE 5
Bronson, FL 74-75 b 2
Bronte 36-37 F 7
Bronte Park 56-57 J 8
Brookings, OR 76-77 A 4
Brookings, SD 72-73 G 3
Brookline, MA 74-75 H 3
Brookneal, VA 74-75 D 6
Brooks Range 70-71 E-H 4
Brooksville, FL 74-75 b 2
Brookton 56-57 C 6
Brookville, OH 74-75 A 5
Brookville, PA 74-75 D 4
Broome 56-57 D 3
Brotas de Macaúbas 78-79 L 7
Brothers, OR 76-77 C 4
Brothers, The – = Jazā'ir al-Ikhwān 62 F 4
Brothers, The – = Samḥah, Darsah 44-45 G 8
Brown, Mount – 24 BC 9
Brown, Point – 58 A 4
Browning, MT 76-77 G 1
Brownsville, OR 76-77 B 3
Brownsville, PA 74-75 CD 4-5
Brownsville, TX 72-73 G 6
Brownsweg 78-79 H 3-4
Brownville Junction, ME 74-75 J 2
Brownwood, TX 72-73 G 5
Broxton, GA 74-75 B 9
Bruay-en-Artois 34-35 J 3
Bruce, Mount – 56-57 C 4
Bruce Rock 56-57 C 6
Bruchsal 33 D 4
Bruck an der Leitha 33 H 4
Bruck an der Mur 33 G 5
Bruges = Brugge 34-35 J 3
Brugge 34-35 J 3
Bruin Peak 76-77 H 6
Bruja, Cerro – 72-73 b 2
Brukkaros, Mount – = Groot Brukkaros 64-65 E 8
Brumado 78-79 L 7
Bruneau, ID 76-77 F 4
Bruneau River 76-77 F 4
Brunei 52-53 F 6
Brunei = Bandar Seri Begawan 52-53 FG 5-6
Brunswick, GA 72-73 K 5
Brunswick, MD 74-75 E 5
Brunswick, ME 74-75 HJ 3
Brunswick, Peninsula – 80 B 8
Brunswick Bay 56-57 D 3
Brunswick Heads 58 LM 2
Bruny Island 56-57 J 8
Bruselas = Bruxelles 34-35 JK 3
Brushy Mountains 74-75 C 6-7
Brusque 80 G 3
Brussel 34-35 JK 3
Brussel = Bruxelles 34-35 JK 3
Brussels = Bruxelles 34-35 JK 3
Bruxelles 34-35 JK 3
Bryan, TX 72-73 G 5
Bryan, WY 76-77 J 5
Bryce Canyon National Park 76-77 GH 7
Brykalansk 38-39 KL 2
Bryson City, TN 74-75 B 7
Brzeg 33 H 3
Bṣaiya, Al- = Al-Buṣaiyah 44-45 EF 4
Bsharri = Basharrī 46-47 G 5
Btaymān, Bi'r – 46-47 H 4
Bua 63 C 6
Buake = Bouaké 60-61 CD 7
Buala 52-53 jk 6
Bū'Amarū 46-47 HJ 5
Bu'ayrāt al-Ḥsūn 60-61 H 2
Būbīyan, Jazīrat – 44-45 FG 5
Bubu 63 C 4
Bucaale 60-61 N 8
Bucak 46-47 D 4
Bucakkışla 46-47 E 4
Bucaramanga 78-79 E 3
Bucarest = Bucureşti 36-37 LM 3
Buccaneer Archipelago 56-57 D 3
Buchan [AUS] 58 J 6
Buchanan [LB] 60-61 B 7
Buchanan, VA 74-75 CD 6
Buchans 70-71 Z 8
Buchara 44-45 JK 3
Buchardo 80 D 4
Bucharest = Bucureşti 36-37 LM 3
Buchon, Point – 76-77 C 8
Buchtarma 42-43 Q 8
Buchtarminskoje vodochranilišče 42-43 PQ 8
Buchyn Mangnaj uul 48-49 EF 4-5
Buckeye, AZ 76-77 G 9
Buckhannon, WV 74-75 C 5
Buckhaven 32 E 3
Buckhorn Lake 74-75 D 2
Buckie 32 E 3
Buckland Tableland 56-57 J 4-5
Buckleboo 56-57 G 6
Buckle Island 24 C 16-17
Buckley, WA 76-77 BC 2
Buckley Bay 24 C 15-16
Bucksport, ME 74-75 J 2
Bucovina 36-37 LM 2
Buco Zau 64-65 D 3
Bucureşti 36-37 LM 3
Budakskij liman 36-37 O 3
Budapest 33 J 5
Budaun 44-45 M 5
Budayr, Al- 46-47 L 7
Budd Land 24 C 12
Bude-Stratton 32 D 6
Búdhardalur 30-31 c 2
Būdhīyah, Jabal – 62 E 3
Budjala 64-65 EF 2
Budva 36-37 H 4
Buea 60-61 F 8
Buena Esperanza, Cabo de – 64-65 E 9
Buenaventura [CO] 78-79 D 4
Buenaventura, Bahía de – 78-79 D 4
Buena Vista [MEX] 76-77 E 10
Buena Vista, VA 74-75 D 6
Buena Vista Lake Bed 76-77 D 8
Buenos Aires [PA] 72-73 b 2
Buenos Aires [RA, ●] 80 E 4
Buenos Aires [RA, ☆] 80 DE 5
Buenos Aires, Lago – 80 B 7
Buen Retiro 72-73 b 3
Buffalo, NY 72-73 L 3
Buffalo, WV 74-75 C 5
Buffalo Hump 76-77 F 3
Buffalo Lake 70-71 NO 5
Bug 33 L 2
Buga 78-79 D 4
Bugant 48-49 K 2
Bugdajly 38-39 KL 8
Bugiri 63 C 2
Bugorkan 42-43 U 5
Bugrino 42-43 H 4
Bugt 48-49 N 2
Bugul'ma 42-43 J 7
Buguruslan 42-43 J 7
Buhăeşti 36-37 M 2
Buḥayrat al-Abyaḍ 60-61 KL 6
Buhemba 63 C 3
Buhl, ID 76-77 F 4
Buhoro 63 B 4
Buin [PNG] 52-53 j 6
Bū'īn-e Zahrā' 46-47 O 5
Buir Nur 48-49 M 2
Buitenzorg = Bogor 52-53 E 8
Buj 42-43 G 6
Bujalance 34-35 EF 10
Bū Jaydūr, Rā's – 60-61 AB 3
Buji 52-53 M 8
Bujnaksk 38-39 J 7
Bujumbura 64-65 G 3
Bukačača 42-43 W 7
Buka Island 52-53 hj 6
Bukama 64-65 G 4
Būkān 46-47 LM 4
Bukavu 64-65 G 3
Bukene 64-65 H 3
Bukit Besi 52-53 D 6
Bukit Bendung 52-53 D 6
Bukittinggi 52-53 CD 7
Bükk 33 K 4-5
Bukoba 64-65 H 3
Bū Kutub 60-61 E 2
Bula [RI] 52-53 K 7
Bulagan = Bulgan 48-49 J 2
Bulan 52-53 H 4
Bulancak 46-47 GH 2
Bulanık 46-47 K 3
Būlāq 62 D 5
Bulawayo 64-65 G 7
Bulaydah 60-61 E 1
Buldan 46-47 C 3
Bulgan [Mongolia, ● Bulgan] 48-49 J 2
Bulgan [Mongolia, ● Chovd] 48-49 G 2
Bulgan [Mongolia, ☆ = 9 ◁] 48-49 J 2
Bulgaria 36-37 K-M 4
Bulgarie 36-37 K-M 4
Bulgarije 36-37 K-M 4
Buli, Teluk – 52-53 J 6
Bulkī 60-61 M 7
Bullaxaar 60-61 a 1
Buller, Mount – 58 H 6
Bullfinch 56-57 C 6
Bulloo Downs 56-57 H 5
Bulloo River 56-57 H 5
Bulls Bay 74-75 D 8
Bulu 52-53 J 6
Buluan 52-53 H 5
Bulucan = Emirhan 46-47 GH 3
Bulukumba 52-53 GH 8
Bulungan 52-53 G 6
Buluntou Hai = Ojorong nuur 48-49 F 2
Bulu Rantekombola 52-53 GH 7
Bumba [ZRE, Bandundu] 64-65 E 4
Bumba [ZRE, Équateur] 64-65 F 2
Bumba = Boumba 60-61 H 8
Buna [EAK] 64-65 J 2
Buna [PNG] 52-53 N 8
Bunbah, Khalīj al- 60-61 J 2
Bunbury 56-57 BC 6
Bundaberg 56-57 K 4
Bundelkhand 44-45 MN 6
Bundi 44-45 M 5
Bundooma 56-57 FG 4
Bundoran 32 B 4
Bunge, zeml'a – 42-43 b 2-3
Bungendore 58 JK 5
Bunger Oasis 24 C 11
Bungo-suidō 48-49 P 5
Bungotakada 50-51 H 6
Bunguran, Pulau – = Pulau Natuna Besar 52-53 E 6
Bunia 64-65 GH 2
Bunkeya 64-65 G 5
Bunnell, FL 74-75 c 2
Bunta 52-53 H 7
Buntok 52-53 FG 7
Bünyan 46-47 F 3
Bunyu, Pulau – 52-53 G 6
Buol 52-53 H 6
Buolkalach 42-43 W 3
Buôn Ma Thuôt = Ban Mê Thuôt 52-53 E 4
Buor-Chaja, guba – 42-43 Z 3
Buor-Chaja, mys – 42-43 Z 3
Buor-Chaja, guba – 42-43 Z 3
Buor-Chaja, mys – 42-43 Z 3
Buqaliq tagh 48-49 G 4
Buquq 48-49 E 3
Būr 60-61 L 7
Bura 64-65 JK 3
Bur Acaba = Buur Hakkaba 60-61 N 8
Buram 60-61 K 6
Burao = Bur'o 60-61 O 7
Būr Atyan = Nawādhību 60-61 A 4
Buraydah 44-45 E 5
Buraymī, Al- 44-45 H 6
Burbank, CA 76-77 DE 8
Burchanbuudaj 48-49 H 2
Burcher 58 H 4
Burchun 48-49 F 2
Burco 60-61 b 2
Burdeau = Mahdīyah 60-61 E 1
Burdekin River 56-57 J 4
Burdur 44-45 BC 3
Burdur Gölü 46-47 CD 4
Burdwan 44-45 O 6
Burdwood, Banc de – 80 DE 8
Burdwood, Banco de – 80 DE 8
Burdwood Bank 80 DE 8
Burē [ETH, Gojam] 60-61 M 6
Burē [ETH, Īlubabor] 60-61 M 7
Bureå 30-31 J 5
Büreen = Büren 48-49 K 2
Bureinskij chrebet 42-43 Z 7-8
Bureja 42-43 Z 7
Büren [Mongolia] 48-49 K 2
Burenchaan [Mongolia, Chentij] 48-49 L 2
Burenchaan [Mongolia, Chövsgöl] 48-49 H 2
Bürencogt 48-49 L 2
Būr Fu'ād = Būr Sādāt 62 E 2
Burg 33 EF 2
Būr Gābo = Buur Gaabo 64-65 K 3
Bur Gao = Buur Gaabo 64-65 K 3
Burgas 36-37 M 4
Burgaski zaliv 36-37 MN 4
Burgaw, NC 74-75 DE 7
Burg el-'Arab = Burj al-'Arab 46-47 C 7
Burgenland 33 H 5
Burgersdorp 64-65 G 9
Burgfjället 30-31 F 5
Burghersdorp = Burgersdrop 64-65 G 9
Bùrgio 36-37 E 7
Burgos 34-35 F 7
Burgsvik 30-31 H 9
Burhaniye 46-47 B 3
Burhanpur 44-45 M 6
Burias Island 52-53 H 4
Buriatos, República Autónoma de los – 42-43 T 7-V 6
Buriatos de Aguinsk, Circunscripción Nacional de los – 42-43 V 7
Buriatos de Ust-Orda, Circunscripción Nacional de los – = 11 ◁ 42-43 T 7
Burica, Punta – 72-73 K 10
Burin Peninsula 70-71 Z 8
Burinšik 38-39 K 6
Buri Ram 52-53 D 3-4
Buriti [BR, Maranhão] 78-79 L 5
Buriti Bravo 78-79 L 6
Buriti dos Lopes 78-79 L 5
Burī Ye-Midir Selatē 60-61 M 5
Burj al-'Arab 62 C 2
Burj al-Haṭṭabah 60-61 F 2
Burj Ban Būl'īd = Qal'at Makmāhūn 60-61 E 3
Burjing = Burchun 48-49 F 2
Burj Luṭfī 60-61 F 3-4
Burj 'Umar Idrīs = Qal'at Flātarz 60-61 EF 3
Burketown 56-57 GH 3
Burkeville, VA 74-75 DE 6
Burkina Faso 60-61 DE 6
Burley, ID 76-77 G 4
Burlingame, CA 76-77 B 7
Burlington 74-75 D 3
Burlington, IA 72-73 H 3
Burlington, NC 74-75 D 6
Burlington, VT 72-73 M 3
Burlington, WA 76-77 BC 1
Burney, CA 76-77 C 5
Burnie 56-57 HJ 8
Burns, OR 76-77 D 4
Burns Lake 70-71 LM 7
Burnsville, WV 74-75 C 5
Burnt Creek 70-71 X 6-7
Burnt River 76-77 DE 3
Burnt River Mountains 76-77 DE 3
Burqah, Khahrat – 46-47 GH 6
Burqān 46-47 M 8
Burra 56-57 G 6
Burrendong Reservoir 58 J 4
Burren Junction 58 J 3
Burrinjuck Reservoir 56-57 J 7
Burro, Serranías del – 72-73 F 6
Burruyacú 80 CD 3
Bursa 44-45 B 2-3
Būr Sādāt 62 E 2
Būr Safāga = Safājah 60-61 L 3
Būr Sa'īd 60-61 L 2
Būr Sūdān 60-61 M 5
Būr Tawfīg 62 E 3
Buru, Pulau – 52-53 J 7
Burullus, Buḥayrat al- 62 D 2
Burūm 44-45 F 8
Burun-Šibertuj, gora – = gora Barun-Šabartuj 42-43 UV 8
Bururi 64-65 G 3
Buryat Autonomous Region 42-43 T 7-V 6
Burye = Burē 60-61 M 6
Bury Saint Edmunds 32 G 5
Buṣaīyah, Al- 44-45 EF 4
Buṣayrah 46-47 J 5
Busayṭā', Al- 46-47 G 7-H 8
Büs Cagaan Nuur = Böön Cagaan nuur 48-49 HJ 2
Būsh 62 D 3
Bushehr 44-45 G 5
Bushire = Bushehr 44-45 G 5
Businga 64-65 F 2
Busira 64-65 E 2-3
Buskerud 30-31 C 7-D 8
Buṣrat ash-Shām 46-47 G 6
Busselton 56-57 BC 6
Busto Arsizio 36-37 C 3
Busuanga Island 52-53 G 4
Busuluk = Buzuluk 42-43 J 7
Buta 64-65 F 2
Bután 44-45 OP 5
Butare 63 B 3
Butembo 63 B 2
Butere 63 C 2
Butha Qi 48-49 N 2
Butiaba 64-65 H 2
Bū Tilimīt 60-61 B 5
Butler, PA 74-75 D 4
Buṭmah 46-47 K 4
Buton, Pulau – 52-53 H 7-8

Buton 163

Butsha 63 B 2
Butsikáki 36-37 J 6
Butte Meadows, CA 76-77 BC 5
Butterworth 52-53 D 5
Butterworth = Gcuwa 64-65 G 9
Butte-Silver Bow, MT 72-73 D 2
Butuan 52-53 HJ 5
Buturlinovka 38-39 GH 5
Buulobarde 60-61 b 3
Buur Gabo 64-65 K 3
Buurhakaba 60-61 N 8
Buur Hakkaba 64-65 K 2
Buwārah, Jabal – 62 F 3
Büyükada, İstanbul- 46-47 C 2
Büyük Ağrı Dağı 44-45 E 2-3
Büyük Köhne 46-47 F 3
Büyük Mahya 46-47 B 2
Büyük Menderes Nehri 44-45 B 3
Buzači, poluostrov – 44-45 G 1-2
Buzău [R, ~] 36-37 M 3
Buzău [R, ●] 36-37 M 3
Buzaymah 60-61 J 4
Bužory 36-37 N 2
Buzuluk 42-43 J 7
Buzzards Bay 74-75 H 4

Byam Martin Channel 70-71 PQ 2
Byam Martin Channel 70-71 PQ 2
Byam Martin Island 70-71 Q 2-3
Byāvar = Beawar 44-45 LM 5
Byawar = Beawar 44-45 LM 5
Býblos = Jubayl 46-47 F 5
Bychawa 33 L 3
Bychov 38-39 EF 5
Bydgoszcz 33 HJ 2
Bygdin 30-31 C 7
Bygland 30-31 BC 8
Byk 36-37 N 2
Bykovo 38-39 J 6
Bylot Island 70-71 V 3
Byrd 24 AB 25
Byrd, Cape – 24 C 29
Byrd Land 24 AB 23-22
Byrock 56-57 J 6
Byron, CA 76-77 C 7
Byron, Cape – 56-57 K 5
Byron Bay 58 LM 2
Byrranga, gory – 42-43 Q 3-V 2
Byske 30-31 J 5
Byssa 42-43 Z 7
Bytom 33 J 3
Bytów 33 H 1

Bzémá = Buzaymah 60-61 J 4
Bzura 33 J 2

C

Caacupé 80 E 3
Caaguazú [PY, ●] 80 EF 3
Caaguazú, Cordillera de – 80 E 3
Caála 64-65 DE 5
Caapucú 80 E 3
Caatinga 78-79 K 8
Caatingas 78-79 L 7-M 6
Caazapá [PY, ●] 80 E 3
Caballería, Cabo de – 34-35 K 8
Caballococha 78-79 E 5
Cabanatuan 52-53 H 3
Cabedelo 78-79 N 6
Cabeza del Buey 34-35 E 9
Cabezas 78-79 G 8
Cabimas 78-79 E 2
Cabinda [Angola, ●] 64-65 D 4
Cabinda [Angola, ☆] 64-65 D 4
Cabinet Mountains 76-77 E 1-F 2
Cabo, Cuenca del – 22-23 K 7
Cabo, Ramal del – 22-23 K 8
Cabo Alto = Cape Dolphin 80 E 8
Cabo Blanco [CR] 72-73 J 10
Cabo Blanco [RA] 80 CD 7
Cabo Branco 78-79 N 6
Cabo Delgado [Moçambique, ∧] 64-65 K 5
Cabo Delgado [Moçambique, ☆] 64-65 JK 5
Cabo Falso [MEX] 72-73 D 7
Cabo Frio [BR, ∧] 78-79 L 9
Cabo Frio [BR, ●] 78-79 L 9
Caboolture 58 L 1
Cabo Pantoja = Pantoja 78-79 DE 5
Cabo Pasado 78-79 C 5
Cabora Bassa 64-65 H 6
Cabo Raso [RA, ●] 80 CD 6
Cabo Raso = Cabo Norte 78-79 K 4
Caborca Heroica 72-73 D 5
Cabo Rojo [MEX] 72-73 G 7
Cabot Strait 70-71 YZ 8
Cabo Verde, Cuenca de – 22-23 GH 4-5
Cabo Verde, Islas – 22-23 H 5
Cabo Verde, Islas – 22-23 H 5
Cabo Verde, Umbral de – 22-23 H 4-5
Cabra 34-35 E 10
Cabra, Monte – 72-73 b 3
Cabrera, Isla – 34-35 J 9
Cabriel 34-35 G 9
Cabrillo, Point – 76-77 AB 6
Cabul = Kābul 44-45 K 4
Cabullona 76-77 J 10
Çaçador 80 F 3
Čačak 36-37 J 4
Caçapava do Sul 80 F 4
Càccia, Capo – 36-37 BC 5
Cacequi 80 F 3
Cáceres [BR] 78-79 H 8
Cáceres [CO] 78-79 D 3
Cáceres [E] 34-35 D 9
Cachar [TJ] 48-49 M 3
Cachegar = Qāshqär 48-49 CD 4
Cachemire = Kashmir 44-45 LM 4
Cache Peak 76-77 G 4
Cacheu 60-61 A 6
Cachi 80 C 3
Cachi, Nevado de – 80 C 2
Cachimbo, Serra do – 78-79 HJ 6
Cachimo 64-65 F 4
Cachoeira [BR ↓ Feira de Santana] 78-79 M 7
Cachoeira do Sul 80 F 3-4
Cachoeiro de Itapemirim 78-79 LM 9
Cachos, Punta – 80 B 3
Caçiporé, Cabo – 78-79 JK 4
Caçiporé, Rio – 78-79 J 4
Çaçmak 46-47 F 4
Cacolo 64-65 E 4-5
Caconda 64-65 DE 5
Cactus Range 76-77 E 7
Caculé 78-79 L 7
Cacuso 64-65 E 4
Cadale 60-61 b 3
Čadan 42-43 R 7
Cadcadde, Raas – 60-61 b 1
Cadena Costera = Coast Mountains, Coast Range 70-71 K 6-M 9
Cadibarrawirracanna, Lake – 58 AB 2
Cádiz 34-35 D 10
Cadiz, CA 76-77 F 8
Cádiz, Golfo de – 34-35 D 10
Čadobec [SU, ~] 42-43 S 6
Čadobec [SU, ●] 42-43 S 6
Čadyr-Lunga 36-37 N 2
Caen 34-35 G 4
Caernarfon 32 D 5
Caesarea 46-47 F 6
Caesarea = Kayseri 44-45 D 3
Caesarea Philippi = Bāniyās 46-47 FG 6
Caetité 78-79 L 7
Cafayate 80 C 3
Cafta = Kafta 60-61 M 6
Cagaan Cherem = Wanli Changcheng 48-49 K 4
Cagaan Cherem = Wanli Changcheng 48-49 K 4
Cagayan de Oro 52-53 HJ 5
Cagayan Islands 52-53 H 5
Cagayan Sulu Island 52-53 GH 5
Čagda 42-43 Z 6
Caggan nuur 48-49 FG 2
Čagil 38-39 L 7
Càgliari 36-37 C 6
Càgliari, Golfo di – 36-37 C 6
Čagoda 42-43 EF 6
Çağrankaya = İkizdere 46-47 J 2
Cag Sum = Dzag 48-49 H 2
Caguán, Río – 78-79 E 4
Caguas 72-73 N 8
Cahama 64-65 DE 6
Cahirciveen 32 AB 6
Cahors 34-35 H 6
Cahuapanas 78-79 D 6
Cahuilla Indian Reservation 76-77 E 9
Cahungula = Caungula 64-65 E 4
Caia [Moçambique] 64-65 J 6
Caiabis, Serra dos – 78-79 H 7
Caiambé 78-79 FG 5
Cai Ban, Đao – 52-53 E 2
Caibarién 72-73 L 7
Caicara [YV] 78-79 F 3
Caicos Islands 72-73 M 7
Caicos Passage 72-73 M 7
Caimito 72-73 b 3
Caimito, Río – 72-73 b 3
Cairari 78-79 K 5
Caird Land 24 B 33-34
Caire, le – = Al-Qāhirah 60-61 KL 2
Cairns 56-57 J 3
Cairo, IL 72-73 J 4
Cairo = Al-Qāhira 60-61 KL 2
Cairo, El – = Al-Qāhira 60-61 KL 2
Caiundo 64-65 E 6
Cajabamba 78-79 D 6
Cajamarca [PE, ●] 78-79 D 6
Cajapió 78-79 KL 5
Cajatambo 78-79 D 7
Cajdam nuur 48-49 M 2
Cajdamyn nuur, Ich – 48-49 GH 4
Cajdamyn nuur, Ich – 48-49 GH 4
Čajek 44-45 L 2
Cajon Pass 76-77 E 8
Cajuás, Ponta dos – 78-79 M 5
Çakıralan 46-47 F 2
Çal = Demirciköy 46-47 C 3
Calabar 60-61 F 7-8
Calabogie 74-75 E 2
Calabozo 78-79 F 3
Calabre = Calàbria 36-37 FG 6
Calàbria 36-37 FG 6
Calada, CA 76-77 F 8
Calafat 36-37 K 3-4
Calafate 80 B 8
Calagua Islands 52-53 H 4
Calahari = Kalahari Desert 64-65 EF 7
Calahorra 34-35 G 7
Calais 34-35 H 3
Calais, Pas de – 34-35 HJ 3
Calais, Pas de – 34-35 HJ 3
Calalaste, Sierra de – 80 C 2-3
Calama [BR] 78-79 G 6
Calama [RCH] 80 C 2
Calamar [CO ↘ Bogotá] 78-79 E 4
Calamian Group 52-53 G 4
Calang 52-53 C 6
Calapan 52-53 H 4
Călăraşi 36-37 M 3
Calatayud 34-35 G 8
Calate = Qalāt 44-45 K 5
Căläţele 36-37 K 2
Calayan Island 52-53 H 3
Calbayog 52-53 HJ 4
Calca 78-79 E 7
Calcanhar, Ponta do – 78-79 M 6-N 5
Calçoene 78-79 J 4
Calcuta = Calcutta 44-45 O 6
Calcutta 44-45 O 6
Caldas da Rainha 34-35 C 9
Caldera 80 B 3
Çaldıran 46-47 K 3
Caldwell, ID 76-77 E 4
Caldwell, OH 74-75 C 5
Calecute = Calicut 44-45 LM 8
Caledon 64-65 EF 9
Caledon Bay 56-57 G 2
Caledonia [CDN, Ontario] 74-75 D 3
Caledonian Canal 32 D 3
Caledonrivier 64-65 G 8-9
Caleta de Vique 72-73 b 3
Caleta Olivia 80 C 7
Caleufú 80 D 5
Calexico, CA 76-77 F 9
Çalgan 46-47 H 4
Calgary 70-71 O 7
Calhoun, TN 74-75 A 7
Calhoun Falls, SC 74-75 B 7
Cali 78-79 D 4
Calicut 44-45 LM 8
Caliente, CA 76-77 D 8
Caliente, NV 72-73 CD 4
California [USA] 72-73 B 3-C 5
California, Golfo de – 72-73 D 5-E 7
California, Gulf of – 72-73 D 5-E 7
Californie = California 72-73 B 3-C 5
Californie, Golfe de – 72-73 D 5-E 7
Californië, Golf van – 72-73 D 5-E 7
Căliman, Munţii – 36-37 L 2
Calimere, Point – 44-45 MN 8
Călineşti 36-37 L 3
Calingasta 80 BC 4
Calipatria, CA 76-77 F 9
Calispell Peak 76-77 E 1
Calistoga, CA 76-77 B 6
Calkini 72-73 H 7
Callabonna, Lake – 56-57 G 5
Callabonna Creek 58 E 2
Callahan, FL 74-75 c 1
Callahan, Mount – 76-77 E 6
Callao 78-79 D 7
Calmucos, República Autónoma de los – 38-39 HJ 6
Caloosahatchee River 74-75 c 3
Caltagirone 36-37 F 7
Caltanissetta 36-37 EF 7
Calulo 64-65 DE 4-5
Caluula 60-61 c 1
Calva, AZ 76-77 HJ 9
Calvados, Côte du – 34-35 G 4
Calvi 36-37 C 4
Calvinia 64-65 EF 9
Calypso, Fosse de la – 28-29 N 8
Calypso, Sima del – 28-29 N 8
Calypsodiep 28-29 N 8
Camabatela 64-65 E 4
Camacupa 64-65 E 5
Camagüey 72-73 L 7
Camagüey, Archipiélago de – 72-73 L 7
Çamalan 46-47 F 4
Camaná 78-79 E 8
Camapuã 78-79 J 8
Camapuã, Sertão de – 78-79 J 8-9
Camaquã 80 F 4
Çamardı 46-47 F 4
Camargo [BOL] 78-79 FG 9
Camargo [MEX] 72-73 E 6
Camargue 34-35 K 7
Camarillo, CA 76-77 D 8
Camariñas 34-35 C 7
Camariñas 34-35 C 7
Camarón [PA] 72-73 b 3
Camarones 80 CD 6
Camas, ID 76-77 G 3
Camas, WA 76-77 B 3
Camas Creek 76-77 GH 3
Camataquí = Villa Abecia 78-79 FG 9
Ca Mau 52-53 DE 5
Ca Mau, Mui – = Mui Bai Bung 52-53 D 5
Cambaia = Khambhat 44-45 L 6
Cambay = Khambhat 44-45 L 6
Cambay, Gulf of – 44-45 L 6
Cambing = Pulau Atauro 52-53 J 8
Cambodja 52-53 DE 4
Camborne 32 D 6
Camboya 52-53 DE 4
Cambrai 34-35 J 3
Cambria, CA 76-77 C 8
Cambrian Mountains 32 D 5-E 6
Cambridge [CDN] 74-75 CD 3
Cambridge [GB] 32 FG 5
Cambridge, ID 76-77 E 3
Cambridge, MA 72-73 NM 3
Cambridge, MD 74-75 E 5
Cambridge, OH 74-75 BC 4
Cambridge Bay 70-71 PQ 4
Cambridge City, OH 74-75 A 5
Cambridge Gulf 56-57 E 2-3
Camden 58 K 5
Camden, AR 72-73 H 5
Camden, ME 74-75 J 2
Camden, NJ 72-73 LM 4
Camden, SC 74-75 C 7
Cameia = Lumeje 64-65 F 5
Çameli 46-47 C 4
Camembert 34-35 H 4
Cameron, AZ 76-77 H 8
Cameron, WV 74-75 C 5
Cameron, Tanah Tinggi – 52-53 D 6
Cameroon 60-61 G 7-8
Camerota 36-37 F 5-6
Cameroun 60-61 G 7-8
Cameroun, Mont – 60-61 F 8
Cameroun Occidental 60-61 FG 7
Cameroun Oriental 60-61 G 7
Camerún 60-61 G 7-8
Cametá 78-79 JK 5
Camiguin Island [RP, Babuyan Channel] 52-53 H 3
Camiguin Island [RP, Mindanao Sea] 52-53 H 5
Camiling 52-53 GH 3
Camino, CA 76-77 C 6
Caminreal 34-35 G 8
Camira = Camiri 78-79 G 9
Camiranga 78-79 K 5
Camiri 78-79 G 9
Camissombo 64-65 EF 4
Çamlıbel 46-47 G 2
Çamlıbel Dağları 46-47 G 3
Çamlıdere [TR, Ankara] 46-47 E 2
çamlıdere [TR, Sanlı Urfa] 46-47 H 4
Camocim 78-79 L 5
Camooweal 56-57 G 3
Camorta Island 44-45 P 9
Campagna 36-37 F 5
Campana, Isla – 80 A 7
Campanario, Cerro – 80 BC 5
Campania 36-37 F 5
Campanie = Campania 36-37 F 5
Campanquiz, Cerros de – 78-79 D 5-6
Campbell, OH 74-75 C 4
Campbellford 74-75 E 2
Campbell Island 24 D 17
Campbell River 70-71 L 7
Campbellton 70-71 X 8
Campbell Town 56-57 J 8
Campeche 72-73 H 8
Campeche, Bahía de – 72-73 GH 7
Campeche, Banc – 72-73 HJ 7
Campeche Bank 72-73 HJ 7
Campeche, Banco de – 72-73 HJ 7
Camperdown [AUS] 58 F 7
Campidano 36-37 C 6
Campiña, La – 34-35 E 10
Campiña del Henares, La – 34-35 F 8
Campina Grande [BR, Amapá] 78-79 MN 6
Campinas 78-79 K 9
Campiña, La – 34-35 E 10
Campiña del Henares, La – 34-35 F 8
Campli 36-37 E 4
Camp Nelson, CA 76-77 D 7
Campo, CA 76-77 E 9
Campo [RFC, ~] 60-61 G 8
Campo [RFC, ●] 60-61 F 8
Campobasso 36-37 F 5
Campo Belo 78-79 KL 9
Campo de Diauarum 78-79 J 7
Campo Duran 80 D 2
Campo Grande [BR] 78-79 J 9
Campo Grande [RA] 80 EF 3
Campo Indian Reservation 76-77 E 9
Campo Maior 34-35 D 9
Campo Maior [BR] 78-79 L 5
Campos [BR, ≅] 78-79 L 7
Campos [BR, ●] 78-79 L 9
Campos, Tierra de – 34-35 E 7-8
Campos Altos [BR, Mato Grosso] 78-79 HJ 9
Campuchea 52-53 DE 4
Camp Verde, AZ 76-77 H 8
Camrose 70-71 O 7
Camulenda 64-65 E 4
Çan [TR, Çanakkale] 46-47 B 2
Çan [TR, Elâzığ] 46-47 J 3
Canada 70-71 M 5-W 7
Canadá 70-71 M 5-W 7
Canada Basin 19 AB 32-33
Cañada de Gómez 80 D 4
Canadees Bekken 19 AB 32-33
Canadian Channel = Jacques Cartier Passage 70-71 Y 7-8
Canadian Channel = Jacques Cartier Passage 70-71 Y 7-8
Canadian National Railways 70-71 PQ 7
Canadian Pacific Railway 70-71 OP 7
Canadian River 72-73 F 4
Çanakkale 44-45 B 2
Çanakkale Boğazı 44-45 B 2-3
Canala 56-57 N 4
Canal du Midi 34-35 HJ 7
Canal Número 11 80 E 5
Canal Viejo de Bahama 72-73 L 7
Canandaigua, NY 74-75 E 3
Cananea 72-73 DE 5
Cananor = Cannanore 44-45 LM 8
Cañar [EC, ●] 78-79 D 5
Canarias, Cuenca de las – 22-23 HJ 4
Canárias, Ilha das – 78-79 L 5
Canarias, Islas – 60-61 A 3
Canarias, Umbral de las – 22-23 HJ 4
Canaries, Bassin des – 22-23 HJ 4
Canaries, Seuil des – 22-23 HJ 4
Canarisch Bekken 22-23 HJ 4
Canarische Drempel 22-23 HJ 4
Canarreos, Archipiélago de los – 72-73 K 7
Canary Basin 22-23 HJ 4
Canary Rise 22-23 HJ 4
Canastota, NY 74-75 EF 3
Canastra, Serra da – [BR, Minas Gerais] 78-79 K 9
Canaveral, FL 74-75 c 2
Canaveral, Cape – 72-73 KL 6
Canavieiras 78-79 M 8
Canbelego 58 H 3
Canberra 56-57 J 7
Canby, CA 76-77 C 5
Canby, OR 76-77 B 3
Canchenjunga = Gangchhendsönga 44-45 O 5
Çandarlı Körfezi 46-47 B 3
Candi = Maha Nuwara 44-45 N 9
Cândido Mendes 78-79 KL 5
Çandili Tepe 46-47 G 3
Çandır 46-47 E 2
Candón 52-53 GH 3
Canelos 78-79 D 5
Cañete [PE] 78-79 D 7
Cangallo [PE] 78-79 DE 7
Cangamba 64-65 E 5
Cangas 34-35 C 7
Cangas de Narcea 34-35 D 7
Cangombe 64-65 E 5
Canguaretama 78-79 MN 6
Cangxien = Cangzhou 48-49 M 4
Cangzhou 48-49 M 4
Caniapiscau, Rivière – 70-71 X 6
Canicatti 36-37 E 7
Canigou, Mont – 34-35 J 7
Canik Dağları 46-47 G 2
Canindé [BR, Ceará] 78-79 M 5
Canisteo, NY 74-75 E 3
Çankırı 44-45 C 2
Cannae 36-37 G 5
Cannanore 44-45 LM 8
Cannes 34-35 L 7
Canning Desert 56-57 D 3
Cann River 58 J 6
Cano = Kano 60-61 F 6
Canoas 80 F 3
Canobie 56-57 H 3
Canon City, CO 72-73 EF 4
Canopus 58 E 4
Caño Quebrado, Río – [PA, Colón] 72-73 a 2
Caño Quebrado, Río – [PA, Panamá] 72-73 b 2-3
Canora 70-71 Q 7
Canowindra 58 J 4
Canso 70-71 Y 8
Canso, Strait of – 70-71 YZ 8
Cansu = Gansu 48-49 G 3-J 4
Canta 78-79 D 7
Cantábrica, Cordillera – 34-35 D-F 7
Cantal 34-35 J 6
Cantal, Plomb du – 34-35 J 6
Cantaura 78-79 G 3
Canterbury 32 G 7
Canterbury Bight 56-57 0 8
Cân Tho' 52-53 E 5
Cantil, CA 76-77 DE 8
Cantilan 52-53 J 5
Cantin, Cap – = Rā's al-Baddūzah 60-61 BC 2
Canto do Buriti 78-79 L 6
Canton, GA 74-75 A 7
Canton, MA 74-75 H 3
Canton, NC 74-75 B 7
Canton, NY 74-75 F 2
Canton, OH 72-73 K 3
Canton, PA 74-75 E 4
Canton = Guangzhou 48-49 LM 7
Cantù 36-37 C 3
Canumã 78-79 H 5
Canumã, Rio – = Rio Sucunduri 78-79 H 6
Canuri = Kanouri 60-61 G 6
Canutama 78-79 G 6
Čany, ozero – 42-43 O 7
Canyon, WY 76-77 H 3
Canyon City, OR 76-77 D 3
Canyon de Chelly National Monument 76-77 J 7-8
Canyon de Chelly National Monument 76-77 J 7-8
Canyon Ferry Dam 76-77 GH 2

164 Butsh

Centreville, MD 74-75 EF 5
Čepca 38-39 K 4
Ceram = Seram 52-53 JK 7
Ceram Sea 52-53 JK 7
Cerbatana, Serranía de la –
 78-79 F 3
Cerbère 34-35 J 7
Cercen = Chärchän 48-49 F 4
Cerdeña = Sardegna
 36-37 C 5
Čerdyn 38-39 L 3
Čeremchovo 42-43 T 7
Čerepanovo 42-43 P 7
Čerepovec 42-43 F 6
Céres [BR] 78-79 JK 8
Ceres [ZA] 64-65 E 9
Ceres, CA 76-77 C 7
Čerevkovo 38-39 J 3
Cerf Island 64-65 M 4
Cerignola 36-37 F 5
Čerkassy 38-39 F 6
Čerkess 46-47 E 2
Čerkessk 38-39 H 7
Čerlak 42-43 N 7
Čermik 46-47 H 3
Čern'achovsk 33 K 1
Černatica 36-37 L 4-5
Černigov 38-39 F 6
Černigovka 42-43 Z 9
Černogorsk 42-43 R 7
Černomorskoje 36-37 OP 3
Černorečje = Dzeržinsk
 42-43 GH 6
Černovskije Kopi, Čita-
 42-43 V 7
Černovskoje 38-39 J 4
Černovcy 38-39 DE 6
Černyševskij 42-43 V 5
Černyševskoje 33 KL 1
Cerralvo, Isla – 72-73 E 7
Cerrigaabo 60-61 b 1
Cerritos 72-73 FG 7
Cerro, El – 79-79 D 7
Cerro Colorado [MEX]
 76-77 F 10
Cerro de Pasco 78-79 D 7
Čerskij 42-43 f 4
Čerskogo, chrebet –
 42-43 V 7
Certaldo 36-37 D 4
Čertež 38-39 L 4
Cervati, Monte – 36-37 F 5
Červen br'ag 36-37 KL 4
Cervera 34-35 H 8
Cervèteri 36-37 E 4
Cèrvia 36-37 E 3
Cesareia = Caesarea 46-47 F 6
Cesena 36-37 DE 3
Cēsis 30-31 L 9
Česká Třebová 33 G 4
České Budějovice 33 G 4
České země 33 F-H 4
Českomoravská vrchovina
 33 GH 4
Çeşme 46-47 B 3
Cessford 70-71 O 7
Cessnock-Bellbird 56-57 K 6
Cestos River 60-61 C 7
Cetinje 36-37 H 4
Çetinkaya 46-47 GH 3
Cetraro 36-37 F 6
Ceuta 60-61 CD 1
Cevennes 34-35 JK 6
Cevizlik = Maçka 46-47 H 2
Ceyhan 46-47 FG 4
Ceyhan Nehri 46-47 G 4
Ceylan = Sri Lanka 44-45 N 9
Ceylanpınar 46-47 HJ 4

Chaaltyn gol 48-49 GH 4
Cha-am [T] 52-53 CD 4
Chaba 48-49 F 2
Chabarovo 42-43 L 4
Chabarovsk 42-43 a 8
Chablis 34-35 J 5
Chachapoyas 78-79 D 6
Chāchārān 72-73 K 4
Chachoengsao 52-53 D 4
Chačmas 38-39 J 7
Chaco 80 D 3
Chaco Austral 80 DE 3
Chaco Boreal 80 DE 2
Chaco Central 80 DE 2-E 3
Chaco River 76-77 J 7
Chadasan 48-49 J 2
Chadzaar 48-49 G 4
Chadchal = Chatgal
 48-49 HJ 1
Chadum 64-65 F 6
Chaeryŏng 50-51 EF 3
Chagan nuur 48-49 G 2
Chagang-do 50-51 EF 2

Chagos 22-23 N 6
Chagres [PA, ~] 72-73 ab 2
Chagres [PA, ●] 72-73 b 2
Chagres, Brazo del –
 72-73 b 2
Chagres, Río – 72-73 bc 2
Chagres Arm – Brazo del
 Chagres 72-73 b 2
Chahär Burjak 44-45 J 4
Chähär Burjak = Chahär
 Burjak 44-45 J 4
Chahär Mahäl-e Bakhteyärï =
 3 ◁ 44-45 G 4
Chahbâ = Shahbä' 46-47 G 6
Chäh Bähär = Bandar-e Chäh
 Bahär 44-45 HJ 5
Ch'aho 50-51 G 2
Chaidamu Pendi = Tsaidam
 48-49 GH 4
Ch'ail-bong 50-51 F 2
Chai Nat 52-53 D 3
Chaîne Pontique 44-45 C-E 2
Chaîne Rocheuse = Rocky
 Mountains 70-71 L 5-P 9
Chaiya 52-53 C 5
Chajarí 80 E 4
Chajdag gol 48-49 EF 3
Chajlar 48-49 M 2
Chajlar = Hailar 48-49 M 2
Chajlar gol = Hailar He
 48-49 MN 2
Chajpudyrskaja guba
 38-39 LM 2
Chajrchan 48-49 J 2
Chajr'uzovo 42-43 e 6
Chaka Nor – Chöch nuur
 48-49 H 4
Chake Chake 63 DE 4
Chäl = Shäl 46-47 N 5
Chala 78-79 E 8
Chalabesa 63 B 5
Cha-lan-tun – Yalu 48-49 N 2
Chalbi Desert 63 D 2
Chalchyn gol 48-49 M 2
Chaleur Bay 70-71 XY 8
Chalhuanca 78-79 E 7
Chálkē 36-37 M 7
Chalkidikḗ 36-37 K 3
Chalkís 36-37 K 4
Challapata 78-79 F 8
Challis, ID 76-77 F 3
Chal'mer-Ju 42-43 L 4
Chalmer-Sede = Tazovskij
 42-43 OP 4
Châlons-sur-Marne 34-35 JK 4
Chalon-sur-Saône 34-35 K 5
Chalosse 34-35 G 7
Chalturin 42-43 H 6
Cham 33 F 4
Chaman 44-45 K 4
Chamba [EAT] 63 D 5
Chamba [IND] 44-45 M 4
Chambal [IND ◁ Kali Sindh]
 44-45 M 5-6
Chambal [IND ◁ Yamuna]
 44-45 M 5-6
Chamberlain Lake 74-75 J 1
Chambersburg, PA
 74-75 DE 4-5
Chambéry 34-35 K 6
Chambeshi 64-65 H 5
Chamchamäl 46-47 L 5
Chamdo = Chhamdo
 48-49 H 5
Chami Choto = Hami
 48-49 G 3
Chamo, Lake – = Tyamo
 60-61 M 7
Champa [IND] 44-45 N 6
Champa [SU] 42-43 X 5
Champagne 34-35 J 5-K 4
Champagny Islands 56-57 D 3
Champaign, IL 72-73 J 3-4
Champāran = Motihari
 44-45 NO 5
Champasak 52-53 DE 4
Champlain, Lake – 72-73 LM 3
Champotón 72-73 H 8
Chanāb = Chenab 44-45 M 4
Chañar 80 C 3
Chañaral [RCH ↘ Copiapó]
 80 B 3
Chañaral, Isla – 80 B 3
Chan Bogd 48-49 K 3
Chancay 78-79 D 7
Chanch 48-49 J 1
Chan-chiang = Zhanjiang
 48-49 L 7
Chanchoengsao 52-53 D 4
Chānda = Chandrapur
 44-45 M 7
Chandalar River 70-71 G 4
Chandeleur Islands 72-73 J 6
Chandigarh 44-45 LM 4

Chandler 70-71 Y 8
Chandler, AZ 76-77 H 9
Chandlers Falls 63 D 2
Chandrapur 44-45 M 7
Chandyga 42-43 a 5
Chang, Ko – [T → Krung
 Thep] 52-53 D 4
Changai = Shanghai 48-49 N 5
Changaj 48-49 H 2
Changajn nuruu 48-49 HJ 2
Changane, Rio – 64-65 H 7
Changara 64-65 H 6
Changbai 50-51 FG 3
Changbai Shan 48-49 O 3
Chang-chia-k'ou =
 Zhangjiakou 48-49 L 3
Changchih = Changzhi
 48-49 L 4
Ch'ang-chih = Changzhi
 48-49 L 4
Changchun 48-49 NO 3
Changde 48-49 L 6
Changdu = Chhamdo
 48-49 H 5
Chang-hai = Shanghai
 48-49 N 5
Changhang 50-51 F 4-5
Changhowŏn 50-51 F 4
Ch'ang-hsing Tao –
 Changxing Dao 50-51 C 3
Changhŭng 50-51 F 5
Changhŭng-ni 50-51 FG 2
Chang Jiang [TJ, ~ ◁ Dong
 Hai] 48-49 K 5-6
Changji Huizu Zizhizhou
 48-49 FG 3
Changjin 50-51 F 2
Changjin-gang 50-51 F 2
Changjin-ho 50-51 F 2
Changjŏn 50-51 G 3
Changkiakow = Zhangjiakou
 48-49 L 3
Chang-kuang-ts'ai Ling =
 Zhangguangcai Ling
 48-49 O 2-3
Changnim-ni 50-51 F 3
Ch'angnyŏng 50-51 G 5
Ch'ang-pai = Changbai
 50-51 FG 2
Ch'ang-pai Shan = Changbai
 Shan 48-49 O 3
Chang-san-ying =
 Zhangsanying 50-51 AB 2
Changsha 48-49 L 6
Changshu 48-49 N 5
Ch'angsŏng = Chŏngsŏng
 50-51 GH 1
Chang Tang = Jang Thang
 48-49 G-J 5
Ch'ang-tê = Anyang
 48-49 LM 4
Ch'ang-tê = Changde
 48-49 L 6
Changteh = Changde
 48-49 L 6
Changting 48-49 M 6
Ch'ang-tu = Chhamdo
 48-49 H 5
Changtutsung = Chhamdo
 48-49 H 5
Ch'angwŏn 50-51 G 5
Changxing Dao [TJ, Liaodong
 Wan] 50-51 C 3
Changyeh = Zhangye
 48-49 J 4
Changyŏn 50-51 NO 4
Changzhi 48-49 L 4
Changzhou 48-49 M 5
Chaniá 36-37 KL 8
Chanión, Kólpos – 36-37 KL 8
Chanka, ozero – 42-43 Z 9
Chankiang = Zhanjiang
 48-49 L 7
Channäb = Chenab 44-45 M 4
Channel Islands 32 E 7
Channel Islands [USA]
 76-77 CD 9
Channel Islands National
 Monument = Anacapa
 Island, Santa Barbara Island
 76-77 D 9
Channel-Port-aux-Basques
 70-71 Z 8
Chanovej 38-39 M 2
Chansi = Shanxi 48-49 L 4
Chantaburi = Chanthaburi
 52-53 D 4
Chantada 34-35 CD 7
Chantajka 42-43 PQ 4
Chantajskoje, ozero –
 42-43 QR 4
Chanten en Mansen, Nationaal
 Gebied der – 42-43 L-P 5
Chan Tengri, pik – 44-45 MN 2
Chanthaburi 52-53 D 4

Chantong = Shandong
 48-49 M 4
Chantrey Inlet 70-71 RS 4
Chanty-Mansijsk 42-43 M 5
Chao'an 48-49 M 7
Chao Hu 48-49 M 5
Chao Phraya, Mae Nam –
 52-53 CD 3-4
Chaor He 48-49 N 2
Chaochow = Chao'an
 48-49 M 7
Chaotung = Zhaotong
 48-49 J 6
Chao-t'ung = Zhaotong
 48-49 J 6
Chaoyang [TJ, Guangdong]
 48-49 M 7
Chaoyang [TJ, Liaoning]
 48-49 MN 3
Ch'ao-yang-chên = Huinan
 48-49 O 3
Chapada da Veadeiros, Parque
 Nacional dos – 78-79 K 7
Chapada Diamantina 78-79 L 7
Chapadinha 78-79 L 5
Chapala, Lago de – 72-73 F 7
Chapčeranga 42-43 V 8
Chapel Hill, NC 74-75 D 7
Chapra 44-45 N 5
Chapčeranga 42-43 V 8
Chaqui 78-79 F 8
Châ'r, Jebel – = Jabal Shā'r
 46-47 GH 5
Charadai 80 E 3
Charagua 78-79 G 8
Charagua, Cordillera de –
 78-79 G 8-9
Charaña 78-79 F 8
Charbin = Harbin 48-49 O 2
Chär Burjak 44-45 J 4
Char Chorin 48-49 J 2
Char Choto 48-49 J 3
Charcas 72-73 F 7
Chärchän 48-49 F 3
Chärchän Darya 48-49 F 4
Charcot, Île – 24 C 29
Chardávol 46-47 M 6
Chardon, OH 74-75 C 4
Charente 34-35 G 5
Char Gov' 48-49 GH 3
Chari 60-61 H 6
Chärïkär 44-45 K 3-4
Char Irčis 48-49 F 2
Charitona Lapteva, bereg –
 42-43 Q 3-R 2
Charity 78-79 H 3
Char'kov 38-39 G 5-6
Charleroi 34-35 K 3
Charles, Cape – 72-73 LM 4
Charles Island 72-73 VW 5
Charleston, SC 72-73 KL 5
Charleston, WV 72-73 K 4
Charleston Peak 76-77 F 7
Charlestown [Saint Kitts und
 Nevis] 72-73 O 8
Charlesville 64-65 F 4
Charleville [AUS] 56-57 J 5
Charleville-Mézières 34-35 K 4
Charlotte, NC 72-73 KL 4-5
Charlotte Amalie 72-73 O 8
Charlotte Harbor 72-73 K 6
Charlottenberg 30-31 E 8
Charlottesville, VA 72-73 L 4
Charlottetown = Roseau
 72-73 O 8
Charlovka 38-39 G 2
Charlton 58 F 6
Charlton Island 70-71 UV 7
Char Narijn uul 48-49 K 3
Char nuur [Mongolia] 48-49 G 2
Char nuur [TJ] 48-49 H 4
Charolais, Monts du –
 34-35 K 5
Charovsk 42-43 G 6
Charqï, Jebel ech- = Jabal ar-
 Ruwäq 46-47 G 5-6
Charqiliq 48-49 F 4
Charsov 42-43 G 6
Charters Towers 56-57 J 3-4
Chartres 34-35 H 5
Char us nuur 48-49 G 2
Chasan 50-51 H 1
Chascomús 80 E 5
Chase City, VA 74-75 D 6
Chasŏng 50-51 F 2
Chassahowitzka Bay 74-75 b 2
Chašuri 38-39 H 7
Chatanga 42-43 TU 3
Chatan gol 48-49 K 3
Chatangskij zaliv 42-43 UV 3
Château-du-Loir 34-35 H 5
Châteaudun 34-35 H 4
Châteaulin 34-35 EF 4
Châteauroux 34-35 H 5

Château-Thierry 34-35 J 4
Châtellerault 34-35 H 5
Chatgal 48-49 HJ 1
Chatham [CDN, New
 Brunswick] 70-71 XY 8
Chatham [CDN, Ontario]
 70-71 U 9
Chatham, NY 74-75 G 3
Chatham, VA 74-75 D 6
Chatham = Isla San Cristóbal
 78-79 B 5
Chatham, Îles – 56-57 Q 8
Chatham, Isla – 80 B 8
Chatham Islands 56-57 Q 8
Chatham Strait 70-71 K 6
Châtillon 36-37 B 3
Châtillon-sur-Seine 34-35 K 5
Chatsworth 74-75 C 2
Chattahoochee River
 72-73 JK 5
Chattanooga, TN 72-73 J 4
Chattarpur = Chhatarpur
 44-45 M 6
Chaumont 34-35 K 4
Chaūn-do 50-51 EF 5
Châu Phu 52-53 E 4
Chautauqua Lake 74-75 D 3
Chaux-de-Fonds, La – 33 C 5
Chavast 44-45 K 2
Chaves 34-35 D 8
Chaves [BR] 78-79 K 5
Chaves, Isla – = Isla Santa
 Cruz 78-79 AB 5
Chavïb Deh 46-47 N 7
Chaviva 78-79 E 4
Chaya – Drayä 48-49 H 5
Ch'a-yü = Dsayul 48-49 H 6
Chazón 80 D 4
Cheat Mountain 74-75 CD 5
Cheat River 74-75 D 5
Cheb 33 F 3
Chebâyesh, Al- = Al-Jaza'ir
 46-47 M 7
Chebir, Uáu el – = Wâdï Bay
 al-Kabïr 60-61 GH 2
Cheboygan, MI 72-73 K 2
Chech, Erg – = 'Irq ash-
 Shaykh 60-61 D 3-4
Chechaouène = Shifshäwn
 60-61 CD 1
Checheno-Ingush Autonomous
 Republic = 5 ◁ 38-39 J 7
Chech'on 50-51 FG 4
Chedâdî, El- = Ash-Shiddädï
 46-47 J 4
Cheduba = Ash-Shaqqät
 60-61 C 3
Chegutu 64-65 GH 6
Cheektowaga, NY 74-75 DE 3
Cheepie 56-57 HJ 5
Chefoo = Yantai 48-49 N 4
Chefu = Yantai 48-49 N 4
Chegga = Ash-Shaqqät
 60-61 C 3
Chehalis, WA 76-77 B 2
Chehalis River 76-77 B 2
Chehel-e Chashmeh, Kühhä-ye
 – 46-47 M 5
Cheju 48-49 O 5
Cheju-do 48-49 NO 5
Cheju-haehyŏp 48-49 O 5
Chekiang = Zhejiang
 48-49 MN 6
Chekkä, Râs – = Rä's ash-
 Shikk'ah 46-47 F 5
Chela, Serra da – 64-65 D 6
Chelan, WA 76-77 CD 2
Chelan, Lake – 76-77 C 1
Chélia, Djebel = Jabal
 Shïlyah 60-61 F 1
Chelleh Khäneh, Küh-e –
 46-47 N 4
Chełm 33 L 3
Chełmińskre, Pojezierze –
 33 J 2
Chełmża 33 J 2
Chelsea, VT 74-75 G 2-3
Cheltenham 32 EF 6
Chelyuskin, Cape – = mys
 Čel'uskin 42-43 UV 2
Chemawa, OR 76-77 B 3
Chemba 64-65 H 6
Chemehuevi Valley Indian
 Reservation 76-77 F 8

Chemnitz 33 F 3
Chemulpo = Inch'ŏn
 48-49 O 4
Chemult, OR 76-77 C 4
Chenab 44-45 M 4
Ch'ên-ch'i = Chenxi 48-49 L 6
Chên-chiang = Zhenjiang
 48-49 M 5
Ch'ên-chou = Yuanling
 48-49 L 6
Cheney, WA 76-77 E 2
Chên-fan = Minqin 48-49 J 4
Ch'êng-chiang = Chengjiang
 48-49 J 7
Chengde 48-49 M 3
Chengdu 48-49 J 5
Chengjiang 48-49 J 7
Chengkiang = Chengjiang
 48-49 J 7
Chengkou 48-49 K 5
Chengmai 48-49 KL 8
Chengteh = Chengde
 48-49 M 3
Chengtu = Chengdu 48-49 J 5
Cheng-Xian = Sheng Xian
 48-49 N 6
Chengzitan 50-51 D 3
Chên-hsi = Bar Köl 48-49 G 3
Chenkiang = Zhenjiang
 48-49 M 5
Chentiin nuruu 48-49 K 2
Chentij = 15 ◁ 48-49 L 2
Chenxi 48-49 L 6
Chen Xian 48-49 L 6
Chenyang = Shenyang
 48-49 NO 3
Chenyuan = Zhenyuan [TJ,
 Yunnan] 48-49 J 7
Chên-yüan = Zhenyuan [TJ,
 Yunnan] 48-49 J 7
Chepes 80 C 4
Cher 34-35 J 5
Cherangani 63 C 2
Cheraw, SC 74-75 CD 7
Cherbourg 34-35 G 4
Cherchen = Chärchän
 48-49 F 4
Cheren = Keren 60-61 M 5
Chergui, Chott ech – = Ash-
 Shatt ash-Sharqï 60-61 DE 2
Cherlen gol 48-49 KL 2
Cherlen gol = Herlen He
 48-49 M 2
Cherrapunj = Cherrapunjee
 44-45 P 5
Cherrapunjee 44-45 P 5
Cherry 56-57 N 2
Cherry Creek, NV 76-77 F 6
Cherson 38-39 F 6
Chesapeake, VA 72-73 LM 4
Chesapeake Bay 72-73 L 4
Cheshire, OR 76-77 B 3
Chesley 74-75 C 2
Chester 32 E 5
Chester, CA 76-77 C 5
Chester, MT 76-77 H 1
Chester, PA 74-75 F 5
Chester, SC 74-75 C 7
Chesterfield 32 F 5
Chesterfield, Île – 64-65 K 6
Chesterfield, Îles – 56-57 L 3
Chesterfield Inlet [CDN, ∪]
 70-71 ST 5
Chesterfield Inlet [CDN, ●]
 70-71 ST 5
Chestertown, MD 74-75 EF 5
Chesuncook Lake 74-75 HJ 1-2
Cheta [SU, ~] 42-43 S 3
Cheta [SU, ●] 42-43 S 3
Chetlat Island 44-45 L 8
Chetumal 72-73 J 8
Chetumal, Bahía de –
 72-73 J 8
Cheviot, The – 32 EF 4
Cheviot Hills 32 E 4
Chewelah, WA 76-77 DE 1
Cheyenne, WY 72-73 F 3
Cheyenne River 72-73 F 3
Chhamdo 48-49 H 5
Chhaprä = Chapra 44-45 N 5
Chhärïkär = Chärïkär
 44-45 K 3-4
Chhatarpur [IND, Madhya
 Pradesh] 44-45 M 6
Chhattisgarh 44-45 N 6
Chhergundo 48-49 H 5
Chhergundo Zhou = Yushu
 Zangzu Zizhizhou
 48-49 GH 5
Chhindvärä = Chhindwara
 [IND ← Seoni] 44-45 M 6

Chhindwara [IND ← Seoni] 44-45 M 6
Chhŏtā Andamān = Little Andaman 44-45 P 8
Chhŏtā Nikōbār = Little Nicobar 44-45 P 9
Chhumar 48-49 G 4-5
Chhushul 48-49 FG 6
Chia-hsing = Jiaxing 48-49 N 5
Chia-i 48-49 MN 7
Chia-li = Lharugö 48-49 G 5
Chia-ling Chiang = Jialing Jiang 48-49 K 5
Chia-mu-szŭ = Jiamusi 48-49 P 2
Chi-an = Ji'an [TJ, Jiangxi] 48-49 LM 6
Chi-an = Ji'an [TJ, Jilin] 50-51 F 2
Chiang-chou = Xinjiang 48-49 L 4
Chiang Dao 52-53 CD 3
Chiange 64-65 D 6
Chiang-hsi = Jiangxi 48-49 LM 6
Chiang Khan 52-53 D 3
Chiang Mai 52-53 CD 3
Chiang Rai 52-53 CD 3
Chiang-su = Jiangsu 48-49 MN 5
Chiapa, Río - = Rio Grande 72-73 H 8
Chiapas 72-73 H 8
Chiari 36-37 CD 3
Chiàvari 36-37 C 3
Chiavenna 36-37 C 2
Chiba 50-51 N 5
Chibabava 64-65 H 7
Chibemba 64-65 DE 6
Chibia 64-65 D 6
Chibinogorsk = Kirovsk 42-43 EF 4
Chibiny 38-39 F 2
Chibougamau 70-71 VW 7-8
Chiburi-jima 50-51 J 5
Chibuto 64-65 H 7
Chicacole = Shrikakulam 44-45 N 7
Chicago, IL 72-73 J 3
Chicapa, Rio - 64-65 F 4
Chic-Chocs, Monts - 70-71 X 8
Chi'ich = Qiqihar 48-49 N 2
Chichagof Island 70-71 J 6
Chichén Itzá 72-73 J 7
Chichester 32 F 6
Chickasha, OK 72-73 G 4-5
Chiclayo 78-79 CD 6
Chico, CA 72-73 B 4
Chico, Rio - [RA, Chubut] 80 C 6
Chico, Rio - [YV] 78-79 F 2
Chico, Río - [RA, Santa Cruz ◁ Bahia Grande] 80 C 7
Chico, Río - [RA, Santa Cruz ◁ Rio Gallegos] 80 C 7
Chicoa 64-65 H 6
Chicoana 80 CD 3
Chiconomo 63 CD 6
Chicopee, MA 74-75 G 3
Chicualacuala 64-65 H 7
Chidley, Cape - 70-71 Y 5
Chiefland, FL 74-75 b 2
Chiehmo = Chärchän 48-49 F 4
Chiemsee 33 F 5
Chien-ch'ang = Jianchang [TJ → Benxi] 50-51 E 2
Chien-ch'ang = Jianchang [TJ ↗ Jinzhou] 50-51 B 2
Ch'ien-chiang = Qianjiang [TJ, Hubei] 48-49 L 5
Chiengi 64-65 G 4
Chiengmai = Chiang Mai 52-53 C 3
Chien-Ho = Jian He [TJ, ~] 50-51 D 2
Chien-ko = Jiange 48-49 JK 5
Chien-ning = Jian'ou 48-49 M 6
Chien-ou = Jian'ou 48-49 M 6
Chien-p'ing = Jianping 50-51 B 2
Chien-shui = Jianshui 48-49 J 7
Ch'ien-wei = Qianwei 50-51 C 2
Chien-yang = Jianyang [TJ, Sichuan] 48-49 JK 5
Chieti 36-37 F 4
Chifeng 48-49 M 3
Chifre, Serra do - 78-79 L 8
Chignik, AK 70-71 E 6
Chigyŏng 50-51 F 3

Chih-chiang = Zhijiang [TJ, Hunan] 48-49 KL 6
Ch'ih-fêng = Chifeng 48-49 M 3
Chih-fu = Yantai 48-49 N 4
Chihkiang = Zhijiang 48-49 KL 6
Chih-li Wan = Bo Hai 48-49 M 4
Chi-hsi = Jixi 48-49 P 2
Chihuahua 72-73 E 6
Chii-san = Chiri-san 50-51 F 5
Chike = Xunke 48-49 O 2
Chikugo 50-51 H 6
Chikwawa 64-65 HJ 6
Chilapa de Alvarez 72-73 G 8
Chilâs 44-45 L 3
Chilca 78-79 D 7
Chilcoot, CA 76-77 CD 6
Chile Basin 22-23 EF 6-7
Chilecito [RA, La Rioja] 80 C 3
Chilete 78-79 D 6
Chili 80 B 5-C 2
Chili, Bassin du - 22-23 E 7-F 6
Chilia, Brațul - 36-37 N 3
Chilibekken 22-23 EF 6-7
Chilibre 72-73 b 2
Ch'i-lien Shan = Qilian Shan 48-49 HJ 4
Chilika Hrada = Chilka Lake 44-45 NO 7
Chililabombwe 64-65 G 5
Chi-lin = Jilin [TJ, ●] 48-49 O 3
Chi-lin = Jilin [TJ, ☆] 48-49 N 2-O 3
Chilivani 36-37 C 5
Chilka Lake 44-45 NO 7
Chilko Lake 70-71 M 7
Chillán 80 B 5
Chill Chainnigh = Kilkenny 32 C 5
Chillicothe, MO 72-73 H 3-4
Chillicothe, OH 72-73 K 4
Chilly, ID 76-77 FG 3
Chiloé, Isla de - 80 AB 6
Chilok 42-43 UV 7
Chilonga 63 B 5-6
Chilongozi 63 BC 6
Chiloquin, OR 76-77 C 4
Chilpancingo de los Bravos 72-73 G 8
Chiltern Hills 32 F 6
Chilung = Kee-lung 48-49 N 6
Chilwa, Lake - 64-65 J 6
Chiman tagh 48-49 FG 4
Chimbas 64-65 H 6
Chimborazo [EC, ▲] 78-79 D 5
Chimbote 78-79 D 6
Chimoio 64-65 H 6
Chimpay 80 C 5
Chimpembe 63 B 5
China, Republiek - 48-49 N 7
China Lake, CA 76-77 E 8
Chinan 50-51 F 5
Chinan = Jinan 48-49 M 4
Ch'in-an = Qin'an 48-49 K 5
Chinandega 72-73 J 9
Chinapa 76-77 HJ 10
China Point 76-77 D 9
Chinbo 50-51 G 4
Chincha Alta 78-79 D 7
Chin-ch'êng = Jincheng 48-49 L 4
Chinchilla 56-57 K 5
Chinchilla de Monte-Aragón 34-35 G 9
Chinchorro, Banco - 72-73 J 8
Chinchow = Jinzhou 48-49 N 3
Chincoteague, VA 74-75 F 6
Chincoteague Bay 74-75 F 5
Chinde 64-65 J 6
Chin-do [ROK, ⊙] 50-51 EF 5
Chindo [ROK, ●] 50-51 F 5
Chindwin Myit 52-53 C 1-2
Chine 48-49 E-K 5
Chine Méridionale, Mer de - 52-53 E 5-G 3
Chine Orientale, Mer de - 48-49 N 6-O 5
Chinese muur 48-49 K 4
Ching-ch'uan = Yinchuan 48-49 JK 4
Ch'ing Hai = Chöch nuur 48-49 H 4
Chinghai = Qinghai 48-49 GH 4
Ching-ho = Jinghe [TJ, ●] 48-49 E 3
Ch'ing-ho-ch'êng = Qinghecheng 50-51 E 2
Ch'ing-ho-mên = Qinghemen 50-51 C 2
Ching-ku = Jinggu 48-49 J 7
Ching-ning = Jingning 48-49 K 4

Chingola 64-65 G 5
Chingombe 63 B 6
Ching-po Hu = Jingbo Hu 48-49 O 3
Ching-t'ai = Jingtai 48-49 J 4
Ch'ing-tao = Qingdao 48-49 N 4
Ch'ing-tui-tzŭ = Qingduizi 50-51 D 3
Ching-tung = Jingdong 48-49 J 7
Ch'ing-yang = Qingyang [TJ, Gansu] 48-49 K 4
Ching-yüan = Jingyuan 48-49 JK 4
Ch'ing-yüan = Qingyuan [TJ, Liaoning] 50-51 E 1
Chinhae 50-51 G 5
Chinhae-man 50-51 G 5
Chinhoyi 64-65 GH 6
Chin-hsien = Jin Xian [TJ, Liaoning ↗ Jinzhou] 50-51 C 2
Chin-hsien = Jin Xian [TJ, Liaoning ↑ Lüda] 48-49 N 4
Chinhsien = Jinzhou 48-49 N 3
Chin-hua = Jinhua 48-49 MN 6
Ch'in-huang-tao = Qinhuangdao 48-49 MN 3-4
Chi-ning = Jining [TJ, Nei Monggol Zizhiqu] 48-49 L 3
Chi-ning = Jining [TJ, Shandong] 48-49 M 4
Chinju 48-49 O 4
Chinko 60-61 J 7
Chinle, AZ 76-77 J 7
Chinle Valley 76-77 J 7
Chin Ling = Qin Ling 48-49 KL 5
Chin-mên Tao 48-49 M 7
Chinnamp'o = Nampo 48-49 NO 4
Chinon 34-35 H 5
Chino Valley, AZ 76-77 G 8
Chinqiuão = Zhenjiang 48-49 M 5
Chinsali 64-65 H 5
Chin-sha Chiang = Jinsha Jiang 48-49 J 6
Chinsura 44-45 O 6
Chinwangtao = Qinhuangdao 48-49 MN 3-4
Chinwetha Pyinnei 52-53 B 2
Ch'in-yang = Qinyang 48-49 L 4
Chinyŏng 50-51 G 5
Chiôco 64-65 H 6
Chiòggia 36-37 E 3
Chios [GR, ⊙] 36-37 L 6
Chios [GR, ●] 36-37 M 6
Chipata 64-65 H 5
Chipili 63 B 5
Chipinge 64-65 H 7
Chipoka 63 C 6
Chiporiro 64-65 H 6
Chiputneticook Lakes 74-75 JK 2
Chiquimula 72-73 HJ 9
Chiquitos, Llanos de - 78-79 G 8
Chira 63 D 2
Chira Bazar 48-49 DE 4
Chiradzi 64-65 H 7
Chirfa 60-61 G 4
Chiricahua National Monument 76-77 J 9-10
Chiricahua Peak 76-77 J 10
Chirikof Island 70-71 EF 6
Chiriqui, Golfo de - 72-73 K 10
Chiriqui, Laguna de - 72-73 K 9-10
Chiri-san 50-51 F 5
Chirripó Grande, Cerro - 72-73 K 10
Chirundu 64-65 G 6
Chisamba 64-65 G 5-6
Chisel Lake 70-71 QR 7
Chi-shih Shan = Amnyemachhen Gangri 48-49 HJ 5
Chishtian Mandi = Chishtiyân Mandī 44-45 L 5
Chishtiyân Mandī 44-45 L 5
Chisimaio = Kismaanyo 64-65 K 3
Chitado 64-65 D 6
Chita-hantō 50-51 L 5
Chitambo 63 B 6
Chitembo 64-65 E 5
Chitogarh = Chittaurgarh 44-45 L 6
Chitose 50-51 b 2

Chitradurga 44-45 M 8
Chitrâl 44-45 L 3
Chitré 72-73 K 10
Chittagong = Châttagâm 44-45 P 6
Chittaldurga = Chitradurga 44-45 M 8
Chittaorgarh = Chittaurgarh 44-45 L 6
Chittaurgarh 44-45 L 6
Chittoor 44-45 M 8
Chittoor = Chittor 44-45 M 8
Chiuchuan = Jiuquan 48-49 H 4
Chiulezi, Rio - 63 D 5-6
Chiumbe, Rio - 64-65 F 4
Chiume 64-65 F 5-6
Ch'iung-chou Hai-hsia = Qiongzhou Haixia 48-49 KL 7
Chiungshan = Qiongshan 48-49 L 8
Ch'iung-tung = Qionghai 48-49 L 8
Chiuta, Lagoa - 64-65 J 5
Chiva [SU] 42-43 L 9
Chivasso 36-37 B 3
Chivay 78-79 E 8
Chivilcoy 80 DE 4
Chivu 64-65 H 6
Chiwanda 64-65 HJ 5
Chiwefwe 63 B 6
Chiweta 64-65 H 5
Chixoy, Rio - 72-73 H 8
Chjargas 48-49 G 2
Chjargas nuur 48-49 GH 2
Chloride, AZ 76-77 F 8
Chmeițiyé = Shmayțiyah 46-47 H 5
Chmelnickij 38-39 E 6
Chobe 64-65 F 6
Chobe National Park 64-65 FG 6
Chocaya 78-79 F 9
Chocca 78-79 D 7
Chochiang = Charqiliq 48-49 F 4
Choch'iwŏn 50-51 F 4
Chöch nuur 48-49 H 4
Chöch Šili 48-49 G 4
Chöch Šili uul 48-49 FG 4
Chocolate Mountains 76-77 F 9
Chocontá 78-79 E 3
Chodžambas 44-45 JK 3
Chodžejli 42-43 K 9
Chodžent = Leninabad 44-45 KL 2-3
Chodzież 33 H 2
Choele-Choel 80 CD 5
Choibalsan = Čojbalsan 48-49 L 2
Choiseul 52-53 j 6
Chojna 33 G 2
Chojnice 33 HJ 2
Chōkai-zan 50-51 MN 3
Chôlamandala = Coromandel Coast 44-45 N 7-8
Cholame, CA 76-77 CD 8
Chold = Chuld 48-49 K 2-3
Cholet 34-35 G 5
Cholgwan 50-51 E 3
Chŏlla-namdo 50-51 F 5
Chŏlla-pukto 50-51 F 5
Cholm 38-39 F 4
Cholmogory 42-43 G 5
Cholmsk 42-43 b 8
Cholodnoje 38-39 N 3
Cholos nuur 48-49 H 4
Ch'ŏlsan 50-51 E 3
Choluteca 72-73 J 9
Choma 64-65 G 6
Chomba 63 D 5
Ch'ŏnan 50-51 F 4
Chon Buri 52-53 D 4
Chŏnch'ŏn 50-51 F 2
Chone 78-79 CD 5
Ch'ŏng'chŏn-gang 50-51 EF 2-3
Chongdjin = Ch'ŏngjin 48-49 OP 3
Chŏnggŏ-dong 50-51 E 3
Ch'ŏngha 50-51 G 4
Ch'ŏngjin 48-49 OP 3
Chongjin = Ch'ŏngjin 48-49 OP 3
Chŏngju 50-51 O 4
Chongming 48-49 N 5
Chongor 48-49 L 2
Chongor = Bajan Adraga 48-49 KL 2
Chongor Oboo Sum = Bajandalaj 48-49 K 3
Chongor Tagh = Qungur tagh 48-49 D 4

Ch'ŏngp'yŏngch'ŏn 50-51 FG 4
Chongqing 48-49 K 6
Ch'ŏngsan-do 50-51 F 5
Chongsŏng = Chongzuo 48-49 K 7
Ch'ŏngsŏktu-ri 50-51 EF 3
Chongsŏng 50-51 GH 1
Chŏngŭp 50-51 F 5
Ch'ŏngyang [ROK] 50-51 F 4
Chongzuo 48-49 K 7
Chŏnju 48-49 O 4
Chonos, Archipiélago de los - 80 AB 6-7
Chonuu 42-43 b 4
Chooloj Gov' 48-49 H 3
Chop'or 38-39 H 5-6
Chorasan = Khorâsân 44-45 H 3-4
Chŏra Sfakion 36-37 L 8
Chordogoj 42-43 W 5
Chor He 48-49 N 2
Chorinsk 42-43 U 7
Chorog 44-45 L 3
Chorrera, La - [PA] 72-73 b 3
Chorsabad = Khorsabad 46-47 K 4
Chŏrwŏn 50-51 F 3
Chŏryŏng-do = Yŏng-do 50-51 G 5
Chorzele 33 K 2
Chorzów 33 J 3
Chosedachard 38-39 L 2
Chösen-kaikyō 48-49 O 5
Chōshi 50-51 N 5
Chos-Malal 80 BC 5
Chosŏn-man = Tonghan-man 48-49 O 4
Choszczno 33 GH 2
Chota 78-79 D 6
Chota Nāgpur 44-45 NO 6
Choteau, MT 76-77 G 2
Chotin 38-39 E 6
Chou Shan = Zhoushan Dao 48-49 N 5-6
Chou-shan Ch'ün-tao = Zhoushan Qundao 48-49 N 5
Chovd [Mongolia, ●] 48-49 G 2
Chovd [Mongolia, ☆ = 3 ◁] 48-49 J 1
Chovd gol 48-49 G 2
Chövsgöl [Mongolia, ●] 48-49 KL 3
Chövsgöl [Mongolia, ☆ = 6 ◁] 48-49 J 1
Chövsgöl nuur 48-49 J 1
Chowan River 74-75 E 6
Chowchilla, CA 76-77 C 7
Christchurch [NZ] 56-57 OP 8
Christian Island 74-75 C 2
Christiansburg, VA 74-75 CD 6
Christianshåb = Qasigiánguir 70-71 a 4
Christie Bay 70-71 O 5
Christmas Creek 56-57 E 3
Christmas Island [AUS] 52-53 E 9
Chromtau 42-43 K 7
Chrudim 33 GH 4
Chrysê 36-37 LM 8
Chrysochûs, Kólpos - 46-47 E 5
Chubb Crater = New Quebec Crater 70-71 VW 5
Chubbuck, CA 76-77 F 8
Chubisgalt = Chövsgöl 48-49 KL 3
Chubsugul = Chövsgöl nuur 48-49 J 1
Chūbu 50-51 LM 4-5
Chubut 80 BC 6
Chubut, Río - 80 C 6
Chucheng = Zhucheng 48-49 MN 4
Chu-chi = Zhuji 48-49 N 6
Ch'ü-ching = Qujing 48-49 J 6
Ch'ü-chou = Qu Xian 48-49 M 6
Chu-chou = Zhuzhou 48-49 L 6
Chuchow = Zhuzhou 48-49 L 6
Ch'üeh-shan = Queshan 48-49 L 5
Chugach Mountains 70-71 GH 5
Chugoku 50-51 HJ 5
Chūgoku-sammyaku 50-51 JK 5
Chuguchak 48-49 E 2
Chügüchak = Tarbagataj 48-49 EF 2
Chuhsien = Qu Xian 48-49 M 6

Ch'u-hsiung = Chuxiong 48-49 J 7
Chü-hua Tao = Juhua Dao 50-51 C 2
Ch'uja-do 50-51 F 6
Chukchi Plateau 19 B 35
Chukchi Sea 19 BC 35-36
Chuki = Zhuji 48-49 N 6
Chukot Autonomous Area 42-43 g-j 4
Chukudu Kraal 64-65 F 7
Chūl, Gardaneh-ye - 46-47 MN 6
Chulaq Aqqan Su 48-49 G 4
Chula Vista, CA 72-73 C 5
Chuld 48-49 K 2-3
Chulga 38-39 M 3
Chü-liu-ho = Juliuhe 50-51 D 1
Chulp'o 50-51 F 5
Chulucanas 78-79 CD 6
Chulumani 78-79 F 8
Chumbicha 80 C 3
Chum Phae 52-53 D 3
Chumphon 52-53 CD 4
Chumsaeng 52-53 D 3
Chumunjin 50-51 G 4
Ch'unch'ŏn 48-49 O 4
Chungam-ni 50-51 G 5
Ch'ungch'ŏng-namdo 50-51 F 4
Ch'ungch'ŏng-pukto 50-51 FG 4
Chüngges 48-49 E 3
Chunghwa 50-51 EF 3
Ch'ungju 50-51 FG 4
Chungking = Chongqing 48-49 K 6
Ch'ung-ming = Chongming 48-49 N 5
Ch'ungmu 50-51 G 5
Chüngsan 50-51 E 3
Chungshan = Zhongshan 48-49 L 7
Chung-tien = Zhongdian 48-49 HJ 6
Chüngüj gol 48-49 GH 2
Chung-wei = Zhongwei 48-49 JK 4
Chunya 64-65 H 4
Chuquibamba 78-79 E 8
Chuquicamata 80 C 2
Chuquisaca = Sucre 78-79 FG 8
Chur 33 D 5
Churchill [CDN] 70-71 RS 6
Churchill, ID 76-77 FG 4
Churchill, Cape - 70-71 S 6
Churchill Falls 70-71 XY 7
Churchill Peak 70-71 LM 6
Churchill River [CDN, Manitoba] 70-71 RS 6
Churchill River [CDN ◁ Hamilton Inlet] 70-71 Y 7
Churu 44-45 LM 5
Chusei-hokudō = Ch'ungch'ŏng-pukto 50-51 FG 4
Chusei-nandō = Ch'ungch'ŏng-namdo 50-51 F 4
Chu-shan = Zhushan 48-49 KL 5
Chusistan = Khūzestân 44-45 F 4
Chuska Mountains 76-77 J 7-8
Chust 38-39 D 6
Chutag 48-49 J 2
Chuučnar 48-49 G 5
Chuvash Autonomous Republic = 4 ◁ 42-43 H 6
Chuwārtah 46-47 L 5
Chuxiong 48-49 J 7
Chuxiong Yizu Zizhizhou 48-49 J 6
Chuy 80 F 4
Chu Yang Sin 52-53 E 4
Chužand 44-45 K 2-L 3
Chužir 42-43 U 7
Chvalynsk 38-39 J 5
Chwārta = Chuwārtah 46-47 L 5
Chypre 44-45 C 3
Čibit 42-43 Q 7
Cibola, AZ 76-77 F 9
Cibuta 76-77 H 10
Çiçekbaba Tepesi 46-47 C 4
Çiçekdağı 46-47 F 3
Cícero Dantas 78-79 M 7
Cicladas 36-37 L 7
Cide 46-47 E 2
Ciechanów 33 K 2
Ciego de Ávila 72-73 L 7
Ciénaga 78-79 DE 2
Cienfuegos 72-73 K 7

Cieza 34-35 G 9
Çifteler 46-47 D 3
Çiftlik = Camlibel 46-47 G 2
Çiftlik = Kelkit 46-47 H 2
Cifuentes 34-35 F 8
Čiganak 42-43 N 8-9
Çığlı 46-47 K 4
Cihanbeyli 46-47 E 3
Cihanbeyli Yaylâsı 46-47 E 3
Čiili 42-43 M 9
Cijara, Embalse de – 34-35 E 9
Cilacap 52-53 E 8
Çıldır 46-47 K 2
Çıldır Gölü 46-47 K 2
Cilo dağı 46-47 KL 4
Cima, CA 76-77 F 8
Cimaltepec 72-73 G 8
Čimbaj 42-43 KL 9
Čimkent 42-43 M 9
Ciml'ansk 38-39 H 6
Ciml'anskoje vodochranilišče 38-39 H 6
Cimmarron River 72-73 F 4
Cimone, Monte – 36-37 D 3
Cîmpina 36-37 LM 3
Cîmpulung 36-37 L 3
Cîmpulung Moldovenesc 36-37 LM 2
Çınar 46-47 J 4
Cinca 34-35 H 8
Cincinnati, OH 72-73 K 4
Çine 46-47 BC 4
Čingaly 42-43 MN 5
Cinnabar Mountain 76-77 E 4
Cinta, Serra da – 78-79 K 6
Cinto, Mont – 36-37 C 4
Cintra = Sintra [BR] 78-79 G 6
Ciotat, la – 34-35 K 7
Čiovo 36-37 G 4
Cipikan 42-43 V 7
Cipó 78-79 M 7
Circeo, Monte – 36-37 E 5
Čirčik 42-43 M 9
Circle, AK 70-71 H 4
Circle Cliffs 76-77 H 7
Circleville, UT 76-77 G 6
Cirebon 52-53 E 8
Cirenaica = Barqah 60-61 J 2
Cirenaica = Barqah 60-61 J 2
Cirene = Shaḥḥāt 60-61 J 2
Ciri, Rio – 72-73 a 3
Cirò Marina 36-37 G 6
Čirpan 36-37 L 4
Cisa, Passo della – 36-37 CD 3
Cisco, UT 76-77 J 6
Cisne, Ilhas del – = Swan Islands 72-73 K 8
Cisneros 78-79 DE 3
Cisterna di Latina 36-37 E 5
Cisternino 36-37 G 5
Čistopol' 42-43 HJ 6
Čita 42-43 V 7
Citlaltépetl 72-73 G 8
Citra, FL 74-75 bc 2
Citrusdal 64-65 EF 9
Citrus Heights, CA 72-73 B 4
Cittanova 36-37 FG 6
Ciucaş 36-37 LM 3
Ciudad Bolívar 78-79 G 3
Ciudad Bolivia 78-79 E 3
Ciudad Camargo = Camargo 72-73 E 6
Ciudad del Carmen 72-73 H 8
Ciudad Delicias = Delicias 72-73 E 6
Ciudadela 34-35 J 8-9
Ciudad Guayana 78-79 G 3
Ciudad Guzmán 72-73 F 8
Ciudad Juárez = Juárez 72-73 E 5
Ciudad Lerdo 72-73 EF 6
Ciudad Linares = Linares 72-73 G 7
Ciudad Madero 72-73 G 7
Ciudad Mante 72-73 G 7
Ciudad Obregón 72-73 DE 6
Ciudad Ojeda 78-79 E 2-3
Ciudad Piar 78-79 G 3
Ciudad Real 34-35 EF 9
Ciudad-Rodrigo 34-35 DE 8
Ciudad Trujillo = Santo Domingo 72-73 MN 8
Ciudad Valles 72-73 G 7
Ciudad Victoria 72-73 G 7
Civa Burnu 46-47 G 2
Civita Castellana 36-37 E 4
Civitanova Marche 36-37 EF 4
Civitavècchia 36-37 D 4
Çivril 46-47 C 3
Čiža 42-43 G 4
Cizre 44-45 E 3
Čkalov = Orenburg 42-43 JK 7
Clacton on Sea 32 G 6
Clain 34-35 H 5
Claire, Lake – 70-71 O 6
Clairton, PA 74-75 CD 4
Clamecy 34-35 J 5
Clan Alpine Mountains 76-77 DE 6
Clanwilliam 64-65 E 9
Clara River 56-57 H 3
Clare [AUS] 56-57 G 6
Claremont, NH 74-75 GH 3
Claremorris 32 B 5
Clarence, Cape – 70-71 S 3
Clarence, Isla – 80 B 8
Clarence Island 24 C 31
Clarence Strait [AUS] 56-57 F 2
Clarion, PA 74-75 D 4
Clarion, Fosse – 22-23 B-D 5
Clarión, Fractura de – 22-23 B-D 5
Clarionbreukzone 22-23 B-D 5
Clarión Fracture Zone 22-23 B-D 5
Clarkdale, AZ 76-77 G 8
Clarke City 70-71 X 7
Clarke Island 56-57 J 8
Clark Fork, ID 76-77 E 1
Clark Fork River 72-73 CD 2
Clark Hill Lake 74-75 B 8
Clarkia, ID 76-77 EF 2
Clark Mountain 76-77 F 8
Clarksburg, WV 72-73 K 4
Clarksdale, MS 72-73 HJ 5
Clarkston, WA 76-77 E 2
Clarksville, TN 72-73 J 4
Clarksville, VA 74-75 D 6
Claxton, GA 74-75 BC 8
Clay, WV 74-75 C 5
Clay Belt 70-71 T-V 7
Claymont, DE 74-75 F 5
Claypool, AZ 76-77 H 9
Clayton, GA 74-75 B 7
Clayton, ID 76-77 F 3
Clayton, NC 74-75 D 7
Clayton, NY 74-75 EF 2
Clearcreek, UT 76-77 H 6
Clearfield, PA 74-75 D 4
Clearfield, UT 76-77 GH 5
Clear Hills 70-71 N 6
Clear Lake 76-77 B 6
Clear Lake Reservoir 76-77 C 5
Clearwater, FL 72-73 C 6
Clearwater Mountains 76-77 F 2-3
Clearwater River [USA] 76-77 E 2
Cleburne, TX 72-73 G 3
Cle Elum, WA 76-77 C 2
Clendenin, WV 74-75 C 5
Clermont [AUS] 56-57 J 4
Clermont, FL 74-75 bc 2
Clermont-Ferrand 34-35 J 6
Cleve 58 C 4
Cleveland, OH 72-73 K 3
Cleveland, TN 72-73 K 4
Cleveland, Mount – 72-73 D 2
Cleveland Heights, OH 74-75 C 4
Clewiston, FL 74-75 c 3
Clifden 32 A 5
Cliff, NM 76-77 J 9
Cliff Lake, MT 76-77 H 3
Cliffs, ID 76-77 E 4
Clifton 56-57 K 5
Clifton, AZ 76-77 J 9
Clifton, NJ 74-75 F 4
Clifton Forge, VA 74-75 D 6
Clifton Hills 56-57 G 5
Clinchco, VA 74-75 B 6
Clinch Mountains 74-75 B 6
Clinch River 74-75 B 6
Clinton [CDN, Ontario] 74-75 C 3
Clinton, IA 72-73 H 3
Clinton, MT 76-77 G 2
Clinton, NC 74-75 D 7
Clinton, SC 74-75 C 7
Clinton, Cape – 56-57 K 4
Clipperton, Fosse de – 22-23 CD 5
Clipperton, Fractura de – 22-23 CD 5
Clipperton, Île – 72-73 E 9
Clippertonbreukzone 22-23 CD 5
Clipperton Fracture Zone 22-23 CD 5
Clisham 32 C 3
Cloates, Point – 56-57 B 4
Clonakilty 32 B 6
Cloncurry 56-57 H 4
Cloncurry River 56-57 H 3
Clonmel 32 BC 5
Cloppenburg 33 CD 2
Cloucester, VA 74-75 E 6
Cloud Peak 72-73 E 3
Clover, VA 74-75 D 6
Cloverdale, CA 76-77 B 6
Cloverdale, NM 76-77 J 10
Clovis, CA 76-77 D 7
Clovis, NM 72-73 F 5
Cluj-Napoca 36-37 KL 2
Cluny 34-35 K 5
Clutha River 56-57 N 9
Clyde 70-71 X 3
Clyde, Firth of – 32 D 4
Clyde Park, MT 76-77 H 3
Clyo, GA 74-75 C 8
Coa 34-35 D 8
Coachella, CA 76-77 E 9
Coachella Canal 76-77 EF 9
Coahuila 72-73 F 6
Coaldale, NV 76-77 E 6
Coalinga, CA 76-77 C 7
Coalville, UT 76-77 H 5
Coari 78-79 G 5
Coari, Rio – 78-79 G 5-6
Coast Mountains 70-71 K 6-M 7
Coast Range 72-73 B 2-C 5
Coatá, Cachoeira do – 78-79 G 6
Coatepec 72-73 G 8
Coatesville, PA 74-75 EF 4-5
Coaticook 74-75 GH 2
Coats Island 70-71 U 5
Coats Land 24 B 33-34
Coatzacoalcos 72-73 H 8
Cobán 72-73 H 8
Çobandede 46-47 JK 3
Cobar 56-57 J 6
Cobargo 58 JK 6
Cobbo = Kobo 60-61 MN 6
Cobe = Kōbe 48-49 PQ 5
Cobh 32 B 6
Cobija 78-79 F 7
Cobleskill, NY 74-75 F 3
Coboconk 74-75 D 2
Cobourg 74-75 DE 3
Cobourg Peninsula 56-57 F 2
Cobre, NV 76-77 F 5
Cobue 63 C 6
Coburg 33 E 3
Coburg, OR 76-77 B 3
Coburg Island 70-71 V 2
Coca 34-35 E 8
Cocanada = Kakinada 44-45 N 7
Cochabamba [BOL, ●] 78-79 F 8
Cochem 33 C 3
Cochi = Kōchi 48-49 P 5
Cochim = Cochin 44-45 M 9
Cochin 44-45 M 9
Cochinchina = Nam Bô 52-53 DE 5
Cochise, AZ 76-77 J 9
Cochran, GA 74-75 B 8
Cochrane [CDN, Ontario] 70-71 U 8
Cochrane River 70-71 Q 6
Cockburn, Canal – 80 B 8
Cockburn Land 70-71 UV 3
Cockeysville, MD 74-75 E 5
Coco, El – 72-73 b 3
Coco, Isla del – 78-79 B 3
Coco, Río – 72-73 K 9
Cocoa, FL 74-75 c 2
Coco Channel 52-53 B 4
Coco Channel 52-53 B 4
Coco Island 64-65 NO 6
Cocolalla, ID 76-77 E 1
Coconino Plateau 76-77 G 7-8
Cocos [AUS] 22-23 O 6
Cocos = Isla del Coco 78-79 B 3
Coco Solo 72-73 b 2
Cocos Rise 22-23 E 5
Cocuy, El – 78-79 E 3
Cod, Cape – 72-73 N 3
Codajás 78-79 G 5
Codera, Cabo – 78-79 F 2
Codihue 80 BC 5
Codó 78-79 L 5
Coen 56-57 H 2
Coesfeld 33 C 3
Coetivy Island 64-65 N 4
Coeur d'Alene, ID 72-73 C 2
Coeur d'Alene Indian Reservation 76-77 E 2
Coeur d'Alene Lake 76-77 E 2
Coffeyville, KS 72-73 G 4
Coffin Bay 56-57 FG 6
Coffin Bay Peninsula 56-57 FG 6
Coffs Harbour 56-57 K 6
Cofrentes 34-35 G 9
Cofu = Kōfu 48-49 Q 4
Cogealac 36-37 N 3
Cognac 34-35 G 6
Çoğun 46-47 F 3
Cohoes, NY 74-75 G 3
Cohuna 56-57 HJ 7
Coi, Sông – = Sông Nhi Ha 52-53 D 2
Coiba, Isla – 72-73 K 10
Coihaique 80 B 7
Coimbatore 44-45 M 8
Coimbra 34-35 C 8
Coin 34-35 E 10
Coipasa, Salar de – 78-79 F 8
Čojbalsan = 18 48-49 L 2
Čojbalsangijn Ajmag = Dornod = 18 ◁ 48-49 LM 2
Cojimies 78-79 C 4
Cojudo Blanco, Cerro – 80 BC 7
Çokak 46-47 G 4
Cokeville, WY 76-77 H 4
Čokurdach 42-43 cd 3
Colac 56-57 H 7
Colapur = Kolhapur 44-45 L 7
Cólar = Kolar Gold Fields 44-45 M 8
Colares 34-35 C 9
Colbeck, Cape – 24 B 20-21
Colbert, WA 76-77 E 2
Colbinabbin 58 G 6
Colca, Río – 78-79 E 8
Colchester 32 G 6
Coldwater 74-75 D 2
Colebrook, NH 74-75 H 2
Colégio = Porto Real do Colégio 78-79 M 6-7
Coleman River 56-57 H 2-3
Çölemerik = Hakkâri 46-47 K 4
Coleraine 32 C 4
Coleraine [AUS] 58 EF 6
Coles, Punta de – 78-79 E 8
Colesburg 64-65 FG 9
Colesville, CA 76-77 D 6
Colfax, CA 76-77 C 6
Colfax, WA 76-77 E 2
Colhué Huapí, Lago – 80 C 7
Colima 72-73 F 8
Colima, Nevado de – 72-73 EF 8
Colinas 78-79 L 6
Coll 32 C 3
Collaguasi 80 C 2
Collarenebri 58 HJ 2
College, AK 70-71 G 4-5
Collie 56-57 C 6
Collier Bay 56-57 D 3
Collingwood [CDN] 56-57 CD 2
Collins, MT 76-77 H 2
Collinson Peninsula 70-71 Q 3-4
Collinsville 56-57 J 4
Colmar 34-35 L 4
Colnett, Bahía – 76-77 E 10
Cologne = Köln 33 C 3
Cololo, Nevado – 78-79 F 7
Colomb-Béchar = Bashshār 60-61 D 2
Colombia 78-79 D-F 4
Colômbia [BR] 78-79 K 9
Colombie 78-79 D-F 4
Colombo = Koḷamba 44-45 M 9
Colón [C] 72-73 K 7
Colón [PA, ●] 72-73 b 2
Colón [PA, ☆] 72-73 ab 2
Colón, Archipiélago de – 78-79 AB 5
Colona 56-57 F 6
Colonia = Köln 33 C 3
Colonia del Sacramento 80 E 4
Colonia 25 de Mayo 80 C 5
Colonia Las Heras = Las Heras 80 C 7
Colonial Beach, VA 74-75 E 5
Colonial Heights, VA 74-75 E 6
Colonia Morelos 76-77 J 10
Colonne, Capo delle – 36-37 G 6
Colonsay 32 C 3
Colorado [USA] 72-73 EF 4
Colorado, Río – [MEX] 72-73 CD 5
Colorado, Río – [RA, La Pampa] 80 C 5
Colorado, Río – [RA, Neuquén] 80 D 5
Colorado, Río – [RA, Río Negro] 80 CD 5
Colorado Desert 76-77 EF 9
Colorado National Monument 76-77 J 6
Colorado Plateau 72-73 DE 4
Colorado River [USA, Colorado] 72-73 E 4
Colorado River [USA, Texas] 72-73 G 5
Colorado River Aqueduct 76-77 F 8
Colorado River Indian Reservation 76-77 F 9
Colorados, Cerros – [RA] 80 C 6
Colorados, Cerros – [RCH] 80 C 3
Colorado Springs, CO 72-73 F 4
Colo River 58 K 4
Colton, UT 76-77 H 6
Columbia, MD 56-57 E 5
Columbia, MO 72-73 H 4
Columbia, NC 74-75 E 7
Columbia, PA 74-75 E 4
Columbia, SC 72-73 K 5
Columbia, Cape – 19 A 25-26
Columbia, District of – 74-75 E 5
Columbia, Mount – 70-71 N 7
Columbia Basin 76-77 D 2
Columbia Británica = British Columbia 70-71 L 6-N 7
Columbia Falls, MT 76-77 FG 1
Columbia Plateau 72-73 C 2-3
Columbia River 72-73 BC 2
Columbia River, WA 76-77 C 2
Columbretes, Islas – 34-35 H 9
Columbus, GA 72-73 K 5
Columbus, MS 72-73 J 5
Columbus, NE 72-73 G 3
Columbus, OH 72-73 K 3-4
Colusa, CA 76-77 BC 6
Colville, WA 76-77 E 1
Colville Indian Reservation 76-77 D 1
Colville River 70-71 EF 4
Comàcchio 36-37 E 3
Comàcchio, Valli di – 36-37 E 3
Comana 36-37 LM 3
Comayagua 72-73 J 9
Combourg 34-35 G 4
Comeau, Baie – 70-71 X 8
Come By Chance 58 J 3
Come By Chance 58 J 3
Comer, GA 74-75 B 7
Comilla = Komillā 44-45 P 6
Comino, Capo – 36-37 CD 5
Comiso 36-37 F 7
Comitán de Domínguez 72-73 H 8
Commerce, GA 74-75 B 7
Committee Bay 70-71 T 4
Commonwealth Range 24 A
Commonwealth Territory 56-57 K 7
Como 36-37 C 3
Como, Lago di – 36-37 C 2-3
Comodoro Rivadavia 80 C 7
Comoé = Komoe 60-61 D 7
Comores 64-65 KL 5
Comores, Archipel des – 64-65 KL 5
Comores, Bassin des – 64-65 L 5
Comores, Cuenca de – 64-65 L 5
Comorin, Cape – 44-45 M 9
Compiègne 34-35 J 4
Comprida, Cachoeira – = Treze Quedas 78-79 H 4
Comprida, Ilha – [BR, São Paulo] 80 G 2-3
Comprida, Lago – = Lagoa Nova 78-79 J 4
Compton, CA 76-77 DE 9
Čona 42-43 V 5
Conakry 60-61 B 7
Conca = Cuenca 78-79 D 5
Concarneau 34-35 EF 5
Conceição [BR, Mato Grosso] 78-79 H 6
Conceição da Barra 78-79 M 8
Conceição do Araguaia 78-79 JK 6
Concelho = Inhambane 64-65 J 7
Concepción [BOL] 78-79 G 8
Concepción [CO, Putumayo] 78-79 DE 4
Concepción [RA, Tucumán] 80 C 3
Concepción [RCH] 80 AB 5
Concepcion, CA 76-77 C 8
Concepción [PY, ●] 80 E 2
Concepción, Canal – 80 AB 8
Concepción, La – 78-79 E 2
Concepción, Río – 76-77 G 10
Concepción del Oro 72-73 F 7
Concepción del Uruguay 80 E 4
Conception, Point – 72-73 B 5
Conchi [RCH, Antofagasta] 80 C 2
Concho, AZ 76-77 J 8
Conchos, Río – 72-73 EF 6
Concord, CA 76-77 BC 7
Concord, NC 74-75 C 7
Concord, NH 72-73 M 3
Concordia [RA] 80 E 4
Côn Đao 52-53 E 5
Conde 78-79 M 7
Condobolin 56-57 J 6
Condon, OR 76-77 C 3
Conejera, Isla – 34-35 J 9
Confusion Range 76-77 G 6
Congo 64-65 D 3-F 2
Congo = Zaïre 64-65 E 3
Congress, AZ 76-77 G 8
Cónia = Konya 44-45 C 3
Conjeeveram = Kanchipuram 44-45 MN 8
Connaught 32 B 4-5
Conneaut, OH 74-75 C 3-4
Connecticut 72-73 M 3
Connecticut River 74-75 G 3-4
Connell, WA 76-77 D 2
Connellsville, PA 74-75 D 4
Conner, MT 76-77 FG 3
Conner, Mount – 56-57 F 5
Connersville, OH 74-75 A 5
Connors Pass 76-77 F 6
Conrad, MT 76-77 H 1
Conselheiro Lafaiete 78-79 L 9
Constância dos Baetas 78-79 G 6
Constanța 36-37 M 3
Constantina = Quṣanṭīn 60-61 F 1
Constantine, Cape – 70-71 DE 6
Constantinople = Istanbul 44-45 BC 2
Constanza = Constanța 36-37 N 3
Constitución 80 B 5
Contact, NV 76-77 F 5
Contamana 78-79 DE 6
Contas, Rio de – 78-79 L 7
Continental, AZ 76-77 H 10
Contratación 78-79 E 3
Contreras, Isla – 80 AB 8
Contwoyto Lake 70-71 OP 4
Conway, NH 74-75 H 3
Conway, SC 74-75 D 8
Coober Pedy 56-57 F 5
Cook 56-57 F 6
Cook, Bahía – 80 B 9
Cook, Mount – [NZ] 56-57 NO 8
Cook Bay 24 C 16
Cooke City, MT 76-77 J 3
Cook Inlet 70-71 F 5-6
Cook Strait 56-57 O 8
Cooktown 56-57 HJ 3
Coolabah 58 H 3
Coolah 58 J 3
Coolamon 58 H 5
Coolgardie 56-57 CD 6
Coolidge, AZ 76-77 H 9
Coolidge Dam 76-77 H 9
Coolin, ID 76-77 E 1
Cooma 56-57 J 7
Coonabarabran 56-57 JK 6
Coonamble 56-57 J 6
Coonana 56-57 D 6
Coonbah 58 EF 4
Coondambo 58 BC 3
Coondapoor 44-45 L 8
Coongoola 56-57 HJ 5
Cooper Creek 56-57 G 5
Cooperstown, NY 74-75 F 3
Coorong, The – 56-57 G 7
Coos Bay 76-77 A 4
Coos Bay, OR 72-73 AB 3
Cootamundra 56-57 J 6
Čop 38-39 D 6
Copahue, Paso – 80 BC 5
Copán 72-73 J 9
Copco, CA 76-77 B 4-5
Copenhagen = København 30-31 DE 10
Copenhague = København 30-31 DE 10
Copiapó 80 BC 3
Copparo 36-37 DE 3
Copperbelt 64-65 G 5
Copper Center, AK 70-71 G 5
Coppermine 70-71 N 4
Coppermine River 70-71 NO 4
Copper River 70-71 GH 5
Copşa Mică 36-37 L 2
Coquilhatville = Mbandaka 64-65 E 2-3
Coquille, OR 76-77 AB 4
Coquille River 76-77 AB 4
Coquimbo [RCH, ●] 80 B 2
Corabia 36-37 L 4
Coracora 78-79 E 7-8
Corail, Grande Barrière de – 56-57 H 1-K 4
Corail, Mer de – 56-57 K-M 3
Coral, Cuenca del – 56-57 K 2

168 Cieza

Coral, Mar del – 56-57 K-M 3
Coral Gables, FL 72-73 KL 6
Coral Harbour 70-71 U 5
Coral Sea 56-57 K-M 3
Coral Sea Basin 56-57 K 2
Coral Sea Islands Territory 56-57 JK 3
Coral Springs, FL 56-57 c 3
Corantijn 78-79 H 4
Corato 36-37 G 5
Corbeil-Essonnes 34-35 HJ 4
Corbières 34-35 J 7
Corbin, KY 72-73 K 4
Corcaigh = Cork 32 B 6
Córcega = Corse 36-37 C 4
Corcoran, CA 76-77 D 7
Corcovado, Volcán – 80 B 6
Corcubión 34-35 C 7
Cordele, GA 74-75 AB 8
Cordillera Azul 78-79 D 6
Cordillera Blanca 78-79 D 6
Cordillera Central [BOL] 78-79 F 8-G 9
Cordillera Central [CO] 78-79 D 4-E 3
Cordillera Central [DOM] 72-73 M 8
Cordillera Central [PE] 78-79 D 6
Cordillera Central [RP] 52-53 H 3
Cordillera Iberica 34-35 F 7-G 8
Cordillera Negra 78-79 D 6
Cordillera Occidental [CO] 78-79 D 3-4
Cordillera Occidental [PE] 78-79 D 6-E 8
Cordillera Oriental [BOL] 78-79 FG 8
Cordillera Oriental [CO] 78-79 D 4-E 3
Cordillera Oriental [DOM] 72-73 N 8
Cordillera Oriental [PE] 78-79 D 5-E 7
Cordillera Penibética 34-35 E 9-G 8
Cordillera Real [EC] 78-79 D 5
Cordillère Bétique = Cordillera Penibética 34-35 E 9-G 8
Córdoba [E] 34-35 E 10
Córdoba [MEX, Veracruz] 72-73 G 8
Córdoba [RA] 80 D 4
Córdoba, Sierra de – [RA] 80 C 4-D 3
Córdova 78-79 DE 7
Cordova, AK 70-71 G 5
Corea del Norte 48-49 O 3-4
Corea del Sur 48-49 OP 4
Corée du Nord 48-49 O 3-4
Corée du Sud 48-49 OP 4
Core Sound 74-75 E 7
Corfield 56-57 H 4
Corfou = Kérkyra 36-37 H 6
Corfu = Kérkyra 36-37 H 6
Coria 34-35 D 8-9
Coria del Rio 34-35 D 10
Coringa Islands 56-57 K 3
Corinne, UT 76-77 G 5
Corinth = Kórinthos 36-37 K 7
Corinthe = Kórinthos 36-37 K 7
Corinto [BR] 78-79 KL 8
Corinto [NIC] 72-73 J 9
Corinto = Kórinthos 36-37 K 7
Corisco, Isla de – 60-61 F 8
Cork 32 B 6
Corleone 36-37 E 7
Corleto Perticara 36-37 FG 5
Çorlu 46-47 B 2
Çorlusuyu Deresi 46-47 B 2
Cormoranes, Rocas – = Shag Rocks 80 H 8
Čormož 38-39 L 4
Čornaja 38-39 L 2
Čornaja [SU, Tajmyrskaja AO] 42-43 Q 3
Cornélio Procópio 80 FG 2
Corner Brook 70-71 Z 8
Corner Inlet 58 H 7
Corning, CA 76-77 B 6
Corning, NY 74-75 E 3
Cornouaille 34-35 EF 4
Cornwall 32 D 6
Cornwall [CDN] 70-71 VW 8
Cornwallis Island 70-71 RS 2-3
Cornwall Island 70-71 RS 2
Corny Point 58 C 5
Coro 78-79 EF 2
Coroatá 78-79 L 5
Corocoro 78-79 F 8
Coroico 78-79 F 8
Coromandel, Côte de – 44-45 N 7-8
Coromandel, Côte de – = Coromandel Coast 44-45 N 7-8
Coromandel, Côte de – = Coromandel Coast 44-45 N 7-8
Coromandel Coast 44-45 N 7-8
Corona, CA 76-77 E 9
Coronado, CA 76-77 E 9
Coronado, Bahía de – 72-73 K 10
Coronados, Islas de – 76-77 E 9
Coronation Gulf 70-71 OP 4
Coronation Island [South Orkneys] 24 CD 32
Coronation Islands 56-57 D 2
Coronel Dorrego 80 DE 5
Coronel Fabriciano 78-79 L 8
Coronel Francisco Sosa 80 CD 5-6
Coronel Galvão = Rio Verde de Mato Grosso 78-79 HJ 8
Coronel Oviedo 78-79 E 2-3
Coronel Pringles 80 D 5
Coronel Rosales 80 D 5
Coronel Suárez 80 D 5
Coropuna, Nudo – 78-79 E 8
Corowa 58 H 5-6
Corozal [BH] 72-73 J 8
Corpus Christi, TX 72-73 G 6
Corpus Christi, TX 72-73 G 6
Corque 78-79 F 8
Corral [RCH] 80 B 5
Corregidor Island 52-53 GH 4
Corrente 78-79 KL 7
Corrente, Rio – [BR, Bahia] 78-79 L 7
Correntes [BR, Mato Grosso] 78-79 HJ 8
Correntina 78-79 KL 7
Corrib, Lough – 32 B 5
Corrientes, Cabo – [CO] 78-79 D 3
Corrientes, Cabo – [MEX] 72-73 E 7
Corrientes, Cabo – [RA] 80 E 5
Corrigin 56-57 C 6
Corry, PA 74-75 D 4
Corse 36-37 C 4
Corse, Cap – 36-37 C 4
Corsica = Corse 36-37 C 4
Corsicana, TX 72-73 G 5
Č'orskogo, chrebet – 42-43 a 4-c 5
Corte 36-37 C 4
Cortez, CO 76-77 J 7
Cortez Mountains 76-77 E 5
Cortina d'Ampezzo 36-37 E 2
Čortkov 38-39 E 6
Cortland, NY 74-75 EF 3
Cortona 36-37 D 4
Çoruh = Artvin 44-45 E 2
Çoruh Nehri 46-47 J 2
Çorum 44-45 CD 2
Corumbá 78-79 H 8
Corumbá, Rio – 78-79 K 8
Coruña, La – 34-35 C 7
Coruña, La – 34-35 C 7
Corvallis, MT 76-77 FG 2
Corvallis, OR 72-73 B 3
Corwin Springs, MT 76-77 H 3
Cosenza 36-37 FG 6
Coshocton, OH 74-75 BC 4
Cosigüina, Punta – 72-73 J 9
Cosigüina, Volcán – 72-73 J 9
Cosmoledo Islands 64-65 L 4
Cosmopolis, WA 76-77 B 2
Cosmos Newberry Aboriginal Reserve 56-57 D 5
Č'ošskaja guba 42-43 H 4
Costa, Cordillera de la – [RCH] 80 B 2-3
Costa, Cordillera de la – [YV] 78-79 FG 3
Costa Brava 34-35 J 8
Costa de Marfil [★] 60-61 CD 7
Costa Grande 72-73 F 8
Costa Rica [CR] 72-73 JK 9-10
Costa Smeralda 24 B 3
Costermansville = Bukavu 64-65 G 3
Cotabato 52-53 H 5
Cotagaita [BOL] 78-79 F 9
Cotahuasi 78-79 E 8
Cotati, CA 76-77 B 6
Coteau des Prairies, Plateau du – 72-73 G 2-3
Coteau du Missouri, Plateau du – 72-73 FG 2
Côteau-Station 74-75 F 2
Côte d'Azur 34-35 L 7
Côte d'Ivoire [★] 60-61 CD 7
Côte Française = French Shore 70-71 Z 7-8
Cotentin 34-35 G 4
Cotonou 60-61 E 7
Cotonu = Cotonou 60-61 E 7
Cotopaxi [EC, ▲] 78-79 D 5
Cotswold Hills 32 EF 6
Cottage Grove, OR 76-77 B 4
Cottageville, SC 74-75 C 8
Cottbus 33 G 3
Cottica 78-79 J 4
Cottonwood, AZ 76-77 GH 8
Cottonwood, CA 76-77 B 5
Cottonwood, ID 76-77 E 2
Cottonwood Creek 76-77 B 5
Cottonwood Wash 76-77 HJ 8
Coudersport, PA 74-75 DE 4
Coulee City, WA 76-77 D 2
Coulee Dam, WA 76-77 D 1-2
Coulman Island 24 B 18
Council, ID 76-77 E 3
Council Bluffs, IA 72-73 GH 3
Council Mountain 76-77 E 3
Courlande 30-31 JK 9
Courtenay [CDN] 70-71 LM 8
Courtrai = Kortrijk 34-35 J 3
Coutances 34-35 G 4
Coveñas 78-79 D 3
Coventry 32 F 5
Coveñas 78-79 D 3
Covilhã 34-35 D 8
Covington, KY 72-73 JK 4
Covington, VA 74-75 CD 6
Cowal, Lake – 56-57 J 6
Cowan, Lake – 56-57 D 6
Cowansville 74-75 G 2
Coward Springs 56-57 G 5
Cowarie 56-57 G 5
Cowell 58 C 4
Cowen, Mount – 76-77 H 3
Cowlitz River 76-77 B 2
Cowra 56-57 J 6
Coxilha Grande 80 F 3
Coxim 78-79 J 8
Cox River 56-57 FG 3
Cox's Bazar = Koks Bāzār 44-45 P 6
Coyote, Arroyo el – 76-77 G 10
Coyotes Indian Reservation, Los – 76-77 E 9
Cozumel 72-73 J 7
Cozumel, Isla de – 72-73 J 7

Crab Creek 76-77 D 2
Cradock 64-65 G 9
Craig, MT 76-77 GH 2
Craig Harbour 70-71 UV 2
Craigmont, ID 76-77 E 2
Craiova 36-37 K 3
Crampel = Ra's al-Mā' 60-61 D 2
Cranbrook 70-71 NO 8
Crane, OR 76-77 D 4
Crane Mountain 76-77 CD 4
Cranston, RI 74-75 H 4
Crary Mountains 24 B 25
Crasna [R, ~] 36-37 K 2
Crasna [R, ●] 36-37 M 2
Crater Lake 72-73 B 3
Crater Lake, OR 76-77 BC 4
Crater Lake National Park 76-77 BC 4
Crateús 78-79 LM 6
Crato [BR] 78-79 M 6
Crau 34-35 K 7
Crauford, Cape – 70-71 TU 3
Cravo Norte 78-79 EF 3
Crawford, GA 74-75 B 8
Crawfordville, FL 74-75 AB 8
Crazy Mountains 76-77 H 2-3
Crazy Peak 76-77 HJ 3
Creedmoor, NC 74-75 D 6
Cree Lake [CDN, ≈] 70-71 P 6
Creil 34-35 J 4
Crema 36-37 C 3
Cremona 36-37 CD 3
Cres [YU, ⊙] 36-37 F 3
Cres [YU, ●] 36-37 F 3
Crescent, OR 76-77 C 4
Crescent, Lake – 76-77 B 1
Crescent City, CA 76-77 A 5
Crescent City, FL 74-75 c 2
Crescent Junction, UT 76-77 J 6
Crescent Lake, OR 76-77 C 4
Cressy 58 F 7
Crestline, NV 76-77 F 7
Creswell, OR 76-77 B 4
Creta = Krētē 36-37 L 8
Crete = Krētē 36-37 L 8
Crète = Krētē 36-37 L 8
Creus, Cabo – 34-35 J 7
Creuse 34-35 H 5
Creusot, le – 34-35 K 5
Crewe 32 E 5
Crewe, VA 74-75 D 6
Cribi = Kribi 60-61 F 8
Crib Point 58 G 7
Crichna = Krishna 44-45 M 7
Crikvenica 36-37 F 3
Crillon, mys – = mys Kriljon 42-43 b 8
Crimea = Krym' 38-39 F 6
Crimée = Krym' 38-39 F 6
Crişana 36-37 JK 2
Crisfield, MD 74-75 F 5-6
Cristobal 72-73 b 2
Crişul Alb 36-37 J 2
Crişul Negru 36-37 JK 2
Crna Gora 36-37 H 4
Crna Reka 36-37 J 5
Croacia 36-37 F-H 3
Croatia 36-37 F-H 3
Croatie 36-37 F-H 3
Crocodile Islands 56-57 FG 2
Croker Island 56-57 F 2
Cromer 32 G 5
Cromwell 56-57 NO 8-9
Crooked Creek 76-77 DE 4
Crooked Island 72-73 M 7
Crooked Island Passage 72-73 LM 7
Crooked River [USA] 76-77 C 3
Crooksville, OH 74-75 B 5
Crookwell 58 J 5
Cross, Cape – = Kaap Kruis 64-65 D 7
Cross City, FL 74-75 b 2
Crossman Peak 76-77 FG 8
Cross River 60-61 F 7-8
Cross Sound 70-71 J 6
Crotone 36-37 G 6
Crowie Creek 58 H 4
Crowley, LA 72-73 H 5-6
Crowley, Lake – 76-77 D 7
Crown King, AZ 76-77 G 8
Crownpoint, NM 76-77 JK 8
Crows Nest 58 L 1
Croydon 56-57 H 3
Croydon, London- 32 FG 7
Crozet 22-23 M 8
Crozet, Dorsal de – 22-23 M 8
Crozet, Seuil des – 22-23 M 8
Crozetdrempel 22-23 M 8
Crozet Ridge 22-23 M 8
Crucero, CA 76-77 EF 8
Cruces, Las – 72-73 b 2
Cruz, Cabo – 72-73 L 8
Cruz Alta [BR] 80 F 3
Cruz del Eje 80 CD 4
Cruzeiro 78-79 L 9
Cruzeiro do Sul 78-79 E 6
Cruzen Island 24 B 22-23
Crystal Bay 74-75 b 2
Crystal Brook 58 CD 4
Crystal River, FL 74-75 b 2

Csongrád 33 K 5

Ctesiphon = Ktesiphon 46-47 L 6

Ču 42-43 N 9
Cuamba 64-65 J 5
Cuando, Rio – 64-65 F 6
Cuando-Cubango 64-65 E 5-F 6
Cuangar 64-65 E 6
Cuango 64-65 E 4
Cuango, Rio – 64-65 E 6
Cuan Long 52-53 DE 5
Cuanza Norte 64-65 DE 4-5
Cuanza Sul 64-65 D 4-5
Cu'a Rao 52-53 DE 3
Cuauhtémoc 72-73 C 6
Cuba 72-73 KL 7
Cubabi, Cerro – 76-77 G 10
Cubal 64-65 D 5
Cubango, Rio – 64-65 E 6
Čubartau = Baršatas 42-43 O 8
Cubuk 46-47 E 2
Cuchi, Rio – 64-65 E 5-6
Cuchilla Grande [ROU] 80 EF 4
Cucui 78-79 F 4
Cucumbi 64-65 E 5
Cucunor = Chöch nuur 48-49 H 4
Cucurpe 76-77 H 10
Cúcuta 78-79 E 3
Cuddalore 44-45 MN 8
Cuddapah 44-45 M 8
Cudgewa 58 HJ 6
Cudi Dağı 46-47 K 4
Čudovo 42-43 E 6
Čudovo 38-39 F 4
Čudskoje ozero 42-43 O 6
Cue 56-57 C 5
Cuenca [E] 34-35 FG 8
Cuenca [EC] 78-79 D 5
Cuenca, Serranía de – 34-35 F 8-G 9
Cuenca Arábiga 22-23 N 5
Cuenca Argelinoprovenzal 28-29 J 8-K 7
Cuenca Argentina 22-23 GH 7-8
Cuenca Atlántico-Índico Antártica 22-23 J-M 9
Cuenca Brasileña 22-23 H 6
Cuenca Canadiense 19 AB 32-33
Cuenca Euroasiática 19 A
Cuenca Ibérica 22-23 HJ 3
Cuenca Índico-Antártica 22-23 O-Q 8
Cuenca Jónica 36-37 GH 7
Cuenca Levantina 44-45 BC 4
Cuenca Mexicana 72-73 HJ 6
Cuenca Norteamericana 22-23 FG 4
Cuenca Pacífico-Antártica 22-23 DE 8-9
Cuenlum = Kunlun Shan 48-49 D-H 4
Cuernavaca 72-73 FG 8
Cuesta Pass 76-77 C 8
Cuevas del Almanzora 34-35 G 10
Cufra, Wāhāt el – = Wāḥāt al-Kufrah 60-61 J 4
Čugujev 38-39 G 6
Cuiabá [BR, Amazonas] 78-79 H 6
Cuiabá [BR, Mato Grosso] 78-79 H 8
Cuiabá, Rio – 78-79 H 8
Cuillin Sound 32 C 3
Cuilo, Rio – 64-65 E 4
Cuima 64-65 E 5
Cuipo 72-73 a 2
Cuito, Rio – 64-65 EF 6
Cuito Cuanavale 64-65 EF 6
Čukotskij, mys – 42-43 l 5
Čukotskij poluostrov 42-43 kl 4
Çukurca 46-47 K 4
Culcairn 56-57 J 7
Culebra [PA] 72-73 b 2
Culgoa River 56-57 J 5
Culiacán 72-73 E 6-7
Culiacán Rosales = Culiacán 72-73 E 6-7
Culion Island 52-53 G 4
Čulkovo 42-43 Q 5
Cúllar de Baza 34-35 F 10
Cullera 34-35 GH 9
Čul'man 42-43 XY 6
Culpeper, VA 74-75 DE 5
Culuene, Rio – 78-79 J 7
Čuluut gol 48-49 J 2
Culver, Point – 56-57 DE 6
Čulym [SU, ~] 42-43 Q 6
Čulym [SU, ●] 42-43 P 6
Cum = Qom 44-45 G 4
Cumae 36-37 EF 5
Cumamoto = Kumamoto 48-49 P 5
Cumaná 78-79 G 2
Cumassia = Kumasi 60-61 D 7
Cumberland, KY 74-75 B 6
Cumberland, MD 72-73 L 4
Cumberland, VA 74-75 DE 6
Cumberland, Cape – 56-57 N 2
Cumberland, Lake – 74-75 A 6
Cumberland Island 74-75 C 9
Cumberland Islands 56-57 JK 4
Cumberland Peninsula 70-71 XY 4
Cumberland Plateau 72-73 J 5-K 4
Cumberland River 72-73 J 4
Cumberland Sound [CDN] 70-71 X 4-Y 5
Cumberland Sound [USA] 74-75 c 1
Cumborah 58 H 2
Cumbre, Paso de la – 80 BC 4
Cumbria 32 F 4
Cumbrian Mountains 32 E 4
Čumikan 42-43 Za 7
Cuminá, Rio – 78-79 H 5
Cummings, CA 76-77 B 6
Cummins 56-57 G 6
Cumpas 76-77 J 10
Çumra 46-47 E 4
Čuna [SU ◁ Angara] 42-43 S 6
Čun'a [SU ◁ Podkamennaja Tunguska] 42-43 ST 5
Cunani 78-79 J 4
Cunco 80 B 5
Cunene 64-65 E 6
Cunene, Rio – 64-65 D 6
Cúneo 36-37 B 3
Çüngüş 46-47 H 3
Cunnamulla 56-57 HJ 5
Cunningham, WA 76-77 D 2
Čuokkarašša 30-31 KL 2
Cupica, Golfo de – 78-79 D 3
Cuprum, ID 76-77 E 3
Curaçá [BR, Amazonas] 78-79 G 6
Curaçá [BR, Bahia] 78-79 LM 6
Curaçao 72-73 N 9
Curacautín 80 B 5
Curanilahue 80 B 5
Čurapča 42-43 Z 5
Curaray, Río – 78-79 D 5
Curdistán = Kordestān 44-45 F 3
Curiapo 78-79 G 3
Curicó 80 B 4
Curitiba 80 G 3
Curlandia 30-31 JK 9
Curlandia 30-31 JK 9
Curlew, WA 76-77 D 1
Curnamona 56-57 GH 6
Currais Novos 78-79 M 6
Currant, NV 76-77 F 6
Currie 56-57 H 7-8
Currie, NV 76-77 F 5
Currituck Sound 74-75 F 6
Curtea-de-Argeş 36-37 L 3
Curtin Springs 56-57 F 5
Curtis Island [AUS] 56-57 K 4
Curtis Island [NZ] 56-57 Q 6
Curuá, Rio – [BR ◁ Rio Iriri] 78-79 J 6
Curuai 78-79 H 5
Curuçá 78-79 K 5
Curup 52-53 D 7
Čurupinsk 36-37 P 2
Cururú 78-79 G 8
Cururupu 78-79 L 5
Curuzú Cuatiá 80 E 3
Curva Grande 78-79 K 5
Curvelo 78-79 L 8
Čusovaja 38-39 L 4
Čusovoj 42-43 K 6
Čust 44-45 L 2
Cut Bank, MT 76-77 GH 1
Cutch = Kutch 44-45 K 6
Cutervo 78-79 D 6
Cutler, CA 76-77 D 7
Cuttaburra Creek 58 G 2
Cuttack 44-45 NO 6
Cu'u Long, Cu'a Sông – 52-53 E 5
Cuvelai 64-65 E 6
Cuvier, Cape – 56-57 B 4
Cuvo, Rio – 64-65 D 5
Cuxhaven 33 D 2
Cuy, El – 80 C 5
Cuyahoga Falls, OH 74-75 C 4
Cuyama River 76-77 C 8
Cuyo Islands 52-53 H 4
Cuyuni River 78-79 G 3
Cuzco [PE, ●] 78-79 E 7

Cyangugu 63 B 3
Cyclades 36-37 L 7
Cyp-Navolok 30-31 PQ 3
Cypress Hills 70-71 OP 8
Cyprus 44-45 C 3
Cyrénaïque = Barqah 60-61 J 2

Czechoslovakia 33 F-K 4
Czersk 33 J 2
Częstochowa 33 JK 3

Ch

Chaaltyn gol 48-49 GH 4
Cha-am [T] 52-53 CD 4
Chaba 48-49 F 2
Chabarovo 42-43 L 4
Chabarovsk 42-43 a 8
Chablis 34-35 J 5
Chačmas 38-39 J 7
Chaco 80 D 3
Chaco Austral 80 DE 3
Chaco Boreal 80 DE 2
Chaco Central 80 D 2-E 3
Chaco River 76-77 J 7
Chachapoyas 78-79 D 6
Chācharān 72-73 K 4
Chachoengsao 52-53 D 4
Chad 60-61 HJ 5
Chadasan 48-49 J 2
Chadchal = Chatgal 48-49 HJ 1
Chadum 64-65 F 6
Chadzaar 48-49 G 4
Chaeryŏng 50-51 EF 3
Chagang-do 50-51 EF 2
Chagan nuur 48-49 L 3
Chaghcharān 44-45 K 4
Chagny 34-35 K 5
Chagos 22-23 N 6
Chagres [PA, ~] 72-73 ab 2
Chagres [PA, ●] 72-73 b 2

Chagr 169

Chagres, Brazo del –
72-73 b 2
Chagres, Río – 72-73 bc 2
Chagres Arm = Brazo del
Chagres 72-73 b 2
Chahâr Burjak 44-45 J 4
Châhâr Burjak = Chahâr
Burjak 44-45 J 4
Chahár Mahâl-e Bakhteyârî =
3 ◁ 44-45 G 4
Chahbâ = Shahbâ' 46-47 G 6
Châh Bâhâr = Bandar-e Châh
Bâhâr 44-45 HJ 5
Ch'aho 50-51 G 2
Chaidamu Pendi = Tsaidam
48-49 GH 4
Ch'ail-bong 50-51 F 2
Chai Nat 52-53 D 3
Chaîne Pontique 44-45 C-E 2
Chaîne Rocheuse = Rocky
Mountains 70-71 L 5-P 9
Chaiya 52-53 C 5
Chajari 80 E 4
Chajdag gol 48-49 EF 3
Chajlar 48-49 M 2
Chajlar = Hailar 48-49 M 2
Chajlar gol = Hailar He
48-49 MN 2
Chajpudyrskaja guba
38-39 LM 2
Chajrchan 48-49 J 2
Chajr'uzovo 42-43 e 6
Chaka Nor = Chöch nuur
48-49 H 4
Chake Chake 63 DE 4
Châl = Shâl 46-47 N 5
Chala 78-79 E 8
Chalabesa 63 B 5
Cha-lan-tun = Yalu 48-49 N 2
Chalbi Desert 63 D 2
Chalchyn gol 48-49 M 2
Chaleur Bay 70-71 XY 8
Chalhuanca 78-79 E 7
Cha-ling Hu = Kyaring Tsho
48-49 H 5
Chálkě 36-37 M 7
Chalkidikě 36-37 K 3
Chalkis 36-37 K 6
Chal'mer-Ju 42-43 L 4
Chalmer-Sede = Tazovskij
42-43 OP 4
Châlons-sur-Marne 34-35 JK 4
Chalon-sur-Saône 34-35 K 5
Chalosse 34-35 G 7
Chalturin 42-43 H 6
Challapata 78-79 F 8
Challis, ID 76-77 F 3
Cham 33 F 4
Chaman 44-45 K 4
Chamba [EAT] 63 D 5
Chamba [IND] 44-45 M 4
Chambal [IND ◁ Kali Sindh]
44-45 M 5-6
Chambal [IND ◁ Yamuna]
44-45 M 5-6
Chamberlain Lake 74-75 J 1
Chambersburg, PA
74-75 DE 4-5
Chambéry 34-35 K 6
Chambeshi 64-65 H 5
Chamchamâl 46-47 L 5
Chamdo = Chhamdo
48-49 H 5
Chami Choto = Hami
48-49 G 3
Chamo, Lake – = Tyamo
60-61 M 7
Champa [IND] 44-45 N 6
Champa [SU] 42-43 X 5
Champagne 34-35 J 5-K 4
Champagny Islands 56-57 D 3
Champaign, IL 72-73 J 3-4
Champâran = Motihari
44-45 NO 3
Champasak 52-53 DE 4
Champlain, Lake – 72-73 LM 3
Champotón 72-73 H 8
Chanâb = Chenab 44-45 M 4
Chan Bogd 48-49 K 3
Chancay 78-79 D 7
Chanch 48-49 J 1
Chan-chiang = Zhanjiang
48-49 L 7
Chanchoengsao 52-53 D 4
Chânda = Chandrapur
44-45 M 7
Chandalar River 70-71 G 4
Chandigarh 44-45 LM 4
Chandler 70-71 Y 8
Chandler, AZ 76-77 H 9
Chandlers Falls 63 D 2
Chandrapur 44-45 M 7
Chandyga 42-43 a 5
Chang, Ko – [T → Krung
Thep] 52-53 D 4

Changai = Shanghai 48-49 N 5
Changaj 48-49 H 2
Changajn nuruu 48-49 HJ 2
Ch'ang-an = Xi'an 48-49 K 5
Changane, Río – 64-65 H 7
Changara 64-65 H 6
Changbai 50-51 FG 2
Changbai Shan 48-49 O 3
Chang-chia-k'ou =
Zhangjiakou 48-49 L 3
Changchih = Changzhi
48-49 L 4
Ch'ang-chih = Changzhi
48-49 L 4
Changchun 48-49 NO 3
Changde 48-49 L 6
Changdu = Chhamdo
48-49 H 5
Chang-hai = Shanghai
48-49 N 5
Changhang 50-51 F 4-5
Changhowön 50-51 F 4
Ch'ang-hsing Tao =
Changxing Dao 50-51 C 3
Changhũng 50-51 F 5
Changhũng-ni 50-51 FG 2
Chang Jiang [TJ, ~ ◁ Dong
Hai] 48-49 K 5-6
Changji Huizu Zizhizhou
48-49 FG 3
Changjin 50-51 F 2
Changjin-gang 50-51 F 2
Changjin-ho 50-51 F 2
Changjon 50-51 G 3
Changkiakow = Zhangjiakou
48-49 L 3
Chang-kuang-ts'ai Ling =
Zhangguangcai Ling
48-49 O 2-3
Changnim-ni 50-51 F 3
Ch'angnyöng 50-51 G 5
Ch'ang-pai = Changbai
50-51 FG 2
Ch'ang-pai Shan = Changbai
Shan 48-49 O 3
Chang-san-ying =
Zhangsanying 50-51 AB 2
Changsha 48-49 L 6
Changshu 48-49 N 5
Char Gov' 48-49 GH 3
Ch'angsŏng = Chongsŏng
50-51 GH 1
Chang Tang = Jang Thang
48-49 E-G 5
Ch'ang-tê = Anyang
48-49 LM 4
Ch'ang-tê = Changde
48-49 L 6
Changteh = Changde
48-49 L 6
Changting 48-49 M 6
Ch'ang-tu = Chhamdo
48-49 H 5
Changtutsung = Chhamdo
48-49 H 5
Ch'angwŏn 50-51 G 5
Changxing Dao [TJ, Liaodong
Wan] 50-51 C 3
Changyeh = Zhangye
48-49 J 4
Changyŏn 48-49 NO 4
Changzhi 48-49 L 4
Changzhou 48-49 M 5
Chaniá 36-37 KL 8
Chaniôn, Kólpos – 36-37 KL 8
Chanka, ozero – 42-43 Z 9
Chankiang = Zhanjiang
48-49 L 7
Channâb = Chenab 44-45 M 4
Channel Islands 32 E 7
Channel Islands [USA]
76-77 CD 9
Channel Islands National
Monument = Anacapa
Island, Santa Barbara Island
76-77 D 9
Channel-Port-aux-Basques
70-71 Z 8
Chanovej 38-39 M 2
Chansi = Shanxi 48-49 L 4
Chantaburi = Chanthaburi
52-53 D 4
Chantada 34-35 CD 7
Chantajka 42-43 PQ 4
Chantajskoje, ozero –
42-43 QR 4
Chanten en Mansen, Nationaal
Gebied der – 42-43 L-P 5
Chan Tengri, pik – 44-45 MN 2
Chanthaburi 52-53 D 4
Chantong = Shandong
48-49 M 4
Chantrey Inlet 70-71 RS 4
Chanty-Mansijsk 42-43 M 5
Chanty y los Mansi,
Circunscripción Nacional de
los – 42-43 L-P 5

Chañar 80 C 4
Chañaral [RCH ↖ Copiapó]
80 B 3
Chañaral, Isla – 80 B 3
Chao'an 48-49 M 7
Chaochow = Chao'an
48-49 M 7
Chao Hu 48-49 M 5
Chao Phraya, Mae Nam –
52-53 CD 3-4
Chaor He 48-49 N 2
Chaotung = Zhaotong
48-49 J 6
Chao-t'ung = Zhaotong
48-49 J 6
Chaoyang [TJ, Guangdong]
48-49 M 7
Chaoyang [TJ, Liaoning]
48-49 MN 3
Ch'ao-yang-chên = Huinan
48-49 NO 3
Chapada da Veadeiros, Parque
Nacional da – 78-79 K 7
Chapada Diamantina 78-79 L 7
Chapadinha 78-79 L 5
Chapala, Lago de – 72-73 F 7
Chapčeranga 42-43 V 8
Chapel Hill, NC 74-75 D 7
Chapra 44-45 N 5
Chaqui 78-79 F 8
Châ'r, Jebel – = Jabal Shâ'r
46-47 GH 5
Charadai 80 E 3
Charagua 78-79 G 8
Charagua, Cordillera de –
78-79 G 8-9
Char Ajrag 48-49 KL 2
Charaña 78-79 F 8
Charbin = Harbin 48-49 O 2
Chãr Burjak 44-45 J 4
Char Chorin 48-49 J 2
Char Choto 48-49 J 3
Chardâvol 46-47 M 6
Chardon, OH 74-75 C 4
Charente 34-35 G 6
Chari 60-61 H 6
Charikâr 44-45 K 3-4
Char Ircis 48-49 F 2
Charita 78-79 H 3
Charitona Lapteva, bereg –
42-43 Q 3-R 2
Charity 78-79 H 3
Char'kov 38-39 G 5-6
Charleroi 34-35 K 3
Charles, Cape – 72-73 LM 4
Charles Island 70-71 VW 5
Charleston, SC 72-73 KL 5
Charleston, WV 72-73 K 4
Charleston Peak 76-77 F 7
Charlestown [Saint Kitts und
Nevis] 72-73 O 8
Charlesville 64-65 F 4
Charleville [AUS] 56-57 J 5
Charleville-Mézières 34-35 K 4
Charlotte, NC 72-73 KL 4-5
Charlotte Amalie 72-73 O 8
Charlotte Harbor 72-73 K 6
Charlottenberg 30-31 E 8
Charlottesville, VA 72-73 L 4
Charlottetown 70-71 Y 8
Charlottetown = Roseau
72-73 O 8
Charlovka 38-39 G 2
Charlton 58 F 6
Charlton Island 70-71 UV 7
Char Narijn uul 48-49 K 3
Char nuur [Mongolia] 48-49 G 2
Char nuur [TJ] 48-49 H 4
Charolais, Monts du –
34-35 K 5
Charovsk 42-43 G 6
Charqí, Jebel ech– = Jabal ar-
Ruwâq 46-47 G 5-6
Charqiliq 48-49 F 4
Charters Towers 56-57 J 3-4
Chartres 34-35 H 4
Char us nuur 48-49 G 2
Charvin = Shanxi 48-49 L 4
Chasan 50-51 H 1
Chascomús 80 E 5
Chase City, VA 74-75 D 6
Chasǒng 50-51 F 2
Chassahowitzka Bay 74-75 b 2
Chašuri 38-39 H 7
Chatanga 42-43 TU 3
Chatangskij zaliv 42-43 UV 3
Chatan gol 48-49 K 3
Châteaubriant 34-35 G 5
Château-du-Loir 34-35 H 5
Châteaudun 34-35 H 4
Châteaulin 34-35 EF 4
Châteauroux 34-35 H 5

Château-Thierry 34-35 J 4
Châtellerault 34-35 H 5
Chatgal 48-49 HJ 1
Chatham [CDN, New
Brunswick] 70-71 XY 8
Chatham [CDN, Ontario]
70-71 U 9
Chatham, NY 74-75 G 3
Chatham, VA 74-75 D 6
Chatham = Isla San Cristóbal
78-79 B 5
Chatham, Îles – 56-57 Q 8
Chatham, Isla – 80 B 8
Chatham Islands 56-57 Q 8
Chatham Strait 70-71 K 6
Châtillon 36-37 B 3
Châtillon-sur-Seine 34-35 K 5
Chatsworth 74-75 C 2
Chattahoochee River
72-73 JK 5
Chattanooga, TN 72-73 J 4
Chattarpur = Chhatarpur
44-45 M 6
Châu Đôc = Châu Phu
52-53 E 4
Chaumont 34-35 K 4
Chaŭn-do 50-51 EF 5
Châu Phu 52-53 E 4
Chautauqua Lake 74-75 D 3
Chaux-de-Fonds, La – 33 C 5
Chavast 44-45 K 2
Chaves 34-35 D 8
Chaves [BR] 78-79 K 5
Chaves, Isla – = Isla Santa
Cruz 78-79 B 5
Chavíb Deh 46-47 N 7
Chaviva 78-79 E 4
Chaya = Drayâ 48-49 H 5
Ch'a-yü = Dsayul 48-49 H 6
Chazón 80 D 4
Cheat Mountain 74-75 CD 5
Cheat River 74-75 D 5
Cheb 33 F 3
Chebâyesh, Al- = Al-Jaza'ir
46-47 M 7
Chebir, Uâu el – = Wâdî Bay
al-Kabîr 60-61 GH 2
Cheboygan, MI 72-73 K 2
Checoslovaquia 33 F-K 4
Chech, Erg – = 'Irq ash-
Shaykh 60-61 D 3-4
Chechaouëne = Shifshâwn
60-61 CD 1
Chechenes e Ingush,
República Autónoma de los
– = 5 ◁ 38-39 J 7
Checheno-Ingush Autonomous
Republic = 5 ◁ 38-39 J 7
Chech'on 50-51 G 4
Chedâdî, El- = Ash-Shiddâdî
46-47 J 4
Cheektowaga, NY 74-75 DE 3
Cheepie 56-57 HJ 5
Chefoo = Yantai 48-49 N 4
Chefu = Yantai 48-49 N 4
Chegga = Ash-Shaqqât
60-61 C 3
Chegutu 64-65 GH 6
Chehalis, WA 76-77 B 2
Chehalis River 76-77 B 2
Chehel-e Chashmeh, Kûhhâ-ye
– 46-47 M 5
Cheikh Ahmad = Shaykh
Ahmad 46-47 J 4
Cheikh Hlâl = Shaykh Hilâl
46-47 G 5
Cheikh Salâh = Shaykh Salâh
46-47 J 4
Cheikh Zerâfâ = Zilâf
46-47 G 6
Cheju 48-49 O 5
Cheju-do 48-49 NO 5
Cheju-haehyŏp 48-49 O 5
Chekiang = Zhejiang
48-49 MN 6
Chekkâ, Râs – = Râ's ash-
Shikk'ah 46-47 F 5
Chela, Serra da – 64-65 D 6
Chelan, WA 76-77 CD 2
Chelan, Lake – 76-77 C 1
Chélia, Djebel – = Jabal
Shîlyah 60-61 F 1
Chê-ling Kuan = Zheling Guan
48-49 L 6
Chełm 33 L 3
Chełmińskre, Pojezierze –
33 J 2
Chełmża 33 J 2
Chelsea, VT 74-75 G 2-3
Cheltenham 32 EF 6
Cheltenham, PA 74-75 F 4
Chelyuskin, Cape – = mys
Čel'uskin 42-43 UV 2

Chelleh Khâneh, Kûh-e –
46-47 N 4
Chemawa, OR 76-77 B 3
Chemba 64-65 H 6
Chemehuevi Valley Indian
Reservation 76-77 F 8
Chemnitz 33 F 3
Chemulpo = Inch'ŏn
48-49 O 4
Chenab 44-45 M 4
Chenab = Shenyang
48-49 NO 3
Ch'ên-ch'i = Chenxi 48-49 L 6
Chên-chiang = Zhenjiang
48-49 M 5
Ch'ên-chou = Yuanling
48-49 L 6
Cheney, WA 76-77 E 2
Chên-fan = Minqin 48-49 J 4
Ch'êng-chiang = Chengjiang
48-49 J 7
Chengde 48-49 M 3
Chengdu 48-49 J 5
Chengjiang 48-49 J 7
Chengkiang = Chengjiang
48-49 J 7
Chengkou 48-49 K 5
Chengmai 48-49 KL 8
Chengteh = Chengde
48-49 M 3
Chengtu = Chengdu 48-49 J 5
Cheng-Xian = Sheng Xian
48-49 N 6
Chengzitan 50-51 D 3
Chên-hsi = Bar Köl 48-49 G 3
Chenkiang = Zhenjiang
48-49 M 5
Chennapaṭṭaṇam = Madras
44-45 N 8
Chensi = Bar Köl 48-49 G 3
Chensi = Shanxi 48-49 L 4
Chentiin nuruu 48-49 K 2
Chentij = 15 ◁ 48-49 L 2
Chenxi 48-49 L 6
Chen Xian 48-49 L 6
Chenyang = Shenyang
48-49 NO 3
Chenyuan = Zhenyuan [TJ,
Yunnan] 48-49 J 7
Chên-yüan = Zhenyuan [TJ,
Yunnan] 48-49 J 7
Chepes 80 C 4
Cher 34-35 J 5
Cherangani 63 C 2
Cheraw, SC 74-75 CD 7
Cherbourg 34-35 G 4
Cherchen = Chärchän
48-49 F 4
Cheren = Keren 60-61 M 5
Chergui, Chott ech – = Ash-
Shaṭṭ ash-Sharqî 60-61 DE 2
Cherlen gol 48-49 KL 2
Cherlen gol = Herlen He
48-49 M 2
Cherrapunj = Cherrapunjee
44-45 P 5
Cherrapunjee 44-45 P 5
Cherry 56-57 N 2
Cherry Creek, NV 76-77 F 6
Cherson 38-39 F 6
Chesapeake, VA 72-73 LM 4
Chesapeake Bay 72-73 L 4
Cheshire, OR 76-77 B 3
Chesley 74-75 C 2
Chester 32 E 5
Chester, CA 76-77 C 5
Chester, MT 76-77 H 1
Chester, PA 74-75 F 4
Chester, SC 74-75 C 7
Chesterfield 32 F 5
Chesterfield, Île – 64-65 K 6
Chesterfield, Îles – 56-57 L 3
Chesterfield Inlet [CDN, ∪]
70-71 ST 5
Chesterfield Inlet [CDN, ●]
70-71 ST 5
Chestertown, MD 74-75 EF 5
Chesuncook Lake 74-75 HJ 1-2
Cheta [SU, ~] 42-43 S 3
Cheta [SU, ●] 42-43 S 3
Chetlat Island 44-45 L 8
Chetumal 72-73 J 8
Chetumal, Bahía de –
72-73 J 8
Cheviot, The – 32 EF 4
Cheviot Hills 32 E 4
Chewelah, WA 76-77 DE 1
Cheyenne, WY 72-73 F 3
Cheyenne River 72-73 F 3

Chhergundo 48-49 H 5
Chhergundo Zhou = Yushu
Zangzu Zizhizhou
48-49 GH 5
Chhibchang Tsho 48-49 G 5
Chhindvârâ = Chhindwara
[IND ← Seoni] 44-45 M 6
Chhindwara [IND ← Seoni]
44-45 M 6
Chhôṭâ Andamân = Little
Andaman 44-45 P 8
Chhôṭâ Nikôbâr = Little
Nicobar 44-45 P 9
Chhumar 48-49 G 4-5
Chhushul 48-49 FG 6
Chia-hsing = Jiaxing 48-49 N 5
Chiai 48-49 M 7
Chia-li = Lharugö 48-49 G 5
Chia-ling Chiang = Jialing
Jiang 48-49 K 5
Chia-mu-szŭ = Jiamusi
48-49 P 2
Chi-an = Ji'an [TJ, Jiangxi]
48-49 LM 6
Chi-an = Ji'an [TJ, Jilin]
50-51 EF 2
Chiang-chou = Xinjiang
48-49 L 4
Chiang Dao 52-53 CD 3
Chiange 64-65 D 6
Chiang-hsi = Jiangxi
48-49 LM 6
Chiang Khan 52-53 D 3
Chiang Mai 52-53 CD 3
Chiang Rai 52-53 CD 3
Chiang-su = Jiangsu
48-49 MN 5
Chiapa, Rio – = Rio Grande
72-73 H 8
Chiapas 72-73 H 8
Chiari 36-37 CD 3
Chiàvari 36-37 C 3
Chiavenna 36-37 C 2
Chiba 50-51 N 5
Chibabava 64-65 H 7
Chibemba 64-65 DE 6
Chibia 64-65 D 6
Chibinogorsk = Kirovsk
42-43 EF 4
Chibiny 38-39 F 2
Chibougamau 70-71 VW 7-8
Chiburi-jima 50-51 J 5
Chibuto 64-65 H 7
Chicacole = Shrikakulam
44-45 N 7
Chicago, IL 72-73 J 3
Chicapa, Rio – 64-65 F 4
Chic-Chocs, Monts –
70-71 X 8
Chickasha, OK 72-73 G 4-5
Chiclayo 78-79 CD 6
Chico, CA 72-73 B 4
Chico, Rio – [RA, Chubut]
80 C 6
Chico, Rio – [YV] 78-79 F 2
Chico, Rio – [RA, Santa Cruz
◁ Bahia Grande] 80 C 7
Chico, Rio – [RA, Santa Cruz
◁ Río Gallegos] 80 C 7
Chicoa 64-65 H 6
Chicoana 80 CD 3
Chiconomo 63 CD 6
Chicopee, MA 74-75 G 3
Chicoutimi 70-71 WX 8
Chicualacuala 64-65 H 7
Ch'i-ch = Qiqihar 48-49 N 2
Chichagof Island 70-71 J 6
Chichén Itzá 72-73 J 7
Chichester 32 F 6
Chi-do 50-51 EF 5
Chidley, Cape – 70-71 Y 5
Chiefland, FL 74-75 b 2
Chiehmo = Chärchän
48-49 F 4
Chiemsee 33 F 5
Chien-ch'ang = Jianchang [TJ
→ Benxi] 50-51 E 2
Chien-ch'ang = Jianchang [TJ
↙ Jinzhou] 50-51 B 2
Ch'ien-chiang = Qianjiang [TJ,
Hubei] 48-49 L 5
Chiengi 64-65 G 4
Chiengmai = Chiang Mai
52-53 C 3
Chien-Ho = Jian He [TJ, ~]
50-51 D 2
Chien-ko = Jiange 48-49 JK 5
Chien-ning = Jian'ou
48-49 M 6
Chien-ou = Jian'ou 48-49 M 6
Chien-p'ing = Jianping
50-51 B 2
Chien-shui = Jianshui
48-49 J 7

Ch'ien-wei = Qianwei 50-51 C 2
Chien-yang = Jianyang [TJ, Sichuan] 48-49 JK 5
Chieti 36-37 F 4
Chifeng 48-49 M 3
Chifre, Serra do – 78-79 L 8
Chignik, AK 70-71 E 6
Chigyŏng 50-51 F 3
Chih-chiang = Zhijiang [TJ, Hunan] 48-49 KL 6
Ch'ih-fêng = Chifeng 48-49 M 3
Chih-fu = Yantai 48-49 N 4
Chihkiang = Zhijiang 48-49 KL 6
Chih-li Wan = Bo Hai 48-49 M 4
Chi-hsi = Jixi 48-49 P 2
Chihuahua 72-73 E 6
Chii-san = Chiri-san 50-51 F 5
Chike = Xunke 48-49 O 2
Chikugo 50-51 H 6
Chikawawa 64-65 HJ 6
Chilapa de Alvarez 72-73 G 8
Chilás 44-45 L 3
Chilca 78-79 D 7
Chilcoot, CA 76-77 CD 6
Chile, Cuenca de – 22-23 E 7-F 6
Chile Basin 22-23 EF 6-7
Chilecito [RA, La Rioja] 80 C 3
Chilete 78-79 D 6
Chili 80 B 5-C 2
Chili, Bassin du – 22-23 E 7-F 6
Chilia, Brațul – 36-37 N 3
Chilibekken 22-23 EF 6-7
Chilibre 72-73 b 2
Ch'i-lien Shan = Qilian Shan 48-49 HJ 4
Chilika Hrada = Chilka Lake 44-45 NO 7
Chililabombwe 64-65 G 5
Chi-lin = Jilin [TJ, ●] 48-49 O 3
Chi-lin = Jilin [TJ, ☆] 48-49 N 2-O 3
Chilivani 36-37 C 5
Chilka Lake = Chilka Lake 44-45 NO 7
Chilko Lake 70-71 M 7
Chiloé, Isla de – 80 AB 6
Chilok 42-43 UV 7
Chilonga 63 B 5-6
Chilongozi 63 BC 6
Chiloquin, OR 76-77 C 4
Chilpancingo de los Bravos 72-73 G 8
Chiltern Hills 32 F 6
Chilung = Kee-lung 48-49 N 6
Chilwa, Lake – 64-65 J 6
Chillán 80 B 5
Chill Chainnigh = Kilkenny 32 C 5
Chillicothe, MO 72-73 H 3-4
Chillicothe, OH 72-73 K 4
Chilly, ID 76-77 FG 3
Chiman tagh 48-49 FG 4
Chimborazo [EC, ▲] 78-79 D 5
Chimbote 78-79 D 6
Chimoio 64-65 H 6
Chimpay 80 C 5
Chimpembe 63 B 5
China, Republiek – 48-49 N 7
China Lake, CA 76-77 E 8
China Meridional, Cuenca de – 52-53 FG 3-4
China Meridional, Mar de – 52-53 E 5-G 3
Chinan 50-51 F 5
Chinan = Jinan 48-49 M 4
Ch'in-an = Qin'an 48-49 K 5
Chinandega 72-73 J 9
China Oriental, Mar de – 48-49 N 6-O 5
Chinapa 76-77 HJ 10
China Point 76-77 D 9
Chinbo 50-51 G 4
Chincoteague, VA 74-75 F 6
Chincoteague Bay 74-75 F 5
Chincha Alta 78-79 D 7
Chin-ch'êng = Jincheng 48-49 L 4
Chinchilla 56-57 K 5
Chinchilla de Monte-Aragón 34-35 G 9
Chinchorro, Banco – 72-73 J 8
Chinchow = Jinzhou 48-49 N 3
Chinde 64-65 J 6
Chin-do [ROK, ☉] 50-51 EF 5
Chindo [ROK, ●] 50-51 F 5
Chindwin Myit 52-53 C 1-2
Chine 48-49 E-K 5
Chine Méridionale, Mer de – 52-53 E 5-G 3

Chine Orientale, Mer de – 48-49 N 6-O 5
Chinese muur 48-49 K 4
Ching-ch'uan = Yinchuan 48-49 JK 4
Ch'ing Hai = Chöch nuur 48-49 H 4
Chinghai = Qinghai 48-49 GH 4
Ching-ho = Jinghe [TJ, ●] 48-49 E 3
Ch'ing-ho-ch'êng = Qinghecheng 50-51 E 2
Ch'ing-ho-mêng = Qinghemen 50-51 C 2
Ching-ku = Jinggu 48-49 J 7
Ching-ning = Jingning 48-49 K 4
Chingola 64-65 G 5
Chingombe 63 B 6
Ching-po Hu = Jingbo Hu 48-49 O 3
Ching-t'ai = Jingtai 48-49 J 4
Ch'ing-tao = Qingdao 48-49 N 4
Ch'ing-tui-tzŭ = Qingduizi 50-51 D 3
Ching-tung = Jingdong 48-49 J 7
Ch'ing-yang = Qingyang [TJ, Gansu] 48-49 K 4
Ching-yüan = Jingyuan 48-49 JK 4
Ch'ing-yüan = Qingyuan [TJ, Liaoning] 50-51 E 1
Chinhae 50-51 G 5
Chinhae-man 50-51 G 5
Chinhoyi 64-65 GH 6
Chin-hsien = Jin Xian [TJ, Liaoning ↗ Jinzhou] 50-51 E 2
Chin-hsien = Jin Xian [TJ, Liaoning ↑ Lüda] 48-49 N 4
Chinhsien = Jinzhou 48-49 N 3
Chin-hua = Jinhua 48-49 MN 6
Ch'in-huang-tao = Qinhuangdao 48-49 MN 3-4
Chi-ning = Jining [TJ, Nei Monggol Zizhiqu] 48-49 L 3
Chi-ning = Jining [TJ, Shandong] 48-49 M 4
Chinju 48-49 O 4
Chinko 60-61 J 7
Chinle, AZ 76-77 J 7
Chinle Valley 76-77 J 7
Ch'in Ling = Qin Ling 48-49 KL 5
Chin-mên Tao 48-49 M 7
Chinnamp'o = Nampo 48-49 NO 4
Chinon 34-35 H 5
Chino Valley, AZ 76-77 G 8
Chinquião = Zhenjiang 48-49 M 5
Chinsali 64-65 H 5
Chin-sha Chiang = Jinsha Jiang 48-49 J 6
Chinsura 44-45 O 6
Chinwangtao = Qinhuangdao 48-49 MN 3-4
Chinwithetha Pyinnei 52-53 B 2
Ch'in-yang = Qinyang 48-49 L 4
Chinyŏng 50-51 G 5
Chiôco 64-65 H 6
Chiòggia 36-37 E 3
Chios [GR, ☉] 36-37 L 6
Chios [GR, ●] 36-37 M 6
Chipata 64-65 H 5
Chipili 63 B 5
Chipinge 64-65 H 7
Chipoka 63 C 6
Chiporiro 64-65 H 6
Chipre 44-45 C 3
Chiputneticook Lakes 74-75 JK 2
Chiquimula 72-73 HJ 9
Chiquitos, Llanos de – 78-79 G 8
Chira 63 D 2
Chira Bazar 48-49 DE 4
Chiraz = Shīrāz 44-45 G 5
Chiredzi 64-65 H 7
Chirfa 60-61 G 4
Chiricahua National Monument 76-77 J 9-10
Chiricahua Peak 76-77 J 10
Chirikof Island 70-71 EF 6
Chiriqui, Golfo de – 72-73 K 10
Chiriqui, Laguna de – 72-73 K 9-10
Chiri-san 50-51 F 5
Chiromo 64-65 J 6
Chirripó Grande, Cerro – 72-73 K 10

Chirundu 64-65 G 6
Chisamba 64-65 G 5-6
Chisel Lake 70-71 QR 7
Chi-shih Shan = Amnyemachhen Gangri 48-49 HJ 5
Chishtian Mandi = Chishtiyān Maṇḍī 44-45 L 5
Chishtiyān Maṇḍī 44-45 L 5
Chisimaio = Kismaanyo 64-65 K 3
Chitado 64-65 D 6
Chita-hantō 50-51 L 5
Chi'-i-t'ai = Qitai 48-49 FG 3
Chitambo 63 B 6
Chitembo 64-65 E 5
Chitogarh = Chittaurgarh 44-45 L 6
Chitose 50-51 b 2
Chitradurga 44-45 M 8
Chitrāl 44-45 L 3
Chitrĕ 72-73 K 10
Chittagong = Châṭṭagām 44-45 P 6
Chittaldurga = Chitradurga 44-45 M 8
Chittaorgarh = Chittaurgarh 44-45 L 6
Chittaurgarh 44-45 L 6
Chittoor 44-45 M 8
Chittoor = Chittor 44-45 M 8
Chiuchuan = Jiuquan 48-49 H 4
Chiulezi, Rio – 63 D 5-6
Chiumbe, Rio – 64-65 F 4
Chiume 64-65 F 5-6
Ch'iung-chou Hai-hsia = Qiongzhou Haixia 48-49 KL 7
Chiungshan = Qiongshan 48-49 L 8
Ch'iung-tung = Qionghai 48-49 L 8
Chiuta, Lagoa – 64-65 J 5
Chiva [SU] 42-43 L 9
Chivasso 36-37 B 3
Chivay 78-79 E 8
Chivilcoy 80 DE 4
Chivu 64-65 H 6
Chiwanda 64-65 HJ 5
Chiwefwe 63 B 6
Chiweta 64-65 H 5
Chixoy, Rio – 72-73 H 8
Chjargas 48-49 G 2
Chjargas nuur 48-49 GH 2
Chloride, AZ 76-77 F 8
Chmeiṭiyé = Shmayṭīyah 46-47 H 5
Chmelnickij 38-39 E 6
Chobe 64-65 F 6
Chobe National Park 64-65 FG 6
Chocaya 78-79 F 9
Chocca 78-79 D 7
Chocolate Mountains 76-77 F 9
Chocontá 78-79 E 3
Chochiang = Charqiliq 48-49 F 4
Choch'iwŏn 50-51 F 4
Chöch nuur 48-49 H 4
Chöch Šili 48-49 G 4
Chöch Šili uul 48-49 FG 4
Chodel = Chuld 48-49 K 2-3
Chodžambas 44-45 JK 3
Chodžejli 42-43 K 9
Chodžent = Leninabad 44-45 KL 2-3
Chodzież 33 H 2
Choele-Choel 80 CD 5
Choibalsan = Čojbalsan 48-49 L 2
Choiseul 52-53 j 6
Chojna 33 G 2
Chojnice 33 HJ 2
Chōkai-zan 50-51 MN 3
Chōlamaṇḍala = Coromandel Coast 44-45 N 7-8
Cholame, CA 76-77 CD 8
Chold = Chuld 48-49 K 2-3
Cholet 34-35 G 5
Cholgwan 50-51 E 3
Cholm 38-39 F 4
Cholmogory 42-43 G 5
Cholmsk 42-43 b 8
Cholodnoje 38-39 N 3
Cholos nuur 48-49 H 4
Ch'ŏlsan 50-51 E 3
Choluteca 72-73 J 9
Chŏlla-namdo 50-51 F 5
Chŏlla-pukto 50-51 F 5
Choma 64-65 G 6
Chomba 63 D 5

Ch'ŏnan 50-51 F 4
Chon Buri 52-53 D 4
Chŏnch'ŏn 50-51 F 2
Chone 78-79 CD 5
Ch'ŏng'ŏn-gang 50-51 EF 2-3
Chongdjin = Ch'ŏngjin 48-49 OP 3
Chŏnggŏ-dong 50-51 E 3
Ch'ŏngha 50-51 G 4
Ch'ŏngjin 48-49 OP 3
Chongjin = Ch'ŏngjin 48-49 OP 3
Chŏngju 48-49 O 4
Chongming 48-49 N 5
Chongor 48-49 L 2
Chongor = Bajan Adraga 48-49 L 2
Chongor Oboo Sum = Bajandalaj 48-49 J 3
Chongor Tagh = Qungur tagh 48-49 D 4
Ch'ŏngp'yŏngch'ŏn 50-51 FG 4
Chongqing 48-49 K 6
Ch'ŏngsan-do 50-51 F 5
Chongshan = Chongzuo 48-49 K 7
Ch'ongsŏktu-ri 50-51 EF 3
Chongsŏng 50-51 GH 1
Chŏngŭp 50-51 F 5
Ch'ŏngyang [ROK] 50-51 F 4
Chongzuo 48-49 K 7
Chŏnju 48-49 O 4
Chonos, Archipiélago de los – 80 AB 6-7
Chonuu 42-43 b 4
Chooloj Gov' 48-49 H 3
Chop'or 38-39 H 5-6
Chor 42-43 Za 8
Chorasan = Khorāsān 44-45 H 3-4
Chŏra Sfakion 36-37 L 8
Chordogoj 42-43 W 5
Chorinsk 42-43 U 7
Chorog 44-45 L 3
Chorrera, La – Chorrera [PA] 72-73 b 3
Chorsabad = Khorsabad 46-47 K 4
Chŏrwŏn 50-51 F 3
Chŏryŏng-do = Yŏng-do 50-51 G 5
Chorzele 33 K 2
Chorzów 33 J 3
Chosedachard 38-39 L 2
Chŏsen-kaikyŏ 48-49 O 5
Chōshi 50-51 N 5
Chos-Malal 80 BC 5
Chosŏn-man = Tonghan-man 48-49 O 4
Choszczno 33 GH 2
Chota 78-79 D 6
Chota Nāgpur 44-45 NO 6
Choteau, MT 76-77 G 2
Chotin 38-39 E 6
Chou Shan = Zhoushan Dao 48-49 N 5-6
Chou-shan Ch'ün-tao = Zhoushan Qundao 48-49 N 5
Chovd [Mongolia, ●] 48-49 G 2
Chovd [Mongolia, ☆ = 3 ◁] 48-49 G 2
Chövsgöl [Mongolia, ●] 48-49 KL 3
Chövsgöl [Mongolia, ☆ = 6 ◁] 48-49 J 1
Chövsgöl nuur 48-49 J 1
Chowan River 74-75 F 6
Chowchilla, CA 76-77 C 7
Christchurch [NZ] 56-57 OP 8
Christian Island 74-75 C 2
Christiansburg, VA 74-75 CD 6
Christianshåb = Qasigiánguir 70-71 ab 4
Christie Bay 70-71 O 5
Christmas Creek 56-57 E 3
Christmas Island [AUS] 52-53 E 1
Chromtau 42-43 K 7
Chrudim 33 GH 4
Chrysê 36-37 LM 8
Chrysochûs, Kólpos – 46-47 E 5
Chuang-ho = Zhuanghe 50-51 D 3
Chubb Crater = New Quebec Crater 70-71 VW 5
Chubbuck, CA 76-77 F 8
Chubisgalt = Chövsgöl 48-49 KL 3
Chubsugul = Chövsgöl nuur 48-49 J 1
Chūbu 50-51 LM 4-5

Chubut 80 BC 6
Chubut, Rio – 80 C 6
Chucheng = Zhucheng 48-49 MN 4
Chu-chi = Zhuji 48-49 N 6
Ch'ü-ching = Qujing 48-49 J 6
Ch'ü-chou = Qu Xian 48-49 M 6
Chu-chou = Zhuzhou 48-49 L 6
Chuchow = Zhuzhou 48-49 L 6
Ch'üeh-shan = Queshan 48-49 L 5
Chugach Mountains 70-71 GH 5
Chūgoku 50-51 HJ 5
Chūgoku-sammyaku 50-51 JK 5
Chuguchak 48-49 E 2
Chügüchak = Tarbagataj 48-49 EF 2
Chuhsien = Qu Xian 48-49 M 6
Ch'u-hsiung = Chuxiong 48-49 J 7
Chü-hua Tao = Juhua Dao 50-51 C 2
Chukchi Plateau 19 B 35
Chukchi Sea 19 BC 35-36
Chukchos, Circunscripción Nacional de los – 42-43 g-j 4
Chukchos, Dorsal de – 19 B 35
Chukchos, Mar de – 19 BC 35-36
Chuki = Zhuji 48-49 N 6
Chukot Autonomous Area 42-43 g-j 4
Chukudu Kraal 64-65 F 7
Chūl, Gardaneh-ye – 46-47 MN 6
Chulaq Aqqan Su 48-49 G 4
Chula Vista, CA 72-73 C 5
Chuld 48-49 K 2-3
Chulga 38-39 M 3
Chü-liu-ho = Juliuhe 50-51 D 1
Chulp'o 50-51 F 5
Chulucanas 78-79 CD 5
Chulumani 78-79 F 8
Chumbicha 80 C 3
Chum Phae 52-53 D 3
Chumphon 52-53 CD 4
Chumsaeng 52-53 D 3
Chumunjin 50-51 G 3
Ch'unch'ŏn 48-49 O 4
Chungam-ni 50-51 G 5
Ch'ungch'ŏng-namdo 50-51 F 4
Ch'ungch'ŏng-pukto 50-51 FG 4
Chüngges 48-49 E 3
Chunghwa 50-51 EF 3
Ch'ungju 50-51 FG 4
Chungking = Chongqing 48-49 K 6
Ch'ung-ming = Chongming 48-49 N 5
Ch'ungmu 50-51 G 5
Chüngsan 50-51 E 3
Chungsan = Zhongshan 48-49 L 7
Chung-tien = Zhongdian 48-49 HJ 6
Chüngüj gol 48-49 GH 2
Chung-wei = Zhongwei 48-49 JK 4
Chunya 64-65 H 4
Chuquibamba 78-79 E 8
Chuquicamata 80 C 2
Chuquisaca = Sucre 78-79 FG 8
Chur 33 D 5
Churchill [CDN] 70-71 RS 6
Churchill, ID 76-77 FG 4
Churchill, Cape – 70-71 S 6
Churchill Falls 70-71 XY 7
Churchill Peak 70-71 LM 6
Churchill River [CDN, Manitoba] 70-71 RS 6
Churchill River [CDN ↗ Hamilton Inlet] 70-71 Y 7
Churu 44-45 LM 5
Chusei-hokudō = Ch'ungch'ŏng-pukto 50-51 FG 4
Chusei-nandō = Ch'ungch'ŏng-namdo 50-51 F 4
Chu-shan = Zhushan 48-49 KL 5
Chusistan = Khūzestān 44-45 F 4
Chuska Mountains 76-77 J 7-8
Chust 38-39 D 6

Chutag 48-49 J 2
Chuučnar 48-49 G 5
Chuŭronjang 50-51 GH 2
Chuvash Autonomous Republic = 4 ◁ 42-43 H 6
Chuvashi, República Autónoma de los – 4 ◁ 42-43 H 6
Chuwārtah 46-47 L 5
Chuxiong 48-49 J 7
Chuxiong Yizu Zizhizhou 48-49 J 6
Chuy 80 F 4
Chu Yang Sin 52-53 E 4
Chužand 44-45 K 2-L 3
Chužir 42-43 U 7
Chvalynsk 38-39 J 5
Chwārta = Chuwārtah 46-47 L 5
Chypre 44-45 C 3

D

Đa, Sông – 52-53 D 2
Ḍab'ah 46-47 G 7
Ḍab'ah, Rā's al-61 K 2
Ḍab'ah, Rā's aḍ- 62 C 2
Ḍabakala 60-61 D 7
Daba Shan 48-49 KL 5
Dabas nuur 48-49 H 4
Dabbâ = Jabal Jarbī 46-47 H 5
Dabbah, Ad- 60-61 KL 5
Dabbūsah, Ad- 46-47 J 7
Dabeiba 78-79 D 3
Dabie Shan [TJ, ▲▲] 48-49 M 5
Dabola 60-61 B 6
Daborow 60-61 b 2
Dąbrowa Tarnowska 33 K 3
Dabuxun Hu = Dabas nuur 48-49 H 4
Dacar = Dakar 60-61 A 6
Dacar, Bir ed – = Bi'r aḍ-Dhikār 60-61 J 3
Dacca = Ḍhāka [BD, ●] 44-45 OP 6
Dachaidan = Tagalgan 48-49 H 4
Dachangshan Dao 50-51 D 3
Dachau 33 E 4
Dachstein 33 F 5
Đắc Lắc, Cao Nguyên – 52-53 E 4
Daday 46-47 E 2
Dade City, FL 74-75 b 2
Dadra and Nagar Haveli 44-45 L 6
Dadu He 48-49 J 5
Daet 52-53 H 4
Dafdaf, Jabal – 62 F 3
Dafinah, Ad- 44-45 E 6
Dagabur = Degeh Bur 60-61 N 7
Dagana 60-61 AB 5
Dağbaşı 46-47 H 4
Dagelet = Ullŭng-do 48-49 P 4
Dagestan, Autonome Republiek – 38-39 J 7
Dagestan, Autonomous Republic – 38-39 J 7
Daggett, CA 76-77 E 8
Daghestán, République Autonome du – 38-39 J 7
Daghgharah, Ad- 46-47 L 6
Dağlıca 46-47 KL 4
Dagö = Hiiumaa 30-31 JK 8
Dagomba 60-61 E 6-7
Dagomys, Soči- 38-39 G 7
Dagua [PNG] 52-53 M 7
Daguestán, República Autónoma del – 38-39 J 7
Daguja 50-51 E 1
Dagverdharnes 30-31 b 2
Dāhānu 44-45 L 6-7
Daḥī, Nafūd ad- 44-45 EF 6
Dahlak = Dehalak Desēt 60-61 N 5
Dahnâ', Ad- 44-45 E 5-F 6
Dahomey = Benin 60-61 E 6-7
Dahrah 60-61 H 3
Ḍahr Walāṭah 60-61 C 5
Dahshûr = Minshāt Dahshūr 62 D 3
Dahūk 46-47 K 4
Dahushan 50-51 D 2
Daimiel 34-35 F 9
Daiō 50-51 L 5
Daipingqiao = Taipingshao 50-51 E 2
Dairen = Dalian 48-49 N 4
Dairût = Dayrūt 60-61 L 3
Dai-sen 50-51 J 5

Dai-Sengen dake 50-51 ab 3
Dais hōji = Kaga 50-51 L 4
Daisy, WA 76-77 DE 1
Daito-jima 48-49 P 6
Daitō-shima 48-49 P 6
Daitō sima = Daitō-shima 48-49 P 6
Dajarra 56-57 G 4
Dakar 60-61 A 6
Dakawa 63 D 4
Daketa Sheṭ 60-61 N 7
Dakhan = Deccan 44-45 M 6-8
Dākhilah, Wāḥāt ad- 60-61 K 3
Dakhlah, Ad- 60-61 A 4
Dakhla Oasis = Wāḥāt ad-Dākhilah 60-61 K 3
Dakka = Ḍhāka 44-45 OP 6
Dakshiṇ Andamān = South Andamān 44-45 P 8
Dakshiṇ Paṭhār = Deccan 44-45 M 6-8
Dala 30-31 bc 2
Dalaba 60-61 B 6
Dalai 48-49 N 2
Dalai Lama Gangri 48-49 GH 5
Dalai Nur 48-49 M 2
Dalaj Nuur = Hulun Nur 48-49 M 2
Dalāk, Kūh-e – 46-47 N 4
Dalälven 30-31 G 7
Dalaman Nehri 46-47 C 4
Dalandzadgad 48-49 JK 3
Dalarna 30-31 EF 7
Da Lat 52-53 E 4
Dalavakasır = Oyalı 46-47 J 4
Dālbandīn 44-45 J 5
Dalby [AUS] 56-57 K 5
Dale 30-31 AB 7
Dale, OR 76-77 D 3
Dale, PA 74-75 D 4
Dalen 30-31 C 8
Dalgaranga, Mount – 56-57 C 5
Dalhousie, Cape – 70-71 KL 3
Dali [TJ, Yunnan] 48-49 HJ 6
Dalian 48-49 N 4
Dalias 34-35 F 10
Dali Baizu Zizhizhou 48-49 HJ 6
Daling He 50-51 C 2
Daljā' 62 D 4
Ḍalkūt = Kharīfūt 44-45 G 7
Dāllah, 'Ayn – 62 B 4
Dallas, OR 76-77 B 3
Dallas, TX 72-73 G 5
Dall Island 70-71 K 7
Dallol Bosso 60-61 E 5-6
Dalmacia = Dalmacija 36-37 F 3-H 4
Dalmacija 36-37 F 3-H 4
Dalmaj, Hawr – 46-47 L 6
Dalmatia = Dalmacija 36-37 F 3-H 4
Dalmatie = Dalmacija 36-37 F 3-H 4
Dal'negorsk 42-43 a 9
Dal'nerečensk 42-43 Za 8
Dal'nij = Lüda-Dalian 48-49 N 4
Daloa 60-61 C 7
Dalqū 60-61 L 4-5
Dalrymple, Mount – 56-57 J 4
Dalton, GA 72-73 JK 5
Dalton, MA 74-75 G 3
Daltonganj 44-45 N 6
Dalton Ice Tongue 24 C 12-13
Dalton in Furness 32 E 4
Dalvik 30-31 d 2
Dalwhinnie 32 DE 3
Daly City, CA 76-77 B 7
Daly River 56-57 F 2
Daly Waters 56-57 F 3
Damā, Wādī – 62 FG 4
Damān 44-45 L 6
Damanhūr 60-61 L 2
Damaq 46-47 N 5
Damar, Pulau – 52-53 J 8
Damara 60-61 H 8
Damaraland 64-65 E 7
Damas = Dimashq 44-45 D 4
Damasco = Dimashq 44-45 D 4
Damascus, VA 74-75 C 6
Damascus = Dimashq 44-45 D 4
Damaturu 60-61 G 6
Damāvand, Kūh-e – 44-45 G 3
Damāzīn, Ad- 60-61 LM 6
Damba 64-65 DE 4
Dambuki 48-49 S 3-T 2
Dam Dam = South Dum Dum 44-45 OP 6
Damdūm, Bi'r – 62 BC 2
Dāmghān 44-45 GH 3
Damietta = Dumyāṭ 60-61 L 2
Damietta Mouth = Maṣabb Dumyāṭ 62 DE 2
Dāmir, Ad- 60-61 L 5
Damīr Qābū 46-47 JK 4
Dammām, Ad- 44-45 FG 5
Damodar 44-45 O 6
Damot 60-61 b 2
Dampier 56-57 C 4
Dampier, Selat – 52-53 K 7
Dampier Archipelago 56-57 C 4
Dampier Downs OC 56-57 D 3
Dampier Land 56-57 D 3
Dāmūr, Ad- 46-47 F 6
Dan, Kap – 70-71 d 4
Dana, Mount – 76-77 D 7
Đa Năng 52-53 E 3
Danbury, CT 74-75 G 4
Danby Lake 76-77 F 8
Dancharia 34-35 G 7
Dandarah 62 E 4
Dandong 48-49 N 3
Danemark 30-31 C-E 10
Danemark, Détroit du – 19 C 20-22
Danforth, ME 74-75 JK 2
Danfu 52-53 h 5
Dange, Rio – 64-65 D 4
Dang Raek, Phanom – 52-53 DE 4
Dangraek, Phnom – = Phanom Dang Raek 52-53 DE 4
Dan Guno 60-61 F 6-7
Daniel, WY 76-77 H 4
Danilov 42-43 G 6
Danişment 46-47 GH 3
Danissa 63 E 2
Danjo-shotō 50-51 G 6
Ḍank 44-45 H 6
Ḍanli 72-73 J 9
Dannemora, NY 74-75 FG 2
Dannevirke 56-57 P 8
Dan River 74-75 CD 6
Danshui = Tan-shui 48-49 N 6
Dansia 78-79 H 4
Dansville, NY 74-75 E 3
Dante, VA 74-75 B 6
Dante = Xaafuun 60-61 c 1
Danube = Dunărea 36-37 M 3
Danubio = Dunărea 36-37 M 3
Danushkodi 44-45 MN 9
Danville, IL 72-73 J 3
Danville, ME 74-75 H 2-3
Danville, VA 72-73 L 4
Dan Xian 48-49 K 8
Dao-Timni 60-61 G 4
Ḍaou, Eḍ- = Aḍ-Ḍaw 46-47 G 5
Dapsang = K 2 44-45 M 3
Dapupan 52-53 GH 3
Daqing Shan 48-49 L 3
Daqmā', Ad- 44-45 FG 6
Daquan 48-49 H 3
Dar'ā 46-47 G 6
Darā, Jazīreh – 46-47 N 7
Dārāb 44-45 GH 5
Darabani 36-37 M 1
Darad = Dardistān 44-45 L 3
Darag = Legaspi 52-53 H 4
Daraj 60-61 G 2
Dār al-Bayḍā', Ad- 60-61 BC 2
Darašun = Veršino-Darasunskij 42-43 VW 7
Darau = Darāw 62 E 5
Darāw 62 E 5
Darb, Ad- 44-45 E 7
Dār Bādām 46-47 M 6
Darband, Kūh-e – 44-45 H 4
Darbandī Khan, Sadd ad- 46-47 L 5
Darbanga = Darbhanga 44-45 O 5
Darbhanga 44-45 O 5
Darbi = Darvi 48-49 G 2
Darby, MT 76-77 FG 2
Darchan 48-49 K 2
Dardanelles = Çanakkale Boğazı 44-45 B 2-3
Dardanelles = Çanakkale Boğazı 44-45 B 2-3
Dardanelos = Çanakkale Boğazı 44-45 B 2-3
Dār Dīshah 46-47 J 5
Dardo = Kangding 48-49 J 5-6
Dâr el Beïḍâ', ed – = Ad-Dār al-Bayḍā' 60-61 BC 2
Darende 46-47 G 3
Dar es Salaam 64-65 JK 4
Dārfūr 60-61 J 6
Dārfūr 60-61 K 5-6
Dargagā, Jebel ed – = Jabal Ardar Gwagwa 62 F 6
Dargan-Ata 44-45 J 2
Dargaville 56-57 O 7
Dargo 58 H 6
Dar Hu = Dalaj Nur 48-49 M 3
Darien, GA 74-75 C 9
Darién [PA, ≅] 72-73 L 10
Darien [PA, ●] 72-73 b 2
Darien = Dalian 48-49 N 4
Darién, Golfo del – 78-79 D 3
Dārigah 46-47 K 5
Dariganga 48-49 L 2
Darjeeling 44-45 O 5
Dārjiling = Darjeeling 44-45 O 5
Darkhazīneh 46-47 N 7
Darling Downs 56-57 JK 5
Darling Range 56-57 C 6
Darling River 56-57 H 6
Darlington 32 EF 4
Darlington, SC 74-75 CD 7
Darlowo 33 H 1
Darmstadt 33 D 4
Darnah 60-61 J 2
Darnick 56-57 H 6
Darnley, Cape – 24 C 7-8
Daroca 34-35 G 8
Darrington, WA 76-77 C 1
Darsah 44-45 G 8
Dart, Cape – 24 B 24
Dartmoor Forest 32 E 6
Dartmouth [CDN] 70-71 Y 9
Dartuch, Cabo – 34-35 J 9
Daru 52-53 M 8
Darūdāb 60-61 M 5
Daruvar 36-37 G 3
Darvaza 44-45 H 2
Darvi 48-49 G 2
Darwešān 44-45 JK 4
Darwin [AUS] 56-57 F 2
Darwin, CA 76-77 E 7
Darwin, Bahía – 80 AB 7
Dās 44-45 G 5
Dashen Terara, Ras – 60-61 M 6
Dashiqiao 50-51 D 2
Dasht 44-45 J 5
Dasht-e Āzādegān 46-47 N 7
Dashtīāri = Polān 44-45 J 5
Dataran Tinggi Cameron = Tanah Tinggi Cameron 52-53 D 6
Datça = Reşadiye 46-47 B 4
Date 50-51 b 2
Datia 44-45 M 5
Datiyā = Datia 44-45 M 5
D'atkovo 38-39 FG 5
Datong [TJ, Shanxi] 48-49 L 3
Datong He 48-49 J 4
Datu, Tanjung – 52-53 E 6
Datu, Teluk – 52-53 EF 6
Datu Piang 52-53 H 5
Dau'an = Al-Huraybah 44-45 F 7
Daudmannsodden 30-31 hj 5
Daugava 30-31 LM 9
Daugava = Severnaja Dvina 42-43 G 5
Daugavpils 30-31 M 10
Daulagiri = Dhaulāgiri 44-45 N 5
Daule, Rio – 78-79 CD 5
Dauna Parma = Dawa 60-61 M 7-8
Dauphin 70-71 QR 7
Dauphiné 34-35 KL 6
Daurskij chrebet = chrebet Čerskogo 42-43 V 7
Dautlatābād = Malāyer 44-45 F 4
Davalguiri = Dhaulagiri 44-45 N 5
Davao 52-53 J 5
Davao Gulf 52-53 J 5
Davenport, IA 72-73 H 3
Davenport, WA 76-77 D 2
Davenport Downs 56-57 H 4
Davenport Range 56-57 FG 4
Davey, Port – 56-57 HJ 8
David 72-73 K 10
David-Gorodok 38-39 E 5
Davidson Mountains 70-71 H 4
Davis, CA 76-77 BC 6
Davis, WV 74-75 D 5
Davis, Détroit de – 70-71 Z 4-5
Davis, Estrecho de – 70-71 Z 4-5
Davis, Straat – 70-71 Z 4-5
Davis Bay 24 C 14
Davis Creek, CA 76-77 C 5
Davis Dam, AZ 76-77 F 8
Davis Sea 24 C 10
Davis Strait 70-71 Z 4-5
Davlekanovo 42-43 JK 7
Davos 33 DE 5
Ḍaw, Aḍ- 46-47 G 5
Dawādimā, Ad- 44-45 EF 6
Dawangjia Dao 50-51 D 3
Dawanle = Dewelē 60-61 N 6
Dawāsir, Wādī ad- 44-45 EF 6
Dawa Weniz 60-61 M 7-8
Dawḥah, Ad- 44-45 G 5
Dawr, Ad- 46-47 KL 5
Dawrah, Baghdād- 46-47 L 6
Dawson 70-71 J 5
Dawson, Isla – 80 BC 8
Dawson Creek 70-71 M 6
Dawson-Lambton Glacier 24 B 33-34
Dawson Range 70-71 J 5
Dawwah 44-45 H 6
Dawwāya = Jamā'at al-Ma'yuf 46-47 M 7
Dax 34-35 G 7
Da Xian 48-49 K 5
Daxue Shan 48-49 J 5-6
Day, FL 74-75 b 1
Dayang Bunting, Pulau – 52-53 C 5
Dayang He 50-51 D 2
Daylesford 58 G 6
Daym Zubayr 60-61 K 7
Dayong 48-49 L 6
Dayr, Ad- 62 E 5
Dayr as-Suryānī 62 CD 2
Dayr az-Zawr 44-45 DE 3
Dayr Ḥāfir 46-47 G 4
Dayr Katrīnah 62 E 3
Dayr Māghar 46-47 H 4
Dayr Mawās 62 D 4
Dayr Samū'īl 62 D 3
Dayrūṭ 60-61 L 3
Dayton, NV 76-77 D 6
Dayton, OH 72-73 K 4
Dayton, WA 76-77 E 2
Daytona Beach, FL 72-73 KL 6
Dayu 48-49 L 6
Da Yunhe [TJ, Jiangsu] 48-49 M 5
Dayville, OR 76-77 D 3
Dazkırı 46-47 CD 4
Dead Indian Peak 76-77 HJ 3
Deadman Bay 74-75 b 2
Dead Sea = Baḥr al-Mayyit 44-45 D 4
Deadwood Reservoir 76-77 F 3
Deal Island 58 cd 1
Deán Funes 80 D 4
Dean River 70-71 L 7
Dearg, Beinn – 32 D 3
Deary, ID 76-77 E 2
Dease Arm 70-71 MN 4
Dease Lake 70-71 KL 6
Dease Strait 70-71 P 4
Death Valley 72-73 C 4
Death Valley, CA 76-77 E 7
Death Valley National Monument 76-77 E 7-8
Deauville 34-35 GH 4
Debar 36-37 J 5
Debark 60-61 M 6
Dębica 33 K 3-4
Dęblin 33 KL 3
Débo, Lac – 60-61 D 5
De Borgia, MT 76-77 F 2
Debre Birhan 60-61 MN 7
Debrecen 33 K 5
Debre Markos 60-61 M 6
Debre Tabor 60-61 M 6
Decamere = Dekemḥarē 60-61 M 5
Decatur, AL 72-73 J 5
Decatur, GA 72-73 K 5
Decatur, IL 72-73 HJ 3-4
Decazeville 34-35 J 6
Decepción, Cabo – = Cape Disappointment 80 J 8-9
Deception 24 C 30
Děčín 33 G 3
Declo, ID 76-77 G 4
Decoto, CA 76-77 BC 7
Deda 36-37 L 2
Dedo, Cerro – 80 B 6
Dédougou 60-61 D 6
Dedza 64-65 H 5
Dee [GB, Cambrian Mts.] 32 E 5
Dee [GB, Grampian Mts.] 32 E 3
Deep Creek Range 76-77 G 5-6
Deep River [USA] 74-75 D 7
Deepwater 58 K 2
Deerfield Beach, FL 74-75 cd 3
Deering, Mount – 56-57 E 5
Deer Lodge, MT 76-77 G 2
Deer Lodge Mountains 76-77 G 2
Deer Lodge Pass 76-77 G 3
Deer Park, WA 76-77 E 2
Deeth, NV 76-77 F 5
Deffa, ed – = Aḍ-Ḍiffah 60-61 J 2
Dêge 48-49 H 5
Degeh Bur 60-61 N 7
Deggendorf 33 F 4
De Grey 56-57 CD 4
De Grey River 56-57 CD 4
Dehalak Desēt 60-61 N 5
Dehgolān 46-47 M 5
Dehkhwareqan = Āzar Shahr 46-47 LM 4
Dehlorān 44-45 F 4
Dehna = Ad Dahnā' 44-45 E 5-F 6
Dehna, Ed- = Ad-Dahnā' 44-45 E 5-F 6
Dehōk = Dahūk 46-47 K 4
Dehong Daizu Zizhizhou = D ◁ 48-49 H 6-7
Dehra Dun 44-45 M 4
Deh Shū 44-45 J 4
Deir, Ed – = Ad-Dayr 62 E 5
Deir es-Suryânî = Dayr as-Suryānī 62 CD 2
Deir ez Zôr = Dayr az-Zawr 44-45 DE 3
Deir Ḥâfir = Dayr Ḥāfir 46-47 G 4
Deir Katerîna = Dayr Katrīnah 62 E 3
Deir Mâghar = Dayr Māghar 46-47 H 4
Deir Mawâs = Dayr Mawās 62 D 4
Deir Samweil = Dayr Samū'īl 62 D 3
Dej 36-37 K 2
Dejnev, Cap – = mys Dežneva 42-43 lm 4
De Jongs, Tanjung – 52-53 L 8
De-Kastri 42-43 ab 7
Dekemhare 60-61 M 5
Dekese 64-65 F 3
Dekoûa, Tell – = Tall adh-Dhakwah 46-47 G 6
Delaimiya, Ad- = Ad-Dulaymīyah 46-47 K 6
De Land, FL 74-75 c 2
Delano, CA 76-77 D 8
Delano Peak 72-73 D 4
Delaware 72-73 LM 4
Delaware Bay 72-73 LM 4
Delaware Reservoir 74-75 B 4
Delaware River 74-75 F 5
Delčevo 36-37 K 4-5
Delegate 58 J 6
Delfi = Delphoi 36-37 K 6
Delfzijl 34-35 L 2
Delgerchet 48-49 L 2
Delger mörön 48-49 H 1-2
Delgo = Delqū 60-61 L 4-5
Delhi [CDN] 74-75 C 3
Delhi [IND] 44-45 M 5
Delhi, NY 74-75 F 3
Delhi = Dili 52-53 J 8
Deli, Pulau – 52-53 DE 8
Delice 46-47 E 3
Deliceırmak 46-47 F 3
Délices 78-79 J 4
Delicias 72-73 E 6
Delījān 46-47 O 5-6
Delingde 42-43 VW 4
Dell, MT 76-77 G 3
Delle, UT 76-77 G 5
Del Mar, CA 76-77 E 9
Delmenhorst 33 CD 2
de Long, proliv – = proliv Longa 42-43 j 3-4
De Longa, ostrova – 42-43 c-e 2
De Long Mountains 70-71 D 4
Deloraine 58 c 2
Dēlos 36-37 L 7
Delphoi 36-37 K 6
Delray Beach, FL 74-75 cd 3
Del Rio 76-77 H 10
Del Rio, TX 72-73 F 6
Delta, UT 76-77 G 6
Delta Mendota Canal 76-77 C 7
Delvinë 36-37 HJ 6
Demachi = Tonami 50-51 L 4
Demavend = Kūh-e Damāvāvand 44-45 G 3
Demba 64-65 F 4
Dembī Dolo 60-61 LM 7
Demchhog 48-49 D 5
Ḍemeir = Ḍumayr 46-47 G 6
Deming, WA 76-77 BC 1
Demini, Rio – 78-79 G 4-5
Demirci 46-47 C 3
Demirciköy = Çal 46-47 C 3
Demirkent 46-47 JK 2
Demirköprü Barajı 46-47 C 3
Demirköy 46-47 BC 2
Demîr Qâboû = Damīr Qābū 46-47 JK 4
Demjanka 42-43 N 6
Demjanskoje 42-43 MN 6
Demmin 33 F 2
Dempo, Gunung – 52-53 D 7
Demta 52-53 M 7
Denakil 60-61 N 6
Denan 60-61 N 7
Denau 44-45 K 3
Denbigh [CDN] 74-75 E 2
Dendang 52-53 E 7
Denemarken 30-31 C-E 10
Denemarken, Straat – 19 C 20-22
Dengkou = Bajan Gol 48-49 K 3
Denham 56-57 B 5
Denia 34-35 H 9
Denial Bay 58 A 4
Denikil = Denakil 60-61 N 6
Deniliquin 56-57 HJ 7
Denio, OR 76-77 D 5
Denison, TX 72-73 G 5
Denizli 44-45 B 3
Denman 58 K 4
Denman Glacier 24 BC 10-11
Denmark 30-31 C-E 10
Denmark 56-57 C 6
Denmark, SC 74-75 C 8
Denmark Strait 19 C 20-22
Denpasar 52-53 FG 8
Dent, ID 76-77 E 2
Denton, MD 74-75 EF 5
Denton, NC 74-75 CD 7
Denton, TX 72-73 G 5
d'Entrecasteaux Islands 52-53 h 6
Denver, CO 72-73 EF 4
Deoghar 44-45 O 6
Deqen 48-49 H 6
Dêqên Zangzu Zizhizhou = B ◁ 48-49 H 6
Değirmenlik 46-47 E 5
Der'â = Dar'ā 46-47 G 6
Dera, Lak – 64-65 K 2
Ḍerah Ghāzī Khān 44-45 L 4
Ḍerah Ismā'īl Khān 44-45 L 4
Derbent 38-39 J 7
Derbesiye = Şenyurt 46-47 J 4
Derby 32 F 5
Derby [AUS] 56-57 D 3
Dereköy = Şerefiye 46-47 G 2
Dereli 46-47 H 2
Derg' = Daraj 60-61 G 2
Derg, Lough – 32 BC 5
Derik 46-47 J 4
Derinkuyu 46-47 F 3
Derkali 63 E 2
Derna = Darnah 60-61 J 2
Derry, NH 74-75 H 3
Derūdêb = Darūdāb 60-61 M 5
Derventa 36-37 G 3
Derwent River 58 c 3
Deržavinsk 42-43 M 7
Desaguadero, Río – [BOL] 78-79 F 8
Deschutes River 76-77 C 3
Desē 60-61 MN 6
Deseado = Puerto Deseado 80 CD 7
Deseado, Cabo – 80 AB 8
Deseado, Río – 80 BC 7
Desenzano del Garda 36-37 D 3
Deseret Peak 76-77 G 5
Deseronto 74-75 E 2
Désert Arabique 60-61 L 3-4
Desertas, Ilhas – 60-61 A 2
Desert Center, CA 76-77 F 9
Deserto Salato = Dasht-e Kavīr 44-45 GH 4
Desful = Dezfūl 44-45 F 4
Desierto Arábigo 60-61 L 3-4
Desierto Líbico 60-61 J 3-L 4
Desierto Sirio 44-45 DE 4
Des Moines, IA 72-73 GH 3
Des Moines River 72-73 GH 3
Desna 38-39 F 5
Desolación, Isla – 80 AB 8
Desolation Canyon 76-77 J 6
Despeñaperros, Puerto de – 34-35 F 9
Despeñaperros, Puerto de – 34-35 F 9
Desroches, Isle – 64-65 MN 4
Dessau 33 F 3
D' Estrees Bay 58 CD 5-6
Destruction Island 76-77 A 2
Desventurados 69 BC 5
Dete 64-65 G 6
Detmold 33 D 3
Detrital Valley 76-77 F 7-8
Detroit, MI 72-73 K 3
Detroit Lake 76-77 B 3
Dettifoss 30-31 e 2
Deva 36-37 K 3
Dévaványa 33 K 5
Deveci Dağları 46-47 FG 2
Develi [TR, Kayseri] 46-47 F 3
Deventer 34-35 L 2
Devils Gate 76-77 D 6
Devil's Hole 32 G 3
Devils Playground 76-77 EF 8
Devin 36-37 L 5

Everett, Mount – 74-75 G 3
Everglades 72-73 K 6
Everglades, FL 74-75 c 4
Everglades National Park 72-73 K 6
Evinayong 60-61 G 8
Evje 30-31 BC 8
Évora 34-35 CD 9
Évreux 34-35 H 4
Evrýchu 46-47 E 5
Evrykhou = Evrýchu 46-47 E 5

Ewan, WA 76-77 E 2
Ewenken, Nationaal Gebied der – 42-43 R-T 5
Ewo 64-65 DE 3

Exaltación [BOL] 78-79 F 7
Excelsior Mountains 76-77 D 6
Exe 32 E 6
Executive Committee Range 24 B 24
Exeter 32 E 6
Exeter, CA 76-77 D 7
Exeter, NH 74-75 H 3
Exmoor Forest 32 E 6
Exmore, VA 74-75 EF 6
Exmouth 32 E 6
Exmouth Gulf [AUS, ◡] 56-57 B 4
Exmouth Gulf [AUS, ●] 56-57 B 4
Expedition Range 56-57 J 4
Extremadura 34-35 D 9-E 8
Exuma Sound 72-73 L 7

Eyasi, Lake – 64-65 HJ 3
Eyjafjardhar 30-31 d 2
Eyjafjördhur 30-31 d 1
Eyl 60-61 b 2
Eynihal = Kale 46-47 CD 4
Eyrarbakki 30-31 c 3
Eyre, Lake – 56-57 G 5
Eyre, Seno – 80 B 7
Eyre Creek 56-57 G 5
Eyre North, Lake – 58 C 2
Eyre Peninsula 56-57 G 6
Eyre South, Lake – 58 C 2

Ezine 46-47 B 3
Ezinepazar = Zigala 46-47 G 2
Ezraa = Izra' 46-47 G 6

F

Fabriano 36-37 E 4
Fachi 60-61 G 5
Fada 60-61 J 5
Fada-Ngourma 60-61 DE 6
Faddeja, zaliv – 42-43 UV 2
Fadejevskij, ostrov – 42-43 b-d 2
Fadghāmī 46-47 J 5
Fadu N'Gurma = Fada-Ngourma 60-61 DE 6
Faenza 36-37 D 3
Færingehavn 70-71 a 5
Faeroe Iceland Ridge 28-29 FG 3
Fafan = Fafen 60-61 N 7
Fafanlap 52-53 K 7
Fafen Shet' 60-61 N 7
Făgăraş 36-37 L 3
Fagatogo 52-53 c 1
Fagernes 30-31 C 7
Fagersta 30-31 FG 7-8
Faguibine, Lac – 60-61 CD 5
Fagundes [BR, Pará] 78-79 H 6
Fahraj 44-45 H 5
Fa'id 62 E 2
Faiḍât = Fayḍât 46-47 HJ 5
Faijum, El – = Al-Fayyūm 60-61 KL 3
Fairbank, AZ 76-77 H 10
Fairbanks, AK 70-71 G 5
Fairbury, NE 72-73 G 3
Fairfax, SC 74-75 C 8
Fairfield, CA 76-77 BC 6
Fairfield, ID 76-77 F 4
Fairfield, ME 74-75 J 2
Fairfield, MT 76-77 H 2
Fairholm, WA 76-77 AB 1
Fair Isle 32 F 2
Fairlie 56-57 NO 8
Fairmont, NC 74-75 D 7
Fairmont, WV 74-75 C 5
Fairport, NY 74-75 E 3
Fairport Harbor, OH 74-75 C 4
Fairview, UT 76-77 H 6
Fairweather, Mount – 70-71 J 6
Faizabad 44-45 N 5
Fajr, Wādī – 44-45 D 5
Fakfak 52-53 K 7
Falam = Hpalam 52-53 B 2
Fălciu 36-37 MN 2
Falcon, Cape – 76-77 A 3
Falcone, Capo – 36-37 BC 5
Falcon Reservoir 72-73 G 6
Falémé 60-61 B 6
Falemé = Falémé 60-61 B 6
Faleşty 36-37 MN 2
Falkenberg [DDR] 33 F 3
Falkenberg [S] 30-31 DE 9
Falkirk 32 E 3-4
Falkland Islands 80 DE 8
Falkland Sound 80 DE 8
Falkonéra 36-37 KL 7
Falköping 30-31 EF 8
Fallbrook, CA 76-77 E 9
Fall Line Hills [USA, Georgia] 74-75 A-C 8
Fallon, NV 72-73 C 4
Fall River, MA 72-73 MN 3
Fall River Mills, CA 76-77 C 5
Falls City, OR 76-77 B 3
Falls Creek 58 H 6
Fallūjah, Al- 46-47 JK 6
Falmouth 32 D 6
Falmouth, MA 74-75 H 4
False Bay = Valsbaai [ZA, Kaapland] 64-65 E 9
False Cape 74-75 c 2
False Point 44-45 O 6
Falster 30-31 E 10
Falsterbo 30-31 E 10
Falterona, Monte – 36-37 DE 4
Fălticeni 36-37 M 2
Falun 30-31 F 7
Famagusta = Gazi Mağusa 44-45 CD 3
Fancheng = Xiangfan 48-49 L 5
Fandre = Vlaanderen 34-35 J 3
Fāngāk = Fānjāq 60-61 L 7
Fangcheng 48-49 L 5
Fānjāq 60-61 L 7
Fanning, Dorsal de las – 22-23 A 5-B 6
Fanning, Dorsale des – 22-23 A 5-B 6
Fanningrug 22-23 A 5-B 6
Fanning Trench 22-23 A 5-B 6
Fanø [DK] 30-31 C 10
Fano [I] 36-37 E 4
Fan Si Pan 52-53 D 2
Fant, Al- 62 D 3
Fanṭâs, Gebel el – = Jabal al-Finṭās 62 D 6
Fâqûs 62 DE 2
Farā', Al- 46-47 J 4
Faraday-Ondiepte 28-29 C 5-6
Faradje 64-65 G 2
Faradofay 64-65 L 8
Farafangana 64-65 L 7
Farāfirah, Al-Qaṣr al- 60-61 K 3
Farāfirah, Wāḥāt al- 60-61 K 3
Farāh 44-45 J 4
Farāh Rōd 44-45 J 4
Farallón, Cabo – = Cabo Santa Elena 72-73 J 9
Farallon Islands 76-77 B 7
Faranah 60-61 BC 6
Farasān, Jazā'ir – 44-45 E 7
Faraulep 52-53 M 5
Farāyid, Jabal al- 62 F 6
Farewell, MI 74-75 A 3
Farewell, Cape – 56-57 O 8
Farewell, Cape – = Kap Farvel 70-71 c 6
Fargo, GA 74-75 B 9
Fargo, ND 72-73 G 2
Fārigh, Wādī al- 60-61 HJ 2-3
Farim 60-61 AB 6
Farina 56-57 G 6
Fāris 44-45 G 6
Farmington, CA 76-77 C 7
Farmington, ME 74-75 HJ 2
Farmington, NM 76-77 J 7
Farmington, UT 76-77 GH 5
Farmville, NC 74-75 E 7
Farmville, VA 74-75 D 6
Farnham [CDN] 74-75 G 2
Faro 34-35 CD 10
Faro [BR] 78-79 H 5
Faro [RFC] 60-61 G 7
Faro, Punta di – 36-37 F 6
Faröer-IJslandrug 28-29 FG 3
Fårön 30-31 H 9
Farquhar Islands 64-65 LM 5
Farrars Creek 56-57 H 4-5
Farrell, PA 74-75 C 4
Farrukhabad 44-45 M 5
Fārs 44-45 G 4-5
Fársala 36-37 K 6
Farshûṭ 62 DE 4
Farson, WY 76-77 J 4
Farsund 30-31 B 8
Fartak, Rā's – 44-45 G 7
Farvel, Kap – 70-71 c 6
Fas 60-61 CD 2
Fasā 44-45 G 5
Fasano 36-37 G 5
Fasham 38-39 K 8
Fâsher, El- = Al-Fâshir 60-61 K 6
Fāshir, Al- 60-61 K 6
Fashn, Al- 60-61 KL 3
Fashoda = Kudūk 60-61 L 6-7
Fáskrúdhsfjördhur 30-31 fg 2
Fastov 38-39 EF 5
Fatagar, Tanjung – 52-53 K 7
Fatahpur = Fatehpur [IND, Rajasthan] 44-45 L 5
Fatehpur [IND, Rajasthan] 44-45 L 5
Fatḥa, Al- = Al-Fatḥah 44-45 E 3
Fatikli = Altınözü 46-47 G 4
Fátima 34-35 C 9
Fatmah, Bi'r – 46-47 K 5
Fatsa 46-47 G 2
Fatuma 63 B 4
Faucilles, Monts – 34-35 K 5-L 4
Făurei 36-37 M 3
Fauro 52-53 j 6
Fauske 30-31 F 4
Faust, UT 76-77 G 5
Favara 36-37 E 7
Faversham 32 G 6
Favignana 36-37 DE 7
Fāw, Al- 46-47 N 7-8
Fawn River 70-71 T 7
Faxaflói 30-31 b 2
Fayala 64-65 E 3
Faya-Largeau 60-61 H 5
Fayḍābād 44-45 KL 3
Fayḍalabad, Shah – 44-45 L 4
Fayḍāt 46-47 HJ 5
Fayetteville, AR 72-73 H 4
Fayetteville, NC 72-73 L 4-5
Fāyid = Fā'id 62 E 2
Faylakah, Jazīrat – 46-47 N 8
Fayṣalīyah, Al- 46-47 KL 7
Faysh Khābūr 46-47 JK 4
Fayum, El – = Al-Fayyūm 60-61 KL 3
Fayyūm, Al- 60-61 KL 3
Fayzabad = Faizabad 44-45 N 5
Fazzān 60-61 GH 3

Fdayrik 60-61 B 4

Fear, Cape – 72-73 L 5
Feather Falls, CA 76-77 C 6
Feather River 76-77 C 6
Featherston 56-57 P 8
Featherville, ID 76-77 F 4
Fécamp 34-35 H 4
Federal 80 E 4
Federal Capital Territory = 1 ◁ 60-61 F 7
Federal Capital Territory = Australian Capital Territory 56-57 J 7
Federick Hills 56-57 G 2
Fedje 30-31 A 7
Fehmarn 33 E 1
Feia, Lagoa – 78-79 L 9
Feijó 78-79 E 6
Feira de Santana 78-79 LM 7
Feisabad = Faizabad 44-45 N 5
Feke 46-47 F 4
Felâhiye 46-47 F 3
Felanitx 34-35 J 9
Feldberg 33 C 5
Feldioara 36-37 L 3
Feldkirch 33 DE 5
Felipe Carillo Puerto 72-73 J 8
Fellin = Viljandi 30-31 L 8
Fellsmere, FL 74-75 c 3
Felton, CA 76-77 B 7
Feltre 36-37 D 2
Femund 30-31 D 6
Femundsenden 30-31 D 7
Fenelon Falls 74-75 D 2
Fénérive = Fenoarivo Atsinanana 64-65 LM 6
Fengári 36-37 L 5
Fengcheng [TJ, Liaoning] 48-49 N 3
Fêng-chieh = Fengjie 48-49 K 5
Fengdu 48-49 K 5-6
Fengjie 48-49 K 5
Fengkieh = Fengjie 48-49 K 5
Fengming Dao 50-51 C 3
Fêng-ming Tao = Fengming Dao 50-51 C 3
Fengning 48-49 M 3
Fengsien = Feng Xian 48-49 K 5
Fengtu = Fengdu 48-49 K 5-6
Feng Xian [TJ, Shaanxi] 48-49 K 5
Fen He 48-49 L 4
Fên Ho = Fen He 48-49 L 4
Feni Islands 52-53 h 5
Fénix, Fosa de las – 22-23 AB 6
Fenoarivo Atsinanana 64-65 LM 6
Fenshui Ling 50-51 D 2-3
Fenyang 48-49 L 4
Feodosija 38-39 G 6-7
Feou-ning = Funing 48-49 MN 5
Férai 36-37 M 5
Ferdows 44-45 H 4
Fère, la – 34-35 J 4
Fergana 44-45 L 2-3
Ferganskaja dolina 44-45 L 2
Ferghana = Fergana 44-45 L 2-3
Fergus 74-75 C 3
Fergus Falls, MN 72-73 GH 2
Fergusson Island 52-53 h 6
Ferkéssédougou 60-61 CD 7
Ferlo 60-61 AB 5
Fermo 36-37 E 4
Fermoselle 34-35 DE 8
Fermoy 32 B 5
Fernandina, FL 74-75 c 1
Fernandina, Isla – 78-79 A 4-5
Fernando de Noronha 78-79 N 5
Fernando de Noronha, Ilha – 78-79 N 5
Fernando Póo, Isla de – = Bioko 60-61 F 8
Ferndale, CA 76-77 A 5
Ferndale, WA 76-77 B 1
Fernlee 58 H 2
Fernley, NV 76-77 D 6
Fernwood, ID 76-77 EF 2
Féróe, Banc des – 28-29 FG 3
Feroe, Banco de las – 28-29 FG 3
Feroe, Dorsal de las – 28-29 FG 3
Féróe, Dorsale des – 28-29 FG 3
Ferrara 36-37 DE 3
Ferreira Gomes 78-79 J 4
Ferreñafe 78-79 D 6
Ferreñafe 78-79 D 6
Ferro = Hierro 60-61 A 3
Ferrol, Peninsula de – 78-79 CD 6
Ferrol de Caudillo, El – 34-35 C 7
Fès = Fās 60-61 CD 2
Feshi 64-65 E 4
Feteşti 36-37 M 3
Fethiye 44-45 B 3
Fethiye Körfezi 46-47 C 4
Fetisovo 44-45 G 2
Fetlar 32 F 1
Feu, Terre de – 80 C 8
Feuilles, Rivière aux – 70-71 W 6
Fevzipaşa 46-47 G 4
Fez = Fās 60-61 CD 2
Fezzan = Fazzān 60-61 GH 3

Fianarantsoa 64-65 L 7
Fichtelgebirge 33 EF 3
Fidenza 36-37 D 3
Fidji 52-53 ab 2
Fidji, Bassin des – 22-23 S 7
Fidji, Îles – = Fiji Islands 52-53 ab 2
Fidji Méridionales, Bassin des – 56-57 OP 4-5
Fidji Septentrional, Cuenca de – 56-57 O 3
Fidji Septentrionales, Bassin du – 56-57 O 3
Fier 36-37 H 5
Fier, Porţile de – 36-37 K 3
Fife Ness 32 E 3
Fifi, Al- 60-61 J 6
Figeac 34-35 J 6
Figueira da Foz 34-35 C 8
Figueras 34-35 J 7
Figuîg = Fiqīq 60-61 D 2
Fiji Basin 22-23 S 7
Fiji Islands 52-53 ab 2
Fijīj = Fiqīq 60-61 D 2
Fiji Meridional, Cuenca de – 56-57 OP 4-5
Fila = Vila 56-57 N 3
Filabres, Sierra de los – 34-35 F 10
Filadélfia [BR, Goiás] 78-79 K 6
Filadelfia [PY] 80 D 2
Filchner-Schelfeis 24 A 30-B 33
Filchner-Schelfeis 24 A 30-B 33
Filer, ID 76-77 F 4
Filiaşi 36-37 K 3
Filiátai 36-37 J 6
Filiatrá 36-37 J 7
Filicudi 36-37 F 6
Filingué 60-61 E 6
Filipevila = Sakīkdah 60-61 F 1
Filipinas 52-53 H 3-J 5
Filipinas, Cuenca de – 22-23 Q 5
Filipinas, Fosa de – 22-23 Q 5
Filippiás 36-37 J 6
Filippijnen 52-53 H 3-J 5
Filippijnenbekken 22-23 Q 5
Filippijnentrog 22-23 Q 5
Filipstad 30-31 EF 8
Fillmore, CA 76-77 D 8
Fillmore, UT 76-77 G 6
Fimi 64-65 E 3
Finch 74-75 F 2
Fındık 46-47 JK 4
Fındıklı 46-47 J 2
Findlay, OH 72-73 K 3
Finger Lakes 72-73 L 3
Fingoè 64-65 H 6
Finike 46-47 D 4
Finisterre, Cabo de – 34-35 BC 7
Finke 56-57 FG 5
Finke River 56-57 G 5
Finland 30-31 L 7-M 4
Finland, Gulf of – 30-31 K 8-M 7
Finlande 30-31 L 7-M 4
Finlande, Golfe de – 30-31 K 8-M 7
Finlandia 30-31 L 7-M 4
Finlandia, Golfo de – 30-31 K 8-M 7
Finlay River 70-71 LM 6
Finnis, Cape – 58 B 4
Finnmark 30-31 K 3-N 2
Finnmarksvidda 30-31 KL 3
Finnskogene 30-31 E 7
Finnsnes 30-31 GH 3
Finschhafen 52-53 N 8
Finse 30-31 B 7
Finse Golf 30-31 K 8-M 7
Finspång 30-31 FG 8
Finsteraarhorn 33 CD 5
Finsterwalde 33 FG 3
Finṭās, Jabal al- 62 D 6
Fiordland National Park 56-57 N 8-9
Fiqīq 60-61 D 2
Fırat Nehri 44-45 D 3
Firebaugh, CA 76-77 C 7
Firenze 36-37 D 4
Firkessedougou = Ferkéssédougou 60-61 CD 7
Firozabad 44-45 M 5
Fīrūzābād [IR, Fārs] 44-45 G 5
Fīrūzābād [IR, Lorestān] 46-47 MN 6
Fishermans Island 74-75 F 6
Fisher Strait 70-71 U 5
Fishguard & Goodwick 32 D 5-6
Fishing Point 74-75 F 6
Fish Lake Valley 76-77 DE 7
Fiskåfjället 30-31 F 5
Fiskenæsset = Qeqertarssuatsiaq 70-71 a 5
Fiskivötn 30-31 c 2
Fitchburg, MA 74-75 GH 3
Fitri, Lac – 60-61 H 6
Fitzgerald, GA 74-75 B 9
Fitzmaurice River 56-57 EF 2
Fitz Roy 80 C 7
Fitz Roy, Monte – 80 B 7
Fitzroy Crossing 56-57 DE 3
Fitzroy River [AUS, Queensland] 56-57 JK 4
Fitzroy River [AUS, Western Australia] 56-57 DE 3
Fitzwilliam Strait 70-71 NO 2
Fiume = Rijeka 36-37 F 3
Five Miles Rapids 76-77 D 2
Fizi 64-65 G 3

Flå 30-31 C 7
Flagstaff, AZ 72-73 D 4
Flagstaff Lake 74-75 H 2
Flaherty Island 70-71 U 6
Flakstadøy 30-31 E 3
Flåm 30-31 B 7
Flamand = Arak 60-61 E 3
Flamborough Head 32 FG 4
Fläming 33 F 2-3
Flaming Gorge Reservoir 76-77 J 5
Flamingo, FL 74-75 c 4
Flamingo, Teluk – 52-53 L 8
Flanders = Vlaanderen 34-35 J 3
Flandes = Vlaanderen 34-35 J 3
Flanigan, NV 76-77 D 5
Flannan Isles 32 BC 2
Flatey 30-31 b 2
Flateyri 30-31 ab 1
Flathead Indian Reservation 76-77 FG 2
Flathead Lake 72-73 CD 2
Flathead Mountains = Salish Mountains 76-77 F 1-2
Flathead River 76-77 F 1
Flattery, Cape – [AUS] 56-57 J 2
Flattery, Cape – [USA] 76-77 A 1
Flat Top Mountain 74-75 C 6
Flèche, la – 34-35 GH 5
Fleetwood 32 E 5
Flekkefjord 30-31 AB 8
Flen 30-31 G 8
Flensburg 33 DE 1
Flers 34-35 G 4
Flesher, MT 76-77 G 2
Fletcher, Seuil – 19 A
Fletcherrug 19 A
Fletcher, Dorsal de – 19 A
Flinders Bay 56-57 BC 6
Flinders Island [AUS, Bass Strait] 56-57 J 7
Flinders Island [AUS, Great Australian Bight] 56-57 F 6
Flinders Ranges 56-57 G 6
Flinders River 56-57 H 3-4
Flin Flon 70-71 Q 7
Flint [GB] 32 E 5
Flint, MI 72-73 K 3
Flora 30-31 A 7
Flora, OR 76-77 E 3
Floreana 78-79 AB 5
Floreana, Isla – 78-79 A 5
Florence, AL 72-73 J 5
Florence, AZ 76-77 H 9
Florence, OR 76-77 A 4
Florence, SC 72-73 L 5
Florence = Firenze 36-37 D 4
Florence Junction, AZ 76-77 H 9
Florencia [CO] 78-79 DE 4
Florencia = Firenze 36-37 D 4
Flores [GCA] 72-73 J 8
Flores [RI] 52-53 H 8
Flores, Las – [RA, Buenos Aires] 80 E 5
Flores, Mar de – 52-53 GH 8
Flores, Mer de – 52-53 GH 8
Flores Sea 52-53 GH 8
Floresta Amazônica 78-79 E-H 6
Floreşty 36-37 MN 2
Floreszee 52-53 GH 8
Floriano 78-79 L 6
Florianópolis 80 G 3
Florida [USA] 72-73 K 5-6
Florida [ROU, ●] 80 E 4
Florida, Cape – 74-75 cd 4
Florida, Straits of – 72-73 K 7-L 6
Florida Bay 72-73 K 7
Florida City, FL 74-75 c 4
Florida Island 52-53 jk 6
Florida Keys 72-73 K 6-7
Floride = Florida 72-73 K 5-6
Flórina 36-37 J 5
Flower Station 74-75 E 2
Floyd, VA 74-75 C 6
Floyd, Mount – 76-77 G 8
Flumendosa 36-37 C 6
Flying Fish, Cape – 24 BC 26
Fly River 52-53 M 8

Foča 36-37 H 4
Foça [TR] 46-47 B 3
Fo-chan = Foshan 48-49 L 7
Fochi 60-61 H 5
Focşani 36-37 M 3
Fòggia 36-37 F 5
Fogo Island 70-71 a 8
Föhr 33 D 1
Foix [F, ≅] 34-35 H 7
Foix [F, ●] 34-35 H 7
Folda [N, Nordland] 30-31 F 4
Folda [N, Nord-Trøndelag] 30-31 D 5
Folégandros 36-37 L 7
Foley Island 70-71 V 4
Folgefonni 30-31 B 7-8
Foligno 36-37 E 4
Folkestone 32 G 6
Folkston, GA 74-75 B 9
Folldal 30-31 CD 6
Folsom, CA 76-77 C 6
Folteşti 36-37 MN 3
Fonda, NY 74-75 F 3
Fond-du-Lac 70-71 PQ 6
Fond du Lac, WI 72-73 J 3
Fond du Lac River 70-71 Q 6
Fondi 36-37 E 5

176 Evere

Fonsagrada 34-35 D 7
Fonseca, Golfo de – 72-73 J 9
Fontainebleau 34-35 J 4
Fonte Boa 78-79 F 5
Fontenelle Reservoir 76-77 HJ 4
Fontur 30-31 fg 1
Fonualei 52-53 c 2
Foochow = Fengdu 48-49 K 5-6
Foochow = Fujian 48-49 MN 6
Foochow = Fuzhou 48-49 MN 6
Foraker, Mount – 70-71 F 5
Forbes 56-57 J 6
Ford, Cape – 56-57 E 2
Ford City, CA 76-77 D 8
Førde 30-31 AB 7
Ford Lake 76-77 F 9
Fords Bridge 56-57 HJ 5
Forécariah 60-61 B 7
Forel, Mont – 70-71 d 4
Forest [CDN] 74-75 B 3
Forestal, La – 80 E 2
Forest City, NC 74-75 BC 7
Forestier Peninsula 58 d 3
Forez, Monts du – 34-35 J 6
Forfar 32 E 3
Forks, WA 76-77 A 1-2
Forlandsundet 30-31 hj 5
Forli 36-37 DE 3
Formentera 34-35 H 9
Formentor, Cabo – 34-35 J 8
Formiga 78-79 K 9
Formosa [BR, Goiás] 78-79 K 8
Formosa [RA, ●] 80 E 3
Formosa = Republiek China 48-49 N 7
Formosa, Estrecho de – = T'ai-wan Hai-hsia 48-49 M 7-N 6
Formosa, Serra – 78-79 HJ 7
Formosa Bay 63 E 3
Formosa Strait = T'ai-wan Hai-hsia 48-49 M 7-N 6
Formose = Taiwan 48-49 N 7
Formose, Détroit de – = T'ai-wan Hai-hsia 48-49 M 7-N 6
Fornæs 30-31 D 9
Forqlôs = Furqlûs 46-47 G 5
Forrest [AUS] 56-57 E 6
Forrest River Aboriginal Reserve 56-57 E 2-3
Forsayth 56-57 H 3
Forsmo 30-31 G 6
Forssa 30-31 K 7
Forster 58 L 4
Fort Albany 70-71 U 7
Fortaleza [BR, Ceará] 78-79 M 5
Fort Apache Indian Reservation 76-77 HJ 8-9
Fort-Archambault = Sarh 60-61 H 7
Fort Bayard = Zhanjiang 48-49 L 7
Fort Benton, MT 76-77 H 2
Fort Bragg, CA 76-77 AB 6
Fort Bragg, NC 74-75 D 7
Fort Bridger, WY 76-77 HJ 5
Fort Bruce = Pībōr 60-61 L 7
Fort Brussaux = Markounda 60-61 H 7
Fort-Charlet = Jannah 60-61 FG 4
Fort Chimo 70-71 X 6
Fort Chipewyan 70-71 OP 6
Fort Collins, CO 72-73 EF 3
Fort-Crampel = Kaga Bandoro 60-61 HJ 7
Fort-Charlet = Jannah 60-61 FG 4
Fort Chimo 70-71 X 6
Fort Chipewyan 70-71 OP 6
Fort-Dauphin = Faradofay 64-65 L 8
Fort Defiance, AZ 76-77 J 8
Fort-de-France 72-73 O 9
Fort de Kock = Bukittinggi 52-53 CD 7
Fort-de-Possel = Possel 60-61 H 7
Fort Dodge, IA 72-73 GH 3
Fort Duquesne = Pittsburg, Pa. 72-73 KL 3
Fort Edward, NY 74-75 G 3
Fort Erie 74-75 D 3
Fortescue River 56-57 C 4
Fort Fairfield, ME 74-75 JK 1
Fort-Flatters = Burj Flātarz 60-61 EF 3
Fort Frances 70-71 S 8
Fort-Gardel = Zaouatallaz 60-61 F 3-4
Fort Good Hope 70-71 L 4
Fort Grey 56-57 H 5
Forth, Firth of – 32 EF 3
Fort Hall, ID 76-77 G 4
Fort Hall = Murang'a 64-65 J 3
Fort Hall Indian Reservation 76-77 GH 4
Fort Hertz = Pūdāō 52-53 C 1
Fort Huachuca, AZ 76-77 H 10
Fortín Falcón 80 DE 2
Fortín Lavalle 80 D 3
Fortín Madrejón 80 D 2
Fortín Pilcomayo 80 DE 2
Fortín Principe de Beira = Principe da Beira 78-79 G 7
Fortín Ravelo 78-79 G 8
Fortín Suárez Arana 78-79 G 8
Fortín Uno 80 CD 5
Fort Jameson = Chipata 64-65 H 5
Fort Johnston = Mangoche 64-65 J 5
Fort Jones, CA 76-77 B 5
Fort Kent, ME 74-75 J 1
Fort Klamath, OR 76-77 BC 4
Fort Knox, KY 72-73 J 4
Fort Lami = N'Djamena 60-61 GH 6
Fort-Lamy = N'Djamena 60-61 GH 6
Fort-Laperrine = Tamanrāsat 60-61 EF 4
Fort Lauderdale, FL 72-73 KL 6
Fort Lewis, WA 76-77 B 2
Fort Liard 70-71 M 5
Fort MacDowell Indian Reservation 76-77 H 9
Fort-Mac-Mahon = Burj Ban Būl'īd 60-61 E 3
Fort MacMurray 70-71 O 6
Fort MacPherson 70-71 JK 4
Fort Madison, IA 72-73 H 3
Fort Maguire 64-65 HJ 5
Fort Manning = Mchinji 64-65 H 5
Fort Meade, FL 74-75 bc 3
Fort Mill, SC 74-75 C 7
Fort Mohave Indian Reservation 76-77 F 8
Fort Myers, FL 72-73 K 6
Fort Nassau = Albany, NY 72-73 LM 3
Fort Nelson 70-71 M 6
Fort Nelson River 70-71 M 6
Fort Norman 70-71 L 4-5
Fort Ogden, FL 74-75 c 3
Fort Peck Lake 72-73 E 2
Fort Pierce, FL 72-73 KL 6
Fort Plain, NY 74-75 F 3
Fort Portal 64-65 H 2
Fort Providence 70-71 N 5
Fort Randolph 72-73 b 2
Fort Reliance 70-71 P 5
Fort Resolution 70-71 O 5
Fortress Mountain 76-77 HJ 3
Fort Rock, OR 76-77 C 4
Fort Rosebery = Mansa 64-65 G 5
Fort Ross, CA 76-77 B 6
Fort-Rousset = Owando 64-65 E 3
Fort Rupert 70-71 V 7
Fort-Saint = Burj al-Haṭṭabah 60-61 F 2
Fort Saint James 70-71 M 7
Fort Saint John 70-71 M 6
Fort Sandeman = Apposai 44-45 K 4
Fort Saskatchewan 70-71 NO 7
Fort Selkirk 70-71 JK 5
Fort Sendeman = Apposai 44-45 K 4
Fort Severn 70-71 T 6
Fort Seward, CA 76-77 B 5
Fort Sherman 72-73 ab 2
Fort Sibut = Sibut 60-61 H 7
Fort Simpson 70-71 M 5
Fort Smith 70-71 OP 5
Fort Smith, AR 72-73 H 4
Fort Smith, District of – 70-71 N-P 5
Fort Stockton, TX 72-73 F 5
Fort Thomas, AZ 76-77 HJ 9
Fort-Trinquet = Bīr Umm Qarayn 60-61 B 3
Fortuna, CA 76-77 AB 5
Fortune Bank 64-65 L 3
Fortune Bay 70-71 Z 8
Fort Vermilion 70-71 NO 6
Fort Victoria = Nyanda 64-65 H 6-7
Fort Wayne, IN 72-73 JK 3
Fort Wingate, NM 76-77 J 8
Fort Worth, TX 72-73 G 5
Fort Yukon, AK 70-71 GH 4
Fosforitnaja 38-39 K 4
Foshan 48-49 L 7
Fosheim Peninsula 70-71 U 1-2
Fosna 30-31 CD 6
Fossano 36-37 BC 3
Fossberg 30-31 BC 7
Fosse Norvégienne 30-31 A 8-C 9
Fosse Péruvienne 78-79 C 6-D 7
Fossil, OR 76-77 C 3
Fougamou 64-65 D 3
Fougères 34-35 G 4
Foula 32 E 1
Foul Bay = Khalīj Umm al-Kataf 62 F 6
Foulpointe = Mahavelona 64-65 LM 6
Foulwind, Cape – 56-57 NO 8
Fouman = Fūman 46-47 N 4
Foumban 60-61 G 7
Foum Taṭâouîn = Taṭāwīn 60-61 G 2
Foundiougne 60-61 A 6
Fourât, El- = Al-Furât 46-47 H 5
Fourcroy, Cape – 56-57 E 2
Fouta Djallon 60-61 B 6
Foveaux Strait 56-57 N 9
Fowler, MT 76-77 H 1
Fowlers Bay 56-57 F 6
Fowling = Fengdu 48-49 K 5-6
Foxe Basin 70-71 UV 4
Foxe Channel 70-71 UV 4-5
Foxe Channel 70-71 UV 4-5
Foxe Peninsula 70-71 V 5
Fox Islands 19 D 35
Foyle, Lough – 32 C 4
Foyn, Cape – 24 C 30
Foynes 32 B 5
Foynøya 30-31 mn 4
Foz do Aripuanã = Novo Aripuanã 78-79 G 6
Foz do Embira = Envira 78-79 EF 6
Foz do Iguaçu 80 F 3
Foz do Riozinho 78-79 E 6
Fragua, La – 80 D 3
Framnesfjella 24 C 7
Franca [BR, São Paulo] 78-79 K 9
Franca Josifa, zeml'a – 42-43 H-M 2
Francavilla Fontana 36-37 GH 5
France 34-35 G 4-K 6
Frances Peak 76-77 J 3-4
Franceville 64-65 D 3
Franche-Comté 34-35 KL 5
Francis Case, Lake – 72-73 FG 3
Francistown 64-65 G 7
François Joseph, Chutes – 64-65 E 4
François Joseph, Chutes – 64-65 E 4
Francquihaven = Ilebo 64-65 F 3
Frankenwald 33 E 3
Frankfort, KY 72-73 K 4
Frankfurt am Main 33 D 3
Frankfurt/Oder 33 G 2
Fränkische Alb 33 E 3-4
Frankland, Cape – 58 c 1
Franklin, NH 74-75 H 3
Franklin, PA 74-75 D 4
Franklin, VA 74-75 E 6
Franklin, WV 74-75 D 5
Franklin Bay 70-71 L 3-4
Franklin Delano Roosevelt Lake 72-73 C 2
Franklin Island 24 B 17-18
Franklin Mountains [CDN] 70-71 L 4-M 5
Franklin Strait 70-71 R 3
Franklinton, NC 74-75 D 6
Franklinville, NY 74-75 DE 3
Frankrijk 34-35 G 4-K 6
Fransfontein 64-65 DE 7
Frans-Guyana 78-79 J 4
Franz Joseph, zeml'a – = zeml'a Franca Josifa 42-43 H-M 2
Frasca, Capo de – 36-37 BC 6
Frascati 36-37 E 5
Fraserburg 64-65 F 9
Fraserburgh 32 EF 3
Fraser Island = Great Sandy Island 56-57 KL 4-5
Fraser Plateau 70-71 M 7
Fraser Range 56-57 D 6
Fraser River 70-71 MN 7
Fray Bentos 80 E 4
Frederica 30-31 CD 10
Frederic Hills 56-57 G 2
Frederick, MD 74-75 E 5
Fredericksburg, VA 74-75 DE 5
Fredericton 70-71 X 8
Frederikshåb = Pâmiut 70-71 ab 5
Frederikshamn = Hamina 30-31 M 7
Frederikshavn 30-31 D 9
Fredonia, AZ 76-77 G 7
Fredonia, NY 74-75 D 3
Fredonyer Peak 76-77 C 5
Fredrikstad 30-31 D 8
Freel Peak 76-77 CD 6
Freemansundet 30-31 l 5
Freetown 60-61 B 7
Freewater, OR 76-77 D 3
Fregenal de la Sierra 34-35 D 9
Freiberg 33 F 3
Freiburg im Breisgau 33 C 4-5
Freire 80 B 5
Freising 33 E 4
Freistadt 33 G 4
Fréjus 34-35 L 7
Fremantle, Perth- 56-57 BC 6
Fremont, CA 76-77 C 7
Fremont, NE 72-73 G 3
Fremont Island 76-77 G 5
Fremont River 76-77 H 6
French Guiana 78-79 J 4
French Island 58 G 7
Frenchman, NV 76-77 D 6
Frenchman Bay 74-75 JK 2
Frenchmans Cap 58 bc 3
French Shore 70-71 Z 7-8
Frentones, Los – 80 D 3
Freshfield, Cape – 24 C 16
Fresno, CA 72-73 BC 4
Freycinet Peninsula 56-57 J 8
Fria 60-61 B 6
Fria, La – 78-79 E 3
Friant, CA 76-77 D 7
Frias 80 CD 3
Fribourg 33 C 5
Friday Harbor, WA 76-77 B 1
Friedrichshafen 33 DE 5
Fries, VA 74-75 C 6
Frijoles 72-73 b 2
Frio, Kaap – 64-65 D 6
Frisco Mountain 76-77 G 6
Frisias Occidentales 34-35 KL 2
Frisias Orientales, Islas – 33 C 2
Frisias Septentrionales, Islas – 33 D 1
Frisones Septentrionales, Bassin du – 33 D 1
Frisonnes Orientales, Îles – 33 C 2
Frisonnes Septentrionales, Îles – 33 D 1
Fritjof Nansen Land = zeml'a Franz Joseph 42-43 H-M 2
Friuli-Venèzia Giulia 36-37 E 2
Friza, proliv – 48-49 S 2
Frobisher Bay [CDN, ∪] 70-71 X 5
Frobisher Bay [CDN, ●] 70-71 X 5
Frohavet 30-31 C 5-6
Frolovo 38-39 H 6
Frome 32 E 6
Frome, Lake – 56-57 GH 6
Frome Downs 56-57 GH 6
Fronteiras 78-79 L 6
Frontera 72-73 H 8
Fronteras 76-77 J 10
Frontignan 34-35 JK 7
Front Range 72-73 E 3-4
Front Royal, VA 74-75 DE 5
Frosinone 36-37 E 5
Frostburg, MD 74-75 D 5
Frostproof, FL 74-75 c 3
Frövi 30-31 F 8
Frøya 30-31 C 6
Frøya, Banc de – 28-29 JK 3
Frøya, Banco de – 28-29 JK 3
Frozen Strait 70-71 U 4
Fruita, CO 76-77 J 6
Fruitland, ID 76-77 E 3
Fruitland, UT 76-77 H 5
Fruška gora 36-37 H 3
Fruto, CA 76-77 B 6
Fu'ād, Bi'r – 62 B 2
Fu'an 48-49 MN 6
Fucheu = Fuzhou 48-49 MN 6
Fu-chien = Fujian 48-49 M 6
Fuchin = Fujin 48-49 P 2
Fu-ch'ing = Fuqing 48-49 MN 6
Fuchow = Fuzhou 48-49 MN 6
Fuchskauten 33 CD 3
Fudai 50-51 NO 2-3
Fuego, Tierra del – 80 C 8
Fuego, Tierra del – 80 C 8
Fuego, Volcán de – 72-73 H 9
Fuente de San Esteban, La – 34-35 DE 8
Fuentes de Oñoro 34-35 D 8
Fuentes de Oñoro 34-35 D 8
Fuerte, Río – 72-73 E 6
Fuerte Bulnes 80 B 8
Fuerte Olimpo 80 E 2
Fuerteventura 60-61 B 3
Fugløy, Banc de – 30-31 HJ 2
Fugløy, Banco de – 30-31 HJ 2
Fuglöy Bank 30-31 HJ 2
Fu-hsien = Fu Xian [TJ, Liaoning] 48-49 N 4
Fu-hsien = Fuxin 48-49 N 3
Fu-hsien Hu = Fuxian Hu 48-49 J 7
Fujairah, Al- = Al-Fujayrah 44-45 H 5
Fujayrah, Al- 44-45 H 5
Fuji 50-51 M 5
Fujian 48-49 M 6
Fu Jiang 48-49 K 5
Fujin 48-49 P 2
Fujinomiya 50-51 M 5
Fujioka 50-51 M 4
Fuji-san 48-49 Q 4-5
Fujisawa 50-51 MN 5
Fuji-Yoshida 50-51 M 5
Fukae = Fukue 50-51 G 6
Fukagawa 50-51 bc 2
Fūkah 62 B 2
Fukien = Fujian 48-49 M 6
Fukuchiyama 50-51 K 5
Fukue 50-51 G 6
Fukue-shima 50-51 G 6
Fukui 48-49 Q 4
Fukuoka [J, Fukuoka] 48-49 OP 5
Fukuoka [J, Iwate] 50-51 N 2
Fukura = Nandan 50-51 K 5
Fukushima [J, Fukushima] 48-49 R 4
Fukushima [J, Hokkaidō] 50-51 b 3
Fukushima [J, Nagano] 50-51 L 5
Fukuyama 50-51 J 5
Fūlah, Al- 60-61 K 6
Fulaikā', Jazīrat – = Jazīrat Faylakah 46-47 N 8
Fulda [D, ~] 33 D 3
Fulda [D, ●] 33 D 3
Fuling 48-49 K 6
Fulton, CA 76-77 B 6
Fulton, NY 74-75 E 3
Fūman 46-47 N 4
Fumban = Foumban 60-61 G 7
Fūmch'ŏn = Kŭmch'on 50-51 F 3
Fumel 34-35 H 6
Funabashi 50-51 MN 5
Funagawa = Oga 50-51 M 3
Funatsu = Kamioka 50-51 L 4
Funchal 60-61 A 2
Fundación 78-79 E 2
Fundão 34-35 D 8
Fundão [BR] 78-79 LM 8
Fundy, Bay of – 70-71 X 8-9
Funhalouro 64-65 HJ 7
Funing [TJ, Jiangsu] 48-49 MN 5
Funtua 60-61 F 6
Fuqing 48-49 MN 6
Furancungo 64-65 H 5
Furano 50-51 c 2
Furāt, Al- 44-45 DE 3
Furāt, Nahr al- 44-45 E 4
Furāt, Shaṭṭ al- 46-47 LM 7
Fūr Ghūrū = Fdayrik 60-61 B 4
Furmanovka [SU, Kazachskaja SSR] 42-43 N 9
Furnas, Represa de – 78-79 K 9
Furneaux Group 56-57 J 7-8
Fūrnoi 36-37 M 7
Furqlūs 46-47 G 5
Fürstenfeld 33 GH 6
Fürstenwalde 33 FG 2
Fürth 33 E 4
Further India 22-23 OP 5
Furubira 50-51 b 2
Furukamappu = Južno-Kuril'sk 42-43 c 9
Furukawa 50-51 N 3
Fury and Hecla Strait 70-71 TU 4
Fusan = Pusan 48-49 OP 4
Fuse = Higasiōsaka 50-51 KL 5
Fushi = Yan'an 48-49 K 4
Fushun 48-49 NO 3
Fushuncheng 50-51 DE 2
Fusien = Fu Xian 48-49 N 4
Fusin = Fuxin 48-49 N 3
Fusong 48-49 O 3
Füssen 33 E 5
Fu-sung = Fusong 50-51 F 1
Futa Djalon = Fouta Djalon 60-61 B 6
Futamata 50-51 L 5
Futaoi-jima 50-51 H 5
Futsing = Fuqing 48-49 MN 6
Futuna 52-53 b 1
Fuwah 62 D 2
Fu Xian [TJ, Liaoning] 48-49 N 4
Fuxian Hu 48-49 J 7
Fuxin 48-49 N 3
Fuyang [TJ, Anhui] 48-49 M 5
Fuyu [TJ, Heilongjiang] 48-49 NO 2
Fuyu [TJ, Jilin] 48-49 NO 2
Fu-yü = Fuyu 48-49 NO 2
Fuyuan 48-49 P 2
Fuzhou [TJ, Fujian] 48-49 MN 6
Fuzhou [TJ, Jianxi] 48-49 M 6
Fuzhoucheng 48-49 N 4
Fiji 52-53 ab 2
Fijibekken 56-57 O 3
Fijibekken 22-23 S 7
Fijieilanden = Fiji Islands 52-53 ab 2
Fyn 30-31 D 10
Fyzabad = Faizabad 44-45 N 5

G

Gaalkacyo 60-61 b 2
Gaarowe = Garoowe 60-61 b 2
Gabbac 60-61 c 2
Gabbs Valley 76-77 DE 6
Gabbs Valley Range 76-77 DE 6
Gabela [Angola] 64-65 DE 5
Gaberones = Gaborone 64-65 FG 7
Gabès = Qābis 60-61 FG 2
Gabilan Range 76-77 C 7
Gabon 64-65 CD 3
Gabón 64-65 CD 3
Gaborone 64-65 FG 7
Gabrovo 36-37 L 4
Gabū 60-61 B 6
Gachsārān 44-45 G 4
Gacko 36-37 H 4
Gadap = Karāchī 44-45 K 6
Gäddede 30-31 F 5
Gadīdah, Al- = Al-Jadīdah [MA] 60-61 C 2
Gadra 44-45 L 5
Gadsden, AL 72-73 J 5
Găeşti 36-37 L 3
Gaeta 36-37 E 5
Gaeta, Golfo di – 36-37 E 5
Gaffney, SC 74-75 C 7
Gagarin 38-39 F 4
Gage, NM 76-77 JK 9
Gagliano del Capo 36-37 GH 6
Gagnoa 60-61 C 7
Gagnon 70-71 X 7
Gago Coutinho = Lungala N'Guimbo 64-65 F 5
Gagra 38-39 GH 7
Gahnpa 60-61 C 7
Gaia = Gayā 44-45 NO 5-6
Gail 33 F 5
Gaima 52-53 M 8
Gaimán 80 C 6
Gainesville, FL 72-73 K 6
Gainesville, GA 72-73 K 5
Gainesville, TX 72-73 G 5
Gairdner, Lake – 56-57 G 6
Gai Xian 50-51 CD 2
Gaizina kalns 30-31 LM 9
Gajny 42-43 J 5
Galadi = Geladī 60-61 O 7
Galán, Cerro – 80 C 3
Galana 64-65 JK 3
Galápagos, Dorsal de las – 22-23 E 5
Galápagos, Îles – = Archipiélago de Colón 78-79 AB 5
Galápagos, Islas – = Archipiélago de Colón 78-79 AB 5
Galápagos, Seuil des – 22-23 E 5
Galapagosdrempel 22-23 E 5
Galapagos Eilanden = Archipiélago de Colón 78-79 AB 5
Galashiels 32 E 4
Galaţi 36-37 MN 3
Galatina 36-37 H 5
Galax, VA 74-75 C 6
Galbeed = Woqooyi-Galbeed 60-61 a 1
Galdhøpiggen 30-31 BC 7
Galela 52-53 J 6

Galel 177

Galena, AK 70-71 E 4-5
Galera, Punta – [EC] 78-79 C 4
Galera, Punta – [RCH] 80 AB 6
Galera Point 72-73 OP 9
Gales 32 E 5-6
Galesburg, IL 72-73 HJ 3
Galeta, Isla – 72-73 b 2
Galeta Island 72-73 b 2
Galeton, PA 74-75 E 4
Galguduud 60-61 b 2-3
Galič [SU, Rossijskaja SFSR] 42-43 G 6
Galicia 34-35 CD 7
Galicie = Galicia 34-35 CD 7
Galicja 33 J-L 4
Galilee, Lake – 56-57 HJ 4
Galipoli = Gelibolu 44-45 B 2
Galiuro Mountains 76-77 H 9
Gālla 44-45 MN 9
Gall'a, ostrov – 42-43 KL 1
Gallabat = Qallābāt 60-61 M 6
Galladi = Geladī 60-61 O 7
Gallatin Gateway, MT 76-77 H 3
Gallatin Peak 76-77 H 3
Gallatin River 76-77 H 3
Galle = Gālla 44-45 MN 9
Gállego, Río – 34-35 G 7
Gallegos, Río – 80 BC 8
Galles, Pays de – 32 E 5-6
Galliate 36-37 C 3
Gallinas, Punta – 78-79 E 2
Gallipoli 36-37 GH 5
Gallipoli = Gelibolu 44-45 B 2
Gallipolis, OH 74-75 B 5
Gällivare 30-31 J 4
Gallo Mountains 76-77 J 8-9
Galloo Island 74-75 E 3
Galloway 32 DE 4
Gallup, NM 72-73 E 4
Galšir 48-49 L 2
Galt, CA 76-77 C 6
Galveston, TX 72-73 H 6
Galveston Bay 72-73 H 6
Gálvez [RA] 80 D 4
Galway 32 B 5
Galway Bay 32 B 5
Gam, Pulau – 52-53 JK 7
Gamane = Bertoua 60-61 G 8
Gāmāsiyāb, Rūd-e – 46-47 MN 5
Gambaga 60-61 D 6
Gambeila = Gambēla 60-61 L 7
Gambēla 60-61 L 7
Gambell, AK 70-71 BC 5
Gambie 60-61 AB 6
Gambie 60-61 B 6
Gamboa 72-73 b 2
Gamboma 64-65 E 3
Gambos 64-65 DE 5
Gamerco, NM 76-77 J 8
Game Reserve Number 1 64-65 EF 6
Gamlakarleby = Kokkola 30-31 K 6
Gamleby 30-31 FG 9
Gamo Gofa 60-61 M 7
Gamova, mys – 50-51 H 1
Gamsah = Jamsah 62 E 4
Gamvik 30-31 N 2
Gana = Ghana 60-61 DE 7
Ganaane, Webi – = Webi Juba 60-61 N 8
Ganado, AZ 76-77 J 8
Gananoque 74-75 E 2
Ganāveh 44-45 FG 5
Ganchhendzönga = Gangchhendsönga 44-45 O 5
Gand = Gent 34-35 JK 3
Ganda 64-65 D 5
Gandajika 64-65 FG 4
Gandak 44-45 NO 5
Gander 70-71 a 8
Gandesa 34-35 H 8
Gandia 34-35 GH 9
Ganga 44-45 M 5
Ganga, Mouths of the – 44-45 OP 6
Gan Gan 80 C 6
Ganganagar 44-45 LM 5
Gangchhendsönga 44-45 O 5
Gange, Bouches du – = Mouths of the Ganga 44-45 OP 6
Gange, Vallée sous-marine du – 44-45 O 6-7
Ganges = Ganga 44-45 M 5
Ganges, Boca del – = Mouths of the Ganga 44-45 OP 6
Ganges, Dorsal del – 44-45 O 6-7
Ganges, Mondingen van de – = Mouths of the Ganga 44-45 OP 6
Ganges Canyon 44-45 O 6-7
Gangesgeul 44-45 O 6-7
Gangīr, Rūdkhāneh ye – 46-47 LM 6
Gangou 50-51 B 2
Gangouzhen = Gangou 50-51 B 2
Gangthog = Gangtok 44-45 O 5
Gangtö Gangri 48-49 G 6
Gangtok 44-45 O 5
Gangtun 50-51 C 2
Gan He 48-49 N 1
Gan Jiang 48-49 LM 6
Gannan Zangzu Zizhizhou 48-49 J 5
Gannett, ID 76-77 FG 4
Gannett Peak 72-73 E 3
Gansos, Banco de los – 42-43 GH 3
Gansu 48-49 G 3-J 4
Ganta = Gahnpa 60-61 C 7
Gantheaume Bay 56-57 B 5
Gan'uškino 38-39 JK 6
Ganxian = Ganzhou 48-49 LM 6
Ganzenbank 42-43 GH 3
Ganzhou 48-49 LM 6
Gao 60-61 D 5
Gao'an 48-49 LM 6
Gaoligong Shan 48-49 H 6
Gaoqiao = Gaoqiaozhen 50-51 C 2
Gaoqiaozhen 50-51 C 2
Gaotai 48-49 H 4
Gaoua 60-61 D 6
Gaoual 60-61 B 6
Gaoxiong = Kaohsiung 48-49 MN 7
Gap 34-35 L 6
Gar, Bir el – = Bi'r al-Qaf 60-61 H 3
Garacad 60-61 bc 2
Garah 58 JK 2
Garamba, Parc national de la – 64-65 GH 2
Garanhuns 78-79 M 6
Gara Samuil 36-37 M 4
Garb, Gebel el – = Jabal Nafusah 60-61 G 2
Garbahaarrey 60-61 N 8
Garba Tula 63 D 2
Garberville, CA 76-77 B 5
Garcias 78-79 J 9
Gard 34-35 K 6-7
Garda 36-37 D 3
Garda, Lago di – 36-37 D 3
Gardelegen 33 E 2
Garden City, KS 72-73 F 4
Garden Grove, CA 76-77 D 9
Garden Valley, ID 76-77 F 3
Gardēz 44-45 K 4
Gardhsskagi 30-31 b 2
Gardiner, ME 74-75 J 2
Gardiner, MT 76-77 H 3
Gardiners Bay 74-75 GH 4
Gardner, MA 74-75 GH 3
Gardnerville, NV 76-77 D 6
Garfield Heights, OH 74-75 C 4
Garfield Mountain 76-77 G 3
Gargaliánoi 36-37 J 7
Gargano 36-37 FG 5
Gargano, Testa del – 36-37 G 5
Gargar 46-47 L 3
Gargar, Īstgāh-e – 46-47 N 7
Gargia 30-31 K 3
Garian = Gharyān 60-61 G 2
Garibaldi, OR 76-77 B 3
Garies 64-65 E 9
Garissa 64-65 JK 3
Garland, NC 74-75 D 7
Garland, UT 76-77 G 5
Garmashīn, 'Ain – = 'Ayn Jarmashīn 62 CD 5
Garmisch-Partenkirchen 33 E 5
Garmsār 38-39 K 8
Garnet, MT 76-77 G 2
Garonne 34-35 G 6
Garoowe 60-61 b 2
Garopaba 80 G 3
Garoua 60-61 G 7
Garrison, MT 76-77 G 2
Garry Lake 70-71 Q 4
Gartempe 34-35 H 5
Gartog 48-49 E 5
Gartok = Gartog 48-49 E 5
Garua = Garoua 60-61 G 7
Gary, IN 72-73 J 3
Garzan = Zok 46-47 J 3
Garze 48-49 J 5
Garze Zangzu Zizhizhou 48-49 HJ 5
Garzón [CO] 78-79 DE 4
Gasan-Kuli 38-39 K 8
Gasan-Kuli 44-45 G 3
Gascogne 34-35 GH 7
Gascogne, Golfe de – 34-35 EF 6
Gascoyne, Mount – 56-57 C 4
Gascoyne River 56-57 C 5
Gashaka 60-61 G 7
Gasmata 52-53 gh 6
Gasparilla Island 74-75 b 3
Gaspé 70-71 Y 8
Gaspé, Cap de – 70-71 Y 8
Gaspésie, Péninsule de – 70-71 XY 8
Gas-san [J] 50-51 MN 3
Gassaway, WV 74-75 C 5
Gaston, OR 76-77 B 3
Gastonia, NC 72-73 K 4
Gastre 80 C 6
Gašuun Gov' 48-49 G 3
Gašuun nuur 48-49 HJ 3
Gat = Ghat 60-61 G 3
Gata, Cabo de – 34-35 FG 10
Gata, Sierra de – 34-35 D 8
Gátas, Akrōtḗrion – 46-47 E 5
Gatčina 42-43 DE 6
Gate City, VA 74-75 B 6
Gateshead 32 EF 4
Gateway, CO 76-77 J 6
Gateway, MT 76-77 F 1
Gateway, OR 76-77 C 3
Gâtinais 34-35 J 4
Gâtine, Hauteurs de – 34-35 G 5
Gatooma = Kadoma 64-65 G 6
Gatrun, el- = Al-Qaṭrūn 60-61 GH 4
Gatun 72-73 b 2
Gatun, Barrage de – = Presa de Gatún 72-73 ab 2
Gatún, Brazo de – 72-73 b 2
Gatún, Esclusas de – 72-73 b 2
Gatún, Lago de – 72-73 b 2
Gatún, Presa de – 72-73 ab 2
Gatún, Río – 72-73 b 2
Gatun Arm = Brazo de Gatún 72-73 b 2
Gatuncillo 72-73 b 2
Gatuncillo, Río – 72-73 b 2
Gatun Dam = Presa de Gatún 72-73 ab 2
Gatun Lake = Lago de Gatún 72-73 b 2
Gatun Locks = Esclusas de Gatún 72-73 b 2
Gatvand 46-47 N 6
Gauani = Gewanī 60-61 N 6
Gauhati 44-45 P 5
Gauja 30-31 L 9
Gaula 30-31 D 6
Gauley Mountain 74-75 C 5
Gaurisankar = Jomotsering 44-45 O 5
Gaurīshankar = Jomotsering 44-45 O 5
Gausta 30-31 C 8
Gausvik 30-31 G 3
Gávdos 36-37 L 8
Gave de Pau 34-35 G 7
Gāveh Rūd 46-47 M 5
Gaviota, CA 76-77 C 8
Gävle 30-31 G 7
Gävleborg 30-31 G 6-7
Gavrilov-Jam 38-39 G 4
Gawdezereh 44-45 J 5
Gawler 56-57 G 6
Gawler Ranges 56-57 G 6
Gawso 60-61 D 7
Gaya [DY] 60-61 E 6
Gaya [IND] 44-45 NO 5-6
Gayaza 63 B 3
Gayndah 56-57 K 5
Gaza 64-65 H 7
Gaza = Ghazzah 44-45 C 4
Gazalkent 42-43 MN 9
Gazelle, CA 76-77 B 5
Gazelle Peninsula 52-53 h 5
Gazi 63 D 4
Gaziantep 44-45 D 3
Gaziantep Ovası 46-47 GH 4
Gazibenli = Yahyalı 46-47 F 3
Gaziler 46-47 K 2
Gazi Mağusa 44-45 CD 3
Gazipaşa 46-47 E 4
Gbarnga 60-61 C 7
Gcuwa 64-65 G 9
Gdańsk 33 J 1
Gdańsk, Baie de – = Zatoka Gdańska 33 J 1
Gdańsk, Bocht van – = Zatoka Gdańska 33 J 1
Gdańsk, Golfo de – = Zatoka Gdańska 33 J 1
Gdańska, Zatoka – 33 J 1
Gdánsk Bay = Zatoka Gdańska 33 J 1
Gdov 38-39 E 4
Gdynia 33 HJ 1
Gearhart Mountain 76-77 C 4
Geba, Rio – 60-61 AB 6
Gebal = Jubayl 46-47 F 5
Gebe, Pulau – 52-53 J 7
Gebeit = Jubayt 60-61 M 4
Gebiz 46-47 D 4
Gebze 46-47 C 2
Gedaref = Al-Qadārif 60-61 M 6
Gedi 64-65 J 3
Gedid, el – = Sabhah 60-61 G 3
Gedikbulak = Canik 46-47 K 3
Gediz 46-47 C 3
Gediz Nehri 46-47 B 3
Gedlegubē 60-61 NO 7
Gēdo [ETH] 60-61 M 7
Gedo [SP] 60-61 N 8
Gedser 30-31 DE 10
Geelong 56-57 H 7
Geelvink Channel 56-57 B 5
Geelvink Channel 56-57 B 5
Geese Bank 42-43 GH 3
Geeveston 56-57 J 8
Gèfyra 36-37 K 5
Gegeen gol = Gen He 48-49 N 1
Geidam 60-61 G 6
Geilo 30-31 C 7
Geiranger 30-31 B 6
Geislingen 33 D 4
Geita 64-65 H 3
Gejiu 48-49 J 7
Gela 36-37 F 7
Geladi 60-61 O 7
Gelai 63 D 3
Gelasa, Selat – 52-53 E 7
Gelendost 46-47 D 3
Gelendžik 38-39 G 7
Gele Zee 48-49 N 4
Gelibolu 44-45 B 2
Gelsenkirchen 33 C 3
Gemas 52-53 D 6
Gemena 64-65 E 2
Gemerek 46-47 G 3
Gemiyanı = Türkeli 46-47 F 2
Gemlik 46-47 C 2
Gemlik Körfezi 46-47 C 2
Gemona del Friuli 36-37 E 2
Gemsa = Jamsah 62 E 4
Gemu Gofa = Gamu Gofa 60-61 M 7
Genale Weniz 60-61 N 7
Genç 46-47 J 3
Geneina, El- = Al-Junaynah 60-61 J 6
General Acha 80 CD 5
General Acha 80 CD 5
General Alvear [RA, Buenos Aires] 80 DE 5
General Alvear [RA, Mendoza] 80 C 4-5
General Belgrano [Antarctica] 24 B 32-33
General Bernardo O'Higgins 24 C 31
General Conesa [RA, Río Negro] 80 CD 6
General Deheza 80 D 4
General Enrique Mosconi 80 D 2
General Güemes 80 CD 2
General Guido 80 E 5
General Juan Madariaga 80 E 5
General La Madrid 80 D 5
General Lavalle 80 E 5
General Lorenzo Vintter 80 D 6
General Machado = Camacupa 64-65 E 5
General Pico 80 D 5
General Pinedo 80 D 3
General Roca 80 C 5
General San Martín [RA, Chaco] 80 E 3
General Santos 52-53 HJ 5
General Toševo 36-37 N 4
General Villamil = Playas 78-79 C 5
General Villegas 80 D 4-5
Gênes = Gènova 36-37 C 3
Genesee, ID 76-77 E 2
Genesee River 74-75 DE 3
Geneseo, NY 74-75 E 3
Geneva, NY 74-75 E 3
Geneva, OH 74-75 C 4
Geneva = Genève 33 C 5
Genève 33 C 5
Genghiz Khan, Wall of – 48-49 LM 2
Gengis Khan, Muralla de – 48-49 LM 2
Gengis Khan, Mur de – 48-49 LM 2
Gen He [TJ, ~] 48-49 N 1
Genhe [TJ, ●] 48-49 N 1
Geničesk 38-39 F 6
Genil 34-35 E 10
Genk 34-35 K 3
Genkai nada 50-51 GH 6
Gennargentu, Monti del – 36-37 C 5-6
Genoa 56-57 J 7
Genoa = Gènova 36-37 C 3
Genootschapseilanden 22-23 B 6-7
Gènova 36-37 C 3
Gènova = Gènova 36-37 C 3
Gènova, Golfo di – 36-37 C 4
Genovesa, Isla – 78-79 B 4
Genrietty, ostrov – 42-43 ef 2
Gent 34-35 JK 3
Genteng 52-53 E 8
Genzan = Wŏnsan 48-49 O 4
Geographe Bay 56-57 BC 6
Geographe Channel 56-57 B 4-5
Geographe Channel 56-57 B 4-5
Geok-Tepe 44-45 H 3
Georga, zeml'a – 42-43 F-H 1
George 64-65 F 9
George, Lake – [AUS] 56-57 JK 7
George, Lake – [EAU] 64-65 H 3
George, Lake – [RWA] 63 B 3
George, Lake – [USA, Florida] 74-75 c 2
George, Lake – [USA, New York] 74-75 G 3
George, Rivière – 70-71 X 6
George Gill Range 56-57 F 4
Georgetown [AUS, Queensland] 56-57 H 3
George Town [AUS, Tasmania] 56-57 J 8
Georgetown [CDN, Ontario] 74-75 D 3
Georgetown [GUY] 78-79 H 3
George Town [MAL] 52-53 CD 5
Georgetown, CA 76-77 C 6
Georgetown, DE 74-75 F 5
Georgetown, ID 76-77 H 4
Georgetown, SC 74-75 D 8
George Washington Birthplace National Monument 74-75 E 5
Georgia 38-39 HJ 7
Georgia 72-73 K 5
Georgia, Strait of – 70-71 M 8
Georgia del Sur = South Georgia 80 J 8
Georgia del Sur, Dorsal de – 24 D 33-E 34
Georgian Bay 70-71 U 8-9
Georgias del Sur, Islas – = South Georgia 80 J 8
Georgië 38-39 HJ 7
Géorgie 38-39 HJ 7
Géorgie du Sud = South Georgia 80 J 8
Géorgie du Sud, Seuil de – 24 D 33-E 34
Georgijevka 42-43 P 8
Georgijevsk 38-39 H 7
Georgijevskoje 38-39 HJ 4
Georgina River 56-57 G 4
Georg von Neumayer 24 B 36
Gera 33 EF 3
Gerais, Chapado dos – 78-79 K 8
Gerais, Chapado dos – 78-79 K 8
Geraldine, MT 76-77 HJ 2
Geraldton [AUS] 56-57 B 5
Geraldton [CDN] 70-71 T 8
Gerasimovka 42-43 N 6
Gercüş 46-47 J 4
Gerdakānehbālā 46-47 M 5
Gerdine, Mount – 70-71 F 5
Gerede 46-47 E 2
Gerede = Beydili 46-47 D 2
Gerede Çayı 46-47 E 2
Gerger 46-47 H 3
Geriş 46-47 D 4
Gerlach, NV 76-77 D 5
Gerlachovský štít 33 JK 4
Gērlogubī = Gedlegubē 60-61 NO 7
Germany 33 D-F 2-4
Germencik 46-47 B 4
Germī 46-47 N 3
Germiston 64-65 G 8
Gerona 34-35 J 8
Gers 34-35 H 7
Gerze 46-47 F 2
Gestro Weniz, Wabē – 60-61 N 7
Gettysburg, PA 74-75 E 5
Getz Ice Shelf 24 B 23-24
Gevar ovası 46-47 L 4
Gevaş 46-47 K 3
Gevgelija 36-37 K 5
Gewanē 60-61 N 6
Geyik Dağları 46-47 E 4
Geyser, MT 76-77 H 2
Geyser, Banc du – 64-65 L 5
Geysir 30-31 c 2
Geyve 46-47 D 2
Gezira, El – = Al-Jazīrah 60-61 L 6
Ghāb, Al- 46-47 G 5
Ghāb, El- = Al-Ghāb 46-47 G 5
Ghāb, Jabal – 46-47 H 5
Ghadai = Ghaday 46-47 M 8
Ghadámes = Ghadāmis 60-61 FG 2-3
Ghadāmis 60-61 FG 2-3
Ghaday 46-47 M 8
Ghadūn, Wādī – 44-45 G 7
Ghaghara 44-45 N 5
Ghallah, Bi'r – 62 E 3
Ghana 60-61 DE 7
Ghānim, Jazīrat – 62 E 4
Ghanzi 64-65 F 7
Gharaq as-Sulṭānī, Al- 62 CD 3
Gharbī, Jabal – 46-47 H 5
Gharbīyah, Al- 62 C 3
Ghardaqah, Al- 60-61 L 3
Ghardāyah 60-61 E 2
Ghārib, Jabal – 60-61 L 3
Gharqābād 46-47 NO 5
Gharyān 60-61 G 2
Ghat 60-61 G 3
Ghāṭ'ā', Al- 46-47 J 5
Ghawdex 36-37 F 7
Ghaydah, Al- [Y ← Sayḥūt] 44-45 FG 7-8
Ghaydah, Al- [Y ↗ Sayḥūt] 44-45 G 7
Ghazāl, 'Ayn al- [ET] 62 E 5
Ghazāl, Bahr al- [Sudan, ~] 60-61 KL 7
Ghazāl, Bahr al- [Sudan, ☆] 60-61 JK 7
Ghazawāṭ, Al- 60-61 D1
Ghazīr = Jazīr 46-47 F 5
Ghaz köl 48-49 G 4
Ghaznī 44-45 K 4
Ghazzah 44-45 C 4
Ghedo = Gēdo 60-61 M 7
Gheorghe Gheorghiu-Dej 36-37 M 2
Gheorghieni 36-37 LM 2
Gherla 36-37 KL 2
Gherlogubi = Gerlogubī 60-61 NO 7
Ghiedo = Gēdo 60-61 M 7
Ghigner = Gīnīr 60-61 N 7
Ghimbi = Gimbī 60-61 M 7
Ghinah, Wādī al- 46-47 G 7-8
Ghōr, El- = Al-Ghūr 46-47 F 7
Ghuja 48-49 E 3
Ghūr, Al- 46-47 F 7
Ghurdaqa, El – = Al-Ghardaqah 60-61 L 3
Ghūryān 44-45 J 4
Giannitsá 36-37 K 5
Giannutri 36-37 D 4
Giant Mountains 33 GH 3
Gia Rai 52-53 E 5
Giarre 36-37 F 7
Gibbon, OR 76-77 D 3
Gibbonsville, ID 76-77 G 3
Gibeil = Jubayl 62 E 3
Gibeon [Namibia, ●] 64-65 E 8
Gibraltar 34-35 E 10
Gibraltar, Détroit de – 34-35 D 11-E 10
Gibraltar, Estrecho de – 34-35 D 11-E 10
Gibraltar, Straat van – 34-35 D 11-E 10
Gibraltar, Strait of – 34-35 D 11-E 10
Gibson Desert 56-57 DE 4
Gīdolē 60-61 M 7
Gien 34-35 J 5
Gießen 33 D 3
Gifu 48-49 Q 4
Giganta, Sierra de la – 72-73 D 6-7
Giglio 36-37 D 4
Giguela 34-35 F 9
Gihān, Rās – = Rā's al-Bālā'im 62 E 3
Giheina = Juhaynah 62 D 4
Gihu = Gifu 48-49 Q 4
Gijón 34-35 E 7
Gila Bend, AZ 76-77 G 9
Gila Cliff 76-77 J 9

178 Galen

Gila Cliff Dwellings National Monument 76-77 J 9
Gila Desert 72-73 D 5
Gila Mountains 76-77 J 9
Gīlān 44-45 FG 3
Gīlān, Sārāb-e – 46-47 LM 5
Gīlān-e Gharb 46-47 LM 5
Gila River 72-73 D 5
Gila River Indian Reservation 76-77 GH 9
Gilbert River [AUS, ~] 56-57 H 3
Gilbert River [AUS, ●] 56-57 H 3
Gilbués 78-79 K 6
Gilf Kebir Plateau = Haḍbat al-Jilf al-Kabīr 60-61 K 4
Gilgandra 56-57 J 6
Gilgat = Gilgit 44-45 L 3
Gilgil 63 CD 3
Gilgit 44-45 L 3
Gillam 70-71 S 6
Gillen, Lake – 56-57 D 5
Gilles, Lake – 58 C 4
Gilmore, ID 76-77 G 3
Gilroy, CA 76-77 G 7
Giluwe, Mount – 52-53 M 8
Gimbala, Jebel – = Jabal Marrah 60-61 JK 6
Gīmbī 60-61 M 7
Gimma = Jīma 60-61 M 7
Gimpu 52-53 GH 7
Ginebra = Genève 33 C 5
Gineifa = Junayfah 62 E 2
Ginevrabotnen 30-31 kl 5
Gîngiova 36-37 KL 4
Gīnīr 60-61 N 7
Ginyer = Gīnīr 60-61 N 7
Giòia del Colle 36-37 G 5
Giovi, Passo dei – 36-37 C 3
Gippsland 56-57 J 7
Girard, OH 74-75 C 4
Girard, PA 74-75 C 3-4
Girardot 78-79 E 4
Giren = Jīma 60-61 M 7
Giresum 38-39 G 7
Giresun 44-45 D 2
Giresun Dağları 46-47 H 2
Girge = Jirjā 60-61 L 3
Giri 64-65 E 2
Giridih 44-45 O 6
Girilambone 58 H 3
Girishk 44-45 J 4
Girne 46-47 E 5
Gironde 34-35 G 6
Girvan 32 D 4
Girvas 30-31 O 4
Gisborne 56-57 P 7
Gisenyi 64-65 G 3
Gislaved 30-31 E 9
Gisr ash-Shughur 46-47 G 5
Gitega 64-65 GH 3
Giuba, Ìsole – 64-65 K 3
Giulianova 36-37 EF 4
Giumbo = Jumbo 64-65 K 3
Giûra 36-37 L 6
Giurgiu 36-37 L 4
Givet 34-35 K 3
Giždūvan 42-43 L 9
Gizeh = Al-Jīzah 60-61 KL 3
Gižiga 42-43 f 5
Gižiginskaja guba 42-43 e 5
Gizmel 46-47 M 5
Gizo 52-53 j 6
Giżycko 33 KL 1

Gjersvik 30-31 E 5
Gjirokastër 36-37 HJ 5
Gjögurtá 30-31 d 1
Gjøvik 30-31 D 7
Gjuhës, Kepi i – 36-37 H 5

Glace Bay 70-71 YZ 8
Glacier Bay National Monument 70-71 J 6
Glacier National Park [USA] 72-73 CD 2
Glacier Peak 76-77 C 1
Glade Park, CO 76-77 J 6
Gladstone [AUS, Queensland] 56-57 K 4
Gladstone [AUS, South Australia] 56-57 G 6
Glady, WV 74-75 D 5
Gláma 30-31 b 2
Glamis, CA 76-77 F 9
Glasgow 32 DE 4
Glassboro, NJ 74-75 F 5
Glauchau 33 F 3
Glazov 42-43 J 6
Gleeson, AZ 76-77 J 10
Gleisdorf 33 GH 5
Glenbrook 58 K 4
Glen Canyon 76-77 H 7
Glencoe [CDN] 74-75 C 3
Glendale, AZ 72-73 D 5
Glendale, CA 72-73 C 5
Glendale, NV 76-77 F 7
Glendale, OR 76-77 B 4
Glenelg River 58 E 6
Glengyle 56-57 GH 4
Glen Innes 56-57 K 5
Glen Lyon, PA 74-75 EF 4
Glen More 32 D 3
Glenmorgan 56-57 JK 5
Glenns Ferry, ID 76-77 F 4
Glenore 56-57 H 3
Glens Falls, NY 74-75 G 3
Glenwood, OR 76-77 B 3
Glenwood, WA 76-77 C 2
Glide, OR 76-77 B 4
Glina 36-37 G 3
Glittertind 30-31 C 7
Gliwice 33 J 3
Globe, AZ 72-73 D 5
Gloggnitz 33 G 5
Głogów 33 GH 3
Glomfjord 30-31 EF 4
Glomma 30-31 D 7
Glommersträsk 30-31 HJ 5
Glória 78-79 M 6
Gloria, La – [CO] 78-79 E 3
Glorieuses, Îles – 64-65 L 5
Gloucester, MA 74-75 H 3
Gloucester City, NJ 74-75 F 5
Glouchester 32 E 6
Glouster, OH 74-75 BC 5
Gloversville, NY 74-75 F 3
Glubokoje 30-31 M 10
Glubokoje [SU, Kazachskaja SSR] 42-43 P 7
Gluchov 38-39 F 5

Gmünd 33 G 4
Gmunden 33 FG 5

Gnaday 46-47 M 8
Gniezno 33 H 2
Gnowangerup 56-57 C 6

Goa 44-45 L 7
Goageb [Namibia, ●] 64-65 E 8
Goaso = Gawso 60-61 D 7
Goba [ETH] 60-61 N 7
Gobabis 64-65 E 7
Gobernador Gregores 80 BC 7
Gobi 48-49 H-L 3
Gobō 50-51 K 6
Godavari 44-45 N 7
Godavari Delta 44-45 N 7
Goddo 78-79 HJ 4
Goddua = Ghuddawah 60-61 G 3
Godfrey Tank 56-57 E 4
Godhavn = Qeqertarssuq 70-71 Za 4
Godoy Cruz 80 BC 4
Gods Lake [CDN, ●] 70-71 S 7
Gods Lake [CDN, ≈] 70-71 S 7
Godthåb = Nûk 70-71 a 5
Godwin Austen, Mount – = K 2 44-45 M 3
Goede Hoop, Kaap de – 64-65 E 9
Goélands, Lac aux – 70-71 Y 6
Goeree 34-35 J 3
Goffs, CA 76-77 F 8
Goggiam = Gojam 60-61 M 6
Gogland, ostrov – 30-31 M 7
Gogra = Ghaghara 44-45 N 5
Gogrial = Qūqriyāl 60-61 K 7
Goiana 78-79 MN 6
Goiandira 78-79 K 8
Goianésia 78-79 K 8
Goiânia 78-79 JK 8
Goiás [BR, ●] 78-79 JK 8
Goiás [BR, ☆] 78-79 J 8-K 7
Goiás, Serra Geral de – 78-79 K 7
Goiatuba 78-79 JK 8
Gojam 60-61 M 6
Gojjam = Gojam 60-61 M 6
Gökbel 46-47 C 4
Gökçeada 46-47 AB 2
Gökırmak 46-47 F 2
Gökova Körfezi 46-47 BC 4
Göksu [TR, ~] 46-47 FG 4
Göksu [TR, ●] 46-47 K 3
Göksun 46-47 G 3
Göksu Nehri 44-45 C 3
Gök Tepe [TR, ▲] 46-47 C 4
Göktepe [TR, ●] 46-47 E 4
Gokwe 64-65 G 6
Gol 30-31 C 7
Golaja Pristan' 36-37 P 2
Golāshkerd 44-45 H 5
Gölbaşı [TR, Adıyaman] 46-47 G 4
Gölbaşı [TR, Ankara] 46-47 E 3
Golconda, NV 76-77 E 5
Gölcük [TR, Kocaeli] 46-47 CD 2
Gołdap 33 L 1
Gold Beach, OR 76-77 A 4
Goldburg, ID 76-77 G 3
Gold Butte, MT 76-77 H 1
Gold Coast 60-61 D 8-E 7
Gold Coast 56-57 K 5
Gold Coast-Southport 58 LM 1
Golden, ID 76-77 F 3
Goldendale, WA 76-77 C 3
Golden Gate 72-73 B 4
Golden Vale 32 BC 5
Goldfield, NV 76-77 E 7
Gold Hill, UT 76-77 G 5
Gold Point, NV 76-77 E 7
Goldsboro, NC 72-73 L 4-5
Goldsworthy, Mount – 56-57 CD 4
Göle 46-47 K 2
Goléa, El- = Al-Gulī'ah 60-61 E 2
Golec-In'aptuk, gora – = gora In'aptuk 42-43 UV 6
Golec-Longdor, gora – = gora Longdor 42-43 W 6
Golela 64-65 H 8
Goleniów 33 G 2
Goleta, CA 76-77 D 8
Golfe Nuevo 80 D 6
Golfe Persique 44-45 FG 5
Golfito 72-73 K 10
Golfo Aranci 36-37 CD 5
Golfo Dulce 72-73 K 10
Golfo Pérsico 44-45 FG 5
Gölhisar 46-47 C 4
Gölköy 46-47 G 2
Göllü = Çoğun 46-47 F 3
Gölmarmara 46-47 BC 3
Golmo 48-49 GH 4
Golodnaja step' = Betpak-Dala 42-43 MN 8
Golog Zangzu Zizhizhou 48-49 HJ 5
Golog Zizhizhou 48-49 HJ 5
Gölören 46-47 E 4
Golpāyegān 44-45 G 4
Gölpazarı 46-47 D 2
Golspie 32 E 2-3
Gol Tappeh 46-47 L 4
Golungo Alto 64-65 D 4
Golyšmanovo 42-43 MN 6
Goma 64-65 G 3
Gomati 44-45 N 5
Gomba 63 D 5
Gombari 63 B 2
Gombe [EAT] 64-65 H 3
Gombe [WAN] 60-61 G 6
Gomel' 38-39 F 5
Gomera 60-61 A 3
Gómez Palacio 72-73 EF 6
Gonābād 44-45 H 4
Gonaïves 72-73 M 8
Gonam [SU, ~] 42-43 Y 6
Gonam [SU, ●] 42-43 Z 6
Gonâve, Golfe de la – 72-73 M 8
Gonâve, Île de la – 72-73 M 8
Gonbād-e Kavus = Gonbad-e Qābūs 44-45 H 3
Gonbad-e Qābūs 44-45 H 3
Gondar = Gonder 60-61 M 6
Gonder [ETH, ●] 60-61 M 6
Gonder [ETH, ☆] 60-61 M 6
Gönen 46-47 B 2
Gongga Shan 48-49 J 6
Gongjiatun = Gangtun 50-51 C 2
Gongoji, Serra do – 78-79 LM 7-8
Gongola 60-61 G 7
Gongola, River – 60-61 G 6
Gongyingzi 50-51 BC 2
Gongzhuling = Huaide 48-49 NO 3
Goniądz 33 L 2
Gonja 63 D 4
Gono-kawa 50-51 J 5
Gonoura 50-51 G 6
Gonzales, CA 76-77 C 7
Gonzanamá 78-79 D 5
Goodenough, Cape – 24 C 13
Goodenough Island 52-53 gh 6
Good Hope, Cape of – 64-65 E 9
Goodhouse 64-65 E 8
Gooding, ID 76-77 F 4
Goodooga 58 HJ 2
Goolgowi 58 G 4
Goomalling 56-57 C 6
Goona = Guna 44-45 M 6
Goondiwindi 56-57 JK 5
Goonyella 56-57 J 4
Goose Bay [CDN, Newfoundland] 70-71 Y 7
Goose Creek 76-77 FG 4-5
Goose Lake [USA] 72-73 B 3
Go Quao 52-53 DE 5
Gor'ačegorsk 42-43 Q 6
Gorakhpoor = Gorakhpur 44-45 N 5
Gorakhpur 44-45 N 5
Gorakpur = Gorakhpur 44-45 N 5
Goram Islands = Kepulauan Seram-Laut 52-53 K 7
Goran, El – = El Ḳoran 60-61 N 7
Gördes 46-47 C 3
Gordion 46-47 DE 3
Gordon, GA 74-75 B 8
Gordon, Lake – 58 bc 3
Gordon Downs 56-57 E 3
Gordonsville, VA 74-75 D 5
Gordonvale 56-57 J 3
Gorē [ETH] 60-61 M 7
Gore [NZ] 56-57 N 9
Goré [Tchad] 60-61 H 7
Gore, Isla – 76-77 F 10
Görele 46-47 H 2
Gore Mountain 74-75 H 2
Gorgān 44-45 GH 3
Gorgān, Rūd-e – 44-45 GH 3
Gorgona, Isla – 78-79 D 4
Gorgora 60-61 M 6
Gori Cheboa 63 E 2
Gori Cheboa 63 E 2
Gorìzia 36-37 E 3
Gorki 38-39 F 5
Gorki [SU, Rossijskaja SFSR Jamalo-Neneckaja AO] 42-43 M 4
Gorki = Gor'kij 42-43 GH 6
Gor'kij = Nižnij Novgorod 42-43 GH 6
Gor'kovskoje vodochranilišče 42-43 GH 6
Görlitz 33 G 3
Gorlovka 38-39 G 6
Gorman, CA 76-77 D 8
Gorna Or'ahovica 36-37 LM 4
Gornji Milanovac 36-37 J 3
Gorno-Altai Autonomous Region = 9 ◁ 42-43 Q 7
Gorno-Altaj, Oblast Autónoma de – = 9 ◁ 42-43 Q 7
Gorno-Altajsk 42-43 Q 7
Gorno-Badachšanskaja Autonome Oblast 44-45 L 3
Gorno-Badachšanskaja Autonome Oblast 44-45 L 3
Gorno-Badachšanskaja Autonomnaja Oblast 44-45 L 3
Gorno-Badachšan, Oblast Autónoma de – 44-45 L 3
Gorno-Badakhshan Autonomous Region 44-45 L 3
Gornozavodsk 42-43 b 8
Gorodok = Zakamensk 42-43 T 7
Goroka 52-53 N 8
Gorom = Gorom-Gorom 60-61 DE 6
Gorom-Gorom 60-61 DE 6
Gorongosa, Serra de – 64-65 HJ 6
Gorontalo 52-53 H 6
Gorrahei = Korahe 60-61 NO 7
Gort 32 B 5
Goryn' 38-39 E 5
Gorzów Wielkopolski 33 GH 2
Gosen [J] 50-51 M 4
Gosford-Woy Woy 56-57 K 6
Goshen, CA 76-77 D 7
Goshen, NY 74-75 F 4
Goshogawara 50-51 MN 2
Goshute Indian Reservation 76-77 F 6
Goslar 33 DE 3
Gospić 36-37 F 3
Gosport 32 F 6
Gostynin 33 J 2
Gosyogahara = Goshogawara 50-51 MN 2
Göta älv 30-31 D 9-E 8
Göta kanal 30-31 EF 8
Götaland 30-31 E-G 9
Göteborg 30-31 D 9
Göteborg och Bohus 30-31 D 8
Gotha 33 E 3
Gotland [S, ⊙] 30-31 H 9
Gotland [S, ☆] 30-31 H 9
Gotland, Fosa de – 30-31 HJ 9
Gotland, Fosse de – 30-31 HJ 9
Gotland Deep 30-31 HJ 9
Gotlanddiep 30-31 HJ 9
Gotō-rettō 48-49 O 5
Gotska Sandön 30-31 HJ 8
Gōtsu 50-51 HJ 5
Göttingen 33 DE 3
Gottwaldov 33 H 4
Goubangzi 50-51 CD 2
Goubéré 60-61 K 7
Goudiry 60-61 B 6
Goudkust 60-61 D 8-E 7
Gough, GA 74-75 B 8
Gouin, Réservoir – 70-71 VW 8
Goulburn 56-57 J 6
Goulburn Islands 56-57 F 2
Gould Bay 24 B 31-32
Goulimîm = Julimīnā 60-61 BC 3
Goundam 60-61 D 5
Gouré 60-61 G 6
Gourma 60-61 E 6
Gourma Rharous 60-61 D 5
Gouro 60-61 H 5
Gouverneur, NY 74-75 F 2
Gōvā = Goa 44-45 L 7
Gov'altaj = 5 ◁ 48-49 H 3
Gov'altajn nuruu 48-49 H 2-J 3
Govena, mys – 42-43 g 6
Goverla 36-37 L 1
Governador Valadares 78-79 L 8
Gowanda, NY 74-75 D 3
Gower Peninsula 32 DE 6
Goya 80 E 3
Göynücek 46-47 F 2
Göynük [TR, Bingöl] 46-47 J 3
Göynük [TR, Bolu] 46-47 D 2
Goz Beïda 60-61 J 6
Goze Delčev 36-37 KL 5
Gozha Tsho 48-49 E 4

Graaff-Reinet 64-65 FG 9
Grã-Canária = Gran Canaria 60-61 A 3
Grace, ID 76-77 H 4
Gracias a Dios, Cabo – 72-73 K 8
Gradaús 78-79 J 6
Gradaús, Serra dos – 78-79 JK 6
Gräddö 30-31 H 8
Grafton 56-57 K 5
Grafton, WV 74-75 CD 5
Graham, NC 74-75 D 6-7
Graham, Mount – 72-73 DE 5
Graham Bell, ostrov – = ostrov Greėm-Bell 42-43 MN 1
Graham Island 70-71 JK 7
Graham Moore, Cape – 70-71 V-X 3
Grahamstad = Grahamstown 64-65 G 9
Grahamstown 64-65 G 9
Grain Coast 60-61 B 7-C 8
Graines, Côte des – 60-61 B 7-C 8
Grajaú 78-79 K 6
Grajaú, Rio – [BR, Maranhão] 78-79 K 5-6
Grajewo 33 L 2
Grambûsa, Akrōtḗrion – 36-37 K 8
Grámmos 36-37 J 5
Grampian Mountains 32 DE 3
Granada [E] 34-35 F 10
Granada [NIC] 72-73 JK 9
Granada [WG] 72-73 O 9
Gran Altiplanicie Central 80 BC 7
Gran Atlas 60-61 CD 2
Gran Bahía Australiana = Great Australian Bight 56-57 E 6-G 7
Gran Bajo [RA, Santa Cruz] 80 C 7
Granby 70-71 W 8
Gran Canaria 60-61 AB 3
Gran Chaco 80 D 3-E 2
Gran Chaco 80 D 3-E 2
Grand Bahama Island 72-73 L 6
Grand Baie Australienne = Great Australian Bight 56-57 E 6-G 7
Grand Ballon 34-35 L 5
Grand Bassa = Buchanan 60-61 B 7
Grand-Bassam 60-61 D 7-8
Grand-Bourg 72-73 OP 8
Grand Canal 32 BC 5
Grand Canyon 72-73 D 4
Grand Canyon, AZ 76-77 GH 7
Grand Canyon National Monument 76-77 G 7
Grand Canyon National Park 72-73 D 4
Grand Cayman 72-73 KL 8
Grand Coulee [USA] 76-77 D 2
Grand Coulee, WA 76-77 D 2
Grand Coulee Dam 72-73 BC 2
Grand Coulee Equalizing Reservoir = Banks Lake 76-77 D 2
Grande Comore = Ngazidja 64-65 K 5
Grande Dépression Centrale 64-65 EF 3
Grande Muraille 48-49 K 4
Grande Prairie 70-71 N 6-7
Grand Erg de Bilma 60-61 G 5
Grand Erg Occidental = Al-'Irq al-Kabīr al-Gharbī 60-61 D 3-E 2
Grand Erg Oriental = Al 'Irq al-Kabīr ash-Sharqī 60-61 F 2-3
Grande-Rivière, la – 70-71 V 7
Grande Rivière à la Balleine 70-71 VW 6
Grande Ronde, OR 76-77 B 3
Grande Ronde River 76-77 E 2-3
Grandes Antilles 72-73 K 7-N 8
Grandes Antillas 72-73 K 7-N 8
Gran Desierto 72-73 D 5
Grandes Landes 34-35 G 6-7
Grande Syrte = Khalīj as-Surt 60-61 H 2
Grand Falls [CDN] 70-71 Za 8
Grand Falls [EAK] 63 D 3
Grand Falls [USA] 76-77 H 8
Grand Falls = Churchill Falls 70-71 XY 7
Grandfather Mountain 74-75 C 6
Grand Forks, ND 72-73 G 2
Grandioznyj, pik – 42-43 RS 7
Grand Island [USA, New York] 74-75 D 3
Grand Island, NE 72-73 G 3
Grand Isle 74-75 G 2
Grand Junction, CO 72-73 DE 4
Grand Khingan 48-49 M 3-W 1
Grand-Lahou 60-61 CD 7-8
Grand Lake [USA, Maine] 74-75 K 2
Grand Météor, Banc du – 22-23 H 4
Grândola 34-35 C 9
Grand Paradiso 36-37 B 3
Grand-Popo 60-61 E 7
Grand Rapids, MI 72-73 J 3
Grand River [CDN] 74-75 CD 3
Grand River [USA, South Dakota] 72-73 F 2
Grand River Valley 76-77 J 6
Grand Teton National Park 76-77 H 3-4
Grand Teton Peak 72-73 D 3
Grand Trunk Pacific Railway = Candian National Railways 70-71 PQ 7
Grand View, ID 76-77 EF 4
Grandview, WA 76-77 D 2
Grand Wash Cliffs 76-77 FG 8
Gran Erg Occidental = Al-'Irq al-Kabīr al-Gharbī 60-61 D 3-E 2
Gran Erg Oriental = Al-'Irq al-Kabīr ash-Sharqī 60-61 F 2-3
Granger, WA 76-77 CD 2
Granger, WY 76-77 J 5
Grängesberg 30-31 F 7
Grangeville, ID 76-77 EF 3
Granite, OR 76-77 D 3
Granite Downs 56-57 F 5
Granite Mountains 76-77 F 8
Granite Peak [USA, Montana] 72-73 E 2
Granite Peak [USA, Utah] 76-77 G 5
Granite Range [USA, Nevada] 76-77 D 5
Granite Springs Valley 76-77 D 5
Graniteville, SC 74-75 C 8
Granja 78-79 L 5
Gran Jingán 48-49 M 3-N 1
Gran Lago Salado = Great Salt Lake 72-73 D 3
Gran Malvina = West Falkland 80 D 8
Gran Muralla 48-49 K 4
Gränna 30-31 F 8
Gran Pampa Pelada 78-79 F 9
Gran Sabana, La – 78-79 G 3
Gran San Bernardo 36-37 B 3
Gran Sasso 36-37 E 4
Grant, FL 74-75 c 3
Grant, MT 76-77 G 3
Grant, Mount – [USA, Clan Alpine Mountains] 76-77 DE 6
Grant, Mount – [USA, Wassuk Range] 76-77 D 6
Grant Land 19 A 25-27
Grant Range 76-77 F 6
Grants, NM 72-73 E 4
Grants Pass, OR 76-77 B 4
Grantsville, UT 76-77 G 5

Grant 179

Grantsville, WV 74-75 C 5
Granville 34-35 G 4
Grasse 34-35 L 7
Grass Lake, CA 76-77 B 5
Grass Valley, CA 76-77 C 6
Grass Valley, OR 76-77 C 3
Grassy 56-57 H 7-8
Grassy Knob 74-75 C 5-6
Gratangen 30-31 GH 3
Gravatá 78-79 M 6
Gravenhage, 's- 34-35 JK 2
Gravenhurst 74-75 D 2
Grave Peak 76-77 F 2
Gravesend 58 JK 2
Gravina di Pùglia 36-37 G 5
Gray 34-35 K 5
Gray, GA 74-75 B 8
Grays Harbor 76-77 AB 2
Graz 33 G 5
Gr'azi 38-39 GH 5
Gr'azovec 38-39 GH 4
Grdelica 36-37 JK 4
Great Abaco Island 72-73 L 6
Great Artesian Basin 56-57 GH 4-5
Great Australian Bight 56-57 E 6-G 7
Great Bahama Bank 72-73 L 6-7
Great Barrier Island 56-57 P 7
Great Barrier Reef 56-57 H 2-K 4
Great Basin 72-73 CD 3-4
Great Bay 74-75 F 5
Great Bear Lake 70-71 MN 4
Great Bear River 70-71 LM 4-5
Great Bend, KS 72-73 FG 4
Great Bitter Lake = Al-Buḥayrat al-Murrat al-Kubrá 62 E 2
Great Dividing Range 56-57 H-K 3-7
Great Driffield 32 FG 4-5
Greater Antilles 72-73 K 7-N 8
Greater Sunda Islands 52-53 E-H 7-8
Great Exuma Island 72-73 L 7
Great Falls [USA] 76-77 H 2
Great Falls, MT 72-73 DE 2
Great Falls, SC 74-75 C 7
Great Inagua Island 72-73 M 7
Great Kei River = Groot Keirivier 64-65 GH 9
Great Khingan Range 48-49 M 3-N 1
Great Lake 56-57 J 8
Great Meteor Seamount 22-23 H 4
Great Namaqua Land = Namaland 64-65 E 8
Great Nicobar 44-45 P 9
Great Northern Pacific Railway 72-73 DE 2
Great Northern Peninsula 70-71 Z 7-8
Great Oyster Bay 58 d 3
Great Peconic Bay 74-75 G 4
Great Plains 72-73 E 2-F 5
Great Ruaha 64-65 J 4
Great Sacandaga Lake 74-75 FG 3
Great Salt Lake 72-73 D 3
Great Salt Lake Desert 72-73 D 3
Great Sandy Desert [AUS] 56-57 DE 4
Great Sandy Desert [USA] 72-73 BC 3
Great Sandy Island 56-57 KL 4-5
Great Slave Lake 70-71 NO 5
Great Smoky Mountains 74-75 B 7
Great Valley 74-75 A 7-F 4
Great Victoria Desert 56-57 EF 5
Great Wall 48-49 K 4
Great Yarmouth 32 GH 5
Grebená 36-37 J 5
Gréboun, Mont – 60-61 F 4-5
Grèce 36-37 J 7-L 5
Grecia 36-37 J 7-L 5
Gredos, Sierra de – 34-35 E 8
Greece 36-37 J 7-L 5
Greeley, CO 72-73 F 3
Greely Fiord 70-71 UV 1
Greem-Bell, ostrov – 42-43 MN 1
Green Bay 72-73 J 2-3
Green Bay, WI 72-73 J 3
Greenbrier River 74-75 CD 5-6
Green Cape 58 K 6
Greencastle, PA 74-75 DE 5
Green Cove Springs, FL 74-75 bc 1-2
Greeneville, TN 74-75 B 6
Greenfield, CA 76-77 C 7
Greenfield, MA 74-75 G 3
Greenhorn Mountains 76-77 D 8
Green Island [AUS] 56-57 J 3
Green Islands 52-53 hj 5
Greenland 19 BC 23
Greenland Basin 22-23 JK 2
Greenland Sea 19 B 20-18
Green Mountains [USA, Vermont] 74-75 G 2-3
Greenock 32 D 4
Green Pond, SC 74-75 C 8
Greenport, NY 74-75 G 4
Green River [USA, Wyoming] 72-73 E 3-4
Green River, UT 76-77 H 6
Green River, WY 76-77 J 5
Green River Basin 72-73 DE 3
Greensboro, GA 74-75 B 8
Greensboro, NC 72-73 L 4
Greensburg, PA 74-75 D 4
Green Swamp 74-75 D 7
Greenville 60-61 C 7-8
Greenville, CA 76-77 C 5
Greenville, FL 74-75 b 1
Greenville, IN 74-75 A 4
Greenville, ME 74-75 HJ 2
Greenville, MS 72-73 HJ 5
Greenville, NC 72-73 L 4
Greenville, PA 74-75 C 4
Greenville, SC 72-73 K 5
Greenville, TX 72-73 GH 5
Greenwich, London- 32 FG 6
Greenwood, MS 72-73 HJ 5
Greenwood, SC 72-73 K 5
Greer, ID 76-77 EF 2
Greer, SC 74-75 B 7
Gregory, Lake – 56-57 GH 5
Gregory Downs 56-57 G 3
Gregory Lake 56-57 E 3-4
Gregory Range 56-57 H 3
Gregory River 56-57 G 3
Greifswald 33 F 1
Grein 33 G 4
Greinerville 63 B 4
Greiz 33 EF 3
Gréko, Akrōtḗrion – 46-47 F 5
Gremicha 42-43 F 4
Grenå 30-31 D 9
Grenade 72-73 O 9
Grenadines 72-73 O 9
Grenen 30-31 D 9
Grenfell [AUS] 58 HJ 4
Grenivík 30-31 de 2
Grenoble 34-35 KL 6
Grenvill, Cape – 56-57 H 2
Gretna, LA 72-73 HJ 6
Grey Islands 70-71 Za 7
Greylock, Mount – 74-75 G 3
Greymouth 56-57 O 8
Grey Range 56-57 H 5
Greytown = Bluefields 72-73 K 9
Gribingui = Ibingui-Économique 60-61 H 7
Gridley, CA 76-77 C 6
Griekenland 36-37 J 7-L 5
Griekwaland-Wes 64-65 F 8
Griffin, GA 72-73 K 5
Griffith 56-57 J 6
Grigoriopol 36-37 N 2
Grim, Cape – 56-57 H 8
Grimari 60-61 HJ 7
Grimes, CA 76-77 C 6
Grimma 33 F 3
Grimsby 32 FG 5
Grimsby [CDN] 74-75 D 3
Grimsey 30-31 d 1
Grimstad 30-31 C 8
Grímsvötn 30-31 e 2
Grindavík 30-31 b 3
Grindsted 30-31 C 10
Grinnell Land 70-71 UV 1-2
Grinnell Peninsula 70-71 RS 2
Griqualand West = Griekwaland-Wes 64-65 F 8
Grodno 38-39 DE 5
Groenland 19 BC 23
Groenland, Bassin du – 22-23 JK 2
Groenland, Mer du – 19 B 20-18
Groenlandbekken 22-23 JK 2
Groenlandia 19 BC 23
Groenlandia, Cuenca de – 22-23 JK 2
Groenlandia, Mar de – 19 B 20-18
Groenlandzee 19 B 20-18
Grœtavær 30-31 FG 3
Groix, Île de – 34-35 F 5
Groll, Crête de – 22-23 H 6
Groll-Ondiepte 22-23 H 6
Groll Seamount 22-23 H 6
Groll, Cima de – 22-23 H 6
Grong 30-31 E 5
Groningen 34-35 L 2
Groningen [SME] 78-79 HJ 3
Groot Barrierrif = Great Barrier Reef 56-57 H 1-K 4
Groot Brittannië en Noordierland 32 F-H 4-5
Groot Brukkaros 64-65 E 8
Groote Eylandt 56-57 G 2
Grootfontein 64-65 E 6
Groot-Karasberge 64-65 E 8
Groot-Karoo 64-65 F 9
Groot Keirivier 64-65 GH 9
Groot Visrivier 64-65 E 8
Grosa, Punta – 34-35 H 9
Gros Morne National Park 70-71 Z 8
Große Antillen 72-73 K 7-N 8
Große Arabische Wüste = Ar-Rub' al-Ḫālī 44-45 F 7-G 6
Große Australische Bucht = Great Australian Bight 56-57 E 6-G 7
Große Bahamabank 72-73 L 6-7
Große Mauer 48-49 K 4
Großenbrode 33 E 1
Große Nefud = An-Nafūd 44-45 E 5
Große Persische Salzwüste = Dasht-e Kavīr 44-45 GH 4
Großer Arber 33 F 3
Großer Bärensee 70-71 MN 4
Großer Beerberg 33 E 3
Großer Chingan = Großer Khingan 48-49 M 3-N 1
Großer Chingan = Großer Khingan 48-49 M 3-N 1
Großer Fischfluß = Groot Visrivier 64-65 E 8
Großer Khingan 48-49 M 3-N 1
Großer Salzsee = Great Salt Lake 72-73 D 3
Großer Sklavensee 70-71 NO 5
Große Sandwüste = Great Sandy Desert 56-57 DE 4
Großes Artesisches Becken = Great Artesin Basin 56-57 GH 4-5
Großes Barrierriff = Great Barrier Reef 56-57 H 2-K 4
Große Sundainseln 52-53 E-H 7-8
Großes Wallriff = Great Barrier Reef 56-57 H 2-K 4
Große Syrte = Khalīj as-Surt 60-61 H 2
Grosseto 36-37 D 4
Große Victoriawüste = Great Victoria Desert 56-57 EF 5
Großglockner 33 F 5
Gros Ventre River 76-77 H 4
Grote Antillen 72-73 K 7-N 8
Grote Australische Bocht = Great Australian Bight 56-57 E 6-G 7
Grote Bahamabank 72-73 L 6-7
Grote Ocean 22-23 Q-T 5-6
Grote Sunda-Eilanden 52-53 GH 8
Grote Syrte = Khalīj as-Surt 60-61 H 2
Grote Xingangebergte 48-49 M 3-N 1
Grotli 30-31 BC 6
Groton, NY 74-75 E 3
Grottoes, VA 74-75 D 5
Grouse, ID 76-77 G 4
Grouse Creek, UT 76-77 G 5
Grouse Creek Mountain 76-77 FG 3
Grove City, PA 74-75 CD 4
Groveland, CA 76-77 CD 7
Grover, WY 76-77 H 4
Grover City, CA 76-77 C 8
Grovont, WY 76-77 H 4
Growler, AZ 76-77 FG 9
Growler Mountains 76-77 G 9
Groznyj 38-39 HJ 7
Grudovo 36-37 M 4
Grudziądz 33 J 2
Grumantbyen 30-31 jk 5
Grumeti 63 C 3
Grumo Appula 36-37 G 5
Grünau [Namibia] 64-65 E 8
Grundarfjördhur 30-31 ab 2
Grundy, VA 74-75 BC 6
Gryfice 33 G 2
Gryllefjord 30-31 G 3
Grytviken 80 J 8
Gṣaiba = Quṣaybah 46-47 J 5
Guacanayabo, Golfo de – 72-73 L 7
Guadalajara [E] 34-35 F 8
Guadalajara [MEX] 72-73 EF 7
Guadalaviar 34-35 G 8
Guadalcanal [Salomonen] 52-53 j 6
Guadalcanar Gela = Guadalcanal 52-53 j 6
Guadalete 34-35 DE 10
Guadalimar 34-35 F 9
Guadalope 34-35 G 8
Guadalquivir 34-35 E 10
Guadalupe [E] 34-35 E 9
Guadalupe [MEX, Nuevo León] 72-73 FG 6
Guadalupe, CA 76-77 C 8
Guadalupe, Isla de – 72-73 C 6
Guadalupe, Sierra de – 34-35 E 9
Guadalupe Mountains [USA ↘ Phoenix] 76-77 J 10
Guadalupe Peak 72-73 F 5
Guadarrama, Sierra de – 34-35 EF 8
Guadeloupe 72-73 O 8
Guadeloupe Passage 72-73 O 8
Guadiana 34-35 D 10
Guadiana Menor 34-35 F 10
Guadix 34-35 F 10
Guadur = Gwādar 44-45 J 5
Guafo, Golfo de – 80 B 6
Guafo, Isla – 80 AB 6
Guai 52-53 L 7
Guainia, Rio – 78-79 F 4
Guaiquinima, Cerro – 78-79 G 3
Guaitecas, Islas – 80 AB 6
Guajará-Mirim 78-79 FG 7
Guajira, Peninsula de – 78-79 E 2
Gualala, CA 76-77 B 6
Gualaquiza 78-79 D 5
Gualeguay 80 E 4
Gualeguaychu 80 E 4
Gualior = Gwalior 44-45 M 5
Guamblin, Isla – 80 A 6
Guaña 78-79 G 4
Guanahani = San Salvador 72-73 M 7
Guanajutao 72-73 F 7
Guanare 78-79 F 3
Guanarito 78-79 F 3
Guandong Bandao 50-51 C 3
Guane 72-73 K 7
Guang'an 48-49 K 5
Guangchang 48-49 M 6
Guangdong 48-49 L 7
Guanghai 48-49 L 7
Guanghua 48-49 L 5
Guangji 48-49 M 6
Guanglu Dao 50-51 D 3
Guangnan 48-49 JK 7
Guangxi Zhuangzu Zizhiqu 48-49 KL 7
Guangyuan 48-49 K 5
Guangzhou 48-49 LM 7
Guangzhou Wan = Zhanjiang Gang 48-49 L 7
Guano Lake 76-77 D 4
Guanshui 50-51 E 2
Guantánamo 72-73 LM 7-8
Guanyun 48-49 MN 5
Guaña 78-79 G 4
Guapi 78-79 D 4
Guaporé = Rondônia 78-79 G 7
Guaporé, Rio – [BR ◁ Rio Mamoré] 78-79 G 7
Guaqui 78-79 F 8
Guarabira 78-79 MN 6
Guaranda 78-79 D 5
Guarapuava 80 F 3
Guaratinguetá 78-79 KL 9
Guaratuba 80 G 3
Guarayos, Llanos de – 78-79 G 8
Guarayos, Llanos de – 78-79 G 8
Guarda 34-35 D 8
Guardafui = 'Asayr 44-45 G 8
Guardo 34-35 E 7
Guarulhos 78-79 K 9
Guasave 72-73 E 6
Guascama, Punta – 78-79 D 4
Guasdualito 78-79 EF 3
Guasipati 78-79 G 3
Guastalla 36-37 D 3
Guatemala [GCA, ●] 72-73 HJ 9
Guatemala [GCA, ★] 72-73 HJ 8
Guatemala, Bassin du – 22-23 DE 5
Guatemala, Cuenca de – 22-23 DE 5
Guatemala Basin 22-23 DE 5
Guatemalabekken 22-23 DE 5
Guaviare, Rio – 78-79 F 4
Guaxupé 78-79 K 9
Guayana Francesa 78-79 J 4
Guayanas, Cuenca de las – 22-23 G 5
Guayaquil 78-79 CD 5
Guayaquil, Golfo de – 78-79 C 5
Guayaramerin 78-79 F 7
Guaymas = Heroica Guaymas 72-73 D 6
Guaymas Heroica 72-73 D 6
Guba 64-65 G 5
Gubacha 42-43 K 6
Guban 60-61 ab 1
Gubanovo = Vereščagino 42-43 JK 6
Gùbbio 36-37 E 4
Guben 33 G 3
Gučin Us 48-49 J 2
Gūḍalūr = Cuddalore 44-45 MN 8
Gudauta 38-39 GH 7
Gudbrandsdal 30-31 CD 7
Gudenå 30-31 CD 9
Gudermes 38-39 J 7
Güdül 46-47 E 2
Gudur 44-45 MN 8
Gūḍūru = Gudur 44-45 MN 8
Guéckédou 60-61 BC 7
Guelma = Qalmah 60-61 F 1
Guelph 70-71 UV 9
Guéné 60-61 E 6
Guéra, Massif de – 60-61 H 6
Gueréda 60-61 J 6
Guéret 34-35 H 5
Guernsey 32 E 7
Guerrero [MEX, ☆] 72-73 FG 8
G'uešovo 36-37 K 4
Guettara, Aïn El – = El Guettâra 60-61 D 4
Guettâra, El – 60-61 D 4
Guezzam, In – = 'Ayn Qazzān 60-61 EF 5
Gugē 60-61 M 7
Gughe = Gugē 60-61 M 7
Guia 78-79 H 8
Guiana Basin 22-23 G 5
Guiana Brasileira 78-79 G-J 4-5
Guichi 48-49 M 5
Guidder = Guider 60-61 G 6-7
Guide 48-49 J 4
Guider 60-61 G 6-7
Guiding 48-49 K 6
Guiers, Lac de – 60-61 AB 5
Guiglo 60-61 C 7
Guildford 32 F 6
Guilin 48-49 KL 6
Guimarães 34-35 C 8
Guimarães [BR] 78-79 L 5
Guimaras Island 52-53 H 4
Guinan Zhou = Qiannon Zizhizhou 48-49 K 6
Guinea, Cuenca de – 22-23 J 5
Guinea, Dorsal de – 22-23 JK 6
Guinea, Golfo de – 60-61 C-F 8
Guinea, Gulf of – 60-61 C-F 8
Guinea Basin 22-23 J 5
Guinea Ecuatorial 60-61 FG 8
Guinea Rise 22-23 JK 6
Guinee 60-61 B 6-C 7
Guinée 60-61 B 6-C 7
Guinée, Bassin de – 22-23 J 5
Guinée, Golfe de – 60-61 C-F 8
Guinee, Golf van – 60-61 C-F 8
Guinée, Seuil de – 22-23 JK 6
Guineebekken 22-23 J 5
Guinee-Bissau 60-61 AB 6
Guinée-Bissau 60-61 AB 6
Guineedrempel 22-23 JK 6
Guinée-Équatoriale 60-61 FG 8
Güines [C] 72-73 K 7
Guingamp 34-35 F 4
Guiping 48-49 KL 7
Guiyang [TJ, Guizhou] 48-49 K 6
Guiyang [TJ, Hunan] 48-49 L 6
Guizhou 48-49 JK 6
Gujarāt 44-45 L 6
Gujerat = Gujarāt 44-45 L 6
Gūjrānwalah 44-45 L 4
Gujrāt 44-45 L 4
Gūk Tappah 46-47 L 5
Gulabarga = Gulburga 44-45 M 7
Gul'ajevo, Archangel'sk- 38-39 H 3
Gul'ajpole 38-39 G 6
Gulargambone 58 J 3
Gulbān aṭ-Ṭaiyārāt, Bīr – = Qulbān aṭ-Ṭayyārāt 46-47 JK 5
Gulbene 30-31 M 9
Gulbin Ka 60-61 F 6
Gülek = Çamalan 46-47 F 4
Gulf Coastal Plain 72-73 G 6-J 5
Gulfport, FL 74-75 b 3
Gulfport, MS 72-73 J 5
Gulgong 58 JK 4
Gulī'ah, Al- = Al-Qulī'ah 60-61 H 1
Gulinīm = Jūlmīnā 60-61 BC 3
Gulistan 42-43 M 9
Güllab Dere 46-47 H 4
Gullbringu-Kjósar 30-31 b 2-c 3
Gullfoss 30-31 d 2
Güllük 46-47 B 4
Güllük Körfezi 46-47 B 4
Gülnar 46-47 E 4
Gulrān 44-45 J 3
Gülşehir 46-47 F 3
Gulu 64-65 H 2
Guma Bazar 48-49 D 4
Gumbiro 63 C 5
Gumma 50-51 M 4
Gumti = Gomati 44-45 N 5
Gümüşane Dağları 46-47 H 2
Gümüşhacıköy 46-47 F 2
Gümüşhane 44-45 D 2
Guna 44-45 M 6
Gunabad = Gonābād 44-45 H 4
Günar = Anaypazari 46-47 E 4
Gunchū = Iyo 50-51 J 6
Gündoğmus 46-47 DE 4
Güney 46-47 C 3
Güney = Kırık 46-47 J 2
Güneydoğu Toroslar 44-45 DE 3
Gungu 64-65 E 4
Gunnbjørn Fjeld 70-71 ef 4
Gunnedah 56-57 K 6
Gunnison, CO 72-73 E 4
Gunnison, UT 76-77 H 6
Gunnison Island 76-77 G 5
Gunt 42-43 L 3
Guntakal 44-45 M 7
Guntur 44-45 MN 7
Guṅṭūru = Guntur 44-45 MN 7
Gunungapi, Pulau – 52-53 J 8
Gunungsitoli 52-53 C 6
Gunzan = Kunsan 48-49 O 4
Gūra = Gurha 44-45 L 5
Guragē 60-61 M 7
Guraghe = Guragē 60-61 M 7
Gurd Abū Muḥarrik 60-61 KL 3
Gurdāspur 44-45 M 4
Gurguéia, Rio – 78-79 L 6
Gūrha = Gurha 44-45 L 5
Gurjev 38-39 K 6
Gurjevsk 42-43 Q 7
Gurk 33 G 5
Gurma = Gourma 60-61 E 6
Gürpınar 46-47 K 3
Gurskøy 30-31 A 6
Gurudaspur = Gurdaspur 44-45 M 4
Gurun [MAL] 52-53 D 5
Gürün [TR] 46-47 G 3
Gurupá 78-79 J 5
Gurupá, Ilha Grande de – 78-79 J 5
Gurupi, Rio – 78-79 K 5
Gurupi, Serra do – 78-79 K 5-6
Gurvansajchan 48-49 K 2
Gusau 60-61 F 6
Gus-Chrustal'nyj 38-39 H 4
Gus-Chrustal'nyj 38-39 H 4
Gusev 33 L 1
Gushan 50-51 D 3
Gusher, UT 76-77 J 5
Gushi 48-49 M 5
Gusinaja, guba – 42-43 cd 3
Gusinaja Zemľa, poluostrov – 42-43 HJ 3
Gustav Adolf land 30-31 l 5
Gustav V land 30-31 kl 4
Gustine, CA 76-77 C 7
Güstrow 33 EF 2
Gutaj 42-43 U 7-8
Gutenko Mountains 24 B 30
Gütersloh 33 CD 3
Guulin 48-49 H 2
Guvāhāṭī = Gauhati 44-45 P 5
Güyan = Kılaban 46-47 K 4
Guyanabekken 22-23 G 5
Guyanas, Macizo de las – 78-79 F 3-J 4
Guyandot River 74-75 BC 5-6
Guyane 78-79 H 3-4
Guyane, Bassin de – 22-23 G 5
Guyane Française 78-79 J 4
Guyanes, Plateau des – = Macizo de las Guyanas 78-79 F 3-J 4
Guyenne 34-35 G-J 6

180 Grant

Guyi = Miluo 48-49 L 6
Guyra 56-57 K 6
Güzelyurt 46-47 E 5
Güzelyurt körfezi 46-47 E 5
Gvalior = Gwalior 44-45 M 5
Gvāliyar = Gwalior 44-45 M 5
Gvardejskoje 38-39 F 6
Gwa 52-53 B 3
Gwabegar 56-57 JK 6
Gwādar 44-45 J 5
Gwai 64-65 G 6
Gwalia 56-57 D 5
Gwalior 44-45 M 5
Gwaliyar = Gwalior 44-45 M 5
Gwanda 64-65 G 7
Gwane 64-65 G 2
Gwda 33 H 2
Gweru 64-65 G 6
Gwydir River 56-57 J 5
Gyamda Dsong 48-49 G 5
Gyangtse 48-49 FG 6
Gyáros 36-37 L 7
Gyda 42-43 O 3
Gydanskaja guba 42-43 O 3
Gydanskij poluostrov 42-43 OP 3-4
Gympie 56-57 K 5
Gyöngyös 33 J 5
Győr 33 H 5
Gypsum Palace 58 G 4
Gýtheion 36-37 K 7
Gyula 33 K 5

H

Haafuun 60-61 c 1
Haafuun, Raas – 44-45 G 8
Haag, Den – = 's-Gravenhage 34-35 JK 2
Haakon VII land 30-31 hj 5
Haapajärvi 30-31 LM 6
Haapamäki 30-31 KL 6
Haapsalu 30-31 KL 8
Haardt 33 CD 4
Haarlem 34-35 JK 2
Hābā, Bi'r – 46-47 H 5
Habana, La – [C, ●] 72-73 K 7
Habārūt 44-45 G 7
Habaswein 63 DE 2
Habay 70-71 N 6
Ḥabbānīyah 46-47 K 6
Ḥabbānīyah, Hawr al- 46-47 K 6
Ḥabbārīyah 46-47 JK 6
Ḥabīb, Wādī – 62 DE 4
Haboro 50-51 b 1
Habrat Najid 46-47 K 7
Hacheim, Bir – = Bi'r al-Ḥukayyim 60-61 J 2
Hachijō-jima 48-49 Q 5
Hachinohe 48-49 R 3
Hachiōji 50-51 M 5
Hachirō-gata 50-51 MN 3
Hachita, NM 76-77 J 10
Hacıbektaş 46-47 F 3
Haciömer 46-47 JK 3
Hacısaklı = Ovacık 46-47 E 4
Hack, Mount – 56-57 G 6
Hackberry, AZ 76-77 G 8
Hadal 'Awāb, Jabal – 62 F 7
Ḥadbarāh 44-45 H 7
Ḥadd, Rā's al- 44-45 HJ 6
Ḥaddār, Al- 44-45 EF 6
Hadejia [WAN, ~] 60-61 F 6
Hadejia [WAN, ●] 60-61 G 6
Ḥadēra 46-47 F 6
Haderslev 30-31 C 10
Hadım 46-47 E 4
Ḥadīṭah, Al- 44-45 F 4
Hadjout 60-61 E 1
Hadley Bay 70-71 P 3
Hadong [ROK] 50-51 FG 5
Ha Đông [VN] 52-53 E 2
Ḥadr, Al- 46-47 K 5
Hadramaut = Ḥaḍramawt 44-45 F 7
Ḥadramaut, Wādī – = Wādī al-Musīlah 44-45 FG 7
Ḥaḍramawt 44-45 F 7
Hadseløy 30-31 EF 3
Hadu 64-65 JK 3
Ḥaḍūr Shu'ayb 44-45 EF 7
Haedo, Cuchilla de – 80 E 4
Haeju 48-49 O 4
Haeju-man 50-51 E 4
Haemi 50-51 F 4
Haenam 50-51 F 5
Haengyŏng 50-51 GH 1
Ḥafar al- Bāṭin, Al- 44-45 F 5
Ḥaffah 46-47 FG 5
Ḥafik 46-47 G 3
Hafızbey 46-47 D 4
Hafnarfjördhur 30-31 bc 2
Haft Gel 44-45 FG 4
Hagadera = Alanga Arba 64-65 JK 2
Hagen 33 C 3
Hagerê Hiwet 60-61 M 7
Hagerman, ID 76-77 F 4
Hagermeister Island 70-71 D 6
Hagerstown, MD 74-75 DE 5
Hagersville 74-75 C 3
Hagfors 30-31 EF 7-8
Hagi 30-31 b 2
Hagi [J] 50-51 H 5
Hagiá 36-37 K 6
Ha Giang 52-53 DE 2
Hágios Evstrátios 36-37 L 6
Hagiwara 50-51 L 5
Hague, Cap de la – 34-35 G 4
Hague, The – = 's-Gravenhage 34-35 JK 2
Haguenau 34-35 L 4
Hagui = Hagi 50-51 H 5
Hagunia, El – = Al-Haqūniyah 60-61 B 3
Hai'an [TJ, Guangdong] 48-49 KL 7
Haibei Zangzu Zizhizhou 48-49 H-J 4
Haicheng 50-51 D 2
Ḥaidarābād 44-45 KL 5
Haiderabad = Hyderābād 44-45 M 7
Haiderbad = Ḥaidarābād 44-45 KL 5
Hai Du'o'ng 52-53 E 2
Haifa = Ḥēfa 44-45 CD 4
Haifeng 48-49 M 7
Haifong = Hai Phong 52-53 E 2
Haikang 48-49 KL 7
Haikou 48-49 L 7-8
Haikow = Haikou 48-49 L 7-8
Ḥā'il 44-45 E 5
Hai-la-êrh = Hailar 48-49 M 2
Hailar 48-49 M 2
Hailar He 48-49 MN 2
Hailey, ID 76-77 F 4
Hailong 48-49 O 3
Hailun 48-49 O 2
Hailuoto 30-31 L 5
Haimen [TJ, Jiangsu] 48-49 N 5
Haimen [TJ, Zhejiang] 48-49 N 6
Haimur Wells = Ābār Ḥaymūr 62 EF 6
Hainan = Hainan Dao 48-49 KL 8
Hainán, Estrecho de – = Qiongzhou Haixia 48-49 KL 7
Hainan Dao 48-49 KL 8
Hainan Strait = Qiongzhou Haixia 48-49 KL 7
Hai-nan Tao = Hainan Dao 48-49 KL 8
Hainan Zangzu Zizhizhou 48-49 H 5-J 4
Hainan Zizhizhou 48-49 K 8
Hainaut 34-35 JK 3
Haines, AK 70-71 JK 6
Haines, OR 76-77 DE 3
Haines City, FL 74-75 c 2
Haines Junction 70-71 J 5
Hai Phong 52-53 E 2
Ḥais = Ḥays 44-45 E 8
Haitan Dao = Pingtan Dao 48-49 MN 6
Haiti 72-73 M 8
Haiti = Hispaniola 72-73 MN 8
Haixi Monggolzu Zangzu Kazakzu Zizhizhou 48-49 GH 4
Haiyā = Ḥayyā 60-61 M 5
Haiyang Dao 50-51 D 3
Hai-yang Tao = Haiyang Dao 50-51 D 3
Haizhou 48-49 M 5
Ḥajar, Al- [Oman] 44-45 H 6
Ḥajara, Al- = Ṣaḥrā' al-Hijārah 46-47 JK 8
Hajdúböszörmény 33 KL 5
Ḥājī Āqa = Bostānābād 46-47 M 4
Hajiki-saki 50-51 M 3
Ḥajir, Jabal – 44-45 G 8
Ḥājī Sa'īd, Kūh-e – 46-47 M 4
Ḥājj 62 FG 3
Ḥajjah 44-45 E 7
Ḥajjār, Al- 60-61 EF 4
Ḥājjīābād 44-45 H 5
Hajnówka 33 L 2
Hajo-do 50-51 F 5
Hajut 60-61 E 1
Hakkârî 46-47 KL 4
Hakkâri 46-47 K 4
Hakkâri Dağları 46-47 K 4
Hakken san 50-51 KL 5
Hakodate 48-49 R 3
Hakui 50-51 L 4
Haku-san [J ↗ Ōno] 50-51 L 4
Haku-san [J ↓ Ōno] 50-51 L 5
Ḥalab 44-45 D 3
Ḥalabān 44-45 E 6
Ḥalabcha = Sirwān 46-47 LM 5
Ḥalabīyah 46-47 H 5
Hala Hu = Char nuur 48-49 H 4
Ḥalā'ib = Ḥalāyb 60-61 M 4
Ḥalāib, Jazā'ir – 62 G 6
Ḥalāl, Gebel – – = Jabal Hilāl 62 EF 2
Ḥalāyb 60-61 M 4
Ḥalbā 46-47 FG 5
Halberstadt 33 E 3
Halden 30-31 D 8
Haldensleben 33 E 2
Hale, Mount – 56-57 C 5
Haleakala Crater 52-53 ef 3
Ḥaleb = Ḥalab 44-45 D 3
Ḥalfāyah, Al- 46-47 M 7
Halfeti 46-47 GH 4
Ḥalfīn, Wādī – 44-45 H 6
Hal Flood Range 24 B 23
Ḥalī = Khay' 44-45 E 7
Haliburton 74-75 D 2
Halicarnassus = Bodrum 46-47 B 4
Hālidah, Bi'r – 62 B 2
Halifax [CDN] 70-71 Y 9
Halifax, VA 74-75 D 6
Halifax Bay 56-57 J 3
Ḥalīl, Al- 46-47 F 7
Ḥalīl Rūd 44-45 H 5
Hall, MT 76-77 G 2
Hall = A 33 E 5
Hall, ostrov – = ostrov Gall'a 42-43 KL 1
Halland 30-31 E 9
Hallandale, FL 74-75 c 4
Halla-san 50-51 F 6
Halle 33 EF 3
Halleck, NV 76-77 F 5
Hällefors 30-31 F 8
Hallein 33 F 5
Halley Bay 24 B 33-34
Hallingdal 30-31 C 7
Hallingskarvet 30-31 BC 7
Hall Lake 70-71 U 4
Hällnäs 30-31 H 5
Hallowell, ME 74-75 J 2
Hall Peninsula 70-71 X 5
Hallsberg 30-31 F 8
Halls Creek 56-57 E 3
Hallstavik 30-31 H 7-8
Halmahera 52-53 J 6
Halmahera, Laut – 52-53 J 7
Halmeu 36-37 K 2
Halmstad 30-31 E 9
Hälsingland 30-31 F 7-G 6
Haltiatunturi 30-31 J 3
Halvmåneøya 30-31 lm 6
Halys = Kızılırmak 44-45 D 3
Hama = Ḥamāâ 46-47 G 5
Ḥamād, Al- 46-47 H 6-J 7
Hamad, Birkat – 46-47 KL 7
Hamada 50-51 HJ 5
Hamadān 44-45 F 3-4
Ḥamāh 44-45 D 3
Hamajima 50-51 L 5
Hamamatsu 48-49 Q 5
Hamamatu = Hamamatsu 48-49 Q 5
Haman = Sarıkaya 46-47 F 3
Hamanaka 50-51 d 2
Hamana ko 50-51 L 5
Hamar 30-31 D 7
Ḥamār, Al- 46-47 M 8
Ḥamar, Dār – 60-61 K 6
Ḥamār, Wādī – 46-47 H 4
Hamas = Ḥamāh 44-45 D 3
Hamasaka 50-51 K 5
Ḥamātah, Jabal – 60-61 LM 4
Hama-Tombetsu 50-51 c 1
Hamatonbetu = Hama-Tombetsu 50-51 c 1
Hambergbreen 30-31 k 6
Hamber Provincial Park 70-71 N 7
Hambourg = Hamburg 33 E 2
Hamburg 33 E 2
Hamburg, CA 76-77 B 5
Hamburg, NY 74-75 D 3
Hamburg, PA 74-75 EF 4
Hamburgo = Hamburg 33 E 2
Hamch'ang 50-51 G 4
Ḥamḍ, Wādī al- 44-45 D 5
Ḥamḍah 44-45 E 7
Ḥamdānīyah, Al- 46-47 G 5
Hämeen lääni 30-31 KL 7
Hämeenlinna 30-31 L 7
Hamelin Pool 56-57 B 5
Hameln 33 D 2
Hamersley Range 56-57 C 4
Ham-gang = Namhan-gang 50-51 F 4
Hamgyŏng-namdo 50-51 FG 2-3
Hamgyŏng-pukto 50-51 G 2-H 1
Hamhŭng 48-49 O 3-4
Hami 48-49 G 3
Ḥamīdīyah 46-47 F 5
Hamilton [AUS] 56-57 H 7
Hamilton [Bermuda Islands] 72-73 O 5
Hamilton [CDN] 70-71 V 9
Hamilton [NZ] 56-57 OP 7
Hamilton, MT 76-77 F 2
Hamilton, NY 74-75 F 3
Hamilton, OH 72-73 K 4
Hamilton, WA 76-77 C 1
Hamilton, Mount – 76-77 F 6
Hamilton, The – 56-57 GH 4
Hamilton City, CA 76-77 BC 6
Hamilton Inlet 70-71 Z 7
Hamilton River 56-57 FG 5
Hamilton River = Churchill River 70-71 Y 7
Hamilton Square, NJ 74-75 F 4
Hamina 30-31 M 7
Ḥamīr, Wādī – [IRQ] 46-47 JK 7
Ḥamīr, Wādī – [Saudi Arabia] 46-47 J 7
Hamitabad = İsparta 44-45 C 3
Hamlet, NC 74-75 D 7
Hamm 33 CD 3
Ḥammāl, Wādī al- = Wādī 'Ajaj 46-47 J 5
Ḥammâm = Makhfir al-Ḥammān 46-47 H 5
Ḥammām, Al- 62 C 2
Ḥammāmāt, Khalīj al- 60-61 G 1
Ḥammār, Hawr al- 44-45 F 4
Hammerdal 30-31 F 6
Hammerfest 30-31 KL 2
Hammett, ID 76-77 F 4
Hammond, IN 72-73 J 3
Hammond, OR 76-77 AB 2
Hammonton, NJ 74-75 F 5
Hampton, FL 74-75 bc 2
Hampton, NH 74-75 H 3
Hampton, OR 76-77 C 4
Hampton, SC 74-75 C 8
Hampton, VA 74-75 E 6
Hampton Tableland 56-57 E 6
Ḥamrā', Al- [Saudi Arabia] 44-45 D 6
Ḥamrā', Al- [SYR] 46-47 G 5
Ḥamrā', Al-Ḥammādat al- 60-61 G 2-3
Ḥamrīn, Jabal – 46-47 KL 5
Ḥamsah, Bi'r al- = Bi'r al-Khamsah 60-61 K 2
Hams Fork 76-77 H 4-5
Ḥāmūl, Al- 62 D 2
Hamun = Daryācheh Sīstān 44-45 HJ 4
Hamur 46-47 K 3
Ḥamza, Al- = Qawām al-Ḥamzah 46-47 L 7
Hanak = Ortahanak 46-47 K 2
Ḥanākīyah, Al- 44-45 E 6
Hanamaki 50-51 N 3
Hanang 64-65 J 3
Hanazura-oki = Sukumo wan 50-51 J 6
Hancheu = Hangzhou 48-49 MN 5
Hancock, NY 74-75 F 3-4
Handa 50-51 L 5
Handae-ri 50-51 FG 2
Handan 48-49 LM 4
Handaq, Al- = Al-Khandaq 60-61 KL 5
Handeni 64-65 J 4
Handrān 46-47 L 4
Hanford, CA 76-77 D 7
Hanford Works United States Atomic Energy Commission Reservation 76-77 D 2
Hangai = Changajn nuruu 48-49 HJ 2
Hangchow = Hangzhou 48-49 MN 5
Hang-hsien = Hangzhou 48-49 MN 5
Hanging Rock 58 H 5
Hängö 30-31 K 8
Hangu 48-49 M 4
Hangzhou 48-49 MN 5
Hani 46-47 J 3
Ḥanīfah, Wādī – 44-45 F 6
Ḥanīyah, Al- 46-47 LM 8
Ḥank, Al- 60-61 C 3-4
Hanko = Hangö 30-31 K 8
Hankou, Wuhan- 48-49 LM 5
Hankow = Wuhan-Hankou 48-49 LM 5
Hanksville, UT 76-77 H 6
Hanku = Hangu 48-49 M 4
Hann, Mount – 56-57 E 3
Hanna 70-71 O 7
Han-Negev 46-47 F 7
Hannibal, MO 72-73 H 3-4
Hannō 50-51 M 5
Hannover 33 D 2
Hanöbukten 30-31 F 10
Ha Nôi 52-53 DE 2
Hanoi = Ha Nôi 52-53 DE 2
Ḥanōt Yōna = Khān Yūnūs 46-47 EF 7
Hanover [CDN] 74-75 C 2
Hanover, NH 74-75 GH 3
Hanover, PA 74-75 E 5
Hanover, VA 74-75 E 6
Hanover, Isla – 80 AB 8
Hansenfjella 24 BC 6
Han Shui 48-49 K 5
Hanson River 56-57 F 4
Hanyang, Wuhan- 48-49 L 5
Hanzhong 48-49 K 5
Haoli = Hegang 48-49 OP 2
Haora 44-45 O 6
Haouach, Ouadi – 60-61 J 5
Haparanda 30-31 KL 5
Hapch'ŏn 50-51 FG 5
Happy Camp, CA 76-77 C 5
Ḥaql 44-45 CD 5
Haqūnīyah, Al- 60-61 B 3
Ḥaraḍ 44-45 F 6
Haramachi 50-51 N 4
Haram Dāgh 46-47 M 4
Haranomachi = Haramachi 50-51 N 4
Hara nur = Char nuur 48-49 G 2
Harardēre = Xarardeere 60-61 b 3
Harare 64-65 H 6
Ḥarāsīs, Jiddat al- 44-45 H 6-7
Hara Ulsa nur = Char us nuur 48-49 G 2
Ḥarawa = Harewa 60-61 N 6-7
Harbin 48-49 O 2
Hardangerfjord 30-31 A 8-B 7
Hardangervidda 30-31 BC 7
Hardeeville, SC 74-75 C 8
Hardey River 56-57 C 4
Harding 64-65 GH 9
Hardvār = Hardwar 44-45 M 4
Hardwār = Hardwar 44-45 M 4
Hardwick, VT 74-75 G 2
Hardy, Peninsula – 80 BC 9
Hardy, Rio – 76-77 F 9
Hareidlandet 30-31 A 6
Ḥarer 60-61 N 7
Ḥarergē 60-61 NO 7
Harewa 60-61 N 6-7
Hargeisa = Hargeysa 60-61 a 2
Hargeysa 60-61 a 2
Hari, Batang – 52-53 D 7
Ḥarīb 44-45 EF 7-8
Haridwar = Hardwar 44-45 M 4
Ḥarim 46-47 G 4
Harima nada 50-51 K 5
Harimgye 50-51 G 4
Harīrōd 44-45 J 4
Ḥāriṭah, Al- 46-47 M 7
Härjedalen 30-31 E 6-F 7
Harlem, GA 74-75 B 8
Harlingen 34-35 K 2
Harlingen, TX 72-73 G 6
Harmal, Al- 46-47 G 5
Harmancık = Çardı 46-47 C 3
Harmanli 36-37 LM 5
Harmanli [TR] 46-47 GH 4
Harmony, ME 74-75 J 2
Harney Basin 72-73 BC 3
Harney Lake 76-77 D 4
Härnösand 30-31 GH 6
Haro 34-35 F 7
Haro, Cabo – 72-73 D 6
Harold Byrd Range 24 A 25-22
Haro Strait 76-77 B 1
Harper 60-61 C 8
Harper, OR 76-77 E 4
Harpers Ferry, WV 74-75 DE 5
Harpster, ID 76-77 F 2-3
Harquahala Mountains 76-77 G 9
Harquahala Plains 76-77 G 9
Ḥarrah, Al- [ET] 62 C 3
Ḥarrah, Al- [Saudi Arabia] 44-45 D 4
Harran [TR] 46-47 H 4
Harrar = Ḥarer 60-61 N 7
Harrawa = Ḥarawa 60-61 N 6-7
Harricana, Rivière – 70-71 V 7-8
Harrington, DE 74-75 F 5
Harrington, WA 76-77 DE 2
Harrington Harbour 70-71 Z 7
Harris 32 C 3
Harris, Dorsal de – = Dorsal de Lomonosov 19 A
Harris, Lake – 58 B 3
Harrisburg, OR 76-77 B 3
Harrisburg, PA 72-73 L 3
Harrismith 64-65 G 8
Harrison, ID 76-77 E 2
Harrison, MT 76-77 H 3
Harrison, Cape – 70-71 Z 7
Harrisonburg, VA 74-75 D 5
Harris Ridge = Lomonosov Ridge 19 A
Harrisrug = Lomonosovrug 19 A
Harriston 74-75 C 3
Harrisville, WV 74-75 C 5
Harrogate 32 F 4-5
Harrow, London- 32 F 6
Harsīn 46-47 M 5
Harşit Deresi 46-47 H 2
Harstad 30-31 FG 3
Harsvik 30-31 D 5
Hart, Cape – 58 D 5-6
Hartenggole He = Chaaltyn gol 48-49 GH 4
Hartford, CT 72-73 M 3
Hartlepool 32 F 4
Hartley = Chegutu 64-65 GH 6
Hartline, WA 76-77 D 2
Hart Mountain 76-77 D 4
Harts Range 56-57 FG 4
Hartsrivier 64-65 FG 8
Hartsville, SC 74-75 CD 7
Hartwell, GA 74-75 B 7
Hartwell Lake 74-75 B 7
Harūj al-Aswad, Al- 60-61 H 3
Hārūnābād [IR] 46-47 N 4
Hārūt Rōd 44-45 J 4
Harvard, CA 76-77 E 8
Harvey 56-57 C 6
Harwell 32 F 6
Harwich 32 G 6
Harwich, MA 74-75 HJ 4
Haryana 44-45 M 5
Harz 33 E 3
Ḥaṣ, Jabal al- 46-47 G 5
'Ḥasā, Al- 44-45 F 5
Ḥasā, Wādī al- [JOR, Al-Karak] 46-47 F 7
Ḥasā, Wādī al- [JOR, Ma'ān] 46-47 G 7
Ḥaṣāḥeiṣa, El – = Al-Ḥuṣayḥiṣah 60-61 L 6
Ḥasakah, Al- 44-45 D 3
Ḥāsana = Hassan 44-45 M 8
Hasançelebi 46-47 GH 3
Hasan Dağı 46-47 EF 3
Hasankale = Pasinler 46-47 J 2-3
Ḥasb, Sha'īb – 44-45 E 4
Hasêtchê, El- = Al-Hasakah 44-45 D 3
Hashemiya, Al- = Al-Hāshimīyah 46-47 L 6
Hāshimīyah, Al- 46-47 L 6
Hashimoto 50-51 K 5
Hashır 46-47 K 4
Hashtpar 46-47 N 4
Hashtrūd 46-47 M 4
Hashun Shamo = Gašuun Gov' 48-49 G 3
Hasib, Sha'ib – = Sha'īb Ḥasb 44-45 E 4
Haskovo 36-37 L 5
Ḥasmat 'Umar, Bi'r – 62 EF 7
Hassa 46-47 G 4
Hassan 44-45 M 8
Hassayampa River 76-77 G 9
Hassel Sound 70-71 R 2
Hasselt 34-35 K 3
Ḥāssī ar-Raml 60-61 E 2
Ḥassi-Inifel = Ḥāssī Īnīfil 60-61 E 2-3
Ḥāssī Īnīfil 60-61 E 2-3
Ḥāssī Mas'ūd 60-61 F 2
Hassi-Messaoud = Ḥāssī Mas'ūd 60-61 F 2
Hassi-R'Mel = Ḥāssī ar-Raml 60-61 E 2
Hässleholm 30-31 EF 9
Hastings [GB] 32 G 6
Hastings [NZ] 56-57 P 7
Hastings, FL 74-75 c 2
Hastings, NE 72-73 G 3
Hasvik 30-31 JK 2
Ḥaṭab, Wādī al- 62 E 7
Hat'ae-do 50-51 E 5
Ḥaṭāṭibah, Al- 62 D 2
Hatay 44-45 D 3
Hatch, UT 76-77 G 7
Haţeg 36-37 K 3
Hatfield [AUS] 58 F 4
Hathras 44-45 M 5
Hatinohe = Hachinohe 48-49 R 3
Hatip 46-47 E 4
Hatizyō zima = Hachijō-jima 48-49 Q 5
Ha-tongsan-ni 50-51 F 3

Hatteras, NC 74-75 F 7
Hatteras, Cape – 72-73 LM 4
Hatteras Island 72-73 LM 4
Hattfjelldal 30-31 F 5
Hattiesburg, MS 72-73 J 5
Haṭṭīyah 46-47 F 8
Hatton 70-71 P 7
Hatvan 33 JK 5
Hat Yai 52-53 D 5
Haud 60-61 NO 7
Haugesund 30-31 A 8
Haukadalur 30-31 c 2
Haukeligrend 30-31 B 8
Haukipudas 30-31 L 5
Haukivesi 30-31 N 6-7
Haukivuori 30-31 M 6-7
Hâurâ = Haora 44-45 O 6
Ḥaurā = Ḥawrah 44-45 F 7
Ḥaurā, Al- = Al-Ḥawrah 44-45 F 8
Hauraki Gulf 56-57 OP 7
Ḥauṣah = Ḥawṣah 46-47 G 8
Hausruck 33 F 3
Haut-Altaï, Région Autonome du – = 9 ◁ 42-43 Q 7
Haut-Atlas 60-61 CD 2
Haute Egypte = Aṣ-Ṣa'īd 60-61 L 3-4
Haute-Guinée 22-23 JK 5
Haute-Kotto 60-61 J 7
Haute-Mbomou 60-61 K 7
Haute-Sangha 60-61 H 8
Hautes Plateaux = Nijād al-'Alī 60-61 D 2-E 1
Haut Plateau d'Amerique = American Highland 24 B 8
Haut-Zaïre 64-65 G 2
Havana = La Habana 72-73 K 7
Havane = La Habana 72-73 K 7
Havasu Lake 76-77 FG 8
Havel 33 F 2
Havelock 74-75 DE 2
Havelock, NC 74-75 E 7
Haverfordwest 32 D 6
Haverhill, MA 74-75 H 3
Haverhill, NH 74-75 GH 3
Haverstraw, NY 74-75 FG 4
Havlíčkův Brod 33 G 4
Havøysund 30-31 L 2
Havre, MT 72-73 DE 2
Havre, le – 34-35 GH 4
Havre de Grace, MD 74-75 EF 5
Havre-Saint-Pierre 70-71 Y 7
Havsa 46-47 B 2
Havza 46-47 F 2
Hawai = Hawaii 52-53 ef 4
Hawai, Dorsal de las – 22-23 AB 4
Hawai, Islas – = Hawaiian Islands 52-53 d 3-e 4
Hawaii 52-53 ef 4
Hawaii, Dorsale des – 22-23 AB 4
Hawaii, Îles – = Hawaiian Islands 52-53 d 3-e 4
Hawaiian Islands 52-53 d 3-e 4
Hawaiian Ridge 22-23 AB 4
Hawaiirug 22-23 AB 4
Ḥawashīyah, Wādī – 62 E 3
Ḥawātah, Al- 60-61 LM 6
Hâwd = Haud 60-61 NO 7
Ḥawḍ, Al- [RIM] 60-61 C 5
Hawera 56-57 OP 7
Hawick 32 E 4
Ḥawīzah, Hawr al- 46-47 M 7
Hawke, Cape – 56-57 K 6
Hawke Bay 56-57 P 7
Hawker 56-57 G 6
Hawkes, Mount – 24 A 32-33
Hawkinsville, GA 74-75 B 8
Ḥawrah 44-45 F 7
Ḥawrah, Al- 44-45 F 8
Ḥawrān, Wādī – 44-45 E 4
Haw River 74-75 D 7
Ḥawṣah 46-47 G 8
Ḥawsh 'Īsá 62 D 2
Ḥawṭah, Al- = Al-Ḥillah 44-45 F 6
Hawthorn, FL 74-75 bc 2
Hawthorne, NV 76-77 D 6
Hay [AUS] 56-57 HJ 6
Haya, La – = s'-Gravenhage 34-35 JK 2
Hayang 50-51 G 5
Haydar Dağı 46-47 DE 4
Hayden, AZ 76-77 H 9
Haye, La – = 's-Gravenhage 34-35 JK 2
Hayes, Mount – 70-71 G 5
Hayes Halvø 70-71 XY 2
Hayes River 70-71 S 6
Hayfork, CA 76-77 B 5
Hay Lake = Habay 70-71 N 6
Haylow, GA 74-75 B 9
Haymana 46-47 E 3
Haymana Yaylâsı 46-47 E 3
Ḥaymūr, Ābār – 62 EF 6
Ḥaymūr, Wādī – 62 E 6
Hayrabolu 46-47 B 2
Hay River [AUS] 56-57 G 4
Hay River [CDN, ~] 70-71 N 6
Hay River [CDN, ●] 70-71 NO 5
Hays 44-45 E 8
Hays, KS 72-73 G 4
Hayshān, Jabal – 62 C 4
Haysī, Bi'r al- 62 F 3
Haystack Mountain 74-75 G 3
Haystack Peak 76-77 G 6
Hayton's Falls 63 CD 3
Hayward, CA 76-77 BC 7
Ḥayy, Al- 44-45 F 4
Hayyā 60-61 M 5
Ḥayy Allāh, Jabal – 62 B 4
Ḥayy Allāh, Jabal – 62 B 4
Ḥayz, Al- 62 C 3-4
Hazak = İdil 46-47 J 4
Hazārān, Kūh-e – = Kūh-e Hezārān 44-45 H 5
Hazard, KY 72-73 K 4
Hazawẓā' 46-47 GH 7
Hazebrouck 34-35 J 3
Hazen, NV 76-77 D 6
Hazen Strait 70-71 OP 2
Hazīm, Al- 46-47 G 7
Ḥazimī, Wādī al- 46-47 J 6
Hazlehurst, GA 74-75 B 9
Hazleton, PA 74-75 F 4
Hazlett, Lake 56-57 E 4
Ḥazm, Al- 62 G 3
Hazo = Kozluk 46-47 J 3
Hazro 46-47 J 3
Hazul, Al- = Al-Huzul 46-47 K 8
Headquarters, ID 76-77 F 2
Heads, The – 76-77 A 4
Healdsburg, CA 76-77 B 6
Healesville 58 GH 6
Heard 22-23 N 8
Hearst 70-71 U 8
Hearst Island 24 BC 30-31
Hebei 48-49 LM 4
Heber, UT 76-77 H 5
Hebgen Lake 76-77 H 3
Hebo, OR 76-77 AB 3
Hebreos, Oblast Autónomo de los – 42-43 Z 8
Hébridas = Outer Hebrides 32 B 3-C 2
Hébrides = Outer Hebrides 32 B 3-C 2
Hebrides, Sea of the – 32 C 3
Hebron [CDN] 70-71 Y 6
Hébron = Al-Halīl 46-47 F 7
Hecate Strait 70-71 K 7
Heceta Head 76-77 A 3
Hechuan 48-49 JK 5
Hecla and Griper Bay 70-71 O 2
Hede 30-31 E 6
He Devil Mountain 76-77 E 3
Hedien = Khotan 48-49 DE 4
Hedjaz 44-45 D 5-6
Hedmark 30-31 D 6-E 7
Heerlen 34-35 KL 3
Hefei 48-49 M 5
Hegang 48-49 OP 2
Heian-hokudō = P'yŏngan-pukto 50-51 E 2-3
Heian-nandō = P'yŏngan-namdo 50-51 EF 3
Ḥeidarābād = Ḥeydarābād 46-47 L 4
Heide 33 D 1
Heidelberg 33 D 4
Ḥeifa 44-45 CD 4
Hei-ho = Aihui 48-49 O 1
Heijo = P'yŏngyang 48-49 NO 4
Heilar He = Chajlar gol 48-49 N 1-2
Heilbronn 33 D 4
Heilong Jiang [TJ, ~] 48-49 O 1
Heilongjiang [TJ, ☆] 48-49 M-P 2
Hei-lung Chiang = Heilong Jiang 48-49 O 1
Hei-lung Chiang = Heilong Jiang 48-49 O 1
Heilung Kiang = Heilong Jiang 48-49 O 1
Heimaey 30-31 c 3
Heinola 30-31 M 7
Heir, El- = Qaṣr al-Ḥayr 46-47 H 5
Heishan 50-51 CD 2
Ḥeisī, Bîr el- = Bi'r al-Ḥaysī 62 F 3
Hekimdağ 46-47 D 3
Hekimhan 46-47 G 3
Hekla 30-31 d 3
Helagsfjället 30-31 E 6
Helder, Den – 34-35 K 2
Helen, Mount – 76-77 E 7
Helena, AR 72-73 H 5
Helena, GA 74-75 B 8
Helena, MT 72-73 D 2
Helendale, CA 76-77 E 8
Helen Reef 52-53 K 6
Heleysund 30-31 I 5
Helgeland 30-31 E 5-F 4
Helgoland 33 C 1
Helikôn 36-37 K 6
Heliopolis = Al-Qahīrah-Miṣr al-Jadīdah 62 DE 2
Helix, OR 76-77 D 3
Hella 30-31 c 3
Helleland 30-31 B 8
Hellepoort = Portes de l'Enfer 64-65 G 4
Hellín 34-35 G 9
Hell-Ville 64-65 L 5
Helmand Rōd 44-45 K 4
Helmond 34-35 KL 3
Helmsdale 32 E 2
Helmstedt 33 E 2
Helmville, MT 76-77 G 2
Helong 48-49 O 3
Helper, UT 76-77 H 6
Helsingborg 30-31 DE 9
Helsingfors = Helsinki 30-31 L 7
Helsingør 30-31 DE 9
Helsinki 30-31 L 7
Helska, Mierzeja – 33 J 1
Ḥelwân = Ḥulwān 60-61 L 3
Hemet, CA 76-77 E 9
Hempstead, NY 74-75 G 4
Henan 48-49 L 5
Henares 34-35 F 8
Henashi-saki 50-51 M 2
Henbury 56-57 F 4
Henchow = Hengyang 48-49 L 6
Hendawashi 63 C 3
Hendaye 34-35 FG 7
Hendek 46-47 D 2
Henderson, KY 72-73 J 4
Henderson, NC 74-75 D 6
Henderson, NV 76-77 F 7
Henderson Bay 74-75 E 2-3
Hendersonville, NC 74-75 B 7
Heng'ang = Hengyang 48-49 L 6
Heng-chan = Hengyang 48-49 L 6
Heng-chou = Heng Xian 48-49 K 7
Hengduan Shan 48-49 H 6
Hengelo 34-35 L 2
Henghsien = Heng Xian 48-49 K 7
Hengshan [TJ, Hunan] 48-49 L 6
Hengshan = Hengyang 48-49 L 6
Hengshui 48-49 LM 4
Heng Xian 48-49 K 7
Hengyang 48-49 L 6
Henik Lake = South Henik Lake 70-71 R 5
Henlopen, Cape – 74-75 F 5
Hennebont 34-35 F 5
Hennesberget 30-31 E 4
Henrietta Maria, Cape – 70-71 U 6
Henriette, ostrov – = ostrov Genrietty 42-43 ef 2
Henrique de Carvalho = Saurimo 64-65 F 4
Henry, Cape – 74-75 F 6
Henry, Mount – 76-77 F 1
Henry Kater Peninsula 70-71 XY 4
Henry Mountains 76-77 H 6-7
Henrys Fork 76-77 H 3-4
Henty 58 H 5
Henzada = Hinthāda 52-53 BC 3
Heppner, OR 76-77 D 3
Heppner Junction, OR 76-77 CD 3
Hepu 48-49 K 7
Heraclea 36-37 G 5
Heraclea = Ereğli 44-45 C 2
Héradhsflói 30-31 fg 2
Héradhsvötn 30-31 d 2
Herákleia = Ereğli 44-45 C 2
Herald, ostrov – 19 B 36
Heras, Las – [RA, Santa Cruz] 80 C 7
Herât 44-45 J 4
Hercegnovi 36-37 H 4
Hereford 32 E 5
Herefoss 30-31 C 8
Hereroland 64-65 EF 7
Herford 33 D 2
Heri Rud = Harī Rūd 44-45 J 4
Herīs 46-47 M 3
Heritage Range 24 B 28-A 29
Herkimer, NY 74-75 F 3
Herlen He 48-49 M 2
Hermanas, NM 76-77 JK 10
Herma Ness 32 F 1
Hermannsburg [AUS] 56-57 F 4
Hermansverk 30-31 B 7
Hermel, el- = Al-Harmal 46-47 G 5
Hermidale 58 H 3
Hermiston, OR 76-77 D 3
Hermite, Isla – 80 C 9
Hermit Islands 52-53 N 7
Hermôn = Jabal as-Saykh 46-47 FG 6
Hérmos = Gediz çayı 46-47 C 3
Hermosillo 72-73 D 6
Hernandarias 80 F 3
Herning 30-31 C 9
Heroica Alvarado = Alvarado 72-73 GH 8
Heroica Matamoros = Matamoros 72-73 G 6
Heroica Puebla de Zaragoza = Puebla de Zaragoza 72-73 G 8
Heroica Veracruz = Veracruz 72-73 GH 8
Heron, MT 76-77 F 1
Herrera 34-35 F 7
Herrera del Duque 34-35 E 9
Herrera de Pisuerga 34-35 EF 7
Herrick 56-57 J 8
Herrington Island 74-75 AB 5-6
Herschel Island 70-71 J 3-4
Hertford 32 FG 6
Hertford, NC 74-75 E 6
Hertogenbosch, 's- 34-35 KL 3
Hervey Bay [AUS, ∪] 56-57 K 4-5
Hervey Bay [AUS, ●] 56-57 K 5
Herzog-Ernst-Bucht 24 B 32-33
Heshjīn 46-47 N 4
Hesperia, CA 76-77 E 8
Hessen 33 D 3
Hesteyri 30-31 b 1
Heuglin, Kapp – 30-31 lm 5
Heves 33 K 5
He Xian [TJ, Guangxi Zhuangzu Zizhiqu] 48-49 L 7
Hexigten Qi 48-49 M 3
Ḥeydarābād 46-47 L 4
Heywood [AUS] 58 EF 7
Hezārān, Kūh-e – 44-45 H 5
Heze 48-49 M 4
Hezelton 70-71 L 6
Hialeah, FL 74-75 c 4
Hiawatha, UT 76-77 H 6
Hibbing, MN 72-73 H 2
Hibbs, Point – 58 b 3
Hichiro-wan = zaliv Terpenija 42-43 b 8
Hickory, NC 74-75 C 7
Hickory, Lake – 74-75 C 7
Hidaka 50-51 c 2
Hidaka-sammyaku 50-51 c 2
Hidalgo [MEX, Hidalgo] 72-73 G 7
Hidalgo del Parral 72-73 EF 6
Hida sammyaku 50-51 L 4-5
Hiddensee 33 F 1
Hienghène 56-57 MN 4
Hierisós 36-37 KL 5
Hieropolis = Manbij 46-47 GH 4
Hierro 60-61 A 3
Higasiôsaka 50-51 KL 5
High Atlas 60-61 CD 2
Highland, WA 76-77 E 2
Highland Peak 76-77 F 7
High Point, NC 72-73 KL 4
High Prairie 70-71 NO 6
High Rock Lake 74-75 CD 7
High Springs, FL 74-75 b 2
Highwood, MT 76-77 H 2
Highwood Peak 76-77 H 2
Hiiraan 60-61 ab 3
Hiiumaa 30-31 JK 8
Ḥijārah, Ṣaḥrā' al- [IRQ] 46-47 L 7
Ḥijārah, Ṣaḥrā' al- [Saudi Arabia] 46-47 JK 8
Ḥijāz, Al- 44-45 D 5-6
Ḥijāzah 62 E 5
Hijo = Tagum 52-53 J 5
Hikari 50-51 H 6
Hiko, NV 76-77 F 7
Hikone 50-51 L 5
Hiko-san 50-51 H 6
Hilāl, Jabal – 62 EF 2
Hilālī, Wādī al- 46-47 J 7
Hildesheim 33 DE 2
Hill, MT 76-77 H 1
Ḥillah, Al- [IRQ] 44-45 E 4
Ḥillah, Al- [Saudi Arabia] 44-45 F 6
Hill City, ID 76-77 F 4
Hillerød 30-31 DE 10
Hillsboro, GA 74-75 B 8
Hillsboro, NC 74-75 D 6
Hillsboro, NH 74-75 H 3
Hillsboro, OR 76-77 B 3
Hillsboro Canal 74-75 c 3
Hillside, AZ 76-77 G 8
Hillston 56-57 HJ 6
Hillsville, VA 74-75 C 6
Hilmänd, Dārya-ye – = Helmand Rōd 44-45 K 4
Hilmar, CA 76-77 C 7
Hilton Head Island 74-75 C 8
Hilts, CA 76-77 B 5
Hilu-Babor = Īlubabor 60-61 LM 7
Hilvan 46-47 H 4
Hilversum 34-35 K 2
Himachal Pradesh 44-45 M 4
Himalaja 44-45 L 4-P 5
Himeji 48-49 P 5
Hime-saki 50-51 M 3
Himezi = Himeji 48-49 P 5
Himi 50-51 L 4
Hinai 50-51 N 2
Hinchinbrook Island [AUS] 56-57 J 3
Hinckley, UT 76-77 G 6
Hindīyah, Al- 46-47 KL 6
Hindūbâgh 44-45 K 4
Hindū Kush 44-45 KL 3
Hindupur 44-45 M 8
Hindupura = Hindupur 44-45 M 8
Hines, FL 74-75 b 2
Hines, OR 76-77 D 4
Hines Creek 70-71 N 6
Hinesville, GA 74-75 C 9
Hinghwa = Putian 48-49 M 6
Hingjen = Xingren 48-49 K 6
Hingol 44-45 K 5
Hingoli 44-45 M 7
Hınıs 46-47 J 3
Hinkley, CA 76-77 E 8
Hinlopenstretet 30-31 kl 5
Hinna = Īmī 60-61 N 7
Hinnøy 30-31 FG 3
Hinojosa del Duque 34-35 E 9
Hinomi-saki 50-51 J 5
Hinş = Dumlu 46-47 J 2
Hinterrhein 33 D 5
Hinthāda 52-53 BC 3
Hinton [CDN] 70-71 N 7
Hinton, WV 74-75 C 6
Hınzır Dağı 46-47 FG 3
Hınzır Dağı 46-47 FG 3
Hippo Regius = Annābah 60-61 F 1
Hiraan = Hiiraan 60-61 ab 3
Hirado 50-51 G 6
Hirado-shima 50-51 G 6
Hirata 50-51 J 5
Hirato jima = Hirado-shima 50-51 G 6
Hiratori 50-51 c 2
Hireimis, Qârat el- = Qārat Huraymis 46-47 B 7
Hirfanlı Barajı 46-47 E 3
Hirgis Nur = Chjargas nuur 48-49 GH 2
Hîrlău 36-37 M 2
Hirono 50-51 N 4
Hiroo 50-51 c 2
Hirosaki 48-49 QR 3
Hiroshima 48-49 P 5
Hirosima = Hiroshima 48-49 P 5
Hirota-wan 50-51 NO 3
Hirr, Wādī al- 46-47 K 7
Hirson 34-35 K 4
Hirtshals 30-31 C 9
Hisaka-jima 50-51 G 6
Hisar 44-45 M 5
Ḥiṣār, Koh-i – 44-45 K 4
Hisarönü 46-47 DE 2
Ḥismā 62 FG 3
Ḥismet 'Umar, Bîr – = Bi'r Ḥasmat 'Umar 62 EF 7
Hispaniola 72-73 MN 8
Hissâr = Hisar 44-45 M 5
Ḥiṣṣar, Kūh-e – = Kōh-i Ḥiṣār 44-45 K 4
Hīt 46-47 K 6
Hita 50-51 H 6
Hitachi 48-49 R 4
Hitachi-Ōta = Hitati-Ōta 50-51 N 4
Hitati = Hitachi 48-49 R 4
Hite, UT 76-77 H 7
Hitoyoshi 50-51 H 6
Hitra 30-31 C 6
Hiuchi-dake 50-51 M 4
Hiuchi-nada 50-51 J 5
Hiw 62 E 4-5
Hiwasa 50-51 K 6
Hizan 46-47 K 3
Hjälmaren 30-31 FG 8
Hjelmelandsvågen 30-31 AB 8
Hjelmsøy 30-31 L 2
Hjørring 30-31 C 9
Hkweibûm 52-53 B 2
Hlaingbwè 52-53 C 3
Hluingbwe = Hlaingbwè 52-53 C 3
Ho 60-61 E 7
Hoa Binh 52-53 DE 2
Hoai Nho'n 52-53 E 4
Hoangho = Huang He 48-49 L 4
Hoang Sa, Quân Đao – 52-53 F 5
Hoarusib 64-65 D 6
Hoback Peak 76-77 H 4
Hobart 56-57 J 8
Hobbs, NM 72-73 F 5
Hobbs Coast 24 B 23
Hobe Sound, FL 74-75 cd 3
Hobetsu 50-51 bc 2
Hobro 30-31 C 9
Hōbsögöl Dalay = Chövsgöl nuur 48-49 J 1
Hobyo 60-61 b 2
Hochgolling 33 FG 5
Hô Chi Minh, Thành Phô – 52-53 E 4
Hochow = Hechuan 48-49 K 5-6
Hochwan = Hechuan 48-49 K 5-6
Hô Chi Minh, Thành Phô – 52-53 E 4
Ḥoddua = Ghuddawah 60-61 G 3
Hodeida = Al-Ḥudaidah 44-45 E 8
Ḥôḍein, Wādī – = Wādī Ḥuḍayn 62 F 6
Hodgdon, ME 74-75 JK 1-2
Hodh = Al-Ḥawḍ 60-61 C 5
Hódmezővásárhely 33 K 5
Hodna, Chott el – = Ash-Shaṭṭ al-Hudnah 60-61 EF 1
Hodna, Chott el – = Ash-Shaṭṭ al-Hudnah 60-61 EF 1
Hoek van Holland, Rotterdam- 34-35 JK 3
Hoengsŏng 50-51 FG 4
Hoeryŏng 50-51 G 1
Hoeyang 50-51 F 3
Hof 33 E 3
Höfdhakaupstadhur 30-31 cd 2
Hofei = Hefei 48-49 M 5
Höfn 30-31 f 2
Hofors 30-31 FG 7
Ḥofrat en Naḥās = Ḥufrat an-Naḥās 60-61 JK 7
Hofsjökull 30-31 d 2
Hofsós 30-31 d 2
Hōfu 50-51 H 5-6
Hofuf = Al-Hufūf 44-45 FG 5
Höganäs 30-31 E 9
Hogan Island 58 c 1
Hogback Mountain [USA, Montana] 76-77 GH 3
Hoge Atlas 60-61 CD 2
Hog Island [USA, Maryland] 74-75 F 6
Hohe Acht 33 C 3
Hohe Acht 33 C 3
Hohe Tauern 33 F 5
Hohhot = Huhehaote 48-49 L 3
Hoh-kai = Ohōtsuku-kai 50-51 cd 1
Ho-hsien = He Xian [TJ, Guangxi Zhuangzu Zizhiqu] 48-49 L 7
Hoifung = Haifeng 48-49 M 7
Hoihong = Haikang 48-49 KL 7
Hoima 64-65 H 2
Hoion = Hai'an 48-49 KL 7
Hokitika 56-57 NO 8
Hokkaidō [J, ⊙] 48-49 RS 3
Hokkaidō [J, ☆] 50-51 bc 2
Hokuoka = Fukuoka 48-49 OP 5
Hokuriku 50-51 L 5-M 4
Holanda = Países Bajos 34-35 K 3-L 2
Hólar 30-31 d 2
Holbæk 30-31 D 10
Holbrook 58 H 5
Holbrook, AZ 76-77 HJ 8
Holbrook, ID 76-77 G 4
Holden, UT 76-77 G 6

182 Hatte

Holguín 72-73 L 7
Höljes 30-31 E 7
Holland = Netherlands 34-35 K 3-L 2
Hollandia = Jayapura 52-53 M 7
Hollick-Kenyon Plateau 24 AB 25-26
Hollidaysburg, PA 74-75 D 4
Hollister, CA 76-77 C 7
Hollister, ID 76-77 F 4
Hollmann, Cape – 52-53 gh 5
Holly Hill, FL 74-75 c 2
Holly Hill, SC 74-75 C 8
Holly Ridge, NC 74-75 E 7
Hollywood, FL 72-73 KL 6
Hollywood, Los Angeles-, CA 72-73 BC 5
Holman Island 70-71 NO 3
Hólmavík 30-31 c 2
Holmes, Mount – 76-77 H 3
Holmestrand 30-31 CD 8
Holmsund 30-31 J 6
Holopaw, FL 74-75 c 2
Holroyd River 56-57 H 2
Holsnøy 30-31 A 7
Holstebro 30-31 C 9
Holsteinsborg = Sisimiut 70-71 Za 4
Holston River 74-75 B 6
Holten, Banc de – 30-31 C 5
Holten, Banco de – 30-31 C 5
Holtville, CA 76-77 F 9
Holung = Helong 50-51 G 1
Holy Cross, AK 70-71 DE 5
Holyhead 32 D 5
Holyoke, MA 74-75 G 3
Holzminden 33 D 3
Hombori 60-61 D 5
Home, OR 76-77 E 3
Home Bay 70-71 XY 4
Homedale, ID 76-77 E 4
Homer, AK 70-71 F 6
Homer, NY 74-75 E 3
Homerville, GA 74-75 B 9
Homestead 56-57 HJ 4
Homestead, FL 74-75 c 4
Homoine 64-65 HJ 7
Homoljske Planine 36-37 J 3
Ḥomra, Al- = Al-Ḥumrah 60-61 L 6
Homra, Hamada el – = Al-Ḥamādat al-Ḥamrā' 60-61 G 2-3
Homs 44-45 D 4
Ḥomṣ = Al-Khums 60-61 GH 2
Hon, Cu Lao – = Cu Lao Thu 52-53 EF 4
Honai 50-51 J 6
Honan = Henan 48-49 L 5
Honaz dağı 46-47 C 4
Honbetsu 50-51 cd 2
Honda 78-79 E 3
Honda Bay 52-53 G 5
Hondo [J] 50-51 H 6
Hondo = Honshū 48-49 PQ 4
Honduras 72-73 J 9
Honduras, Cabo de – 72-73 JK 8
Honduras, Golfe de – 72-73 J 8
Honesdale, PA 74-75 F 4
Honey Lake 76-77 C 5
Honfleur 34-35 H 4
Hongarije 33 H-K 5
Hongch'ŏn 50-51 FG 4
Hong-do 50-51 E 5
Hong He [TJ, Yunnan] 48-49 J 7
Honghe Hanizu Yizu Zizhizhou 48-49 J 7
Honghu [TJ, ●] 48-49 L 6
Hongjiang 48-49 KL 6
Hong Kong 48-49 LM 7
Hongluoxian 50-51 C 2
Hongmoxian = Hongluoxian 50-51 C 2
Hongrie 33 H-K 5
Hongshui He 48-49 K 6-7
Hongsŏng 50-51 F 4
Hongū 50-51 K 6
Hongueda, Détroit d' 70-71 XY 8
Honguedo, Détroit de – 70-71 XY 8
Hongwŏn 50-51 FG 2-3
Honiara 52-53 jk 6
Honjo 50-51 MN 3
Honningsvåg 30-31 LM 2
Honshū 48-49 PQ 4
Honshu, Cresta Meridional de – 48-49 R 5-6
Honshu Méridional, Seuil de – 48-49 R 5-6
Honshu Méridional, Seuil de – 48-49 R 5-6
Honsyū = Honshū 48-49 PQ 4
Hood = Isla Española 78-79 B 5
Hood, Mount – 72-73 B 2
Hood Canal 76-77 B 2
Hood Point 56-57 CD 6
Hood River, OR 76-77 C 3
Hoog-Altaj, Autonome Gebied – = 9 ◁ 42-43 Q 7
Hooker, Bi'r – 62 D 2
Hooker Creek 56-57 F 3
Hook Island 56-57 J 4
Hoonah, AK 70-71 JK 6
Hoopa, CA 76-77 B 5
Hoopa Valley Indian Reservation 76-77 AB 5
Hooper, UT 76-77 G 5
Hoover Dam 72-73 D 4
Hopa 46-47 J 2
Hope, AR 72-73 H 5
Hope, AZ 76-77 G 9
Hope, Ben – 32 D 2
Hopedale 70-71 YZ 6
Hopeh = Hebei 48-49 LM 4
Hope Island 74-75 C 2
Hopen 19 B 16
Hopes Advance, Cape – 70-71 X 5
Hopetoun [AUS, Victoria] 56-57 H 7
Hopetoun [AUS, Western Australia] 56-57 D 6
Hopetown 64-65 F 8
Hopewell, VA 74-75 E 6
Hopi Indian Reservation 76-77 H 7-8
Hopkins, Lake – 56-57 E 4
Hopkinsville, KY 72-73 J 4
Hopland, CA 76-77 B 6
Hoppo = Hepu 48-49 K 7
Hopu = Hepu 48-49 K 7
Ho-p'u = Hepu 48-49 K 7
Hoquiam, WA 76-77 AB 2
Hōrān, Wādī – = Wādī Ḥawrān 44-45 E 4
Horasan 46-47 K 2
Hörby 30-31 E 10
Hordaland 30-31 A 8-B 7
Hordio = Hurdiyo 44-45 G 8
Horlick Mountains 24 A 26-27
Hormoz 44-45 H 5
Hormoz, Tangeh – 44-45 H 5
Horn [IS] 30-31 bc 1
Horn, Îles – 52-53 b 1
Hornafjördhur 30-31 f 2
Hornavan 30-31 GH 4
Hörnefors 30-31 H 6
Hornell, NY 74-75 E 3
Horn Mountains [CDN] 70-71 MN 5
Hornos, Cabo de – 80 CD 9
Hornsea 32 FG 5
Hornsund 30-31 jk 6
Hornsundtind 30-31 k 6
Horobetsu 50-51 b 2
Horonobe 50-51 bc 1
Horqueta 80 E 2
Horseheads, NY 74-75 E 3
Horsens 30-31 CD 10
Horse Shoe Bend, ID 76-77 EF 4
Horse Springs, NM 76-77 JK 9
Horsham [AUS] 56-57 H 7
Horten 30-31 D 8
Horton River 70-71 M 4
Horzum-Armutlu = Gölhisar 46-47 C 4
Hoşeima, el – = Al-Ḥusaymah 60-61 D 1
Ḥoseinābād = Īlām 44-45 F 4
Ḥoseynābād 46-47 M 5
Hoseyniyeh 46-47 MN 6
Hoshingo Mdogo 63 DE 3
Ḥôsh 'Īsá = Ḥawsh 'Īsá 62 D 2
Hospitalet de Llobregat 34-35 J 8
Hospitalet de Llobregat 34-35 J 8
Hosta Butte 76-77 JK 8
Hoste, Isla – 80 C 9
Hot 52-53 C 3
Hotamış Gölü 46-47 E 4
Hotan = Khotan 48-49 DE 4
Hot Creek Valley 76-77 E 6
Hotien = Khotan 48-49 DE 4
Hoting 30-31 G 5
Hot Springs, AR 72-73 H 5
Hot Springs, MT 76-77 F 2
Hot Springs, NC 74-75 B 7
Hot Springs, VA 74-75 D 6
Hottah Lake 70-71 N 4
Houlton, ME 74-75 JK 1
Houma 48-49 L 4
Houma, LA 72-73 H 6
Ḥoumaïmá, Bîr – = Bi'r Ḥumaymah 46-47 HJ 5
Houndé 60-61 D 6
Houston, TX 72-73 G 5-6
Houtman Abrolhos 56-57 B 5
Ḥouẓ Solṭān, Daryācheh – 46-47 O 5
Ḥouz Solṭān, Karavānsarā-ye – = Daryācheh Ḥouẓ Solṭān 46-47 O 5
Hover, WA 76-77 D 2
Hovrah = Haora 44-45 O 6
Howar = Wādī Huwār 60-61 K 5
Howe, ID 76-77 G 4
Howe, Cape – 56-57 K 7
Howick [CDN] 74-75 G 2
Howrah = Haora 44-45 O 6
Hoy 32 E 2
Høyanger 30-31 B 7
Hōyokaiko = Bungo-suidō 48-49 P 5
Hoyran gölü 46-47 D 3
Höytiäinen 30-31 N 6
Hozat 46-47 H 3
Hpā'an 52-53 C 3
Hpalam 52-53 B 2
Hpyū 52-53 C 3
Hradec Králové 33 GH 3
Hrochei La 48-49 DE 5
Hron 33 J 4
Hrvatska 36-37 F-H 3
Hsay Walad 'Alī Bābī 60-61 B 5
Hsia-ho = Xiahe 48-49 J 4
Hsia-kuan = Xiaguan 48-49 J 6
Hsia-mên = Xiamen 48-49 M 7
Hsi-an 48-49 K 5
Hsi-an = Xi'an 48-49 K 5
Hsiang-kang = Hong Kong 48-49 LM 7
Hsiang-yang = Xiangyang 48-49 L 5
Hsiang-yang-chên = Xiangyangzhen 50-51 E 1
Hsiao-ch'ang-shan Tao = Xiaochang-shan Dao 50-51 D 3
Hsiao-ling Ho = Xiaoling He 50-51 C 2
Hsia-tung = Xiadong 48-49 H 3
Hsi-ch'ang = Xichang [TJ, Sichuan] 48-49 J 6
Hsi Chiang = Xi Jiang 48-49 L 7
Hsi-ch'uan = Xichuan 48-49 L 5
Hsi Chiang = Xi Jiang 48-49 L 7
Hsien-hs'ien = Xian Xian 48-49 M 4
Hsien-yang = Xianyang 48-49 K 5
Hsi-fêng-k'ou = Xifengkou 50-51 B 2
Hsi-hsien = She Xian 48-49 M 5-6
Hsi-hsien = Xi Xian [TJ, Shanxi] 48-49 L 4
Hsi-hu = Wusu 48-49 EF 3
Hsi-liao Ho = Xar Moron He 48-49 MN 3
Hsin-chiang = Xinjiang Uygur Zizhiqu 48-49 D-F 3
Hsinchu 48-49 N 6-7
Hsing-ch'êng = Xingcheng 50-51 C 2
Hsing-jên = Xingren 48-49 K 6
Hsing-ning = Xingning 48-49 M 7
Hsin-hai-lien = Haizhou 48-49 M 5
Hsin-hsiang = Xinxiang 48-49 LM 4
Hsin-hua = Xinhua 48-49 L 6
Hsi-ning = Xining 48-49 J 4
Hsin-kao Shan = Yu Shan 48-49 N 7
Hsinking = Changchun 48-49 NO 3
Hsin-liao Ho = Xiliao He 48-49 N 3
Hsin-li-t'un = Xinlitun 50-51 CD 1-2
Hsin-lo = Xinle 48-49 LM 4
Hsin-min = Xinmin 50-51 D 1-2
Hsin-pin = Xinbin 50-51 E 2
Hsin-ts'ai = Xincai 48-49 LM 5
Hsin-tu = Xindu 48-49 L 7
Hsin-yang = Xinyang 48-49 LM 5
Hsi-ta-ch'uan = Xidachuan 50-51 FG 2
Hsüan-hua = Xuanhua 48-49 LM 3
Hsüan-wei = Xuanwei 48-49 J 6
Hsuchang = Xuchang 48-49 L 5
Hsü-chou = Xuzhou 48-49 M 5
Hsūmbārabūm 52-53 C 1
Hsün-hua = Xunhua 48-49 J 4
Htāwei 52-53 C 4
Hua'an 48-49 M 6
Huab 64-65 D 7
Huachi [PE] 78-79 D 5
Huachinera 76-77 J 10
Huacho 78-79 D 7
Huacrachuco 78-79 D 6
Huagaruancha 78-79 DE 7
Hua-hsien = Hua Xian [TJ, Henan] 48-49 LM 4
Huai'an 48-49 MN 5
Huai-chi = Huaiji 48-49 L 7
Huaide 48-49 NO 3
Huai He 48-49 M 5
Huaiji 48-49 L 7
Huainan 48-49 M 5
Huaining = Anqing 48-49 M 5
Huaiyin 48-49 M 5
Huai-yin = Qingjiang 48-49 M 5
Hualian = Hua-lien 48-49 N 7
Hua-lien 48-49 N 7
Huallaga, Rio – 78-79 D 6
Huallanca 78-79 D 6
Hualpai Indian Reservation 76-77 G 8
Hualpai Mountains 76-77 G 8
Huambo 64-65 E 5
Hu'a Mu'o'ng 52-53 D 2-3
Huancabamba 78-79 CD 6
Huancané [PE] 78-79 F 8
Huancavelica [PE, ●] 78-79 DE 7
Huancayo 78-79 DE 7
Huanchaca, Serrania de – 78-79 G 7
Huangbai 50-51 F 2
Huang He 48-49 L 4
Huang He = Chatan gol 48-49 K 3
Huang He = Ma Chhu 48-49 J 4
Huangheyan 48-49 H 5
Huang Ho = Chatan gol 48-49 K 3
Huang Ho = Huang He 48-49 L 4
Huang Ho = Ma Chhu 48-49 J 4
Huang-ho-yen = Huangheyan 48-49 H 5
Huang-hsien = Huang Xian 48-49 MN 4
Huanghuadian 50-51 D 2
Huang-hua-tien = Huanghuadian 50-51 D 2
Huangnan Zangzu Zizhizhou 48-49 J 4-5
Huangshi 48-49 LM 5
Huangshijiang = Huangshi 48-49 LM 5
Huang-t'u-liang-tzŭ = Huangtuliangzi 50-51 B 2
Huangtuliangzi 50-51 B 2
Huanguelén 80 D 5
Huang Xian 48-49 MN 4
Huangyuan = Thangkar 48-49 J 4
Huan-jên = Huanren 50-51 E 2
Huanren 50-51 E 2
Huanta 78-79 E 7
Huánuco [PE, ●] 78-79 D 6-7
Huara 80 BC 1-2
Huaráz 78-79 D 6
Huari 78-79 E 6
Huarmey 78-79 D 7
Huascaran = Nevado Huascaran 78-79 D 6
Huascaran, Nevado – 78-79 D 6
Huasco 80 B 3
Hua Shan 48-49 L 5
Huatabampo 72-73 DE 6
Huauchinango 72-73 G 7
Hua Xian [TJ, Henan] 48-49 LM 4
Ḥubāra, Wādī – = Wādī al-Asyūṭī 62 D 4
Hubbaḷi = Hubli-Dhawad 44-45 M 7
Hubbard, Mount – 70-71 J 5
Hubei 48-49 KL 5
Hubli-Dhawad 44-45 M 7
Huch'ang 50-51 F 2
Hu-chou = Wuxing 48-49 MN 5
Huchuento, Cerro – 72-73 E 7
Ḥudaybū = Ṭamrīdah 44-45 GH 8
Ḥudaydah, Al- 44-45 E 8
Ḥuḍayn, Wādī – 62 F 6
Huddersfield 32 F 5
Hudiksvall 30-31 G 7
Hudnah, Ash-Shaṭṭ al- 60-61 EF 1
Hudson, NY 74-75 FG 3
Hudson, Bahia de – 70-71 S-U 5-6
Hudson, Baie d' 70-71 S-U 5-6
Hudson, Cerro – 80 B 7
Hudson, Détroit d' 70-71 WX 5
Hudson, Estrecho de – 70-71 WX 5
Hudson, Surco del – 74-75 GH 5
Hudson, Vallée sous-marine de l' 74-75 GH 5
Hudson Bay 70-71 S-U 5-6
Hudson Canyon 74-75 GH 5
Hudson Falls, NY 74-75 G 3
Hudsongeul 74-75 GH 5
Hudson Mountains 24 B 27
Hudson River 72-73 M 3
Hudson Strait 70-71 WX 5
Huê 52-53 E 3
Huedin 36-37 K 2
Huelva 34-35 D 10
Huércal-Overa 34-35 FG 10
Huesca 34-35 G 7
Huéscar 34-35 F 10
Ḥufrat an-Naḥās 60-61 JK 7
Hufūf, Al- 44-45 FG 5
Hughenden 56-57 H 4
Huhehaote 48-49 L 3
Huibplato 64-65 E 8
Hŭich'ŏn 48-49 O 3
Hui-chou = She Xian 48-49 M 5-6
Huíla [Angola, ●] 64-65 D 6
Huíla [Angola, ☆] 64-65 DE 5
Huila, Nevado del – 78-79 D 4
Huinan 48-49 O 3
Hui-tsê = Huize 48-49 J 6
Huittinen 30-31 K 7
Hui Xian 48-49 JK 5
Huixtla 72-73 H 8
Huiyang 48-49 LM 7
Huize 48-49 J 6
Ḥukayyim, Bi'r al- 60-61 J 2
Hûker, Bîr – = Bi'r Hooker 62 D 2
Hŭksan-chedo 50-51 E 5
Hŭksan-jedo = Hŭksan-chedo 50-51 E 5
Hukui = Fukui 48-49 Q 4
Hukuntsi 64-65 F 7
Hukusima = Fukushima 48-49 R 4
Hulan 48-49 O 2
Ḥulayfā' 44-45 E 5
Hull 70-71 V 8
Hull, Kingston upon – 32 FG 5
Hull Mountain 76-77 B 6
Hulu = Ulu 52-53 HJ 6
Huludao 50-51 C 2
Hulun = Hailar 48-49 M 2
Hulun Nur 48-49 M 2
Hulun nuur 48-49 M 2
Hu-lu-tao = Huludao 50-51 C 2
Ḥulwān 60-61 L 3
Huma 48-49 O 1
Hu-ma-êrh Ho = Huma He 48-49 NO 1
Huma He 48-49 NO 1
Humahuaca 80 C 2
Humaitá [BR] 78-79 G 6
Humansdorp 64-65 FG 9
Ḥumayḍah, Al- 62 F 3
Ḥumaym 44-45 GH 6
Ḥumaymah, Bi'r – 46-47 HJ 5
Humbe 64-65 D 6
Humber 32 G 5
Humberto de Campos 78-79 L 5
Humboldt [CDN] 70-71 PQ 7
Humboldt, AZ 76-77 GH 8
Humboldt, NV 76-77 D 5
Humboldt, Mount – 56-57 N 4
Humboldt Bay 76-77 A 5
Humboldt Gletscher 70-71 Y 2
Humboldtkette 48-49 H 4
Humboldt Range 76-77 D 5
Humboldt River 72-73 C 3
Humboldt Salt Marsh 76-77 DE 6
Hume, Lake – 56-57 J 7
Humedad, Isla – 72-73 a 2
Humenné 33 KL 4
Humpata 64-65 D 6
Humphrey, ID 76-77 GH 3
Humphreys, Mount – 76-77 D 7
Humphreys Peak 72-73 D 4
Humptulips, WA 76-77 B 2
Ḥumrah, Al- 60-61 L 6
Hums, Al- = Al-Khums 60-61 GH 2
Humurgân = Sürmene 46-47 J 2
Hūn 60-61 H 3
Húnaflói 30-31 c 1-2
Hunan 48-49 L 6
Hun Chiang = Hun Jiang 50-51 E 2
Hunchun 48-49 P 3
Hun Chiang = Hun Jiang 50-51 E 2
Hunedoara 36-37 K 3
Hungary 33 H-K 5
Hung-chiang = Hongjiang 48-49 KL 6
Hungerford [AUS] 58 G 2
Hung Ho = Hong He [TJ, Yunnan] 48-49 J 7
Hung Hu = Honghu 48-49 L 6
Hungkiang = Hongjiang 48-49 KL 6
Hŭngnam 48-49 O 4
Hungría 33 H-K 5
Hungry Horse Reservoir 76-77 G 1
Hung-shui Ho = Hongshui He 48-49 K 6-7
Hun He 50-51 D 2
Hun Ho = Hun He 50-51 D 2
Hunjani 64-65 H 6
Hun Jiang [TJ, ~] 50-51 E 2
Hunjiang [TJ, ●] 50-51 F 2
Ḥunkurāb, Rā's – 62 F 5
Hunsrück 33 C 3-4
Hunte 33 D 2
Hunter, Dorsal de – 56-57 OP 4
Hunter, Île – 56-57 O 4
Hunter, Seuil – 56-57 OP 4
Hunterdrempel 56-57 OP 4
Hunter Island [AUS] 56-57 H 8
Hunter River 58 K 4
Hunters, WA 76-77 DE 1
Huntingdon 32 F 5
Huntingdon [CDN] 74-75 FG 2
Huntingdon, PA 74-75 DE 4
Hunting Island 74-75 C 8
Huntington, OR 76-77 E 3
Huntington, UT 76-77 H 6
Huntington, WV 72-73 K 4
Huntington Beach, CA 76-77 DE 9
Huntsville, AL 72-73 J 5
Huntsville, TX 72-73 GH 5
Hunyung 50-51 H 1
Hunzā = Bāltit 44-45 L 3
Huon Gulf 52-53 N 8
Huon Peninsula 52-53 N 8
Hupeh = Hubei 48-49 KL 5
Hūrānd 46-47 M 3
Huraybah, Al- 44-45 F 7
Huraymis, Qārat – 62 B 2
Hurd, Cape – 74-75 BC 2
Hurdiyo 60-61 c 1
Hure Qi 48-49 N 3
Huribgah = Khurībgah 60-61 C 2
Hurjādah = Al-Ghardaqah 60-61 L 3
Hurley, NM 76-77 J 9
Hurma Çayı 46-47 G 3
Huron, CA 76-77 C 7
Huron, SD 72-73 G 3
Huron, Lake – 72-73 K 2-3
Hurricane, UT 76-77 G 7
Húsavík 30-31 e 1
Ḥuṣayḥiṣah, Al- 60-61 L 6
Ḥusaymah, Al- 60-61 D 1
Ḥusaynīyah, Al- 44-45 EF 7
Hüseyinli = Kızılırmak 46-47 EF 2
Huşi 36-37 MN 2
Huskisson 58 K 5
Huskvarna 30-31 F 9
Husum 33 D 1
Hutanopan 52-53 CD 6
Hutchinson, KS 72-73 G 4
Hutchinsons Island 74-75 cd 3
Hutch Mountain 76-77 H 8
Huutokoski 30-31 M 6
Hüvek = Bozova 46-47 H 4
Huwar, Wādī – 60-61 K 5
Huy 34-35 K 3
Hüyük 46-47 D 4
Huzgan 46-47 MN 7
Huzhou = Wuxing 48-49 MN 5
Huzi san = Fuji-san 48-49 Q 4-5
Huzul, Al- 46-47 K 8
Hvalsbakur 30-31 g 2
Hval Sund 70-71 WX 2
Hvammsfjördhur 30-31 bc 2
Hvammstangi 30-31 c 2
Hvar 36-37 G 4
Hveragerdhi 30-31 c 2
Hvitá [IS, Árnes] 30-31 c 2

Hvitá [IS, Mýra] 30-31 c 2
Hvitárvatn 30-31 d 2
Hvolsvöllur 30-31 cd 3

Hwaak-san 50-51 F 3-4
Hwach'ŏn 50-51 F 3
Hwach'ŏn-ni 50-51 FG 3
Hwaian = Huai'an 48-49 MN 5
Ḥwaiza, Hōr al- = Hawr al-Ḥawīzah 46-47 M 7
Hwange 64-65 G 6
Hwanggan 50-51 FG 4
Hwanghae-namdo 50-51 E 3-4
Hwanghae-pukto 50-51 EF 3
Hwangho = Huang He 48-49 L 4
Hwanghsien = Huang Xian 48-49 MN 4
Hwangju 50-51 EF 3
Hwangyuan = Thangkar 48-49 J 4
Hwap'yŏng 50-51 F 2
Hwasun 50-51 F 5
Hweichow = She Xian 48-49 M 5-6
Hweitseh = Huize 48-49 J 6

Hijaz 44-45 D 5-6
Hybla 74-75 E 2
Hyden 56-57 C 6
Hyde Park, VT 74-75 G 2
Hyder, AZ 76-77 G 9
Hyderabad 44-45 M 7
Hyderabad = Ḥaidarābād 44-45 KL 5
Hyères 34-35 L 7
Hyères, Îles d' 34-35 L 7
Hyesanjin 48-49 O 3
Hyltebruk 30-31 E 9
Hyndman, PA 74-75 D 5
Hyndman Peak 76-77 FG 4
Hyōgo 50-51 K 5
Hyŏnch'on 50-51 G 2
Hyŏpch'ŏn = Hapch'ŏn 50-51 FG 5
Hyrra-Banda = Ira Banda 60-61 J 7
Hyrum, UT 76-77 H 5
Hyrynsalmi 30-31 N 5
Hyūga 50-51 H 6
Hyvinkää 30-31 L 7

Ḥzimī, Wādī al- = Wādī al-Ḥazimī 46-47 J 6

I

Iaco, Rio – 78-79 EF 7
Iaçu 78-79 L 7
Iakoutie, République Autonome de – 42-43 U-b 4
Ialomiţa 36-37 M 3
Ialu = Yalu Jiang 50-51 EF 2
Iamalo-Nenets, District National des – 42-43 M-O 4-5
Iaşi 36-37 M 2
Iaundé = Yaoundé 60-61 G 8
Iavello = Yabēlo 60-61 M 7-8

Iba [RP] 52-53 G 3
Ibadan 60-61 E 7
Ibagué 78-79 DE 4
Ibar 36-37 J 4
Ibaraki 50-51 N 4
Ibarra 78-79 D 4
Ibarreta 80 E 3
Ibb 44-45 E 8
Iberá, Esteros del – 80 E 3
Iberian Basin 22-23 HJ 3
Iberisch Bekken 22-23 HJ 3
Iberville, Lac d' 70-71 W 6
Ibi [WAN] 60-61 F 7
Ibiá 78-79 J 8
Ibib, Wādī – 62 F 6
Ibicaraí 78-79 M 7-8
Ibicuí, Rio – 80 E 3
Ibicuy 80 E 4
Ibingui-Économique 60-61 H 7
Ibipetuba 78-79 KL 7
Ibiza [E, ⊙] 34-35 H 9
Ibiza [E, ●] 34-35 H 9
Ibjīlī 60-61 F 3
Ibn Hānī, Rā's – 46-47 F 5
Ibn Şuqayh, 'Uqlat – 46-47 M 8
Ibo 63 E 6
Ibo = Sassandra 60-61 C 7
Ibotirama 78-79 L 7
'Ibrā 44-45 H 6
Ibrāhīm, Jabal – 44-45 E 6
Ibrāhīmīyah, Qanāl al- 62 D 3
'Ibrī 44-45 H 6
Ibsāwī, 'Ayn – 62 B 4
Ibshawāy 62 D 3

Ibu 52-53 J 6
Ibusuki 50-51 H 7

Iča [SU] 42-43 e 6
Ica [PE, ●] 78-79 D 7
Içá, Rio – 78-79 F 5
Icabarú 78-79 G 4
Içana 78-79 F 4
Içana, Rio – 78-79 F 4
Icatu 78-79 L 5
İçel 46-47 EF 4
İçel 44-45 C 3
Iceland 30-31 c-f 2
Iceland Basin 28-29 CD 4
Iceland Jan Mayen Ridge 28-29 F 2
Ichang = Yichang 48-49 L 5
Ich Chogosoor 48-49 GH 5
Ichibusa-yama 50-51 H 6
Ichihara 50-51 N 5
Ichikawa 50-51 MN 5
Ichinohe 50-51 N 2
Ichinomya 50-51 L 5
Ichinoseki 48-49 QR 4
Ich'ŏn [North Korea] 50-51 F 3
Ich'ŏn [ROK] 48-49 O 4
Ichow = Linyi 48-49 M 4
Ichun = Yichun [TJ, Heilongjiang] 48-49 O 2
Ichun = Yichun [TJ, Jiangxi] 48-49 LM 6
Ičinskaja sopka = Velikaja Ičinskaja sopka 42-43 e 6
Ičinskaja Sopka, vulkan – 42-43 e 6
İçme 46-47 H 3
Icy Cape 70-71 D 3

Ichang = Yichang 48-49 L 5
Ich Chogosoor 48-49 GH 5
Ichibusa-yama 50-51 H 6
Ichihara 50-51 N 5
Ichikawa 50-51 MN 5
Ichinohe 50-51 N 2
Ichinomya 50-51 L 5
Ichinoseki 48-49 QR 4
Ich'ŏn [North Korea] 50-51 F 3
Ich'ŏn [ROK] 48-49 O 4
Ichow = Linyi 48-49 M 4
Ichun = Yichun [TJ, Heilongjiang] 48-49 O 2
Ichun = Yichun [TJ, Jiangxi] 48-49 LM 6

Ida = Kaz dağ 46-47 B 3
Idad, Qārat al – 62 C 3
Idah 60-61 F 7
Idaho 72-73 C 2-D 3
Idaho City, ID 76-77 F 4
Idaho Falls, ID 72-73 D 3
Idanha, OR 76-77 BC 3
Idar-Oberstein 33 C 4
'Idd, Al- 44-45 G 6
'Idd al-Ghanam 60-61 J 6
Idel' 38-39 F 3
Idē Óros 36-37 L 8
Iderijn gol 48-49 HJ 2
Idfū 60-61 L 4
'Idhaim, Nahr al- = Shaţţ al-'Uzaym 46-47 L 5
Idi 52-53 C 5-6
İdil 46-47 J 4
Idiofa 64-65 E 4
'Idīsât, El – = Al-'Udaysât 62 E 5
Idkū, Buḥayrat – 62 D 2
Idlib 44-45 D 3
Idrī 60-61 G 3
Idria, CA 76-77 C 7
Idrica 30-31 N 9
Idrija 36-37 EF 2
İdris Dağı 46-47 E 2

Ieper 34-35 J 3
Ierápetra 36-37 L 8
Ierland 32 BC 5
Ierse Zee 32 D 5
Iesi 36-37 E 4

Ifakara 64-65 J 4
Ifalik 52-53 MN 5
Ifanadiana 64-65 L 7
Ife 60-61 EF 7
Iferouâne 60-61 F 5
Iffley 56-57 H 3
Ifni 60-61 B 3
Iforas, Adrar des – 60-61 E 4-5

Igalula 64-65 H 4
Iganga 64-65 H 2
Igarapava 78-79 K 9
Igarapé-Açu 78-79 K 5
Igarapé-Mirim 78-79 K 5
Igarité 78-79 L 7
Igarka 42-43 Q 4
Iğdır 46-47 KL 3
Ighil-Izane = Ghālizān 60-61 E 1

Ighil M'Goun = Ighil M'Gūn 60-61 C 2
Ighil M'Gūn 60-61 C 2
Igidi, Erg – = Şaḥrā' al-Īgīdī 60-61 CD 3
Iglèsias 36-37 C 6
Iglesiente 36-37 C 6
'Igma, Gebel el- = Jabal al-'Ajmah 60-61 L 3
Ignacio, CA 76-77 B 6
İğneada Burun 46-47 C 2
Igo, CA 76-77 B 5
Igomo 64-65 H 4
Igra 38-39 K 4
Igrim 42-43 L 5
Igrumaro 63 C 4
Iguaçu, Rio – 80 F 3
Igualada 34-35 H 8
Iguala de la Independencia 72-73 G 8
Iguape 80 G 2
Iguatu 78-79 M 6
Iguazú, Cataratas del – 80 F 3
Iguéla 64-65 C 3
Igula 63 C 4

Ihosy 64-65 L 7
İhsangazi 46-47 E 2
İhsaniye 46-47 D 3
I-hsien = Yi Xian [TJ, Liaoning] 50-51 C 2
Ihtiman 36-37 KL 4

Iida 50-51 L 5
Iida = Suzu 50-51 L 4
Iīde-san 50-51 M 4
Iijoki 30-31 LM 5
Iisalmi 30-31 M 6
Iizuka 50-51 H 6

Ijara 64-65 K 3
Ījīdī, Şaḥrā' al- 60-61 CD 3
Ijjill, Kidyat – 60-61 B 4
IJssel 34-35 KL 2
IJsselmeer 34-35 K 2

Ik 38-39 K 4
Ikaalinen 30-31 K 7
Ikanga 63 D 3
Ikaría 36-37 LM 7
Ikeda [J, Hokkaidō] 50-51 c 2
Ikeda [J, Shikoku] 50-51 JK 5-6
Ikeja 60-61 E 7
Ikela 64-65 F 3
Ikelemba 64-65 E 2
Ikerre 60-61 F 7
Ikhîl 'm Goûn = Ighil M'Gūn 60-61 C 2
Ikhwân, Gezir el- = Jazā'ir al-Ikhwān 62 F 4
Ikhwân, Jazā'ir al- 62 F 4
Iki 50-51 G 6
Iki suidō 50-51 GH 6
Ikitsuki-shima 50-51 G 6
İkizdere 46-47 J 2
Ikkerre 60-61 F 7
Ikoma 64-65 H 3
Ikonde 63 B 4
Ikonium = Konya 44-45 C 3
Ikopa 64-65 L 6
Ikoto = Ikutu 63 C 1
Ikpikpuk River 70-71 F 3-4
Ikr'anoje 38-39 J 6
Ikungi 63 C 4
Ikungu 63 C 4
Ikuno 50-51 K 5
Ikushumbetsu 50-51 bc 2
Ikutha 63 D 3
Ikutu 63 C 1

Ilagan 52-53 H 3
Ilāhābād = Allahabad 44-45 N 5
Īlām 44-45 F 4
Ilan = Yilan 48-49 OP 2
Ilangali 64-65 HJ 4
Ilanskij 42-43 S 6
Ilaro 60-61 E 7
Ilay, Wādī – 62 F 7
Ilchuri Alin = Yilehuli Shan 48-49 NO 1
Ilebo 64-65 F 3
Ileckaja Zaščita = Sol'-Ileck 42-43 JK 7
Île-de-France 34-35 HJ 4
Ilek [SU, ~] 38-39 K 5
Ileret 63 D 1
Île Royale = Cape Breton Island 70-71 X-Z 8
Îles Anglo-Normandes = Channel Islands 32 E 7
Îles Britanniques 28-29 F 5-G 4
Îles Canaries = Islas Canarias 60-61 A 3
Îles Eoliennes = Isole Eòlie o Lipari 36-37 F 6
Ilesha 60-61 EF 7
Îles Ioniennes 36-37 H 6-J 7

'Ilfag = 'Afag 46-47 L 6
Ilford 70-71 RS 6
Ilfracombe 32 D 6
Ilgaz 46-47 E 2
Ilgaz Dağlar 46-47 EF 2
Ilgin 46-47 DE 3
Ilha Grande [BR, Rio de Janeiro] 78-79 L 9
Ilha Grande = Ilha das Sete Quedas 80 EF 2-3
Ilha Grande ou das Sete Quedas 78-79 HJ 9
Ilha Mexiana 78-79 K 4-5
Ilhas Desertas 60-61 A 2
Ílhavo 34-35 C 8
Ilhéus 78-79 M 7
Ili [SU] 42-43 O 8
Ili [TJ] 48-49 E 3
Iliamna Lake 70-71 E 6
Iliamna Volcano 70-71 EF 5
Iliç 46-47 H 3
Iligan 52-53 H 5
Ilihuli Shan = Ilchuri Alin 48-49 NO 1
Ilion 44-45 B 3
Ilion, NY 74-75 F 3
Ilijč 42-43 M 9
Ilijč'ovsk 36-37 O 2
Iljinskij [SU ↑ Južno-Sachalinsk] 42-43 b 8
Illampur, Nevado – 78-79 F 8
Illapel 80 B 4
Iller 33 E 4
Illimani, Nevado de – 78-79 F 8
Illinois 72-73 HJ 3
Illinois Peak 76-77 F 2
Illinois River 72-73 HJ 3-4
Illīzī 60-61 F 3
Illubabor = Īlubabor 60-61 LM 7
Il'men', ozero – 42-43 E 6
Ilo 78-79 E 8
Ilo, Rada de – 78-79 E 8
Iloilo 52-53 H 4
Ilorin 60-61 E 7
Il'pyrskij 42-43 f 5-6
Īlubabor 60-61 LM 7
Ilūkste 30-31 LM 9-10
Ilula 63 C 3
Ilwaco, WA 76-77 AB 2
Ilwaki 52-53 J 8
İlyas Burnu 46-47 AB 2
Iłża 33 K 3

Illampur, Nevado – 78-79 F 8
Illapel 80 B 4
Iller 33 E 4
Illimani, Nevado de – 78-79 F 8
Illinois 72-73 HJ 3
Illinois Peak 76-77 F 2
Illinois River 72-73 HJ 3-4
Illīzī 60-61 F 3
Illubabor = Īlubabor 60-61 LM 7

Imabari 50-51 J 5-6
Imabetsu 50-51 N 2
Imagane 50-51 ab 2
Imaichi 50-51 M 4
Imajō 50-51 KL 5
Imandra, ozero – 42-43 E 4
Imari 50-51 GH 6
Imataca, Serranía de – 78-79 G 3
Imatra 30-31 N 7
Imatra vallinkoski 30-31 N 7
Imazu 50-51 KL 5
Imbâbah 62 D 2
Imbaimadai 78-79 G 3
Imbros = İmroz 46-47 A 2
Imeri, Serra – 78-79 F 4
Imfal = Imphal 44-45 P 6
Īmī 60-61 N 7
Imilac 80 C 2
Imja-do 50-51 E 5
Imjin-gang 50-51 F 3
Imlay, NV 76-77 DE 5
Immokalee, FL 74-75 c 3
Immyŏng-dong 50-51 G 2
Imnaha River 76-77 E 3
Imo 60-61 F 7
Ímola 36-37 D 3
Imotski 36-37 G 4
Imperatriz 78-79 K 6
Impéria 36-37 C 4
Imperial, CA 76-77 F 9
Imperial Dam 76-77 F 9
Imperial Valley 72-73 CD 5
Impfondo 64-65 E 2
Imphal 44-45 P 6
Imp'o 50-51 FG 5
İmralı Adası 46-47 C 2
İmranlı 46-47 GH 3
İmroz 46-47 A 2
Imthān 46-47 G 6

Imuruan Bay 52-53 G 4
Imwŏnjin 50-51 G 4

In'a 42-43 b 6
Ina [J] 50-51 LM 5
Inanwatan 52-53 K 7
Iñapari 78-79 EF 7
In'aptuk, gora – 42-43 UV 6
Inari [SF, ●] 30-31 M 3
Inari [SF, ≈] 30-31 MN 3
Inawashiro 50-51 MN 4
Inawashiro ko 50-51 MN 4
Inca 34-35 J 9
İnce Burun 44-45 C 2
İncekum Burnu 46-47 EF 4
İncesu 46-47 F 3
Inch'ŏn 50-51 F 4
İncili = Karasu 46-47 D 2
İncir burun 46-47 G 2
Incudine, l' 36-37 C 5
Indaor = Indore 44-45 M 6
Indaur = Indore 44-45 M 6
Inde [≈] 22-23 NO 4
Inde [★] 44-45 L-N 6
Independence, CA 76-77 D 7
Independence, MO 72-73 H 4
Independence, OR 76-77 B 3
Independence Mountains 76-77 EF 5
Independence Valley 76-77 F 5
Independencia [MEX] 76-77 F 9
Independencia, Islas – 78-79 D 7
Inderagiri, Sungai – 52-53 D 7
Index, WA 76-77 C 2
India 44-45 L-N 6
India, Bassas da – 64-65 JK 7
Indiana 72-73 J 3-4
Indiana, PA 74-75 D 4
Indianapolis, IN 72-73 J 4
Indian Lake [USA, Ohio] 74-75 AB 4
Indian Mountain 76-77 H 4
Indian Ocean 22-23 NO 6-7
Indian Peak 76-77 G 6
Indian River [USA, Florida] 72-73 K 6
Indian Springs, NV 76-77 F 7
Indian Valley, ID 76-77 E 3
Índico Central, Cuenca del – 22-23 NO 6
Índico Central, Dorsal del – 22-23 N 5-7
Índico Meridional, Dorsal de – 22-23 OP 8
Índico Sudoccidental, Cuenca del – 22-23 MN 7
Índico Sudoriental, Cuenca del – 22-23 OP 7
Indiga 42-43 HJ 4
Indigirka 42-43 bc 4
Indio, CA 76-77 E 9
Indio, Rio – 72-73 c 2
Índios, Cachoeira dos – 78-79 G 4
Indische Oceaan 22-23 NO 6-7
Indisch Zuidpolairbekken 22-23 O-Q 8
Indispensable Strait 52-53 k 6
Indo = Sindh 44-45 L 4
Indo, Dorsal de – 44-45 K 6
Indochina 22-23 OP 5
Indonesia 52-53 D-K 7
Indonesië 52-53 D-K 7
Indonésie 52-53 D-K 7
Indore 44-45 M 6
Indostán 44-45 M 5-O 6
Indramaiu = Indramayu 52-53 E 8
Indramayu 52-53 E 8
Indravati 44-45 N 7
Indre 34-35 H 5
Indre Arna 30-31 AB 7
Indūra = Nizamabad 44-45 M 7
Indus = Sengge Khamba 48-49 DE 5
Indus = Sindh 44-45 L 4
Indus, Vallée sous-marine de l' 44-45 K 6
Indus Canyon 44-45 K 6
Indusgeul 44-45 K 6
İnebolu 46-47 E 2
İnegöl 46-47 C 2
Inerie, Gunung – 52-53 H 8
Ineul 36-37 L 2
İnevi = Cihanbeylı 46-47 E 3
In-Ezzane = 'Ayn 'Azzān 60-61 G 4
Infernão, Cachoeira do – 78-79 G 6
I-n-Gall 60-61 F 5
Ingende 64-65 E 3
Ingeniero Jacobacci 80 BC 6
Ingersoll 74-75 C 3
Ingham 56-57 J 3
Inglaterra 32 E-G 5

Ingle, CA 76-77 C 7
Inglefield Bredning 70-71 XY 2
Inglefield Land 70-71 XY 2
Inglewood 56-57 K 5
Inglewood, CA 76-77 D 9
Ingólfshöfdhi 30-31 ef 3
Ingolstadt 33 EF 3
Ingøy 30-31 KL 2
Ingrid Christensen land 24 BC 8
Ingrid Christensen land 24 BC 8
Ingul 36-37 P 2
Ingulec 38-39 F 6
Inhambane [Moçambique, ●] 64-65 J 7
Inhambane [Moçambique, ☆] 64-65 HJ 7
Inhambupe 78-79 M 7
Inhaminga 64-65 HJ 6
Inharrime 64-65 J 7
Inhung-ni 50-51 F 3
Inirida, Rio – 78-79 F 4
Inishowen Peninsula 32 C 4
Injune 56-57 J 5
Inkerman 56-57 H 3
Inkom, ID 76-77 GH 4
Inland Sea = Seto-naikai 48-49 P 5
Inn 33 E 5
Innamincka 58 E 1
Inner Mongolian Autonomous Region 48-49 K 3-M 2
Inner Sound 32 D 3
Innisfail [AUS] 56-57 J 3
Innoshima 50-51 J 5
Innsbruck 33 E 5
Innymnej, gora – 42-43 kl 4
Ino 50-51 J 6
Inomino-misaki 50-51 J 6
Inongo 64-65 E 3
İnönü 46-47 D 3
Inoucdjouac 70-71 V 6
Inowrocław 33 HJ 2
Inquisivi 78-79 F 8
Inscription, Cape – 56-57 B 5
Insein = Inzein 52-53 C 3
Inta 42-43 KL 4
Interlaken 33 CD 5
Inthanon, Doi – 52-53 C 3
Intiyaco 80 DE 3
Inubō saki 50-51 N 5
Inútil, Bahía – 80 BC 8
Inuvik 70-71 K 4
Inuvik, District of – 70-71 KL 4-5
Invercargill 56-57 NO 9
Inverell 56-57 K 5
Inverleigh 56-57 H 3
Inverness 32 DE 3
Inverness, FL 74-75 b 2
Inverurie 32 EF 3
Inverway 56-57 EF 3
Investigator Group 58 AB 4
Investigator Strait 56-57 FG 7
Inyangani 64-65 H 6
Inyokern, CA 76-77 DE 8
Inyo Mountains 76-77 DE 7
Inza [SU, ●] 42-43 H 7
Inzein 52-53 C 3
Inzia 64-65 E 4

Iñapari 78-79 EF 7

Iōánnina 36-37 J 6
Iō-jima 50-51 H 7
Iokanga 38-39 G 2
Iolotan' 44-45 J 3
Iona, ID 76-77 H 4
Ione, CA 76-77 C 6
Ione, OR 76-77 D 3
Ione, WA 76-77 E 1
Ionian Basin 36-37 GH 7
Ionian Islands 36-37 H 6-J 7
Ionian Sea 36-37 GH 7
Iónioi Nēsoi 36-37 H 6-J 7
Ionisch Bekken 36-37 GH 7
Ionische Zee 36-37 GH 7
Ionti = Joontoy 64-65 K 3
Iony, ostrov – 42-43 b 6
Íos 36-37 L 7
Iosser 38-39 K 3
Iowa 72-73 H 3

Ipadu, Cachoeira – 78-79 F 4
Ipameri 78-79 K 8
Iparia 78-79 E 6
Ipatovo 38-39 H 6
Ipel' 33 J 4
Ipiaú 78-79 M 7
Ipin = Yibin 48-49 JK 6
Ipiranga [BR, Amazonas ↗ Benjamin Constant] 78-79 F 5
Ipixuna 78-79 KL 5
Ipixuna, Rio – [BR ◁ Rio Purus] 78-79 G 6

184 Hvitá

ooh 52-53 D 6
oorâ [BR, Goiás] 78-79 J 8
opy 60-61 J 7
osala 46-47 B 2
oswich [GB] 32 G 5
oswich, Brisbane- 56-57 K 5
ou 78-79 L 5
oueiras 78-79 L 5

qlīt 62 E 5
quique 80 B 2
quitos 78-79 E 5

ra Banda 60-61 J 7
racoubo 78-79 J 3
rago-suidō 50-51 L 5
rago-zaki 50-51 L 5
rak = Arāk 44-45 F 4
rala [PY] 80 EF 3
rán 44-45 F-H 4
ran, Hoogland van –
22-23 MN 4
rán, Meseta de – 22-23 MN 4
ran, Plateau d' 22-23 MN 4
ran, Plateau of – 22-23 MN 4
rānshāh 46-47 M 4
rānshahr 44-45 HJ 5
rapa 78-79 G 2
rapuato 72-73 F 7
raq 44-45 D-F 4
Irâq Arabī 46-47 L 6-M 7
rarrarene = Irharharān
60-61 F 3
rati 80 F 3
rawadi = Erāwadī Myit
52-53 C 2
razú, Volcán – 72-73 K 9
rbeni väin 30-31 JK 9
rbid 44-45 D 4
rbit 42-43 L 6
recê 78-79 L 7
reland 32 BC 5
rene 80 D 5
Irgalem = Yirga 'Alem
60-61 M 7
Irgiz [SU, ~] 38-39 M 6
Irgiz [SU, ●] 42-43 L 8
Irharharān 60-61 F 3
Irhyang-dong 50-51 GH 2
Iri 50-51 F 4-5
Irian, Teluk – = Teluk
Cenderawasih 52-53 KL 7
Irian Jaya 52-53 K 7-L 8
Irian Occidental 52-53 K 7-L 8
Iriba 60-61 J 5
Iriga 52-53 H 4
Iringa 64-65 J 4
Iriomote-jima 48-49 N 7
Iriomote zima = Iriomote-jima
48-49 N 7
Iriri, Rio – 78-79 J 5
Irish Sea 32 D 5
Irituia 78-79 K 5
Irkutsk 42-43 TU 7
Irlanda 32 BC 5
Irlanda, Mar de – 32 D 5
Irlanda del Norte 32 CD 4
Irlande 32 BC 5
Irlande, Mer d' 32 D 5
Irlande du Nord 32 CD 4
Irmak 46-47 E 3
Irminger, Mar de – 70-71 d-f 5
Irminger, Mer d' 70-71 d-f 5
Irmingerzee 70-71 d-f 5
Iro, Lac – 60-61 HJ 7
Īrōḍ = Erode 44-45 M 8
Iron Baron 58 C 4
Irondequoit, NY 74-75 E 3
Iron Knob 56-57 G 6
Iron Mountain 76-77 G 7
Ironside, OR 76-77 DE 3
Ironton, OH 74-75 B 5
Ironwood, MI 72-73 HJ 2
Iroquois Falls 70-71 U 8
Irō saki 50-51 M 5
'Irq, Al- 60-61 J 3
'Irqah 44-45 F 8
'Irq al-Gharbī al-Kabīr, Al-
60-61 D 3-E 2
'Irq ash-Sharqī al-Kabīr, Al-
60-61 F 2-3
Irrawaddy = Erāwadī Myit
52-53 C 2
Irtyš 42-43 N 6
Irtyšskoje 42-43 NO 7
Irumu 64-65 G 2
Irún 34-35 G 7
Iruya 80 CD 2
Irwin, ID 76-77 H 4
Irwŏl-san 50-51 G 4

Īs, Jabal – 62 F 6
Isabela 52-53 H 5
Isabela, Isla – 78-79 A 5
Isabella, CA 76-77 D 8
Isabella, Cordillera – 72-73 J 9
Isabella Lake 76-77 D 8
Isachsen 70-71 Q 2
Isachsen, Cape – 70-71 OP 2
Ísafjardhardjúp 30-31 b 1
Ísafjördhur 30-31 b 1
Isahara = Isahaya 50-51 GH 6
Isahaya 50-51 GH 6
Isangi 64-65 F 2
Isar 33 F 4
'Isāwīyah, Al- 44-45 D 4
Isāwuwan, 'Irq – 60-61 F 3
Ischia 36-37 E 5
Ise [J] 50-51 L 5
Iseo 36-37 D 3
Isère 34-35 K 6
Isère, Pointe – 78-79 J 3
Išerim, gora – 42-43 K 5
Isèrnia 36-37 F 5
Iset' 42-43 L 6
Ise-wan 50-51 L 5
Iseyin 60-61 E 7
Isezaki 50-51 M 4
Isfahan = Eşfahān 44-45 G 4
İsfendiyar dağları 44-45 CD 2
Isfjorden 30-31 j 5
I-shan = Yishan 48-49 K 7
Ishibashi 50-51 N 3
Ishigaki-shima 48-49 NO 7
Ishikari 50-51 b 2
Ishikari gawa 50-51 b 2
Ishikari-wan 50-51 b 2
Ishikawa 50-51 L 4
Ishinomaki 50-51 N 3
Ishinomaki wan 50-51 N 3
Ishioka 50-51 N 4
Ishizuchino san 50-51 J 6
Isigaki sima = Ishigaki-shima
48-49 NO 7
Isigny-sur-Mer 34-35 G 4
Işık Dağı 46-47 E 2
Isil'kul' 42-43 N 7
Išim [SU, ~] 42-43 M 7
Išim [SU, ●] 42-43 M 6
Išimbaj 42-43 K 7
Isimbira 63 BC 4
Išimskaja ravnina 42-43 N 6-7
Isiolo 64-65 J 2
Isiro 64-65 G 2
Isisford 56-57 H 4
Isispynten 30-31 mn 5
Iskandar 42-43 M 9
Iskandarīyah, Al- 60-61 KL 2
Iskar 36-37 L 4
Iskardū = Skardū 44-45 M 3
İskele = Karataş 46-47 F 4
İskenderun 44-45 D 3
İskenderun Körfezi 46-47 F 4
İskilip 46-47 F 2
Iskitim 42-43 P 7
Iskushuban 60-61 bc 1
Isla-Cristina 34-35 D 10
İslâhiye 46-47 G 4
Islāmābād 44-45 L 4
Islāmābād = Anantnag
44-45 M 4
Islamorada, FL 74-75 c 4
Island City, OR 76-77 E 3
Islande 30-31 c-f 2
Island Falls, ME 74-75 J 1-2
Islandia 30-31 c-f 2
Islandia, Cuenca de –
28-29 CD 4
Island Lagoon 56-57 G 6
Island Lake [CDN, ≈]
70-71 RS 7
Island Mountain, CA 76-77 B 5
Island Park, ID 76-77 H 3
Island Park Reservoir 76-77 H 3
Island Pond, VT 74-75 GH 2
Islands, Bay of – [NZ]
56-57 OP 7
Isla Nueva 80 C 9
Islas Anglo-Normandas =
Channel Islands 32 E 7
Islas Británicas 28-29 F 5-G 4
Islas Jónicas 36-37 H 6-J 7
Islay 32 C 4
Isle 34-35 H 6
Isle au Haut 74-75 J 2-3
Isle Royale 72-73 J 2
Isleton, CA 76-77 C 6
Ismā'īlīyah, Al- 60-61 L 2
Ismetpaşa = Yeşilyurt
46-47 H 3
Isnā 60-61 L 3
Isohama = Ōarai 50-51 N 4
Isoka 64-65 H 5
Ispahán = Eşfahān 44-45 G 4
İsparta 44-45 C 3
Isperih 36-37 M 4
İspir 46-47 J 2
Israël 44-45 CD 4
Israelite Bay 56-57 DE 6
Issano 78-79 H 3
Issaouane, Erg – = 'Irq
Isāwuwan 60-61 F 3
Issoudun 34-35 HJ 5
Issyk-Kul' 44-45 M 2
Issyk-Kul', ozero – 48-49 M 3
Iṣṭabl, Bi'r – 62 B 2
Istāda-Moqur, Ab-e –
44-45 K 4
İstanbul 44-45 BC 2
Istiaia 36-37 K 6
Istiwā'ī, Al- 60-61 KL 7
Istmina 78-79 D 3
Istria 36-37 EF 3
Istria = Istra 36-37 EF 3
Istrie = Istra 36-37 EF 3

Itabaianinha 78-79 M 7
Itabaina 78-79 M 6
Itaberaba 78-79 L 7
Itaberai 78-79 JK 8
Itabuna 78-79 M 7
Itacaiúnas, Rio – 78-79 JK 6
Itacaré 78-79 M 7
Itacoatiara 78-79 H 5
Itacolomi, Pico – 78-79 L 9
Itaetê 78-79 L 7
Itaguatins 78-79 K 6
Itai 80 G 2
Itaipava, Cachoeira – [BR, Rio
Araguaia] 78-79 K 6
Itaipava, Cachoeira – [BR, Rio
Xingu] 78-79 J 5
Itaituba 78-79 H 5
Itajai 80 G 3
Itajubá 78-79 K 9
Itajuipe 78-79 LM 7
Itaka 42-43 W 7
Italia 36-37 C 3-F 5
Itália 34-35 DE 10
Italië 36-37 C 3-F 5
Italie 36-37 C 3-F 5
Italy 36-37 C 3-F 5
Itambé 78-79 L 8
Itany 78-79 J 4
Itaocara 78-79 L 9
Itapaci 78-79 JK 7
Itapajé 78-79 LM 5
Itapebi 78-79 M 8
Itapemirim 78-79 LM 9
Itapetinga 78-79 LM 8
Itapetininga 80 G 2
Itapeva 80 G 2
Itapicuru, Rio – [BR, Bahia]
78-79 M 7
Itapicuru, Rio – [BR,
Maranhão] 78-79 L 5
Itapicuru, Serra – 78-79 KL 6
Itapicurumirim 78-79 L 5
Itapipoca 78-79 M 5
Itapira 78-79 K 9
Itaqui 80 E 3
Itarsi 44-45 M 6
Itasca, Lake – 72-73 G 2
Itatuba 78-79 G 6
Itawa = Etawah 44-45 M 5
Itebero 63 AB 3
Itende 63 C 4
Ithaca, NY 72-73 L 3
Itháke 36-37 J 6
Ithrā = Itrah 46-47 G 7
Itigi 64-65 H 4
Itimbiri 64-65 F 2
Itinoseki = Ichinoseki
48-49 QR 4
Itiquira 78-79 J 8
Itiquira, Rio – 78-79 H 8
Itiruçu 78-79 L 7
Itiúba 78-79 M 7
'Itmâniya, El- = Al-
'Uthmānīyah 62 DE 4
Itō 50-51 M 5
Itoigawa 50-51 L 4
Itoikawa = Itoigawa 50-51 L 4
Itrah 46-47 G 7
Itrī, Jabal – 62 F 7
Itṣā 62 D 3
Itsjang = Yichang 48-49 L 5
I-tu = Yidu [TJ, Shandong]
48-49 M 4
Ituaçu 78-79 L 7
Itui, Rio – 78-79 E 6
Itula 64-65 G 3
Itumbiara 78-79 K 8
Ituni Township 78-79 H 3
Itupiranga 78-79 JK 6
Ituri 64-65 G 2
Iturup, ostrov – 42-43 c 8
Ituxi, Rio – 78-79 F 6
Itzehoe 33 D 1-2

Iva, SC 74-75 B 7
Ivai, Rio – 80 F 2
Ivajlovgrad 36-37 M 5
Ivalo 30-31 M 3
Ivalojoki 30-31 M 3
Ivangorod 30-31 N 8
Ivanhoe 56-57 H 6
Ivano-Frankovsk 38-39 DE 6
Ivanovka 36-37 O 2
Ivanovo [SU, Rossijskaja SFSR
Ivanovo] 42-43 FG 6
Ivanuškova = Koršunovo
42-43 U 6
Ivaščenkovo = Čapajevsk
42-43 HJ 7
Ivdel' 42-43 L 5
Ivenec 30-31 M 11
Iversen, Banc d' 42-43 EF 3
Iversen, Banco de –
42-43 EF 3
Ivigtût 70-71 b 5
Ivindo 64-65 D 2
Ivinheima, Rio – 78-79 J 9
Ivohibe 64-65 L 7
Ivoire, Côte d' [≅] 60-61 CD 8
Ivoorkust [≅] 60-61 CD 8
Ivoorkust [★] 60-61 CD 7
Ivrea 36-37 B 3
İvrindi 46-47 B 3
Ivuna 63 C 5

Iwadate 50-51 MN 2
Iwaizumi 50-51 NO 3
Iwaki 50-51 N 4
Iwaki yama 50-51 N 2
Iwakuni 50-51 J 5
Iwamizawa 48-49 R 3
Iwanai 50-51 b 2
Iwanowo = Ivanovo 42-43 FG 6
Iwanuma 50-51 N 3
Iwata 50-51 LM 5
Iwate [J, ●] 50-51 N 3
Iwate [J, ☆] 50-51 N 2-3
Iwate-yama 50-51 N 3
Iwo 60-61 E 7
Iwō-jima = Iō-jima 50-51 H 7
Iwŏn 50-51 G 2

Ixiamas 78-79 F 7
Ixopo 64-65 GH 9
Ixtepec 72-73 G 8

I-yang = Yiyang [TJ, Hunan]
48-49 L 6
Iyo 50-51 J 6
Iyomishima 50-51 J 6
Iyonada 50-51 HJ 6

Izabal, Lago de – 72-73 HJ 8
Izalco 72-73 H 9
Izashiki = Sata 50-51 H 7
Izbat ash-Shaykh 62 C 5
Izberbaš 38-39 J 7
Iževsk 42-43 J 6
Izkī 44-45 H 6
Ižma [SU, ~] 42-43 J 5
Ižma [SU, ●] 42-43 J 4
Izmail 38-39 E 6
İzmir 44-45 B 3
İzmir Körfezi 46-47 B 3
İzmit = Kocaeli 44-45 BC 2
İzmit Körfezi 46-47 C 2
İznik 46-47 C 2
İznik Gölü 46-47 C 2
Izozog, Bañados de –
78-79 G 8
Izozog, Bañados de –
78-79 G 8
Izra' 46-47 G 6
Izu hantō 50-51 M 5
Izuhara 50-51 G 5
Izumi 50-51 H 6
Izumo 50-51 J 5
Izu-shotō 48-49 QR 5
Izu syotō = Izu-shotō
48-49 QR 5
Izvestij CIK, ostrova –
42-43 OP 2

J

Ja = Dja 60-61 G 8
Jāb, Tall – 46-47 G 6
Jabal, Bahr al- 60-61 L 7
Jabalayn, Al- 60-61 L 6
Jabal Lubnān = 2 [RL, ☆ ◁]
46-47 F 6
Jabalón 34-35 F 9
Jabalpur 44-45 MN 6
Jabjabah, Wādī – 62 E 7
Jablah 46-47 F 5
Jablanica [AL] 36-37 J 5
Jablanica [BG] 36-37 L 4
Jablanica [YU] 36-37 G 4
Jablunkovský průsmyk 33 J 4
Jabung, Tanjung – 52-53 DE 7
Jabuticabal 78-79 K 9
Jaca 34-35 G 7
Jacaré, Rio – [BR, Bahia]
78-79 L 6-7
Jacarei 78-79 K 9
Jáchal = San José de Jáchal
80 C 4
Jachhen 48-49 E 5
Jáchymov 33 F 3
Jaciparaná 78-79 G 6
Jackman Station, ME 74-75 H 2
Jackson, CA 76-77 C 6
Jackson, MI 72-73 JK 3
Jackson, MS 72-73 HJ 5
Jackson, MT 76-77 G 3
Jackson, OH 74-75 B 5
Jackson, TN 72-73 J 4
Jackson, WY 76-77 H 4
Jackson, ostrov – = ostrov
Džeksona 42-43 H-K 1
Jackson Head 56-57 N 8
Jackson Lake 76-77 H 4
Jackson Mountains 76-77 D 5
Jacksonville, FL 72-73 KL 5
Jacksonville, NC 74-75 E 7
Jacksonville, OR 76-77 B 4
Jacksonville Beach, FL
74-75 C 9
Jäckvik 30-31 G 4
Jacmel 72-73 M 8
Jacobina 78-79 L 7
Jacob Lake, AZ 76-77 GH 7
Jacques Cortier, Détroit de –
70-71 Y 7-8
Jacuipe, Rio – 78-79 LM 7
Jacumba, CA 76-77 EF 9
Jacundá 78-79 K 5
Jadā, Sha'īb – = Sha'īb al-
Judā' 46-47 LM 7-8
Jadaf, Wādī al- 44-45 E 4
Jadaf al-Jadaf 46-47 J 6
Jaddī, Wādī – 60-61 E 2
Jade 33 D 2
Jadīda, el – = Al-Jadīdah
60-61 C 2
Jadīdah, Al- [ET] 62 C 5
Jadīdah, Al- [MA] 60-61 G 2
Jadīd Rā's al-Fīl 60-61 K 6
Jadotville = Likasi 64-65 G 5
Jadrin 38-39 J 4
Jādū 60-61 G 2
Jaén 34-35 F 10
Jæren 30-31 A 8
Jaesalmēr = Jaisalmer
44-45 KL 5
Jafa, Tēl Avive – = Tel-Avīv-
Yafō 44-45 C 4
Ja'farābād [IR] 44-45 F 3
Jaffa, Cape – 58 D 6
Jaffatin = Jazā'ir Jiftūn 62 EF 4
Jaffna = Yāpanaya 44-45 MN 9
Jafr, Al- [JOR, ~] 46-47 G 7
Jafr, Al- [JOR, ●] 44-45 D 4
Jafr, El- = Al-Jafr 44-45 D 4
Jafū, Ḥāssī – 60-61 E 2
Jagdalpur 44-45 N 7
Jaghbūb, Al- 60-61 J 3
Jaghiagh, Wādī – 46-47 J 4
Jaghjagh, Ouâdî – = Wādī
Jaghiagh 46-47 J 4
Jagodnoje 42-43 cd 5
Jagog Tsho 48-49 F 5
Jagst 33 DE 4
Jagtial 44-45 M 7
Jagua, La – 78-79 E 3
Jaguarão 80 F 4
Jaguarari 78-79 LM 7
Jaguaribe, Rio – 78-79 M 6
Jagüé, Rio del – 80 C 3
Jahrah, Al- 44-45 F 5
Jahrom 44-45 G 5
Jaicós 78-79 L 6
Jailolo 52-53 J 6
Jaipur 44-45 M 5
Jaisalmer 44-45 KL 5
Jaja 42-43 Q 6
Jajah, Al- 62 D 5
Jājarm 44-45 H 3
Jajce 36-37 G 3
Jakan, mys – 42-43 j 4
Jakarta 52-53 E 8
Jakasia, Oblast Autónomo de
– = 10 ◁ 42-43 R 7
Jakobshavn = Jlullssat
70-71 ab 4
Jakobstad 30-31 JK 6
Jakoeten Autonome Republiek
42-43 U-b 4
Jakša 42-43 K 5
Jakutsk 42-43 Y 5
Jaladah, Al- 44-45 F 7
Jalālābād 44-45 KL 4
Jalālat al-Baḥrīyah, Jabal al-
62 DE 3
Jalālat al-Qiblīyah, Jabal al-
62 E 3
Jalāl Kōt = Jalālābād
44-45 KL 4
Jalāmīd, Al- 46-47 HJ 7
Ja'lan 44-45 H 6
Jalandar = Jullundur
44-45 LM 4
Jalandhar = Jullundur
44-45 LM 4
Jalapa Enríquez 72-73 GH 8
Jalawlā' 46-47 L 5
Jalgāńv = Jālgaon [IND ←
Bhusawal] 44-45 M 6
Jālgaon [IND ← Bhusawal]
44-45 M 6
Jalhāk, Al- 60-61 L 6
Jalīb, Maqarr al- 46-47 J 6
Jalībah 46-47 M 7
Jalib Shahab 46-47 M 7
Jalingo 60-61 G 7
Jalisco 72-73 EF 7
Jallekān 46-47 N 6
Jālna 44-45 M 7
Jalon, Rio – 34-35 G 8
Jalo Oasis = Wāḥāt Jālū
60-61 J 3
Jalpug, ozero – 36-37 N 3
Jalta 38-39 F 7
Jalu = Yalu Jiang 50-51 EF 2
Jālū, Wāḥāt – 60-61 J 3
Jamaame 60-61 N 8
Jamaat 48-49 E 2
Jamā'at al-Ma'yuf 46-47 M 7
Jamaica 72-73 L 8
Jamaica Channel 72-73 L 8
Jamaica Channel 72-73 L 8
Jamaïque 72-73 L 8
Jamakhaṅḍī = Jamkhandi
44-45 LM 7
Jamal, poluostrov –
42-43 MN 3
Jamal-Nenets, Circunscripción
Nacional de los –
42-43 M-O 4-5
Jamal-Nentsen, Nationaal
Gebied der –
42-43 M-O 4-5
Jamantau, gora – 42-43 K 7
Jamanxim, Rio – 78-79 H 6
Jamari, Rio – 78-79 G 6
Jambi [RI, ●] 52-53 D 7
Jambi [RI, ☆ = 5 ◁] 52-53 D 7
Jambol 36-37 M 4
Jambongan, Pulau –
52-53 G 5
Jambūr 46-47 L 5
Jambuto 38-39 O 2
Jamdena, Pulau – = Pulau
Yamdena 52-53 K 8
James, Baie – 70-71 UV 7
James Bay 70-71 UV 7
James Ranges 56-57 F 4
James River [USA ◁
Chesapeake Bay] 72-73 L 4
James River [USA ◁ Missouri
River] 72-73 G 2
Jamestown [AUS] 58 D 4
Jamestown, ND 72-73 G 2
Jamestown, NY 72-73 L 3
Jamkhandi 44-45 LM 7
Jamm 30-31 MN 8
Jammerbugt 30-31 C 9
Jammu 44-45 LM 4
Jammu and Kashmir
44-45 LM 3-4
Jamnā = Yamuna 44-45 MN 5
Jāmnagar 44-45 L 6
Jampol' 38-39 E 6
Jāmpūr 44-45 KL 5
Jamsah 62 E 4
Jämsankoski 30-31 L 7
Jamshedpur 44-45 NO 6
Jamsk 42-43 de 6
Jämtland 30-31 E-G 6
Jämtlands Sikås 30-31 F 6
Jamursba, Tanjung = Tanjung
Yamursba 52-53 K 7
Jana 42-43 Z 4
Janaperi, Rio – 78-79 G 4
Janaúba 78-79 L 8
Janaucu, Ilha – 78-79 JK 4
Janaul 42-43 JK 6
Jandaq 44-45 GH 4
Jandiatuba, Rio – 78-79 F 5-6
Jandowae 56-57 K 5
Janesville, CA 76-77 C 5
Jangarej 42-43 L 4
Jangijul' 42-43 M 9
Jang Thang 48-49 E-G 5
Jangtsekiang = Chang Jiang
48-49 K 5-6
Jang-tse-tjiang = Chang Jiang
48-49 K 5-6
Jānī Beyglū 46-47 M 3
Janīn 46-47 F 6
Jan Mayen 19 B 19-20
Jan Mayen, Dorsal de –
28-29 F 2
Jan Mayen, Dorsale de –
28-29 F 2
Jan Mayen, Plataforma de –
28-29 H 1-2

Jan Mayen, Seuil de – 28-29 H 1-2
Jan-Mayendrempel 28-29 H 1-2
Jan Mayen Ridge 28-29 H 1-2
Jannah 60-61 FG 4
Jano-Indigirskaja nizmennost' 42-43 Z-c 3
Janos 76-77 J 10
Jánoshalma 33 J 5
Janskij 42-43 Za 4
Janskij zaliv 42-43 Za 3
Jantarnyj 33 J 1
Jantra 36-37 M 4
Januária 78-79 KL 8
Jao-ho = Raohe 48-49 P 2
Jaonpur = Jaunpur 44-45 N 5
Jao-yang Ho = Raoyang He 50-51 D 2
Japan Basin 50-51 J-L 2
Japans Bekken 50-51 J-L 2
Japan Sea 48-49 P 4-Q 3
Japanse Zee 48-49 P 4-Q 3
Japan Trench 22-23 R 4
Japantrog 22-23 R 4
Japón 48-49 P 5-Q 3
Japon 48-49 P 5-Q 3
Japón, Cuenca del – 50-51 J-L 2
Japón, Fosa del – 22-23 R 4
Japon, Fosse du – 22-23 R 4
Japón, Mar de – 48-49 P 4-Q 3
Japon, Mer du – 48-49 P 4-Q 3
Japurá, Rio – 78-79 F 5
Jara, La – 34-35 E 9
Jarâbulus 46-47 GH 4
Jarādah 60-61 D 2
Jaraguari 78-79 HJ 8-9
Jaransk 42-43 H 6
Jarārah, Wādī – 62 F 6
Jarāwī, Al- 46-47 H 7
Jarbah, Jazīrat – 60-61 G 2
Jarbidge, NV 76-77 F 5
Jarcevo [SU, Jenisej] 42-43 R 5
Jarcevo [SU ↗ Smolensk] 38-39 F 4
Jardines de la Reina 72-73 L 7
Jarega 38-39 K 3
Jarensk 42-43 H 5
Jari, Rio – 78-79 J 5
Jarīd, Shaṭṭ al- 60-61 F 2
Jarīr, Wādī – 44-45 E 5-6
Jarkand = Yarkand 48-49 D 4
Jarkov = Char'kov 38-39 G 5-6
Jarkovo 42-43 M 6
Jarmashīn, 'Ayn – 62 CD 5
Jarny 34-35 K 4
Jarocin 33 H 2-3
Jarok, ostrov – 42-43 a 3
Jaroslavl' 42-43 FG 6
Jarosław 33 L 3-4
Järpen 30-31 E 6
Jarrāḥī, Rūd-e – 46-47 N 7
Jarroto 38-39 O 2
Jar-Sale 42-43 MN 4
Jartum = Al-Kharṭūm 60-61 L 5
Jartum = Al-Kharṭūm 60-61 L 5
Jaru 78-79 G 7
Järvenpää 30-31 L 7
Jāsk 44-45 H 5
Jašma 38-39 H 2
Jasnyj 42-43 Y 7
Jasonhalvøy 24 C 30-31
Jason Islands 80 D 8
Jasper [CDN, Alberta] 70-71 N 7
Jasper [CDN, Ontario] 74-75 F 2
Jasper, FL 74-75 b 1
Jasper National Park 70-71 N 7
Jaṣṣān 46-47 L 6
Jastrebac 36-37 J 4
Jászberény 33 JK 5
Jatai [BR ↙ Rio Verde] 78-79 J 8
Jatapu, Rio – 78-79 H 5
Játiva 34-35 G 9
Jatobá 78-79 JK 5
Jat Potī = Kārēz 44-45 K 4
Jaú 78-79 K 9
Jaú, Rio – 78-79 G 5
Jau'aliyāt, Jebel el- = Jabal al-Aḍiriyāt 46-47 G 7
Jauf, Al- = Al-Jawf 44-45 DE 5
Jauf, El – = Al-Jawf 60-61 J 4
Jauja 78-79 DE 7
Jaunde = Yaoundé 60-61 G 8
Jaunjelgava 30-31 L 9
Jaunpur 44-45 N 5
Java [RI] 52-53 EF 8
Java, Fosse de – 22-23 P 6
Java, Mar de – 52-53 EF 8
Java, Mer de – 52-53 EF 8
Java Head = Tanjung Layar 52-53 DE 8
Javaj, poluostrov – 42-43 NO 3
Javalambre 34-35 G 8
Javari, Rio – 78-79 E 6
Java Sea 52-53 EF 8
Javatrog 22-23 P 6
Javazee 52-53 EF 8
Javhār = Jawhār 44-45 L 7
Javlenka 42-43 M 7
Javor 36-37 HJ 4
Jawa 52-53 EF 8
Jawa = Java 52-53 EF 8
Jawa Barat = 11 ◁ 52-53 E 8
Jaw'alīyāt, Jabal al- 46-47 G 7
Jawa Tengah = 12 ◁ 52-53 E 8
Jawa Timur = 14 ◁ 52-53 F 8
Jawf, Al- [LAR] 60-61 J 4
Jawf, Al- [Saudi Arabia] 44-45 DE 5
Jawf, Al- [Y] 44-45 EF 7
Jawhār 44-45 L 7
Jawhar [ETH] 60-61 ab 3
Jawor 33 H 3
Jaxartes = Syrdarja 44-45 K 2
Jaya, Gunung – 52-53 L 7
Jayapura 52-53 M 7
Jayawijaya, Pegunungan – 52-53 LM 7
Jāyid 46-47 J 6
Jaypur = Jaipur 44-45 M 5
Jaypura = Jeypore 44-45 N 7
Jaza'ir, Al- [DZ] 60-61 E 1
Jaza'ir, Al- [IRQ] 46-47 M 7
Jazīr 46-47 F 5
Jazīra, Al- = Arḍ al-Jazīrah 44-45 E 3-F 4
Jazīrah, Al- [IRQ] 46-47 J 5
Jazīrah, Al- [Sudan] 60-61 L 6
Jazīrah, Arḍ al- 44-45 E 3-F 4
Jāz Mūreyān, Hāmūn-e – 44-45 H 5
Jazzīn 46-47 F 6

Jean, NV 76-77 F 8
Jeanette, ostrov – = ostrov Žanetty 42-43 ef 2
Jebaïl = Jubayl 46-47 F 5
Jebba 60-61 E 7
Jebel, Bahr el – = Bahr al-Jabal 60-61 L 7
Jebelein, El- = Al-Jabalayn 60-61 L 6
Jeblé = Jablah 46-47 F 5
Jécori 76-77 J 1
Jeddah = Jiddah 44-45 D 6
Jędrzejów 33 K 3
Jefferson, MT 76-77 GH 2
Jefferson, OH 74-75 C 4
Jefferson, OR 76-77 B 3
Jefferson, Mount – [USA, Nevada] 76-77 E 6
Jefferson, Mount – [USA, Oregon] 76-77 C 3
Jefferson City, MO 72-73 H 4
Jeffersonville, GA 74-75 B 8
Jeffrey, Abysse de – 56-57 F 7
Jeffrey, Fosa – 56-57 F 7
Jeffrey Depth 56-57 F 7
Jeffreydiep 56-57 F 7
Jefremov 38-39 G 5
Jegorjevsk 42-43 FG 6
Jegyrjach 42-43 M 5
Jēhlam = Jihlam 44-45 L 4
Jehlum = Jihlam 44-45 L 4
Jehol = Chengde 48-49 M 3
Jejsk 38-39 G 6
Jēkabpils 30-31 L 9
Jekaterinburg 42-43 L 6
Jekaterinovka [SU, Primorskij Kraj] 50-51 J 1
Jekubābād 44-45 K 5
Jelabuga 38-39 K 4
Jelec 38-39 G 5
Jelenia Góra 33 GH 3
Jelfa = Jilfah 60-61 E 2
Jelgava 30-31 KL 9
Jelizavety, mys – 42-43 b 7
Jelizovo [SU, Rossijskaja SFSR] 42-43 e 7
Jema = Djema 60-61 K 7
Jemaja, Pulau – 52-53 DE 6
Jemanželinsk 38-39 M 5
Jembiani 63 DE 4
Jemeck 42-43 G 5
Jena 33 E 3
Jenakijevo 38-39 G 6
Jenašimskij Polkan, gora – 42-43 RS 6
Jeneponto 52-53 G 8
Jenisej 42-43 Q 4
Jenisejsk 42-43 R 6
Jenisejskij kr'až 42-43 R 5-6
Jenisejskij zaliv 42-43 OP 3
Jenkins, KY 74-75 B 6
Jenkiu = Renqiu 48-49 M 4
Jenner, CA 76-77 B 6
Jennings, MT 76-77 F 1
Jenny Lind Island 70-71 Q 4
Jensen, UT 76-77 J 5
Jensen Beach, FL 74-75 cd 3
Jens Munk Island 70-71 UV 4
Jens Munks Ø 70-71 cd 5
Jenud = Gorē 60-61 M 7
Jen'uka 42-43 X 6
Jeol = Chengde 48-49 M 3
Jepara 52-53 F 8
Jequié 78-79 L 7
Jequitaí 78-79 L 8
Jequitinhonha, Rio – 78-79 L 8
Jerâblous = Jarābulus 46-47 GH 4
Jerâda = Jarādah 60-61 D 2
Jerantut 52-53 D 6
Jerba = Jazīrat Jarbah 60-61 G 2
Jerbogač'on 42-43 U 5
Jérémie 72-73 M 8
Jeremoabo 78-79 M 6-7
Jerevan 38-39 H 7
Jerez de García Salinas 72-73 F 7
Jerez de la Frontera 34-35 DE 10
Jerez de los Caballeros 34-35 D 9
Jergeni 38-39 H 6
Jericho [AUS] 56-57 J 4
Jericho = Arīḥa 46-47 F 7
Jerilderie 58 G 5
Jermak 42-43 O 7
Jermakovskoje 42-43 R 7
Jermentau 42-43 N 7
Jermī 46-47 L 4
Jerofej Pavlovič 42-43 X 7
Jerome, AZ 76-77 G 8
Jerome, ID 76-77 F 4
Jeropol 42-43 g 4
Jersey 32 E 7
Jersey City, NJ 72-73 M 3-4
Jersey Shore, PA 74-75 E 4
Jerumenha 78-79 L 6
Jérusalem = Yĕrūshālayim 44-45 CD 4
Jerusalén = Yĕrūshālayim 44-45 CD 4
Jeruzalem = Yĕrūshālayim 44-45 CD 4
Jervis Bay 56-57 K 7
Jervois Range 56-57 G 4
Jesenice 36-37 EF 2
Jesenik 33 H 3
Jesil' 42-43 M 7
Jessalange 63 D 5
Jessaur = Jessore 44-45 O 6
Jessej 42-43 T 4
Jesselton = Kota Kinabalu 52-53 FG 5
Jesso = Hokkaidō 48-49 RS 3
Jessore 44-45 O 6
Jestro, Webi – = Weyb 60-61 N 7
Jesup, GA 74-75 BC 9
Jesús María [RA] 80 D 4
Jevpatorija 38-39 F 6
Jewish Autonomous Region 42-43 Z 8
Jeypore 44-45 N 7
Jezzîn = Jazzīn 46-47 F 6

Jhang Maghiana = Jhang-Maghiyāṇh 44-45 L 4
Jhang-Maghiyāṇh 44-45 L 4
Jhānsi 44-45 M 5
Jharsuguda 44-45 NO 6
Jharsugura = Jharsuguda 44-45 NO 6
Jhelum = Jihlam 44-45 L 4

Jiali = Lharugö 48-49 G 5
Jiali = Qionghai 48-49 L 8
Jialing Jiang 48-49 K 5
Jiamusi 48-49 P 2
Ji'an [TJ, Jiangxi] 48-49 LM 6
Ji'an [TJ, Jilin] 50-51 EF 2
Jianchang [TJ → Benxi] 50-51 E 2
Jianchang [TJ ← Jinzhou] 50-51 B 2
Jiangdu = Yangzhou 48-49 M 5
Jiange 48-49 JK 5
Jiangling 48-49 L 5
Jiangmen 48-49 L 7
Jiangsu 48-49 MN 5
Jiangxi 48-49 LM 6
Jian He [TJ, ~] 50-51 D 2
Jian'ou 48-49 M 6
Jianping 50-51 B 2
Jianshui 48-49 J 7
Jianyang [TJ, Fujian] 48-49 M 6
Jianyang [TJ, Sichuan] 48-49 JK 5
Jiao Xian 48-49 M 4
Jiaozou 48-49 L 4
Jiaxing 48-49 N 5
Jiayi = Chiayi 48-49 MN 7
Jiayuguan 48-49 H 4
Jibhalanta = Uliastaj 48-49 H 2
Jibou 36-37 K 2
Jičín 33 G 3
Jidaidat Ḥāmir = Judayyīat Ḥāmir 46-47 J 7
Jidāmī, B'īr al- 62 E 4
Jiddah 44-45 D 6
Jiddī, Jabal al- 62 E 2
Jido 44-45 P 5
Jidole = Gīdolē 60-61 M 7
Jiekkevarre 30-31 H 3
Iiešjavrre 30-31 L 3
Jiftūn, Jazā'ir – 62 EF 4
Jiggithai Tsho 48-49 F 4
Jihlam [PAK, ~] 44-45 L 4
Jihlam [PAK, ●] 44-45 L 4
Jihlava 33 G 4
Jijiga 60-61 N 7
Jijili 60-61 F 1
Jil, Al- 46-47 KL 7
Jilava, Bucureşti- 36-37 M 5
Jilemutu 48-49 N 1
Jilfah, Al- 60-61 E 2
Jilf al-Kabīr, Haḍbat al- 60-61 K 4
Jilib 60-61 N 8
Jilīb Bākūr = Qalīb Bākūr 46-47 L 8
Jilidah, Al- = Al-Jaladah 44-45 F 6-7
Jilin [TJ, ●] 48-49 O 3
Jilin [TJ, ☆] 48-49 N 2-O 3
Jiljila, Hōr al- = Hawr al-Jiljilah 46-47 L 6
Jiljilah, Hawr al- 46-47 L 6
Jill, Al- = Al-Jil 46-47 KL 7
Jilong = Chilung 48-49 N 6
Jīma 60-61 M 7
Jimaja = Pulau Jemaja 52-53 DE 6
Jimāl, Wādī – 62 F 5
Jimbolia 36-37 J 3
Jiménez [MEX, Chihuahua] 72-73 F 6
Jimma = Jīma 60-61 M 7
Jinah 62 D 5
Jinan 48-49 M 4
Jincheng 48-49 L 4
Jindabyne 58 J 6
Jingbo Hu 48-49 O 3
Jingchuan 48-49 K 4
Jingdezhen 48-49 M 6
Jingdong 48-49 J 7
Jinggu 48-49 J 7
Jinghe [TJ, ●] 48-49 E 3
Jinghong 48-49 J 7
Jingning 48-49 K 4
Jingshi = Jinshi 48-49 L 6
Jingtai 48-49 J 4
Jingyu 50-51 F 1
Jingyuan 48-49 JK 4
Jingzhen = Xinchengbu 48-49 K 4
Jinhua 48-49 MN 6
Jiniiang = Quanzhou 48-49 MN 6-7
Jining [TJ, Nei Monggol Zizhiqu] 48-49 L 3
Jining [TJ, Shandong] 48-49 M 4
Jinja 64-65 H 2
Jinmen = Kinmen Dao 48-49 M 7
Jinmu Jiao = Jintu Jiao 48-49 KL 8
Jinotega 72-73 J 9
Jinsen = Inch'ŏn 48-49 O 4
Jinsha Jiang 48-49 J 6
Jinshi 48-49 L 6
Jintu Jiao 48-49 KL 8
Jinxi [TJ, Liaoning] 50-51 C 2
Jin Xian [TJ, Liaoning ↑ Dalian] 48-49 N 4
Jin Xian [TJ, Liaoning ↗ Jinzhou] 50-51 C 2
Jinzhou 48-49 N 3
Jiparaná, Rio – 78-79 G 6-7
Jipijapa 78-79 C 5
Jirays, Jabal – 62 F 7
Jiren = Jima 60-61 M 7
Jirgalanta = Chovd 48-49 G 2
Jiriid = Kiridh 60-61 b 2
Jirjā 60-61 L 3
Jīroft 44-45 H 5
Jirwān 44-45 G 6
Jishi Shan = Amnyemachhen Gangri 48-49 HJ 5
Jisr ech Chaghoûr = Gisr ash-Shughūr 46-47 G 5
Jisr ech Chaghoûr = Gisr ash-Shughūr 46-47 G 5
Jiu 36-37 K 3
Jiujiang [TJ, Jiangxi] 48-49 M 6
Jiuquan 48-49 H 4
Jiwā', Al- 44-45 G 6
Jīwānī 44-45 J 5-6
Jixi [TJ, Heilongjiang] 48-49 P 2
Jīzah, Al- [ET] 60-61 KL 3
Jīzah, Al- [JOR] 46-47 FG 7
Jīzah, El- = Al-Jīzah 46-47 FG 7
Jīzān 44-45 E 7
Jizl, Wādī al- 44-45 D 5
Jlaiba = Jalībah 46-47 M 7
Jlullssat 70-71 ab 4

Joaçaba 80 F 3
Joana Peres 78-79 JK 5
Joanna Spring 56-57 DE 4
João 78-79 J 5
João de Almeida = Chibia 64-65 D 6
João Pessoa 78-79 N 6
Joaquim Felício 78-79 KL 8
Joaquin V. González 80 D 3
Jobal Island = Jazā'ir Qaysūm 62 EF 4
Job Peak 76-77 D 6
Jo-ch'iang = Charqiliq 48-49 F 4
Jocolí 80 C 4
Joden, Autonome Oblast der – 42-43 Z 8
Jodhpur 44-45 L 5
Jodpur = Jodhpur 44-45 L 5
Joegoslavië 36-37 H 4-J 5
Joensuu 30-31 NO 6
Joerg Plateau 24 B 29-30
Jofane 64-65 H 7
Jofra Oasis, el – = Wāḥāt al-Jufrah 60-61 GH 3
Jõgeva 30-31 LM 8
Jögödseer Chijd = Erdenecagaan 48-49 LM 2
Jögödseer Chijd = Erdenecagaan 48-49 LM 2
Jogyakarta = Yogyakarta 52-53 EF 8
Jōhana 50-51 L 4
Johanna Island = Ndzuwani 64-65 KL 5
Johannesburg 64-65 G 8
Johi [GUY] 78-79 H 4
John Day, OR 76-77 D 3
John Day River 76-77 C 3
Johnsonburg, PA 74-75 D 4
Johnson City, NY 74-75 F 3
Johnson City, TN 72-73 K 4
Johnsonville, SC 74-75 D 8
Johnston, SC 74-75 C 8
Johnston, Lakes – 56-57 D 6
Johnstown, NY 74-75 FG 3
Johnstown, PA 72-73 L 3-4
Johor Baharu 52-53 DE 6
Jõhvi 30-31 M 8
Joinvile 80 G 3
Joinville, Île – 24 C 31
Jōkāu = Jūkāw 60-61 L 7
Jokkmokk 30-31 HJ 4
Joko = Yoko 60-61 G 7
Jokohama = Yokohama 48-49 QR 4
Jökulsa á Brú 30-31 f 2
Jökulsá á Fjöllum 30-31 ef 2
Jolfā 44-45 F 3
Joliet, IL 72-73 J 3
Joliette 70-71 W 8
Joló 52-53 H 5
Joló Island 52-53 H 5
Jomotsering 44-45 O 5
Jomu 63 C 3
Jonava 30-31 KL 10
Jonesboro, AR 72-73 H 4
Jonesport, ME 74-75 K 2
Jones Sound 70-71 TU 2
Jongkha 48-49 F 6
Joniškis 30-31 KL 9
Jonköping 30-31 EF 9
Jönköpings län 30-31 EF 9
Jonquière 70-71 WX 8
Jonzac 34-35 G 6
Joontoy 64-65 K 3
Joowhar = Jawhar 60-61 ab 3
Joplin, MO 72-73 H 4
Joplin, MT 76-77 H 1
Jordan 44-45 D 4
Jordan = Nahr ash-Sharī'ah 46-47 F 6-7
Jordan Creek 76-77 E 4
Jordania 44-45 D 4
Jordanië 44-45 D 4
Jordanie 44-45 D 4
Jordan Valley, OR 76-77 E 4
Jorhat 44-45 PQ 5
Jörn 30-31 J 5
Jos 60-61 F 7
José de San Martín 80 BC 6
Joseph, OR 76-77 E 3
Joseph, Lac – 70-71 XY 7
Joseph, Lake – 74-75 D 2
Joseph Bonaparte Gulf 56-57 E 2
Joseph City, AZ 76-77 H 8
Joshua Tree, CA 76-77 E 8
Joshua Tree National Monument 72-73 CD 5
Joškar-Ola 42-43 H 6
Joson Bulag = Altaj 48-49 H 2
Jos Plateau 60-61 E 6-7
Josselin 34-35 F 5
Jostedalsbreen 30-31 B 7
Jotunheimen 30-31 BC 7
Joûniyé = Jūnīyah 46-47 F 6
Joutsa 30-31 LM 7
Jow Kār 46-47 N 5

Juan Aldama 72-73 F 7
Juan A. Pradere 80 D 5
Juan de Fuca, Strait of – 70-71 LM 8
Juan de Nova 64-65 K 6
Juan Díaz 72-73 c 2
Juan Fernández 69 BC 6
Juan Fernández, Dorsal de las islas – 22-23 E 7
Juan Fernandez, Seuil de – 22-23 E 7
Juan Fernández Ridge 22-23 E 7
Juan Fernandezrug 22-23 E 7
Juan Gallegos, Isla – 72-73 b 2
Juan José Castelli 80 DE 3
Juanjui 78-79 D 6
Juankoski 30-31 N 6
Juan Stuven, Isla – 80 A 7
Juárez [MEX ↑ Chihuahua] 72-73 E 5
Juárez, Sierra de – 72-73 C 5
Juatinga, Ponta do – 78-79 L 9
Juazeiro 78-79 L 6
Juazeiro do Norte 78-79 M 6
Jūbā 60-61 L 8
Juba, Webi – 60-61 N 8
Jubab, Qar'at – 46-47 J 5
Jubail, Al- = Al-Jubayl al-Baḥrī 44-45 FG 5
Jubal, Madiq – = Jazīrat Shadwan 60-61 LM 3
Jubayl [ET] 62 E 3
Jubayl [RL] 46-47 F 5
Jubayl al-Baḥrī, Al- 44-45 FG 5
Jubayt 60-61 M 4
Jubba = Jubbah 46-47 K 6
Jubbada Hoose 64-65 K 3
Jubbada Hoose = 4 ◁ 60-61 N 8
Jubbade Dhexe 60-61 N 8
Jubbah 46-47 K 6
Jubbulpore = Jabalpur 44-45 MN 6
Jubeil = Jubayl 46-47 F 5
Jubilee Lake 56-57 E 5
Júcar 34-35 G 9
Jucás 78-79 LM 6
Juchitán de Zaragoza 72-73 GH 8
Judā', Sha'īb al- 46-47 L 8-M 7
Judayyīdat-Ar'ar 44-45 DE 4
Judayyīdat Ḥāmir 46-47 J 7
Judenburg 33 G 5
Judino = Petuchovo 42-43 M 6
Judith, Point – 74-75 H 4
Judith Bassin 76-77 HJ 2
Judoma 42-43 a 6
Jufrah, Wāḥāt al- 60-61 GH 3
Jug 38-39 J 3
Juggernaut = Purī 44-45 O 7
Jugiong 58 J 5
Jugorskij poluostrov 42-43 L 4
Jugorskij Šar, proliv – 42-43 L 4-M 3
Juhaym 46-47 L 8
Juhaynah 62 D 4
Juhua Dao 50-51 C 2
Juifs, Province des – 42-43 Z 8
Juikin = Ruijin 48-49 M 6
Juiz de Fora 78-79 KL 9
Jujuy 80 C 2
Jujuy = San Salvador de Jujuy 80 CD 2
Jukagirskoje ploskogorje 42-43 de 4
Jukao = Rugao 48-49 N 5
Jūkāw 60-61 L 7
Jukta 42-43 TU 5
Julaca 78-79 F 9
Juli 78-79 F 8
Juliaca 78-79 E 8
Julia Creek 56-57 H 4
Julian, CA 76-77 E 9
Julian Alps 36-37 EF 2

Julianehåb = Qaqortoq 70-71 b 5
Jülich 33 C 3
Juliuhe 50-51 D 1
Jullundur 44-45 LM 4
Jūlmīnā [MA, Aghādīr] 60-61 BC 3
Julundur = Jullundur 44-45 LM 4
Jumaima, Al- = Al-Jumaymah 46-47 KL 8
Jumaymah, Al- 46-47 KL 8
Jumbe Salim's 63 D 5
Jumbilla 78-79 D 6
Jumbo 64-65 K 3
Jumbo, Raas – 64-65 K 3
Jumilla 34-35 G 9
Jumna = Yamuna 44-45 MN 5
Junagadh 44-45 KL 6
Junagarh = Junagadh 44-45 KL 6
Junayfah 62 E 2
Junaynah 60-61 J 6
Junction, UT 76-77 G 6
Junction City, KS 72-73 G 4
Jundah 56-57 H 4
Jundtion City, OR 76-77 B 3
Juneau, AK 70-71 K 6
Junee 58 H 5
June Lake, CA 76-77 D 7
Junggharīyā 48-49 EF 2
Jungo, NV 76-77 D 5
Juniata River 74-75 E 4
Junín [RA, Buenos Aires] 80 D 4
Junín [PE, ●] 78-79 D 7
Junín de los Andes 80 BC 5
Juniper Mountains 76-77 G 8
Jūnīyah 46-47 F 6
Juniye = Jūnīyah 46-47 F 6
Junsele 30-31 G 6
Junten = Sunch'ŏn 48-49 O 4-5
Juntura, OR 76-77 DE 4
Jupiá, Represa de – 78-79 J 9
Jūr, Nahr – 60-61 K 7
Jūr, Nahr el – = Nahr Jūr 60-61 K 7
Jura [CH] 33 BC 5
Jura [GB] 32 D 3-4
Jura, Sound of – 32 D 4
Jurab = Djourab 60-61 H 5
Juraiba, Al- = Al-Juraybah 46-47 KL 8
Juraybah, Al- 46-47 KL 8
Jurbarkas 30-31 K 10
Jurdī, Wādī – 62 E 4
Jurf ad-Darāwish 46-47 FG 7
Jurf ed Darāwish = Jurf ad-Darāwish 46-47 FG 7
Jurga 42-43 P 6
Juribej 38-39 NO 2
Jurien Bay 56-57 B 6
Juries, Los – 80 D 3
Jurjevec 42-43 G 6
Jurjev-Pol'skij 38-39 G 4
Jurjurah 60-61 EF 1
Jurmala 30-31 K 9
Jūrqāy, Jabal – 60-61 JK 6
Juruá, Rio – 78-79 F 6
Juruena 78-79 H 7
Juruena, Rio – 78-79 H 6-7
Jur'ung-Chaja 42-43 VW 3
Jur'ung-Chaja 42-43 VW 3
Jur'uzan' 38-39 L 5
Juškozero 42-43 E 5
Jussey 34-35 K 5
Justo Daract 80 CD 4
Jutai, Rio – 78-79 F 5
Jüterbog 33 F 2-3
Jūṭhī Antarīp = False Point 44-45 O 6
Jutiapa 72-73 HJ 9
Juticalpa 72-73 J 9
Jutland 30-31 C 10-D 9
Jutlandia 30-31 C 10-D 9
Juuka 30-31 N 6
Juva 30-31 MN 7
Juventud, Isla de la – 72-73 K 7
Juwārah, Al- 44-45 H 7
Ju Xian 48-49 M 4
Juža 38-39 H 4
Jūzān 46-47 N 5
Južna Morava 36-37 JK 4
Južno-Kuril'sk 42-43 c 9
Južno-Sachalinsk 42-43 bc 8
Južnyj, mys – 42-43 e 6
Južnyj An'ujskij chrebet = An'ujskij chrebet 42-43 fg 4
Južnyj Bug 38-39 F 6
Južnyj Ural 42-43 K 7-L 6
Južsib 42-43 L 7
Jyekunde = Chhergundo 48-49 H 5
Jylland 30-31 C 10-D 9
Jyväskylä 30-31 L 6

K

K 2 44-45 M 3
K XVIII, Dorsal – 22-23 O 7
K XVIII, Dorsale – 22-23 O 7
K XVIII Ridge 22-23 O 7
K XVIII-Rug 22-23 O 7
Kaamanen 30-31 M 3
Kaapbekken 22-23 K 7
Kaapdrempel 22-23 K 8
Kaapdrempel 22-23 K 8
Kaapland 64-65 FG 9
Kaapplato 64-65 F 8
Kaapprovinsie = Kaapland 64-65 FG 9
Kaapstad 64-65 E 9
Kaap Verdebekken 22-23 GH 4-5
Kaap Verdedrempel 22-23 H 4-5
Kaaschka 44-45 HJ 3
Kabaena, Pulau – 52-53 H 8
Kabahaydar 46-47 H 4
Kabála [GR] 36-37 L 5
Kabala [WAL] 60-61 B 7
Kabale 64-65 GH 3
Kabalo 64-65 G 4
Kabambare 64-65 G 3
Kabango 63 B 5
Kabansk 42-43 U 7
Kabardino-Balkar Autonomous Republic = 3 ◁ 38-39 H 7
Kabardino-Balkarische Autonome Republiek = 3 ◁ 38-39 H 7
Kabardino-Balkars, République Autonome des – = 3 ◁ 38-39 H 7
Kabardinos y Balkares, República Autónoma de los – = 3 ◁ 38-39 H 7
Kabare [RCB] 64-65 G 3
Kabarei 52-53 K 7
Kabarnet 63 CD 2
Kabba 60-61 F 7
Kåbdalis 30-31 J 4
Kabelega Falls 64-65 H 2
Kabelega Falls National Park 64-65 H 2
Kaberamaido 63 C 2
Kabia, Pulau – = Pulau Selayar 52-53 H 8
Kabin Buri 52-53 D 4
Kabinda 64-65 FG 4
Kabinda = Cabinda 64-65 D 4
Kabīr, Wāw al- 60-61 H 3
Kabīr, Zāb al- 46-47 K 4
Kabīr Kūh 44-45 F 4
Kabkābīyah 60-61 J 6
Kabo 60-61 H 7
Kabobo 63 B 4
Kaboel = Kabul 44-45 K 4
Kabompo 64-65 F 5
Kabongo 64-65 FG 4
Kaboul = Kabul 44-45 K 4
Kabudārāhang 46-47 N 5
Kābul 44-45 K 4
Kabunda 63 B 6
Kaburuan, Pulau – 52-53 J 6
Kābuwītā 60-61 L 8
Kabwe 64-65 G 5
Kachchh = Kutch 44-45 K 6
Kacheliba 63 C 2
Ka-Chem = Malyj Jenisej 42-43 RS 7
Kachgar = Qäshqär 48-49 CD 4
Kachin Pyinnei 52-53 C 1-2
Kachovka 38-39 F 6
Kachovskoje vodochranilišče 38-39 FG 6
K'achta 42-43 U 7
Kaçkar Daği 46-47 J 2
Kačug 42-43 U 7
Ka-Chem = Malyj Jenisej 42-43 RS 7
Kadaingdi 52-53 C 3
Kadaingti = Kadaingdi 52-53 C 3
Kadan Kyûn 52-53 C 4
Kaḍappa = Cuddapah 44-45 M 8
Kade [GH] 60-61 D 7
Kadeï 60-61 H 8
Kadhdhāb, Sinn al- 62 DE 6
Kadıköy, İstanbul- 46-47 C 2
Kadiköy Deresi 46-47 B 2-3
Kadina 58 CD 4-5
Kadınhanı 46-47 E 3
Kadirli 46-47 FG 4
Kadmat Island 44-45 L 8
Ka-do 50-51 E 3
Kadoma 64-65 G 6
Kadugli = Kāduqlī 60-61 KL 6
Kaduna [WAN, ●] 60-61 F 6
Kāduqlī 60-61 KL 6
Kadykčan 42-43 C 5
Kaech'i-ri 50-51 G 2
Kaesŏng 48-49 O 4
Kāf 44-45 D 4
Kāf, Al- 60-61 F 1
Kafan 38-39 J 8
Kafanchan 60-61 F 7
Kafērevs, Akrōtērion – 36-37 L 6
Kaffrine 60-61 AB 6
Kafr ash-Shaykh 62 D 2
Kafr az-Zayyāt 62 D 2
Kafta = Keftiya 60-61 M 6
Kafu 64-65 H 2
Kafue [Z, ~] 64-65 G 6
Kafue [Z, ●] 64-65 G 6
Kafue Flats 64-65 G 6
Kafue National Park 64-65 G 5-6
Kafulwa 63 B 5
Kaga 50-51 L 4
Kaga Bandoro 60-61 HJ 7
Kagan 44-45 J 3
Kagawa 50-51 JK 5
Kagera 64-65 H 3
Kagera, Parc national de la – 64-65 H 3
Kagera Magharibi 64-65 H 3
Kagi = Chiayi 48-49 MN 7
Kağızman 46-47 K 2
Kagmār = Kajmār 60-61 L 6
Kagoro 60-61 F 7
Kagoshima 48-49 OP 5
Kagoshima wan 50-51 H 7
Kagosima = Kagoshima 48-49 OP 5
Kagul 38-39 E 6
Kahama 64-65 H 3
Kahayan, Sungai – 52-53 F 7
Kahemba 64-65 E 4
Kahia 64-65 G 4
Kahlā [IR] 46-47 N 5
Kahler Asten 33 D 3
Kahlotus, WA 76-77 D 2
Kahoku-gata 50-51 L 4
Kahoolawe 52-53 e 3
Kahramanmaraş 44-45 D 3
Kâhta 46-47 H 4
Kai, Kepulauan – 52-53 K 8
Kaiama 60-61 E 7
Kaibab Indian Reservation 76-77 G 7
Kaibab Plateau 76-77 G 7
Kaidong = Tongyu 48-49 N 3
Kaieteur Falls 78-79 GH 3
Kaifeng 48-49 LM 5
K'ai-fong = Kaifeng 48-49 LM 5
Kaihwa = Wenshan 48-49 JK 7
Kai Kecil 52-53 K 8
Kaikohe 56-57 O 7
Kaikoura 56-57 O 8
Kailas Gangri = Kailash Gangri 48-49 E 5
Kailash Gangri 48-49 E 5
Kailu 48-49 N 3
Kaimana 52-53 K 7
Kaimon-dake 50-51 H 7
Kainan 50-51 K 5
Kainantu 52-53 N 8
Kainji Dam 60-61 EF 6-7
Kainsk = Kujbyšev 42-43 O 6
Kaipara Harbour 56-57 O 7
Kaiparowits Plateau 76-77 H 7
Kairiru 52-53 M 7
Kaïrouan = Al-Qayrawān 60-61 FG 1
Kairuku 52-53 N 8
Kaisariyah = Caesarea 46-47 F 6
Kaiser Peak 76-77 D 7
Kaiserslautern 33 CD 4
Kaiser-Wilhelm II.-Land 24 C 9-10
Kaishū = Haeju 48-49 O 4
Kaitaia 56-57 O 7
Kaitangata 56-57 NO 9
Kaitum älv 30-31 HJ 4
Kaizanchin = Hyesanjin 48-49 O 3
Kajaani 30-31 MN 5
Kajabbi 56-57 H 4
Kajakī 44-45 JK 4
Kajang [RI] 52-53 H 8
Kajiado 64-65 J 3
Kajmār 60-61 L 6
Kajnar [SU, Kazachskaja SSR] 42-43 O 8
Kākā 60-61 L 6
Kakamas 64-65 F 8
Kakamega 64-65 HJ 2
Kakarka = Sovetsk 42-43 H 6
Kakata 60-61 B 7
Kakbil = Karaoğlan 46-47 H 3
Kake 50-51 J 5
Kakegawa 50-51 LM 5
Kakelwe 63 B 4
Kakia 64-65 F 7-8
Kakinada 44-45 N 7
Käkisalmi = Prioz'orsk 42-43 DE 5
Kakogawa 50-51 K 5
Kakonko 63 B 3
Kakšaal-Too, chrebet – 44-45 M 2
Kakuda 50-51 N 4
Kakulu 63 AB 4
Kakuma 64-65 HJ 2
Kakunodate 50-51 N 3
Kala 63 B 5
Kala, El – = Al-Qal'ah 60-61 F 1
Kalabahi 52-53 H 8
Kalabo 64-65 F 6
Kalábryta 36-37 K 6
Kalābsha 60-61 L 4
Kalač 38-39 H 5
Kalač-na-Donu 38-39 H 6
Kaladar 74-75 E 2
Ka Lae 52-53 e 4
Kalahari = Kalahari Desert 64-65 EF 7
Kalahari Desert 64-65 EF 7
Kalahari Gemsbok National Park 64-65 F 8
Kalakan 42-43 W 6
Kalama, WA 76-77 B 2-3
Kalamáta 36-37 JK 7
Kalamazoo, MI 72-73 J 3
Kalambo Falls 64-65 H 4
Kalampáka 36-37 JK 6
Kalan = Tunceli 44-45 DE 3
Kalančak 36-37 P 2
Kalangali 63 C 4
Kalannie 56-57 C 6
Kalanshiyu, Sarīr – = Sarīr Qalanshū 60-61 J 3
Kalaotao, Pulau – 52-53 H 8
Kalar 42-43 W 6
Kalaraš 36-37 N 2
Kalasin [RI] 52-53 F 6
Kalasin [T] 52-53 D 3
Kalat = Qalāt 44-45 K 5
Kalāt, Jabal – 62 F 6
Kalâtdlit nunât 70-71 b 2-c 5
Kalāt-i Ghilzay = Qalāt 44-45 K 4
Kal'azin 38-39 G 4
Kale [TR, Antalya] 46-47 CD 4
Kale [TR, Denizli] 46-47 C 4
Kale [TR, Gümüşane] 46-47 H 2
Kalecik 46-47 E 2
Kalecik = Kabahaydar 46-47 H 4
Kalehe 64-65 G 3
Kalemie 64-65 G 4
Kalemma 63 CD 3
Kale Sultanie = Çanakkale 44-45 B 2
Kaletwa 52-53 B 2
Kalevala 42-43 E 4
Kalewa 52-53 BC 2
Kaleybar 46-47 M 3
Kálfafell 30-31 de 2-3
Kálfafellstadhur 30-31 f 2
Kalgan = Zhangjiakou 48-49 L 3
Kalgoorlie 56-57 D 6
Kalhāt 44-45 H 6
Kali = Sangha 64-65 E 2-3
Kaliakra, nos – 36-37 N 4
Kalibo 52-53 H 4
Kalikata = Calcutta 44-45 O 6
Kalima 64-65 G 3
Kalimantan 52-53 F 7-G 6
Kalimantan Barat = 7 ◁ 52-53 F 7
Kalimantan Selatan = 9 ◁ 52-53 G 7
Kalimantan Tengah = 8 ◁ 52-53 F 7
Kalimantan Timur = 10 ◁ 52-53 G 6
Kalinin = Tver' 42-43 EF 6
Kaliningrad 33 K 1
Kalinkoviči 38-39 EF 5
Kalinku 63 C 5
Kalisizo 63 BC 3
Kalispell, MT 72-73 CD 2
Kalisz 33 J 3
Kalisz Pomorski 33 GH 2
Kaliua 64-65 H 3-4
Kalix älv 30-31 JK 4
Kalkan 46-47 C 4
Kalkfeld 64-65 E 7
Kalkfontein = Karasburg 64-65 E 8
Kalkrand 64-65 E 7
Kallafo = Ḳelafo 60-61 N 7
Kallaste 30-31 M 8
Kallipolis = Gelibolu 44-45 B 2
Kallsjön 30-31 E 6
Kalmar 30-31 G 9
Kalmar län 30-31 FG 9
Kalmarsund 30-31 G 9
Kalmouks, République Autonome des – 38-39 HJ 6
Kalmukken Autonome Republiek 38-39 HJ 6
Kalmyk Autonomous Republic 38-39 HJ 6
Kalmykovo 42-43 J 8
Kaloko 64-65 G 4
Kalola 63 B 5
Kalomo 64-65 G 6
Kalonje 63 B 6
Kalpeni Island 44-45 L 8
Kal Sefīd 46-47 M 5
Kaluga 38-39 G 5
Kalulaui = Kahoolawe 52-53 e 3
Kalundborg 30-31 D 10
Kalundu 63 B 3
Kalungwishi 63 B 5
Kaluš 38-39 D 6
Kalutara 44-45 MN 9
Kalvarija 30-31 K 10
Kálymnos 36-37 M 7
Kama [RCB] 64-65 G 3
Kama [SU, ~] 42-43 J 6
Kamae 50-51 HJ 6
Kamaeura = Kamae 50-51 HJ 6
Kamaishi 48-49 R 4
Kamaishi wan 50-51 NO 3
Kamaisi = Kamaishi 48-49 R 4
Kamalampakea 63 B 4
Kaman [TR] 46-47 E 3
Kamarān 44-45 E 7
Kamba [ZRE] 64-65 F 3
Kambalnaja Sopka, vulkan – 42-43 e 7
Kambia 60-61 B 7
Kambing, Pulau – = Pulau Atauro 52-53 J 8
Kambodja 52-53 DE 4
Kambove 64-65 G 5
Kamčatka, poluostrov – 42-43 e 6-7
Kamčatskij poluostrov 42-43 fg 6
Kamčatskij zaliv 42-43 f 6
Kamčija 36-37 M 4
Kamchatka, Peninsula de – = Kamčatka 42-43 e 6-7
Kamela, OR 76-77 D 3
Kamenec-Podol'skij 38-39 E 6
Kamenjak, Rt – 36-37 E 3
Kamenka [SU, Rossijskaja SFSR Mezenskaja guba] 42-43 G 4
Kamenka [SU → Tambov] 38-39 H 5
Kamen'-na-Obi 42-43 OP 7
Kamennogorsk 30-31 NO 7
Kamennomostskij 38-39 GH 7
Kamenskoje 42-43 fg 5
Kamensk-Šachtinskij 38-39 GH 6
Kamensk-Ural'skij 42-43 LM 6
Kamenz 33 FG 3
Kameoka 50-51 K 5
Kameroen 60-61 G 7-8
Kameshli = Al-Qāmishlīyah 44-45 E 3
Kāmēt 44-45 M 4
Kamiah, ID 76-77 EF 2
Kamień Pomorski 33 G 2
Kamiiso 50-51 b 3
Kamikawa 50-51 c 2
Kami-Koshiki-shima 50-51 G 7
Kāmil, Al- 44-45 H 6
Kamilīn, Al- 60-61 L 5
Kamina 64-65 FG 4
Kaminokuni 50-51 ab 3
Kaminoshima 50-51 G 5
Kaminoyama 50-51 N 3
Kami-Sihoro 50-51 c 2
Kāmit, Jabal – 62 B 6
Kamitsushima 50-51 G 5
Kamituga 63 AB 3
Kamiyaku 50-51 H 7
Kāmlīn, El- = Al-Kamilīn 60-61 L 5
Kamloops 70-71 MN 7
Kammuri yama 50-51 HJ 5
Kamniokan 42-43 V 6
Kamo [J] 50-51 M 4
Kamoenai 50-51 ab 2
Kamortā Drīp = Camorta Island 44-45 P 9
Kamp 33 G 4
Kampala 64-65 H 2
Kampar 52-53 D 6
Kampemha 63 AB 5
Kamp'o 50-51 G 5
Kampo = Campo 60-61 F 8
Kampolombo, Lake – 64-65 G 5
Kampot 52-53 D 4
Kampulu 63 B 5
Kampung Pasir Besar 52-53 D 6
Kamskoje vodochranilišče 42-43 K 6
Kamtchatka, Presqu'île de – = Kamčatka 42-43 e 6-7
Kamtchatka Peninsula = Kamčatka 42-43 e 6-7
Kamtsjatka = Kamčatka 42-43 e 6-7
Kamudi [EAK] 63 D 3
Kamui-misaki 50-51 ab 2
Kāmyārān 46-47 M 5
Kamyšin 38-39 HJ 5
Kamyšlov 42-43 L 6
Kan [SU] 42-43 S 6-7
Kanaal, Het – 32 E 7-F 6
Kanaal-Eilanden = Channel Islands 32 E 7
Kanaaupscow, Rivière – 70-71 VW 7
Kanab, UT 76-77 G 7
Kanab Creek 76-77 G 7
Kanagawa 50-51 M 5
Kanā'is, Rā's al- 62 BC 2
Kanala = Canala 56-57 N 4
Kan'ān 46-47 L 6
Kananga 64-65 F 4
Kanarraville, UT 76-77 G 7
Kanaš 42-43 H 6
Kanawha River 74-75 BC 5
Kanazawa 48-49 Q 4
Kanchanaburi 52-53 C 4
Kancheepuram = Kanchepuram 44-45 MN 8
Kanchenjunga = Gangchhendsönga 44-45 O 5
Kanchibia 63 B 5
Kānchipuram = Kanchepuram 44-45 MN 8
Kanchow = Zhangye 48-49 J 4
Kandahār = Qandahār 44-45 K 4
Kandalakša 42-43 EF 4
Kandalakšskij zaliv 42-43 EF 4
Kandangan 52-53 FG 7
Kandavu 52-53 a 2
Kandi [DY] 60-61 E 6
Kandıra 46-47 D 2
Kandla 44-45 L 6
Kandos 56-57 JK 6
Kandreho 64-65 L 6
Kandūleh 46-47 M 5
Kandulu 63 D 5
Kandy = Maha Nuwara 44-45 N 9
Kane, PA 74-75 D 4
Kane Basin 70-71 WX 2
Kanem 60-61 H 6
Kanevskaja 38-39 G 6
Kaneyama 50-51 M 4
Kang 64-65 F 7
Kangal 46-47 G 3
Kangar 52-53 D 5
Kangaroo Island 56-57 G 7
Kangāvar 46-47 M 5
Kangding 48-49 J 5-6
Kangean, Pulau – 52-53 G 8
Kangerdlugssuaq [Grönland, ∪] 70-71 ef 4
Kangerdlugssuaq [Grönland, ●] 70-71 ab 4
Kangetet 64-65 J 2
Kanggye 48-49 O 3
Kanggyŏng 50-51 F 4
Kanghwa 50-51 F 4
Kanghwa-do 50-51 EF 4
Kanghwa-man 50-51 E 4
Kangjin 50-51 F 5
Kangnŭng 48-49 OP 4
Kango 64-65 D 2
Kangsŏ 50-51 E 3
Kangwŏn-do [North Korea] 50-51 F 3
Kangwŏn-do [ROK] 50-51 G 4
Kan Ho = Gan He 48-49 N 1
Kaniama 64-65 FG 4
Kaniapiskau Lake 70-71 W 7
Kaniet Islands 52-53 N 7
Kānī Masī 46-47 K 4
Kanin, poluostrov – 42-43 GH 4
Kanin Nos [SU, ●] 38-39 H 2

Kanin 187

Kanin Nos, mys – 42-43 G 4
Kanireş = Karlıova 46-47 J 3
Kanita 50-51 N 2
Kankakee, IL 72-73 J 3
Kankan 60-61 C 6
Kankō = Hamhŭng 48-49 O 3-4
Kankō = Hŭngnam 48-49 O 4
Kankossa = Kankūssah 60-61 B 5
Kan-kou-chên = Gango 50-51 B 2
Kankūssah 60-61 B 5
Kankyō-hokudō = Hamgyŏng-pukto 50-51 G 2-H 1
Kankyō-nandō = Hamgyŏng-namdo 50-51 FG 2-3
Kaṇṇanūr = Cannanore 44-45 LM 8
Kannapolis, NC 74-75 C 7
Kannus 30-31 K 6
Kano [WAN, ●] 60-61 F 6
Kanoji 50-51 J 5
Kanona 63 B 6
Kanosh, UT 76-77 G 6
Kanouri 60-61 G 6
Kanoya 50-51 H 7
Kanpur 44-45 MN 5
Kansas 72-73 FG 4
Kansas City, KS 72-73 GH 4
Kansas City, MO 72-73 H 4
Kansas River 72-73 G 4
Kansk 42-43 S 6
Kansŏng 50-51 G 3
Kansu = Gansu 48-49 G 3-J 4
Kantalahti = Kandalakša 42-43 EF 4
Kantara = Al-Qanṭarah 62 E 2
Kantchari 60-61 E 6
Kantō 50-51 MN 4
Kantō sammyaku 50-51 M 4-5
Kanuma 50-51 M 4
Kanuri = Kanouri 60-61 G 6
Kanyākumārī Antarīp = Cape Comorin 44-45 M 9
Kanyama 63 B 2
Kanye 64-65 FG 7-8
Kanzanlı 46-47 F 4
Kao-an = Gao'an 48-49 LM 6
Kao-hsiung 48-49 MN 7
Kaokoveld 64-65 D 6-7
Kaolack 60-61 A 6
Kao-li-kung Shan = Gaoligong Shan 48-49 H 6
Kaosiung = Kao-hsiung 48-49 MN 7
Kaotai = Gaotai 48-49 H 4
Kaouar 60-61 G 5
Kap'a-do 50-51 F 6
Kapagere 52-53 N 8-9
Kapanga 64-65 F 4
Kapatu 63 B 5
Kapčagajskoje vodochranilišče 42-43 O 9
Kapela 36-37 F 3
Kapenguria 63 C 2
Kapfenberg 33 G 5
Kapıdağı Yarımadası 46-47 BC 2
Kapinnie 58 B 5
Kapiri Mposhi 64-65 G 5
Kapit 52-53 F 6
Kāpōētā = Kābuwītā 60-61 L 8
Kapona 64-65 G 4
Kapongolo 63 AB 4
Kapos 33 J 5
Kaposvár 33 HJ 5
K'appesel'ga 38-39 F 3
Kapsan 50-51 FG 2
Kapsowar 63 CD 2
Kapsukas 30-31 K 10
Kapuas, Sungai – [RI, Kalimantan Barat] 52-53 F 6
Kapunda 58 D 5
Kapuskasing 70-71 U 8
Kapustin Jar 38-39 J 6
Kaputar, Mount – 58 JK 3
Kaputir 63 C 2
Kapverde 20-21 H 5
Kara = Ust'-Kara 42-43 LM 4
Kara, Mar de – 42-43 K 3-R 2
Kara, Mer de – 42-43 K 3-R 2
Karaali 46-47 E 3
Karababa Dağı 46-47 FG 3
Kara-Bau 38-39 K 6
Karabekaul 44-45 JK 3
Karabiga 46-47 B 2
Kara-Bogaz-Gol 38-39 K 7
Kara-Bogaz-Gol, zaliv – 44-45 G 2
Karabük 44-45 C 2
Karaburun [TR] 46-47 B 3
Karabutak 42-43 L 8
Karaca = Şiran 46-47 H 2
Karacabey 46-47 C 2
Karaca Dağ [TR, Ankara] 46-47 E 3
Karacadağ [TR, Konya] 46-47 E 4
Karaçadağ [TR, Sanlı Urfa ▲▲] 46-47 H 4
Karacadağ [TR, Sanlı Urfa ●] 46-47 H 4
Karacaköy 46-47 C 2
Karacasu 46-47 C 4
Karachayevo-Cherkess Autonomous Region = 2 ◁ 38-39 H 7
Karāchī 44-45 K 6
Karaçurun = Hilvan 46-47 H 4
Karachai y Cherkeses, Oblast Autónoma de los – = 2 ◁ 38-39 H 7
Karachayevo-Cherkess Autonomous Region = 2 ◁ 38-39 H 7
Karachi 44-45 K 6
Karadağ 46-47 E 4
Karadeniz Boğazı = Boğazici 44-45 BC 2
Karadoğan = Kıbrısak 46-47 DE 2
Karafuto = Sachalin 42-43 b 7-8
Karagajly 42-43 NO 8
Karaganda 42-43 NO 8
Karagije, vpadina – 38-39 K 7
Karaginskij, ostrov – 42-43 fg 6
Karaginskij zaliv 42-43 fg 6
Karagoua 60-61 G 6
Karahallı 44-45 C 3
Karahasanlı 46-47 F 3
Kāraikkāl = Karajkal 44-45 MN 8
Karaisalı = Çeceli 46-47 F 4
Karaj 44-45 G 3
Karajkal 44-45 MN 8
Karak, Al- 44-45 D 4
Karakallı = Özalp 46-47 KL 3
Karakeçi 46-47 H 4
Karakeçili 46-47 E 3
Karakelong, Pulau – 52-53 J 6
Karakoçan 46-47 HJ 3
Karakoram 44-45 L 3-M 4
Karakoram Pass = Qaramurun davan 44-45 MN 3
Kara Korē 60-61 MN 6
Karakorum = Char Chorin 48-49 J 2
Karaköse = Ağrı 44-45 E 3
Karakumskij kanal 44-45 J 3
Karakumy 44-45 HJ 3
Karam = Karin 60-61 O 6
Karaman 44-45 C 3
Karaman = Çameli 46-47 C 4
Karamian, Pulau – 52-53 F 8
Karamürsel 46-47 C 2
Karamyševo 30-31 N 9
Karand 46-47 M 5
Karaoğlan 46-47 H 3
Karapınar 46-47 E 4
Karas, Pulau – 52-53 K 7
Karasburg 64-65 E 8
Kara Sea 42-43 K 3-R 2
Kara Shar = Qara Shahr 48-49 F 3
Karasjok 30-31 L 3
Karasjokka 30-31 L 3
Karasu [TR, ~] 46-47 J 3
Karasu [TR, ●] 46-47 D 2
Karasu = Hizan 46-47 K 3
Karasu = Salavat 46-47 F 2
Karasu-Aras Dağları 44-45 E 2-3
Karasuk 42-43 O 7
Karataş 46-47 F 4
Karataş Burnu 46-47 F 4
Karatau 42-43 N 9
Karatau, chrebet – 42-43 MN 9
Karatobe 42-43 J 8
Karatsjai-Tsjerkessen Autonome Oblast = 2 ◁ 38-39 H 7
Karatsu 50-51 G 6
Karaul 42-43 P 3
Karaussa Nor = Char us nuur 48-49 G 2
Karawang 52-53 E 8
Karawayn, Bi'r – 62 C 4
Karayazı 46-47 JK 3
Karayün 46-47 G 3
Karažal 42-43 N 8
Karbalā' 44-45 E 4
Karcag 33 K 5
Kardeljevo 36-37 G 4
Kardítsa 36-37 JK 6
Kärdla 30-31 K 8
Kărdžali 36-37 L 5
Kareeberge 64-65 F 9
Kareima = Kuraymah 60-61 L 5
Karelia 28-29 P 2-3
Karelian Autonomous Republic 42-43 E 4-5
Karelië 28-29 P 2-3
Karelische Autonome Republiek 42-43 E 4-5
Karelstad = Charlesville 64-65 F 4
Karema 64-65 H 4
Karen = Karin Pyinnei 52-53 C 3
Karesuando 30-31 JK 3
Karet = Qārrāt 60-61 C 4
Kārēz 44-45 K 4
Kargamıs 46-47 G 4
Kargapazarı Dağları 46-47 J 2
Kargat 42-43 P 6
Kargi [EAK] 63 D 2
Kargı [TR] 46-47 F 2
Kargopol' 42-43 F 5
Karhula 30-31 M 7
Kariba, Lake – 64-65 G 6
Kariba Dam 64-65 G 6
Kariba Gorge 64-65 GH 6
Kariba-yama 50-51 ab 2
Karibib 64-65 E 7
Karigasniemi 30-31 LM 3
Karima = Kuraymah 60-61 L 5
Karimata, Kepulauan – 52-53 E 7
Karimata, Selat – 52-53 E 7
Karimunjawa, Kepulauan – 52-53 EF 8
Karin 60-61 O 6
Karin Pyinnei 52-53 C 3
Karis 30-31 KL 7-8
Karische Zee 42-43 K 3-R 2
Karisimbi, Mont – 64-65 G 3
Kariya 50-51 L 5
Karjaa = Karis 30-31 KL 8
Karjepolje 38-39 H 2
Karkaar 60-61 b 2
Karkar Island 52-53 N 7
Karkheh, Rūd-e – 46-47 N 6-7
Karkinitskij zaliv 38-39 F 6
Karkkila 30-31 KL 7
Karkonosze 33 GH 3
Karkūk = Kirkūk 44-45 EF 3
Karla-Aleksandra, ostrov – 42-43 H-K 1
Karl Alexander, ostrov – = ostrov Karla Aleksandra 42-43 H-K 1
Karlıova 46-47 J 3
Karl-Marx-Stadt = Chemnitz 33 F 3
Karlobag 36-37 F 3
Karlovac 36-37 F 3
Karlovy Vary 33 F 3
Karlsborg 30-31 F 8
Karlshamn 30-31 F 9
Karlskoga 30-31 F 8
Karlskrona 30-31 FG 9
Karlsruhe 33 D 4
Karlstad 30-31 EF 8
Karmah 60-61 L 5
Karmøy 30-31 A 8
Karnak, Al- 62 E 5
Karnal 44-45 M 5
Karnataka 44-45 M 7-8
Karnobat 36-37 M 4
Kärnten 33 FG 5
Karnūlu = Kurnool 44-45 M 7
Karoi 64-65 G 6
Karokobe = Karukubī 63 B 2
Karonga 64-65 H 4
Karoonda 58 DE 5
Kārōra = Kārūrah 60-61 M 5
Karosa 52-53 G 7
Karpaşa 46-47 EF 5
Kárpathos [GR, ⊙] 36-37 M 8
Kárpathos [GR, ●] 36-37 M 8
Karpeddo 63 D 2
Karpenēsion 36-37 JK 6
Karpinsk 38-39 LM 4
Karpinsk = Krasnoturjinsk 42-43 L 5-6
Karrats Fjord 70-71 Za 3
Kars 44-45 E 2
Karsakpaj 42-43 M 8
Kärsava 30-31 MN 9
Karši 44-45 K 3
Karşiyaka, İzmir- 46-47 B 3
Karskije Vorota, proliv – 42-43 J-L 3
Kartal, İstanbul- 46-47 C 2
Kartaly 42-43 KL 7
Karthage 60-61 G 1
Karukubī 63 B 2
Karumba 56-57 H 3
Karumwa 63 C 3
Kārūn, Rūd-e – 44-45 FG 4
Karungi 30-31 K 4-5
Karungu 63 C 3
Kārūrah 60-61 M 5
Karviná 33 J 4
Karwar 44-45 L 8
Karyai 36-37 KL 5
Karymkary 42-43 M 5
Kaş 44-45 BC 3
Kasa = Ui-do 50-51 E 5
Kasaba 63 B 5
Kasaba = Kiği 46-47 J 3
Kasaba = Turgutlu 46-47 BC 3
Kasache 63 C 6
Kasai [ZRE] 64-65 E 3
Kasai-Occidental 64-65 EF 3-4
Kasai-Oriental 64-65 FG 3-4
Kasaji 64-65 F 5
Kasama 64-65 H 5
Kasan = Kazan' 42-43 HJ 6
Kasanda 63 BC 2
Kasane 64-65 FG 6
Kasanga 64-65 H 4
Kasaoka 50-51 J 5
Kasba Lake 70-71 Q 5
Kaseda 50-51 H 7
Kasempa 64-65 FG 5
Kasenga 64-65 G 5
Kasenyi 64-65 GH 2
Kasese 64-65 GH 2-3
Kasha 63 E 3
Kāshān 44-45 G 4
Kashghariya 48-49 DE 4
Kashi 48-49 D 4
Kashi = Qāshqār 48-49 CD 4
Kashima 50-51 GH 6
Kashing = Jiaxing 48-49 N 5
Kashishi 63 B 6
Kashiwazaki 50-51 LM 4
Kashkān, Rūdkhāneh-ye – 46-47 N 6
Kāshmar 44-45 H 3-4
Kashmir 44-45 LM 4
Kashmor 44-45 O 5
Kashqar = Qāshqār 48-49 CD 4
Kash Rūd = Khāsh Rōd 44-45 J 4
Kasigao 63 D 3
Kasimov 42-43 G 7
Kašin 38-39 G 4
Kašira 38-39 G 5
Kasirota = Pulau Kasiruta 52-53 J 7
Kasiruta, Pulau – 52-53 J 7
Kasivobara = Severo-Kuril'sk 42-43 de 7
Kaskinen = Kaskö 30-31 J 6
Kaskö 30-31 J 6
Kasongan 52-53 F 7
Kasongo 64-65 G 3
Kasongo-Lunda 64-65 E 4
Kásos 36-37 M 8
Kaspische Zee 44-45 F 2-G 3
Kasrık = Kirkgeçit 46-47 K 3
Kassai = Kasai 64-65 E 3
Kassalā 60-61 M 5
Kassándra 36-37 K 5-6
Kassel 33 D 3
Kasserine = Al-Qasrayn 60-61 F 1-2
Kastamonu 44-45 CD 2
Kastamum = Kastamonu 44-45 CD 2
Kastéllion 36-37 K 8
Kastellórizon = Mégistē 46-47 C 4
Kastoria 36-37 J 5
Kastornoje 38-39 G 5
Kasulu 64-65 H 3
Kasumiga ura 50-51 N 5
Kasungu 64-65 H 5
Kasungu National Park 63 C 6
Kasur = Qaṣūr 44-45 L 4
Kataba 64-65 FG 6
Katahdin, Mount – 72-73 MN 2
Kaṭaka = Cuttack 44-45 NO 6
Katako-Kombe 64-65 F 3
Katakumba 64-65 F 4
Katami sammyaku 50-51 c 1-2
Katana 63 B 3
Katanga 42-43 T 5-6
Katanga = Shaba 64-65 FG 4
Katangli 42-43 b 7
Katanning 56-57 C 6
Katav-Ivanovsk 42-43 K 7
Katāwāz = Zarghūn Shahr 44-45 K 4
Katchall Island 44-45 P 9
Katenga 64-65 G 4
Katera 63 BC 3
Katerîna, Gebel – = Jabal Katrīnah 60-61 L 3
Katerinē 36-37 K 5
Kates Needle 70-71 KL 6
Katete 64-65 H 5
Kathā 52-53 C 2
Katherine 56-57 F 2
Kāthiāwār 44-45 K 6
Kathlambagebirge = Drakensberge 64-65 G 9-H 8
Kathmandu = Kātmāndu 44-45 NO 5
Kathua 63 D 3
Kati 60-61 C 6
Katif, El- = Al-Qaṭīf 44-45 F 5
Katihar 44-45 O 5
Katiola 60-61 CD 7
Katmai, Mount – 70-71 F 6
Katmai National Monument 70-71 EF 6
Kātmāndu 44-45 NO 5
Káto Achaîa 36-37 J 6
Káto Achaîa 36-37 J 6
Katomba 56-57 JK 6
Katonga 63 B 2-3
Katoomba 58 JK 4
Katoomba = Blue Mountains 56-57 JK 6
Katowice 33 J 3
Katrancık Dağı 46-47 D 4
Katrīnah, Jabal – 60-61 L 3
Katrineholm 30-31 G 8
Katsina 60-61 F 6
Katsina Ala 60-61 F 7
Katsuda 50-51 N 4
Katsumoto 50-51 G 6
Katsuura 50-51 N 5
Katsuyama 50-51 L 4
Katta = Katsuta 50-51 N 4
Kattakurgan 44-45 K 2-3
Kattegat 30-31 D 9
Katwe 63 B 3
Kau, Teluk – 52-53 J 6
Kauai 52-53 e 3
Kauai Channel 52-53 e 3
Kauai Channel 52-53 e 3
Kaufbeuren 33 E 5
Kauhajoki 30-31 JK 6
Kaukauveld 64-65 F 6
Kauliranta 30-31 KL 4
Kaulun = Kowloon 48-49 LM 7
Kaunas 30-31 K 10
Kaura Namoda 60-61 F 6
Kautokeino 30-31 KL 3
Kavajë 36-37 H 5
Kavak [TR, Samsun] 46-47 FG 2
Kavak [TR, Sivas] 46-47 G 3
Kaval'kan 42-43 a 6
Kavaratti 44-45 L 8
Kavaratti Island 44-45 L 8
Kavardhā = Kawardha 44-45 N 6
Kavarna 36-37 N 4
Kavieng 52-53 h 5
Kavīr, Dasht-e – 44-45 GH 4
Kavīr-e Lūt 42-43 J 5
Kavirondo Gulf 63 C 3
Kavu 63 B 4
Kaw 78-79 J 4
Kawagoe 50-51 M 5
Kawaguchi 50-51 MN 4-5
Kawaharada = Sawata 50-51 M 3-4
Kawamata 50-51 N 4
Kawambwa 64-65 GH 4
Kawanoe 50-51 J 5-6
Kawardha 44-45 N 6
Kawasaki 48-49 QR 4
Kawashiri-misaki 50-51 H 5
Kawewe 63 AB 5
Kawich Range 76-77 E 6-7
Kawimbe 64-65 H 4
Kawlin 52-53 C 2
Kawm Umbū 60-61 L 4
Kawn Ken = Khon Kaen 52-53 D 3
Kawthaung 52-53 C 4
Kaya [HV] 60-61 D 6
Kaya [J] 50-51 K 5
Kaya [RI] 52-53 G 6
Kayadibi = Salmanlı 46-47 F 3
Kayak Island 70-71 H 6
Kayambi 64-65 H 4
Kayā Pyinnei 52-53 C 3
Kaya-san 50-51 G 5
Kayenta, AZ 76-77 H 7
Kayes 60-61 B 6
Kayhaydi 60-61 B 5
Kaymas 46-47 D 2
Kaynar 46-47 G 3
Kaynaslı 46-47 D 2
Kayoa, Pulau – 52-53 J 6
Kaypak 46-47 G 4
Kayseri 44-45 D 3
Kaysville, UT 76-77 GH 5
Kayuagung 52-53 DE 7
Kazachskaja guba 38-39 K 7
Kazachskij melkosopočnik 42-43 M-P 7-8
Kazachstan 42-43 J-P 8
Kazachstan = Aksaj 42-43 J 7
Kazačinskoje [SU, Jenisej] 42-43 R 6
Kazačinskoje [SU, Kirenga] 42-43 U 6
Kazačje 42-43 a 3
Kazajstán 42-43 J-P 8
Kazakhie, Steppe de – = Kazachskij Melkosopočnik 42-43 M-P 79
Kazakhstan 42-43 J-P 8
Kazamoto = Katsumoto 50-51 G 6
Kazan' [SU, Tatarskaja ASSR] 42-43 HJ 6
Kazan [TR] 46-47 E 2
Kazandağ 46-47 K 3
Kazandžik 44-45 GH 3
Kazanlak 36-37 L 4
Kazan River 70-71 Q 5
Kazanskoje [SU, Zapadno-Sibirskaja nizmennost'] 42-43 M 6
Kazatin 38-39 E 6
Kazbek, gora – 38-39 H 7
Kāzerūn 44-45 G 5
Kazi-Magomed 38-39 J 7
Kāẓimīyah, Baghdād-Al- 46-47 L 6
Kazimoto 63 D 5
Kazincbarcika 33 K 4
Kazumba 64-65 F 4
Kazungula 64-65 G 6
Kazvin = Qazvīn 44-45 FG 3
Kazym 38-39 N 3
Kazym [SU, Chanty-Mansijskaja AO] 42-43 M 5
Kbaisa = Kubaysah 46-47 K 6
Kea 36-37 L 7
Keams Canyon, AZ 76-77 H 8
Kearney, NE 72-73 G 3
Keban 46-47 H 3
Keban Barajı 46-47 H 3
Kebāng 44-45 PQ 5
Kebbi = Sokoto 60-61 EF 6
Kébémer 60-61 A 5
Kebkābiya = Kabkābīyah 60-61 J 6
Kebnekajse 30-31 H 4
Kebumen 52-53 E 8
Keçiborlu 46-47 D 4
Kecskemét 33 J 5
Kėdainiai 30-31 L 10
Keddie, CA 76-77 C 5-6
Kedia d'Idjil = Kidyat Ijjill 60-61 B 4
Kediri 52-53 F 8
Kédougou 60-61 B 6
Keele Peak 70-71 KL 5
Keeler, CA 76-77 E 7
Keele River 70-71 L 5
Keeling, Bassin de – 22-23 OP 6
Keeling, Cuenca de – 22-23 OP 6
Keeling Basin 22-23 OP 6
Keelingbekken 22-23 OP 6
Kee-lung 48-49 N 6
Keelung = Kee-lung 48-49 N 6
Keene, NH 74-75 G 3
Keeseville, NY 74-75 G 2
Keetmanshoop 64-65 E 8
Keewatin, District of – 70-71 RS 4-5
Kefa 60-61 M 7
Kefallēnia 36-37 J 6
Kéfalos 36-37 M 7
Kefamenanu 52-53 HJ 8
Kefar Ata = Qiryat-Ata' 46-47 F 6
Keferdiz 46-47 G 4
Kefil, Al- = Al-Kifl 46-47 L 6
Kēfisiá 36-37 KL 6
Keflavík 30-31 b 2-3
Ķeftiya 60-61 M 6
Kegueur Terbi 60-61 H 4
Kehl 33 CD 4
Kei 63 B 2
Keiki-dō = Kyŏnggi-do 50-51 F 4
Keila 30-31 L 8
Keishō-hokudō = Kyŏngsang-pukto 50-51 G 4
Keishō-nandō = Kyŏngsang-namdo 50-51 FG 5
Keitele 30-31 LM 6
Keith 32 E 3
Keith [AUS] 56-57 GH 7
Keith Arm 70-71 M 4
Keitū = Keytū 46-47 N 5
Kejvy 38-39 G 2
Kelafo 60-61 N 7
Keles 46-47 C 3
Kelford, NC 74-75 E 6
Kelifely, Causse du – 64-65 KL 6
Kelil'vun, gora – 42-43 g 4
Kelkit 46-47 H 2

188 Kanin

Kelkit Çayı 46-47 G 2
Kellé 64-65 D 2-3
Keller Lake 70-71 M 5
Kellett, Cape – 70-71 L 3
Kelleys Islands 74-75 B 4
Kellogg, ID 76-77 EF 2
Kelloselkä 30-31 N 4
Kelmė 30-31 K 10
Kélo 60-61 H 7
Kelowna 70-71 N 7-8
Kelso [ZA] 64-65 H 9
Kelso, CA 76-77 F 8
Kelso, WA 76-77 B 2
Keltische Zee 32 C 6
Kelton Pass 76-77 G 5
Kelulun He = Herlen He 48-49 M 2
Kelvin, AZ 76-77 H 9
Kem' [SU, ●] 42-43 E 4
Kemä 48-49 H 6
Ké Macina 60-61 C 6
Kemah 46-47 H 3
Kemaliye 46-47 H 3
Kemaliye = Vakfıbekir 46-47 H 2
Kemalpaşa [TR, Artvin] 46-47 J 2
Kemalpaşa [TR, İzmir] 46-47 B 3
Kemanai = Towada 50-51 N 2
Kembalpur 44-45 L 4
Kembolcha 60-61 MN 6
Kemer [TR, Antalya] 46-47 D 4
Kemer [TR, Burdur] 46-47 D 4
Kemer [TR, Muğla] 46-47 C 4
Kemer = Eskiköy 46-47 D 4
Kemerovo 42-43 PQ 6
Kemi 30-31 L 5
Kemijärvi [SF, ●] 30-31 M 4
Kemijärvi [SF, ≈] 30-31 MN 4
Kemijoki 30-31 L 4-5
Kemijoki = Kem' 42-43 E 4
Kemmerer, WY 76-77 H 5
Kémo-Ibingui 60-61 H 7
Kemp Land 24 C 6
Kemp Peninsula 24 B 31
Kempsey 56-57 K 6
Kempten 33 E 5
Kemptville 74-75 EF 2
Kena = Qinā 60-61 L 3
Kenai, AK 70-71 F 5
Kenai Mountains 70-71 F 6-G 5
Kenai Peninsula 70-71 FG 5
Kenamo 70-71 L 7
Kenansville, FL 74-75 c 3
Kenbridge, VA 74-75 DE 6
Kendal 32 E 4
Kendari 52-53 H 7
Kendawangan 52-53 F 7
Kēndrāpaḍā = Kendrapara 44-45 O 6
Kendrāpāra 44-45 O 6
Kendrick, ID 76-77 E 2
Kendu 63 C 3
Kenema 60-61 B 7
Kenge 64-65 D 3
Kengtung = Kyöngdôn 52-53 CD 2
Kenhardt 64-65 F 8
Kéniéba 60-61 B 6
Kenitra = Al-Q'nitrah 60-61 C 2
Kenmare [IRL, ~] 32 A 6
Kenmare [IRL, ●] 32 B 6
Kenmore, NY 74-75 D 3
Kennebec River 74-75 HJ 2
Kennebunk, ME 74-75 H 3
Kennedy, Mount – 70-71 J 5
Kennedy Channel 70-71 WX 1-2
Kennedy Channel 70-71 WX 1-2
Kennewick, WA 76-77 D 2
Kenney Dam 70-71 M 7
Keno Hill 70-71 JK 5
Kenora 70-71 S 8
Kenosha, WI 72-73 J 3
Kenova, WV 74-75 B 5
Kent 32 G 6
Kent, OH 74-75 C 4
Kent, OR 76-77 C 3
Kent, WA 76-77 B 2
Kentau 42-43 M 9
Kent Group 58 cd 1
Kent Peninsula 70-71 P 4
Kentucky 72-73 JK 4
Kentucky Lake 72-73 J 4
Kenya 64-65 JK 2
Kenya, Mount – 64-65 J 2-3
Keokuk, IA 72-73 H 3
Kepce Dağları 46-47 K 4
Kępno 33 J 3
Keppel Bay 56-57 K 4
Kepsut 46-47 C 3
Kerala 44-45 M 8-9
Kerang 56-57 H 7
Kerasûs = Giresun 44-45 D 2
Kerava 30-31 L 7
Kerbi = Poliny-Osipenko 42-43 a 7
Kerby, OR 76-77 B 4
Kerč 38-39 G 6
Kerčel 38-39 M 4
Kerčenskij proliv 38-39 G 6-7
Kerema 52-53 N 8
Kerempe Burnu 46-47 E 1
Keren 60-61 M 5
Kerga 38-39 J 3
Kerguelen 22-23 N 8
Kerguelen, Grande Dorsale des – 22-23 N 8-J 9
Kerguelen, Plataforma de las – 22-23 N 8-J 9
Kerguelen-Gaussberg Ridge 22-23 N 8-J 9
Kerguelen-Gaussbergrug 22-23 N 8-J 9
Kericho 63 C 3
Kerinci, Gunung – 52-53 D 7
Kerio 63 D 2
Keriske 42-43 Z 4
Keriya 48-49 E 4
Keriya Darya 48-49 E 4
Kerkenna, Îles – = Arkhbīl Qarqannah 60-61 G 2
Kerki 44-45 K 3
Kérkyra [GR, ⊙] 36-37 H 6
Kérkyra [GR, ●] 36-37 H 6
Kerling 30-31 de 2
Kerlingarfjöll 30-31 d 2
Kerma = Karmah 60-61 L 5
Kermadec, Fosse des – 56-57 Q 6-7
Kermadec, Îles – 56-57 PQ 6
Kermadec Islands 56-57 PQ 6
Kermadec-Tonga, Fosa de – 56-57 Q 6-7
Kermadec-Tonga, Fosse de – 22-23 T 6-7
Kermadec Tonga Trench 22-23 T 6-7
Kermadec Tongatrog 22-23 T 6-7
Kermadec Trench 56-57 Q 6-7
Kermadectrog 56-57 Q 6-7
Kermān 44-45 H 4
Kerman, CA 76-77 CD 7
Kermānshāh = Bākhtarān 44-45 F 4
Kermānshāhān = 1 ◁ 44-45 F 4
Kerme Körfezi 46-47 B 4
Kern River 76-77 D 8
Kernville, CA 76-77 D 8
Kérouané 60-61 C 7
Kershaw, SC 74-75 C 7
Kerulen = Cherlen gol 48-49 L 2
Keşan 46-47 B 2
Kesânê = Keşan 46-47 B 2
Keşap 46-47 H 2
Kesennuma 50-51 NO 3
Keshan 48-49 O 2
Keshvar, Īstgāh-e – 46-47 N 6
Keskin 46-47 E 3
Keski-Suomen lääni 30-31 L 6
Kestenga 30-31 OP 5
Kesten'ga 42-43 E 4
Keszthely 33 H 5
Ket' 42-43 P 6
Keta 60-61 E 7
Keta, ozero – 42-43 QR 4
Ketapang [RI, Kalimantan] 52-53 EF 7
Ketchikan, AK 70-71 K 6
Ketchum, ID 76-77 F 4
Kete Krachi 60-61 DE 7
Kętrzyn 33 K 1-2
Kettharin Kyûn 52-53 C 4
Kettle Falls, WA 76-77 DE 1
Kettle River Range 76-77 D 1
Ketumbaine 63 D 3
Keulen = Köln 33 C 3
Kevin, MT 76-77 H 1
Kevir = Dasht-e Kavīr 44-45 GH 4
Keweenaw Peninsula 72-73 J 2
Kewir = Dasht-e Kavīr 44-45 GH 4
Kexholm = Prioz'orsk 42-43 DE 5
Key Largo 74-75 cd 4
Key Largo, FL 74-75 c 4
Keyser, WV 74-75 D 5
Keysville, VA 74-75 D 6
Keytū 46-47 N 5
Key West, FL 72-73 K 7
Kežma 42-43 T 6
Kežmarok 33 K 4
Khaanzuur, Raas – = Raas Khansiir 60-61 ab 1
Khabīr, Zāb al- = Zāb al-Kabīr 46-47 K 4
Khabra Najid = Habrat Najid 46-47 K 7
Khābūr, Nahr al- 44-45 E 3
Khābūrah, Al- 44-45 H 6
Khādim, Shūshat al- 62 B 3
Khāf, Rūd – = Khvāf 44-45 J 4
Khaibar = Shurayf 44-45 D 5
Khairabad 44-45 N 5
Khakass Autonomous Region = 10 ◁ 42-43 R 7
Khakassie, Région Autonome des – = 10 ◁ 42-43 R 7
Khalafābād 46-47 N 7
Khâlda, Bîr – = Bi'r Hālidah 46-47 B 7
Khalīj as-Sintirā', Al- 60-61 A 4
Khalīj-e Fārs, Banāder va Jazāyer-e – = 5 ◁ 44-45 G 5
Khalîl, El- = Al-Halīl 46-47 F 7
Khaliq tau 48-49 E 3
Khāliş, Al- 46-47 L 6
Khalkhāl 46-47 N 4
Khalūf, Al- 44-45 H 6
Kham 48-49 H 5
Khamāsīn, Al- 44-45 EF 6
Khambat = Khambhat 44-45 L 6
Khambhat 44-45 L 6
Khambhāt nī Khāḍī = Gulf of Cambay 44-45 L 6
Khamir 44-45 E 7
Khāmis, Al-Jandal al- 60-61 L 5
Khampa Dsong 48-49 F 6
Khamsa, Bîr el- = Bi'r al-Khamsah 60-61 K 2
Khamsah, Bi'r al- 60-61 K 2
Khān al-Baghdādī 46-47 K 6
Khānaqīn = Khāniqīn 46-47 L 5
Khān az-Zabīb 46-47 G 7
Khandaq, Al- 60-61 KL 5
Khandaq, El- = Al-Khandaq 60-61 KL 5
Khaṇḍavā = Khandwa 44-45 M 6
Khandwa 44-45 M 6
Khan ez Zābib = Khān az-Zabīb 46-47 G 7
Khangai = Changajn nuruu 48-49 HJ 2
Khāniqīn 44-45 F 4
Khānpūr [PAK, Sindh] 44-45 KL 5
Khanshalah 60-61 F 1
Khansiir, Raas – 60-61 ab 1
Khantan = Kuantan 52-53 D 6
Khanty-Mansi Autonomous Area 42-43 L-P 5
Khanty-Mansis, District National des – 42-43 L-P 5
Khān Yūnūs 62 EF 2
Khanzi 64-65 F 7
Khanzi = Ghanzi 64-65 F 7
Khānzūr, Ras – = Raas Khaanzuur 60-61 ab 1
Kharāb, Al- 44-45 EF 7
Kharagpur [IND, West Bengal] 44-45 O 6
Kharan Kalat = Khārān Qalāt 44-45 K 5
Khārān Qalāt 44-45 K 5
Kharaz, Jabal – 44-45 E 8
Kharbin = Harbin 48-49 O 2
Khârga, El- = Al-Khārijah 60-61 L 3
Khârga, Wâḥât el- = Al-Wāḥāt al-Khārijah 60-61 KL 3-4
Kharīfūt 44-45 G 7
Khārijah, Al- 60-61 L 3
Khārijah, Al-Wāḥāt al- 60-61 KL 3-4
Kharīṭ, Wādī al- 62 EF 5
Kharîṭ, Wâdî el- = Wādī al-Kharīṭ 62 EF 5
Kharj, Al- 44-45 F 6
Khārk, Jazīreh-ye – 44-45 FG 5
Kharkheh, Rūd-e – 46-47 M 6
Kharkov = Char'kov 38-39 G 5-6
Khar Rūd 46-47 N 5
Khartoem = Al-Khartūm 60-61 L 5
Khartoum = Al-Khartūm 60-61 L 5
Kharṭūm, Al- 60-61 L 5
Khartūm Baḥrī, Al- 60-61 L 5
Kharṭūm Baḥrī, El- = Al-Kharṭūm Baḥrī 60-61 L 5
Khaṣab, Al- 44-45 H 5
Khashm al-Qirbah 60-61 LM 6
Khāsh Rōd 44-45 J 4
Khaṭâṭba, El- = Al-Haṭāṭibah 62 D 2
Khaṭṭ, Wād al- 60-61 B 3
Khawr al-Amaīyah 46-47 N 8
Khawr al-Fakkān 44-45 H 5
Khawr Rūrī 44-45 G 7
Khay' 44-45 E 7
Khaybar, Ḥarrat – 44-45 DE 5
Kḥāybar, Kotal – 44-45 L 4
Khayrpūr [PAK, Punjab] 44-45 K 5
Khazhung Tsho 48-49 F 5
Khāzir, Nahr al- 46-47 K 4
Khazir Su = Nahr al-Khāzir 46-47 K 4
Khechmâ = Al-Bogham 46-47 J 5
Khedir, Al- = Khiḍr Dardash 46-47 L 7
Khemarat 52-53 DE 3
Khem Belder = Kyzyl 42-43 R 7
Khenachich, El – 60-61 D 4
Khenchela = Khanshalah 60-61 F 1
Khentei Nuruu = Chentin nuruu 48-49 K 2
Khiḍr Dardash 46-47 L 7
Khīrābād = Khairabad 44-45 N 5
Khirr, Wādī al- 44-45 E 4
Khnâchich, El – 60-61 D 4
Khobdo = Chovd 48-49 G 2
Khobso Gol = Chövsgöl nuur 48-49 J 1
Khökh Nuur = Chöch nuur 48-49 H 4
Khomām 46-47 NO 4
Khomas Highland = Khomasplato 64-65 E 7
Khomasplato 64-65 E 7
Khomeyn 46-47 NO 6
Khondāb 46-47 N 5
Khong, Mae Nam – 52-53 D 3
Khong Sedone = Muang Khôngxédon 52-53 E 3
Khon Kaen 52-53 D 3
Khor 38-39 L 9
Khorāsān 44-45 H 3-4
Khorāsān, Kavīre – = Dasht-e Kavīr 44-45 GH 4
Khorat = Nakhon Ratchasima 52-53 D 3-4
Khōrmāl = Hūrmāl 46-47 LM 5
Khorramābād [IR, Lorestān] 44-45 FG 4
Khorramābād [IR, Māzandarān] 46-47 O 4
Khorramshahr 44-45 F 4
Khorsabad 46-47 K 4
Khosrovī 46-47 L 5
Khosrowābād [IR, Hamadān] 46-47 N 5
Khosrowābād [IR, Kordestan] 46-47 M 5
Khotan 48-49 DE 4
Khotan darya 48-49 E 3-4
Khourîbga = Khurībqah 60-61 C 2
Khowst 44-45 KL 4
Khuẓdar 44-45 K 5
Khuff 44-45 E 6
Khükhe Noor = Chöch nuur 48-49 H 4
Khums, Al- 60-61 GH 2
Khurasan = Khorāsān 44-45 H 3-4
Khurayş 44-45 F 5
Khurībqah 60-61 C 2
Khūriyā Mūriyā, Jazā'ir – 44-45 H 7
Khurmah, Al- 44-45 E 6
Khūrmāl 46-47 LM 5
Khurr, Wādī al- = Wādī al-Khirr 46-47 K 7
Khushāb 44-45 L 4
Khūzestān 44-45 F 4
Khvāf 44-45 J 4
Khvoy 44-45 EF 3
Khwāf = Khvāf 44-45 J 4
Khyber Pass = Kotal Kḥāybar 44-45 L 4
Khyetentshering 48-49 G 5
Kiabakari 63 C 3
Kiama 58 K 5
Kiambi 64-65 G 4
Kiamusze = Jiamusi 48-49 P 2
Kian = Ji'an 48-49 LM 6
Kiangning = Nanjing 48-49 M 5
Kiangsi = Jiangxi 48-49 LM 6
Kiangsu = Jiangsu 48-49 MN 5
Kiantajärvi 30-31 N 5
Kiaohsien = Jiao Xian 48-49 M 4
Kiawah Island 74-75 CD 8
Kiayukwan = Jiuquan 48-49 H 4
Kibaha = Bagamoyo 64-65 J 4
Kibale 63 B 2
Kibali 64-65 GH 2
Kibamba 64-65 G 3
Kibangou 64-65 D 3
Kibau 64-65 HJ 4
Kibaya 64-65 J 4
Kiberashi 63 D 4
Kiberege 64-65 J 4
Kibiti 63 D 4
Kiboko 63 D 3
Kibombo 64-65 G 3
Kibondo 64-65 H 3
Kıbrıscık 46-47 DE 2
Kibungu 64-65 H 3
Kibuye 63 AB 5
Kibwezi 64-65 J 3
Kičevo 36-37 J 5
Kichčik 42-43 de 7
Kicking Horse Pass 70-71 NO 7
Kidal 60-61 E 5
Kidatu 64-65 J 4
Kidepo National Park 64-65 H 2
Kidete 63 D 4
Kidira 60-61 B 6
Kidston 56-57 H 3
Kiel 33 E 1
Kielce 33 K 3
Kieler Bucht 33 E 1
Kiên Hung = Go Quao 52-53 DE 5
Kienning = Jian'ou 48-49 M 6
Kienshui = Jianshui 48-49 J 7
Kierunavaara 30-31 J 4
Kiestinki = Kesten'ga 42-43 E 4
Kieta 52-53 j 6
Kiev = Kijev 38-39 F 5
Kiëv = Kijev 38-39 F 5
Kīfah 60-61 B 5
Kiffa = Kīfah 60-61 B 5
Kifl, Al- 46-47 L 6
Kifrī 46-47 L 5
Kigali 64-65 GH 3
Kiganga 63 C 4
Kiği 46-47 J 3
Kigoma 64-65 G 3
Kigosi 63 B 3
Kıgzı = Gürpınar 46-47 K 3
Kiha = Kwiha 60-61 MN 6
Kihelkonna 30-31 JK 8
Kihindi 63 D 5
Kihnu 30-31 K 8
Kihowera 63 D 5
Kihti = Skiftet 30-31 J 7
Kihurio 63 D 4
Kii hantō 48-49 Q 5
Kii sammyaku 50-51 KL 5-6
Kii-suidō 48-49 PQ 5
Kijang 50-51 G 5
Kijev 38-39 F 5
Kijevka [SU, Kazachskaja SSSR] 42-43 N 7
Kijevka [SU, Rossijskaja SFSR] 50-51 J 1
Kijevskoje vodochranilišče 38-39 F 5
Kikinda 36-37 J 3
Kikombo 63 CD 4
Kikonai 50-51 B 3
Kikori 52-53 M 8
Kikwit 64-65 E 4
Kil 30-31 E 8
Kilauea Crater 52-53 ef 4
Kilbuck Mountains 70-71 E 5-D 6
Kilchu 50-51 G 2
Kilcoy 56-57 K 5
Kil'din 38-39 FG 2
Kildinstroj 30-31 PQ 3
Kildonan 64-65 H 6
Kilembe 63 B 2
Kilgore, ID 76-77 GH 3
Kilifi 64-65 JK 3
Kilija 36-37 N 3
Kilimanjaro [EAT, ▲] 64-65 J 3
Kilimanjaro [EAT, ☆] 64-65 J 3
Kilimatinde 64-65 HJ 4
Kilin = Jilin 48-49 N 2-O 3
Kilis 46-47 G 4
Kilkee 32 AB 5
Kilkenny 32 C 5
Kilkis 36-37 K 5
Killarney 32 B 5
Killarney 58 L 2
Killiecrankie Pass 32 E 3
Killin 32 D 3
Killinek Island 70-71 Y 5
Killington Peak 74-75 G 3
Killybegs 32 B 4
Kilmarnock 32 DE 4
Kil'mez 38-39 K 4
Kilmore 58 G 6
Kilo 63 B 2
Kilombero 64-65 J 4
Ki-long = Chilung 48-49 N 6
Kilosa 64-65 J 4
Kilossa = Kilosa 64-65 J 4
Kilpisjärvi 30-31 J 3
Kilrea 32 C 4
Kilrush 32 B 5
Kiltān Island 44-45 L 8
Kilwa 64-65 G 4
Kilwa, Khirbat – 46-47 G 8
Kilwa Kisiwani 64-65 JK 4
Kilwa-Kissiwni = Kilwa Kisiwani 64-65 JK 4
Kilwa Kivinje 64-65 JK 4
Kilwa-Kiwindje = Kilwa Kivinje 64-65 JK 4
Kimaam 52-53 L 8
Kimali 63 C 3
Kimama, ID 76-77 G 4
Kimasozero 30-31 O 5
Kimba 58 C 4
Kimbe 52-53 gh 6
Kimbe Bay 52-53 h 6
Kimberley [AUS] 56-57 E 3
Kimberley [CDN] 76-77 EF 1
Kimberley [ZA] 64-65 FG 8
Kimberly, NV 76-77 F 6
Kimchaek 48-49 OP 3
Kimch'ŏn 48-49 O 4
Kimhandu 63 D 4
Kimje 50-51 F 5
Kimkang = Chengmai 48-49 KL 8
Kimōlos 36-37 L 7
Kimpoku san 50-51 LM 3
Kimry 42-43 F 6
Kimuenza 64-65 E 3
Kinabalu, Gunung – 52-53 G 5
Kinchinjunga = Gangchhendsönga 44-45 O 5
Kindersley 70-71 P 7
Kindia 60-61 B 6
Kindu 64-65 G 3
Kinel' 42-43 J 7
Kinešma 42-43 G 6
King and Queen Court House, VA 74-75 E 6
Kingchow = Jiangling 48-49 L 5
Kingchwan = Jingchuan 48-49 K 4
King City, CA 76-77 C 7
King Edward VIIIth Gulf 24 C 6-7
King George Vth Land 24 BC 15-16
King George VIth Sound 24 B 29-30
King George Island 24 CD 30-31
King George Sound 56-57 CD 7
King Hill, ID 76-77 F 4
Kingisepp [SU, Luga] 30-31 N 8
Kingisepp [SU, Saaremaa] 30-31 K 8
King Island [AUS] 56-57 H 7
Kingku = Jinggu 48-49 J 7
King Lear 76-77 D 5
King Leopold Ranges 56-57 DE 3
Kingman, AZ 76-77 FG 8
King Mountain [USA, Oregon] 76-77 D 4
Kingoonya 56-57 G 6
King Oscar Land 70-71 TU 2
Kings Canyon National Park 76-77 D 7
Kingscote 56-57 G 7
Kingscourt 32 C 5
Kingsland, GA 74-75 C 9
King's Lynn 32 FG 5
Kings Mountain, NC 74-75 C 7
King Sound 56-57 D 3
Kings Peaks 72-73 DE 3
Kingsport, TN 74-75 B 6
Kings River 76-77 CD 7
Kingston [CDN] 70-71 Y 9
Kingston [JA] 72-73 L 8
Kingston [NZ] 56-57 N 9
Kingston, NY 74-75 FG 4
Kingston, PA 74-75 EF 4
Kingston, WA 76-77 B 2
Kingston Peak 76-77 EF 8
Kingston SE 56-57 G 7
Kingston upon Hull 32 FG 5
Kingstown 72-73 O 9
Kingstown [IRL] 32 CD 5
Kingstree, SC 74-75 D 8
Kingsville, TX 72-73 G 6
King William Island 70-71 R 4
King William's Town 64-65 G 9
Kingwood, WV 74-75 D 5
Kingyang = Qingyang 48-49 K 4
Kingyuan = Yishan 48-49 K 7
Kinhwa = Jinhua 48-49 MN 6
Kınık 46-47 B 3
Kinkala 64-65 D 3

Kinka 189

Kinkazan tō 50-51 NO 3
Kinmen Dao = Chin-mên Tao 48-49 M 7
Kinmount 74-75 D 2
Kinnaird's Head 32 F 3
Kinneret, Yam – 44-45 D 4
Kino kawa 50-51 K 5
Kinomoto = Kumano 50-51 L 6
Kinosaki 50-51 K 5
Kinross 32 E 3
Kinsale 32 B 6
Kinshasa 64-65 E 3
Kinsien = Jin Xian 48-49 N 4
Kinston, NC 72-73 L 4
Kintampo 60-61 D 7
Kin-tcheou = Jinzhou 48-49 N 3
Kintinku 63 C 4
Kintop 52-53 G 7
Kintyre 32 D 4
Kinyangiri 63 C 4
Kinyatī 63 C 1
Kioesjoedrempel 48-49 P 6-Q 7
Kios = Gemlik 46-47 C 2
Kioshan = Queshan 48-49 L 5
Kioto = Kyōto 48-49 PQ 4
Kipembawe 64-65 H 4
Kipengere 63 C 5
Kipeta 63 B 5
Kipili 64-65 H 4
Kipini 64-65 K 3
Kiptopeke, VA 74-75 F 6
Kipushi 64-65 G 5
Kirakira 52-53 k 7
Kiraz 46-47 C 3
Kırbaşı 46-47 DE 2-3
Kirenga 42-43 U 6
Kirensk 42-43 U 6
Kirghizie 44-45 LM 2
Kirgiezië 44-45 LM 2
Kirgis Nor = Chjargas nuur 48-49 GH 2
Kirgizia 44-45 LM 2
Kirgiz Kizilsu Zizhizhou 48-49 CD 3-4
Kirgizskij chrebet 44-45 LM 2
Kirguizistán 44-45 LM 2
Kiri 64-65 E 3
Kiribati 20-21 S 6
Kiridh 60-61 b 2
Kırık 46-47 J 2
Kırıkhan 46-47 G 4
Kırıkkale 44-45 C 2-3
Kirillov 42-43 F 6
Kirin = Jilin [TJ, ●] 48-49 O 3
Kirin = Jilin [TJ, ☆] 48-49 N 2-O 3
Kirin-do 50-51 E 4
Kirishima-yama 50-51 H 7
Kirit = Jiriid 60-61 O 7
Kiriwina Islands = Trobriand Islands 52-53 h 6
Kırka 46-47 D 3
Kırkağaç 46-47 BC 3
Kirkcaldy 32 E 3
Kirkcudbright 32 DE 4
Kirkenes 30-31 O 3
Kırkgeçit = Kasrık 46-47 K 3
Kirkjuból 30-31 g 2
Kirkland, WA 76-77 BC 2
Kirkland Lake 70-71 U 8
Kırklareli 44-45 B 2
Kirksville, MO 72-73 H 3
Kirkūk 44-45 EF 3
Kirkwall 32 E 2
Kirkwood 64-65 FG 9
Kirlangıç burnu = Gelıdonya burnu 46-47 D 4
Kirman = Kermān 44-45 H 4
Kirmir Çayı 46-47 E 2
Kırobası 46-47 EF 4
Kirongwe 63 DE 4
Kirov [SU ↑ Br'ansk] 38-39 F 5
Kirov = Vjatka 42-43 HJ 6
Kirovabad 38-39 J 7
Kirovakan 38-39 HJ 7
Kirovograd 38-39 F 6
Kirovsk [SU, Rossijskaja SFSR Murmansk] 42-43 EF 4
Kirovskij [SU, Kazachskaja SSR] 42-43 O 9
Kirovskij [SU, Rossijskaja SFSR ↖ Petropavlovsk-Kamčatskij] 42-43 de 7
Kirs 42-43 J 6
Kırşehir 44-45 C 3
Kīrthar, Koh – 44-45 K 5
Kirthar Range = Koh Kīrthar 44-45 K 5
Kirtland, NM 76-77 J 7
Kiruna 30-31 HJ 4
Kiruru 52-53 KL 7
Kiryū 50-51 M 4
Kisa 30-31 F 8-9
Kisabi 63 B 4-5
Kisakata 50-51 M 3
Kisaki 63 D 4
Kisale, Lac – 64-65 G 4
Kisangani 64-65 G 2
Kisangire 64-65 J 4
Kisar, Pulau – 52-53 J 8
Kisarawe 64-65 J 4
Kisarazu 50-51 MN 5
Kisel'ovsk 42-43 Q 7
Kisen = Hŭich'ŏn 48-49 O 3
Kisengwa 64-65 G 4
Kisenyi = Gisenyi 64-65 G 3
Kish 46-47 L 6
Kīsh, Jazīreh-ye – 44-45 G 5
Kishb, Ḥarrat al- 44-45 E 6
Kishiwada 50-51 K 5
Kishm = Qeshm [IR, ≅] 44-45 H 5
Kishm = Qeshm [IR, ●] 44-45 H 5
Kisigo 63 C 4
Kisii 64-65 H 3
Kisiju 63 D 4
Kišin'ov 38-39 E 6
Kısır Dağı 46-47 K 2
Kiska Island 19 D 1
Kiskunfélegyháza 33 JK 5
Kiskunhalas 33 J 5
Kislovodsk 38-39 H 7
Kismaanyo 64-65 K 3
Kismayu = Kismaanyo 64-65 K 3
Kiso gawa 50-51 L 5
Kiso sammyaku 50-51 L 5
Kisreka 30-31 O 5
Kissangire = Kisangire 64-65 J 4
Kissaraing Island = Kettharin Kyûn 52-53 C 4
Kissenje = Gisenyi 64-65 G 3
Kissenji = Gisenyi 64-65 G 3
Kisserawe = Kisarawe 64-65 J 4
Kissidougou 60-61 BC 7
Kissimmee, FL 74-75 c 2
Kissimmee, Lake – 74-75 c 2-3
Kissimmee River 74-75 c 3
Kistna = Krishna 44-45 M 7
Kistufell 30-31 f 2
Kisumu 64-65 HJ 3
Kisvárda 33 KL 4
Kiswere 63 D 5
Kita 60-61 C 6
Kita Daitō-jima 48-49 P 6
Kita-Daitō zima = Kita-Daitō-jima 48-49 P 6
Kitagō 50-51 H 7
Kitai = Qitai 48-49 FG 3
Kita-Ibaraki 50-51 N 4
Kitakami 50-51 N 3
Kitakami gawa 48-49 R 4
Kitakami kōti 50-51 N 2-3
Kitakata 50-51 MN 4
Kita-Kyūshū 48-49 OP 5
Kita-Kyûsyû = Kita-Kyūshū 48-49 OP 5
Kitale 64-65 J 2
Kitami 48-49 R 3
Kita ura 50-51 N 4
Kitčan 42-43 Y 5
Kitchener 70-71 U 9
Kitee 30-31 O 6
Kitega = Gitega 64-65 GH 3
Kitendwe 63 B 4
Kitengela Game Reserve 63 D 3
Kitgum 64-65 H 2
Kitimat 70-71 L 7
Kitimeot, District of – 70-71 N-S 4
Kitinen 30-31 LM 3
Kitsuki 50-51 H 6
Kittanning, PA 74-75 D 4
Kittery, ME 74-75 H 3
Kitthareng = Kettharin Kyûn 52-53 C 4
Kittilä 30-31 L 4
Kitty Hawk, NC 74-75 F 6
Kitu 63 A 4
Kitui 64-65 J 3
Kituku 63 B 4
Kitumbini 63 DE 5
Kitunda 64-65 H 4
Kitwe 64-65 G 5
Kitzbühel 33 EF 5
Kitzingen 33 E 4
Kiuchuan = Jiuquan 48-49 H 4
Kiukiang = Jiujiang 48-49 M 6
Kiunga 52-53 M 8
Kiung-chow = Qiongshan 48-49 L 8
Kiungchow Hai-hsia = Qiongzhou Haixia 48-49 KL 7
Kiuruvesi 30-31 M 6
Kiushiu = Kyūshū 48-49 P 5
Kiu-Shu, Dorsal de – 48-49 P 6-Q 7
Kivalo 30-31 L 5-M 4
Kivu 64-65 G 3
Kivu, Lac – 64-65 G 3
Kiyāt = Khay' 44-45 E 7
Kıyıköy 46-47 C 2
Kizel 42-43 K 6
Kizema 38-39 HJ 3
Kiziba 63 C 2
Kızılcahamam 46-47 E 2
Kızılçakcak = Akkaya 46-47 K 2
Kızılırmak [TR, ~] 44-45 D 3
Kızılırmak [TR, ●] 46-47 EF 2
Kızılkoca = Şefaatli 46-47 F 3
Kizilsu Kirgiz Zizhizhou 48-49 C 4-D 3
Kızıltepe 46-47 J 4
Kızılveran = Uğurludağ 46-47 F 2
Kızılyaka 46-47 E 4
Kizl'ar 38-39 J 7
Kizl'arskij zaliv 38-39 J 7
Kızören 46-47 E 3
Kizyl-Arvat 44-45 H 3
Kizyl-Atrek 44-45 G 3
Kjækan 30-31 K 3
Kjerringøy 30-31 EF 4
Kjøllefjord 30-31 MN 2
Kjøpsvik 30-31 G 3
Kladno 33 FG 3
Kladovo 36-37 K 3
Klagenfurt 33 G 5
Klaipėda 30-31 J 10
Klamath, CA 76-77 A 5
Klamath Falls, OR 72-73 B 3
Klamath Mountains 72-73 B 3
Klamath River 72-73 B 3
Klamono 52-53 K 7
Klapper = Pulau Deli 52-53 DE 8
Klarälven 30-31 E 7
Klatovy 33 F 4
Klaver = Klawer 64-65 E 9
Klawer 64-65 E 9
Klay = Bomi Hills 60-61 B 7
Kl'az'ma 38-39 H 4
Kleine Antillen 72-73 N 9-O 8
Kleine Nefud = Ad-Dahnā' 44-45 E 5-F 6
Kleine Paternosterinseln = Kepulauan Balabalangan 52-53 G 7
Kleiner Khingan = Xiao Hinggan Ling 48-49 O 1-2
Kleiner Sklavensee 70-71 NO 6
Kleine Sunda-Eilanden 52-53 GH 8
Kleine Sundainseln 52-53 GH 8
Klein-Karoo 64-65 F 9
Klerksdorp 64-65 G 8
Kleve 33 BC 3
Klickitat, WA 76-77 C 3
Klickitat River 76-77 C 2-3
Klin 42-43 F 6
Klincy 38-39 F 5
Klinovec 33 F 3
Klintehamn 30-31 GH 9
Klippan 30-31 E 9
Kłodzko 33 H 3
Klondike 70-71 HJ 5
Klong, Mae – = Mae Nam Khong 52-53 D 3
Klosterneuburg 33 GH 4
Kluane Lake 70-71 J 5
Kluane National Park 70-71 HJ 5
Kl'učevskaja sopka = Velikaja Kl'učevskaja sopka 42-43 f 6
Kl'učevskaja Sopka, vulkan – 42-43 f 6
Kl'uči 42-43 f 6
Kluczbork 33 HJ 3
Kmeit = Al-Kumayt 46-47 M 6
Knabengruver 30-31 B 8
Kneža 36-37 L 4
Knin 36-37 FG 3
Knjaževac 36-37 K 4
Knob Lake = Schefferville 70-71 X 7
Knolls, UT 76-77 G 5
Knōssós 36-37 L 8
Knowles, Cape – 24 B 30-31
Knox Land 24 C 11
Knoxville, TN 72-73 K 4
Knud Rasmussen Land 19 B 25-A 21
Knysna 64-65 F 9
Ko, gora – 42-43 a 8
Kob'aj 42-43 Y 5
Kobayashi 50-51 H 6-7
Kobdo = Chovd 48-49 G 2
Kōbe 48-49 PQ 5
København 30-31 DE 10
Kobin = Beşiri 46-47 J 4
Koblenz 33 C 3
Kobo 60-61 MN 6
Kobrin 38-39 D 5
Kobroor, Pulau – 52-53 KL 8
Kobrur = Pulau Kobroor 52-53 KL 8
Kobuk River 70-71 E 4
Koca Çay 46-47 C 3
Kocaeli 44-45 C 4
Koca ırmak 46-47 E 2
Kočani 36-37 K 5
Kocapinar = Ömerin 46-47 JK 4
Koçarlı 46-47 B 4
Kočečum 42-43 ST 4
Kočevje 36-37 F 3
Kōch'ang 50-51 F 5
Kochchi-Kaṇayannūr = Cochin 44-45 M 9
Kōchi 48-49 P 5
Koch Island 70-71 V 4
Ko-chiu = Gejiu 48-49 J 7
Kochow = Maoming 48-49 L 7
Koch Peak 76-77 H 3
Kochtel = Kohtla 42-43 D 6
Kočki 42-43 P 7
Kodiak, AK 70-71 F 6
Kodiak Island 70-71 F 6
Kōdikkarai Antarīp = Point Calimere 44-45 MN 8
Kodima 38-39 H 3
Kodino 42-43 F 5
Kodōk = Kūdūk 60-61 L 6-7
Kodomari-misaki 50-51 MN 2
Koefra oasen = Wāḥāt al -Kufrah 60-61 J 4
Koerilen 48-49 S 3-T 2
Koerilentrog 19 D 2-E 3
Koerland 30-31 JK 9
Koes 64-65 E 8
Koesan 50-51 FG 4
Koettlitz Glacier 24 B 15-16
Koeweit 44-45 F 5
Kofa Mountains 76-77 FG 9
Kofiau, Pulau – 52-53 JK 7
Koforidua = Karimana 60-61 DE 7
Kōfu 48-49 Q 4
Koga 50-51 M 4
Kogane-saki = Henashi-saki 50-51 M 2
Køge 30-31 DE 10
Kōgen-dō = Kangwŏn-do 50-51 F 3-G 4
Kogilnik 36-37 N 2
Kogota 50-51 N 3
Kōgūm-do 50-51 F 5
Kogunsan-kundo 50-51 EF 5
Kohāṭ 44-45 L 4
Kohima 44-45 P 5
Koh Kong 52-53 D 4
Kohler Range 24 B 25
Kohtla-Järve 30-31 M 8
Kohtla-Järve 42-43 D 6
Kōhu = Kōfu 48-49 Q 4
Koide 50-51 M 4
Koidu 60-61 B 7
Koidu-Sefadu 60-61 B 7
Kōisanjaq = Kūysanjaq 46-47 L 4
Koitere 30-31 O 6
Kōje 50-51 G 5
Kōje-do 50-51 G 5
Kojgorodok 42-43 HJ 5
Kojp, gora – 38-39 L 3
Kōkai = Kanggye 48-49 O 3
Kōkai-hokudō = Hwanghae-pukto 50-51 EF 3
Kōkai-nandō = Hwanghae-namdo 50-51 E 3-4
Kokand 44-45 L 2-3
Kokaral, ostrov – 42-43 L 8
Kokatha 58 B 3
Kokčetav 42-43 MN 7
Kōk-dong = Irhyang-dong 50-51 GH 2
Kokemäenjoki 30-31 JK 7
Kokenau 52-53 L 7
Kokiu = Gejiu 48-49 J 7
Kok-Jangak 44-45 L 2
Kokkola 30-31 K 6
Koknese 30-31 L 9
Kokoda 52-53 N 8
Kōkō Kyûn 52-53 B 4
Kokomo, IN 72-73 JK 3
Koko Noor = Chöch nuur 48-49 H 4
Kokonselkä 30-31 N 7
Kokpekty 42-43 P 8
Kokšaal-Tau, chrebet – = chrebet Kakšaal-Too 44-45 M 2
Koksan 50-51 F 3
Koks Bazar 44-45 P 6
Kök shal 48-49 D 3
Koksoak, Rivière – 70-71 X 6
Koksŏng 50-51 F 5
Kōk Tappa = Gūk Tappah 46-47 L 5
Kokubo = Kokubu 50-51 H 7
Kokubu 50-51 H 7
Kōl = Aligarh 44-45 M 5
Kola [SU, ~] 30-31 P 3
Kola [SU, ●] 42-43 E 4
Kola, Pulau – 52-53 KL 8
Kolaka 52-53 H 7
Koḷamba 44-45 MN 9
Kolanjīn = Kulanjīn 46-47 N 5
Kolar 44-45 M 8
Kolar Gold Fields 44-45 M 8
Kolari 30-31 KL 4
Kōlāru = Kolar 44-45 M 8
Kolašin 36-37 H 4
Kolbio 64-65 K 3
Kolbuszowa 33 KL 3
Kol'čugino = Leninsk-Kuzneckij 42-43 Q 6-7
Kolda 60-61 B 6
Kolding 30-31 C 10
Kole 64-65 F 3
Kolepom, Pulau – = Pulau Yos Sudarsa 52-53 L 8
Kolgujev, ostrov – 42-43 GH 4
Kolhapur 44-45 L 7
Koli 30-31 N 6
Kolin 33 G 3-4
Kolkasrags 30-31 K 9
Kōllam = Quilon 44-45 M 9
Kollumúli 30-31 fg 2
Köln 33 C 3
Kolno 33 K 2
Koło 33 J 2
Kołobrzeg 33 GH 1
Kologriv 42-43 G 6
Kolokani 60-61 C 6
Kolombangara 52-53 j 6
Kolombo = Koḷamba 44-45 MN 9
Kolomna 38-39 GH 4
Kolonedale 52-53 H 7
Kolosovka 42-43 N 6
Kolossia 63 CD 2
Kolpaševo 42-43 P 6
Kol'skij poluostrov 42-43 EF 4
Kölük = Kâhta 46-47 H 4
Kolwezi 64-65 FG 5
Kolyma 42-43 de 4
Kolymskaja nizmennost' 42-43 de 4
Kolymskoje nagorje 42-43 e 4-f 5
Kom 36-37 K 4
Komadugu Gana 60-61 G 6
Komadugu Yobe 60-61 G 6
Komaga-dake 50-51 b 2
Komagane 50-51 LM 5
Komaga take 50-51 M 4
K'o-mai = Kemä 48-49 H 6
Komandorskije ostrova 42-43 f 6-g 7
Komárom 33 J 5
Komatipoort 64-65 H 8
Komatsu 50-51 L 4
Komatsujima = Komatsushima 50-51 K 5-6
Komatsushima 50-51 K 5-6
Kombol = Kombot 52-53 H 6
Kombolcha = Kembolcha 60-61 MN 6
Kombot 52-53 H 6
Kome [EAT] 63 C 3
Kome [EAU] 63 C 3
Komi, República Autónoma de los – 42-43 JK 5
Komi Autonome Republiek 42-43 JK 5
Komi Autonomous Republic 42-43 JK 5
Komilla 44-45 P 6
Kominternovskoje 36-37 O 2
Komi-Permjaken, Nationaal Gebied der – = 1 ◁ 42-43 J 6
Komi-Permyak Autonomous Area = 1 ◁ 42-43 J 6
Komis, République Autonome des – 42-43 JK 5
Komis-Permiaks, District National des – = 1 ◁ 42-43 J 6
Komi y los Permiacos, Circunscripción Nacional de los – = 1 ◁ 42-43 J 6
Kommunarsk 38-39 GH 6
Kommunizma, pik – 44-45 L 3
Komodo, Pulau – 52-53 G 8
Komoé 60-61 D 7
Kôm Ombō = Kawm Umbū 60-61 L 4
Komono 64-65 D 3
Komoran, Pulau – 52-53 L 8
Komorenbekken 64-65 L 5
Komoro 50-51 M 4
Komotēnē 36-37 L 5
Kompong Cham 52-53 E 4
Kompong Chhnang 52-53 D 4
Kompong Cham 52-53 E 4
Kompong Chhnang 52-53 D 4
Kompong Kleang 52-53 DE 4
Kompong Som 52-53 D 4
Kompong Speu 52-53 D 4
Kompong Thom 52-53 DE 4
Komrat 36-37 N 2
Komsa 42-43 Q 5
Komsomolec 42-43 L 7
Komsomolec, ostrov – 42-43 P-R 1
Komsomolec, zaliv – 38-39 K 6
Komsomolec, zaliv – 44-45 G 1
Komsomol'skij [SU, Komi ASSR] 42-43 KL 4
Komsomol'sk-na-Amure 42-43 a 7
Komsomol'skoj Pravdy, ostrova – 42-43 U-W 2
Kŏmun-do 50-51 F 5
Kömür Burun 46-47 AB 3
Komusan 50-51 G 1
Kona 60-61 D 6
Konakovo 38-39 G 4
Konārak [IR] 44-45 HJ 5
Koncha = Kontcha 60-61 G 7
Konche darya 48-49 F 3
Konda 42-43 M 6
Kondinskoje 42-43 M 6
Kondinskoje = Okt'abr'skoje 42-43 M 5
Kondoa 64-65 J 3
Kondolole 64-65 G 2
Kondopoga 42-43 EF 5
Koné 56-57 M 4
Konec-Kovdozero 30-31 O 4
Konečnaja 42-43 O 7
Kong, Mae Nam – 52-53 D 3
Kong, Mé – 52-53 E 4
Kong Christian den IX[s] Land 70-71 de 4
Kong Christian den X[s] Land 19 B 21-22
Kong Christian den IX[s] Land 70-71 de 4
Kong Christian den X[s] Land 19 B 21-22
Kong Frederik den VI[s] Kyst 70-71 c 5
Kong Frederik den VIII[s] Land 19 B 21
Kongju 50-51 F 4
Kong Karls land 30-31 mn 5
Kong Leopold og Dronning Astrid land 24 BC 9
Kongolo 64-65 G 4
Kongōr = Kunkūr 60-61 L 7
Kongpo 48-49 G 6
Kongsberg 30-31 C 8
Kongsøya 30-31 n 5
Kongsvinger 30-31 DE 7
Kongwa 64-65 J 4
Kŏnha-dong 50-51 F 2
Koni, poluostrov – 42-43 d 6
Konin 33 J 2
Konjic 36-37 GH 4
Könkämä älv 30-31 J 3
Konken = Khon Kaen 52-53 D 3
Konkiep = Goageb 64-65 E 8
Konna = Kona 60-61 D 6
Konoša 42-43 G 5
Konotop 38-39 F 5
Konšakovskij Kamen 38-39 L 4
Konstanz 33 D 5
Kontagora 60-61 F 6
Kontcha 60-61 G 7
Kontiomäki 30-31 N 5
Kontum 52-53 E 4
Konur = Sulakyurt 46-47 E 2
Konya 44-45 C 3
Konya Ovası 46-47 E 4
Konza 63 D 3
Kookynie 56-57 D 5
Kooloonong 58 F 5
Koonibba 58 AB 3
Koorowatha 58 J 5
Koosharem, UT 76-77 H 6
Kootenai = Kootenay 70-71 N 8
Kootenai Falls 76-77 F 1
Kootenai River 72-73 C 2
Kootenay 70-71 N 8
Kopaonik 36-37 J 4
Kópasker 30-31 ef 1
Kópavogur 30-31 bc 2
Kopejsk 42-43 L 6-7

190 Kinka

Koper 36-37 EF 3
Kopervik 30-31 A 8
Köping 30-31 FG 8
Koporje 30-31 N 8
Koppang 30-31 D 7
Kopparberg 30-31 EF 7
Koppeh Dāgh 44-45 HJ 3
Kopperå 30-31 D 6
Koprivnica 36-37 G 2
Köprü Irmağı 46-47 D 4
Koraalbekken 56-57 K 2
Koraalzee 56-57 K-M 3
Korab 36-37 J 5
Korahē 60-61 NO 7
Koraka burnu 46-47 B 3
Kor'akskaja sopka = vulkan Kor'akskaja Sopka 42-43 ef 7
Kor'akskaja Sopka, vulkan – 42-43 ef 7
Kor'akskoje nagorje 42-43 j-f 5
Koram = Korem 60-61 M 6
Koran, El – 60-61 N 7
Korapun 52-53 h 6
Korarou, Lac – 60-61 D 5
Korat = Nakhon Ratchasima 52-53 D 3-4
Kor'ažma 38-39 J 3
Korbiyāy, Jabal – 62 F 6
Korbu, Gunung – 52-53 D 5-6
Korçë 36-37 J 5
Korčino 42-43 P 7
Korčula 36-37 G 4
Kordestān 44-45 D 3
Kordofān = Kurdufān al-Janūbīyah 60-61 KL 6
Korem 60-61 M 6
Koret 64-65 F 2
Korf 42-43 g 5
Korhogo 60-61 C 7
Koriak, Circunscripción Nacional de los – 42-43 g 5-e 6
Koriaks, District Nacional des – 42-43 g 5-e 6
Korinthiakòs Kólpos 36-37 JK 6
Kórinthos 36-37 K 7
Kőrishegy 33 HJ 5
Kōriyama 48-49 QR 4
Korjaken, Nationaal Gebied der – 42-43 g 5-e 6
Korkino 42-43 L 7
Korkodon 42-43 de 5
Korkuteli = Dösemeatlı 46-47 CD 4
Korla 48-49 F 3
Kornat 36-37 F 4
Kornsjø 30-31 DE 8
Koro [FJI] 52-53 a 2
Köroğlu Dağları 44-45 C 2
Köroğlu Tepesi 46-47 DE 2
Korogwe 64-65 J 4
Koromo = Toyota 50-51 L 5
Korṓneia, Límnē – 36-37 K 5
Korong Vale 58 F 6
Koror 52-53 KL 5
Körös 33 K 5
Koro Sea 52-53 ab 2
Korosko = Wādī Kuruskū 62 E 6
Korosten' 38-39 E 5
Koro Toro 60-61 H 5
Korpilombolo 30-31 JK 4
Korppoo 30-31 JK 7
Korsakov 42-43 b 8
Korsør 30-31 D 10
Koršunovo 42-43 UV 6
Kortī = Kūrtī 60-61 L 5
Kortrijk 34-35 J 3
Koruçam Burnu 46-47 E 5
Korumburra 58 GH 7
Koryak Autonomous Area 42-43 g 5-e 6
Kōs [GR, ⊙] 36-37 M 7
Kōs [GR, ●] 36-37 M 7
Kosa 38-39 KL 4
Košaba 38-39 K 7
Koš-Agač 42-43 Q 7-8
Kosaka 50-51 N 2
Kō-saki 50-51 G 5
Koščagyl 44-45 G 1
Koscian 33 H 2
Kościerzyna 33 HJ 1
Kosciusko, Mount – 56-57 J 7
Köse 46-47 H 2
Kösedağ Tepesi 46-47 GH 2
K'o-shan = Keshan 48-49 O 2
K'o-shih = Qāshqār 48-49 CD 4
Koshiki-rettō 50-51 G 7
Kōshū = Kwangju 48-49 O 4
Kōsī = Aruṇ 44-45 O 5
Kōsī = Sapt Kosi 44-45 O 5
Kosī, Sūn – 44-45 O 5
Košice 33 K 4
Kosju 42-43 KL 4
Koški [SU] 42-43 M 3
Koslan 42-43 H 5
Kosmos, WA 76-77 BC 2
Koso Gol = Chövsgöl nuur 48-49 J 1
Kosŏng [North Korea] 48-49 O 4
Kŏsŏng [ROK] 50-51 G 5
Kosŏng-ni 50-51 F 6
Kosovo 36-37 J 4
Kosovo polje 36-37 J 4
Kosovska Mitrovica 36-37 J 4
Kōstī = Kūstī 60-61 L 6
Kostino [SU ↓ Igarka] 42-43 Q 4
Kostroma [SU, ●] 42-43 G 6
Kostrzyn 33 G 2
Koszalin 33 H 1
Kőszeg 33 H 5
Kota [IND] 44-45 M 5
Kotaagung 52-53 D 8
Kota Baharu 52-53 D 5
Kotabaru 52-53 G 7
Kotabaru = Jayapura 52-53 M 7
Kota Belud 52-53 G 5
Kotabumi 52-53 DE 7
Kotah = Kota 44-45 M 5
Kota Kinabalu 52-53 FG 5
Kota Kota 64-65 H 5
Kotamubagu 52-53 HJ 6
Kotatengah 52-53 D 6
Kotel 36-37 M 4
Kotel'nič 42-43 H 6
Kotel'nikovo 38-39 H 6
Kotel'nyj, ostrov – 42-43 Za 2-3
Kothráki = Kythréa 46-47 E 5
Kotido 64-65 H 2
Kotka 30-31 M 7
Kotlas 42-43 H 5
Kotooka 50-51 N 2
Kotor 36-37 H 4
Kotor Varoš 36-37 G 3
Kotovsk [SU ↘ Tambov] 38-39 H 5
Kotovsk [SU ↑ Tiraspol'] 38-39 EF 6
Koṭrī [PAK] 44-45 K 5
Kottagudem 44-45 N 7
Kotte = Sri Jayawardanapura 44-45 N 9
Kotto 60-61 J 7
Kotuj 42-43 T 3
Kotujkan 42-43 U 3
Kotzebue, AK 70-71 D 4
Kotzebue Sound 70-71 CD 4
Kouango 60-61 HJ 7
Kouba = Kelta 60-61 H 5
Koudougou 60-61 D 6
Koufra, Oasis de – = Wāḥāt al-Kufrah 60-61 J 4
Koufra, Oasis de – = Wāḥāt al-Kufrah 60-61 J 4
Kouilou 64-65 D 3
Koukdjuak River 70-71 W 4
Koula-Moutou 64-65 D 3
Koulen 52-53 DE 4
Koulikoro 60-61 C 6
Koumass = Kumasi 60-61 D 7
Koumra 60-61 H 7
Koungheul 60-61 B 6
Kounradskij 42-43 O 8
Kou-pang-tzŭ = Goubangzi 50-51 CD 2
Koupéla 60-61 D 6
Kouriles 48-49 S 3-T 2
Kouriles, Fosse des – 19 D 2-E 3
Kourou 78-79 J 3
Kouroussa 60-61 BC 6
Koutiala 60-61 C 6
Kouvola 30-31 M 7
Kouyou 64-65 DE 3
Kovdor 42-43 DE 4
Kovdozero 30-31 OP 4
Kovel' 38-39 D 5
Kovero 30-31 O 6
Kovik 70-71 V 5
Kovrov 42-43 G 6
Koweit 44-45 F 5
Kowŏn 48-49 O 4
Kōyaṁpattūr = Coimbatore 44-45 M 8
Köyceğiz 46-47 C 4
Kōyikōṭa = Calicut 44-45 LM 8
Koyukuk River 70-71 EF 4
Koyulhisar 46-47 GH 2
Köyyeri 46-47 G 3
Kozaklı 46-47 F 3
Kozan 46-47 F 4
Kozánē 36-37 J 5
Kozara 36-37 G 3
Kozi 63 DE 3
Koźle 33 HJ 3
Kozloduj 36-37 K 4
Kozluk 46-47 J 3
Koz'mino [SU ↘ Nachodka] 50-51 J 1
Koz'modemjansk 38-39 J 4
Kōzu-shima 50-51 M 5
Kožva 42-43 K 4
Kpalimé 60-61 E 7
Kpandu 60-61 DE 7
Kra, Isthme de – = Kho Khot Kra 52-53 CD 4
Kra, Istmo de – = Kho Khot Kra 52-53 CD 4
Kra, Istmus of – = Kho Khot Kra 52-53 CD 4
Kra, Kho Khot – 52-53 CD 4
Krabi 52-53 C 5
Kra Buri 52-53 C 4
Kragerø 30-31 C 8
Kragujevac 36-37 J 3
Krakatau = Pulau Anak Krakatau 52-53 DE 8
Kraków 33 JK 3
Kralendijk 72-73 N 9
Kraljevo 36-37 J 4
Kramatorsk 38-39 G 6
Kramfors 30-31 G 6
Kranidion 36-37 K 7
Kranj 36-37 F 2
Krapina 36-37 FG 2
Kras 36-37 EF 3
Krasavino 42-43 GH 5
Kraskino 50-51 H 1
Kraslava 30-31 M 10
Kraśnik 33 KL 3
Krasnoarmejsk 38-39 HJ 5
Krasnoarmejsk [SU, Kazachskaja SSR] 42-43 MN 7
Krasnoarmejskij 38-39 H 6
Krasnodar 38-39 G 6
Krasnograd 38-39 G 6
Krasnogvardejsk 44-45 K 3
Krasnogvardejsk = Gatčina 42-43 DE 6
Krasnoj Armii, proliv – 42-43 ST 1
Krasnojarsk 42-43 R 6
Krasnoje 38-39 H 4
Krasnoje Selo 30-31 NO 8
Krasnokamensk 42-43 W 7-8
Krasnokamsk 42-43 K 6
Krasnookt'abr'skij 38-39 HJ 6
Krasnosel'kup 42-43 OP 4
Krasnoturjinsk 42-43 L 5-6
Krasnoufimsk 42-43 K 6
Krasnoural'sk 42-43 L 6
Krasnousolskij 38-39 L 5
Krasnovišersk 42-43 K 5
Krasnovodsk 44-45 G 2-3
Krasnovodskaja guba 38-39 K 8
Krasnovodskoje plato 44-45 G 2
Krasnoznamenskoje 42-43 M 7
Krasnyj = Možga 42-43 J 6
Krasnyj Čikoj 42-43 UV 7
Krasnyje Okny 36-37 N 2
Krasnyj Jar 38-39 J 6
Krasnyj Liman 38-39 G 6
Krasnyj Luč 38-39 G 6
Krasnystaw 33 L 3
Kratié 52-53 E 4
Kraulshavn = Nûgssuaq 70-71 YZ 3
Krawang = Karawang 52-53 E 8
Krečetovo 38-39 G 3
Krefeld 33 BC 3
Kremenčug 38-39 FG 6
Kremenčugskoje vodochranilišče 38-39 F 6
Kremnica 33 J 4
Krems 33 G 4
Krenachich, El – = El Khenachich 60-61 D 4
Krenachich, Oglat – = Oglat Khenachich 60-61 D 4
Krĕnē = Çeşme 46-47 B 3
Kresta, zaliv – 42-43 k 4
Krestcy 38-39 F 4
Krestovaja guba 42-43 H-K 3
Krestovyj, pereval – 38-39 HJ 7
Krĕtē 36-37 L 8
Kribi 60-61 F 8
Kričev 38-39 F 5
Kriós, Akrōtḗrion – 36-37 K 8
Krishna 44-45 M 7
Krishna Delta 44-45 N 7
Kristiansand 30-31 BC 8
Kristianstad 30-31 F 9-10
Kristianstads län 30-31 E 9-F 10
Kristiansund 30-31 B 6
Kristiinankaupunki = Kristinestad 30-31 J 6
Kristineberg 30-31 H 5
Kristinehamn 30-31 EF 8
Kristinestad 30-31 J 6
Kriva Palanka 36-37 JK 4
Krivoj Rog 38-39 F 6
Križevci [YU, Bilo gora] 36-37 G 2
Krk 36-37 F 3
Krnov 33 HJ 3
Krohnwodoke = Nyaake 60-61 C 8
Kroksfjardharnes 30-31 c 2
Kronoberg 30-31 EF 9
Kronockaja sopka = Velikaja Kronockaja sopka 42-43 ef 7
Kronockaja Sopka, vulkan – 42-43 ef 7
Kronockij, mys – 42-43 f 7
Kronockij zaliv 42-43 f 7
Kronoki 42-43 f 7
Kronprins Christians Land 19 AB 20-21
Kronprins Christians Land 19 AB 20-21
Kronprinsesse Mærtha land 24 B 35-1
Kronprins Frederiks Bjerge 70-71 de 4
Kronprins Olav land 24 C 5
Kroonstad 64-65 G 8
Kropotkin 38-39 H 6
Krosno 33 K 4
Krosno Odrzańskie 33 G 2-3
Krotoszyn 33 H 3
Kruger National Park 64-65 H 7-8
Krugersdorp 64-65 G 8
Krui 52-53 D 8
Kruis, Kaap – 64-65 D 7
Krujë 36-37 HJ 5
Krung Thep 52-53 D 4
Kruševac 36-37 J 4
Kruševo 36-37 J 5
Krymsk 38-39 G 7
Krymskije gory 38-39 F 7-G 6
Krynica 33 K 4
Krzyż 33 H 2
Ksar-el-Boukhari = Qaṣr al-Bukharī 60-61 E 1
Ksar el Kebir = Al-Qṣar al-Kabīr 60-61 C 1
Ksar es Seghir = Al-Qaṣr aṣ-Ṣaghīr 60-61 D 2
Ksar es Souk = Al-Qaṣr as-Sūq 60-61 K 2
Ksenjevka 42-43 WX 7
Ksyl-Orda = Kzyl-Orda 42-43 M 8-9
Ktesiphon 46-47 L 6
Kuala Belait 52-53 F 6
Kuala Berang 52-53 D 5-6
Kuala Kangsar 52-53 CD 6
Kualakapuas 52-53 F 7
Kuala Kerai 52-53 D 5
Kualalangsa 52-53 C 6
Kuala Lumpur 52-53 D 6
Kuala Merang 52-53 D 5
Kuala Perlis 52-53 CD 5
Kuala Selangor 52-53 D 6
Kuala Trengganu 52-53 DE 5
Kuancheng 50-51 B 2
Kuandian 50-51 E 2
Kuang-an = Guang'an 48-49 K 5
Kuang-ch'ang = Guangchang 48-49 M 6
Kuangchou = Guangzhou 48-49 L 7
Kuang-chou Wan = Zhanjiang Gang 48-49 L 7
Kuang-hai = Guanghai 48-49 L 7
Kuang-hsi = Guangxi Zhuangzu Zizhiqu 48-49 KL 7
Kuang-hsin = Shangrao 48-49 M 6
Kuang-lu Tao = Guanglu Dao 50-51 D 3
Kuang-nan = Guangnan 48-49 JK 7
Kuango = Kwango 64-65 E 3-4
Kuangsi = Guangxi Zhuangzu Zizhiqu 48-49 KL 7
Kuangtung = Guangdong 48-49 L 7
Kuang-yüan = Guangyuan 48-49 K 5
Kuantan 52-53 D 6
Kuantan, Batang – = Sungai Inderagiri 52-53 D 7
K'uan-tien = Kuandian 50-51 E 2
Kuan-tung Pan-tao = Guandong Bandao 50-51 C 3
Kuan-yün = Guanyun 48-49 MN 5
Kuba [SU] 38-39 J 7
Kuban 38-39 G 6
Kubango = Rio Cubango 64-65 E 6
Kubaysah 46-47 K 6
Kubbar, Jazīrat – 46-47 N 8
Kubbum 60-61 J 6
Kubokawa 50-51 J 6
Kučevo 36-37 J 3
Kucha 48-49 E 3
Kuche = Kucha 48-49 E 3
Kuchengtze = Qitai 48-49 FG 3
Kuching 52-53 F 6
Kuchinoerabu-jima 50-51 GH 7
Kuchino-shima 50-51 G 7
Küçük Ağrı Dağı 46-47 L 3
Küçüksu = Kotum 46-47 K 3
Küçükyozgat = Elma dağı 46-47 E 3
Kudamatsu 50-51 H 5-6
Kudat 52-53 G 5
Kuddla = Kandla 44-45 L 6
Kudirkos Naumiestis 30-31 K 10
Kudō = Taisei 50-51 ab 2
Kudūk 60-61 L 6-7
Kudymkar 42-43 JK 6
Kuei-ch'ih = Guichi 48-49 M 5
Kueichou = Guizhou 48-49 JK 6
Kuei-lin = Guilin 48-49 KL 6
Kuei-p'ing = Guiping 48-49 KL 7
Kuei-tê = Guide 48-49 J 4
Kuei-ting = Guiding 48-49 K 6
Kuei-yang = Guiyang [TJ, Guizhou] 48-49 K 6
Kuei-yang = Guiyang [TJ, Hunan] 48-49 L 6
Kūfah, Al- 46-47 L 6
Kufra = Wāḥāt al-Kufrah 60-61 J 4
Kufra, Oasis de – = Wāḥāt al-Kufrah 60-61 J 4
Kufrah, Wāḥāt al- 60-61 J 4
Kufra Oasis = Wāḥāt al-Kufrah 60-61 J 4
Küfre = Sirvan 46-47 K 3
Kufstein 33 F 5
Kūh, Pīsh-e – 46-47 M 6
Kūhak 44-45 J 5
Kuh dağı = Kazandağ 46-47 K 3
Kūhdasht 46-47 M 6
Kūhīn 46-47 N 4
Kuhmo 30-31 NO 5
Kuito 64-65 E 5
Kuitozero 30-31 O 5
Kuiu Island 70-71 K 6
Kuivaniemi 30-31 L 5
Kuja 42-43 G 4
Kujal'nickij liman 36-37 O 2
Kujang-dong 50-51 EF 3
Kujawy 33 J 2
Kujbyšev 42-43 O 6
Kujbyšev = Samara 42-43 HJ 7
Kujbyševka-Vostočnaja = Belogorsk 42-43 YZ 7
Kujbyševskoje vodochranilišče 42-43 HJ 7
Kuji 48-49 R 3
Kujto, ozero – 42-43 E 5
Kujumba 42-43 S 5
Kukarka = Sovetsk 42-43 H 6
Kukawa 60-61 G 6
Kuke 64-65 F 7
Kuku Noor = Chöch nuur 48-49 H 4
Kula [BG] 36-37 K 4
Kula [TR] 46-47 C 3
Kula [YU] 36-37 H 3
Kul'ab 44-45 K 3
Kulagino 38-39 K 6
Kulal 63 D 2
Kulaly, ostrov – 38-39 J 7
Kulambangra = Kolombangara 52-53 j 6
Kulanjīn 46-47 N 5
Kular, chrebet – 42-43 Z 4
Kulaura 44-45 P 6
Kuldiga 30-31 J 9
Kulebaki 38-39 H 4
Kulgera 56-57 F 5
Kulha Gangri 48-49 G 6
Kulhakangri = Kulha Gangri 48-49 G 6
Kulikoro = Koulikoro 60-61 C 6
Kulja = Ghulja 48-49 E 3
Kullen 30-31 E 9
Küllük = Güllük 46-47 B 4
Kulmbach 33 E 3
Kulp 46-47 J 3
Kul'sary 42-43 J 8
Kultuk 42-43 T 7
Kulu 46-47 E 3
Kulumadau 52-53 h 6
Kulunda 42-43 OP 7
Kulundinskaja ravnina 42-43 O 7
Kulwin 58 F 5
Kum = Qom 44-45 G 4
Kuma 38-39 J 6-7
Kuma [J] 50-51 J 6
Kumagaya 50-51 M 4
Kumai, Teluk – 52-53 F 7
Kumaishi 50-51 ab 2
Kumalar Dağı 46-47 D 3
Kumamba, Kepulauan – 52-53 LM 7
Kumamoto 48-49 P 5
Kumano 50-51 L 6
Kumano-nada 50-51 L 5-6
Kumanovo 36-37 JK 4
Kumasi 60-61 D 7
Kumaun 44-45 M 4
Kumayt, Al- 46-47 M 6
Kumba 60-61 F 8
Kumbakale 52-53 j 6
Kumbakonam 44-45 MN 8
Kumbe 52-53 LM 8
Kŭmch'on 50-51 F 3
Kŭmch'ŏn = Kimch'ŏn 48-49 O 4
Kumertau 42-43 K 7
Kŭm-gang 50-51 F 4
Kŭmgang-san 50-51 FG 3
Kŭmhwa 50-51 F 3
Kumini-dake 50-51 H 6
Kŭmje = Kimje 50-51 F 5
Kumla 30-31 F 8
Kumluca 46-47 D 4
Kŭmnyŏng 50-51 F 6
Kŭmo-do 50-51 FG 5
Kumo-Manyčskaja vpadina 38-39 HJ 6
Kumon Range = Kūmûn Taungdan 52-53 C 1
Kumphawapi 52-53 D 3
Kŭmsan 50-51 F 4
Kumul = Hami 48-49 G 3
Kūmûn Taungdan 52-53 C 1
Kunašir, ostrov – 42-43 c 9
Kunayt, Al- 46-47 M 6
Kunda 30-31 M 8
Kundabwika Falls 63 B 5
Kuṅḍāpura = Condapoor 44-45 L 8
Kundelungu 64-65 G 4-5
Kundelungu, Parc National de – 63 AB 5
Kundiawa 52-53 M 8
Kundur, Pulau – 52-53 D 6
Kunduz 44-45 K 3
Kunene 64-65 DE 6
K'ung'o-Ala-Too, chrebet – 42-43 O 9
Kungrad 42-43 K 9
Kungsbacka 30-31 DE 9
Kungu 64-65 E 2
Kungur 42-43 K 6
Kung-ying-tsŭ = Gongyingzi 50-51 BC 2
Kunie = Île des Pins 56-57 N 4
Kunjirap Daban 48-49 D 4
Kunkūr 60-61 L 7
Kûnlôn 52-53 C 2
Kunlun Shan 48-49 D-H 4
Kunming 48-49 J 6
Kunovat 38-39 N 3
Kunsan 48-49 O 4
Kunsan-man 50-51 F 5
Kuntillā, Al- 62 F 3
K'ŭnyŏnp'yŏng-do = Tae-yŏnp'yŏng-do 50-51 E 4
Kuolajarvi 38-39 EF 2
Kuopio 30-31 M 6
Kupa 36-37 FG 3
Kupang 52-53 H 9
Kup'ansk 38-39 G 6
Kupino 42-43 O 7
Kupiškis 30-31 L 10
Kupreanof Island 70-71 K 6
Kura 38-39 J 8
Kurahashi-jima 50-51 J 5
Kurashiki 50-51 J 5
Kuraymah 60-61 L 5
Kurayoshi 50-51 JK 5
Kurchahan Hu = Chagan nuur 48-49 L 3
Kurdistan = Kordestān 44-45 F 3
Kurdufān 60-61 K 5-L 6
Kure [J] 48-49 P 5
Küre [TR] 46-47 E 2
Kurejka [SU, ~] 42-43 QR 4
Kurejka [SU, ●] 42-43 PQ 4
Kurgan 42-43 M 6

Kurga 191

Kurganinsk 38-39 GH 6-7
Kurgan-T'ube 44-45 KL 3
Kuria Muria Island = Jazā'ir Khūrīyā Mūrīyā 44-45 H 7
Kurikka 30-31 JK 6
Kurikoma yama 50-51 N 3
Kuriles 48-49 S 3-T 2
Kuriles, Fosa de las – 19 D 2-E 3
Kuril Islands 48-49 S 3-T 2
Kuril'sk 42-43 c 8
Kuril'skije ostrova 48-49 S 3-T 2
Kuril Trench 19 D 2-E 3
Kürkcü = Sarıkavak 46-47 E 4
Kurkur 62 E 6
Kurle = Korla 48-49 F 3
Kurleja 42-43 WX 7
Kurmuk 60-61 L 6
Kurnool 44-45 M 7
Kurobe 50-51 L 4
Kuroishi 50-51 N 2
Kuromatsunai 50-51 b 2
Kurosawajiri = Kitakami 50-51 N 3
Kuro-shima 50-51 G 7
Kuršėnai 30-31 K 9-10
Kursī 46-47 J 4
Kursk 38-39 G 5
Kurskaja kosa 33 K 1
Kurskij zaliv 33 K 1
Kuršumlija 36-37 J 4
Kurşunlu [TR, Çankırı] 46-47 E 2
Kurtalan 46-47 J 4
Kurthasanlı 46-47 E 3
Kūrtī 60-61 L 5
Kurtoğlu Burnu 46-47 C 4
Kurucaşile 46-47 E 2
Kuruçay 46-47 H 3
Kuruman 64-65 F 8
Kurume [J, Kyūshū] 50-51 H 6
Kurumkan 42-43 V 7
Kuruṇegala 44-45 MN 9
Kurun-Ur'ach 42-43 a 6
Kurupukari 78-79 H 4
Kuruskū, Wādī – 62 E 6
Kuryongp'o 50-51 G 5
Kuşadası 46-47 B 4
Kuşadası Körfezi 46-47 B 4
Kusakaki-shima 50-51 G 7
Kusatsu 50-51 KL 5
Kusaybah, Bi'r – 60-61 K 4
Kuščʼovskaja 38-39 GH 6
Kuş Gölü 46-47 BC 2
Ku-shan = Gushan 50-51 D 3
Kushih = Gushi 48-49 M 5
Kushikino 50-51 GH 7
Kushima 50-51 H 7
Kushimoto 50-51 K 6
Kushiro 48-49 RS 3
Kūshkak 46-47 NO 5
Kushui 48-49 G 3
Kusiro = Kushiro 48-49 RS 3
Kuška 44-45 J 3
Kuskokwim Bay 70-71 D 6
Kuskokwim Mountains 70-71 EF 5
Kuskokwim River 70-71 DE 5
Kuşluyan = Gölköy 46-47 G 2
Kušmurun 42-43 LM 7
Kusnezk = Kuzneck 42-43 H 7
Kusŏng 50-51 E 2-3
Kustanaj 42-43 LM 7
K'ustendil 36-37 K 4
Küstenkanal 33 CD 2
Kūstī 60-61 L 6
Kusu 50-51 H 6
Kušum 38-39 K 5
K'us'ur 42-43 Y 3
Kušva 42-43 K 6
Kūt, Al- 44-45 F 4
Kut, Ko – 52-53 D 4
Kūt 'Abdollāh 46-47 N 7
Kütahya 44-45 BC 3
Kutai 52-53 G 6
Kutaisi 38-39 H 7
Kut-al-Imara = Al-Kūt 44-45 F 4
Kutaradja = Banda Aceh 52-53 BC 5
Kutch 44-45 K 6
Kutch, Gulf of – 44-45 KL 6
Kutch, Rann of – 44-45 KL 6
Kutchan 50-51 b 2
Kutcharo-ko 50-51 d 2
Kutina 36-37 G 3
Kutno 33 J 2
Kutsing = Qujing 48-49 J 6
Kutu 64-65 E 3
Kutum 60-61 J 6
Kutunbul, Jabal – 44-45 E 7
Kuusalu 30-31 L 8
Kuusamo 30-31 N 5
Kuusankoski 30-31 M 7
Kuvandyk 42-43 K 7
Kuwana 50-51 L 5
Kuwayt, Al- 44-45 F 5
Kūysanjaq 46-47 L 4
Kuyucak 46-47 C 4
Kuz'movka 42-43 QR 5
Kuzneck 42-43 H 7
Kuzneckij Alatau 42-43 Q 6-7
Kuzneck-Sibirskij = Novokuzneck 42-43 Q 7
Kuznetsk = Kuzneck 42-43 H 7
Kuzomen' 42-43 F 4
Kuzucubelen 46-47 EF 4

Kvænangen 30-31 J 2
Kvaløy 30-31 KL 2
Kvalsund 30-31 KL 2
Kvalvågen 30-31 k 6
Kvarken 30-31 J 6
Kvarner 36-37 F 3
Kvarnerić 36-37 F 3
Kverkfjöll 30-31 ef 2
Kvigtind 30-31 EF 5
Kvikne 30-31 D 6
Kvitøya 30-31 no 4

Kwa 64-65 E 3
Kwair, Al- = Al-Quwayr 46-47 K 4
Kwakhanai 64-65 F 7
Kwale 63 D 4
Kwamouth 64-65 E 3
Kwa Mtoro 63 CD 4
Kwandang 52-53 H 6
Kwangan = Guang'an 48-49 K 5
Kwangando 63 D 3
Kwangchang = Guangchang 48-49 M 6
Kwangch'on 50-51 F 4
Kwangchow = Guangzhou 48-49 L 7
Kwangju 48-49 O 4
Kwango 64-65 E 3-4
Kwangsi = Guangxi Zhuangzu Zizhiqu 48-49 KL 7
Kwangtung = Guangdong 48-49 L 7
Kwangyuan = Guangyuan 48-49 K 5
Kwania, Lake – 63 C 2
Kwanmo-bong 50-51 G 2
Kwanto = Kantō 50-51 MN 4
Kwanyun = Guanyun 48-49 MN 5
Kwanza, Rio – 64-65 E 4-5
Kwara 60-61 E 6-F 7
Kwatta 44-45 K 4
Kwazulu [ZA, ≅] 64-65 H 8
Kweiang = Guiyang 48-49 K 6
Kweichih = Guichi 48-49 M 5
Kweichow = Fengjie 48-49 K 5
Kweichow = Guizhou 48-49 JK 6
Kweichu = Guiyang 48-49 K 6
Kweilin = Guilin 48-49 KL 6
Kweiping = Guiping 48-49 KL 7
Kweiteh = Shangqiu 48-49 LM 5
Kweiyang = Guiyang 48-49 K 6
Kwekwe 64-65 G 6
Kwenge 64-65 E 4
Kwenlun = Kunlun Shan 48-49 D-H 4
Kwesang-bong 50-51 G 2
Kwethluk, AK 70-71 DE 5
Kwidzyn 33 J 2
Kwigillingok, AK 70-71 D 6
Kwiha 60-61 MN 6
Kwilu 64-65 E 3
Kwinana 56-57 BC 6
Kwonghoi = Guanghai 48-49 L 7

Kyaiktō 52-53 C 3
Kyaka 63 B 3
Kyancutta 56-57 G 6
Kyaring Tsho [TJ, Qinghai] 48-49 H 5
Kyaring Tsho [TJ, Xizang Zizhiqu] 48-49 F 5
Kyaukhsī 52-53 C 2
Kyaukse = Kyaukhsī 52-53 C 2
Kydōniai = Ayvacık 46-47 B 3
Kyebang-san 50-51 G 4
Kyezīmanzan 52-53 C 2
Kykládes 36-37 L 7
Kykládes Nēsoi 36-37 L 7
Kyle of Lochalsh 32 D 3
Kyllēnē 36-37 J 7
Kýmē 36-37 L 6
Kymen lääni 30-31 MN 7
Kymijoki 30-31 M 7
Kynuna 56-57 H 4
Kyoga, Lake – 64-65 H 2
Kyōga-saki 50-51 K 5
Kyogle 58 L 2
Kyŏmip'o = Songnim 48-49 O 4
Kyŏngan-ni 50-51 F 4
Kyŏngdôn 52-53 CD 2
Kyŏnggi-do 50-51 F 4
Kyonghŭng 50-51 H 1
Kyŏngju 48-49 OP 4
Kyŏngnyŏlbi-yŏlto 50-51 E 4
Kyŏngsan 50-51 G 5
Kyŏngsang-pukto 50-51 G 4
Kyŏngsan-namdo 50-51 FG 5
Kyŏngsŏng 50-51 GH 2
Kyŏngsŏng = Sŏul 48-49 O 4
Kyŏngwŏn 50-51 H 1
Kyōto 48-49 PQ 4
Kyparissia 36-37 J 7
Kyparissiakòs Kólpos 36-37 J 7
Kyrá Panagia 36-37 KL 6
Kyrksæterøra 30-31 C 6
Kyrkslätt 30-31 L 7
Kyrönjoki 30-31 K 6
Kyštovka 42-43 O 6
Kyštym 42-43 L 6
Kýthēra 36-37 K 7
Kythēron, Stenòn – 36-37 K 7-8
Kýthnos 36-37 L 7
Kytyl-Žura 42-43 Y 5
Kyŭgôk 52-53 C 2
Kyūshū 48-49 P 5
Kyushu, Seuil des – 48-49 P 6-Q 7
Kyushu Ridge 48-49 P 6-Q 7
Kyūshū sammyaku 50-51 H 6
Kyūsyū = Kyūshū 48-49 P 5
Kywong 58 H 5
Kyzyl 42-43 R 7
Kyzyl-Kija 44-45 L 2-3
Kyzylkum 42-43 LM 9
Kyzyl-Mažalyk 42-43 QR 7
Kyzyl-Suu 44-45 L 3

Kzyl-Orda 42-43 M 9

L

Laa 33 H 4
La'ā', Al- = Al-Lu'ā'ah 46-47 L 7
Laascaanood 60-61 b 2
Laasqoray 60-61 b 1
Laas Warwar 60-61 bc 2
La Barge, WY 76-77 HJ 4
Labbezanga 60-61 E 5-6
Labe 33 G 3
Labé [Guinea] 60-61 B 6
La Belle, FL 74-75 c 3
Labin 36-37 F 3
Labinsk 38-39 H 7
Labis 52-53 D 6
La Blanquilla, Isla – 78-79 G 2
Laboulaye 80 D 4
Labrador, Bassin du – 22-23 G 3
Labrador, Coast of – 70-71 YZ 6-7
Labrador, Cuenca del – 22-23 G 3
Labrador, Mar del – 70-71 Y-a 5-6
Labrador, Mer du – 70-71 Y-a 5-6
Labrador Basin 22-23 G 3
Labradorbekken 22-23 G 3
Labrador City 70-71 X 7
Labrador Peninsula 70-71 V 6-Y 7
Labrador Sea 70-71 Y-a 5-6
Labradorzee 70-71 Y-a 5-6
Lábrea 78-79 G 6
Labuan 52-53 FG 5
Labuan, Pulau – 52-53 FG 5
Labuha 52-53 J 7
Labuhan 52-53 E 8
Labuhanbajo 52-53 GH 8
Labuhanbilik 52-53 CD 6
Labytnangi 42-43 M 4
Lača, ozero – 38-39 G 3
Laccadive Islands 44-45 L 9
Lacepede Islands 56-57 D 3
Lacey, WA 76-77 B 2
Lachlan River 56-57 HJ 6
Lacio = Latium 36-37 E 4-5
Lackawanna, NY 74-75 D 3
Lac Mégantic 56-57 H 2
Lacolle 74-75 G 2
Lacombe 70-71 O 7
Laconia, NH 74-75 H 3
Lacoochee, FL 74-75 b 2
Lacq 34-35 G 7
Lacrosse, WA 76-77 E 2
La Crosse, WI 72-73 H 3
Lac Superior = Lake Superior 72-73 HJ 2
Ladakh 44-45 M 4
Ladakh Range 44-45 M 3-4
Lādhiqīyah, Al- 44-45 CD 3
La Digue Island 64-65 N 3
Lādik 46-47 FG 2
Ladiqiya, El- = Al-Lādhiqīyah 44-45 CD 3
Ladismith 64-65 F 9
Ladožskoje ozero 42-43 E 5
L'ady 30-31 N 8
Ladybrand 64-65 G 8
Lady Franklinfjord 30-31 k 4
Lady Newnes Ice Shelf 24 B 18-17
Ladysmith [ZA] 64-65 G 8
Lae 52-53 N 8
La Encantada, Cerro de – 72-73 C 5
Lærdalsøyri 30-31 BC 7
Læsø 30-31 D 9
Lafayette, IN 72-73 J 3
Lafayette, LA 72-73 H 5-6
Lafia 60-61 F 7
Lafiagi 60-61 EF 7
Lagan 30-31 E 9
Lagarfljót 30-31 f 2
Lagarterito 72-73 b 2
Lagarto = Palmas Bellas 72-73 a 2
Lågen 30-31 CD 7
Laghouat = Al-Aghwāṭ 60-61 E 2
Lågneset 30-31 j 6
Lago Argentino 80 B 8
Lagodei, El- = Qardho 44-45 F 9
Lago Maggiore 36-37 C 2-3
Lagonegro 36-37 FG 5
Lago Novo 78-79 J 4
Lagos [P] 34-35 C 10
Lagos [WAN] 60-61 E 7
Lagosa 64-65 GH 4
Lagos Amorgas = Al-Buḥayrat al-Murrat al-Kubrá 62 E 2
Lagos de Moreno 72-73 F 7
Lago Superior = Lake Superior 72-73 HJ 2
Lagowa, El – = Al-Laqawah 60-61 K 6
Lågøya 30-31 k 4
La Grande, OR 76-77 D 3
Lagrange 56-57 D 3
La Grange, GA 72-73 JK 5
La Grange, NC 74-75 E 7
Laguna [BR] 80 G 3
Laguna, La – [PA ↑ Panamá] 72-73 b 2
Laguna, La – [PA ← Panamá] 72-73 b 3
Laguna Beach, CA 76-77 DE 9
Laguna Dam 76-77 FG 9
Laguna Mountains 76-77 E 9
Lagunas [PE] 78-79 DE 6
Lagunas [RCH] 80 BC 2
Laguna Superior 72-73 H 8
Laguna Yema 80 D 2
Lahad Datu 52-53 G 5-6
Laham [RI] 52-53 G 6
Lahat 52-53 D 7
Lāhawr 44-45 L 4
Lahewa 52-53 C 6
Laḥij 44-45 EF 8
Lāhījān 44-45 FG 3
Lahn 33 D 3
Laholm 30-31 E 9
Laholms bukten 30-31 E 9
Lahontan Reservoir 76-77 D 6
Lahore = Lāhawr 44-45 L 4
Lahti 30-31 LM 7
Laï 60-61 H 7
Lai Châu 52-53 D 2
Lai Châu 52-53 D 2
Laidley 58 L 1
Lai HKa = Lechā 52-53 C 2
Lailā = Laylā 44-45 F 6
Lailān = Laylān 46-47 L 5
Laingsburg 64-65 EF 9
Laipo = Lipu 48-49 KL 7
Laisamis 63 D 2
Laiyuan 48-49 LM 4
Lai-yüan = Laiyuan 48-49 LM 4
Lajā', Al- 46-47 G 6
Lajes [BR, Rio Grande do Norte] 78-79 M 6
Lajes [BR, Santa Catarina] 80 F 3
Lajkovac 36-37 HJ 3
La Jolla, CA 76-77 E 9
Lajtamak 42-43 M 6
La Junta, CO 72-73 F 4
Lake, WY 76-77 H 3
Lake Bolac 58 F 6
Lake Butler, FL 74-75 b 1
Lake Cargelligo 56-57 J 6
Lake Charles, LA 72-73 H 5
Lake City, FL 74-75 b 1
Lake City, SC 74-75 D 8
Lake Charles, LA 72-73 H 5
Lakefield [AUS] 56-57 H 2-3
Lake George, NY 74-75 FG 3
Lake Grace 56-57 C 6
Lake Harbour 70-71 WX 5
Lake Havasu City, AZ 76-77 F-G 8
Lake King 56-57 CD 6
Lakeland, FL 72-73 K 6
Lakeland, GA 74-75 B 9
Lake Mead National Recreation Area 76-77 FG 7-8
Lake Oswego, OR 76-77 B 3
Lake Placid, FL 74-75 c 3
Lake Placid, NY 72-73 M 3
Lake Pleasant, NY 74-75 F 3
Lakeport, CA 76-77 B 6
Lake Range 76-77 D 5
Lakes Entrance 58 HJ 6
Lakeside, AZ 76-77 J 8
Lakeside, OR 76-77 A 4
Lakeside, UT 76-77 G 5
Lakeside, VA 74-75 E 6
Lake Toxaway, NC 74-75 B 7
Lakeview, MI 74-75 A 3
Lakeview, OR 76-77 C 4
Lake Wales, FL 74-75 c 3
Lakewood, NJ 74-75 F 4
Lakewood, NY 74-75 D 3
Lakewood, OH 74-75 BC 4
Lake Worth, FL 72-73 KL 6
Lakhadsweep 44-45 L 8
Lakhnaū = Lucknow 44-45 MN 5
Lakōnikòs Kólpos 36-37 K 7
Laksefjord 30-31 M 2
Lakselv 30-31 L 2
Lakṣhadvīp = Lakshadweep 44-45 L 8
Lâlapaşa 46-47 B 2
Lalaua 64-65 J 5
Lālī 46-47 N 6
Lalībela 60-61 M 6
Lambaréné 64-65 D 3
Lambasa 52-53 a 2
Lambayeque [PE, ●] 78-79 CD 6
Lambert Glacier 24 B 8
Lambi Kyūn 52-53 C 4
Lambton, Cape – 70-71 M 3
Lāmding = Lumding 44-45 P 5
Lamé 60-61 G 7
Lamego 34-35 D 8
La Mesa, CA 76-77 E 9
Lamèzia Terme 36-37 FG 6
Lamía 36-37 K 6
L'amin 42-43 N 5
Lamo = Lamu 64-65 K 3
Lamoille, NV 76-77 F 5
La Moine, CA 76-77 B 5
Lamona, WA 76-77 D 2
Lamon Bay 52-53 H 4
Lamont, CA 76-77 D 8
Lamont, ID 76-77 H 3-4
Lamotrek 52-53 N 5
Lampa [PE] 78-79 EF 8
Lampang 52-53 C 3
Lampedusa 36-37 E 8
Lampedusa, Ìsola – 60-61 G 1
Lampi Island = Lambi Kyūn 52-53 C 4
Lampung 52-53 DE 7
Lamu [EAK] 64-65 K 3
Lanai 52-53 e 3
Lanao, Lake – 52-53 HJ 5
Lancang Jiang 48-49 HJ 7
Lancaster 32 E 4
Lancaster, CA 76-77 DE 8
Lancaster, NH 74-75 H 2
Lancaster, PA 74-75 EF 4
Lancaster, SC 74-75 C 7
Lancaster Sound 70-71 TU 3
Lancheu = Lanzhou 48-49 JK 4
Lanchou = Lanzhou 48-49 JK 4
Lanchow = Lanzhou 48-49 JK 4
Lanciano 36-37 F 4
Lancun 48-49 N 4
Landau 33 D 4
Landeck 33 E 5
Landego 30-31 EF 4
Landerneau 34-35 E 4
Lander River 56-57 F 4
Landrum, SC 74-75 B 7
Landsberg am Lech 33 E 4
Land's End 32 CD 6
Land's End [CDN] 70-71 LM 2
Landshut 33 F 4
Landskrona 30-31 E 10
Landsort, Fosa de – 30-31 H 8
Landsort, Fosse du – 30-31 H 8
Landsortdiep 30-31 H 8
Langchhen Khamba 48-49 DE 5
Langchung = Langzhong 48-49 JK 5
Langeland 30-31 D 10
Langerūd 46-47 O 4
Langjökull 30-31 cd 2
Langkawi, Pulau – 52-53 C 5
Langlois, OR 76-77 A 4
Langon 34-35 G 6
Langøy 30-31 F 3
Langres 34-35 K 5
Langres, Plateau de – 34-35 K 5
Langsa 52-53 C 6
Lang Shan = Char Narijn uul 48-49 K 3
Lang So'n 52-53 E 2
Langtans udde 24 C 31
Languedoc 34-35 J 7-K 6
Langzhong 48-49 JK 5
Lanín, Volcán – 80 B 5
Lannion 34-35 F 4
Lansdale, PA 74-75 F 4
Lansing, MI 72-73 K 3
Lan-ts'ang Chiang = Lancang Jiang 48-49 HJ 7
Lan-ts'ang Chiang = Lancang Jiang 48-49 HJ 7
Lan-ts'un = Lancun 48-49 N 4
Lanusei 36-37 C 6
Lan Yü 48-49 N 7
Lanzarote 60-61 B 3
Lanzhou 48-49 JK 4
Laoag 52-53 GH 3
Laodicea = Al-Lādhiqīyah 44-45 CD 3
Laoha He 50-51 B 2
Lao-ha Ho = Laoha He 50-51 B 2
Laohekou = Guanghua 48-49 L 5
Laohushan 50-51 BC 2
Lao Kay 52-53 D 2
Laon 34-35 J 4
Laora 52-53 H 7
Laos 52-53 D 2-3
Laoshan 48-49 N 4
Lao-t'ieh-shan-hsi Chiao = Laotieshanxi Jiao 50-51 C 3
Lao-t'ieh-shan-hsi Chiao = Laotieshanxi Jiao 50-51 C 3
Lapa 80 FG 3
La Panza Range 76-77 CD 8
La Paz, Bahía de – 72-73 DE 7
Laperuza, proliv – 42-43 b 8
Lápēthos = Lapta 46-47 E 5
Lapine, OR 76-77 C 4
Lapin lääni 30-31 L-N 4
Lapinlahti 30-31 MN 6
Lapland 30-31 F 5-N 3
Laplandskij zapovednik 30-31 OP 4
La Plata, MD 74-75 E 5
Laponia 30-31 F 5-N 3
Laponie 30-31 F 5-N 3
Laporte, PA 74-75 E 4
Lapovo 36-37 J 3
Lappajärvi 30-31 KL 6
Lappeenranta 30-31 N 7
Lappi 30-31 L 5
Laprida [RA, Buenos Aires] 80 D 5
Lâpseki 46-47 B 2
Lapta 46-47 E 5
Laptev, Mar de – 42-43 V 2-a 3
Laptev, Mer du – 42-43 V 2-a 3
Laptev Sea 42-43 V 2-a 3
Laptevzee 42-43 V 2-a 3
Lapua 30-31 K 6
Lapush, WA 76-77 A 2
Łapy 33 L 2
Laqawah, Al- 60-61 K 6
Lāqīyat 60-61 K 4
Lār [IR] 44-45 G 5
Larache = Al-'Arā'ish 60-61 C 1
Laramie, WY 72-73 EF 3
Laramie Range 72-73 E 3
Laranjeiras do Sul 80 F 3
Larantuka 52-53 H 8
Larat, Pulau – 52-53 K 8
Lärbro 30-31 H 9
Lare 63 D 2
Laredo, TX 72-73 G 6
Lārestān 44-45 GH 5
Largeau = Faya-Largeau 60-61 H 5
Largo, FL 74-75 b 3
Largo Remo, Isla – 72-73 b 2
Largo Remo Island 72-73 b 2
Lariang 52-53 G 7
Larino 36-37 F 5
Lárisa 36-37 K 6

192 Kurga

Laristan = Lārestān 44-45 GH 5
Larjak 42-43 OP 5
Lārkānah 44-45 K 5
Larnaca = Lárnax 44-45 C 4
Lárnax 44-45 C 4
Larne 32 D 4
Larrey Point 56-57 C 3
Larrimah 56-57 F 3
Lars Christensen land 24 BC 7
Lars Christensen land 24 BC 7
Larsen is-shelf 24 C 30-31
Larvik 30-31 D 8
Lasa = Lhasa 48-49 G 6
La Sal, UT 76-77 J 6
Las Aves, Islas – 78-79 F 2
Las Cruces, NM 72-73 E 5
Lāsgird = Lāsjerd 44-45 G 3
Lāshe Iowayn 44-45 J 4
Lashio = Lāshō 52-53 C 2
Lashkar = Gwalior 44-45 M 5
Lashkar Gāh 44-45 JK 4
Lashkar Satma 48-49 F 4
Lāshō 52-53 C 2
La Silveta, Cerro – 80 B 8
Lasíthion 36-37 L 8
Lāsjerd 44-45 G 3
Las Minas, Bahía – 72-73 b 2
Lasolo, Teluk – 52-53 H 7
Lassance 78-79 KL 8
Lassen Peak 72-73 B 3
Lassen Volcanic National Park 76-77 C 5
Lastoursville 64-65 D 3
Lastovo 36-37 G 4
Las Vegas, NM 72-73 EF 4
Las Vegas, NV 72-73 C 4
Las Vegas Bombing and Gunnery Range 76-77 EF 7
Latacunga 78-79 D 5
Latady Island 24 BC 29
Latakia = Al-Lādhiqīyah 44-45 CD 3
Late 52-53 c 2
Latina 36-37 E 5
La Tortuga, Isla – 78-79 FG 2
Latrobe 58 c 2
Latrobe, PA 74-75 D 4
Latvia 30-31 K-M 9
Lauderdale 58 c 3
Lauenburg/Elbe 33 E 2
Laughlan Islands 52-53 h 6
Lau Group 52-53 b 2
Launceston [AUS] 56-57 J 8
Launceston [GB] 32 D 6
Laura 56-57 H 3
Laurel, DE 74-75 F 5
Laurel, MD 74-75 E 5
Laurel, MS 72-73 J 5
Laurel, OH 74-75 A 5
Laurel Hill 74-75 D 4-5
Laurens, SC 74-75 BC 7
Laurentides, Parc provincial des – 70-71 W 8
Laurie Island 24 C 32
Laurinburg, NC 74-75 D 7
Lauritsala 30-31 N 7
Lausanne 33 C 5
Lausitzer Gebirge 33 G 3
Laut, Pulau – [RI, Kepulauan Natuna] 52-53 E 6
Laut, Pulau – [RI, Selat Makasar] 52-53 G 7
Laut Kecil, Kepulauan – 52-53 G 7-8
Lautoka 52-53 a 2
Lava Bads 76-77 JK 8
Lava Beds [USA, Oregon ↘ Cedar Mountains] 76-77 E 4
Lava Beds [USA, Oregon ← Harney Basin] 76-77 C 4
Lava Beds [USA, Oregon ↘ Steens Mountain] 76-77 D 4
Lava Beds National Monument 76-77 C 5
Laval [CDN] 70-71 VW 8
Laval [F] 34-35 G 4
Lavapié, Punta – 80 AB 5
Laveaga Peak 76-77 C 7
Lavelanet 34-35 HJ 7
La Verkin, UT 76-77 G 7
Laverton 56-57 D 5
Lavongai = New Hanover 52-53 gh 5
Lavonia, GA 74-75 B 7
Lavrador = Labrador Peninsula 70-71 V 6-Y 7
Lavras 78-79 L 9
Lávrion 36-37 KL 7
Lawa 78-79 J 4
Lawen, OR 76-77 D 4
Lawers, Ben – 32 DE 3
Lawit, Gunung – [RI] 52-53 F 6
Lawowa 52-53 H 7
Lawqah 46-47 K 8
Lawra 60-61 D 6
Lawrence, MA 74-75 H 3
Lawrence, NY 74-75 G 4
Lawrenceburg, OH 74-75 A 5
Lawrenceville, VA 74-75 E 6
Laws, CA 76-77 D 7
Lawton, OK 72-73 G 5
Lawz, Jabal al- 44-45 D 5
Laxå 30-31 F 8
Lāyalpūr = Faisalābād 44-45 L 4
Layar, Tanjung – 52-53 DE 8
Laylā 44-45 F 6
Laylān 46-47 L 5
Layton, UT 76-77 G 5
Lazarev 42-43 ab 7
Lazarevskoje, Soči- 38-39 G 7
Lázio 36-37 E 4-5
Lead, SD 72-73 F 3
Leadore, ID 76-77 G 3
Leaksville, NC 74-75 D 6
Leamington, UT 76-77 GH 6
Leavenworth, WA 76-77 C 2
Leavitt Peak 76-77 D 6
Łeba 33 H 1
Lebádeia 36-37 K 6
Lebam, WA 76-77 B 2
Lebanon 48-49 D 4
Lebanon, NH 74-75 GH 3
Lebanon, OR 76-77 B 3
Lebanon, PA 74-75 E 4
Leb'ažje [SU, Kazachskaja SSR] 42-43 O 7
Leb'ažje [SU, Rossijskaja SFSR] 42-43 M 6
Lebedin 38-39 F 5
Lebesby 30-31 M 2
Lébithia 36-37 M 7
Lebo 64-65 F 2
Lèbôn 52-53 B 2
Lębork 33 H 1
Lebrija 34-35 DE 10
Lebú 80 B 5
Lecce 36-37 H 5
Lecco 36-37 C 3
Lech 33 E 4
Lechā 52-53 C 2
Lectoure 34-35 H 7
Leduc 70-71 O 7
Lee, MA 74-75 G 3
Leeds 32 F 5
Leer 33 C 2
Leesburg, FL 74-75 bc 2
Leesburg, ID 76-77 FG 3
Leesburg, VA 74-75 E 5
Leeton 56-57 J 6
Leeuwarden 34-35 KL 2
Leeuwin, Cape – 56-57 B 6
Leeuwin, Dorsal de – 56-57 A 8-B 7
Leeuwin, Seuil – 56-57 A 8-B 7
Leeuwindrempel 56-57 A 8-B 7
Leeuwin Rise 56-57 A 8-B 7
Lee Vining, CA 76-77 D 7
Leeward Islands 72-73 O 8
Lefini 64-65 E 3
Lefka 46-47 E 5
Lefroy, Lake – 56-57 D 6
Legaspi 52-53 H 4
Legaupi = Legaspi 52-53 H 4
Leghorn = Livorno 36-37 CD 4
Legnica 33 GH 3
Le Grand, Cape – 56-57 D 6
Leh 44-45 M 4
Lehi, UT 76-77 GH 5
Lehliu 36-37 M 3
Lehrte 33 DE 2
Lehututu 64-65 F 7
Leiah = Leya 44-45 L 4
Leibnitz 33 G 5
Leicester 32 F 5
Leichhardt Range 56-57 J 4
Leichhardt River 56-57 GH 3
Lei-chou Pan-tao = Leizhou Bandao 48-49 L 7
Leiden 34-35 K 2
Leie 34-35 J 3
Leigh Creek 56-57 G 6
Leikanger 30-31 A 6
Leine 33 D 3
Leinster 32 C 5
Leipsói 36-37 M 7
Leipzig 33 F 3
Leiranger 30-31 F 4
Leiria 34-35 C 9
Leisler, Mount – 56-57 EF 4
Leitha 33 H 5
Leith Harbour 80 J 8
Leiyang 48-49 L 6
Leizhou Bandao 48-49 L 7
Lejâå, El- = Al-Lajā' 46-47 G 6
Lek 34-35 K 3
Leka 30-31 D 5
Lekef = Al-Kāf 60-61 F 1
Lekemti = Nekemtē 60-61 M 7
Leksand 30-31 F 7
Leksozero 30-31 O 6
Leksula 52-53 J 7
Lel = Lêh 44-45 M 4
Leland Elk Rapids, MI 74-75 A 2
Leleque 80 B 6
Lelingluang 52-53 K 8
Lemahabang 52-53 E 8
Léman 33 C 5
Le Marie, Estrecho de – 80 C 9-D 8
Lembale 63 BC 4
Lemesós 44-45 C 4
Lemhi, ID 76-77 G 3
Lemhi Range 76-77 G 3
Lemhi River 76-77 G 3
Lemju 38-39 K 3
Lemland 30-31 J 8
Lemmenjoen kansallispuisto 30-31 LM 3
Lemmon, Mount – 76-77 H 9
Lḗmnos 36-37 L 6
Lemoore, CA 76-77 CD 7
Lemvig 30-31 C 9
Lena [SU] 42-43 W 5-6
Lena, OR 76-77 D 3
Lençóis 78-79 L 7
Lenda 63 B 2
Lendery 42-43 E 5
Lenger 42-43 MN 9
Lengerskij = Georgijevka 42-43 P 8
Lengua de Vaca, Punta – 80 B 4
Lenina, pik – 44-45 L 3
Leninabad 44-45 KL 2-3
Leninakan 38-39 H 7
Leningrad 42-43 E 5-6
Lenino = Leninsk-Kuzneckij 42-43 Q 6-7
Leninogorsk 42-43 P 7
Leninsk-Kuzneckij 42-43 Q 6-7
Leninskoje 38-39 J 4
Lenkoran 38-39 J 8
Lennep, MT 76-77 H 2
Lennox, Isla – 80 C 9
Lenoir, NC 74-75 C 7
Lens 34-35 J 3
Lensk 42-43 V 5
Lentini 36-37 F 7
Léo 60-61 D 6
Leoben 33 G 5
Leominster, MA 74-75 GH 3
León [MEX] 72-73 F 7
León [NIC] 72-73 J 9
León [E, ≅] 34-35 E 7-8
León [E, ●] 34-35 E 7
León, Cerro del – 72-73 G 8
Leon, Montes de – 34-35 D 7
León, Pays de – 34-35 E 4
Leonardtown, MD 74-75 E 5
Leonardville 64-65 E 7
Leongatha 58 G 7
Leonídion 36-37 K 7
Leonora 56-57 D 5
Léopold II, Lac – = Mai Ndombe 64-65 E 3
Léopoldville = Kinshasa 64-65 E 3
Leovo 36-37 MN 2
Lepar, Pulau – 52-53 E 7
Lepel 38-39 E 5
Leper Colony = Balboa Heights 72-73 b 3
Lephepe 64-65 FG 7
Lépi = Caála 64-65 DE 5
Leping 48-49 M 6
Lepsy 42-43 O 8
Leptis magna 60-61 GH 2
Lequeitio 34-35 F 7
Lêr = Līr 60-61 KL 7
Léré [Tchad] 60-61 G 7
Lérida 34-35 H 8
Lérida [CO, Vaupés] 78-79 E 4
Lerma 34-35 F 7-8
Léros 36-37 M 7
Le Roy, MI 74-75 A 2
Le Roy, NY 74-75 DE 3
Le Roy, WY 76-77 H 5
Lerwick 32 F 1
Lésbos 36-37 L 6
Leščevo = Charovsk 42-43 G 6
Leshan 48-49 J 6
Lesistyje Karpaty 33 KL 4
Leskovac 36-37 J 4
Leslie, ID 76-77 G 4
Lesnoj [SU, Vjatka] 42-43 J 6
Lesnoj = Umba 42-43 J 6
Lesnoj Umba 42-43 EF 4
Lesosibirsk 42-43 R 6
Lesozavodsk 42-43 Za 8
Lesozavodskij 30-31 P 4
Lesser Antilles 72-73 N 9-O 8
Lesser Sunda Islands 52-53 GH 8
Lešukonskoje 42-43 H 5
Leszno 33 H 3
Letaba [ZA, ~] 64-65 H 7
Lethbridge 70-71 O 8
Lethem 78-79 H 4
Leti, Kepulauan – 52-53 J 8
Letiahau 64-65 F 7
Leticia 78-79 EF 5
Letland 30-31 K-M 9
Letnij bereg 38-39 G 2-3
Letonia 30-31 K-M 9
Letpadan = Letpandan 52-53 C 3
Letpandan 52-53 C 3
Lettonie 30-31 K-M 9
Leuser, Gunung – 52-53 C 6
Leuven 34-35 K 3
Levan, UT 76-77 H 6
Levanger 30-31 D 6
Levant, Bassin du – 44-45 BC 4
Levantine Basin 44-45 BC 4
Levantijns Bekken 44-45 BC 4
Lèvanzo 36-37 DE 6
Levent 46-47 G 3
Leveque, Cape – 56-57 D 3
Leverett Glacier 24 A 24-22
Leverkusen 33 C 3
Levice 33 J 4
Levick, Mount – 24 B 16-17
Levin 56-57 P 8
Lévis 70-71 W 8
Levittown, PA 74-75 F 4
Lévka = Lefka 46-47 E 5
Levkà Órē 36-37 KL 8
Levkás [GR, ⊙] 36-37 J 6
Levkás [GR, ●] 36-37 J 6
Levkōsia 44-45 C 3
Levski 36-37 L 4
Levskigrad 36-37 L 4
Lewes, DE 74-75 F 5
Lewis, Butt of – 32 C 2
Lewis, Isle of – 32 C 2
Lewisburg, PA 74-75 E 4
Lewisburg, WV 74-75 C 6
Lewis Pass 56-57 O 8
Lewis Range 72-73 D 2
Lewis River 76-77 BC 2
Lewiston, ID 72-73 C 2
Lewiston, ME 72-73 MN 3
Lewiston, UT 76-77 H 5
Lewistown, PA 74-75 DE 4
Lexington, KY 72-73 K 4
Lexington, NC 74-75 CD 7
Lexington, VA 74-75 D 6
Lēxúrion 36-37 J 6
Leyah 44-45 L 4
Leydsdorp 64-65 H 7
Leyte 52-53 J 4
Leżajsk 33 L 3
Lezhë 36-37 H 5
L'gov 38-39 G 5
Lha Ri 48-49 E 5
Lharugö 48-49 G 5
Lhasa 48-49 G 6
Lhatse Dsong 48-49 F 6
Lhokkruet 52-53 BC 6
Lhokseumawe 52-53 C 5
Lhunpo Gangri 48-49 EF 5-6
Liangjiadian 50-51 CD 3
Liangshan Yizu Zizhizhou 48-49 J 6
Liangshan Zizhizhou 48-49 J 6
Liang Xiang 48-49 LM 4
Liangxiangzhen 48-49 LM 4
Lianhua 48-49 L 6
Lianjiang [TJ, ● Guangdong] 48-49 KL 7
Lianping 48-49 LM 7
Lianshanguan 50-51 D 2
Lianyungang 48-49 MN 5
Liaocheng 48-49 LM 4
Liao-chung = Liaozhong 50-51 D 2
Liaodong Bandao 48-49 N 4
Liaodong Wan 48-49 MN 3-4
Liao He 50-51 D 1
Liao Ho = Liao He 50-51 D 1
Liaoning 48-49 MN 3
Liaosi = Liaoxi 48-49 N 3
Liaotung = Liaodong Bandao 48-49 N 4
Liaoxi 48-49 N 3
Liaoyang 48-49 N 3
Liaoyuan 48-49 NO 3
Liaoyuan = Shuangliao 48-49 N 3
Liard River 70-71 M 5
Liaunim = Liaoning 48-49 MN 3
Liban 48-49 D 4
Libano 48-49 D 4
Libby, MT 76-77 F 1
Libby Reservoir 76-77 F 1
Libebe = Andara 64-65 F 6
Libenge 64-65 E 2
Liberal, KS 72-73 F 4
Liberec 33 G 3
Libéria 60-61 BC 7
Liberia, Ramal de – 22-23 J 5
Libéria, Seuil du – 22-23 J 5
Liberia Basin 22-23 J 5
Liberiadrempel 22-23 J 5
Liberty, NY 74-75 F 4
Liberty, OH 74-75 A 5
Liberty, WA 76-77 C 2
Libia 60-61 G-J 3
Libië 60-61 G-J 3
Libische Woestijn 60-61 J 3-L 4
Libourne 34-35 GH 6
Libreville 64-65 CD 2
Libya 60-61 G-J 3
Libyan Desert 60-61 J 3-L 4
Libye 60-61 G-J 3
Libye, Désert de – 60-61 J 3-L 4
Licantén 80 B 4
Licata 36-37 E 7
Lice 46-47 J 3
Lichangshan Liedao 50-51 D 3
Li-ch'ang-shan Lieh-tao = Lichangshan Liedao 50-51 D 3
Li-chiang = Lijiang 48-49 J 6
Lichinga 64-65 J 5
Lichtenburg 64-65 FG 8
Licosa, Punta – 36-37 F 5
Lida 38-39 E 5
Lida, NV 76-77 E 7
Lidām, Al- = Al-Khamāsīn 44-45 EF 6
Lidingö 30-31 H 8
Lidinon, Akrōtḗrion – 36-37 L 8
Lidköping 30-31 E 8
Lido di Òstia, Roma- 36-37 DE 5
Liechtenstein 33 D 5
Liège 34-35 K 3
Lieja = Liège 34-35 K 3
Lieksa 30-31 NO 6
Lielupe 30-31 KL 9
Lielvārde 30-31 L 9
Lienartville 64-65 G 2
Lien-chiang = Lianjiang [TJ, Guangdong] 48-49 KL 7
Lien-hua = Lianhua 48-49 L 6
Lienhwa = Lianhua 48-49 L 6
Lien-shan-kuan = Lianshanguan 50-51 D 2
Lienyunkang = Lianyungang 48-49 MN 5
Lienz 33 F 5
Liepāja 30-31 J 9
Liezen 33 FG 5
Lifi Mahuida 80 C 6
Līfīyah, Al- 46-47 K 7
Lifou, Île – 56-57 N 4
Lifu = Île Lifou 56-57 N 4
Lifubu 63 B 5
Liganga 63 C 5
Light, Cape – 24 B 30-31
Lightning Ridge 58 HJ 2
Ligonha, Rio – 64-65 J 6
Ligua, La – 80 B 4
Ligùria 36-37 B 4-C 3
Liguria, Mar de – 36-37 BC 4
Ligurian Sea 36-37 BC 4
Ligurie = Ligùria 36-37 B 4-C 3
Ligurische Zee 36-37 BC 4
Lihir Group 52-53 h 5
Lihua = Litang 48-49 J 5
Lihula 30-31 K 8
Lijiang 48-49 J 6
Likasi 64-65 G 5
Likati 64-65 F 2
Likely, CA 76-77 C 5
Likiang = Lijiang 48-49 J 6
Likoma Island 64-65 HJ 5
Likoto 64-65 F 3
Likouala [RCB ◁ Sangha] 64-65 E 2
Likouala [RCB ◁ Zaïre] 64-65 E 2
Likuala = Likouala [RCB ◁ Sangha] 64-65 E 2
Likuala = Likouala [RCB ◁ Zaïre] 64-65 E 2
Likupang 52-53 J 6
Liland 30-31 G 3
Lille 34-35 J 3
Lille Bælt 30-31 CD 10
Lille-Ballangen 30-31 G 3
Lillehammer 30-31 D 7
Lillesand 30-31 C 8
Lillestrøm 30-31 D 7-8
Lilongwe [MW, ~] 63 C 6
Lilongwe [MW, ●] 64-65 H 5
Lilydale 58 c 2
Lim 36-37 H 4
Lima [P] 34-35 C 8
Lima, MT 76-77 G 3
Lima, OH 72-73 K 3
Lima [PE, ●] 78-79 D 7
Lima = Dsayul 48-49 H 6
Limão, Cachoeira do – 78-79 J 6
Lima Reservoir 76-77 GH 3
Limassol = Lemesós 44-45 C 4
Limay, Río – 80 C 5
Limay Mahuida 80 C 5
Limbang 52-53 FG 6
Limbaži 30-31 L 9
Limbe 60-61 F 8
Limburg 33 D 3
Limchow = Hepu 48-49 K 7
Limeira 78-79 K 9
Limerick 32 B 5
Limfjorden 30-31 D 9
Limia 34-35 C 8-D 7
Li Miao Zhou = Hainan Zangzu Zizhizhou 48-49 K 8
Liminka 30-31 L 5
Limkong = Lianjiang 48-49 KL 7
Limmen Bight 56-57 G 2
Limnē 36-37 K 6
Limoges 34-35 H 6
Limoges [CDN] 74-75 F 2
Limón 72-73 K 9-10
Limón, Bahía – 72-73 b 2
Limon Bay 72-73 b 2
Limousin 34-35 HJ 6
Limoux 34-35 J 7
Limpia, Laguna – [RA ↖ Resistencia] 80 DE 3
Limpopo 64-65 G 7
Lin 36-37 J 5
Linan = Jianshui 48-49 J 7
Linares [CO] 78-79 D 4
Linares [E] 34-35 F 9
Linares [MEX] 72-73 G 7
Linares [RCH] 80 B 5
Lincang 48-49 HJ 7
Lin-chiang = Linjiang [TJ, Jilin] 48-49 O 3
Lin-ch'ing = Linqing 48-49 M 4
Linchow = Hepu 48-49 K 7
Linchuan = Fuzhou 48-49 MN 6
Lincoln [GB] 32 F 5
Lincoln [RA] 80 D 4
Lincoln, CA 76-77 C 6
Lincoln, ME 74-75 J 2
Lincoln, NE 72-73 G 3
Lincoln, NH 74-75 GH 2
Lincoln Sea 19 A 24-25
Lincolnton, NC 74-75 C 7
Lind, WA 76-77 D 2
Lindau 33 D 5
Linde [SU] 42-43 X 4
Lindesberg 30-31 F 8
Lindesnes 30-31 B 9
Lindi [EAT] 64-65 J 4-5
Lindi [ZRE] 64-65 G 2
Lindian 48-49 NO 2
Líndos 36-37 N 7
Lindsay 74-75 D 2
Lindsay, CA 76-77 D 7
Linea, La – 34-35 E 10
Linfen 48-49 L 4
Lingao 48-49 K 8
Lingayen Gulf 52-53 GH 3
Linge [BUR] 52-53 C 2
Lingeh = Bandar-e Lengeh 44-45 GH 5
Lingen 33 C 2
Lingga, Kepulauan – 52-53 DE 7
Lingga, Pulau – 52-53 DE 7
Lingling 48-49 L 6
Lingmar 48-49 F 5-6
Linguère 60-61 AB 5
Lingyuan 50-51 B 2
Ling-yüan = Lingyuan 50-51 B 2
Lingyun 48-49 K 7
Linhai 48-49 N 6
Linhares 78-79 LM 8
Linh Cam 52-53 E 3
Linhe 48-49 K 3
Lin-ho = Linhe 48-49 K 3
Lin-hsi = Linxi 48-49 M 3
Lin-hsia = Linxia 48-49 J 4
Lini = Linyi [TJ ↗ Xuzhou] 48-49 M 4
Linjiang [TJ, Jilin] 48-49 O 3
Linköping 30-31 FG 8
Linkou 48-49 OP 2
Linkow = Linkou 48-49 OP 2
Linli 48-49 L 6
Linn, Mount – 76-77 B 5
Linné, Kapp – 30-31 j 5
Linnhe, Loch – 32 D 3
Linosa 36-37 E 8
Linosa, Ìsola – 60-61 G 1

Linos 193

Linqing 48-49 M 4
Lins 78-79 JK 9
Linsia = Linxia 48-49 J 4
Linsin = Linxia 48-49 J 4
Lintan 48-49 J 5
Lintao 48-49 J 4
Lintien = Lindian 48-49 NO 2
Lintsing = Linqing 48-49 M 4
Linxi 48-49 M 3
Linxia 48-49 J 4
Linxia Huizu Zizhizhou = A ◁ 48-49 J 4
Linyanti 64-65 F 6
Linyi [TJ, Shandong ↗ Xuzhou] 48-49 M 4
Linyu = Shanhaiguan 50-51 BC 2
Linz 33 FG 4
Lion, Golf du – 34-35 JK 7
Liouesso 64-65 DE 2
Lípari 36-37 F 6
Lipeck 38-39 G 5
Lipez, Cordillera de – 78-79 F 9
Lipin Bor 38-39 G 3
Liping 48-49 K 6
Lipljan 36-37 J 4
Lipno 33 J 2
Lipova 36-37 J 2
Lippe 33 C 3
Lippstadt 33 D 3
Lipu 48-49 KL 7
Līr 60-61 KL 7
Lira 64-65 H 2
Liranga 64-65 E 3
Lisala 64-65 F 2
Līsār 46-47 N 3
Lisboa 34-35 C 9
Lisbon, OH 74-75 C 4
Lisbon = Lisboa 34-35 C 9
Lisbonne = Lisboa 34-35 C 9
Lisburn 32 CD 4
Lisburne, Cape – 70-71 C 4
Lishi 48-49 L 4
Lishih = Lishi 48-49 L 4
Lishui [TJ, Zhejiang] 48-49 MN 6
Lisičansk 38-39 G 6
Lisieux 34-35 H 4
Lisle, NY 74-75 EF 3
Lismore [AUS] 56-57 K 5
Lismore [IRL] 32 C 5
Lista 30-31 B 8
Lister, Mount – 24 B 17
Listowel 74-75 C 3
Listowel 32 B 5
Litan 48-49 J 5
Litang 48-49 K 7
Līṭānī, Nahr al- 46-47 F 6
Litchfield, CA 76-77 CD 5
Līth, Al- 44-45 E 6
Lithgow 56-57 JK 6
Lithuania 30-31 KL 10
Litke 42-43 ab 7
Litóchōron 36-37 K 5
Litoměřice 33 G 3
Litomyšl 33 GH 4
Litouwen 30-31 KL 10
Litovko 42-43 Za 8
Little Andaman 44-45 P 8
Little Belt Mountains 76-77 H 2
Little Cayman 72-73 KL 8
Little Colorado River 72-73 DE 5
Little Desert, The – 58 E 6
Little Falls, NY 74-75 F 3
Littlefield, AZ 76-77 G 7
Little Humboldt River 76-77 E 5
Little Lake, CA 76-77 E 8
Little Mecatina River 70-71 YZ 7
Little Minch 32 C 3
Little Nicobar 44-45 P 9
Little Pee Dee River 74-75 D 7-8
Little Rock, AR 72-73 H 5
Littlerock, CA 76-77 DE 8
Little Rock, WA 76-77 B 2
Little Rock Mountains 76-77 J 1-2
Little Ruaha 63 C 4-5
Little Smoky Valley 76-77 F 6
Little Snake River 76-77 J 5
Littleton, NC 74-75 DE 6
Littleton, NH 74-75 H 2
Little Valley, NY 74-75 D 3
Little Wood River 76-77 FG 4
Lituania 30-31 KL 10
Lituanie 30-31 KL 10
Litunde 63 CD 6
Liu-chia-tzū = Liujiazi 50-51 C 2
Liuchow = Liuzhou 48-49 K 7
Liuhe [TJ, Jilin] 50-51 E 1
Liu-ho = Liuhe [TJ, Jilin] 50-51 E 1
Liujiazi 50-51 C 2
Liurbao 50-51 D 2
Liuwa Plain 64-65 F 5
Liuzhou 48-49 K 7
Live Oak, FL 74-75 b 1
Livermore, CA 76-77 C 7
Livermore, Mount – 72-73 F 5
Livermore Falls, ME 74-75 HJ 2
Liverpool 32 E 5
Liverpool Bay [CDN] 70-71 L 3-4
Liverpool Range 56-57 JK 6
Livingston, MT 76-77 H 3
Livingstone 64-65 G 6
Livingstone Memorial 64-65 GH 5
Livingstone Mountains 64-65 H 4-5
Livingstonia 63 C 5
Livingstonia = Chiweta 64-65 H 5
Livingston Island 24 CD 30
Livno 36-37 G 4
Livny 38-39 G 5
Livonia 30-31 L 9-M 8
Livonie 30-31 L 9-M 8
Livorno 36-37 CD 4
Livourne = Livorno 36-37 CD 4
Liwale 64-65 J 4
Lī Yūbū 60-61 K 7
Lizarda 78-79 K 6
Lizard Head Peak 76-77 J 4
Lizard Point 32 D 7
Ljubljana 36-37 F 2
Ljungan 30-31 G 6
Ljungby 30-31 E 9
Ljusdal 30-31 FG 7
Ljusnan 30-31 F 6-7
Ljusne 30-31 G 7
Llamellín 78-79 D 6
Llandrindod Wells 32 E 5
Llanes 34-35 E 7
Llangefni 32 D 5
Llano 76-77 H 10
Llano Estacado 72-73 F 5
Llanquihue, Lago – 80 B 6
Llata 78-79 D 6
Llerena 34-35 DE 9
Lleyn Peninsula 32 D 5
Llobregat 34-35 H 7-8
Llorena, Punta – = Punta San Pedro 72-73 K 10
Lloyd Bay 56-57 H 2
Lloydminster 70-71 OP 7
Llullaillaco, Volcán – 80 C 2-3
Loa, UT 76-77 H 6
Loa, Río – 80 BC 2
Loange 64-65 F 3-4
Loango 64-65 D 3
Lobata 52-53 H 7
Lobatse 64-65 FG 8
Lobaye 60-61 H 8
Lobería [RA, Buenos Aires] 80 E 5
Lobito 64-65 D 5
Lob nuur 48-49 G 3
Lobstick Lake 70-71 Y 7
Lobva 38-39 LM 4
Loche, La – 70-71 P 6
Loch Garman = Wexford 32 C 5
Lochgilphead 32 D 3
Lo-ch'ing = Yueqing 48-49 N 6
Lochnagar 32 E 3
Lochsa River 76-77 F 2
Lock 58 BC 4
Lockes, NV 76-77 F 6
Lockhart 58 H 5
Lockhart River Aboriginal Reserve 56-57 H 2
Lock Haven, PA 74-75 E 4
Lockport, NY 74-75 D 3
Lôc Ninh 52-53 E 4
Locri 36-37 G 6
Lod 46-47 F 7
Lodejnoje Pole 38-39 FG 3
Lodi 36-37 C 3
Lodi, CA 76-77 C 6
Lodi = Aynı 46-47 JK 4
Lødingen 30-31 F 3
Lodja 64-65 F 3
Lodwar 64-65 J 2
Łódź 33 J 3
Loei 52-53 D 3
Lofa River 60-61 B 7
Lofoten 30-31 E 3-4
Lofoten, Bassin des – 28-29 JK 1
Lofoten, Cuenca de las – 28-29 JK 1
Lofoten Basin 28-29 JK 1
Lofotenbekken 28-29 JK 1
Lofthus 30-31 B 7
Lofty Range, Mount – 56-57 G 6
Lofusa = Lufusā 63 C 2
Logan, OH 74-75 B 5
Logan, UT 72-73 D 3
Logan, WV 74-75 BC 6
Logan, Mount – [CDN, Yukon Territory] 70-71 HJ 5
Logandale, NV 76-77 F 7
Logan Mountains 70-71 L 5
Logansport, IN 72-73 J 3
Loge, Rio – 64-65 D 4
Logojsk 30-31 M 10
Logone 60-61 H 7
Logroño 34-35 F 7
Logroño 34-35 F 7
Løgstør 30-31 C 9
Lohardaga 44-45 N 6
Lōhārḍaggā = Lohardaga 44-45 N 6
Lōhit = Luhit 44-45 Q 5
Lohja 30-31 KL 7
Lohtaja 30-31 K 5
Lohumbo 63 C 3
Loibl 33 G 5
Loikaw = Lûykau 52-53 C 3
Loimaa 30-31 K 7
Loir 34-35 G 5
Loire 34-35 H 5
Loiya 63 C 2
Loja [E] 34-35 E 10
Loja [EC, ●] 78-79 D 5
Loji 52-53 J 7
Lo-jung = Luorong 48-49 K 7
Loka = Lūkā 63 B 1
Lokan tekojärvi 30-31 MN 3
Lokichoggio 63 C 1
Lokila = Lukilā 63 C 1
Lokitaung 64-65 HJ 2
Lokka 30-31 MN 4
Lokoja 60-61 F 7
Lokolo 64-65 EF 3
Loksa 30-31 LM 8
Loks Land 70-71 Y 5
Lōl, Nahr – = Nahr Lūl 60-61 K 7
Lola, Mount – 76-77 C 6
Loleta, CA 76-77 A 5
Lolgorien 63 C 3
Loliondo 63 C 3
Lol Laikumaiki 63 D 4
Lolland 30-31 D 10
Lolmuryoi 63 D 4
Lolo 64-65 D 3
Lolo, MT 76-77 F 2
Lolobau 52-53 h 5
Loloda 52-53 J 6
Lolui 63 C 3
Lom [BG] 36-37 K 4
Lom [RFC] 60-61 G 7
Loma, MT 76-77 H 1-2
Lomadi 52-53 C 3
Lomami 64-65 FG 3
Loma Mountains 60-61 B 7
Lomas [PE] 78-79 E 8
Lombard, MT 76-77 H 2
Lombarda, Serra – 78-79 J 4
Lombardia 36-37 C 3-D 2
Lombardie = Lombardia 36-37 C 3-D 2
Lomblem = Pulau Lomblen 52-53 H 8
Lomblen, Pulau – 52-53 H 8
Lombok, Pulau – 52-53 G 8
Lombok, Selat – 52-53 G 8
Lomé 60-61 E 7
Lomela [ZRE, ~] 64-65 F 3
Lomela [ZRE, ●] 64-65 F 3
Lomié 60-61 G 8
Lomitas, Las – 80 D 2
Lomond, Ben – [AUS] 58 cd 2
Lomond, Loch – 32 D 3
Lomonosov 38-39 E 4
Lomonosov, Dorsal de – 19 A
Lomonosovka 42-43 M 7
Lomonosov Ridge 19 A
Lomonosovrug 19 A
Lomonossov, Crête de – 19 A
Lompoc, CA 76-77 C 8
Lom Sak 52-53 D 3
Łomża 33 L 2
Loncoche 80 B 5
Londen = London 32 G 6
Londlani 63 C 3
London [CDN] 70-71 UV 9
London [GB] 32 G 6
Londonderry 32 C 4
Londonderry, Cape – 56-57 E 2
Londonderry, Islas – 80 B 9
Londres = London 32 G 6
Londrina 80 FG 2
Lone Mountain 76-77 E 7
Lone Pine, CA 76-77 DE 7
Lonerock, OR 76-77 D 3
Lonetree, WY 76-77 H 5
Longa [Angola] 64-65 E 5
Longa, proliv – 42-43 j 3-4
Long Bay 72-73 L 5
Long Beach, CA 72-73 BC 5
Longboat Key 74-75 b 3
Long Branch, NJ 74-75 FG 4
Longchuan [TJ, Dehong Daizu Zizhizhou] 48-49 H 7
Long Creek, OR 76-77 D 3
Longdor, gora – 42-43 W 6
Long Eddy, NY 74-75 F 4
Longford 56-57 J 8
Longford 32 BC 5
Longhua 48-49 M 3
Longido 63 D 3
Longiram 52-53 G 6-7
Long Island [BS] 72-73 LM 7
Long Island [CDN] 70-71 UV 7
Long Island [PNG] 52-53 N 7-8
Long Island [USA] 72-73 M 3-4
Long Island Sound 74-75 G 4
Longjing 50-51 G 1
Longling 48-49 H 7
Longmalinau 52-53 G 6
Longmire, WA 76-77 C 2
Longnan 48-49 LM 7
Longnawan 52-53 FG 6
Longonot 63 D 3
Long Point [CDN, Ontario] 74-75 CD 3
Long Point Bay 74-75 CD 3
Longqi = Zhangzhou 48-49 M 7
Longquan 48-49 M 6
Long Range Mountains 70-71 Z 7-8
Longreach 56-57 H 4
Longs Peak 72-73 E 3
Long Valley [USA, California] 76-77 D 7
Long Valley [USA, Nevada] 76-77 D 5
Longview, TX 72-73 GH 5
Longview, WA 72-73 B 2
Longxi 48-49 J 4-5
Long Xuyên 52-53 DE 4
Longyearbyen 30-31 jk 5
Longyou 48-49 M 6
Longzhen 48-49 O 2
Lonja 36-37 G 3
Lønsdal 30-31 F 4
Lons-le-Saunier 34-35 K 5
Lookout, Cape – [USA, North Carolina] 72-73 L 5
Lookout, Cape – [USA, Oregon] 76-77 A 3
Lookout Mountain 76-77 E 3
Lookout Mountains [USA, Washington] 76-77 BC 2-3
Lookout Pass 76-77 F 2
Loolmalasin 63 CD 3
Loongana 56-57 E 6
Loop Head 32 A 5
Lopatina, gora – 42-43 b 7
Lopatino = Volžsk 42-43 H 6
Lopatka, mys – 19 D 3
Lop Buri 52-53 D 4
Loperot 63 C 2
Lopez, Cap – 64-65 C 3
López Collada 76-77 FG 10
Loping = Leping 48-49 M 6
Lop Noor = Lob nuur 48-49 G 3
Lopori 64-65 F 2
Lopphavet 30-31 JK 2
Lopt'uga 38-39 J 3
Lopydino 38-39 K 3
Lōra, Hāmūn-e – 44-45 JK 5
Lora Creek 56-57 FG 5
Lora del Río 34-35 E 10
Lorain, OH 72-73 K 3
Loralai = Lorālāy 44-45 K 4
Lorālāy 44-45 K 4
Lorca 34-35 G 10
Lord Howe Island 56-57 LM 6
Lord Howe Islands = Ontong Java Islands 52-53 j 6
Lord Howe Rise 56-57 M 5-7
Lord Mayor Bay 70-71 ST 4
Lordsburg, NM 76-77 J 9
Lorena 78-79 KL 9
Lorengau 52-53 N 7
Lorestān 44-45 F 4
Loreto [BOL] 78-79 G 8
Loreto [BR, Maranhão] 78-79 K 6
Loreto [CO] 78-79 EF 5
Loreto [MEX, Baja California Norte] 72-73 D 6
Lorian Swamp 64-65 JK 2
Lorica 78-79 D 3
Lorı dere 46-47 HJ 2
Lorient 34-35 F 5
Loris, SC 74-75 D 7
Lorne, Firth of – 32 CD 3
Loro 78-79 F 4
Loros, Los – 80 BC 3
Lörrach 33 C 5
Lorraine 34-35 KL 4
Lorugumu 63 C 2
Los Alamos, CA 76-77 C 8
Los Alamos, NM 72-73 E 4
Los Angeles, CA 72-73 BC 5
Los Angeles Aqueduct 76-77 DE 8
Los Banos, CA 76-77 C 7
Los Gatos, CA 76-77 C 7
Lošinj 36-37 F 3
Los Molinos, CA 76-77 BC 5
Los Monjes, Islas – 78-79 EF 2
Los Roques, Islas – 78-79 F 2
Lossiemouth 32 E 3
Los Testigos, Islas – 78-79 G 2
Lost Hills, CA 76-77 D 8
Lost River Range 76-77 FG 3-4
Lost Trail Pass 76-77 G 3
Lot 34-35 H 6
Lota 80 B 5
Lotagipi Swamp 64-65 HJ 2
Lothair, MT 76-77 H 1
Lotharingen 34-35 KL 4
Lotmozero 30-31 NO 3
Lotta 38-39 EF 2
Louang Namtha 52-53 D 2
Louangphrabang 52-53 D 3
Loubnān, Jabal – = Jabal Lubnān [RL, ▲▲] 46-47 FG 5-6
Loubomo 64-65 D 3
Louchi 42-43 E 4
Loudéac 34-35 F 4
Loudonville, OH 74-75 BC 4
Louga 60-61 A 5
Lougheed Island 70-71 PQ 2
Louisa, VA 74-75 DE 5
Louisbourg 70-71 Z 8
Louisburg, NC 74-75 D 6
Louisiade, Archipel de – 52-53 h 7
Louisiade Archipelago 52-53 h 7
Louisiana 72-73 H 5
Louis Trichardt 64-65 GH 7
Louisville, GA 74-75 B 8
Louisville, KY 72-73 JK 4
Loulan = Loulanyiyi 48-49 F 3
Loulanyiyi 48-49 F 3
Loulé 34-35 C 10
Loup River 72-73 G 3
Lourdes 34-35 G 7
Lourenço Marques = Maputo 64-65 H 8
Lourenço Marques, Baía de – = Baía do Maputo 64-65 H 8
Lousia, KY 74-75 B 5
Louth 32 FG 5
Louth [AUS] 56-57 HJ 6
Louvain = Leuven 34-35 K 3
Louviers 34-35 H 4
Lovászi 33 H 5
Lovat' 38-39 F 4
Loveč 36-37 L 4
Lovelock, NV 76-77 D 5
Lovenia, Mount – 76-77 H 5
Loviisa = Lovisa 30-31 M 7
Lovingston, VA 74-75 D 6
Lovisa 30-31 M 7
Lovl'a 38-39 JK 4
Lovozero 38-39 G 2
Lóvua 64-65 F 5
Low, Cape – 70-71 T 5
Lowa 64-65 G 3
Lowell, ID 76-77 F 2
Lowell, MA 72-73 M 3
Lowell, OR 76-77 B 4
Lower California 76-77 F 10
Lower Guinea 22-23 K 5-6
Lower Hutt 56-57 OP 8
Lower Lake 76-77 CD 5
Lower Lake, CA 76-77 B 6
Lower Lough Erne 32 BC 4
Lower Peninsula 72-73 JK 3
Lower Woolgar 56-57 H 3
Lowestoft 32 GH 5
Łowicz 33 J 2
Lowlands 32 D 4-E 3
Lowman, ID 76-77 F 3
Low Rocky Point 58 b 3
Lowville, NY 74-75 F 3
Loxton 58 E 5
Loyalton, CA 76-77 C 6
Loyang = Luoyang 48-49 L 5
Loyauté, Îles – 56-57 N 4
Lozère 34-35 J 6
Loznica 36-37 H 3
Lozva 38-39 M 3-4
Lu'ā'ah, Al- 46-47 L 7
Luacano 64-65 F 5
Luachimo 64-65 F 4
Luala 64-65 G 4
Lualaba 64-65 G 4
Luama 64-65 G 3
Luambe 63 C 6
Lu'an 48-49 M 5
Luanda 64-65 D 4
Luando, Rio – 64-65 E 5
Luang, Khao – [T ← Nakhon Si Thammarat] 52-53 CD 5
Luang, Thale – 52-53 D 5
Luanginga, Rio – 64-65 F 5
Luangue, Rio – 64-65 E 4
Luangwa 64-65 H 5
Luangwa Valley Game Reserve 64-65 H 5
Luanping 48-49 M 3
Luanshya 64-65 G 5
Luan Xian 48-49 M 4
Luapula 64-65 G 5
Luarca 34-35 D 7
Luatizi, Rio – 63 D 6
Luau 64-65 F 5
Lubań 33 G 3
Lubānas ezers 30-31 M 9
Lubandaye 63 B 4
Lubang Islands 52-53 G 4
Lubango 64-65 D 5
Lubbock, TX 72-73 F 5
L'ubča 38-39 E 5
Lübeck 33 E 2
Lubefu [ZRE, ~] 64-65 F 3
Lubefu [ZRE, ●] 64-65 F 3
L'ubercy 38-39 G 4
Lubero 64-65 G 3
Lubika 63 B 4
Lubilash 64-65 F 4
Lubin 33 H 3
L'ubinskij 42-43 N 6
Lublin 33 L 3
Lubliniec 33 J 3
Lubnān, Jabal – 46-47 FG 5-6
Lubnān al-Janūbī = 3 ◁ 3 46-47 F 6
Lubnān ash-Sharqī, Jabal – 46-47 G 5-6
Lubnān ash-Shimālī = 1 ◁ 1 46-47 G 5
Lubny 38-39 F 5-6
L'ubotin 38-39 G 6
Lubudi [ZRE, ~] 64-65 FG 4
Lubudi [ZRE, ●] 64-65 G 4
Lubukklinggau 52-53 D 7
Lubuksikaping 52-53 CD 6
Lubumbashi 64-65 G 5
Lubutu 64-65 G 3
Lubwe 63 B 5
Lucania, Mount – 70-71 HJ 5
Lucas, Punta – = Cape Meredith 80 D 8
Lucca 36-37 D 4
Lucena [E] 34-35 E 10
Lucena [RP] 52-53 H 4
Lučenec 33 J 4
Lucera 36-37 F 5
Lucerne Lake 76-77 E 8
Lucerne Valley, CA 76-77 E 8
Lucheringo 63 CD 6
Lu-chou = Hefei 48-49 M 5
Luchow = Lu Xian 48-49 K 6
Luchuan 48-49 KL 7
Luchwan = Luchuan 48-49 KL 7
Lucia, CA 76-77 C 7
Lucin, UT 76-77 G 5
Lucipara, Kepulauan – 52-53 J 8
Lucira 64-65 D 5
Luck 38-39 DE 5
Luckenwalde 33 F 2
Lucknow [IND] 44-45 MN 5
Lüderitz [Namibia] 64-65 DE 8
Lüderitzbaai 64-65 DE 8
Ludhiana 44-45 M 4
Ludhiyānā = Ludhiana 44-45 M 4
L'udinovo 38-39 F 5
Ludlow, CA 76-77 EF 8
Ludogorie 36-37 M 4
Ludowici, GA 74-75 C 9
Ludus 36-37 KL 2
Ludvika 30-31 F 7
Ludwigsburg 33 D 4
Ludwigshafen 33 CD 4
Ludwigslust 33 E 2
Ludza 30-31 M 9
Luebo 64-65 F 4
Luele, Rio – 64-65 F 4
Luemba 63 B 3
Luembe, Rio – 64-65 F 4
Luena 64-65 F 5
Luena, Rio – 64-65 F 5
Luena Flats 64-65 F 5
Lufeng 48-49 M 7
Lufira 64-65 G 4-5
Lufkin, TX 72-73 H 5
Lufusā 63 C 2
Luga [SU, ~] 42-43 D 6

194 Linqi

Luga [SU, ●] 42-43 D 6
Lugano 33 D 5
Luganville 56-57 N 3
Lugard's Falls 63 D 3
Lugela 64-65 J 6
Lugenda, Rio – 64-65 J 5
Lugh Ferrandi = Luuq 60-61 N 8
Lugo [E] 34-35 D 7
Lugo [I] 36-37 D 3
Lugoj 36-37 JK 3
Luhayyah, Al- 44-45 E 7
Luhit 44-45 Q 5
Luhsien = Lu Xian 48-49 K 6
Luiana, Rio – 64-65 F 6
Luichow = Haikang 48-49 KL 7
Luik = Liège 34-35 K 3
Luilaka 64-65 F 3
Luimneach = Limerick 32 B 5
Luirojoki 30-31 M 4
Luís Correira 78-79 L 5
Luishia 64-65 G 5
Luiza 64-65 F 4
Luján [RA, Buenos Aires] 80 E 4
Lujenda = Rio Lugenda 64-65 J 5
Lujiapuzi 50-51 D 2
Lūkā 63 B 1
Lukanga 63 B 6
Lukanga Swamp 64-65 G 5
Lukašek 42-43 Z 7
Lukenie 64-65 E 3
Lukenie Supérieure, Plateau de la – 64-65 F 3
Lukilā 63 C 1
Lukimwa 63 D 5
Lukolela 64-65 E 3
Lukovit 36-37 L 4
Łuków 33 L 3
Lukuga 64-65 G 4
Lukuledi 63 D 5
Lukulu 63 B 6
Lukusashi 63 B 6
Lūl, Nahr – 60-61 K 7
Luleå 30-31 JK 5
Lule älv 30-31 J 4-5
Lulébargas = Lüleburgaz 46-47 B 2
Lüleburgaz 46-47 B 2
Lulonga 64-65 E 2
Lulua 64-65 F 4
Luluabourg = Kananga 64-65 F 4
Luma 63 D 6
Lumbala 64-65 F 5
Lumber River 74-75 D 7
Lumberton, NC 72-73 L 5
Lumbo 64-65 K 5-6
Lumding 44-45 P 5
Lumege = Cameia 64-65 F 5
Lumeje 64-65 F 5
Lumu 52-53 G 7
Lumut 52-53 D 5
Lün 48-49 K 2
Luna, NM 76-77 J 9
Lund 30-31 E 10
Lund, NV 76-77 F 6
Lund, UT 76-77 G 6-7
Lunda 64-65 EF 4
Lundazi [Z, ~] 63 C 6
Lundazi [Z, ●] 64-65 H 5
Lundi [ZW, ~] 64-65 H 7
Lundi [ZW, ●] 64-65 H 7
Lundy 32 D 6
Lüneburg 33 E 2
Lüneburger Heide 33 DE 2
Lunenburg 70-71 Y 9
Lunéville 34-35 L 4
Lunga [Z] 64-65 G 5
Lunga Game Reserve 64-65 FG 5
Lungala N'Guimbo 64-65 EF 5
Lung-chên = Longzhen 48-49 O 2
Lung-chiang = Qiqihar 48-49 N 2
Lung-ching-ts'un = Longjing 50-51 G 1
Lung-chuan = Suichuan 48-49 L 6
Lung-hsi = Longxi 48-49 J 4-5
Lung-hua = Longhua 50-51 AB 2
Lunglê = Lungleh 44-45 P 6
Lungleh 44-45 P 6
Lungling = Longling 48-49 H 7
Lung-nan = Longnan 48-49 LM 7
Lungsi = Longxi 48-49 J 4-5
Lungué-Bungo, Rio – 64-65 F 5
Lungyu = Longyou 48-49 M 6
Luni [IND, ~] 44-45 L 5
Luninec 38-39 E 5
Lunsemfwa 64-65 GH 5
Luntai = Buquq 48-49 E 3
Luofu 63 B 3
Luombwa 63 B 6
Luongo 63 B 5
Luorong 48-49 K 7
Luoyang 48-49 L 5
Luozi 64-65 D 3
Lupa 63 C 5
Lupilichi 63 C 5
Łupkowska, Przełęcz – 33 L 4
Luputa 64-65 F 4
Luray, VA 74-75 D 5
Lurio 63 E 6
Lúrio, Rio – 64-65 JK 5
Luristan = Lorestān 44-45 F 4
Lusaka 64-65 G 6
Lusambo 64-65 F 3
Lusenga Flats 64-65 G 4
Lu Shan [TJ, Jiangxi] 48-49 M 6
Lushnjë 36-37 H 5
Lushoto 64-65 J 3
Lüshun 48-49 MN 4
Lusien = Lu Xian 48-49 K 6
Luso = Moxico 64-65 EF 5
Lūṭ, Dasht-e – 44-45 H 4
Lutembwe 63 C 6
Luton 32 F 6
Lutong 52-53 F 6
Lutunguru 63 B 3
Lützow-Holm bukt 24 C 4-5
Luuq 60-61 N 8
Luvua 64-65 G 4
Luwegu 64-65 J 4
Luwingu 64-65 GH 5
Luwu 52-53 GH 7
Luwuk 52-53 H 7
Luxembourg 34-35 KL 4
Luxembourg [★] 34-35 KL 4
Luxemburgo [★] 34-35 KL 4
Lu Xian 48-49 K 6
Luxor = Al-Uqṣur 60-61 L 3
Lüyang 50-51 C 2
Lûykau 52-53 C 3
Lûylin 52-53 C 2
Luz [BR] 78-79 K 8
Luza 38-39 J 3
Luza [SU, ●] 42-43 H 5
Luzern 33 CD 5
Luzón 52-53 H 3
Luzón, Détroit de – 52-53 H 2
Luzón Strait 52-53 H 2

L'vov 38-39 D 5-6

Lwanhsien = Luan Xian 48-49 M 4
Lwela 63 B 5

Lyantonde 63 B 3
Lycksele 30-31 H 5
Lydda = Lod 46-47 F 7
Lydell Wash 76-77 G 7
Lydenburg 64-65 GH 8
Lijfland 30-31 L 9-M 8
Lykwati 63 C 4
Lyle, WA 76-77 C 3
Lyme Bay 32 E 6
Łyna 33 K 2
Lynch, KY 74-75 B 6
Lynchburg, VA 72-73 L 4
Lynches River 74-75 CD 7
Lynden, WA 76-77 B 1
Lyndhurst 58 D 3
Lyndonville, VT 74-75 GH 2
Lyngenfjord 30-31 J 2-3
Lyngseiden 30-31 HJ 3
Lynn, MA 74-75 H 3
Lynndyl, UT 76-77 G 6
Lynn Lake 70-71 Q 6
Lyon 34-35 K 6
Lyons, GA 74-75 B 8
Lyons, NY 74-75 E 3
Lyons River 56-57 C 4
Lysá hora 33 J 4
Lysekil 30-31 D 8
Lyskovo 42-43 GH 6
Łyso gory 33 K 3
Lys'va 42-43 K 6
Lyswa = Lys'va 42-43 K 6

Ll

Llamellín 78-79 D 6
Llandrindod Wells 32 E 5
Llanes 34-35 E 7
Llangefni 32 D 5
Llano 76-77 H 10
Llano Estacado 72-73 F 5
Llanquihue, Lago – 80 B 6
Llata 78-79 D 6

Llerena 34-35 DE 9
Lleyn Peninsula 32 D 5
Llobregat 34-35 H 7-8
Llorena, Punta – = Punta San Pedro 72-73 K 10
Lloyd Bay 56-57 H 2
Lloydminster 70-71 OP 7

Llullaillaco, Volcán – 80 C 2-3

M

Mâ, Wâd al- 60-61 C 4
Ma'abûs = Tazarbū 60-61 J 3
Maagdeneilanden 72-73 NO 8
Malloûla = Ma'lūlā 46-47 G 6
Ma'ân 44-45 D 4
Ma'anīyah, Al- 44-45 E 4
Maanselkä 30-31 L 3-N 4
Maarianhamina = Mariehamn 30-31 HJ 7
Ma'ārīk, Wādī – 46-47 H 7
Ma'arrah, Al- 46-47 G 4
Ma'arrat an-Nū'mān 46-47 G 5
Maas 34-35 K 3
Maastricht 34-35 K 3
Ma'azzah, Jabal – 62 E 2
Mababe Depression 64-65 F 6
Mabalane 64-65 H 7
Mabana 63 B 2
Mabang Gangri 48-49 DE 5
Mabaruma 78-79 H 3
Mabogwe 63 B 4
Mabroûk 60-61 D 5
Mabruck = Mabroûk 60-61 D 5
Mabton, WA 76-77 CD 2
Mabuki 64-65 H 3
Mača 42-43 W 6
Macá, Monte – 80 B 7
Macaé 78-79 L 9
MacAlester, OK 72-73 GH 5
MacAllen, TX 72-73 G 6
Macalogne 63 C 6
MacAlpine Lake 70-71 PQ 4
MacAllen, TX 72-73 G 6
Macao = Macau 48-49 L 7
Macapá [BR, Amapá] 78-79 J 4
Macar = Gebiz 46-47 D 4
Macará 78-79 CD 5
Maçaranduba, Cachoeira – 78-79 J 4-5
Macarani 78-79 LM 8
MacArthur, OH 74-75 B 5
MacArthur River 56-57 G 3
Macas 78-79 D 5
Macau [BR] 78-79 M 5-6
Macau [Macau] 48-49 L 7
Macaúba 78-79 J 7
Macayari 78-79 E 4
MacBee, SC 74-75 C 7
MacCall, ID 76-77 EF 3
MacCammon, ID 76-77 G 4
Macchu Picchu 78-79 E 7
MacClellanville, SC 74-75 D 8
Macclenny, FL 74-75 b 1
Macclesfield, Banc de – 53-53 FG 3
Macclesfield, Banco de – 52-53 FG 4
Macclesfield Bank 52-53 FG 3
MacClintock, ostrov – = ostrov Mak-Klintoka 42-43 H-K 1
MacClintock Channel 70-71 Q 3
MacClintock Channel 70-71 Q 3
MacCloud, CA 76-77 BC 5
Maccluer, Teluk – = Teluk Berau 52-53 K 7
MacClure, PA 74-75 E 4
MacClure Strait 70-71 MN 2-3
MacColl, SC 74-75 D 7
MacComb, MS 72-73 H 5
MacConnellsburg, PA 74-75 DE 5
MacConnelsville, OH 74-75 C 5
MacCook, NE 72-73 F 3
MacCormick, SC 74-75 BC 8
MacDermitt, NV 76-77 DE 5
Macdhui, Ben – 32 DE 3
MacDonald 22-23 N 8
Macdonald, Lake – [AUS] 56-57 E 4
MacDonald, Lake – [CDN] 76-77 FG 1
MacDonald Peak 76-77 G 2
Macdonnell Ranges 56-57 F 4
MacDouall Peak 56-57 F 5
MacDougall Sound 70-71 R 2-3
MacDowell Peak 76-77 GH 9
Macédoine 36-37 JK 5
Macedonia 36-37 JK 5
Maceió 78-79 MN 6
Macenta 60-61 C 7
Macerata 36-37 E 4
Macfarlane, Lake – 56-57 G 6
MacGaffey, NM 76-77 J 8
MacGill, NV 76-77 F 6
MacGrath, AK 70-71 EF 5
MacGuire, Mount – 76-77 F 3
Machachi 78-79 D 5
Machačkala 38-39 J 7
Machaila 64-65 H 7
Machakos 64-65 J 3
Machala 78-79 CD 5
Machambet 38-39 K 6
Machaneng 64-65 G 7
Machanga 64-65 J 7
Macharadze 38-39 H 7
Machattie, Lake – 56-57 GH 4
Machaze 64-65 H 7
Ma Chha 48-49 HJ 5
Ma Chhu [TJ] 48-49 J 4
Machias, ME 74-75 K 2
Machilipatnam 44-45 N 7
Machiques 78-79 E 2-3
Macia [Moçambique] 64-65 H 8
Macias Nguema = Bioko 60-61 F 8
Măcin 36-37 N 3
Macina 60-61 CD 6
Mack, CO 76-77 J 6
Maçka 46-47 H 2
Mackay 56-57 J 4
Mackay, ID 76-77 G 4
Mackay, Lake – 56-57 E 4
MacKay Lake [CDN, Northwest Territories] 70-71 O 5
MacKeesport, PA 72-73 KL 3
Mackenzie [GUY] 78-79 H 3
Mackenzie Bay 70-71 J 4
MacKenzie Bridge, OR 76-77 BC 3
Mackenzie Highway 70-71 N 6
Mackenzie King Island 70-71 OP 2
Mackenzie Mountains 70-71 J 4-L 5
Mackenzie River 70-71 KL 4
Mackinac, Straits of – 74-75 A 2
MacKinlay 56-57 H 4
MacKinley, Mount – 70-71 F 5
Mackinnon Road 64-65 JK 3
MacKittrick, CA 76-77 D 8
Macksville 56-57 K 6
Maclean [AUS] 56-57 K 5
Maclear 64-65 G 9
Macleay River 58 L 3
MacLennan 70-71 N 6
Macleod, Lake – 56-57 BC 4
MacLeod Bay 70-71 OP 5
MacLoughlin Peak 76-77 B 4
MacMechen, WV 74-75 C 5
MacMinnville, OR 76-77 B 3
MacMurdo 24 B 16-17
MacMurdo Sound 24 B 17
MacNary, AZ 76-77 J 8
Macomia 64-65 JK 5
Mâcon [F] 34-35 K 5
Macon, GA 72-73 K 5
Macondo 64-65 F 5
Macqarie Ridge 22-23 Q 8
Macquarie, Dorsal de la – 22-23 Q 8
Macquarie, Dorsale de – 22-23 Q 8
Macquarie, Lake – 58 KL 4
Macquarie Harbour 56-57 HJ 8
Macquarie Islands 24 D 16
Macquarie Range 56-57 JK 5
Macquarie River [AUS, New South Wales] 56-57 J 6
Macquarie River [AUS, Tasmania] 58 c 2-3
Macquarierug 22-23 Q 8
MacRae, GA 74-75 B 8
MacRoberts, KY 74-75 B 6
MacRobertson Land 24 BC 6-7
MacTavish Arm 70-71 N 4
MacTier 74-75 CD 2
Macumba, The – 56-57 G 5
Macusani 78-79 E 7
MacVivar Arm 70-71 MN 4-5
Ma Chha 48-49 HJ 5
Ma Chhu [TJ] 48-49 J 4
Mā'dabā 46-47 F 7
Madadi 60-61 J 5
Madagascar 64-65 K 7-L 6
Madagascar, Bassin de – 22-23 M 7
Madagascar, Cuenca de – 22-23 M 7
Madagascar, Dorsal de – 22-23 M 7
Madagascar, Dorsale de – 22-23 M 7
Madagascar Basin 22-23 M 7
Madagascar Ridge 22-23 M 7
Madagaskarbekken 22-23 M 7
Madagaskarrug 22-23 M 7
Madā'in Ṣāliḥ 44-45 D 5
Maḍakalapūwa 44-45 N 9
Madama 60-61 G 4
Madan 36-37 L 5
Madang 52-53 N 8
Madanīyīn 60-61 FG 2
Madaoua 60-61 F 6
Madawaska River 74-75 E 2
Maddalena 36-37 C 5
Madden, Lago – 72-73 b 2
Madden, Presa de – 72-73 b 2
Madden Dam = Presa de Madden 72-73 b 2
Madden Lake = Lago Madden 72-73 b 2
Madeira 60-61 A 2
Madeira = Arquipélago da Madeira 60-61 A 2
Madeira, Arquipélago da – 60-61 A 2
Madeira, Rio – 78-79 G 6
Madeleine, Îles de la – 70-71 Y 8
Madeline, CA 76-77 C 5
Madeline Plains 76-77 C 5
Maden [TR, Bayburt] 46-47 J 2
Maden [TR, Elâzığ] 46-47 H 3
Maden Adası = Alibey Adası 46-47 B 3
Madenhanları = Maden 46-47 J 2
Madera 72-73 E 6
Madera, CA 76-77 CD 7
Madhya Andamân = Middle Andaman 44-45 P 8
Madhya Pradesh 44-45 MN 6
Madibira 63 C 5
Madidi, Rio – 78-79 F 7
Madimba 64-65 E 3-4
Madina do Boé = Boé 60-61 B 6
Madīnah, Al- [IRQ] 46-47 M 7
Madīnah, Al- [Saudi Arabia] 44-45 DE 6
Madīnat ash-Sha'ab 44-45 EF 8
Madingou 64-65 D 3
Madison, FL 74-75 b 1
Madison, GA 74-75 B 8
Madison, ME 74-75 HJ 2
Madison, WI 72-73 HJ 3
Madison, WV 74-75 C 5
Madison Range 76-77 H 3
Madison River 76-77 H 3
Madiun 52-53 F 8
Madjerda, Quèd – = Wādī Majradah 60-61 F 1
Madley, Mount – 56-57 D 4
Madoc 74-75 E 2
Mado Gashi 64-65 J 2
Madona 30-31 LM 9
Madonie 36-37 EF 7
Madra Dağı 46-47 B 3
Madrakah, Rā's al- 44-45 H 7
Madras 44-45 N 8
Madras, OR 76-77 C 3
Madrâs = Tamil Nadu 44-45 M 8-9
Madrasta = Madras 44-45 N 8
Madre, Laguna – 72-73 G 6-7
Madre de Dios [PE, ●] 78-79 EF 7
Madre de Dios, Isla – 80 A 8
Madre de Dios, Rio – 78-79 F 7
Madrid 34-35 EF 8
Mad River 76-77 B 5
Madrona, Sierra – 34-35 EF 9
Madura 56-57 E 6
Madura = Madurai 44-45 M 9
Madura = Pulau Madura 52-53 F 8
Madura, Pulau – 52-53 F 8
Madurai 44-45 M 9
Mádytos = Eceabat 46-47 AB 2
Maê = Mahe 44-45 M 8
Maebashi 50-51 M 4
Maengbu-san 50-51 F 2
Mae Sai 52-53 CD 2
Mae Sariang 52-53 C 3
Maestra, Sierra – 72-73 L 7-8
Maevatanana 64-65 L 6
Maewo 56-57 N 3
Maffra 58 H 7
Mafia Channel 63 D 4-5
Mafia Channel 63 D 4-5
Mafia Island 64-65 JK 4
Mafikeng 64-65 FG 8
Mafra [BR] 80 FG 3
Mafraq, Al- 46-47 G 6
Mafupa 64-65 G 5
Magadan 42-43 CD 6
Magadi 64-65 J 3
Magadi, Lake – 63 D 3
Magadoxo = Muqdiisho 60-61 O 8
Magallanes, Estrecho de – 80 AB 8
Magangué 78-79 E 3
Mağara = Höketçe 46-47 G 3
Mağara = Kırobası 46-47 EF 4
Magaria 60-61 F 6
Magburaka 60-61 B 7
Magdagači 42-43 Y 7
Magdalena [BOL] 78-79 G 7
Magdalena [MEX, Sonora] 76-77 H 10
Magdalena, Bahía – 72-73 D 7
Magdalena, Isla – 80 B 6
Magdalena, Llano de la – 72-73 D 6-7
Magdalena, Llano de la – 72-73 D 6-7
Magdalena, Rio – [CO] 78-79 E 2-3
Magdalena, Rio – [MEX] 72-73 D 5
Magdalen Islands = Îles de la Madeleine 70-71 Y 8
Magdeburg 33 E 2
Magelang 52-53 EF 8
Magerøy 30-31 M 2
Magga Range 24 B 35-36
Maghāghah 62 D 3
Maghayrā', Al- 44-45 G 6
Maghrah, Al- [ET, ≅] 62 C 2
Maghrah, Al- [ET, ●] 62 C 2
Magi = Maji 60-61 M 7
Magic Reservoir 76-77 F 4
Màglie 36-37 H 5
Magna, UT 76-77 GH 5
Magnesia = Manisa 44-45 B 3
Magnetic Island 56-57 J 3
Magnitogorsk 42-43 KL 7
Magnor 30-31 DE 7-8
Mágoè 64-65 H 6
Magosa = Gazi Mağusa 44-45 CD 3
Maguari, Cabo – 78-79 K 4-5
Magude 64-65 H 7-8
Mağusa Körfezi 46-47 EF 5
Magwe 52-53 BC 2
Mahābād 44-45 F 3
Mahābhārat Lekh 44-45 NO 5
Mahabo 64-65 KL 7
Maha Chana Chai 52-53 DE 3
Maha Chana Chai 52-53 DE 3
Mahagi 64-65 H 2
Mahaicony Village 78-79 H 3
Mahajamba, Helodranon'i – 64-65 L 5-6
Mahajanga 64-65 L 6
Mahakam, Sungai – 52-53 G 6-7
Mahalapye 64-65 G 7
Maḥallat al-Kubra, Al- 60-61 L 2
Mahanadi 44-45 N 6
Mahanadi Delta 44-45 O 7
Mahanoro 64-65 L 6
Maha Nuwara 44-45 N 9
Maharashtra [IND, ≅] 44-45 M 7
Mahārī, Al- = Al-Muhārī 46-47 L 7
Mahārī, Sha'īb al- 46-47 KL 7
Maḥārīq, Al- 62 D 5
Maha Sarakham 52-53 D 3
Mahato 63 E 5
Maḥaṭṭat 1 62 E 7
Maḥaṭṭat 2 62 EF 7
Maḥaṭṭat 3 62 EF 7
Maḥaṭṭat 4 62 F 7
Mahavelona 64-65 LM 6
Mahawa 44-45 M 9
Mahd adh-Dhahab 44-45 E 6
Mahdia 78-79 H 3
Mahdīyah, Al- [TN] 60-61 G 1
Mahe 44-45 M 8
Mahé Island 64-65 N 3
Mahendra Parvata = Eastern Ghats 44-45 M 8-N 7
Mahenge 64-65 J 4
Mahēsāṇā = Mehsāna 44-45 L 6
Māhī = Mahe 44-45 M 8
Mahia, El – 60-61 D 4
Mahia Peninsula 56-57 P 7
Mahindi 63 D 5
Maḥmūdīyah, Al- 46-47 L 6
Mahmudiye 46-47 D 3
Māhneshān 46-47 M 4
Maho = Mahawa 44-45 M 9
Mahogany Mountain 76-77 E 4
Mahón 34-35 K 9
Mahuta 63 D 5
Maiándros = Büyük Menderes nehri 46-47 B 4
Maichaila 64-65 H 7
Maicuru, Rio – 78-79 J 5
Maidān = Maydān 46-47 L 5
Maïdân Akbas = Maydān Ikbis 46-47 G 4

Maïdâ 195

Maidī = Maydī 44-45 E 7
Maidstone 32 G 6
Maiduguri 60-61 G 6
Maiella 36-37 F 4
Maigaiti = Marqat Bazar 48-49 D 4
Maigualida, Serranía de – 78-79 F 3-G 4
Maijdi 44-45 P 6
Mai-kai-t'i = Marqat Bazar 48-49 D 4
Maiko 64-65 G 2-3
Maiko, Parc national de – 64-65 G 3
Maikona 63 D 2
Maikoor, Pulau – 52-53 K 8
Maimacheng = Altanbulag 48-49 K 1-2
Maimansingh 44-45 OP 5-6
Main 33 D 4
Ma'īn [Y] 44-45 EF 7
Mai Ndombe 64-65 E 3
Maine [F] 34-35 GH 4
Maine [USA] 72-73 MN 2
Maine, Gulf of – 72-73 N 3
Mainemenē = Menemen 46-47 B 3
Maïné-Soroa 60-61 G 6
Mainland [GB, Orkney] 32 DE 2
Mainland [GB, Shetland] 32 F 1
Maintirano 64-65 K 6
Mainz 33 D 3-4
Maipo, Volcán – 80 C 4
Maipú [RA, Buenos Aires] 80 E 5
Maipures 78-79 F 3
Maiquetía 78-79 F 2
Maisarī, Al- = Al-Maysarī 46-47 H 7
Maisí, Cabo – 72-73 M 7
Maisome 63 C 3
Maisūru = Mysore 44-45 M 8
Mait = Mayd 44-45 F 8
Maitland 56-57 K 6
Maitland, Lake – 56-57 D 5
Maíz, Islas del – 72-73 K 9
Maizuru 48-49 Q 4
Maja [SU, ~] 42-43 Za 6
Maja [SU, ●] 42-43 Z 5
Majagual 78-79 E 3
Majal, Bi'r – 62 E 6
Majarr al-Kabīr, Al- 46-47 M 7
Majdal = Ashqĕlōn 46-47 F 7
Majene 52-53 G 7
Majevica 36-37 H 3
Maji 60-61 M 7
Maji Moto 64-65 H 4
Majkain 42-43 O 7
Majkop 38-39 H 7
Majma'ah 44-45 F 5
Majn 42-43 h 5
Majngy-Pil'gyn = Mejnypil'gyno 42-43 j 5
Majoli 78-79 H 4
Major Pablo Lagerenza 80 DE 1
Majradah, Wādī – 60-61 F 1
Majunga = Mahajanga 64-65 L 6
Makah Indian Reservation 76-77 A 1
Makalle = Mekelē 60-61 M 6
Makampi 63 C 5
Makanya 63 D 4
Makarov 42-43 b 8
Makarska 36-37 G 4
Makasar = Ujung Pandang 52-53 G 8
Makasar, Selat – 52-53 G 6-7
Makat 42-43 J 8
Makedonía 36-37 JK 5
Makedonija 36-37 JK 5
Makejevka 38-39 G 6
Make-jima 50-51 H 7
Makeni 60-61 B 7
Makgadikgadi Salt Pan 64-65 FG 7
Makhfīr al-Ḥammān 46-47 H 5
Makhiruq, Wādī el- = Wādī al-Makhrūq 46-47 G 7
Makhmūr 46-47 K 5
Makhrūq, Khashm al- 46-47 J 7
Makhrūq, Wādī al- 46-47 G 7
Makian, Pulau – 52-53 J 6
Makīlī, Al- 60-61 J 2
Makinsk 42-43 MN 7
Makinson Inlet 70-71 UV 2
M'akit 42-43 d 5
Makka = Makkah 44-45 DE 6
Makkah 44-45 DE 6
Makkaur 30-31 O 2
Mak-Klintoka, ostrov – 42-43 H-K 1
Maklakovo 42-43 R 6
Maklakovo = Lesosibirsk 42-43 R 6
Makó 33 K 5
Makoko 63 C 4
Makokou 64-65 D 2
Makoua 64-65 DE 2-3
Makounda = Markounda 60-61 H 7
Makragéfyra = Uzunköprü 46-47 B 2
Makran = Mokrān 44-45 HJ 5
Makrāna 44-45 L 5
Makrónēsos 36-37 L 7
Maks al-Baḥrī, Al- 62 CD 5
Maks al-Qiblī, Al- 60-61 L 4
Maks el-Baharî = Al-Maks al-Baḥrī 62 CD 5
Makteir = Maqṭayr 60-61 BC 4
Mākū 46-47 L 3
Mākū Chāy 46-47 L 3
Mākū Chāy 46-47 L 3
Makumbako 63 C 5
Makumbi 64-65 EF 4
Makurazaki 50-51 GH 7
Makurdi 60-61 F 7
Makuyuni 63 D 3
Mala = Malaita 52-53 k 6
Malabar, Côte de – = Malabar Coast 44-45 L 8-M 9
Malabar Coast 44-45 L 8-M 9
Malabo 60-61 F 8
Malacca = Malaiische Halbinsel 52-53 C 5-D 6
Malacca, Détroit de – 52-53 CD 6
Malacca, Estrecho de – 52-53 CD 6
Malacca, Peninsule de – 52-53 C 5-D 6
Malacca, Strait of – 52-53 CD 6
Malad City, ID 76-77 G 4
Maladeta 34-35 H 7
Málaga 34-35 E 10
Málaga [CO] 78-79 E 3
Malagarasi [EAT, ~] 64-65 H 3
Malagarasi [EAT, ●] 63 B 4
Malaija = Melayu 52-53 D 6
Malaita 52-53 k 6
Malaja In'a 42-43 c 5
Malaja Ob' 42-43 M 5-L 4
Malaja Višera 42-43 E 6
Malakāl 60-61 L 7
Mālākaṇḍ 44-45 L 4
Malakka 52-53 C 5-D 6
Malakka, Straat – 52-53 CD 6
Mala Krsna 36-37 J 3
Malalaling 64-65 F 8
Malang 52-53 F 8
Malange 64-65 E 4
Malangen 30-31 H 3
Mälaren 30-31 G 8
Malargüe 80 C 5
Malartic 70-71 V 8
Malasia 52-53 D-F 6
Malaspina 80 C 6-7
Malaspina Glacier 70-71 H 5-6
Malatia = Malatya 44-45 D 3
Malatya 44-45 D 3
Malatya Dağları 46-47 G 4-H 3
Malāvī 46-47 MN 6
Malawi, Lake – 64-65 H 5
Malayagiri 44-45 O 6
Malayalam Coast = Malabar Coast 44-45 L 8-M 9
Malaya Parvata = Eastern Ghats 44-45 M 8-N 7
Malay Archipelago 22-23 O 5-Q 6
Malāyer 44-45 F 4
Malāyer, Rūdkhāneh-ye – 46-47 N 5
Malay Peninsula 52-53 C 5-D 6
Malayu = Melayu 52-53 D 6
Malazgirt 46-47 K 3
Malbon 56-57 H 4
Malbooma 58 AB 3
Malbork 33 J 1-2
Malcèsine 36-37 D 3
Malden, MA 74-75 H 3
Maldivas 22-23 N 5
Maldive Islands 22-23 N 5
Maldives 22-23 N 5
Maldonado [ROU, ●] 80 F 4
Maldonado, Punta – 72-73 FG 8
Male [Malediven] 20-21 N 5
Maléas, Akrōtḗrion – 36-37 K 7
Malebo, Pool – 64-65 E 3
Mālēgāṅv = Malegaon 44-45 LM 6
Mālegaon = Malegaon 44-45 LM 6
Maleise Archipel 22-23 O 5-Q 6
Maleisië 52-53 D-F 6
Male Karpaty 33 H 4
Malek Kandī 46-47 M 4
Malekula 56-57 N 3
Malela 64-65 G 3
Malema 64-65 J 5
Malen'ga 38-39 G 3
Malghīr, Shaṭṭ – 60-61 F 2
Malgrat 34-35 J 8
Malḥah 46-47 K 5
Malheur Lake 76-77 D 4
Malheur River 76-77 E 4
Mali [RMM] 60-61 C 6-D 5
Malije Derbety 38-39 HJ 6
Malik, Qūr al- 62 BC 5
Malik, Wādī al- 60-61 KL 5
Malıköy 46-47 E 3
Mali Kyûn 52-53 C 4
Malimba, Monts – 63 B 4
Malin 38-39 E 5
Malin, OR 76-77 C 4
Malinau = Longmalinau 52-53 G 6
Malindi 64-65 K 3
Malines = Mechelen 34-35 K 3
Malin Head 32 C 4
Malinyi 63 CD 5
Malipo 48-49 J 7
Malita 52-53 HJ 5
Malkara 46-47 B 2
Małkinia Górna 33 L 2
Mallacoota Inlet 58 JK 6
Mallaig 32 D 3
Mallakastër 36-37 HJ 5
Mallapunyah 56-57 G 3
Mallawī 62 D 4
Mallès Venosta 36-37 D 2
Mallicolo = Malekula 56-57 N 3
Mallīt 60-61 K 6
Mallorca 34-35 J 9
Mallow 32 B 5
Malmberget 30-31 J 4
Malmedy 34-35 L 3
Malmesbury [ZA] 64-65 E 9
Malmö 30-31 E 10
Malmöhus 30-31 E 9-10
Malmyž 38-39 JK 4
Maloca 78-79 H 4
Malojaroslavec 38-39 FG 4
Maloje Karmakuly 42-43 HJ 3
Malole 63 B 5
Malombe, Lake – 64-65 J 5
Malone, NY 74-75 F 2
Malonga 64-65 F 5
Malouines, Îles – = Falkland Islands 80 DE 8
Malovata 36-37 N 2
Måløy 30-31 A 7
Malpelo, Isla – 78-79 C 4
Malta 36-37 EF 8
Malta, ID 76-77 G 4
Maltahöhe 64-65 E 7
Malte 36-37 EF 8
Maltepe = Manyas 46-47 B 2
Malu 52-53 k 6
Maluku = 22 ⊲ 52-53 J 7
Ma'lūlā 46-47 G 6
Malumba 64-65 G 3
Malumteken 52-53 h 5
Malung 30-31 E 7
Malūt 60-61 L 6
Malvan 44-45 L 7
Malwa 44-45 M 6
Malwinas, Islas – = Falkland Island 80 DE 8
Malya 63 C 3
Malyj Jenisej 42-43 RS 7
Malyj Kavkaz 38-39 HJ 7
Malyj L'achovskij, ostrov – 42-43 bc 3
Malyj Nimnyr 42-43 Y 6
Malyj Tajmyr, ostrov – 42-43 UV 2
Malyj Uzen' 38-39 J 6
Mama 42-43 V 6
Mamahatun = Tercan 46-47 J 3
Mamasa 52-53 G 7
Mambasa 64-65 G 2
Mamberamo, Sungai – 52-53 L 7
Mambere = Carnot 60-61 H 8
Mambirima Falls 63 B 6
Mambone = Nova Mambone 64-65 J 7
Mamfe 60-61 F 7
Māmī, Rā's – 44-45 GH 8
Mammola 36-37 G 6
Mammoth, AZ 76-77 H 9
Mammoth Hot Springs, WY 76-77 H 3
Mamonovo 33 JK 1
Mamoré, Río – 78-79 FG 7-8
Mamou 60-61 B 6
Mampawah 52-53 E 6
Mampi = Sepopa 64-65 F 6
Mampong 60-61 D 7
Mamry, Jezioro – 33 K 1
Mamuju 52-53 G 7
Man [CI] 60-61 C 7
Man, Isle of – 32 DE 4
Mana [Guyane Française, ●] 78-79 J 3
Manaas 48-49 F 3
Manacapuru 78-79 G 5
Manacor 34-35 J 9
Manado 52-53 H 6
Managua 72-73 J 9
Managua, Lago de – 72-73 J 9
Manakara 64-65 L 7
Manāmah, Al- 44-45 G 5
Manambaho 64-65 KL 6
Manambolo 64-65 K 6
Manam Island 52-53 N 7
Manamo, Caño – 78-79 G 3
Manamo, Caño – 78-79 G 3
Mananara [RM, ~] 64-65 L 7
Mananara [RM, ●] 64-65 L 6
Mananjary 64-65 L 7
Manantenina 64-65 L 7
Manantiales 80 BC 8
Manapouri, Lake – 56-57 N 9
Manāqil, Al- 60-61 L 6
Manār, Jabal al- 44-45 EF 8
Manas, gora – 42-43 N 9
Mānasārovar = Mapham Tsho 48-49 E 5
Manāṣif, Al- 46-47 J 5
Manasquan, NY 74-75 FG 4
Manaus 78-79 H 5
Man'auung Kyûn 52-53 B 3
Manavgat 46-47 D 4
Manbij 46-47 G 4
Mancha, La – 34-35 F 9
Manchan 48-49 G 2
Manche 32 E 7-F 6
Manchester [GB] 32 EF 5
Manchester, CT 74-75 G 4
Manchester, NH 72-73 MN 3
Manchester, VT 74-75 G 3
Manchouli = Manzhouli 48-49 M 2
Manchuria = Manzhou 48-49 N-P 2
Máncora 78-79 C 5
Máncora = Puerto Máncora 78-79 C 5
Mancos, CO 76-77 J 7
Mancha, Canal de la – 32 E 7-F 6
Manchuria 48-49 N-P 2
Mand, Rūd-e – = Rūd-e Mond 44-45 G 5
Manda [EAT, Iringa] 64-65 HJ 5
Manda [EAT, Mbeya] 63 C 4
Mandab, Bāb al- 44-45 E 8
Mandabe 64-65 K 7
Mandal 30-31 B 8-9
Mandal [Mongolia] 48-49 K 2
Mandalay = Mandale 52-53 C 2
Mandale 52-53 C 2
Mandalgov' 48-49 JK 2
Mandalī 46-47 L 6
Mandal Ovoo 48-49 JK 3
Mandalya Körfezi 46-47 B 4
Mandalyat = Selimiye 46-47 B 4
Mandaon 52-53 H 4
Mandar 52-53 G 7
Mandar, Teluk – 52-53 G 7
Mandara, Monts – 60-61 G 6-7
Mándas 36-37 C 6
Mandasor 44-45 LM 6
Māṇḍavī = Mandvi 44-45 K 6
Mandchourie 48-49 N-P 2
Mandeb, Bab al- = Bāb al-Mandab 44-45 E 8
Mandeb, Bab el – = Bāb al-Mandab 44-45 E 8
Mandi 44-45 M 4
Mandidzudzure 64-65 H 6-7
Mandimba 64-65 J 5
Mandingues, Monts – 60-61 C 6
Mandioli, Pulau – 52-53 J 7
Mandla 44-45 N 6
Mandria 46-47 E 5
Mandritsara 64-65 L 6
Mandsaor = Mandsaur 44-45 LM 6
Mandsaur 44-45 LM 6
Mandui = Māndvi 44-45 K 6
Mandurah 56-57 BC 6
Mandùria 36-37 G 5
Mandvi [IND, Gujarat ↙ Bhuj] 44-45 K 6
Mānesht, Kūh-e – 46-47 M 6
Manfalūṭ 62 D 4
Manfredònia 36-37 FG 5
Manfredònia, Golfo di – 36-37 FG 5
Manga [BR] 78-79 L 7
Manga [RN] 60-61 G 6
Mangabeiras, Chapada das – 78-79 K 6-L 7
Mangabeiras, Chapada das – 78-79 K 6-L 7
Mangai 64-65 E 3
Mangalia 36-37 N 4
Mangalmé 60-61 HJ 6
Mangalore 44-45 L 8
Mangaḷūru = Mangalore 44-45 L 8
Mangas, NM 76-77 J 8
Manggar 52-53 E 7
Manggyŏng-dong 50-51 GH 1
Mangi 64-65 G 2
Mangkalihat, Tanjung – 52-53 GH 6
Manglares, Cabo – 78-79 CD 4
Mango 60-61 E 6
Mangoche 64-65 J 5
Mangoky 64-65 K 7
Mangole, Pulau – 52-53 J 7
Mangoli = Pulau Mangole 52-53 J 7
Mangrove, Punta – 72-73 F 8
Mangueigne 60-61 J 6
Mangueira, Lagoa – 80 F 4
Mangueni, Plateau de – 60-61 G 4
Mangui 48-49 O 1
Manguinho, Ponta do – 78-79 M 7
Mangyai 48-49 G 4
Mangyšlak, plato – 44-45 G 2
Mangyšlakskij zaliv 38-39 J 6-K 7
Manhattan, KS 72-73 G 4
Manhattan, MT 76-77 H 3
Manhattan, NV 76-77 E 6
Manhattan Beach, CA 76-77 D 9
Manhuaçu 78-79 L 9
Maní [CO] 78-79 E 4
Mani [TJ] 48-49 F 5
Mānī', Wādī al- 46-47 J 5-6
Mania 64-65 L 7
Maniamba 64-65 HJ 5
Manica [Moçambique, ●] 64-65 H 6
Manica [Moçambique, ☆] 64-65 H 6-7
Manicaland 64-65 H 6
Manicoré 78-79 G 6
Manicouagan, Rivière – 70-71 X 7-8
Maniema 63 AB 4
Manika, Plateau de la – 64-65 G 4-5
Manila 52-53 H 3-4
Manila, UT 76-77 HJ 5
Manila Bay 52-53 GH 4
Manilla 58 K 3
Manipur [IND, ☆] 44-45 P 5-6
Manipur = Imphal 44-45 P 6
Manisa 44-45 B 3
Manislee River 74-75 A 2
Manitoba 70-71 Q-S 6
Manitoba, Lake – 70-71 R 7
Manitoulin Island 70-71 U 8
Manitouwadge 70-71 T 8
Manitowoc, WI 72-73 J 3
Manītsoq 70-71 Za 4
Maniwaki 70-71 V 8
Manizales 78-79 D 3
Manja 64-65 K 7
Manjacaze 64-65 H 7-8
Manjīl 46-47 N 4
Manjimup 56-57 C 6
Manjra 44-45 M 7
Mankato, MN 72-73 H 3
Mankono 60-61 C 7
Mankoya 64-65 F 5
Manna 52-53 D 7
Mannahill 58 DE 4
Mannar, Golfe de – 44-45 M 9
Mannar, Gulf of – 44-45 M 9
Mannār Khārī = Gulf of Mannar 44-45 M 9
Mannheim 33 D 4
Manning, SC 74-75 CD 8
Mannington, WV 74-75 C 5
Man'niyah, Al- = Al-Ma'anīyah 44-45 E 4
Manokwari 52-53 K 7
Manombo 64-65 K 7
Manono 64-65 G 4
Manp'ojin 50-51 F 2
Manqalah 60-61 L 7
Manresa 34-35 HJ 8
Mans, le – 34-35 H 4-5
Mansa [ZRE] 64-65 G 5
Mansalar = Pulau Mursala 52-53 C 6
Mansaya = Masaya 72-73 J 9
Mansel Island 70-71 U 5
Manseriche, Pongo de – 78-79 D 5
Mansfield [AUS] 58 H 6
Mansfield [GB] 32 F 5
Mansfield, OH 72-73 K 3
Mansfield, PA 74-75 E 4
Mansfield, WA 76-77 D 2
Manso, Rio – 78-79 J 7-8
Manṣūrābād = Mehrān 46-47 M 6
Manṣūrah, Al- [ET] 60-61 L 2
Manṣūrīyah, Al- 46-47 L 5
Manta 78-79 C 5
Manta, Bahía de – 78-79 C 5
Mantalingajan, Mount – 52-53 G 5
Mantaro, Río – 78-79 E 7
Manteca, CA 76-77 C 7
Manteco, El – 78-79 G 3
Manteo, NC 74-75 F 7
Mantes-la-Jolie 34-35 H 4
Manti, UT 76-77 H 6
Mantiqueira, Serra da – 78-79 KL 9
Mantoue = Mantova 36-37 D 3
Mantova 36-37 D 3
Mantsjoerije 48-49 N-P 2
Mänttä 30-31 L 6
Mantung 58 E 5
Manturovo 38-39 HJ 4
Mäntyharju 30-31 M 7
Mäntyluoto 30-31 J 7
Mantzikert = Malazgirt 46-47 K 3
Manú 78-79 E 7
Manuelito, NM 76-77 J 8
Manuelzinho 78-79 HJ 6
Manuk, Pulau – 52-53 K 8
Mānūk, Tall – 46-47 H 6
Manukau 56-57 OP 7
Manukau Harbour 56-57 O 7
Manus 52-53 N 7
Manyara, Lake – 64-65 J 3
Manyas 46-47 B 2
Manyč 38-39 H 6
Manyonga 63 C 3-4
Manyoni 64-65 H 4
Manzanares [E, ~] 34-35 F 8
Manzanares [E, ●] 34-35 F 9
Manzanillo [C] 72-73 L 7
Manzanillo [MEX] 72-73 EF 8
Manzanillo, Punta – 72-73 L 9-10
Manzanza 63 B 4
Manzay 44-45 KL 4
Manzhouli 48-49 M 2
Manzikert = Malazgirt 46-47 K 3
Manzilah, Al- 62 DE 2
Manzilah, Buḥayrat al- 62 DE 2
Manzini 64-65 H 8
Manzovka = Sibircevo 42-43 Z 9
Mao [Tchad] 60-61 H 6
Maoka = Cholmsk 42-43 b 8
Maoke, Pegunungan – 52-53 LM 7
Maoming 48-49 L 7
Mapaga 52-53 G 7
Mapai 64-65 H 7
Mapare 64-65 NO 6
Mapham Tsho 48-49 E 5
Mapham Yumtsho = Mapham Tsho 48-49 E 5
Mapi 52-53 L 8
Mapia, Kepulauan – 52-53 KL 6
Mapichi, Serranía de – 78-79 F 3-4
Mapimí, Bolsón de – 72-73 F 6
Ma-p'ing = Liuzhou 48-49 K 7
Mapinhane 64-65 HJ 7
Mapire 78-79 G 3
Mapiripan, Salto – 78-79 E 4
Mapleton, OR 76-77 AB 3
Mapoon Aboriginal Reserve 56-57 H 2
Mappi = Mapi 52-53 L 8
Maprik 52-53 M 7
Mapuera, Rio – 78-79 H 5
Mapula 63 D 6
Maputo [Moçambique, ●] 64-65 H 8
Maputo, Baía do – 64-65 H 8
Ma'qalā' 44-45 F 5
Ma'qil, Al- 46-47 M 7
Maqinchao 80 C 6
Maqnā 62 F 3
Maqṭayr 60-61 BC 4
Maquan He = Tsangpo 48-49 EF 6
Maquela do Zombo 64-65 DE 4
Maqueze 64-65 H 7
Maqwa', Al- 46-47 M 8
Mar, Serra do – 80 G 2-3
Mara [EAT, ~] 64-65 H 3
Mara [EAT, ●] 63 C 3
Mara [EAT, ☆] 64-65 HJ 3
Maraā 78-79 F 5
Marabá 78-79 K 6

196 Maidī

Marabitanas 78-79 F 4
Maracá, Ilha – 78-79 G 4
Maracá, Ilha de – 78-79 JK 4
Maracaibo 78-79 F 2
Maracaibo, Lago de – 78-79 E 2-3
Maracaju 78-79 H 9
Maracaju, Serra de – 78-79 H 9-J 8
Maracanã [BR, Pará] 78-79 K 5
Maracay 78-79 F 2
Marādah 60-61 H 3
Maradi 60-61 F 6
Mar Adriático 36-37 E 3-H 5
Ma'rafāy, Jabal – 62 F 6
Mara Game Reserve 64-65 HJ 3
Marāghah, Al- 62 D 4
Marāgheh 44-45 F 3
Marahuaca, Cerro – 78-79 FG 4
Marajó, Baía de – 78-79 K 4-5
Marajó, Ilha de – 78-79 JK 5
Marākand 46-47 L 3
Maralal 64-65 J 2
Maral Bashi 48-49 D 3-4
Maralinga 56-57 F 6
Mar Amarillo 48-49 N 4
Maramasike 52-53 k 6
Maramba = Livingstone 64-65 G 6
Marambaia, Restinga da – 78-79 L 9
Marampa 60-61 B 7
Maran [MAL] 52-53 D 6
Mārān = Mohājerān 46-47 N 5
Marana, AZ 76-77 H 9
Maranboy 56-57 F 2
Marand 46-47 L 3
Marandellas = Marondera 64-65 H 6
Maranguape 78-79 M 5
Maranhão 78-79 KL 5-6
Maranoa River 56-57 J 5
Marañón, Río – 78-79 DE 5
Marañón, Río – 78-79 DE 5
Mar Arábigo 44-45 JK 7
Mar Argentino 80 D 7-E 5
Maraş = Kahramanmaraş 44-45 D 3
Maraşalçakmak = Ovacıg 46-47 H 3
Mărăşeşti 36-37 M 3
Maratha = Maharashtra [IND, ≅] 44-45 M 7
Maratha = Maharashtra [IND, ☆] 44-45 L 7-M 6
Marathón 36-37 KL 6
Marathon [CDN] 70-71 T 8
Marathon, FL 74-75 c 4
Maratua, Pulau – 52-53 G 6
Marau [RI] 52-53 F 7
Marauni 52-53 k 7
Maraviė = Morava 33 G-J 4
Marawī 60-61 L 5
Mar'ayt 44-45 G 7
Mar Báltico 30-31 G 10-J 8
Marbella 34-35 E 10
Mar Blanco 42-43 FG 4
Marble Bar 56-57 CD 4
Marble Canyon, AZ 76-77 H 7
Marble Gorge 76-77 H 7
Marble Hall 64-65 G 8
Marburg 33 D 3
Marcali 33 H 5
Marcaria 36-37 D 3
Marcas = Marche 36-37 E 4
Mar Caspio 44-45 F 2-G 3
Marcelino 78-79 F 5
Marcellus, WA 76-77 D 2
Marcha [SU, ~] 42-43 W 5
Marcha [SU, ●] 42-43 X 5
Marche 34-35 HJ 5
Marche 36-37 E 4
Marchena 34-35 E 10
Marchena, Isla – 78-79 AB 4
Marches = Marche 36-37 E 4
Mar Chiquita, Laguna – 80 D 4
Marcoule 34-35 K 6
Marcus Baker, Mount – 70-71 G 5
Marcus-Necker, Dorsal de – 22-23 R 4-T 5
Marcus Necker, Dorsale de – 22-23 R 4-T 5
Marcus Necker Ridge 22-23 R 4-T 5
Marcus Neckerrug 22-23 R 4-T 5
Marcy, Mount – 74-75 FG 2-3
Mar Chiquita, Laguna – 80 D 4
Mardān 44-45 L 4
Mar del Norte 32 F-J 3
Mar del Plata 80 E 5
Mardin 44-45 E 3
Mardin Dağları 46-47 J 4
Marė, Île – 56-57 N 4
Mare, Muntele – 36-37 K 2
Marebe = Mā'rib 44-45 F 7
Maree, Loch – 32 D 3
Mareeba 56-57 HJ 3
Mareeg = Mereeg 60-61 b 3
Mar Egeo 36-37 L 5-M 7
Maremma 36-37 D 4
Maréna 60-61 B 6
Marengo, WA 76-77 DE 2
Marengo = Ḥajut 60-61 E 1
Marèttimo 36-37 DE 7
Marfa', Al- = Al-Maghayrā' 44-45 G 6
Marfil, Costa de – [≅] 60-61 CD 8
Margarita 80 D 3
Margarita, Isla de – 78-79 G 2
Margeride, Monts de la – 34-35 J 6
Margherita 63 B 2
Margherita = Jamaame 64-65 K 2
Margherita, Lake – = Abaya 60-61 M 7
Margilan 44-45 L 2
Mārgo, Dasht-i – 44-45 J 4
Margoh, Dasht-e – = Dasht-e Marg 44-45 J 4
Marguerite, Baie – 24 C 29-30
Mari, República Autónoma de los – = 3◁ 42-43 H 6
Maria Chiquita 72-73 b 2
Maria Chiquita 72-73 b 2
Maria Elena 80 BC 2
Maria Enrique, Altos de – 72-73 bc 2
Maria Island [AUS, Northern Territory] 56-57 G 2
Maria Island [AUS, Tasmania] 56-57 J 8
Mariakani 63 D 3
Maria Madre, Isla – 72-73 E 7
Maria Magdalena, Isla – 72-73 E 7
Mariana Basin 22-23 R 5
Marianao 72-73 K 7
Marianas, Cuenca de las – 22-23 R 5
Marianas, Fosa de las – 22-23 R 5
Mariana Trench 22-23 R 5
Marianenbekken 22-23 R 5
Marianentrog 22-23 R 5
Mariannes, Bassin des – 22-23 R 5
Mariannes, Fosse des – 22-23 R 5
Mariano Machado = Ganda 64-65 D 5
Mariánské Lázně 33 F 4
Marías, Islas – 72-73 E 7
Marias Pass 72-73 D 2
Marias River 76-77 H 1
Mari Autonome Republiek = 3 ◁ 42-43 H 6
Mari Autonomous Republic = 3◁ 42-43 H 6
Maria van Diemen, Cape – 56-57 O 6
Mariazell 33 G 5
Ma'rib 44-45 F 7
Maribor 36-37 F 2
Marica [BG, ~] 36-37 L 4
Marica [BG, ●] 36-37 LM 4
Maricopa, AZ 76-77 G 9
Maricopa, CA 76-77 D 8
Maricopa Indian Reservation 76-77 G 9
Maricourt 70-71 W 5
Marīdī 60-61 KL 8
Mariê, Rio – 78-79 F 5
Marie-Galante 72-73 OP 8
Mariehamn 30-31 HJ 7
Marie Louise Island 64-65 MN 4
Mariental 64-65 E 7
Mariestad 30-31 E 8
Marietta, GA 72-73 K 5
Marietta, OH 74-75 C 5
Mariinsk 42-43 Q 6
Marii Prončiščevoj, buchta – 42-43 VW 2
Mariis, République Autonome des – = 3◁ 42-43 H 6
Marília 78-79 JK 9
Marina, Île – = Santo 56-57 MN 3
Marina di Gioiosa Iònica 36-37 G 6
Marinduque Island 52-53 H 4
Marinette, WI 72-73 J 2
Maringa [ZRE] 64-65 F 2
Mar Interior = Seto-naikai 48-49 P 5
Marion 24 E 4
Marion, MT 76-77 F 1
Marion, NC 74-75 BC 7
Marion, SC 74-75 D 7
Marion, VA 74-75 C 6
Marion, Lake – 74-75 C 8
Marion Island 24 E 4
Maripa 78-79 FG 3
Maripasoula 78-79 J 4
Mariposa, CA 76-77 D 7
Marīr, Jazīrat – 62 FG 6
Mariscal Estigarribia 80 D 2
Marismas, Las – 34-35 D 10
Marīwān 46-47 M 5
Mārīyah, Al- 44-45 G 6
Marj, Al- 60-61 J 2
Marjaayoûn = Marj'uyūn 46-47 F 6
Märjamaa 30-31 L 8
Marjan = Wāza Khwā 44-45 K 4
Marjevka 42-43 M 7
Mar Jónico 36-37 GH 7
Marj'uyūn 46-47 F 6
Marka [SP] 60-61 NO 8
Markādā' 46-47 J 5
Markazī 44-45 E 3-F 4
Markdale 74-75 C 2
Markham 74-75 D 3
Markham, WA 76-77 AB 2
Markham, Mount – 24 A 15-16
Markkēri = Mercara 44-45 M 8
Markleeville, CA 76-77 CD 6
Markounda 60-61 H 7
Markovo [SU, Čukotskaja AO] 42-43 gh 5
Marktredwitz 33 EF 3-4
Marlborough [AUS] 56-57 JK 4
Marlinton, WV 74-75 CD 5
Marlo 58 J 6
Marmagab 44-45 L 7
Marmande 34-35 H 6
Marmara Adası 44-45 B 2
Marmara Denizi 44-45 B 2
Marmarâs = Marmaris 46-47 C 4
Marmarica = Barqat al-Baḥrīyah 60-61 JK 2
Marmaris 46-47 C 4
Mar Mediterraneo 28-29 J 8-O 9
Marmelos, Rio dos – 78-79 G 6
Mar Menor 34-35 G 10
Marmet, WV 74-75 C 5
Marmolada 36-37 DE 2
Mar Muerto = Baḥr al-Mayyit 44-45 D 4
Marne 34-35 JK 4
Marne au Rhin, Canal de la – 34-35 K 4
Maroantsētra 64-65 LM 6
Maroc 60-61 C 3-D 2
Marondera 64-65 H 6
Maroni 78-79 J 3-4
Maroona 58 F 6
Maros [RI] 52-53 GH 7-8
Marosvasarhely = Tîrgu Mureş 36-37 L 2
Maroua 60-61 G 6
Marovoay 64-65 L 6
Marowijne [SME, ~] 78-79 J 3-4
Marqat Bazar 48-49 D 4
Marquesas Keys 74-75 b 4
Marquette, MI 72-73 J 2
Marrah, Jabal – 60-61 JK 6
Marrâkech = Marrākush 60-61 C 2
Marrākush 60-61 C 2
Marrawah 56-57 H 8
Marree 56-57 G 5
Mar Rojo 44-45 D 5-7
Marromeu 64-65 J 6
Marruecos 60-61 C 3-D 2
Marrupa 64-65 J 5
Marsā 'Alam 62 F 5
Marsā al-Burayqah 60-61 HJ 2
Marsabit 64-65 J 2
Marsabit Game Reserve 63 D 2
Marsala 36-37 E 7
Marsā Sha'b 60-61 M 4
Marsa Sūsa = Sūsah 60-61 J 2
Marseille 34-35 K 7
Marsfjället 30-31 F 5
Marshall, NC 74-75 B 7
Marshall, TX 72-73 H 5
Marshall, Fosse des – 22-23 S 5
Marshall, Îles – 22-23 S 5
Marshall, Mount – 74-75 D 5
Marshall Trench 22-23 S 5
Marshalltrog 22-23 S 5
Marshall, Fosa de las – 22-23 S 5
Marshfield = Coos Bay, OR 72-73 AB 3
Mars Hill, ME 74-75 JK 1
Marsing, ID 76-77 E 4
Marstrand 30-31 D 9
Martaban = Môktama 52-53 C 3
Martensøya 30-31 I 4
Marthaguy Creek 58 H 3
Martha's Vineyard 72-73 MN 3
Martigny 33 C 5
Martigues 34-35 K 7
Martim Vaz, Ilhas – 78-79 O 9
Martin 33 J 4
Martinique 72-73 OP 9
Martin Peninsula 24 B 25-26
Martin Point 70-71 H 3
Martinsburg, WV 74-75 DE 5
Martinsdale, MT 76-77 H 2
Martins Ferry, OH 74-75 C 4
Martinsville, VA 74-75 D 6
Mar Tirreno 36-37 D-F 6
Marton [NZ] 56-57 OP 8
Martos 34-35 EF 10
Martre, Lac la – 70-71 MN 5
Martuk 42-43 K 7
Marua = Maroua 60-61 G 6
Marugame 50-51 J 5
Marui 52-53 M 7
Maruim 78-79 M 7
Marungu 64-65 GH 4
Marvão 34-35 D 9
Mārvāṛ = Marwar [IND, ≅] 44-45 L 5
Mārvāṛ = Marwar [IND, ●] 44-45 L 5
Marvine, Mount – 76-77 H 6
Marwar [IND, ≅] 44-45 L 5
Marwar [IND, ●] 44-45 L 5
Marx 38-39 J 5
Mary 44-45 J 3
Maryborough [AUS, Queensland] 56-57 K 5
Maryborough [AUS, Victoria] 56-57 HJ 7
Mary Kathleen 56-57 GH 4
Maryland [USA] 72-73 L 4
Mary Rvier 56-57 F 2
Marysvale, UT 76-77 GH 6
Marysville, WA 76-77 BC 1
Maryūṭ, Buḥayrat – 62 CD 2
Maryvale 56-57 HJ 3
Maryville, CA 76-77 C 6
Marzo, Cabo – 78-79 D 3
Marzu, Kūh-e – 46-47 M 6
Marzūq 60-61 G 3
Marzūq, Ṣaḥrā' – 60-61 G 3-4
Masai Mara Game Reserve 63 C 3
Masai Steppe 64-65 J 3
Masaka 64-65 H 3
Masalembu Besar, Pulau – 52-53 FG 8
Masampo = Masan 48-49 O 4-5
Masan 48-49 O 4-5
Masandam, Rā's – 44-45 H 5
Maṣarah, Al- 62 C 5
Masardis, ME 74-75 J 1
Masasi 64-65 J 5
Masavi 78-79 G 8
Masaya 72-73 J 9
Masbat = Masbate 52-53 H 4
Masbate 52-53 H 4
Mascara = Mū'askar 60-61 E 1
Mascareignes, Bassin des – 22-23 M 6
Mascarene Basin 22-23 M 6
Mascarene Islands 64-65 M 7-O 6
Mascarene Plateau 22-23 MN 6
Mascareñas, Cuenca de las – 22-23 M 6
Mascareñas, Dorsal de las – 22-23 MN 6
Mascate = Masqaṭ 44-45 H 6
Maserti = Ömerli 46-47 J 4
Maseru 64-65 G 8
Mashala 64-65 F 3-4
Mashash, Bi'r – = Bi'r Mushāsh 46-47 G 7
Mashhad 44-45 HJ 3
Mashike 50-51 b 2
Māshkel, Hāmūn-i – 44-45 J 5
Mashonaland North 64-65 GH 6
Mashonaland South 64-65 GH 6
Mashrā' ar-Raqq 60-61 K 7
Mashraqī Bangāl 44-45 O 5-P 6
Mashrūkah, Qārat al- 62 C 2
Mashū-ko 50-51 d 2
Mašigina, guba – 42-43 HJ 3
Masīlah, Wādī al- 44-45 F 7
Masi-Manimba 64-65 E 3
Masin 52-53 L 8
Masindi 64-65 H 2
Maṣīrah, Jazīrat al- 44-45 HJ 6
Maṣīrah, Khalij al- 44-45 H 6-7
Masisi 63 B 3
Masjed Soleymān 44-45 FG 4
Maskanah 46-47 GH 4-5
Maskarenenbekken 22-23 M 6
Maskarenenrug 22-23 MN 6
Maskate = Masqaṭ 44-45 H 6
Masoala, Cap – 64-65 M 6
Mason, WY 76-77 HJ 4
Mason City, IA 72-73 H 3
Masqaṭ 44-45 H 6
Maṣr el-Gedîda = Al-Qahīrah-Miṣr al-Jadīdah 62 D 2
Massa 36-37 D 3
Massachusetts 72-73 M 3
Massachusetts Bay 72-73 MN 3
Massakori = Massakory 60-61 H 6
Massakory 60-61 H 6
Massa Marittima 36-37 D 4
Massangena 64-65 H 7
Massango 64-65 E 4
Massangulo 63 C 6
Massasi = Masasi 64-65 J 5
Massaua = Mitsiwa 60-61 MN 5
Massena, NY 74-75 F 2
Massenya 60-61 H 6
Masset 70-71 K 7
Massif Central 34-35 J 6
Massillon, OH 74-75 C 4
Massina = Macina 60-61 CD 6
Massinga 64-65 J 7
Masson Island 24 C 10
Mastabah 44-45 D 6
Masterton 56-57 P 8
Mastung 44-45 K 5
Mastūrah 44-45 D 6
Masuda 50-51 H 5
Māsūleh 46-47 N 4
Maṣyāf 46-47 G 5
Matabeleland 64-65 G 6-7
Mata da Corda, Serra da – 78-79 K 8
Matadi 64-65 D 4
Matagalpa 72-73 J 9
Matagami 70-71 V 8
Matagamon, ME 74-75 J 1
Matagorda Bay 72-73 GH 6
Matagorda Island 72-73 G 6
Maṭāi = Maṭāy 62 D 3
Mataj 42-43 O 8
Matala 64-65 E 5
Matam 60-61 B 5
Matamoros [MEX, Coahuila] 72-73 F 6
Matamoros [MEX, Tamaulipas] 72-73 G 6
Matancillas 80 B 4
Matandu 63 D 5
Matane 70-71 X 8
Matanzas 72-73 K 7
Matão, Serra do – 78-79 J 6
Matapalo, Cabo – 72-73 K 10
Mataporquera 34-35 E 7
Mātara [CL] 44-45 N 9
Mataram 52-53 G 8
Matarani 78-79 E 8
Mataranka [AUS] 56-57 F 2
Mataró 34-35 J 8
Matatiele 64-65 G 9
Maṭāy 62 D 3
Mategua 78-79 G 7
Matehuala 72-73 F 7
Matemo 63 E 6
Matera 36-37 G 5
Mátészalka 33 KL 4-5
Matetsi 64-65 G 6
Mâṭeur = Māṭir 60-61 FG 1
Mather, CA 76-77 D 7
Mathews, VA 74-75 E 6
Mathura 44-45 M 5
Mati 52-53 J 5
Matías Hernández 72-73 bc 2
Matimana 63 D 5
Matimbuka 64-65 J 5
Matinicus Island 74-75 J 3
Māṭir 60-61 FG 1
Maṭlā', Al- 46-47 M 8
Matlock, WA 76-77 B 2
Matočkin Šar 42-43 KL 3
Matočkin Šar, proliv – 42-43 KL 3
Mato Grosso [BR, Mato Grosso] 78-79 HJ 7
Mato Grosso, Planalto do – 78-79 HJ 7
Mato Grosso do Sul 78-79 HJ 8-9
Matombo 63 D 4
Matope 64-65 HJ 6
Matopo Hills 64-65 G 7
Matosinhos 34-35 C 8
Mátra 33 JK 5
Matra = Mathura 44-45 M 5
Maṭraḥ 44-45 H 6
Maṭrūḥ 60-61 K 2
Maṭrūḥ = Marsá Maṭrūḥ 60-61 K 2
Maṭrūḥ, Marsà – 62 B 2
Matsue 48-49 P 4
Matsumae 50-51 ab 3
Matsumoto 50-51 LM 4
Matsunami = Suzu 50-51 L 4
Matsusaka 50-51 KL 5
Ma-tsu Tao 48-49 MN 6
Matsuyama 50-51 J 6
Mattagami River 70-71 U 7-8
Mattamuskeet Lake 74-75 EF 7
Mattawamkeag, ME 74-75 JK 2
Matterhorn [USA] 76-77 F 5
Matthew, Île – 56-57 O 4
Matthews Peak 64-65 J 2
Maṭṭī, Sabkhat – 44-45 G 6
Matua 52-53 F 7
Matucana 78-79 D 7
Matue = Matsue 48-49 P 4
Matuku 52-53 ab 2
Matumoto = Matsumoto 48-49 Q 4
Matundu 64-65 F 2
Matura = Mathura 44-45 M 5
Maturín 78-79 G 2-3
Matuyama = Matsuyama 48-49 P 5
Maúa [Moçambique] 64-65 J 5
Maubeuge 34-35 JK 3
Maud, Banc de – 24 C 1
Maude 58 G 5
Maudlow, MT 76-77 H 2
Maud Seamount 24 C 1
Maués 78-79 H 5
Maués-Açu, Rio – 78-79 H 5
Mauhan 52-53 C 2
Maui 52-53 e 3
Maulamyaing 52-53 C 3
Maullín 80 B 6
Maumere 52-53 H 8
Maun [RB] 64-65 F 6
Mauna Kea 52-53 e 4
Mauna Loa 52-53 e 4
Maungdaw 52-53 B 2
Maunoir, Lac – 70-71 M 4
Maupin, OR 76-77 C 3
Maurice 64-65 N 7
Maurice, Lake – 56-57 EF 5
Mauricio 64-65 N 7
Mauritania 60-61 BC 4-5
Mauritanië 60-61 BC 4-5
Mauritanie 60-61 BC 4-5
Maury Mountains 76-77 C 3
Mava 52-53 M 8
Mavago 64-65 J 5
Mavinga 64-65 EF 6
Mawa 64-65 G 2
Mawhūb 62 C 5
Mawhun = Mauhan 52-53 C 2
Mawson 24 C 7
Maximo 63 D 6
Maxville 74-75 F 2
Maxville, MT 76-77 G 2
Maxwell, CA 76-77 B 6
May, ID 76-77 G 3
Maya, Pulau – 52-53 E 7
Mayādīn 46-47 J 5
Mayaguana Island 72-73 M 7
Mayagüez 72-73 N 8
Mayama 64-65 DE 3
Maya Mountains 72-73 J 8
Mayang-do 50-51 G 2-3
Mayanja 63 BC 2
Mayapán 72-73 J 7
Maydān 46-47 L 5
Maydān Ikbis 46-47 G 4
Maydena 56-57 J 8
Maydh 60-61 b 1
Maydī 44-45 E 7
Mayenne [F, ~] 34-35 G 4-5
Mayenne [F, ●] 34-35 G 4
Mayer, AZ 76-77 G 8
Mayesville, SC 74-75 C 7-8
Mayfield, ID 76-77 F 4
Maymana 44-45 JK 3
Maymyo = Memyō 52-53 C 2
Maynard, WA 76-77 B 2
Maynas 78-79 DE 5
Mayo, FL 74-75 b 1-2
Mayodan, NC 74-75 CD 6
Mayo Landing 70-71 JK 5
Mayor, El – 76-77 F 9
Mayotte 64-65 K 5
Mayoumba 64-65 CD 3
May Point, Cape – 74-75 F 5
Mayrhofen 33 EF 5
Maysarī, Al- 46-47 H 7
Maysville, NC 74-75 E 7
Mayu, Pulau – 52-53 J 6
Mayunga 64-65 G 3
Mayville, NY 74-75 D 3
Mayyit, Baḥr al- 44-45 D 4
Mazabuka 64-65 G 6
Mazagan = Al-Jadīdah 60-61 C 2
Mazagão 78-79 J 5
Mazáka = Kayseri 44-45 D 3

Mazák 197

Mazamet 34-35 J 7
Mazan = Villa Mazán 80 C 3
Māzandarān 44-45 GH 3
Mazār, Al- 46-47 F 7
Mazara del Vallo 36-37 DE 7
Mazār-i-Sharīf 44-45 K 3
Mazarrón 34-35 G 10
Mazarrón, Golfo de – 34-35 G 10
Mazar tagh 48-49 D 4
Mazatenango 72-73 H 9
Mazatlán 72-73 E 7
Mazatzal Peak 76-77 H 8
Mažeikiai 30-31 K 9
Mazgirt 46-47 H 3
Mazhafah, Jabal – = Jabal Buwārah 62 F 3
Mazıdağı 46-47 J 4
Mazirbe 30-31 JK 9
Mazoco 63 C 5
Mazr'a, Al- 46-47 F 7
Māzū 46-47 N 6
Mazurskie, Pojezierze – 33 K 2-L 1

Mbabane 64-65 H 8
Mbaikï 60-61 H 8
Mbala 64-65 H 4
Mbalabala 64-65 GH 7
Mbale 64-65 H 2
M'Balmayo 60-61 G 8
Mbamba Bay 63 C 5
Mbandaka 64-65 E 2-3
Mbanga 60-61 FG 8
Mbanza Congo 64-65 D 4
Mbanza Ngungu 64-65 D 3-4
Mbarangandu [EAT, ~] 63 D 5
Mbarangandu [EAT, ●] 63 D 5
Mbarara 64-65 H 3
Mbari 60-61 J 7
M'Bé 64-65 E 3
Mbemkuru 64-65 JK 4
Mbenkuru 63 D 5
Mbeya [EAT, ▲] 63 C 5
Mbeya [EAT, ●] 64-65 H 4
M'Bigou 64-65 D 3
Mbin 60-61 F 8
M'Binda 64-65 D 3
Mbindera 63 D 5
Mbinga 63 C 5
Mbini [Äquatorial-Guinea, ☆] 60-61 G 8
Mbizi 64-65 H 7
Mbogo's 63 C 4
Mbomou 60-61 J 7-8
M'Boro 63 AB 2
Mbour 60-61 A 6
Mbozi 63 C 5
Mbud 60-61 B 5
Mbuji-Mayi 64-65 F 4
Mbulu 63 C 3
Mburu 63 C 5
Mburucuyá 80 E 3

Mcensk 38-39 G 5
Mchinga 64-65 JK 4
Mchinji 64-65 H 5

Mdaina, Al- = Al-Madīnah 46-47 M 7
Mdandu 63 C 5

Meacham, OR 76-77 D 3
Mead, WA 76-77 E 2
Mead, Lake – 72-73 D 4
Meade Peak 76-77 H 4
Meadow Lake 70-71 P 7
Meadow Valley Range 76-77 F 7
Meadow Valley Wash 76-77 F 7
Meadville, PA 74-75 CD 4
Meaford 74-75 C 2
Mealy Mountains 70-71 Z 7
Meandro = Büyük Menderes nehri 46-47 B 4
Mearim, Rio – 78-79 L 5
Meaux 34-35 J 4
Mebote 64-65 H 7
Mebreije, Rio – = Rio Mebridege 64-65 D 4
Mebridege, Rio – 64-65 D 4
Meca = Makkah 44-45 DE 6
Meca, La – = Makkah 44-45 DE 6
Mecca, CA 76-77 EF 9
Mecca = Makkah 44-45 DE 6
Mechanicsburg, PA 74-75 E 4
Mechanicville, NY 74-75 G 3
Meched = Mashhad 44-45 HJ 3
Mechelen 34-35 K 3
Méchéria = Mishrīyah 60-61 DE 2
Mecidiye 46-47 B 3
Meçitözü 46-47 F 2
Mecklenburg 33 EF 2
Mecklenburger Bucht 33 EF 1

Mecque, la – = Makkah 44-45 DE 6
Mecsek 33 J 5
Mecúfi 64-65 K 5
Mecula 64-65 J 5
Medan 52-53 C 6
Médanos [RA, Buenos Aires ●] 80 D 5
Medanosa, Punta – 80 CD 7
Mededsia 44-45 C 3
Medellín [CO] 78-79 D 3
Medellín [RA] 80 D 3
Medelpad 30-31 FG 6
Medenîn = Madanīyīn 60-61 FG 2
Medford, MA 74-75 H 3
Medford, OR 72-73 B 3
Medgidia 36-37 N 3
Mediano 34-35 H 7
Mediaş 36-37 L 2
Medical Lake, WA 76-77 DE 2
Medicanceli 34-35 F 8
Medicine Bow Peak 72-73 EF 3
Medicine Hat 70-71 O 7
Medina, OH 74-75 BC 4
Medina del Campo 34-35 E 8
Medina de Rioseco 34-35 E 8
Medina-Sidonia 34-35 DE 10
Médine = Al-Madīnah 44-45 DE 6
Medinipur 44-45 O 6
Mediterranean Sea 28-29 J 8-O 9
Medjdel, El- = Ashqĕlōn 46-47 F 7
Mednogorsk 42-43 K 7
Mednyi, ostrov – 19 D 2
Médoc 34-35 G 6
Medvedica 38-39 H 5-6
Medvežij ostrova 42-43 f 3
Medvežjegorsk 42-43 EF 5
Meekatharra 56-57 C 5
Meerut 44-45 M 5
Mēga [ETH] 60-61 M 8
Mega [RI] 52-53 K 7
Mégalē Préspa, Límnē – 36-37 J 5
Megalópolis 36-37 JK 7
Megálo Sofráno 36-37 M 7
Mégantic 74-75 H 2
Mégara 36-37 K 6-7
Meghalaya 44-45 P 5
Megion 42-43 O 5
Mégistē 46-47 C 4
Megler, WA 76-77 B 2
Megrega 42-43 E 5
Mehadia 36-37 K 3
Mehdia = Mahdīyah 60-61 E 1
Meherrin River 74-75 E 6
Mehrabān 46-47 M 3-4
Mehrān 46-47 M 6
Mehsāna 44-45 L 6
Meia Ponte, Rio – 78-79 K 8
Meighen Island 70-71 RS 1
Meihekou = Shanchengzhen 50-51 EF 1
Meikhtīlā 52-53 BC 2
Meiktila = Meikhtīlā 52-53 BC 2
Meiling Guan = Xiaomei Guan 48-49 LM 6
Meiningen 33 E 3
Meißen 33 F 3
Mei Xian 48-49 M 7
Mejicana, Cumbre de – 80 C 3
Mejillones 80 B 2
Mejnypil'gyno 42-43 j 5
Meka Galla 63 D 2
Mekambo 64-65 D 2
Mekelē 60-61 M 6
Mekerrhane, Sebkra – = Sabkhat Mukrān 60-61 E 3
Meknès = Miknās 60-61 C 2
Mekran = Mokrān 44-45 HJ 5
Mékrou 60-61 E 6
Melagênai 30-31 M 10
Melah, Yam ham – 46-47 F 7
Melaka [MAL, ●] 52-53 D 6
Melaka, Selat – 52-53 CD 6
Melanesia 22-23 Q 5-S 6
Melanesië 22-23 Q 5-S 6
Mélanésie 22-23 Q 5-S 6
Mělas 36-37 L 7
Melayu 52-53 D 6
Melba, ID 76-77 E 4
Melbourne [AUS] 56-57 H 7
Melbourne, FL 74-75 c 2
Melbu 30-31 F 3
Melchers, Kapp – 30-31 m 6
Melchor, Isla – 80 AB 7
Melchor Múzquiz 72-73 F 6
Meldrim, GA 74-75 C 8
Melendiz Dağları 46-47 F 3
Melenki 38-39 H 4
Mélèzes, Rivière aux – 70-71 W 6

Melfi 36-37 F 5
Melfi [Tchad] 60-61 H 6
Melfort 70-71 Q 7
Melik, Wadi el – = Wādī al-Malik 60-61 KL 5
Melili 63 CD 6
Melilia = Melilla 60-61 D 1
Melilla 60-61 D 1
Melimoyu, Monte – 80 B 6
Melinde = Malindi 64-65 K 3
Melipilla 80 B 4
Melitene = Malatya 44-45 D 3
Melito di Porto Salvo 36-37 FG 7
Melitopol' 38-39 FG 6
Melk 33 G 4
Mellerud 30-31 E 8
Mellīț = Mallīț 60-61 K 6
Mellizo Sur, Cerro – 80 B 7
Mělník 33 G 3
Mel'nikovo [SU ← Tomsk] 42-43 P 6
Melo [ROU] 80 F 4
Meloco 63 D 6
Melrhir, Chott – = Shaṭṭ Malghīr 60-61 F 2
Melrhir, Chott – = Shaṭṭ Malghīr 60-61 F 2
Melrose, MT 76-77 G 3
Melsetter = Mandidzudzure 64-65 H 6-7
Meltaus 30-31 L 4
Melton Mowbray 32 F 5
Meluco 63 D 6
Melun 34-35 J 4
Melunga 64-65 E 6
Melūț = Malūț 60-61 L 6
Melville, MT 76-77 HJ 2
Melville, Cape – 56-57 HJ 2
Melville, Lake – 70-71 YZ 7
Melville Bay 56-57 G 2
Melville Bugt 70-71 X-Z 2
Melville Hills 70-71 M 4
Melville Island [AUS] 56-57 F 2
Melville Island [CDN] 70-71 N-P 2
Melville Peninsula 70-71 U 4
Melville Sound = Viscount Melville Sound 70-71 O-Q 3
Memala 52-53 F 7
Memba 64-65 K 5
Memboro 52-53 G 8
Memmingen 33 DE 5
Memphis 60-61 L 3
Memphis, TN 72-73 HJ 4
Memphremagog, Lac – 74-75 GH 2
Memuro 50-51 c 2
Memyō 52-53 C 2
Menado = Manado 52-53 H 6
Ménaka 60-61 E 5
Menam = Mae Nam Chao Phraya 52-53 CD 3-4
Menan Khong 52-53 D 3
Menarandra 64-65 KL 7-8
Menard, MT 76-77 H 3
Menbij = Manbij 46-47 G 4
Mende 34-35 J 6
Mendez [EC] 78-79 D 5
Mendī [ETH] 60-61 M 7
Mendi [PNG] 52-53 M 8
Mendocino, CA 76-77 AB 6
Mendocino, Cape – 72-73 AB 3
Mendocino, Fractura de – 22-23 BC 4
Mendocino, Gradin de – 22-23 BC 4
Mendocino Fracture Zone 22-23 BC 4
Mendocino Range 76-77 AB 5
Mendocinotrap 22-23 BC 4
Mendol, Pulau – 52-53 D 6
Mendong Gonpa 48-49 F 5
Mendota, CA 76-77 C 7
Mendoza [PA] 72-73 b 2
Mendoza [RA, ●] 80 C 4
Méné 64-65 E 2
Mene de Mauroa 78-79 E 2
Menemen 46-47 B 3
Mengen [TR] 46-47 E 2
Mengene Dağı 46-47 KL 3
Menggala 52-53 E 7
Mengkoka, Gunung – = Pulau Penyeler 52-53 H 7
Mengtze = Mengzi 48-49 J 7
Mengulek, gora – 42-43 Q 7
Mengzi 48-49 J 7
Menindee 56-57 H 6
Menindee Lake 58 EF 4
Menongue 64-65 E 5
Menorca 34-35 K 8
Men'šikova, mys – 42-43 KL 3
Mentakab 52-53 D 6
Mentawai, Kepulauan – 52-53 CD 7

Mentok 52-53 DE 7
Menton 34-35 L 7
Menzelinsk 38-39 K 4
Menzies 56-57 D 5
Menzies, Mount – 24 B 6-7
Meoqui 72-73 E 6
Meponda 63 C 6
Meppel 34-35 KL 2
Meppen 33 C 2
Meqdādiya, Al- = Al-Miqdādīyah 46-47 L 6
Mequinenza 34-35 GH 8
Mer Adriatique 36-37 E 3-H 5
Meramangye, Lake – 56-57 F 5
Merano 36-37 D 2
Merapoh 52-53 D 6
Mēraṭh = Meerut 44-45 M 5
Meratus, Pegunungan – 52-53 G 7
Merauke 52-53 LM 8
Mer Baltique 30-31 G 10-J 8
Merbein 58 EF 5
Mer Blanche 42-43 FG 4
Merca = Marka 64-65 KL 2
Mercan Dağları 46-47 H 3
Mercara 44-45 M 8
Mer Caspienne 44-45 F 2-G 3
Merced, CA 72-73 BC 4
Mercedario, Cerro – 80 BC 4
Mercedes [RA, Buenos Aires] 80 DE 4
Mercedes [RA, Corrientes] 80 E 3
Mercedes [RA, San Luis] 80 C 4
Mercedes [ROU] 80 E 4
Mercedes, Las – 78-79 F 3
Merced River 76-77 C 7
Mer Celtique 32 C 6
Mercimekkale 46-47 J 3
Mercy, Cape – 70-71 Y 5
Merdenik = Göle 46-47 K 2
Meredit, Cabo – = Cape Meredith 80 D 8
Meredith, Cape – 80 D 8
Mereeg 60-61 b 3
Mer Egee 36-37 L 5-M 7
Meregh = Mareeg 64-65 L 2
Meregh = Mereeg 60-61 b 3
Merena = Santo 56-57 MN 3
Merga = Nukhaylah 60-61 K 5
Mergui = Myeik 52-53 C 4
Merguï, Archipel de – = Myeik Kyûnzu 52-53 C 4
Mergui, Archipiélago de – = Myeik Kyûnzu 52-53 C 4
Meriç = Büyük Doğanca 46-47 B 2
Meriç Nehri 46-47 B 2
Merida [E] 34-35 D 9
Mérida [MEX] 72-73 J 7
Mérida [YV] 78-79 E 3
Mérida, Cordillera de – 78-79 EF 3
Meriden, CT 74-75 G 4
Meridian, ID 76-77 E 4
Meridian, MS 72-73 J 5
Merimbula 58 JK 6
Meringur 56-57 H 6
Mer Intérieure = Seto-naikai 48-49 P 5
Mer Ionienne 36-37 GH 7
Merir 52-53 K 6
Mer Jaune 48-49 N 4
Merke [SU] 42-43 N 9
Merket Bazar = Marqat Bazar 48-49 D 4
Mer Ligurienne 36-37 BC 4
Merlin, OR 76-77 B 4
Merluna 56-57 H 2
Mer Mediteranée 28-29 J 8-O 9
Mermer 46-47 J 3
Mer Morte = Baḥr al-Mayyit 44-45 D 4
Merna, WY 76-77 H 4
Mer Noire 38-39 E-G 7
Merowê = Marawī 60-61 L 5
Merq, el- = Al-Marj 60-61 J 2
Merredin 56-57 C 6
Merrick 32 D 4
Merrill, OR 76-77 C 4
Merrimack River 74-75 H 3
Merrit 70-71 M 7
Merriwa 58 JK 4
Mer Rouge 44-45 D 5-7
Merseburg 33 EF 3
Mersin = İcel 44-45 C 3
Mersing 52-53 D 6
Mers-les-Bains 34-35 H 3
Merthyr Tydfil 32 DE 6
Merti 63 D 2
Mer Tyrrhénienne 36-37 D-F 6
Mertz Glacier 24 C 15
Meru [EAK] 64-65 J 2-3
Meru [EAT] 64-65 J 3
Meru National Park 63 D 2

Merv 44-45 J 3
Merv = Mary 44-45 J 3
Merwar = Marwar 44-45 L 5
Merzifon 46-47 F 2
Mesa, AZ 72-73 D 5
Mesabi Range 72-73 H 2
Mesa Central = Mesa de Anáhuac 72-73 FG 7-8
Mesagne 36-37 GH 5
Mesarya 46-47 E 5
Mesa Verde National Park 76-77 J 7
Mescit Dağı 46-47 J 2
Mescit Dağları 46-47 J 2
Mescitli = Söylemez 46-47 JK 3
Meščura 38-39 K 3
Meseta del Norte 72-73 F 6
Meshhed = Mashhad 44-45 HJ 3
Meshkīn Shar 46-47 M 3
Meshra' er Req = Mashrā' ar-Raqq 60-61 K 7
Meskené = Maskanah 46-47 GH 4-5
Mesmiyé = Al-Mismīyah 46-47 G 6
Mesolóngion 36-37 J 6
Mesopotamia 44-45 E 3-F 4
Mesopotamia [RA] 80 E 3-4
Mesopotamië 44-45 E 3-F 4
Mésopotamie 44-45 E 3-F 4
Mesquite, NV 76-77 F 7
Messalo, Rio – 64-65 J 5
Messḗnē [GR, ●] 36-37 JK 7
Messḗnē [GR, ∅] 36-37 J 7
Messēniakòs Kólpos 36-37 JK 7
Messina 36-37 F 6
Messina [ZA] 64-65 GH 7
Messina, Stretto di – 36-37 F 6-7
Messinge 63 C 5
Messojacha 42-43 O 4
Mestre, Venèzia- 36-37 E 3
Mesudiye 46-47 G 2
Meta, Rio – 78-79 E 3
Meta Incognita Peninsula 70-71 X 5
Metairie, LA 72-73 H 6
Metalici, Munţii – 36-37 K 2
Metaline Falls, WA 76-77 E 1
Metán 80 D 3
Metangula 64-65 HJ 5
Metaponto 36-37 G 5
Metarica 63 D 6
Metema 60-61 M 6
Meteor, Abysse – 22-23 HJ 8
Meteor, Banco del – 22-23 H 4
Meteor, Fosa de – 22-23 HJ 8
Metéōra 36-37 J 6
Meteorbank 22-23 H 4
Meteor Crater 76-77 H 8
Meteor Depth 22-23 HJ 8
Meteordiep 22-23 HJ 8
Methow River 76-77 CD 1
Mê Thuôt = Ban Me Thuôt 52-53 E 4
Mḗthymna 36-37 LM 6
Metinic Island 74-75 J 3
Metković 36-37 GH 4
Metlakatla, AK 70-71 KL 6
Metlaouî, El – = Al-Mitlawī 60-61 F 2
Metolius, OR 76-77 C 3
Metorica 63 D 6
Métsobon 36-37 J 6
Metter, GA 74-75 B 8
Mēṭṭur Kuḷam = Stanley Reservoir 44-45 M 8
Metuge 63 E 6
Metulla 46-47 F 6
Metundo 63 E 5
Metz 34-35 L 4
Meulaboh 52-53 C 6
Meureudu 52-53 C 5
Meuse 34-35 K 4
Mexcala, Rio – = Rio Balsas 72-73 F 8
Mexicaans Bekken 72-73 HJ 6
Mexicali 72-73 C 5
Mexican Hat, UT 76-77 J 7
Mexico 72-73 E 6-G 8
México 72-73 E 6-G 8
Mexico, ME 74-75 H 2
México [MEX, ●] 72-73 G 8
Mexico, Fosa de – 22-23 DE 5
México, Golfo de – 72-73 HJ 7
Mexico, Gulf of – 72-73 HJ 7
Mexico Basin 72-73 HJ 6
Mexico Bay 74-75 E 3
México City = México 72-73 G 8
Mexicotrog 72-73 HJ 7
Mexique 72-73 E 6-G 8

Mexique, Bassin du – 72-73 HJ 6
Mexique, Golfe du – 72-73 HJ 7
Meyâdîn = Mayādīn 46-47 J 5
Meyāndowab = Mīāndowāb 46-47 M 4
Meyāneh 44-45 F 3
Meyāneh, Kūreh-ye – 46-47 M 5
Meydān Dāgh 46-47 MN 4
Meydān-e Naftūn 46-47 N 7
Meyersdale, PA 74-75 D 5
Mezdra 36-37 KL 4
Meždurečenskij 42-43 MN 6
Meždušarskij, ostrov – 42-43 HJ 3
Mezen' [SU, ~] 42-43 H 5
Mezen' [SU, ●] 42-43 GH 4
Mézenc, Mont – 34-35 JK 6
Mezenskaja guba 42-43 G 4
Mežirečje 36-37 L 1
Mezőkövesd 33 K 5

Mfūlū 60-61 KL 7
Mfwanganu 63 C 3

Mia, Wed – = Wādī Miyāh 60-61 EF 2
Miagas, Pulau – 52-53 J 5
Miajadas 34-35 E 9
Miajlar 44-45 KL 5
Miami, AZ 76-77 H 9
Miami, FL 72-73 K 6
Miami Beach, FL 72-73 KL 6
Miami Canal 72-73 K 6
Miami Shores, FL 74-75 cd 4
Mīāndou Āb = Mīāndowāb 46-47 M 4
Miandrivazo 64-65 L 6
Mianwali = Miyānwālī 44-45 L 4
Mian Xian 48-49 K 5
Mianyang [TJ, Sichuan] 48-49 J 5
Miaodao Qundao 48-49 N 4
Miao Liedao = Miaodao Qundao 48-49 N 4
Miass [SU, ●] 42-43 L 7
Miastko 33 H 1-2
Miaws, Bi'r – 62 F 6
Micay 78-79 D 4
Michajlovka 38-39 J 6
Michajlovskij 42-43 OP 7
Michalitsion = Karacabey 46-47 C 2
Michalovce 33 KL 4
Michelson, Mount – 70-71 GH 4
Michigan 72-73 J 2-K 3
Michigan, Lake – 72-73 J 2-3
Michipicoten Island 70-71 T 8
Michoacán 72-73 F 8
Micronesia [⊙] 22-23 R-T 5
Micronesia [★] 52-53 MN 5
Micronesië [⊙] 22-23 R-T 5
Micronésie [⊙] 22-23 R-T 5
Micronesië [★] 52-53 MN 5
Micronésie [★] 52-53 MN 5
Mičurin 36-37 MN 4
Mičurinsk 38-39 GH 5
Mida 63 DE 3
Midáeion = Eskişehir 44-45 C 2-3
Midai, Pulau – 52-53 E 6
Midas, NV 76-77 E 5
Mid Atlantic Ridge 22-23 H 5-3
Middelburg [ZA, Kaapland] 64-65 FG 9
Middelburg [ZA, Transvaal] 64-65 GH 8
Middelfart 30-31 CD 10
Middellandse Zee 28-29 J 8-O 9
Midden Atlas = Al-Aṭlas al-Mutawassiț 60-61 CD 2
Midden Siberisch Bergland 42-43 R-W 4-5
Middle Alkali Lake 76-77 CD 5
Middle America Trench 22-23 DE 5
Middle Andaman 44-45 P 8
Middle Atlas = Al-Aṭlas al-Mutawassiț 60-61 CD 2
Middlebury, VT 74-75 G 2
Middle East, The – 22-23 NO 4
Middle Fork John Day River 76-77 D 3
Middle Fork Salmon River 76-77 F 3
Middleport, OH 74-75 B 5
Middlesboro, KY 72-73 JK 4
Middlesbrough 32 F 4
Middleton, ID 76-77 E 4
Middleton Island 70-71 GH 6
Middleton Reef 56-57 L 5
Middletown, NY 74-75 F 4
Middletown, NJ 56-57 F 4

198 Mazam

Middle West 72-73 F-J 3
Midhdharidhrah, Al- 60-61 A 5
Midhsandur 30-31 c 2
Midia = Midye 46-47 C 2
Mid Indian Basin 22-23 NO 6
Midland 74-75 CD 2
Midland, CA 76-77 F 9
Midland, TX 72-73 F 5
Midnapore = Medinipur 44-45 O 6
Midnapur = Medinipur 44-45 O 6
Midongy-atsimo 64-65 L 7
Midsayap 52-53 HJ 5
Midvale, ID 76-77 E 3
Midvale, UT 76-77 H 5
Midville, GA 74-75 B 8
Midyān II 62 F 3
Midyat 46-47 J 4
Midžor 36-37 K 4
Mie 50-51 L 5
Międzyrec Podlaski 33 L 3
Mielec 33 K 3
Mienhsien = Mian Xian 48-49 K 5
Mien-yang = Mianyang [TJ, Sichuan] 48-49 J 5
Miercurea-Ciuc 36-37 L 2
Mieres 34-35 DE 7
Mīēso 60-61 N 7
Mifflintown, PA 74-75 E 4
Migamuwa 44-45 M 9
Migdal Ashqĕlōn = Ashqĕlon 46-47 F 7
Migdal Gad = Ashqĕlōn 46-47 F 7
Mīghān, Kavīr-e – 46-47 N 5
Migole 63 CD 4
Miguel Alves 78-79 L 5
Miguel Calmon 78-79 LM 7
Mihajlovgrad 36-37 K 4
Mihalgazi 46-47 D 2
Mihalıççık 46-47 D 3
Mihara 50-51 J 5
Miho wan 50-51 J 5
Miïto = Moyto 60-61 H 6
Mijares 34-35 G 8-9
Mijriyyah, Al- 60-61 B 5
Mikata 50-51 K 5
Mikawa wan 50-51 L 5
Miki 50-51 K 5
Mikindani 64-65 K 5
Mikkaichi = Kurobe 50-51 L 4
Mikkeli 30-31 M 7
Miknās 60-61 C 2
Mikumi 63 D 4
Mikumi National Park 63 D 4
Mikun' 42-43 HJ 5
Mikuni 50-51 KL 4
Mila = Mīlah 60-61 F 1
Milaan = Milano 36-37 C 3
Milagro, El – 80 C 4
Mīlah 60-61 F 1
Milāḥah, Wādī – 62 E 4
Milājerd 46-47 N 5
Milan, WA 76-77 E 2
Milan = Milano 36-37 C 3
Milán = Milano 36-37 C 3
Milano 36-37 C 3
Milas 46-47 B 4
Milazzo 36-37 F 6
Milbridge, ME 74-75 K 2
Mildura 56-57 H 6
Mīleh, Kūh-e – 46-47 M 6
Milepa 63 D 5
Miles 56-57 JK 5
Miles, WA 76-77 D 2
Miles City, MT 72-73 E 2
Milet 46-47 B 4
Miletos = Milet 44-45 B 3
Miletus = Milet 44-45 B 3
Milford, CA 76-77 C 5
Milford, DE 74-75 F 5
Milford, MA 74-75 H 3
Milford, NH 74-75 H 3
Milford, PA 74-75 F 4
Milford, UT 76-77 G 6
Milford Sound [NZ, ∪] 56-57 N 8
Milgis 63 D 2
Milḥ, Qurayyāt al- 46-47 G 7
Milicz 33 H 3
Miling 56-57 C 6
Milk, Wādī el – = Wādī al-Malik 60-61 KL 5
Mil'kovo 42-43 ef 7
Milk River 72-73 E 2
Millau 34-35 J 6
Mill City, OR 76-77 B 3
Milledgeville, GA 74-75 B 8
Millegan, MT 76-77 H 2
Mille Lacs Lake 72-73 H 2
Millen, GA 74-75 C 8
Millerovo 38-39 H 6
Miller Peak 76-77 H 10
Millersburg, OH 74-75 BC 4
Millersburg, PA 74-75 E 4
Millerton Lake 76-77 D 7
Millevaches, Plateau de – 34-35 HJ 6
Millican, OR 76-77 C 4
Millicent 56-57 GH 7
Millinocket, ME 74-75 J 2
Mill Island 24 C 11
Millmerran 56-57 K 5
Millville, NJ 74-75 F 5
Milne Bay 52-53 h 7
Milo [Guinea] 60-61 C 7
Milo, ME 74-75 J 2
Milo, OR 76-77 B 4
Milton, OR 76-77 D 3
Milton, PA 74-75 E 4
Milton, WV 74-75 B 5
Miluo 48-49 L 6
Milverton 74-75 C 3
Milwaukee, WI 72-73 J 3
Milwaukee, Abysse de – 72-73 N 8
Milwaukee Depth 72-73 N 8
Milwaukeediep 72-73 N 8
Milwaukeetiefe 72-73 N 8
Milwaukie, OR 76-77 B 3
Mimitsu 50-51 H 6
Mimongo 64-65 D 3
Mina, NV 76-77 DE 6
Minā' al-Aḥmadī 46-47 N 8
Min' 'Abd Allāh 46-47 N 8
Min' 'Abd Allāh 46-47 N 8
Mina de São Domingos 34-35 D 10
Minahasa 52-53 H 6
Minakami 50-51 M 4
Minam, OR 76-77 E 3
Minamata 48-49 P 5
Minami Daitō-jima 48-49 P 6
Minami-Daitō zima = Minami-Daitō-jima 48-49 P 6
Minamitane 50-51 H 7
Minas 80 EF 4
Minas Cué 80 E 2
Minas de Riotinto 34-35 DE 10
Minas Gerais 78-79 KL 8-9
Minatitlán 72-73 H 8
Minato = Nakaminato 50-51 N 4
Min Chiang = Min Jiang [TJ, Sichuan] 48-49 J 5-6
Min-ch'in = Minqin 48-49 J 4
Min Chiang = Min Jiang [TJ, Sichuan] 48-49 J 5-6
Mindanao 52-53 J 5
Mindanao Sea 52-53 HJ 5
Mindanau = Mindanao 52-53 J 5
Minden 33 D 2
Minden, NV 76-77 D 6
Minderoo 56-57 C 4
Mindoro 52-53 GH 4
Mindoro Strait 52-53 GH 4
Mindra, Vîrful – 36-37 KL 3
Mine 50-51 H 5
Mineiga, Bîr – = Bi'r Munayjah 62 F 6
Mineola, NY 74-75 G 4
Miner, MT 76-77 H 3
Mineral, CA 76-77 C 5
Mineral, WA 76-77 B 2
Mineral Mountains 76-77 G 6
Mineral'nyje Vody 38-39 H 7
Minersville, UT 76-77 G 6
Minerva, OH 74-75 C 4
Minervino Murge 36-37 FG 5
Mingan Passage = Jacques Cartier Passage 70-71 Y 7-8
Mingary 58 E 4
Mingečaur 38-39 J 7
Mingečaurskoje vodochranilišče 38-39 J 7
Mingenew 56-57 C 5
Mingfeng = Niya Bazar 48-49 E 4
Mingo Junction, OH 74-75 C 4
Mingoya 63 D 5
Minho [P, ~] 34-35 C 7
Minho [P, ≅] 34-35 C 8
Minhow = Fuzhou 48-49 MN 6
Min-hsien = Min Xian 48-49 J 5
Minicoy Island 44-45 L 9
Minidoka, ID 76-77 G 4
Minigwal, Lake – 56-57 D 5
Minikkōy Dvīp = Minicoy Island 44-45 L 9
Minilya River 56-57 BC 4
Ministro João Alberto 78-79 J 7
Minja 38-39 L 4
Min Jiang [TJ, Fujian] 48-49 M 6
Min Jiang [TJ, Sichuan] 48-49 J 5-6
Minkébé 64-65 D 2
Minle 48-49 J 4
Min-lo = Minle 48-49 J 4
Minna 60-61 F 7
Minneapolis, MN 72-73 GH 2-3
Minnesota 72-73 H 2-3
Minnesota River 72-73 H 3
Minnipa 58 B 4
Miño 34-35 D 7
Mino 50-51 L 5
Mino-Kamo 50-51 L 5
Minot, ND 72-73 F 2
Minqin 48-49 J 4
Min Shan 48-49 J 5
Minshât Dahshûr 62 D 3
Minsk 38-39 E 5
Minto, Lac – 70-71 V 5
Minto Inlet 70-71 N 3
Minūf 62 D 2
Minusinsk 42-43 R 7
Min Xian 48-49 J 5
Minyā, Al- 60-61 KL 3
Miño 34-35 D 7
Miqdādīyah, Al- 46-47 L 6
Mira 36-37 DE 3
Mīrā', Wādī al- 46-47 HJ 7
Miracema do Norte 78-79 K 6
Mirador [BR] 78-79 KL 6
Miraflores [PA] 72-73 b 2
Miraflores, Esclusas de – 72-73 b 3
Miraflores Locks = Esclusas de Miraflores 72-73 b 3
Miramar 80 E 5
Miramar, Isla – 76-77 F 10
Mirampéllu, Kólpos – 36-37 LM 8
Miranda [BR] 78-79 H 9
Miranda, Rio – 78-79 H 9
Miranda de Ebro 34-35 F 7
Miranda do Douro 34-35 D 8
Mirande 34-35 H 7
Mirandela 34-35 D 8
Mirándola 36-37 D 3
Mirapinima 78-79 G 5
Mirbāṭ 44-45 GH 7
Mirêar, Gezîret – = Jazīrat Marīr 62 FG 6
Mirgorod 38-39 F 5-6
Miri 52-53 F 6
Mirim, Lagoa – 80 F 4
Miriti 78-79 H 6
Mīrjāveh 44-45 J 5
Mirnyj [Antarctica] 24 C 10
Mirnyj [SU] 42-43 V 5
Mirtağ = Mutki 46-47 J 3
Miryang 50-51 G 5
Mirzapur 44-45 N 5-6
Misāḥah, Bi'r – 60-61 K 4
Mīsān 46-47 M 6
Mish'āb, Al- 44-45 F 5
Mīshāb, Kūh-e – 46-47 L 3
Mishan 48-49 P 2
Mishbīh, Jabal – 60-61 L 4
Mi-shima 50-51 H 5
Misima 52-53 h 7
Misión, La – 76-77 E 9
Misiones [RA] 80 EF 3
Miskito, Cayos – 72-73 K 9
Miskolc 33 K 4
Misli = Gölcük 46-47 F 3
Mismāḥ, Tall al- 46-47 G 6
Mismār 60-61 M 5
Mismīyah, Al- 46-47 G 6
Misool, Pulau – 52-53 K 7
Misore = Mysore 44-45 M 8
Miṣr, Al- 60-61 KL 3
Miṣr al-Jadīdah, Al-Qāhirah- 62 DE 2
Misrātah 60-61 H 2
Miṣr Baḥrī 62 DE 2
Miṣr el-Gedîda = Al-Qāhirah-Miṣr al-Jadīdah 62 DE 2
Mısrıç = Kurtalan 46-47 J 4
Missale 63 C 6
Missinaibi River 70-71 U 7
Mississauga 74-75 D 3
Mississippi 72-73 J 5
Mississippi River 72-73 H 3
Mississippi River Delta 72-73 J 6
Missoula, MT 72-73 D 2
Missouri 72-73 H 3-4
Missouri River 72-73 G 3
Mistassini, Lac – 70-71 W 7
Mistassini, Lac – 70-71 W 7
Mistelbach 33 H 4
Misumi 50-51 H 6
Misurāta = Misrātah 60-61 H 2
Mita, Punta de – 72-73 E 7
Mitai 50-51 H 6
Mitchell [AUS] 56-57 J 5
Mitchell [CDN] 74-75 C 3
Mitchell, OR 76-77 CD 3
Mitchell, SD 72-73 G 3
Mitchell, Mount – 72-73 K 4
Mitchell River [AUS, ~] 56-57 H 3
Mitchell River [AUS, ●] 56-57 H 3
Miteja 63 D 5
Mithrâw 44-45 KL 5
Mi'tiq, Gebel – = Jabal Mu'tiq 62 E 4
Mīt Jamr 62 D 2
Mitlawī, Al- 60-61 F 2
Mito 48-49 R 4
Mitowa 63 D 5
Mitre 56-57 O 2
Mitre, Península – 80 CD 8
Mitsinjo 64-65 L 6
Mitsio, Nosy – 64-65 L 5
Mitšiwa 60-61 MN 5
Mitsuke 50-51 M 4
Mitsumata 50-51 c 2
Mitsushima 50-51 G 5
Mittellandkanal 33 CD 2
Mitú 78-79 EF 4
Mitumba, Chaîne des – 64-65 G 4-5
Mitumba, Chaîne des – 64-65 G 4-5
Mitumba, Monts – 64-65 G 3
Mitwaba 64-65 G 4
Mityana 63 BC 2
Mitzic 64-65 D 2
Mitzusawa 48-49 QR 4
Miyagi 50-51 N 3
Miyāh, Wādī – 60-61 EF 2
Miyāh, Wadī al- 62 E 5
Miyāh, Wādī al- = Wādī Jarīr 44-45 E 5-6
Miya kawa 50-51 L 5
Miyake-jima 48-49 QR 5
Miyake zima = Miyake-jima 48-49 QR 5
Miyako 50-51 N 3
Miyako-jima 48-49 O 7
Miyakonojō 48-49 P 5
Miyakonozyō = Miyakonojō 48-49 P 5
Miyako wan 50-51 NO 3
Miyako zima = Miyako-jima 48-49 O 7
Mīyāneh = Meyāneh 44-45 F 3
Miyanoura = Kamiyaku 50-51 H 7
Miyānwālī 44-45 L 4
Miyazaki 48-49 P 5
Miyazu 50-51 K 5
Miyet, Baḥr el- = Baḥr al-Mayyit 44-45 D 4
Miyoshi 50-51 J 5
Mizar = Karakeçi 46-47 H 4
Mizdah 60-61 G 2
Mizen Head 32 AB 6
Mizil 36-37 M 3
Mizoram 44-45 P 6
Mizque 78-79 FG 8
Mizusawa 48-49 QR 4
Mjölby 30-31 F 8
Mjøsa 30-31 D 7
Mkata 63 D 4
Mkhili = Al-Makīlī 60-61 J 2
Mkobela 63 D 5
Mkokotoni 63 D 4
Mkondoa 63 D 4
Mkonga 63 CD 4
Mkulwe 63 C 5
Mkuranga 63 D 4
Mkushi 63 B 6
Mladá Boleslav 33 G 3
Mladenovac 36-37 J 3
Mlangali 63 C 5
Mława 33 K 2
Mlayḥān, Bi'r – 46-47 H 4
Mligazi 63 D 4
Mljet 36-37 G 4
Mmabatho = Mafikeng 64-65 FG 8
Moa, Pulau – 52-53 J 8
Moab, UT 76-77 J 6
Mōāb, Jabal – 46-47 F 7
Moa Island 56-57 H 2
Moala 52-53 a 2
Moamba 64-65 H 8
Moapa, NV 76-77 F 7
Moba [ZRE] 64-65 G 4
Mobaye 60-61 J 8
Moberly, MO 72-73 H 4
Mobile, AL 72-73 J 5
Mobile Bay 72-73 J 5
Mobutu-Sese-Seko, Lac – 64-65 H 2
Moca = Al-Mukhā 44-45 E 8
Moca = Al-Mukhā 44-45 E 8
Mocajuba 78-79 K 5
Moçambique [Moçambique, ●] 64-65 K 6-7
Moçambique, Canal de – 64-65 K 7-5
Moçâmedes 64-65 D 6
Mocha = Al-Mukhā 44-45 E 8
Mocha, Isla – 80 B 5
Mochis, Los – 72-73 E 6
Möch Sar'dag uul 48-49 HJ 1
Mochudi 64-65 G 7
Mocimboa da Praia 64-65 JK 5
Mocksville, NC 74-75 C 7
Moclips, WA 76-77 A 2
Mocoa 78-79 D 4
Moçoró 78-79 M 6
Mocuba 64-65 J 6
Modane 34-35 L 6
Mòdena 36-37 D 3
Modena, UT 76-77 FG 7
Modesto, CA 72-73 BC 4
Mòdica 36-37 F 7
Modjamboli 64-65 F 2
Modoc Lava Bed 76-77 C 5
Modriča 36-37 H 3
Moengo 78-79 J 3
Moenkopi Wash 76-77 H 7
Moermanskdrempel 42-43 EF 2
Moe-Yallourn 56-57 J 7
Moffen 30-31 j 4
Mogadiscio = Muqdisho 60-61 O 8
Mogadisho = Muqdiisho 64-65 L 2
Mogadishu = Muqdisho 60-61 O 8
Mogador = Aṣ-Ṣawīrah 60-61 BC 2
Mogalakwenarivier 64-65 G 7
Mogami gawa 50-51 MN 3
Mogdy 42-43 Z 7
Moghān, Dasht-e – 44-45 F 3
Mogil'ov 38-39 F 5
Mogil'ov-Podolskij 38-39 E 6
Mogincual 64-65 K 6
Mogoča [SU, ●] 42-43 WX 7
Mogočin 42-43 P 6
Mogollon Mountains 76-77 J 9
Mogollon Rim 76-77 H 8
Mogororo = Mongororo 60-61 J 6
Moguer 34-35 D 10
Mogzon 42-43 V 7
Mohács 33 J 6
Mohājerān 46-47 N 5
Mohammadia = Muḥammadīyah 60-61 DE 1
Mohammed, Ras – = Rā's Muḥammad 60-61 LM 4
Moḥammerah = Khorramshar 44-45 F 4
Mohawk, AZ 76-77 G 9
Mohawk River 74-75 F 3
Mohe 48-49 N 1
Mohéli = Mwali 64-65 K 5
Mohican, Cape – 70-71 C 5
Mohilla = Mwali 64-65 K 5
Mohn, Kapp – 30-31 m 5
Mo-ho = Mohe 48-49 N 1
Mohon Peak 76-77 G 8
Mohoro 64-65 J 4
Mointy = Mojynty 42-43 N 8
Mo i Rana 30-31 F 4
Moira River 74-75 E 2
Mõisaküla 30-31 L 8
Moisie, Rivière – 70-71 X 7
Moissac 34-35 H 6
Moïssala 60-61 H 7
Mojave, CA 76-77 DE 8
Mojave Desert 72-73 C 4
Mojave River 76-77 E 8
Mojero 42-43 T 4
Moji das Cruzes 78-79 KL 9
Mojo, Pulau – = Pulau Moyo 52-53 G 8
Mojokerto 52-53 F 8
Mojynkum, peski – 42-43 MN 9
Mojynty 42-43 N 8
Mōka 50-51 MN 4
Mokai 56-57 P 7
Mokambo 64-65 G 5
Mokelumne Aqueduct River 76-77 C 6-7
Mokolo 60-61 G 6
Mokp'o 48-49 O 5
Mokrān 44-45 HJ 5
Môktama 52-53 C 3
Môktama Kwe 52-53 C 3
Moktok-to = Kyŏngnyŏlbi-yŏlto 50-51 E 4
Mola di Bari 36-37 G 5
Molalla, OR 76-77 B 3
Molat 36-37 F 3
Moldary = Konečnaja 42-43 O 7
Moldavia [≅] 36-37 M 2-3
Moldavia [★] 38-39 E 6
Moldavië [≅] 36-37 M 2-3
Moldavie [≅] 36-37 M 2-3
Moldavië [★] 38-39 E 6
Moldavie [★] 38-39 E 6
Molde 30-31 B 6
Moldova 36-37 M 2
Moldovița 36-37 L 2
Mole Creek 58 bc 2
Molepolole 64-65 FG 7
Molfetta 36-37 G 5
Molina de Segura 34-35 G 9
Moline, IL 72-73 HJ 3
Moliro 64-65 GH 4
Molise 36-37 F 5
Mollakendi 46-47 H 3
Mollālar 46-47 M 4
Mollendo 78-79 E 8
Mollera, zaliv – 42-43 HJ 3
Mölndal 30-31 DE 9
Molócue 64-65 J 6
Molodečno 38-39 E 5
Molodežnaja 24 C 5
Molodogvardejskoje 42-43 N 7
Molokai 52-53 e 3
Moloma 38-39 J 4
Molong 56-57 J 6
Molopo 64-65 F 8
Molotovsk = Nolinsk 42-43 HJ 6
Molotovsk = Severodvinsk 42-43 FG 5
Moloundou 60-61 H 8
Molu, Pulau – 52-53 K 8
Molucas, Mar de las – 52-53 HJ 6-7
Moluccas 52-53 J 6-8
Molucca Sea 52-53 HJ 6-7
Molukkenzee 52-53 HJ 6-7
Molundu = Moloundou 60-61 H 8
Moluques 52-53 J 6-8
Moluques, Mer des – 52-53 HJ 6-7
Moma [Moçambique] 64-65 J 6
Moma [SU] 42-43 bc 4
Momba 63 C 5
Mombasa 64-65 JK 3
Mombetsu 48-49 R 3
Mombongo 64-65 F 2
Momboyo 64-65 E 3
Momčilgrad 36-37 L 5
Mōminābād = Ambajogai 44-45 M 7
Momskij chrebet 42-43 b 4-c 5
Møn 30-31 E 10
Mona 72-73 N 8
Mona, UT 76-77 GH 6
Mona, Canal de la – 72-73 N 8
Mònaco 34-35 L 7
Monaco [MC, ●] 34-35 L 7
Monaco [MC, ★] 34-35 L 7
Monaghan 32 C 4
Monahans, TX 72-73 F 5
Monapo 64-65 K 5-6
Monarch, MT 76-77 H 2
Monashee Mountains 70-71 N 7
Monbetsu 50-51 bc 2
Monča Guba = Mončegorsk 42-43 DE 4
Monção [BR] 78-79 K 5
Mončegorsk 42-43 DE 4
Mönchchaan 48-49 L 2
Mönch Chajrchan uul 48-49 FG 2
Mönchengladbach 33 BC 3
Monchique, Serra de – 34-35 C 10
Moncks Corner, SC 74-75 CD 8
Monclova 72-73 F 6
Moncton 70-71 XY 8
Mönch Chajrchan uul 48-49 FG 2
Mond, Rūd-e – 44-45 G 5
Mondego 34-35 CD 8
Mondego, Cabo – 34-35 C 8
Mondo 63 CD 4
Mondoñedo 34-35 D 7
Mondoñedo 34-35 D 7
Mondovì 36-37 BC 3
Mondragon 34-35 K 6
Moné Lávras 36-37 L 5
Monembasia 36-37 K 7
Moneron, ostrov – 42-43 b 8
Monessen, PA 74-75 D 4
Moneta, VA 74-75 D 6
Monfalcone 36-37 E 3
Monforte de Lemos 34-35 D 7
Monga [EAT] 63 D 5
Monga [ZRE] 64-65 F 2
Mongala 64-65 EF 2
Mongalla = Manqalah 60-61 L 7
Mongbwalu 63 B 2
Möngbyat 52-53 CD 2
Möngdôn 52-53 C 2
Mongers Lake 56-57 C 5
Monggŭmp'o-ri 50-51 E 3
Monghyr = Munger 44-45 O 5
Mongo [Tchad] 60-61 H 6
Mongolia 46-47 H-L 2

Mongo 199

Mulanje, Mount – 64-65 J 6
Mūlayit Taung 52-53 C 3
Muldoon, ID 76-77 G 4
Muleba 63 BC 3
Mule Creek, NM 76-77 J 9
Mulgubi 50-51 G 2
Mulhacén 34-35 F 10
Mulhouse 34-35 L 5
Muli = Vysokogornyj 42-43 ab 7
Mulka 58 D 2
Mull 32 CD 3
Mullan, ID 76-77 EF 2
Mullan Pass 72-73 D 2
Mullens, WV 74-75 C 6
Muller, Pegunungan – 52-53 F 6
Müllerberg 30-31 I 6
Mullewa 56-57 C 5
Mullingar 32 C 5
Mullins, SC 74-75 D 7
Mulobezi 64-65 FG 6
Multān 44-45 L 4
Mulu, Gunung – 52-53 FG 6
Mulucas 52-53 J 6-8
Mulula, Wed – = Wādī al-Mūlūyah 60-61 D 2
Mulūṣī, Bi'r al- 46-47 J 6
Mulūṣī, Shādir al- 46-47 HJ 6
Mūlūyah, Wādī al- 60-61 D 2
Muluzia 63 B 5
Mulymja 42-43 LM 5
Mumbaī = Bombay 44-45 L 7
Mumbwa 64-65 G 6
Mumeng 52-53 N 8
Mumpu, Mount – 63 B 6
Mumra 38-39 J 6
Mun, Mae Nam – 52-53 D 3
Muna [SU] 42-43 W 4
Muna, Pulau – 52-53 H 8
Munasarowar Lake = Mapham Tsho 48-49 E 5
Munayjah, Bi'r – 62 F 6
München 33 EF 4
Munch'ŏn 50-51 F 3
Muncie, IN 72-73 JK 3
Münden 33 D 3
Mundiwindi 56-57 CD 4
Mundo, Río – 34-35 F 9
Mundrabilla 56-57 E 6
Mundubbera 56-57 JK 5
Mungallala Creek 56-57 J 5
Mungana 56-57 H 3
Mungari 64-65 H 6
Mungbere 64-65 G 2
Munger 44-45 O 5
Mungindi 56-57 J 5
Munhango 64-65 E 5
Munich = München 33 EF 4
Munkfors 30-31 EF 8
Munksund 30-31 JK 5
Muñoz Gamero, Península – 80 B 8
Munsan 50-51 F 4
Munsfjället 30-31 F 5
Münster [D] 33 C 2-3
Munster [IRL] 32 B 5
Munte 52-53 G 6
Muntok = Mentok 52-53 DE 7
Muñoz Gamero, Península – 80 B 8
Muodoslompolo 30-31 K 4
Mu'o'ng Khoua 52-53 D 2
Mu'o'ng Pak Beng 52-53 D 2-3
Muong Plateau = Cao Nguyên Trung Phân 52-53 E 4
Mu'o'ng Sen, Đeo – 52-53 DE 3
Muonio 30-31 KL 4
Muonio älv 30-31 K 4
Mup'vŏng-ni = Chŏnch'ŏn 50-51 F 2
Muqayshit 44-45 G 6
Muqayyar, Al- = Ur 44-45 F 4
Muqdisho 60-61 O 8
Muqsim, Jabal – 62 EF 6
Muqur = Moqur 44-45 K 4
Mur 33 FG 5
Mura 36-37 FG 2
Murādābād = Moradabad 44-45 MN 5
Muradiye [TR, Manisa] 46-47 B 3
Muradiye [TR, Van] 46-47 KL 3
Murakami 50-51 M 3
Murallón, Cerro – 80 B 7
Mūrān [IR] 46-47 N 7
Murang'a 64-65 J 3
Mur'anyo = Bandar Murcaayo 60-61 bc 1
Muraši 42-43 H 6
Murat Dağı 44-45 B 3
Murat Dağları = Şerafettin Dağları 46-47 J 3
Murathüyügü = Musabeyli 46-47 G 4
Murat nehri 44-45 E 3
Muravera 36-37 CD 6
Murayama 50-51 N 3
Muraywad, Al- 46-47 L 8
Murchison, Cape – 70-71 S 3
Murchison Falls = Kabelega Falls 64-65 H 2
Murchison Falls National Park = Kabelega Falls National Park 64-65 H 2
Murchisonfjord 30-31 k 4-5
Murchisonfjorden 30-31 kl 4
Murchison River 56-57 C 5
Murcia [E, ≅] 34-35 G 9-10
Murcia [E, ●] 34-35 G 9-10
Murdochville 70-71 XY 8
Murdock, FL 74-75 b 3
Mureş 36-37 K 2-3
Murfreesboro, NC 74-75 E 6
Murfreesboro, TN 72-73 J 4
Murgab [SU, ~] 44-45 J 3
Murgab [SU, ●] 44-45 L 3
Murge 36-37 G 5
Murghāb Rōd 44-45 JK 3-4
Murgon 56-57 K 5
Muriaé 78-79 L 9
Müritz 33 F 2
Murmansk 42-43 EF 4
Murmansk, Plataforma de – 42-43 EF 2
Murmanskij bereg 38-39 G 2
Murmansk Rise 42-43 EF 2
Murmaši 42-43 E 4
Muro, Capo di – 36-37 C 5
Muro Lucano 36-37 FG 5
Murom 42-43 G 6
Muromcevo 42-43 O 6
Muroran 48-49 R 3
Muros 34-35 C 7
Muroto 50-51 JK 6
Muroto zaki 50-51 K 6
Murphy, ID 76-77 E 4
Murphy, TN 74-75 A 7
Murr, Bi'r – 62 D 6
Murrat al-Kubrá, Al-Buḥayrat al- 62 E 2
Murrat el-Kubrá, Buḥeirat el – = Al-Buḥayrat al-Murrat al-Kubrá 62 E 2
Murray, Fosse de – 22-23 BC 4
Murray, Fractura de – 22-23 BC 4
Murray, Lake – [PNG] 52-53 M 8
Murray, Lake – [USA] 74-75 C 7
Murraybreukzone 22-23 BC 4
Murray Bridge 58 D 5
Murray Fracture Zone 22-23 BC 4
Murray River [AUS] 56-57 H 6-7
Murrumbidgee River 56-57 HJ 6
Murrumburrah 58 J 5
Mursala, Pulau – 52-53 C 6
Murtaf'āt Tāsīlī 60-61 F 3
Murtoa 58 F 6
Murupara 56-57 P 7
Murupu 78-79 G 4
Murvāṛā = Murwara 44-45 N 6
Murwara 44-45 N 6
Murwillumbah 56-57 K 5
Murzūq = Marzūq 60-61 G 3
Murzúq, Edeien el- = Ṣaḥrā' Marzūq 60-61 G 3-4
Mürzzuschlag 33 G 5
Muş 44-45 E 3
Mūsā, Khūr-e – 46-47 N 7-8
Muşa Ali Terara 60-61 N 6
Musabeyli 46-47 G 4
Musā'idah 46-47 M 7
Musala 36-37 K 4
Musan 48-49 OP 3
Mūsā Qal'a 44-45 JK 4
Musay'īd 44-45 G 5-6
Musayyib, Al- 46-47 L 6
Musazade = Arhavi 46-47 J 2
Muscat = Masqaṭ 44-45 H 6
Muscongus Bay 74-75 J 3
Musgrave 56-57 H 2
Musgrave Ranges 56-57 F 5
Mushā 62 D 4
Mushāsh, Bi'r – 46-47 G 7
Mushie 64-65 E 3
Mushkābād = Ebrāhīmābād 46-47 O 5
Mushora = Mushūrah 46-47 K 4
Mushūrah 46-47 K 4
Musi, Air – 52-53 D 7
Mūṣil, Al- 44-45 E 3
Musinia Peak 76-77 H 6
Musisi 63 C 4
Mūsiyān 46-47 M 6
Muskat = Masqaṭ 44-45 H 6
Muskegon, MI 72-73 J 3
Muskingum River 74-75 BC 5
Muskogee, OK 72-73 GH 4
Muskoka, Lake – 74-75 D 2
Muslimīyah 46-47 G 4
Musmār = Mismār 60-61 M 5
Musoma 64-65 H 3
Musoshi 63 AB 5
Muş ovası 46-47 J 3
Mussali, Mount – = Muşa Ali 60-61 N 6
Mussanāt, Al- 46-47 M 8
Mussau 52-53 N 7
Musselburgh 32 E 4
Musselshell River 72-73 E 2
Mussende 64-65 E 5
Mussuma 64-65 F 5
Mustafa Kemalpaşa 46-47 C 2-3
Mustaghānam 60-61 DE 1
Musters, Lago – 80 BC 7
Mustla 30-31 L 8
Mustvee 30-31 M 8
Musu-dan 50-51 GH 2
Muswellbrook 56-57 K 6
Mūṭ [ET] 60-61 K 3
Mut [TR] 46-47 E 4
Muta 63 A 3
Mutankiang = Mudanjiang 48-49 OP 3
Mutare 64-65 H 6
Muthanna, Al- 46-47 L 7
Mu'tiq, Jabal – 62 E 4
Mutis, Gunung – 52-53 H 8
Mutki 46-47 J 3
Muṭlah = Al-Maṭlā' 46-47 M 8
Mutsamudu 64-65 KL 5
Mutshatsha 64-65 F 5
Mutsu 50-51 N 2
Mutsu-wan 50-51 N 2
Muttra = Mathurā 44-45 M 5
Muwaffaqīyah, Al- 46-47 L 6
Muwayḥ, Al- 44-45 E 6
Muwayliḥ, Al- 62 F 4
Muxima 64-65 D 4
Muyinga 64-65 GH 3
Muyumba 64-65 G 4
Muẓaffarābād 44-45 LM 4
Muẓaffargaṛh 44-45 L 4-5
Muzaffarnagar 44-45 M 5
Muzaffarpur 44-45 NO 5
Muži 42-43 L 4
Muz tagh 48-49 E 4
Muz tagh ata 48-49 D 4
Mvuma 64-65 GH 6
Mwali 64-65 K 5
Mwambwa 63 C 5
Mwanamundia 63 DE 3
Mwanza [EAT] 64-65 H 3
Mwanza [ZRE] 64-65 G 4
Mwatate 63 D 3
Mwaya 64-65 H 4
Mwazya 63 BC 5
Mweka 64-65 F 3
Mwene-Ditu 64-65 F 4
Mwenga 64-65 G 3
Mwenzo 63 C 5
Mweru, Lake – 64-65 G 4
Mweru Swamp 64-65 G 4
Mwingi 63 D 3
Mwinilunga 64-65 FG 5
Mwitikira 63 C 4
Myan'aung 52-53 BC 3
Myanmar 52-53 BC 3
Myeik 52-53 C 4
Myeik Kyûnzu 52-53 C 4
Myingyan 52-53 BC 2
Myitkyīnā 52-53 C 1
Mykénai 36-37 K 7
Mýkonos 36-37 L 7
Myla 38-39 K 2
Mymensingh = Maimansingh 44-45 OP 6
Mynämäki 30-31 JK 7
Mynaral 42-43 N 8
Myohyang-sanmaek 50-51 E 3-F 2
Myōkō-zan 50-51 LM 4
Myŏngch'ŏn 50-51 GH 2
Mýra 30-31 c 2
Myrdal 30-31 B 7
Mýrdalsjökull 30-31 d 3
Mýrdalssandur 30-31 d 3
Myre 30-31 F 3
Mýrina 36-37 L 6
Myrthle 74-75 D 2
Myrtle Beach, SC 74-75 D 8
Myrtle Creek, OR 76-77 B 4
Myrtleford 58 H 6
Myrtle Point, OR 76-77 AB 4
Mysen 30-31 D 8
mys Kriljon 42-43 b 8
Myślenice 33 JK 4
Mysovsk = Babuškin 42-43 U 7
Mys Vchodnoj 42-43 QR 3
Mys Želanija 42-43 MN 2
My Tho 52-53 E 4
Mytilēnē 36-37 M 6
Myton, UT 76-77 HJ 5
Mývatn 30-31 e 2
Mziha 64-65 J 4
Mzimba 64-65 H 5
Mzuzu 63 C 5

N

Naab 33 F 4
Na'âg, Gebel – = Jabal Ni'āj 62 E 6
Na'ām, Bi'r an- 46-47 G 7
Na'ām, Maqarr an- 46-47 HJ 7
Nā'am Zarqat 62 F 6
Naantali 30-31 JK 7
Naas 32 C 5
Näätämöjoki 30-31 MN 3
Naauwpoort = Noupoort 64-65 FG 9
Nābah, Bi'r – 62 E 7
Nabč 48-49 G 4
Nâbeul = Nābul 60-61 G 1
Nabiac 58 L 4
Nabilatuk 63 C 2
Nabire 52-53 L 7
Nabīsar 44-45 KL 5-6
Nabk, An- [Saudi Arabia] 46-47 G 7
Nabk, An- [SYR] 44-45 D 4
Nāblus = Nābulus 46-47 F 6
Nabq 62 F 3
Nābul 60-61 G 1
Nābulus 46-47 F 6
Nacaca 63 D 5
Naçala 64-65 K 5
Nacfa = Nakfa 60-61 M 5
Naches, WA 76-77 C 2
Nachičevan' 38-39 J 8
Nachingwea 64-65 J 5
Nachitsjevan Autonome Republiek = 10 ◁ 38-39 J 8
Nachodka 42-43 Z 9
Nachrači = Kondirskoje 42-43 M 6
Nacka 30-31 H 8
Naco, AZ 76-77 HJ 10
Nacololo 63 D 6
Nacozari de Gracia 72-73 DE 5
Nachičevan, República Autónoma de – = 10 ◁ 38-39 J 8
Nådendal = Naantali 30-31 JK 7
Nadeždinsk = Serov 42-43 L 6
Nadhatah, An- 46-47 J 6
Nadiād 44-45 L 6
Nadjaf, An- = An-Najaf 44-45 E 4
Nadjd = Najd 44-45 E 5-6
Nādiac 36-37 J 2
Nadoa = Dan Xian 48-49 K 8
Nadqān 44-45 G 6
Nadvoicy 38-39 F 3
Nadym 38-39 O 2
Næstved 30-31 DE 10
Nafada 60-61 G 6
Nafīshah 62 DE 2
Naft, Āb i – 46-47 L 6
Naft-e Sefīd 46-47 N 7
Naft-e Shāh 46-47 L 5-6
Naft Hānah 46-47 L 5
Naft Khāna = Naft Hānah 46-47 L 5
Nafūd, An- 44-45 E 5
Nafusah, Jabal – 60-61 G 2
Naga 52-53 H 4
Nagahama [J, Ehime] 50-51 J 6
Nagahama [J, Shiga] 50-51 L 5
Nagai 50-51 MN 3
Nagaland 44-45 P 5
Nagano 48-49 Q 4
Naganohara 50-51 M 4
Nagaoka 48-49 Q 4
Nāgaur = Nagaur 44-45 L 5
Nagapattinam 44-45 MN 8
Naga Pradesh = Nagaland 44-45 P 5
Nagara gawa 50-51 L 5
Nagar Aveli = Dadra and Nagar Haveli 44-45 L 6
Nāgarkōyil = Nāgercoil 44-45 M 9
Nagar Pārkar 44-45 KL 6
Nagasaki 48-49 O 5
Naga-shima [J, ⊙] 50-51 GH 6
Nagashima [J, ●] 50-51 L 5
Nagato 50-51 H 5
Nagaur 44-45 L 5
Nag Chhu 48-49 G 5
Nagchhu Dsong 48-49 G 5
Nagchhukha = Nagchhu Dsong 48-49 G 5
Nag Chhu 48-49 G 5
Nāgercoil 44-45 M 9
Nāgīshōt = Nāqīshūt 60-61 L 8
Nagorno-Karabag, Oblast Autónoma de – = 9 ◁ 38-39 J 7-8
Nagorno-Karabagh, Région Autonome de – = 9 ◁ 38-39 J 7-8
Nagorno-Karabagh Autonome Oblast = 9 ◁ 38-39 J 7-8
Nagorno-Karabagh Autonomous Region = 9 ◁ 38-39 J 7-8
Nagornyj 42-43 Y 6
Nagoya 48-49 Q 4
Nagpur 44-45 M 6
Nagura, Ras en – = Rā's an-Naqurah 46-47 F 6
Naguun Mörön 48-49 NO 1-2
Nagykanizsa 33 H 5
Nagykőrös 33 JK 5
Nagyvárad = Oradea 36-37 JK 2
Naha 48-49 O 6
Nahanni National Park 70-71 LM 5
Nahari 50-51 JK 6
Nahariya = Nahariyya 46-47 F 6
Nahariyya 46-47 F 6
Nahāvand 46-47 N 5
Nāhid, Bi'r – 62 C 2
Nahuel Huapi, Lago – 80 B 6
Nahungo 63 D 5
Nahunta, GA 74-75 BC 9
Nain [CDN] 70-71 Y 6
Nā'īn [IR] 44-45 G 4
Naindi 52-53 a 2
Naini Tal 44-45 M 5
Nain Singh Range = Nganglong Gangri 48-49 E 5
Nairn 32 E 3
Nairobi 64-65 J 3
Naissaar 30-31 L 8
Naivasha 64-65 J 3
Najaf, An- 44-45 E 4
Najafābād 44-45 G 4
Najd 44-45 E 5-6
Naj' Ḥammādī 62 DE 4-5
Najin 48-49 P 3
Najran 44-45 E 7
Naju 50-51 F 5
Nakadōri-shima 50-51 G 6
Naka gawa 50-51 K 6
Nakajō 50-51 M 3
Nakaminato 50-51 N 4
Nakamura 50-51 J 6
Nakamura = Sōma 50-51 N 4
Nakano 50-51 M 4
Nakano-shima 50-51 J 4
Nakano-umi 50-51 J 5
Nakasato 50-51 N 2
Naka-Shibetsu 50-51 d 2
Nakasongola 63 C 2
Nakatane 50-51 H 7
Nakatsu 50-51 H 6
Nakatsukawa 50-51 L 5
Nakatsukawa = Nakatsugawa 50-51 L 5
Nakatu 50-51 H 6
Nakfa 60-61 M 5
Nakhichevan, Autonomous Republic = 10 ◁ 38-39 J 8
Nakhichevan, République Autonome de – = 10 ◁ 38-39 J 8
Nakhilī, Bi'r – 46-47 K 5
Nakhl 62 E 3
Nakhlāy, Bi'r – 62 D 6
Nakhon Lampang = Lampang 52-53 C 3
Nakhon Pathom 52-53 CD 4
Nakhon Phanom 52-53 D 3
Nakhon Ratchasima 52-53 D 3-4
Nakhon Sawan 52-53 CD 3
Nakhon Si Thammarat 52-53 CD 5
Nakina 70-71 T 7
Nakło nad Notecią 33 H 2
Naknek, AK 70-71 E 6
Nakonde 63 C 5
Nakskov 30-31 D 10
Naktong-gang 50-51 G 5
Nakuru 64-65 J 3
Nāl 44-45 K 5
Nalajch 48-49 K 2
Nal'čik 38-39 H 7
Nallıhan 46-47 D 2
Nālūt 60-61 G 2
Namacurra 64-65 J 6
Na'mah, An- 60-61 C 5
Namak, Daryācheh – 44-45 G 4
Namak-e Mīghan, Kavīre – 46-47 H 4
Namakwaland 64-65 E 8
Namakzār-e Khwāf 44-45 HJ 4
Namaland 64-65 E 8
Na'mān, Jazīrat an – = Jazīrat an-Nu'mān 62 F 4
Namanga 64-65 J 3
Namangan 44-45 L 2
Na'mānīyah, An- 46-47 L 6
Namanyere 64-65 H 4
Namapa 64-65 JK 5
Namarrói 64-65 J 6
Namasagali 64-65 H 2
Namasakata 63 D 5
Namatanai 52-53 h 5
Namatele 63 D 5
Nambanje 63 D 5
Nam Bô 52-53 DE 5
Nambour 56-57 K 5
Năm Căn 52-53 D 5
Nam Choed Yai = Kra Buri 52-53 C 4
Namch'ŏnjŏm 50-51 F 3
Namcy 42-43 Y 5
Nam Choed Yai = Kra Buri 52-53 C 4
Nam Đinh 52-53 E 2-3
Namerikawa 50-51 L 4
Nametil 64-65 JK 6
Nam-gang 50-51 F 3
Namhae-do 50-51 G 5
Namhan-gang 50-51 F 4
Namhoi = Foshan 48-49 L 7
Namib = Namibwoestyn 64-65 D 6-E 8
Namib Desert = Namibwoestyn 64-65 D 6-E 8
Namibie 64-65 E 7
Namib-Naukluft Park 64-65 DE 7
Namibwoestyn 64-65 D 6-E 8
Namjabarba Ri 48-49 H 6
Namlea 52-53 J 7
Namling Dsong 48-49 FG 6
Namoi River 56-57 JK 6
Namous, Ouèd en – = Wādī an-Nāmūs 60-61 D 2
Nampa, ID 72-73 C 3
Nampala 60-61 C 5
Nampo 48-49 NO 4
Namp'ot'ae-san 50-51 G 2
Nampula 64-65 JK 6
Namsen 30-31 E 5
Namsi 50-51 E 3
Namsos 30-31 DE 5
Nam Tsho 48-49 G 5
Namuli, Serra – 64-65 J 6
Namuling Zong = Namling Dsong 48-49 FG 6
Namulo 63 D 6
Namuno 63 D 6
Namur 34-35 K 3
Nāmūs, Wādī an- 60-61 D 2
Namus, Wau en – = Wāw an-Nāmūs 60-61 H 4
Nāmūs, Waw an- 60-61 H 4
Namutoni 64-65 E 6
Namwala 64-65 G 6
Namwŏn 50-51 F 5
Nan 52-53 D 3
Nan, Mae Nam – 52-53 D 3
Nana Candungo 64-65 F 5
Nanae 50-51 b 3
Nanaimo 70-71 M 8
Nanam 50-51 GH 2
Nana-Mambéré 60-61 GH 7
Nanango 56-57 K 5
Nanao [J] 50-51 L 4
Nanao wan 50-51 L 4
Nanau 63 E 1
Nanay, Río – 78-79 E 5
Nancha 48-49 O 2
Nanchang 48-49 LM 6
Nanchang = Nanchong 48-49 JK 5
Nancheng 48-49 M 6
Nan-ching = Nanjing [TJ, Jiangsu] 48-49 M 5
Nanchino = Nanjing 48-49 M 5
Nanchong 48-49 JK 5
Nanchung = Nanchong 48-49 JK 5
Nancy 34-35 L 4
Nanda Devi 44-45 MN 4
Nandan 50-51 K 5
Nanded 44-45 M 7
Nandeir = Nanded 44-45 M 7
Nandi 52-53 a 2
N'andoma 42-43 G 5
Nandurbār 44-45 L 6
Nandyal 44-45 M 7
Nangade 63 DE 5
Nanga Eboko 60-61 G 8

Nanga 201

Nangah Pinoh 52-53 F 7
Nan-gang = Nam-gang 50-51 F 3
Nāngā Parbat 44-45 LM 3-4
Nangatayap 52-53 F 7
Nang'-ch'ien = Nangqian 48-49 H 5
Nangnim-sanmaek 50-51 F 2
Nangqian 48-49 H 5
Nan Hai 48-49 L 8-M 7
Nanhai = Foshan 48-49 L 7
Nan-hsiung = Nanxiong 48-49 LM 6
Nanjing [TJ, Jiangsu] 48-49 M 5
Nankhu 48-49 G 3
Nanking = Nanjing 48-49 M 5
Nankoku 50-51 JK 6
Nanlaoye Ling 50-51 E 2-F 1
Nan Ling [TJ, ▲▲] 48-49 L 6-7
Nanling [TJ, ●] 48-49 M 5
Nanning 48-49 K 7
Nannup 56-57 C 6
Nanpan Jiang 48-49 JK 7
Nanping [TJ, Fujian] 48-49 M 6
Nanping [TJ, Hubei] 48-49 L 6
Nanripo 63 D 6
Nansei-shotō 48-49 NO 6-7
Nansei syotō = Nansei-shotō 48-49 NO 6-7
Nansen Sound 70-71 ST 1
Nan Shan 48-49 HJ 4
Nansio 64-65 H 3
Nantai-san 50-51 M 4
Nan-tch'ang = Nanchang 48-49 LM 6
Nan-tch'eng = Nancheng 48-49 M 6
Nan-tch'ong = Nanchong 48-49 JK 5
Nantes 34-35 G 5
Nanticoke, PA 74-75 EF 4
Nantong 48-49 N 5
Nantsang = Nanchang 48-49 LM 6
Nantucket, MA 74-75 HJ 4
Nantucket Island 72-73 N 3
Nantucket Sound 74-75 H 4
Nantung = Nantong 48-49 N 5
Nanty Glo, PA 74-75 D 4
Nanuque 78-79 LM 8
Nanusa, Kepulauan – 52-53 J 6
Nanxiong 48-49 LM 6
Nanyang 48-49 L 5
Nanyi = Nancha 48-49 O 2
Nanyuki 64-65 J 2
Nanzheng = Hanzhong 48-49 K 5
Nao, Cabo de la – 34-35 H 9
Naoconane Lake 70-71 W 7
Naoetsu 50-51 LM 4
Naōgata = Nōgata 50-51 H 6
Naoli He 48-49 P 2
Nao-li Ho = Naoli He 48-49 P 2
Naos, Isla – 72-73 bc 3
Naouá = Nawá 46-47 FG 6
Napa, CA 76-77 B 6
Napaku 52-53 G 6
Napanee 74-75 E 2
Napanwainami 52-53 L 7
Napas 42-43 P 6
Nape 52-53 DE 3
Napels = Nàpoli 36-37 EF 5
Napier [NZ] 56-57 P 7
Napier, Mount – 56-57 EF 3
Napier Mountains 24 C 6
Naples, FL 72-73 K 6
Naples, NY 74-75 E 3
Napo, Río – 78-79 E 5
Nápoles = Nàpoli 36-37 EF 5
Nàpoli 36-37 E 5
Nàpoli, Golfo di – 36-37 EF 5
Naqàda = Naqādah 62 E 5
Naqādah 62 E 5
Naqadeh 46-47 L 4
Nāqishūt 60-61 L 8
Naqūrah, Rā's an- 46-47 F 6
Nara [J] 50-51 KL 5
Nårā [PAK] 44-45 K 5
Nara [RMM] 60-61 C 5
Naracoorte 56-57 GH 7
Naradham 58 GH 4
Naranjas, Punta – 78-79 C 3
Narathiwat 52-53 DE 2
Narâyanganj 44-45 OP 6
Narbadā = Narmada 44-45 LM 6
Narbonne 34-35 J 7
Nardò 36-37 GH 5
Narembeen 56-57 C 6
Narew 33 K 2
Nåri 44-45 K 5
Narinda, Helodranon'i – 64-65 L 5
Narjan-Mar 42-43 JK 4

Narli 46-47 G 4
Narmada 44-45 LM 6
Narman 46-47 JK 2
Narodnaja, gora – 42-43 L 5
Naro-Fominsk 38-39 FG 4
Narok 64-65 J 3
Narooma 56-57 JK 7
Narrabri 56-57 JK 6
Narragansett Bay 74-75 H 4
Narrandera 56-57 J 6
Narran Lake 58 H 2
Narran River 58 H 2
Narrogin 56-57 C 6
Narromine 56-57 J 6
Narrows, OR 76-77 D 4
Narrows, VA 74-75 C 6
Narssaq 70-71 bc 5
Narssarssuaq 70-71 bc 5
Narugo 50-51 N 3
Narungombe 63 D 5
Naru-shima 50-51 G 6
Naruto 50-51 K 5
Narva [SU, ~] 30-31 M 8
Narva [SU, ●] 42-43 D 6
Narva laht 30-31 M 8
Narvik 30-31 G 3
Narvskoje vodochranilišče 30-31 N 8
Narwa = Narva 42-43 D 6
Narym 42-43 P 6
Naryn [SU, Kirgizskaja SSR ~] 44-45 L 2
Naryn [SU, Kirgizskaja SSR ●] 44-45 L 2
Naryn [SU, Rossijskaja SFSR] 42-43 S 7
Naryn = Taš-Kumyr 44-45 L 2
Narynkol 44-45 MN 2
Nasafjell 30-31 F 4
Nasarawa [WAN, Plateau] 60-61 F 7
Nasaret = Nazẹrat 46-47 F 6
Nåsåud 36-37 L 2
Naschitti, NM 76-77 J 7
Nåshik = Nasik 44-45 L 6-7
Nashua, NH 74-75 H 3
Nashville, GA 74-75 B 9
Nashville, TN 72-73 J 4
Našice 36-37 H 3
Nāsijärvi 30-31 KL 7
Nasik 44-45 L 6-7
Nåsir, An- 60-61 L 7
Nasir, Jabal an- 60-61 F 4
Nāsiriyah [IRQ] 44-45 F 4
Nasiyah, Jabal – 62 E 6
Nasondoye 64-65 FG 5
Nayoro 50-51 c 1
Nayoro = Gornozavodsk 42-43 b 8
Nazare 34-35 C 9
Nazaré [BR, Amazonas] 78-79 F 4
Nazaré [BR, Bahia] 78-79 M 7
Nazaré = Nazẹrat 46-47 F 6
Nazareth = Nazẹrat 46-47 F 6
Nazareth-Bank 64-65 O 5
Nazca 78-79 DE 7
Nazca, Dorsal de – 22-23 E 7-F 6
Nazca, Seuil de – 22-23 E 7-F 6
Nazca Ridge 22-23 F 7-E 6
Nazcarug 22-23 E 7-F 6
N'azepetrovsk 38-39 LM 4
Nazẹrat 46-47 F 6
Nazija 38-39 F 4
Nazilli 46-47 C 4
Nazimiye 46-47 HJ 3
Nazimovo = Novonazimovo 42-43 QR 6
Nazino 42-43 OP 5-6
Năzlū Rūd 46-47 L 4
Nazombe 63 D 5
Nazrēt 60-61 M 7
Nazwá 44-45 H 6
Nazyvajevsk 42-43 N 6
Nazzah 62 D 4

Nchanga 63 AB 6
Nchelenge 63 B 5

Ndabala 63 B 6
N'daghâmshah, Sabkhat – 60-61 AB 5
Ndai 52-53 k 6
Ndala 63 C 4
Ndalatando 64-65 DE 4
Ndali 60-61 E 7
Ndélé 60-61 J 7
N'Dendé 64-65 D 3
Ndeni 52-53 l 7
N'djamena 60-61 GH 6
Ndola 64-65 G 5
Nduye 63 B 2
Ndye 63 B 2
Ndzuwani 64-65 KL 5

Natural Bridges National Monument 76-77 HJ 7
Naturaliste, Cape – 56-57 B 6
Naturita, CO 76-77 J 6
Nauja Vilejka, Vilnius-30-31 LM 10
Naukarr 56-57 FG 2
Naulavaraa 30-31 N 6
Naulila 64-65 DE 6
Nā'ūr 46-47 F 6
Nåusa 36-37 JK 5
Nauvo 30-31 JK 7
Nava de Ricomalillo, La – 34-35 E 9
Navajo, AZ 76-77 J 8
Navajo Indian Reservation 76-77 HJ 7-8
Navajo Mountain 76-77 H 7
Navan 32 C 5
Navangar = Jāmnagar 44-45 L 6
Navarin, mys – 42-43 jk 5
Navarino, Isla – 80 C 9
Navarra 34-35 G 7
Navassa Island 72-73 LM 8
Naver 32 D 2
Navia 34-35 D 7
Navoi 42-43 M 9
Navojoa 72-73 E 6
Navolato 72-73 E 7
Návpaktos 36-37 JK 6
Návplion 36-37 K 7
Navrongo 60-61 D 6
Navşar = Şemdinli 46-47 L 4
Nawá 46-47 FG 6
Nawa = Naha 48-49 O 6
Nawābshāh 44-45 K 5
Nawādhibu 60-61 A 4
Nawākshūt 60-61 A 5
Nawari = Nahari 50-51 JK 6
Nawāşif, Harrat – 44-45 E 6
Nawfaliyah, An- 60-61 H 2
Naws, Rā's – 44-45 H 7
Naxos [I] 36-37 F 7
Náxos [GR, ☉] 36-37 L 7
Náxos [GR, ●] 36-37 L 7
Nayarit 72-73 EF 7
Näy Band [IR, Banāder va Jazāyer-e Khalīj-e Fārs] 44-45 G 5
Näy Band [IR, Khorāsān] 44-45 H 4
Näy Band, Ra's-e – 44-45 G 5

Neagh, Lough – 32 C 4
Neah Bay, WA 76-77 A 1
Neale, Lake – 56-57 F 4
Neales, The – 56-57 G 5
Neápolis [GR, Grámmos] 36-37 J 5
Neápolis [GR, Pelopónnēsos] 36-37 K 7
Near Islands 19 D 1
Nebek, En- = An-Nabk 44-45 D 4
Nebine Creek 56-57 J 5
Nebit-Dag 44-45 GH 3
Nebo, Mount – 76-77 H 6
Nebraska 72-73 FG 3
Nebrodie, Monti – 36-37 F 7
Neckar 33 D 4
Necochea 80 E 5
Neder-Californie 76-77 F 10
Neder-Guinee 22-23 K 5-6
Nederland 34-35 K 3-L 2
Needle Peak 76-77 E 8
Needles, CA 76-77 F 8
Neepawa 70-71 R 7
Nefoussa, Djebel – = Jabal Nafusah 60-61 G 2
Nefud = An-Nafūd 44-45 E 5
Nefud, En- = An-Nafūd 44-45 E 5
Negade = Naqādah 62 E 5
Negapatam = Nagapattinam 44-45 MN 8
Negeb = Han-Negev 46-47 F 7
Negélē 60-61 MN 7
Negerpynten 30-31 I 6
Neggio = Nejo 60-61 M 7
Neghilli = Negélē 60-61 MN 7
Negoiu 36-37 L 3
Negomane 63 D 5
Negombo = Mīgamuwa 44-45 M 9
Negotin 36-37 K 3
Negribreen 30-31 k 5
Negros 52-53 H 5
Negru Vodă 36-37 N 4
Negueve = Han-Negev 46-47 F 7
Nehalem, OR 76-77 B 3
Nehbandān 44-45 HJ 4
Nehe 48-49 NO 2
Neiafu 52-53 c 2
Nei-chiang = Neijiang 48-49 JK 6
Neihart, MT 76-77 H 2
Neijiang 48-49 JK 6
Neikiang = Neijiang 48-49 JK 6
Nei Menggu = Nei Monggol Zizhiqu 48-49 K 3-M 2
Neimenggu, Région Autonome – 48-49 K 3-M 2
Neineva 46-47 JK 5
Neiße 33 G 3
Neiva 78-79 DE 4
Neja 42-43 G 6
Nejd = Najd 44-45 E 5-6
Nejo 60-61 M 7
Nejto 38-39 NO 1-2
Nekemtē 60-61 M 7
Nekropolis 62 E 5
Nekso 30-31 F 10
Nelidovo 38-39 F 4
Nel'kan 42-43 Za 6
Nellore 44-45 MN 8
Nellūru = Nellore 44-45 MN 8
Nel'ma 42-43 ab 8
Nelson [CDN] 70-71 N 8
Nelson [NZ] 56-57 O 8
Nelson [RA] 80 D 4
Nelson, AZ 76-77 G 8
Nelson, CA 76-77 C 6
Nelson, Estrecho – 80 AB 8
Nelson, NY 74-75 E 3
Nelson Forks 70-71 M 6
Nelson Island 70-71 C 5
Nelson River 70-71 RS 6
Nelsonville, OH 74-75 B 5
Nelspruit 64-65 H 8
Nemah, WA 76-77 B 2
Neman 30-31 J 10
Ne'māniya, An- = An-Na'mānīyah 44-45 L 6
Nemenčinė 30-31 L 10
Nemira, Muntele – 36-37 M 2
Nemours = Ghazawat 60-61 D 1
Nemrut Daği 46-47 JK 3
Nemunas 30-31 K 10
Nemuro 48-49 S 3
Nemuro-kaikyō 50-51 d 1-2
Nemuro wan 50-51 d 2
Nenagh 32 BC 5
Nenana, AK 70-71 FG 5

Nenets, Circunscripción Nacional de los – 42-43 J-L 4
Nenets, District National des – 42-43 J-L 4
Nenets Autonomous Area 42-43 J-L 4
Nen Jiang [TJ, ~] 48-49 N 2
Nenjiang [TJ, ●] 48-49 O 2
Nen Jiang = Naguun Mörön 48-49 NO 1-2
Nentsen, Nationaal Gebied der – 42-43 J-L 4
Neola, UT 76-77 H 5
Neosho River 72-73 G 4
Nepa 42-43 U 6
Nephi, UT 76-77 GH 6
Nephin 32 B 4
Nepoko 64-65 G 2
Nerbudda = Narmada 44-45 LM 6
Nerča 42-43 W 7
Nerčinsk 42-43 W 7
Nerčinskij Zavod 42-43 W 7
Nerechta 38-39 H 4
Neretva 36-37 H 4
Neriquinha = N'Riquinha 64-65 F 6
Neris 30-31 L 10
Ñermete, Punta – 78-79 C 6
Nerojka, gora – 42-43 KL 5
Nerskoje ploskogorje 42-43 c 5
Ner'ungri 42-43 XY 6
Nes' 38-39 HJ 2
Nesebâr 36-37 MN 4
Neskaupstadhur 30-31 fg 2
Nesna 30-31 E 4
Ness, Loch – 32 D 3
Néstos 36-37 L 5
Nesttun, Bergen- 30-31 AB 7
Nesviž 30-31 M 11
Nêtanya 46-47 F 6
Nethany = Nêtanya 46-47 F 7
Netherdale 56-57 J 4
Netherlands 34-35 K 3-L 2
Nettilling Lake 70-71 W 4
Neubrandenburg 33 F 2
Neuchâtel 33 C 5
Neuchâtel, Lac de – 33 C 5
Neufchâteau [B] 34-35 K 4
Neufchateau [F] 34-35 KL 4
Neufchâtel-en-Bray 34-35 H 4
Neumarkt 33 E 4
Neumünster 33 DE 1
Neunkirchen [A] 33 H 5
Neunkirchen [D] 33 C 4
Neuquén [RA, ●] 80 C 5
Neuruppin 33 F 2
Neuschwabenland 24 B 36-2
Neuse River 74-75 E 7
Neusiedler See 33 H 5
Neustrelitz 33 F 2
Neu-Ulm 33 E 4
Neuwied 33 CD 3
Neva 38-39 F 4
Nevada 72-73 CD 4
Nevada City, CA 76-77 C 6
Nevado, Cerro el – 80 C 5
Nevado, Sierra del – 80 C 5
Neve, Serra da – 64-65 D 5
Nevel' 38-39 EF 4
Never 42-43 XY 7
Nevers 34-35 J 5
Nevinnomyssk 38-39 H 7
Nevis 72-73 O 8
Nevis, Ben – 32 D 3
Nevjansk 42-43 KL 6
Nevşehir 44-45 C 3
Newala 64-65 J 5

New Castile = Castilla la Nueva 34-35 E 9-F 8
Newcastle [AUS] 56-57 K 6
Newcastle [GB] 32 D 4
Newcastle [ZA] 64-65 GH 8
New Castle, OH 74-75 A 5
New Castle, PA 74-75 C 4
Newcastle, VA 74-75 C 6
Newcastle Bay 56-57 H 2
Newcastle upon Tyne 32 EF 4
Newcastle Waters 56-57 F 3
Newcomb, NM 76-77 J 7
Newcomerstown, OH 74-75 C 4
Newdale, ID 76-77 H 4
Newdegate 56-57 C 6
New Delhi 44-45 M 5
New England [USA] 72-73 M 3-N 2
New England Range 56-57 K 5-6
Newenham, Cape – 70-71 D 6
Newfane, VT 74-75 G 3
Newfondland Basin 22-23 GH 3
Newfoundland [CDN, ☉] 70-71 Za 8
Newfoundland [CDN, ☆] 70-71 Y 6-Z 8
Newfoundland Bank 22-23 G 3
Newfoundlandbekken 22-23 GH 3
Newfoundlanddrempel 22-23 G 3-H 4
Newfoundland-Ondiepte 22-23 G 3
Newfoundland Ridge 22-23 G 3-H 4
New Georgia 52-53 j 6
New Georgia Group 52-53 j 6
New Georgia Sound = The Slot 52-53 j 6
New Glasgow 70-71 Y 8
New Guinea 52-53 L 7-M 8
New Guinea Rise 52-53 M 5-6
Newhalem, WA 76-77 C 1
Newhall, CA 76-77 D 8
New Hampshire 72-73 M 3
New Hanover [PNG] 52-53 gh 5
Newhaven [GB] 32 G 6
New Haven, CT 72-73 M 3
New Hebrides 56-57 N 2-O 3
New Hebrides Basin 56-57 MN 3
New Hebrides Trench 56-57 N 3-4
New Iberia, LA 72-73 H 5-6
New Ireland 52-53 h 5
New Jersey 72-73 M 3
New Kensington, PA 74-75 D 4
New Kowloon 48-49 LM 7
New Lexington, OH 74-75 BC 5
New Liskeard 70-71 UV 8
New London, CT 74-75 GH 4
Newman, CA 76-77 C 7
Newmarket [CDN] 74-75 D 2
New Martinsville, WV 74-75 C 5
New Meadows, ID 76-77 E 3
New Mexico 72-73 EF 5
New Norfolk 56-57 J 8
New Orleans, LA 72-73 HJ 5-6
New Philadelphia, OH 74-75 C 4
New Pine Creek, OR 76-77 C 4
New Plymouth 56-57 O 7
Newport [GB, I. of Wight] 32 F 6
Newport [GB, Severn] 32 E 6
Newport, KY 72-73 K 4
Newport, ME 74-75 J 2
Newport, NH 74-75 GH 3
Newport, OR 76-77 A 3
Newport, RI 74-75 H 4
Newport, TN 74-75 B 6-7
Newport, VT 74-75 GH 2
Newport, WA 76-77 E 1
Newport News, VA 72-73 L 4
New Providence Island 72-73 L 6
Newquay 32 D 6
New Rochelle, NY 74-75 G 4
Newry 32 CD 4
New Siberian Islands = Novosibirskije ostrova 42-43 Z-f 2
New Smyrna Beach, FL 74-75 c 2
New South Wales 56-57 H-K 6
Newton, KS 72-73 G 4
Newton, MA 74-75 H 3
Newton, NC 74-75 C 7
Newton, NJ 74-75 F 4
Newton Falls, NY 74-75 F 2
Newtontoppen 30-31 k 5
Newtownards 32 D 4
New Westminster 70-71 MN 8
New York 72-73 LM 3
New York, NY 72-73 M 3-4

New York Mountains 76-77 F 8
New Zealand 56-57 N 8-O 7
Neyed = Najd 44-45 E 5-6
Neyrīz 44-45 G 5
Neyshābūr 44-45 H 3
Nezametnyj = Aldan 42-43 XY 6
Nežin 38-39 F 5
Nezperce, ID 76-77 EF 2
Nez Perce Indian Reservation 76-77 EF 2

Ngabang 52-53 EF 6
Ngamdo Tsonag Tsho 48-49 G 5
Ngami, Lake – 64-65 F 7
Nganghouei = Anhui 48-49 M 5
Nganglaring Tso = Nganglha Ringtsho 48-49 EF 5
Nganglong Gangri 48-49 E 5
Ngangtha Ringtsho 48-49 EF 5
Ngangtse Tsho 48-49 F 5
Ngan-yang = Anyang 48-49 LM 4
Ngao 52-53 CD 3
Ngaoundéré 60-61 G 7
Ngara 63 B 3
Ngau 52-53 a 2
Ngaumdere = Ngaoundéré 60-61 G 7
Ngaundere = Ngaoundéré 60-61 G 7
Ngazidja 64-65 K 5
Ngerengere 63 D 4
Ngiro, Ewaso – 64-65 J 3
Ngiva 64-65 E 6
Ngoc Linh 52-53 E 3
Ngoko 64-65 E 2
Ngomba 63 C 5
Ngong 64-65 J 3
Ngoring Tsho 48-49 H 4-5
Ngorongoro Crater 64-65 HJ 3
N'Gounié 64-65 D 3
Ngoura 60-61 H 6
Ngouri 60-61 H 6
Ngourti 60-61 G 5
Ngoywa 64-65 H 4
Ngozi 63 B 3
Nguigmi 60-61 G 6
Ngulu 52-53 L 5
Ngunza 64-65 D 5
N'Guri = Ngouri 60-61 H 6
Nguru 60-61 G 6

Nha Trang 52-53 EF 4
Nhecolândia 78-79 H 8
Nhi Ha, Sông – 52-53 D 2
Nhill 56-57 H 7

Niafounké 60-61 D 5
Niagara Falls 72-73 KL 3
Niagara Falls, NY 72-73 L 3
Niagara River 74-75 D 3
Niah 52-53 F 6
Ni'āj, Jabal – 62 E 6
Niamey 60-61 E 6
Niangara 64-65 G 2
Nia-Nia 64-65 G 2
Nianqingtanggula Shan = Nyanchhenthanglha 48-49 G 5-6
Nias, Pulau – 52-53 C 6
Niassa 64-65 J 5
Niassa = Malawi 64-65 HJ 5
Nibāk 44-45 G 6
Nibe 30-31 C 9
Niblinto 80 B 5
Nicaragua 72-73 JK 9
Nicaragua, Lago de – 72-73 JK 9
Nicaro 72-73 L 7
Nice 34-35 L 7
Nichinan 50-51 H 7
Nicholson [AUS] 56-57 E 3
Nicholson River 56-57 G 3
Nickel = Nikel' 42-43 E 4
Nickol Bay 56-57 C 4
Nicobar Islands 44-45 P 9
Nicolás, Canal – 72-73 KL 7
Nicomedia = İzmit 44-45 BC 2
Nico Pérez 80 EF 4
Nicosia 36-37 F 7
Nicosie = Levkōsia 44-45 C 3
Nicoya 72-73 J 9
Nicoya, Golfo de – 72-73 J 9
Nicoya, Peninsula de – 72-73 J 9-10
Nida 33 K 3
Nī Dillī = New Delhi 44-45 M 5
Nido, El – 52-53 G 4
Niebüll 33 D 1
Niedere Tauern 33 FG 5
Niederösterreich 33 GH 4
Niedersachsen 33 C-E 2
Niemba [ZRE, ~] 63 B 4
Niemba [ZRE, ●] 63 B 4
Nienburg 33 D 2
Nienchentangla = Nyanchhenthanglha 48-49 F 6-G 5
Nieuw Amsterdam [SME] 78-79 HJ 3
Nieuw-Antwerpen = Nouvelle-Anvers 64-65 EF 2
Nieuw-Caledonië 56-57 MN 3
Nieuw-Castillië = Castilla la Nueva 34-35 E 9-F 8
Nieuwe Hebriden 56-57 N 2-O 3
Nieuwe Hebriden Bekken 56-57 MN 3
Nieuwe Hebriden Bekken 56-57 MN 3
Nieuwe Hebridentrog 56-57 N 3-4
Nieuw-Guinea 52-53 L 7-M 8
Nieuw Guineadrempel 52-53 M 5-6
Nieuw Nickerie 78-79 H 3
Nieuwoudtville 64-65 E 9
Nieuwsiberische Eilanden = Novosibirskije ostrova 42-43 Z-f 2
Nieuw-Zeeland 56-57 N 8-O 7
Nieuw-Zeelandrug 56-57 M 5-7
Nieves = Nevis 72-73 O 8
Niffur = Nippur 46-47 L 6
Nifīsha = Nafīshah 62 DE 2
Niğde 44-45 CD 3
Niger 60-61 FG 5
Niger [RN, ☆] 60-61 F 7
Niger, Bouches du – 60-61 F 8
Niger, Mouths of the – 60-61 F 7-8
Niger, River – 60-61 E 6
Nighthawk, WA 76-77 D 1
Nigrita 36-37 K 5
Nihah 46-47 J 2
Nihonmatsu = Nihommatsu 50-51 N 4
Niigata 48-49 Q 4
Niihama 50-51 J 5-6
Niihau 52-53 de 3
Niimi 50-51 J 5
Nii-shima 50-51 M 5
Niitsu 50-51 M 4
Nijād al-'Alī 60-61 D 2-E 1
Nijamābād = Nizamabad 44-45 M 7
Nijmegen 34-35 KL 3
Nikel' 42-43 E 4
Nikēphorion = Ar-Raqqah 44-45 DE 3
Nikhaib, An- = Nukhayb 44-45 E 4
Nikheila, En – = An Nuhaylah 62 D 4
Nikito-Ivdel'skoje = Ivdel' 42-43 L 5
Nikki 60-61 E 6-7
Nikolajev 38-39 F 6
Nikolajevsk = Pugač'ov 42-43 HJ 7
Nikolajevskij 38-39 J 5
Nikolajevsk-na-Amure 42-43 b 7
Nikol'sk [SU, Severnyje uvaly] 42-43 H 6
Nikol'skij 42-43 M 8
Nikol'skoje [SU, Komandorskije ostrova] 42-43 fg 6
Nikomēdeia = İzmit 44-45 BC 2
Nikonga 63 B 3-4
Nikopol 36-37 L 4
Nikopol' 38-39 F 6
Nikosia = Levkōsia 44-45 C 3
Nīk Pey 46-47 N 4
Niksar 46-47 G 2
Nikšić 36-37 H 4
Nīl, Bahr an- 60-61 L 3-4
Nila, Pulau – 52-53 JK 8
Nīlagiri = Nilgiri Hills 44-45 M 8
Nīl al-Abyaḍ, An- 60-61 L 6
Nīl al-Azraq, An- 60-61 L 6
Niland, CA 76-77 F 9
Nile = Baḥr an-Nīl 60-61 L 3-4
Nile Bleu = Abay 60-61 M 6
Niles, OH 74-75 C 4
Nilo = Baḥr an-Nīl 60-61 L 3-4
Nimba, Mont – 60-61 C 7
Nimega = Nijmegen 34-35 KL 3
Nimègue = Nijmegen 34-35 KL 3
Nîmes 34-35 JK 7
Nimmitabel 58 J 6
Nimnyrskij = Malyj Nimnyr 42-43 Y 6
Nimrod, MT 76-77 G 2
Nimūlī 60-61 L 8
Nīnawá 46-47 JK 5
Nīnawá = Ninive 46-47 K 4
Nindigully 58 J 2
Nine Degree Channel 44-45 L 9
Nine Degree Channel 44-45 L 9
Nineve = Ninive 44-45 E 3
Ninfas, Punta – 80 D 6
Ning'an 48-49 OP 3
Ningbo 48-49 N 6
Ningcheng 50-51 B 2
Ningde 48-49 M 6
Ningdu 48-49 M 6
Ningguo 48-49 M 5
Ninghsia, Autonomes Gebiet 48-49 H 3-K 4
Ning-hsiang = Ningxiang 48-49 L 6
Ninghsien = Ning Xian 48-49 K 4
Ninghua 48-49 M 6
Ninghwa = Ninghua 48-49 M 6
Ning-po = Ningbo 48-49 N 6
Ningsia Autonomous Region 48-49 JK 3-4
Ningteh = Ningde 48-49 M 6
Ninguta = Ning'an 48-49 OP 3
Ningxia 48-49 H 3-K 4
Ningxia, Región Autónoma de – 48-49 JK 3-4
Ningxiahui, Région Autonome – 48-49 JK 3-4
Ningxia Huizu Zizhiqu 48-49 JK 3-4
Ning Xian 48-49 K 4
Ningxiang 48-49 L 6
Ninh Giang 52-53 E 2
Ninh Hoa [VN ↑ Nha Trang] 52-53 EF 4
Ninigo Group 52-53 M 7
Ninive 44-45 E 3
Ninjintangla Shan = Nyanchhenthanglha 48-49 G 5-6
Ninnis Glacier 24 C 16-15
Ninua = Ninive 44-45 E 3
Niobrara River 72-73 F 3
Niokolo Koba, Parc national du – 60-61 B 6
Nioro du Rip 60-61 A 6
Nioro du Sahel 60-61 C 5
Niort 34-35 G 5
Nipawin 70-71 Q 7
Nipepe 63 D 6
Nipigon 70-71 T 8
Nipigon, Lake – 70-71 ST 8
Nipissing, Lake – 70-71 UV 8
Nippur 46-47 L 6
Nipton, CA 76-77 F 8
Niquelândia 78-79 K 7
Nīr 46-47 N 3
Nirasaki 50-51 M 5
Niriz, Daryacheh i – = Daryâcheh Bakhtegān 44-45 G 5
Niš 36-37 JK 4
Nişāb 44-45 E 5
Niṣāb, An – = Anṣāb 44-45 F 8
Nišava 36-37 K 4
Niscemi 36-37 F 7
Nishinomiya 50-51 K 5
Nishinoomote 50-51 H 7
Nishino shima 50-51 J 4
Nishio 50-51 L 5
Nishisonoki hantō 50-51 G 6
Nishiyama 50-51 M 4
Nishtawn 44-45 G 7
Nishtūn = Nishtawn 44-45 G 7
Nisia Floresta 78-79 MN 6
Nisibin = Nusaybin 44-45 E 3
Nisibis = Nusaybin 44-45 E 3
Nisko 33 KL 3
Nissan 30-31 E 9
Nisser 30-31 C 8
Nisutlin Plateau 70-71 K 5
Nisyros 36-37 M 7
Nītaure 30-31 L 9
Niterói 78-79 L 9
Nitra 33 J 4
Nitro, WV 74-75 C 5
Niuafo'ou 52-53 b 2
Niuatoputapu 52-53 c 2
Niva 30-31 P 4
Nivernais 34-35 J 5
Nivskij 42-43 E 4
Niya Bazar 48-49 E 4
Niyut, Gunung – 52-53 E 6
Niza = Nice 34-35 L 7
Nizamabad 44-45 M 7
Nizamghāṭ 44-45 Q 5
Nizam Sagar 44-45 M 7
Nizip 46-47 G 4
Nizke Tatry 33 JK 4
Nizkij, mys – 42-43 hj 5
Nižn'aja Kamenka 38-39 JK 2
Nižn'aja Peša 42-43 H 4
Nižn'aja Tunguska 42-43 TU 5
Nižn'aja Tura 42-43 K 6
Nižneangarsk 42-43 UV 6
Nižneilimsk 42-43 T 6
Nižneimbatskoje 42-43 QR 5
Nižnekamsk 42-43 J 7
Nižneleninskoje 42-43 Z 8
Nižneudinsk 42-43 S 7
Nižnevartovsk 42-43 O 5
Nižnije Sergi 38-39 L 4
Nižnij Lomov 38-39 H 5
Nižnij Novgorod 42-43 GH 6
Nižnij Tagil 42-43 KL 6
Nižnij Trajanov val 36-37 N 3

Njala = Mono 60-61 E 7
Njardhvik 30-31 b 3
Njassa = Lake Malawi 64-65 H 5
Njombe [EAT, ~] 64-65 H 4
Njombe [EAT, ●] 64-65 HJ 4
Nkata Bay = Nkhata Bay 64-65 H 5
Nkhata Bay 64-65 H 5
Nkiôna 36-37 K 6
Nkongsamba 60-61 FG 8
Nkréko, Ákra – = Akrōtḗrion Gréko 46-47 F 5
Nkululu 63 C 4

Noanama 78-79 D 4
Noatak, AK 70-71 D 4
Noatak River 70-71 DE 4
Nobeoka 48-49 P 5
Nockatunga 58 F 1
Nófilia, en – = An-Nawfalīyah 60-61 H 2
Nogajskaja step' 38-39 J 7
Nogal = Nugal 44-45 F 9
Nogales [MEX] 76-77 J 10
Nogales, AZ 72-73 D 5
Nogales Heroica 72-73 D 5
Nogat 33 J 1
Nōgata 50-51 H 6
Noginsk 38-39 G 4
Nogoyá 80 DE 4
Noheji 50-51 N 2
Noir, Isla – 80 B 8
Noirmoutier, Île de – 34-35 F 5
Nojima-saki 50-51 MN 5
Nojon 48-49 J 3
Nokia 30-31 K 7
Nok Kuṇdī 44-45 J 5
Nola [RCA] 60-61 H 8
Nolinsk 42-43 HJ 6
Nomamisaki 50-51 GH 7
Nome, AK 70-71 C 5
No-min Ho = Nuomin He 48-49 N 2
Nõmme, Tallinn- 30-31 L 8
Nomo-saki 50-51 G 6
Nong'an 48-49 NO 3
Nong Khai 52-53 D 3
Nongoma 64-65 H 8
Nonni = Nen Jiang 48-49 O 1-2
Nonsan 50-51 F 4
Noord-Amerika 22-23 DE 3
Noordamerikaans Bekken 22-23 FG 4
Noordatlantische Rug 22-23 H 5-3
Noordaustralisch Bekken 56-57 C 2
Noordbandabekken 52-53 HJ 7
Noordelijke IJszee 19 AB 32-5
Noord-Ierland 32 CD 4
Noord-Korea 48-49 O 3-4
Noordossetische Autonome Republiek = 4 ◁ 38-39 H 7
Noordpacifisch Bekken 22-23 AB 3-4
Noordpacifisch Bekken 22-23 ST 3-4
Noordwestaustralisch Bekken 22-23 OP 6
Noordwestpacifisch Rug 22-23 S 3-4
Noordzee 32 F-J 3
Noordzeekanal 34-35 K 2
Noormarkku 30-31 JK 7
Noors Bekken 22-23 JK 2
Noorse Geul 30-31 A 8-C 9
Noorvik, AK 70-71 DE 4
Noorweegse Zee 19 C 19-B 17
Noorwegen 30-31 C 7-L 2
Nootka Island 70-71 L 8
Noqui 64-65 D 4
Nora 30-31 F 8
Norah 60-61 MN 5
Nòrcia 36-37 E 4
Nord, Canal du – 32 CD 4
Nord, Mer du – 32 F-J 3
Nordaustlandet 30-31 k-m 5
Nordcross, GA 74-75 A 8
Norden 33 C 2
Nordenškel'da, archipelag – 42-43 RS 2
Nordenškel'da, zaliv – 42-43 JK 2
Nordenskiøldbukta 30-31 l 4
Nordenskiøld land 30-31 jk 6
Nordfjord 30-31 AB 7
Nordfjorden 30-31 j 5
Nordfriesische Inseln 33 D 1
Nordhausen 33 E 3
Nordhorn 33 C 2
Nordhur-Ísafjardhar 30-31 b 1-2
Nordhur-Múla 30-31 f 2
Nordhur-Thingeyjar 30-31 ef 1-2
Nordkapp [N] 30-31 LM 2
Nordkapp [Svalbard] 30-31 k 4
Nordkinn 30-31 MN 2
Nordkjosbotn 30-31 HJ 3
Nordland 30-31 E 5-G 3
Nördliche Dwina = Severnaja Dvina 42-43 G 5
Nördlicher Ural = Severnyj Ural 42-43 K 5-6
Nördlingen 33 E 4
Nordos Çayı 46-47 K 3
Nordostrundingen 19 A 18-20
Nord-Ostsee-Kanal 33 D 1-2
Nord-Ouest, Territoire du – = Northwest Territories 70-71 M-U 4
Nord-Ouest Australien, Bassin du – 22-23 OP 6
Nord-Ouest Indien, Dorsale du – 22-23 N 5-6
Nordre Kvaløy 30-31 H 2
Nordre Strømfjord 70-71 a 4
Nordrhein-Westfalen 33 CD 3
Nord-Trøndelag 30-31 DE 5
Nordvik 42-43 V 3
Nordwestindische Rug 22-23 N 5-6
Nore 30-31 C 7
Norfolk, NE 72-73 G 3
Norfolk, VA 72-73 LM 4
Norfolk, Dorsal de – 56-57 N 6-7
Norfolk, Seuil – 56-57 N 6-7
Norfolkdrempel 56-57 N 6-7
Norfolk Island 56-57 N 5
Norfolk Ridge 56-57 N 6-7
Norheimsund 30-31 AB 7
Nori 42-43 N 4
Norikura dake 50-51 L 4
Noril'sk 42-43 Q 4
Norische Alpen 33 FG 5
Norlina, NC 74-75 D 6
Norman, OK 72-73 G 4
Normanby 32 F 4
Normanby Island 52-53 h 7
Normandie 34-35 GH 4
Norman River 56-57 H 3
Normanton [AUS] 56-57 H 3
Norman Wells 70-71 KL 4
Noroeste, Territorios del – = Northwest Territories 70-71 M-U 4
Norquinćo 80 B 6
Norra Bergnäs 30-31 H 4
Norra Storfjället 30-31 FG 5
Norrbotten [S, ≅] 30-31 J 5-K 4
Norrbotten [S, ☆] 30-31 G-K 4
Nørresundby, Ålborg- 30-31 CD 9
Norris, MT 76-77 H 3
Norristown, PA 74-75 F 4
Norrköping 30-31 G 8
Norrland 30-31 F-J 5
Norrtälje 30-31 H 8
Norseman 56-57 D 6
Norsk 42-43 Y 7
Nortbruk, ostrov – 42-43 GH 2
Norte, Cabo – 78-79 K 4
Norte, Canal del – = North Channel 32 CD 4
Norte, Canal do – 78-79 JK 4
Norte, Punta – 80 D 6
Norte, Serra do – 78-79 H 7
North, SC 74-75 C 8
North, Cape – [CDN, Nova Scotia] 70-71 YZ 8
North Adams, MA 74-75 G 3
Northallerton 32 F 4
Northam [AUS] 56-57 C 6
Northam [ZA] 64-65 G 8
North America 22-23 DE 3
North American Basin 22-23 FG 4
Northampton 32 FG 5
Northampton [AUS] 56-57 B 5
Northampton, MA 74-75 G 3
North Andaman 44-45 P 8
North Arm 70-71 NO 5
North Augusta, SC 74-75 BC 8
North Australian Basin 56-57 C 2
North Banda Basin 52-53 HJ 7
North Battleford 70-71 P 7
North Bay 70-71 UV 8
North Belcher Islands 70-71 U 6
North Bend, OR 76-77 A 4
North Bend, WA 76-77 C 2
Northbrook, ostrov – = ostrov Nortbruk 42-43 GH 2
North Bruny Island 58 cd 3
North Canadian River 72-73 FG 4
North Cape [NZ] 56-57 O 6
North Caribou Lake 70-71 ST 7
North Carolina 72-73 KL 4
North Channel 32 CD 4
North Channel [CDN] 70-71 U 8
North Charleston, SC 74-75 D 8
Northcliffe 56-57 C 6
North Creek, NY 74-75 FG 3
North Channel 32 CD 4
North Channel [CDN] 70-71 U 8
North Charleston, SC 74-75 D 8
North Dakota 72-73 FG 2
North East, PA 74-75 CD 3
North East Carry, ME 74-75 HJ 2
North Eastern 64-65 K 2-3
Northeast Providence Channel 72-73 L 6
Northeast Providence Channel 72-73 L 6
Northeim 33 DE 3
Northern [MW] 63 C 5-6
Northern [Z] 64-65 H 4
Northern Ireland 32 CD 4
Northern Pacific Railway 72-73 EF 2
Northern Territory 56-57 FG 3-4
Northfield, VT 74-75 G 2
North Fiji Basin 56-57 O 3
North Foreland 32 GH 6
North Fork, CA 76-77 D 7
North Fork, ID 76-77 FG 3
North Fork Clearwater River 76-77 F 2
North Fork Feather River 76-77 C 5-6
North Fork Humboldt River 76-77 F 5
North Fork John Day River 76-77 D 3
North Fork Mountain 74-75 D 5
North Fork Payette River 76-77 E 3
North Horr 64-65 J 2
North Island [NZ] 56-57 P 7
North Island [USA] 74-75 D 8
North Korea 48-49 O 3-4
North Las Vegas, NV 76-77 F 7
North Little Rock, AR 72-73 H 4-5
North Miami, FL 74-75 cd 4
North Minch 32 C 3-D 2
North New River Canal 74-75 c 3
North Ossetian Autonomous Republic = 4 ◁ 38-39 H 7
North Pacific Basin 22-23 AB 3-4
North Palisade 72-73 C 4
North Pass 72-73 J 6
North Platte, NE 72-73 F 3
North Platte River 72-73 F 3
Northport, WA 76-77 E 1
North Powder, OR 76-77 DE 3
North Rona 32 D 2
North Ronaldsay 32 EF 2
North Santiam River 76-77 B 3
North Saskatchewan River 70-71 OP 7
North Sea 32 F-J 3
North Stradbroke Island 56-57 K 5
North Stratford, NH 74-75 H 2
North Taranaki Bight 56-57 O 7
North Tonawanda, NY 74-75 D 3
North Truchas Peak 72-73 E 4
North Uist 32 BC 3
Northumberland Islands 56-57 JK 4
Northumberland Strait 70-71 Y 8
North Umpqua River 76-77 B 4
Northwest Australian Basin 22-23 OP 6
North West Cape 56-57 B 4
North Western 64-65 FG 5
North-West-Frontier 44-45 L 3-4
Northwest Highlands 32 D 2-3

North 203

Northwest Indian Ridge 22-23 N 5-6
Northwest Pacific Basin 22-23 ST 3-4
Northwest Pacific Ridge 22-23 S 3-4
Northwest Passage 70-71 J-L 3
Northwest Territories 70-71 M-U 4
North Wilkesboro, NC 74-75 C 6
North York 74-75 D 3
Norton, VA 74-75 B 6
Norton Sound 70-71 D 5
Noruega 30-31 C 7-L 2
Noruega, Canal de – 30-31 A 8-C 9
Noruega, Cuenca de – 22-23 JK 2
Noruega, Mar de – 19 C 19-B 17
Norvège 30-31 C 7-L 2
Norvège, Mer de – 19 C 19-B 17
Norvegia, Kapp – 24 B 34-35
Norwalk, CT 74-75 G 4
Norway 30-31 C 7-L 2
Norway, ME 74-75 H 2
Norway House 70-71 R 7
Norwegian Basin 22-23 JK 2
Norwegian Bay 70-71 ST 2
Norwegian Trench 30-31 A 8-C 9
Norwich 32 G 5
Norwich [CDN] 74-75 C 3
Norwich, CT 74-75 GH 4
Norwich, NY 74-75 F 3
Norwood, NC 74-75 C 7
Norwood, NY 74-75 F 2
Noshiro 48-49 QR 3
Nosiro = Noshiro 48-49 QR 3
Nossob 64-65 E 7
Nosy-Bé 64-65 L 5
Nosy-Varika 64-65 L 7
Notch Peak 76-77 G 6
Noteć 33 G 2
Noto 36-37 F 7
Noto [J] 50-51 L 4
Notodden 30-31 C 8
Noto hantō 48-49 Q 4
Noto-jima 50-51 L 4
Notoro-ko 50-51 d 1
Notre Dame, Monts – 70-71 WX 8
Notre Dame Bay 70-71 Z 8-a 7
Nottawasaga Bay 74-75 C 2
Nottaway, Rivière – 70-71 V 7
Nottingham 32 F 5
Nottingham Island 70-71 VW 5
Nottoway River 74-75 E 6
Nouadhibou = Nawādhību 60-61 A 4
Nouakchott = Nawākshūt 60-61 A 5
Nouméa 56-57 N 4
Noupoort 64-65 FG 9
Nouveau Brunswick = New Brunswick 70-71 X 8
Nouveau-Québec 70-71 V-X 6
Nouveau-Québec, Cratère du – 70-71 VW 5
Nouvelle Amsterdam 22-23 NO 7
Nouvelle Angleterre = New England 72-73 M 3-N 2
Nouvelle-Anvers 64-65 EF 2
Nouvelle-Calédonie 56-57 MN 3
Nouvelle-Castille = Castilla la Nueva 34-35 E 9-F 8
Nouvelle-Ecosse = Nova Scotia 70-71 X 9-Y 8
Nouvelle-Guinée 52-53 L 7-M 8
Nouvelle-Guinée, Seuil de – 52-53 M 5-6
Nouvelle-Hébrides, Bassin de – 56-57 MN 3
Nouvelle-Hébrides, Fosse des – 56-57 N 3-4
Nouvelles-Hébrides 56-57 N 2-O 3
Nouvelle Sibérie, Îles – = Novosibirskije ostrova 42-43 Z-f 2
Nouvelle-Zélande 56-57 N 8-O 7
Nouvelle-Zemble, Gouttière de la – 42-43 K 3-L 2
Novabad 44-45 L 3
Nova Chaves = Muconda 64-65 F 5
Nova Cruz 78-79 MN 6
Nova Chaves = Muconda 64-65 F 5
Nova Freixo = Cuamba 64-65 J 5
Nova Gaia 64-65 E 4-5
Nova Gradiška 36-37 GH 3
Nova Iguaçu 78-79 L 9
Novaja Buchara = Kagan 44-45 J 3
Novaja Kazanka 38-39 J 6
Novaja L'al'a 38-39 M 4
Novaja Odessa 36-37 OP 2
Novaja Pis'm'anka = Leninogorsk 42-43 J 7
Novaja Sibir', ostrov – 42-43 de 3
Novaja Zeml'a 42-43 J 3-L 2
Nova Lamego = Gabú 60-61 B 6
Nova Lima 78-79 L 8-9
Nova Lisboa = Huambo 64-65 E 5
Nova Lusitânia 64-65 H 6
Nova Mambone 64-65 J 7
Novara 36-37 C 3
Nova Scotia 70-71 X 9-Y 8
Nova Sofala 64-65 HJ 7
Novato, CA 76-77 B 6
Novaya Zemlya Trough 42-43 K 3-L 2
Nova Zagora 36-37 LM 4
Nova Zemblageul 42-43 K 3-L 2
Nové Zámky 33 J 4
Novgorod 42-43 E 6
Novgorod-Severskij 38-39 F 5
Novi Bečej 36-37 J 3
Novigrad 36-37 E 3
Novi Pazar [BG] 36-37 M 4
Novi Pazar [YU] 36-37 M 4
Novi Sad 36-37 HJ 3
Novoagansk 42-43 O 5
Novoaleksandrovskaja 38-39 H 6
Novoaltajsk 42-43 PQ 7
Novoanninskij 38-39 H 5
Novobiril'ussy 42-43 QR 6
Novobogatinskoje 38-39 K 6
Novočerkassk 38-39 GH 6
Novograd-Volynskij 38-39 E 5
Novogrudok 38-39 E 5
Novo Hamburgo 80 FG 3
Novojerudinskij 42-43 RS 6
Novokazalinsk 42-43 L 8
Novokujbyševsk 38-39 JK 5
Novokuzneck 42-43 Q 7
Novolazarevskaja 24 B 1
Novo-Mariinsk = Anadyr' 42-43 j 5
Novo Mesto 36-37 F 3
Novomoskovsk 38-39 GH 5
Novonazimovo 42-43 QR 6
Novonikolajevsk = Novosibirsk 42-43 P 6-7
Novo Redondo = N'Gunza Kabolo 64-65 D 5
Novorossijk 38-39 G 7
Novošachtinsk 38-39 G 6
Novosibirsk 42-43 P 6-7
Novosibirskije ostrova 42-43 Z-f 2
Novosokol'niki 38-39 EF 4
Novos'olovo 42-43 R 6
Novotroick 42-43 K 7
Novo-Troickij Promysel = Balej 42-43 W 7
Novoukrainka 38-39 F 6
Novo-Urgenč = Urgenč 42-43 L 9
Novouzensk 38-39 J 5
Novozybkov 38-39 F 5
Novska 36-37 G 3
Novyj Bor 38-39 K 2
Novyj Bug 38-39 F 6
Novyje Karymkary 42-43 MN 5
Novyj Karymkary = Karymkary 42-43 M 5
Novyj Margelan = Fergana 44-45 L 2-3
Novyj Port 42-43 MN 4
Novyj Tevriz 42-43 O 6
Nowa Sól 33 G 3
Nowbarān 46-47 N 5
Nowe 33 J 2
Nowgorod = Novgorod 42-43 E 6
Nowkash 46-47 MN 6
Nowra 56-57 K 6
Now Shar 38-39 K 8
Nowy Korczyn 33 K 3
Nowy Sącz 33 K 4
Nowy Targ 33 K 4
Noxon, MT 76-77 F 1-2
Noya 34-35 C 7
Noyon 34-35 J 4
N'Riquinha = Lumbala 64-65 F 6
Nsanje 64-65 J 6
Nsefu 63 BC 6
Nsukka 60-61 F 7
Ntcheu 64-65 HJ 5
Nuanetsi = Mwenezi 64-65 GH 7
Nūbah, An- 60-61 K-M 4-5
Nūbah, Jibāl an- 60-61 KL 6
Nubia, Desierto de – 60-61 LM 4
Nubie, Désert de – 60-61 LM 4
Nubieber, CA 76-77 C 5
Nubische Woestijn 60-61 LM 4
Nūbiya = An-Nubah 60-61 K-M 4-5
Nu Chiang = Nag Chhu 48-49 G 5
Nu Chiang = Nag Chhu 48-49 G 5
Nueces River 72-73 G 6
Nueltin Lake 70-71 R 5
Nueva Antioquia 78-79 EF 3
Nueva Bretaña-Bougainville, Fosa de – 52-53 h 6
Nueva Caledonia 56-57 MN 3
Nueva Casas Grandes 72-73 E 5
Nueva Delhi = New Delhi 44-45 M 5
Nueva Escocia = Nova Scotia 70-71 X 9-Y 8
Nueva Germania 80 E 2
Nueva Guinea 52-53 L 7-M 8
Nueva Guinea, Dorsal de – 52-53 M 5-6
Nueva Inglaterra = New England 72-73 M 3-N 2
Nueva Providencia 72-73 b 2
Nueva Rosita 72-73 F 6
Nueva San Salvador 72-73 HJ 9
Nuevas Hébridas 56-57 N 2-O 3
Nuevas Hébridas, Cuenca de – 56-57 MN 3
Nuevas Hébridas, Fosa de – 56-57 N 3-4
Nueva Siberia, Islas de – = Novosibirskije ostrova 42-43 Z-f 2
Nueva York = New York, NY 72-73 M 3-4
Nueva Zelanda 56-57 N 8-O 7
Nueva Zelanda, Dorsal de – 56-57 M 5-7
Nueva Zembla, Dorsal de – 42-43 K 3-L 2
Nueve de Julio [RA, Buenos Aires] 80 D 5
Nuevo Chagres 72-73 ab 2
Nuevo Chagres 72-73 ab 2
Nuevo Emperador 72-73 b 2
Nuevo Laredo 72-73 FG 6
Nuevo León 72-73 F 7-G 6
Nuevo Rocafuerte 78-79 D 5
Nuevo San Juan 72-73 b 2
Nuffar = Nippur 46-47 L 6
Nugaal 60-61 b 2
Nugruş, Gebel – = Jabal Nuqruş 62 F 5
Nûgssuaq 70-71 YZ 3
Nûgssuaq Halvø 70-71 a 3
Nuguria Islands 52-53 hj 5
Nuhaylah, An- 62 D 4
Nuhu Cut 52-53 K 8
Nuhūd, An- 60-61 K 6
Nuhurowa = Kai Kecil 52-53 K 8
Nuhu Rowa = Kai Kecil 52-53 K 8
Nuhu Tjut = Nuhu Cut 52-53 K 8
Nuhu Yut = Nuhu Cut 52-53 K 8
Nui Đeo 52-53 E 2
N'uja [SU, ~] 42-43 V 5
N'uja [SU, ●] 42-43 W 5
Nu Jiang = Nag Chhu 48-49 G 5
Nujiang Lisuzu Zizhizhou = C ◁ 48-49 H 6
Nûk 70-71 a 5
Nukey Bluff 58 BC 4
Nukhayb 44-45 E 4
Nukhaylah 60-61 K 5
Nukheila, Bîr – = Nukhaylah 60-61 K 5
Nukumanu Islands 52-53 jk 5
Nukus 42-43 KL 9
N'ukža 42-43 X 6-7
Nulato, AK 70-71 E 5
Nullagine 56-57 D 4
Nullarbor 56-57 EF 6
Nullarbor Plain 56-57 EF 6
Num, Meos – 52-53 KL 7
Numakunai = Iwate 50-51 N 3
Numan 60-61 G 7
Nu'mān, Jazīrat an- 62 F 4
Numancia 34-35 F 8
Numata [J, Gunma] 50-51 M 4
Numata [J, Hokkaidō] 50-51 bc 2
Numazu 50-51 M 5
Numedal 30-31 C 7-8
Numeia = Nouméa 56-57 N 4
Numero 1 Station = Maḥaṭṭat 1 62 D 7
Numero 2 Station = Maḥaṭṭat 2 62 DE 7
Numero 3 Station = Maḥaṭṭat 3 62 DE 7
Numero 4 Station = Maḥaṭṭat 4 62 E 7
Numfoor, Pulau – 52-53 KL 7
Numto 42-43 MN 5
Numurkah 58 G 6
Nun Chiang = Nen Jiang 48-49 O 1-2
Nun Chiang = Nen Jiang 48-49 O 1-2
Nundle 58 K 3
Nungan = Nong'an 48-49 NO 3
Nungo 64-65 J 5
Nunivak Island 70-71 C 6
Nuomin He 48-49 N 2
Nuoro 36-37 C 5
Nuqrat as-Salmān = As-Salmān 46-47 L 7
Nuqruş, Jabal – 62 F 5
Nura 42-43 N 7
Nuratau, chrebet – 42-43 M 9
N'urba 42-43 W 5
Nur Dağları 46-47 G 4
Nūrestān 44-45 KL 3-4
Nurhak Dağı 46-47 G 3
Nurmes 30-31 N 6
Nürnberg 33 E 4
Nusa Tenggara Barat = 16 ◁ 52-53 G 8
Nusa Tenggara Timur = 17 ◁ 52-53 H 8
Nusaybin 44-45 E 3
Nuşf, Bi'r an- 62 B 2
Nushagak River 70-71 E 5-6
Nu Shan 48-49 H 6
Nūshkī 44-45 K 5
Nutak 70-71 Y 6
Nutrias = Puerto de Nutrias 78-79 EF 3
Nutzotin Mountains 70-71 H 5
Nuwara Eliya 44-45 N 9
Nuwaybi' al-Muzayyinah 62 F 3
Nuweiba' = Nuwaybi' al-Muzayyinah 62 F 3
Nuyts Archipelago 56-57 F 6

Nxai Pan National Park 64-65 FG 6

Nyaake 60-61 C 8
Nya Chhu = Yalong Jiang 48-49 HJ 5
Nya Chhu = Yalong Jiang 48-49 HJ 5
Nyahanga 64-65 H 3
Nyakahanga 64-65 H 3
Nyālā 60-61 J 6
Ny Ålesund 30-31 hj 5
Nyalikungu 63 C 3
Nyamandhlovu 64-65 G 6
Nyambiti 64-65 H 3
Nyāmlīl 60-61 K 7
Nyamtumbu 64-65 J 5
Nyanchhenthanglha [TJ, ▲▲] 48-49 F 6-G 5
Nyanchhenthanglha [TJ, ⇆] 48-49 G 5-6
Nyanga 64-65 D 3
Nyanji 63 BC 6
Nyanza [EAK] 64-65 H 2-3
Nyanza [RU] 63 B 4
Nyanza [RWA] 63 B 3
Nyasa = Lake Malawi 64-65 H 5
Nyaunglebin 52-53 C 3
Nyawalu 63 AB 3
Nyborg 30-31 D 10
Nybro 30-31 F 9
Nyda 42-43 N 4
Nyenchentanglha = Nyanchhenthanglha 48-49 F 6-G 5
Nyeri [EAK] 64-65 J 3
Nyeri [EAU] 63 B 2
Ny Friesland 30-31 k 5
Nyika Plateau 64-65 H 4-5
Nyira Gonga 63 B 3
Nyírbátor 33 KL 5
Nyíregyháza 33 K 5
Nyiri Desert 63 D 3
Nyiro, Uoso – = Ewaso Ngiro 64-65 J 3
Nyiru, Mount – 64-65 J 2
Nyítra = Nitra 33 J 4
Nykarleby 30-31 K 6
Nykøbing Falster 30-31 DE 10
Nykøbing Mors 30-31 C 9
Nykøbing Sjælland 30-31 D 9-10
Nyköping 30-31 G 8
Nijl = Baḥr an-Nīl 60-61 L 3-4
Nyland = Uusimaa 30-31 KL 7
Nylstroom 64-65 G 7
Nymagee 58 H 4
Nymboida 58 L 2
Nymburk 33 G 3
Nynäshamn 30-31 GH 8
Nyngan 56-57 J 6
Nyong 60-61 G 8
Nyonga 64-65 H 4
Nyrud 30-31 N 3
Nysa 33 H 3
Nysa Kłodzka 33 H 3
Nyslott = Savonlinna 30-31 N 7
Nyssa, OR 76-77 E 4
Nystad = Uusikaupunki 30-31 J 7
Nytva 42-43 JK 6
Nyūdō-saki 50-51 M 2
Nyunzu 64-65 G 4

Nzega 64-65 H 3
Nzérékoré 60-61 C 7
N'Zeto 64-65 D 4
Nzoia 63 C 2
Nzoro 63 B 2

Ñ

Ñermete, Punta – 78-79 C 6

O

Oahe, Lake – 72-73 F 2
Oahu 52-53 e 3
Oakbank 56-57 H 6
Oak City, UT 76-77 G 6
Oakdale, CA 76-77 C 7
Oakey 56-57 K 5
Oak Harbor, WA 76-77 B 1
Oak Hill, FL 74-75 c 2
Oak Hill, WV 74-75 C 5-6
Oakland, CA 72-73 B 4
Oakland, MD 74-75 D 5
Oakland, OR 76-77 B 4
Oaklands 58 GH 5
Oakley, ID 76-77 FG 4
Oakover River 56-57 D 4
Oakridge, OR 76-77 B 4
Oak Ridge, TN 72-73 K 4
Oakville 74-75 D 3
Oamaru 56-57 O 9
Oarai 50-51 N 4
Oasis, CA 76-77 DE 7
Oasis, NV 76-77 F 5
Oates Land 24 B 16-17
Oatlands [AUS] 58 cd 3
Oatman, AZ 76-77 F 8
Oaxaca 72-73 G 8
Oaxaca de Juárez 72-73 GH 8

Ob' 42-43 NO 5
Oba [Vanuatu] 56-57 N 3
Obama 50-51 K 5
Oban 32 D 3
Oban [NZ] 56-57 N 9
Obara = Ōchi 50-51 J 5
Obdorsk = Salechard 42-43 M 4
Obeidh, El- = Al-Ubayyiḍ 60-61 KL 6
Oberá 80 F 3
Obere Tunguska = Angara 42-43 S 6
Oberhausen 33 C 3
Oberösterreich 33 F-H 4
Oberpfälzer Wald 33 F 4
Oberstdorf 33 E 5
Obi, Pulau – 52-53 J 7
Óbidos [BR] 78-79 HJ 5
Obihiro 48-49 R 3
Objačevo 42-43 H 5
Obkeik, Jebel – = Jabal 'Ubkayk 60-61 M 4
Oblačnaja, gora – 42-43 Za 9
Oblučje 42-43 Z 8
Obo 60-61 K 7
Oboa 63 C 2
Obock 60-61 N 6
Obojan 38-39 G 5
Obok = Obock 60-61 N 6
Obonai = Tazawako 50-51 N 3
Oboz'orskij 38-39 H 3
Obra 33 G 2
Obrenovac 36-37 HJ 3
Obrian Peak = Trident Peak 76-77 D 5
Obrovac 36-37 F 3
Obruk = Kızören 46-47 E 3
Obruk Yaylâsı 46-47 E 3
Obščij Syrt 42-43 H-K 7
Obskaja guba 42-43 N 3-4
Obuasi 60-61 D 7
Obuchi = Rokkasho 50-51 N 2

Očakov 36-37 O 2
Ocala, FL 72-73 K 6
Očamčire 38-39 H 7
Ocaña [CO] 78-79 E 3
Ocaña = E 34-35 F 9
Ocaña [CO] 78-79 E 3
Ocaña = E 34-35 F 9
Océan Arctique 19 AB 32-5
Océan Atlantique 22-23 G 4-J 7
Ocean City, MD 74-75 F 5
Ocean City, NJ 74-75 F 5
Ocean Falls 70-71 L 7
Oceanlake, OR 76-77 AB 3
Océano Atlantico 22-23 G 4-J 7
Océano Glacial Ártico 19 AB 32-5
Océano Índico 22-23 NO 6-7
Océano Indien 22-23 NO 6-7
Océano Pacifico 22-23 Q-T 5-6
Océan Pacifique 22-23 Q-T 5-6
Oceanside, CA 72-73 C 5
Ocean Strip 76-77 A 2
Ocha 42-43 b 7
Óchĕ 36-37 L 6
Ochiai = Dolinsk 42-43 b 8
Ochogbo = Oshogbo 60-61 EF 7
Ŏch'ŏng-do 50-51 E 4
Och'onjang 50-51 G 2
Ochota 42-43 b 5
Ochotsk 42-43 b 6
Ochotsk, Zee van – 42-43 b-d 6-7
Ochotskij Perevoz 42-43 a 5
Ocilla, GA 74-75 B 9
Ockelbo 30-31 G 7
Ocmulgee National Monument 74-75 B 8
Ocmulgee River 74-75 B 8-9
Oconee River 74-75 B 8
Ocotlán 72-73 F 7
Ocracoke Island 74-75 F 7

Ocha 42-43 b 7
Óchĕ 36-37 L 6
Ochiai = Dolinsk 42-43 b 8
Ochogbo = Oshogbo 60-61 EF 7
Ŏch'ŏng-do 50-51 E 4
Och'onjang 50-51 G 2
Ochota 42-43 b 5
Ochotsk 42-43 b 6
Ochotsk, Mar de – 42-43 b-d 6-7
Ochotsk, Zee van – 42-43 b-d 6-7
Ochotskij Perevoz 42-43 a 5

Oda [GH] 60-61 D 7
Ōda [J] 50-51 J 5
Ōda, Hōr – = Hawr Awdah 46-47 M 7
'Ōda, Jebel – = Jabal Ūdah 60-61 M 4
Ódáðahraun 30-31 e 2
Ŏdaejin 50-51 GH 2
Ōdate 50-51 N 2
Odawara 50-51 M 5
Odaym 46-47 H 5
Odda 30-31 B 7
Odemira 34-35 C 10
Ödemis 46-47 BC 3
Odendaalsrus 64-65 G 8
Odense 30-31 D 10
Odenwald 33 D 4
Oder 33 G 2
Oderzo 36-37 E 3
Odessa [SU] 38-39 F 6
Odessa, TX 72-73 F 5
Odessa, WA 76-77 D 2
Odienné 60-61 C 7
Odioñgan 52-53 H 4
Odioñgan 52-53 H 4
Ŏdomari = Korsakov 42-43 b 8
Odorheiul Secuiesc 36-37 L 2
Odra 33 H 3
Odum, GA 74-75 B 9
Odweeyne = Oodweyne 60-61 b 2
Odzala 64-65 DE 2
Oedmoerten Autonome Republiek = 2 ◁ 42-43 J 6
Oeganda 64-65 H 2
Oekraine 38-39 E-G 6
Oelan Bator = Ulaanbaatar 48-49 K 2

204 North

Oenpelli 56-57 F 2
Oeral 28-29 V 3-U 4
Oe-raro-do 50-51 F 5
Oermiameer = Urmia 44-45 F 3
Oest-Orda-Boerjaten, Nationaal Gebied der = 11 ◁ 42-43 T 7
Oeyŏn-do 50-51 F 4
Oezbekistan 44-45 J 2-K 3

Of 46-47 J 2
Ôfanto 36-37 F 5
Offenbach 33 D 3
Offenburg 33 CD 4
Ofooué 64-65 D 3
Ofotfjord 30-31 G 3
Ōfunato 50-51 NO 3

Oga 50-51 M 3
Ōgada 50-51 J 6
Ogadēn 60-61 NO 7
Oga hantō 50-51 M 3
Ōgaki 50-51 L 5
Ogasawana 54 RS 7
Ogasawara, Fosa de – 22-23 R 4
Ogashi 50-51 N 3
Ogashi tōge 50-51 MN 3
Ōgawara 50-51 N 3-4
Ogawara ko 50-51 N 2
Ogbomosho 60-61 E 7
Ogden, UT 72-73 D 3
Ogdensburg, NY 72-73 LM 3
Ogeechee River 74-75 BC 8
Ogi 50-51 M 4
Ogida = Hinai 50-51 N 2
Ogilby, CA 76-77 F 9
Ogilvie Mountains 70-71 J 4-5
Ôglio 36-37 CD 3
Ognon 34-35 KL 5
Oğnut = Göynük 46-47 J 3
Ogoja 60-61 F 7
Ogoki River 70-71 T 7
Ogon'ok 42-43 ab 6
Ogooué 64-65 D 3
Ogr = 'Uqr 60-61 K 6
Ogre 30-31 L 9
Ogué = Ogooué 64-65 D 3
Ogulin 36-37 F 3
Ogun 60-61 E 7
Ogurčinskij, ostrov – 44-45 G 3
Oğuzeli 46-47 G 4

Ohakune 56-57 P 7
Ōhara 50-51 N 5
Ōhata 50-51 N 2
Ohazama 50-51 N 3
O'Higgins [RCH] 80 BC 2
Ohio 72-73 K 3
Ohio River 72-73 J 4
Ohopoho 64-65 D 6
Ohōtuku-kai 50-51 cd 1
Ohře 33 G 3
Ohrid 36-37 J 5
Ohridsko Ezero 36-37 J 5
Ohuam 60-61 H 7
Ōhunato 50-51 NO 3

Oiapoque 78-79 J 4
Oiapoque, Rio – 78-79 J 4
Oies, Banc des – 42-43 GH 3
Ōi gawa 50-51 M 5
Oil City, PA 72-73 L 3
Oildale, CA 76-77 D 8
Oio = Oyo 60-61 E 7
Oise 34-35 J 4
Ōita 50-51 H 6

'Ōja, Al- = Al-'Awjā 46-47 M 8
Ojai, CA 76-77 D 8
Ojem = Oyem 60-61 G 8
Ojika-shima 50-51 G 6
Ojinaga 72-73 EF 6
Ojiya 50-51 M 4
Ojm'akon 42-43 b 5
Ojm'akonskoje nagorje 42-43 b 5
Ojo de Agua = Villa Ojo de Agua 80 D 3
Öjöngö Nuur = Ojorong nuur 48-49 F 2
Ojorong nuur 48-49 F 2
Ojos del Salado, Nevado – 80 C 3
Ojrot-Tura = Gorno-Altajsk 42-43 Q 7
Ojtal = Merke 42-43 N 9

Oka 38-39 G 5
Oka [SU ◁ Bratskoje vodochranilišče] 42-43 T 7
Oka [SU ◁ Volga] 42-43 G 6
Okaba 52-53 L 8
Okahandja 64-65 E 7
Okaloacoochee Slough 74-75 c 3
Okanagan Lake 70-71 MN 8
Okano 64-65 D 2
Okanogan, WA 76-77 D 1
Okanogan Range 76-77 CD 1
Okanogan River 76-77 D 1
Okaukuejo 64-65 E 6
Okavango 64-65 E 6
Okavango Basin 64-65 F 6
Ōkawara = Ōgawara 50-51 N 3-4
Okaya 50-51 LM 4
Okayama 48-49 P 5
Okazaki 50-51 L 5
Okeechobee, FL 74-75 c 3
Okeechobee, Lake – 72-73 K 6
Okefenokee Swamp 72-73 K 5
Okene 60-61 F 7
Oketo 50-51 c 2
Okha 44-45 K 6
Okhotsk, Mer d' 42-43 b-d 6-7
Okhotsk, Sea of – 42-43 b-d 6-7
Oki 48-49 P 4
Okinawa 48-49 O 6
Okinawa-guntō 48-49 O 6
Okino Daitō-jima 48-49 P 7
Okino-Daitō zima = Okino-Daitō-jima 48-49 P 7
Okino-shima 50-51 J 6
Okino-Tori-shima 48-49 Q 7
Okino-Tori sima = Okino-Tori-shima 48-49 Q 7
Okkang-dong 50-51 E 2
Oklahoma 72-73 G 4
Oklahoma City, OK 72-73 G 4
Okok 63 C 2
Okombahe 64-65 DE 7
Okoppe 50-51 c 1
Okoyo 64-65 DE 3
Øksfjordjøkelen 30-31 JK 2
Oksovskij 38-39 G 3
Okstindan 30-31 F 5
Okt'abr'sk [SU, Kazachskaja SSR] 42-43 K 8
Okt'abr'skaja magistral' 38-39 F 4
Okt'abr'skij [SU, Rossijskaja SFSR Baškirskaja ASSR] 42-43 JK 7
Okt'abr'skij [SU, Rossijskaja SFSR chrebet Džagdy] 42-43 Y 7
Okt'abr'skoje [SU, Chanty-Mansijskaja AO] 42-43 M 5
Okt'abr'skoj Revol'ucii, ostrov – 42-43 Q-S 2
Oktember'an 38-39 H 7
Ōkuchi 50-51 H 6
Okujiri-shima 50-51 a 2
Okulovka 38-39 F 4

Ola [SU, Rossijskaja SFSR] 42-43 d 6
Ola, ID 76-77 E 3
Olaf Prydz bukt 24 C 8
Ólafsfjördhur 30-31 d 1
Ólafsvik 30-31 ab 2
Olancha Peak 76-77 D 7
Öland 30-31 G 9
Olanga 30-31 NO 4
Olary 56-57 GH 6
Olavarría 80 DE 5
Òlbia 36-37 C 5
Ol'chon, ostrov – 42-43 U 7
Ol'chovskij = Art'omovsk 42-43 R 7
Olcott, NY 74-75 D 3
Old Castile = Castilla la Vieja 34-35 E 8-F 7
Oldcastle 32 C 5
Old Chitambo = Livingstone Memorial 64-65 GH 5
Old Crow 70-71 J 4
Old Chitambo = Livingstone Memorial 64-65 GH 5
Oldeani [EAT, ▲] 64-65 HJ 3
Oldeani [EAT, ●] 64-65 J 3
Oldenburg 33 CD 2
Old Faithful, WY 76-77 H 3
Old Forge, NY 74-75 F 3
Old Gumbiro 64-65 J 4-5
Oldham 32 EF 5
Ol Doinyo Lengai 63 C 3
Old Orchard Beach, ME 74-75 HJ 3
Old Town, ME 74-75 J 2
Old Woman Mountains 76-77 F 8
Öldzijt 48-49 J 2
Olean, NY 74-75 D 3
Olecko 33 L 1
Ölegey = Ölgij 48-49 FG 2
Olene, OR 76-77 C 4
Olenegorsk 38-39 FG 2
Olenij, ostrov – [SU, Karasee] 42-43 O 3
Olen'ok [SU, ~] 42-43 X 3
Olen'ok [SU, ●] 42-43 V 4
Olen'okskij zaliv 42-43 WX 3
Olen'ovka 36-37 P 3
Oléron, Île d' 34-35 G 6
Oleśnica 33 H 3
Ol'ga 42-43 a 9
Olga, Mount – 56-57 EF 5
Olgastretet 30-31 m 5
Ölgij 48-49 FG 2
Olhão 34-35 D 10
Olib 36-37 F 3
Olifantsrivier [Namibia] 64-65 E 7-8
Olifantsrivier [ZA, Transvaal] 64-65 G 7
Olimarao 52-53 MN 5
Olinda 78-79 N 6
O-Ling Hu = Ngoring Tsho 48-49 H 4-5
Olio 56-57 H 4
Oliva 34-35 GH 9
Oliva, Cordillera de – 80 BC 3
Olivares de Júcar 34-35 F 9
Olivenza 34-35 D 9
Olkusz 33 J 3
Ollagüe 80 C 2
Ollas Arriba 72-73 b 3
Ollita, Cordillera de – 80 B 4
Olmos [PE] 78-79 CD 6
Olney, MT 76-77 F 1
Olofström 30-31 F 9
Oloj 42-43 f 4
Ol'okma 42-43 X 5-6
Ol'okminsk 42-43 WX 5
Ol'okminskij stanovik 42-43 W 7-X 6
Ol'okmo-Čarskoje ploskogorje 42-43 WX 6
Olomouc 33 H 4
Ölön = Lün 48-49 K 2
Olongapo 52-53 GH 4
Oloron-Sainte-Marie 34-35 G 7
Olot 34-35 J 7
Olov'annaja 42-43 W 7
Öls nuur 48-49 G 4
Olsztyn 33 K 2
Olt 36-37 L 3
Olten 33 C 5
Oltenița 36-37 M 3
Olteț 36-37 KL 3
Oltu 46-47 JK 2
Olur 46-47 K 2
Ol'utorskij, mys – 42-43 h 6
Ol'utorskij poluostrov 42-43 h 5
Ol'utorskij zaliv 42-43 g 5-6
Olvera 34-35 E 10
Olympia [GR] 36-37 J 7
Olympia, WA 72-73 B 2
Olympic Mountains 76-77 AB 2
Olympic National Park 76-77 A 2
Ólympos [CY] 46-47 E 5
Ólympos [GR, ▲] 36-37 K 5-6
Ólympos [GR, ●] 36-37 M 8
Olympus, Mount – 76-77 B 2
Olyphant, PA 74-75 F 4

Ollagüe 80 C 2
Ollas Arriba 72-73 b 3
Ollita, Cordillera de – 80 B 4

Om' 42-43 O 6
Ōma 50-51 N 2
Ōmachi 50-51 L 4
Omae-zaki 50-51 M 5
Ōmagari 50-51 N 3
Om Ager = Om Hajer 60-61 M 6
Omagh 32 C 4
Omaha, NE 72-73 G 3
Omak, WA 76-77 D 1
Omak Lake 76-77 D 1
Omán 44-45 H 6-7
Oman, Bassin d' 44-45 H 7-J 6
Omán, Cuenca de – 44-45 H 7-J 6
'Oman, Daryā-ye – = Golf von Oman 44-45 HJ 6
Oman, Golfe d' 44-45 HJ 6
Omán, Golfo de – 44-45 HJ 6
Oman, Golf van – 44-45 HJ 6
Oman, Gulf of – 44-45 HJ 6
Omanbekken 44-45 H 7-J 6
Omar, WV 74-75 B 6
Omaruru 64-65 E 7
Ōma-saki 50-51 N 2
Omate 78-79 E 8
Ombella-Mpoko 60-61 H 7-8
Ombepera 64-65 D 6
Omboué 64-65 C 3
Ombrie = Umbria 36-37 DE 4
Ombrone 36-37 D 4
Ombu = Umbu 48-49 F 5
Ombuctá 80 D 5
Omčak 42-43 c 5
Omdurmân = Umm Durmān 60-61 L 5
O-mei Shan = Emei Shan 48-49 J 6
Omeo 58 HJ 6
Ömerli 46-47 J 4
Ometepe, Isla de – 72-73 J 9
Omgon, mys – 42-43 e 6
Om Hajer 60-61 M 6
Ōminato 50-51 N 2
Omineca Mountains 70-71 LM 6
Omiš 36-37 G 4
Ōmi-shima 50-51 H 5
Ōmiya 50-51 M 4-5
Ommanney Bay 70-71 Q 3
Ömnödelger 48-49 KL 2
Ömnögov' = 14 ◁ 48-49 K 3
Omo Bottego = Omo 60-61 M 7
Omoloj 42-43 Z 3
Omolon [SU, ~] 42-43 e 4-f 5
Omolon [SU, ●] 42-43 e 5
Ōmon 50-51 J 5
Omono-gawa 50-51 N 3
Omo Weniz 60-61 M 7
Omsk 42-43 N 7
Omsukčan 42-43 de 5
Ōmu 48-49 R 3
Omul 36-37 L 3
Ōmura 50-51 G 6
Omuramba Omatako 64-65 E 6-7
Ōmura wan 50-51 G 6
Omuta 48-49 OP 5
Omutninsk 42-43 J 6

Ona, FL 74-75 bc 3
Onagawa 50-51 N 3
Onahama = Iwaki 50-51 N 4
Onalaska, WA 76-77 B 2
Onancock, VA 74-75 EF 6
Onangué, Lac – 64-65 CD 3
Onaqui, UT 76-77 G 5
Onch'on-ni = Onyang 50-51 F 4
Oncócua 64-65 D 6
Ondangua 64-65 E 6
Ondo 60-61 EF 7
Öndörchaan 48-49 L 2
Onega [SU, ~] 42-43 F 5
Onega [SU, ●] 42-43 F 5
Oneida, NY 74-75 F 3
Oneida Lake 74-75 EF 3
Onekotan, ostrov – 19 E 3
Oneonta, NY 74-75 F 3
Onežskaja guba 42-43 F 5
Onežskij poluostrov 42-43 F 5
Onežskoje ozero 42-43 EF 5
Ongerup 56-57 C 6
Ongijn gol 48-49 J 2
Ongjin 48-49 NO 4
Ongole 44-45 MN 7
Ōngŭlu = Ongole 44-45 MN 7
Onib, Khōr – = Khawr Unib 62 F 7
Onilahy 64-65 KL 7
Onitsha 60-61 F 7
Onjŏng 50-51 EF 2
Onjŏng-ni 50-51 E 3
Ōno [J, Fukui] 50-51 L 5
Onoda 50-51 H 5-6
Onomichi 50-51 J 5
Onon gol 48-49 L 2
Onslow 56-57 C 4
Onslow Bay 72-73 L 5
Onsong 50-51 GH 1
Ontake san 50-51 L 5
Ontario 70-71 S 7-V 8
Ontario, CA 76-77 E 8
Ontario, OR 76-77 E 3
Ontario, Lake – 72-73 L 3
Ontario Peninsula 70-71 UV 9
Ontong Java Islands 52-53 j 6
Onverwacht 78-79 H 3

Oodnadatta 56-57 G 5
Oodweyne 60-61 b 2
Ooldea 56-57 F 6
Ooratippra 56-57 G 4
Oos-Londen 64-65 G 9
Oostaustralisch Bekken 22-23 RS 8
Oost-Carolinenbekken 22-23 R 5
Oostchinese Zee 48-49 N 6-O 5
Oostelijke Grote Erg = Al-'Irq al-Kabīr ash-Sharqī 60-61 F 2-3
Oostende 34-35 J 3
Oostenrijk 33 E-G 5
Oosterschelde 34-35 JK 3
Oostpacifische Drempel 22-23 D 6-7
Oostsiberische Drempel 19 B 36-1
Oostsiberische Zee 42-43 c-j 3
Oostzee 30-31 G 10-J 8

Opal, WY 76-77 H 5
Opala [SU] 42-43 e 7
Opala [ZRE] 64-65 F 3
Opal City, OR 76-77 C 3
Oparino 42-43 H 6
Opatija 36-37 EF 3
Opava 33 H 4
Ophir, AK 70-71 E 5
Ophir, OR 76-77 A 4
Ophira 62 F 4
Ophthalmia Range 56-57 CD 4
Opienge 64-65 G 2
Opočka 38-39 E 4
Opole 33 HJ 3
Opole Lubelskie 33 KL 3
Oppa gawa 50-51 N 3
Oppdal 30-31 C 6
Oppeid 30-31 F 3
Opper-Guinee 22-23 JK 5
Oppland 30-31 C 6-D 7
Opunake 56-57 O 7
Oputo 76-77 J 10

'Oqr = 'Uqr 60-61 K 6
Oquitoa 76-77 H 10

Or, Côte d' 60-61 D 8-E 7
Or, Côte d' 34-35 K 5
'Or, Wâdî – = Wādī Ur 62 D 6-7
Oradea 36-37 JK 2
Öræfajökull 30-31 e 2
Orahovica 36-37 GH 3
Or'ahovo 36-37 KL 4
Oraibi, AZ 76-77 H 8
Oramar = Dağlıca 46-47 KL 4
Orán = San Ramón de la Nueva Orán 80 CD 2
Oran = Wahrān 60-61 D 1
Orange [AUS] 56-57 J 6
Orange [F] 34-35 K 6
Orange, CA 76-77 E 9
Orange, TX 72-73 H 5
Orange, VA 74-75 DE 5
Orange = Oranje-Vrystaat 64-65 G 8
Orange = Oranje-Vrystaat 64-65 G 8
Orange, Cabo – 78-79 J 4
Orange, Ilha de – 60-61 A 6
Orangeburg, SC 72-73 K 5
Orange Cliffs 76-77 H 6
Orange Free State = Oranje-Vrystaat 64-65 G 8
Orange Park, FL 74-75 bc 1
Orange River = Oranjerivier [ZA, ~] 64-65 F 8
Orangeville 74-75 CD 3
Orani [RP] 52-53 GH 4
Oranje = Oranjerivier 64-65 DE 8
Oranje Gebergte 78-79 HJ 4
Oranje Gebergte = Pegunungan Jayawijaya 52-53 LM 7
Oranjerivier [ZA, ~] 64-65 F 8
Oranjestad 72-73 NM 9
Oranje-Vrystaat 64-65 G 8
Orawia 56-57 N 9
Orbetello 36-37 D 4
Orbost 56-57 J 7
Örbyhus 30-31 G 7
Orcadas 24 CD 32
Orchard, ID 76-77 EF 4
Orchard Homes, MT 76-77 F 2
Orchila, Isla – 78-79 F 2
Orchómenos 36-37 K 6
Orchon gol 48-49 J 2
Ördene 48-49 L 3
Orderville, UT 76-77 G 7
Ordi, el – = Dunqulah 60-61 KL 5
Ord Mountain 76-77 E 8
Ordos 48-49 K 4
Ord River 56-57 E 3
Ordu 44-45 D 2
Ordu = Yayladağı 46-47 FG 5
Ordžonikidze 38-39 HJ 7
Orealla 78-79 H 3
Oreana, NV 76-77 D 5
Örebro [S, ●] 30-31 F 8
Örebro [S, ☆] 30-31 F 8
Oregon 72-73 BC 3
Oregon Butte 76-77 E 2
Oregon City, OR 76-77 B 3
Oregon Inlet 74-75 F 7
Öregrund 30-31 H 7
Orem, UT 76-77 H 5
Ören [TR] 46-47 BC 4
Orenburg 42-43 JK 7
Örencik 46-47 C 3
Orense 34-35 D 7
Öresund 30-31 E 10
Orfa = Urfa 44-45 D 3
Orfánu, Kólpos – 36-37 KL 5
Organ Pipe Cactus National Monument 72-73 D 5
Orgejev 36-37 N 2
Orhaneli 46-47 C 3
Orhangazi 46-47 C 2
Orick, CA 76-77 A 5
Orient, WA 76-77 D 1
Oriental, NC 74-75 E 7
Oriente [C] 72-73 LM 7
Orihuela 34-35 G 9
Orillia 70-71 V 9
Orinoco, Delta del – 78-79 G 3
Orinoco, Llanos del – 78-79 E 4-F 3
Orinoco, Llanos del – 78-79 E 4-F 3
Orinoco, Río – 78-79 F 3
Orissa 44-45 N 7-O 6
Oristano 36-37 C 6
Orivesi [SF, ●] 30-31 L 7
Orivesi [SF, ≈] 30-31 N 6
Oriximiná 78-79 H 5
Orizaba 72-73 G 8
Orizaba, Pico de – = Citlaltépetl 72-73 G 8
Orkanger 30-31 C 6
Orkney 32 EF 2
Orland, CA 76-77 B 6
Orlando, FL 72-73 K 6
Orléanais 34-35 HJ 4-5
Orléans 34-35 HJ 5
Orléansville = Al-Asnām 60-61 E 1
Orlik 42-43 S 7
Orlinga 42-43 U 6
Orlov = Chalturin 42-43 H 6
Ormārā 44-45 JK 5
Ormoc 52-53 HJ 4
Ormond Beach, FL 74-75 c 2
Ormsby 74-75 DE 2
Orne 34-35 G 4
Örnsköldsvik 30-31 H 6
Oro, Costa de – 60-61 D 8-E 7
Oročen 42-43 Y 6
Orocué 78-79 E 4
Orodara 60-61 CD 6
Orofino, ID 76-77 EF 2
Or'ol 38-39 G 5
Orongo gol 48-49 F 2
Orono, ME 74-75 J 2
Oronoque 78-79 H 4
Orontes = Nahr al-'Āṣī 46-47 G 5
Orope 78-79 E 3
Oroquieta 52-53 H 5
Oro-ri 50-51 F 2
Oros 78-79 M 6
Orosei 36-37 C 5
Orosháza 33 K 5
Orosi, Volcán – 72-73 JK 9
Orotukan 42-43 d 5
Orovada, NV 76-77 DE 5
Oroville, CA 76-77 C 6
Oroville, WA 76-77 D 1
Oroya, La – 78-79 D 7
Orroroo 58 D 4
Orrville, OH 74-75 C 4
Orsa [S] 30-31 F 7
Orša [SU] 38-39 EF 5
Orsk 42-43 K 7
Orşova 36-37 K 3
Ørsta 30-31 AB 6
Ortabağ 46-47 K 4
Ortaca 46-47 C 4
Ortahanak = Hanak 46-47 K 2
Ortaköy [TR, Çorum] 46-47 F 2
Ortaköy [TR, Niğde] 46-47 EF 3
Ortegal, Cabo – 34-35 CD 7
Orthez 34-35 G 7
Ortigueira 34-35 CD 7
Orting, WA 76-77 BC 2
Ortlès 36-37 D 2
Ortona 36-37 F 4
Orūmīyeh 44-45 E 3
Orūmīyeh, Daryâcheh-ye – = Urmia 44-45 E 3
Orumo 63 C 2
Oruro [BOL, ●] 78-79 F 8
Orust 30-31 D 8
Orvieto 36-37 DE 4
Orville Escarpment 24 B 29-30

Oš [SU] 44-45 L 2
Osa 38-39 L 4
Osa [ZRE] 63 AB 3
Osa, Peninsula de – 72-73 JK 10
Osage River 72-73 H 4
Ōsaka 48-49 Q 5
Ōsaka wan 50-51 K 5
Osâm 36-37 L 4
Osan 50-51 F 4
Ošarovo 42-43 S 5

Panamá [PA, ☆] 72-73 a 3-b 2
Panamá, Bahía de – 72-73 bc 3
Panamá, Canal de – 72-73 b 2
Panama, Canal de – = Canal de Panamá 72-73 b 2
Panamá, Golfo de – 72-73 L 10
Panamá, Istmo de – 72-73 L 9-10
Panama Canal = Canal de Panamá 72-73 b 2
Panama City, FL 72-73 JK 5-6
Panamá Viejo 72-73 c 2
Panamint Range 76-77 E 7
Panamint Valley 76-77 E 7-8
Panao 78-79 D 6
Panaon Island 52-53 HJ 5
Pana Tinani 52-53 h 7
Panay 52-53 H 4
Pancake Range 76-77 EF 6
Pančevo 36-37 J 3
Panda 64-65 H 7
Pandharpur 44-45 LM 7
Pandie Pandie 56-57 GH 5
Pándormos = Bandırma 44-45 B 2
P'andž 44-45 K 3
Panevėžys 30-31 KL 10
Panfilov 42-43 OP 9
Pangaîon 36-37 KL 5
Pangala 64-65 BC 2
Pangalanes, Canal des – 64-65 L 6-7
Pangani [EAT, ~] 64-65 J 3
Pangani [EAT, ● Morogoro] 63 D 4
Pangani [EAT, ● Tanga] 63 C 5
Pangbei = Erlian 48-49 L 3
Pangeo 52-53 J 6
Pangi 64-65 G 3
Pangkajene 52-53 G 7
Pangkalpinang 52-53 E 7
Pangnirtung 70-71 XY 4
Panguitch, UT 76-77 G 7
Pangutaran Group 52-53 GH 5
Panhandle 70-71 JK 6
Paniai, Danau – 52-53 L 7
Panié, Mount – 56-57 M 4
Pänj = P'andž 44-45 K 3
Panjāb 44-45 K 4
Panjāb = Punjab [IND] 44-45 LM 4
Panjāb = Punjab [PAK] 44-45 L 4
Panjang 52-53 E 8
Panjang, Hon – 52-53 D 5
Panjgūr 44-45 J 5
Panjim = Panaji 44-45 L 7
Panjwīn 46-47 L 5
Pankshin 60-61 FG 7
Panlı 46-47 E 3
P'anmunjŏm 50-51 F 3-4
Panna 44-45 N 6
Panoche, CA 76-77 C 7
Pánō Lévkara 46-47 E 5
Panshan 50-51 D 2
Pantanal Mato-Grossense 78-79 H 8
Pantano, AZ 76-77 H 9-10
Pantar, Pulau – 52-53 H 8
Pantelleria [I, ⊙] 36-37 E 7
Pantelleria [I, ●] 36-37 DE 7
Pantoja 78-79 DE 5
Pantokrátōr 36-37 H 6
Pánuco, Río – 72-73 G 7
Panyu = Guangzhou 48-49 LM 7
Pao, El – [YV, Bolívar] 78-79 G 3
Paochi = Baoji 48-49 K 5
Pao-ching = Baojing 48-49 K 6
Pao-ch'ing = Shaoyang 48-49 L 6
Paoki = Baoji 48-49 K 5
Pàola 36-37 FG 6
Paoning = Langzhong 48-49 JK 5
Paoshan = Baoshan [TJ, Yunnan] 48-49 HJ 6
Paoteh = Baode 48-49 L 4
Pao-ting = Baoding 48-49 LM 4
Paotow = Baotou 48-49 KL 3
Paotsing = Baojing 48-49 K 6
Paotsing = Baoqing 48-49 P 2
Paoying = Baoying 48-49 M 5
P'aozero 38-39 EF 2
Pápa 33 H 5
Papagayo, Golfo del – 72-73 J 9
Papago Indian Reservation 76-77 GH 9-10
Papantla de Olarte 72-73 G 7
Papatoetoe 56-57 OP 7
Paphos = Páfos 46-47 E 5
Pa-pien Chiang = Babian Jiang 48-49 J 7
Pa-pien Chiang = Babian Jiang 48-49 J 7
Papikion 36-37 L 5
Papilė 30-31 K 9
Papouasie et Nouvelle-Guinée 52-53 MN 7-8
Papua, Gulf of – 52-53 MN 8
Papua New Guinea 52-53 MN 7-8
Papua-Nieuw-Guinea 52-53 MN 7-8
Papúa-Nueva Guinea 52-53 MN 7-8
Pâques, Île de – 22-23 D 7
Pará [BR] 78-79 J 5
Pará = Belém 78-79 K 5
Pará, Dorsal de – 22-23 GH 5
Pará, Rio do – 78-79 JK 5
Para, Seuil de – 22-23 GH 5
Parabel' 42-43 P 6
Paraburdoo 56-57 C 4
Paracale 52-53 H 4
Paracas, Península – 78-79 D 7
Paracatu 78-79 K 8
Paracels, Îles – = Quân Đao Tây Sa 52-53 EF 3
Parachilna 58 D 3
Paraćin 36-37 J 4
Paracuru 78-79 M 5
Parada, Punta – 78-79 D 8
Paraday, Montes de – 28-29 C 5-6
Paraday Seamount Group 28-29 C 5-6
Paradise, CA 76-77 C 6
Paradise, MT 76-77 F 2
Paradise, NV 76-77 F 7
Paradise Valley, NV 76-77 E 5
Parádrempel 22-23 GH 5
Paragould, AR 72-73 H 4
Paragua, La – 78-79 G 3
Paraguá, Río – [BOL] 78-79 G 7
Paragua, Río – [YV] 78-79 G 3
Paraguai, Rio – 78-79 H 9
Paraguaipoa 78-79 E 2
Paraguaná, Península de – 78-79 F 2
Paraguari [PY, ●] 80 E 3
Paraguay, Río – 80 E 2
Paraíba 78-79 M 6
Paraíba, Rio – 78-79 M 6
Parainen = Pargas 30-31 K 7
Paraiso [PA] 72-73 b 2
Parakou 60-61 E 7
Paramaribo 78-79 HJ 3
Paramirim 78-79 L 7
Paramonga 78-79 D 7
Paramušir, ostrov – 42-43 de 7
Paraná [RA] 80 DE 4
Paranã [BR, ●] 78-79 K 7
Paraná [BR, ☆] 80 FG 2
Paraná, Río – [RA] 80 E 3-4
Paraná, Rio – [BR ◁ Río de la Plata] 78-79 J 9
Paranã, Rio – [BR ◁ Rio Tocantins] 78-79 K 7
Paranaguá 80 G 3
Paranaíba 78-79 J 8
Paranaíba, Rio – 78-79 JK 8
Paranapanema, Rio – 78-79 J 9
Paranapiacaba, Serra do – 78-79 G 2-3
Paranavaí 80 F 2
Parandak, Īstgāh-e – 46-47 O 5
Paranjang 50-51 F 4
Parapol'skij dol 42-43 fg 5
Pará Rise 22-23 GH 5
Parata, Pointe della – 36-37 BC 5
Paratinga 78-79 L 7
Paraúna 78-79 JK 8
Parbati 44-45 M 5
Parbatipur 44-45 O 5
Parbig 42-43 P 6
Parchim 33 EF 2
Parc national de la Komoé 60-61 D 7
Parczew 33 L 3
Pardo, Rio – [BR, Planalto Brasileiro] 78-79 L 8
Pardo, Rio – [BR ◁ Rio Paraná] 78-79 J 9
Pardubice 33 GH 3
Parecis, Campos dos – 78-79 H 7
Parecis, Chapada dos – 78-79 GH 7
Parecis, Chapada dos – 78-79 GH 7
Parelhas 78-79 M 6
Pare Mountains 63 D 3-4
Parentis-en-Born 34-35 G 6
Parepare 52-53 G 7
Parga 36-37 J 6
Pargas 30-31 K 7
Paria, Golfo de – 78-79 G 2
Paria, Península de – 78-79 G 2
Pariaman 52-53 CD 7
Paria River 76-77 H 7
Paricutín, Volcán – 72-73 F 8
Parika 78-79 H 3
Parima, Sierra – 78-79 G 4
Pariñas, Punta – 78-79 C 5
Parintins 78-79 H 5
Pariñas, Punta – 78-79 C 5
Parīpārit Kyūn 52-53 B 4
Paris 34-35 J 4
Paris, ID 76-77 H 4
Paris, TX 72-73 GH 5
Paris = Paris 34-35 J 4
Parkano 30-31 K 6
Park City, UT 76-77 H 5
Parkdale, OR 76-77 C 3
Parker, AZ 76-77 FG 8
Parker Dam, CA 76-77 F 8
Parkersburg, WV 72-73 K 4
Parkes 56-57 J 6
Park Range 72-73 E 3-4
Park Valley, UT 76-77 G 5
Parlākimidi 44-45 NO 7
Parma 36-37 D 3
Parma, ID 76-77 E 4
Parma, OH 74-75 C 4
Parnaguá 78-79 L 7
Parnaíba 78-79 L 5
Parnaíba, Rio – 78-79 L 5
Parnassós 36-37 K 6
Párnēs 36-37 K 6
Párnōn 36-37 K 7
Pärnu [SU, ~] 30-31 L 8
Pärnu [SU, ●] 30-31 KL 8
Paromaj 42-43 b 7
Parona = Fındık 46-47 JK 4
Paroo Channel 56-57 H 6
Paroo Channel 56-57 H 6
Paroo River 58 G 2
Páros 36-37 L 7
Parowan, UT 76-77 G 7
Parr, SC 74-75 C 7
Parral 80 B 5
Parramore Island 74-75 F 6
Parras de la Fuente 72-73 F 6
Parry, Cape – 70-71 M 3
Parry Bay 70-71 U 4
Parry Island 74-75 C 2
Parry Islands 70-71 M-R 2
Parryøya 30-31 kl 4
Parsa = Persepolis 44-45 G 5
Parsnip River 70-71 M 6-7
Parsons, KS 72-73 G 4
Parsons, WV 74-75 D 5
Parța Jebel 36-37 J 3
Pårtefjället 30-31 GH 4
Parthenay 34-35 GH 5
Partinico 36-37 E 6
Partizansk 42-43 Z 9
Paru, Rio – [BR] 78-79 J 5
Pārvatī = Parbati 44-45 M 5
Parvatipurom 44-45 N 7
Parijs = Paris 34-35 J 4
Pasadena, CA 72-73 C 5
Pasadena, TX 72-73 GH 6
Pasaje 78-79 D 5
Pasajes de San Juan 34-35 FG 7
Pascagoula, MS 72-73 J 5
Paşcani 36-37 M 2
Pasco, WA 76-77 D 2
Pascua, Isla de – 22-23 D 7
Pascua, Plataforma de la isla de – 22-23 C-E 7
Pasewalk 33 FG 2
Pashāwar 44-45 KL 4
Pashchimī Bangāl = West Bengal 44-45 O 6
Pashid Haihsia 48-49 N 7
P'asina 42-43 QR 3
Pasinler 46-47 J 2-3
P'asino, ozero – 42-43 QR 4
P'asinskij zaliv 42-43 PQ 3
Pasir Besar = Kampung Pasir Besar 52-53 D 6
Paskenta, CA 76-77 B 6
Pasley, Cape – 56-57 D 6
Pašman 36-37 F 4
Pasnī 44-45 J 5
Paso, El – 78-79 E 3
Paso de Indios 80 BC 6
Paso de los Libres 80 E 3
Paso de los Toros 80 EF 4
Paso Robles, CA 76-77 C 8
Passau 33 F 4
Pàssero, Capo – 36-37 F 7
Passo Fundo 80 F 3
Passos 78-79 K 9
Pastaza, Río – 78-79 D 5
Pasto 78-79 D 4
Pastora Peak 76-77 J 7
Pasvalys 30-31 KL 9
Pasvikelv 30-31 NO 3
Patagonia 80 B 8-C 6
Patagonia, AZ 76-77 H 10
Patagonia, Plataforma de – 22-23 FG 8
Patagonian Shelf 22-23 FG 8
Patagónica, Cordillera – 80 B 8-5
Patagonisch Plat 22-23 FG 8
Pātan [Nepal] 44-45 NO 5
Patane = Pattani 52-53 D 5
Patang = Batang 48-49 H 6
Patargān, Daqq-e – 44-45 J 4
Patchewollock 58 EF 5
Patchogue, NY 74-75 G 4
Paternò 36-37 F 7
Pateros, WA 76-77 D 1-2
Paterson, NJ 74-75 F 4
Paterson, WA 76-77 D 2-3
Pathum Thani 52-53 CD 4
Patía, Río – 78-79 D 4
Patiala 44-45 M 4
Patience Well 56-57 E 4
P'atigorsk 38-39 H 7
Paṭiyālā = Patiala 44-45 M 4
Pátmos 36-37 M 7
Patna 44-45 O 5
Patnos 46-47 K 3
Patomskoje nagorje 42-43 V 6-W 6
Patos [BR, Paraíba] 78-79 M 6
Patos, Lagoa dos – 80 F 4
Patquia 80 C 4
Pátrai 36-37 J 6
Patraïkòs Kólpos 36-37 J 6-7
Patreksfjördhur 30-31 ab 2
Patricia [CDN, ≅] 70-71 S-U 7
Patricio Lynch, Isla – 80 A 7
Patrocínio 78-79 K 8
Patta Island 64-65 K 3
Pattani 52-53 D 5
Patten, ME 74-75 J 2
Patterson, CA 76-77 C 7
Patterson, GA 74-75 B 9
Patti 36-37 F 6
Pattiá 78-79 D 4
Patton, PA 74-75 D 4
Patu 78-79 M 6
Patuca, Punta – 72-73 K 8
Patuca, Río – 72-73 J 9-K 8
Patung = Badong 48-49 KL 5
Pau 34-35 G 7
Pau d'Arco 78-79 K 6
Pauillac 34-35 G 6
Paulina, OR 76-77 D 3
Paulina Mountains 76-77 C 4
Paulis = Isiro 64-65 G 2
Paulista [BR, Pernambuco] 78-79 MN 6
Paulista [BR, Zona litigiosa] 78-79 L 8
Paulistana 78-79 L 6
Paulo Afonso, Cachoeira de – 78-79 M 6
Paungde = Paungdī 52-53 BC 3
Paungdī 52-53 BC 3
Pavant Mountains 76-77 G 6
Pavêh 46-47 M 5
Pavia 36-37 C 3
Pavino 38-39 J 4
Pavlodar 42-43 O 7
Pavlovac 36-37 G 3
Pavlovo 38-39 H 4
Pavlovskaja 38-39 GH 6
Pavo, GA 74-75 B 9
Pavullo nel Frignano 36-37 D 3
Pavuvu = Russell Islands 52-53 j 6
Pavy 30-31 N 8-9
Pawleys Island, SC 74-75 D 8
Pawtucket, RI 74-75 H 4
Páxoi 36-37 J 6
Payakumbuh 52-53 D 7
Payette, ID 76-77 E 3
Payette River 76-77 E 3-4
Payne, Lac – 70-71 W 6
Payne Bay = Bellin 70-71 WX 5
Paynes Creek, CA 76-77 BC 5
Paysandú [ROU, ●] 80 E 4
Pays-Bas 34-35 K 3-L 2
Payson, AZ 76-77 H 8
Payson, UT 76-77 GH 5
Payún, Cerro – 80 BC 5
Paz, La – [MEX, Baja California Sur] 72-73 DE 7
Paz, La – [RA, Entre Ríos] 80 DE 4
Paz, La – [RA, Mendoza] 80 C 4
Paz, La – [BOL, ●] 78-79 F 8
Paž'a 38-39 L 3
Pazar 46-47 J 2
Pazar = Şorba 46-47 E 2
Pazarbası Burnu 46-47 D 2
Pazarcık 46-47 G 4
Pazarcık = Pazaryeri 46-47 C 2-3
Pazardžik 36-37 KL 4
Pazaryeri [TR, Bilecik] 46-47 C 2-3
Pčinja 36-37 J 4-5
Peace River [CDN, ~] 70-71 MN 6
Peace River [CDN, ●] 70-71 N 6
Peach Springs, AZ 76-77 G 8
Peacock Bay 24 B 26-27
Peake Creek 58 B 1-2
Peak Hill [AUS, New South Wales] 58 J 4
Peak Hill [AUS, Western Australia] 56-57 C 5
Peale, Mount – 72-73 DE 4
Pearce, AZ 76-77 J 10
Pearl Harbor 52-53 e 3
Pearl River 72-73 H 5
Pearson, GA 74-75 B 9
Peary Channel 70-71 R 2
Peary Channel 70-71 R 2
Peary Land 19 A 21-23
Pebane 64-65 J 6
Pebas 78-79 E 5
Peć 36-37 J 4
Peças, Ilha das – 80 G 3
Pečenga [SU, ●] 42-43 E 4
Pechabun = Phetchabun 52-53 CD 3
Pechawar = Pashāwar 44-45 KL 4
Pêcheurs, Presq'île des – = poluostrov Rybačij 42-43 EF 4
Pečora [SU, ~] 42-43 K 5
Pečora [SU, ●] 42-43 K 4
Pecoraro, Monte – 36-37 FG 6
Pečorskaja guba 42-43 JK 4
Pečorskaja magistral' 42-43 JK 5
Pečory 30-31 M 9
Pecos, TX 72-73 F 5
Pecos River 72-73 F 5
Pécs 33 HJ 5
Pedder, Lake – 58 bc 3
Pedee, OR 76-77 B 3
Pedernales [EC] 78-79 CD 4
Pedernales [YV] 78-79 G 3
Pederneira, Cachoeira – 78-79 FG 6
Pedra Azul 78-79 L 8
Pedras Negras 78-79 G 7
Pedregal [PA] 72-73 c 2
Pedreiras 78-79 KL 5
Pedrera, La – 78-79 EF 5
Pedro, Point – = Pēduru Tuḍuwa 44-45 N 9
Pedro Afonso 78-79 K 6
Pedro Cays 72-73 L 8
Pedro de Valdivia 80 BC 2
Pedro II 78-79 L 5
Pedro Juan Caballero 80 E 2
Pedro Miguel 72-73 b 2
Pedro Miguel, Esclusas de – 72-73 b 2
Pedro Miguel Locks = Esclusas de Pedro Miguel 72-73 b 2
Pedro R. Fernández 80 E 3
Pēduru Tuḍuwa [CL, ∧] 44-45 N 9
Peebinga 56-57 H 6
Peebles 32 E 4
Pee Dee River 72-73 L 5
Peekskill, NY 74-75 G 4
Peel River 70-71 JK 4
Peel Sound 70-71 R 3
Peene 33 F 2
Peera Peera Poolanna Lake 56-57 G 5
Pegasus Bay 56-57 O 8
Pegram, ID 76-77 H 4
Pègū 52-53 C 3
Pehpei = Beipei 48-49 K 6
Pehuajó 80 D 5
Peian = Bei'an 48-49 O 2
Pei-chên = Beizhen 50-51 C 2
Peighambar Dāgh = Peyghambar Dāgh 46-47 N 4
Pei-hai = Beihai 48-49 K 7
P'ei-hsien = Pei Xian 48-49 M 5
Peine 33 E 2
Pei-ngan = Bei'an 48-49 O 2
Peipei = Beipei 48-49 K 6
Pei-p'iao = Beipiao 50-51 C 2
Peiping = Beijing 48-49 LM 3-4
Peiraiévs 36-37 K 7
Pei Shan = Bei Shan 48-49 GH 3
Peixe 78-79 K 7
Pei Xian [TJ ↖ Xuzhou] 48-49 M 5
Pekalongan 52-53 EF 8
Pekan 52-53 D 6
Pekanbaru 52-53 D 6
Pekín = Beijing 48-49 LM 3-4
Pékin = Beijing 48-49 LM 3-4
Pekul'nej, chrebet – 42-43 hj 4
Peleaga 36-37 K 3
Peleduj 42-43 V 6
Pelée, Montagne – 72-73 O 8
Pelēnaion 36-37 LM 6
Peleng, Pulau – 52-53 H 7
Pēlion 36-37 K 6
Pelješac 36-37 G 4
Pelkosenniemi 30-31 MN 4
Pello 30-31 L 4
Pelly Bay 70-71 S 4
Pelly Mountains 70-71 K 5
Pelly River 70-71 K 5
Peloncillo Mountains 76-77 J 9
Pelopónnēsos 36-37 JK 7
Peloritani, Monti – 36-37 F 6-7
Pelotas 80 F 4
Pelotas, Rio – 80 F 3
Pelusium 62 E 2
Pelusium, Bay of – = Khalīj aṭ-Ṭīnah 62 E 2
Pelvoux 34-35 L 6
Pelym [SU, ~] 42-43 L 5
Pelym [SU, ●] 42-43 L 6
Pemadumcook Lake 74-75 J 2
Pemalang 52-53 EF 8
Pemangkat 52-53 E 6
Pematangsiantar 52-53 C 6
Pemba [EAT] 64-65 JK 4
Pemba [Moçambique] 64-65 K 5
Pemba [Z] 64-65 G 6
Pemberton [AUS] 56-57 C 6
Pembina 70-71 NO 7
Pembroke 32 D 6
Pembroke [CDN] 72-73 L 2
Pembroke, GA 74-75 C 8
Peña, Sierra de la – 34-35 G 7
Peñafiel 34-35 EF 8
Peñagolosa 34-35 G 8
Peña Negra, Punta – 78-79 C 5
Peña Nevada, Cerro – 72-73 FG 7
Penang = George Town 52-53 CD 5
Peñarroya 34-35 G 8
Peñarroya-Pueblonuevo 34-35 E 9
Peñas, Cabo de – 34-35 E 7
Peñas, Golfo de – 80 AB 7
Peñas, Punta – 78-79 G 2
Penawawa, WA 76-77 E 2
Penck, Cape – 24 C 9
Pendembu 60-61 B 7
Pender Bay 56-57 D 3
Pendjab = Punjab [IND] 44-45 LM 4
Pendjab = Punjab [PAK] 44-45 L 4
Pendleton, OR 72-73 C 2
Pend Oreille Lake 76-77 E 1-2
Pend Oreille River 76-77 E 1
Pendroy, MT 76-77 GH 1
Pendžikent 44-45 K 3
Pēneiós 36-37 K 6
Penetanguishene 74-75 CD 2
Penganga 44-45 M 7
Penge [ZRE, Haut-Zaïre] 63 AB 2
Penge [ZRE, Kasai-Oriental] 64-65 FG 4
Penghu Liedao = Penghu Lieh-tao 48-49 M 7
Penghu Lieh-tao 48-49 M 7
Penglai 48-49 N 4
Pengra Pass 76-77 BC 4
Pengze 48-49 M 6
Penida, Nusa – 52-53 FG 8
Peninsula Malaya 52-53 C 5-D 6
Peñíscola 34-35 H 8
Penitente, Serra do – 78-79 K 6
Penki = Benxi 48-49 N 3
Penmarch, Pointe de – 34-35 E 5
Penne 36-37 EF 4
Penn Hills, PA 56-57 D 4
Pennine Chain 32 E 4-F 5
Pennine Chain 32 E 4-F 5
Pennsylvania 72-73 KL 3
Penn Yan, NY 74-75 E 3

Penny Highland 70-71 X 4
Penny Strait 70-71 R 2
Penobscot Bay 74-75 J 2
Penobscot River 74-75 J 2
Penong 56-57 F 6
Penrith 32 E 4
Pensa = Penza 42-43 GH 7
Pensacola, FL 72-73 J 5
Pensacola Mountains 24 A 33-34
Pentecost Island 56-57 N 3
Pentecost River 56-57 E 3
Penticton 70-71 N 8
Pentland Firth 32 E 2
Penyu, Kepulauan – 52-53 J 8
Penza 42-43 GH 7
Penzance 32 CD 6
Penžina 42-43 g 5
Penžinskaja guba 42-43 f 5
Peña, Sierra de la – 34-35 G 7
Peñafiel 34-35 EF 8
Peñagolosa 34-35 G 8
Peña Negra, Punta – 78-79 C 5
Peña Nevada, Cerro – 72-73 FG 7
Peñarroya 34-35 G 8
Peñarroya-Pueblonuevo 34-35 E 9
Peñas, Cabo de – 34-35 E 7
Peñas, Golfo de – 80 AB 7
Peñas, Punta – 78-79 G 2
Peñíscola 34-35 H 8
Peoria, AZ 76-77 G 9
Peoria, IL 72-73 HJ 3
Pepel 60-61 B 7
Peperkust 60-61 B 7-C 8
Pequeni, Rio – 72-73 bc 2
Pequeñas Antillas 72-73 N 9-O 8
Pequop Mountains 76-77 F 5
Perälä 30-31 JK 6
Perche 34-35 H 4
Percival Lakes 56-57 DE 4
Perdido, Monte – 34-35 GH 7
Pereguete, Rio – 72-73 b 3
Pereira 78-79 D 4
Pereira, Cachoeira – 78-79 H 5
Pereira d'Eça = N'Giva 64-65 E 6
Perekop 38-39 F 6
Perelik 36-37 L 5
Peremul Par 44-45 L 8
Pereslavl'-Zalesskij 38-39 G 4
Perevoz [SU ↗ Bodajbo] 42-43 W 6
Pergamino 80 D 4
Pergamon 46-47 B 3
Pergamos = Pergamon 46-47 B 3
Perhonjoki 30-31 KL 6
Péribonca, Rivière – 70-71 W 7-8
Perico 80 CD 2
Périgord 34-35 H 6
Perigoso, Canal – 78-79 K 4
Périgueux 34-35 H 6
Perija, Sierra de – 78-79 E 2-3
Perim Island = Barīm 44-45 E 8
Periquito, Cachoeira do – 78-79 G 6
Peri Suyu 46-47 J 3
Perito Moreno 80 BC 7
Perlas, Archipiélago de las – 72-73 KL 10
Perlas, Punta de – 72-73 K 9
Perm' 42-43 K 6
Permskoje = Komsomol'sk-na-Amure 42-43 a 7
Pernambuco 78-79 LM 6
Pernambuco = Recife 78-79 N 6
Pernik 36-37 K 4
Péronne 34-35 J 4
Peron Peninsula 56-57 B 5
Pérou 78-79 D 5-E 7
Pérou, Bassin du – 22-23 E 6
Pérouse, proliv la – = proliv Laperuza 42-43 b 8
Perovsk = Kzyl-Orda 42-43 M 9
Perpignan 34-35 J 7
Perrégaux = Muḥammadīyah 60-61 DE 1
Perrine, FL 74-75 c 4
Perris, CA 76-77 E 9
Perry, FL 74-75 b 1
Perry, NY 74-75 DE 3
Perse = Iran 44-45 F-H 4
Perşembe 46-47 G 2
Persepolis 44-45 G 5
Perseverancia 78-79 G 7
Persia = Iran 44-45 F-H 4
Persian Gulf 44-45 FG 5
Pertek 46-47 H 3
Perth [AUS, Tasmania] 58 c 2
Perth [AUS, Western Australia] 56-57 BC 6
Perth [CDN] 74-75 E 2
Perth [GB] 32 E 3
Perth Amboy, NJ 74-75 F 4
Perú 78-79 D 5-E 7
Perú [RA] 80 D 5
Perú, Cuenca del – 22-23 E 6
Perú, Fosa del – 78-79 C 6-D 7
Peru Basin 22-23 E 6
Perubekken 22-23 E 6
Peru Chile Trench 78-79 C 6-D 7
Peru Chile Trench 78-79 C 6-D 7
Perùgia 36-37 E 4
Peruibe 80 G 2
Perutrog 78-79 C 6-D 7
Pervari = Hashır 46-47 K 4
Perveri 46-47 GH 4
Pervomajsk 38-39 EF 6
Pervoural'sk 42-43 KL 6
Pervyj Kuril'skij proliv 42-43 de 7
Perzië = Iran 44-45 F-H 4
Perzische Golf 44-45 FG 5
Pèsaro 36-37 E 4
Pescadero, CA 76-77 B 7
Pescadores = Penghu Liehtao 48-49 M 7
Pesčanyj, ostrov – 42-43 WX 3
Pescara 36-37 F 4
Peschici 36-37 FG 5
Peshawar = Pashāwar 44-45 KL 4
Peshwar = Pashāwar 44-45 KL 4
Peštera 36-37 KL 4
Petah Tiqua = Pētaḥ Tiqwa 46-47 F 6
Pētaḥ Tiqwa 46-47 F 6
Petaliôn, Kólpos – 36-37 L 7
Petaluma, CA 76-77 B 6
Petauke 64-65 H 5
Petén, El – 72-73 H 8
Peterborough 32 FG 5
Peterborough [AUS, South Australia] 56-57 GH 6
Peterborough [AUS, Victoria] 58 F 7
Peterborough [CDN] 70-71 V 9
Peterborough, NH 74-75 GH 3
Peterhead 32 F 3
Petermann Ranges 56-57 E 4-F 5
Peter Pond Lake 70-71 P 6
Petersburg, AK 70-71 K 6
Petersburg, VA 72-73 L 4
Petersburg, WV 74-75 D 5
Petersburg = Sankt-Peterburg 42-43 E 5-6
Petilia Policastro 36-37 G 6
Petites Antilles 72-73 N 9-O 8
Petitjean = Sīdī Qāsim 60-61 CD 2
Petit Manan Point 74-75 K 2
Petitot River 70-71 M 5-6
Peto 72-73 J 7
Petorca 80 B 4
Petra [JOR] 46-47 F 7
Petra, ostrova – 42-43 VW 2
Petra I, ostrov – 24 C 27
Petra Velikogo, zaliv – 42-43 Z 9
Petre, Point – 74-75 E 3
Petrič 36-37 K 5
Petrified Forest National Monument 76-77 J 8
Pétriou = Chachoengsao 52-53 D 4
Petroaleksandrovsk = Turtkul' 42-43 L 9
Petrodvorec 30-31 O 8
Petrograd = Leningrad 42-43 E 5-6
Petrolândia 78-79 M 6
Petrólea 78-79 E 3
Petrolia, CA 76-77 A 5
Petrolina [BR, Pernambuco] 78-79 L 6
Petropavlovka 42-43 TU 7
Petropavlovsk 42-43 MN 7
Petropavlovsk-Kamčatskij 42-43 ef 7
Petrópolis 78-79 L 9
Petroşeni 36-37 K 3
Petroskoi = Petrozavodsk 42-43 EF 5
Petrovaradin 36-37 HJ 3
Petrovka [SU, Vladivostok] 50-51 J 1
Petrovsk 38-39 J 5
Petrovskij Zavod = Petrovsk-Zabajkal'skij 42-43 U 7
Petrovsk-Zabajkal'skij 42-43 U 7
Petrozavodsk 42-43 EF 5
Petrun 38-39 LM 2
Petuchovo 42-43 M 6
Peumo 80 B 4
Pevek 42-43 gh 4
Peyghambar Dāgh 46-47 N 4
Peza 38-39 J 2
Pézenas 34-35 J 7

Pfaffenhofen 33 E 4
Pfarrkirchen 33 F 4
Pforzheim 33 D 4

Phalodi 44-45 L 5
Phaltan 44-45 LM 7
Phangan, Ko – 52-53 CD 5
Phanggong Tsho 48-49 DE 5
Phan Rang 52-53 EF 4
Phan Thiet 52-53 E 4
Phatthalung 52-53 D 5
Phaykkhaphum Phisai 52-53 D 3
Phelps Lake 74-75 E 7
Phenix City, AL 72-73 J 5
Phetchabun 52-53 CD 3
Phetchaburi 52-53 CD 4
Philadelphia [ET] 62 D 3
Philadelphia, PA 72-73 LM 3-4
Philip Island 56-57 N 5
Philippe-Thomas = Al-Mittawī 60-61 F 2
Philippeville 34-35 K 3
Philippeville = Sakīkdah 60-61 F 1
Philippi, WV 74-75 CD 5
Philippine Basin 22-23 Q 5
Philippines 52-53 H 3-J 5
Philippines, Bassin des – 22-23 Q 5
Philippines, Fosse des – 22-23 Q 5
Philippine Trench 22-23 Q 5
Philipsburg, MT 76-77 G 2
Philipsburg, PA 74-75 D 4
Philip Smith Mountains 70-71 GH 4
Phillipi, Lake – 56-57 G 4
Phillip Island 58 G 7
Phillippines 52-53 H 3-J 5
Phillips, ME 74-75 H 2
Phillipsburg, NJ 74-75 F 4
Phillips Mountains 24 B 22-23
Philo, CA 76-77 B 6
Phippsøya 30-31 kl 4
Phitsanulok 52-53 D 3
Phnom Penh 52-53 D 4
Pho, Laem – 52-53 D 5
Phoenix, AZ 72-73 D 5
Phoenix, Fosse des – 22-23 AB 6
Phoenix Trench 22-23 AB 6
Phoenixtrog 22-23 AB 6
Phoenixville, PA 74-75 EF 4
Phôngsaly 52-53 D 2
Phosphate Hill 56-57 GH 4
Phra Chedi Sam Ong 52-53 C 3-4
Phra Chedi Sam Ong 52-53 C 3-4
Phra Nakhon Si Ayutthaya 52-53 D 4
Phu Diên Châu 52-53 E 3
Phu Diên Châu 52-53 E 3
Phuket 52-53 C 5
Phuket, Ko – 52-53 C 5
Phu Ly 52-53 E 2
Phum Rovieng 52-53 E 4
Phunakha 44-45 OP 5
Phu Quôc, Dao – 52-53 D 4
Phu Tho 52-53 DE 2

Piacá 78-79 K 6
Piacenza 36-37 C 3
Piangil 56-57 H 7
Pianosa, Ìsola – 36-37 D 4
Piaseczno 33 K 2
Piatra 36-37 L 3
Piatra-Neamţ 36-37 M 2
Piauí 78-79 L 6
Piauí, Rio – 78-79 L 6
Piave 36-37 E 2
Piazza Armerina 36-37 F 7
Pībōr = Bībūr 60-61 L 7
Pībōr, Nahr – = Nahr Bībūr 60-61 L 7
Picabo, ID 76-77 F 4
Picacho, AZ 76-77 H 9
Picacho, CA 76-77 F 9
Picardie 34-35 HJ 4
Pichanal 80 CD 2
Pichi Ciego 80 C 4
Pichieh = Bijie 48-49 K 6
Pichilemú 80 B 4
Pichtovka 42-43 P 6
Pickens, SC 74-75 B 7
Pickle Crow 70-71 ST 7
Pico, El – 78-79 G 8
Picola 58 G 5
Picos 78-79 L 6
Pico Truncado 80 C 7
Picton [CDN] 74-75 E 2-3
Picton [NZ] 56-57 O 8
Picton, Mount – 58 bc 3
Picui 78-79 M 6
Picún Leufú 80 BC 5
Pidurutalāgala 44-45 N 9
Pie de Palo 80 C 4
Piedmont 72-73 K 5-L 4
Piedmont, SC 74-75 B 7
Piedmont, WV 74-75 D 5
Piedra del Águila 80 BC 6
Piedras 78-79 CD 5
Piedras, Río – [PA] 72-73 b 2
Piedras, Río de las – 78-79 E 7
Piedras Negras 72-73 F 6
Pieksämäki 30-31 M 6
Pielinen 30-31 N 6
Piemonte 36-37 BC 3
Pierce, ID 76-77 F 2
Piercy, CA 76-77 B 6
Pierre, SD 72-73 F 3
Pierson, FL 74-75 c 2
Piešt'any 33 HJ 4
Pietarsaari = Jakobstad 30-31 JK 6
Pietermaritzburg 64-65 H 8
Pietersburg 64-65 G 7
Pietrasanta 36-37 CD 4
Pietrosul [R ↙ Borşa] 36-37 L 2
Pietrosul [R ↙ Vatra Dornei] 36-37 L 2
Pigailoe 52-53 N 5
Pigeon Point 76-77 B 7
Pigŭm-do 50-51 E 5
Pihtipudas 30-31 LM 6
Pihyŏn 50-51 E 2
Piippola 30-31 LM 5
Pija, Sierra de – 72-73 J 8
Pikelot 52-53 N 5
Pikes Peak 72-73 F 4
Piketberg 64-65 E 9
Pikeville, KY 74-75 B 6
Pikou 50-51 D 3
Piła 33 H 2
Pilão Arcado 78-79 L 7
Pilar [PY] 80 E 3
Pilares de Nacozari 76-77 J 10
Pilas Group 52-53 H 5
Pilawa 33 K 3
Pilcaniyeu 80 BC 6
Pilcomayo, Rio – [BR] 80 D 2
Pil'gyn 42-43 jk 4
Pilica 33 K 3
Pillar, Cape – 56-57 J 8
Pilot Mountain, NC 74-75 C 6
Pilot Peak [USA, Absaroka Range] 76-77 HJ 3
Pilot Peak [USA, Gabbs Valley Range] 76-77 E 6
Pilot Peak [USA, Toano Range] 76-77 FG 5
Pilot Rock, OR 76-77 D 3
Piltene 30-31 JK 9
Pim 42-43 N 5
Pimba 56-57 G 6
Pimenta Bueno 78-79 G 7
Pimienta, Costa de la – 60-61 B 7-C 8
Piña [PA] 72-73 a 2
Pinaleno Mountains 76-77 HJ 9
Pinamelayan 52-53 H 4
Pinang = George Town 52-53 CD 5
Pınar = Ören 46-47 BC 4
Pınarbaşı 46-47 G 3
Pinar del Río 72-73 K 7
Pınarhisar 46-47 B 2
Pîncota 36-37 J 2
Pindaré, Rio – 78-79 K 5
Píndos Óros 36-37 J 5-6
Pine, ID 76-77 F 4
Pine Bluff, AR 72-73 H 5
Pine City, WA 76-77 E 2
Pine Creek [AUS] 56-57 F 2
Pine Creek [USA] 76-77 E 5
Pinedale, WY 76-77 J 4
Pine Forest Mountains 76-77 D 5
Pinega 42-43 G 5
Pine Hills 72-73 J 5
Pine Island 74-75 b 3
Pine Island Bay 24 B 26
Pine Islands 74-75 c 4
Pine Point 70-71 O 5
Pinerolo 36-37 B 3
Pine Valley Mountains 76-77 G 7
Ping, Mae Nam – 52-53 C 3
P'ing-ch'üan = Pingquan 50-51 B 2
Pingdong = Ping-tung 48-49 N 7
P'ing-hsiang = Pingxiang 48-49 L 6
P'ing-hsien = Pingxiang 48-49 K 7
Pingle [TJ] 48-49 L 7
P'ing-leang = Pingliang 48-49 K 4
Pingliang 48-49 K 4
Pingliang = Pingtung 48-49 N 7
Pinglo = Pingle 48-49 L 7
P'ing-lo = Pingluo 48-49 K 4
Pingluo 48-49 K 4
Pingquan 50-51 B 2
Pingree, ID 76-77 G 4
Pingrup 56-57 C 6
Pingsiang = Pingxiang 48-49 L 6
Pingtan Dao 48-49 MN 6
Ping-tung 48-49 N 7
Pingwu 48-49 J 5
Pingxiang [TJ, Guangxi Zhuangzu Zizhiqu] 48-49 K 7
Pingxiang [TJ, Jiangxi] 48-49 L 6
Pinhal 78-79 K 9
Pinheiro 78-79 KL 5
Pini, Pulau – 52-53 C 6
Pinjarra 56-57 C 6
Pinkiang = Harbin 48-49 O 2
Pinnacles National Monument 76-77 C 7
Pinnaroo 56-57 H 7
Pinón, Monte – 72-73 b 2
Pinos, Mount – 76-77 D 8
Pinos, Point – 76-77 BC 7
Pinrang 52-53 G 7
Pins, Îles de – 56-57 N 4
Pins, Pointe aux – 74-75 C 3
Pinsk 38-39 E 5
Pinta, Isla – 78-79 A 4
Pintada [BR, Rio Grande do Sul] 80 F 4
Pintados 80 BC 2
Pintas, Sierra de – 76-77 F 10
Pinto [RA] 80 D 3
Piña [PA] 72-73 a 2
Pioche, NV 76-77 F 7
Piombino 36-37 D 4
Pioneer Mountains 76-77 G 3
Pioner, ostrov – 42-43 QR 2
Pionki 33 K 3
Piorini, Lago – 78-79 G 5
Piorini, Rio – 78-79 G 5
Piotrków Trybunalski 33 J 3
Pipérion 36-37 L 6
Pipinas 80 E 5
Piquetberg = Piketberg 64-65 E 9
Piquiri, Rio – 80 F 2
Piracanjuba 78-79 JK 8
Piraçununga 78-79 K 9
Piracuruca 78-79 L 5
Piraeus = Peiraiévs 36-37 K 7
Piraí do Sul 80 G 2
Pirajuí 78-79 K 9
Pīr 'Alī Emāmzādeh 46-47 N 6
Piran 36-37 E 3
Piran = Dicle 46-47 J 3
Pirané 80 E 3
Piranhas 78-79 M 6
Piranhas, Rio – [BR, Rio Grande do Norte] 78-79 M 6
Pirapora 78-79 L 8
Pir'atin 38-39 F 5
Piratuba 80 F 3
Pirée, le – = Peiraiévs 36-37 K 7
Pireo, El – = Peiraiévs 36-37 K 7
Pirin 36-37 K 5
Pirinçlik 46-47 H 4
Pirineos 34-35 G-J 7
Piripiri 78-79 L 5
Pirmasens 33 C 4
Pirna 33 F 3
Piro-bong 50-51 G 3
Pirot 36-37 K 4
Pirpintos, Los – 80 D 3
Pirtleville, AZ 76-77 J 10
Piru 52-53 J 7
Pisa 36-37 D 4
Pisagua 80 B 1
Pisco 78-79 D 7
Pisco, Bahía de – 78-79 D 7
Písek 33 G 4
Pisgah, Mount – 76-77 C 3
Pishan = Guma Bazar 48-49 D 4
P'i-shan = Guma Bazar 48-49 D 4
Pispek = Frunze 42-43 NO 9
Pisticci 36-37 G 5
Pistòia 36-37 D 3-4
Pistol River, OR 76-77 A 4
Pisuerga 34-35 E 7
Pisz 33 K 2
Pita 60-61 B 6
Piteå 30-31 J 5
Pite älv 30-31 HJ 5
Piteşti 36-37 L 3
Pit-Gorodok 42-43 RS 6
Pithara 56-57 C 6
Piti, Cerro – 80 C 2
Pitigliano 36-37 D 4
Pitiquito 76-77 G 10
Pitk'ajarvi 30-31 NO 3
Pit River 76-77 BC 5
Pitt Island [CDN] 70-71 KL 7
Pitt Island [NZ] 56-57 Q 8
Pittsboro, NC 74-75 D 7
Pittsburg, CA 76-77 C 6
Pittsburg, KS 72-73 H 4
Pittsburgh, PA 72-73 KL 3
Pittsfield, MA 74-75 G 3
Pittsfield, ME 74-75 J 2
Pittston, PA 74-75 F 4
Pittsworth 58 K 1
P'i-tzŭ-wo = Pikou 50-51 D 3
Piuka = Bifuka 50-51 c 1
Piura [PE, ●] 78-79 CD 6
Piute Peak 76-77 D 8
Piva 36-37 H 4
Pivka 36-37 F 3
Pizzo 36-37 FG 6

Pjagina, poluostrov – 42-43 de 6

Placentia Bay 70-71 Za 8
Placerville, CA 76-77 C 6
Placetas 72-73 L 7
Plácido de Castro 78-79 F 7
Plains, MT 76-77 F 2
Plainview, TX 72-73 F 5
Planada, CA 76-77 CD 7
Planaltina 78-79 K 8
Planalto Brasileiro 78-79 KL 8
Plantation, FL 56-57 c 3
Plant City, FL 74-75 b 2-3
Plasencia 34-35 D 8
Plast 42-43 L 7
Plaster City, CA 76-77 EF 9
Plastun 42-43 a 9
Plata, Isla de la – 78-79 C 5
Plata, La – [CO] 78-79 D 4
Plata, La – [RA] 80 E 5
Plata, Río de la – 80 EF 5
Plateau 60-61 F 7
Plateau Central = Cao Nguyên Trung Phân 52-53 E 4
Plateau Continental Patagonien 22-23 FG 8
Platen, Kapp – 30-31 lm 4
Platinum, AK 70-71 D 6
Platte Island 64-65 N 4
Platte River [USA, Nebraska] 72-73 FG 3
Plattsburgh, NY 72-73 LM 3
Plauen 33 F 3
Playas 78-79 C 5
Plaza Huincul 80 BC 5
Pleasant, Mount – 74-75 D 6
Pleasant Grove, UT 76-77 H 5
Pleasant Valley, OR 76-77 E 3
Pleasant View, WA 76-77 DE 2
Pleasantville, NJ 74-75 FG 5
Pleihari 52-53 F 7
Pleiku 52-53 E 4
Plenița 36-37 K 3
Plenty, Bay of – [NZ, ◡] 56-57 P 7
Pleseck 42-43 G 5
Pleszew 33 HJ 3
Pleven 36-37 L 4
Plitvice 36-37 F 3
Plitvička Jezera 36-37 FG 3
Pljevlja 36-37 H 4
Płock 33 JK 2
Ploieşti 36-37 LM 3
Plomo, El – 76-77 GH 10
Plovdiv 36-37 L 4
Plumas, Las – 80 C 6
Plummer, ID 76-77 E 2
Plumtree 64-65 G 7
Plungė 30-31 J 10
Plush, OR 76-77 D 4
Plymouth 32 DE 6
Plymouth, CA 76-77 C 6
Plymouth, MA 74-75 H 4
Plymouth, NC 74-75 E 7
Plymouth, NH 74-75 GH 3
Plymouth, PA 74-75 EF 4
Plzeň 33 F 4

Po 36-37 D 3
Pô [HV] 60-61 D 6
Pobè 60-61 E 7
Pobeda, gora – 42-43 c 4

208 Penny

Pobedino 42-43 b 8
Pobedy, pik – 44-45 MN 2
Pocatello, ID 72-73 D 3
P'och'ŏn 50-51 F 4
Pochval'nyj 42-43 cd 4
Pocklington Reef 52-53 j 7
Poções 78-79 LM 7
Pocomoke City, MD 74-75 F 5
Pocomoke Sound 74-75 EF 6
Poconé 78-79 H 8
Poços de Caldas 78-79 K 9
Podborovje 38-39 FG 4
Podgornoje 42-43 P 6
Podkamennaja Tunguska 42-43 R 5
Podkova 36-37 L 5
Podol'sk 38-39 G 4
Podor 60-61 AB 5
Podporožje 42-43 EF 5
Podravska Slatina 36-37 GH 3
Podtesovo 42-43 R 6
Po-êrh-t'a-la Chou = Bortala Monggol Zizhizhou 48-49 E 2-3
Po-êrh-t'a-la Chou = Bortala Monggol Zizhizhou 48-49 E 2-3
Pofadder 64-65 EF 8
Poggibonsi 36-37 D 4
Pogibi 42-43 b 7
Pogyndeno 42-43 fg 4
P'oha-dong 50-51 GH 2
Po Hai = Bo Hai 48-49 M 4
Po-hai Hai-hsia = Bohai Haixia 48-49 N 4
P'ohang 48-49 OP 4
Pohjanmaa 30-31 K 6-M 5
Pohjois-Karjalan lääni 30-31 N 6
Pohsien = Bo Xian 48-49 LM 5
Point Arena, CA 76-77 AB 6
Pointe-à-Pitre 72-73 O 8
Pointe-Noire 64-65 D 3
Point Harbor, NC 74-75 F 6
Point Lake 70-71 O 4
Point Marion, PA 74-75 D 5
Point Pleasant, NJ 74-75 FG 4-5
Point Pleasant, WV 74-75 BC 5
Point Roberts, WA 76-77 B 1
Poitevin, Marais – 34-35 G 5
Poitiers 34-35 H 5
Poitou 34-35 GH 5
Poivre, Côte du – = Malabar Coast 44-45 L 8-M 9
Poix 34-35 HJ 4
Pojarkovo 42-43 Y 8
Pokataroo 58 J 2
Pokhara 44-45 N 5
Poko 64-65 G 2
Pokrovsk 42-43 Y 5
Pokrovsk-Ural'skij 42-43 K 5
Polacca Wash 76-77 H 8
Pola de Siero 34-35 E 7
Polān [IR] 44-45 J 5
Poland 33 H-L 3
Pol'arnoje 42-43 c 3
Pol'arnyj 38-39 F 2
Pol'arnyj Ural 42-43 LM 4
Polathane = Akçaabat 46-47 H 2
Polatlı 44-45 C 3
Polcirkeln 30-31 J 4
Polesje 38-39 DE 5
Poleskoj 38-39 M 4
Polessk 33 K 1
Põlgyo 50-51 F 5
Poli 60-61 G 7
Poli = Boli 48-49 P 2
Policastro, Golfo di – 36-37 F 5-6
Polillo Islands 52-53 H 3-4
Polinesia 22-23 A 5-6
Poliny Osipenko 42-43 a 7
Pólis 46-47 E 5
Polk, PA 74-75 CD 4
Pollensa 34-35 J 9
Pollino 36-37 G 5-6
Pollock, ID 76-77 E 3
Polmak 30-31 N 2
Polock 38-39 E 4
Pologi 38-39 G 6
Pologne 33 H-L 3
Polonia 33 H-L 3
Polonio, Cabo – 80 F 4
Polousnyj kr'až 42-43 bc 4
Polson, MT 76-77 FG 2
Poltava 38-39 F 6
Poltorack = Aščhabad 44-45 HJ 3
Põltsamaa 30-31 LM 8
Poluj 42-43 M 4
Poluj = Pospolnj 42-43 MN 4
Polunočnoje 42-43 L 5
Polýaigos 36-37 L 7
Polýchnitos 36-37 LM 6
Polýgyros 36-37 K 5
Polynesia 22-23 A 5-6
Polynesië 22-23 A 6-7
Polynésie 22-23 A 5-6
Poma, La – 80 C 2
Pomarão 34-35 D 10
Pomasi, Cerro de – 78-79 E 8
Pombal 34-35 C 9
Pombal [BR] 78-79 M 6
Pombetsu = Honbetsu 50-51 cd 2
Pomerania 33 G 2-H 1
Poméranie 33 G 2-H 1
Pomeroy, OH 74-75 BC 5
Pomeroy, WA 76-77 E 2
Pommeren 33 G 2-H 1
Pommersche Bucht 33 FG 1
Pomona, CA 76-77 E 8-9
Pomorie 36-37 MN 4
Pompano Beach, FL 74-75 cd 3
Pompeji 36-37 F 5
Pompeys Pillar, MT 76-77 JK 2
Pomut 38-39 N 3
Ponca City, OK 72-73 G 4
Ponce 72-73 N 8
Ponce de Leon Bay 74-75 c 4
Pondicheri = Pondicherry 44-45 MN 8
Pondicherry 44-45 MN 8
Pond Inlet [CDN, ∪] 70-71 VW 3
Pond Inlet [CDN, ●] 70-71 V 3
Pondo Dsong 48-49 G 5
Pondosa, CA 76-77 C 5
Pondosa, OR 76-77 E 3
Ponferrada 34-35 D 7
Pong 52-53 CD 3
Pongnim-ni = Põlgyo 50-51 F 5
Pongola [ZA, ~] 64-65 H 8
Ponoj [SU, ~] 38-39 G 2
Ponoj [SU, ●] 42-43 FG 4
Ponta Albina 64-65 D 6
Ponta de Pedras 78-79 JK 5
Ponta Grossa [BR, Amapá] 78-79 K 4
Ponta Grossa [BR, Paraná] 80 F 3
Ponta Porã 78-79 HJ 9
Pontarlier 34-35 KL 5
Pontchartrain, Lake – 72-73 HJ 5
Ponte de Pedra [BR ↖ Diamantino] 78-79 H 7
Ponte-Leccia 36-37 C 4
Ponte Nova 78-79 L 9
Pontes-e-Lacerda 78-79 H 8
Pontevedra 34-35 C 7
Ponthierville = Ubundu 64-65 FG 3
Pontiac, MI 72-73 K 3
Pontianak 52-53 E 7
Pontic Mountains 44-45 C-E 2
Pontisch Gebergte 44-45 C-E 2
Pontivy 34-35 F 4
Ponto, Montes del – 44-45 C-E 2
Pontoise 34-35 HJ 4
Pontrèmoli 36-37 CD 3
Pony, MT 76-77 GH 3
Ponza 36-37 E 5
Ponziane, Ísole – 36-37 E 5
Poochera 58 B 4
Poole 32 E 6
Poona = Pune 44-45 L 7
Pooncarie 56-57 H 6
Poopó 78-79 F 8
Poopó, Lago de – 78-79 F 8
Popa = Pulau Kofiau 52-53 JK 7
Popayán 78-79 D 4
Popigaj 42-43 UV 3
Popilta Lake 58 E 4
Poplar Bluff, MO 72-73 H 4
Popocatépetl 72-73 G 8
Popokabaka 64-65 E 4
Popondetta 52-53 N 8
Popovo 36-37 M 4
Poprad [CS, ~] 33 K 4
Poprad [CS, ●] 33 K 4
Pŏpsŏngp'o 50-51 F 5
Porālī 44-45 K 5
Porangatu 78-79 K 7
Porbandar 44-45 K 6
Porbunder = Porbandar 44-45 K 6
Porchov 38-39 E 4
Porcupine Mountain 70-71 Q 7
Porcupine River 70-71 H 4
Pordenone 36-37 E 2-3
Pore 78-79 E 3
Pori 30-31 J 7
Porjus 30-31 HJ 4
Porlamar 78-79 G 2
Pornic 34-35 F 5
Poronajsk 42-43 b 8
Poroshiri-dake 50-51 c 2
Porosozero 38-39 F 3
Porpoise Bay 24 C 13
Porsangerfjord 30-31 LM 2
Porsangerhalvøya 30-31 L 2
Porsgrunn 30-31 CD 8
Porsuk Çayı 46-47 D 3
Portachuelo 78-79 G 8
Portadown 32 C 4
Portage, UT 76-77 G 5
Portage-la-Prairie 72-73 R 8
Port Alberni 70-71 LM 8
Port Albert [AUS] 58 H 7
Portalegre 34-35 D 9
Portales, NM 72-73 F 5
Port Alfred 64-65 G 9
Port Allegany, PA 74-75 DE 4
Port Allegany, PA 74-75 DE 4
Port Angeles, WA 76-77 B 1
Port Antonio 72-73 L 8
Port Arthur 58 cd 3
Port Arthur, TX 72-73 H 6
Port Arthur = Lüshun 48-49 MN 4
Port Augusta 56-57 G 6
Port-au-Prince 72-73 M 8
Port-Bergé 64-65 L 6
Port Blair 44-45 P 8
Port-Bou 34-35 J 7
Port Brega = Marsá al-Burayqah 60-61 H 2
Port Burwell [CDN, Ontario] 74-75 C 3
Port Burwell [CDN, Quebec] 70-71 XY 5
Port Cartier 70-71 X 7
Port Chalmers 56-57 O 9
Port Colborne 74-75 D 3
Port Curtis 56-57 K 4
Port Chalmers 56-57 O 9
Port Darwin 80 E 8
Port Dunford = Buur Gaabo 64-65 K 3
Portel [BR] 78-79 J 5
Port Elizabeth 64-65 G 9
Port Erin 32 D 4
Porterville 64-65 EF 9
Porterville, CA 76-77 D 7-8
Port Essington 70-71 KL 7
Port-Étienne = Nawādhību 60-61 A 4
Port Fairy 56-57 H 7
Port-Francqui = Ilebo 64-65 F 3
Port Fu'ad = Būr Sādāt 62 E 2
Port-Gentil 64-65 C 3
Port Harcourt 60-61 F 8
Port Hardy 70-71 L 7
Port Harrison = Inoucdjouac 70-71 V 6
Port Hedland 56-57 C 4
Port Henry, NY 74-75 G 2-3
Port Herald = Nsanje 64-65 J 6
Porthill, ID 76-77 E 1
Port Hope 74-75 D 2-3
Port Hueneme, CA 76-77 D 8
Port Huron, MI 72-73 K 3
Portimão 34-35 C 10
Port Jefferson, NY 74-75 G 4
Port Jervis, NY 74-75 F 4
Port Keats 56-57 EF 2
Port Kembla, Wollongong- 56-57 K 6
Port Kenney 56-57 F 6
Port Lairge = Waterford 32 C 5
Portland [AUS, New South Wales] 58 JK 4
Portland [AUS, Victoria] 56-57 H 7
Portland [CDN] 74-75 EF 2
Portland, ME 72-73 MN 3
Portland, OR 72-73 B 2
Portland = Dyrhólaey 30-31 d 3
Portland, Bill of – 32 EF 6
Portland, Cape – 58 c 2
Portland Promontory 70-71 UV 6
Port Laoise 32 C 5
Port Lincoln 56-57 FG 6
Port Loko 60-61 B 7
Port Louis 64-65 N 7
Port-Lyautey = Al-Q'nitrah 60-61 C 2
Port Macdonnell 58 DE 7
Port Macquarie 58 L 3
Port Mathurin 64-65 O 6
Port Mayaca, FL 74-75 c 3
Port Moresby 52-53 N 8
Port Musgrave 56-57 H 2
Port Natal = Durban 64-65 H 8
Port Neill 58 C 5
Port Nelson [CDN, ∪] 70-71 S 6
Port Nelson [CDN, ●] 70-71 S 6
Port Nolloth 64-65 E 8
Port Norris, NJ 74-75 F 5
Porto 34-35 C 8
Porto Acre 78-79 F 6
Porto Alegre [BR, Rio Grando do Sul] 80 FG 4
Porto Alexandre 64-65 D 6
Porto Alexandre, Parque National de – 64-65 D 6
Porto Amboim 64-65 D 5
Porto Amélia = Pemba 64-65 K 5
Porto Artur 78-79 HJ 7
Portobelo [PA] 72-73 b 1
Porto Caneco 78-79 HJ 7
Porto Conceição 78-79 H 8
Porto de Más 78-79 H 8
Porto de Môs [BR] 78-79 J 5
Porto Empèdocle 36-37 E 7
Portoferràio 36-37 CD 4
Porto Franco 78-79 K 6
Port of Spain 72-73 O 9
Portogruaro 36-37 E 3
Porto Guaira 80 F 2
Portola, CA 76-77 C 6
Pörtom 30-31 J 6
Porto Mendes 80 F 2
Porto Nacional 78-79 K 7
Porto-Novo [DY] 60-61 E 7
Port Orchard, WA 76-77 B 2
Porto Real do Colégio 78-79 M 6-7
Port Orford, OR 76-77 A 4
Porto Rico, Fosse de – 22-23 FG 4
Porto Santana 78-79 J 5
Porto Santo 60-61 AB 2
Porto São José 80 F 2
Porto Seguro 78-79 M 8
Porto Tolle 36-37 E 3
Porto Tòrres 36-37 C 5
Porto União 80 F 3
Porto-Vecchio 36-37 C 5
Porto Velho 78-79 G 6
Portoviejo 78-79 C 5
Porto Walter 78-79 E 6
Portpatrik 32 D 4
Port Phillip Bay 56-57 H 7
Port Pirie 56-57 G 6
Port Radium 70-71 NO 4
Port Rowan 74-75 C 3
Port Royal = Annapolis Royal 70-71 XY 9
Port Royal Sound 74-75 C 8
Port Safâga = Safājah 60-61 L 3
Port Said = Būr Sa'īd 60-61 L 2
Port Shepstone 64-65 H 9
Portsmouth [GB] 32 F 6
Portsmouth, NH 72-73 MN 3
Portsmouth, OH 72-73 K 4
Portsmouth, VA 72-73 L 4
Port Stanley 74-75 C 3
Port Stanley = Stanley 80 E 8
Port Sūdān = Būr Sūdān 60-61 M 5
Port Talbot 32 DE 6
Port Tewfik = Būr Tawfīq 62 E 3
Porttipahdan tekojärvi 30-31 LM 3-4
Port Townsend, WA 76-77 B 1
Portugalete 34-35 E 7
Portugália = Luachimo 64-65 F 4
Portugues, El – 78-79 D 6
Portuguesa, Río – 78-79 F 3
Port-Vendres 34-35 J 7
Port Victoria [AUS] 58 C 5
Port Victoria [EUA] 64-65 H 2-3
Port Vladimir 38-39 FG 2
Port Wakefield 58 CD 5
Port Weld 52-53 CD 6
Porvoo = Borgå 30-31 LM 7
Posadas [RA] 80 E 3
Posad-Pokrovskoje 36-37 OP 2
Poshan = Boshan 48-49 M 4
Posio 30-31 N 4
Posjet 42-43 Z 9
Poso 52-53 H 7
Posof 46-47 K 2
Posŏng 48-49 O 5
Pospoluj 42-43 MN 4
Posse 78-79 K 7
Post, OR 76-77 C 3
Post Falls, ID 76-77 E 2
Postmasburg 64-65 F 8
Postojna 36-37 F 3
Poston, AZ 76-77 F 8
Potchefstroom 64-65 G 8
Potenza 36-37 F 5
Potgietersrus 64-65 G 7
Potholes Reservoir 76-77 D 2
Poti 38-39 H 7
Potiskum 60-61 G 6
Potlatch, ID 76-77 E 2
Pot Mountain 76-77 F 2
Potomac River 74-75 E 5
Potosí [BOL, ●] 78-79 F 8
Potrerillos [RCH] 80 C 3
Potsdam 33 F 2
Potsdam, NY 74-75 F 2
Pottstown, PA 74-75 F 4
Pottsville, PA 74-75 E 4
Pottuvil = Potuvil 44-45 N 7
Pötürge 46-47 H 3
Potuvil 44-45 N 7
Poughkeepsie, NY 72-73 LM 3
Pouilles = Pùglia 36-37 FG 5
Poŭn 50-51 F 4
Pouso Alegre [BR, Mato Grosso] 78-79 H 7
Pouso Alegre [BR, Minas Gerais] 78-79 K 9
Póvoa de Varzim 34-35 C 8
Povorino 38-39 H 5
Povraz adası = Alibey adası 46-47 B 3
Povungnituk 70-71 V 6
Powder River [USA, Montana] 72-73 E 2
Powder River [USA, Oregon] 76-77 E 3
Powell, Lake – 72-73 D 4
Powell Butte, OR 76-77 C 3
Powell River 70-71 M 8
Power, MT 76-77 H 2
Powers, OR 76-77 AB 4
Poxoréu 78-79 J 8
Poyang Hu 48-49 M 6
Pozantı 46-47 F 4
Požarevac 36-37 J 3
Poza Rica 72-73 G 7
Požeg 38-39 KL 3
Poznań 33 H 2
Pozo Almonte 80 C 2
Pozoblanco 34-35 E 9
Pozo Colorado 80 E 2
Pozo Hondo [RA] 80 D 3
Pozzallo 36-37 F 7
Pozzuoli 36-37 EF 5

Pra [WG] 60-61 D 7
Praag = Praha 33 G 3
Prachuap Khiri Khan 52-53 CD 4
Praděd 33 H 3
Prades 34-35 J 7
Prado [BR] 78-79 M 8
Praga = Praha 33 G 3
Prague = Praha 33 G 3
Prague = Praha 33 G 3
Praha 33 G 3
Praião, Cachoeira do – 78-79 K 8
Prainha [BR, Amazonas] 78-79 G 6
Prainha [BR, Pará] 78-79 J 5
Prairie, ID 76-77 F 4
Prairie City, OR 76-77 D 3
Prairies 70-71 Q 7-R 9
Pran Buri 52-53 CD 4
Pranhita 44-45 MN 7
Praskoveja 38-39 HJ 7
Praslin Island 64-65 N 3
Prasonēsion, Akrōtērion – 36-37 MN 8
Prata [BR, Pará] 78-79 K 5
Pratas = Dongsha Qundao 48-49 LM 7
Prato 36-37 D 4
Prawle, Point – 32 E 6
Přebeza 36-37 J 6
Precordillera 80 C 3-4
Predeal, Pasul – 36-37 L 3
Predivinsk 42-43 R 6
Pregol'a 33 K 1
Preiļi 30-31 M 9
Premuda 36-37 F 3
Prenzlau 33 FG 2
Přerov 33 H 4
Prescott 74-75 F 2
Prescott, AZ 72-73 D 5
Presidencia Roque Sáenz Peña 80 D 3
Presidencia Roque Sáenz Peña 80 D 3
Presidente Dutra 78-79 L 6
Presidente Epitácio 78-79 J 9
Presidente Hermes 78-79 G 7
Presidente Prudente 78-79 J 9
Presidio, TX 72-73 F 6
Prešov 33 K 4
Prespansko Ezero 36-37 J 5
Presque Isle, ME 72-73 N 2
Prestea 60-61 D 7
Preston 32 E 5
Preston, CA 76-77 B 6
Preston, ID 76-77 H 4
Prestonsburg, KY 74-75 B 6
Prestwick 32 DE 4
Preto, Rio – [BR ◁ Rio Grande] 78-79 K 7
Preto, Rio – [BR ◁ Rio Paracatu] 78-79 K 8
Pretoria 64-65 G 8
Prey Veng 52-53 E 4
Priargunsk 42-43 WX 7
Pribilof Islands 19 D 35-36
Příbram 33 G 4
Pribrežnyj chrebet 42-43 Za 6
Price, UT 72-73 D 4
Price River 76-77 H 6
Prichard, AL 72-73 J 5
Prichard, ID 76-77 EF 2
Priego de Córdoba 34-35 E 10
Priekulė 30-31 J 9
Prienai 30-31 K 10
Prieska 64-65 F 8
Priest Lake 76-77 E 1
Priest Rapids Reservoir 76-77 CD 2
Priest River, ID 76-77 E 1
Prijedor 36-37 G 3
Prikumsk 38-39 H 7
Prilep 36-37 J 5
Priluki 38-39 F 5
Primorsk 30-31 N 7
Primorskij chrebet 42-43 TU 7
Primorsko-Achtarsk 38-39 G 6
Primorsko-Achtarsk 38-39 G 6
Prince Albert 70-71 P 7
Prince Albert Mountains 24 B 16-17
Prince Albert National Park 70-71 P 7
Prince Albert Peninsula 70-71 NO 3
Prince Albert Sound 70-71 NO 3
Prince Alfred, Cape – 70-71 KL 3
Prince Charles Island 70-71 V 4
Prince Charles Range 24 B 7
Prince Charles Island 70-71 V 4
Prince Charles Range 24 B 7
Prince Edward Bay 74-75 E 2-3
Prince Edward Island 70-71 Y 8
Prince Edward Islands 24 E 4
Prince Edward Peninsula 74-75 E 2-3
Prince Frederick, MD 74-75 E 5
Prince George 70-71 M 7
Prince Gustaf Adolf Sea 70-71 P 2
Prince Island = Pulau Panaitan 52-53 DE 8
Prince of Wales, Cape – 70-71 C 4-5
Prince of Wales Island [AUS] 56-57 H 2
Prince of Wales Island [CDN] 70-71 QR 3
Prince of Wales Island [USA] 70-71 JK 6
Prince of Wales Island = Wales Island 70-71 T 4
Prince of Wales Strait 70-71 N 3
Prince Patrick Island 70-71 M 2
Prince Regent Inlet 70-71 ST 3
Prince Rupert 70-71 KL 7
Princess Anne, MD 74-75 F 5
Princess Charlotte Bay 56-57 H 2
Princess Charlotte Bay 56-57 H 2
Princess Elizabeth Land 24 BC 8-9
Princess Royal Island 70-71 L 7
Princeton, CA 76-77 BC 6
Princeton, NJ 74-75 F 4
Princeton, WV 74-75 C 6
Prince William Sound 70-71 G 5
Príncipe, Ilha do – 60-61 F 8
Principe da Baira 78-79 G 7
Principe da Beira 78-79 G 7
Prineville, OR 76-77 C 3
Prins Christian Sund 70-71 c 5-d 6
Prins Christian Sund 70-71 c 5-d 6
Prinsesse Astrid land 24 B 1-2
Prinsesse Ragnhild land 24 B 3
Prins Harald land 24 B 4-C 5
Prinzregent-Luitpold-Land 24 B 33-34
Prior, Cabo – 34-35 C 7
Priozersk = Prioz'orsk 42-43 DE 5
Prioz'orsk 42-43 DE 5
Prip'at 38-39 EF 5
Pripol'arnyj Ural 42-43 KL 4-5
Priština 36-37 J 4
Privas 34-35 K 6
Priverno 36-37 E 5
Prividencia, Isla de – 78-79 C 2
Privol'noje 36-37 OP 2

Privo 209

Quang Tri 52-53 E 3
Quang Yên 52-53 E 2
Quantico, VA 74-75 E 5
Quanxian = Quanzhou 48-49 KL 6
Quanzhou [TJ, Fujian] 48-49 MN 6-7
Quanzhou [TJ, Guangxi Zhuangzu Zizhiqu] 48-49 KL 6
Qu'Appelle River 70-71 Q 7
Quartu Sant'Èlena 36-37 C 6
Quartzsite, AZ 76-77 FG 9
Qubayyât, Al- 46-47 G 5
Qûchân 44-45 H 3
Quchaq Bai 48-49 D 4
Qûchghâr 44-45 F 3
Quds, Al- 46-47 F 7
Quealy, WY 76-77 J 5
Queanbeyan 56-57 JK 7
Québec [CDN, ●] 70-71 W 8
Quebec [CDN, ☆] 70-71 V-Y 7
Quebracho 80 E 4
Quedal, Cabo – 80 AB 6
Quedlinburg 33 E 3
Queen Alexandra Range 24 A 17-15
Queen Charlotte 70-71 K 7
Queen Charlotte Islands 70-71 K 7
Queen Charlotte Sound 70-71 KL 7
Queen Charlotte Strait 70-71 L 7
Queen Charlotte 70-71 K 7
Queen Charlotte Islands 70-71 K 7
Queen Charlotte Sound 70-71 KL 7
Queen Charlotte Strait 70-71 L 7
Queen Elizabeth Islands 70-71 N-U 2
Queen Elizabeth National Park = Ruwenzori National Park 64-65 GH 3
Queen Mary Coast = Queen Mary Land 24 C 10
Queen Mary Land 24 C 10
Queen Maud Gulf 70-71 Q 4
Queen Maud Land = Dronning Maud land 24 B 36-4
Queen Maud's Range = Dronning Maud fjellkjede 24 A
Queens Channel 56-57 E 2
Queenscliff 58 G 7
Queens Channel 56-57 E 2
Queensland 56-57 G-J 4
Queenstown [AUS] 56-57 HJ 8
Queenstown [NZ] 56-57 N 8
Queenstown [ZA] 64-65 G 9
Queets, WA 76-77 A 2
Quela 64-65 E 4
Quelimane 64-65 J 6
Quelpart = Cheju-do 48-49 NO 5
Quemado, NM 76-77 J 8
Quemoy = Chin-mên Tao 48-49 M 7
Que Que = Kwekwe 64-65 G 6
Queras, Rio – 72-73 a 3
Quercy 34-35 H 6
Querétaro 72-73 FG 7
Querobabi 76-77 H 10
Quesada 34-35 F 10
Queshan 48-49 L 5
Quesnel 70-71 M 7
Quetta = Kwatta 44-45 K 4
Quezaltenango 72-73 H 9
Quezon City 52-53 H 4
Quffah, Wâdî al- 62 E 6
Quiaca, La – 80 CD 2
Quiansu = Jiangsu 48-49 LM 6
Quibala 64-65 DE 5
Quibaxe 64-65 D 4
Quibdó 78-79 D 3
Quiberon 34-35 F 5
Quijotoa, AZ 76-77 GH 9
Quilcene, WA 76-77 B 2
Quilimari 80 B 4
Quillacollo 78-79 F 8
Quillagua 80 BC 2
Quill Lakes 70-71 Q 7
Quillota 80 B 4
Quilon 44-45 M 9
Quilpie 56-57 H 5
Quimbele 64-65 E 4
Quimili 80 D 3
Quimper 34-35 E 4-5
Quimperle 34-35 F 5
Quinault, WA 76-77 B 2
Quinault Indian Reservation 76-77 AB 2
Quince Mil 78-79 EF 7
Quincy, CA 76-77 C 6
Quincy, IL 72-73 H 4
Quincy, MA 74-75 H 3
Quincy, WA 76-77 D 2
Quines 80 C 4
Qui Nho'n 52-53 EF 4
Quinn River 76-77 E 5
Quinn River Crossing, NV 76-77 DE 5
Quintanar de la Orden 34-35 F 9
Quintana Roo 72-73 J 7-8
Quiongdong = Quionghai 48-49 L 8
Quirima 64-65 E 5
Quirimba, Ilhas – 64-65 K 5
Quirindi 58 K 3
Quissanga 64-65 K 5
Quissico 64-65 HJ 7
Quiterajo 63 E 5
Quitman, GA 74-75 B 9
Quito 78-79 D 5
Quitovac 76-77 G 10
Quixadá [BR, Ceará] 78-79 M 5
Quixeramobim 78-79 M 5-6
Qujiang = Shaoguan 48-49 L 6-7
Qujing 48-49 J 6
Qûlâshgird = Golâshkerd 44-45 H 5
Qulay'ah, Râ's al- 46-47 N 8
Qulayb, Bi'r – 62 EF 5
Qulbân aṭ-Ṭayyârât 46-47 JK 5
Qulbân Layyah 46-47 M 8
Quleib, Bîr – = Bi'r Qulayb 62 EF 5
Qûlonjî 46-47 L 4
Qum = Qom 44-45 G 4
Qum darya 48-49 F 3
Qum Köl 48-49 F 4
Qum tagh 48-49 G 4
Qumush 48-49 F 3
Qunâytirah 46-47 FG 6
Qundûz = Kunduz 44-45 K 3
Qunfudhah, Al- 44-45 DE 7
Qungur tagh 48-49 D 4
Quoram = Korem 60-61 M 6
Quorn [AUS] 56-57 G 6
Qûqrîyâl 60-61 K 7
Qurayni, Al- 44-45 GH 6
Quraytû 46-47 L 5
Qurayyah, Al- 62 FG 3
Qurayyah, Wâdî – 62 F 2
Qurbah 60-61 M 1
Qurdûd 60-61 KL 6-7
Qûrénâ = Shaḥḥât 60-61 J 2
Qurnah, Al- 46-47 M 7
Quruq Tagh 48-49 F 3
Qûş 62 E 5
Quşaybah 46-47 J 5
Quşay'ir 44-45 G 7-8
Quşayr, Al- [ET] 60-61 L 3
Quşayr, Al- [IRQ] 46-47 L 7
Quşayr, Al- [SYR] 46-47 G 5
Qushrân 44-45 D 6
Qushui = Chhushul 48-49 FG 6
Qûşîyah, Al- 62 D 4
Qusṭanṭîn 60-61 F 1
Quṭayfah, Al- 46-47 G 6
Quwârib, Al- 60-61 A 5
Quwaymât, Al- 46-47 GH 6
Quwayr, Al- 46-47 K 4
Quwayrah, Al- 46-47 F 8
Quwaysinâ 62 D 2
Qu Xian 48-49 M 6
Qûyûn, Jazîreh – 46-47 L 4
Qytet Stalin 36-37 HJ 5

R

Raab 33 G 5
Raahe 30-31 L 5
Ra'an, Ar- 46-47 J 8
Raanes Peninsula 70-71 T 2
Raas, Pulau – 52-53 FG 8
Rab 36-37 F 3
Raba 33 H 5
Raba [RI] 52-53 G 8
Rabaçal 34-35 D 8
Rabat [M] 36-37 F 7
Rabat = Ar-Ribâṭ 60-61 C 2
Rabaul 52-53 h 5
Râb'i, Al-Jandal ar – 60-61 L 5
Râbigh 44-45 D 6
Rabun Bald 74-75 B 7
Raccoon Mountains = Sand Mountains 72-73 J 5
Race, Cape – 70-71 a 8
Râchayâ = Râshayyâ 46-47 FG 6
Rach Gia 52-53 DE 4-5
Rachov 38-39 D 6
Racht = Rasht 44-45 FG 3
Racibórz 33 J 3
Racine, WI 72-73 J 3
Radâ' [Y] 44-45 EF 8
Radama, Nosy – 64-65 L 5
Rădăuţi 36-37 L 2
Radford, VA 74-75 C 6
Radîsîyat Baḥrî, Ar- 62 E 5
Radkersburg 33 GH 5
Radom 33 K 3
Radomsko 33 JK 3
Radøy 30-31 A 7
Radstock, Cape – 58 AB 4
Rae 70-71 NO 5
Rae Bareli 44-45 N 5
Raeford, NC 74-75 D 7
Rae Isthmus 70-71 T 4
Rae Strait 70-71 RS 4
Rafaela 80 D 4
Rafael del Encanto 78-79 E 5
Rafai 60-61 J 7-8
Rafḥah 44-45 E 5
Rafsanjân 44-45 H 4
Raft River 76-77 G 4
Raft River Mountains 76-77 G 5
Râgâ = Râjâ 60-61 K 7
Ragaing Pyinnei 52-53 B 2
Ragaing Yôma 52-53 B 2-3
Ragged Island 74-75 J 3
Ragozino = Novyj Tevriz 42-43 O 6
Ragunda 30-31 FG 6
Ragusa 36-37 F 7
Ragusa = Dubrovnik 36-37 GH 4
Raha 52-53 H 7
Rahâb, Ar- = Ar-Rihâb 46-47 L 7
Rahad, Ar- 60-61 L 6
Rahad, Nahr ar- 60-61 L 6
Rahad al-Bardî 60-61 J 6
Rahaeng = Tak 52-53 C 3
Rahaṭ, Ḥarrat – 44-45 DE 6
Raḥḥâlîyah, Ar- 46-47 K 6
Râhjerd 46-47 O 5
Raḥmat, Âb-e – 46-47 N 6
Raiâitît, Wâdî – = Wâdî Rayâytît 62 F 6
Raichur 44-45 M 7
Raidat aş Şai'ar = Raydat aş-Şay'ar 44-45 F 7
Raidestós = Tekirdağ 44-45 B 2
Raigarh 44-45 N 6
Railroad Pass 76-77 E 6
Railroad Valley 76-77 F 6-7
Rainbow 58 EF 5
Rainbow Bridge National Monument 76-77 H 7
Rainier, OR 76-77 B 2
Rainier, Mount – 72-73 BC 2
Rainy Lake 72-73 H 2
Raippaluoto 30-31 J 6
Raipur [IND, Madhya Pradesh] 44-45 N 6
Râjâ 60-61 K 7
Rajada 78-79 L 6
Rajahmundry 44-45 N 7
Rajakoski 30-31 N 3
Râjamahêndri = Rajahmundry 44-45 N 7
Rajang [RI, ~] 52-53 F 6
Rajapalaiyam 44-45 M 9
Râjapâlayam = Rajapalaiyam 44-45 M 9
Rajasthan 44-45 LM 5
Rajčichinsk 42-43 YZ 8
Rajeputana = Rajasthan 44-45 LM 5
Rajkot 44-45 L 6
Rajputâna = Rajasthan 44-45 LM 5
Râjshâhî 44-45 O 6
Rakaia 56-57 O 8
Rakasdal 48-49 E 5
Rakata = Pulau Anak Krakatau 52-53 DE 8
Rakhshân 44-45 JK 5
Rakiura = Stewart Island 56-57 N 9
Rakops 64-65 F 7
Rakovnik 33 F 3
Raksakiny 42-43 NO 5
Rakvere 30-31 M 8
Raleigh, NC 72-73 L 4
Raleigh Bay 74-75 EF 7
Râm, Jabal – 46-47 F 8
Ramâdî, Ar- 44-45 E 4
Ramah 70-71 Y 6
Ramah, NM 76-77 J 8
Ramalho, Serra do – 78-79 KL 7
Râm Allâh 46-47 F 7
Râm Allâh 46-47 F 7
Raman [TR] 46-47 J 4
Ramapo, Abysse de – 48-49 R 5
Ramapo, Fosa de – 48-49 R 5
Ramapo Deep 48-49 R 5
Ramapodiep 48-49 R 5
Rambi 52-53 b 2
Rambrè 52-53 B 3
Rambrè Kyûn 52-53 B 3
Ramḍâ', Ar- 46-47 L 8
Râmhormoz 46-47 N 7
Rami, 'Ayn ar- 62 B 2
Ramla 46-47 F 7
Ramona, CA 76-77 E 9
Rampur [IND, Uttar Pradesh] 44-45 MN 5
Ramree = Rambrè 52-53 B 3
Ramree Island = Rambrè Kyûn 52-53 B 3
Ramseur, NC 74-75 D 7
Ramsey 32 DE 4
Ramsgate 32 G 6
Ramthâ, Ar- 46-47 FG 6
Ramu River 52-53 N 8
Raṇ, Môṭuṇ – = Rann of Kutch 44-45 KL 6
Rancagua 80 BC 4
Rânchi 44-45 O 6
Ranco, Lago – 80 B 6
Rand 58 H 5
Randazzo 36-37 F 7
Randers 30-31 CD 9
Randijaur 30-31 HJ 4
Randolph, UT 76-77 H 5
Randsburg, CA 76-77 DE 8
Randsfjord 30-31 D 7
Rânêbanûra = Ranibennur 44-45 M 8
Rāṇēbanūru = Ranibennur 44-45 M 8
Ranebennur = Ranibennur 44-45 M 8
Rangárvalla 30-31 cd 3
Rangeley, ME 74-75 H 2
Rangely, CO 76-77 J 5
Rangiora 56-57 O 8
Rangôn = Yangon 52-53 BC 3
Rangôn Taing 52-53 C 3
Rangoon = Yangôn 52-53 BC 3
Rangoon = Yangôn 52-53 BC 3
Rangsang, Pulau – 52-53 D 6
Rangûn = Yangôn 52-53 BC 3
Ranibennur 44-45 M 8
Rânîyah 46-47 L 4
Rank 60-61 L 6
Rankins Springs 56-57 J 6
Ransiki 52-53 K 7
Rantau, Pulau – 52-53 D 6
Rantauprapat 52-53 CD 6
Rânya = Rânîyah 46-47 L 4
Ranyah, Wâdî – 44-45 E 6
Rache 48-49 P 2
Raoui, Erg er – = 'Irq ar-Rawî 60-61 D 3
Raoyang He 50-51 D 2
Rapallo 36-37 C 3
Raper, Cape – 70-71 XY 4
Rapid City, SD 72-73 F 3
Râpina 30-31 M 8
Rapla 30-31 L 8
Rappahannock River 74-75 E 6
Rapti [IND] 44-45 N 5
Raqqah, Ar- 44-45 DE 3
Râqûbah 60-61 H 3
Raquette Lake 74-75 F 3
Raquette River 74-75 F 2
Raša 36-37 EF 3
Râ's al-'Ayn 46-47 J 4
Râ's al-Ḥikmah 62 BC 2
Râ's al-Khaymah 44-45 GH 5
Ra's al-Wâd 60-61 E 1
Râ's an-Naqb 44-45 D 4-5
Rasappa = Riṣâfah 46-47 H 5
Râ's as-Sidr 62 E 3
Râ's at-Tannûrah 44-45 G 5
Râ's Ba'labakk 46-47 G 5
Râ's Duqm 44-45 H 7
Raseiniai 30-31 K 10
Râs el 'Aïn = Râ's al-'Ayn 46-47 J 4
Râ's Ghârib 62 E 3
Rashâd 60-61 L 6
Râshayyâ = Abû Adî 46-47 FG 6
Rashîd 62 D 2
Rashîd, Maşabb – 62 D 2
Râshidah, Ar- 62 C 5
Rashîdîyah, Ar- 60-61 D 2
Rashin = Najin 48-49 P 3
Rasht 44-45 FG 3
Raška 36-37 J 4
Rason Lake 56-57 D 5
Rass, Ar- 44-45 E 5
Rass-el-Oued = Ra's al-Wâd 60-61 E 1
Rasskazovo 38-39 H 5
Rastatt 33 D 4
Rastigaissa 30-31 LM 3
Rasu, Monte – 36-37 C 5
Râs Za'farâna = Az-Za'farânah 62 E 3
Rata, Ilha – 78-79 N 5
Ratchaburi 52-53 C 4
Rathenow 33 F 2
Rathlin Island 32 C 4
Rätische Alpen 33 DE 5
Rat Islands 19 D 1
Ratka, Wâdî ar- = Wâdî ar-Ratqah 46-47 J 5-6
Ratlam 44-45 LM 6
Ratnagiri [IND, Maharashtra] 44-45 L 7
Raton, NM 72-73 F 4
Ratqah, Wâdî ar- 46-47 J 5-6
Rättvik 30-31 F 7
Raualpindi = Râwalpindî 44-45 L 4
Rauch 80 E 5
Raudhamelur 30-31 bc 2
Raudhatayn 46-47 M 8
Raufarhöfn 30-31 f 1
Rauma 30-31 J 7
Raumo = Rauma 30-31 J 7
Raurkela = Rourkela 44-45 NO 6
Rausu 50-51 d 1-2
Ravalli, MT 76-77 F 2
Ravalpindi = Râwalpindî 44-45 L 4
Ravânsar 46-47 M 5
Râvar 44-45 H 4
Rava-Russkaja 38-39 DE 5
Ravena = Ravenna 36-37 E 3
Ravendale, CA 76-77 CD 5
Ravenna 36-37 E 3
Ravenna, OH 74-75 C 4
Ravenne = Ravenna 36-37 E 3
Ravensburg 33 D 5
Ravenshoe 56-57 HJ 3
Ravensthorpe 56-57 D 6
Ravenswood, WV 74-75 C 5
Râvî 44-45 L 4
Râwah 46-47 JK 5
Râwalpindî 44-45 L 4
Rawa Mazowiecka 33 K 3
Rawândûz 46-47 L 4
Rawḍah, Ar- 62 D 4
Rawî, 'Irq ar- 60-61 D 3
Rawicz 33 H 3
Rawlinna 56-57 E 6
Rawlins, WY 72-73 E 3
Rawlinson Range 56-57 E 4-5
Rawson [RA, Chubut] 80 CD 6
Rawwâfah, Ar- 62 G 4
Ray, Cape – 70-71 Z 8
Raya, Bukit – 52-53 F 7
Rayachuru = Raichur 44-45 M 7
Rayâq 46-47 G 6
Rayât 46-47 L 4
Rayâytît, Wâdî – 62 F 6
Rây Barêlî = Rae Bareli 44-45 N 5
Raydat aş-Şay'ar 44-45 F 7
Râygaṛh = Raigarh 44-45 N 6
Raymond, CA 76-77 D 7
Raymond, WA 76-77 B 2
Raymond Terrace 58 KL 4
Raymondville, TX 72-73 G 6
Ray Mountains 70-71 F 4
Raynesford, MT 76-77 H 2
Rayong 52-53 D 4
Râypur = Raipur [IND, Madhya Pradesh] 44-45 N 6
Raz, Pointe du – 34-35 E 4
R'azan' 38-39 GH 5
Râzân [IR, Bâkhtarân] 46-47 N 5
Razan [IR, Lorestân] 46-47 N 6
Razazah, Hawr ar- 46-47 KL 6
Razdel'naja 38-39 F 6
Razdolinsk 42-43 R 6
Razeh 46-47 N 6
Razelm, Lacul – 36-37 N 3
Razgrad 36-37 M 4
R'ažsk 38-39 H 5
R'dayif, Ar- = Ar-Rudayyif 60-61 F 2
Ré, Île de – 34-35 G 5
Reading [GB] 32 F 6
Reading, PA 72-73 L 3
Read Island 70-71 O 4
Real del Castillo 76-77 E 9-10
Realicó 80 CD 4-5
Réam 52-53 D 4
Rebbenesøy 30-31 GH 2
Rebecca, Lake – 56-57 D 6
Rebia, Umm er – = Nahr Umm ar-Rabî' 60-61 C 2
Rebiána = Ribyânah 60-61 J 4
Reboledo 80 EF 4
Reboly 38-39 F 3
Rebun-jima 48-49 QR 2
Recalde 80 D 5
Recherche, Archipelago of the – 56-57 D 6
Recherche, Archipel de la – 56-57 D 6
Rechô Taung 52-53 C 4
Recht = Rasht 44-45 FG 3
Rečica 38-39 EF 5
Recife 78-79 N 6
Reconquista 80 DE 3
Recreo [RA, La Rioja] 80 CD 3
Reḍâ'iyeh = Orûmiyeh 44-45 EF 3
Reḍâ'iyeh, Daryâcheh – = Urmia 44-45 F 3
Red Bank, NJ 74-75 F 4
Red Bluff, CA 72-73 B 3
Red Butte 76-77 GH 8
Redcliffe, Brisbane- 56-57 K 5
Red Cliffs 58 F 5
Red Deer 70-71 O 7
Red Deer River [CDN, Alberta] 70-71 O 7
Reddick, FL 74-75 b 2
Redding, CA 72-73 B 3
Redeyef, Er – = Ar-R'dayif 60-61 F 2
Red Hill 56-57 HJ 7
Red Hills [USA, Alabama] 72-73 J 5
Red House, NV 76-77 E 5
Red Lake [USA] 72-73 G 2
Red Lake [CDN, ●] 70-71 S 7
Redlands, CA 76-77 E 8-9
Red Lion, PA 74-75 E 5
Redmond, OR 76-77 C 3
Red Mountain [USA, California] 76-77 B 5
Red Mountain [USA, Montana] 76-77 G 2
Red Mountain, CA 76-77 E 8
Rednitz 33 E 4
Redon 34-35 F 5
Redonda, Ponta – 78-79 M 5
Redondela 34-35 C 7
Redondo Beach, CA 76-77 D 9
Red River 72-73 H 5
Red River of the North 72-73 G 2
Redrock, AZ 76-77 H 9
Redrock, NM 76-77 J 9
Red Rocks Point 56-57 E 6
Red Sea 44-45 D 5-7
Red Springs, NC 74-75 D 7
Red Tank 72-73 b 2
Reḍvandeh 46-47 N 4
Redwood City, CA 76-77 B 7
Redwood Valley, CA 76-77 B 6
Ree, Lough – 32 C 5
Reed City, MI 74-75 A 3
Reedley, CA 76-77 D 7
Reedsport, OR 76-77 AB 4
Reefton 56-57 O 8
Reese River 76-77 E 6
Refâ'î, Ar- = Ar-Rifâ'î 46-47 M 7
Refaniye 46-47 H 3
Regen 33 F 4
Regência 78-79 M 8
Regência, Ponta de – 78-79 M 8
Regensburg 33 EF 4
Reggane = Rijân 60-61 E 3
Règgio di Calàbria 36-37 FG 6
Règgio nell'Emilia 36-37 D 3
Regina [CDN] 70-71 Q 7
Régina [Guyane Française] 78-79 J 4
Registan = Rîgestân 44-45 JK 4
Registro 80 G 2
Regresso, Cachoeira – 78-79 HJ 5
Reguengos de Monsaraz 34-35 D 9
Reh 48-49 M 3
Rehoboth 64-65 E 7
Rehoboth Beach, DE 74-75 F 5
Rĕḥôvôt 46-47 F 7
Rei = Rey 46-47 O 5
Reichle, MT 76-77 G 3
Reid 56-57 E 6
Reidsville, NC 74-75 D 6
Reigate 32 FG 6
Reihoku 50-51 GH 6
Reims 34-35 JK 4
Reina Adelaida, Archipiélago – 80 AB 8
Reina Isabel, Islas de la – 70-71 N-U 2
Reina Maud, Banco de la – 24 C 1
Reindeer Lake 70-71 Q 6

Reind 211

Reine Elizabeth, Îles de la – 70-71 N-U 2
Reinosa 34-35 E 7
Reino Unido de Gran Bretaña e Irlanda del Norte 32 F-H 4-5
Reinøy 30-31 H 2-3
Reisa 30-31 J 3
Rejaf = Rijâf 63 B 1
Relem, Cerro – 80 B 5
Reliance, WY 76-77 J 5
Rélizane = Ghâlizân 60-61 E 1
Remansão 78-79 JK 5
Remanso 78-79 L 6
Remarkable, Mount – 56-57 G 6
Remédios [BR, Fernando de Noronha] 78-79 N 5
Remeshk 44-45 H 5
Remington, VA 74-75 E 5
Rémire 78-79 J 3-4
Remiremont 34-35 KL 4
Remote, OR 76-77 B 4
Rems 33 D 4
Remscheid 33 C 3
Remsen, NY 74-75 F 3
Rena 30-31 D 7
Renascença 78-79 F 5
Rendova Island 52-53 j 6
Rendsburg 33 DE 1
Rênéia 36-37 L 7
Rengat 52-53 D 7
Reni 38-39 E 6
Renk = Al-Rank 60-61 L 6
Renmark 56-57 H 6
Rennell Island 52-53 k 7
Rennes 34-35 G 4
Rennick Glacier 24 C 16-17
Reno [I] 36-37 DE 3
Reno, ID 76-77 G 3
Reno, NV 72-73 C 4
Renos, Lago de los – 70-71 Q 6
Renoville, CA 76-77 EF 8
Renovo, PA 74-75 E 4
Renqiu 48-49 M 4
Rensselaer, NY 74-75 FG 3
Renton, WA 76-77 B 2
Reo 52-53 H 8
Republic, WA 76-77 D 1
República Centroafricana 60-61 HJ 7
República Dominicana 72-73 MN 7-8
Republican River 72-73 G 3
République Centrafricaine 60-61 HJ 7
République Dominicaine 72-73 MN 7-8
Repulse Bay [AUS] 56-57 JK 4
Repulse Bay [CDN, ∪] 70-71 T 4
Repulse Bay [CDN, ●] 70-71 TU 4
Repunshiri = Rebun-jima 50-51 b 1
Requena 34-35 G 9
Requena [PE] 78-79 E 6
Reşadiye [TR, Bitlis] 46-47 K 3
Reşadiye [TR, Muğla] 46-47 B 4
Reşadiye [TR, Tokat] 46-47 G 2
Reşadiye Yarımadası 46-47 BC 4
Reşâfé, Er- = Riṣâfah 46-47 H 5
Resa'iya = Orūmīyeh 44-45 EF 3
Reschenpaß 33 E 5
Reserve, NM 76-77 J 9
Resht = Rasht 44-45 FG 3
Resistencia 80 DE 3
Reşița 36-37 J 3
Resolute 70-71 S 3
Resolution Island 70-71 Y 5
Rethel 34-35 K 4
Réthymnon 36-37 L 8
Reus 34-35 H 8
Reuss 33 D 5
Reut 36-37 N 2
Reutlingen 33 D 4
Revā = Narmada 44-45 LM 6
Reval = Tallinn 42-43 CD 5
Revda [SU, Srednij Ural] 42-43 KL 6
Revelstoke 70-71 N 7
Revillagigedo, Islas de – 72-73 D 8
Revillagigedo Island 70-71 KL 6
Rĕvīvīm 46-47 F 7
Revoil-Beni-Ounif = Banī Wanīf 60-61 D 2
Rewâ = Narmada 44-45 LM 6
Rewda = Revda 42-43 KL 6
Rex, Mount – 24 B 29
Rexburg, ID 76-77 H 4
Rexford, MT 76-77 F 1
Rey, Isla del – 72-73 L 10
Reyes, Point – 76-77 B 6-7
Reyhanlı 46-47 G 4
Reykhólar 30-31 b 2
Reykholt 30-31 c 2
Reykjanes 30-31 b 3
Reykjanes, Dorsal de – 22-23 H 2-3
Reykjanes, Seuil de – 22-23 H 2-3
Reykjanes Ridge 22-23 H 2-3
Reykjanesrug 22-23 H 2-3
Reykjavik 30-31 bc 2
Reynolds, ID 76-77 E 4
Reynolds Range 56-57 F 4
Reynoldsville, PA 74-75 D 4
Reynosa 72-73 G 6
Rezā'īyeh = Orūmīyeh 44-45 EF 3
Rēzekne 30-31 M 9
Rezina 36-37 N 2
Rhein 33 C 3
Rheine 33 C 2
Rheinland-Pfalz 33 CD 3-4
Rhin = Rhein 33 C 3
Rhine = Rhein 33 C 3
Rhino Camp 64-65 H 2
Rhode Island [USA, ⊙] 74-75 H 4
Rhode Island [USA, ☆] 72-73 MN 3
Rhodopë 36-37 KL 5
Rhodope 36-37 KL 5
Rhodope Mountains 36-37 KL 5
Rhön 33 DE 3
Rhondda 32 E 6
Rhone [CH] 33 C 5
Rhône [F] 34-35 K 6
Rhône au Rhin, Canal du – 34-35 L 4-5
Riaad = Ar-Riyāḍ 44-45 F 6
Riachão 78-79 K 6
Riad, Er- = Ar-Riyāḍ 44-45 F 6
Riang 44-45 P 5
Riau = 4 ◁ 52-53 D 6
Riau, Kepulauan – 52-53 DE 6
Ribadeo 34-35 D 7
Ribas do Rio Pardo 78-79 J 9
Ribaṭ, Ar- 60-61 C 2
Ribatejo 34-35 C 9
Ribauè 64-65 J 5-6
Ribe 30-31 C 10
Ribeira 34-35 C 7
Ribeirão [BR, Pernambuco] 78-79 MN 6
Ribeirão [BR, Rondônia] 78-79 FG 7
Ribeirão Preto 78-79 K 9
Ribeiro Gonçalves 78-79 KL 6
Riberalta 78-79 F 7
Ribyānah 60-61 J 4
Ribyānah, Ṣaḥrā' – 60-61 J 4
Riccione 36-37 E 3-4
Rice, CA 76-77 F 8
Riceboro, GA 74-75 C 9
Rice Lake 74-75 DE 2
Richard's Bay 64-65 H 8
Richardson Mountains 70-71 J 4
Richfield, ID 76-77 FG 4
Richfield, UT 76-77 GH 6
Richford, VT 74-75 G 2
Richgrove, CA 76-77 D 8
Richland, WA 72-73 C 2
Richland Balsam 74-75 B 7
Richlands, VA 74-75 C 6
Richmond [AUS] 56-57 H 4
Richmond [ZA, Kaapland] 64-65 F 9
Richmond [ZA, Natal] 64-65 G 9-H 8
Richmond, CA 72-73 B 4
Richmond, IN 72-73 JK 3-4
Richmond, VA 72-73 L 4
Richmond Gulf 70-71 V 6
Richmond Hill, GA 74-75 C 9
Richwood, WV 74-75 C 5
Ridder = Leninogorsk 42-43 P 7
Riddle, ID 76-77 EF 4
Riddle, OR 76-77 B 4
Rideau Lake 74-75 E 2
Ridgecrest, CA 76-77 E 8
Ridgeland, SC 74-75 C 8
Ridgetown 74-75 C 3
Ridgeway, SC 74-75 C 7
Ridgway, PA 74-75 D 4
Riding Mountain National Park 70-71 Q 7
Ridīsiya, Er- = Ar-Radīsīyat Baḥrī 62 E 5
Rıdvan = Alenz 46-47 J 4
Riesa 33 F 3
Riesco, Isla – 80 B 8
Riesi 36-37 F 7
Rietfontein 64-65 F 8
Rieth, OR 76-77 D 3
Rieti 36-37 E 4
Rīf = Ar-Rīf 60-61 CD 1-2
Rīf, Ar- 60-61 CD 1-2
Rīf, er – = Ar-Rīf 60-61 CD 1-2
Rifā'ī, Ar- 46-47 M 7
Rifstangi 30-31 ef 1
Rift Valley 64-65 J 2
Riga 30-31 KL 9
Riga, Golfe d' = Rīgas Jūras Līcis 30-31 KL 9
Riga, Golfo de – = Rīgas Jūras Līcis 30-31 KL 9
Riga, Golf van – = Rīgas Jūras Līcis 30-31 KL 9
Riga, Gulf of – = Rīgas Jūras Līcis 30-31 KL 9
Rīgas Jūras Līcis 30-31 KL 9
Rigby, ID 76-77 H 4
Rīgestān 44-45 JK 4
Riggins, ID 76-77 E 3
Rigo 52-53 N 8
Rigolet 70-71 Z 7
Rihāb, Ar- 46-47 L 7
Riihimäki 30-31 L 7
Riiser-Larsen halvøy 24 C 4-5
Rijāf 63 B 1
Rījān 60-61 E 3
Rijeka 36-37 F 3
Rijpfjord 30-31 l 4
Rikeze = Zhigatse 48-49 F 6
Rikorda, ostrov – 50-51 H 1
Riksgränsen 30-31 GH 3
Rikubetsu 50-51 c 2
Rikuzen-Takada 50-51 NO 3
Rila 36-37 K 4-5
Rīm, Bi'r – 62 B 2
Rimah, Wādī ar- 44-45 E 5
Rimāl, Ar- = Ar-Rub' al-Khālī 44-45 F 7-G 6
Rimini 36-37 E 3
Rîmnicu Sărat 36-37 M 3
Rîmnicu Vîlcea 36-37 L 3
Rimouski 70-71 X 8
Rim Rocky Mountains 76-77 C 4
Rin = Rhein 33 C 3
Rinca, Pulau – 52-53 G 8
Rinconada 80 C 2
Rin'gang = Riāng 44-45 P 5
Ringerike-Hønefoss 30-31 CD 7
Ringkøbing 30-31 BC 9
Ringling, MT 76-77 H 2
Ringvassøy 30-31 H 3
Riñihue [RCH, ●] 80 B 5-6
Rinjani, Gunung – 52-53 G 8
Riñihue [RCH, ●] 80 B 5-6
Rio Abajo 72-73 bc 2
Riobamba 78-79 D 5
Rio Blanco [BR] 78-79 G 7
Rio Branco [BR, Amazonas] 78-79 F 6
Rio Branco [BR, Rio Branco] 78-79 G 4-5
Río Bravo del Norte 72-73 E 5-F 6
Río Chico [RA, Santa Cruz ●] 80 C 7
Rio Claro [TT] 72-73 O 9
Rio Claro [BR, Goiás ◁ Rio Araguaia] 78-79 J 8
Rio Claro [BR, Goiás ◁ Rio Paranaíba] 78-79 J 8
Río Cuarto [RA, ●] 80 D 4
Río Chico [RA, Santa Cruz ●] 80 C 7
Rio de Janeiro [BR, ●] 78-79 L 9
Rio de Janeiro [BR, ☆] 78-79 LM 9
Rio do Sul 80 G 3
Rioekioetrog 48-49 O 7-P 6
Rio Grande [BR, Minas Gerais] 78-79 K 8-9
Rio Grande [BR, Rio Grande do Sul] 80 F 4
Río Grande [MEX] 72-73 H 8
Río Grande [RA, Tierra del Fuego ●] 80 C 8
Rio Grande [USA, Texas] 72-73 FG 6
Río Grande [BOL, ~] 78-79 G 8
Río Grande [NIC, ~] 72-73 JK 9
Rio Grande, Ramal de – 22-23 GH 7
Rio Grande, Seuil du – 22-23 GH 7
Rio Grande de Santiago 72-73 F 7
Rio Grande do Norte 78-79 M 6
Rio Grande do Norte = Natal 78-79 MN 6
Rio Grande do Sul 80 F 3-4
Rio Grandedrempel 22-23 GH 7
Rio Grande Rise 22-23 GH 7
Riohacha 78-79 E 2
Rioja [PE] 78-79 D 6
Rioja, La – [E] 34-35 F 7
Rioja, La – [RA, ●] 80 C 3
Rio Largo 78-79 MN 6
Río Mayo [RA, ●] 80 BC 7
Río Mulatos 78-79 F 8
Río Muni = Mbini 60-61 G 8
Rio Negro [BR, Amazonas] 78-79 G 5
Rio Negro [BR, Mato Grosso] 78-79 H 8
Rio Negro [BR, Paraná ●] 80 F 3
Río Negro [RA, Río Negro ~] 80 D 5-6
Río Negro [RA, Río Negro ☆] 80 C 6
Río Negro [ROU, ~] 80 EF 4
Río Negro, Embalse del – 80 E 4
Rio Negro, Pantanal do – 78-79 H 8
Rio Pardo de Minas 78-79 L 8
Río Primero [RA, ●] 80 D 4
Rio Real 78-79 M 7
Río Sonora 72-73 D 6
Riosucio [CO, ●] 78-79 D 3
Río Tercero [RA, ●] 80 D 4
Riou-Kiou, Fosse des – 48-49 O 7-P 6
Riouw Archipel = Kepulauan Riau 52-53 DE 6
Rio Verde [BR, Goiás ●] 78-79 J 8
Río Verde [MEX, Oaxaca] 72-73 G 8
Río Verde [PY] 80 E 2
Río Verde [RCH] 80 B 8
Rio Verde [BR, Goiás ◁ Represa de São Simão] 78-79 J 8
Rio Verde [BR, Mato Grosso ◁ Rio Paraná] 78-79 J 9
Rio Verde [BR, Mato Grosso ◁ Rio Teles Pires] 78-79 H 7
Rio Verde de Mato Grosso 78-79 HJ 8
Riparia, WA 76-77 DE 2
Ripley, CA 76-77 F 9
Ripley, NY 74-75 D 3
Ripley, WV 74-75 C 5
Ripoll 34-35 J 7
Riṣāfah 46-47 H 5
Rīṣām 'Anayzah 62 E 2
Rīṣānī, Ar- 60-61 D 2
Risasi 64-65 G 3
Rishiri suidō 50-51 b 1
Rishiri tō 48-49 QR 2
Ri'shôn Lĕẓiyyôn 46-47 F 7
Rising Sun, OH 74-75 A 5
Risiri 50-51 b 1
Risle 34-35 H 4
Risør 30-31 C 8
Ristikent 30-31 O 3
Ritscherhochland 24 B 36
Ritter, Mount – 72-73 C 4
Rittman, OH 74-75 BC 4
Ritzville, WA 76-77 D 2
Riukiu = Ryūkyū 48-49 N 7-O 6
Riu-Kiu, Fosa de – 48-49 O 7-P 6
Riva 36-37 D 3
Rivadavia [RA, Buenos Aires] 80 D 5
Rivadavia [RA, Salta] 80 D 2
Rivadavia [RCH] 80 B 3
Rivalensundet 30-31 mn 5
Rivera [RA] 80 D 5
Rivera [ROU, ●] 80 E 4
Riverbank, CA 76-77 C 7
River Cess 60-61 BC 7
Riverdale, CA 76-77 D 7
Riverhead, NY 74-75 G 4
Riverina 56-57 HJ 6-7
Rivers 60-61 F 7-8
Riversdal 64-65 F 9
Riversdale = Riversdal 64-65 F 9
Riverside, CA 72-73 C 5
Riverside, OR 76-77 DE 4
Riverton [AUS] 56-57 G 6
Riviera Beach, FL 74-75 cd 3
Rivière-du-Loup 70-71 WX 8
Rivoli 36-37 B 3
Rivungo 64-65 F 6
Riyad = Ar-Riyāḍ 44-45 F 6
Riyāḍ, Ar- 44-45 F 6
Rize 44-45 E 2
Rize Dağları 46-47 J 2
Rizzuto, Cabo – 36-37 G 6
Rjukan 30-31 C 8
R'kîz, Ar- 60-61 AB 5
R'kîz, Lac – = Ar-R'kîz 60-61 AB 5
Roan Cliffs 76-77 J 6
Roanne 34-35 K 5
Roanoke, VA 72-73 KL 4
Roanoke Island 74-75 F 7
Roanoke Rapids, NC 74-75 E 6
Roanoke River 72-73 L 4
Roatán, Isla de – 72-73 J 8
Robāṭ 46-47 M 5
Robbins Island 58 b 2
Robe [NZ] 58 D 6
Robe, Mount – 58 E 3
Roberts, ID 76-77 GH 4
Roberts Creek Mountain 76-77 E 6
Robertsfors 30-31 J 5
Robertson, WY 76-77 HJ 5
Robertson Bay 24 BC 17-18
Robertsons øy 24 C 31
Robertsport 60-61 B 7
Robertstown 58 D 4
Roberval 70-71 W 8
Robinette, OR 76-77 E 3
Robinson Crusoe 69 C 6
Robinson Island 24 C 30
Robinson Range 56-57 C 5
Robinson River 56-57 G 3
Robinvale 56-57 H 6
Robla, La – 34-35 E 7
Robson, Mount – [CDN, ▲] 70-71 N 7
Roca, Cabo da – 34-35 C 9
Roçadas = Xangongo 64-65 E 6
Roçalgate = Râs al-Ḥadd 44-45 HJ 6
Rocamadour 34-35 HJ 6
Rocas, Atol das – 78-79 N 5
Rocas Negras = Black Rock 80 H 8
Rocha [ROU, ●] 80 F 4
Rochefort 34-35 G 5-6
Rochelle, la – 34-35 G 7
Rochester, MN 72-73 H 3
Rochester, NH 74-75 H 3
Rochester, NY 72-73 L 3
Roche-sur-Yon, la – 34-35 G 5
Rock, The – 58 H 5
Rockall 28-29 EF 4
Rockall Plateau 28-29 E 4
Rockall, Ramal de – 28-29 E 4
Rock Creek, OR 76-77 CD 3
Rock Creek [USA ◁ Clark Fork River] 76-77 G 2
Rockefeller Plateau 24 AB 23-24
Rockford, IL 72-73 HJ 3
Rockhampton 56-57 JK 4
Rock Hill, SC 72-73 K 4-5
Rockingham [AUS] 56-57 BC 6
Rockingham, NC 74-75 CD 7
Rockingham Bay 56-57 J 3
Rock Island, IL 72-73 HJ 3
Rock Island, WA 76-77 CD 2
Rock Lake 76-77 E 2
Rockland, ID 76-77 G 4
Rockland, ME 74-75 J 2-3
Rocklands Reservoir 56-57 H 7
Rockport, WA 76-77 C 1
Rock Springs, AZ 76-77 GH 8
Rock Springs, WY 72-73 E 3
Rockstone 78-79 H 3
Rockville, MD 74-75 E 5
Rockville, OR 76-77 E 4
Rockwood, PA 74-75 D 5
Rocky Mount, NC 74-75 E-6-7
Rocky Mount, VA 74-75 D 6
Rocky Mountain 76-77 G 2
Rocky Mountain National Park 72-73 EF 3
Rocky Mountains 70-71 L 5-P 9
Rocky Mountain Trench 70-71 L 6-N 7
Rocky Point [USA, California] 76-77 A 5
Rôḍá, Er- = Ar-Rawḍah 62 D 4
Roda, la – 34-35 F 9
Rodalquilar 34-35 FG 10
Rødberg 30-31 C 7
Rødby Havn 30-31 D 10
Rode Bekken = Sichuan Pendi 48-49 JK 5-6
Rodeo 80 BC 4
Rodeo, NM 76-77 J 10
Rodez 34-35 J 6
Rode Zee 44-45 D 5-7
Rodney 74-75 C 3
Ródopes 36-37 KL 5
Ródos [GR, ⊙] 36-37 N 7
Ródos [GR, ●] 36-37 N 7
Rodosto = Tekirdağ 44-45 B 2
Rodrigues [Mascarene Islands] 22-23 N 6-7
Rodrigues [MS] 64-65 O 6
Roebourne 56-57 C 4
Roebuck Bay 56-57 D 3
Roemelië = Rumelija 36-37 LM 4
Roemenië 36-37 K-M 2
Roermond 34-35 K 3
Roeselare 34-35 J 3
Roe's Welcome Sound 70-71 T 4-5
Rogač'ov 38-39 EF 5
Rogagua, Lago – 78-79 F 7
Rogaland 30-31 B 8
Rogerson, ID 76-77 F 4
Rogersville, TN 74-75 B 6
Rognan 30-31 F 4
Rogoaguado, Lago – 78-79 F 7
Rogue River 76-77 A 4
Rogue River Mountains 76-77 AB 4
Roha-Lalibela = Lalībela 60-61 M 6
Rohan 34-35 F 4
Rohṛī 44-45 K 5
Rohtak 44-45 M 5
Rojas 80 D 4
Rokkasho 50-51 N 2
Rokugō-saki = Suzu misaki 50-51 L 4
Rolla 30-31 G 3
Rolla, MO 72-73 H 4
Rolleston 56-57 J 4
Rolvsøy 30-31 K 2
Rom 30-31 B 8
Rom [EAU] 63 C 2
Roma 36-37 E 5
Roma [AUS] 56-57 J 5
Romain, Cape – 74-75 D 8
Romaine, Rivière – 70-71 Y 7
Roman 36-37 M 2
Romana, La – 72-73 J 8
Romanche Deep 22-23 J 6
Romanchediep 22-23 J 6
Romang, Pulau – 52-53 J 8
Românî = Rummânah 62 E 2
Romania 36-37 K-M 2
Romano, Cape – 74-75 bc 4
Romano, Cayo – 72-73 L 7
Romanovka [SU, Bur'atskaja ASSR] 42-43 V 7
Romans-sur-Isère 34-35 K 6
Roman Wall 32 E 4
Romanzof, Cape – 70-71 C 5
Romblon 52-53 H 4
Rome, GA 72-73 J 5
Rome, NY 72-73 LM 3
Rome, OR 76-77 E 4
Rome = Roma 36-37 E 5
Romilly-sur-Seine 34-35 J 4
Romney, WV 74-75 D 5
Romny 38-39 F 5
Rømø 30-31 C 10
Romsdal 30-31 BC 6
Romsdalfjord 30-31 B 6
Ronan, MT 76-77 FG 2
Roncador, Serra do – 78-79 J 7
Roncador Reef 52-53 j 6
Roncesvalles 34-35 G 7
Ronceverte, WV 74-75 C 6
Ronda 34-35 E 10
Rondane 30-31 C 7
Rondón = Puerto Rondón 78-79 E 3
Rondônia [BR, ●] 78-79 G 7
Rondônia [BR, ☆] 78-79 G 7
Rondonópolis 78-79 HJ 8
Ronge, la – 70-71 P 6
Ronge, Lac la – 70-71 Q 6
Rongui 63 E 5
Ron Ma, Mui – 52-53 E 3
Rønne 30-31 F 10
Ronne Bay 24 B 29
Ronneby 30-31 F 9
Roof Butte 76-77 J 7
Roosendaal en Nispen 34-35 K 3
Roosevelt, UT 76-77 HJ 5
Roosevelt, WA 76-77 C 3
Roosevelt, Rio – 78-79 G 6-7
Roosevelt Island 24 AB 20-21
Roper River 56-57 F 2
Roper Valley 56-57 F 2-3
Ropi 30-31 J 3
Roquefort-sur-Soulzon 34-35 J 7
Roraima 78-79 GH 4
Roraima, Mount – 78-79 G 3
Røros 30-31 D 6
Rørvik 30-31 D 5
Rosa 64-65 H 4
Rosalia, WA 76-77 E 2
Rosamond, CA 76-77 D 8

212 Reine

Rosamond Lake 76-77 DE 8
Rosário [BR] 78-79 L 5
Rosario [RA, Santa Fe] 80 DE 4
Rosario, Río del – 76-77 H 10
Rosario de la Frontera 80 D 3
Rosário do Sul 80 EF 4
Rosário Oeste 78-79 HJ 7
Rosarito [MEX, Baja California Norte ↓ Tijuana] 76-77 E 9
Rosas 34-35 J 7
Roscoe, NY 74-75 F 4
Roscoff 34-35 EF 4
Roscommon 32 BC 5
Roseau 72-73 O 8
Rosebery 56-57 HJ 8
Roseboro, NC 74-75 D 7
Roseburg, OR 76-77 B 4
Roşeireş, Er- = Ar-Ruşayriş 60-61 LM 6
Rosenheim 33 EF 5
Rose River 56-57 G 2
Rosetown 70-71 P 7
Rosetta = Rashīd 62 D 2
Rosetta Mouth = Maşabb Rashīd 62 D 2
Rosette = Rashīd 62 D 2
Rose Wood 58 L 1
Rosignano Marittimo 36-37 CD 4
Rosignol 78-79 H 3
Roşiori-de-Vede 36-37 L 3-4
Roskilde 30-31 E 10
Roslavl' 38-39 F 5
Roslyn, WA 76-77 C 2
Ross 56-57 O 8
Ross, Mar de – – = Ross Sea 24 B 20-18
Ross, Mer de – – = Ross Sea 24 B 20-18
Rossano 36-37 G 6
Rossel Island 52-53 hi 7
Ross Ice Shelf 24 AB 20-17
Ross Island [Antarctica, Ross Sea] 24 B 17-18
Ross Island [Antarctica, Weddell Sea] 24 C 31
Ross Island [CDN] 70-71 R 7
Rosslare 32 CD 5
Rosso 60-61 A 5
Rossoš' 38-39 GH 5
Ross River 70-71 K 5
Ross Sea 24 B 20-18
Røssvatn 30-31 E 5
Røssvik 30-31 FG 4
Rossville 56-57 HJ 3
Rostock 33 F 1
Rostov 42-43 FG 6
Rostov-na-Donu 38-39 GH 6
Rota 34-35 D 10
Rote, Pulau – 52-53 H 9
Rothaargebirge 33 D 3
Rothbury 32 EF 4
Rothenburg 33 DE 4
Rothesay 32 D 4
Roto 56-57 J 6
Rotondo, Mont – 36-37 C 4
Rotorua 56-57 P 7
Rotterdam 34-35 JK 3
Rotti = Pulau Rote 52-53 H 9
Roubaix 34-35 J 3
Rouen 34-35 H 4
Roulers = Roeselare 34-35 J 3
Roumanie 36-37 K-M 2
Roumélie = Rumelija 36-37 LM 4
Round Island 64-65 N 6
Round Mountain 56-57 K 6
Round Mountain, NV 76-77 E 6
Round Valley Indian Reservation 76-77 B 6
Rounga, Dar – 60-61 J 6-7
Rourkela 44-45 NO 5
Rousay 32 E 2
Rouses Point, NY 74-75 G 2
Roussillon 34-35 J 7
Rouţbé, El- = Ar-Ruţbah 46-47 G 6
Rouyn 70-71 V 8
Rovaniemi 30-31 L 4
Rovdino 38-39 H 3
Rovereto 36-37 D 3
Rovigo 36-37 D 3
Rovinj 36-37 E 3
Rovkuly 30-31 O 5
Rovno 38-39 E 5
Rovuma, Rio – 64-65 J 5
Rowley Island 70-71 UV 4
Rowley Shoals 56-57 C 3
Rowuma = Rio Rovuma 64-65 J 5
Rox, NV 76-77 F 7
Roxas 52-53 H 4
Roxboro, NC 74-75 D 6
Roxburgh [NZ] 56-57 N 9

Roy, UT 76-77 G 5
Royal Canal 32 C 5
Royal Society Range 24 B 15-16
Royan 34-35 G 6
Royaume-Uni 32 F-H 4-5
Røykenvik 30-31 D 7
Royston, GA 74-75 B 7
Rozewie, Przylądek – 33 J 1
Rožňava 33 K 4
Roztocze 33 L 3

Rtiščevo 38-39 H 5

Ruacana Falls 64-65 DE 6
Ruaha National Park 63 C 4
Ruanda = Rwanda 64-65 GH 3
Ruapehu 56-57 P 7
Rubā'ī, Ash-Shallāl ar- = Al-Jandal ar-Rāb'i 60-61 L 5
Rub' al-Khālī = Ar-Rub'al-Khālī 44-45 F 7-G 6
Rub' al-Khālī, Ar- 44-45 F 7-G 6
Rubcovsk 42-43 P 7
Rubeho 63 D 4
Rubesibe 50-51 c 2
Rubi 64-65 G 2
Rubia, La – 80 D 4
Rubondo 63 BC 3
Ruby, AK 70-71 EF 5
Ruby Lake 76-77 F 5
Ruby Mountains 76-77 F 5
Ruby Range [USA] 76-77 FG 3
Ruby Valley 76-77 F 5
Ruchlovo = Skovorodino 42-43 XY 7
Rudall 58 BC 4
Rudayyif, Ar- 60-61 F 2
Rūdbār 46-47 N 4
Rudensk 30-31 M 11
Rudewa 63 C 5
Rudnaja Pristan' 42-43 a 9
Rudnyj 42-43 L 7
Rudog 48-49 D 5
Rudol'fa, ostrov – 42-43 JK 1
Rūd Sar 46-47 O 4
Rudyard, MT 76-77 H 1
Ruffec 34-35 GH 5
Rufino 80 D 4
Rufisque 60-61 A 5-6
Rufiji 64-65 J 4
Rufunsa 64-65 GH 6
Rugao 48-49 N 5
Rugby 32 F 5
Rugozero 38-39 F 3
Ruhnu 30-31 K 9
Ruhr 33 D 3
Ruhudji 63 D 5
Ruhuhu 63 C 5
Ruijin 48-49 M 6
Ruivo, Pico – 60-61 A 2
Ruiz, Nevado del – 78-79 DE 4
Rujewa 63 C 5
Rūjiena 30-31 L 9
Rujm Tal'at al-Jamā'ah 46-47 F 7
Rukhaimīyah, Ar- = Ar-Rukhaymīyah 46-47 L 8
Rukhaymīyah, Ar- 46-47 L 8
Ruki 64-65 E 2-3
Rukungiri 63 B 3
Rukuru 63 C 5
Rukwa 64-65 H 4
Rukwa, Lake – 64-65 H 4
Rum 32 C 3
Ruma 36-37 H 3
Rumāh, Ar- 44-45 F 5
Rumahui 52-53 k 7
Rumania 36-37 K-M 2
Rumaylah, Ar- 46-47 M 7
Rumaythah, Ar- 46-47 L 7
Rumbalara 56-57 FG 5
Rumberpon, Pulau – 52-53 KL 7
Rumbīk 60-61 K 7
Rum Cay 72-73 M 7
Rumelia = Rumelija 36-37 LM 4
Rumelija 36-37 LM 4
Rumford, ME 74-75 H 2
Rummānah 62 E 2
Rumoe = Rumoi 50-51 b 2
Rumoi 48-49 R 3
Rumorosa 76-77 EF 9
Rumpi 63 C 5
Rumula 56-57 HJ 3
Rumuruti 63 CD 2
Rundu 64-65 E 6
Runga, Dar – – = Dar Rounga 60-61 J 6-7
Rungu 63 AB 2
Rungwa [EAT, ~] 63 C 4
Rungwa [EAT, ●] 64-65 H 4
Rungwa East 63 BC 4
Rungwe Mount 64-65 H 4
Runton Range 56-57 D 4

Ruo Shui 48-49 HJ 3
Ruoxi 48-49 M 6
Rupat, Pulau – 52-53 D 6
Rupert, ID 76-77 G 4
Rupert, Rivière de – 70-71 VW 7
Rupert House = Fort Rupert 70-71 V 7
Ruppert Coast 24 B 21-22
Ruq'ī, Ar- 46-47 M 8
Rūrkalā = Rourkela 44-45 NO 5
Rurrenabaque 78-79 F 7
Rusanovo 38-39 KL 1
Rusanovo 42-43 JK 3
Rusape 64-65 H 6
Ruşayriş, Ar- 60-61 LM 6
Ruse 36-37 LM 4
Ruşetu 36-37 M 3
Rusia 42-43 L-g 4
Rusland 42-43 L-g 4
Russas 78-79 M 5
Russell [NZ] 56-57 OP 7
Russell Island 70-71 R 3
Russell Islands 52-53 j 6
Russell Range 56-57 D 6
Russenes 30-31 L 2
Russia 42-43 L-g 4
Russian River 76-77 B 6
Russie 42-43 L-g 4
Russisi = Ruzizi 64-65 G 3
Russkij, ostrov – [SU, p-ov Tajmyr] 42-43 RS 2
Russkij, ostrov – [SU, Vladivostok] 42-43 Z 9
Russkij Zavorot, mys – 42-43 JK 4
Rustâq, Ar- 44-45 H 6
Rustavi 38-39 HJ 7
Rustenburg 64-65 G 8
Ruston, LA 72-73 H 5
Rutana 64-65 GH 3
Rutanzige 64-65 G 3
Ruţbah, Ar- [IRQ] 44-45 DE 4
Ruţbah, Ar- [SYR] 46-47 G 6
Ruth, NV 76-77 F 6
Rutherfordton, NC 74-75 C 7
Ruthin 32 E 5
Rutland, VT 72-73 M 3
Rutshuru 64-65 G 3
Ruvo di Pùglia 36-37 G 5
Ruvu [EAT, ~] 64-65 J 4
Ruvu [EAT, ●] 63 D 4
Ruvu = Pangani 64-65 J 3
Ruvuma [EAT, ~] 63 C 5
Ruvuma [EAT, ☆] 64-65 J 5
Ruvuvu 63 B 3
Ruwâq, Jabal ar- 46-47 G 5-6
Ruwenzori 64-65 G 2
Ruwenzori National Park 64-65 GH 3
Ruwu = Pangani 64-65 J 3
Ruzajevka 42-43 GH 7
Ruzizi 64-65 G 3
Ružomberok 33 J 4

Rwanda 64-65 GH 3
Rwashamaire 63 B 3

Ryanggang-do 50-51 FG 2
Rybačij 33 K 1
Rybačij, poluostrov – 42-43 EF 4
Rybinsk 42-43 F 6
Rybinskoje vodochranilišče 42-43 FG 6
Rybnica 38-39 E 6
Rybnik 33 J 3
Ryderwood, WA 76-77 B 2
Rye Patch Reservoir 76-77 D 5
Ryke Yseøyane 30-31 m 6
Rijn = Rhein 33 C 3
Ryōtsu 50-51 M 3
Rypin 33 J 2
Ryškany 36-37 M 2
Ryūkyū 48-49 N 7-O 6
Ryukyu Trench 48-49 O 7-P 6

Rzeszów 33 KL 3
Ržev 38-39 FG 4

S

Sá [BR] 78-79 L 8
Saale 33 E 3
Saalfeld 33 E 3
Saar 33 C 4
Saarbrücken 33 C 4
Saaremaa 30-31 K 8
Saarijärvi 30-31 L 6

Saariselkä 30-31 MN 3
Saarland 33 C 4
Saarlouis 33 C 4
Saba ['Westindien] 72-73 O 8
Sabaa, Gebel es – = Qârat as-Sab'ah 60-61 H 3
Šabac 36-37 H 3
Sabadell 34-35 J 8
Sabae 50-51 KL 5
Sabah 52-53 G 5
Sab'ah, Qârat as- 60-61 H 3
Sabaki = Galana 64-65 JK 3
Sabana, Archipiélago de – 72-73 KL 7
Sabanalarga [CO, Atlántico] 78-79 DE 2
Sabang [RI, Aceh] 52-53 C 5
Şabanözü 46-47 E 2
Sabari 44-45 N 7
Şabâyâ, Jabal – 44-45 E 7
Šab' Biyâr 46-47 G 6
Şabbūrah 46-47 G 5
Sabhah 60-61 G 3
Sabhah, As- 46-47 H 5
Sabi 64-65 H 7
Sabile 30-31 K 9
Sabinas 72-73 F 6
Sabinas Hidalgo 72-73 F 6
Sabine land 30-31 k 5
Sabine Peninsula 70-71 OP 2
Sabine River 72-73 H 5
Sabini, Monti – 36-37 E 4
Şābirīyah, Aş- 46-47 M 8
Sable 56-57 M 3
Sable-ri 60-61 J 7
Sable, Cape – [CDN] 70-71 XY 9
Sable, Cape – [USA] 72-73 K 6
Sable Island [CDN] 70-71 Z 9
Sable Island [PNG] 52-53 hj 5
Sables-d'Olonne, les – 34-35 FG 5
Saboûrá = Şabbūrah 46-47 G 5
Sabrina Land 24 C 12-13
Sabun 42-43 P 5
Sabuncu 46-47 D 3
Sabuncupinar = Sabuncu 46-47 D 3
Şabyâ', Aş- 44-45 E 7
Säbzawār = Shīndand 44-45 J 4
Sabzewār 44-45 H 3
Sacaba 78-79 F 8
Sacaca 78-79 F 8
Sacajawea Peak 76-77 E 3
Sacami, Lac – 70-71 V 7
Sacanta 80 D 4
Sacedi-Arabië 44-45 D 5-F 6
Sachalin 42-43 b 7-8
Sachalinskij zaliv 42-43 b 7
Sach'ang-ni 50-51 F 2
Sacharvan 38-39 KL 2
Sachigo River 70-71 S 6-7
Sachisbaz 44-45 K 3
Šachtinsk 42-43 N 8
Šachty 38-39 H 6
Sachunja 42-43 GH 6
Šack 38-39 H 5
Sackets Harbor, NY 74-75 EF 3
Saco, ME 74-75 H 3
Sacramento, CA 76-77 C 6
Sacramento, Pampa del – 78-79 D 6
Sacramento Mountains 72-73 EF 5
Sacramento River 72-73 B 3-4
Sacramento Valley 72-73 B 3-4
Sa'dah 44-45 E 7
Sada-misaki 50-51 HJ 6
Sadani 46-47 J 4
Saddle Mountain 76-77 G 4
Saddle Mountains 76-77 CD 2
Saddle Peak 76-77 H 3
Sa Dec 52-53 E 4
Sadıkali = Karahasanlı 46-47 F 3
Sadiya 44-45 Q 5
Sa'dīyah, As- 46-47 L 5
Sa'dīyah, Hawr as- 46-47 M 6
Sado 34-35 C 10
Sado 48-49 Q 4
Şadr, Wādī – 62 F 3
Šadrinsk 42-43 LM 6
Sæby 30-31 D 9
Saeki = Saiki 50-51 HJ 6
Şafā, Aş- 46-47 G 6
Şafā, Tulūl aş- 46-47 G 6
Şafad = Żefat 44-45 D 4
Safafir 46-47 G 4
Şafah, Aş- 46-47 J 4
Safājā 60-61 L 3
Safâjâ, Jazîrat – 62 F 4

Safaji Island = Jazīrat Safājah 62 F 4
Şafayn, 'Ard – 46-47 H 5
Safěd Kôh, Selselae – 44-45 JK 4
Saff, Aş- 62 D 3
Saffāf, Birkat as- 46-47 M 7
Saffāf, Hôr as- = Birkat as-Saffāf 46-47 M 7
Saffānīyah 44-45 F 5
Şaffār Kalay 44-45 J 4
Säffle 30-31 E 8
Safford, AZ 76-77 J 9
Saffron Walden 32 G 5-6
Şāfī 60-61 FG 2
Säfīd, Kūh-e – = Kūh-e Sefīd 46-47 M 5-N 6
Säfīd Kuh = Selselae Safēd Kôh 44-45 JK 4
Säfīd Rūd = Sefid Rūd 46-47 N 4
Safīrah 46-47 G 4
Şāfītā' 46-47 G 5
Safranbolu 46-47 E 2
Saga 48-49 P 5
Sagae 50-51 MN 3
Sagaing = Sitkaing 52-53 D 2
Sagaing = Sitkaing Taing 52-53 B 2-C 1
Sagami nada 48-49 Q 4-R 5
Saganoseki 50-51 HJ 6
Şagany, ozero – 36-37 NO 3
Sagar [IND, Maharashtra] 44-45 M 6
Sagarmatha 48-49 F 6
Sagavanirktok River 70-71 G 3-4
Sage, WY 76-77 H 5
Sage Zong = Sakha Dsong 48-49 F 6
Saghīr, Zāb aş- 46-47 K 5
Saghru, Jebel – – = Jabal Sārū 60-61 C 2
Sagī', Har – 46-47 F 7
Saginaw, MI 72-73 K 3
Saginaw Bay 72-73 K 3
Sagiz 42-43 JK 8
Şagonar 42-43 R 7
Sagra 34-35 F 10
Sagra, La – 34-35 EF 8
Sagres 34-35 C 10
Saguaro National Monument 76-77 H 9
Saguenay, Rivière – 70-71 WX 8
Sagunto 34-35 GH 9
Sahagún 34-35 E 7
Sahand, Kūh-e – 46-47 M 4
Saharan Atlas 60-61 D 2-F 1
Saharanpur 44-45 M 4
Sahara Occidental 60-61 A 4-B 3
Sahara Well 56-57 D 4
Saharunpore = Saharanpur 44-45 M 4
Sahbā', Wādī aş- 44-45 F 6
Sahel = Sāhil 60-61 BC 5
Sahhāt = Shahhāt 60-61 J 2
Sāhīl 60-61 BC 5
Sāhīwāl 44-45 L 4
Şahn, Aş- 46-47 K 7
Şahneh 46-47 M 5
Şahrā, Bi'r – 62 C 6
Şahrā, Jabal – 62 EF 4
Şahrā' al-Gharbīyah, Aş- 62 BC 4
Sahuarita, AZ 76-77 H 10
Sahuayo de José Maria Morelos 72-73 F 7-8
Sahyādri = Western Ghats 44-45 L 6-M 8
Saibai Island 52-53 M 8
Sai Buri 52-53 D 5
Saiburi = Alor Setar 52-53 CD 5
Saigó 50-51 J 4
Saigón = Thàn Phô Hô Chi Minh 52-53 E 4
Saihūt = Sayhūt 44-45 G 7
Saijo 50-51 J 6
Saikai National Park = Gotō-rettō 50-51 G 6
Saiki 50-51 HJ 6
Šaim 42-43 L 5
Saima 50-51 E 2
Saimaa 30-31 MN 7

Sai-ma-chi = Saima 50-51 E 2
Saimbeyli 46-47 FG 3
Sā'īn Dezh 46-47 M 4
Sainjang 50-51 F 2
Sāīn Qal'eh = Shāhīn Dezh 46-47 M 4
Saint Albans, VT 74-75 G 2
Saint Albans, WV 74-75 BC 5
Saint-Amand-Mont-Rond 34-35 J 5
Saint-André, Cap – 64-65 K 6
Saint Andrews, SC 74-75 CD 8
Saint Anthony 70-71 Za 7
Saint Anthony, ID 76-77 H 4
Saint Arnaud 58 F 6
Saint Augustin, Baie de – 64-65 K 7
Saint-Augustine, FL 72-73 KL 6
Saint Austell 32 D 6
Saint-Avold 34-35 L 4
Saint Barthélemy 72-73 O 8
Saint-Boniface 70-71 R 8
Saint-Brieuc 34-35 F 4
Saint Catharines 70-71 UV 9
Saint Catherines Island 74-75 C 9
Saint Charles, ID 76-77 H 4
Saint Charles, MO 72-73 H 4
Saint Charles, Cape – 70-71 Za 7
Saint Clair, Lake – 70-71 U 9
Saint Clairsville, OH 74-75 C 4
Saint Cloud, FL 74-75 c 2
Saint Cloud, MN 72-73 H 2
Saint Croix 72-73 O 8
Saint Charles, ID 76-77 H 4
Saint Charles, MO 72-73 H 4
Saint Charles, Cape – 70-71 Za 7
Saint Christopher y Nevis 72-73 O 8
Saint David Islands = Kepulauan Mapia 52-53 KL 6
Saint David's Head 32 CD 6
Saint-Denis [F] 34-35 J 4
Saint-Denis [Réunion] 64-65 N 7
Saint-Dié 34-35 L 4
Saint-Dizier 34-35 K 4
Sainte-Agathe-des-Monts 70-71 VW 8
Saint Elias, Mount – 70-71 H 5
Saint Elias Mountains 70-71 J 5-6
Saint-Élie 78-79 J 3-4
Sainte-Lucie 72-73 O 8
Sainte-Marie [CDN] 74-75 H 1
Sainte-Marie [Gabon] 64-65 D 3
Sainte-Marie [Martinique] 72-73 O 9
Sainte-Marie, Cap – 64-65 L 8
Sainte-Marie, Île – – = Nosy Boraha 64-65 M 6
Saintes 34-35 G 6
Saint-Étienne 34-35 JK 6
Saint-Flour 34-35 J 6
Saint Francis, ME 74-75 J 1
Saint Francis River 72-73 H 4
Saint François, Lac – 74-75 H 2
Saint Francois Island 64-65 M 4
Saint-Gaudens 34-35 H 7
Saint George [AUS] 56-57 J 5
Saint George, GA 74-75 B 9
Saint George, SC 74-75 C 8
Saint George, UT 76-77 G 7
Saint George, Point – 76-77 A 5
Saint-Georges [Guyane Française] 78-79 J 4
Saint George's [WG] 72-73 O 9
Saint-Georges, Canal – = Saint George's Channel 32 C 6-D 5
Saint George's Channel 32 C 6-D 5
Saint George's Channel [PNG] 52-53 h 5-6
Saint George's Channel 32 C 6-D 5
Saint George's Channel [PNG] 52-53 h 5-6
Saint-Gilles-sur-Vie 34-35 FG 5
Saint-Girons 34-35 H 7
Saint Govan's Head 32 D 6
Saint Helena 66 F 10
Saint Helena, CA 76-77 BC 6
Saint Helena Bay = Sint Helenabaai 64-65 E 9
Saint Helena Range 76-77 B 6
Saint Helena Sound 74-75 CD 8
Saint Helens 32 E 5
Saint Helens [AUS] 58 d 2
Saint Helens, OR 76-77 B 3
Saint Helens, WA 76-77 B 2

Saint Helens, Mount – 76-77 BC 2
Saint Helens Point 58 d 2
Saint Helier 32 E 7
Saint-Hyacinthe 70-71 W 8
Saint Ignatius, MT 76-77 FG 2
Saint James, Cape – 70-71 K 7
Saint-Jean 70-71 W 8
Saint-Jean, Lac – 70-71 W 8
Saint-Jean-de-Luz 34-35 FG 7
Saint Joe River 76-77 E 2
Saint John [CDN] 70-71 X 8
Saint John, Lake – = Lac Saint Jean 70-71 W 8
Saint John River 70-71 X 8
Saint John's [CDN] 70-71 a 8
Saint John's [Westindien] 72-73 O 8
Saint Johns, AZ 76-77 J 8
Saint Johns = Saint-Jean 70-71 W 8
Saint Johnsbury, VT 74-75 G 2
Saint Johns River 74-75 c 1-2
Saint Joseph, MO 72-73 GH 4
Saint Joseph, Lake – 70-71 ST 7
Saint-Joseph-d'Alma = Alma 70-71 W 8
Saint Joseph Island [SY] 64-65 M 4
Saint-Junien 34-35 H 6
Saint Kilda 32 B 3
Saint Laurent 70-71 W 8
Saint-Laurent, Fleuve – 70-71 W 8-9
Saint-Laurent, Golfe du – = Gulf of Saint Lawrence 70-71 Y 8
Saint Lawrence [AUS] 56-57 J 4
Saint Lawrence, Gulf of – 70-71 Y 8
Saint Lawrence Island 70-71 BC 5
Saint Lawrence River 70-71 X 8
Saint-Lô 34-35 G 4
Saint-Louis [SN] 60-61 A 5
Saint Louis, MO 72-73 H 4
Saint Lucia, Lake – = Sint Luciameer 64-65 H 8
Saint Magnus Bay 32 EF 1
Saint-Malo 34-35 FG 4
Saint Maries, ID 76-77 E 2
Saint-Marin 36-37 E 4
Saint Martin [⊙] 72-73 O 8
Saint Martins Bay 74-75 A 1-2
Saint Mary Lake 76-77 G 1
Saint Mary Peak 56-57 G 6
Saint Marys [AUS] 56-57 J 8
Saint Mary's [CDN, Ontario] 74-75 C 3
Saint Marys, GA 74-75 C 9
Saint Marys, PA 74-75 D 4
Saint Marys, WV 74-75 C 5
Saint Marys River [USA] 72-73 K 2
Saint Mathieu, Pointe – 34-35 E 4
Saint Matthew 42-43 I 5
Saint Matthew Island 70-71 B 5
Saint Matthew Island = Zādetkyī Kyûn 52-53 C 5
Saint Matthews, SC 74-75 C 8
Saint Matthias Group 52-53 NO 7
Saint-Maurice, Rivière – 70-71 W 8
Saint Michael, AK 70-71 D 5
Saint Michaels, AZ 76-77 J 8
Saint-Nazaire 34-35 F 5
Saint-Omer 34-35 HJ 3
Saintonge 34-35 G 6
Saint Paul [CDN] 70-71 O 7
Saint Paul [Saint Paul] 22-23 NO 7
Saint Paul, MN 72-73 H 2
Saint Paul, VT 74-75 B 6
Saint Paul River 60-61 BC 7
Saint Pauls, NC 74-75 D 7
Saint Peter Port 32 E 7
Saint Petersburg, FL 72-73 K 6
Saint-Pierre et Miquelon 70-71 Za 8
Saint Pierre Island 64-65 LM 4
Saint-Quentin 34-35 J 4
Saint-Raphaël 34-35 L 7
Saint Regis, MT 76-77 F 2
Saint-Sébastien, Cap – 64-65 L 5
Saint Simons Island 74-75 C 9
Saint Simons Island, GA 74-75 C 9
Saint Stephens, SC 74-75 D 8
Saint Thomas [CDN] 74-75 C 3
Saint Thomas [Westindien] 72-73 NO 8
Saint-Tropez 34-35 L 7
Saint Vincent, Gulf – 56-57 G 6-7
Saint Vincent en de Grenadinen 72-73 O 9
Saio = Dembī Dolo 60-61 LM 7
Saishū = Cheju-do 50-51 F 6
Saitama 50-51 M 4
Saiteli = Kadinhanı 46-47 E 3
Saito 50-51 H 6
Sai'wun = Say'ūn 44-45 F 7
Sajak 42-43 O 8
Sajama, Nevado de – 78-79 F 8
Sajano-Šušenskoje vodochranilišče 44-45 R 7
Sajarī, Bi'r – 46-47 H 6
Saji-dong 50-51 G 2
Šajmak 44-45 L 3
Sajnšand 48-49 KL 3
Sajo 33 K 4
Sajram nuur 48-49 DE 3
Saka 63 D 3
Sakai 48-49 Q 5
Sakaide 50-51 JK 5
Sakaiminato 50-51 J 5
Sakākah 44-45 E 4-5
Sakakawea, Lake – 72-73 F 2
Sakamachi = Arakawa 50-51 M 3
Sakania 64-65 G 5
Sakarya 46-47 D 2
Sakarya 44-45 C 2
Sakarya Nehri 44-45 C 2
Sakata 48-49 Q 4
Sakavi = Mercimekkale 46-47 J 3
Sakawa 50-51 J 6
Sakchu 50-51 E 2
Saketa 52-53 J 7
Sakha Dsong 48-49 F 6
Sakht-Sar 46-47 O 4
Saki 38-39 F 6
Sakīkdah 60-61 F 1
Sakinohama 50-51 K 6
Sakishima-guntō 48-49 NO 7
Sakisima guntō = Sakishima-guntō 48-49 NO 7
Sâkkâne, 'Erg I-n- 60-61 D 4
Sakon Nakhon 52-53 B 3
Sakonnet Point 74-75 H 4
Sakovlevskoje = Privolžsk 42-43 N 5
Sakrivier [ZA, ●] 64-65 EF 9
Sal 38-39 H 6
Sala 30-31 G 8
Salacgrīva 30-31 KL 9
Sala Consilina 36-37 F 5
Salada, Laguna – [MEX] 76-77 F 9
Saladillo [RA, Buenos Aires] 80 DE 5
Salado, Río – [RA, Santa Fe] 80 D 3
Salado, Valle del – 72-73 F 7
Salaga 60-61 D 7
Salah, In- = 'Ayn Ṣāliḥ 60-61 E 3
Salāhuddīn 46-47 KL 5
Salair 42-43 PQ 7
Salairskij kr'až 42-43 PQ 7
Salajar = Pulau Selayar 52-53 H 8
Salal 60-61 H 6
Ṣalālah 44-45 G 7
Salālah, Jabal – 62 F 7
Salamanca 34-35 E 8
Salamanca, NY 74-75 D 3
Salamat, Bahr – 60-61 H 6-7
Salāmatābād 46-47 M 5
Salamaua 52-53 N 8
Salamis 36-37 K 7
Salamīyah 46-47 G 5
Salang = Ko Phuket 52-53 C 5
Salantai 30-31 J 9
Salatan, Cape – = Tanjung Selatan 52-53 F 7
Salatiga 52-53 F 8
Salavat 42-43 K 7
Salaverry 78-79 D 6
Salawati, Pulau – 52-53 K 7
Salazar = Ndalatando 64-65 DE 4
Saldanha [ZA] 64-65 E 9
Saldus 30-31 K 9
Sale [AUS] 56-57 J 7
Salé = Slā 60-61 C 2
Salé, Grand Lac – = Great Salt Lake 72-73 D 3
Salechard 42-43 M 4
Saleh, Teluk – 52-53 G 8
Ṣāleḥābād [IR ↖ Hamadān] 46-47 N 5
Ṣāleḥābād [IR ↙ Īlām] 46-47 M 6
Salem [IND] 44-45 M 8
Salem, FL 74-75 b 2
Salem, MA 74-75 H 3
Salem, NJ 74-75 F 5
Salem, OH 74-75 C 4
Salem, OR 72-73 B 2
Salem, VA 74-75 C 6
Salem, WV 74-75 C 5
Salemi 36-37 E 7
Sälen 30-31 E 7
Salentina 36-37 GH 5
Salerno 36-37 F 5
Salerno, Golfo di – 36-37 F 5
Salford 32 E 5
Salgótarján 33 J 4
Salgueiro 78-79 M 6
Salibabu, Pulau – 52-53 J 6
Salida, CO 72-73 E 4
Ṣalīf, Aṣ- 44-45 E 7
Ṣāliḥīyah, Aṣ- [ET] 62 DE 2
Ṣāliḥīyah, Aṣ- [SYR] 46-47 J 5
Salihli 46-47 C 3
Salima 64-65 HJ 5
Ṣalīmah, Wāḥat – 60-61 K 4
Salina, KS 72-73 G 4
Salina, UT 76-77 H 6
Salina, Isola – 36-37 F 6
Salina, La – 76-77 G 10
Salina Cruz 72-73 G 8
Salinas [BR] 78-79 L 8
Salinas [EC] 78-79 C 5
Salinas, CA 72-73 B 4
Salinas, Cabo de – 34-35 J 9
Salinas, Punta de – 78-79 D 7
Salinas Grandes [RA ↖ Córdoba] 80 C 4-D 3
Salinas River 76-77 C 7-8
Saline Valley 76-77 E 7
Salinópolis 78-79 K 4-5
Salisbury 32 EF 6
Salisbury, CT 74-75 G 3-4
Salisbury, MD 72-73 LM 4
Salisbury, NC 72-73 KL 4
Salisbury = Harare 64-65 H 6
Salisbury, ostrov – = ostrov Salsberi 42-43 HJ 1
Salisbury Island 70-71 VW 5
Salish Mountains 76-77 F 1-2
Saljany 38-39 J 8
Šalkar 38-39 K 5
Šalkar, ozero – 38-39 K 5
Ṣalkhad 46-47 G 6
Salkum, WA 76-77 B 2
Salla 30-31 N 4
Salley, SC 74-75 C 8
Sallyana 44-45 N 5
Sal'm, ostrov – 42-43 KL 2
Salmah, Jabal – 44-45 E 5
Salmān, As- 46-47 L 7
Salmanlı 46-47 F 3
Salmanlı = Kaymas 46-47 D 2
Salmān Pāk 46-47 L 6
Salmās 46-47 L 3
Salmi 42-43 E 5
Salmon, ID 76-77 FG 3
Salmon Creek Reservoir 76-77 F 4
Salmon Falls 76-77 F 4
Salmon Falls Creek Lake 76-77 F 4
Salmon Gums 56-57 D 6
Salmon River [USA, Idaho] 72-73 CD 2
Salmon River Mountains 72-73 C 3-D 2
Salo 30-31 K 7
Salomón [⊙] 52-53 h 6-k 7
Salomón [★] 52-53 kl 7
Salomon, Bassin des – 52-53 h 6
Salomón, Cuenca de las – 52-53 h 6
Salomon, Îles – [⊙] 52-53 h 6-k 7
Salomon, Îles – [★] 52-53 kl 7
Salomón, Mar de las – 52-53 hj 6
Salomon, Mer des – 52-53 hj 6
Salomonbekken 52-53 h 6
Salomoneilanden [⊙] 52-53 h 6-k 7
Salomoneilanden [★] 52-53 kl 7
Salomonzee 52-53 hj 6
Salonga 64-65 F 3
Salonga Nord, Parc national de la – 64-65 F 3
Salonga Sud, Parc national de la – 64-65 F 3
Salónica = Thessaloníkē 36-37 K 5
Salonika = Thessaloníkē 36-37 K 5
Salonique = Thessaloníkē 36-37 K 5
Salonta 36-37 JK 2
Salor 34-35 D 9
Salpausselkä 30-31 L-O 7
Salsacate 80 CD 4
Salsberi, ostrov – 42-43 HJ 1
Sal'sk 38-39 H 6
Salso 36-37 E 7
Salsomaggiore Terme 36-37 C 3
Salṭ, As- 46-47 F 6
Salta [RA, ●] 80 CD 2
Salten 30-31 F 4-G 3
Saltfjord 30-31 EF 4
Salt Flat, TX 72-73 EF 5
Saltillo 72-73 FG 6
Salt Lake, NM 76-77 J 8
Salt Lake City, UT 72-73 D 3
Salt Lakes 56-57 CD 5
Salt Marsh = Lake MacLeod 56-57 B 4
Salto [RA] 80 DE 4
Salto [ROU, ●] 80 E 4
Salto, El – 72-73 E 7
Salto da Divisa 78-79 LM 8
Salto Grande, Embalse – 80 E 4
Saltoluokta 30-31 H 4
Salton, CA 76-77 F 9
Saltón, El – 80 B 7
Salton Sea 72-73 CD 5
Salt River [USA, Arizona] 72-73 D 5
Salt River Indian Reservation 76-77 H 9
Saltspring Island 76-77 B 1
Saltville, VA 74-75 C 6
Saluda, SC 74-75 BC 7-8
Saluen 48-49 H 6
Saluen = Thanlwin Myit 52-53 C 2-3
Salûm, As- 60-61 K 2
Saluzzo 36-37 B 3
Salvador 78-79 M 7
Salwá Baḥrī 62 E 5
Salyānā = Sallyana 44-45 N 5
Salzach 33 F 4-5
Salzbrunn 64-65 E 7
Salzburg [A, ●] 33 F 5
Salzburg [A, ☆] 33 F 5
Salzgitter 33 E 2-3
Salzwedel 33 E 2
Sam 38-39 L 6
Sama de Langreo 34-35 E 7
Samāh, Bi'r – 46-47 L 8
Samālūṭ 62 D 3
Samaná, Bahía de – 72-73 N 8
Samānalakanda 44-45 N 9
Samandağı 46-47 F 4
Samangān 44-45 K 3
Samani 48-49 R 3
Samar 52-53 J 4
Samara [SU, Rossijskaja SFSR ~] 42-43 J 7
Samara [SU, Rossijskaja SFSR ●] 42-43 HJ 7
Samarai 52-53 gh 7
Samarga 42-43 ab 8
Samarinda 52-53 G 7
Samarkand 44-45 K 3
Samarkand = Temirtau 42-43 N 7
Sāmarrā' 44-45 E 4
Samāwah, As- 44-45 EF 4
Sambala 64-65 F 4
Sambaliung 52-53 G 6
Sambalpore = Sambalpur 44-45 N 6
Sambalpur 44-45 N 6
Sambas 52-53 E 6
Sambava 64-65 M 5
Sambhal 44-45 M 5
Samboja 52-53 G 7
Sambongi = Towada 50-51 N 2
Sambor 38-39 D 6
Sambor [K] 52-53 E 4
Samborombón, Bahía – 80 E 5
Sambre 34-35 K 3
Samch'ŏk 48-49 OP 4
Samch'ŏnp'o 50-51 FG 5
Samdŭng 50-51 F 3
Same [EAT] 64-65 J 3
Samfya 63 B 5
Samḥah 44-45 G 8
Samīm, Umm as- 44-45 H 6
Samnagjin 50-51 G 5
Samoa, CA 76-77 A 5
Samoa, Îles – = Samoa Islands 52-53 c 1
Samoa Islands 52-53 c 1
Samora = Zamora de Hidalgo 72-73 F 7-8
Sámos [GR, ⊙] 36-37 M 7
Sámos [GR, ●] 36-37 M 7
Samosir, Pulau – 52-53 C 6
Samothrákē 36-37 L 5
Sampacho 80 CD 4
Sampang 52-53 F 8
Samper de Calanda 34-35 G 8
Sampit 52-53 F 7
Sampit, Teluk – 52-53 F 7
Samrah = Mazıdağı 46-47 J 4
Samrong 52-53 D 4
Samsø 36-37 D 10
Samsu 50-51 G 2
Samsun 44-45 D 2
Samtredia 38-39 H 7
Samuel, Mount – 56-57 F 3
Samui, Ko – 52-53 D 5
Samur 38-39 J 7
Samutlu = Temelli 46-47 E 3
Samut Prakan 52-53 D 4
San 33 L 3
San [RMM] 60-61 CD 6
Sanā [Y, Hadramawt] 44-45 FG 7
Ṣan'ā' [Y, Tihāmah] 44-45 EF 7
Sana [YU] 36-37 G 3
Sanaag 60-61 b 2
Sānabād 46-47 N 4
Ṣanabū 62 D 4
SANAE 24 b 36-1
Ṣanāfīr, Jazīrat – 62 F 4
Sanaga 60-61 G 8
San Agustín [RA, Buenos Aires] 80 E 5
San Agustin, Cape – 52-53 J 5
Sanām, As- 44-45 G 6
Sanām, Jabal – 46-47 M 7
San Ambrosio 69 C 5
Sanana, Pulau – 52-53 J 7
Sanandaj 44-45 F 3
San Andreas, CA 76-77 C 6
San Andrés [CO, ⊙] 72-73 KL 9
San Andres Mountains 72-73 E 5
San Andres Tuxtla 72-73 GH 8
San Angel 78-79 E 2-3
San Angelo, TX 72-73 FG 5
San Anselmo, CA 76-77 B 7
San Antonio [RCH] 80 B 4
San Antonio, TX 72-73 G 6
San Antonio, Cabo – [C] 72-73 K 7
San Antonio de Caparo 78-79 E 3
San Antonio del Mar 76-77 E 10
San Antonio de los Cobres 80 C 2
San Antonio Oeste 80 CD 6
San Antonio Peak 76-77 E 8
San Ardo, CA 76-77 C 7
Sanāw 44-45 G 7
Sanbalpur = Sambalpur 44-45 N 6
San Benedetto del Tronto 36-37 EF 4
San Benedicto, Isla – 72-73 DE 8
San Benito, TX 72-73 G 6
San Benito Mountain 76-77 C 7
San Bernardino, CA 72-73 CD 5
San Bernardino Mountains 76-77 E 8
San Bernardo [RCH] 80 BC 4
San Blas, Cape – 72-73 J 6
San Blas, Cordillera de – 72-73 L 10
San Blas, Punta – 72-73 L 10
San Borja 78-79 F 7
San Buenaventura = Ventura, CA 76-77 D 8
San Carlos [RCH] 80 B 5
San Carlos [RP, Luzón] 52-53 GH 3
San Carlos [RP, Negros] 52-53 H 4
San Carlos [YV, Cojedes] 78-79 F 3
San Carlos, AZ 76-77 H 9
San Carlos, Estrecho de – = Falkland Sound 80 DE 8
San Carlos Bay 74-75 bc 3
San Carlos de Bariloche 80 B 6
San Carlos de Bolívar 80 D 5
San Carlos de Puno 78-79 EF 8
San Carlos de Río Negro 78-79 F 4
San Carlos de Zulia 78-79 E 3
San Carlos Indian Reservation 76-77 HJ 9
San Carlos Lake 76-77 H 9
San Clemente, CA 76-77 E 9
San Clemente Island 72-73 BC 5
San Cristóbal [CO] 78-79 E 5
San Cristóbal [RA] 80 D 4
San Cristóbal [Salomonen] 52-53 k 7
San Cristóbal [YV] 78-79 E 3
San Cristóbal, Isla – 78-79 B 5
San Cristóbal de las Casas 72-73 H 8
San Cristobal Wash 76-77 G 9
San Cristoval = San Cristóbal 52-53 k 7
Sancti-Spíritus [C] 72-73 L 7
Sand 30-31 AB 8
Ṣandafā' 62 D 3
Sandai 52-53 F 7
Sandakan 52-53 G 5
Sandane 30-31 AB 7
Sandanski 36-37 K 5
Sanday 32 EF 2
Sandefjord 30-31 D 8
Sanders, AZ 76-77 J 8
Sandersville, GA 74-75 B 8
Sandfontein 64-65 EF 7
Sandhornøy 30-31 EF 4
Sandia 78-79 F 7
San Diego, CA 72-73 C 5
San Diego, Cabo – 80 CD 8
San Diego Aqueduct 76-77 E 9
Sandıklı 46-47 CD 3
Sand Key 74-75 b 3
Sand Mountains 72-73 J 5
Sandnes 30-31 A 8
Sandoa 64-65 F 4
Sandomierz 33 K 3
San Donà di Piave 36-37 E 3
Sandover River 56-57 FG 4
Sandoway = Thandwe 52-53 B 3
Sandpoint, ID 76-77 E 1
Sandringham 56-57 G 4
Sandstone 56-57 C 5
Sand Tank Mountains 76-77 G 9
Sandur 30-31 ab 2
Sandveld [Namibia] 64-65 EF 7
Sandviken 30-31 G 7
Sandwich du Sud, Fosse du – 24 D 34
Sandwich del Sur, Dorsal de las – 24 D 34
Sandy, NV 76-77 F 8
Sandy Cape [AUS, Queensland] 56-57 K 4
Sandy Cape [AUS, Tasmania] 58 ab 2
Sandy City, UT 72-73 D 3
Sandy Creek 76-77 J 4-5
Sandy Hills 72-73 GH 5
Sandy Hook 74-75 G 4
Sandy Key 74-75 c 4
Sandy Lake [CDN, ≈ Ontario] 70-71 S 7
Sandy Ridge 74-75 B 6
Sandy River 76-77 BC 3
San Estanislao 80 E 2
San Esteban de Gormaz 34-35 F 8
San Felipe [CO] 78-79 F 4
San Felipe [RCH] 80 B 4
San Felipe [YV] 78-79 F 2
San Felipe, Punta – 76-77 F 10
San Felipe de Puerto Plata = Puerto Plata 72-73 M 8
San Feliu de Guíxols 34-35 J 8
San Félix [Desventurados] 69 B 5
San Félix [RCH] 69 BC 5
San Fernando [E] 34-35 D 10
San Fernando [RA] 80 E 4
San Fernando [RCH] 80 B 4
San Fernando [TT] 72-73 L 9
San Fernando [YV] 78-79 F 3
San Fernando, CA 76-77 D 8
San Fernando [RP ↖ Baguio] 52-53 GH 3
San Fernando [RP ↖ Manila] 52-53 H 3
San Fernando de Atabapo 78-79 F 4
San Fernando del Valle de Catamarca 80 C 3
Sånfjället 30-31 E 6
Sanford, FL 72-73 K 6
Sanford, ME 74-75 H 3
Sanford, NC 74-75 D 7
San Francisco [RA] 80 D 4
San Francisco, CA 72-73 AB 4
San Francisco Bay 76-77 B 7
San Francisco de la Caleta 72-73 bc 3
San Francisco del Oro 72-73 E 6
San Francisco del Parapetí 78-79 G 8-9
San Francisco de Macorís 72-73 MN 8
San Francisco Peaks 76-77 GH 8
San Francisco Plateau 72-73 D 4-E 5
San Francisco River 76-77 J 9
San Francisco Solano, Punta – 78-79 D 3
Sangā 52-53 C 2
Sanga = Sangha 64-65 E 2-3
San Gabriel [EC] 78-79 D 4

214 Saint

San Gabriel Mountains 76-77 DE 8
Sangagchhö Ling 48-49 G 6
Šangaly 38-39 H 3
Sangar 42-43 Y 5
Sangários = Sakarya nehri 44-45 C 2
Sangasār 46-47 L 4
Sangay 78-79 D 5
Sangeang, Pulau – 52-53 GH 8
Sanger, CA 76-77 D 7
Sanggau 52-53 F 6
Sangha 64-65 E 2-3
Sang-i Māsha 44-45 K 4
San Giovanni in Persiceto 36-37 D 3
Sangir, Kepulauan – 52-53 J 6
Sangir, Pulau – 52-53 J 6
Sangju 50-51 G 4
Sangkulirang 52-53 G 6
Sangkulirang, Teluk – 52-53 G 6
Sāngli 44-45 LM 7
Sangmélima 60-61 G 8
Sangonera, Río – 34-35 G 10
San Gorgonio Mountain 76-77 E 8
Sangre, La – 76-77 H 10
Sangre de Cristo Range 72-73 E 4
Sangre Grande 72-73 OP 9
Sangue, Rio do – 78-79 H 7
Sangymgort 42-43 M 5
Sanibel Island 74-75 b 3
San Ignacio [PY] 80 E 3
San Ignacio [BOL ↗ La Paz] 78-79 F 7
San Ignacio [BOL ↗ Santa Cruz] 78-79 G 8
Saniquellie 60-61 C 7
San Isidro [RA] 80 E 4
Sanitatas 64-65 D 6
Sanīyah, Hawr as- 46-47 M 7
San Jacinto, CA 76-77 E 9
San Jacinto Mountains 76-77 E 9
San Javier [BOL, Santa Cruz] 78-79 G 8
San Javier [RA, Misiones] 80 EF 3
San Jerónimo, Serranía de – 78-79 D 3
Sanjō 50-51 M 4
San Joaquin [BOL] 78-79 FG 7
San Joaquin River 72-73 BC 4
San Joaquin Valley 72-73 BC 4
San Jorge, Canal de – = Saint George's Channel 32 C 6-D 5
San Jorge, Golfo – 80 CD 7
San Jorge, Golfo de – 34-35 H 8
San José [CR] 72-73 K 9-10
San José [GCA] 72-73 H 9
San José [PA] 72-73 b 3
San José [RP] 52-53 H 3
San Jose, CA 72-73 B 4
San José [ROU, ●] 80 E 4
San José, Isla – [MEX] 72-73 DE 6
San José, Isla – = Weddell Island 80 D 8
San José de Buenavista 52-53 H 4
San José de Chiquitos 78-79 G 8
San José de Chiquitos 78-79 G 8
San José de Jáchal 80 C 4
San José de las Salinas 80 CD 4
San José del Cabo 72-73 E 7
San José del Guaviare 78-79 E 4
San José de Ocuné 78-79 E 4
San Juan [PE] 78-79 DE 8
San Juan [Puerto Rico] 72-73 N 8
San Juan [RA, ●] 80 C 4
San Juan, Cabo – [Äquatorial-Guinea] 60-61 F 8
San Juan, Cabo – [RA] 80 D 8
San Juan, Río – [NIC] 72-73 K 9
San Juan Archipelago 76-77 B 1
San Juan Bautista 34-35 H 9
San Juan Bautista 80 E 3
San Juan Bautista = Villahermosa 72-73 H 8
San Juan de Guía, Cabo de – 78-79 DE 2
San Juan del Norte = Bluefields 72-73 K 9
San Juan del Norte, Bahía de – 72-73 K 9
San Juan de los Morros 78-79 F 3
San Juan Mountains 72-73 E 4
San Juan River 72-73 E 4
San Justo [RA, Santa Fe] 80 D 4
Sankisen 50-51 cd 2
Sankt Gallen 33 D 5
Sankt Gotthard 33 D 5
Sankt Michel = Mikkeli 30-31 MN 7
Sankt Moritz 33 DE 5
Sankt-Peterburg 42-43 E 5-6
Sankt Pölten 33 G 4
Sankuru 64-65 F 3
San Lázaro, Cabo – 72-73 D 7
Sanlı Urfa 44-45 D 3
San Lorenzo [EC] 78-79 D 4
San Lorenzo [PY] 80 E 3
San Lorenzo [RA, Santa Fe] 80 D 4
San Lorenzo [YV, Zulia] 78-79 E 3
San Lorenzo [BOL ↙ Riberalta] 78-79 F 7
San Lorenzo [BOL ↑ Tarija] 78-79 FG 9
San Lorenzo, Cabo de – 78-79 C 5
San Lorenzo, Cerro – 80 B 7
San Lorenzo, Isla – [PE] 78-79 D 7
San Lorenzo, Sierra de – 34-35 F 7
Sanlúcar de Barrameda 34-35 D 10
San Lucas, CA 76-77 C 7
San Lucas, Cabo – 72-73 E 7
San Luis [RA, ●] 80 C 4
San Luis, Sierre de – [YV] 78-79 EF 2
San Luis Obispo, CA 72-73 B 4
San Luis Obispo Bay 76-77 C 8
San Luis Potosí 72-73 FG 7
San Manuel, AZ 76-77 H 9
San Marco, Capo – 36-37 BC 6
San Marcos [RCH] 80 B 4
San Marcos, TX 72-73 G 6
San Marino [RSM, ●] 36-37 E 4
San Marino [RSM, ★] 36-37 E 4
San Martín [BOL] 78-79 G 7-8
San Martín [RA, La Rioja] 80 C 3
San Martín, Lago – 80 B 7
San Martín, Río – 78-79 G 8
San Mateo, CA 72-73 B 4
San Mateo Peak 72-73 E 5
San Matías, Golfo – 80 D 6
San-mên-hsia = Sanmenxia 48-49 L 5
Sanmenxia 48-49 L 5
San Miguel [ES] 72-73 J 9
San Miguel [MEX] 76-77 H 10
San Miguel, AZ 76-77 H 10
San Miguel, CA 76-77 C 8
San Miguel, Río – [BOL] 78-79 G 7-8
San Miguel de Huachi 78-79 F 8
San Miguel del Monte 80 E 5
San Miguel de Tucumán 80 CD 3
San Miguel Island 76-77 C 8
San Miguelito [PA] 72-73 bc 3
San Miguel River 76-77 JK 6-7
Sannār 60-61 L 6
San Narciso 52-53 GH 3
San Nicolás de los Arroyos 80 D 4
San Nicolas Island 72-73 BC 5
Sannikova, proliv – 42-43 ab 3
Sanniquellie = Saniquellie 60-61 C 7
Sannohe 50-51 N 2
Sannūr, Wādī – 62 D 3
Sanok 33 L 4
San Pablo [RP] 52-53 H 4
San Pablo Bay 76-77 B 6
San Pedro [RA, Buenos Aires] 80 E 4
San Pedro [RA, Santiago del Estero] 80 C 3
San Pedro [PY, ●] 80 E 2
San Pedro [BOL, Santa Cruz ↗ Santa Cruz] 78-79 G 8
San Pedro [BOL, Santa Cruz ↑ Trinidad] 78-79 G 7
San Pedro, Punta – [CR] 72-73 K 10
San Pedro, Sierra de – 34-35 D 9
San Pedro, Volcán – 78-79 F 9
San Pedro Channel 76-77 D 9
San Pedro Channel 76-77 D 9
San Pedro de las Colonias 72-73 F 6
San Pedro de Macorís 72-73 N 8
San Pedro Mártir, Sierra – 72-73 CD 5
San Pedro River 76-77 H 9
San Pedro Sula 72-73 J 8
San Pietro 36-37 BC 6
San Quintín, Cabo – 72-73 C 5
San Rafael [RA] 80 C 4
San Rafael, CA 72-73 B 4
San Rafael, Río – 76-77 EF 10
San Rafael del Encanto 78-79 E 5
San Rafael Mountains 76-77 CD 8
San Rafael River 76-77 H 6
San Rafael Swell 76-77 H 6
San Ramón de la Nueva Orán 80 CD 2
San Remo 36-37 BC 4
San Román, Cabo – 78-79 EF 2
San Rosendo 80 B 5
San Salvador [BS] 72-73 M 7
San Salvador [ES] 72-73 HJ 9
San Salvador, Isla – 78-79 A 5
San Salvador de Jujuy 80 CD 2
Sansanding 60-61 CD 6
Sansanné-Mango = Mango 60-61 E 6
San Sebastián 34-35 FG 7
San Sebastián [RA] 80 C 8
San Sebastián de la Gomera 60-61 A 3
San Severo 36-37 F 5
San Silvestre [YV] 78-79 EF 3
San Simeon, CA 76-77 C 8
San Simon, AZ 76-77 J 9
Sansing = Yilan 48-49 OP 2
Santa Ana [CO, Guainía] 78-79 F 4
Santa Ana [ES] 72-73 HJ 9
Santa Ana [MEX] 72-73 D 5
Santa Ana, CA 72-73 C 5
Santa Ana [BOL ↖ Trinidad] 78-79 F 7
Santa Ana Mountains 76-77 E 9
Santa Bárbara [MEX] 72-73 E 6
Santa Bárbara [RCH] 80 B 5
Santa Barbara, CA 72-73 BC 5
Santa Bárbara [YV ↙ Maturín] 78-79 G 3
Santa Bárbara [YV → San Cristóbal] 78-79 E 3
Santa Bárbara [YV → San Fernando de Atabapo] 78-79 F 4
Santa Bárbara, Serra de – 78-79 J 9
Santa Barbara Channel 76-77 CD 8
Santa Barbara Channel 76-77 CD 8
Santa Barbara Island 76-77 D 9
Santa Catalina [RA, Jujuy] 80 C 2
Santa Catalina = Catalina 80 C 3
Santa Catalina, Gulf of – 76-77 DE 9
Santa Catalina Island 72-73 BC 5
Santa Catarina 80 FG 3
Santa Catarina, Ilha de – 80 G 3
Santa Catarina, Valle de – 76-77 EF 10
Santa Clara [C] 72-73 KL 7
Santa Clara [CO] 78-79 EF 5
Santa Clara, CA 72-73 B 4
Santa Cruz [BR, Rio Grande do Norte] 78-79 M 6
Santa Cruz [RA, Santa Cruz] 80 BC 7
Santa Cruz, CA 72-73 B 4
Santa Cruz [BOL, ●] 78-79 G 8
Santa Cruz, Îles – = Santa Cruz Islands 52-53 l 7
Santa Cruz, Isla – [EC] 78-79 AB 5
Santa Cruz Cabrália 78-79 M 8
Santa Cruz de Barahona = Barahona 72-73 M 8
Santa Cruz de la Palma 60-61 A 3
Santa Cruz de Tenerife 60-61 A 3
Santa Cruz do Sul 80 F 3
Santa Cruz Island 72-73 BC 5
Santa Cruz Islands 52-53 l 7
Santa Cruz Mountains 76-77 BC 7
Santa Cruz River 76-77 H 9
Santa Elena [BOL] 78-79 G 9
Santa Elena [PE] 78-79 E 5
Santa Elena, Cabo – 72-73 J 9
Santa Elena de Uairén 78-79 G 4
Santa Fe, NM 72-73 E 4
Santa Fe [RA, ●] 80 D 4
Santa Fé do Sul 78-79 J 9
Santa Fe Pacific Railway 72-73 F 4
Santa Filomena 78-79 K 6
Santa Genoveva = Cerro las Casitas 72-73 E 7
Santa Helena [BR, Maranhão] 78-79 K 5
Santa Helena [BR, Pará] 78-79 H 5-6
Santai 48-49 JK 5
Santa Inés [BR, Bahia] 78-79 LM 7
Santa Inés, Isla – 80 B 8
Santa Isabel [RA, La Pampa] 80 C 5
Santa Isabel [Salomonen] 52-53 jk 6
Santa Isabel = Malabo 60-61 F 8
Santa Isabel, Ilha Grande de – 78-79 L 5
Santa Isabel, Sierra – 76-77 F 10
Santa Isabel do Araguaia 78-79 K 6
Santa Isabel do Morro 78-79 J 7
Santa Lucía 72-73 O 8
Santa Lucia Range 76-77 C 7-8
Santaluz [BR, Bahia] 78-79 M 7
Santa Margarita, CA 76-77 C 8
Santa Margarita, Isla – 72-73 D 7
Santa Margherita Ligure 36-37 C 3
Santa Maria [BR, Amazonas] 78-79 H 5
Santa Maria [BR, Rio Grande do Sul] 80 EF 3
Santa María [PE, Loreto] 78-79 E 5
Santa María [RA] 80 C 3
Santa Maria [Vanuatu] 56-57 N 2
Santa Maria [Z] 63 B 5
Santa Maria, CA 72-73 B 5
Santa Maria, Cabo de – 34-35 CD 10
Santa Maria, Cabo de – = Cap Sainte-Marie 64-65 L 8
Santa María Asunción Tlaxiaco 72-73 G 8
Santa Maria das Barreiras 78-79 JK 6
Santa María de Ipire 78-79 F 3
Santa Maria di Leuca, Capo – 36-37 H 6
Santa Marta [CO] 78-79 DE 2
Santa Marta, Sierra Nevada de – 78-79 E 2
Santa Monica, CA 72-73 BC 5
Santana 78-79 L 7
Santana, Coxilha da – 80 E 3-F 4
Santana, Ilha de – 78-79 L 5
Santana do Livramento 80 EF 4
Santander 34-35 F 7
Santander [CO, Cauca] 78-79 D 4
Sant'Antioco [I, ⊙] 36-37 BC 6
Sant'Antioco [I, ●] 36-37 BC 6
Santañy 34-35 J 9
Santañy 34-35 J 9
Santa Paula, CA 76-77 D 8
Santa Pola, Cabo de – 34-35 GH 9
Santarém [BR] 78-79 J 5
Santarem [P] 34-35 C 9
Santaren Channel 72-73 L 7
Santaren Channel 72-73 L 7
Santa Rita [BR, Paraíba] 78-79 MN 6
Santa Rita [YV, Zulia] 78-79 E 2
Santa Rita, NM 76-77 J 9
Santa Rita do Araguaia 78-79 J 8
Santa Rito do Weil 78-79 F 5
Santa Rosa [BR, Acre] 78-79 EF 6
Santa Rosa [BR, Rio Grande do Sul] 80 F 3
Santa Rosa [CO, Guainía] 78-79 EF 4
Santa Rosa [PE] 78-79 E 5
Santa Rosa [RA, La Pampa] 80 CD 5
Santa Rosa [RA, Mendoza] 80 C 4
Santa Rosa [RA, San Luis] 80 C 4
Santa Rosa, CA 72-73 B 4
Santa Rosa [BOL, Beni ↘ Riberalta] 78-79 F 7
Santa Rosa de Copán 72-73 J 9
Santa Rosa del Palmar 78-79 G 8
Santa Rosa Island [USA, California] 72-73 B 5
Santa Rosalía [MEX] 72-73 D 6
Santa Rosa Range 76-77 E 5
Santa Rosa Wash 76-77 GH 9
Šantarskije ostrova 42-43 a 6-7
Santa Sylvina 80 DE 3
Santa Tecla = Nueva San Salvador 72-73 HJ 9
Santa Vitória do Palmar 80 F 4
Santa Ynez, CA 76-77 CD 8
Santee River 74-75 D 8
San Telmo 76-77 EF 10
Sant'Eufèmia, Golfo di – 36-37 FG 6
Santiago [BR] 80 EF 3
Santiago [DOM] 72-73 M 7
Santiago [PA] 72-73 K 10
Santiago de Chile 80 B 4
Santiago de Chuco 78-79 D 6
Santiago de Cuba 72-73 L 7-8
Santiago de Chile 80 B 4
Santiago de Chuco 78-79 D 6
Santiago del Estero [RA, ●] 80 CD 3
Santiago di Compostela 34-35 CD 7
Santiago Ixcuintla 72-73 EF 7
Santiagoma 78-79 H 8
Santiago Papasquiaro 72-73 EF 6-7
Santiam Pass 76-77 BC 3
Santigi 52-53 H 6
Santo 56-57 MN 3
Santo Amaro 78-79 M 7
Santo André 78-79 K 9
Santo André = Isla de San Andrés 72-73 KL 9
Santo Ângelo 80 EF 3
Santo António [São Tomé und Príncipe] 60-61 F 8
Santo Antônio, Cachoeira – [BR, Rio Madeira] 78-79 FG 6
Santo Antônio de Jesus 78-79 LM 7
Santo António do Zaire = Soyo 64-65 D 4
Santo Corazón 78-79 H 8
Santo Domingo [DOM] 72-73 MN 8
Santo Domingo, Río – [MEX] 72-73 G 8
Santo Domingo de Guzmán = Santo Domingo 72-73 MN 8
Santo Domingo Tehuantepec 72-73 G 8
Santoña 34-35 F 7
Santoña 34-35 F 7
Santorínē = Thēra 36-37 L 7
Santos 78-79 K 9
Santo Tomás [PE] 78-79 E 7
Santo Tomás, Punta – 76-77 E 10
Santo Tomé [RA, Corrientes] 80 E 3
Sanup Plateau 76-77 G 8
San Valentín, Cerro – 80 B 7
San Vicente 72-73 O 9
San Vicente [ES] 72-73 J 9
San Víctor 80 E 4
San Vito, Capo – 36-37 E 6
San Xavier Indian Reservation 76-77 H 9-10
Sanya = Ya Xian 48-49 KL 8
San Yanaro 78-79 EF 4
San Ysidro, CA 76-77 E 9
Sanza Pombo 64-65 E 4
São Bernardo 78-79 L 5
São Borja 80 EF 3
São Carlos [BR, São Paulo] 78-79 K 9
São Domingos [Guinea-Bissau] 60-61 A 6
São Félix do Xingu 78-79 J 6
São Filipe 78-79 M 7
São Francisco, Rio – [BR, Pernambuco] 78-79 LM 6
São Francisco do Sul 80 G 3
São Gabriel 80 EF 4
São Gotardo 78-79 KL 8
Sao Hill 63 C 5
São Jerónimo, Serra de – 78-79 J 8
Sao João, Ilhas de – 78-79 L 5
São João do Piauí 78-79 L 6
São José do Rio Preto [BR, São Paulo] 78-79 JK 9
São José dos Campos 78-79 KL 9
São Luís 78-79 L 5
São Marcos, Baía de – 78-79 L 5
São Mateus [BR, Espírito Santo] 78-79 M 8
São Miguel do Araguaia 78-79 JK 7
São Miguel do Tapuio 78-79 L 6
Saona, Isla – 72-73 N 8
Saône 34-35 K 5
São Paulo [BR, ⊙] 20-21 H 5
São Paulo [BR, ☆] 78-79 JK 9
São Paulo de Olivença 78-79 F 5
São Raimundo Nonato 78-79 L 6
São Romão [BR, Amazonas] 78-79 F 6
São Romão [BR, Minas Gerais] 78-79 KL 8
São Roque, Cabo de – 78-79 MN 6
São Sebastião, Ilha de – 78-79 KL 9
São Sebastião, Ponta – 64-65 J 7
São Simão, Represa de – 78-79 JK 8
São Tomé [São Tomé und Príncipe] 60-61 F 8
São Tomé, Cabo de – 78-79 LM 9
São Tomé, Ilha – 60-61 F 8-9
São Tomé and Principe 60-61 F 8-9
São Tomé en Principe 60-61 F 8-9
São Tomé et Principe 60-61 F 8-9
São Tomé y Príncipe 60-61 F 8-9
Şaouîra, eş – = Aş-Şawīrah 60-61 BC 2
Saoura, Ouèd – = Wādī as-Sāwrah 60-61 D 2-3
São Vicente [BR, São Paulo] 78-79 K 9
São Vicente, Cabo de – 34-35 C 10
Sápai 36-37 L 5
Sapanjang, Pulau – 52-53 G 8
Sapateiro, Cachoeira do – 78-79 H 5
Sape [RI] 52-53 G 8
Sapele 60-61 EF 7
Sapelo Island 74-75 C 9
Şaphane Dağı 46-47 C 3
Sapiéntza 36-37 J 7
Saposoa 78-79 D 6
Sapphire Mountains 76-77 G 2-3
Sappho, WA 76-77 AB 1
Sapporo 48-49 QR 3
Sapri 36-37 F 5
Sapt Kosi 44-45 O 5
Sapudi, Pulau – 52-53 FG 8
Sapulpa, OK 72-73 G 4
Sapwe 63 B 5
Saqasiq, Es- = Az-Zaqāzīq 60-61 KL 2
Sāqīyat al-Ḥamrā', As- 60-61 B 3
Şaqqārah 62 D 3
Saqqez 44-45 F 3
Sarab 38-39 K 9
Sarāb [IR, Ādharbayejān-e Khāvarī] 46-47 M 4
Saraburi 52-53 D 4
Sarafutsu 50-51 c 1
Saraguro 78-79 D 5
Sarajevo 36-37 H 4
Sarala 42-43 Q 7
Saramabila 63 AB 4
Saramati 44-45 P 5
Saran' [SU, Kazachskaja SSR] 42-43 N 8
Sāran = Chhapra 44-45 N 5
Saranac Lake, NY 74-75 F 2
Saranda 63 C 4
Sarandë 36-37 HJ 6
Sarandí del Yi 80 EF 4
Sarangani Bay 52-53 HJ 5
Sarangani Islands 52-53 HJ 5
Saranlay = Sarinleey 60-61 N 8
Saranpaul' 42-43 L 5
Saransk 42-43 GH 7
Saránta Ekklēsies = Kırklareli 44-45 B 2
Sarapul 42-43 J 6
Sarapul'skoje 42-43 a 8
Sarārāt Sayyāl, Bi'r – 62 F 6
Sarāskand = Hashtrūd 46-47 M 4
Sarasota, FL 72-73 K 6
Sarata 36-37 N 2-3
Saratoga Springs, NY 72-73 M 3

Sarat 215

Saratov 38-39 HJ 5
Saratovskoje vodochranilišče 38-39 J 5
Sarāvān [IR] 44-45 J 5
Saravan [LAO] 52-53 E 3
Sarawak 52-53 F 6
Saray 46-47 B 2
Sarāyah 46-47 F 5
Sarayköy 46-47 C 4
Sarayönü 46-47 E 3
Sarayü = Ghaghara 44-45 N 5
Sār Cham 46-47 MN 4
Sār Cham 46-47 MN 4
Sardaigne = Sardegna 36-37 C 5
Sardalas 60-61 G 3
Sardarshahar = Sardārshahr 44-45 L 5
Sardarshahr 44-45 L 5
Sar Dasht [IR, Khūzestān] 46-47 N 6
Sar Dasht [IR, Kordestān] 46-47 L 4
Sardegna 36-37 C 5
Sardes 46-47 C 3
Sardinia = Sardegna 36-37 C 5
Sardis, GA 74-75 BC 8
Sard Rūd 46-47 LM 3
Sare 63 C 3
Sarek nationalpark 30-31 GH 4
Sarektjåkko 30-31 G 4
Sar-e Pol-e Dhahāb 46-47 LM 5
Sare Pul 44-45 K 3
Sargasses, Mer des – 72-73 N-P 6
Sargasso Sea 72-73 N-P 6
Sargassozee 72-73 N-P 6
Sargazos, Mar de los – 72-73 N-P 6
Sargho, Djebel – = Jabal Şaghrŭ’ 60-61 C 2
Sargoda = Sargodhā 44-45 L 4
Sargodhā 44-45 L 4
Sargon, Dur – = Khorsabad 46-47 K 4
Sarhadd 44-45 L 3
Şarhrŏ’, Jbel – = Jabal Şaghrŭ’ 60-61 C 2
Sārī 44-45 G 3
Saria 36-37 M 8
Sáric 76-77 H 10
Sarıgöl 46-47 C 3
Sarıkamış 46-47 K 2
Sarıkavak 46-47 E 4
Sarıkavak = Kumluca 46-47 D 4
Sarıkaya 46-47 F 3
Sarıkaya = Gömele 46-47 D 2
Sarikei 52-53 F 6
Sarina 56-57 J 4
Sarinleey 60-61 N 8
Sarıoğlan 46-47 FG 3
Sarir 60-61 J 3
Sarī Tappah 46-47 KL 5
Sarıyar Barajı 46-47 D 2
Sarıyer, İstanbul- 46-47 C 2
Sarız = Köyyeri 46-47 G 3
Šarja 42-43 H 6
Sarjū = Ghaghara 44-45 N 5
Sark 32 E 7
Şarkı Karaağaç 46-47 D 3
Şarkışla 46-47 G 3
Šarkovščina 30-31 MN 10
Šarkovskij 38-39 F 4
Sarlat 34-35 H 6
Şärmäşag 36-37 K 2
Sarmi 52-53 L 7
Sarmiento 80 BC 7
Sär mörön 48-49 MN 3
Särna 30-31 E 7
Sarneh 46-47 M 6
Sarnia 70-71 U 9
Sarny 38-39 E 5
Sarolangun 52-53 D 7
Saroma-ko 50-51 c 1
Saronikòs Kólpos 36-37 K 7
Saros Körfezi 46-47 B 2
Sarpa 38-39 J 6
Šar Planina 36-37 J 4-5
Sarpsborg 30-31 D 8
Sar Qal’ah 46-47 L 5
Sarrah, Ma’tan as- 60-61 J 4
Sarre, La – 70-71 V 8
Sarrebourg 34-35 L 4
Sarreguemines 34-35 L 4
Sarria 34-35 D 7
Sarro, Djebel – = Jabal Şaghrŭ’ 60-61 C 2
Šar Uul, Altay 48-49 F 2
Sartang 42-43 Z 4
Sartène 36-37 C 5
Sarthe 34-35 G 5
Sârū, Jabal – 60-61 C 2
Saruhan = Manisa 44-45 B 2

Saruhanlı 46-47 B 3
Sārūq Chāy 46-47 M 4
Sārūq Chāy 46-47 M 4
Saruyama-zaki 50-51 L 4
Saryč, mys – 38-39 F 7
Saryjesik-Alytau 42-43 O 8
Sarykamyšskaja kotlina 38-39 L 7
Šaryngol 48-49 K 2
Saryozek 42-43 O 9
Sarysu 42-43 M 8
Sarytaš 38-39 K 7
Sary-Taš [SU, Tadžikskaja SSR] 44-45 L 3
Sasebo 48-49 O 5
Saskatchewan 70-71 PQ 6-7
Saskatchewan River 70-71 Q 7
Saskatoon 70-71 P 7
Saskylach 42-43 VW 3
Sason 46-47 J 3
Sasovo 38-39 H 5
Sassafras Mountain 74-75 B 7
Sassandra [CI, ~] 60-61 C 7
Sassandra [CI, ●] 60-61 C 7-8
Sâssari 36-37 C 5
Saßnitz 33 FG 1
Sastobe 42-43 MN 9
Sasyk, ozero – 36-37 NO 3
Sasykkol’, ozero – 42-43 P 8
Sata 50-51 H 7
Satadougou 60-61 B 6
Satakunta 30-31 JK 7
Sata-misaki 48-49 OP 5
Satara 44-45 L 7
Satawal 52-53 N 5
Satif 60-61 F 1
Satilla River 74-75 C 9
Satırlar = Yeşilova 46-47 C 4
Satka 42-43 KL 6
Satlaj 44-45 L 4
Satlaj = Langchhen Khamba 48-49 DE 5
Sátleg = Satlaj 44-45 L 4
Satoraljaúghely 33 K 4
Satpura Range 44-45 L-N 6
Satsuma-hantŏ 50-51 GH 7
Sattahip 52-53 D 4
Saţţēt 60-61 C 2
Satu Mare 36-37 K 2
Sauce [RA] 80 E 3-4
Sauda 30-31 B 8
Sauda, Jebel er – = Jabal as-Sawdâ 60-61 GH 3
Saûde 78-79 L 7
Saudhárkrókur 30-31 d 2
Saudi-Arabia 44-45 D 5-F 6
Saugeen River 74-75 C 2
Saugerties, NY 74-75 FG 3
Saugor = Sagar 44-45 M 6
Sâûjbolâgh = Mahābād 44-45 F 3
Saukorem 52-53 K 7
Saûl 78-79 J 4
Šaul’der 42-43 M 9
Sault-Sainte-Marie 70-71 U 8
Sault Sainte Marie, MI 72-73 JK 2
Saumlaki 52-53 K 8
Saumur 34-35 G 5
Şauqirah, Ghubbat – – Dawhat as-Sawqirah 44-45 H 7
Saura, Wed – = Wâdï Sâwrah 60-61 D 2-3
Saurâshtra 44-45 KL 6
Saurimo 64-65 F 4
Sausalito, CA 76-77 B 7
Sautar 64-65 E 5
Sauzal, El – 76-77 E 10
Sava 36-37 J 3
Savage River 58 b 2
Savai’i 52-53 c 1
Savalou 60-61 E 7
Savannah, GA 72-73 KL 5
Savannah Beach, GA 74-75 C 8
Savannah River 72-73 K 5
Savannakhêt 52-53 DE 3
Savari = Sabari 44-45 N 7
Savé [DY] 60-61 E 7
Save [F] 34-35 H 7
Sâveh 44-45 G 3-4
Savigliano 36-37 BC 3
Savo 30-31 M 6-7
Savoie 34-35 L 5-6
Sâvojbolâgh = Mahābād 44-45 F 3
Savona 36-37 C 3
Savonlinna 30-31 N 7
Şavşat 46-47 K 2
Sävsjö 30-31 F 9
Savu = Pulau Sawu 52-53 H 9
Savu, Mer de – 52-53 H 8

Savukoski 30-31 N 4
Savur 46-47 J 4
Savu Sea 52-53 H 8
Şawāb, Wâdī as- 46-47 J 5
Sawahlunto 52-53 D 7
Sawara 50-51 N 5
Sawata 50-51 M 3-4
Sawdâ, Jabal as- 60-61 GH 3
Sawdirī 60-61 K 6
Şawhaţ 60-61 H 3
Şawîrah, Aş- 60-61 BC 2
Sawknah 60-61 GH 3
Sawqirah 44-45 H 7
Sawqirah, Dawhat as- 44-45 H 7
Şawrah, Aş- 62 F 4
Sâwrah, Wâdī – 60-61 D 2-3
Sawtooth Mountains 76-77 FG 3-4
Sawtooth Range 76-77 C 1-2
Sawu, Mar de – 52-53 H 8
Sawu, Pulau – 52-53 H 9
Sawuzee 52-53 H 8
Şawwân, ‘Arḑ aş- 46-47 G 7
Saxton, PA 74-75 DE 4
Say 60-61 E 6
Sayaboury = Muang Xaignabouri 52-53 D 3
Saya de Malha Bank 64-65 O 5
Şaydâ [RL] 44-45 CD 4
Sayhŭt 44-45 G 7
Saykh, Jabal as- 46-47 FG 6
Saylac 60-61 N 6
Sayn Shanda = Sajnšand 48-49 KL 3
Sayo = Dembī Dolo 60-61 LM 7
Şayq, Wâdī – 44-45 F 8
Sayre, PA 74-75 E 4
Say’ûn 44-45 F 7
Sazanit 36-37 H 5
Sāzin 46-47 N 5

Sba, Wad – – Nahr Sībū 60-61 CD 2
S’bū’, Wâd – – Nahr Sībū 60-61 CD 2

Scafell Pike 32 E 4
Scalloway 32 F 1
Scandinavië 28-29 K 4-N 1
Scandinavie 28-29 K 4-N 1
Scandinavie 28-29 K 4-N 1
Scapa Flow 32 E 2
Scappoose, OR 76-77 B 3
Scarborough 32 FG 4
Scarborough [TT] 72-73 OP 9
Ščeglovsk = Kemerovo 42-43 PQ 6
Scerpeddi, Punta – 36-37 C 6
Schaffhausen 33 D 5
Schebschi Mountains 60-61 G 7
Schefferville 70-71 X 7
Schelde 34-35 J 3
Schell Creek Range 76-77 F 6
Schenectady, NY 72-73 LM 3
Schiza 36-37 J 7
Schleswig 33 D 1
Schleswig-Holstein 33 D 1-E 2
Schlüchtern 33 DE 3
Schmidt Island = ostrov Šmidta 42-43 QR 1
Schotland 32 D 3-E 4
Schouten Island 58 d 3
Schouwen 34-35 J 3
Schrag, WA 76-77 D 2
Schuckmannsburg 64-65 F 6
Schurz, NV 76-77 D 6
Schwabach 33 E 4
Schwäbische Alb 33 D 5-E 4
Schwäbisch Gmünd 33 DE 4
Schwäbisch Hall 33 DE 4
Schwandorf 33 F 4
Schwaner, Pegunungan – 52-53 F 7
Schwarze Elster 33 FG 3
Schwarzer Volta = Black Volta 60-61 D 7
Schwarzwald 33 D 4-5
Schwatka Mountains 70-71 EF 4
Schweinfurt 33 E 3
Schweizergletscher 24 B 32-33
Schwerin 33 E 2
Schwyz 33 D 5
Sciacca 36-37 C 3
Scicli 36-37 F 7
Scilly, Isles of – 32 C 3
Scipio, UT 76-77 G 6
Scone 58 e 5
Scoresby Land 19 B 21

Scoresby Sund [Grönland, ∪] 19 B 20-21
Scoresbysund [Grönland, ●] 19 B 20-21
Scotia, CA 76-77 AB 5
Scotia, Dorsal del – 22-23 G 8
Scotia, Seuil de la – 22-23 G 8
Scotia Ridge 22-23 G 8
Scotiarug 22-23 G 8
Scotland 32 D 3-E 4
Scotland Neck, NC 74-75 E 6
Scotstown 74-75 H 2
Scott 24 B 17-18
Scott, Cape – 70-71 L 7
Scott, Mount – [USA → Crater Lake] 72-73 B 3
Scott, Mount – [USA ↓ Pengra Pass] 76-77 BC 4
Scott Glacier [Antarctica, Dronning Maud fjellkjede] 24 A 21-23
Scott Glacier [Antarctica, Knox Land] 24 C 11
Scott Inlet 70-71 WX 3
Scott Island 24 C 19
Scott Range 24 C 5-6
Scott Reef 56-57 D 2
Scottsbluff, NE 72-73 F 3
Scottsdale 56-57 J 8
Scottsville, VA 74-75 D 6
Scranton, PA 72-73 LM 3
Ščuč’a 38-39 N 2
Ščučinsk 42-43 MN 7
Scunthorpe 32 FG 5
Seferihisar 46-47 B 3
Sefīd, Kūh-e – 46-47 M 5-N 6
Sefid Rûd 46-47 N 4
Sefton, Restinga de – 69 BC 6
Segendy 38-39 K 7
Segesta 36-37 E 7
Segeža 42-43 EF 5
Segguedim = Séguédine 60-61 G 4
Sego, UT 76-77 J 6
Segorbe 34-35 G 9
Ségou 60-61 C 6
Segovary 38-39 H 3
Segovia 34-35 E 8
Segovia, Rio – = Río Coco 72-73 K 9
Segozero 38-39 F 3
Segré 34-35 G 5
Segre, Río – 34-35 H 8
Segu = Ségou 60-61 C 6
Séguédine 60-61 G 4
Séguéla 60-61 C 7
Seguin, TX 72-73 G 6
Segura, Río – 34-35 G 9
Segura, Sierra de – 34-35 F 9-10
Sehirköy = Şarköy 46-47 B 2
Sehit Nusretbey 46-47 H 4
Seiland 30-31 K 2
Seinäjoki 30-31 K 6
Seine 34-35 H 4
Seine, Baie de la – 34-35 G 4
Seishin = Ch’öngjin 48-49 OP 3
Seishū = Ch’öngju 48-49 O 4
Seistan = Sīstān 44-45 J 4
Seiyit, Sararât – = Bi’r Sararât Sayyâl 62 F 6
Sejm 38-39 F 5
Sejmčan 42-43 d 5
Sejny 33 L 1
Sejrī, Bîr – = Bi’r Sajarī 46-47 H 6
Seke 64-65 F 2
Sekenke 64-65 H 3
Şeki 38-39 J 7
Sekiu, WA 76-77 A 1
Sekondi-Takoradi 60-61 D 7-8
Selah, WA 76-77 C 2
Selatan, Tanjung – 52-53 F 7
Selawik, AK 70-71 DE 4
Selawik Lake 70-71 DE 4
Selayar, Pulau – 52-53 H 8
Selbu 30-31 D 6
Selby 32 F 5
Seldovia, AK 70-71 F 6
Selemdža 42-43 YZ 7
Selemiyé = Salamīyah 46-47 G 5
Selendi 46-47 C 3
Selenge [Mongolia, ●] 48-49 K 2
Selenge [Mongolia, ☆ = 11 ◁] 48-49 K 2
Selenga mörön 48-49 J 2
Selenn’ach 42-43 a 4
Selenodolsk = Zelenodol’sk 42-43 HJ 6

Şebinkarahisar 46-47 H 2
Sebring, FL 74-75 c 3
Sebta = Ceuta 60-61 CD 1
Sebuku, Pulau – 52-53 G 6
Sebuku, Teluk – 52-53 G 6
Seburi-yama 50-51 H 6
Secen Chaan = Öndörchaan 48-49 L 2
Secen Chaan = Öndörchaan 48-49 L 2
Sechuan = Sichuan 48-49 J 5-6
Sechura 78-79 C 6
Sechura, Bahía de – 78-79 C 6
Secunderabad 44-45 M 7
Sedan 34-35 K 4
Sedan [AUS] 56-57 G 6
Sedel’nikovo 42-43 O 6
Sêdôk 38-39 H 7
Sêdôm 46-47 F 7
Sedona, AZ 76-77 H 8
Sedov, Fosse – 19 A
Sedova, pik – 42-43 J 3
Sedovdiep 19 A
Sedow, Fosa de – 19 A
Seeheim [Namibia] 64-65 E 8
Seeis 64-65 H 3
Seeley Lake, MT 76-77 G 2
Sefadu = Koidu-Sefadu 60-61 B 7

Seletyteniz, ozero – = ozero Siletiteniz 42-43 N 7
Seleucia = Silifke 44-45 C 3
Seleucia Pieria = Samandağ 46-47 F 5
Selfoss 30-31 c 3
Selibabi 60-61 B 6
Seliger, ozero – 38-39 F 4
Seligman, AZ 76-77 G 8
Selim 46-47 K 2
Selīma, Wâhat es – – Wâhat Şalīmah 60-61 K 4
Selimiye 46-47 B 4
Seling Tsho 48-49 FG 5
Selinus 36-37 E 7
Seliphug Gonpa 48-49 E 5
Seljord 30-31 C 8
Selkirk [CDN] 70-71 R 7
Selkirk Mountains 70-71 N 7-8
Selleck, WA 76-77 C 2
Sells, AZ 76-77 H 10
Selma, AL 72-73 J 5
Selma, CA 76-77 D 7
Selma, NC 74-75 D 7
Selous Game Reserve 64-65 J 4
Selukwe 64-65 H 6
Selva 80 D 3
Selvagens, Ilhas – 60-61 A 2
Selvas 69 DE 3
Selway River 76-77 F 2
Selwyn 56-57 H 4
Selwyn Mountains 70-71 KL 5
Selwyn Range 56-57 GH 4
Seman 36-37 H 5
Semarang 52-53 F 8
Semau, Pulau – 52-53 H 9
Sembodja = Samboja 52-53 G 7
Şemdinli 46-47 L 4
Semenanjung 52-53 K 7
Semeru, Gunung – 52-53 F 8
Semeuluë, Pulau – = Pulau Simeulue 52-53 BC 6
Semeyen = Simên 60-61 M 6
Semipalatinsk 42-43 OP 7
Semirara Islands 52-53 H 4
Semka = Sangâ 52-53 C 2
Semmering 33 GH 5
Semnān [IR, ●] 44-45 G 3
Semnan [IR, ☆] 44-45 GH 3
Semois 34-35 K 4
Šemonaicha 42-43 P 7
Sem’onov 38-39 H 4
Semu 63 C 3
Senador Pompeu 78-79 LM 6
Senaisla = Sunaysilah 46-47 J 5
Sena Madureira 78-79 F 6
Senanga 64-65 F 6
Šenber 42-43 M 8
Sendai [J, Kagoshima] 50-51 GH 7
Sendai [J, Miyagi] 48-49 R 4
Sene = Pru 60-61 D 7
Seneca, OR 76-77 D 3
Seneca, SC 74-75 B 7
Seneca Falls, NY 74-75 E 3
Seneca Lake 74-75 E 3
Sénégal 60-61 AB 6
Sénégal [SN, ~] 60-61 B 5
Sénégal [SN, ★] 60-61 AB 6
Sengejskij, ostrov – 42-43 HJ 4
Sengge Khamba 48-49 DE 5
Sengilej 38-39 J 5
Sengwe 64-65 G 6
Senhor do Bonfim 78-79 L 7
Senigàllia 36-37 E 4
Senijân 46-47 N 5
Senirkent 46-47 D 3
Senj 36-37 F 3
Senja 30-31 G 3
Senkaku-shotó 48-49 N 6
Senkaku syotó = Senkaku-shotó 48-49 N 6
Šenkursk 42-43 G 5
Senlis 34-35 J 4
Senmonorom 52-53 E 4
Sennār = Sannâr 60-61 L 6
Seno 52-53 DE 3
Sens 34-35 J 4
Senta 36-37 HJ 3
Sentery 64-65 G 4
Sentinel, AZ 76-77 G 9
Sentinel Range 24 B 28
Sento-Sé 78-79 L 6
Senyurt 46-47 J 4
Seo de Urgel 34-35 H 7
Seoni 44-45 M 6
Seoul = Sôul 48-49 O 4
Separ, NM 76-77 J 9
Separation Well 56-57 D 4
Separ Shâhâbâd 46-47 MN 5
Šepetovka 38-39 E 5

Sepik River 52-53 M 7
Sepone 52-53 E 3
Sepopa 64-65 F 6
Sep'o-ri 50-51 F 3
Sept-Îles 70-71 X 7-8
Sequim, WA 76-77 B 1
Sequoia National Park 72-73 C 4
Serachs 44-45 J 3
Şerafettin Dağları 46-47 J 3
Seram [RI] 52-53 JK 7
Seram, Mar de – 52-53 JK 7
Seram, Mer de – 52-53 JK 7
Seram-Laut, Kepulauan – 52-53 K 7
Serampore 44-45 O 6
Seramzee 52-53 JK 7
Serang 52-53 E 8
Serâyâ = Sarâyah 46-47 F 5
Serbia 36-37 H 3-J 4
Serbie 36-37 H 3-J 4
Serbka 36-37 O 2
Serdar = Kaypak 46-47 G 4
Serdéles = Sardalas 60-61 G 3
Serdobsk 38-39 HJ 5
Serebr'ansk 42-43 P 8
Serefiye 46-47 G 2
Şereflikoçhişar 46-47 E 3
Seremban 52-53 D 6
Serena, La – [E] 34-35 E 9
Serena, La – [RCH] 80 B 3
Serengeti National Park 64-65 HJ 3
Serengeti Plain 63 C 3
Serenje 64-65 GH 5
Sergeja Kirova, ostrova – 42-43 QR 2
Sergijev Posad 42-43 F 6
Serginskij 42-43 LM 5
Sergiopolis = Rişâfah 46-47 H 5
Sergipe 78-79 M 7
Seria 52-53 F 6
Seribu, Kepulauan – 52-53 E 7-8
Sérifos 36-37 L 7
Serik 46-47 D 4
Seringa, Serra da – 78-79 J 6
Şerkaly 42-43 M 5
Šerlovaja Gora 42-43 W 7
Sermata, Pulau – 52-53 J 8
Sermilik 70-71 d 4
Serov 42-43 L 6
Serowe 64-65 G 7
Serpa 34-35 D 10
Serpa Pinto = Menongue 64-65 E 5
Serpeddì, Punta – 36-37 C 6
Serpiente, Boca de la – 78-79 G 2-3
Serpuchov 38-39 G 5
Serra Geral [BR, Santa Catarina] 80 F 3
Serra Geral [BR, Rio Grande do Sul ↖ Porto Alegre] 80 F 3
Sérrai 36-37 K 5
Serrana Bank = Banco Serrana 78-79 CD 2
Serra Talhada 78-79 M 6
Serrezuela 80 C 4
Serrinha [BR ↑ Feira de Santana] 78-79 M 7
Sertânia 78-79 M 6
Sertão 78-79 L 7-M 6
Serua, Pulau – 52-53 K 8
Serule 64-65 G 7
Serxü 48-49 H 5
Sese Islands 64-65 H 3
Sesepe 52-53 J 7
Sesfontein 64-65 D 6
Sesheke 64-65 FG 6
Sesimbra 34-35 C 9
Sessa Aurunca 36-37 EF 5
Sestroreck 42-43 DE 5
Setana 48-49 Q 3
Sète 34-35 J 7
Sétéia 36-37 M 8
Sete Quedas, Salto das – [BR, Rio Teles Pires] 78-79 H 6
Setermoen 30-31 H 3
Setesdal 30-31 B 8
Sétif = Saṭīf 60-61 F 1
Seto 50-51 L 5
Seto-naikai 48-49 P 5
Seṭṭât = Saṭṭât 60-61 C 2
Setté Cama 64-65 C 3
Sette-Daban, chrebet – 42-43 a 5
Setúbal 34-35 C 9
Setúbal, Baia de – 34-35 C 9
Seuil Neo-zélandais 56-57 M 5-7
Seuil Sibérien Oriental 19 B 36-1
Seul = Sŏul 48-49 O 4
Seul, Lac – 70-71 S 7
Sevan 38-39 H 7
Sevan, ozero – 38-39 J 7
Sevastopol' 38-39 F 7
Seven Emu 56-57 G 3
Seven Islands = Sept-Îles 70-71 X 7-8
Severn 32 E 6
Severnaja 42-43 QR 4
Severnaja Dvina 42-43 G 5
Severnaja Semlja = Severnaja Zeml'a 42-43 ST 1-2
Severnaja Sos'va 42-43 L 5
Severnaja Zeml'a 42-43 ST 1-2
Severnoje [SU ↑ Samara] 42-43 O 6
Severn River 70-71 T 6-7
Severnyj 42-43 LM 4
Severnyj čink = Donyztau 42-43 K 8
Severnyje uvaly 42-43 HJ 5-6
Severnyj Ural 42-43 K 5-6
Severobajkal'sk 44-45 UV 6
Severo-Bajkal'skoje nagorje 42-43 UV 6
Severodoneck 38-39 GH 6
Severodvinsk 42-43 FG 5
Severo-Jenisejskij 42-43 RS 5
Severo-Kuril'sk 42-43 de 7
Severo-Sibirskaja nizmennost' 42-43 P-X 3
Severouralsk 38-39 LM 3
Sevier Desert 76-77 G 6
Sevier Lake 76-77 G 6
Sevier River 72-73 D 4
Sevierville 74-75 B 7
Sevilla 34-35 E 10
Sevlievo 36-37 L 4
Sèvre 34-35 G 5
Sevsib 42-43 M 6
Sewa 60-61 B 7
Seward, AK 70-71 G 5-6
Seward Peninsula 70-71 CD 4
Sewell, Lake – = Canyon Ferry Reservoir 76-77 H 2
Seychellen 64-65 L-N 4
Seychelles 66 M 8
Seychelles 64-65 L-N 4
Seydhisfjördhur 30-31 fg 2
Seydişehir 46-47 D 4
Seyhan = Adana 44-45 D 3
Seyhan Nehri 44-45 D 3
Seyitgazi 46-47 D 3
Seyla' = Saylac 60-61 N 6
Seymour [AUS] 58 G 6
Seymour, IN 72-73 JK 4
Seyne-sur-Mer, la – 34-35 K 7
Sezze 36-37 E 5
Sfax = Şafâqis 60-61 FG 2
Sfîntu Gheorghe 36-37 LM 3
Sfîntu Gheorghe, Braţul – 36-37 N 3
Sfîre = Safîrah 46-47 G 4
Sfoûk = Sufûq 46-47 J 4
Sha Alam 52-53 D 6
Shaanxi 48-49 K 4-5
Shaba 64-65 FG 4
Shabakah, Ash- [IRQ, ≅] 46-47 K 7
Shabakah, Ash- [IRQ, ●] 46-47 K 7
Shabani = Zvishavane 64-65 GH 7
Shabb, Ash- 62 C 6
Shabeelle, Webi – 60-61 N 8
Shabellaha Dhexe = 5 ◁ 60-61 b 3
Shabellaha Hoose = 3 ◁ 60-61 N 8
Shabēlle, Webi – = Wabē Shebelē Weniz 60-61 N 7
Shabunda 64-65 G 3
Shabwah 44-45 F 7
Shackleton Ice Shelf 24 C 10
Shackleton Inlet 24 A 19-17
Shackleton Range 24 A 35-1
Shādegān 46-47 N 7
Shafter, CA 76-77 D 8
Shafter, NV 76-77 F 5
Shag Rocks 80 H 8
Shaguotun 50-51 C 2
Shāh, Godār-e – 46-47 MN 5
Shahabad [IND, Maisuru] 44-45 M 7
Shahāmī 46-47 H 6
Shāhān, Kūh-e – 46-47 LM 5
Shaḥan, Wādī – = Wādī Shiḥan 44-45 G 7
Shahbā 46-47 G 6
Shahbā', Ḥarrat ash- 46-47 G 6-7
Shahdād 44-45 H 4
Shahdād, Namakzār-e – 44-45 H 4
Shāhī 44-45 G 3
Shāhī 38-39 K 8
Shahidulla Mazar 48-49 D 4
Shahpura 44-45 L 5
Shahrak 44-45 J 4
Shahr-e Bābak 44-45 GH 4
Shahredā 44-45 G 4
Shahr-e Kord 44-45 G 4
Shahrestānbālā 46-47 NO 4
Shāh Rūd [IR, ~] 46-47 NO 4
Shāhrūd [IR, ●] 44-45 GH 3
Shāhzand 46-47 N 6
Shā'ib al-Banāt, Jabal – 60-61 L 3
Sha'īt, Wādī – 62 E 5
Shajahanpur 44-45 MN 5
Shajianzi 50-51 E 2
Shaka, Ras – 63 E 3
Shakar Bolāghī = Qara Būteh 46-47 M 4
Shakh yar 48-49 E 3
Shaki 60-61 E 7
Shakir, Jazīrat – 60-61 LM 3
Shakotan misaki 50-51 b 2
Shāl 46-47 N 5
Shalaamboot 60-61 N 8
Shala Hayik 60-61 M 7
Shalar, Nahr – 46-47 L 5
Shalar Rūd = Nahr Shalar 46-47 L 5
Shallāl, Ash- [ET, ~] 60-61 L 3
Shallāl, Ash- [ET, ●] 60-61 L 3
Shallotte, NC 74-75 D 7-8
Shāmah, Ash- = Al-Ḥarrah 46-47 GH 7
Shamālī, Ash- 60-61 KL 5
Shāmbā 60-61 L 7
Shāmīyah, Ash- 46-47 L 7
Shammar, Jabal – 44-45 E 5
Shamo = Gobi 48-49 H-K 3
Shamokin, PA 74-75 E 4
Shamrock, FL 74-75 b 2
Shāmshīr = Pāveh 46-47 M 5
Shamva 64-65 H 6
Sha'nabī, Jabal ash- 60-61 F 1-2
Shanchengzhen 50-51 EF 1
Shandan 48-49 J 4
Shandī 60-61 L 5
Shandish, MI 74-75 AB 3
Shandong 48-49 M 4
Shandong Bandao 48-49 MN 4
Shangani 64-65 G 6
Shangbangcheng 50-51 B 2
Shang-chia-ho = Shangjiahe 50-51 E 2
Shang-ch'iu = Shangqiu 48-49 LM 5
Shangchuan Dao 48-49 L 7
Shangcigang = Beijingzi 50-51 DE 3
Shanghai 48-49 N 5
Shanghang 48-49 M 6-7
Shanghsien = Shang Xian 48-49 KL 5
Shangjao = Shangrao 48-49 M 6
Shangjiahe 50-51 E 2
Shangkiu = Shangqiu 48-49 LM 5
Shangqiu 48-49 LM 5
Shangrao 48-49 M 6
Shang Xian 48-49 KL 5
Shangzhi 48-49 O 2
Shanhaiguan 48-49 MN 3
Shan-hai-kuan = Shanhaiguan 50-51 BC 2
Shan-hsi = Shaanxi 48-49 L 4-5
Shaniko, OR 76-77 C 3
Shannon 32 B 5
Shannon Airport 32 B 5
Shannon Ø 19 B 20
Shannontown, SC 74-75 CD 8
Shan Pyinnei 52-53 C 2
Shanshan 48-49 G 3
Shansi = Shanxi 48-49 L 4
Shan-tan = Shandan 48-49 J 4
Shantou 48-49 M 7
Shantow = Shantou 48-49 M 7
Shantung = Shandong 48-49 M 4
Shanwa 63 C 3
Shanxi 48-49 L 4
Shanyin 48-49 L 4
Shaoguan 48-49 L 6-7
Shaohsing = Shaoxing 48-49 N 5-6
Shaotze = Wan Xian 48-49 K 5
Shaowu 48-49 M 6
Shaoxing 48-49 N 5-6
Shaoyang 48-49 L 6
Shaqlāwah 46-47 L 4
Shaqqar 60-61 C 3
Shaqrā' 44-45 F 5
Shār, Jabal – [Saudi Arabia] 62 F 4
Shā'r, Jabal – [SYR] 46-47 GH 5
Sharafkhāneh 46-47 LM 3
Sharāh, Ash- 46-47 F 7
Sharbithāt, Rā's ash- 44-45 H 7
Sharbot Lake 74-75 E 2
Shari 50-51 d 2
Shari = Chari 60-61 H 6
Shārī', Bahr ash- = Buhayrat Shārī 46-47 L 5
Shārī, Buhayrat – 46-47 L 5
Sharī'ah, Nahr ash- 46-47 F 6-7
Shārib, Ma'tan – 62 C 2
Shari-dake 50-51 d 2
Shāriqah, Ash- 44-45 GH 5
Shark Bay 56-57 B 5
Sharmah, Ash- 62 F 3-4
Sharmah, Wādī ash- = Wādī Ṣadr 62 F 3
Sharm ash-Shaykh 62 F 4
Sharm esh-Sheikh = Sharm ash-Shayh 62 F 4
Shar Mörön = Chatan gol 48-49 K 3
Sharon, PA 72-73 KL 3
Sharqāṭ, Ash- 46-47 K 5
Sharqī, Ash- 60-61 GH 6
Sharqī, Ash-Shaṭṭ ash- 60-61 DE 2
Sharqi, Jebel esh – = Jabal Lubnān ash-Sharqī 46-47 G 5-6
Sharrukīn, Dur – = Khorsabad 46-47 K 4
Shāsh, 'Irq ash- 60-61 D 3-4
Shashemenē 60-61 M 7
Shashi 48-49 L 5-6
Shasta, Mount – 72-73 B 3
Shasta Lake 76-77 B 5
Shaṭrah, Ash- 46-47 LM 7
Shau = Wādī Huwār 60-61 K 5
Shaubak, Esh- = Ash-Shawbak 46-47 F 7
Shawatun = Shaguotun 50-51 C 2
Shawbak, Ash- 46-47 F 7
Shawinigan Sud 70-71 W 8
Shawnee, OK 72-73 G 4
Shaw River 56-57 C 4
Shāwshāw, Jabal – 62 C 5
Shawville 74-75 E 2
Sha Xian 48-49 M 6
Shaykh Aḥmad 46-47 J 4
Shaykh Hilāl 46-47 G 5
Shaykh Sa'd 46-47 M 6
Shaykh Ṣalāḥ 46-47 J 4
Shaykh 'Uthmān, Ash- 44-45 EF 8
Shayōg = Shyog 44-45 M 3-4
Shāẓī, Wādī ash- 46-47 J 7
Shea 78-79 H 4
She'aiba, Ash- = Ash-Shu'aybah 46-47 M 7
Sheaville, OR 76-77 E 4
Shebelē Weniz, Webī – 60-61 N 7
Sheboygan, WI 72-73 J 3
Sheenjek River 70-71 H 4
Sheep Peak 76-77 F 7
Sheep Range 76-77 F 7
Sheffield [AUS] 58 c 2
Sheffield [GB] 32 F 5
Shefoo = Yantai 48-49 N 4
Sheḥamī = Shaḥāmī 46-47 H 6
Shê-hsien = She Xian [TJ, Anhui] 48-49 M 5-6
Shekhar Dsong 48-49 F 6
Shelār 46-47 N 6
Shelburne [CDN, Ontario] 74-75 CD 2
Shelburne Bay 56-57 H 2
Shelby, MT 76-77 H 1
Shelby, NC 72-73 K 4
Shelikof Strait 70-71 EF 6
Shell Creek [USA, Colorado] 76-77 J 5
Shelley, ID 76-77 GH 4
Shellharbour, Wollongong- 56-57 K 6
Shelter Cove, CA 76-77 A 5
Shelton, WA 76-77 B 2
Shenāfiya, Ash- = Ash-Shināfīyah 46-47 L 7
Shenandoah, PA 74-75 EF 4
Shenandoah, VA 74-75 D 5
Shenandoah Mountains 74-75 D 5
Shenandoah National Park 74-75 DE 5
Shenandoah River 74-75 DE 5
Shendam 60-61 FG 7
Shendī = Shandī 60-61 L 5
Sheng Xian 48-49 N 6
Shenmu 48-49 L 4
Shensa Dsong 48-49 FG 5
Shensi = Shaanxi 48-49 K 4-5
Shenton, Mount – 56-57 D 5
Shenyang 48-49 NO 3
Sheopuri = Shivpuri 44-45 M 5
Shepparton 56-57 HJ 7
Sherbro Island 60-61 B 7
Sherbrooke [CDN, Quebec] 70-71 W 8
Shereik = Ash-Shurayk 60-61 L 5
Sherī'ah, Nahr esh- = Nahr ash-Sharī'ah 46-47 F 6-7
Sheridan, MT 76-77 GH 3
Sheridan, OR 76-77 B 3
Sheridan, WY 72-73 E 3
Sheridan, Mount – 76-77 H 3
Sherman, TX 72-73 G 5
Sherman Inlet 70-71 R 4
Sherman Mills, ME 74-75 JK 2
Sherman Mountain 76-77 EF 5
Sherridon 70-71 Q 6
Sheṭhātha = Shithāthah 46-47 K 6
Shetland 32 FG 1
Shewa 60-61 M 7
She Xian [TJ, Anhui] 48-49 M 5-6
Sheykh Ḥoseyn 46-47 N 7
Shibām 44-45 F 7
Shibarghān 44-45 K 3
Shibata 50-51 M 4
Shibecha 50-51 d 2
Shibetsu [J ↑ Asahikawa] 50-51 c 1
Shibetsu [J ↖ Nemuro] 50-51 d 2
Shibicha, Ash- = Ash-Shabakah 46-47 K 7
Shībīgā 52-53 C 1
Shībīn al-Kawn 62 D 2
Shībīn al-Qanāṭir 62 D 2
Shib Kūh 44-45 G 5
Shibushi 50-51 H 7
Shibushi-wan 50-51 H 7
Shibutami = Tamayama 50-51 N 3
Shicheng Dao 50-51 D 3
Shickshock, Monts – = Monts Chic-Choqs 70-71 X 8
Shidād, Umm ash- = Sabkhat Abā ar-Rūs 44-45 GH 6
Shiddādī, Ash- 46-47 J 4
Shīdīyah, Ash- 46-47 FG 8
Shifshāwn 60-61 CD 1
Shiga 50-51 KL 5
Shigatse = Zhigatse 48-49 F 6
Shiḥan, Wādī – 44-45 G 7
Shih-ch'êng Tao = Shicheng Dao 50-51 D 3
Shih-ch'ien = Shiqian 48-49 K 6
Shih-ch'ü = Serxü 48-49 H 5
Shihchuan = Shiquan 48-49 K 5
Shihnan = Enshi 48-49 K 5
Shih-p'ing = Shiping 48-49 J 7
Shiḥr, Ash- 44-45 F 8
Shihtsien = Shiqian 48-49 K 6
Shijiazhuang 48-49 L 4
Shikārpūr 44-45 K 5
Shikhartse = Zhigatse 48-49 F 6
Shikine-chima 50-51 M 5
Shikk'ah, Rā's ash- 46-47 F 5
Shikoku 48-49 P 5
Shikoku sammyaku 50-51 JK 6
Shikotan-tō 48-49 S 3
Shikotsu-ko 50-51 b 2
Shilaong = Shillong 44-45 P 5
Shilchar = Silchar 44-45 P 6
Shilif [DZ, ~] 60-61 E 1
Shilif [DZ, ●] 60-61 E 1
Shillington, PA 74-75 EF 4
Shillong 44-45 P 5
Shiloguṛī = Siliguri 44-45 O 5
Shilong = Shajianzi 50-51 E 2
Shīlyah, Jabal – 60-61 F 1
Shimabara 50-51 H 6
Shimabara hantō 50-51 H 6
Shimada 50-51 M 5
Shima-hantō 50-51 L 5
Shimālīyah, Ash- = Ash-Shamālī 60-61 KL 5
Shimane 50-51 HJ 5
Shimizu 48-49 Q 4-5
Shimizu = Tosashimizu 50-51 J 6
Shimlā = Simla 44-45 M 4
Shimminato 50-51 L 4
Shimo = Kyūshū 48-49 P 5
Shimoda 50-51 M 5
Shimodate 50-51 MN 4
Shimoga 44-45 LM 8
Shimokita-hantō 48-49 R 3
Shimo-Koshiki-chima 50-51 G 7
Shimoni 64-65 JK 3
Shimonoseki 48-49 P 5
Shimono-shima 50-51 G 5
Shimoyaku = Yaku 50-51 H 7
Shimo-Yūbetsu 50-51 cd 1
Shimushiru = ostrov Simušir 42-43 d 8
Shimushu = ostrov Šumšu 42-43 e 7
Shin, Loch – 32 D 2
Shināfīyah, Ash- 46-47 L 7
Shinano gawa 50-51 M 4
Shināṣ 44-45 H 6
Shināy, Bi'r – 62 F 6
Shinbwīyan 52-53 C 1
Shīndand 44-45 J 4
Shindidāy, Jabal – 62 G 6
Shingbwiyang = Shinbwīyan 52-53 C 1
Shingishu = Sinŭiju 48-49 NO 3
Shingletown, CA 76-77 C 5
Shingu 50-51 KL 6
Shinjiang = Xinjiang Uyghur Zizhiqu 48-49 D-G 3
Shinji-ko 50-51 J 5
Shinjō 48-49 QR 4
Shinko = Chinko 60-61 J 7
Shinkolobwe 64-65 G 5
Shin-nan = Enshi 48-49 K 5
Shinnston, WV 74-75 C 5
Shinqīṭi 60-61 B 4
Shinshān, Sabkhat – 60-61 B 4
Shinshū = Chinju 48-49 O 4
Shinyanga 64-65 H 3
Shiobara 50-51 MN 4
Shiogama 50-51 N 3
Shiono-misaki 50-51 K 6
Shioya-misaki 50-51 N 4
Shiping 48-49 J 7
Shippensburg, PA 74-75 DE 4
Shiprock, NW 76-77 J 7
Shiqian 48-49 K 6
Shiqq, Ḥāssī – 60-61 B 3
Shiquan 48-49 K 5
Shiquan He = Sengge Khamba 48-49 DE 5
Shirahama 50-51 K 6
Shirakami-saki 50-51 MN 2
Shirakawa 50-51 N 4
Shirane-san 50-51 LM 5
Shiranuka 50-51 cd 2
Shiraoi 50-51 b 2
Shirataka 50-51 MN 3
Shīrāz 44-45 G 5
Shiraze-hyōga 24 B 4-5
Shirbīn 62 D 2
Shire 64-65 HJ 6
Shiretoko hantō 50-51 d 1-2
Shiretoko-misaki 50-51 d 1
Shīrīn Sū 46-47 N 5
Shiritoru = Makarov 42-43 b 8
Shiriya-saki 50-51 N 2
Shiroishi 50-51 N 3-4
Shirotori 50-51 L 5
Shirqāṭ, Ash- = Ash-Sharqāṭ 46-47 K 5
Shishikui 50-51 K 6
Shishmaref, AK 70-71 CD 4
Shitai 48-49 M 5
Shithāthah 46-47 K 6
Shivālak Pahāṛiyān = Siwālik Range 44-45 M 4-N 5
Shivamagga = Shimoga 44-45 LM 8
Shivpuri 44-45 M 5
Shivwits Indian Reservation 76-77 FG 7
Shivwits Plateau 76-77 G 7
Shiwa Ngandu 63 BC 5
Shizukawa 50-51 N 3
Shizunai 50-51 c 2
Shizuoka 50-51 LM 5
Shkodër 36-37 H 4
Shkumbîn 36-37 H 5
Shmayṭīyah 46-47 H 5
Shoa = Shewa 60-61 M 7
Shōbara 50-51 J 5
Shōdo-shima 50-51 K 5
Shodu 48-49 H 5
Shokambetsu-dake 50-51 b 2
Shokotsu 50-51 c 1
Sholāpur = Solapur 44-45 M 7
Shōra, Ash- = Ash-Shūr'a 46-47 K 5
Shorapur 44-45 M 7
Shortland Island 52-53 hj 6
Shoshone, CA 76-77 EF 8
Shoshone, ID 76-77 F 4
Shoshone Falls 76-77 FG 4
Shoshone Mountain 76-77 E 7
Shoshone Mountains 72-73 C 3-4
Shō-Tombetsu 50-51 c 1
Shott el Jerid = Shaṭṭ al-Jarīd 60-61 F 2
Shoup, ID 76-77 F 3

Shoup 217

Showak = Shuwak 60-61 M 6
Show Low, AZ 76-77 H 8
Shreveport, LA 72-73 H 5
Shrewsbury 32 E 5
Shrīkākulam = Srikakulam 44-45 M 7
Shrirampur = Serampore 44-45 O 6
Shrīrangam = Srirangam 44-45 M 8
Shrīvardhan = Srivardhan 44-45 L 7
Shuaiba = Ash-Shu'aybah 46-47 M 7
Shuangcheng 48-49 NO 2
Shuang-ch'êng = Shuangcheng 48-49 NO 2
Shuangliao 48-49 N 3
Shu'aybah, Ash- 46-47 M 7
Shu'bah, Ash- 46-47 L 8
Shufu = Qāshqār 48-49 CD 4
Shugra = Shuqrā 44-45 F 8
Shuguri Falls 63 D 5
Shuifeng Supong Hu = Supung Hu 50-51 E 2
Shuikou 48-49 M 6
Shūkāt ath-Thalātha, Rā's ash- 60-61 D 1
Shumagin Islands 70-71 DE 6
Shumlūl, Ash- = Ma'qalā' 44-45 F 5
Shungnak, AK 70-71 EF 4
Shunking = Nanchong 48-49 JK 5
Shunsen = Ch'unch'ŏn 48-49 O 4
Shunteh = Xingtai 48-49 L 4
Shuqrā' 44-45 F 8
Shūr, Āb-e – 46-47 N 7
Shūr'a, Ash- 46-47 K 5
Shurayf 44-45 D 5
Shurayk 60-61 L 5
Shurugwi 64-65 GH 6
Shūsh 46-47 N 6
Shushan = Susa 46-47 N 6
Shūshtar 44-45 F 4
Shuwak 60-61 M 6
Shuwayyib, Ash- 46-47 MN 7
Shuyang 48-49 M 5
Shuzenji 50-51 M 5
Shwangcheng = Shuangcheng 48-49 NO 2
Shwangliao = Liaoyuan 48-49 NO 3
Shwebō 52-53 C 2
Shyog 44-45 M 3-4
Shyopur = Shivpuri 44-45 M 5

Sīāh, Kūh-e – = Kūh-e Marzu 46-47 M 6
Siāhdehān = Tākestān 46-47 NO 4
Siakwan = Xiaguan 48-49 J 6
Sialcote = Siyālkoṭ 44-45 LM 4
Sialkot = Siyālkoṭ 44-45 LM 4
Siam = Thaïlande 52-53 CD 3
Siam = Thailandia 52-53 CD 3
Sian = Xi'an 48-49 K 5
Siangfan = Fangcheng 48-49 L 5
Siangtan = Xiangtan 48-49 L 6
Siangyang = Xiangyang 48-49 L 5
Siapa, Rio – 78-79 FG 4
Siargao Island 52-53 J 4-5
Siau, Pulau – 52-53 J 6
Šiauliai 30-31 K 10
Sībah, As- 46-47 N 7
Siba'ī, Jabal as- 62 EF 5
Sibā'īyah, As- 62 E 5
Şibaj 42-43 K 7
Šibenik 36-37 FG 4
Siberia 42-43 N-W 5
Siberia Central, Meseta de – 42-43 R-W 4-5
Siberia Oriental, Mar de – 42-43 c-j 3
Siberia Oriental, Ramal de – 19 B 36-1
Siberië 42-43 N-W 5
Sibérie 42-43 N-W 5
Sibérie Centrale, Plateau de – 42-43 R-W 4-5
Sibérie Orientale, Mer de – 42-43 c-j 3
Siberut, Pulau – 52-53 C 7
Siberut, Selat – 52-53 C 7
Sibī 44-45 K 5
Sibir'akova, ostrov – 42-43 OP 3
Sibircevo 42-43 Z 9
Sibiti [EAT] 63 C 3
Sibiti [RCA] 64-65 D 3
Sibiu 36-37 KL 3
Sibolga 52-53 C 6
Sibu 52-53 F 6
Sibū, Nahr – 60-61 CD 2
Sibū 'Gharb, As- 62 E 6
Sibutu Group 52-53 G 6
Sibuyan Island 52-53 H 4
Sibuyan Sea 52-53 H 4
Sibyŏn-ni 50-51 F 3
Sicasica 78-79 F 8
Sicasso = Sikasso 60-61 C 6
Sichang = Xichang 48-49 J 6
Sichem = Nābulus 46-47 F 6
Sichota-Alin = Sichotė Alin' 42-43 a 8-Z 9
Sichotė Alin' 42-43 a 8-Z 9
Šichrany = Kanaš 42-43 H 6
Sichuan 48-49 J 5-6
Sichwan = Xichuan 48-49 L 5
Sicile = Sicilia 36-37 EF 7
Sicilia 36-37 EF 7
Sicily = Sicilia 36-37 EF 7
Sicuani 78-79 E 7
Sīdamo 60-61 MN 8
Sidamo-Borana = Sīdamo 60-61 MN 8
Sidaogou 50-51 F 2
Sideby 30-31 J 6
Sidērókastron 36-37 K 5
Sideros, Akrōtērion – 36-37 M 8
Sīdī Abd'ar Rahman 62 C 2
Sīdī Ban al-'Abbās 60-61 DE 1
Sīdī Barrānī 60-61 K 2
Sidi-bel-Abbès = Sīdī Ban al-'Abbās 60-61 DE 1
Sīdī Mirwân 60-61 JK 1
Sīdī Qāsim 60-61 CD 2
Sīdī Sālim 62 D 2
Sidley, Mount – 24 B 24
Sidney 76-77 B 1
Sidney, OH 74-75 A 4
Sidr, As- 60-61 H 2
Sidr, Wādī – 62 E 3
Sidra = As-Surt 60-61 H 2-3
Sidra, Golfo de – = Khalīj as-Surt 60-61 H 2
Sidra, Gulf of – = Khalīj as-Surt 60-61 H 2
Sidra, Khalig – = Khalīj as-Surt 60-61 H 2
Sidrolândia 78-79 HJ 9
Siedlce 33 L 2
Sieg 33 C 3
Siegen 33 D 3
Siemiatycze 33 L 2
Siem Reap 52-53 D 4
Siena 36-37 D 4
Sienyang = Xianyang 48-49 K 5
Sieradz 33 J 3
Sierpc 33 JK 2
Sierra Blanca Peak 72-73 E 5
Sierra Colorada 80 C 6
Sierra de Outes 34-35 C 7
Sierra Gorda 80 C 2
Sierra Grande [RA, Río Negro ●] 80 C 6
Sierra Lenona, Ramal de – 22-23 HJ 5
Sierra Leona 60-61 B 7
Sierra Leona, Cuenca de – 22-23 HJ 5
Sierra Leone, Bassin de – 22-23 HJ 5
Sierra Leone, Seuil de – 22-23 HJ 5
Sierra Leone Basin 22-23 HJ 5
Sierra Leonebekken 22-23 HJ 5
Sierra Leonedrempel 22-23 HJ 5
Sierra Leone Rise 22-23 HJ 5
Sierra Madre [MEX] 72-73 H 8
Sierra Madre [RP] 52-53 H 3
Sierra Madre del Sur 72-73 FG 8
Sierra Madre Mountains 76-77 CD 8
Sierra Madre Occidental 72-73 E 5-F 7
Sierra Madre Oriental 72-73 F 6-G 7
Sierra Morena 34-35 D 10-E 9
Sierra Nevada 34-35 F 10
Sierra Nevada [USA] 72-73 BC 4
Sierra Pinta 76-77 G 9
Sierras Pampeanas 80 C 3
Siesta Key 74-75 b 3
Sifnos 36-37 L 7
Sifton Pass 70-71 LM 6
Sig 38-39 F 2
Sighetul Marmatiei 36-37 KL 2
Sighişoara 36-37 L 2
Sigli 52-53 C 5
Siglufjördhur 30-31 d 1
Signal Peak 76-77 FG 9
Signy 24 C 32
Sigoor 63 C 2
Sigtuna 30-31 GH 8
Siguiri 60-61 C 6
Sigulda 30-31 L 9
Sigurd, UT 76-77 H 6
Sihsien = She Xian 48-49 M 5-6
Sihsien = Xi Xian [TJ, Shanxi] 48-49 L 4
Siilinjärvi 30-31 M 6
Siinai = Sīnā' 60-61 L 3
Siirt 44-45 E 3
Sijerdijelach Jur'ach = Batamaj 42-43 YZ 5
Sijiazi = Laohushan 50-51 BC 2
Sikandarābād = Secunderabad 44-45 M 7
Sikao 52-53 C 5
Sikasso 60-61 C 6
Sikefti = Albayrak 46-47 KL 3
Sikem = Nābulus 46-47 F 6
Sikhim = Sikkim 44-45 O 5
Sikhiu 52-53 D 4
Siking = Xi'an 48-49 K 5
Sikinos 36-37 L 7
Sikkim 44-45 O 5
Sikoku = Shikoku 48-49 P 5
Sikotan tō = Shikotan-tō 48-49 S 3
Sikt'ach 42-43 X 4
Sikyṓn 36-37 K 7
Sil 34-35 D 7
Sila, La – 36-37 G 6
Silasjaure 30-31 G 3-4
Şile 46-47 C 2
Šilega 42-43 GH 5
Siler City, NC 74-75 D 7
Silesia 33 G-J 3
Silésie 33 G-J 3
Siletiteniz, ozero – 42-43 N 7
Silezië 33 G-J 3
Silfke = Silifke 44-45 C 3
Silgarhi Doti 44-45 N 5
Silhat 44-45 P 5-6
Silhouette Island 64-65 MN 3
Silifke 44-45 C 3
Siligir 42-43 V 4
Siliguri 44-45 O 5
Silistra 36-37 M 3
Silivri 46-47 C 2
Siljan 30-31 F 7
Šilka 42-43 W 7
Šilkan 42-43 c 6
Silkeborg 30-31 C 9
Silleiro, Cabo – 34-35 C 7
Sillyŏng 50-51 G 4
Silopi 46-47 K 4
Siltou 60-61 H 5
Šilutė 30-31 J 10
Silvan 46-47 J 3
Silverbell, AZ 76-77 H 9
Silverbow, MT 76-77 G 2-3
Silver City 72-73 b 2
Silver City, ID 76-77 E 4
Silver City, NM 72-73 E 5
Silver City, UT 76-77 G 6
Silver Creek 76-77 D 4
Silver Creek, NY 74-75 D 3
Silver Lake, CA 76-77 EF 8
Silver Lake, OR 76-77 C 4
Silverpeak, NV 76-77 E 7
Silver Peak Range 76-77 E 7
Silverton 56-57 H 6
Silverton, OR 76-77 B 3
Silves 34-35 C 10
Silvies River 76-77 D 4
Silwa Baḥarī = Salwá Baḥrī 62 E 5
Simanggang 52-53 F 6
Simanovsk 42-43 Y 7
Simao 48-49 J 7
Simav 46-47 C 3
Simav Çayı 46-47 C 3
Simbillâwein, Es- = As-Sinbillāwayn 62 DE 2
Simbirsk = Ujanovsk 42-43 H 7
Simcoe 74-75 CD 3
Simcoe, Lake – 70-71 V 9
Simēn 60-61 M 6
Simeulue, Pulau – 52-53 BC 6
Simferopol' 38-39 F 7
Simḥām, Jabal as- 44-45 GH 7
Simingan = Samangān 44-45 K 3
Simiti 78-79 E 3
Simi Valley, CA 76-77 D 8
Simiyu 63 C 3
Simizu = Shimizu 48-49 Q 4-5
Simla 44-45 M 4
Simms, MT 76-77 GH 2
Simnij bereg 38-39 H 2
Simokita hantō = Shimokita-hantō 48-49 R 3
Simola 30-31 MN 7
Simonoseki = Shimonoseki 48-49 P 5
Simonstad 64-65 E 9
Simonstown = Simonstad 64-65 E 9
Simplício Mendes 78-79 L 6
Simplon 33 CD 5
Simpson Desert 56-57 G 4-5
Simpson Islands 70-71 O 5
Simpson Peninsula 70-71 T 4
Simpson Strait 70-71 R 4
Simrishamn 30-31 F 10
Simular = Pulau Simeulue 52-53 BC 6
Simušir, ostrov – 48-49 T 2
Sīnā' [ET] 60-61 L 3
Sinabang 52-53 C 6
Sinadhapo = Dhuusa Maareeb 60-61 b 2
Sinai = Sīnā' 60-61 L 3
Sinai, Peninsula de – = Sīnā' 60-61 L 3
Sinaï, Presqu'île du – = Sīnā' 60-61 L 3
Sinai Peninsula = Sīnā' 60-61 L 3
Sinaloa 72-73 E 6-7
Sinan 48-49 K 6
Sinanju 50-51 E 3
Sinanpaşa 46-47 CD 3
Sinaûen = Sināwan 60-61 G 2
Sināwan 60-61 G 2
Sinbillāwayn, As- 62 DE 2
Sincan 46-47 GH 3
Sincanlı = Sinanpaşa 46-47 CD 3
Sincelejo 78-79 DE 3
Sinch'ang 50-51 G 2
Sinch'ang-ni 50-51 F 3
Sincheng = Xingren 48-49 K 6
Sinch'ŏn 50-51 E 3
Sincik 46-47 H 3
Sinclair, Lake – 74-75 B 8
Sind 44-45 M 5
Sind = Sindh 44-45 K 5
Sinda = Sindh 44-45 K 5
Sindangbarang 52-53 E 8
Sindelfingen 33 D 4
Sindh 44-45 K 5
Sındıran = Yenice 46-47 E 3
Sındırğı 46-47 C 3
Sin-do 50-51 DE 3
Šindy = Sajmak 44-45 L 3
Sinelnikovo 38-39 G 6
Sines 34-35 C 10
Sines, Cabo de – 34-35 C 10
Singah = Sinjah 60-61 L 6
Si-ngan = Xi'an 48-49 K 5
Singapore 52-53 DE 6
Singapore, Strait of – 52-53 DE 6
Singapour 52-53 DE 6
Singaraja 52-53 G 8
Singatoka 52-53 a 2
Sing Buri 52-53 D 3-4
Singen 33 D 5
Singida 64-65 H 3
Singkawang 52-53 E 6
Singkep, Pulau – 52-53 DE 7
Singkil 52-53 C 6
Singleton 56-57 K 6
Singleton, Mount – 56-57 F 4
Singora = Songkhla 52-53 D 5
Sin'gosan 50-51 F 3
Singtai = Xingtai 48-49 L 4
Sin'gye 50-51 F 3
Sinhbhūm = Singhbhum 44-45 NO 6
Sin-hiang = Xinxiang 48-49 LM 4
Sinhsien = Xin Xian 48-49 L 4
Sining = Xining 48-49 J 4
Siniscola 36-37 CD 5
Sinjah 60-61 L 6
Sinjai 52-53 GH 8
Sinjār 46-47 J 4
Sinjār, Jabal – 46-47 JK 4
Sin-kalp'ajin 50-51 F 2
Sinkāt 60-61 M 5
Sinkiang = Xinjiang 48-49 L 4
Sinkiang = Xinjiang Uygur Zizhiqu 48-49 D-F 3
Sinlo = Xinle 48-49 LM 4
Sinmak 50-51 F 3
Sinmi-do 50-51 E 3
Sinmin = Xinmin 50-51 D 1-2
Sinnamary [Guyane Française, ●] 78-79 J 3
Sinneh = Sanandaj 44-45 F 3
Sinhhabhūm = Singhbhum 44-45 NO 6
Sinnūris 62 D 3
Sinnyŏng = Sillyŏng 50-51 G 4
Sinoe = Greenville 60-61 C 7-8
Sinola = Chinhoyi 64-65 GH 6
Sinop 44-45 D 2
Sinope = Sinop 44-45 D 2
Sinoquipe 76-77 H 10
Sinp'o 48-49 O 3-4
Sinquim = Xi'an 48-49 K 5
Sinsiang = Xinxiang 48-49 LM 4
Sintang 52-53 F 6
Sint Eustatius 72-73 O 8
Sint Helenabaai 64-65 E 9
Sintjiang = Xinjiang Uygur Zizhiqu 48-49 D-F 3
Sint Luciameer 64-65 H 8
Sintra 34-35 C 9
Sintra [BR] 78-79 G 6
Sintsai = Xincai 48-49 LM 5
Sinwŏn-ni 50-51 E 3
Sinyang = Xinyang 48-49 LM 5
Sinzyō = Shinjō 48-49 QR 4
Sió 33 J 5
Sioma 64-65 F 6
Sion 33 C 5
Sioux City, IA 72-73 GH 3
Sioux Falls, SD 72-73 G 3
Sioux Lookout 70-71 S 7
Šipčenski prohod 36-37 LM 4
Siphaqeni 64-65 GH 9
Siphaqeni 64-65 GH 9
Siping 48-49 N 3
Sipitang 52-53 G 5-6
Siple, Mount – 24 B 24
Sipolilo = Chiporiro 64-65 H 6
Sipora, Pulau – = Pulau Sipura 52-53 C 7
Sip Sông Châu Thai 52-53 D 2
Sip Sông Châu Thai 52-53 D 2
Sipura, Pulau – 52-53 C 7
Siquijor Island 52-53 H 5
Siquisique 78-79 F 2
Šira [SU] 42-43 QR 7
Sira [N, ~] 30-31 B 8
Sira [N, ●] 30-31 B 8
Siracuas 80 D 2
Siracusa 36-37 F 7
Šir'ajevo 36-37 O 2
Siran 46-47 H 3
Sir Edward Pellew Group 56-57 G 3
Siret [R, ~] 36-37 M 3
Siret [R, ●] 36-37 M 2
Sirḥān, Wādī as- 44-45 D 4
Siria 44-45 D 4
Sirirskaja ravnina 42-43 L-P 5-6
Sir James MacBrien, Mount – 70-71 KL 5
Sīrjān 44-45 H 5
Sırkıntı 46-47 F 4
Şırnak 46-47 K 4
Sirr, Nafūd as- 44-45 E 5-F 6
Sirsa 44-45 LM 5
Sirte = Khalīj Surt 60-61 H 2
Sirte, Gulf of – = Khalīj Surt 60-61 H 2
Sir Thomas, Mount – 56-57 EF 5
Sirtica = As-Surt 60-61 H 2-3
Şirvan 46-47 K 3
Sīrvān, Rūd-e – 46-47 M 5
Sirwān 46-47 LM 5
Sirwān, Ābī – 46-47 L 5
Sirya = Zeytinlik 46-47 JK 2
Sisak 36-37 G 3
Si Sa Ket 52-53 D 3-4
Sishen 64-65 F 8
Sisimiut 70-71 Za 4
Siskiyou, OR 76-77 B 4
Siskiyou Mountains 76-77 B 4-5
Sisophon 52-53 D 4
Sīstān 44-45 J 4
Sīstān, Daryācheh – 44-45 HJ 4
Sīstān va Balūchestān 44-45 H 4-J 5
Sisteron 34-35 K 6
Sisters, OR 76-77 C 3
Sithōnia 36-37 K 5-6
Sítio da Abadia 78-79 K 7
Sitka, AK 70-71 J 6
Sitkaing 52-53 C 2
Sitkaing Taing 52-53 B 2-C 1
Šitkino 42-43 S 6
Sittwe 52-53 B 2
Siunī = Seoni 44-45 M 6
Siuslaw River 76-77 B 4
Siut = Asyūṭ 60-61 L 3
Sivaki 42-43 Y 7
Sīvand 44-45 G 4
Sivas 44-45 D 3
Sivaslı 46-47 C 3
Šiveluč, vulkan – 42-43 f 6
Siverek 46-47 H 4
Sivrice 46-47 H 3
Sivrihisar 46-47 D 3
Sivučij, mys – 42-43 fg 6
Sīwah 60-61 K 3
Sīwah, Wāḥāt – 60-61 K 3
Siwālik Range 44-45 M 4-N 5
Siwni = Seoni 44-45 M 6
Siyāh Chaman 46-47 M 4
Siyāh Chaman 46-47 M 4
Siyāl, Jazā'īr – 62 G 6
Siyālkoṭ 44-45 LM 4

Sjöbo 30-31 EF 10
Sjøvegan 30-31 GH 3
Sjuøyane 30-31 l 4

Skadarsko jezero 36-37 H 4
Skadovsk 36-37 P 2
Skagafjardhar 30-31 d 2
Skagafjördhur 30-31 c 1-d 2
Skagen 30-31 D 9
Skagerrak 30-31 B 9-D 8
Skagit River 76-77 C 1
Skagway, AK 70-71 JK 6
Skaland 30-31 G 3
Skálar 30-31 f 1
Skálholt 30-31 cd 2
Skalistyj Golec, gora – 42-43 WX 6
Skanderborg 30-31 CD 9
Skåne 30-31 E 10
Skanör 30-31 E 10
Skara 30-31 E 8
Skaraborg 30-31 EF 8
Skardū 44-45 M 3
Skarżysko-Kamienna 33 K 3
Skeena Mountains 70-71 L 6
Skeena River 70-71 L 6
Skegness 32 G 5
Skeidharársandur 30-31 e 3
Skellefteå 30-31 J 5
Skellefte älv 30-31 H 5
Skelleftehamn 30-31 JK 5
Skene 30-31 E 9
Skerkij Banco – 36-37 D 7
Ski 30-31 D 8
Skíathos 36-37 K 6
Skidaway Island 74-75 C 9
Skien 30-31 C 8
Skierniewice 33 K 3
Skiftet 30-31 J 7
Skikda = Sakīkdah 60-61 F 1
Skipskjølen 30-31 NO 2
Skive 30-31 C 9
Skjalfandafljót 30-31 e 2
Skjálfandi 30-31 e 1
Skjervøy 30-31 J 2
Skjold 30-31 H 3
Sklad 42-43 X 3
Skobelev = Fergana 44-45 L 2-3
Skógafoss 30-31 cd 3
Skolpen, Banc de – 42-43 F 3
Skolpen, Banco de – 42-43 F 3
Skolpen Bank 42-43 F 3
Skönvik 30-31 G 6
Skópelos 36-37 K 6
Skopin 38-39 G 5
Skopje 36-37 J 4-5
Skövde 30-31 EF 8
Skovorodino 42-43 XY 7
Skowhegan, ME 74-75 J 2
Skudeneshavn 30-31 A 8
Skukuza 64-65 H 8
Skul'any 36-37 M 2
Skull Valley, AZ 76-77 G 8
Skull Valley Indian Reservation 76-77 G 5
Skuodas 30-31 JK 9
Skuratova, mys – 42-43 LM 3
Skutari, İstanbul- = İstanbul-Üsküdar 44-45 BC 2
Skutskär 30-31 GH 7
Skwierzyna 33 G 2
Skye 32 C 3
Skykomish, WA 76-77 C 2
Skyring, Seno – 80 B 8
Skyrópula 36-37 KL 6
Skýros 36-37 L 6

Slå 60-61 C 2
Slagelse 30-31 D 10
Slagnäs 30-31 H 5
Slancy 30-31 N 8
Slănic 36-37 L 3
Slatina 36-37 L 3
Slatoust = Zlatoust 42-43 K 6
Slav'anka 50-51 H 1
Slav'ansk 38-39 G 6
Slav'ansk-na-Kubani 38-39 G 6
Slave Coast 60-61 E 7
Slavenkust 60-61 E 7
Slave River 70-71 O 5-6
Slavgorod [SU, Rossijskaja SFSR] 42-43 O 7
Slavkov u Brna 33 H 4
Slavonija 36-37 GH 3
Slavonska Požega 36-37 GH 3
Slavonski Brod 36-37 GH 3
Sławno 33 H 1
Sleetmute, AK 70-71 E 5
Slide Mountain 74-75 F 3

218 Showa

Sliema 36-37 F 8
Sligeach = Sligo 32 B 4
Sligo 32 B 4
Slite 30-31 H 9
Sliten = Zlītan 60-61 GH 2
Sliven 36-37 M 4
Slivnica 36-37 K 4
Slobodčikovo 38-39 J 3
Slobodskoj 42-43 HJ 6
Slobodskoj 38-39 K 4
Slobodzeja 36-37 NO 2
Slobozia 36-37 M 3
Slonim 38-39 E 5
Slot, The – 52-53 j 6
Slough 32 F 6
Sloûk = Sulūk 46-47 H 4
Slovakia 33 JK 4
Slovaquie 33 JK 4
Slovenia 36-37 F 3-G 2
Slovénie 36-37 F 3-G 2
Slovenské rudohorie 33 JK 4
Slovenija 36-37 F 3-G 2
Slowakije 33 JK 4
Sluck 38-39 E 5
Sl'ud'anka 42-43 T 7
Slunj 36-37 F 3
Słupsk 33 H 1

Småland 30-31 EF 9
Small, ID 76-77 G 3
Small Point 74-75 J 3
Smallwood Réservoir 70-71 Y 7
S'marah 60-61 B 3
Smederevo 36-37 J 3
Smela 38-39 F 6
Smeru = Gunung Semeru 52-53 F 8
Smethport, PA 74-75 D 4
Šmidta, ostrov – 42-43 QR 1
Smiley, Cape – 24 B 29
Smiltene 30-31 LM 9
Smith [CDN] 70-71 O 6-7
Smith Arm 70-71 M 4
Smithers 70-71 L 7
Smithfield, NC 74-75 D 7
Smithfield, UT 76-77 H 5
Smithfield, VA 74-75 E 6
Smith Island [CDN] 70-71 V 5
Smith Island [USA] 74-75 E 8
Smith River 76-77 H 2
Smith River, CA 76-77 A 5
Smiths Creek Valley 76-77 E 6
Smith's Falls 70-71 V 9
Smiths Ferry, ID 76-77 EF 3
Smith Sound 70-71 W 2
Smithton 56-57 HJ 8
Smithtown 58 L 3
Smjörfjöll 30-31 f 2
Smögen 30-31 D 8
Smoke Creek Desert 76-77 D 5
Smoky Bay 58 A 4
Smoky Cape 58 L 3
Smoky Hill River 72-73 FG 4
Smoky Mountains 76-77 F 4
Smoky River 70-71 N 7
Smøla 30-31 B 6
Smol'an 36-37 L 5
Smolensk 38-39 F 5
Smólikas 36-37 J 5
Smoot, WY 76-77 H 4
Smyrne = İzmir 44-45 B 3

Snaefell [GB] 32 D 4
Snæfell [IS] 30-31 f 2
Snæfellsjökull 30-31 ab 2
Snæfellsnes 30-31 b 2
Snag 70-71 HJ 5
Snake Range 76-77 F 6
Snake River [USA ◁ Columbia River] 72-73 C 2
Snake River Canyon 76-77 E 3
Snake River Plains 72-73 D 3
Snake Valley 76-77 G 6
Snåsa 30-31 E 5
Śniardwy, Jezioro – 33 K 2
Śnieżka 33 GH 3
Snigir'ovka 38-39 F 6
Snøhetta 30-31 C 6
Snohomish, WA 76-77 BC 2
Snoqualmie Pass 76-77 C 2
Snota 30-31 C 6
Snøtind 30-31 E 4
Snowdon 32 DE 5
Snowdrift 70-71 OP 5
Snowflake, AZ 76-77 H 8
Snow Hill, MD 74-75 F 5
Snow Hill Island 24 C 31
Snow Road 74-75 E 2
Snowshoe Peak 76-77 F 1
Snowtown 58 CD 4
Snowville, UT 76-77 G 5
Snowy, Mount – 74-75 F 3
Snowy Mountains 56-57 J 7
Snowy River 58 J 6
Snyder, TX 72-73 F 5

Soalala 64-65 KL 6
Soanierana-Ivongo 64-65 LM 6
Soan-kundo 50-51 F 5
Soap Lake, WA 76-77 D 2
Soasiu 52-53 J 6
Soavinandriana 64-65 L 6
Sobaek-sanmaek 50-51 F 5-G 4
Sōbāṭ, Nahr – = As-Sūbāṭ 60-61 L 7
Sobolevo [SU, p-ov Kamčatka] 42-43 e 7
Sobo-zan 50-51 H 6
Sobozo 60-61 GH 4
Sobrado [BR] 78-79 J 6
Sobral [BR, Ceará] 78-79 L 5
Socha 78-79 E 3
Sochaczew 33 K 2
Soche = Yarkand 48-49 D 4
Sŏch'ŏn 50-51 F 4
Sochor, gora – 42-43 TU 7
Soči 38-39 G 7
Sociedad, Islas de la – 22-23 B 6-7
Société, Îles de la – 22-23 B 6-7
Society Islands 22-23 B 6-7
Socompa, Volcán – 80 C 2
Socorro [CO] 78-79 E 3
Socorro, Isla – 72-73 DE 8
Socoto = Sokoto 60-61 EF 6
Socotra = Suquṭrā' 44-45 G 8
Socuéllamos 34-35 F 9
Sódá, Gebel es – = Jabal as-Sawdā' 60-61 GH 3
Soda Lake 76-77 F 8
Sodankylä 30-31 LM 4
Soda Springs, ID 76-77 H 4
Soddu = Sodo 60-61 M 7
Söderhamn 30-31 G 7
Söderköping 30-31 G 8
Södermanland 30-31 G 8
Södertälje 30-31 GH 8
Sōdirī = Sawdirī 60-61 K 6
Sodo 60-61 M 7
Sodom = Sĕdōm 46-47 F 7
Sodus, NY 74-75 E 3
Soedan [≅] 60-61 C-K 6
Soedan [★] 60-61 J-L 6
Soekmekaar 64-65 G 7
Soela väin 30-31 K 8
Soest 33 D 3
Sofala, Baia de – 64-65 HJ 7
Sofia 64-65 L 6
Sofia = Sofija 36-37 K 4
Sofija 36-37 K 4
Sofijsk 42-43 Z 7
Sofporog 30-31 O 5
Soga 63 D 4
Sogamoso 78-79 E 3
Soğanlı Çayı 46-47 E 2
Sogndalstrand 30-31 B 8
Sognefjord 30-31 AB 7
Sogn og Fjordane 30-31 AB 7
Söğüt 46-47 D 2-3
Söğütlü Çayı 46-47 G 3
Sogwip'o 50-51 F 6
Sôhâg = Sawhāj 60-61 L 3
Sŏhan-man 48-49 NO 4
Sohano 52-53 h 6
Sohar = Ṣuḥār 44-45 H 6
So-hŭksan-do 50-51 E 5
Soissons 34-35 J 4
Sōja 50-51 J 5
S'ojacha 38-39 NO 1
S'ojacha [SU, ●] 42-43 N 3
Šojna [SU] 42-43 G 4
Sŏjosŏn-man = Sŏhan-man 48-49 NO 4
Šokal'skogo, ostrov – 42-43 NO 3
Šokal'skogo, proliv – 42-43 RS 2
Söke 44-45 B 3
Sokhna = Sawknah 60-61 GH 3
Sokodé 60-61 E 7
Sokol 42-43 G 6
Sokółka 33 L 2
Sokolo 60-61 C 6
Sokołów Podlaski 33 L 2
Sokoto [WAN, ~] 60-61 E 6
Sokoto [WAN, ●] 60-61 EF 6
Sokotra = Suquṭrā' 44-45 G 8
Sŏkpā 52-53 C 3
Sŏk-to 50-51 E 3
Sol, Costa del – 34-35 E 10
Solai 64-65 J 2-3
Solaklı = Of 46-47 J 2
Solapur 44-45 M 7
Soldedad 78-79 DE 2
Soledad [YV] 78-79 G 3
Soledad, CA 76-77 C 7
Soledad, Isla – = East Falkland 80 E 8
Solesmes 34-35 G 5
Soleymān, Takht-e – 46-47 O 4
Solfonn 30-31 B 8
Solhan 46-47 J 3
Solihull 32 F 5
Solikamsk 42-43 K 6
Sol'-Ileck 42-43 JK 7
Solimões, Rio – 78-79 G 5
Solingen 33 C 3
Sollefteå 30-31 G 6
Sóller 34-35 J 9
Sollum = As-Salûm 60-61 K 2
Sol-lun = Solon 48-49 N 2
Solna 30-31 GH 8
Solo = Surakarta 52-53 F 8
Sologne 34-35 HJ 5
Šologoncy 42-43 VW 4
Solok 52-53 D 7
Solomon Basin 52-53 h 6
Solomoneilanden [★] 52-53 kl 7
Solomon Islands [⊙] 52-53 h 6-k 7
Solomon Sea 52-53 hj 6
Solončak Šalkarteniz 42-43 L 8
Solong Cheer = Sulan Cheer 48-49 K 3
Solong Cheer = Sulan Cheer 48-49 K 3
Solor, Pulau – 52-53 H 8
Solothurn 33 C 5
Soloveckije ostrova 42-43 F 4
Šolta 36-37 G 4
Solṭānābād = Arāk 44-45 F 4
Solṭānīyeh 46-47 N 4
Soltau 33 DE 2
Soluch = Sulūq 60-61 J 2
Solun 48-49 N 2
Solvay, NY 74-75 E 3
Sölvesborg 30-31 F 9
Sol'vyčegodsk 42-43 H 5
Solway Firth 32 DE 4
Solwezi 64-65 G 5
Sōma [J] 50-51 N 4
Soma [TR] 46-47 B 3
Somabhula 64-65 G 6
Somalia, Cuenca de – 22-23 M 5-6
Somali Basin 22-23 M 5-6
Somalibekken 22-23 M 5-6
Somalië 60-61 N 8-O 7
Somalie 60-61 N 8-O 7
Somalies, Bassin des – 22-23 M 5-6
Sombor 36-37 H 3
Sombrero, El – [YV] 78-79 F 3
Şomcuta Mare 36-37 K 2
Somero 30-31 K 7
Somers, MT 76-77 F 1
Somerset, PA 74-75 D 4-5
Somerset East = Somerset-Oos 64-65 FG 9
Somerset Island 70-71 S 3
Somerset-Oos 64-65 FG 9
Somersworth, NH 74-75 H 3
Somerton, AZ 76-77 F 9
Somerville, MA 74-75 H 3
Somerville, NJ 74-75 F 4
Someş 36-37 K 2
Somesbar, CA 76-77 B 5
Somme 34-35 H 3
Somuncurá, Meseta de – 80 C 6
Son [IND] 44-45 N 6
Sŏnch'ŏn 50-51 E 3
Sonda, Fosa de la – 22-23 P 6
Sonda, Grandes islas de la – 52-53 E-H 7-8
Sonda, Pequeñas islas de la – 52-53 GH 8
Sonde, Grandes Îles de la – 52-53 E-H 7-8
Sonde, Îles de la – 22-23 O 5-Q 6
Sonde, Petites Îles de la – 52-53 GH 8
Sønderborg 30-31 CD 10
Sondershausen 33 E 3
Søndre Kvaløy 30-31 GH 3
Søndre Strømfjord 70-71 a 4
Søndre Strømfjord = Kangerdlugssuaq 70-71 ab 4
Sòndrio 36-37 CD 2
Sŏngch'on 50-51 F 3
Songea 64-65 J 5
Songhua Hu 48-49 O 3
Songhua Jiang 48-49 O 2
Sŏnghwan 50-51 F 4
Songjiang 48-49 N 5
Songjiangzhen 50-51 F 1
Sŏngjin = Kim Chak 48-49 OP 3
Songjŏng-ni 50-51 F 5
Songkhla 52-53 D 5
Songkla = Songkhla 52-53 D 5
Sŏngnae-ri = Inhung-ni 50-51 F 3
Songnim 48-49 O 4
Songo 64-65 DE 4
Songpan 48-49 J 5
Songwe 63 C 5
Sonhat 44-45 N 6
Sonkovo 42-43 F 6
Sonkovo 38-39 G 4
Sonmiani = Sonmiyānī 44-45 K 5
Sonmiyāni 44-45 K 5
Sonmiyānī, Khalīj – 44-45 J 6-K 5
Sonneberg 33 E 3
Sono, Rio do – [BR, Goiás] 78-79 K 6-7
Sonoma, CA 76-77 B 6
Sonoma Range 76-77 E 5
Sonora 72-73 DE 6
Sonora, AZ 76-77 H 9
Sonora, CA 76-77 C 6-7
Sonora Peak 76-77 D 6
Sonoyta, Rio – 76-77 G 10
Sonqor 46-47 M 5
Sonsón 78-79 DE 3
Sonsonate 72-73 HJ 9
Sonsorol 52-53 K 5
Soperton, GA 74-75 B 8
Sŏp'o-ri 50-51 FG 2
Sopot 33 J 1
Sopron 33 H 5
Sor 34-35 C 9
Sora 36-37 E 5
Sŏrak-san 50-51 G 3
Sōrath = Jūnāgaḍh 44-45 KL 6
Sorbas 34-35 FG 10
Sorel 70-71 W 8
Sorell 58 cd 3
Sorell, Cape – 56-57 HJ 8
Sorell, Lake – 58 c 2
Soren Arwa = Selat Yapen 52-53 L 7
Sørfonna 30-31 lm 5
Sòrgono 36-37 C 5
Sorgun = Büyük Köhne 46-47 F 3
Sōrhād = Sarhade Wākhān 44-45 L 3
Soria 34-35 F 8
Sørkapp 30-31 k 6
Sørkapp land 30-31 k 6
Sørkjosen 30-31 J 3
Sorø 30-31 D 10
Sorocaba 80 G 2
Soročinsk 42-43 J 7
Soroka = Belomorsk 42-43 EF 5
Sorol 52-53 M 5
Sorong 52-53 K 7
Soroti 64-65 H 2
Sørøy 30-31 K 2
Sørøysund 30-31 K 2
Sorraia 34-35 C 9
Sorrento 36-37 F 5
Sør-Rondane 24 B 2-3
Sorsele 30-31 G 5
Sorsogon 52-53 HJ 4
Sortavala 42-43 E 5
Sortland 30-31 F 3
Sør-Trøndelag 30-31 CD 6
Sørvågen 30-31 E 4
Sörve 30-31 JK 9
Sŏsan 50-51 F 4
Sosnogorsk 42-43 JK 5
Sosnovka 38-39 H 5
Sosnovo 30-31 NO 7
Sosnovo-Oz'orskoje 42-43 V 7
Sosnowiec 33 J 3
Šostka 38-39 F 5
Sŏsura 50-51 H 1
Sos'va 38-39 M 4
Sos'va [SU, Chanty-Mansijskaja AO] 42-43 L 5
Sos'va [SU ↘ Serov] 42-43 L 6
So-tch'ê = Yarkand 48-49 D 4
Sotkamo 30-31 N 5
Sotra 30-31 A 7
Souanké 64-65 D 2
Soûâr = Aṣ-Ṣuwār 46-47 J 5
Soubré 60-61 C 7
Soudan [≅] 60-61 C-K 6
Soudan [★] 60-61 J-L 6
Soufrière 72-73 O 9
Souillac 34-35 H 6
Souk-Ahras = Sūq Aḥrās 60-61 F 1
Sŏul 48-49 O 4
Sources, Mont aux – 64-65 G 8
Soure [BR] 78-79 K 5
Souris River 70-71 Q 8
Sousa 78-79 M 6
Soûssâ = Sūssah 46-47 J 5
Sousse = Sūsah 60-61 G 1
South Africa 64-65 F-H 8
South Alligator River 56-57 F 2
South Alligator River 56-57 F 2
South America 22-23 FG 6
Southampton [GB] 32 F 6
Southampton, NY 74-75 GH 4
Southampton Island 70-71 TU 5
South Andaman 44-45 P 8
South Aulatsivik Island 70-71 YZ 6
South Australia 56-57 E-G 5-6
South Australia Basin 22-23 PQ 8
South Banda Basin 52-53 J 8
South Bend, IN 72-73 JK 3
South Bend, WA 76-77 B 2
South Boston, VA 74-75 D 6
South Branch Potomac River 74-75 D 5
South Bruny Island 58 cd 3
South Carolina 72-73 K 5
South Charleston, WV 74-75 BC 5
South China Basin 52-53 FG 3-4
South China Sea 52-53 E 5-G 3

South Charleston, WV 74-75 BC 5
South China Basin 52-53 FG 3-4
South China Sea 52-53 E 5-G 3

South Dakota 72-73 FG 3
South Dum Dum 44-45 OP 6
South East Cape 56-57 J 8
Southeast Indian Basin 22-23 OP 7
South East Point 58 H 7
Southend [CDN] 70-71 PQ 6
Southend-on-Sea 32 G 6
Southern [Z] 64-65 G 6
Southern Alps 56-57 NO 8
Southern Cross 56-57 CD 6
Southern Indian Lake 70-71 R 6
Southern Pacific Railway 72-73 EF 5
Southern Pine Hills = Pine Hills 72-73 J 5
Southern Pines, NC 74-75 D 7
Southern Uplands 32 DE 4
South Fiji Basin 56-57 OP 4-5
South Fork Clearwater River 76-77 F 3
South Fork Flathead River 76-77 G 2
South Fork John Day River 76-77 D 3
South Fork Mountains 76-77 B 5
South Fork Owyhee River 76-77 E 4-5
South Fork Salmon River 76-77 F 3
South Gate, CA 76-77 DE 9
South Georgia 80 J 8
South Georgia Ridge 24 D 33-E 34
South Henik Lake 70-71 R 5
South Hill, VA 74-75 D 6
South Honshu Ridge 48-49 R 5-6
South Horr 64-65 J 2
South Indian Ridge 22-23 OP 8
South Island 56-57 OP 8
South Korea 48-49 OP 4
South Mountain 74-75 E 4-5
South Nahanni River 70-71 LM 5
South Ogden, UT 76-77 H 5
South Orkneys 24 C 32
South Ossetian Autonomous Region = 7 ◁ 38-39 H 7
South Pacific Basin 24 D 21-19
South Pacific Ridge 24 D 22-C 20
South Paris, ME 74-75 H 2
South Pass [USA, Louisiana] 72-73 J 6
South Pass [USA, Wyoming] 72-73 E 3
South Plate River 72-73 F 3
Southport [AUS] 58 c 3
Southport, NC 74-75 DE 7-8
South Portland, ME 74-75 HJ 3
South Ronaldsay 32 EF 2
South Sandwich Islands 24 CD 34
South Sandwich Trench 24 D 34
South Saskatchewan River 70-71 OP 7
South Shetlands 24 C 30
South Shields 32 F 4
South Taranaki Bight 56-57 O 7
South Tent 76-77 H 6
South Tyrol 36-37 D 2
South Uist 32 BC 3
South Umpqua River 76-77 B 4
Southwest Africa = Namibia 64-65 E 7
South West Cape [AUS] 58 bc 3
Southwest Cape [NZ] 56-57 N 9
Southwest Cay 72-73 KL 9
Southwest Indian Basin 22-23 MN 7
Southwest Pass [USA, Mississippi River Delta] 72-73 J 6
South Williamsport, PA 74-75 E 4
Soutpansberge 64-65 GH 7
Souzel 78-79 J 5
Sovetsk 33 K 1
Sovetsk [SU, Vjatka] 42-43 H 6
Sovetskaja Gavan' 42-43 ab 8
Sōya [J, Hokkaidō] 50-51 b 1
Sōya-kaikyō 48-49 R 2
Sōya misaki 50-51 bc 1
Söylemez 46-47 JK 3
Soyo 64-65 D 4
Sozopol 36-37 MN 4

Spain 34-35 D 7-G 9
Spalato = Split 36-37 G 4
Spalding 32 FG 5
Spalding [AUS] 58 D 4
Spalding, ID 76-77 E 2
Spangle, WA 76-77 E 2
Spanish Fork, UT 76-77 H 5
Spanish Head 32 D 4
Spanish Town 72-73 L 8
Spanje 34-35 D 7-G 9
Spanta, Akrōtḗrion – 36-37 KL 8
Sparbu 30-31 D 6
Sparks, GA 74-75 B 9
Sparks, NV 76-77 D 6
Sparta, GA 74-75 B 8
Sparta, NC 74-75 C 6
Sparta = Spártē 36-37 K 7
Spartanburg, SC 72-73 K 4-5
Spártē 36-37 K 7
Spartivento, Capo – [I, Calábria] 36-37 G 7
Spartivento, Capo – [I, Sardegna] 36-37 G 6
Spassk = Kujbyšev 42-43 HJ 7
Spassk = Spassk-Dal'nij 42-43 Z 9
Spassk-Dal'nij 42-43 Z 9
Speke Gulf 64-65 H 3
Spencer, ID 76-77 G 3
Spencer, NC 74-75 C 7
Spencer, WV 74-75 C 5
Spencer, Cape – [AUS] 56-57 G 7
Spencer Gulf 56-57 G 6
Spessart 33 D 3-4
Spětsai 36-37 K 7
Spey 32 E 3
Speyer 33 D 4
Spèzia, La – 36-37 C 3
Spezzano Albanese 36-37 G 6
Spicer Islands 70-71 UV 4
Spilimbergo 36-37 E 2
Spīn Buldak 44-45 K 4
Spirit Lake, ID 76-77 E 1-2
Spirit Lake, WA 76-77 BC 2
Spitsbergen 30-31 k 6-o 5
Spittal 33 F 5
Spitzberg = Svalbard 34-35 k-m 6
Split 36-37 G 4
Splügen 33 D 5
Spokane, WA 72-73 C 2
Spokane Indian Reservation 76-77 DE 2
Spokane River 76-77 DE 2
Spokojnyj 42-43 YZ 6
Špola 38-39 F 6
Spoleto 36-37 E 4
Sporades 36-37 M 6-8
Sporyj Navolok, mys – 42-43 M-O 2
Spotted Range 76-77 F 7
Sprague, WA 76-77 DE 2
Sprague River 76-77 C 4
Sprague River, OR 76-77 C 4
Spratly Islands = Quần Đao Hoang Sa 52-53 F 5
Spray, OR 76-77 D 3
Spree 33 G 3
Spreewald 33 F 2-G 3
Spremberg 33 G 3
Sprengisandur 30-31 de 2
Spring Bay 76-77 G 5
Springbok 64-65 E 8
Springdale, MT 76-77 HJ 3
Springdale, NV 76-77 E 7
Springdale, UT 76-77 G 7
Springdale, WA 76-77 DE 1
Springerville, AZ 76-77 J 8
Springfield, GA 74-75 C 8

Sprin 219

Springfield, ID 76-77 G 4
Springfield, IL 72-73 HJ 4
Springfield, MA 72-73 M 3
Springfield, MO 72-73 H 4
Springfield, OH 72-73 K 3-4
Springfield, OR 76-77 B 3
Springfield, VT 74-75 G 3
Spring Hope, NC 74-75 DE 7
Spring Mountains 76-77 F 7
Springs 64-65 G 8
Springsure 56-57 J 4
Spring Valley [USA] 76-77 F 6
Springville, NY 74-75 D 3
Springville, UT 76-77 H 5
Spruce Knob 72-73 KL 4
Spruce Mountain 76-77 F 5
Spruce Pine, NC 74-75 BC 6-7
Spry, UT 76-77 G 7
Spur Lake, NM 76-77 J 8-9

Squaw Valley, CA 72-73 BC 4
Squillace, Golfo di – 36-37 G 6

Srbija 36-37 H 3-J 4
Sredinnyj chrebet 42-43 f 6-e 7
Sredna gora 36-37 L 4
Srednekolymsk 42-43 d 4
Sredne-Sibirskoje ploskogorje 42-43 R-W 4-5
Srednij Ural 42-43 KL 6
Sredsib 42-43 L 7-P 7
Śrem 33 H 2
Sremska Mitrovica 36-37 H 3
Sremska Rača 36-37 H 3
Sretensk 42-43 W 7
Srê Umbell 52-53 D 4
Sri Jayawardanapura 44-45 N 9
Srikakulam 44-45 M 7
Srinagar 44-45 LM 4
Srirangam 44-45 M 8
Srivardhan 44-45 L 7
Środa Wielkopolski 33 HJ 2

Sseu-p'ing = Siping 48-49 N 3
Ssongea = Songea 64-65 J 5

Staaten River 56-57 H 3
Stachanov 38-39 G 6
Stack Skerry 32 D 2
Stade 33 D 2
Städjan 30-31 E 7
Stadlandet 30-31 A 6
Stafford 32 E 5
Staked Plain = Llano Estacado 72-73 F 5
Stalina, pik – = pik Kommunizma 44-45 L 3
Stalinabad = Dušanbe 44-45 K 3
Stalino = Ošarovo 42-43 S 5
Stalinsk = Novokuzneck 42-43 Q 7
Stalowa Wola 33 L 3
Stambul = İstanbul 44-45 BC 2
Stamford [AUS] 56-57 H 4
Stamford, CT 74-75 G 4
Stampriet 64-65 E 7
Stamsund 30-31 EF 3
Stanbury Mountains 76-77 G 5
Standerton 64-65 GH 8
Stanford, MT 76-77 H 2
Stanislaus River 76-77 C 6-7
Stanke Dimitrov 36-37 K 4
Stanley [AUS] 58 b 2
Stanley [Falkland Islands] 80 E 8
Stanley, ID 76-77 F 3
Stanley, Mount – 56-57 F 4
Stanley Pool = Pool Malebo 64-65 E 3
Stanley Reservoir 44-45 M 8
Stanleyville = Kisangani 64-65 G 2
Stann Creek 72-73 J 8
Stanovoj chrebet 42-43 X-Z 6
Stanovoje nagorje 42-43 VW 6
Stanthorpe 58 KL 2
Stanwood, WA 76-77 B 1
Stapi 30-31 b 2
Star, NC 74-75 D 7
Starachowice 33 K 3
Staraja Buchara = Buchara 44-45 JK 3
Staraja Russa 42-43 E 6
Stara Pazova 36-37 J 3
Stara Zagora 36-37 L 4
Stargard Szczeciński 33 G 2
Starigrad 36-37 F 3
Starke, FL 74-75 bc 2
Starkey, ID 76-77 E 3
Starnberg 33 E 4-5
Starnberger See 33 E 5
Starobel'sk 38-39 G 6
Starogard Gdański 33 HJ 2
Staroizborsk 30-31 MN 9
Starokonstantinov 38-39 E 6
Starominskaja 38-39 G 6
Starotitarovskaja 38-39 G 6-7
Staryj Oskol 38-39 G 5
Staßfurt 33 E 3
Staszów 33 K 3
State College, PA 74-75 DE 4
Staten Island 74-75 FG 4
Statenville, GA 74-75 B 9
Statesboro, GA 74-75 C 8
Statesville, NC 72-73 K 4
Stauffer, OR 76-77 C 4
Staunton, VA 72-73 KL 4
Stavanger 30-31 A 8
Stavern 30-31 CD 8
Stavropol' 38-39 H 6
Stavropol' = Togliatti 42-43 H 7
Stavrós 36-37 K 5
Stawell 56-57 H 7
Steamboat, NV 76-77 D 6
Steele Island 24 B 30-31
Steelpoort 64-65 GH 7
Steelton, PA 74-75 E 4
Steenkool = Bintuni 52-53 K 7
Steensby Inlet 70-71 V 3
Steens Mountain 76-77 D 4
Steenstrups Gletscher 70-71 Za 2
Steep Point 56-57 B 5
Ștefănești 36-37 M 2
Stefansson Island 70-71 OP 3
Steflești 36-37 K 3
Stege 30-31 E 10
Steiermark 33 G 5
Steinen, Rio – 78-79 J 7
Steinhatchee, FL 74-75 b 2
Steinkjer 30-31 DE 5
Steinnest 30-31 m 6
Steins, NM 76-77 J 9
Stellaland 64-65 F 8
Stellenbosch 64-65 EF 9
Stendal 33 E 2
Stensele 30-31 G 5
Stepanakert 38-39 J 8
Stephanie, Lake – = Thew Bahir 60-61 M 8
Stephenville 70-71 YZ 8
Stepn'ak 42-43 N 7
Sterkstroom 64-65 G 9
Sterling, CO 72-73 F 3
Sterlitamak 42-43 K 7
Steubenville, OH 72-73 K 3
Stevenson, WA 76-77 BC 3
Stevenson, The – 56-57 FG 5
Stevensville, MT 76-77 FG 2
Stewart, AK 70-71 KL 6
Stewart, NV 76-77 D 6
Stewart, Isla – 80 B 8-9
Stewart Island 56-57 N 9
Stewart Islands 52-53 k 6
Stewart River [CDN, ∽] 70-71 JK 5
Stewart River [CDN, ●] 70-71 J 5
Steyr 33 G 4
Stikine Mountains = Cassiar Mountains 70-71 KL 6
Stikine Plateau 70-71 K 6
Stikine River 70-71 KL 6
Stillwater Mountains 76-77 DE 6
Stimson, Mount – 76-77 G 1
Stinear Nunataks 24 BC 7
Štip 36-37 K 5
Stirling City, CA 76-77 C 6
Stirling Range 56-57 C 6
Stites, ID 76-77 EF 2
Stjernøy 30-31 K 2
Stjørdalshalsen 30-31 D 6
Stobi 36-37 J 5
Stockerau 33 G 4
Stockett, MT 76-77 H 2
Stockholm 30-31 GH 8
Stockholm, ME 74-75 JK 1
Stockholms län 30-31 GH 8
Stockport 32 E 5
Stocks, Cima de – 78-79 N 7
Stocks, Crête de – 78-79 N 7
Stocks-Ondiepte 78-79 N 7
Stocks Seamount 78-79 N 7
Stockton, CA 72-73 BC 4
Stockton on Tees 32 F 4
Stojba 42-43 Z 7
Stoke on Trend 32 EF 5
Stokes Point 58 ab 2
Stokkseyri 30-31 c 3
Stokksnes 30-31 f 2
Stolac 36-37 GH 4
Stolbcy 30-31 M 11
Stolbovoj, ostrov – 42-43 Za 3
Ston 36-37 G 4
Stonehaven 32 EF 3
Stonehenge 32 EF 6
Stonehenge [AUS] 56-57 H 4
Stone Mountains 74-75 C 6
Stoner, CO 76-77 J 7
Stonington 24 C 30
Stonington, ME 74-75 J 2-3
Stony Creek, VA 74-75 E 6
Stonyford, CA 76-77 B 6
Stony Point [USA] 74-75 E 3
Stony River 70-71 EF 5
Stopnica 33 K 3
Stora Lulevatten 30-31 HJ 4
Stora Sjöfallet 30-31 H 4
Stora-Sjöfallets nationalpark 30-31 GH 4
Storavan 30-31 H 5
Stord 30-31 A 8
Store Bælt 30-31 D 10
Støren 30-31 CD 6
Storfjord 30-31 B 6
Storfjordbotn 30-31 LM 2
Storfjorden 30-31 k 6
Storlien 30-31 E 6
Storm Bay 56-57 J 8
Stornorrfors 30-31 HJ 6
Stornoway 32 CD 2
Storøya 30-31 n 4
Storoževsk 42-43 J 5
Storsjön 30-31 E 6
Storuman [S, ●] 30-31 G 5
Storuman [S, ≈] 30-31 G 5
Stosch, Isla – 80 A 7
Straatsburg = Strasbourg 34-35 L 4
Strabane 32 C 4
Straight Cliffs 76-77 H 7
Strakonice 33 FG 4
Stralsund 33 F 1
Strand 64-65 E 9
Stranda 30-31 c 1-2
Stranraer 32 D 4
Strasbourg 34-35 L 4
Stratford [AUS] 58 H 7
Stratford [CDN] 70-71 U 9
Stratford, CA 76-77 D 7
Stratford, CT 74-75 G 4
Stratford on Avon 32 F 5
Strathgordon 58 bc 3
Strathmore 32 E 3
Strathroy 74-75 C 3
Stratonis Turris = Caesarea 46-47 F 6
Stratton, ME 74-75 H 2
Straubing 33 F 4
Strawberry Mountains 76-77 D 3
Strawberry River 76-77 H 5
Streaky Bay [AUS, ∪] 56-57 F 6
Streaky Bay [AUS, ●] 56-57 FG 6
Streich Mound 56-57 D 6
Strelka-Čun'a 42-43 T 5
Strelna 38-39 G 2
Strenči 30-31 LM 9
Stresa 36-37 C 3
Strevell, ID 76-77 G 4
Strickland River 52-53 M 8
Stroeder 80 D 6
Strofádes 36-37 J 7
Strómboli 36-37 F 6
Strömstad 30-31 D 8
Strömsund 30-31 F 6
Ströms Vattudal 30-31 F 5-6
Stronsay 32 EF 2
Stroud 32 EF 6
Stroudsburg, PA 74-75 F 4
Struer 30-31 C 9
Strugi Krasnyje 30-31 M 8
Struma 36-37 K 5
Strumica 36-37 K 5
Stryj 38-39 D 6
Strymōn 36-37 K 5
Strzelecki Creek 58 E 2
Strzelno 33 HJ 2
Stuart, FL 74-75 c 3
Stuart, VA 74-75 C 6
Stuart Island 70-71 D 5
Stuart Lake 70-71 M 7
Stuart Range 56-57 FG 5
Stubbenkammer 33 FG 1
Studenica 36-37 J 4
Stumpy Point, NC 74-75 F 7
Stung Treng 52-53 E 4
Stupino 38-39 G 4-5
Stura di Demonte 36-37 B 3
Sturge Island 24 C 17
Sturt, Mount – 56-57 H 5
Sturt Creek 56-57 E 3
Sturt Desert 56-57 H 5
Sturt Plain 56-57 F 3
Stutterheim 64-65 G 9
Stuttgart 33 D 4
Stykkishólmur 30-31 b 2
Stylis 36-37 K 6
Styr' 38-39 E 5

Suâkin = Sawâkîn 60-61 M 5
Suan 50-51 F 3
Süanhua = Xuanhua 48-49 LM 3
Suanhwa = Xuanhua 48-49 LM 3
Su-ao 48-49 N 7
Su'ao = Su-ao 48-49 N 7
Šubarkuduk 42-43 K 8
Sūbāṭ, Bahr as- 60-61 L 7
Sūbāṭ, Nahr as- 60-61 L 7
Subayhah 46-47 H 7
Subiaco 36-37 E 5
Sublett, ID 76-77 G 4
Subotica 36-37 HJ 2
Subugo 63 C 3
Suceava 36-37 LM 2
Suchaj nuur 48-49 GH 4
Suchana 42-43 W 4
Süchbaatar [Mongolia, ●] 48-49 JK 1
Suchbaatar [Mongolia, ☆ = 17] 48-49 L 2
Sucheng = Su Xian 48-49 M 5
Su-chia-t'un = Sujiatun 50-51 D 2
Su-ch'ien = Suqian 48-49 M 5
Suchiniči 38-39 FG 5
Suchoj Liman 36-37 O 2
Suchona 42-43 G 6
Suchou = Xuzhou 48-49 M 5
Su-chou = Yibin 48-49 JK 6
Suchow = Xuzhou 48-49 M 5
Suchow = Yibin 48-49 JK 6
Suchumi 38-39 H 7
Sucre [BOL] 78-79 FG 8
Sucuaro 78-79 F 4
Sucunduri, Rio – 78-79 H 6
Sucuriú, Rio – 78-79 J 8
Sûd = As-Sudd 60-61 L 7
Sudáfrica, República de – 64-65 F-H 8
Sudán [≅] 60-61 C-K 6
Sudán [★] 60-61 J-L 6
Sudayr 44-45 EF 5
Sudbury [CDN] 70-71 U 8
Sudd, As- 60-61 L 7
Suddie 78-79 H 3
Sud-Est Indien, Bassin du – 22-23 OP 7
Sud-Est Indien, Dorsale du – 22-23 OP 8
Suðhavík 30-31 b 1
Suðhur-Múla 30-31 f 2
Suðhur-Thingeyjar 30-31 ef 2
Sudirman, Pegunungan – 52-53 L 7
Südlicher Ural = Južnyj Ural 42-43 K 7-L 6
Sudong-ni = Changhang 50-51 F 4-5
Sud-Ouest Indien, Bassin du – 22-23 MN 7
Sudr = Rā's as-Sidr 62 E 3
Sudr, Wâdî – = Wādī Sidr 62 E 3
Sue = Nahr Sūī 60-61 K 7
Sueca 34-35 G 9
Suecia 30-31 F 9-J 10
Suède 30-31 F 9-J 10
Suez = As-Suways 60-61 L 3
Sūfān, Qulbān as- 46-47 H 8
Sūfeyān 46-47 LM 3
Suffolk, VA 74-75 E 6
Suflion 36-37 LM 5
Sufu = Qäshqär 48-49 CD 4
Ṣufūq 46-47 J 4
Šuga 42-43 N 4
Sugarloaf Mountain 74-75 HJ 2
Sugiyasu 50-51 H 6
Suğla Gölü 46-47 DE 4
Suguta 63 D 2
Sūhāj = Sawhaṭ 60-61 L 3
Ṣuḥār 44-45 H 6
Suhelīpād = Suheli Par 44-45 L 8
Suheli Par 44-45 L 8
Suhl 33 E 3
Su-hsien = Su Xian 48-49 M 5
Ṣuhut 46-47 D 3
Suichuan 48-49 L 6
Sui-chung = Suizhong 50-51 C 2
Suichwan = Suichuan 48-49 L 6
Suide 48-49 KL 4
Suifenhe 48-49 OP 3
Suihsien = Sui Xian [TJ, Hubei] 48-49 L 5
Suihua 48-49 O 2
Suihwa = Suihua 48-49 O 2
Suilai = Manaas 48-49 F 3
Suir 32 C 5
Suisse 33 CD 5
Suiteh = Suide 48-49 KL 4
Sui Xian [TJ, Hubei] 48-49 L 5
Suiyuan 48-49 K 4-L 3
Sui-yüan = Suiyuan 48-49 K 4-L 3
Suiza 33 CD 5
Suizhong 50-51 C 2
Šuja [SU, Ivanovo] 42-43 G 6
Sujiatun 50-51 D 2
Sukabumi 52-53 E 8
Sukadana 52-53 EF 7
Sukagawa 50-51 MN 4
Sukaraja = Marau 52-53 F 7
Sukch'ŏn 50-51 E 3
Sukhe Bator = Süchbaatar 48-49 JK 1
Ṣukhnah, Aṣ- 46-47 H 5
Sūki, As- 60-61 L 6
Sukkertoppen = Manîtsoq 70-71 Za 4
Sukses 64-65 E 7
Sukulu 63 C 2
Sukumo 50-51 J 6
Sukumo wan 50-51 J 6
Sul, Canal do – 78-79 K 4-5
Sula, MT 76-77 FG 3
Sula [SU, ∼] 38-39 F 6
Sula [SU, ●] 38-39 K 2
Sula, Kepulauan – 52-53 HJ 7
Sulak 38-39 J 7
Sulakyurt 46-47 E 2
Sulan Cheer 48-49 K 3
Sulan Cheer 48-49 K 3
Sula Sgeir 32 C 2
Sulawesi 52-53 G 7-H 6
Sulawesi Selatan = 21 ◁ 52-53 G 7
Sulawesi Tengah = 19 ◁ 52-53 H 6
Sulawesi Tenggara = 20 ◁ 52-53 H 7
Sulawesi Utara = 18 ◁ 52-53 H 6
Sulaymân, Kohistân – 44-45 KL 4-5
Sulaymānīyah 44-45 EF 3
Sulaymīyah, As- 44-45 F 6
Sulayyil, As- 44-45 F 6
Ṣulb, Aṣ- 44-45 F 5
Šul'ca 38-39 J 3
Sule He 48-49 H 4
Sule Skerry 32 D 2
Süleymanlı 46-47 G 4
Sulima 60-61 B 7
Sulina 36-37 N 3
Sulina, Braţul – 36-37 N 3
Sulitjelma [N, ▲] 30-31 G 4
Sulitjelma [N, ●] 30-31 FG 4
Šuljereckoje 38-39 F 3
Sullana 78-79 C 5
Šul'mak = Novabad 44-45 L 3
Sulmona 36-37 E 4-5
Su-lo Ho = Sule He 48-49 H 4
Sulphur, NV 76-77 D 5
Sulphurdale, UT 76-77 G 6
Sultanabad = Arâk 44-45 F 4
Sultandağı 46-47 D 3
Sultan Dağları 46-47 D 3
Sultan Hamud 63 D 3
Sultanhisar 46-47 C 4
Sultanpur [IND, Uttar Pradesh] 44-45 N 5
Sulu, Mar de – 52-53 GH 5
Sulu, Mer de – 52-53 GH 5
Sulu Archipelago 52-53 H 5
Suluca = Suluova 46-47 F 2
Sulūk 46-47 H 4
Sülüklü 46-47 E 3
Sul'ukta 44-45 KL 3
Suluova 46-47 F 2
Sulūq 60-61 J 2
Sulu Sea 52-53 GH 5
Suluzee 52-53 GH 5
Sulzberger Bay 24 B 21-22
Šumadija 36-37 J 3-4
Sūmār 46-47 L 6
Sumas, WA 76-77 BC 1
Sumatera Barat = 3 ◁ 52-53 D 7
Sumatera Selatan = 6 ◁ 52-53 D 7
Sumatera Tengah = Riau = 4 ◁ 52-53 D 6
Sumatera Utara = 2 ◁ 52-53 C 6
Sumaúma 78-79 G 6
Sumba [RI] 52-53 G 9
Sumba, Selat – 52-53 GH 8
Sumbawa 52-53 G 8
Sumbawa Besar 52-53 G 8
Sumbawanga 64-65 H 4
Sumbe 63 C 3
Sümber 48-49 K 2
Sumbu 63 B 5
Sumbu Game Reserve 63 B 5
Sumburgh Head 32 F 2
Šumen 36-37 M 4
Šumerl'a 38-39 J 4
Sumgait 38-39 JK 7
Šumicha 42-43 L 6
Sumisu-jima 48-49 R 5
Sumisu zima = Sumisu-jima 48-49 R 5
Ṣummān, Aṣ- [Saudi Arabia ↑ Ar-Riyāḍ] 44-45 F 5
Ṣummān, Aṣ- [Saudi Arabia ↘ Ar-Riyāḍ] 44-45 F 6
Summer Lake 76-77 C 4
Summer Lake, OR 76-77 C 4
Summerville, SC 74-75 CD 8
Summerville, WV 74-75 C 5
Summit 72-73 b 2
Summit, CA 76-77 E 8
Summit, OR 76-77 B 3
Summit Lake Indian Reservation 76-77 D 5
Summit Mountain 76-77 E 6
Šumoto 50-51 K 5
Šumperk 33 H 3-4
Sumprabum = Hsûmbârabûm 52-53 C 1
Sumpter, OR 76-77 DE 3
Sumter, SC 72-73 KL 5
Sumy 38-39 FG 5
Suna [EAT] 63 C 4
Sunagawa 50-51 b 2
Sunan 50-51 E 3
Sunato 63 DE 6
Sunaysilah 46-47 J 5
Sunburst, MT 76-77 H 1
Sunbury, PA 74-75 E 4
Suncho Corral 80 D 3
Sunch'ŏn [North Korea] 50-51 E 3
Sunch'ŏn [ROK] 48-49 O 4-5
Sunchow = Guiping 48-49 KL 7
Suncook, NH 74-75 H 3
Sunda, Selat – 52-53 E 8
Sundar Ban = Sundarbans 44-45 OP 6
Sundarbans 44-45 OP 6
Sunda Trench 22-23 P 6
Sundbyberg 30-31 G 8
Sunderbunds = Sundarbans 44-45 OP 6
Sunderland 32 F 4
Sunderland [CDN] 74-75 D 2
Sündiken Dağları 46-47 D 2-3
Sundown [AUS] 56-57 F 5
Sundsvall 30-31 GH 6
Sungaidareh 52-53 D 7
Sungai Patani 52-53 CD 5
Sungaipenuh 52-53 D 7
Sungari 48-49 N 2-O 3
Sungari Reservoir = Songhua Hu 48-49 O 3
Sung-chiang = Songjiang 48-49 N 5
Sung hua Chiang = Songhua Jiang 48-49 N 2-O 3
Sung hua Chiang = Songhua Jiang 48-49 N 2-O 3
Süngjibaegam 50-51 G 2
Sungkiang = Songjiang 48-49 N 5
Sungu 64-65 E 3
Sungurlu 46-47 F 2
Sunhwa = Xunhua 48-49 J 4
Súnion, Atrōtḗrion – 36-37 KL 7
Sunke = Xunke 48-49 O 2
Sunnagyn, chrebet – = Aldano-Učurskij chrebet 42-43 Y 6
Sunndalsøra 30-31 C 6
Sunniland, FL 74-75 c 3
Sunnūris = Sinnūris 62 D 3
Sunnyside, UT 76-77 H 6
Sunnyside, WA 76-77 CD 2
Sunnyvale, CA 76-77 B 7
Suno saki 50-51 M 5
Sun River 76-77 GH 2
Sunset Country 58 E 5
Suntar 42-43 W 5
Suntar-Chajata, chrebet – 42-43 ab 5
Suntar-Chajata, chrebet – 42-43 ab 5
Suntsar 44-45 J 5
Sun Valley, ID 76-77 F 4
Sunyani 60-61 D 7
Suojarvi 42-43 E 5
Suojarvi 38-39 F 3
Suokonmäki 30-31 KL 6
Suolahti 30-31 LM 6
Suomen selkä 30-31 K-N 6
Suomussalmi 30-31 N 5
Suō nada 50-51 H 6
Suonenjoki 30-31 M 6
Supai, AZ 76-77 G 7
Superior, AZ 76-77 H 9
Superior, MT 76-77 F 2
Superior, WI 72-73 H 2
Superior, Lake – 72-73 HJ 2
Suphan Buri 52-53 CD 4
Süphan Dağı 46-47 K 3

220 Sprin

Supiori 52-53 KL 7
Sup'ung-chŏsuji 50-51 E 2
Şupung Hu 48-49 NO 3
Šupunskij, mys – 42-43 f 7
Sūq Aḥrās 60-61 F 1
Suq ash-Shuyūkh 46-47 M 7
Suqian 48-49 M 5
Suquṭrā' 44-45 G 8
Şūr [Oman] 44-45 H 6
Şur [RL] 46-47 F 6
Sur, Point – 76-77 BC 7
Sura, Raas – = Raas Surud 60-61 b 1
Šurab 44-45 L 2
Surabaia = Surabaya 52-53 F 8
Surabaya 52-53 F 8
Surakarta 52-53 F 8
Şūrān 46-47 G 5
Surat [AUS] 56-57 J 5
Surat [IND] 44-45 L 6
Surate = Surat 44-45 L 6
Surat Thani 52-53 CD 5
Sūrdāsh 46-47 L 5
Surf, CA 76-77 C 8
Surgut [SU, Chanty-Mansijskaja AO] 42-43 N 5
Surgut [SU, Samara] 42-43 J 7
Surguticha 42-43 PQ 5
Surigao 52-53 J 5
Surin 52-53 D 4
Sürmene 46-47 J 2
Surnadalsøra 30-31 C 6
Surprise Valley 76-77 CD 5
Surt 60-61 H 2
Surt, Khalīj – 60-61 H 2
Surt, Saḥrā' – 60-61 H 2-3
Surtsey 30-31 C 3
Sürüç 46-47 H 4
Surud, Raas – 60-61 b 1
Suruga wan 50-51 M 5
Surulangun 52-53 D 7
Šuryškary 42-43 M 4
Susa 36-37 B 3
Susa [IR] 46-47 N 6
Susa [J] 50-51 H 5
Susa = Sūsah 60-61 G 1
Sušac 36-37 G 4
Sūsah [LAR] 60-61 J 2
Sūsah [TN] 60-61 G 1
Susaki 50-51 J 6
Susami 50-51 K 6
Susan = Susa 46-47 N 6
Susanville, CA 72-73 B 3
Suşehri 46-47 GH 2
Sušice 33 F 4
Susitna River 70-71 FG 5
Susquehanna, PA 74-75 EF 4
Susquehanna River 74-75 E 5
Susques 80 C 2
Sūssah 46-47 J 5
Sussey 32 FG 6
Susuman 42-43 cd 5
Susurluk 46-47 C 3
Sütçüler 46-47 D 4
Sutherland [ZA] 64-65 EF 9
Sutherlin, OR 76-77 B 4
Sutlej = Satlaj 44-45 L 4
Sutsien = Suqian 48-49 M 5
Sutter Creek, CA 76-77 C 6
Sutton, WV 74-75 C 5
Suttsu 50-51 ab 2
Suur väin 30-31 K 8
Suva 52-53 a 2
Suvorovo 36-37 N 3
Suwa 50-51 M 4
Suwa-ko 50-51 M 4-5
Suwałki 33 L 1
Suwannee River 74-75 b 2
Suwannee Sound 74-75 b 2
Şuwār, Aş- 46-47 J 5
Şuwaybit, As- 46-47 H 6
Suwaydā', As- 44-45 D 4
Suwayḥ 44-45 HJ 6
Suwayqīyah, Hawr as- 46-47 LM 6
Şuwayr 46-47 J 7
Şuwayrah, Aş- 46-47 L 6
Suways, As- 60-61 L 2-3
Suways, Khalīj as- 60-61 L 3
Suways, Qanat as- 60-61 L 2
Suweis, Es- = As-Suways 60-61 L 2-3
Suweis, Khalîg es – = Khalīj as-Suways 60-61 L 3
Suweis, Qanât es- = Qanat as-Suways 60-61 L 2
Suwŏn 48-49 P 4
Şuwwān, 'Arḍ eş- = 'Arḍ aş-Şawwān 46-47 G 7
Su Xian 48-49 M 5
Suxima = Tsushima 50-51 G 5
Sūy, Nahr – 60-61 K 7
Suzaka 50-51 M 4
Suzhou 48-49 N 5
Suzu 50-51 L 4
Suzuka 50-51 L 5
Suzu misaki 50-51 L 4
Svalbard 34-35 k-m 6
Svalbard 30-31 k 6-o 5
Svappavaara 30-31 J 4
Svartenhuk Halvø 70-71 Za 3
Svartisen 30-31 EF 4
Sv'atoj Nos, mys – 42-43 ab 3
Svatovo 38-39 G 6
Svay Rieng 52-53 E 4
Sveagruva 30-31 k 6
Svealand 30-31 E-G 7
Svedala 30-31 E 10
Sveg 30-31 F 6
Svelvik 30-31 CD 8
Švenčionėliai 30-31 M 10
Svendborg 30-31 D 10
Svenskøya 30-31 mn 5
Šventoji 30-31 L 10
Sverdlovsk = Jekaterinburg 42-43 L 6
Sverdrup, ostrov – 42-43 O 3
Sverdrup Islands 70-71 P-T 2
Svetac 36-37 F 4
Svetlaja 42-43 a 8
Svetlograd 38-39 H 6
Svetlyj [SU → Orsk] 42-43 L 7
Svetozarevo 36-37 J 3-4
Svilengrad 36-37 LM 5
Svir 30-31 M 10
Svir [SU, ~] 42-43 EF 5
Svirsk 42-43 T 7
Svištov 36-37 L 4
Svobodnyj [SU ↑ Belogorsk] 42-43 YZ 7
Svolvær 30-31 F 3
Swaib, As- = Ash-Shuwayyib 46-47 MN 7
Swaibit, As- = As-Suwaybit 46-47 H 6
Swain Reefs 56-57 K 4
Swainsboro, GA 74-75 B 8
Şwaira, Aş- = Aş-Şuwayrah 46-47 L 6
Swakopmund 64-65 D 7
Swale 32 F 4
Swallow Islands 52-53 l 7
Swanage 32 F 6
Swan Hill 56-57 H 7
Swan Hills 70-71 N 7
Swan Range 76-77 G 2
Swan River [CDN, ●] 70-71 Q 7
Swansea 32 DE 6
Swansea, SC 74-75 C 8
Swans Island 74-75 J 2-3
Swanton, VT 74-75 G 2
Swartberge 64-65 F 9
Swāt 44-45 L 3-4
Swatow = Shantou 48-49 M 7
Swaziland 64-65 H 8
Sweden 30-31 F 9-J 10
Sweetgrass, MT 76-77 GH 1
Sweet Home, OR 76-77 B 3
Sweetwater, TX 72-73 FG 5
Swellendam 64-65 F 9
Świdnica 33 H 3
Świdwin 33 GH 2
Świebodzin 33 G 2
Świecie 33 HJ 2
Swift Current 70-71 P 7-8
Swinburne, Cape – 70-71 R 3
Swindon 32 F 6
Swinoujście 33 G 2
Switzerland 33 CD 5
Sybaris 36-37 G 6
Sychem = Nābulus 46-47 F 6
Sydney [AUS] 56-57 K 6
Sydney [CDN] 70-71 Y 8
Syene = Aswān 60-61 L 4
Syktyvkar 42-43 J 5
Sylarna 30-31 E 6
Sylhet = Silhat 44-45 P 6
Sylt 33 D 1
Sylva, NC 74-75 B 7
Sylvania, GA 74-75 C 8
Sylvan Pass 76-77 H 3
Sylvester, GA 74-75 B 9
Sym 42-43 Q 5
Sýmē 36-37 M 7
Syndassko 42-43 UV 3
Syowa 24 C 4-5
Syracuse, NY 72-73 LM 3
Syracuse = Siracusa 36-37 F 7
Syrdarja 42-43 M 9
Syria 44-45 D 4
Syriam = Thanlyin 52-53 C 3
Syrian Desert 44-45 DE 4
Syrië 44-45 D 4
Syrie 44-45 D 4
Syrie, Désert de – 44-45 DE 4
Syrische Woestijn 44-45 DE 4
Syrjanowsk = Zyr'anovsk 42-43 PQ 8
Sýrna 36-37 M 7
Sýros 36-37 L 7
Sysert' 38-39 M 4
Sysladobsis Lake 74-75 JK 2
Sysola 38-39 K 3
Sysran = Syzran' 42-43 N 7
Sytynja 42-43 YZ 4
Syzran' 42-43 N 7
Szamos 36-37 K 2
Szamotuły 33 H 2
Szczecin 33 G 2
Szczecinek 33 H 2
Szczytno 33 K 2
Szechuan = Sichuan 48-49 J 6-K 5
Szeged 33 JK 5
Székesfehérvár 33 J 5
Szekszárd 33 J 5
Szemao = Simao 48-49 J 7
Szeming = Xiamen 48-49 M 7
Szentes 33 K 5
Szeping = Siping 48-49 N 3
Szeskie Wzgórza 33 L 1
Szolnok 33 K 5
Szombathely 33 H 5
Szŭ-mao = Simao 48-49 J 7
Szŭ-p'ing = Siping 48-49 N 3
Szŭ-tao-kou = Sidaogou 50-51 F 2

T

Ta = Da Xian 48-49 K 5
Tabaco 52-53 H 4
Tābah, Bi'r – 62 F 3
Tabajé, Ponta – 78-79 LM 5
Tabankort 60-61 D 5
Tabar Islands 52-53 h 5
Tabarka = Ṭabarqah 60-61 F 1
Ṭabarqah 60-61 F 1
Ṭabas 44-45 H 4
Tabasco 72-73 H 8
Tabašino 38-39 J 4
Tabatinga [BR, Amazonas] 78-79 F 5
Taber 70-71 O 7
Taberg 30-31 EF 9
Tablas Island 52-53 H 4
Table, Île de la – = Đao Cai Ban 52-53 E 2
Table Mountain 76-77 G 3
Taboga 72-73 b 3
Taboga, Isla – 72-73 bc 3
Taboguilla, Isla – 72-73 bc 3
Tábor 33 G 4
Tabora 64-65 H 4
Tabor City, NC 74-75 D 7
Tabory 38-39 M 4
Tabou 60-61 C 8
Tabris = Tabrīz 44-45 F 3
Tabrīz 44-45 F 3
Tabu-dong 50-51 G 4
Tabūk 44-45 D 5
Täby 30-31 GH 8
Tabyn-Bogdo-Ola = gora Tavan Bogdo Ula 48-49 F 2
Tacau = Kaohsiung 48-49 MN 7
Ta-ch'ang-shan Tao = Dachangshan Dao 50-51 D 3
Tacheng = Chuguchak 48-49 E 2
T'a-ch'êng = Chuguchak 48-49 E 2
Tachia 48-49 MN 7
Tachibana-wan 50-51 GH 6
Tachikawa 50-51 M 5
Ta-ch'ing Shan = Daqing Shan 48-49 L 3
Tachnoj 42-43 TU 7
Tachta 42-43 a 7
Tachta-Bazar 44-45 J 3
Tachtabrod 42-43 M 7
Tachtojamsk 42-43 de 5
Ta-ch'üan = Daquan 48-49 H 3
Tacloban 52-53 HJ 4
Tacna [PE, ●] 78-79 E 8
Tacoma, WA 72-73 B 2
Taconic Range 74-75 G 3-4
Tacora, Volcán – 80 C 1
Tacuarembó [ROU, ●] 80 EF 4
Tadami gawa 50-51 M 4
Tademaït, Plateau du – = Haḍbah Tādmayt 60-61 E 3
Tādipatri = Tadpatri 44-45 M 7-8
Tadjikie 44-45 KL 3
Tadjoura 60-61 N 6
Tadjoura, Golfe de – 60-61 N 6
Tādmāyt, Haḍbah – 60-61 E
Tadmur 44-45 D 4
Tadoussac 70-71 X 8
Tadpatri 44-45 M 7-8
Tadum = Tradum 48-49 E 6
Tadzhikistan 44-45 KL 3
Tadzikistán 44-45 KL 3
Tadzjikistan 44-45 KL 3
T'aean 50-51 F 4
T'aebaek-san 50-51 G 4
T'aebaek-sanmaek 48-49 O 4
Taebu-do 50-51 F 4
T'aech'ŏn 50-51 E 3
Taech'ŏng-do 50-51 E 4
Taedong-gang 50-51 EF 3
Taegu 48-49 O 4
Tae-hŭksan-do 50-51 E 5
Taehwa-do 50-51 E 3
Taejŏn 48-49 O 4
Taejŏng 50-51 EF 6
Tae-muŭi-do 50-51 EF 4
Ta-êrh Hu = Dalaj Nur 48-49 M 3
T'aet'an 50-51 E 3
Tae-yŏnp'yŏng-do 50-51 E 4
Tafalla 34-35 G 7
Tafaraut = Ṭarfāyah 60-61 B 3
Tafâsasat, Wādī – 60-61 F 4
Tafassasset, Ouèd – = Wādī Tafâsasat 60-61 F 4
Tafassasset, Ténéré du – 60-61 FG 4
Tafdasat 60-61 F 3-4
Ṭafīlah, Aṭ- 46-47 F 7
Tafí Viejo 80 C 3
Tafresh 46-47 N 5
Tafresh, Kūh-e – 46-47 NO 5
Taft, CA 76-77 D 8
Taftān, Kūh-e – 44-45 J 5
Tagalgan 48-49 H 4
Taganrog 38-39 G 6
Taganrogskij zaliv 38-39 G 6
Tâgâu 52-53 C 2
Tagawa = Takawa 50-51 H 6
Tagbilaran 52-53 H 5
Tag-Dheer = Togdheer 60-61 b 2
Tāghīt 60-61 D 2
Tagil 38-39 M 4
Tagiúra = Tājūrā' 60-61 G 2
Tăgu = Taegu 48-49 O 4
Taguatinga [BR, Distrito Federal] 78-79 K 8
Taguatinga [BR, Goiás] 78-79 K 7
Tagula 52-53 h 7
Tagum 52-53 J 5
Tahan, Gunung – 52-53 D 6
Tahara 50-51 L 5
Tahat 60-61 F 4
Tahoe, Lake – 72-73 BC 4
Tahoe City, CA 76-77 C 6
Tahoe Valley, CA 76-77 CD 6
Tahola, WA 76-77 A 2
Tahoua 60-61 F 6
Taḥrīr, At- 62 CD 2
Ta-hsien = Da Xian 48-49 K 5
Ta-hsüeh Shan = Daxue Shan 48-49 J 5-6
Ṭahṭā 60-61 L 3
Tahtacı = Borlu 46-47 C 3
Tahtalı Dağı 46-47 D 4
Tahtali Dağlar 46-47 F 4-G 3
Ta-hu = Tachia 48-49 MN 7
Tahulandang, Pulau – 52-53 J 6
Tahuna 52-53 HJ 6
Ta-hu-shan = Dahushan 50-51 D 2
Taï 60-61 C 7
Tai'an [TJ, Liaoning] 50-51 D 2
Tai'an [TJ, Shandong] 48-49 M 4
Taibai Shan 48-49 K 5
Taibei = Taipei 48-49 N 6-7
Taichū = Taichung 48-49 MN 7
Taichung 48-49 MN 7
T'ai-chung = Taichung 48-49 MN 7
Taiden = Taejŏn 48-49 O 4
Taidong = Taitung 48-49 N 7
Ṭā'if, Aṭ- 44-45 E 6
Taigu 48-49 L 4
Taihang Shan 48-49 LM 4
Taihe [TJ, Jiangxi] 48-49 L 6
Taihei yō 50-51 K 7-O 3
Taihing = Taixing 48-49 N 5
Taiho = Taihe [TJ, Jiangxi] 48-49 L 6
Taihoku = Tai-pei 48-49 N 6-7
Tai Hu [TJ, ≈] 48-49 MN 5
Taiki 50-51 c 2
Taiku = Taigu 48-49 L 4
Taikyu = Taegu 48-49 O 4
Tailai 48-49 N 2
T'ai-lai = Tailai 48-49 N 2
Tailem Bend 56-57 GH 7
Taim 80 F 4
Tain 32 D 3
Tai-nan 48-49 MN 7
T'ai-nan = Tai-nan 48-49 MN 7
Tainão = Tai-nan 48-49 MN 7
Tainaron, Akrōtḗrion – 36-37 K 7
Taipale 30-31 N 6
Taipeh = Tai-pei 48-49 N 6-7
Tai-pei 48-49 N 6-7
Taiping [MAL] 52-53 CD 5-6
Taipingshao 50-51 E 2
Taiping Yang 48-49 O 8-R 5
Taipinsan = Miyako-jima 48-49 O 7
Taisei 50-51 ab 2
Taisha 50-51 J 5
Taishun 48-49 MN 6
Ta'iss = Ta'izz 44-45 E 8
Taitao, Cabo – 80 A 7
Taitao, Peninsula de – 80 AB 7
T'ai-tchong = Tai-chung 48-49 MN 7
Taitō = Tai-tung 48-49 N 7
Tai-tung 48-49 N 7
T'ai-tzŭ Ho = Taizi He 50-51 D 2
Taivalkoski 30-31 N 5
Taivassalo 30-31 JK 7
Taiwa 50-51 N 3
Taiwán 48-49 N 7
Taïwan 48-49 N 7
T'ai-wan Hai-hsia 48-49 M 7-N 6
Taiwan Haixia = T'ai-wan Hai-hsia 48-49 M 7-N 6
T'ai-wan Shan 48-49 N 7
Taixing 48-49 N 5
Taiyuan 48-49 L 4
T'ai-yüan = Taiyuan 48-49 L 4
Taizhong = Taichung 48-49 MN 7
Taizhou 48-49 MN 5
Taizi He 50-51 D 2
Ta'izz 44-45 E 8
Tāj, At- 60-61 J 4
Taj, El – = At-Tāj 60-61 J 4
Tajarḥī 60-61 G 4
Tajdžinar nuur 48-49 GH 4
Tajga 42-43 PQ 6
Tajgonos, mys – 42-43 ef 5
Tajgonos, poluostrov – 42-43 f 5
Tajima 50-51 M 4
Tajis 44-45 G 8
Tajitos 76-77 G 10
Tajmura 42-43 ST 5
Tajmyr, Circunscripción Nacional de – 42-43 P-U 3
Tajmyr, ozero – 42-43 TU 3
Tajmyr, poluostrov – 42-43 R-U 2
Tajo 34-35 F 8
Tajšet 42-43 S 6
Tajsir 48-49 H 2
Tajumulco, Volcán de – 72-73 H 8
Tajuña 34-35 F 8
Tajuña 34-35 F 8
Tajūrā' 60-61 G 2
Tak 52-53 C 3
Takāb 46-47 M 4
Takaba 63 E 2
Takachiho = Mitai 50-51 H 6
Takada 48-49 Q 4
Takada = Bungotakada 50-51 H 6
Takada = Rikuzen-Takata 50-51 NO 3
Takahagi 50-51 N 4
Takahashi 50-51 J 5
Takahashi-gawa 50-51 J 5
Takahe, Mount – 24 B 25-26
Takalar 52-53 G 8
Takamatsu 48-49 PQ 5
Takamatu = Takamatsu 48-49 PQ 5
Takamori 50-51 H 6
Takanabe 50-51 H 6
Takao = Kao-hsiung 48-49 MN 7
Takaoka 48-49 Q 4
Takapuna 56-57 O 7
Takasaki 48-49 Q 4
Takataka 52-53 k 6
Takawa 50-51 H 6
Takayama 50-51 L 4
Takefu 50-51 KL 5
Takemachi = Taketa 50-51 H 6
Takengon 52-53 C 6
Takéo 52-53 D 4
Take-shima [J, Ōsumi shotō] 50-51 H 7
Take-shima [J ↖ Oki] 50-51 HJ 4
Tākestān 46-47 NO 4
Taketa 50-51 H 6
Takhlīs, Bi'r – 62 CD 6
Ta Khmau 52-53 DE 4
Takht-e Jämshīd = Persepolis 44-45 G 4
Takikawa 50-51 b 2
Takinoue 50-51 c 1
Takiyuak Lake 70-71 O 4
Takla Lake 70-71 LM 6
Takla Makan 48-49 D-F 4
Takla Makan Chöli 48-49 D-F 4
Takla Makan Chöli 48-49 D-F 4
Tako-bana 50-51 J 5
Takoma Park, MD 74-75 E 5
Takua Pa 52-53 C 5
Tākwayat, Wādī – 60-61 E 4
Takyu = Taegu 48-49 O 4
Talā [ET] 62 D 2
Talacasto 80 C 4
Talaimannar = Taleimannarama 44-45 MN 9
Talak 60-61 EF 5
Tālaqān 46-47 O 4
Talara 78-79 C 5
Talas 42-43 N 9
Talasea 52-53 gh 6
Talaud, Kepulauan – 52-53 J 6
Talavera de la Reina 34-35 E 8-9
Talawdī 60-61 L 6
Talbingo 58 J 5
Talbot, Cape – 56-57 E 2
Talbot, Mount – 56-57 E 5
Talca 80 B 5
Talcahuano 80 AB 5
Taldy-Kurgan 42-43 OP 8
Taleimannarama 44-45 MN 9
Tal-e Khosravī = Yasūj 44-45 G 4
Talent, OR 76-77 B 4
Tale Sap = Thale Luang 52-53 D 5
Tali = Dali [TJ, Yunnan] 48-49 HJ 6
Taliabu, Pulau – 52-53 HJ 7
Talica 38-39 M 4
Ta-lien = Dalian 48-49 N 4
Talimā 78-79 H 4
Ta-ling Ho = Daling He 50-51 G 2
Taliwang 52-53 G 8
Talju, Jabal – 60-61 K 6
Talkeetna Mountains 70-71 G 5
Talkheh Rūd 46-47 M 4
Talladega, AL 72-73 J 5
Tall 'Afar 46-47 K 4
Tallahassee, FL 72-73 K 5
Tall al-Abyaḍ 46-47 H 4
Tall as-Sam'ān 46-47 H 4
Tall Bisah 46-47 G 5
Tall Ḥalaf 46-47 HJ 4
Tallin = Tallinn 42-43 CD 6
Tallinn 42-43 CD 6
Tallinn 30-31 KL 8
Tall Kalakh 46-47 G 5
Tall Kayf 46-47 K 4
Tall Kujik 46-47 JK 4
Tall Tāmir 46-47 J 4
Tall 'Uwaynāt 46-47 JK 4
Tal'menka 42-43 PQ 7
Talnach 42-43 QR 4
Talo = Nantong 48-49 N 5
Talōdī = Talawdī 60-61 L 6
Talovaja 38-39 GH 5
Talsi 30-31 K 9
Taltal 80 B 3
Taltson River 70-71 O 5
Talvār, Rūdkhāneh – 46-47 MN 5
Talvik 30-31 K 2
Talwood 58 J 2
Talyawalka Creek 58 F 3-4
Tamādah 60-61 E 4
Tamale 60-61 D 7
Tamana [J] 50-51 H 6
Tamano 50-51 JK 5
Tamanrāsat 60-61 EF 4
Tamanrâsat, Wādī – 60-61 E 4
Tamaqua, PA 74-75 F 4
Tamarugal, Pampa del – 80 C 1-2
Tamási 33 HJ 5
Tamatave = Toamasina 64-65 LM 6
Tamaulipas 72-73 G 6-7
Tamayama 50-51 N 3
Tambach 63 CD 2
Tambacounda 60-61 B 6
Tambaqui 78-79 G 6
Tambej 42-43 N 3
Tambo, El – [CO, Cauca] 78-79 D 4
Tambo, Río – [PE ◁ Río Ucayali] 78-79 E 7
Tambohorano 64-65 K 6
Tambora, Gunung – 52-53 G 8
Tamboritha, Mount – 58 H 6
Tambov 38-39 H 5
Tamč 48-49 G 2

Tam Cag Bulak = Tamsagbulag 48-49 M 2
Tamdybulak 42-43 L 9
Tâmega 34-35 D 8
Támesis = Thames 32 G 6
Tamgak, Monts – 60-61 F 5
Tamiahua, Laguna de – 72-73 G 7
Tamiami Canal 74-75 c 4
Tamil Nadu 44-45 M 8-9
Ta'mīn, At- 46-47 KL 5
Tāmir'z'qīd 60-61 AB 5
Tamise = Thames 32 G 6
Tāmīyah 62 D 3
Tam Ky 52-53 E 3
Tammerfors = Tampere 30-31 K 7
Tammisaari = Ekenäs 30-31 K 7
Tampa, FL 72-73 K 6
Tampa Bay 72-73 K 6
Tampelan, Kepulauan – 52-53 E 6
Tampere 30-31 KL 7
Tampico 72-73 G 7
Tampin 52-53 D 6
Tampoketsa, Plateau du – = Causse du Kelifely 64-65 KL 6
Ṭamrīdah 44-45 G 8
Tamsagbulag 48-49 M 2
Tāmshikiṭ 60-61 BC 5
Tamud = Thamūd 44-45 F 7
Tamworth [AUS] 56-57 K 6
Tamyang 50-51 F 5
Tana [EAK] 64-65 JK 3
Tana [Vanuatu] 56-57 N 3
Tana [N, ∼] 30-31 M 2-3
Tana [N, ●] 30-31 N 2
Tanabat 52-53 C 6
Tanabe 50-51 K 6
Tanabu = Mutsu 50-51 N 2
Tanacross, AK 70-71 H 5
Ta-n-Adar 60-61 F 5
Tanafjord 30-31 N 2
Tanaga Island 19 D 36-1
Tanágra 36-37 K 6
Ṭana Hayik 60-61 M 6
Tanahbala, Pulau – 52-53 C 7
Tanahgrogot 52-53 G 7
Tanahjampea, Pulau – 52-53 H 8
Tanahkadukung 52-53 H 9
Tanahmasa, Pulau – 52-53 C 6-7
Tanah Menah 52-53 D 5
Tanahmerah 52-53 LM 8
Tanakeke, Pulau – 52-53 G 8
Tanami 56-57 E 3
Tanami Desert 56-57 F 3
Tanana, AK 70-71 F 4
Tananarive = Antananarivo 64-65 L 6
Tanana River 70-71 G 5
Tân Ấp 52-53 E 3
Tànaro 36-37 B 3
Ṭanburah 60-61 K 7
Tanchavur = Thanjavar 44-45 MN 8
Tanch'ŏn 50-51 G 2
Tanchow = Dan Xian 48-49 K 8
Tancitaro, Pico de – 72-73 F 8
Tandag 52-53 J 5
Tandaho = Tendaho 60-61 N 6
Ţăndărei 36-37 M 3
Tandil 80 E 5
Tandou Lake 58 EF 4
Tanega-shima 48-49 P 5
Tanega sima = Tanega-shima 48-49 P 5
Tanew 33 L 3
Tanezrouft = Tānīzruft 60-61 DE 4
Tanf, Jabal at- 46-47 H 6
Tanga 64-65 J 4
Tangail = Ṭangāyal 44-45 O 6
Tanga Islands 52-53 h 5
Tanganyika, Lake – 64-65 G 3-H 4
Tangar = Thangkar 48-49 J 4
Tangará 80 F 3
Tangāyal 44-45 O 6
T'ang-chan = Tangshan 48-49 M 4
Tanger = Ṭanjah 60-61 C 1
Tanggela Youmu Hu = Thangra Yumtsho 48-49 EF 5
Tanggu 48-49 M 4
Tangier Sound 74-75 EF 5-6
Tangjin 50-51 F 4
Tang La [TJ, Himalaya ⇆] 48-49 F 6
Tang La [TJ, Tanglha] 48-49 G 5
Tangla = Tanglha 48-49 FG 5
Tanglha 48-49 FG 5
Tangshan 48-49 M 4
Tangshancheng 50-51 DE 2
Tanguj 42-43 T 6
Tangyuan 48-49 O 2
Tanhsien = Dan Xian 48-49 K 8
Tanimbar, Kepulauan – 52-53 K 8
Taninthārī 52-53 C 4
Taninthārī Taing 52-53 C 4
Tānīzruft 60-61 DE 4
Ṭanjah 60-61 C 1
Tanjay 52-53 H 5
Tanjong Malim 52-53 D 6
Tanjor = Thanjavur 44-45 MN 8
Tanjung 52-53 G 7
Tanjungbalai 52-53 CD 6
Tanjungkarang 52-53 DE 8
Tanjungkarang-Telukbetung = Bandar Lampung 52-53 DE 8
Tanjungpandan 52-53 E 7
Tanjungpinang 52-53 DE 6
Tanjungpura 52-53 C 6
Tanjungredep 52-53 G 6
Tanlovo 42-43 NO 4
Tännäs 30-31 E 6
Tannūmah, At- 46-47 MN 7
Tannu-Ola, chrebet – 42-43 R 7
Tanoé 60-61 D 7
Tanoût 60-61 F 6
Tanque, AZ 76-77 J 9
Tan-shui 48-49 N 6
Tansīft, Wādī – 60-61 C 2
Ṭanṭā 60-61 KL 2
Tanyang 50-51 G 4
Tanyeri 46-47 HJ 3
Tanzania 64-65 HJ 4
Tanzanie 64-65 HJ 4
Taoan 48-49 N 2
Tao'an = Baicheng 48-49 N 2
T'ao-chou = Lintan 48-49 J 5
Taormina 36-37 F 7
Taos, NM 72-73 E 4
Taoudenni 60-61 D 4
Taourirt = Tāwrīrt 60-61 D 2
Tapa 30-31 L 8
Tapachula 72-73 H 9
Tapajós, Rio – 78-79 H 5
Tapaktuan 52-53 C 6
Ta-pa Shan = Daba Shan 48-49 KL 5
Tapat, Pulau – 52-53 J 7
Tapauá 78-79 FG 6
Tapauá, Rio – 78-79 F 6
Tapepo 63 B 4
Taperoá [BR, Bahia] 78-79 M 7
Tapeta 60-61 C 7
Tāpī = Tapti 44-45 M 6
Ta-pieh Shan = Dabie Shan 48-49 M 5
Tapini 52-53 N 8
Tapirapecó, Sierra – 78-79 FG 4
Tappahannock, VA 74-75 E 5-6
Tappi-saki 50-51 MN 2
Tappita = Tapeta 60-61 C 7
Tapti 44-45 M 6
Tapuaenuku 56-57 O 8
Ta-pu-hsün Hu = Dabas nuur 48-49 H 4
Tapuruquara 78-79 FG 5
Taqṭaq 46-47 L 5
Taquari Novo, Rio – 78-79 H 8
Tara 36-37 H 4
Tara [AUS] 56-57 K 5
Tara [SU, ∼] 42-43 O 6
Tara [SU, ●] 42-43 N 6
Tarabuco 78-79 FG 8
Ṭarābulus 60-61 GH 2
Ṭarābulus al-Gharb 60-61 G 2
Ṭarābulus ash-Shām 44-45 CD 4
Tarago 58 J 5
Tarahumara, Sierra – 72-73 E 6
Tarāī = Terei 44-45 NO 5
Tarakan 52-53 G 6
Taraklı 46-47 D 2
Taraklija 36-37 N 3
Taralga 58 JK 5
Taram Darya = Tarim darya 48-49 E 3
Taran, mys – 33 JK 1
Tarangire National Park 63 D 3-4
Tàranto 36-37 G 5
Tàranto, Golfo di – 36-37 G 5
Tarapoto 78-79 D 6
Taraquá 78-79 F 4
Tarare 34-35 K 6
Tarascon 34-35 K 7
Tarasovo 38-39 J 2
Tarat, Ouèd – = Wādī Tarāt 60-61 F 3
Tarāt, Wādī – 60-61 F 3
Tarauacá 78-79 E 6
Tarauacá, Rio – 78-79 E 6
Tarayfāwī 46-47 J 7
Tarazona 34-35 G 8
Tarbagataij, chrebet – 42-43 PQ 8
Tarbagataj 48-49 EF 2
Tarbaj 63 E 2
Tarbes 34-35 H 7
Tarboro, NC 74-75 E 7
Tarchankut, mys – 36-37 OP 3
Tarcoola 56-57 FG 6
Tarcoon 58 H 3
Tardoire 34-35 H 6
Tardoki-Jani, gora – 42-43 a 8
Taree 56-57 K 6
Tareja = Ust'-Tareja 42-43 R 3
Tärendö 30-31 JK 4
Tarente = Tàranto 36-37 G 5
Tarento = Tàranto 36-37 G 5
Tareraimbu, Cachoeira – 78-79 J 6
Ṭarfā', Wādī aṭ- 62 D 3
Ṭarfāwī, Bi'r – [ET] 62 C 6
Ṭarfāwī, Bi'r – [IRQ] 46-47 K 5
Ṭarfāyah [MA, ●] 60-61 B 3
Ṭarfāyah, Qārat aṭ- 62 BC 2
Tarfāyah, Rā's – 60-61 B 3
Targhee Pass 76-77 H 3
Tîrgovişte 36-37 M 4
Tarhit = Tāghīt 60-61 D 2
Tarhūnah [DZ] 60-61 G 2
Tarian Ganga = Dariganga 48-49 L 2
Tarīf 44-45 G 6
Tarifa 34-35 E 11
Tarifa, Punta de – 34-35 DE 10
Tarija [BOL, ●] 78-79 G 9
Tarīm 44-45 F 7
Tarim darya 48-49 E 3
Tarime 63 C 3
Tarkio, MT 76-77 F 2
Tarko-Sale 42-43 O 5
Tarkwa 60-61 D 7
Tarlac 52-53 H 3
Ṭārmīyah, Aṭ- 46-47 KL 6
Tarn 34-35 H 7
Tärna 30-31 F 5
Tarnów 33 K 3
Ṭārom 44-45 GH 5
Taroom 56-57 JK 5
Târoûdânt = Tārūdānt 60-61 C 2
Tarpon Springs, FL 74-75 b 2
Tarquinia 36-37 D 4
Tarragona 34-35 H 8
Tarrakoski 30-31 J 3
Tar River 74-75 E 7
Tarso = Tarsus 46-47 F 4
Tarso Emissi = Kégueur Terbi 60-61 H 4
Tarsus 46-47 F 4
Tarsusırmağı 46-47 F 4
Tartagal [RA, Salta] 80 D 2
Tartār, Wādī at- 46-47 K 5
Tartaria, Estrecho de – 42-43 b 7-a 8
Tartaria, República Autónoma de – = 6 ◁ 42-43 J 6
Tartarie, Manche de – 42-43 b 7-a 8
Tartas [SU] 42-43 O 6
Ṭarṭīn, Bi'r – 46-47 J 5
Tartu 30-31 M 8
Ṭarṭūs 44-45 D 4
Tārūdānt 60-61 C 2
Tarūfāwī, Bi'r – 46-47 K 6
Tarumizu 50-51 H 7
Tarutino 36-37 N 2
Tarutung 52-53 C 6
Tarvisio 36-37 E 2
Tašauz 42-43 K 9
Tasāwah 60-61 G 3
Taşçı = Bakırdağı 46-47 F 3
Tasejevo 42-43 RS 6
Taşeli Yaylâsı 46-47 E 4
Tashichhö Dsong = Thimbu 44-45 OP 5
Tashigong = Zhaxigang 48-49 DE 5
Tashi Gonpa 48-49 G 5
Ta-shih-ch'iao = Dashiqiao 50-51 D 2
Tashijong Dsong 44-45 P 5
Tashilhumpo = Zhaxilhünbo 48-49 F 6
Ṭashk, Daryācheh – 44-45 GH 5
Tash Qurghan 48-49 D 4
Tasikmalaja 52-53 E 8
Taškent 42-43 M 9
Tasköprü 46-47 F 2
Tasköprü = Hekimdağ 46-47 D 3
Taš-Kumyr 44-45 L 2
Tas-Kystabyt 42-43 bc 5
Taşlıcay 46-47 K 3
Tasman, Mar de – 56-57 K-N 7
Tasman, Mer de – 56-57 K-N 7
Tasman Bay 56-57 O 8
Tasman Head 58 cd 3
Tasmania 56-57 HJ 8
Tasmania, Dorsal de – 22-23 R 8
Tasmanie = Tasmania 56-57 HJ 8
Tasmanie, Seuil de – 22-23 R 8
Tasman Land 56-57 D 3-E 2
Tasman Peninsula 58 d 3
Tasman Rise 22-23 R 8
Tasmanrug 22-23 R 8
Tasman Sea 56-57 K-N 7
Tasmanzee 56-57 K-N 7
Taşova 46-47 G 2
Tassili n'Ajjer = Murtaf'āt Tāsīlī 60-61 F 3
Taštagol 42-43 Q 7
Taštyp 42-43 Q 7
Tasūj 46-47 L 3
Tata 33 J 5
Tatabánya 33 HJ 5
Tatar Autonomous Region = 6 ◁ 42-43 J 6
Tatarbunary 36-37 N 3
Tataren Autonome Republiek = 6 ◁ 42-43 J 6
Tatarensont 42-43 b 7-a 8
Tatars, République Autonome des – = 6 ◁ 42-43 J 6
Tatarsk 42-43 NO 6
Tatar Strait 42-43 b 7-a 8
Tātā'ū, Rūd-e – 46-47 LM 4
Taṭāwīn 60-61 G 2
Tateoka = Murayama 50-51 N 3
Tateyama 50-51 M 5
Tateyamahōjō = Tateyama 50-51 M 5
Tathlina Lake 70-71 N 5
Tathlīth 44-45 E 7
Tathlīth, Wādī – 44-45 E 6-7
Tatlīt = Tathlīth 44-45 E 7
Tatnam, Cape – 70-71 ST 6
Ta-t'ong = Datong 48-49 L 3
Tatran 48-49 EF 4
Tatry 33 JK 4
Tatsaitan = Tagalgan 48-49 H 4
Tatsuno 50-51 K 5
Tatta = Ṭhaṭṭha 44-45 K 6
Tatung = Datong [TJ, Shanxi] 48-49 L 3
Ta-t'ung Ho = Datong He 48-49 J 4
Tatvan 46-47 K 3
Tau 30-31 AB 8
Tauá 78-79 L 6
Taubaté 78-79 KL 9
Tauberbischofsheim 33 DE 4
Taujskaja guba 42-43 cd 6
Taukum 42-43 O 9
Taumarunui 56-57 OP 7
Taumaturgo 78-79 E 6
Taungdwingyī 52-53 BC 2-3
Taunggyī 52-53 C 2
Taungngū 52-53 C 3
Taunton 32 E 6
Taunton, MA 74-75 H 4
Taunus 33 D 3
Taupo 56-57 P 7
Taupo, Lake – 56-57 P 7
Tauragė 30-31 JK 10
Tauranga 56-57 P 7
Taurirt = Tāwrīrt 60-61 D 2
Tauro 44-45 C 3
Taurovo 42-43 N 6
Taurus Mountains 44-45 C 3
Taushqan Darya = Kök shal 48-49 D 3
Tauz 38-39 J 7
Ṭavālesh, Kūhha-ye – 46-47 MN 3
Tavan Bogdo Ula, gora – 48-49 F 2
Tavares, FL 74-75 c 2
Tavas 46-47 C 4
Tavastehus = Hämeenlinna 30-31 L 7
Tavda [SU, ∼] 42-43 L 6
Tavda [SU, ●] 42-43 M 6
Taveta 64-65 J 3
Taveuni 52-53 b 2
Tavira 34-35 D 10
Tavolara 36-37 CD 5
Tavoliere 36-37 F 5
Tavoy = Htāwei 52-53 C 4
Tavoy Island = Mali Kyūn 52-53 C 4
Tavşanlı 46-47 C 3
Tavua 52-53 a 2
Ta-wa = Dawa 50-51 D 2
Ta-wang-chia Tao = Dawangjia Dao 50-51 D 3
Tawau 52-53 G 6
Ṭawīl, Bi'r – 60-61 L 4
Ṭawīl, Sabkhat aṭ- 46-47 J 5
Ṭawīlah, Juzur – 62 EF 4
Tawile Island = Juzur Ṭawīlah 62 EF 4
Tawi-tawi Island 52-53 GH 5
Ṭawkar 60-61 M 5
Tāwrīrt 60-61 D 2
Ṭāwūq 46-47 L 5
Ṭāwūq Chāy 46-47 L 5
Ṭāwūq Chāy 46-47 L 5
Tāwurghā', Sabkhat – 60-61 H 2
Tawzar 60-61 F 2
Taxco de Alarcón 72-73 FG 8
Tay 32 E 3
Tay, Firth of – 32 E 3
Tayabamba 78-79 D 6
Tayan 52-53 F 7
Ta-yang Ho = Dayang He 50-51 D 2
Ṭayb al-Fāl 46-47 J 5
Tayeeglow 60-61 ab 3
Taÿgetos 36-37 K 7
Tayishan = Guanyun 48-49 MN 5
Taylorsville, NC 74-75 C 6-7
Taymā' 44-45 D 5
Tayna 63 B 3
Tây Ninh 52-53 E 4
Ṭayr, Jabal aṭ- 44-45 E 7
Tây Sa, Quân Đao – 52-53 EF 3
Taytay 52-53 GH 4
Ta-yü = Dayu 48-49 L 6
Tayung = Dayong 48-49 L 6
Taz 42-43 OP 4
Tazădīt 60-61 B 4
Tāzah 60-61 D 2
Tazarbū 60-61 J 3
Tāzārīn 60-61 CD 2
Tazarine = Tāzārīn 60-61 CD 2
Tazawako 50-51 N 3
Tázerbó = Tazarbū 60-61 J 3
Tazewell, VA 74-75 C 6
Tazovskaja guba 42-43 NO 4
Tazovskij 42-43 OP 4
Tazovskij poluostrov 42-43 NO 4
Tbilisi 38-39 H 7
Tchad 60-61 HJ 5
Tchad, Lac – 60-61 G 6
Tch'ang-cha = Changsha 48-49 L 6
Tchang-kia-k'eou = Zhangjiakou 48-49 L 3
Tch'ang-tch'ouen = Changchun 48-49 NO 3
Tchan-kiang = Zhanjiang 48-49 L 7
Tchécoslovaquie 33 F-K 4
Tchéliouskine, Cap – = mys Čel'uskin 42-43 UV 2
Tch'eng-tö = Chengde 48-49 M 3
Tch'eng-tou = Chengdu 48-49 J 5
Tcherkesses, Région Autonome des – = 2 ◁ 38-39 H 7
Tchertchen = Chärchän 48-49 F 4
Tchetcheno-Ingouches, République Autonome des – = 5 ◁ 38-39 J 7
Tchibanga 64-65 D 3
Tchien = Zwedru 60-61 C 7
Tchin Tabaraden 60-61 F 5
Tchong King = Chongqing 48-49 K 6
Tchouktchis, District National des – 42-43 g-j 4
Tchouktchis, Mer des – 19 BC 35-36
Tchouktchis, Seuil des – 19 B 35
Tchouvaches, République Autonome des – = 4 ◁ 42-43 H 6
Tczew 33 J 1
Te Anau, Lake – 56-57 N 9
Teano 36-37 F 5
Tea Tree 56-57 F 4
Te Awamutu 56-57 OP 7
Tebas = Thêbai 36-37 K 6
Tebas = Thêbai [ET] 60-61 L 3
Tebessa = Tibissah 60-61 F 1
Tebingtinggi [RI, Sumatera Selatan] 52-53 D 7
Tebingtinggi [RI, Sumatera Utara] 52-53 CD 6
Tebulosmta, gora – 38-39 J 7
Tecate 72-73 C 5
Tecer Dağları 46-47 G 3
Techis 48-49 E 3
Tecka 80 B 6
Tecomán 72-73 F 8
Tecuala 72-73 E 7
Tecuci 36-37 M 3
Tedeini, In – = 'Ayn Tādīn 60-61 E 4
Tedžen 44-45 J 3
Tees 32 EF 4
Tefé 78-79 G 5
Tefé, Rio – 78-79 F 5
Tefedest = Tafdasat 60-61 F 3-4
Tefenni 46-47 C 4
Tegal 52-53 E 8
Tégerhi = Tajarhī 60-61 G 4
Tegernsee 33 EF 5
Teguantepeque = Santo Domingo Tehuantepec 72-73 G 8
Tegucigalpa 72-73 J 9
Tegul'det 42-43 Q 6
Tehachapi, CA 76-77 D 8
Tehachapi Mountains 76-77 D 8
Tehachapi Pass 76-77 D 8
Tehama, CA 76-77 B 5
Tehek Lake 70-71 R 4
Teherán = Tehrān 44-45 G 3
Téhéran = Tehrān 44-45 G 3
Tehrān 44-45 G 3
Tehuacán 72-73 G 8
Tehuantepec, Golfo de – 72-73 GH 8
Tehuantepec, Istmo de – 72-73 GH 8
Teide, Pico de – 60-61 A 3
Teixeira da Silva = Bailundo 64-65 E 5
Tejkovo 38-39 H 4
Tejo 34-35 C 9
Tejon Pass 72-73 C 4-5
Tekağaç Burun 46-47 B 4
Te Kao 56-57 O 6
Teke [TR, ≅] 46-47 CD 4
Teke [TR, ●] 46-47 C 2
Teke Burnu 46-47 B 3
Tekeli 42-43 O 9
Tekeli Dağı 46-47 G 2
Tekirdağ 44-45 B 2
Tekman 46-47 J 3
Tekoa, WA 76-77 E 2
Tekouiât, Ouèd – = Wādī Tākwayat 60-61 E 4
Te Kuiti 56-57 OP 7
Tel 44-45 N 6
Tela 72-73 J 8
Tēla = Tel 44-45 N 6
Telanaipura = Jambi 52-53 D 7
Telavi 38-39 J 7
Telefomin 52-53 M 8
Telegraph Creek 70-71 K 6
Telegraph Point 58 L 3
Telemark 30-31 BC 8
Telemsès = Tlemcès 60-61 EF 5
Telenešty 36-37 N 2
Teleno, El – 34-35 D 7
Telescope Peak 76-77 E 7
Teles Pires, Rio – 78-79 H 6
Telford 32 E 5
Télig 60-61 D 4
Telijn nuur 48-49 F 2
Télimélé 60-61 B 6
Teljō, Jebel – = Jabal Talju 60-61 K 6
Tell Abyad = Tall al-Abyaḍ 46-47 H 4
Tell Atlas 60-61 D 2-E 1
Tell Bīs = Tall Bisah 46-47 G 5
Teller, AK 70-71 CD 4
Tell Ḥalaf = Tall Ḥalaf 46-47 HJ 4
Tell Kalakh = Tall Kalakh 46-47 G 5
Tell Kôttchak = Tall Kujik 46-47 JK 4
Tell Sem'ân = Tall as-Sam'ān 46-47 H 4
Telocaset, OR 76-77 E 3
Telok Anson = Teluk Intan 52-53 CD 6
Telok Betong = Bandar Lampung 52-53 DE 8
Teloloapan 72-73 FG 8
Tēlos 36-37 M 7
Tel'posiz, gora – 42-43 K 5
Telsen 80 C 6
Telšiai 30-31 K 10
Telukbetung = Tanjungkarang 52-53 DE 8
Telukdalam 52-53 C 6
Teluk Intan 52-53 CD 6
Tema 60-61 DE 7
Temassinine = Burj 'Umar Idrīs 60-61 EF 3

Tembellaga = Timboulaga 60-61 F 5
Tembenči 42-43 S 4
Tembilahan 52-53 D 7
Temblor Range 76-77 D 8
Temecula, CA 76-77 E 9
Temelli 46-47 E 3
Temesvár = Timişoara 36-37 J 3
Téminos, Laguna de – 72-73 H 8
Temir 42-43 K 8
Temirtau [SU, Kazachskaja SSR] 42-43 N 7-8
Temirtau [SU, Rossijskaja SFSR] 42-43 Q 7
Témiscaming 70-71 V 8
Temnikov 42-43 G 7
Temora 56-57 J 6
Témpē 36-37 K 6
Tempe, AZ 76-77 GH 9
Tempe, Danau – 52-53 GH 7
Tèmpio Pausània 36-37 C 5
Temple, TX 72-73 G 5
Temple Bay 56-57 H 2
Temporal, Cachoeira – 78-79 J 7
Temuco 80 B 5
Tena [CO] 78-79 D 5
Tenabo, NV 76-77 E 5
Tenabo, Mount – 76-77 E 5
Tenali 44-45 N 7
Tenasserim = Taninthārī 52-53 C 4
Tenasserim = Taninthārī Taing 52-53 C 4
Tenda, Colle di – 36-37 B 3
Tendaho 60-61 N 6
Ten Degree Channel 44-45 P 8
Ten Degree Channel 44-45 P 8
Tendrovskaja kosa 36-37 OP 2
Tendūf 60-61 C 3
Tendürek Daği 46-47 KL 3
Tenedos = Bozcaada 46-47 AB 3
Ténéré 60-61 FG 4-5
Tenerife [E] 60-61 A 3
Ténès = Tanas 60-61 E 1
Tenf, Jebel – = Jabal at-Tanf 46-47 H 6
Tenga, Kepulauan – 52-53 G 8
Tengarong 52-53 G 7
Tengchong 48-49 H 6-7
Tengchung = Tengchong 48-49 H 6-7
Tenggeli Hai = Nam Tsho 48-49 G 5
Tenghsien = Teng Xian 48-49 M 4
Tengiz, ozero – 42-43 M 7
Tengréla = Tingréla 60-61 C 6
Tengri Nuur = Nam Tsho 48-49 G 5
Teng Xian 48-49 M 4
Teniente, El – 80 BC 4
Teniente Matienzo 24 C 30-31
Tenino, WA 76-77 B 2
Tenke 64-65 G 5
Tenkodogo 60-61 DE 6
Tennant, CA 76-77 C 5
Tennant Creek 56-57 FG 3
Tennessee 72-73 JK 4
Tennessee River 72-73 J 4-5
Tennille, GA 74-75 B 8
Tēnos 36-37 L 7
Tenosique de Pino Suárez 72-73 H 8
Tenryū gawa 50-51 L 5
Tensift, Ouèd – = Wad Tansīft 60-61 C 2
Ten Sleep 76-77 K 3-4
Tenterfield 56-57 K 5
Ten Thousand Islands 72-73 K 6
Tenyueh = Tengchong 48-49 H 6-7
Teocaltiche 72-73 F 7
Teófilo Otoni 78-79 L 8
Teotepec, Cerro – 72-73 FG 8
Tepa 52-53 J 8
Tepasto 30-31 L 3-4
Tepatitlán de Morelos 72-73 F 7
Tepe = Karakoçan 46-47 HJ 3
Tepeköy = Torbalı 46-47 B 3
Tepic 72-73 EF 7
Teplice 33 E 3
Tepoca, Bahía de – 76-77 G 10
Tepoca, Cabo – 76-77 G 10
Teques, Los – 78-79 F 2
Tēqūma 46-47 F 7
Ter 34-35 J 8
Téra 60-61 E 6
Tera 34-35 D 8
Teradomari 50-51 M 4
Terai 44-45 NO 5
Terang 58 F 7
Terangan = Pulau Trangan 52-53 K 8
Tercan 46-47 J 3
Terek 38-39 J 7
Terengganu, Kuala – 52-53 DE 5
Teresina 78-79 L 6
Teresinha 78-79 J 4
Teressa Island 44-45 P 9
Terhazza [RMM, ≅] 60-61 CD 4
Terhazza [RMM, ∅] 60-61 CD 4
Teriberka [SU, ●] 42-43 F 4
Termas, Las – 80 CD 3
Terme 46-47 G 2
Termet = Termit 60-61 G 5
Termez 44-45 K 3
Tèrmini Imerese 36-37 E 7-F 6
Termit 60-61 G 5
Tèrmoli 36-37 F 4-5
Ternate 52-53 J 6
Ternej 42-43 a 8
Terni 36-37 E 4
Ternopol' 38-39 E 6
Terpenija, mys – 42-43 bc 8
Terpenija, zaliv – 42-43 b 8
Terrace 70-71 L 7
Terracina 36-37 E 5
Terråk 30-31 E 5
Terranova = Newfoundland 70-71 Za 8
Terranova = Newfoundland 70-71 Za 8
Terranova, Banco de – 22-23 G 3
Terranova, Cuenca de – 22-23 GH 3
Terranova, Ramal de – 22-23 G 3-H 4
Terrassa 34-35 HJ 8
Terrebonne, OR 76-77 C 3
Terre Clarie 24 C 14
Terre Haute, IN 72-73 J 4
Terrell, TX 72-73 G 5
Terre-Neuve = Newfoundland 70-71 Za 8
Terre-Neuve, Banc de – 22-23 G 3
Terre-Neuve, Bassin de – 22-23 GH 3
Terre-Neuve, Seuil de – 22-23 G 3-H 4
Terreton, ID 76-77 G 4
Tersakan Gölü 46-47 E 3
Terskej Ala-Too, chrebet – 44-45 M 2
Teruel 34-35 G 8
Terutao, Ko – 52-53 C 5
Tesaua = Tasāwah 60-61 G 3
Teseney 60-61 M 5-6
Teshekpuk Lake 70-71 F 3
Teshikaga 50-51 d 2
Teshio 48-49 R 3
Teshio dake 50-51 c 2
Teshio-gawa 50-51 bc 1
Teshio-santi 50-51 bc 1
Tesijn gol 48-49 H 2
Tesino = Ticino 33 D 5
Tesio = Teshio 48-49 R 3
Teslin 70-71 K 5
Teslin Lake 70-71 K 5
Teslin River 70-71 K 5
Tessalit 60-61 E 4
Tessaoua 60-61 F 6
Teste, la – 34-35 G 6
Tetas, Punta – 80 B 2
Tete [Moçambique, ●] 64-65 H 6
Tete [Moçambique, ☆] 64-65 H 6
Tētērē 42-43 T 5
Teterev 38-39 E 5
Teteven 36-37 L 4
Tetonia, ID 76-77 H 4
Teton Mountains 76-77 H 3-4
Teton River 76-77 H 2
Tetouan = Tiṭwān 60-61 CD 1
Tetovo 36-37 J 4-5
Tetuán = Tiṭwān 60-61 CD 1
Tet'uche-Pristan' = Rudnaja Pristan' 42-43 a 9
Tet'uši 42-43 H 6-7
Tet'uši 38-39 J 5
Teuco, Río – 80 D 2-3
Teulada 36-37 C 6
Teun, Pulau – 52-53 J 8
Teuri-tō 50-51 b 1
Teutoburger Wald 33 C 2-D 3
Tèvere 36-37 E 4
Tēverya 46-47 F 6
Tevriz 42-43 N 6
Texarkana, AR 72-73 H 5
Texarkana, TX 72-73 GH 5
Texas [AUS] 56-57 K 5
Texas [USA] 72-73 FG 5
Texas City, TX 72-73 GH 6
Texel 34-35 K 2
Texoma, Lake – 72-73 G 5
Tezaua = Tasāwah 60-61 G 3
Teziutlán 72-73 G 7-8
Tezpur 44-45 P 5
Thabazimbi 64-65 G 7
Thabt, Gebel eth – = Jabal ath-Thabt 62 EF 3
Thabt, Jabal ath- 62 EF 3
Thadôn [BUR, Karin Pyinnei] 52-53 C 3
Thailand, Golf van – 52-53 D 4-5
Thailand, Gulf of – 52-53 D 4-5
Thaïlande 52-53 CD 3
Thaïlande, Golfe de – 52-53 D 4-5
Thailandia 52-53 CD 3
Thailandia, Golfo de – 52-53 D 4-5
Thaj, Ath- 44-45 F 5
Thakhek 52-53 DE 3
Thākurgāon 44-45 O 5
Thal [PAK] 44-45 L 4
Thālith, Al-Jandal ath- 60-61 KL 5
Thallon 58 J 2
Thalmann, GA 74-75 C 9
Thames 32 G 6
Thames [NZ] 56-57 P 7
Thames River 74-75 C 3
Thamūd 44-45 F 7
Thandwe 52-53 B 3
Thangkar 48-49 J 4
Thangool 56-57 K 4
Thangra Tsho = Thangra Yumtsho 48-49 EF 5
Thangra Yumtsho 48-49 EF 5
Thanh Hoa 52-53 E 3
Thanjavur 44-45 MN 8
Thanlwin Myit 52-53 C 2-3
Thanlyin 52-53 C 3
Thapsacus = Dibsah 46-47 GH 5
Thar 44-45 L 5
Thar, Dhāṭ yā = Great Indian Desert 44-45 L 5
Thargomindah 56-57 H 5
Tharsis 34-35 D 10
Tharthār, Bahr ath – = Munkhafad ath-Tharthār 44-45 E 4
Tharthār, Munkhafad ath- 44-45 E 4
Tharthār, Wādī ath- 46-47 K 5
Tharwānīyah = Ath-Tharwānīyah 44-45 GH 6
Tharwānīyah, Ath- 44-45 GH 6
Thásos [GR, ⊙] 36-37 L 5
Thásos [GR, ●] 36-37 L 5
Thatcher, AZ 76-77 HJ 9
Thaton = Thadôn 52-53 C 3
Thaṭṭhah 44-45 K 6
Thayne, WY 76-77 H 4
Thāzī 52-53 C 2
Thbeng 52-53 DE 4
Thbeng Meanchey 52-53 DE 4
Thēbai [ET] 60-61 L 3
Thēbai [GR] 36-37 K 6
Thebe = Thēbai 60-61 L 3
Thebes = Thēbai 36-37 K 6
Thèbes = Thēbai 36-37 K 6
Thebes = Thēbai [ET] 60-61 L 3
The Dalles, OR 76-77 C 3
Theems = Thames 32 G 6
Thelon Game Sanctuary 70-71 PQ 5
Thelon River 70-71 Q 5
Theodore 56-57 JK 4-5
Theodore Roosevelt Lake 76-77 H 9
The Pas 70-71 Q 7
Thēra 36-37 L 7
Thermaïkòs Kólpos 36-37 K 5-6
Thermopýlai 36-37 K 6
Theron Range 24 AB 34-36
Theronsville = Pofadder 64-65 EF 8
Thessalía 36-37 JK 6
Thessalonikē 36-37 K 5
Thetford 32 G 5
Thetford Mines 70-71 W 8
Thiel Mountains 24 A
Thielsen, Mount – 76-77 BC 4
Thiers 34-35 J 6
Thiès 60-61 A 6
Thika 63 D 3
Thikombia 52-53 b 2
Thimbu 44-45 OP 5
Thingvallavatn 30-31 c 2
Thingvellir 30-31 c 2
Thio 56-57 N 4
Thionville 34-35 KL 4
Thisted 30-31 C 9
Thistilfjördhur 30-31 f 1
Thistle, UT 76-77 H 5-6
Thistle Island 56-57 G 7
Thjórsá 30-31 d 2
Thlèta Madârî, Berzekh – = Râ's ash-Shūkāt ath-Thalātha 60-61 D 1
Thlewiaza River 70-71 R 5
Thmail = Thumayl 46-47 K 6
Thogdoragpa 48-49 F 5
Thogjalung 48-49 E 5
Thomas, WV 74-75 D 5
Thomasville, GA 72-73 K 5
Thomasville, NC 74-75 C 7
Thompson 70-71 R 6
Thompson, UT 76-77 HJ 6
Thompson Falls, MT 76-77 F 2
Thompson Peak [USA, Colorado] 76-77 B 5
Thompson Peak [USA, Montana] 76-77 F 2
Thompson's Falls 63 D 2-3
Thomson, GA 74-75 B 8
Thomson, Abysse de – 56-57 K 6
Thomson, Fosa – 56-57 K 6
Thomson Deep 56-57 K 6
Thomsondiep 56-57 K 6
Thon Buri, Krung Thep- 52-53 CD 4
Thong Pha Phum 52-53 C 4
Thonon-les-Bains 34-35 L 5
Thoreau, NM 76-77 JK 8
Thørisvatn 30-31 de 2
Thornton, WA 76-77 E 2
Thorp, WA 76-77 C 2
Thórshöfn 30-31 f 1
Thousand Islands 74-75 EF 2
Thousand Islands = Kepulauan Seribu 52-53 E 7-8
Thousand Spring Creek 76-77 F 5
Thowa 64-65 J 3
Thrákē 36-37 LM 5
Three Creek, ID 76-77 F 4
Three Forks, MT 76-77 H 3
Three Hummock Island 58 bc 2
Three Kings Islands 56-57 O 6
Threemile Rapids 76-77 F 3
Three Pagodas Pass = Phra Chedi Sam Ong 52-53 C 3-4
Three Points, Cape – 60-61 D 8
Three Rivers = Trois-Rivières 70-71 W 8
Three Sisters [USA] 76-77 C 3
Three Springs 56-57 BC 5
Thu, Cu Lao – 52-53 EF 4
Thubby = Abū Ẓabī 44-45 G 6
Thule = Qânâq 70-71 W-X 2
Thumayl 46-47 K 6
Thumb, WY 76-77 H 3
Thun 33 C 5
Thunder Bay [CDN] 70-71 ST 8
Thuqb al-Ḥājj 46-47 L 8
Thüringen 33 E 3
Thüringer Wald 33 E 3
Thurloo Downs 58 F 2
Thurso 32 E 2
Thurston Island 24 BC 26-27
Thyatera = Akhisar 46-47 BC 3
Thyatira = Akhisar 46-47 BC 3
Thykkvibær 30-31 c 3
Thysville = Mbanza-Ngungu 64-65 D 4
Tiahuanacu 78-79 F 8
Tianguá 78-79 L 5
Tianjin 48-49 M 4
Tian Shan 48-49 C-G 3
Tianshui 48-49 JK 5
Tianzhuangtai 50-51 CD 2
Tiaret = Tiyārat 60-61 E 1
Tiassalé 60-61 CD 7
Tīb 60-61 G 1
Ṭīb, Rā's aṭ- = Rā's Ādhār 60-61 G 1
Tibaji 80 F 2
Tibastī, Sarīr – 60-61 H 4
Tibati 60-61 G 7
Ṭīb el Fâl = Ṭayb al-Fāl 46-47 J 5
Tibell, Wādī – = Wādī at-Tubal 46-47 J 6
Tiber = Tèvere 36-37 E 4
Tiberias = Tēverya 46-47 F 6
Tibesti 60-61 H 4
Tibet = Xizang 48-49 E-H 5
Tibet, Plateau of – = Jang Thang 48-49 E-G 5
Tibet, Región Autónoma del – 48-49 E-H 5
Tibissah 60-61 F 1
Tibnī 46-47 H 5
Tibooburra 56-57 H 5
Tibre = Tèvere 36-37 E 4
Tiburón, Isla – 72-73 D 6
Tichborne 74-75 E 2
Tichitt = Tīshīt 60-61 C 5
Tichon'kaja Stancija = Birobidžan 42-43 Z 8
Tichoreck 38-39 GH 6
Tichvin 42-43 E 6
Ticino 33 D 5
Ticonderoga, NY 74-75 G 3
Ticul 72-73 J 7
Tidaholm 30-31 EF 8
Tidikelt = Tidikilt 60-61 E 3
Tidioute, PA 74-75 D 4
Tidjikja = Tijiqjah 60-61 B 5
Tidore, Pulau – 52-53 J 6
Tidra, Île – 60-61 A 5
Tiechang 50-51 EF 2
T'ieh-ling = Tieling 50-51 DE 1
Tieling 50-51 DE 1
T'ien-chia-an = Huainan 48-49 M 5
T'ien-chin = Tianjin 48-49 M 4
T'ien-chouei = Tianshui 48-49 JK 5
T'ien-chuang-t'ai = Tianzhuangtai 50-51 CD 2
Tienkiaan = Huainan 48-49 M 5
Tien Shan 48-49 C-G 3
Tienshui = Tianshui 48-49 JK 5
Tiensjan 48-49 C-G 3
Tientsin = Tianjin 48-49 M 4
Tiên Yên 52-53 E 2
Tierp 30-31 G 7
Tierra Blanca [MEX, Veracruz] 72-73 G 8
Tiétar 34-35 E 8
Tieton, WA 76-77 C 2
Tifariti = Atfārītī 60-61 B 3
Tiffany Mountain 76-77 CD 1
Tifore, Pulau – 52-53 J 6
Tifton, GA 74-75 B 9
Tigieglo = Tayeegle 64-65 K 2
Tigil' 42-43 e 6
Tigra = Tigrē 60-61 MN 6
Tigray 60-61 MN 6
Tigre = Nahr Dijlah 44-45 E 3
Tigrē = Tigray 60-61 MN 6
Tigre, Dent du – = Dông Voi Mêp 52-53 E 3
Tigre, El – [MEX] 76-77 J 10
Tigre, El – [YV] 78-79 G 3
Tigre, Rio – [EC] 78-79 D 5
Tigui 60-61 H 5
Tīh, Jabal at- 60-61 L 3
Tīh, Ṣaḥrā' at- 60-61 L 2
Tiham = Tihāmah 44-45 D 6-E 8
Tihāmah 44-45 D 6-E 8
Ti-hua = Ürümchi 48-49 F 3
Tihwa = Ürümchi 48-49 F 3
Tiirismaa 30-31 L 7
Tijiqjah 60-61 B 5
Tijoca 78-79 K 5
Tijuana 72-73 C 5
Tikal 72-73 J 8
Tikopia 56-57 N 2
Tikrīt 46-47 K 5
Tiksi 42-43 Y 3
Tikšozero 30-31 OP 4
Tilamuta 52-53 H 6
Tilbeşar ovası 46-47 G 4
Tilburg 34-35 K 3
Tilcara 80 CD 2
Tilemsès 60-61 EF 5
Tilemsi 60-61 E 5
Tiličiki 42-43 g 5
Tilimsān 60-61 D 2
Tillabéry 60-61 E 6
Tillamook, OR 76-77 B 3
Tillamook Bay 76-77 AB 3
Tillery, Lake – 74-75 CD 7
Tillia 60-61 E 5
Tillsonburg 74-75 C 3
Tilpa 56-57 H 6
Tīmā 62 D 4
Timaná 78-79 D 4
Timanskij kr'až 42-43 J 5-H 4
Timar 46-47 K 3
Timaru 56-57 O 8
Timaševsk 38-39 G 6
Timassah 60-61 H 3
Timassanin = Burj 'Umar Idrīs 60-61 EF 3
Timbédra = Tinbadghah 60-61 C 5
Timber, OR 76-77 B 3
Timber Mountain 76-77 F 6
Timbo [Guinea] 60-61 B 6
Timboulaga 60-61 F 5
Timia 60-61 F 5
Timimoun = Tīmīmūn 60-61 E 3
Tīmīmūn 60-61 E 3
Timiş 36-37 J 3
Timişoara 36-37 J 3
Ti-m-Merhsoï, Oued – 60-61 F 5
Timmins 70-71 U 8
Timmonsville, SC 74-75 D 7
Timmoudi = Tīmmūdī 60-61 D 3
Timon 78-79 L 6
Timor 52-53 H 9-J 8
Timor, Fosa de – 52-53 J 8
Timor, Fosse de – 52-53 J 8
Timor, Mar de – 56-57 E 2
Timor, Mer de – 56-57 E 2
Timor Sea 56-57 E 2
Timor Timur = 23 ◁ 52-53 J 8
Timortrog 52-53 J 8
Timor Trough 52-53 J 8
Timorzee 56-57 E 2
Timošino 38-39 FG 3
Timpahute Range 76-77 F 7
Timsāḥ, Buḥayrat at- 62 E 2
Ţinah, Khalīj aṭ- 62 E 2
Tinakula 52-53 kl 7
Ti-n-Asselak 60-61 E 5
Tinbadghah 60-61 C 5
Tindouf = Tindūf 60-61 C 3
Tindouf, Sebkra de – = Sabkhat Tindūf 60-61 C 3
Tindūf 60-61 C 3
Tindūf, Sabkhat – 60-61 C 3
Tineo 34-35 D 7
Tin Essalak = Ti-n-Asselak 60-61 E 5
Tingha 58 K 2-3
Tinghīrt, Hammadat – = Ḥammādat Tinrīrt 60-61 FG 3
Ting-hsi = Dingxi 48-49 J 4
Ting-hsin = Dingxin 48-49 H 3
Tingling Shan = Qin Ling 48-49 KL 5
Tingo María 78-79 D 6
Tingréla 60-61 C 6
Tingri Dsong 48-49 F 6
Tingsryd 30-31 F 9
Tinguipaya 78-79 F 8
Tingvoll 30-31 BC 6
Tingwon 52-53 g 5
Ting-yüan-ying = Bajan Choto 48-49 JK 4
Tinjil, Pulau – 52-53 E 8
Tinkisso 60-61 BC 6
Tinnevelly = Tirunelveli 44-45 M 9
Tinnīn, 'Ayn – 62 C 4
Tinogasta 80 C 3
Tinrhert, Hamada de – = Ḥammādat Tinrīrt 60-61 FG 3
Tinrīrt, Ḥammādat – 60-61 FG 3
Tinsukia 44-45 Q 5
Tīn Tarābīn, Wādī – 60-61 F 4
Tintina 80 D 3
Tintinara 58 E 5
Tio, El – 80 D 4
Tioman, Pulau – 52-53 DE 6
Tionesta, CA 76-77 C 5
Tionesta, PA 74-75 D 4
Tipperary 32 BC 5
Tipton, CA 76-77 D 7
Tipton, Mount – 76-77 F 8
Tiracambu, Serra de – 78-79 K 5
Tīrān, Jazīrat – 62 F 4
Tirana = Tiranë 36-37 HJ 5
Tiranë 36-37 HJ 5
Tiraspol' 38-39 EF 6
Tirbande Turkestān 44-45 JK 3
Tire 46-47 B 3
Tirebolu 46-47 H 2
Tiree 32 C 3
Tiree Passage 32 C 3
Tîrgovişte 36-37 L 3
Tîrgu Cărbuneşti 36-37 KL 3
Tîrgu Jiu 36-37 K 3
Tîrgu Mureş 36-37 L 2
Tîrgu Neamţ 36-37 LM 2
Tirich Mīr 44-45 L 3
Tirikuṇāmalaya 44-45 N 9
Tirl'anskij 38-39 L 5
Tirnabos 36-37 K 6
Tirol 33 EF 5
Tirso 36-37 C 6
Tiruchchendur = Tiruchendur 44-45 M 9
Tiruchchirāppalli = Tiruchirapalli 44-45 M 8
Tiruchendur 44-45 M 9
Tiruchirapalli 44-45 M 8
Tirukkunamalai = Tirikuṇāmalaya 44-45 N 9
Tirunelveli 44-45 M 9
Tirupati 44-45 M 8
Tiruvanatapuraṁ = Trivandrum 44-45 M 9
Tisa 36-37 J 3
Tisdale 70-71 Q 7
Tīshīt 60-61 C 5

Tīshī 223

Trinity River [USA, California] 76-77 B 5
Trinity River [USA, Texas] 72-73 G 5
Tripdi = Ṭarābulus al-Gharb 60-61 G 2
Tripoli = Ṭarābulus al-Gharb 60-61 G 2
Tripolis 36-37 K 7
Tripolitaine = Ṭarābulus 60-61 GH 2
Tripura 44-45 P 6
Trishshivaperūr = Trichur 44-45 M 8
Trivandrum 44-45 M 9
Trnava 33 H 4
Trobriand Islands 52-53 h 6
Trofors 30-31 E 5
Trogir 36-37 FG 4
Troglav 36-37 G 4
Tròia [I] 36-37 F 5
Troick [SU ↓ Čel'abinsk] 42-43 L 7
Troickoje [SU, Rossijskaja SFSR] 42-43 a 8
Troicko-Pečorsk 42-43 K 5
Troickosavsk = K'achta 42-43 U 7
Trois-Rivières 70-71 W 8
Trojan 36-37 L 4
Trojanski prohod 36-37 L 4
Trollhättan 30-31 E 8
Trolltindan 30-31 B 6
Trombetas, Rio – 78-79 H 5
Tromelin, Île – 64-65 M 6
Troms 30-31 G-J 3
Tromsø 30-31 H 3
Tron 30-31 D 6
Trona, CA 76-77 E 8
Tronador, Monte – 80 B 6
Trondheim 30-31 D 6
Trondheimfjord 30-31 CD 6
Tróodos 44-45 C 4
Tropic, UT 76-77 GH 7
Trosa 30-31 G 8
Trotus 36-37 M 2
Troûmbâ = Turumbah 46-47 J 4
Trout Creek 76-77 D 4
Trout Creek, MT 76-77 EF 2
Trout Creek, UT 76-77 G 6
Trout Lake [CDN, Northwest Territories] 70-71 MN 5
Trout Lake [CDN, Ontario] 70-71 S 7
Trouwers Island = Pulau Tinjil 52-53 E 8
Trowbridge 32 EF 6
Troy, AL 72-73 J 5
Troy, ID 76-77 E 2
Troy, MT 76-77 F 1
Troy, NC 74-75 D 7
Troy, NY 72-73 M 3
Troy, OR 76-77 E 3
Troy, PA 74-75 E 4
Troyes 34-35 K 4
Truckee, CA 76-77 CD 6
Truckee River 76-77 D 6
Trudante = Tārūdānt 60-61 C 2
Trujillo [E] 34-35 DE 9
Trujillo [Honduras] 72-73 J 8
Trujillo [PE] 78-79 CD 6
Trujillo [YV] 78-79 EF 3
Trumbull, Mount – 76-77 G 7
Trung Bộ 52-53 D 3-E 4
Trung Phân, Cao Nguyên – 52-53 E 4
Trung Phân, Plateau de – = Cao Nguyên Trung Phân 52-53 E 4
Truro 32 D 6
Truro [CDN] 70-71 Y 8
Trutnov 33 GH 3
Truva 44-45 B 3
Truxilho = Trujillo 72-73 J 8
Trysil 30-31 DE 7
Trysilelv 30-31 DE 7

Tsabong 64-65 F 8
Tsaidam 48-49 GH 4
Tsai-Dam = Tsaidam 48-49 GH 4
Tsala Apopka Lake 74-75 bc 2
Tsamkong = Zhanjiang 48-49 L 7
Tsangpo 48-49 EF 6
Tsangwu = Wuzhou 48-49 L 7
Tsaratanana [RM, ▲] 64-65 L 5
Tsaratanana [RM, ●] 64-65 L 6
Tsau 64-65 F 7
Tsavo [EAK, ~] 63 D 3
Tsavo [EAK, ●] 64-65 J 3
Tsavo National Park 64-65 J 3
Ts'ê-lo = Chira Bazar 48-49 DE 4
Tses 64-65 E 8
Tsethang 48-49 G 6
Tsetserlig = Cecerleg 48-49 J 2
Tshaidam 48-49 GH 4
Tshela 64-65 D 3-4
Tshikapa 64-65 EF 4
Tshimbo 63 B 4
Tshing Hai = Chöch nuur 48-49 H 4
Tshipa = Katakumba 64-65 F 4
Tshofa 64-65 FG 4
Tsho Ngonpo = Chöch nuur 48-49 H 4
Tshopo 64-65 G 2
Tshuapa 64-65 F 3
Tshungu, Chutes – 64-65 FG 2
Tshungu, Chutes – 64-65 FG 2
Tshwane 64-65 F 7
Tsiafajavona 64-65 L 6
Tsienkiang = Qianjiang 48-49 L 5
Tsihombe 64-65 KL 8
Tsinan = Jinan 48-49 M 4
Tsincheng = Jincheng 48-49 L 4
Tsinchow = Tianshui 48-49 JK 5
Tsinghai = Qinghai 48-49 GH 4
Tsinghu = Jinghe 48-49 E 3
Tsingkiang = Qingjiang [TJ, Jiangsu] 48-49 M 5
Tsingkiang = Qingjiang [TJ, Jiangxi] 48-49 M 6
Tsingtau = Qingdao 48-49 N 4
Tsining = Jining 48-49 M 4
Tsining = Xining 48-49 J 4
Tsinyang = Qinyang 48-49 L 4
Tsiroanomandidy 64-65 L 6
Tsitsihar = Qiqihar 48-49 N 2
Tsivory 64-65 L 7
Tsjaad 60-61 HJ 5
Tsjakassen, Autonome Oblast der – = 10 ◁ 42-43 R 7
Tsjechoslowakije 33 F-K 4
Tsjeljoeskin, Kaap – = mys Čel'uskin 42-43 UV 2
Tsjetsen-Ingoesjen Autonome Republiek = 5 ◁ 38-39 J 7
Tsjoektsjen, Nationaal Gebied der – 42-43 g-j 4
Tsjoektsjendrempel 19 B 35
Tsjoektsjenzee 19 BC 35-36
Tsjoevasjen, Autonome Republiek = 4 ◁ 42-43 H 6
Tsorlû = Çorlu 46-47 B 2
Tsu 48-49 Q 5
Tsubame 50-51 M 4
Tsuchiura 50-51 N 4
Tsugaru kaikyō 48-49 R 3
Tsukigata 50-51 b 2
Tsukumi 50-51 H 6
Tsuma = Saito 50-51 H 6
Tsumeb 64-65 E 6
Tsungming = Chongming 48-49 N 5
Tsuno-shima 50-51 H 5
Tsunyi = Zunyi 48-49 K 6
Tsuruga 50-51 KL 5
Tsurugi san 50-51 JK 6
Tsurumi-zaki 50-51 J 6
Tsuruoka 50-51 M 3
Tsurusaki 50-51 HJ 6
Tsushima 48-49 O 5
Tsushima-kaikyō 48-49 OP 5
Tsuyama 50-51 JK 5
Tsuyung = Chuxiong 48-49 J 7

Tu = Tibesti 60-61 H 4
Tu = Tsu 48-49 Q 5
Tua 34-35 D 8
Tuamotu, Bassin des – 22-23 BC 7
Tuamotu, Cuenca de las – 22-23 BC 7
Tuamotu Basin 22-23 BC 7
Tuapse 38-39 G 7
Tubac, AZ 76-77 H 10
Tuba City, AZ 76-77 H 7
Tubal, Wādī at- 46-47 J 6
Tuban 52-53 F 8
Tubarão 80 G 3
Tubau 52-53 F 6
Ṭubayq, Jabal aṭ- 44-45 D 5
Tübingen 33 D 4
Tubmanburg 60-61 B 7
Tubqāl, Jabal – 60-61 C 2
Ṭubruq 60-61 J 2
Tubutama 76-77 H 10
Tucacas 78-79 F 2
Tucano 78-79 M 7
Tucavaca 78-79 H 8
Tucholskie, Bory – 33 HJ 2
Tucker Bay 24 B 18
Tuckerton, NJ 74-75 FG 5
Tucson, AZ 72-73 D 5
Tucson Mountains 76-77 H 9
Tucumán = San Miguel de Tucumán 80 CD 3
Tucumcari, NM 72-73 F 4
Tucunuco 80 C 4
Tucupita 78-79 G 3
Tucuruí 78-79 K 5
Tudela 34-35 G 7
Tuela 34-35 D 8
Tufanbeyli 46-47 G 3
Tufi 52-53 N 8
Tugaru kaikyō = Tsugaru-kaikyō 48-49 R 3
Tugela [ZA, ~] 64-65 H 8
Tuggurt = Tūjurt 60-61 EF 2
Tugh Fafan = Fafen 60-61 N 7
Tughghūrt = Tūjurt 60-61 EF 2
Tugt 48-49 L 3-4
Tuguegarao 52-53 H 3
Tugur 42-43 a 7
Tuht = Yaprakli 46-47 E 2
Tujmazy 42-43 JK 7
Tūjurt 60-61 EF 2
T'ukalinsk 42-43 N 6
Tukangbesi, Kepulauan – 52-53 H 8
Tukayyid 46-47 L 8
Tūkrah 60-61 HJ 2
Tuktoyaktuk 70-71 JK 4
Tukums 30-31 K 9
Tukuyu 64-65 H 4
Tula [EAK] 63 D 3
Tulagi 52-53 jk 6
Tulancingo 72-73 G 7
Tulare, CA 72-73 C 4
Tulare Lake 72-73 C 4
Tulare Lake Area 76-77 D 8
Tularosa Mountains 76-77 J 9
Tulcán 78-79 D 4
Tulcea 36-37 N 3
Tul'čin 38-39 E 6
Tuléar = Toliary 64-65 K 7
Tulelake, CA 76-77 C 5
Tule River 76-77 D 7
Tule River Indian Reservation 76-77 D 7-8
T'ul'gan 42-43 K 7
T'ul'gan 38-39 L 5
Tuli 64-65 G 7
Tūljā 60-61 EF 2
Tūl Karm 46-47 F 6
Tullamore 58 H 4
Tulle 34-35 HJ 6
Tullibigeal 58 GH 4
Tully 56-57 J 3
Tuloma 38-39 F 2
Tulpan 42-43 K 5
Tulsa, OK 72-73 G 4
Tulsa = La Barge, WY 76-77 HJ 4
Tuluá 78-79 D 4
Tulufan = Turpan 48-49 F 3
Tulūl, Dīrat at- 46-47 G 6
Tulūl ash-Shaḥm 46-47 FG 8
Tulun 42-43 ST 7
Tuma 38-39 H 4
Tumacacori National Monument 76-77 H 10
Tumaco 78-79 D 4
Tumaco, Rada de – 78-79 CD 4
Tuman-gang 50-51 G 1
Tumany 42-43 e 5
Tumba, Lac – 64-65 E 3
Tumbarumba 56-57 J 7
Tumbes [EC, ●] 78-79 C 5
Ṭumbī 60-61 L 7
Tumboni 64-65 J 3
Tumby 58 C 5
T'umen' [SU] 42-43 M 6
Tumen [TJ] 48-49 O 3
Tumen Jiang 50-51 G 1
Tumkur 44-45 M 8
Tumkūru = Tumkur 44-45 M 8
Ṭummō, Jabal – 60-61 G 4
Tumpat 52-53 D 5
Tumu 60-61 D 6
Tumucumaque, Serra do – 78-79 HJ 4
Tumureng 78-79 G 3
Tumut 58 J 5
Tunaydah 62 C 5
Tunceli 44-45 DE 3
Tuncelin 46-47 H 3
Tünchel 48-49 K 2
Tundrino 42-43 N 5
Tunduma 64-65 H 4
Tunduru 64-65 J 5
Tundža 36-37 M 4
Tunesië 60-61 F 1-G 2
T'ung 42-43 W 4
Tungaru = Tunqarū 60-61 L 6
Tung-chou = Nantong 48-49 N 5
Tungchow = Nantong 48-49 N 5
T'ung-ch'uan = Tongchuan 48-49 K 4
Tungchwan = Huize 48-49 J 6
Tungchwan = Santai 48-49 JK 5
Tung-fang = Dongfang 48-49 K 8
Tung Hai = Dong Hai 48-49 NO 5-6
Tunghsien = Tong Xian 48-49 M 3-4
Tunghua = Tonghua 48-49 O 3
Tungjen = Tongren 48-49 K 6
Tung-kuan = Dongguan 48-49 LM 7
T'ung-kuan = Tongguan 48-49 L 5
T'ung-liao = Tongliao 48-49 N 3
Tunglu = Tonglu 48-49 M 5-6
T'ung-p'u = Tongphu 48-49 H 5
Tungshan = Xuzhou 48-49 M 5
Tung-shêng = Dongsheng 48-49 K 4
Tungtai = Dongtai 48-49 N 5
Tung-t'ing Hu = Dongting Hu 48-49 L 6
Tun-hua = Dunhua 48-49 O 3
Tun-huang = Dunhuang 48-49 GH 3
Tunhwang = Dunhuang 48-49 GH 3
Tunicia 60-61 F 1-G 2
Tūnis 60-61 FG 1
Tunisi, Canale di – 36-37 D 7
Tunisia 60-61 F 1-G 2
Tunisie 60-61 F 1-G 2
Tunj 60-61 K 7
Tunja 78-79 E 3
Tūnjah 60-61 L 7
Tunkhannock, PA 74-75 EF 4
Tunnsjø 30-31 E 5
Tunqarū 60-61 L 6
Tunuyan, Sierra de – 80 C 4
Tunxi 48-49 M 6
Tuoketuo = Tugt 48-49 L 3
Tuokexun = Toksun 48-49 F 3
Tuolumne, CA 76-77 CD 7
Tuolumne River 76-77 CD 7
Tuoppajärvi = Topozero 42-43 E 4
Tuosuo Hu = Tos nuur 48-49 H 4
Tupã 78-79 JK 9
Tūp Āghāj 46-47 M 4
Tupanciretã 80 F 3
Tupelo, MS 72-73 J 5
Tupik 38-39 F 4
Tupik [SU ↑ Mogoča] 42-43 WX 7
Tupinambaranas, Ilha – 78-79 H 5
Tupiza 78-79 F 9
Tupper Lake, NY 74-75 F 2
Tupungato, Cerro – 80 BC 4
Tuque, la – 70-71 W 8
Túquerres 78-79 D 4
Ṭūr, Aṭ- 60-61 L 3
Tura [SU, ~] 42-43 L 6
Tura [SU, ●] 42-43 ST 5
Turabah 44-45 E 6
Turan 42-43 R 7
Turan = Turanskaja nizmennost' 42-43 K 9-L 8
Turanskaja nizmennost' 42-43 K 9-L 8
Ṭurayf 44-45 D 4
Turbat 44-45 J 5
Turbi 63 D 2
Turbio, El – 80 B 8
Turbo 78-79 D 3
Turda 36-37 K 2
Ṭūreh 46-47 N 5
Turek 33 J 2
Turgaj [SU, ~] 42-43 L 8
Turgaj [SU, ●] 42-43 L 8
Turgajskaja ložbina 42-43 L 7
Türgen Echin uul 48-49 FG 2
Türgen Echin uul 48-49 FG 2
Turgut 46-47 DE 3
Turgutlu 46-47 BC 3
Turhal 46-47 G 2
Türi 30-31 L 8
Turia 34-35 G 9
Turiaçu 78-79 K 5
Turiaçu, Baía de – 78-79 KL 5
Turij Rog 42-43 Z 8
Turin = Torino 36-37 BC 3
Turinsk 42-43 L 6
Ṭūrīt 60-61 L 8
Turka 33 L 4
Turkana 63 C 2
Turkana, Lake – 64-65 J 2
Türkeli 46-47 F 2
Turkestan 42-43 M 9
Turkey 44-45 B-E 3
Turkistan 48-49 B-F 4
Türkmen Dağı 46-47 D 3
Turkménie 44-45 HJ 2-3
Turkmenistán 44-45 HJ 2-3
Turkmen-Kala 44-45 J 3
Türkoğlu 46-47 G 4
Turksib 42-43 P 7
Turks Islands 72-73 M 7
Turku 30-31 K 7
Turkwel 64-65 J 2
Turkije 44-45 B-E 3
Turlock, CA 76-77 C 7
Turneffe Islands 72-73 J 8
Turner, WA 76-77 E 2
Turnhout 34-35 K 3
Turnu Măgurele 36-37 L 4
Turnu Roșu, Pasul – 36-37 KL 3
Turo 63 DE 3
Tuross Head 58 K 6
Turpan 48-49 F 3
Turqino, Pico – 72-73 L 8
Turquestán 42-43 M 9
Turquía 44-45 B-E 3
Turquie 44-45 B-E 3
Tursāq 46-47 L 6
Turtkul' 42-43 L 9
Turuchansk 42-43 Q 4
Turugart = Torugart Davan 44-45 L 2
Turumbah 46-47 J 4
Turun ja Poorin lääni 30-31 K 6-7
Turut = Ṭorūd 44-45 H 3
Turijn = Torino 36-37 BC 3
Tuscaloosa, AL 72-73 J 5
Tuscarora, NV 76-77 E 5
Tusenøyane 30-31 l 6
Tu Shan = Du Shan [TJ, ▲] 50-51 B 2
Tuside = Pic Toussidé 60-61 H 4
Tusima = Tsushima 48-49 O 5
Tusima kaikyō = Tsushima-kaikyō 48-49 OP 5
Tussey Mountain 74-75 DE 4-5
Tustna 30-31 B 6
Tutak 46-47 K 3
Tuticorin 44-45 M 9
Tutončana 42-43 R 4
Tutrakan 36-37 M 3-4
Tuttlingen 33 D 4-5
Tūttukkuḍi = Tuticorin 44-45 M 9
Tutubu 63 C 4
Tutuila 52-53 c 1
Tutupaca, Volcán – 78-79 E 8
Tuul gol 48-49 JK 2
Tuva, República Autónoma de los – 42-43 RS 7
Tuva Autonomous Republic 42-43 RS 7
Ṭuwāl 'Aba' 46-47 H 4
Ṭuwāt, At- 60-61 DE 3
Ṭuwayq, Jabal – 44-45 F 6
Ṭuwaythah 60-61 K 6
Tuwut 60-61 L 7
Tuxpan [MEX, Nayarit] 72-73 E 7
Tuxpán de Rodriguez Cano 72-73 G 7
Tuxtla Gutiérrez 72-73 H 8
Tùy 34-35 C 7
Tuy An 52-53 E 4
Tuy Hoa 52-53 EF 4
Tūyserkān 46-47 N 5
Tuyun = Duyun 48-49 K 6
Tuz Gölü 44-45 C 3
Ṭuz Khurmātū 46-47 L 5
Tuzla 36-37 H 3
Tuzla [TR] 46-47 F 4
Tuzluca 46-47 K 2
Tūzlū Gol = Kavīr-e Mīghān 46-47 N 5
Tuzly 36-37 O 3

Tvedestrand 30-31 C 8
Tver' 42-43 EF 6

Tweed 74-75 E 2
Tweed 32 E 4
Tweedsmuir Provincial Park 70-71 L 7
Twentynine Palms, CA 76-77 EF 8
Twilight Cove 56-57 E 6
Twin Bridges, MT 76-77 GH 3
Twin Falls, ID 72-73 CD 3
Twin Heads 56-57 E 4
Twin Islands 70-71 UV 7
Twin Peaks 76-77 F 3
Twodot, MT 76-77 HJ 2
Two Harbors, MN 72-73 HJ 2

Tyamo Hayiķ 60-61 M 7
Tyborøn 30-31 BC 9
Tyentya 60-61 M 7
Tyew Bahir 60-61 M 8
Tygda 42-43 Y 7
Tygh Valley, OR 76-77 C 3
Tyler, TX 72-73 GH 5
Tylösand 30-31 E 9
Tym 42-43 P 6
Tymfrêstós 36-37 JK 6
Tymovskoje 42-43 b 7
Tympákion 36-37 L 8
Tynda 42-43 XY 6
Tynemouth 32 F 4
Tynset 30-31 D 6
Tyōsen kaikyō = Chōsen-kaikyō 48-49 O 5
Tyrell, Lake – 56-57 H 7
Tyrifjord 30-31 CD 7
Tyrma 42-43 Z 7
Tyrol = Tirol 33 EF 5
Tyrol du Sud 36-37 D 2
Tyrone, PA 74-75 D 4
Tyros = Ṣūr 46-47 F 6
Tyrrell, Lake – 58 F 5
Tyrrheense Zee 36-37 D-F 6
Tyrrhenian Sea 36-37 D-F 6
Tysnesøy 30-31 A 7-8

Tzaneen 64-65 H 7
Tzechung = Zizhong 48-49 JK 5-6
Tzekung = Zigong 48-49 JK 6
Tzŭ-hu = Bajan Choto 48-49 JK 4
Tzŭ-kung = Zigong 48-49 JK 6

U

Uaçari, Serra – 78-79 H 4
Uaco Cungo 64-65 E 5
Uaddán = Waddān 60-61 H 3
Uadi-Halfa = Wādī Ḥalfā 60-61 L 4
Uagadugu = Ouagadougou 60-61 D 6
Ualega = Welega 60-61 LM 7
Uancheu = Wenzhou 48-49 N 6
Uanle Uen = Wanleweeyn 64-65 K 2
Uarangal = Warangal 44-45 MN 7
Uaso Nyiro 63 D 2
Uatumã, Rio – 78-79 H 5
Uauá 78-79 M 6
Uáu en-Námûs = Wāw an-Nāmūs 60-61 H 4
Uaupés 78-79 F 5
Uaupés, Rio – 78-79 F 4
Uaxactún 72-73 J 8

Ubá 78-79 L 9
Ubá, Salto do – 80 F 2
Ubaitaba 78-79 M 7
Ubangi 64-65 E 2
Ubari = Awbārī 60-61 G 3
'Ubári, Edeien- = Ṣaḥrā' Awbārī 60-61 G 3
Ubari, Edeyin – = Ṣaḥrā' Awbārī 60-61 G 3
Ubaye 34-35 L 6
'Ubaylah, Al- 44-45 G 6
Ubayyiḍ, Al- 60-61 KL 6
Ubayyid, Bi'r al- 62 BC 4
Ubayyiḍ, Wādī al- 46-47 K 6
Ube 48-49 P 5
Úbeda 34-35 F 9
Ubekendt Ø 70-71 a 3
Uberaba 78-79 K 8
Uberlândia 78-79 K 8
Ubiña, Peña – 34-35 DE 7
Ubiña, Peña – 34-35 DE 7
'Ubkayk, Jabal – 60-61 M 4
Ubsa Nur = Uvs nuur 48-49 G 1
Ubundu 64-65 FG 3

Učaly 38-39 LM 5
Ucami 42-43 S 5
Ucayali, Río – 78-79 D 6
Uchiko 50-51 J 6
Uchinoko = Uchiko 50-51 J 6
Uchinoura 50-51 H 7
Uchiura-wan 50-51 b 2
Uchta [SU, Komi ASSR] 42-43 J 5
Uchta = Kalevala 42-43 E 4
Üchturpan 48-49 DE 3
Ucrania 38-39 E-G 6
Učur 42-43 Z 6

Uchiko 50-51 J 6
Uchinoko = Uchiko 50-51 J 6
Uchinoura 50-51 H 7
Uchiura-wan 50-51 b 2

Uchiu 225

Uchta [SU, Komi ASSR] 42-43 J 5
Uchta = Kalevala 42-43 E 4

Uda [SU ◁ Čuna] 42-43 S 7
Uda [SU ◁ Selenga] 42-43 UV 7
Uda [SU ◁ Udskaja guba] 42-43 Z 7
Ūdah, Jabal – 60-61 M 4
Udaipur [IND ↗ Ahmadabad] 44-45 L 6
'Udaysāt, Al- 62 E 5
Udbina 36-37 FG 3
Uddevalla 30-31 DE 8
Uddjaur 30-31 GH 5
Udine 36-37 E 2
Udipi = Udupi 44-45 L 8
Uḍīsā = Orissa 44-45 N 7-O 6
Udjidji = Ujiji 64-65 G 3-4
Udmurt Autonomous Republic = 2 ◁ 42-43 J 6
Udmurtos, República Autónoma de los – = 2 ◁ 42-43 J 6
U-do 50-51 F 6
Udon Thani 52-53 D 3
Udskaja guba 42-43 a 7
Udupi 44-45 L 8
Udža 42-43 W 3

Uebonti 52-53 H 7
Ueda 50-51 M 4
Uele 64-65 F 2
Uèlen 70-71 BC 4
Uelzen 33 E 2
Uengan, mys – 42-43 LM 3
Ueno 50-51 L 5
Uere 64-65 G 2

Ufa [SU, ~] 42-43 K 6
Ufa [SU, ●] 42-43 K 7

Ugalla 64-65 H 4
Uglič 42-43 F 6
Ugljan 36-37 F 3
Ugogo 64-65 HJ 4
Ugol'nyj = Beringovskij 42-43 j 5
Ugoma 63 B 3-4
Uguay 80 E 3
Uğurludağ 46-47 F 2

Uha 64-65 H 3
Uha-dong 48-49 O 3
Uhrichsville, OH 74-75 C 4

Ui-do 50-51 E 5
Uíge 64-65 DE 4
Uijŏngbu 50-51 F 4
Uiju 50-51 E 2
Uil 38-39 K 6
Uil [SU, ●] 42-43 J 8
Uintah and Ouray Indian Reservation [USA ↓ East Tavaputs Plateau] 76-77 J 6
Uintah and Ouray Indian Reservation [USA ↓ Uinta Mountains] 76-77 HJ 5
Uinta Mountains 72-73 DE 3
Uisŏng 50-51 G 4
Uitenhage 64-65 FG 9

Uj 42-43 L 7
Ujandina 42-43 b 4
Ujar 42-43 R 6
Ujda = Ūjdah 60-61 D 2
Ūjdah 60-61 D 2
Ujedinenija, ostrov – 42-43 OP 2
Uji-guntō 50-51 G 7
Ujiji 64-65 G 3-4
Ujjaen = Ujjain 44-45 M 6
Ujjain 44-45 M 6
Ujung Pandang 52-53 G 8

Ukara 63 C 3
'Ukāsh, Wādī – 46-47 J 5-6
Ukerewe Island 64-65 H 3
Ukiah, CA 72-73 B 4
Ukiah, OR 76-77 D 3
Ukimbu 64-65 H 4
Ukmergė 30-31 L 10
Ukonongo 64-65 H 4
Ukumbi 64-65 H 4
Uku-shima 50-51 G 6
Ukwama 63 C 5

Ula 46-47 C 4
'Ulā', Al- 44-45 D 5
Ulaanbaatar 48-49 K 2
Ulaan Choto = Ulan Hot 48-49 N 2
Ulaan Choto = Ulan Hot 48-49 N 2
Ulaangom 48-49 G 1-2
Ulaan mörön [TJ ◁ Dre Chhu] 48-49 G 5
Ulaan uul 48-49 G 5
Ulala = Gorno-Altajsk 42-43 Q 7
Ulamba 64-65 F 4
Ulan = Dulaan Chijd 48-49 H 4
Ulán Bator = Ulaanbaatar 48-49 K 2
Ulan-Burgasy, chrebet – 42-43 UV 7
Ulan Gom = Ulaangom 48-49 G 1-2
Ulan Hot 48-49 N 2
Ulankom = Ulaangom 48-49 G 1-2
Ulan-Udė 42-43 U 7
Ulapes 80 C 4
Ulaş 46-47 G 3
Ulastai = Uljastaj 48-49 H 2
Ulawa 52-53 k 6
Ul'ba 42-43 P 7
Ulchin 50-51 G 4
Ulcinj 36-37 H 5
Uldza = Bajan Uul 48-49 L 2
Üldzejt = Öldzijt 48-49 J 2
Uldz gol 48-49 L 2
Uleåborg = Oulu 30-31 L 5
Ule Lhee 52-53 C 5
Ulete 64-65 J 4
Ulety 42-43 V 7
Ulhasnagar 44-45 L 7
Uliassutai = Uliastaj 48-49 H 2
Uliastaj 48-49 H 2
Ulijasutai = Uliastaj 48-49 H 2
Ulindi 64-65 G 3
Ulingan 52-53 N 7
Ulja 42-43 b 6
Uljanovsk 42-43 H 7
Uljinskij chrebet 42-43 ab 6
Ulladulla 56-57 K 7
Ullsfjord 30-31 HJ 3
Ullŭng-do 48-49 P 4
Ullyul 50-51 E 3
Ulm 33 D 4
Ulm, MT 76-77 H 2
Ulmarra 58 L 2
Uløy 30-31 J 3
Ulsan 48-49 OP 4
Ulster 32 C 4
Ulster Canal 32 C 4
Ulu [RI] 52-53 J 6
Ulu [SU] 42-43 Y 5
Ulúa, Río – 72-73 J 8
Uluabat Gölü 46-47 C 2
Ulubey 46-47 C 3
Ulubey 46-47 G 2
Ulubey [TR, Ordu] 46-47 G 2
Uluborlu 46-47 D 3
Uluçınar 46-47 FG 4
Uludağ 46-47 C 2-3
Ulugh Muz tagh 48-49 F 4
Uluguru Mountains 64-65 J 4
Ulukışla 46-47 F 4
Ulus 46-47 E 2
Ulutau, gora – 42-43 M 8
Ulverstone 58 bc 2
'Ulyā, Qaryat al- 44-45 F 5
Ulyastai = Uliastaj 48-49 H 2
Ulytau 42-43 M 8

Ulladulla 56-57 K 7
Ullsfjord 30-31 HJ 3
Ullŭng-do 48-49 P 4
Ullyul 50-51 E 3

Umala 78-79 F 8
Umal'tinskij 42-43 Z 7
Uman' 38-39 F 6
Umanak = Umánaq 70-71 ab 3
Umanak Fjord 70-71 Za 3
Umánaq 70-71 ab 3
'Umarī, Qā'al – 46-47 G 7
Umatilla Indian Reservation 76-77 D 3
Umatilla River 76-77 D 3
Umba [SU, ●] 42-43 J 6
Umboi 52-53 N 8
Umbria 36-37 DE 4
Umbu [TJ] 48-49 F 5
Umeå 30-31 HJ 6
Ume älv 30-31 H 5
Umm ad-Durūs, Sabkhat – 60-61 B 4
Umm al-'Abīd 60-61 H 3
Umm al-Kataf, Khalīj – 62 F 6
Umm al-Qaywayn 44-45 GH 5
Umm ar-Rabī', Nahr – 60-61 C 2
Umm aṭ-Ṭuyūr al-Fawqānī, Jabal – 62 F 6
Umm aṭ-Ṭūz 46-47 K 5
Umm Badr 60-61 K 6
Umm Ball 60-61 K 6
Umm Bishtīt, Bi'r – 62 FG 6
Umm Bujmah 62 E 3
Umm Durmān 60-61 L 5
Umm el-'Abid 60-61 H 3
Umm Hajer = Om Hajer 60-61 M 6
Umm Ḥibāl, Bi'r – 62 E 6
Umm 'Inab, Jabal – 62 E 4
Umm Kaddādah 60-61 K 6
Umm Karār, Tall – 46-47 H 6
Umm Keddâda = Umm Kaddādah 60-61 K 6
Umm Laǧǧ = Umm Lajj 44-45 D 5
Umm Lajj 44-45 D 5
Umm Naqqāṭ, Jabal – 62 EF 5
Umm Qaṣr 46-47 M 7
Umm Quṣur, Jazīrat – 62 F 3-4
Umm Rashrash = Ēlat 44-45 C 4
Umm Ruwābah 60-61 L 6
Umm Sa'īd, Bi'r – 62 EF 3
Umm Shāghir, Jabal – 62 D 6
Umnak Island 19 D 35-36
Umniati 64-65 G 6
Umpqua River 76-77 AB 4
'Umshaymin, Al- 46-47 H 6
Ŭmsŏng 50-51 F 4
Umtali = Mutare 64-65 H 6
Umtata 64-65 G 9
Umvuma = Mvuma 64-65 H 6
Umzimvubu 64-65 GH 9

Una 36-37 G 3
Una [BR] 78-79 M 8
'Unāb, Wādī el- = Wādī al-'Unnāb 46-47 G 7-8
Unac 36-37 G 3
Unadilla, GA 74-75 AB 8
Unai 78-79 K 8
'Unaizah = 'Unayzah 44-45 E 5
Unalakleet, AK 70-71 D 5
Unalaska Island 19 D 35
Unango 63 C 6
'Unayzah [JOR] 46-47 FG 7
'Unayzah [Saudi Arabia] 44-45 E 5
'Unayzah, Jabal – 44-45 DE 4
Uncía 78-79 F 8
Uncompahgre Peak 72-73 E 4
Uncompahgre Plateau 76-77 JK 6
Underbool 58 E 5
Undurkhan = Öndörchaan 48-49 L 2
Uneča 38-39 F 5
Uneiuxi, Rio – 78-79 F 5
Unga Island 70-71 D 6
Ungava 70-71 V-X 6
Ungava, Péninsule d' 70-71 VW 5
Ungava Bay 70-71 X 6
Ungava Crater = New Quebec Crater 70-71 VW 5
Ungeny 36-37 MN 2
Unggi 50-51 H 1
União 78-79 L 5
União dos Palmares 78-79 MN 6
Unib, Khawr – 62 F 7
Unije 36-37 EF 3
Unimak Island 19 D 35
Unini, Rio – 78-79 G 5
Unión [RA] 80 C 5
Union, OR 76-77 E 3
Union, SC 74-75 C 7
Union, WV 74-75 C 6
Unión, La – 34-35 G 10
Unión, La – [ES] 72-73 J 9
Unión, La – [PE, Huánuco] 78-79 D 6-7
Unión, La – [RCH] 80 B 6
Union, Mount – 76-77 G 8
Union City, PA 74-75 CD 4
Union Creek, OR 76-77 B 4
Union Pacific Railway 72-73 E 3
Union Point, GA 74-75 B 8
Uniontown, PA 74-75 D 5
Unionville, NV 76-77 DE 5
United Arab Emirates 44-45 G 6-H 5
United Kingdom 32 F-H 4-5
United Provinces = Uttar Pradesh 44-45 MN 5
United States 72-73 D-K 4
United States Atomic Energy Commission Reservation = National Reactor Testing Station 76-77 G 4
Unity, ME 74-75 J 2
University Heights, OH 74-75 C 4
Unjamwesi = Unyamwezi 64-65 H 3-4
'Unnāb, Wādī al- 46-47 G 7-8
Unsan 50-51 E 2-3
Unsan-ni 50-51 EF 3
Unst 32 F 1
Unstrut 33 E 3
Unyamwezi 64-65 H 3-4
Ünye 46-47 G 2
Unža 38-39 H 4
Unže Pavinskaja 38-39 MN 4

Uolkitte = Welkītē 60-61 M 7
Uollega = Welega 60-61 LM 7
Uozu 50-51 L 4

Upanda, Serra – 64-65 DE 5
Upemba, Lac – 64-65 G 4
Upemba, Parc national de l' 64-65 G 4
Upernavik 70-71 Z 3
Upington 64-65 F 8
Upolokša 30-31 O 4
Upolu 52-53 c 1
Upper Darby, PA 74-75 F 4-5
Upper Egypt = Aṣ-Ṣa'īd 60-61 L 3-4
Upper Guinea 22-23 JK 5
Upper Klamath Lake 76-77 BC 4
Upper Lake 76-77 C 5
Upper Lake, CA 76-77 B 6
Upper Peninsula 72-73 J 2
Upper Seal Lake = Lac d'Iberville 70-71 W 6
Uppland 30-31 G 7-H 8
Uppsala [S, ●] 30-31 G 8
Uppsala [S, ☆] 30-31 GH 7
Upstart Bay 56-57 J 3

'Uqaylah, Al- 60-61 H 2
'Uqayr, Al- 44-45 FG 5
Uqṣur, Al- 60-61 L 3

Ur 44-45 F 4
Ur, Wādī – 62 D 6-7
Urabá, Golfo de – 78-79 D 3
Urabá, Isla – 72-73 bc 3
Urakawa 50-51 c 2
Ural, MT 76-77 F 1
Ural [SU, ~] 42-43 J 8
Urales 28-29 V 3-U 4
Uralla 58 K 3
Uralmed'stroj = Krasnoural'sk 42-43 L 6
Urals 28-29 V 3-U 4
Ural'sk 42-43 J 7
Urana 58 GH 5
Urandangi 56-57 G 4
Urandi 78-79 L 7
Uranium City 70-71 P 6
Uraricoera, Rio – 78-79 G 4
Ura-T'ube 44-45 K 3
Uravan, CO 76-77 J 6
Urawa 48-49 QR 4
'Uray'irah 44-45 F 5
'Urayyiḍah, Bi'r – 62 DE 3
Urbana, La – 78-79 F 3
Urbino 36-37 E 4
Urbión, Picos de – 34-35 F 8
Urcos 78-79 E 7
Urda 38-39 J 6
Urdžar 42-43 P 8
Uren' 38-39 J 4
Ureparapara 56-57 N 2
Ures 72-73 DE 6
'Urf, Jabal al- 62 E 4
Urfa = Sanlı Urfa 44-45 D 3
Urfa Yaylâsı 46-47 H 4
'Urf Umm Rashīd 62 F 5
Urga 42-43 K 9
Urga = Ulaanbaatar 48-49 K 2
Urgenč 42-43 L 9
Ürgüp 46-47 F 3
Uribe 78-79 E 4
Uribia 78-79 E 2
Urickij [SU, Kazachskaja SSR] 42-43 M 7
Urim = Ur 44-45 F 4
Urīsā = Orissa 44-45 N 7-O 6
Urla 44-45 B 3
Urmannyj 42-43 M 5
Urmia 44-45 F 3
Urmia = Reḍā'iyeh 44-45 EF 3
Urmia, Lac – = Urmia 44-45 F 3
Urmia, Lago de – = Urmia 44-45 F 3
Ursatjevskaja = Chavast 44-45 K 2
Ursine, NV 76-77 F 6-7
Urt Mörön = Chadzaar 48-49 G 4
Uruaçu 78-79 K 7
Uruana 78-79 JK 8
Uruapan del Progreso 72-73 F 8
Urubamba 78-79 E 7
Urubamba, Rio – 78-79 E 7
Urucará 78-79 H 5
Uruçuí 78-79 L 6
Uruçuí, Serra do – 78-79 K 7-L 6
Urucurituba 78-79 H 5
Uruguai, Rio – 80 F 3
Uruguaiana 80 E 3
Uruguay, Río – [RA ◁ Río de la Plata] 80 E 3
Uruguay, Salto Grande del – 80 F 3
Urūm aṣ-Ṣuğrah 46-47 G 4
Urumbi 78-79 F 4
Ürümchi 48-49 F 3
Urumchi = Ürümchi 48-49 F 3
Urundi = Burundi 64-65 GH 3
Urunga 58 L 3
Ur'ung-Chaja = Jur'ung-Chaja 42-43 VW 3
Ur'ung-Chaja = Jur'ung-Chaja 42-43 VW 3
Urup, ostrov – 48-49 S 2
Uruppu = ostrov Urup 42-43 cd 8
'Urūq al-Mu'tariḍah, Al- 44-45 G 6-7
Uruša 42-43 X 7
Uruyén 78-79 G 3
Urville, Île d' 24 C 31
Urville, Mer d' 24 C 14-15
Urziceni 36-37 M 3
Uržum 42-43 HJ 6

Usa 42-43 K 4
Usagara 64-65 J 4
Uşak 44-45 B 3
Usakos 64-65 DE 7
Ušakova, ostrov – 42-43 OP 1
Usambara Mountains 63 D 4
Usango 63 C 4
Usborne, Mount – 80 E 8
Usedom 33 F 1-G 2
Usengo 63 B 4
Usetsu = Noto 50-51 L 4
Usevia 63 B 4
'Usfān 44-45 D 6
Ushero 63 BC 4
Ushibuka 50-51 GH 6
Ushirombo 63 BC 3
Ushuaia 80 C 8
Usk, WA 76-77 E 1
Üsküdar, İstanbul- 44-45 BC 2
Usman' 38-39 GH 5
Usoke 63 C 4
Usolje = Usolje-Sibirskoje 42-43 T 7
Usolje-Sibirskoje 42-43 T 7
Usolje-Solikamskoje = Berezniki 42-43 JK 6
Ussagara = Usagara 64-65 J 4
Ussuri = Wusuli Jiang 48-49 P 2
Ussurijsk 42-43 Z 9
Ussurijskij zaliv 50-51 HJ 1
Ust'-Abakanskoje = Abakan 42-43 R 7
Ust'-Barguzin 42-43 UV 7
Ust'-Bol'šereck 42-43 de 7
Ust'-Čaun 42-43 h 4
Ust'-Cil'ma 42-43 J 4
Ust'-Čižapka 42-43 OP 6
Ustica 36-37 E 6
Ust'-Ilimsk 42-43 T 6
Ust'-Ilyč 38-39 L 3
Ústí nad Labem 33 FG 3
Ust'-Išim 42-43 N 6
Ustje-Agapy = Agapa 42-43 Q 3
Ust'-Juribej 42-43 MN 4
Ustka 33 H 1
Ust'-Kamčatsk 42-43 f 6
Ust'-Kamenogorsk 42-43 OP 7-8
Ust'-Kan 42-43 PQ 7
Ust'-Kara 42-43 G 4
Ust'-Karabula 42-43 S 6
Ust'-Karsk 42-43 W 7
Ust'-Kulom 42-43 JK 5
Ust'-Kut 42-43 U 6
Ust'-Luga 38-39 E 4
Ust'-Maja 42-43 Z 5
Ust'-Muja 42-43 W 6
Ust'-Nem 38-39 KL 3
Ust'-Nera 42-43 b 5
Uštobe 42-43 O 8
Ust'-Orda = Ust'-Ordynskij 42-43 TU 7
Ust-Orda-Burjaten, Nationalkreis der – = 10 ◁ 42-43 T 7
Ust'-Ordynskij 42-43 TU 7
Ust-Ordynsky-Buryat Autonomous Area = 11 ◁ 42-43 T 7
Ust'-Oz'ornoje 42-43 Q 6
Ust'-Port 42-43 PQ 4
Ust'-Ščug'or 42-43 K 5
Ust Sysolsk = Syktyvkar 42-43 J 5
Ust'-Tareja 42-43 R 3
Ust'-Tatta 42-43 Za 5
Ust'-Tym 42-43 OP 6
Ust'-Ulagan 42-43 Q 7
Ust'-Ura 38-39 HJ 3
Ust'urt, plato – 42-43 K 9
Ust'-Usa 42-43 K 4
Ust'-Vym' 38-39 K 3
Usu-dake 50-51 b 2
Usuki 50-51 HJ 6
Usule 63 C 4
Usumacinta, Río – 72-73 H 8
Usumbura = Bujumbura 64-65 G 3
Usure 63 C 4
Usuyŏng 50-51 EF 5
Usu zan 50-51 b 2

Utah 72-73 DE 4
Utah Lake 72-73 D 3
Utasinai 50-51 c 2
Utegi 63 C 3
Ute Mountain Indian Reservation 76-77 J 7
Utena 30-31 L 10
Utengule 63 C 5
Ute Peak 76-77 J 7
Utete 64-65 J 4
'Uthmānīyah, Al- 62 DE 4
U Thong 52-53 C 4
Utiariti 78-79 H 7
Utica, NY 72-73 LM 3
Utica, OH 74-75 B 4
Utiel 34-35 G 9
Utiura-wan 48-49 R 3
Utrecht 34-35 K 2
Utrera 34-35 E 10
Utrillas 34-35 G 8
Utsjoki 30-31 M 3
Utsunomiya 48-49 QR 4
Uttaradit 52-53 D 3
Uttar Andamān = North Andaman 44-45 P 8
Uttar Pradesh 44-45 MN 5
Utunomiya = Utsunomiya 48-49 QR 4
Utupua 52-53 l 7

Uu = Wuhu 48-49 M 5
Uudenmaan lääni 30-31 K-M 7
Uusikaarlepyy = Nykarleby 30-31 K 6
Uusikaupunki 30-31 J 7
Uusimaa 30-31 KL 7

Uva 38-39 K 4
Uvalde, TX 72-73 G 6
Uvarovo 38-39 H 5
Uvat 42-43 M 6
Uvéa 52-53 b 1
Uvea = Île Ouvéa 56-57 N 4
Uvel'skij 38-39 M 5
Uvinza 64-65 H 3-4
Uvira 64-65 G 3
Uvs = 2 ◁ 48-49 G 2
Uvs nuur 48-49 G 1

Uwajima 48-49 P 5
'Uwayjā', Al- 44-45 G 6
Uwayl 60-61 K 7
'Uwaynāt, Jabal al- 60-61 K 4
'Uwaynidhīyah, Jazīrat al- 62 FG 4
'Uwayqilah, Ma'āṭin – 62 BC 2
'Uwayriḍ, Ḥarrat al- 44-45 D 5
Uwaysit 46-47 GH 7
Uwazima = Uwajima 48-49 P 5
Uwimbi 64-65 HJ 4
Uwinsa = Uvinza 64-65 H 3-4

Uxbridge 74-75 D 2
Uxmal 72-73 J 7

Uyowa 63 BC 4
Uyuni 78-79 F 9
Uyuni, Salar de – 78-79 F 9

Už 38-39 E 5
'Uzaym, Shaṭṭ al- 46-47 L 5
'Uzayr, Al- 46-47 M 7
Uzbekistan 44-45 J 2-K 3
Uzbekistán 44-45 J 2-K 3
Uzboj 38-39 L 8
Uzboj 44-45 H 2-3
Uzgen 44-45 L 2
Užgorod 38-39 D 6
Uzlovaja 38-39 G 5
Uzunköprü 46-47 B 2
Uzun Yaylâ 46-47 G 3
Užur 42-43 QR 6

V

Vääkiö 30-31 N 5
Vaala 30-31 M 5
Vaaldam 64-65 G 8
Vaal River = Vaalrivier 64-65 G 8
Vaalrivier 64-65 G 8

226 Uchta

Vaalwater 64-65 G 7
Vaasa 30-31 J 6
Vác 33 J 5
Vacamonte, Punta – 72-73 b 3
Vacaria 80 F 3
Vacaville, CA 76-77 BC 6
Vach [SU] 42-43 O 5
Vachš 44-45 K 3
Vader, WA 76-77 B 2
Vadheim 30-31 A 7
Vaḍhvān = Wadhwan 44-45 L 6
Vadodara 44-45 L 6
Vadsø 30-31 NO 2
Vadstena 30-31 F 8
Vaduz 33 D 5
Værøy 30-31 E 4
Vafs 46-47 N 5
Vaga 38-39 H 3
Vagaj 42-43 M 6
Vågåmo 30-31 C 7
Vaggeryd 30-31 EF 9
Vågsfjord 30-31 G 3
Váh 33 H 4
Vaigat 70-71 a 3
Vajdaguba 30-31 OP 3
Vajgač 38-39 LM 1
Vajgač, ostrov – 42-43 KL 3
Vakaga 60-61 J 7
Vakfıkebir 46-47 H 2
Valachia 36-37 LM 3
Valachie 36-37 LM 3
Valadim = Mavago 64-65 J 5
Valais 33 C 5
Valaquia 36-37 LM 3
Valcheta 80 C 6
Valdagno 36-37 D 3
Valdajskaja vozvyšennost' 38-39 F 4
Val d'Aosta 36-37 B 3
Valdemārpils 30-31 JK 9
Valdemarsvik 30-31 G 8
Valdepeñas 34-35 F 9
Valdepeñas 34-35 F 9
Valderaduey 34-35 E 7-8
Valdés, Península – 80 D 6
Valdesa, La – 72-73 b 3
Valdez, AK 70-71 G 5
Valdia = Weldya 60-61 M 6
Valdivia [RCH] 80 B 5
Val-d'Or 70-71 V 8
Valdosta, GA 72-73 K 5
Valdres 30-31 C 7
Vale, OR 76-77 E 3-4
Valea-lui-Mihai 36-37 K 2
Vålebru 30-31 D 7
Valença 34-35 C 7-8
Valença [BR, Bahia] 78-79 M 7
Valença = Valencia 78-79 F 2
Valença do Piauí 78-79 L 6
Valence 34-35 K 6
Valencia [YV] 78-79 F 2
Valencia [E, ≅] 34-35 G 8-9
Valencia [E, ●] 34-35 GH 9
Valencia, Golfo de – 34-35 H 9
Valencia, Lago de – 78-79 F 2
Valencia de Alcántara 34-35 D 9
Valencia de Don Juan 34-35 E 7
Valenciennes 34-35 J 3
Valentim, Serra do – 78-79 L 6
Valentin 42-43 Za 9
Valenza 36-37 C 3
Valera 78-79 E 3
Valga 30-31 M 9
Valier, MT 76-77 G 1
Valjevo 36-37 H 3
Valka 30-31 LM 9
Valkeakoski 30-31 L 7
Valladolid 34-35 E 8
Valladolid [MEX] 72-73 J 7
Valle, AZ 76-77 G 8
Vallecito Mountains 76-77 E 9
Valle de la Pascua 78-79 FG 3
Valledupar 78-79 E 2
Valle Grande [BOL] 78-79 G 8
Valle Hermoso [MEX] 72-73 G 6
Vallejo, CA 72-73 B 4
Vallenar 80 B 3
Valletta 36-37 F 8
Valley, WY 76-77 J 3
Valley Falls, OR 76-77 C 4
Valleyfield 70-71 VW 8
Valley Pass 76-77 FG 5
Valls 34-35 H 8
Valmiera 30-31 L 9
Valmy, NV 76-77 E 5
Valnera 34-35 F 7
Vals, Tanjung – 52-53 L 8
Valsbaai [ZA, Kaapland] 64-65 E 9
Valsetz, OR 76-77 B 3
Valujki 38-39 G 5
Valverde [E] 60-61 A 3
Valverde del Camino 34-35 D 10
Vamizi 63 E 5
Vammala 30-31 K 7
Van 44-45 E 3
Vanavara 42-43 T 5
Van Buren, ME 74-75 JK 1
Vanceboro, ME 74-75 K 2
Vanceboro, NC 74-75 E 7
Vancouver 70-71 M 8
Vancouver, WA 72-73 B 2
Vancouver Island 70-71 L 8
Vandemere, NC 74-75 E 7
Vandenberg Air Force Base 76-77 C 8
Vanderlin Island 56-57 G 3
Van Diemen, Cape – 56-57 EF 2
Van Diemen Gulf 56-57 F 2
Vāndrā = Bandra 44-45 L 7
Vänern 30-31 E 8
Vänersborg 30-31 E 8
Vanga = Shimoni 64-65 JK 3
Vangaindrano 64-65 L 7
Van Gölü 44-45 E 3
Vangunu 52-53 j 6
Vanikoro Islands 52-53 l 7
Vanimo 52-53 M 7
Vankarem 42-43 k 4
van Keulenfjord 30-31 jk 6
van Mijenfjord 30-31 jk 6
Vännäs 30-31 HJ 6
Vannes 34-35 F 5
Vannøy 30-31 HJ 2
Vanrhynsdorp 64-65 EF 9
Vanrook 56-57 H 3
Vansbro 30-31 EF 7
Vansittart Bay 56-57 E 2
Vansittart Island 70-71 U 4
Vanua Lava 56-57 N 2
Vanua Levu 52-53 b 2
Vanuatu 56-57 N 2-O 3
Vanwyksvlei 64-65 F 9
Vanzevat 42-43 M 5
Vanžil'-Kynak 42-43 P 5
Varakļāni 30-31 M 9
Vārānasi 44-45 N 5
Vārangal = Warangal 44-45 MN 7
Varangerbotn 30-31 N 2
Varangerfjord 30-31 NO 2-3
Varanger halvøya 30-31 NO 2
Varaždin 36-37 FG 2
Varazze 36-37 C 3
Varberg 30-31 DE 9
Vardar 36-37 K 5
Varde 30-31 C 10
Vardhā = Wardha [IND, ~] 44-45 M 6
Vardhā = Wardha [IND, ●] 44-45 M 6
Vardø 30-31 O 2
Varella, Cap – = Mui Diêu 52-53 EF 4
Vareš 36-37 H 3
Varese 36-37 C 3
Varfolomejevka 42-43 Z 9
Varginha 78-79 K 9
Varillas 80 B 2
Varillas, Las – 80 D 4
Varjegan = Novoangarsk 42-43 O 5
Varkaus 30-31 MN 6
Värmland 30-31 E 8
Värmlandsnäs 30-31 E 8
Varna 36-37 MN 4
Värnamo 30-31 F 9
Varnek 42-43 KL 4
Varnville, SC 74-75 C 8
Varsinais Suomi 30-31 JK 7
Varšipel'da 38-39 G 3
Varsovie = Warszawa 33 KL 2
Varsovie = Warszawa 33 KL 2
Varto 46-47 J 3
Varvarovka 36-37 O 2
Varzuga 38-39 G 2
Vasa = Vaasa 30-31 J 6
Vaşcău 36-37 K 2
Vashon Island 76-77 B 2
Vasknarva 30-31 M 8
Vaskojoki 30-31 LM 3
Vaslui 36-37 MN 2
Vassar 74-75 B 3
Vastan = Gevaş 46-47 K 3
Västerås 30-31 FG 8
Västerbotten [S, ≅] 30-31 H 6-J 5
Västerbotten [S, ☆] 30-31 F-J 5
Västerdalälven 30-31 EF 7
Västergötland 30-31 E 9-F 8
Västernorrland 30-31 GH 6
Västervik 30-31 G 9
Västmanland 30-31 FG 8
Vasto 36-37 F 4
Vas'ugan 42-43 O 6
Vas'uganje 42-43 N 5-O 6
Vasvár 33 H 5
Vaté, Île – = Efate 56-57 N 3
Vaticaanstad 36-37 DE 5
Vatican 36-37 DE 5
Vatican City 36-37 DE 5
Vaticano, Ciudad del – 36-37 DE 5
V'atka 42-43 H 6
V'atka = Kirov 42-43 HJ 6
Vatnajökull 30-31 e 2
Vatomandry 64-65 LM 6
Vatra Dornei 36-37 L 2
V'atskije Pol'any 42-43 HJ 6
Vättern 30-31 F 8
Vaughn, MT 76-77 H 2
Vaupés, Río – 78-79 E 4
Vava'u Group 52-53 c 2
Växjö 30-31 F 9
V'azemskij 42-43 Za 8
V'az'ma 38-39 F 4
Veadeiros, Chapada dos – 78-79 K 7-8
Veadeiros, Chapada dos – 78-79 K 7-8
Vedea 36-37 L 3
Vedia 80 D 4
Vega 30-31 D 5
Vega, La – [DOM] 72-73 MN 8
Vega de Granada 34-35 EF 10
Vegreville 70-71 O 7
Veis = Veys 46-47 N 7
Vejer de la Frontera 34-35 DE 10
Vejle 30-31 C 10
Veka Vekalla = Vella Lavella 52-53 j 6
Vela, Cabo de la – 78-79 E 2
Vela de Coro, La – 78-79 F 2
Velay 34-35 JK 6
Velebit 36-37 F 3
Vélez-Málaga 34-35 EF 10
Velhas, Rio das – 78-79 L 8
Velho = Mágoè 64-65 H 6
Velikaja 38-39 E 4
Velikaja [SU ◁ Anadyrskij zaliv] 42-43 h 5
Velikaja Aleksandrovka 36-37 P 2
Velikaja Ičinskaja sopka = vulkan Ičinskaja Sopka 42-43 e 6
Velikaja Kambalnaja sopka = vulkan Kambalnaja Sopka 42-43 e 7
Velikaja Kl'učevskaja sopka = vulkan Kl'učevskaja Sopka 42-43 f 6
Velikaja Kor'akskaja sopka = vulkan Kor'akskaja Sopka 42-43 ef 7
Velikaja Kronockaja sopka = vulkan Kronockaja Sopka 42-43 ef 7
Velikije Luki 38-39 EF 4
Velikij Šiveluč = vulkan Šiveluč 42-43 f 6
Velikij Ust'ug 42-43 GH 5
Veliko Târnovo 36-37 L 4
Veliž 38-39 F 4
Velkomstpynten 30-31 j 5
Vella Lavella 52-53 j 6
Velletri 36-37 E 5
Vellore 44-45 M 8
Velluga 42-43 H 6
Velmerstot 33 D 3
Vel'sk 42-43 G 5
Vēlūr = Vellore 44-45 M 8
Vemdalen 30-31 EF 6
Venado, Isla – 72-73 b 3
Venado Tuerto 80 D 4
Venator, OR 76-77 DE 4
Vendas Novas 34-35 C 9
Vendée 34-35 G 5
Vendôme 34-35 H 5
Venecia = Venèzia 36-37 E 3
Veneta, OR 76-77 B 3-4
Venetie, AK 70-71 G 4
Venetië = Venèzia 36-37 E 3
Veneto 36-37 DE 3
Venèzia 36-37 E 3
Venèzia, Golfo di – 36-37 E 3
Venezuela 78-79 FG 3
Venezuela, Golfo de – 78-79 E 2
Vēngangā = Wainganga 44-45 MN 6-7
Vengerovo 42-43 O 6
Vengurla 44-45 L 7
Vēṅgurlēṅ = Vengurla 44-45 L 7
Venice, FL 74-75 b 3
Venice = Venèzia 36-37 E 3
Venise = Venèzia 36-37 E 3
Venosa 36-37 F 5
Venta 30-31 K 9
Venta de Baños 34-35 E 8
Venta de Baños 34-35 E 8
Ventana, Sierra de la – 80 D 5
Ventnor 32 F 6
Ventoux, Mont – 34-35 K 6
Ventspils 30-31 J 9
Ventuari, Río – 78-79 F 3
Ventura, CA 76-77 D 8
Vera [RA] 80 D 3
Vera, La – 34-35 E 8
Verá, Laguna – 80 E 3
Veracruz [MEX, ●] 72-73 GH 8
Veracruz [MEX, ☆] 72-73 G 7-8
Veranópolis 80 F 3
Verāval 44-45 KL 6
Vercelli 36-37 C 3
Verchn'aja Amga 42-43 Y 6
Verchn'aja Salda 38-39 M 4
Verchn'aja Tojma 42-43 GH 5
Verchnedvinsk 30-31 MN 10
Verchneimbatsk 42-43 QR 5
Verchneje Adimi 50-51 H 1
Verchne Ozernaja 42-43 f 6
Verchneudinsk = Ulan-Udè 42-43 U 7
Verchneural'sk 42-43 KL 7
Verchneusinkoje 42-43 RS 7
Verchnevil'ujsk 42-43 X 5
Verchnij Baskunčak 38-39 J 6
Verchnij Trajanov val 36-37 N 2
Verchnij Ufalej 42-43 KL 6
Verchojansk 42-43 Za 4
Verchojanskij chrebet 42-43 Y 4-Z 5
Verdalsøyra 30-31 DE 6
Verden 33 D 2
Verde River 76-77 H 8
Verdi, NV 76-77 CD 6
Verdon 34-35 L 7
Verdon-sur-Mer, le – 34-35 G 6
Verdun 34-35 K 4
Vereeniging 64-65 G 8
Vérendrye, Parc provincial de la – 70-71 V 8
Verenigde Arabische Emiraten 44-45 G 6-H 5
Verenigde Staten 72-73 D-K 4
Vereščagino [SU ↓ Igarka] 42-43 QR 5
Vereščagino [SU ← Krasnokamsk] 42-43 JK 6
Verín 34-35 D 8
Verkola 38-39 J 3
Verlegenhuken 30-31 jk 4
Vermilion 70-71 O 7
Vermilion Cliffs 76-77 G 7
Vermillion, OH 74-75 B 4
Vermont 72-73 M 3
Vernal, UT 76-77 J 5
Vernon 34-35 H 4
Vernon [CDN, British Colombia] 70-71 N 7
Vernon, AZ 76-77 J 8
Vernon, NV 76-77 D 5
Vernon, TX 72-73 FG 5
Vernon = Onaqui, UT 76-77 G 5
Vernonia, OR 76-77 B 3
Vernyj = Alma-Ata 42-43 O 9
Vero Beach, FL 74-75 cd 3
Verona 36-37 D 3
Versailles 34-35 HJ 4
Versailles, OH 74-75 A 5
Veršino-Darasunskij 42-43 VW 7
Verviers 34-35 KL 3
Vervins 34-35 JK 4
Vescovato 36-37 C 4
Veselí nad Lužnicí 33 G 4
Veselinovo 36-37 O 2
Vesjegonsk 42-43 F 6
Vesoul 34-35 KL 5
Vest-Agder 30-31 B 8
Vesterålen 30-31 FG 3
Vestfjorden 30-31 E 4-F 3
Vestfold 30-31 CD 8
Vestfonna 30-31 l 4
Vestmannaeyjar 30-31 c 3
Vestspitsbergen 30-31 j-l 5
Vestur-Bardhastrandar 30-31 ab 2
Vestur-Húnavatn 30-31 cd 2
Vestur-Ísafjardhar 30-31 b 1-2
Vestur-Skaftafell 30-31 de 3
Vestvågøy 30-31 EF 3
Vesùvio 36-37 F 5
Veszprem 33 HJ 5
Vetlanda 30-31 F 9
Vetralla 36-37 DE 4
Vevay, OH 74-75 A 5
Veynes 34-35 K 6
Veyo, UT 76-77 G 7
Veys 46-47 N 7
Vézère 34-35 H 6
Vezirköprü 46-47 F 2
Viacha 78-79 F 8
Viana [BR, Maranhão] 78-79 K 5
Viana del Bollo 34-35 D 7
Viana do Castelo 34-35 C 8
Viangchan 52-53 D 3
Vianópolis 78-79 K 8
Viarèggio 36-37 CD 4
Viborg 30-31 C 9
Viborg = Vyborg 42-43 DE 5
Vibo Valentia 36-37 FG 6
Vic 34-35 J 8
Vicente, Point – 76-77 D 9
Vicenza 36-37 D 3
Vichada, Río – 78-79 F 4
Vichy 34-35 J 5
Vicksburg, AZ 76-77 FG 9
Vicksburg, MS 72-73 HJ 5
Victor, ID 76-77 H 4
Victor, MT 76-77 F 2
Victor Harbor 56-57 G 7
Victoria [AUS] 56-57 HJ 7
Victoria [CDN] 70-71 M 8
Victoria [HK] 48-49 LM 7
Victoria [RA] 80 DE 4
Victoria [RCH, Araucanía] 80 B 5
Victoria [SY] 64-65 MN 3
Victoria [ZW] 64-65 H 7
Victoria, TX 72-73 G 6
Victoria = Labuan 52-53 FG 5
Victoria, Île – = Victoria Island 70-71 O-Q 3
Victoria, Lake – [AUS] 58 E 4
Victoria, Lake – [≈] 64-65 H 3
Victoria, Mount – 52-53 N 8
Victoria, Mount – = Tomaniive 52-53 a 2
Victoria and Albert Mountains 70-71 VW 1-2
Victoria de Durango 72-73 F 7
Victoria de las Tunas 72-73 L 7
Victoria Island [CDN] 70-71 O-Q 3
Victoria Land 24 B 17-15
Victoria Point = Kawthaung 52-53 C 4
Victoria River 56-57 EF 3
Victoria River Downs 56-57 F 3
Victoria Strait 70-71 QR 4
Victoria-Wes 64-65 F 9
Victoria West = Victoria-Wes 64-65 F 9
Victorica 80 C 5
Victorino 78-79 F 4
Victorville, CA 76-77 E 8
Vičuga 42-43 G 6
Vidal, CA 76-77 F 8
Vidalia, GA 74-75 B 8
Vidim 42-43 T 6
Vidin 36-37 K 3-4
Vidio, Cabo – 34-35 DE 7
Vidisha 44-45 M 6
Vidra 36-37 M 3
Viedma 80 D 6
Viedma, Lago – 80 B 7
Vieille Castille = Castilla la Vieja 34-35 E 8-F 7
Viejo, Cerro – 76-77 G 10
Viena = Wien 33 H 4
Vienna, GA 74-75 B 8
Vienna, WV 74-75 C 5
Vienna = Wien 33 H 4
Vienne [F, ~] 34-35 H 5
Vienne [F, ●] 34-35 K 6
Vienne = Wien 33 H 4
Vientiane = Viangchan 52-53 D 3
Vientos, Los – 80 BC 2
Vientos, Paso de los – 72-73 M 7-8
Vieques 72-73 N 8
Vierges, Îles – 72-73 NO 8
Vierwaldstätter See 33 D 5
Vierzon 34-35 J 5
Viesīte 30-31 L 9
Vieste 36-37 G 5
Viêt Tri 52-53 E 2
Vietnam 52-53 D 2-E 4
Vigan 52-53 GH 3
Vigia 78-79 K 5
Vigía, El – 78-79 E 3
Vignola 36-37 D 3
Vigo 34-35 C 7
Vihren 36-37 K 5
Viipuri = Vyborg 42-43 DE 5
Viitasaari 30-31 LM 6
Vijayanagaram = Vizianagaram 44-45 NO 7
Vijayawada 44-45 N 7
Vik 30-31 d 3
Vika 30-31 M 4
Viking 70-71 O 7
Vikna 30-31 D 5
Vikøyri 30-31 B 7
Vila [Vanuatu] 56-57 N 3
Vila Arriaga = Bibala 64-65 D 5
Vila Artur de Paiva = Cubango 64-65 E 5
Vila Bela da Santíssima Trindade 78-79 H 7-8
Vila Cabral = Lichinga 64-65 J 5
Vila Coutinho 64-65 H 5
Vila da Maganja 64-65 J 6
Vila de Aljustrel = Cangamba 64-65 E 5
Vila de Aviz = Oncócua 64-65 D 6
Vila de João Belo = Xai Xai 64-65 H 8
Vila de Manica = Manica 64-65 H 6
Vila de Sena 64-65 HJ 6
Vila Fontes = Caia 64-65 J 6
Vila Franca de Xira 34-35 C 9
Vila Gouveia = Catandica 64-65 H 6
Vila Henrique de Carvalho = Saurimo 64-65 F 4
Vilaine 34-35 F 5
Vila João de Almeida = Chibia 64-65 D 6
Vilaller 34-35 H 7
Vila Macedo do Cavaleiros = Andulo 64-65 E 5
Vila Marechal Carmona = Uíge 64-65 E 4
Vila Mariano Machado = Ganda 64-65 D 5
Vilanculos 64-65 J 7
Viļāni 30-31 M 9
Vila Norton de Matos = Balombo 64-65 D 5
Vila Nova do Seles 64-65 D 5
Vila Paiva Couceiro = Gambos 64-65 DE 5
Vila Pereira d'Eça = Ngiva 64-65 E 6
Vila Pery = Manica 64-65 H 6
Vila Real 34-35 D 8
Vila Real de Santo António 34-35 D 10
Vilar Formoso 34-35 D 8
Vila Salazar = Ndalatando 64-65 DE 4
Vila Teixeira da Silva = Bailundo 64-65 E 5
Vila Teixeira de Sousa = Luau 64-65 EF 5
Vila Velha [BR, Espírito Santo] 78-79 LM 9
Vila Viçosa 34-35 D 9
Vilcabamba, Cordillera – 78-79 E 7
Vil'čeka, zeml'a – 42-43 L-N 1
Vilejka 38-39 E 5
Vil'gort = Vyl'gort [SU, Syktyvkar] 42-43 HJ 5
Vilhelmina 30-31 G 5
Vilhena 78-79 G 7
Vilija 38-39 E 5
Viljandi 30-31 L 8
Vil'kickogo, ostrov – [SU, Gydanskij p-ov] 42-43 NO 3
Vil'kickogo, ostrov – [SU, Novosibirskije o-va] 42-43 de 2
Vil'kickogo, proliv – 42-43 S-U 2
Villa Abecia 78-79 FG 9
Villa Ángela 80 D 3
Villa Bella 78-79 F 7
Villablino 34-35 D 7
Villacañas 34-35 F 9
Villacarillo 34-35 F 9
Villach 33 F 5
Villacidro 36-37 C 6
Villa Cisneros = Ad-Dakhlah 60-61 A 4
Villada 34-35 E 7
Villa de Cura 78-79 F 2-3
Villa de María 80 D 3
Villa Dolores 80 C 4
Villa Federal = Federal 80 E 4
Villafranca del Bierzo 34-35 D 7
Villafranca de los Barros 34-35 DE 9
Villafranca del Penedès 34-35 H 8
Villa Frontera 72-73 F 6
Villagarcía de Arosa 34-35 C 7
Villàgio Duca degli Abruzzi = Joowhar 64-65 L 2
Villaguay 80 E 4
Villahermosa [MEX] 72-73 H 8
Villajoyosa 34-35 GH 9
Villa María 80 D 4
Villa Mazán 80 C 3
Villamil 78-79 A 5
Villa Montes 78-79 G 9
Villanova i la Geltrú 34-35 HJ 8
Villanueva de Córdoba 34-35 E 9

Villa 227

Waynesboro, PA 74-75 E 5
Waynesboro, VA 74-75 D 5
Waynesburg, PA 74-75 CD 5
Waynesville, NC 74-75 B 7
Waza 60-61 G 6
Wāzakhwā 44-45 K 4
Wāzīrābād = Balkh 44-45 K 3
Wazz, Al- 60-61 L 5
Wazzān 60-61 C 2
We, Pulau – 52-53 BC 5
Weaverville, CA 76-77 B 5
Webbe Shibeli = Wābi Shebelē 60-61 N 7
Webster, MA 74-75 GH 3
Webster Springs, WV 74-75 C 5
Weda 52-53 J 6
Weddell, Mer de – = Weddell Sea 24 BC 32-34
Weddell Island 80 D 8
Weddell Sea 24 BC 32-34
Weddellzee = Weddell Sea 24 BC 32-34
Weddell, Mar de – = Weddell Sea 24 BC 32-34
Wedel Jarlsberg land 30-31 j 6
Weed, CA 76-77 B 5
Weedon Centre 74-75 H 2
Weedville, PA 74-75 D 4
Weeksbury, KY 74-75 B 6
Weenusk = Winisk 70-71 T 6
Wee Waa 56-57 J 6
Wegener-Inlandeis 24 B 36-1
Weichang 48-49 M 3
Weiden 33 EF 4
Weifang 48-49 MN 4
Weihai 48-49 N 4
Wei He [TJ ◁ Hai He] 48-49 M 4
Wei He [TJ ◁ Huang He] 48-49 K 5
Weilmoringle 58 H 2
Weimar 33 E 3
Weining 48-49 JK 6
Weipa 56-57 H 2
Weirton, WV 74-75 C 4
Weiser, ID 76-77 E 3
Weiser River 76-77 E 3
Weiße Elster 33 F 3
Weißenfels 33 E 3
Weißer Volta = White Volta 60-61 D 7
Weißes Meer 42-43 FG 4
Weiss Knob 74-75 D 5
Weiyang = Huiyang 48-49 LM 7
Wejh = Al-Wajh 44-45 D 5
Welbourn Hill 56-57 F 5
Welch, WV 74-75 C 6
Weldon, NC 74-75 E 6
Weldya 60-61 M 6
Welega 60-61 LM 7
Welel, Tulu – 60-61 LM 7
Welkītē 60-61 M 7
Welkom 64-65 G 8
Welland [CDN] 74-75 D 3
Welland Canal 74-75 D 3
Wellesley Islands 56-57 GH 3
Wellington [AUS] 56-57 JK 6
Wellington [CDN] 74-75 D 3
Wellington [NZ] 56-57 OP 8
Wellington, NV 76-77 D 6
Wellington, OH 74-75 B 4
Wellington, Isla – 80 AB 7
Wellington Channel 70-71 S 2-3
Wells, NV 72-73 C 3
Wells, Lake – 56-57 D 5
Wellsboro, PA 74-75 E 4
Wellsford 56-57 OP 7
Wells Gray Provincial Park 70-71 MN 7
Wells next the Sea 32 G 5
Wellston, OH 74-75 B 5
Wellsville, NY 74-75 E 3
Wellton, AZ 76-77 FG 9
Welo 60-61 MN 6
Wels 33 FG 4
Welshpool 32 E 5
Wellington Channel 70-71 S 2-3
Wembere 64-65 H 3-4
Wenatchee, WA 72-73 BC 2
Wenatchee Mountains 76-77 C 2
Wenchow = Wenzhou 48-49 N 6
Wendel, CA 76-77 CD 5
Wendell, ID 76-77 F 4
Wendell, NC 74-75 D 7
Wenden, AZ 76-77 G 9
Wendling, OR 76-77 B 3
Wendover, UT 76-77 FG 5
Wenen = Wien 33 H 4
Wenshan 48-49 JK 7
Wenshan Zhuangzu Miaozu Zizhizhou 48-49 JK 7
Wên-su = Aqsu 48-49 E 3
Wentworth 56-57 H 6
Wenzhou 48-49 N 6
Wepener 64-65 G 8
Werdēr [ETH] 60-61 O 7
Wernecke Mountains 70-71 JK 5
Wernigerode 33 E 3
Werra 33 D 3
Werribee, Melbourne- 58 FG 6
Werris Creek 56-57 K 6
Wesel 33 C 3
Weser 33 D 2
Weserbergland 33 D 2-3
Wesleyville, PA 74-75 CD 3
Wessel, Cape – 56-57 G 2
Wessel Islands 56-57 G 2
Westall, Point – 58 AB 4
Westaustralian Basin 22-23 P 7
Westaustralisch Bekken 22-23 P 7
West Bengal 44-45 O 6
Westbrook, ME 74-75 H 3
West Butte 76-77 H 1
West Caroline Basin 22-23 QR 5
West-Carolinenbekken 22-23 QR 5
West Columbia, SC 74-75 C 8
Westerland 33 D 1
Westerly, RI 74-75 H 4
Western [EAK] 64-65 H 2
Western [Z] 64-65 F 6
Western Australia 56-57 C-E 4-5
Western Dvina = Daugava 30-31 LM 9
Western Ghats 44-45 L 6-M 8
Western Port 56-57 HJ 7
Westernport, MD 74-75 D 5
Western Sahara 60-61 A 4-B 3
Western Shoshone Indian Reservation 76-77 E 4-5
Westerschelde 34-35 J 3
Westerwald 33 CD 3
West European Basin 22-23 HJ 3
Westeuropees Bekken 22-23 HJ 3
West Falkland 80 D 8
Westfall, OR 76-77 E 3-4
Westfield, MA 74-75 G 3
Westfield, NY 74-75 D 3
Westfield, PA 74-75 E 4
West Frisian Islands 34-35 KL 2
Westgate 56-57 J 5
Westham, London- 32 FG 6
West Haven, CT 74-75 G 4
West Ice Shelf 24 C 9
West-Indië 72-73 LM 7
West Indies 72-73 LM 7
West Irian 52-53 K 7-L 8
West Jefferson, NC 74-75 C 6
Westlake, OR 76-77 A 4
Westlicher Großer Erg = Al-'Irq al-Gharbī al-Kabīr 60-61 D 3-E 2
Westlicher Sajan = Zapadnyj Sajan 42-43 Q-S 7
West Memphis, AR 72-73 H 4
Westminster, MD 74-75 D 5
Westmorland, CA 76-77 F 9
West Mountain 74-75 FG 3
West Nicholson 64-65 GH 7
Weston [CDN] 74-75 D 3
Weston [MAL] 52-53 G 5
Weston, ID 76-77 GH 4
Weston, OR 76-77 D 3
Weston, WV 74-75 C 5
Weston-super-Mare 32 E 6
West Palm Beach, FL 72-73 KL 6
West Point [AUS] 56-57 F 7-G 6
West Point, NY 74-75 G 4
West Point, VA 74-75 E 6
Westport [IRL] 32 AB 5
Westport [NZ] 56-57 O 8
Westport, CA 76-77 AB 6
Westport, OR 76-77 B 2
Westray 32 E 2
West-Sahara 60-61 A 4-B 3
West Scotia Basin 22-23 G 8
West Union, WV 74-75 C 5
West Virginia 72-73 KL 4
Westwater, UT 76-77 J 6
Westwood, CA 76-77 C 5
West Wyalong 58 H 4
West Yellowstone, MT 76-77 H 3
Wetar, Pulau – 52-53 J 8
Wetaskiwin 70-71 NO 7
Wete 64-65 JK 4
Weti = Wete 64-65 JK 4
Wetmore, OR 76-77 D 3
Wetter = Pulau Wetar 52-53 J 8
Wewak 52-53 M 7
Wexford 32 C 5
Weyb = Wabē Gestro Weniz 60-61 N 7
Weyburn 70-71 Q 8
Weymouth 32 EF 6
Weymouth, Cape – 56-57 HJ 2
Weyprecht, Kapp – 30-31 l 5
Whakatane 56-57 P 7
Whaleback, Mount – 56-57 CD 4
Whales, Bay of – 24 B 19-20
Whalsay 32 F 1
Whangarei 56-57 OP 7
Wheatland, CA 76-77 C 6
Wheeler, OR 76-77 AB 3
Wheeler Peak [USA, Nevada] 72-73 CD 4
Wheeler Peak [USA, New Mexico] 72-73 E 4
Wheeler Ridge, CA 76-77 D 8
Wheeling, WV 72-73 KL 4-5
Whewell, Mount – 24 B 17-18
Whichaway Nunataks 24 A 34-1
Whidbey, Point – 58 B 5
Whidbey Island 76-77 B 1
Whiporie 58 L 2
Whitby [CDN] 74-75 D 3
White, Lake – 56-57 E 4
White Bay 70-71 Z 7
White Bird, ID 76-77 EF 3
White City, FL 74-75 c 3
White Cliffs 56-57 H 6
Whiteface Mountain 74-75 FG 2
Whitefish, MT 76-77 F 1
Whitefish Range 76-77 F 1
Whitehall, MT 76-77 GH 3
Whitehall, NY 74-75 G 3
Whitehaven 32 DE 4
Whitehorse 70-71 JK 5
White Horse, CA 76-77 C 5
White Horse Pass 76-77 FG 5
Whitemark 58 cd 2
White Mountain, AK 70-71 D 5
White Mountains [USA, California] 76-77 D 7
White Mountains [USA, New Hampshire] 74-75 H 2
Whiteoak Swamp 74-75 E 7
White Pine, MT 76-77 F 2
White Pine Mountains 76-77 F 6
White Plains, NY 74-75 FG 4
White River [CDN, Yukon Territory] 70-71 H 5
White River [USA, Arkansas] 72-73 H 4
White River [USA, California] 76-77 F 7
White River [USA, South Dakota] 72-73 F 3
White River Valley 76-77 F 6
White Salmon, WA 76-77 C 3
White Springs, FL 74-75 b 1
White Sulphur Springs, MT 76-77 H 2
White Swan, WA 76-77 C 2
Whiteville, NC 74-75 D 7
Whitewater Baldy 72-73 E 5
Whitfield 58 H 6
Whithorn 32 DE 4
Whiting, NJ 74-75 F 5
Whitmire, SC 74-75 C 7
Whitmore Mountains 24 A
Whitney, OR 76-77 DE 3
Whitney, Mount – 72-73 C 4
Whitsunday Island 56-57 JK 4
Whittier, AK 70-71 G 5
Whittlesea 58 G 6
Wholdaia Lake 70-71 PQ 5
Whyalla 56-57 G 6
Wiang Phran = Mae Sai 52-53 CD 2
Wichian Buri 52-53 D 3
Wichita, KS 72-73 G 4
Wichita Falls, TX 72-73 FG 5
Wick 32 E 2
Wickenburg, AZ 76-77 G 8-9
Wickersham, WA 76-77 BC 1
Wickham, Cape – 58 b 1
Wicklow 32 CD 5
Wicklow Mountains 32 C 5
Widen, WV 74-75 C 5
Widgiemooltha 56-57 D 6
Wi-do 50-51 F 5
Widyan, Al- 44-45 E 4
Więcbork 33 H 2
Wieluń 33 J 3
Wien 33 G 4
Wiener Neustadt 33 GH 5
Wienerwald 33 GH 4
Wieprz 33 L 3
Wiesbaden 33 CD 3
Wiese Island = ostrov Vize 42-43 O 2
Wigadēn 60-61 NO 7
Wigan 32 E 5
Wight, Isle of – 32 F 6
Wijdefjorden 30-31 j 5
Wilborn, MT 76-77 G 2
Wilbourn Hill 58 B 1
Wilbur, WA 76-77 D 2
Wilcannia 56-57 H 6
Wilczek, zeml'a – = zeml'a Vil'čeka 42-43 L-N 1
Wilczek land = zeml'a Vil'čeka 42-43 L-N 1
Wild Horse Reservoir 76-77 F 5
Wildwood, FL 74-75 bc 2
Wildwood, NJ 74-75 F 5
Wilgena 58 B 3
Wilhelm, Mount – 52-53 M 8
Wilhelmina Gebergte 78-79 H 4
Wilhelmøya 30-31 l 5
Wilhelmshaven 33 CD 2
Wilkes 24 C 12
Wilkes Barre, PA 72-73 L 3
Wilkes Land 24 BC 12-14
Wilkie 70-71 P 7
Wilkinsburg, PA 74-75 D 4
Wilkinson Lakes 56-57 F 5
Willacoochee, GA 74-75 B 9
Willamette River 72-73 B 3
Willandra Billabong Creek 58 G 4
Willapa Bay 76-77 AB 2
Willard, UT 76-77 GH 5
Willcox, AZ 76-77 HJ 9
Willemstad [NA] 72-73 N 9
Willeroo 56-57 F 3
William Creek 56-57 G 5
Williams, AZ 76-77 G 8
Williams, CA 76-77 B 6
Williams Lake 70-71 M 7
Williamson, WV 74-75 B 6
Williamsport, PA 72-73 L 3
Williamston, NC 74-75 E 6-7
Willimantic, CT 74-75 G 4
Willis Group 56-57 K 3
Williston 64-65 F 9
Williston, FL 74-75 b 2
Williston, ND 72-73 F 2
Williston, SC 74-75 C 8
Willits, CA 76-77 B 6
Willoughby, OH 74-75 C 4
Willow 70-71 F 5
Willow Creek [USA, California] 76-77 C 5
Willow Creek [USA, Oregon] 76-77 D 3
Willowlake River 70-71 MN 5
Willowmore 64-65 F 9
Willow Ranch, CA 76-77 C 5
Willows, CA 76-77 B 6
Willsboro, NY 74-75 G 2
Willunga 58 D 5
Wilmington [AUS] 58 D 4
Wilmington, DE 72-73 LM 4
Wilmington, NC 72-73 L 5
Wilsall, MT 76-77 H 3
Wilson, NC 72-73 L 4
Wilson, NY 74-75 D 3
Wilson Bluff 56-57 EF 6
Wilson Creek, WA 76-77 D 2
Wilson Creek Range 76-77 F 6
Wilson River 56-57 H 5
Wilsons Promontory 56-57 J 7
Wilton River 56-57 F 2
Wiluna 56-57 D 5
Wimbledon, London- 32 F 6
Wimmera 56-57 H 7
Wina = Ouina 60-61 G 7
Winburg 64-65 G 8
Winchester 32 F 6
Winchester [CDN] 74-75 F 2
Winchester, ID 76-77 E 2
Winchester, VA 72-73 L 4
Winchester Bay, OR 76-77 A 4
Windber, PA 74-75 D 4
Windesi 52-53 K 7
Windhoek 64-65 E 7
Windorah 56-57 H 5
Wind River Indian Reservation 76-77 J 4
Wind River Range 72-73 DE 3
Windsor [AUS] 58 K 4
Windsor [CDN, Ontario] 70-71 U 9
Windsor [GB] 32 F 6
Windsor, NC 74-75 E 6
Windsor, VT 74-75 G 3
Windward Islands [Westindien] 72-73 O 9
Winfield, KS 72-73 G 4
Winisk 70-71 T 6
Winisk Lake 70-71 T 7
Winisk River 70-71 T 7
Winkelman, AZ 76-77 H 9
Winlock, WA 76-77 B 2
Winneba 60-61 D 7
Winnemucca, NV 72-73 C 3
Winnemucca Lake 76-77 D 5
Winning 56-57 B 4
Winnipeg 70-71 R 7
Winnipeg, Lake – 70-71 R 7
Winnipegosis, Lake – 70-71 R 7
Winnipeg River 70-71 RS 7
Winnipesaukee, Lake – 74-75 H 3
Winnsboro, SC 74-75 C 7
Winona, AZ 76-77 H 8
Winona, MN 72-73 H 3
Winona, WA 76-77 DE 2
Winschoten 34-35 L 2
Winslow, AZ 72-73 DE 4
Winslow, ME 74-75 J 2
Winsted, CT 74-75 G 4
Winston, MT 76-77 GH 2
Winston, OR 76-77 B 4
Winston-Salem, NC 72-73 KL 4
Winterberg 33 D 3
Winter Garden, FL 74-75 c 2
Winterhaven, CA 76-77 F 9
Winter Haven, FL 74-75 c 2
Winter Park, FL 74-75 c 2
Winters, CA 76-77 C 6
Winterthur 33 D 5
Winthrop, ME 74-75 HJ 2
Winthrop, WA 76-77 C 1
Winton [AUS] 56-57 H 4
Winton [NZ] 56-57 N 9
Winton, WA 76-77 C 2
Winton, WY 76-77 J 5
Winyah Bay 74-75 D 8
Wirāj, Wādī al- 62 D 3
Wirrulla 56-57 FG 6
Wiscasset, ME 74-75 J 2
Wisconsin 72-73 H 2-J 3
Wisconsin River 72-73 HJ 3
Wisdom, MT 76-77 G 3
Wiseman, AK 70-71 FG 4
Wisła 33 K 3
Wislana, Mierzeja – 33 J 1
Wislany, Zalew – 33 J 1
Wisłok 33 KL 4
Wisłoka 33 K 4
Wismar 33 E 2
Wissel, Danau – = Danau Paniai 52-53 L 7
Wissembourg 34-35 LM 4
Wissmann, Chutes – 64-65 EF 4
Wissmann, Chutes – 64-65 EF 4
Wiswila 63 AB 5
Witbank 64-65 GH 8
Withernsea 32 FG 5
Witjasdiep 48-49 S 3
Witputs 64-65 E 8
Wit-Rusland 38-39 EF 5
Wittenberg 33 F 3
Wittenberge 33 EF 2
Wittenoom Gorge 56-57 C 4
Witte Zee 42-43 FG 4
Wittlich 33 C 4
Wittmann, AZ 76-77 G 9
Wittstock 33 F 2
Witu 64-65 JK 3
Witvlei 64-65 E 7
Wiwŏn 50-51 F 2
Wkra 33 JK 2
Włocławek 33 J 2
Włodawa 33 L 3
Wodonga 58 H 6
Wohlthatmassiv 24 B 2
Wokam, Pulau – 52-53 KL 8
Wolcott, NY 74-75 E 3
Woleai 52-53 M 5
Wolf Creek, MT 76-77 G 2
Wolf Creek, OR 76-77 B 4
Wolfenbüttel 33 E 2
Wolff, Chutes – 64-65 F 4
Wolff, Chutes – 64-65 F 4
Wolfsburg 33 E 2
Wolin 33 G 2
Wolkitte = Welkītē 60-61 M 7
Wollaston, Islas – 80 C 9
Wollaston Lake 70-71 PQ 6
Wollaston Peninsula 70-71 NO 3-4
Wollega = Welega 60-61 LM 7
Wollo = Welo 60-61 MN 6
Wollogorang 56-57 G 3
Wollongong 56-57 K 6
Wołów 33 H 3
Wolseley [AUS] 56-57 GH 7
Wolstenholme 70-71 VW 5
Wolstenholme, Cape – 70-71 VW 5
Wolsztyn 33 GH 2
Wolverhampton 32 E 5
Wonder, OR 76-77 B 4
Wŏngsŏng-dong 50-51 DE 3
Wŏnju 48-49 O 4
Wonosari 52-53 F 8
Wŏnsan 48-49 O 4
Wonthaggi 56-57 HJ 7
Woocalla 58 C 3
Wood, Mount – [USA] 76-77 J 3
Wood Bay 24 B 17-18
Woodbine, GA 74-75 C 9
Wood Buffalo National Park 70-71 O 6
Woodburn, OR 76-77 B 3
Woodbury, NJ 74-75 F 5
Woodend 58 G 6
Woodfjorden 30-31 j 5
Woodlake, CA 76-77 D 7
Woodland, CA 76-77 BC 6
Woodland, WA 76-77 B 3
Woodlark Island 52-53 h 6
Woodroffe, Mount – 56-57 F 5
Woodruff, SC 74-75 BC 7
Woodruff, UT 76-77 H 5
Woods, Lake – 56-57 F 3
Woods, Lake of the – 70-71 R 8
Woodsfield, OH 74-75 C 5
Woodside 56-57 J 7
Woodside, UT 76-77 H 6
Woodstock [AUS] 56-57 H 3
Woodstock [CDN, Ontario] 74-75 C 3
Woodstock, VA 74-75 D 5
Woodstock, VT 74-75 G 3
Woodsville, NH 74-75 GH 2
Woodville 56-57 P 8
Woodward, OK 72-73 G 4
Woolgoolga 58 L 3
Wooltana 58 DE 3
Woomera 56-57 G 6
Woonsocket, RI 74-75 GH 4
Wooramel River 56-57 C 5
Wooster, OH 74-75 C 4
Woqooyi Galbeed 60-61 a 1
Worcester [GB] 32 E 5
Worcester [ZA] 64-65 EF 9
Worcester, MA 72-73 M 3
Worcester Range 24 B 17-15
Worden, OR 76-77 BC 4
Workington 32 E 4
Worms 33 CD 4
Worthing 32 FG 6
Wou-han = Wuhan 48-49 L 5
Wou-hou = Wuhu 48-49 M 5
Wour 60-61 H 4
Wou-tcheou = Wuzhou 48-49 L 7
Wowoni, Pulau – 52-53 H 7
Wrangel, ostrov – = ostrov Vrangel'a 42-43 hj 3
Wrangell, AK 70-71 K 6
Wrangell Mountains 70-71 H 5
Wrath, Cape – 32 D 2
Wrens, GA 74-75 B 8
Wright, Lake – 56-57 EF 5
Wrightson, Mount – 76-77 H 10
Wrightsville, GA 74-75 B 8
Wrigley 70-71 M 5
Wrigley Gulf 24 B 24
Wrocław 33 H 3
Września 33 HJ 2
Wschowa 33 H 3
Wubin 56-57 C 5-6
Wuchang 48-49 O 3
Wuchang, Wuhan- 48-49 LM 5
Wu Chiang = Wu Jiang [TJ, ~] 48-49 K 6
Wu-chou = Wuzhou 48-49 L 7
Wuchow = Wuzhou 48-49 L 7
Wuchuan [TJ, Guizhou] 48-49 K 6
Wuchuan [TJ, Nei Monggol Zizhiqu] 48-49 L 3
Wu-chung-pao = Wuzhong 48-49 K 4
Wu Chiang = Wu Jiang [TJ, ~] 48-49 K 6
Wudaogou 50-51 EF 1
Wudi 48-49 M 4
Wudu 48-49 J 5
Wugang 48-49 L 6
Wuhan 48-49 L 5
Wu hei 48-49 K 4
Wu-hsi = Wuxi 48-49 MN 5
Wuhu 48-49 M 5
Wu-i Shan = Wuyi Shan 48-49 M 6
Wu Jiang [TJ, ~] 48-49 K 6
Wujin = Changzhou 48-49 MN 5
Wukari 60-61 F 7
Wuli 48-49 K 7
Wuliang Shan 48-49 J 7
Wuling He 48-49 P 2
Wulumuqi = Ürümchi 48-49 F 3
Wunstorf 33 D 2

Wunst 229

Wupatki National Monument 76-77 GH 8
Wuppertal 33 C 3
Wŭqbá, Al- = Al-Waqbá 46-47 L 8
Wur = Wour 60-61 H 4
Wurno 60-61 EF 6
Wŭruq, Rã's - - Rã's ash-Shŭkât ath-Thalâtha 60-61 D 1
Würzburg 33 DE 4
Wushi [TJ ↓ Shaoguan] 48-49 L 7
Wushi = Üchturpan 48-49 DE 3
Wusi = Wuxi 48-49 MN 5
Wusu 48-49 EF 3
Wusuli Jiang 48-49 P 2
Wutai Shan 48-49 L 4
Wuti 48-49 M 4
Wutongqiao 48-49 J 6
Wu-tu = Wudu 48-49 J 5
Wuvulu 52-53 M 7
Wuwei [TJ, Gansu] 48-49 J 4
Wuxi 48-49 MN 5
Wuxian = Suzhou 48-49 N 5
Wuxing 48-49 MN 5
Wuxue = Guangji 48-49 M 6
Wuyiling 48-49 OP 2
Wuying 48-49 OP 2
Wuyi Shan 48-49 M 6
Wuyuan [TJ, Nei Monggol Zizhiqu] 48-49 K 3
Wu-yüan = Wuyuan [TJ, Nei Monggol Zizhiqu] 48-49 K 3
Wuyun 48-49 O 2
Wu-yün = Wuyun 48-49 O 2
Wuz, El = Al-Wazz 60-61 L 5
Wuzhang = Wuchang 48-49 O 3
Wuzhong 48-49 K 4
Wuzhou 48-49 L 7

Wyandra 56-57 HJ 5
Wyangala Reservoir 56-57 J 6
Wye 32 E 5
Wynbring 56-57 F 6
Wyndham 56-57 E 3
Wynniatt Bay 70-71 O 3
Wynyard [AUS] 56-57 HJ 8
Wyoming 72-73 D-F 3
Wyoming Peak 76-77 H 4
Wyoming Range 76-77 H 4
Wytheville, VA 74-75 C 6

X

Xadded 60-61 b 1
Xa-doai 52-53 E 3
Xai-Xai 64-65 H 8
Xalapa = Jalapa Enríquez 72-73 D-E 7
Xalin 60-61 b 2
Xalisco = Jalisco 72-73 EF 7
Xam Nua 52-53 D 4
Xangongo 64-65 E 6
Xánthē 36-37 L 5
Xanxerê 80 F 3
Xapuri 78-79 F 7
Xarardheere 60-61 b 3
Xar Moron He 48-49 MN 3
Xauen = Shifshawn 60-61 CD 1
Xavantes, Serra dos - 78-79 K 7

Xcan 72-73 J 7

Xiachuan Dao 48-49 L 7
Xiadong 48-49 H 3
Xiaguan [TJ, Yunnan] 48-49 J 6
Xiahe 48-49 J 4
Xiamen 48-49 M 7
Xi'an 48-49 K 5
Xiangfan 48-49 L 5
Xianggang = Hong Kong 48-49 LM 7
Xiang Jiang 48-49 L 6
Xiangkhouang 52-53 D 3
Xiangtan 48-49 L 6
Xiangxi Zizhizhou 48-49 KL 6
Xiangyang 48-49 L 5
Xiangyangchen 50-51 E 1
Xianning 48-49 LM 6
Xian Xian 48-49 M 4
Xianyang 48-49 K 5
Xiaochangshan Dao 50-51 D 3
Xiao Hinggan Ling 48-49 O 1-2
Xiaoliangshan 50-51 D 1
Xiaoling He 50-51 C 2
Xiaomei Guan 48-49 LM 6
Xichang 48-49 J 6

Xichuan 48-49 L 5
Xicoco = Shikoku 48-49 P 5
Xidachuan 50-51 FG 2
Xiegar Zong = Shekhar Dsong 48-49 F 6
Xiengmai = Chiang Mai 52-53 CD 3
Xifengkou 50-51 B 2
Xigezi = Zhigatse 48-49 F 6
Xiguit Qi 48-49 N 2
Xi Jiang 48-49 L 7
Xiliao He 48-49 N 3
Xilin Hot 48-49 M 3
Ximo = Kyūshū 48-49 P 5
Ximucheng 50-51 D 2
Xinbin 50-51 E 2
Xincai 48-49 LM 5
Xinchengbu 48-49 K 4
Xindi 50-51 B 2
Xindi = Honghu 48-49 L 6
Xindu 48-49 J 5
Xingang = Tanggu 48-49 M 4
Xingcheng 50-51 C 2
Xingning 48-49 M 7
Xingren 48-49 K 6
Xingtai 48-49 L 4
Xingu [BR, Amazonas] 78-79 F 6
Xingu, Rio - 78-79 J 6
Xinhua 48-49 L 6
Xining 48-49 J 4
Xinjiang [TJ, ●] 48-49 L 4
Xinjiang = Xinjiang Uygur Zizhiqu 48-49 D-F 3
Xinjiang Uygur Zizhiqu 48-49 D-F 3
Xinjin 50-51 CD 3
Xinjiulong = New Kowloon 48-49 LM 7
Xinkai He 48-49 N 3
Xinle 48-49 LM 4
Xinlitun 50-51 CD 1-2
Xinmin 48-49 N 3
Xinxian [TJ, Shanxi] 48-49 L 4
Xinxiang 48-49 LM 4
Xinyang 48-49 LM 5
Xinzhangzi 50-51 AB 2
Xinzhu = Hsinchu 48-49 N 7
Xiongyuecheng 50-51 CD 2
Xiquexique 78-79 L 7
Xiraz = Shīrãz 44-45 G 5
Xishuangbanna Daizu Zizhizhou - E ◁ 48-49 J 7
Xiuyan 50-51 D 2
Xi Xian [TJ, Shanxi] 48-49 L 4
Xizang, Région Autonome - 48-49 E-H 5
Xizhong Dao 50-51 C 3

Xolapur = Sholapur 44-45 M 7
Xuan'en 48-49 KL 5-6
Xuanhua 48-49 LM 3
Xuanwei 48-49 J 6
Xuchang 48-49 L 5
Xuddur 60-61 a 3
Xuguit Qi 48-49 N 2
Xunhua 48-49 J 4
Xunke 48-49 O 2
Xunyuecheng = Xiongyuecheng 50-51 CD 2
Xuyan = Xiuyan 50-51 D 2
Xuzhou 48-49 M 5

Y/IJ

Yaak, MT 76-77 F 1
Ya'an 48-49 J 6
Yaapeet 58 EF 5
Yaballo = Yabĕlo 60-61 M 7-8
Yabĕlo 60-61 M 7-8
Yabrïn 44-45 F 6
Yachats, OR 76-77 A 3
Yacheng 48-49 K 8
Ya-chou = Ya'an 48-49 J 6
Yacolt, WA 76-77 B 3
Yacuiba 78-79 G 9
Yafi 52-53 D 2
Yafō, Tel-Avïv- 44-45 C 4
Yagda = Erdemli 46-47 F 4
Yağmurdere 46-47 HJ 2
Yahiko 50-51 M 4
Yahila 64-65 F 2
Yahuma 64-65 F 3
Yahyalı 46-47 F 3
Yaichau = Ya Xian 48-49 KL 8
Yaizu 50-51 M 5
Yakarta = Jakarta 52-53 E 8
Yakima, WA 72-73 BC 2
Yakima Indian Reservation 76-77 C 2
Yakima Ridge 76-77 CD 2
Yakima River 76-77 CD 2

Yakishiri-jima 50-51 b 1
Yako 60-61 D 6
Yakoko = Yapehe 64-65 FG 3
Yakt, MT 76-77 F 1
Yaku 50-51 H 7
Yakumo 50-51 b 2
Yaku sima = Yaku-shima 48-49 P 5
Yakutat, AK 70-71 HJ 6
Yakutat Bay 70-71 HJ 6
Yakut Autonomous Republic 42-43 U-b 4
Yakutia, República Autónoma - 42-43 U-b 4
Yala [BUR] 52-53 D 5
Yale Point 76-77 J 7
Yalgoo 56-57 C 5
Yalinga 60-61 J 7
Yalnızçam Dağları 46-47 JK 2
Yaloké 60-61 H 7
Yalong Jiang 48-49 J 6
Yalova 46-47 C 2
Yalu 48-49 N 2
Yalu Cangpu Jiang = Tsangpo 48-49 EF 6
Ya-lu Chiang = Yalu Jiang 50-51 EF 2
Ya-lu Chiang = Yalu Jiang 50-51 EF 2
Yalu He 48-49 N 2
Ya-lu Ho = Yalu He 48-49 N 2
Yalu Jiang 48-49 O 3
Ya-lung Chiang = Yalong Jiang 48-49 J 6
Ya-lung Chiang = Yalong Jiang 48-49 J 6
Yalvaç 46-47 D 3
Yamada 50-51 NO 3
Yamada = Nankoku 50-51 JK 6
Yamaga 50-51 H 6
Yamagata 48-49 QR 4
Yamaguchi 50-51 HJ 5
Yamakuni 50-51 H 6
Yamalo-Nenets Autonomous Area 42-43 M-O 4-5
Yamanashi 50-51 M 5
Yamarna Aboriginal Reserve 56-57 DE 5
Yamasaki 50-51 K 5
Yamato 50-51 K 5
Yamato, Banc de - 48-49 PQ 4
Yamato, Banco de - 48-49 PQ 4
Yamato Bank 48-49 PQ 4
Yamato-sammyaku 24 B 4
Yambéring 60-61 B 6
Yambí, Mesa de - 78-79 E 4
Yămbïyŭ 60-61 K 8
Yambu = Kâtmându 44-45 NO 5
Yamdena, Pulau - 52-53 K 8
Yamethin = Yamïthin 52-53 C 2
Yamïthin 52-53 C 2
Yamma Yamma, Lake - 56-57 H 5
Yammu = Jammu 44-45 LM 4
Yamsay Mountain 76-77 C 4
Yamuduozuonake Hu = Ngamdo Tsonag Tsho 48-49 G 6
Yamuna 44-45 MN 5
Yamursba, Tanjung - 52-53 K 7
Yanac 58 E 6
Yanagawa 50-51 H 6
Yanai 50-51 HJ 6
Yanam 44-45 N 7
Yanan = Yan'an 48-49 K 5
Yanaoca 78-79 E 7
Yanaon = Yanam 44-45 N 7
Yan'an 48-49 K 5
Yanbian 48-49 J 6
Yanbian Chaoxianzu Zizhizhou 48-49 OP 3
Yanbian Chaoxianzu Zizhizhou 48-49 OP 3
Yanbian Zizhizhou 50-51 GH 1
Yanbu' al-Baḥr 44-45 D 6
Yancheng [TJ, Jiangsu] 48-49 N 5
Yanchuan 48-49 KL 4
Yandama Creek 58 E 2
Yandeerra Aboriginal Reserve 56-57 C 4
Yangambi 64-65 FG 2
Yangang-do = Ryanggang-do 50-51 FG 2
Yang-chiang = Yangjiang 48-49 L 7
Yangchuan = Yangquan 48-49 L 4
Yangdök 50-51 F 3
Yangdong Tsho 48-49 G 6
Yanggu [ROK] 50-51 FG 3
Yangi Hisar 48-49 CD 4

Yangjiang 48-49 L 7
Yangjŏng-ni 50-51 F 4
Yangkiang = Yangjiang 48-49 L 7
Yangon 52-53 BC 3
Yangp'yŏng 50-51 F 4
Yangquan 48-49 L 4
Yangsan 50-51 G 5
Yangshuling 50-51 B 2
Yangsi 50-51 E 3
Yang Tsé Kiang = Chang Jiang 48-49 K 5-6
Yang-tse-Kiang = Chang Jiang 48-49 K 5-6
Yangyang 48-49 O 4
Yangzhou 48-49 M 5
Yanina = Iốánnina 36-37 J 6
Yanji 48-49 O 3
Yanjing 48-49 H 6
Yankton, SD 72-73 G 3
Yanku = Taiyuan 48-49 L 4
Yanna 56-57 J 5
Yanonge 64-65 F 2
Yanqi = Qara Shahr 48-49 F 3
Yantabulla 58 G 2
Yantai 48-49 N 4
Yanxi 48-49 L 6
Yao 60-61 H 6
Yaoganhutun = Yaoqianhu 50-51 D 2
Yaolo 64-65 F 2
Yaoqianhu 50-51 D 2
Yaoundé 60-61 G 8
Yapehe 64-65 FG 3
Yapen, Pulau - 52-53 L 7
Yapen, Selat - 52-53 L 7
Yap Islands 52-53 L 5
Yapraklı 46-47 E 2
Yaqui, Rio - 72-73 E 6
Yaquina Head 76-77 A 3
Yaraka 56-57 H 4
Yaralıgoz Dağı 46-47 EF 2
Yarangüme = Tavas 46-47 C 4
Yardımcı Burnu 46-47 D 2
Yari, Rio - 78-79 E 4
Yariga-take 48-49 Q 4
Yarkand 48-49 D 4
Yarkand darya 48-49 D 4-E 3
Yarmouth 72-73 X 9
Yarnell, AZ 76-77 G 8
Yarra 56-57 J 7
Yarram 56-57 J 7
Yarraman 56-57 K 5
Yarras 58 L 3
Yarrawonga 58 GH 6
Yarumal 78-79 D 3
Yasanyama 60-61 J 8
Yasawa Group 52-53 a 2
Yashima 50-51 J 6
Yashiro-jima 50-51 J 6
Yass 50-51 J 7
Yasugi 50-51 J 5
Yasŭj 44-45 G 4
Yasun Burun 46-47 GH 2
Yatağan 46-47 C 4
Yatakala 60-61 E 6
Yathkyed Lake 70-71 R 5
Yatsuga take 50-51 M 4-5
Yatsushiro 50-51 H 6
Yatsushiro-wan 50-51 H 6
Yatta Plateau 63 D 3
Yaunde = Yaoundé 60-61 G 8
Yauyos 78-79 D 7
Yavari, Rio - 78-79 E 5
Yavello = Yabĕlo 60-61 M 7-8
Yavi 46-47 K 3
Yavı = Çat 46-47 J 3
Yavi, Cerro - 78-79 F 3
Yavuzeli 46-47 G 4
Yawatahama 50-51 J 6
Yaxchilán 72-73 H 8
Ya Xian 48-49 KL 8
Yay 60-61 L 6
Yay, Nahr - 63 B 1
Yayako = Palamut 46-47 B 3
Yayladağı 46-47 FG 5
Yayo 60-61 H 5
Yayuan 50-51 F 2
Yazd 44-45 G 4
Yazlıka Dağları 46-47 K 4
Yazoo River 72-73 H 5

Yell 32 F 1
Yellowhead Pass 70-71 N 7
Yellowknife 70-71 O 5
Yellow Pine, ID 76-77 F 3
Yellow Sea 48-49 N 4
Yellowstone Lake 72-73 D 3
Yellowstone National Park 72-73 D 3
Yellowstone River 72-73 E 2
Yellowtail Reservoir 76-77 JK 3
Yelwa 60-61 EF 6
Yemassee, SC 74-75 C 8
Yemen 44-45 E 7-8
Yémen 44-45 E 7-8
Yemişenbükü = Taşova 46-47 G 2
Yenangyaung 52-53 BC 2
Yenda 60-61 DE 7
Yengejeh 46-47 N 4
Yengī Kand 46-47 MN 4
Yenibaşak 46-47 J 3
Yeniçağa 46-47 DE 2
Yenice 46-47 E 3
Yenice [TR, Çanakkale] 46-47 B 3
Yenice [TR, Mersin] 46-47 F 4
Yeniceırmağı 46-47 FG 3
Yenidoğan, Ankara- 46-47 E 2
Yeni Erenköy 46-47 EF 5
Yeniköy = Şavşat 46-47 K 2
Yenimahalle, Ankara- 46-47 E 2-3
Yenipazar 46-47 BC 4
Yenişehir 46-47 C 2
Yenişehir, Ankara- 46-47 E 3
Yeniyol = Borçka 46-47 JK 2
Yenki = Qara Shahr 48-49 F 3
Yenki = Yanji 48-49 O 3
Yenpien = Yanbian 48-49 J 6
Yenping = Nanping 48-49 M 6
Yentai = Yantai 48-49 N 4
Yeo Lake 56-57 D 5
Yeovil 32 E 6
Yeppoon 56-57 K 4
Yerington, NV 76-77 D 6
Yerköy 46-47 F 3
Yerna Tsho 48-49 F 5
Yerqiang = Yarkand 48-49 D 4
Yerupaja 78-79 D 7
Yĕrŭshãlayim 44-45 CD 4
Yesan 50-51 F 4
Yeşildere 46-47 E 4
Yeşilhisar 46-47 F 3
Yesilırmak 44-45 D 2
Yeşilova 46-47 C 4
Yeşilyurt 46-47 H 3
Yesso = Hokkaidō 48-49 RS 3
Yeste 34-35 F 9
Yetman 58 K 2
Yeu, Île de - 34-35 F 5
Yeungkong = Yangjiang 48-49 L 7
Yew Mountain 74-75 C 5
Ye Xian [TJ, Shandong] 48-49 MN 4
Yezd = Yazd 44-45 G 4

Yhú 80 E 2

Yi'allaq, Gebel - - = Jabal Yu'alliq 62 E 2
Yibin 48-49 JK 6
Yichang 48-49 L 5
Yicheng [TJ, Hubei] 48-49 L 5
Yichun [TJ, Heilongjiang] 48-49 O 2
Yichun [TJ, Jiangxi] 48-49 LM 6
Yidda = Jiddah 44-45 D 6
Yidu [TJ, Hubei] 48-49 L 5
Yidu [TJ, Shandong] 48-49 M 4
Yiershi 48-49 MN 2
Yiğit Dağı 46-47 L 4
Yığlıca 46-47 D 2
Yilan 48-49 OP 2
Yıldız Dağı 46-47 G 2
Yıldız Dağları 46-47 BC 2
Yıldızeli 46-47 G 3
Yilehuli Shan 48-49 NO 1
Yinchuan 48-49 JK 4
Yindu He = Sengge Khamba 48-49 E 5
Yingchuan 48-49 K 4
Yingde 48-49 L 7
Yinghai = Yangi Hisar 48-49 CD 4
Yingkou 48-49 N 3
Ying-k'ou = Yingkou 48-49 N 3

Yingkow = Yingkou 50-51 CD 2
Yingpan 50-51 E 2
Yingshan [TJ → Nanchong] 48-49 K 5
Yingtan 48-49 M 6
Ying-tê = Yingde 48-49 L 7
Yining = Ghulja 48-49 E 3
Yinkow = Yingkou 48-49 N 3
Yinxian = Ningbo 48-49 N 6
Yi-pin = Yibin 48-49 JK 6
Yirga Alem 60-61 M 7
Yirül 60-61 L 7
Yishan [TJ, ●] 48-49 K 7
Yi-tcheou = Linyi 48-49 M 4
Yitu = Yidu 48-49 M 4
Yi Xian [TJ, Liaoning] 48-49 N 3
Yixian = Ye Xian 48-49 LM 4
Yiyang [TJ, Hunan] 48-49 L 6

Yläne 30-31 K 7
Ylikita 30-31 N 4
Ylivieska 30-31 L 5
Ylläständuri 30-31 KL 4
Yochow = Yueyang 48-49 L 6
Yodoe 50-51 J 5
Yogan, Cerro - 80 BC 3
Yogyakarta [RI, ●] 52-53 EF 8
Yogyakarta [RI, ☆ = 13 ◁] 52-53 EF 8
Yoichi 50-51 b 2
Yokadouma 60-61 H 8
Yōkaichiba 50-51 N 4
Yokkaichi 48-49 Q 5
Yokkaiti = Yokkaichi 48-49 Q 5
Yoko 60-61 G 7
Yokohama 48-49 QR 4
Yokosuka 48-49 QR 4
Yokote 48-49 QR 4
Yola 60-61 G 7
Yolombo 64-65 F 3
Yom, Mae Nam - 52-53 CD 3
Yonago 50-51 J 5
Yonan 50-51 EF 4
Yoncalla, OR 76-77 B 4
Yŏnch'ŏn 50-51 F 3
Yoneshiro-gawa 50-51 N 2
Yonezawa 48-49 QR 4
Yŏngam 50-51 F 5
Yongamp'o 50-51 E 3
Yong'an 48-49 M 6
Yŏngch'ŏn 50-51 G 5
Yongdeng 48-49 J 4
Yŏngdŏk 50-51 G 4
Yŏngdong 50-51 F 4
Yonggok-tang 50-51 E 2
Yŏnghae 50-51 G 4
Yongha-ri 50-51 F 3
Yŏnghŭng 50-51 F 3
Yŏnghŭng-do 50-51 EF 4
Yŏngil-man 50-51 G 4
Yongji 48-49 L 5
Yongjia = Wenzhou 48-49 N 6
Yŏngju 50-51 G 4
Yongling 50-51 E 2
Yŏngsan 50-51 G 5
Yongtai 48-49 M 6
Yŏngwŏl 50-51 G 4
Yŏngwŏn 50-51 F 3
Yongxiu 48-49 LM 6
Yŏngyu 50-51 E 3
Yonkers, NY 72-73 M 3
Yonne 34-35 J 5
York 32 F 5
York [AUS] 56-57 C 6
York, PA 72-73 L 3-4
York, SC 74-75 C 7
York, Cape - 56-57 H 2
York, Kap - 70-71 X 2
Yorke Peninsula 56-57 G 6
Yorke Town 56-57 G 6-7
York Factory 70-71 S 6
York River 74-75 E 6
Yorkshire 32 F 4
York Sound 56-57 DE 2
Yorkton 70-71 Q 7
Yorktown, VA 74-75 E 6
Yosemite National Park 76-77 D 7
Yosemite National Park, CA 72-73 C 4
Yoshida 50-51 J 6
Yoshii-gawa 50-51 K 5
Yoshino-gawa 50-51 JK 5
Yosō-do 50-51 F 6
Yŏsu 48-49 O 5
Yos Sudarsa, Pulau - 52-53 L 8
Yost, UT 76-77 G 5
Yŏsu 48-49 O 5
Yotaú 78-79 G 8
Yŏtei-dake 50-51 b 2

Youghal 32 C 6
Yougoslavie 36-37 H 4-J 5
Youkounkoun 60-61 B 6
Young [AUS] 56-57 J 6
Young, AZ 76-77 H 8
Younghusband, Lake –
58 BC 3
Younghusband Penisland
58 D 5-6
Young Island 24 C 16-17
Youngstown, OH 72-73 KL 3
Younts Peak 76-77 J 4
Yowl Islands = Kepulauan Ayu
52-53 K 6
Yoyang = Yueyang 48-49 L 6
Yŏyu 50-51 F 4
Yozgat 44-45 CD 3
Ypres = Ieper 34-35 J 3
Ypsárion 36-37 L 5
Yreka, CA 76-77 B 5
Ysabel = Santa Isabel
52-53 jk 6
Ysabel Channel 52-53 NO 7
Ysabel Channel 52-53 NO 7
IJsland 30-31 c-f 2
IJslandbekken 28-29 CD 4
IJsland-Jan-Mayenrug
28-29 F 2
IJssel 34-35 KL 2
IJsselmeer 34-35 K 2
Ystad 30-31 E 10
Yu'alliq, Jabal – 62 E 2
Yuan'an 48-49 L 6
Yüan Chiang = Hong He
48-49 J 7
Yüan Chiang = Yuan Jiang
48-49 L 6
Yüan-chou = Yichun
48-49 LM 6
Yuanchow = Zhijiang
48-49 KL 6
Yüan Chiang = Hong He
48-49 J 7
Yüan Chiang = Yuan Jiang
48-49 L 6
Yuan Jiang [TJ, ~] 48-49 L 6
Yuanling 48-49 L 6
Yüan-ling = Yuanling 48-49 L 6
Yuanmou 48-49 J 6
Yuanping 48-49 L 4
Yuba City, CA 72-73 B 4
Yūbari 48-49 R 3
Yuba River 76-77 C 6
Yūbetsu 50-51 d 2
Yubo = Lī Yūbū 60-61 K 7
Yucatán 72-73 J 7
Yucatan, Bassin du –
72-73 JK 8
Yucatán, Canal de – 72-73 J 7
Yucatán, Cuenca del –
72-73 JK 8
Yucatán, Península de –
72-73 HJ 8
Yucatan Basin 72-73 JK 8
Yucatánbekken 72-73 JK 8
Yucca, AZ 76-77 F 8
Yuci 48-49 L 4
Yudian = Keriya 48-49 E 4
Yüeh-yang = Yueyang
48-49 L 6
Yueqing 48-49 N 6
Yueyang 48-49 L 6
Yugoslavia 36-37 H 4-J 5
Yuhuang 48-49 M 4
Yuhuang Ding 48-49 M 4
Yukarı Doğancılar = Alaplı
46-47 D 2
Yukarı Hadım = Hadım
46-47 E 4
Yukarı ova 46-47 FG 4
Yukon, Territoire de – =
Yukon Territory 70-71 JK 4-5
Yukon Plateau 70-71 J 5
Yukon River 70-71 H 4
Yukon Territory 70-71 JK 4-5
Yüksekkum = Köyceğiz
46-47 C 4
Yüksekova 46-47 L 4
Yukuduma = Yokadouma
60-61 H 8
Yukuhashi 50-51 H 6
Yulee, FL 74-75 c 1
Yule River 76-77 C 4
Yulin [TJ, Guangxi Zhuangzu
Zizhiqu] 48-49 L 7
Yulin [TJ, Shaanxi] 48-49 KL 4
Yü-lin = Yulin [TJ, Guangxi
Zhuangzu Zizhiqu] 48-49 L 7
Yü-lin = Yulin [TJ, Shaanxi]
48-49 KL 4
Yulongxue Shan 48-49 J 6

Yü-lung Shan = Yulongxue
Shan 48-49 J 6
Yuma, AZ 72-73 D 5
Yuma Desert 76-77 F 9
Yuma Indian Reservation
76-77 F 9
Yumari, Cerro – 78-79 F 4
Yumen 48-49 H 4
Yumurtalik 46-47 F 4
Yuna 56-57 BC 5
Yunak 46-47 D 3
Yungan = Yong'an 48-49 M 6
Yungas 78-79 FG 8
Yungchang = Baoshan
48-49 HJ 6
Yung-chi = Yongji 48-49 L 5
Yung-chou = Lingling
48-49 L 6
Yungki = Jilin 48-49 O 3
Yung-ning = Yongning
48-49 J 6
Yungtai = Yongtai 48-49 M 6
Yung-têng = Yongdeng
48-49 J 4
Yung-tien-ch'êng = Yongdian
50-51 E 2
Yungxiao 48-49 M 7
Yunhe = Lishui 48-49 MN 6
Yün-lin 48-49 MN 7
Yunnan 48-49 HJ 7
Yunnan = Kunming 48-49 J 6
Yunsiao = Yunxiao 48-49 M 7
Yunta 58 D 4
Yunxiao 48-49 M 7
Yura-gawa 50-51 K 5
Yurimaguas 78-79 D 6
Yurung darya 48-49 DE 4
Yûsef, Bahr – = Bahr Yusuf
62 D 3
Yü Shan [RC] 48-49 N 7
Yushu 48-49 O 3
Yushu = Chhergundo
48-49 H 5
Yushu Zangzu Zizhizhou
48-49 GH 5
Yusuf, Bahr – 62 D 3
Yūsufīyah, Al- 46-47 KL 6
Yü-tien = Keriya 48-49 E 4
Yuty 80 E 3
Yutze = Yuci 48-49 L 4
Yuzawa [J, Akita] 50-51 N 3
Yuzawa [J, Niigata] 50-51 M 4

Z

Zaaltajn Gov' 48-49 H 3
Zaanstad 34-35 K 2
Zabajkal'sk 42-43 W 8
Zabarjad, Jazīrat – 62 FG 6
Zabdānī 46-47 G 6
Zāb-e Kūchek, Rūd-e –
46-47 L 4
Zabīd 44-45 E 8
Žabljak 36-37 H 4
Zabok 36-37 FG 2
Zabol 44-45 J 4
Zabū, Az- 62 C 3
Zaburunje 38-39 K 6
Zacatecas 72-73 F 7
Zadar 36-37 F 3
Zafar = Zufār 44-45 G 7
Za'farānah, Az- 62 E 3
Zafer Burnu 46-47 F 5
Zafra 34-35 D 9
Żagań 33 G 3
Zagazig, Ez- = Az-Zaqāzīq
60-61 KL 2
Zaghartā 46-47 F 5
Zagnanado 60-61 E 7
Zāğôrâ = Zākūrah 60-61 C 2
Zagorsk = Sergijev Posad
42-43 F 6
Zagreb 36-37 FG 3
Zāgros, Kūhhā-ye –
44-45 F 3-4
Žagubica 36-37 J 3
Zagura = Zākūrah 60-61 C 2
Zāhedān 44-45 J 5
Zahļah 46-47 F 5
Zahrān 44-45 E 7
Żahrān, Az- 44-45 FG 5
Zaidam = Tshaidam
48-49 GH 4
Zaire [Angola] 64-65 D 4
Zaïre [ZRE, ~] 64-65 G 3
Zaïre [ZRE, ★] 64-65 FG 3
Zaječar 36-37 JK 4
Zajsan 42-43 P 8
Zajsan, ozero – 42-43 P 8
Zakamensk 42-43 T 7

Zākhū 44-45 E 3
Zako 60-61 J 7
Zakopane 33 JK 4
Zakouma 60-61 HJ 6
Zakroczym 33 K 2
Zākūrah 60-61 C 2
Zákynthos [GR, ⊙] 36-37 J 7
Zákynthos [GR, ●] 36-37 J 7
Zala 33 H 5
Zalabīyah 46-47 HJ 5
Zalaegerszeg 33 H 5
Zalău 36-37 K 2
Zālinjay 60-61 J 6
Zaļtan 60-61 H 3
Žambaj 38-39 K 6
Zambeze, Rio – 64-65 H 6
Zambezi 64-65 GH 6
Zambézia 64-65 H 6
Zambia 64-65 G 6-H 5
Zambie 64-65 G 6-H 5
Zamboanga 52-53 H 5
Zamboanga Peninsula
52-53 H 5
Zamfara, River – 60-61 F 6
Zammār 46-47 K 4
Zamora 34-35 E 8
Zamora, CA 76-77 BC 6
Zamora [EC, ●] 78-79 D 5
Zamora de Hidalgo 72-73 F 7-8
Zamość 33 L 3
Zamzam, Wâdî – 60-61 G 2
Žanadarja 42-43 L 9
Zanaga 64-65 D 3
Zanapa 46-47 F 4
Žanatas 42-43 MN 9
Záncara 34-35 F 9
Zanesville, OH 72-73 K 4
Žanetty, ostrov – 42-43 ef 2
Zang = Xizang Zizhiqu
48-49 EF 5
Zanján 44-45 F 3
Zanjänrüd 46-47 MN 4
Žanterek 38-39 K 6
Zanthus 56-57 D 6
Zanulje 38-39 J 3
Zanzibar 64-65 JK 4
Zanzibar and Pemba
64-65 JK 4
Zanzibar Island 64-65 JK 4
Zaouatallaz 60-61 F 3
Zaouia-el-Kahla = Burj 'Umar
Idrīs 60-61 EF 3
Zap = Çiğli 46-47 K 4
Zapadnaja Dvina 38-39 EF 4
Zapadna Morava 36-37 HJ 4
Zapadno-Sibirskaja ravnina
42-43 L-Q 5-6
Zapadnyj Sajan 42-43 Q-S 7
Zapala 80 BC 5
Zapaleri, Cerro – 80 C 2
Zapiga 80 BC 1
Zapokrovskij 42-43 W 7
Zaporožje 38-39 FG 6
Zaqāzīq, Az- 60-61 KL 2
Zara 46-47 G 3
Zara = Zadar 36-37 F 3
Zaragoza 34-35 G 8
Zarand-e Kohneh 46-47 O 5
Zarasai 30-31 LM 10
Zárate 80 E 4
Zaraza 78-79 F 3
Zarbāţiya = Zurbāţīyah
46-47 LM 6
Zareq 46-47 N 5
Zarghūn Shahr 44-45 K 4
Zaria 60-61 F 6
Zarisberge 64-65 E 7-8
Žarkamys 42-43 K 8
Žarma 42-43 OP 8
Żarmyš 38-39 K 7
Zarqā', Az- 46-47 G 6
Zarrīnābād 46-47 N 5
Zarrīneh Rūd 46-47 LM 4
Zarskoje Selo = Puškin
42-43 DE 4
Zaruşat = Arpaçay 46-47 K 2
Żary 33 G 3
Žaryk 42-43 N 8
Žašejek [SU ↙ Kandalakša]
30-31 O 4
Žašejek [SU ↑ Kandalakša]
30-31 P 4
Žaškov 38-39 F 6
Zasla 30-31 M 10
Zatab ash-Shamah 46-47 GH 7
Żataj 42-43 YZ 7
Žatec 33 F 3
Żatišje 36-37 NO 2
Zatoka 38-39 F 6
Záuiet el Beidâ' = Al-Baydā'
60-61 J 2
Zavety Iljiča 42-43 ab 8
Zavidovići 36-37 GH 3
Zavitinsk 42-43 Y 7
Zāviyeh 46-47 L 3

Zavodoukovsk 42-43 M 6
Zavolžje 42-43 G 6
Zawi 64-65 GH 6
Zawia = Az-Zāwīyah 60-61 G 2
Zawīlah 60-61 H 3
Zāwīyah, Az- 60-61 G 2
Zâwīyah, Jabal az- 46-47 G 5
Zâwiyat al-Muthniyān 62 B 2
Zâwiyat aţ-Ţarfâyah 62 B 1-2
Zâwiyat Shammâs 62 B 1-2
Zawr, Az- 46-47 N 8
Zayb, Bi'r – 46-47 K 6
Zaydūn, Wādī – 62 E 5
Zaytūn, Az- 62 AB 3
Zbąszyn 33 GH 2
Ždanov 38-39 G 6
Zdolbunov 38-39 E 5
Zduńska Wola 33 J 3
Zebedânî = Zabdânī 46-47 G 6
Zeebrugge, Brugge- 34-35 J 3
Zeehan 56-57 HJ 8
Zeerust 64-65 G 8
Zêfat 44-45 D 4
Zeghortâ = Zaghartā
46-47 F 5
Zeidûn, Wâdî – = Wādī
Zaydūn 62 E 5
Zeil, Mount – 56-57 F 4
Zeila = Seyla' 60-61 N 6
Zeitz 33 EF 3
Zeja [SU, ~] 42-43 Y 7
Zeja [SU, ●] 42-43 Y 7
Zejskoje vodochranilišče
42-43 Y 7
Zelebiyé = Zalabīyah
46-47 HJ 5
Zelenga 38-39 J 6
Zelenoborskij 30-31 P 4
Zelenodol'sk 42-43 HJ 6
Zelenogorsk 30-31 NO 7
Zelenogradsk 33 K 1
Železnik 36-37 J 3
Zeleznik, WA 76-77 C 2
Železnodorožnyj [SU, Komi
ASSR] 42-43 J 5
Železnogorsk 38-39 G 5
Zelinograd = Celinograd
42-43 MN 7
Zella = Zillah 60-61 H 3
Zembra, Djezîra – – Al-
Jāmūr al-Kabīr 60-61 M 1
Zemcy 38-39 F 4
Zemio 60-61 JK 7
Zemmâr = Zammār 46-47 K 4
Zemongo 60-61 J 7
Zempoaltepec, Cerro –
72-73 GH 8
Zemun, Beograd- 36-37 HJ 3
Zemzen, Uâdî – = Wādī
Zamzam 60-61 G 2
Zenia, CA 76-77 B 5
Zenica 36-37 G 3
Zenshū = Chŏnju 48-49 O 4
Zephyrhills, FL 74-75 bc 2
Zeravšan 44-45 K 3
Zeravšanskij chrebet 44-45 K 3
Zerbst 33 F 2-3
Žerdevka 38-39 H 5
Zesfontein = Sesfontein
64-65 D 6
Zevgári, Akrôtêrion –
46-47 E 5
Zeydikān = Zidikān 46-47 K 3
Zeytin Burnu 46-47 F 5
Zeytinlik 46-47 JK 2
Zêzere 34-35 CD 9
Zgierz 33 J 3
Zhahang = Tsethang
48-49 G 6
Zhaling Hu = Kyaring Tsho
48-49 F 5
Zhangguangcai Ling
48-49 O 2-3
Zhangjiakou 48-49 L 3
Zhangling 48-49 N 1
Zhangsanying 50-51 AB 2
Zhangye 48-49 J 4
Zhangzhou 48-49 M 7
Zhangzi Dao 50-51 D 3
Zhanjiang 48-49 L 7
Zhanjiang Gang 48-49 L 7
Zhaotong 48-49 J 6
Zhaxigang 48-49 DE 5
Zhaxilhünbo 48-49 F 6
Zhejiang 48-49 MN 6
Zheling Guan 48-49 L 6
Zhengzhou 48-49 LM 5
Zhenhai 48-49 N 5-6
Zhenjiang 48-49 M 5
Zhenxi = Bar Köl 48-49 G 3
Zhenyuan [TJ, Guizhou]
48-49 K 6

Zhenyuan [TJ, Yunnan]
48-49 J 7
Zhigatse 48-49 F 6
Zhijiang [TJ, Hunan] 48-49 KL 6
Zhongdian 48-49 HJ 6
Zhongshan 48-49 L 7
Zhongwei 48-49 JK 4
Zhongyang Shanmo =
Chungyang Shanmo
48-49 N 7
Zhoujiakou = Zhoukou
48-49 LM 5
Zhoukou 48-49 LM 5
Zhoushan Qundao 48-49 N 5
Zhuanghe 50-51 D 3
Zhuhe = Shangzhi 48-49 O 2
Zhuji 48-49 N 6
Zhushan 48-49 KL 5
Zhuzhou 48-49 L 6
Zībār, Az- 46-47 KL 4
Zibo 48-49 M 4
Zidani most 36-37 F 2
Zidikān 46-47 K 3
Zielona Góra 33 GH 2-3
Ziftá 62 D 2
Zigala 46-47 G 2
Žigalovo 42-43 U 7
Žigansk 42-43 X 4
Zigong 48-49 JK 6
Ziguey 60-61 H 6
Ziguinchor 60-61 A 6
Zihu = Bajan Choto
48-49 JK 4
Zijin 48-49 M 7
Zikhrōn-Ya'aqov 46-47 F 6
Zilâf 46-47 G 6
Zilair 42-43 K 7
Zile 46-47 F 2
Zillah 60-61 H 3
Zillah, WA 76-77 C 2
Ziltī, Az- 44-45 EF 5
Zima 42-43 T 7
Zimbabwe 64-65 H 7
Zimbabwe [★] 64-65 GH 6
Zimkān, Āb-e – 46-47 LM 5
Zimme = Chiang Mai
52-53 CD 3
Zimnicea 36-37 L 4
Zinder 60-61 F 6
Zion National Monument
76-77 G 7
Zion National Park 76-77 G 7
Zipaquirá 78-79 E 3-4
Žirje 36-37 F 4
Zirrâh, Gaud-e –
Gawdezereh 44-45 J 5
Zi Shui 48-49 L 6
Zistersdorf 33 H 4
Žitomir 38-39 E 5
Zittau 33 G 3
Ziway Hayik 60-61 M 7
Ziyamet 46-47 F 5
Zizhong 48-49 JK 5-6
Zizō-zaki 50-51 J 5
Zlatica 36-37 KL 4
Zlatograd 36-37 L 5
Zlatoust 42-43 K 6
Zlatoustovsk 42-43 Za 7
Zlin = Gottwaldov 33 G 4
Zlītan 60-61 GH 2
Złobin 38-39 F 5
Złoczew 33 J 3
Złotów 33 H 2
Zmeinogorsk 42-43 P 7
Zmeinyj ostrov 38-39 F 6
Žmerinka 38-39 E 6
Znamenka 38-39 F 6
Znamensk 33 K 1
Znojmo 33 GH 4
Zóbuè 64-65 H 6
Žochova, ostrov – 42-43 de 2
Zohreh, Rūd-e – 46-47 N 7
Zola Chây 46-47 L 3-4
Zola Chây 46-47 L 3-4
Zoločev 38-39 DE 6
Zolotaja Gora 42-43 XY 7
Zomba 64-65 J 6
Zombi Nzoro 63 B 2
Zongo 64-65 E 2
Zonguldak 44-45 C 2
Zongwe 63 AB 4
Zonūz 46-47 L 3
Zorra, Isla – 72-73 b 2
Zorzor 60-61 C 7
Zouar 60-61 H 4
Zoutpansberge =
Soutpansberge 64-65 GH 7

Zuar = Zouar 60-61 H 4
Zubaydīyah, Az- 46-47 L 6
Zubayr, Az- 46-47 M 7
Zubayr, Jabal – 62 E 4
Zubayr, Jazā'ir az- 44-45 E 7-8
Zubayr, Khawr az- 46-47 MN 7
Zubova Pol'ana 38-39 H 5
Zuénoula 60-61 C 7
Zuera 34-35 G 8
Zufār 44-45 G 7
Żug 33 D 5
Zugdidi 38-39 H 7
Zugspitze 33 E 5
Zuid-Afrika 64-65 F-H 8
Zuid-Amerika 22-23 FG 6
Zuid-Antillenbekken 22-23 G 8
Zuidatlantische Rug
22-23 J 6-8
Zuidaustralisch Bekken
22-23 PQ 8
Zuid-Bandabekken 52-53 J 8
Zuidchinees Bekken
52-53 FG 3-4
Zuidchinese Zee 52-53 E 5-G 3
Zuid-Georgië = South
Georgia 80 J 8
Zuid-Georgiëdrempel
24 D 33-E 34
Zuid-Honsjoerug 48-49 R 5-6
Zuidindische Rug 22-23 OP 8
Zuid-Korea 48-49 OP 4
Zuidoostindisch Bekken
22-23 OP 7
Zuidossetisch Autonome
Oblast = 7 ◁ 38-39 H 7
Zuidpacifisch Bekken
24 D 21-19
Zuidpacifische Rug
24 D 22-C 20
Zuid-Sandwichtrog 24 D 34
Zuidwest-Afrika = Namibie
64-65 E 7
Zuidwestindisch Bekken
22-23 MN 7
Zuila = Zawīlah 60-61 H 3
Zújar 34-35 E 9
Zujevo, Orechovo- 42-43 FG 6
Zujewka 38-39 K 4
Žukovka 38-39 F 5
Zukur 60-61 N 6
Zumba 78-79 D 5
Zumbo 64-65 GH 6
Zumūl, Umm az- 44-45 GH 6
Zungeru 60-61 F 7
Zuni, NM 76-77 J 8
Zuni Indian Reservation
76-77 J 8
Zuni Mountains 76-77 JK 8
Zunyi 48-49 K 6
Županja 36-37 H 3
Zūq, Ḥāssī – 60-61 B 4
Zuqar = Zukur 60-61 N 6
Zūrābād 46-47 L 3
Zurbāţīyah 46-47 LM 6
Zürich 33 D 5
Zürichsee 33 D 5
Zuru 60-61 F 6
Zurzuna = Çıldır 46-47 K 2
Zuwārah 60-61 G 2
Zvishavane 64-65 H 7
Zvolen 33 J 4
Zvornik 36-37 H 3
Zwai, Lake – – = Ziway
60-61 M 7
Zwarte Zee 38-39 E-G 7
Zweden 30-31 F 9-J 10
Zwedru 60-61 C 7
Zweibrücken 33 C 4
Zwettl 33 G 4
Zwickau 33 F 3
Zwiesel 33 F 3
Zwitserland 33 CD 5
Zwolle 34-35 L 2
Zyōhana 50-51 L 4
Zyōzankei 50-51 b 2
Zyr'anka 42-43 cd 4
Zyr'anovsk 42-43 PQ 8
Żyrardów 33 K 2